P9-DCF-056

Business Law
Principles and Cases

Business Law

Principles and Cases

HAROLD F. LUSK, S.J.D.
Late of the
Indiana University Foundation

CHARLES M. HEWITT, J.D., D.B.A.
Indiana University

JOHN D. DONNELL, J.D., D.B.A
Indiana University

A. JAMES BARNES, J.D.
Beveridge, Fairbanks, and Diamond

1978 Fourth U.C.C. Edition

RICHARD D. IRWIN, INC. Homewood, Illinois 60430
Irwin-Dorsey Limited Georgetown, Ontario L7G 4B3

ISBN 0-256-02021-3
Library of Congress Catalog Card No. 77–085808
Printed in the United States of America

6 7 8 9 0 K 5 4 3 2 1 0

Preface

This edition represents a major revision of a textbook that has been a leader in its field since the first edition appeared in 1935. Approximately one half of the text cases have been replaced with current cases and considerable rewriting has been done to bring it up to date, to make it more readable, and to add new topics. Problem cases at the end of the chapters have also been replaced with recent cases. An entirely new chapter on employment law discusses not only the Labor Management Relations Act but the Civil Rights Act, OSHA, ERISA, and other important areas of government regulation of employment relations. Marvin F. Hill, Jr., of the University of Northern Illinois, contributed a major portion of the material in this chapter. Tort coverage has again been expanded. The chapter on constitutional law has been extensively rewritten and moved toward the back of the book because many students found this important area difficult to grasp at the beginning of law study. Much of the textual coverage of the Uniform Commercial Code has been rewritten to simplify and clarify as well as to update. The material covering the antitrust laws has been expanded to include recent amendments and recent cases in this vital area. The material on wills has been expanded into a full chapter concerning wills, trusts, and estates.

In our judgment, students can best gain an understanding of the legal environment of business by studying law in action as it affects business. This necessarily involves an understanding of the Uniform Commercial Code, which has now been adopted in all the states and territories, and the court-developed law of contracts, torts, and property, and also an understanding of the major federal statutes regulating business such as the Sherman Act, the Federal Trade Commission Act, the securities laws, the Labor Management Relations Act, and the Occupational Safety and Health Act. It also requires a comprehension of the work of the federal agencies, such as the FTC, the SEC, and the NLRB, which through their rule-making power are responsible for perhaps the largest segment of the legal environment of business.

Our goal has been to include discussion of the areas of law most pertinent to the operation of most businesses. The breadth of subjects covered permits use of the book as the text for two or three standard length courses. Even if only one course is offered, the variety of topics covered permits the instructor or the student working on his or her own to choose those that appear most relevant to the objectives of the course or of the individual student. It will be noted that most of the subject matter covered by the CPA examination is included, so that the book may be used in its entirety in preparation for that examination.

Despite many changes and additions, the text still follows the general pattern developed through eight editions by its original author, Harold F. Lusk. We mourn Harold's death at age 82 on September 28, 1976. He put the same sustained effort and care into his teaching and other university commitments as he did into his books. His life will always remain an inspiration to us.

We remain, as before, eager to receive criticisms of the text and suggestions from both instructors and students. Those submitted by users of the last edition are too numerous to acknowledge here but are much appreciated. Not all suggestions have been adopted, in part because they are frequently conflicting. This proved true also of the suggestions of those who reviewed the last edition or who read parts of the manuscript for this edition, including Herbert M. Bohlman of Arizona State University; Robert R. Garrett of American River College; Tom Gossman of Western Michigan University; J. Kirkland Grant of the College of Law, University of South Carolina; Dugald W. Hudson of Georgia State University; Barry Roberts of the University of North Carolina; Jeff Speno of the University of Delaware; Alvin Stauber of Florida State University; and our colleague Michael B. Metzger of Indiana University. Much indebted as we are to them, we made the final judgments, so that responsibility for whatever errors there may be remains ours only.

We also wish to express appreciation for their important contributions to the text and the supplementary teaching aids to our research assistants including Craig Benson, William McCullough, Mike Wade, Steve Reed, and Linda Ritchie; to our secretaries Joan Wenzel, Janice Siler, Mmemae Spencer, Elaine Kunz, and Sarah Jane Hughes; and to our teaching colleagues both in Bloomington and Indianapolis.

We are pleased to be able again to offer a student workbook thoroughly revised by Phillip J. Scaletta of Purdue University and Thomas W. Dunfee of the University of Pennsylvania. Other supplementary aids to instructors using the text include a teacher's manual and a test manual, both completely revised for use with this edition.

February 1978

Charles M. Hewitt, Jr.
John D. Donnell
A. James Barnes

Contents

PART II
Crimes and Torts

PART III
Contracts

PART IV
Agency and Employment Law

PART VII
Property

Appendixes

PART I

The American Legal System

1

The Nature of Law and Its Development

A Society of Laws. A shaft of black diorite unearthed in 1901 is the first great monument to man's continuing search for justice. It records the code of Babylon's King Hammurabi . . . a list of crimes and penalties demanding, in essence, an eye for an eye and a tooth for a tooth. Five centuries later, the Mosaic Code still echoed this harsh doctrine. But by the Sixth Century A.D. Justinian's Code was shifting the emphasis from punishment to due process, ruling that a man was innocent until proved guilty. In 1215, England's nobles forced King John to sign the Magna Carta, which recognized such basic rights as that to a fair trial. Over the centuries the law continued to grow, adapting to the changing needs of society as it progressed, from the Napoleonic Code of 1804, which legalized the reforms of the French Revolution, to the civil rights decisions of today's U.S. Supreme Court. The search for justice still goes on, attempting to fulfill the promise made by Hammurabi 4,000 years ago: "The oppressed . . . shall read the writing . . . and he shall find his right."[1]

Concepts of Law

Defining Law. Ancient as the concept is, it is most difficult to develop a useful and meaningful definition of law. Legal scholars and other "experts" are not in agreement, particularly if the effort goes beyond a relatively simple dictionary definition.

At this point it may be more helpful to the student who is studying law for the first time merely to point out some erroneous ideas as to what law is. A police officer is part of "the law" but neither he nor the courts completely encompass what is meant by this term. Although a statute passed by a legislature may properly be called a law, statutes are only a small part of the law. Nor is law just a system of rules of conduct and the methods used for their enforcement. Indeed, it is more accurate to conceive of law as a process by

[1] S. N. Kramer, *Cradle of Civilization* (New York: Time Inc., 1967), p. 170.

which numerous functions needed by society are carried out than as a body of rules. Law may also be viewed as a system of many interacting parts of which rules are only one aspect.

It is suggested that instead of seeking a definition of law to learn at this point, the student read the introductory chapters of this textbook with the objective of learning as much as possible about law in general in order to gain a better understanding of the text and cases which follow.

Legal Philosophy. From time immemorial people have discussed the nature of law, its sources and its functions, as well as that even more illusive concept, "justice." Writings are available by the thousands, including statements from the great philosophers of the ages such as Plato, Aristotle, and St. Thomas Aquinas, down to Roscoe Pound of recent times.

Until one has gained some familiarity with the materials of the law and more particularly some appreciation of the difficulties judges face as they deal with specific fact situations and seek to justify their decisions in specific disputes, a discussion of legal theories may be relatively meaningless. On the other hand, some general notion of the concepts of the law expounded by some of the great legal thinkers who have helped to shape our law is likely to be useful to the student as one reads a case and seeks to understand the judge's opinion.

Pound, perhaps the most widely acclaimed American legal philosopher, distinguishes and briefly outlines 12 different concepts of law in his *Introduction to the Philosophy of Law.*[2] However, there are four basic concepts, some encompassing several of those identified by Pound, which reappear most frequently in the writings of scholars as well as entering into the thinking of judges as they decide specific disputes.

Law as What Is Right. The first of these concepts is that law is "what is right" in a moral sense, whether the notion of right is derived directly from a divine source or from the nature of humans. This concept suggests that laws may be bad because they are inconsistent with properly reasoned deductions from God's revealed will or assumptions concerning the inherent nature of people. Under this concept improvement of the law, and therefore of the society of people, may come from better reasoning and/or new revelations. Critics of this view question the existence of any fixed code of right and wrong. They also question the ability of any person to set out such a code, because as anthropologist Ruth Benedict says, no person ". . . ever looks at the world with pristine eyes. [Each person] sees it edited by a definite set of customs and ways of thinking."[3]

---

[2] Roscoe Pound, *Introduction to the Philosophy of Law* (New Haven, Conn.: Yale University Press, 1922), pp. 26–30, paperback edition.

[3] Ruth Benedict, *Patterns of Culture* (Boston: Houghton Mifflin Co., Mentor Books, 1934), p. 18.

Law as Custom. Another concept is that law is a historical accretion, developed over ages from the traditions and customs of a society, which reflects the peculiar nature of the people interacting with a particular environment. Some of the thinkers emphasizing this concept of law have visualized legal development as the unfolding of some basic idea. For example, Sir Henry Maine noted that under the rigid class hierarchy system that characterized feudalism nearly all legal rights and duties that a person had depended upon one's position in the hierarchy—or status. The feudal structure was shattered by the expansion of trade and industry which involved the use of contract. This led to Maine's famous generalization that the history of law is the progress from status to contract.

Law as Command. A third basic concept of the law is that it is a body of rules which are essentially the commands of a political entity, backed by sanctions imposed by that entity. Under this view it is the will of the ruler or the ruling group rather than reason or morality which shapes and defines the law, and the influence of group character and tradition is minimized.

Law as Social Planning. A fourth concept of law emphasizes its purpose rather than its source and views law as a means of social control which seeks to balance conflicting claims and values of the society and its various elements. Pound, the leader of the group called the sociological school of jurists, says:

> Sociological jurists seek to enable and to compel lawmaking, whether legislative or judicial or administrative, and also the development, interpretation, and application of legal precepts, to take more complete and intelligent account of the social facts upon which law must proceed and to which it is to be applied. . . . (They) insist that we must look at law functionally. We must inquire how it operates, since the life of law is in its application and enforcement.[4]

Schools of Jurisprudence. Although, of course, legal scholars differ in the emphasis which they give to these four general concepts, the outstanding thinkers are frequently classified as belonging to a group which can be identified according to which of these concepts seems uppermost in their thinking. The metaphysical or natural law theory adherents stress the concept of law as "what is right." The historical group stresses the second concept, custom and tradition; the analytical group or positivists stress the third or imperative theory; and the sociological school is the name given to those holding the fourth concept. As Roscoe Pound points out, these differences stem from concentration on different processes or phenomena which are lumped together as law. The precepts or rules are the focus of the analytical school. The technique of the law or the way judges find a basis for their decisions, which tends to be particularly tradition bound and slow to change, is the central

[4] Roscoe Pound, *Jurisprudence* (St. Paul, Minn.: West Publishing Co., 1959), 1:350–52.

focus of the historical school. The metaphysical or natural law schools concentrate primarily on the ideal element of the law, that is, what the law ought to be. As has been indicated, the sociological school focuses on the balancing of conflicting interests in society so as to achieve social ends.

Many legal scholars are convinced that no theory or group of theories can adequately describe law. Some, often called the realists, prefer to focus on law as a process. For example, Llewellyn says:

> Actual disputes call for someone to do something about them. First, so that there may be peace . . . and secondly, so that the dispute may really be put to rest. . . . This doing of something about disputes, this doing of it reasonably, is the business of the law. And the people who have the doing in charge, whether they be judges or sheriffs or clerks or jailers or lawyers, are officials of the law. *What these officials do about disputes is, to my mind, the law itself.*[5]

SUMMARY

Writings of many great people have discussed the nature of law. Four major concepts can be identified. They are: (1) law is what is right, (2) law is custom, (3) law is the command of the ruler, and (4) law is an attempt at social planning.

Functions and Limits of Law

Changing Functions through Time. If law cannot be adequately defined by theory, can it at least be described in terms of the major functions law has performed for society? Roscoe Pound traced the development of law from ancient to modern times.[6] He concluded that in terms of major functions performed, the law has evolved through four stages.

In the first stage, found in primitive societies, the major function of law is to keep the peace. In more advanced societies, represented by Greek and Roman law and also by the law of medieval England where landholding was the major interest, the prime function of law tends to shift to maintenance of the status quo. Pound characterizes this stage as, "An idea of justice as a device to . . . keep each man in his appointed groove and thus prevent friction with his fellows." The third stage was a product of the Age of Enlightenment, the appeal of reason against authority. Legal theory then shifted to the view that justice is a device to secure a maximum of individual self-assertion, especially through freedom of contract. Similar ideas developed

---

[5] K. N. Llewellyn, *The Bramble Bush* (New York: Oceana Publications, Inc., 1960), p. 12.

[6] Roscoe Pound, "Liberty of Contract," 18 *Yale L. J.* 454 (1909).

in religion, philosophy, politics, and economics and came as the emphasis in economic activity shifted from agriculture to trade and manufacture. Finally, the fourth and current stage emphasizes social justice. This is the stage that Pound himself helped to usher in.

The law today still performs the earlier functions, but also others. Nine of the functions performed by modern law will be discussed briefly. The list that follows is not all-inclusive; others could be added. Note that some of these functions are at times in conflict with others, as, for example, the maximizing of individual self-assertion often may be inconsistent with the promotion of social justice. Much of the law protecting the environment requires the imposition of legal restrictions on the choices and property rights of individuals.

Peace Keeping. One of the important functions of modern legal systems is keeping of the peace. Disruptions of the equilibrium in highly interdependent modern societies tend to spread and tend to penalize innocent nonparticipants. In addition, rising standards of education tend to militate against self-help and any form of unjustifiable injurious conduct by any members of society. Criminal law and tort law seek to maintain the peace and to punish or penalize those who disturb the social order. Tort law also seeks to provide reimbursement for the members of society who suffer losses due to the dangerous or unreasonable conduct of others.

Influence and Enforce Standards of Conduct. Although legal standards often differ from moral standards, the law frequently influences or shapes the social consensus concerning standards of morality. Price-fixing agreements by business, for example, were neither criminal nor immoral until after the passage of the Sherman Act in 1890. The failure of the National Prohibition experiment, however, would seem to indicate that there are limits on the power of law to shape and influence the moral standards of society.

The law sets standards as to what constitutes reasonable or acceptable performance of legal duties. For business this has meant that as more careful or efficient processes have been developed these improved processes tend to establish new higher legal standards for judging business conduct. Thus the modern businessperson must exercise a great deal more care in making, advertising, and distributing a product than did counterparts of the last century.

Maintenance of the Status Quo. Cohen gave an example of law functioning to maintain the status quo when he analyzed the British law of real property:

> . . . back of the complicated law of settlement, fee-tails, copyhold estates, of the heir-at-law, of the postponement of women, and other feudal incidents, there was a great and well founded fear that by simplifying and modernizing the real property law of England the land might become more marketable. Once land becomes fully marketable it can no longer be counted on to remain in the hands of the landed aristocratic families; and this means the destinies of the British Empire. For if American experience has demonstrated anything, it is that the continued leadership by great families cannot be as well founded on a money as on a land

economy. The same kind of talent which enables Jay Gould to acquire dominion over certain railroads enables Mr. Harriman to take it away from his sons. From the point of view of an established land economy, a money economy thus seems a state of perpetual war instead of a social order where son succeeds father. . . .[7]

To the extent that zoning laws are enacted to protect the status quo for property owners, they can be taken as modern examples of the law performing this function. The repetitiveness of change in modern society undoubtedly makes it much more difficult for the law to operate in this way.

Facilitate Orderly Change. A more important function of modern law is to facilitate orderly change in order to meet the changing needs of a dynamic society. American law paradoxically functions so as to preserve stability in the law and yet to permit and facilitate change. Indeed, Whitehead states that, "The art of progress is to preserve order amidst change, and to preserve change amidst order."[8] Justice Holmes once stated that, "Every important principle is in fact at bottom the result of views of public policy." Subsequent chapters will disclose how the courts have initiated policy changes in many vital areas. These court-made changes have been especially important in antitrust, product liability, and other areas of vital concern to people in business.

Maximum Individual Self-Assertion. Although the concept of political democracy goes back to the Greeks, the ideas of individual freedom in terms of a minimum of external restraints was formalized into economic theory and had maximum impact on the law during the 19th century. Ideas of personal freedom of thought, dress, and private activity have had greater impact in the last half of this century, perhaps in response to the greater concentration of a growing population. Freedom for the individuals in society, however, must always be defined in relative terms. The total absence of restrictions means anarchy where no rights are recognized or protected by law. In legal terms absolute rights cannot exist because legal rights cannot be defined except in terms of the corresponding legal duties imposed upon others.

In absolute terms a businessperson's "right" to run one's factory on one's own land as one pleases could become the duty of society to accept foul odors, loud noises, and perhaps even physical damage to property. The unlimited right to strike could mean the legal duty of society to tolerate the stoppage of essential public services.

Facilitate Planning and the Realization of Reasonable Expectations. In a modern industrial society business managers must, within limits, be able to plan ahead. This involves not only a basis for predicting the risks and consequences of alternative courses of action, but, also, some means for planning and seeing that reasonable expectations are realized. Tort law, insurance

[7] Morris R. Cohen, "Property and Sovereignty," 13 *Cornell Law Quarterly* (1927) pp. 8, 10.

[8] A. N. Whitehead, *Process and Reality* (New York: The Macmillian Co., 1929), p. 515.

law, sales law, contract law, and other areas provide a basic legal framework to facilitate both the prediction of risks and the effectuation of economic plans.

Promotion of Social Justice. Since the turn of the century the emphasis has shifted toward the positive use of governmental powers as a means of affording all citizens equal access to the benefits of our economic and political life. Congress has passed legislation establishing a social security system, welfare for the poor, and medical payments for the old. Statutes requiring businesses to give equal opportunities in hiring and promotion have sought to overcome historical patterns of discrimination. Courts too have tended more and more to protect the disadvantaged. The U.S. Supreme Court decisions requiring school desegregation and the furnishing of legal counsel to impoverished persons accused of crime are examples of efforts to make the legal system operate more nearly in accord with our creed of equal justice for all.

Provision of Compromise Solutions. In a special sense American law usually functions so as to avoid extremes which, according to Aristotle, is the true path to justice. Freund summarizes this when he says of the U.S. Supreme Court:

> By avoiding absolutes, by testing general maxims against concrete particulars, by deciding only in the context of specific controversies, by accommodating between polar principles, by holding itself open to reconsideration of dogma, the Court at its best provided à symbol of reconciliation. Perhaps it is this blend of idealism and pragmatism that constitutes, in the end, the most notable characteristic of the judicial process.[9]

Provision of Checks against Power. Schwartz argues, "The true American contribution to human progress has not been in technology, economics, or culture; it has been in the development of law as a check upon power."[10] In the last century the law focused on protecting individuals from the arbitrary exercise of power by public officials and agencies. In this century the law has broadened its focus so as to restrict as well the arbitrary exercise of power by private organizations.

Limits on the Law. Although legal rules have been created concerning most aspects of our vital relationships, there are definite limits not only as to what law can do but also limits as to what the law will try to do. Some of these limits are imposed by the Constitution. Other limits have been self-imposed by the courts. The courts generally will refuse to deal with trifling or insignificant matters. Considerations of public expense and the prestige of the court system probably are behind this policy. In addition, the courts have evolved various hands-off policies in certain areas of the law such as

---

[9] Paul A. Freund, "The Supreme Court," Harold J. Berman (ed.), *Talks on American Law* (New York: Random House, Inc., Vintage Books edition, 1961), pp. 83–84.

[10] Bernard Schwartz, *Law in America* (New York: McGraw-Hill Book Co., 1974), p. 7.

certain types of internal family disputes, political questions, and social insults or affronts. The Supreme Court recently reversed its long-standing policy of keeping hands off state voting district decisions on the basis that equalizing voting rights justified dealing with the political issues.[11]

Historically, American courts have refused to answer hypothetical questions or to give advisory opinions by the requirement that there must be a bona fide case or controversy before the court. By refusing to address themselves to hypothetical or feigned questions the courts both avoid unseen pitfalls and preserve maximum flexibility for the real controversies that may eventually arise.

For similar reasons American courts will not address themselves to moot issues. An issue becomes moot if later events render any decision by the court meaningless in regard to a specific case. A student applied for admission to a law school and was not accepted although his test scores and grades were better than those of some of the minority students admitted under special programs. The student sued, claiming that he had suffered reverse discrimination in violation of his rights under the 14th Amendment's Equal Protections Clause. While his case was being appealed to the Supreme Court he was admitted to the same law school and was in his senior year when the case finally reached the Court. The Court refused to rule on the constitutional issues raised on the ground of mootness.[12]

In a democracy, at least, there is another important limitation on the law. If any particular legal rule that specifies conduct is to have its intended effect, at least the great majority of those persons affected by it must believe the rule to be reasonable and fair or at least be willing to follow it voluntarily. Even authoritarian regimes find it difficult to enforce rules which are generally perceived to be unnecessary and unjust by those to whom they apply.

The *Goss* case, which follows, illustrates the court developing compromise rules where idealism comes into conflict with practicality. The case also demonstrates an application of perhaps the most important constitutional limitation on the exercise of governmental authority, the Due Process Clause. This and other constitutional law concepts applicable to criminal law, and to the regulation of business are discussed more extensively in Chapters 3 and 48.

SUMMARY

The main functions of modern law include: peace keeping; influencing and enforcing standards of conduct; maintaining the status quo; facilitating orderly change; providing for maximum individual self-assertion; facilitating planning

---

[11] The leading case is *Baker v. Carr,* 396 U.S. 186 (1962).

[12] *De Funis v. Odegaard,* 416 U.S. 312 (1974).

and the realization of reasonable expectations; promotion of social justice; the provision of compromise solutions; and the provisions of checks against power.

The Constitution limits the application of law. Other limits have been self-imposed by the courts themselves, such as refusal to deal with insignificant matters, hypothetical questions, and moot issues. Rules of conduct which are not accepted as reasonable and fair by most people affected are likely to be difficult to enforce.

Goss v. Lopez

419 U.S. 565 (U.S. Sup. Ct. 1975)

Suit brought by suspended students (plaintiffs) against the Columbus, Ohio Public School System and certain officials thereof (defendants). The defendants petitioned the U.S. Supreme Court for a review of adverse decisions in the lower courts. Affirmed.

Following a period of unrest, nine high school students (plaintiffs) were suspended from classes without an administrative hearing for periods up to ten days each. The suspended students sought a declaration that school regulations unconstitutionally permitted public school officials to deprive them of their rights to an education without a hearing of any kind in violation of the Due Process Clause of the 14th Amendment.

MR. JUSTICE WHITE. Defendants contend that because there is no constitutional right to an education at public expense, the Due Process Clause does not protect against expulsions from the public school system. This position misconceives the nature of the issue and is refuted by prior decisions. The 14th Amendment forbids the State to deprive any person of life, liberty or property without due process of law. Protected interests in property are normally "not created by the Constitution. Rather, they are created and their dimensions are defined" by an independent source such as state statutes or rules entitling the citizen to certain benefits. . . . Having chosen to extend the right to an education to people of plaintiffs' class generally, Ohio may not withdraw that right on grounds of misconduct absent fundamentally fair procedures to determine whether the misconduct has occurred.

We do not believe that school authorities must be totally free from notice and hearing requirements if their schools are to operate with acceptable efficiency. Students facing temporary suspension have interests qualifying for protection of the Due Process Clause, and due process requires, in connection with a suspension of ten days or less, that the student be given oral or written notice of the charges against him and, if he denies them, an explanation of the evidence the authorities have and an opportunity to present his side of the story. The clause requires at least these rudimentary precautions against unfair or mistaken findings of misconduct and arbitrary exclusion from school.

We stop short of construing the Due Process Clause to require, countrywide, that hearings in connection with short suspensions must afford the student the opportunity to secure counsel, to confront and cross-examine witnesses supporting the charge or to call his own witnesses to verify his version of the incident. Brief disciplinary suspensions are almost countless. To impose in each such case even truncated trial type procedures might well overwhelm administrative facilities in many places and, by diverting resources, cost more than it would save in educational effectiveness.

On the other hand, requiring effective notice and informal hearing permitting the student to give his version of the events will provide a meaningful hedge against erroneous action. At least the disciplinarian will be alerted to the existence of disputes about facts and arguments about cause and effect. He may then determine himself to summon the accuser, permit cross-examination and allow the student to present his own witnesses. In any event, his discretion will be more informed and we think the risk of error substantially reduced.

Sources of American Law

English Common Law. The English legal system was developed by the Normans after their conquest in 1066. The body of law known as the "common law" developed in the two or three centuries following the Conquest. It acquired its name from the desire of William the Conqueror and his successors to unite England under their rule. One device to accomplish this was to replace the varying bodies of custom or law of each locality with a uniform or "common" system administered by the king's personal followers in his name.

This body of rules called the common law grew from the decisions of judges in settling actual disputes, the judges following the determinations of their predecessors and fellow judges in similar situations. Very early, a strong legal profession grew up in England, and legal apprentices (later law students) began to compile records of the decisions in the royal courts. These earlier decisions or precedents were then used by lawyers to support their clients' petitions for relief and by judges to justify their decisions. Thus, the rule of *stare decisis*—a Latin phrase meaning to "let the decision stand"—developed, and once a court had decided a dispute, it would decide later cases which were similar in the same way—at least until changing circumstances called for the creation of a new precedent.

Equity. The law of equity and the Court of Chancery grew out of the Norman Kings' Council as did the common law. Under the Normans the chancellor was the most powerful executive officer of the king and the chief law member of the King's Council. He not only issued writs which permitted an aggrieved person to bring an action in a common-law court, but he himself, as a personal representative of the king, heard pleas which the common-law courts were unable to handle. Procedure, too, at least in the earlier period, was more flexible in chancery. So a separate body of law, equity, with a separate court, the Court of Chancery, gradually developed. Equity had precedence over the common law because its decrees applied to the person of the defendant and disobedience to a decree was a contempt of court.

The remedies in equity were also more flexible. While a judgment of a law court was limited to money damages or recovery of property, courts of equity, for example, would grant an injunction (a decree forbidding the defendant to do some act, even a prohibition against pursuing a cause of action in a common-law court), specific performance (ordering the defendant to perform his contract), reformation (rewriting a contract or instrument to conform to the actual intent of the parties), or partition (to divide disputed property). It might be said that the common-law courts emphasized form, while the chancery courts were more interested in the merits of the case and the justice of the decision. Another distinction was that juries were not used in equity.

Although some states still have separate courts of chancery, in most of the states the same judges sit, often at separate periods, both as law judges and chancellors. In most states and in the federal courts the distinction between law and equity has been all but eliminated.

The Law Merchant. Even before the Middle Ages trading cities existed throughout Europe and the merchants and traders established their own courts and developed a set of rules which were international in origin and application governing trade and commerce. These courts existed outside of established systems of courts. It was in these courts that our law of sales of goods, negotiable instruments and other commercial law developed. It was not until the eighteenth century that the law merchant and the merchants' courts were absorbed into the common law. This area of the law represents a good example of law based on traditions and customs.

Adoption of English Law by the United States. Although English law also included royal decrees and later statutes enacted by Parliament, the decisions rendered through the centuries by the law courts and by the merchants' courts constituted the bulk of English law. It was this body of law and the English legal system which came to this continent with the first English settlers and its use became solidified during the colonial period of English rule.

As additional states were admitted to the Union, they, too, except for Louisiana, adopted the English legal system. Louisiana, as a French colony, had previously adopted and it continues to base its law upon the French civil law which culminated in the Code Napoléon, which, in turn, had its roots in the Justinian Code of Rome. Roman law also has influenced the law of California and Texas through their Spanish heritage (Spain's law also is based upon Roman law).

Some states have codified, that is, enacted as statutes, large parts of the common law, particularly in the criminal law area. More recently a large part of the common law rules and older statutes governing commercial transactions have been superceded by the adoption of the Uniform Commercial Code in all states. These tendencies towards more uniformity and towards codification represent a basic trend in modern law.

SUMMARY

The newly organized states of the United States adopted the English legal system and generally followed English common law and the law merchant insofar as they were applicable to American conditions. However, Louisiana adopted the French civil law system, and the laws of Texas and California also have been influenced by the civil law which is based on Roman law. The trend toward more uniformity in the law as a result of codification is a basic trend in modern law.

Sources of Current Law in the United States

Fifty-one Legal Systems. Basic to an understanding of the American legal system is appreciation of the fact that there are 51 different systems. In addition to the federal court system there are 50 different state court systems each, for the most part, applying its own body of law.[13]

Constitutions. A constitution, federal or state, is the basic source of law for the jurisdiction. Constitutions not only specify the structure of the government and outline the powers of its principal officers and subdivisions, but they also allocate power between levels of government—between federal and state in the United States Constitution and between state and local governmental bodies in state constitutions. In addition, constitutions contain limitations upon governmental power which proscribe certain governmental actions and certain kinds of laws. The best known example of such proscriptions is the Bill of Rights of the United States Constitution.[14]

The federal Constitution is written in broad and general language. Some of the state constitutions are much more detailed and specific, with the result that they have been amended much more frequently than the federal Constitution. The latter has only 26 amendments, the first 10 of which were adopted immediately following ratification of the basic document. Since the federal Constitution is the supreme law within the United States, any provision of

[13] The District of Columbia also has its own separate system.

[14] Constitutional law related to criminal law is discussed in Chapter 3. The constitutional background related to the regulation of business is discussed in Chapter 48.

a state constitution which conflicts with the federal document is of no force and effect; likewise, a state or federal statute conflicting with the Constitution is unenforceable.

Treaties. According to the United States Constitution, treaties made by the President with heads of foreign governments that have been ratified by the Senate are "the Supreme Law of the Land." Although there has been considerable debate concerning the wisdom of the Founders in drafting this section and as to its proper interpretation, it has not had a very great impact upon our domestic law. Nevertheless, treaties have not infrequently been the basis for holding either a state of federal statute inoperative.

Statutes. The major responsibility for changing the law of a jurisdiction belongs to the legislature. It can see a need for rules governing a new situation—for example, the dangers of radiation—and enact or "pass" a statute or "law" to prohibit or control certain uses of radioactive materials. The legislature can establish a new agency of government to administer the statute, or it can abolish an existing government agency. The legislature can repeal an outdated or unsatisfactory statute, and it can also change the common or judge-made law by superseding it with a statute which changes the rule. For example, a number of state legislatures have recently established "no fault" plans for providing damages to those injured in automobile accidents, a system which supersedes, at least in part, the centuries old common-law tort liability system.

One of the major advantages of the legislative process as compared to the common-law method of law development is the opportunity for all interested persons and groups to be heard. In the development of legal rules through the settlement of disputes in court, only the disputants and their lawyers are permitted to try to influence the judge, although occasionally the judge may permit other interested parties to file a legal argument or "brief" as an *amicus curiae,* or friend of the court, in cases likely to have an impact much broader than the parties to the lawsuit. A second advantage is that the legislators are always directly elected by the people and are more likely to be responsive to the public will. Also a broader range of viewpoints than among judges is likely to emerge in the election of legislative representatives.

Ordinances. State governments have many subsidiary units to which the state, by statute, delegates certain functions. Some of these, such as water or school districts, have rather specific and limited functions. Others, such as counties, municipalities, and townships, exercise a number of governmental functions. Legislative enactments of municipalities are called ordinances, and this term is sometimes applied also to such enactments of other political subdivisions. Ordinances are enforceable provided they do not exceed the legislative power conferred by the state legislature upon the subordinate legislative body nor violate constitutions of the state or federal governments.

Administrative Regulations. Although included as part of the executive branch of government, administrative agencies such as the Federal Trade Commission and the Securities and Exchange Commission and the state commerce or utility commissions also contribute to the body of law of their respective jurisdictions. Indeed, in 1952 Justice Jackson asserted,

> The rule of administrative bodies probably has been the most significant legal trend of the last century and perhaps more values today are affected by their decisions than by those of all the courts, review of administrative decisions apart.[15]

Starting with the predecessor to the Veterans Administration in 1789, the number and size of the administrative agencies established by acts of Congress have increased steadily.

The federal agencies with which business is most frequently involved, other than those mentioned above, include the National Labor Relations Board, the Environmental Protection Agency, and the one upon which most of the others have been modeled—the Interstate Commerce Commission, which was established in 1887. They have not only the power to issue regulations which have the force of law but also the power to initiate proceedings under those regulations (and also usually under certain statutes), to investigate, prosecute, and make a decision or adjudicate the matter. In deciding cases the administrative agency also may establish new rules. However, in most cases the agency must go into the courts to enforce its orders.

This concentration of functions—legislative, prosecutive, and adjudicative—in a single agency has been much criticized. However, the advantages of specialization and consequent expertise, of continuous rather than case-by-case development of policy through rule making and adjudication, and of the simpler procedures generally followed are claimed to outweigh the risks of abuse of the powers granted. The Administrative Procedure Act of 1946 was enacted to require the agencies to keep these functions separate within the agency, to follow fair procedures, and to afford better protection of the rights of persons appearing before them.

In recent times two principal criticisms have been leveled against the regulatory agencies. First, some argue that the costs of regulation are too high and may, in fact, exceed any real public benefits achieved. Second, some contend that at least some of the agencies are overly concerned with protecting the interests of those being regulated and not enough concerned with protecting the public interest.

Executive Orders. The President, governor, or mayor may also make law if, as is frequently the case, that person is delegated the right by the legislative body to issue executive orders to effectuate the purposes of a statute

---

[15] *FTC v. Ruberoid Co.,* 343 U.S. 470, 487 (1952).

or ordinance. For example, the President has issued a number of executive orders implementing various federal civil rights acts. These have accomplished such things as racially integrating the armed services and forbidding the federal government from purchasing from firms that discriminate on the basis of race.

SUMMARY

There are 50 state legal systems as well as a federal system. The law which they apply is derived from a number of sources. The fundamental law is the constitution of the jurisdiction, state or federal, and the United States Constitution, which supercedes all state constitutions and other sources of law. Under the Constitution, treaties with foreign nations are also the "Law of the Land."

The English common law serves as a basis for the law of each jurisdiction (except Louisiana) but a major part of the law now is statutory. The major role in changing the law is that of the legislature, and it has advantages over the common-law method of law development in that it provides a means for all interested parties to make their interests known to the legislators, who being popularly elected, may be more responsive to the public will and have a wider range of viewpoints than judges.

Subsidiary governmental units, such as cities and counties, have such powers as are granted by the state legislature. Their ordinances have the force of law if enacted within the granted powers. Administrative regulations, decisions of administrative bodies, and official orders by executive officers such as the President or a governor also may become part of the law.

Questions

1. How would you briefly explain the functions of our law to a visitor from Moscow?
2. Can you think of a function that law performs for society in addition to those discussed in the text?
3. Why is the concept of law merely as a set of rules inadequate?
4. Max Weber, the philosopher, argues that it is important that law not embrace all human relationships, at least leaving some leeway so that ethical choices are possible. Do you agree?
5. The voting district of a Chicago alderman, Russo, was redrawn by the opposition party virtually assuring his defeat. Russo sues to have the change rescinded. He alleges improper political motivation by the elected representatives. Must the boundary lines be redrawn?
6. Does the Due Process Clause require that formal hearings be held for all types of disciplinary proceedings affecting people?
7. Why have administrative agencies grown so rapidly since the turn of the century?

2

Courts and Procedures

The Courts as Lawmakers

Deciding Controversies. When there is a dispute between two persons, it is the function of the appropriate court, when asked to resolve it, to apply the applicable law to decide whether the petitioning party (plaintiff) is entitled to what he or she claims, such as money damages for some injury to plaintiff's person or property suffered as a result of the activities of the other person (defendant). There may be one or more statutes or, possibly, even governmental agency regulations which apply. If so, it or they will be applied, but frequently, however, there are none. Such a state of affairs would not permit the court to abdicate its function. It still must decide the controversy, and it then relies upon the previous decisions of the appellate courts in the same state in similar situations. It derives rules of conduct developed in the earlier cases—the precedents—to decide the present controversy.

If the controversy involves a new situation, the court's job is more difficult. For example, the old common-law rule that a landowner owned the space under his land to the center of the earth and above it to the heavens served well enough to resolve disputes between landowners and power companies seeking to string wires to serve their customers. It did not, however, appear to be satisfactory when the landowner complained of airplanes flying overhead, and the courts modified the old rule so as to balance society's interest in developing the new invention and the interest of the individual landowner. Even the modified rule was later subject to revision in a case where a landowner was granted an injunction against one who used an airplane to attempt to cause precipitation through chemical seeding of clouds over the plaintiff's land.[1] In these new situations courts often will not wait for legislative action. A decision is made, and in rendering it the court makes new law.

[1] See *Southwest Weather Research v. Rounsaville,* 320 S.W.2d 211 (Tex. Ct. Civ. App. 1959). The court granted the plaintiff an injunction.

Interpreting Enacted Law. Even when there is a pertinent statute the court cannot always go to the statute books and find a clear answer as to whether the plaintiff or the defendant is right. It is very difficult and frequently impossible to draft a statute that is not ambiguous when applied to a specific controversy. Legislators may intentionally enact a statute that uses broad and general terms because they feel incapable of foreseeing the variety of situations to which they might later like to see it applied. The Sherman Act, discussed in Chapter 50, is a prime example of this kind of statute. In addition, drafters and promoters of legislation may also choose to use rather unspecific or unclear wording because they think it more likely that the bill will be passed in that form than if it is made more specific. In addition, it should be pointed out that even when people seek to be precise and specific, their words are frequently susceptible to more than one meaning, especially when applied to an unforeseen situation.

If statutory wording is so vague, ambiguous or contradictory that the court cannot reasonably construe the language, the court may strike down the legislation utilizing constitutional law doctrines requiring various minimum levels of specificity and clarity for legislation. In many instances, however, the courts utilize legal rules and doctrines in order to fill gaps and resolve ambiguities and conflicts.

The four principal approaches utilized by the courts in interpreting legislation are as follows:

1. *Literal.* Ordinary words are given their customary and ordinary meaning. Technical words are given their technical meaning.
2. *Purposive.* An attempt is made to ascertain the intent of those enacting the legislation. The words are construed to give effect to this intent.
3. *Precedent based.* Past cases and laws are referred to in order to establish support for various meanings attributed to the words.
4. *Policy based.* The court adopts an interpretation consistent with its own view of the public interest considerations involved. As an example, the court may declare that public policy supports free competition and therefore any statute granting a particular trade or industry an exemption to the antitrust laws must be narrowly construed.

The courts frequently adopt a combination of these approaches in rationalizing a particular statutory interpretation. In the *Peterson* case, which follows, the court rejected literal construction on policy grounds.

Courts in the final analysis, therefore, determine what the law is even where a legislature has spoken. This observation is also true of administrative (agency) regulations and even of constitutions. As Justice Charles Evans Hughes once said of the United States Constitution and the Supreme Court, "The Constitution is what the Judges say it is."

Judicial Review. The federal courts have another power, one which does not appear in the Constitution but which was exercised by Chief Justice John Marshall in 1803 in the famous case of *Marbury v. Madison.* It is called the power of judicial review and under it the courts have claimed successfully the right to declare that an act by either of the other two branches of government is unconstitutional and, therefore, unenforceable. The Supreme Court has on a number of occasions declared regulations of the administrative agencies and acts of Congress unconstitutional. It has also held acts of governmental officials unconstitutional, and in a few cases has held an act of the President to be unconstitutional. State laws and actions by state officials may also be found to conflict with the United States Constitution. It is this power of judicial review, now well established and accepted even though not always popular in particular cases, which leads commentators to say that the judiciary is the first among the three equal branches of government. State courts also exercise the power of judicial review.

Limits on Courts. The power of judicial review, however, does not give judges free reign to indulge their biases and predilections. First, judges in all but the court of final resort, state or federal (and it is the United States Supreme Court when a matter of interpretation of the federal Constitution is involved), may be overruled by a higher court upon appeal. Second, there is self-restraint. Judges are expected to base their decisions on precedents under the doctrine of *stare decisis,* thus maintaining continuity and a considerable amount of consistency in "judge-made law." Although a court—even a trial court—may refuse to follow a precedent which seems clearly applicable, this is a very rare occurrence. If it is a trial court, the decision is quite certain to be appealed, and if it is the highest appellate court, it will feel bound to justify its action in terms of new conditions or a previous error. Third, appeal courts generally publish opinions in which they carefully explain the rationale leading to their decision. Fourth, appellate judges sit in groups of from three to nine or more, depending upon the court. Biases are, therefore, likely to be cancelled out to a greater or lesser extent depending upon the similarity of backgrounds of the judges. A fifth restraint is that in many states some or all judges are elected. However, the federal judiciary is appointed for life and in a number of states the judges are appointed, and if they stand for election at all, it is infrequently and the voters can only remove. Under this system, if a judge is defeated a successor is appointed, not elected.

SUMMARY

The courts not only continue to make law as the English courts did by deciding disputes but they determine the meaning of constitutions, statutes, and administrative regulations. They also have the power of judicial review which permits them to declare unconstitutional federal and state statutes, regulations of government agencies and even the acts of governmental officials, including the President. The four principal construction rationales utilized by the courts are: *literal, purposive, precedent based,* and *policy based.* There are a number of restraints on the freedom of judges to decide cases as they might wish, varying for different courts. They include: (1) right of appeal (except in the highest court); (2) tradition and their oath of office; (3) necessity of appeal courts to publish a written opinion; (4) multiple judge courts on appeal; and (5) need to be reelected.

Peterson v. Romero

542 P.2d 434 (Ct. App. N.M. 1975)

An action for damages was brought by Peterson (plaintiff) arising from an automobile collision between Romero, age 18, (defendant) and Peterson. Romero brought Hertz Corporation in as a party co-defendant and sought indemnification from Hertz. Summary judgment for Hertz was appealed by Romero. Affirmed.

Romero sought indemnification from Hertz pursuant to terms of the auto rental contract he had entered into with Hertz despite the fact that the contract expressly provided that only persons 21 years or older were authorized to operate the leased autos. Romero contended that a New Mexico statute which states, "any person who has reached his 18th birthday shall be considered to have reached his majority and is an adult for all purposes the same as if he had reached his 21st birthday," has the effect of altering the contract so as to allow 18 year olds not only to operate Hertz autos; but also to qualify for indemnity under the rental contract provisions protecting those 21 years or older.

SUTIN, JUDGE. The statute is broad when it states that defendant "is an adult for all purposes the same as if he had reached his 21st birthday." What is meant by the phrase "for all purposes"? We believe that the phrase "for all purposes" does not bar the right of parties to a contract to agree that "of full age" may be stipulated to mean 21 years.

The intent of the legislature is clear. Subsection B declared that the purpose of the statute was to substitute the age of 18 for the age of 21 when any prior special law fixed an adult age of 21 years, subject to the specific exception of liquor control.

"For all purposes" means that when a prior special law fixes the age of 21 years, a person of the age of 18 years is an adult, and subject to the provisions of the special law, "for all purposes" of that special law.

We can find no analogical or interpretive basis for the contention that "for all purposes" means that a person 18 years of age is an adult in every phase of law, including the law of contracts and the modification of contracts.

"The phrase 'for any purpose' . . . is not all-encompassing, but is restricted to a reasonable construction by the context of the entire statute and the purposes of the act." *Pacific Insurance Co., Ltd. v. Oregon Auto Ins. Co. (1971).* The Hawaiian Court held that where the interpretation of the phrase "for any purpose" was totally inconsistent with the purposes of the Act as well as unreasonable and absurd, a departure from a literal construction is justified even in the absence of statutory ambiguity.

We hold that a reasonable construction of § 13–13–1 (A) should not lead to the unreasonable and absurd result that the contract language "of full age (21 years)" means "18 years." Romero was not covered by the Hertz rental agreement.

How Judges Find the Law—Judicial Procedures

Trial Judges. The trial judge is bound to apply the law of the jurisdiction, and if there is a jury the judge must instruct it properly as to what the law is. There may be an applicable provision of the state or federal Constitution or a statute which will clearly apply and decide the case once the facts are determined. In such a situation, the attorneys will each argue for (and submit proposed instructions if there is a jury) the interpretation that is most favorable to their particular clients. The judge must then determine, perhaps making an independent study, what he believes to be the correct interpretation and so instruct the jury. If there is no applicable statute or constitutional provision, then the attorneys, and ultimately the judge, must determine the law from earlier decided cases, as described above. Indeed, prior cases decided by appeals courts of the jurisdiction will also be looked to for an authoritative interpretation of a statute or constitution provision.

Appeal Courts. The function of appeal courts is to correct errors of law made by inferior courts and, particularly for the supreme court or whatever the highest court of the jurisdiction is called, to declare authoritatively what the law is. The supreme court has all of the difficulties of interpreting the law that the trial court has, and its role is much more important because it has the final word, subject only to a change by the legislature or overruling by the court in a later case.

Much has been written on how judges, especially appeals court judges, decide cases. Obviously, it is not a mechanical process, and all judges do not approach the task in the same way. Indeed, it can be a highly creative process and much of it is intuitive. Some understanding of the process should be helpful to anyone reading the cases in this text or trying to understand a news account of a recent decision of the U.S. Supreme Court.

Because of the doctrine of *stare decisis*, the first step in deciding a case where there is no applicable statute is to seek prior decisions involving substantially similar facts. Since it is seldom that the facts will be precisely the same, there is room for some discretion and even imagination in selecting the facts of the present case which are fundamental to the decision and thus in determining what kinds of cases offer precedents upon which the judge may rely.

A celebrated example of analogizing from differing fact precedents was Justice Cardozo's opinion in *Buick v. MacPherson.*[2] Buick was sued by a customer who had been injured because of a defective wheel on a new car purchased by the plaintiff through a dealer. The common law precedents at that time did not permit recovery against manufacturers where the injured customers had dealt with the manufacturers through independent dealers. There was, however, an exception rule allowing recovery against manufacturers which distributed poisonous or highly dangerous products through dealers. Cardozo argued persuasively that defectively made automobiles were like poisonous products and recovery should be allowed. His decision was influential in changing the law in the product liability area. Edward H. Levi says, "The problem for the law is: when will it be just to treat different cases as though they were the same?"[3]

The second step is to abstract from these precedents a rule that states the law as it has developed through those cases. Sometimes the cases that might be used as precedent differ not only as to facts but also as to the rules or principles applied. The judge then has a choice among differing fact and differing rule cases for the purpose of deriving the rule to be applied to the current case. The third and final step then is to apply the derived rule.

Judges are required under the doctrine of *stare decisis* to consider precedents within the same jurisdiction, but they may choose to "distinguish" (that is, find they don't apply because the present case differs in some material fact) the case or, in the case of the highest appeals court, even overrule them. They may or may not follow a precedent from another jurisdiction, according to whether the judges find the reasoning in the opinion persuasive.

SUMMARY

The task of the trial judge in applying or instructing the jury as to the law of the jurisdiction is frequently difficult whether one is applying a statutory or constitutional provision or finding precedents among earlier decided cases. Even statutes can be ambiguous and their applicability uncertain.

The same difficulty inheres in the task of the appeals court. There the judges tend to follow a three-step process: (1) select as precedents cases which

---

[2] 111 N.E. 1050 (N.Y. 1916). See Chapter 37 for an extended discussion of product liability.

[3] *An Introduction to Legal Reasoning* (Chicago: University of Chicago Press, 1948), p. 3.

have involved similar facts; (2) determine from them a rule of law which would explain how they were decided; and (3) apply that rule to the present case. The process is not a mechanical one but can involve great creativity on the part of the judge in determining what facts to emphasize in seeking similar cases as precedents.

Federal Court System

Jurisdiction. No court has authority to hear every sort of dispute that might be brought to it. Some are specialized as to subject matter; for example, tax courts only handle taxation cases. Other courts are courts of general jurisdiction and are authorized to try a broad range of cases. Every court serves only some geographic area; citizens of California cannot bring a dispute arising in California to a Nevada court, nor can a dispute involving Canadians arising in Canada be appealed to the United States Supreme Court. Minor state courts may have their authority to hear cases—their jurisdiction—limited to disputes of less than some sum of money, such as $1,000.

Article III of the Constitution establishes the Supreme Court and leaves to Congress the duty of establishing such additional courts as it feels are desirable. Under this article federal courts may hear cases arising under the Constitution, federal statutes and treaties, admiralty cases, controversies to which the United States is a party or between states or between a state and citizens of another state. Also, the federal courts have jurisdiction to hear cases between citizens of different states. Thus, most of the case load of the federal courts falls into two categories of cases: those involving a federal question and those involving diversity of citizenship. Cases involving federal statutes, including crimes defined by federal law, and claiming violation of rights granted by the Constitution are federal questions. Diversity of citizenship exists when one of the parties on one side of the suit is from a different state from any of the parties on the opposing side. For this purpose a corporation is treated as a citizen of the state of its incorporation or of the state in which it has its principal or general office if that is a different state. Congress has restricted the federal courts in civil (noncriminal) cases involving either a federal question or diversity of citizenship to those in which the amount in controversy exceeds $10,000 exclusive of interest and costs.

Federal courts have exclusive jurisdiction over patents, copyrights, bankruptcy, crimes defined by federal law, and a few other matters. They have concurrent jurisdiction with the state courts over the broad area of general civil actions involving diversity of citizenship, that is, a plaintiff can choose either the federal or a state court. If he chooses a state court the defendant may have the case removed to the federal court if the jurisdictional amount ($10,000) is involved.

District Court. With a few exceptions the district court is the court of original jurisdiction in the federal system. It is here that suits are started, and it is here that issues of fact are determined. There is at least one United States District Court for each state and the more populated states have two or more districts. There may be one or more judges assigned to a district depending upon the case load.

Court of Appeals. There are 11 United States Courts of Appeal, one serving the District of Columbia alone because so many cases involving the federal government arise there. Ordinarily appeals from United States District Courts are taken to the court of appeals for the region in which the district court is located. The court of appeals also has jurisdiction to review directly certain orders of administrative agencies such as the Securities and Exchange Commission and the Federal Trade Commission. Courts of appeal hear most cases in panels of three judges but some matters may be heard *en banc,* that is, by all of the judges of that circuit.

The function of a court of appeals is to review the work of the district court. To be granted an appeal, a party who is discontented with the judgment of the trial court, the appellant, must allege that an error of law was made during the course of the trial. Such an error might be an erroneous ruling on a motion or an incorrect statement of the law made in an instruction to the jury. The court of appeals reviews the record of the case, reads the briefs, hears the arguments of the attorneys for the parties to the suit, and decides the issues raised on the appeal. If no material error has been committed, the judgment of the district court will be affirmed. If material error has been committed, the court of appeals may grant a judgment for the appellant, thus disposing of the case; or it may set aside the judgment of the lower court and send the case back for retrial, that is, the case is reversed and remanded. In some instances, the judgment of the lower court may be affirmed in part and reversed in part.

Supreme Court. Whether a case decided by a federal court may be reviewed by the Supreme Court is determined by statute and the Court's own rules. There are two procedures by which review is obtainable—by appeal and by writ of certiorari. The latter is entirely discretionary with the court, and review is granted usually to resolve conflicts between prior decisions of different courts of appeal or in questions of legal importance to the nation. Even where a party is entitled to appeal, the Court may grant a motion to affirm a case coming from a federal court or a motion to dismiss a state court case without a hearing.

Review may be had on appeal from a court of appeals of cases where that court has held a state statute to be unconstitutional or in conflict with laws (or treaties) of the United States. Review of the court of appeals' decision may be had by writ of certiorari in other criminal and civil cases. Also, a court of appeals may certify a case to the Supreme Court when it desires instructions. In such a situation the Court may give instructions or decide the entire case. Where a matter is required to be heard by a three-judge district court, appeal may be taken directly to the Supreme Court. Such courts are required, for example, to hear actions seeking to enjoin enforcement of a federal or state statute on the ground the statute is unconstitutional. The federal government may also request such a court to hear an enforcement action brought under the Sherman Act.

The Supreme Court may also review on appeal a final judgment of the highest court in a state when the state court has decided a case on the ground that a federal statute or treaty is invalid or when the state court has held a state statute valid despite the claim of the losing party that the statute is in conflict with the Constitution or laws of the United States. The Supreme Court may also take cases from the highest state court by writ of certiorari where a right is claimed under the Constitution or where the validity of a federal statute is in question.

Original jurisdiction is given to the Supreme Court in cases affecting ambassadors and consuls of foreign countries and where a state is sued by another state.

Special Courts. The federal court system also includes several special courts. The Court of Claims is established to hear claims against the United States, although district courts may also hear such cases. There is also a Customs Court to hear controversies over the imposition of duties on imported goods and a Court of Customs and Patent Appeals, which hears appeals from the customs courts and appeals from the Patent Office involving patents and trademarks. Bankruptcy proceedings are heard by the district courts.

Administrative Agencies. In addition, there are numerous quasi-judicial bodies within the government agencies. Usually, the governing body of the agency acts as the final point of appeal within the agency. This is true for the Interstate Commerce Commission (ICC), the National Labor Relations Board (NLRB), the Securities and Exchange Commission (SEC), the Federal Trade Commission (FTC), and several others.

SUMMARY

The Constitution establishes and gives specific jurisdiction to the Supreme Court but leaves to Congress the jurisdiction and organization of lower courts. In the federal system the district court is the trial court. A dissatisfied party who claims the trial court made an error of law may take an appeal to the court of appeals, although under certain circumstances appeal may be taken directly to the Supreme Court. The function of an appeals court is to correct errors of law. Cases can go to the Supreme Court either on appeal or a writ of certiorari. Even where a party is entitled to an appeal under the statutes defining the jurisdiction of the Supreme Court, the Court may refuse to grant a hearing and may decide the case on motion. It has full discretion as to whether to grant a writ of certiorari. The Supreme Court is granted original jurisdiction by the Constitution in certain cases, such as suits of one state against another.

State Courts

Jurisdiction. The states have general jurisdiction over controversies arising between the citizens of the state. They have jurisdiction over all controversies involving the title to land, other than federally-owned land, which is within their borders, and they have jurisdiction over all crimes committed within the state, except crimes against the federal government. The various courts of the state system have whatever jurisdiction is conferred on them by the constitution and statutes of the state. The names of the various courts and the way they are organized varies widely between the different states but the following brief description will provide a general understanding of their nature.

Inferior Courts. A very large volume of cases involving minor violations of criminal statutes and civil controversies involving relatively small amounts of money are handled in courts which keep no transcript of the testimony and proceedings, that is, they are not courts of record. Such courts may be called a justice of the peace (j.p.) court in rural areas or municipal court in towns and cities. The judge or judicial officer may not be a trained lawyer. Some cities have a small claims court where the claimant may argue his own case and procedure is informal. If an appeal is taken, there must be a trial *de novo;* that is, since there is no record there will be a new trial in a court of record.

Trial Courts. State courts of record having jurisdiction to hear criminal and civil cases without limit as to penalty or amount of damages are usually called circuit, superior, district or county courts. Their geographic jurisdiction is often a county. In the more populous states, and areas within those states, special courts are often established to handle particular types of cases, such as domestic relations courts, probate courts, and juvenile courts.

State Appeals Courts. In most states there is only one court having general appellate jurisdiction, usually called the supreme court. Some states have two appellate courts. Where there are two courts, the intermediate court is usually called the court of appeals. It may be provided that certain cases can be appealed from the intermediate court to the supreme court and that some types of cases may be appealed to the highest court directly from the trial court. New York's nomenclature is confusing since there the highest court is called the court of appeals and the intermediate court is the supreme court, one division of which also serves as a trial court.

SUMMARY

The court systems of the states vary considerably but include inferior courts such as those of justices of the peace and municipal courts. Trial courts of general jurisdiction are often called circuit or county courts. Some states have two levels of appeals courts, others only one. Where there are two tiers it may be provided that appeals in certain types of cases may be taken directly to the highest court, usually called the supreme court.

Procedure

The Adversary System. Disputes are settled by courts under what is known as the adversary system. In this system the judge's role is viewed not only as unbiased but also as essentially passive.

It is the lawyer's job to present a client's version of the facts, to convince the judge (or jury if one is used) that they are true and to undermine confidence in the other party's allegations to the extent they are inconsistent. The lawyer seeks to persuade the judge that that lawyer's interpretation of the law applicable to the case is the correct one, and proposes jury instructions which state the law in the light most favorable to the client's case. If there is no jury the lawyer seeks to present the judge with a line of reasoning which, if accepted, will result in a decision favoring the lawyer's client. It is believed that this competition between counsel in presenting their competing versions of the facts and conceptions of the law will result in the judge, or jury, sorting out the facts and the judge finding the soundest view of the law. Proponents believe that the principal advantage of the adversary system rests in the fact that it limits the role and power of judges. The facts and issues are developed by the competing parties and the system makes it more difficult for a judge to control the outcome of the case.

However, the judge does not have to be entirely passive. The judge is responsible for the correct application of the law and may ignore the legal reasoning of both of the opposing attorneys and base rulings and decisions wholly on a personal study of the law. Also, the judge may ask questions of witnesses and suggest types of evidence to be presented. In certain types of disputes, especially in domestic relations matters, judges assume much more of the initiative and may even change character completely and engage in attempts at mediation.

The Functions of Procedure. There is a large body of law which establishes the rules and standards for determining disputes in the courts. Much of this law is complex and technical. However, knowledge of some of the basic principles of the law of procedure is necessary if the student is to understand the reports of cases included in this text and for people to be able to cooperate effectively with their lawyers when they become parties to a legal controversy.

The law of procedure varies in different jurisdictions and in different types of cases. For example, the procedure followed in a criminal case is somewhat different from that applicable to a civil case. Equity, probate, and admiralty cases have still different rules. The following discussion pertains to procedure in civil cases such as an action for breach of contract.

Complaint, Summons, and Answer. In general, the first step in a civil law suit occurs when a person claiming legal injury files a complaint in a court of proper jurisdiction. The court then causes the issuance of a summons to the named defendant or defendants. The summons notifies the defendant that suit has been started against him by the named plaintiff. The form of the summons in general use states briefly the nature of the suit and the time within which the defendant must enter an appearance, which can be done through an attorney.

The rules relative to the service of the summons vary widely. At common law and generally in civil law cases the summons is served on the defendant personally by the sheriff or a deputy within the territorial limits of the court's jurisdiction. For instance, a summons issued out of a circuit or district court having jurisdiction over a county would have to be served on the defendant within the boundaries of that county. In some states the summons may be left at the defendant's residence or place of business; and in a few states, service may be made by mail. Other rules relative to service apply in cases such as divorce suits or suits to quiet title to land.

In order that the defendant may know the claims of the plaintiff and be prepared to defend against those claims, the plaintiff is required to file a complaint (also called a declaration or a petition). Under the rules generally in force, the plaintiff's complaint must state in separate, numbered paragraphs the plaintiff's claim in full. Any matter omitted from the complaint is not a part of the plaintiff's case; and evidence, in the case of trial, is not admissible to prove material facts not stated in the complaint. The complaint will also state the remedy requested by the plaintiff. In a civil law case the remedy requested is usually a stated sum of money as damages. It is of the utmost importance that the plaintiff state all the facts of his case to his attorney, since the omission of material facts from the complaint may be fatal to the plaintiff's case.

The defendant who wishes to defend, must, within the permitted time, file an answer, which responds to the plaintiff's complaint paragraph by paragraph. The allegations may be admitted or denied, or the plaintiff may be left to his proof. The defendant may, in addition, state an affirmative defense to the plaintiff's case. For example, suppose the plaintiff bases his suit on a contract. The defendant may admit the contract but set up, by way of affirmative defense, facts which, if established, would prove that the defendant was induced to enter into the contract by fraudulent representations made by the plaintiff. The defendant might also counterclaim for damages based on these allegations of fraud. If the defendant sets up an affirmative defense, he must state facts supporting it. The plaintiff then has a duty to make an answer (called a reply).

The complaint and answer (called "pleadings") serve a twofold purpose: they inform the parties of their relative claims, fulfilling the constitutional requirement of "notice," and they form the basis for the trial of the case. Only those points which are matters in dispute or issues in the case will be considered on the trial of the case. Points which are not stated in the pleadings and points admitted in the pleadings are not issues in the case, and no evidence will be admitted to prove such points. If a material point has been omitted from the pleadings, the trial judge may, after proper motion has been made, permit an amendment of the pleadings and allow the omitted matter to be added.

Discovery and Pretrial Hearing. The trend in legal procedure has been away from legal technicalities toward simplification, greater flexibility, and emphasis upon the merits of the case. One important development with this purpose is "discovery procedure." In civil cases (suits between private parties) rules of procedure adopted by the federal courts and by many of the states in the last few decades give the parties access to the facts upon which the other party relies. This permits a lawyer, in the presence of the opposing lawyer, to interrogate the other party's witnesses under oath prior to trial and to obtain copies of pertinent documents and other data. In an injury case the defendant would be permitted to choose a physician to examine the plaintiff and to have copies of such potentially pertinent evidence as X-rays and photographs. The pretrial interrogations, called depositions, may be used to impeach the testimony of the witness at the trial, if there should be discrepancies. Either party may make use of depositions to bring into the trial testimony from a person who cannot be present in person.

Another recent procedural device of great importance is the pretrial conference during which the opposing attorneys are required to sit down with the judge to try to get agreement, a "stipulation," on as many of the pertinent facts as possible so that the time required to establish legal proof of them through witnesses in court may be eliminated. Also, the judge will encourage the parties to try to settle the case by coming to an agreement disposing of the dispute so that it need not go to trial. Both efforts are directed at clearing the increasingly congested calendars of most courts so as to shorten the time between the filing of the pleadings (the complaint and answer) of the parties and the conclusion of the trial. Simplification of pleading procedure serves the same purpose as well as putting more emphasis on merit than form.

Trial of Case. When the pleadings are complete and the issues determined, the case will be set for trial. The parties will decide whether or not they wish a trial by jury. If a jury is desired, it must then be selected and sworn in, after which the attorneys will usually make statements to it, outlining the claims their clients make in regard to the controversy. The witnesses for the plaintiff will then be sworn, examined, and cross-examined. When all the evidence of the plaintiff has been presented, plaintiff's attorney will so indicate, and the attorney for the defendant will take charge.

At this point the defendant's attorney may make a motion asking the judge to direct a judgment for the defendant. If the judge decides that the plaintiff has offered no evidence that would justify the granting of the remedy requested, the motion will be granted and the trial will end at this point. However, if the judge believes that the plaintiff has offered any evidence that would support a judgment, the motion will be denied, and the trial will continue.

The defendant's witnesses will then be sworn and examined on direct examination by the defendant's attorney and cross-examined by the plaintiff's attorney. When all the testimony of the witnesses has been heard, the case is ready to be presented to the jury. At this point in the trial, either the defendant's attorney or the plaintiff's attorney, or both, may make a motion for a directed verdict. If both attorneys make motions for a directed verdict, the case will not, under the rules of procedure generally followed, be presented to the jury but will be decided by the judge. If only one motion for a directed verdict is made, the judge will deny the motion unless he feels that no credible evidence has been offered which would justify the jury in finding for the other party. If no motion for a directed verdict is made, or if such motion is made and denied, the case will be presented to the jury for its consideration.

The attorneys will sum up the case and give their arguments to the jury, and the judge will instruct the jury as to the law which applies in the case. In the instructions the judge must not, under the laws of most states, comment on the weight of the evidence or credibility of the witnesses, but must confine instructions to expounding the rules of law which the jury should apply in reaching its verdict.

Where the amount of the plaintiff's loss is in dispute, the jury not only finds for one of the parties but if it finds for the plaintiff, its verdict will state the amount of the recovery. The attorney for the losing party may make a motion for a judgment notwithstanding the verdict. If the judge finds no competent evidence to support the verdict, or decides that the law requires the opposite result, the motion will be granted; otherwise it will be denied.

If the verdict is not set aside, the judge will enter a judgment based on the verdict. The defeated party may make a motion for a new trial. This gives the trial judge an opportunity to correct material errors which may have been made during the trial; however, such motions are usually denied. If the unsuccessful party thinks a material error was committed during the trial, that party may appeal the case.

If there is no jury, the judge is the finder of facts. Upon appeal those findings of fact, as in the case of those of a jury, are accepted as correct unless the appeal court finds no competent evidence supporting a finding of fact.

Procedure in Administrative Agencies. The procedure followed in administrative agencies is more informal than that followed in the courts. In general, the staff or field investigators employed by the agency investigate suspected and reported violations of the regulatory law over which the agency has jurisdiction. If, after reading the report of the field investigations, the members of the agency decide that there has been a violation, a hearing is held before the members of the agency. The agency will impose sanctions if the accused is found guilty. The accused does have the right to appeal to the courts; but under the terms of the act creating the agency, this right is usually limited. In general, no appeal is allowed if the decision involves only the discretionary powers of the persons rendering the decision. However, the court will, as a general rule, hear and determine an appeal if it is based on the ground that the person making the decision acted capriciously or was guilty of discrimination, or that the subject matter of the case was not within the scope of the powers vested in the agency.

Class Actions. When a number of people have a right or claim against the same defendants growing out of the same or substantially the same event or transaction, courts have long permitted some of them to maintain an action for the benefit of all. An example might be a preferred shareholder bringing an action in behalf of all holders of that security seeking the payment of a dividend. The number of class actions by shareholders (as well as consumers, environmentalists, and others) has greatly increased since Rule 23 of the Federal Rules of Civil Procedure was amended in 1966 and many states relaxed their requirements for class actions.

Rule 23 requires: (1) that there be questions of law and fact which are common to all members of the class, (2) that the class be so large that it be impracticable to force them to join as parties, (3) that the claims of the representatives of the class be typical of the class, and (4) that the plaintiff(s) must fairly and adequately represent the class (for example, must have suffered the wrong complained of, have no interests adverse to the class, and have competent counsel).

Any recovery in a class action is distributed to members of the entire class, according to such rules and procedures as may be established by the court. The Supreme Court has made it more difficult for class actions to be brought by interpreting Rule 23 so as to require that the class action plaintiff give actual notice of suit to all members of the represented class where such members can be "identified through reasonable efforts."

SUMMARY

American courts operate under what is known as the adversary system. The determination of liability (or guilt or innocence in criminal cases) is made through a contest in which the attorney for each party tries to persuade the jury (or judge if he is the trier of fact) what are the true facts and the judge what the appropriate rules of law are. The law of procedure provides a complex body of rules by which this contest is conducted.

In a noncriminal case the suit begins with the serving of a summons on the defendant which requires him to appear in court on or before a certain time. A complaint stating the plaintiff's claim must also be given to the defendant who must serve an "answer" on the plaintiff. The purpose of these documents, called the pleadings, is to inform the parties of the relative claims and the trial is limited to those claims.

Class actions provide a procedure for consolidating many similarly based actions into one suit enabling a small group of plaintiffs to represent a larger group.

Arbitration and Other Dispute Settlement Methods

Arbitration. Arbitration is a method of settling disputes which is available as an alternative to the court system. The parties to the dispute select a person or persons who may or may not have been trained in the law, to hear and determine the dispute. Most disputes arising under labor contracts, many involving exports and imports, and a small proportion of other commercial contracts are resolved by arbitration.

Frequently, the parties have agreed as part of the contract into which they have entered to submit any dispute arising out of the contract to arbitration. Procedure in arbitration is usually more informal than in a court and technical rules of evidence are not applied. However, frequently the arbitrator will render a written award.

The principal advantages claimed for arbitration are: (1) disposition of the dispute is usually much quicker—perhaps days instead of months or even years; (2) an arbitrator may be chosen who has considerable familiarity with the technical background of the dispute; (3) since procedure tends to be informal the parties need not employ lawyers to represent them (although they frequently do); and (4) the time required of executives to be witnesses and other costs are likely to be much less than in a trial.

Other methods. The rapidly increasing case load of the courts has given rise to proposals to remove whole classes of disputes from the courts. A number of people, including Chief Justice Burger,[4] have proposed using an administrative process such as is used under workmen's compensation statutes for compensating those injured in automobile accidents and other cases involving negligence. Some suggest that cases involving professional malpractice and product liability claims, where presently insurance costs are skyrocketing, should also be handled outside of the court system. Critics of the tort system point out that although a few of the injured get very large judgments or settlements, determination is long delayed and many claimants get nothing or very little. Basically, critics argue that the costs of settling disputes utilizing existing procedures and institutions are too high and that better alternatives are available.

Questions and Problem Case

1. To what extent does the doctrine of *stare decisis* make the decision in a lawsuit predictable?
2. Which of the four principal construction approaches were adopted by the court in the *Peterson* case?
3. Discuss some of the advantages and disadvantages of the adversary system.
4. Some legal scholars' opinions are that procedure is at the heart of law. What are some of the important functions of legal procedure?
5. Eisen claimed that on a purchase and sale of odd lot shares on the New York Stock Exchange, he was illegally overcharged 5 percent. It appears that there are over 6 million people who were likewise overcharged; 2.5 million can be easily identified. Eisen wants to file a class action, but is fearful that pursuant to Rule 23, he would have to give individual notice to 2.5 million people. The cost of such notice would be prohibitive. Must Eisen provide actual notice to each of the 2.5 million potential claimants?

---

[4] "The Direction of the Administration of Justice," 62 *Am. Bar Ass'n J.* (1976), p. 727.

PART II

Crimes and Torts

3

Crimes

Crimes

Introduction. The criminal law area includes not only law designed to punish conduct harmful to the interests of society; but also, law designed to give maximum protection to the innocent. In order for a crime to be committed there must be a preexisting law which defines the prohibited conduct in terms which a reasonable person can understand. Various parts of criminal law apply to the detection, apprehension, prosecution, and subsequent punishment of criminal law offenders.

Nature of Crime. A crime may be defined to be any act done by an individual which is considered a wrong by society and for the commission of which the law has provided that the wrongdoer shall make satisfaction to the public. The term *wrong* as used in its popular sense includes violation of moral or ethical standards, failure to perform social duties imposed by the group of which the individual is a member, and many other acts. However, under the legal definition of crime, such conduct is not necessarily classed as criminal. It is not criminal unless it is condemned by law and unless the wrongdoer is subject to punishment imposed by the state, in which case the state will bring an action in its own name against the wrongdoer. One of the difficult problems confronting society is where to draw the line between that conduct which is so socially undesirable that it should be punished as criminal and that conduct which should be merely treated as a breach of a social duty with only civil liability, or perhaps with no legal liability at all being imposed. Which conduct will be held to be criminal and punishable as such will depend on the values and attitudes of the particular society at a given time.

The fact that the definition of criminal conduct changes over time should not be taken to preclude the existence of a large degree of historical continuity in the criminal law area. Almost all societies have considered treason, murder, theft, and certain sex offenses as crimes; however, the nature and severity of the penalty imposed for the commission of these crimes has varied from country to country and from time to time. At one time in England, and in some countries today, any expression of disagreement with the policies of the rulers of the country was treason; and in England prior to the reform of the criminal law, the death penalty was imposed as punishment for substantially all crimes. During the early colonial period here in America, blasphemy and witchcraft were punished as crimes.

In the common law serious crimes involving moral turpitude, such as arson, rape, and murder, were classed as felonies. Today the term *felony* has no definite meaning except where it has been defined by statute. Generally, however, felonies are punishable by confinement in penitentiaries for substantial periods of time. Misdemeanors are lesser crimes, such as traffic offenses, breaches of the peace, and petty larceny; these generally are punishable by fines or by limited periods of confinement in city or county jails.

Procedure in Criminal Cases. In the United States, criminal law is recognized as a separate division of the law. The rules of procedure followed in the trial of criminal cases differ in important respects from those followed in the trial of civil cases. For example, in criminal cases the accused is presumed to be innocent, and guilt must be proven by the state beyond a reasonable doubt.

This presumption of innocence and other principles of our criminal law are grounded on the belief that our criminal law system should function so as to give maximum protection to the rights of innocent people charged with crimes even if this results in fewer guilty people being apprehended and punished.

If the verdict of the jury in a criminal case is "not guilty," the state cannot obtain a reversal by appeal, but the accused can always appeal as a matter of right. All criminal cases are brought in the name of the state, as, for instance, *State v. John Brown,* or *United States v. John Brown* in the event the crime is punishable by the federal government.

Scope of Criminal Law. It is the function of the legislature to define the criminal act and to state the punishment to be imposed on those guilty of the commission of such act. It is the function of the court to determine whether or not the accused is guilty and, if so, to impose the penalty set out in the criminal statute. In performing this function, the court must interpret the criminal statute, determine its scope, and decide whether or not the crime of which the party is accused comes within the provisions of the statute. It is the function of the prosecutor to investigate the case, prepare the indictment, and present the facts to the court.

Essentials of a Crime. At common law, two elements were considered essential to criminal liability: the criminal act accompanied by criminal intent (*mens rea*). Today, as a general rule, those acts which are declared to be crimes will be defined by the criminal statutes. Establishing the fact that a criminal act has been committed is, in most criminal cases, a relatively simple matter. Also, the identity of the person or persons who are guilty of performing the criminal act may be established with a reasonable degree of certainty by direct evidence. However, the accompanying criminal intent cannot be established by direct evidence. Intent is a state of mind.

Intent is established through the use of legal standards, and the standard applied is that of the "ordinary man." That is, what would one be justified in assuming that an ordinary man would have intended if he had been in the position of the accused and had acted as the accused did? If one voluntarily does a criminal act, he will be held to have intended the natural and probable consequences of his act.

Capacity to Commit a Crime. With the exception of certain exempt classes, all persons are held to be responsible for their criminal conduct. In general, minors and persons who are insane or intoxicated are not held to be criminally liable, because they do not have mental capacity to entertain the criminal intent which is an essential element of crime. However, self-induced intoxication offers only limited protection against punishment.

In regard to minors the common law concept of a minor's liability for crime has been replaced by a new theory. The age at which a person is considered a minor under the criminal law is, in many states, 16 or 17 years. Juvenile courts have been established in almost every state, new administrative procedures have been set up, and new methods of dealing with juveniles have been adopted. The prevailing philosophy is that a minor is not a criminal and that it is the duty of society to guide an erring minor and to help the minor develop into a desirable citizen.

There are many stages of insanity. The generally accepted rule is that if the person committing the criminal act was, at the time the act was committed, incapable of distinguishing right from wrong or, incapable of understanding the nature and consequences of one's act, one cannot be held criminally liable for one's conduct. In some states the courts have held that if the criminal act was done under an irresistible impulse, the person committing the act will not be criminally liable. If the accused, after the commission of the criminal act, becomes insane and, as a result of this insanity, is incapable of aiding in the conduct of his or her defense, the prosecution will be postponed or dismissed. A person who becomes insane after conviction but before sentence will not be sentenced until sanity has been regained. As a general rule, the insane person who has committed a crime will be confined in a mental hospital.

Business Crimes

Corporate Crimes. Although corporate officials and employees are subject to criminal law as "natural" persons, corporations are "artificial" persons created by law and cannot harbor the criminal intent required for conviction of many crimes. Corporations are subject to fines and the modern trend is to make corporations subject to more and heavier criminal penalties for specifically prohibited conduct. In extreme situations they may have their charters revoked.

In 1910, Woodrow Wilson noted some of the public policy difficulties that are still being debated in this area when he said:

> You cannot punish corporations. Fines fall upon the wrong persons; more heavily upon the innocent than upon the guilty; as much upon those who knew nothing whatever of the transactions for which the fine is imposed as upon those who originated and carried them through—upon the stockholders and customers rather than upon the men who direct the policy of the business. If you dissolve the offending corporation, you throw great undertakings out of gear.[1]

It is estimated that so-called "white-collar" crimes now cost the public in excess of $40 billion annually.[2] The term "white-collar" usually refers to the respected status of the culprit in the community. The Department of Justice defines this type of crime by its typical characteristics as being nonviolent, involving deceit, corruption, or breach of trust.[3] Despite the huge losses suffered by innocent victims, business, and the public at large, the penalties imposed on white-collar criminals traditionally have been significantly less severe than have been the penalties for other types of crimes. Furthermore, many of the crimes in this area go undetected or unreported because white-collar crime is much less visible.

Fraudulent Acts. Many of the crimes related to business transactions entail some fraudulent conduct. In some states, it is a crime for an officer of a bank knowingly to overdraw one's own account with the bank without the written consent of the board of directors; and in some states, it is a crime for a banker or broker to receive deposits while insolvent. In substantially all states, it is a crime to obtain property by fraudulent pretenses, to issue fraudulent checks, to make false credit statements, to make false statements in advertisements, and to convey property for the purpose of defrauding one's

---

[1] For an extended treatment of the difficulties in holding corporations legally accountable along with suggested remedial laws see Christopher D. Stone, *Where the Law Ends* (New York: Harper and Row, Pub., 1976). For discussion of the criminal liability of corporations and corporate officers see Chapter 27.

[2] "White-Collar Justice" (759 *ATRR Spec. Rep., Part II,* April 13, 1976), p. 2.

[3] Mark J. Green focuses on corporate crimes as the "least excusable" type of "white-collar" crimes. He defines four distinct subcategories of corporate crime: commercial bribery, antitrust crimes, product and health crimes (knowingly selling dangerous products or polluting), and financial crimes. *Ibid.,* p. 2.

creditors. The giving of short weights or measures is generally declared to be a criminal act.

Forgery. The crime of forgery pertains to the making of false writings. In general, the definition of the crime is sufficiently broad to include the false and fraudulent making or alteration of any writing which, if genuine, would, or on its face might, have some legal effect upon the rights of others. Forgery is usually thought of as the signing of another's name to negotiable instruments, but the crime is much broader than this. It includes counterfeiting, changing trademarks, falsifying public records, and altering wills, deeds, leases, or any other legal document. In fact, it includes all falsification of or tampering with any document of any kind or nature which is of legal significance.

Criminal Law and the Fourth and Fifth Amendments. The Fourth Amendment provides:

> The right of the people to be secure in their persons, houses, papers, and effects, against unreasonable searches and seizures, shall not be violated, and no Warrants shall issue, but upon probable cause, supported by Oath or affirmation, and particularly describing the place to be searched, and the persons or things to be seized.

The Fourth Amendment protects individuals from unreasonable searches and seizures. The basic purpose is to protect a person's right of privacy from overzealous intrusion by governmental investigatory activities. In general, evidence obtained in violation of Fourth Amendment rights cannot be introduced as evidence in a criminal case against the person whose rights were violated.[4] Search warrants, if properly drawn and utilized, may legalize or justify governmental intrusions of various types depending on the nature of the intrusion, the wording of the warrant, and the presence of probable cause to justify issuance of the warrant.

There may be valid searches and seizures of evidence made without warrants as an incident to a lawful arrest, or where the person affected has voluntarily given his or her consent.[5] As a general rule, however, a search of a person or property without either consent or a properly drawn and issued warrant is "unreasonable" under the Fourth Amendment. For example, the search of locked luggage without either the consent of the owner or a warrant is an unreasonable search.

The Fifth Amendment provides:

> No person shall be held to answer for a capital, or otherwise infamous crime, unless on a presentment or indictment of a Grand Jury, except in cases arising in the land or naval forces, or in the Militia, when in actual service in time of War or public danger; nor shall any

---

[4] This is known as the "exclusionary evidence" rule.

[5] The protection these amendments provide against unreasonable governmental intrusions in regard to business and private papers is discussed at the end of this chapter. An extended discussion of the important constitutional law concepts and principles relating to the regulation of business is found in Chapter 48.

person be subject for the same offense to be twice put in jeopardy of life or limb; nor shall be compelled in any criminal case to be a witness against himself, nor be deprived of life, liberty, or property, without due process of law; . . . .

Indictment by grand jury is required as a preliminary step designed to reduce the possibility that innocent persons may be brought to trial for serious federal crimes. Grand jury indictment is not generally required before trial of crimes under state law.

The protection against double jeopardy means that no person, natural or artificial, can be tried for the same crime by the same jurisdiction more than once. If a person kidnaps a child, takes the child across a state line, and then murders the child at least four separate crimes would be involved. Kidnapping laws would be violated in both states, murder laws in one state, and the federal criminal code (Lindberg Act) would be violated. The defendant could be tried for all of these separate crimes arising out of the same activities without any double jeopardy rights being infringed.

Due Process clauses protect persons, both natural and artificial, from the laws and acts of public officials, both state and federal, which are essentially arbitrary. Due Process requires that criminal statutes define the prohibited conduct with a reasonable degree of clarity so that a person of ordinary intelligence would have fair notice. The application of the Due Process clause to the regulation of business is discussed in detail in Chapter 48.

The privilege against self-incrimination found in the Fifth Amendment applies to both federal and state proceedings because the Court has held that its protections are incorporated into the Fourteenth Amendment via the Due Process Clause. A witness in any civil or criminal federal or state proceeding can assert the privilege and remain silent. This is true even where such person is not a party to the action.

The accused can be compelled to give nontestimonial evidence such as fingerprints, urine, or voice samples; but involuntary evidence obtained by a stomach pump was held to exceed the bounds of propriety and could not be used against the defendant. A witness who is granted immunity against prosecution can be compelled to testify.

Decisions Protecting the Accused. Justice Holmes expressed a basic philosophy of the American criminal law system when he said: ". . . and for my part I think it less evil that some criminals should escape than that the government should play an ignoble part." In a series of landmark decisions after World War II, the U.S. Supreme Court clarified and expanded the constitutional guarantees of people accused of crimes.

Some of these decisions established the following principles.

1. A suspect charged with a federal crime must be taken before a magistrate without "unnecessary delay" or any confession obtained will not be admissible.

2. Illegally obtained evidence may not be admitted in either federal or state courts.
3. Any indigent person charged with a crime the punishment for which may involve a prison sentence has a right to be represented by court appointed counsel.
4. The Fifth Amendment protection against self-incrimination applies to both state and federal criminal proceedings.
5. When police questioning begins to focus on the accused for accusatory rather than for investigative purposes, the accused must be permitted to consult with counsel.
6. The police must advise the accused of his right to remain silent and his right to counsel prior to any questioning. This is designated as giving a "Miranda" warning.
7. An indigent defendant cannot be confined beyond the maximum sentence specified by statute because of inability to pay the monetary portion of the sentence.
8. Capital punishment statutes which permit room for caprice, whim, and discrimination are unconstitutional as representing cruel and unusual punishment prohibited under the Eighth Amendment.
9. A state prison regulation which permits indigent prisoners to have only a very limited access to law books was found to be unconstitutional on the ground that it denied such prisoners reasonable access to the courts.[6]

Possibly reflecting growing national concern over the crime rate, it appears that the Burger Court may be redefining or at least reexamining some of the rights claimed by persons charged with or convicted of crimes. For example, the Court has:

1. Expanded the circumstances under which an officer could legally make a search as an incident to an arrest.
2. Narrowed the application of the exclusionary evidence rule by permitting the use of evidence illegally obtained for purposes of impeaching testimony.
3. Limited the rights of prisoners in regard to hearings taking away "good-time" credit or imposing solitary confinement.
4. Narrowed the requirement for a *Miranda* warning by admitting evidence taken during a pre-Miranda interrogation.

---

[6] These principles were established in the following cases: *Mallory v. United States,* 354 U.S. 449 (1948); *Mapp v. Ohio,* 367 U.S. 643 (1961); *Gideon v. Wainwright,* 372 U.S. 335 (1963); *Malloy v. Hogan,* 378 U.S. 1 (1964); *Escobedo v. Illinois,* 378 U.S. 478 (1964); *Miranda v. Arizona,* 384 U.S. 436 (1966); *Williams v. Illinois,* 399 U.S. 235 (1970); *Furman v. Georgia,* 408 U.S. 238 (1972); and *Younger v. Gilmore,* 404 U.S. 15 (1971).

5. Ruled that the state does not have to provide indigents counsel for discretionary appeals to state or federal courts, and otherwise narrowed the circumstances under which the state must provide legal counsel.[7]

In addition to defining rights for those accused of crimes, the Supreme Court in recent years has declared unconstitutional many long-standing criminal statutes. Examples include various vagrancy, obscenity, and anti-demonstration statutes stricken for vagueness, or overbreadth on due process and/or First Amendment grounds; and abortion statutes stricken as being violative of due process.[8]

SUMMARY

A crime is a wrong forbidden by law which is subject to punishment by the state and which the state prosecutes in its own name. Not all wrongs are punishable as crimes. What conduct will be held to be criminal and punishable will depend on the attitude of society at a given time. Many acts are declared to be criminal today which were unknown or were not so declared 50 or 75 years ago.

With the exception of certain exempt classes, all persons are held responsible for their criminal conduct. Infants, insane persons, and others who do not have the mental capacity to entertain a criminal intent cannot be held criminally liable.

The long term trend has been to broaden the rights of those accused of crimes. Recent decisions, however, suggest that the current Court may be somewhat more concerned with the effective enforcement of criminal law and perhaps less in sympathy with the rights of those accused or convicted of crimes.

City of Columbus v. Rogers

324 N.E.2d 563 (Sup. Ct. Ohio 1975)

Rogers (defendant) was arrested and convicted for violating a Columbus, Ohio, ordinance prohibiting the public appearance of any person "in a dress not belonging to his or her sex, or in an indecent or lewd dress." Rogers

---

[7] These principles were established in the following cases: *U.S. v. Robinson,* 414 U.S. 218 (1973); *Gustafson v. Florida,* 414 U.S. 260 (1973); *U.S. v. Calandra,* 414 U.S. 338 (1974); *Wolff v. McDonnell,* 418 U.S. 539 (1974); *Michigan v. Tucker,* 417 U.S. 433 (1974); *Ross v. Moffitt,* 417 U.S. 600 (1974); and *United States v. MacCollom* 426 U.S. 317 (1976).

[8] The *Rogers* case in the text is an example of the former group while *Roe v. Wade,* 410 U.S. 113 (1973) is an abortion decision.

appealed challenging the ordinance on the ground that it was unconstitutionally vague under the Due Process Clause. Reversed.

O'NEILL, CHIEF JUSTICE. Section 2343.04 of the Columbus City Codes reads:

"No person shall appear upon any public street or other public place in a state of nudity or in a dress not belonging to his or her sex, or in an indecent or lewd dress."

In holding a Cincinnati ordinance prohibiting prowling unconstitutional in *Cincinnati v. Taylor* (1973), it was said:

> Section 910–P10 is unconstitutionally void for vagueness, because it does not provide adequate standards by which activity can be determined as legal or illegal.
>
> The standard is inadequate ". . . to give a person of ordinary intelligence fair notice that his contemplated conduct is forbidden by the statute. The underlying principle is that no man shall be held criminally responsible for conduct which he could not reasonably understand to be proscribed."
>
> The ordinance is also inadequate in providing guidelines for law enforcement officials charged with its enforcement. Such boundless discretion granted by the ordinance encourages arbitrary and capricious enforcement of the law. . . .

Modes of dress for both men and women are historically subject to changes in fashion. At the present time, clothing is sold for both sexes which is so similar in appearance that "a person of ordinary intelligence" might not be able to identify it as male or female dress. In addition, it is not uncommon today for individuals to purposely, but innocently, wear apparel which is intended for wear by those of the opposite sex.

Once it is recognized that present-day dress may not be capable of being characterized as being intended for male or female wear by a "person of ordinary intelligence," the constitutional defect in the ordinance becomes apparent.

The Fourth and Fifth Amendments and Business Papers. In 1886 the Supreme Court noted the interrelationship between the Fourth and Fifth Amendments in regard to business papers saying:

> We have already noticed the intimate relation between the two amendments. They throw great light on each other. For the "unreasonable searches and seizures" condemned in the Fourth Amendment are almost always made for the purpose of compelling a man to give evidence against himself, which in criminal cases is condemned in the Fifth Amendment; and compelling a man "in a criminal case to be a witness against himself," which is condemned in the Fifth Amendment, throws light on the question as to what is an "unreasonable search and seizure" within the meaning of the Fourth Amendment. And we have been unable to perceive that the seizure of a man's private books and papers to be used in evidence against him is substantially different from compelling him to be a witness against himself.[9]

---

[9] *Boyd v. U.S.*, 116 U.S. 616 (1886).

A few years later (1911) the Court ruled that corporate records were not protected by the Fifth Amendment. In 1921, the Court made another exception to the *Boyd* ruling in regards to documents which were being used in carrying out crimes. The government was said to share a property interest in such "instrumentality of crime" papers that was greater than the defendant's right of privacy.[10] Later cases narrowed the protection of private papers still further by narrowly defining private papers to include only those papers in which the defendant has a "reasonable expectation" of privacy.[11] Business records usually are viewed as "transactional" not personal and, hence, are not subject to protection under this "expectation" test. The protection clearly does not apply to records required by law which are to be prepared for inspection by an outsider such as the government.

Personal diaries and letters retained in the possession of the defendant appear to be about the only types of documents now subject to constitutional protection. This protection continues even if the defendant turns such papers over to an attorney after being charged with a crime. The case which follows illustrates an area of protection afforded to business papers where such papers were not seized as "instrumentalities of crime" and where no proper warrant had been issued.

G.M. Leasing Corp. v. United States

429 U.S. 338 (U.S. Sup. Ct. 1977)

The IRS (defendant) levied assessments on G.M. Leasing Corp. (plaintiff) for nonpayment of taxes and seized certain automobiles parked in front of the building out of which G.M. operated. In addition, the IRS made a warrantless forced entry into the building and seized certain books and records. G.M. then sued the IRS seeking return of the automobiles, and suppression of the evidence obtained on the ground that the IRS activities violated G.M.'s Fourth Amendment rights. The Court of Appeals ruled in favor of IRS on all counts. Affirmed in part and reversed in part.

MR. JUSTICE BLACKMUN. The seizures of the automobiles in this case took place on public streets, parking lots, or other open places, and did not involve any invasion of privacy. In *Murray's Lessee v. Hoboken Land & Improv. Co.,* (1856), this Court held that a judicial warrant is not required for the seizure of a debtor's land in satisfaction of a claim of the United States.

---

[10] *Gouled v. U.S.,* 235 U.S. 292 (1921).

[11] "Note, Papers, Privacy, and the Fourth and Fifth Amendments: A Constitutional Analysis," 69 *N.W.L. Rev.* 626 (1974). In *Andreson v. Maryland,* 427 U.S. 463 (1976), the Court held that certain drafts and memoranda the defendant had made in his own handwriting and kept in his possessions were subject to discovery by search warrant.

The seizure in *Murray's Lessee* was made through a transfer of title which did not involve an invasion of privacy. The warrantless seizures of the automobiles in this case are governed by the same principles and therefore were not unconstitutional.

The seizure of the books and records, however, involved intrusion into the privacy of G.M.'s offices. Significantly, the Court has said:

> [O]ne governing principle, justified by history and by current experience, has consistently been followed: except in certain carefully defined classes of cases, a search of private property without proper consent is 'unreasonable' unless it has been authorized by a valid search warrant.

The IRS does not contend that business premises are not protected by the Fourth Amendment. Such a proposition could not be defended in light of this Court's clear holdings to the contrary. Nor can it be claimed that corporations are without some Fourth Amendment rights.

The Court, of course, has recognized that a business, by its special nature and voluntary existence, may open itself to intrusions that would not be permissible in a purely private context. Thus, in *United States v. Biswell,* (1972), a warrantless search of a locked storeroom during business hours, pursuant to the inspection procedure authorized by the Gun Control Act of 1968, 18 U.S.C. § 923(g), was upheld:

> When a dealer chooses to engage in this pervasively regulated business and to accept a federal license, he does so with the knowledge that his business records, firearms, and ammunition will be subject to effective inspection.

In the present case, however, the intrusion into plaintiff's privacy was not based on the nature of its business, its license, or any regulation of its activities. Rather, the intrusion is claimed to be justified on the ground that G.M.'s assets were seizable to satisfy tax assessments. This involves nothing more than the normal enforcement of the tax laws, and we find no justification for treating G.M. differently in these circumstances simply because it is a corporation.

It is one thing to seize without a warrant property resting in an open area or seizable by levy without an intrusion into privacy, and it is quite another thing to effect a warrantless seizure of property, even that owned by a corporation, situated on private premises to which access is not otherwise available for the seizing officer.

Problem Cases

1. The defendant students engaged in a demonstration and were convicted under a Cincinnati ordinance which made it a criminal offense for "three or more persons to assemble . . . on any sidewalks . . . and there conduct themselves in a manner annoying to persons passing by. . . ." The defendants appealed contending that the ordinance was unconstitutionally vague and overly broad under the Due Process Clause. Are the defendants correct?

2. Kim, suspected of engaging in gambling operations, was observed by federal agents while in the privacy of his own apartment making numerous phone calls and reading the "J. K. Sports Journal," allegedly used in the gambling operation. The observations of the agents were made from a quarter of a mile away, with the aid of an 800 millimeter telescope. No unaided surveillance method was possible under the circumstances. No warrant had been obtained for this method of surveillance. Were Kim's Fourth Amendment rights violated?
3. Schmerber was arrested while driving under the influence of alcohol. At the time of his arrest, the officer directed that a blood sample be taken to ascertain alcohol content. The test was performed over Schmerber's objections; the analysis indicated intoxication. Schmerber was eventually convicted on the basis of this evidence. Schmerber contends that the blood test was inadmissible because it violated his Fifth Amendment priviledge against self-incrimination. Is the analysis of the blood sample admissible?
4. Marchetti engaged in the gambling business. He was arrested and convicted for violating a federal statute that required him to register with the IRS, stating the nature of his gambling business, and the names and addresses of his agents and employees. The statute also required Marchetti to keep a daily record of gambling receipts and to pay a tax on the proceeds. The information that was to be filed in the registration statement was widely available to both federal and state law enforcement agencies. The applicable state law made any gambling illegal. Marchetti claims that the federal obligation to register violated his constitution right against self-incrimination. Does Marchetti have a valid defense?
5. Beattie turned some business papers over to his accountant but later recovered them when he learned that he was being investigated by the IRS. The IRS subpoenaed the papers but Beattie refused to turn them over claiming rights against self-incrimination under the Fifth Amendment. Will Beattie prevail?
6. Couch was proprietress of her own business and delivered daily account records to her accountant. These records were used to prepare cumulative records and tax returns. IRS subpoenaed the accountant who then turned the papers over to Couch's attorney. IRS brought suit to get the papers and Couch raised the Fifth Amendment protection against self-incrimination as a defense. Is this a good defense?

4

Intentional Torts

Introduction

Nature of Torts. The basis of a person's liability in tort is breach of a duty owed to another member of society. In the development of the law of torts the courts at first recognized the duty of a person to refrain from an intentional aggression on another. At a somewhat later time, they began to recognize the duty of a person when engaged in a course of conduct to act with due care with respect to consequences which might reasonably be anticipated. As society became increasingly industrialized and urbanized, personal contacts, and interdependencies increased, and the duties owed by members of society increased accordingly.

For the most part the law of torts is based on concepts of legal standards of conduct. Each member in society is under a legal duty, in daily activities, to follow a course of conduct which does not fall below the social standards recognized in the community. If a person, without any legal defense or justification, harms or interferes with the legally recognized interests of others as a result of conduct falling below recognized social standards, such person will be held liable. The interests protected from unjustifiable interference include those related to physical integrity, freedom of movement, peace of mind, privacy, freedom of thought and action, and the acquisition and use of property and services essential to material well-being.

The protection of these and other interests inevitably involves a balancing process for public policy and the law. If the law protects physical integrity to an extreme, societal interests in freedom of movement may be unduly burdened with legal risks. If the law protects peace of mind, privacy, and interests in a good reputation to an extreme, freedom of speech and freedom of press might be unduly restrained.[1]

A leading authority on tort law lists the following factors as worthy of special mention in determining whether or not given conduct causing harm to others may result in liability under tort law: (1) the moral aspect of the defendant's conduct; (2) the convenience of administration if liability is attached; (3) the defendant's capacity to bear the loss; (4) the preventive or deterrent benefits to be derived from imposing liability; and (5) the motive or purpose underlying the defendant's conduct.[2] If a particular type of conduct causes harm to others and one or more of these factors suggests logical reasons for holding persons engaged in such conduct liable, it is likely that the conduct will be classed as tortious.

In general, torts may be classified as intentional torts, negligence, and conduct giving rise to strict liability. Intentional torts may be subdivided into intentional interference with the person and intentional interference with property rights.

Elements of Torts. A tort is a breach of a duty, other than a duty created by contract, for which the wrongdoer is liable in damages to the injured party. If the conduct of the defendant is found to be willful or malicious the jury may award penalty or *punitive* damages exceeding the actual damages suffered by the injured plaintiff.

The concept of duty under tort law shifts with social developments. In general, culpable conduct which causes injury to another person is an essential element of tort liability. Under some circumstances, failure to act may be a tort, but the law usually does not impose liability on a person who fails to play the part of the Good Samaritan. Base ingratitude, cruel refusal of kindness, and discourtesy are not the basis of tort liability. One of the objectives of our society is to assure to each individual in society the greatest degree of freedom consistent with a like degree of freedom for others. Our law of torts aids materially in the accomplishment of this objective. If we legalize all relationships the law would leave little room for voluntary ethical choices.

SUMMARY

The basis of a person's liability in tort is breach of a duty owed to a fellow member of society, which breach causes harm to such member. For the most part the law of torts is based on standards of conduct. If a person

---

[1] For a detailed discussion of the role of tort law in balancing conflicting societal interests, see William L. Prosser, *Law of Torts,* 4th ed. (St. Paul, Minn.: West Publishing Co., 1972), p. 15.

[2] *Ibid.,* p. 16.

fails to maintain the accepted standard of conduct and, as a result of such failure, another is injured, such person will be required to answer for the resulting damage unless he or she can establish a legal justification for the harm inflicted.

Interference with Personal Rights

Assault and Battery. An assault is the intentional act of putting another person in immediate apprehension for his or her physical safety. Actual physical contact is not an element of an assault, and neither is fear. For example, if Addison threatens Berry and shoots at Berry but misses her, Addison is liable to Berry in tort. Berry has not been physically injured and she may not have been frightened, but she was apprehensive that she would be injured.

Battery is the intentional touching of another without justification or without the consent of that person. This does not mean that a tort results every time one person touches another. In our everyday activities, especially in crowded cities, there are many physical contacts between persons which are not torts, since such contacts cannot be classed as intentional interference with the person of another.

False Imprisonment. False imprisonment is the intentional confining of another for an appreciable time within limits fixed by the one causing the confinement. Unless the one confined is aware of the confinement and has not consented to it, the act is not false imprisonment. Suppose a private detective mistakenly thinks a customer in a store is a shoplifter and, over the protests of the customer, locks him in the manager's office until the manager returns from lunch about an hour later. In such a case the customer, if not guilty, may have a right of action against the store owner for false imprisonment.

Because of the rising cost of shoplifting, now estimated to exceed $3 billion per year, nearly all states have adopted "Merchant Protection" legislation. This legislation usually allows a merchant to detain a suspected shoplifter provided there is reasonable cause for suspicion and provided the detention is carried out in a reasonable way.

Defamation. Closely related to the protection of the person's body is the protection of the person's reputation and good name. The twin torts of libel and slander are based on defamation. A distinction is made between libel and slander, in that libel is written defamation whereas slander is oral defamation.

In both libel and slander the basis of the tort is the publication of statements which hold a person up to hatred, contempt, or ridicule. By publication is meant that the defamatory statements must have been made to one other than the defamed party. If you accuse a person to his face or write him a personal letter, these acts do not constitute publishing your statements. From a legal standpoint, statements made by one spouse to the other are not considered published. The courts have generally held that the dictation of a letter to a stenographer or the communication of statements by one corporate officer to another is publication, although a minority of courts do not so hold. If defamatory statements are made to the defamed person and overheard by another, the courts have held that this constitutes publication. A person who repeats or republishes defamatory statements is liable even though that person reveals the source of the statements.

Damages are presumed where libel is concerned unless the written statement is not defamatory on its face. For example, a false written announcement that W. C. Baker had married Miss Phelps would not be defamatory on its face even though Baker was married to someone else at the time.

Slander, however, is not actionable without proof of damages unless the false utterances can be classed as defamation *per se.* At common law, the following four types of false utterances fell into *per se* categories: (*a*) charges that anyone had committed or had been imprisoned for a serious crime; (*b*) reporting that anyone had a loathesome communicable disease; (*c*) suggest that the plaintiff committed improprieties in the practice of his or her trade or profession; and (*d*) imputing lack of chastity to a woman.

Truth is a complete defense to a defamation suit. In addition, false statements may be either absolutely privileged or conditionally privileged. Statements made by members of Congress on the floor of Congress, official papers filed in court proceedings, statements made by judges or attorneys during a trial are examples where absolute privilege usually attaches. Reports made between corporate officials concerning matters pertinent to their jobs and credit bureau reports may be qualifiedly or conditionally privileged. Conditional privileges may be lost if the defendant has acted out of malicious motives or has abused or exceeded the privilege by the nature of his or her conduct.

False and defamatory statements published in the media concerning public figures are privileged if made without malice.[3] In order to show malice the plaintiff must prove that the defendant had either actual knowledge of falsity or a reckless disregard for the truth. Negligence in collecting or publishing the information does not defeat the privilege. "Public figures" under this rule are defined as those who thrust themselves into the forefront of public controversy, as distinguished from being merely well known or even notorious people. Private persons suing the media for defamation need not prove malice

---

[3] *New York Times v. Sullivan,* 376 U.S. 254 (1964) was the seminal case aimed at encouraging more public discussion of matters of legitimate public concern.

unless the law of the state where the suit is brought so requires. Many states require only proof of negligent publication of defamatory material where "private" people bring suit.

Malicious Prosecution and Abuse of Process. Tort cases involving malicious prosecution are closely related to cases involving abuse of civil process. In the former, the plaintiff sues alleging that the defendant "maliciously" instigated criminal proceedings against the plaintiff which were later terminated in the plaintiff's favor. In the latter, the defendant employed civil proceedings to harass or injure the plaintiff.

The presence of probable cause (grounds for reasonable suspicion) usually will excuse the defendant from liability in a malicious prosecution suit because of the broad public interest in encouraging people to report suspected criminal conduct. The plaintiff must prove both the absence of probable cause and the presence of malice on the part of the defendant. Malice means that the defendant acted with an improper motive. The bringing of a lawsuit for ulterior motives, such as to ruin the defendant financially rather than for the relief asked in the complaint of the plaintiff, may constitute abuse of process even if the suit is successful. In abuse of process suits the courts are balancing the interests of society in permitting wide use of civil process against the interests of people who are unduly harassed by persons with improper motives.

Right of Privacy. A fairly recent development in the tort area is the granting of a remedy for the invasion of privacy. The boundaries in this area are not definitely determined, but the law is primarily concerned with the protection of a mental interest, such as freedom from mental anguish resulting from the invasion of one's privacy. The cases granting relief have involved: the use, without permission, of a picture of a person for advertising purposes; intrusion upon a person's physical solitude, such as by wire-tapping; the public disclosure of private facts; and, the giving of publicity which places a person in a false light in the public eye. A person who is currently in the public eye does not have the right of privacy in matters published concerning him if such matters would be classed as news.

Infliction of Mental Distress. Historically, the courts have been hesitant to grant redress for alleged mental injuries for fear of opening the floodgates to fictitious claims. Modern medical science has established the fact that traumatic experiences involving strong emotions such as rage, shock, fright, or shame can induce physical changes which can be detected. As a result, modern courts are more receptive to claims involving claimed mental injuries of various types. The courts try to contain this new type of liability by imposing requirements that the conduct causing the distress must be "outrageous" and in the case of negligent infliction of emotional distress, there must be proof of actual physical injury of a substantial and serious nature.

SUMMARY

The safety of the person is important to any society, and the wrongful interference with the person is a tort. Assault is the intentional act of putting a person in apprehension of physical injury. Battery is the intentional act of touching another without the consent of that person and without justification. False imprisonment is the intentional act of confining another for an apprecia-ble time within limits fixed by the one causing the confinement.

Closely associated to these are the torts of libel, slander, malicious prosecu-tion, and the invasion of the right of privacy. Libel and slander are the defama-tion of character or good name. Libel is written, and slander is spoken. The basis of both libel and slander is the publication of false statements which hold one up to hatred, contempt, or ridicule. "Public figures" are accorded less protection than are "private" persons. Invasion of privacy involves using a person's picture for advertising without consent, unwarranted publicity, and other similar acts which cause a person mental anguish. The intentional infliction of emotional distress may create tort liability where there is outra-geous misconduct. The trend in tort law is for the courts to recognize new theories for tort liability thus making the law more sensitive to additional types of harms.

Southwest Drug Stores of Mississippi, Inc. v. Garner

195 So.2d 837 (Sup. Ct. Miss. 1967)

Mrs. Garner (plaintiff) sued Southwest Drug Stores of Mississippi, Inc. (defendant), for damages for false imprisonment and slander. The jury returned a verdict for Mrs. Garner for $8,000. Southwest appealed. Affirmed.

Mrs. Garner and her sister stopped at Southwest Drug Store in the Gardiner Shopping Center in Laurel. They went into the drugstore, leaving her father, who was ill, in the car in the parking lot in front of the drugstore.

While Mrs. Garner was at the cosmetic counter looking at soap, Ratcliff, the store manager, approached her and asked if he could help her. She told him she wanted a bar of soap, and he said he would have one of the ladies wait on her. With the assistance of the saleslady Mrs. Garner found the soap, and with the saleslady went to the cashier and paid for it. She received a sales ticket and the soap was placed in a small paper bag.

Mrs. Garner's sister continued to shop, since she also wanted some soap. Mrs. Garner told her that she would go to the car to see about their father and would take some of the sister's packages with her. She walked out of the store, and before she reached the car Ratcliff hurried after her, calling in a loud voice to stop.

She testified that he said to her in a rude and loud manner, "Hey, wait there. . . . You stop there, I want to see what you got in that little bag. You stole a bar of soap." Mrs. Garner said further, "And I looked at him, I said, 'You mean you're accusing me of stealing this soap.' I pulled the soap out. He says, 'Yes, you stole the soap, and let's prove it, let's go back.' "

Mrs. Garner said a number of people were close by and heard the words, but that she did not know any of them. Ratcliff did not put a hand on her or her belongings, but he did demand that she return to the store.

When they got back in the store Mrs. Garner asked the cashier if she had bought the soap, and the cashier told her that she had paid for the soap. She told the cashier that Ratcliff was accusing her of stealing the soap. She then began to cry and was embarrassed. Mrs. Garner said the incident made her sick and she had to go to the family doctor twice.

INZER, JUSTICE. Southwest Drug urges that the lower court erred in not granting a requested peremptory instruction. They argue that the proof shows a qualified privilege existed and it was not exceeded; that Ratcliff investigated what he believed to be a case of shoplifting upon probable cause in a reasonable manner, and therefore under the laws of Mississippi such an investigation was privileged and no action was maintainable thereon. The statute relied upon is Mississippi Code Annotated section 2374–04 (Supp. 1964), which reads as follows:

> If any person shall commit or attempt to commit the offense of shoplifting, as defined herein, or if any person shall wilfully conceal upon his person or otherwise any unpurchased goods, wares or merchandise held or owned by any store or mercantile establishment, the merchant or any employee thereof or any peace or police officer, acting in good faith and upon probable cause based upon reasonable grounds therefor, may question such person, in a reasonable manner for the purpose of ascertaining whether or not such person is guilty of shoplifting as defined herein. Such questioning of a person by a merchant, merchant's employee or peace or police officer shall not render such merchant, merchant's employee or peace or police officer civilly liable for slander, false arrest, false imprisonment, malicious prosecution, unlawful detention or otherwise in any case where such merchant, merchant's employee, or peace or police officer acts in good faith and upon reasonable grounds to believe that the person questioned is committing or attempting to commit the crime of shoplifting as defined in this act.

Southwest argues that Ratcliff had observed Mrs. Garner and believed by her actions that she was committing an act of shoplifting; that her actions gave him probable cause to investigate, and that he acted in good faith and upon an occasion of privilege in carrying out his duties to protect his employer's property.

Although the occasion was one of qualified privilege, the privilege was lost by the manner in which it was exercised. Mrs. Garner testified, and the jury found that she was wrongfully accused of stealing in a rude and loud voice in the presence of other people outside the place of business. Granting that Ratcliff had reason to believe that Mrs. Garner had put a bar of soap in her purse and left the store without paying for it, and that he had probable cause to make inquiry, still he was careless and negligent in his method of ascertaining whether Mrs. Garner had paid for the soap.

Martin v. Griffin

549 P.2d 85 (Sup. Ct. Okla. 1976)

Action for damages for defamation brought by Martin (plaintiff), the owner of a pet store, against Griffin Television, Inc. (defendant). Judgment for Martin reversed for retrial because of erroneous instructions given in regard to the damages awarded.

A customer called in a complaint to a voluntarily staffed "Call for Action" program reporting that Martin was failing to operate his pet shop in an acceptable manner. The newscaster for the defendant's TV station utilized the customer complaint as a basis for several news stories.

LAVENDER, JUDGE. In *New York Times Co. v. Sullivan,* (1964), the U.S. Supreme Court held that the standard of liability for a media defendant in a defamation action brought by a public official was actual malice, defined as a statement made "with knowledge that it was false or with reckless disregard of whether it was false or not." The New York Times standard was extended from public officials to public figures in *Curtis Publishing Co. v. Butts,* (1967). Its application was broadened to matters of public interest in *Rosenbloom v. Metromedia,* (1971).

However, in *Gertz v. Robert Welch, Inc.* (1974), the Court refused to constitutionally require the extension of the New York Times standard to media defamation of private persons if an issue of general or public interest was involved. The *Gertz* decision seeks a balance of competing values between the legitimate state interest of compensating individuals for harm inflicted by defamatory falsehoods and the constitutionally guaranteed freedoms of speech and press with a need to avoid self-censorship by the news media. The balance was struck by allowing the states to define for themselves the appropriate standard of liability of the news media for defamatory falsehoods that injure a private individual, provided that liability is not imposed without fault.

Basic to *Gertz* and to the present case is the determination whether the plaintiff is a private individual or a public official or figure. Using the general guidelines suggested by *Gertz,* we believe that the pet store owner must be characterized as a private individual. He did not voluntarily inject himself into this particular public controversy nor did he attempt to engage the public's attention to influence the outcome of a public issue.

With the pet store owner determined to be a private individual, *Gertz* necessitates the defining for Oklahoma of a standard of liability for news media defamation injurious to private individuals. The Oklahoma Bill of Rights, Const. Art. II Section 22, provides in part: "Every person may freely speak, write or publish his sentiments on all subjects, being responsible for the abuse of that right." We conclude that reasonable balance between the right of a news media and the right of the private individual is best achieved by a negligence test. 76 O.S. 1971 Section 5(a) provides in part: "Everyone is responsible, not only for the result of his willful acts, but also for an injury occasioned to another by his want of ordinary care or skill in the management of his property or person. . . ." Ordinary care is that degree of care which ordinarily prudent persons engaged in the same kind of business usually exercise under similar circumstances, and the failure to exercise such ordinary care would be negligence.

El Meson Espanol v. NYM Corp.

521 F.2d 737 (2d Cir. 1975)

El Meson Espanol (plaintiff), a corporate owner of a restaurant, brought a libel action against NYM Corporation (defendant), and it appealed from a judgment for the defendant. Affirmed.

The November 5, 1973, issue of *New York Magazine* contained an article which stated:

> They [i.e. cocaine dealers] are still out there across the Hudson River, too—in Elizabeth, in West New York, in Union City. Late at night in Union City, bars like El Tropicano at 49th Street and Hudson Avenue and restaurants like El Meson Espanol at 4018 Bergenline Avenue become good places to meet a connection.

GURFEIN, CIRCUIT JUDGE. While a corporation enjoys the same right to plead general damages as do individuals, since it has no character to be affected by a libel it can only be protected against false and malicious statements affecting its credit or property. While the complaint, averring injury to "reputation," would be more appropriate pleading a libel against a natural person, we construe the pleading liberally as including injury to the property of the corporation.

At the threshold we are met by the established New York doctrine that a publication defamatory of a place or product is not a libel against its owner unless the owner himself is accused of a disreputable conduct. *Kennedy v. Press Publishing Co.* (1886) and other cases.

In *Kennedy,* the article charged that the plaintiff's saloon in Coney Island was a resort for improper characters and that the influence was bad. In *Maglio v. New York Herald Co.* (1904), the article charged that the Roma Hotel kept by plaintiff Maglio was harboring a murderer. In both cases, the court held no cause of action was stated. In *Richman v. New York Herald Tribune,* (1957), the court held that even if the defamatory matter is libelous *per se* with respect to a proprietary hospital, it is not defamatory of its owner in the absence of a statement charging the plaintiff with personal misconduct or reprehensible character.

The quoted passage, tested by a "fair" not a broad reading, judged in its full context as it must be, cannot be read to accuse the plaintiff corporation of "knowing" acquiescence or participation in narcotics activity on its premises.

Vogel v. W. T. Grant Co.

327 A.2d 133 (Sup. Ct. Penn. 1974)

Vogel and others (plaintiffs) brought a class action against W. T. Grant Co. (defendant) for violation of right of privacy. Vogel appealed from a judgment for Grant. Affirmed.

The plaintiffs were credit customers of Grant whose accounts had not been kept up to date. They alleged that Grant, in order to coerce payment, has, by contacting third parties, engaged in a systematic program of harassment. This "program" allegedly violated their right to privacy.

ROBERTS, JUSTICE. Since 1890 when Samuel Warren and Louis Brandeis published their famous article, *"The Right to Privacy,"* violation of this right has been steadily accepted as an actionable tort. Plaintiffs based their claim of invasion of privacy upon Grant's practice of contacting individuals not in privity to the debtor-creditor relationship. Specifically, both Vogel and Smith alleged, and Grant admitted, that a form letter had been sent to plaintiffs' respective employers. Further, Grant contacted various of their relatives. There were no allegations that the calls were offensive or made at inconvenient hours.

Unreasonable publicity given to the existence of a debt has often been held to constitute an invasion of privacy.

The *Restatement (Second) of Torts* has parsed the holdings of these and other cases and arrived at an accurate formulation of the tort of invasion of privacy. *Section 652D,* titled *Publicity Given to Private Life,* states:

> One who gives publicity to matters concerning the private life of another, of a kind highly offensive to a reasonable man, is subject to liability to the other for invasion of his privacy.

The crux of the tort developed in these cases and described in section 652D is publicity. Without it there is no actionable wrong. The classic example of unreasonable publicity given to a lawful debt is found in *Brents v. Morgan* (1927). There an automobile repairman placed in a show window of his garage a five by eight-foot notice calling attention to a customer's overdue account. The court concluded that despite the truth of the notice's assertion, publication of the debt could constitute an actionable invasion of plaintiff's right to privacy. And publication, the court found, had been accomplished by disclosing the existence of the debt to the public at large.

In *Brents,* as in many later debt collection cases, the court applied a three-part test in determining whether the right to privacy had been violated: publicity which is unreasonable must be given to a private fact. If there is no publicity, or if it is only what would normally be considered reasonable, or if the fact publicized is not a private one, there has been no actionable invasion of privacy.

As Dean Prosser has perceptively noted:

The disclosure . . . must be a public disclosure, and not a private one; there must be, in other words, publicity. It is an invasion of his rights to publish in a newspaper that the plaintiff did not pay his debts, or to post a notice to that effect in a window on the public street, or to cry it aloud in the highway, but not to communicate the fact to the plaintiff's employer, or to any other individual, or even to a small group. . . .

The American Law Institute has adopted a similar view.

'Publicity' means that the matter is made public, by communicating it to the public at large, or to so many persons that the matter must be regarded as substantially certain to become one of public knowledge.

We conclude that here there has been no such publicity. We need not now determine how many outside parties must be notified to make a creditor's disclosures rise to the level of publication. We hold only that in these circumstances notification of two or four third parties is not sufficient to constitute publication.

Wehrman v. Liberty Petroleum Co.

382 S.W.2d 56 (Ct. App. Mo. 1964)

Wehrman (plaintiff) sued Liberty (defendant) for false arrest. The trial court jury brought in a verdict of $100 actual and $7,500 punitive damages and Liberty appealed. Affirmed.

Wehrman bought some gasoline from a Liberty station and began to have engine trouble. He complained to the station manager, Brown, and was told that water was in the gasoline and that the company would reimburse Wehrman $9.10 for the gas and expense he had incurred. That afternoon Wehrman had to spend another $4.05 getting his car fixed. He told Brown and Brown told him to write the company. After two weeks Wehrman asked Brown for his check but Brown was busy so Wehrman had his tank filled for $2.65 while waiting.

Brown thereupon told Wehrman that he would never get paid, and demanded payment of $2.65 for the gas. Wehrman replied that he hadn't come in to buy, that the sale had been solicited, that if Brown wanted the gas he could drain it out of his tank, or that Brown could deduct the amount from what was owed Wehrman. Brown said, ". . . 'I'm telling you for the last time it's pay or get off.' . . ." Wehrman said, ". . . 'Well, I'll get off.' . . ."

Brown then called the police and reported that Wehrman had bought gas without paying for it. He did not give any background facts. Wehrman was arrested for larceny but was released after about one hour.

DOERMER, JUDGE. Liberty argues that all Brown did was to give the police information of the occurrence, and points to a line of cases, beginning with the decision of this court in 1877 in *Lark* v. *Bande,* which holds that the mere giving of wrong information to the police, even though it results in an arrest, cannot be the basis of an action for false arrest and imprisonment. . . . We are of the opinion, however, that a different rule should prevail where the informant knowingly and deliberately gives the police an incomplete and biased version of the occurrence which induces them to believe that another is a thief, and results in the latter's unwarranted arrest. It seems to us that from such evidence the jury could reasonably find that the informant instigated the arrest by stimulating or goading the police to take such action.

In the instant case, had Brown fully reported to the police *all* of the facts known to him we would have no hesitancy in holding that any arrest which followed could not be said to have been instigated by him. But Brown's own testimony, as well as that of Wehrman's, shows that the information which Brown gave to the police was incomplete, inaccurate, and highly misleading.

Public Finance Corp. v. Davis

343 N.E.2d 226 (Ct. App. Ill., 1976)

Action to collect a debt brought against Davis (defendant) who had borrowed money from Public Finance Corporation (plaintiff) and later was unable to meet the payments as they became due. Davis counterclaimed for damages for intentional infliction of emotional distress and appealed from a dismissal of her counterclaim. Affirmed.

Davis claimed that Public Finance harassed her with frequent phone calls and visits to her home. Public Finance also informed her friends that the debt was owing and on one occasion contacted Davis while she was visiting her seriously ill daughter in the hospital.

Public Finance induced Davis to write a payment check knowing at the time that she had no funds and later phoned an acquaintance reporting that Davis was writing bad checks.

EBERSPACHER, JUSTICE. The *Restatement* defines outrageous conduct causing severe emotional distress in the following manner:

(1) One who by extreme and outrageous conduct intentionally or recklessly causes severe emotional distress to another is subject to liability for such emotional distress, and if bodily harm to the other results from it, for such bodily harm.

The gravamen of the tort is "extreme and outrageous conduct." As set forth in *Comment d,* "Liability has been found only where the conduct has been so outrageous in character, and so extreme in degree, as to go beyond all possible bounds of decency, and to be regarded as atrocious, and utterly intolerable in a civilized community." (*Restatement of Torts* 2d, § 46, *Comment d.*) While *Comment f* notes that "The extreme and outrageous character of the conduct may arise from the actor's knowledge that the other is peculiarly susceptible to emotional distress, by reason of some physical or mental condition or peculiarity," it continues by noting that, "it must be emphasized again, however, that major outrage is essential to the tort; and the mere fact that the actor knows that the other will regard the conduct as insulting, or will have his feelings hurt, is not enough." (*Restatement of Torts* 2d, § 56, *Comment f.*) *Comment g* reiterates that "That actor is never liable, for example, where he has done no more than to insist upon his legal rights in a permissible way, even though he is well aware that such insistence is certain to cause emotional distress." Finally, *Comment h* accurately reflects the role of the trial court in determining the sufficiency of the pleadings; "It is for the court to determine, in the first instance, whether the defendant's conduct may reasonably be regarded as so extreme and outrageous as to permit recovery, or whether it is necessarily so."

Applying the foregoing principles to the pleadings filed by Davis we find that she failed to state a cause of action under the theory of intentional infliction of severe emotional distress upon which her pleadings were framed. While we find that Davis' pleadings were sufficient to allege her particular susceptibility and Public Finance's notice thereof, we are unable to find within such pleadings any allegations of fact which may reasonably be regarded as a "major outrage," i.e., "so extreme or outrageous as to permit recovery." Albeit two of the allegations contained in Davis' amended counterclaim, Public Finance's second call while Davis waited at the hospital and Public Finance's disclosure of Davis having written a bad check, approach the requisite degree of extreme and outrageous conduct necessary for recovery, and should not be condoned, we cannot say that they are "so extreme in degree, as to go beyond all possible bounds of decency, and to be regarded as atrocious, and utterly intolerable in a civilized community."

Rights of Property

Nature of Property Rights. Historically rights associated with the acquisition and use of private property have occupied a high position in Anglo-American law. In cases of tortious interference with property rights, any action brought to recover damages, as a general rule, is brought by the party in possession rather than by the owner. However, an action for trespass may be brought by the owner of land that is leased to another if the nature of the trespass is such that it results in damage to the owner's reversionary interests. The recognized torts against property are trespass to land, trespass to personal property, and conversion.

Trespass to Land. Any entry by a person onto the land in the possession of another, or the causing of anything to enter onto the land of another, or the remaining on the land or the permitting of anything to remain on the land in the possession of another is a trespass to that land unless permission is given or unless the entry is privileged. Actual pecuniary harm to the land is not an essential element of the tort. The interference with the right of possession is sufficient injury on which to base a suit. If no harm is done, only nominal damages can be recovered.

Walking across land in the possession of another, throwing water against a building in the possession of another, shooting across land in possession of another, or damming a stream and thus causing the water to back up on land in possession of another are trespasses to land. In fact, any interference with land in possession of another may be a trespass whether it is of short or long duration and whether or not pecuniary harm results. If no harm is done, it is a technical interference with the property rights of the possessor.

The early cases laid down the rule that the right to land extended from the center of the earth to the heavens. This rule has been modified since the advent of aircraft. Today the temporary invasion of the air space over the land by aircraft is privileged, provided it is done in a reasonable manner and in conformity with legislative requirements. The operation of aircraft, at the present time, is considered an extrahazardous activity; and if anything is dropped from an aircraft, or if a forced landing is made, the aviator is liable for any actual harm which results. The trend in the law is to impose greater duties on landowners to keep their premises in a reasonably safe condition thus giving more emphasis to the safety of people rather than the protection of property rights.

Trespass to Personal Property. Any intentional intermeddling with personal property which is in the possession of another is a trespass if the intermeddling does harm to the property or deprives the possessor of the use of the property for an appreciable time unless it is privileged or is done with the consent of the possessor. Suppose Adams moves an automobile a few feet to enable him to park his own automobile. He is not liable for trespass. However, if, as a joke, Adams moves the automobile around the corner, and the owner, although he uses reasonable diligence, cannot find it for some time, say an hour or more, Adams is liable for trespass. As a general rule, if one intermeddles with the personal property of another and the property is harmed in no way, no trespass has been committed. However, if the property is personal to the owner, say, for instance, an undergarment, and the owner refuses to use the property after the intermeddling, a trespass has been committed even though the property has not been damaged physically.

Conversion. A conversion is an unlawful dominion over, or the unlawful appropriation of, the personal property of another. A conversion takes place when a distinct act of dominion is wrongfully exerted over another's personal property in denial of, or inconsistent with, the other's ownership or rights therein. Generally, the gist of a conversion is the wrongful deprivation of a person's personal property to the possession of which he is entitled. A person who unlawfully takes goods from the possession of another is guilty of conversion even though he mistakenly thought he was entitled to the possession of the goods. A person who wrongfully sells, pledges, mortgages, leases, or uses the goods of another is guilty of conversion. A person is guilty of conversion if he wrongfully, even though by mistake, delivers goods of one person to another who is not entitled to the possession of the goods. In the case of a conversion of goods the owner, or the one entitled to the possession of the goods, is entitled to recover the reasonable value of the goods from the one guilty of the conversion.

Deceit (Fraud). The tort of deceit, included in the broader term "fraud," is based on injury resulting from a misrepresentation of a material fact, knowingly made with intent to deceive, which is justifiably relied on to the injury of the defrauded party.[4] The keystone of the tort is misrepresentation of a material fact; but misrepresentation is also the basis for equitable relief in fraud cases, and it also plays a major role in quasi contract and restitution cases. There is no clear line of demarcation between these fields. A misrepresentation may be the basis for the rescission of a contract, relief in equity, recovery in quasi contract, or the remedy of restitution in law; but as a general rule, misrepresentation standing alone cannot be the basis for recovery of damages in tort.

Five elements are considered as essential to a recovery in deceit. There must be (1) misrepresentation of a material fact, (2) knowingly made or made in disregard of the truth of the representation, (3) with the intent to induce action, (4) justifiably relied on, and (5) injury must result. The misrepresentation must be of an existing or past fact. A statement of opinion or a prediction of future events generally cannot be the basis of the tort of deceit. The person making the statement must know that it is false or must know that he does not have sufficient information to make a positive statement. An honest mistake of fact is not actionable. Intent is tested objectively, and a person is held to have intended the usual and normal results of his acts. If the party to whom the statement is made knows it is false or under the circumstances should

---

[4] Fraud as it relates to contracts is discussed extensively in Chapter 9.

know that it is false, he cannot recover in deceit. The relation of the parties and their experience and intelligence will be considered in determining whether a person has justifiably relied on a false representation. If no injury has resulted from the false representation, there can be no recovery in tort.

SUMMARY

The torts for interfering with property rights are trespass to land, trespass to personal property, and conversion. Any wrongful interference with the possession of land is a trespass. Likewise, wrongful intermeddling with the possession of personal property is a trespass. Conversion is, basically, such a serious interference with a person's right to control or to dispose of personal property that the party who interferes is generally required to pay full value for the property and take title to it. Deceit is based on misrepresentation of a material fact knowingly made with the intent to mislead, justifiably relied on to one's injury. Through deceit one gains a wrongful economic advantage of another.

McKinsey v. Wade

220 S.E.2d 30 (Ct. App. Ga. 1975)

Action for wrongful death of McKinsey brought by his mother (plaintiff) against Wade (defendant). The plaintiff appealed from an adverse ruling. Reversed.

Robert McKinsey, a 16 year old, was killed by the explosion of a dynamite charge in a booby-trapped cigarette machine located on the premises of Wade's liquor store. It was admitted by Mrs. McKinsey that Robert McKinsey was burglarizing the vending machine. Wade admitted setting the booby-trap, but contended that, due to prior burglaries, he was merely attempting to protect his property by scaring vandals.

EVANS, JUDGE. The duty of the property owner is not to wilfully or intentionally injure a trespasser.

The defendant may be guilty of a crime, either murder or some degree of manslaughter in this instance, but that question is not before us in a criminal prosecution as this is civil action.

The wrongful death statute (Code Ch. 105–13) clearly provides for the recovery for the full value of the life of a human being resulting from a crime or criminal negligence. The law does not provide that if the human being is killed while in the performance of an unlawful act there shall be no recovery.

What is a mantrap? In *Crosby v. Savannah Electric Co.* it is held:

The doctrine of mantrap or pitfall is rested upon the theory that the owner is expecting a trespasser or a licensee and has prepared the premises to do him injury. A typical example is the setting of a spring or trap gun to stop or prevent depredations by animals or humans. . . .

What wrong did the defendant commit? He had an abandoned and malignant heart; he set a deathtrap with dynamite, never testing it to determine how many innocent persons might be killed if within 100 to 200 yards of it, and thus sought to protect his several dollars in the vending machine. He had a conscious indifference to consequences, and by all the tried-and-tested rules of our laws, he was guilty of wilful and wanton negligence. There need be no actual intent by defendant; his conscious indifference to consequences is all that is required to characterize his negligence as wilful and wanton conduct.

Where a party's negligence is wilful and wanton, he is debarred from pleading that the other party was a trespasser, or was negligent or was a wrongdoer.

Business Torts

Economic Relations. The modern courts recognize various types of interferences with economic relations as torts, but much of this area is now covered by various trade regulation laws. Business torts and trade regulations laws are discussed beginning with Chapter 49.

Problem Cases

1. Fabish purchased a new book at a book store and then entered Montgomery Ward in order to shop. An employee of Montgomery Ward thought she saw Fabish take the book off a shelf and Fabish was detained for about one hour before he was able to clear himself. Fabish repeatedly requested that he be allowed to call the store where he had purchased the book. These requests were denied. Fabish sued for false imprisonment and the jury awarded him $3,300 compensatory damages and $5,000 punitive damages. Montgomery Ward appealed, asking that the punitive damages be set aside for lack of evidence of wilful or malicious conduct. Should the damages be reduced?
2. Smith was detained by an employee of Brookshire Bros., Inc., on shoplifting charges. Smith had placed a jar of cold cream in the outside pocket of her purse while in the store, but had made no move to approach the checkout lanes or to leave the store. She was taken to the local police station by an officer, fingerprinted, and booked. Charges were ultimately dismissed against her. Later it was revealed that Brookshire Bros. had an informal agreement with police providing that the police would automatically arrest anyone identified by store employees as a shoplifter. Smith filed suit for malicious prosecution. Can Smith recover?
3. Mrs. Cantrell's husband was killed, along with 43 others, when a bridge collapsed. Five months later Forest City Publishing Co. sent a reporter to interview Mrs. Cantrell. The reporter instead interviewed four minor children of Mrs. Cantrell's at a time when she was not present. The reporter's article stated that Mrs. Cantrell would not talk of the

accident and that she "wears the same mask of nonexpression she wore at the funeral," as well as other inaccuracies. Will Mrs. Cantrell's suit for invasion of privacy prevail?

4. Neff, a private citizen, was in the dugout with a group of fans prior to a professional football game. A photographer for *Sports Illustrated* magazine was present preparing to take pictures of the upcoming game. Upon hearing for whom the photographer worked, Neff and his group began to request the photographer to photograph them, which he did. All of these fans, including Neff, made no objection to the picture taking. One rather embarrassing picture of Neff with his pants unzipped was published in a book, although Neff was not mentioned by name nor is the precise football game involved mentioned in it. Neff sued the owner of *Sports Illustrated* claiming an invasion of his right of privacy due to the publication of his picture. Should he recover?

5. The Gary *Post Tribune* published several articles concerning an electrical fire at the home of Easley which caused the death of his two small children. Aafco Heating and Air Conditioning Co. had installed a furnace in the home of Easley three weeks before the fire. The articles reported that Aafco had failed to obtain a permit before installation and that a fire official observed that the furnace probably caused an electrical overload which ignited the fire. Aafco filed a $250,000 libel complaint against the *Post Tribune Co.* alleging that the articles were factually incorrect and that it had lost business because of the stories. The *Post Tribune Co.* admitted "some errors" in the facts but denied malice or intentional falsity. Is the newspaper liable to Aafco for publishing defamatory material?

6. Mark Peth and Mary Peth were engaged in the collection business and were employed by Dr. Lydic to collect a $197 debt that Joan Housh owed Dr. Lydic.

   The Peths called Housh on the telephone many times in the course of a day with regard to this collection and called her at her place of employment three times within 15 minutes on March 19, 1954. As a result, her employer told her on March 19, 1954, that unless this collection is "straightened up" on or before March 23, 1954, that Housh would be discharged from her employment.

   The Peths also called the Supervisor of Music of the Dayton Public Schools and called the Housh's landlord regarding the collection claiming that she did not pay her bills and inquiring as to her earnings. Two weeks prior to filing her suit, the Peths called Housh at her place of residence eight or nine times a day dunning her for this collection, giving her notices and warnings and called her as late as 11:45 P.M. Housh sued Lydic and the Peths claiming that their conduct constituted an invasion of her right of privacy. Is Housh entitled to damages?

7. Van Dorn, an internationally known, professional race car driver, brought suit against T. L. Parker Tobacco Co. for invasion of privacy, alleging that the defendant had misappropriated his "likeness" in a nationally televised advertisement. Parker legally obtained a "stock" photograph of Van Dorn seated in his automobile, which could be immediately identified by its number "7," its color, and by its unique front pinstripes. In retouching the photograph Parker changed "7" to "75" and added the name of its tobacco to the sides of the automobile. Although Van Dorn himself was unrecognizable in the final advertisement, the pinstripes and color of the automobile had not been removed or changed by Parker. The advertisement made no reference to Van Dorn by name. Will the court award damages to Van Dorn based on the alleged invasion of privacy by Parker through the misappropriation of his "likeness?"

8. *Time Magazine* erroneously reported that a Firestone tire heir and his wife had been divorced on the grounds of extreme cruelty and adultery. The official ground for divorce

was a lack of "domestication." In a libel suit by Alice Firestone against Time, Inc., Time asserted a defense that Alice was a public figure, hence subject to the *New York Times* rule that actual malice must be proved. Must she prove malice?

9. "Black History: Stolen, Lost, or Strayed?" was a documentary produced and shown by the Columbia Broadcasting System and narrated by a well-known black entertainer, Bill Cosby. Cosby, in narrative commentary, said:

   "The tradition of the lazy, stupid, crap-shooting, chicken-stealing idiot was popularized by an actor named Lincoln Boles. The cat made $2 million in five years in the middle 30s. It's too bad he was as good as he was. The character he played was planted in a lot of people's heads and they remember it the rest of their lives as clear as an auto accident."

   In a suit against CBS, Boles claims that the reference to him was a defamation of character because he is neither "lazy" nor "stupid" and because the characters he portrayed in movies were never crap-shooters or chicken stealers. CBS claims that its commentary is fair and accurate. Can Boles win?

10. About July 18, 1971, Heuer and Wiese entered into an oral contract whereby Heuer agreed to sell and Wiese agreed to buy for $600 a clover crop then standing on Heuer's field. Heuer was to cut the crop when directed by Wiese. Heuer cut the crop on July 31, 1971. After Heuer had cut the crop, he notified Wiese by letter to remove the crop by August 10, 1971. Wiese failed to remove the crop by August 10, 1971, and a week later Heuer took possession of the cut crop and with a chopper cut the crop up on his field. On September 25, 1971, Heuer brought suit against Wiese to recover the unpaid balance of the purchase price of the crop and Wiese filed a counterclaim for damages for the conversion of the crop by Heuer. Who will prevail?

5

Negligence and Strict Liability

Negligence

Nature of Negligence. In the law of torts, negligence occupies a position midway between intentional tort and strict liability. Each person in society should be given the maximum freedom of action consistent with the like freedom of other persons. If a person is given freedom to act, that person is legally bound to give due consideration to the rights and welfare of other members of society and to exercise such a degree of self-control that his or her acts are not injurious to others. Each member of society owes a duty to refrain from following a course of action which will result in harm to another.

To recover damages for negligence, a person must establish that (1) the defendant has been guilty of negligent conduct toward the plaintiff and (2) that plaintiff has suffered an injury as a result of such conduct. Negligence without resulting injury is not actionable.

Standards of Conduct. The presence or absence of negligence is determined by applying standards of conduct to the facts of the case. The standard which has been adopted is the conduct of a reasonable man of ordinary prudence under the same or similar circumstances. This standard is flexible and serves as a measuring stick in the infinite variety of situations arising in the negligence cases. It also satisfies the requirement that a standard be external and objective and that, as far as possible, it be the same for all persons. The standard is one which must be applied by the jury, or by the court in the absence of a jury. Since negligence is based on conduct, the court, in applying the standard, attempts to put itself in the place of the actor and to pose the following questions: "Did the actor, in the light of the existing conditions, act like a reasonable man of ordinary prudence? Should he, as a reasonable and prudent man, have foreseen the danger of harm and prevented it?"

Ignorance, honest mistakes, and physical defects of a person do not relieve a person from his or her responsibility to persons whom he or she has injured. Under the law of negligence, each member of society is required to act in such a manner that he does not create unreasonable risks which endanger the person or property of others. To have negligence, there must be a recognizable risk, and the conduct of the person causing the injury must be unreasonable in relation to the foreseeable risk. That is, his personal conduct must be below the accepted standard, which is the conduct of a reasonable and prudent person under the circumstances.

Negligent Infliction of Emotional Distress. A growing number of states now permit recovery of damages for negligent infliction of emotional distress. The courts are afraid that the floodgates of litigation might be opened unless relief is limited to extreme situations. Mere proof of mental anguish caused by the defendant's negligence is not enough. In addition, the plaintiff must prove some actual physical harm (e.g., loss of weight or sleeplessness), if the plaintiff is to recover. Some courts require that the plaintiff must have been in a position of proximity to the danger created by the defendant's conduct.

Special Duties Imposed by Law. Special duties of care may be imposed by statutes. The wording of the statute and the intent of the legislature controls in such circumstances. This is treated later in the chapter as a form of strict liability.

Special duties of care may be created by the relationship between the parties. Common carriers, with a few exceptions, are absolute insurers of goods being shipped, and innkeepers at common law were held strictly accountable for any loss or damage to the personal effects of guests.

Under the doctrine of *respondeat superior* employers have a form of strict liability for the harm caused by agents or employees acting in the line and scope of authority. Duties may increase or decrease depending upon how particular hazards or risks are created. For example, business proprietors may not be liable for injuries to customers caused by "natural conditions" such as wet and slippery entrances during a rain storm.

Proximate Cause. When a person has acted affecting others, it may be impossible to trace to the ultimate end all the consequences of the act. Therefore, it is necessary to place a limit on a person's responsibility for the results of his or her acts. Early in the development of the law of negligence the court adopted the rule that a person would not be held liable unless his or her act was the "proximate cause" of the injury. The choice of language was unfortunate because it connotes proximity in time and place. Some courts have held that the person is not liable unless the harm is the natural and probable consequence of his act or unless the resulting harm is foreseeable. Other courts have held that the act must have been a substantial factor in producing the harm. In all but a limited number of cases the question of "proximate cause" will be a question of fact for the jury; or for the judge in the absence of a jury, to solve by the application of good common sense to the facts of each case.

Defenses. There are two principal defenses to a tort action for damages for negligence, namely, assumption of risk and contributory negligence. A person may, either by express agreement or by conduct, enter into a relation with another whereby some risks are assumed. He may indicate his willingness to assume the risks of the known or foreseeable dangers, thereby relieving the other party from any legal responsibility for injuries of this type.

In many cases, no express agreement to assume risks exists, but the assumption of the risks is implied from the conduct of the parties and from the surrounding circumstances. By voluntarily entering into a relationship which involves obvious danger, it may be taken as an assumption of the risks of the situation and relieve the other party from legal responsibility. If a person goes to a ball game, he or she may have assumed the risk of being hit by a ball. On the other hand, the ball park management may have installed defective netting on the backstop thus creating an unreasonable risk of being hit. If the person had no knowledge of this risk the defense would not be available. Ordinarily, a person will be held to have assumed only those risks which are known or which are forseeable and which are voluntarily assumed.

Each person in society is required to exercise a reasonable degree of caution and to look out for himself. If one does not exercise a reasonable degree of caution and this failure combined with the negligence of another results in an injury, neither party can recover damages from the other. Each party has been negligent, and their combined negligence has caused the injury. If either party sues in tort for damages for negligence, the other party can set up "contributory negligence," which would be a complete defense under the common law rules. Contributory negligence is not a defense to intentional torts or to suits based upon strict liability. Any person faced with an emergency created by the negligence of another is required to exercise only that degree of care that could be expected of a reasonable person in an emergency. In general, the contributory negligence of third parties cannot be used as a defense against nonnegligent plaintiffs.

The trend is to narrow the scope of defenses and immunities in negligence cases. A growing number of states now allow plaintiffs guilty of contributory negligence to recover based on the doctrine of comparative negligence. The jury is instructed to determine the extent each party was at fault. If the jury finds the plaintiff suffered $6,000 in damages and was 20 percent at fault for the accident, the plaintiff is allowed to recover $4,800. Common law immunities such as those for state and municipal governmental activities, charitable institutions, and intra-family litigation seem to be gradually disappearing in nearly all jurisdictions.

Last Clear Chance. This doctrine applies where a plaintiff through initial negligence exposes himself to a risk of harm but then is helpless to avoid the harm, and the defendant has a last clear chance to avoid the harm but fails to do so. Under these circumstances the plaintiff is allowed to recover in spite of the fact that plaintiff's initial negligence was a contributing cause. Prosser suggests that the "last clear chance" doctrine is more a matter of dissatisfaction with the defense of contributory negligence than anything else.[1]

Res Ipsa Loquitur. The injured plaintiff normally has the sometimes difficult burden of proving how and when the defendant was negligent. The so-called *res ipsa* doctrine permits a plaintiff to establish a prima facie case of negligence simply by showing that: (*a*) the event which injured him would not ordinarily occur in the absence of negligence, and (*b*) the defendant was in exclusive charge or control of the instrumentalities causing the harm. The Latin words *res ipsa loquitur* translated mean "the thing speaks for itself" and where the doctrine is held to apply the defendant must defend himself against the prima facie case thus made or run the risk of having a judgment rendered against him.

SUMMARY

Liability for negligence is based on a breach of duty to refrain from following a course of action which will result in foreseeable harm to another. The standard of conduct in determining a person's duty to fellow members of society is the conduct of a reasonable man of ordinary prudence under the same or similar circumstances. A growing number of states permit recovery for negligent infliction of emotional distress.

The courts have attempted to place some ultimate limits on the scope of a person's liability for negligent conduct. One theory for the limitation of liability is the theory of "proximate cause," that is, recovery is possible only if the injury is the direct and foreseeable result of the negligent act.

The principal defenses to liability for negligence are (1) assumption of risk, and (2) contributory negligence. The *last clear chance* doctrine permits an injured plaintiff to recover under some circumstances even though guilty of contributory negligence.

The doctrine *res ipsa loquitur* in effect shifts the evidentiary burden from the plaintiff to the defendant. The defendant must rebut the prima facie case

[1] William L. Prosser, *Handbook of the Law of Torts,* 4th ed. (St. Paul, Minn.: West Publishing Co., 1972), p. 428.

the plaintiff makes when the plaintiff proves his injury falls under circumstances where the doctrine applies.

Special affirmative duties of care may be created by the existence of economic relationships or may be created by statute. The trend in negligence law is towards the imposition of greater duties of care.

Jiffy Markets, Inc. v. Vogel

340 F.2d 495 (8th Cir. 1965)

This was an action brought by Vogel (plaintiff) who received extensive lacerations as the result of walking into and through a large glass panel which formed the front of the building in which Jiffy Markets, Inc. (defendant) operated a supermarket. Vogel sued Jiffy and won a judgment in the federal district court and Jiffy appealed. Affirmed.

MATTHES, CIRCUIT JUDGE. There were no signs or markings of any kind on the glass panels on the night of the litigated occurrence and the glass was spotlessly clean. Vogel stopped his automobile with the front facing the vending machine. He turned off the lights, got out of the automobile 18 or 20 feet from the front of the store and proceeded toward the building intending to enter the store and make a purchase. From the testimony, the jury was warranted in finding that as Vogel approached the store he was walking at a normal gait and with his head up; that although he was looking ahead, he did not see the glass or its bordering metal frame and saw no reflections from lights or identifying marks of any kind on the glass. He did not realize until he crashed through the glass that what he thought was the entrance to the store was, in fact, a solid plate-glass panel.

Inasmuch as the litigated incident occurred in the State of Kansas, we look to the law of that state for ascertainment of the duty imposed on the proprietor of a business establishment toward his patron or business invitee. Both parties cite and rely upon *Little v. Butner* (1960). That case teaches that the business proprietor is under a duty to use care to keep in a reasonably safe condition the premises where guests or customers may be expected to come and go; if there is a dangerous place on the premises, the proprietor must safeguard those who come lawfully thereon by warning them of the condition and risk involved: "The true ground of liability is his *superior knowledge* over that of business invitees of the dangerous condition and his failure to give warning of the risk . . . however, he is not an insurer against all accidents which may befall them upon the premises."

Jiffy contends that under all of the evidence favorable to Vogel and giving to Vogel the benefit of all reasonable inferences, it conclusively appears that Jiffy did not breach any duty toward Vogel; that Jiffy was not guilty of any actionable negligence, and the issue of liability should not have been presented to the jury. To support this contention, Jiffy invokes and presses upon us the "superior knowledge" test enunciated in *Little.* It insists (*a*) that the evidence clearly showed that the glass panels constituted an accepted method of construction, and the presence of the glass was clearly observable to a person in the exercise of ordinary care for his own safety; (*b*) that there was no duty on the part of Jiffy to warn Vogel of the claimed hazardous condition (glass panels) because the evidence conclusively established that the condition was apparent and would have been seen by Vogel if he had been giving reasonable attention to the surrounding physical conditions.

We are not so persuaded. To be sure, transparent plate glass is recognized as suitable and safe material for use in construction of buildings, indeed, it is common knowledge that such glass is used rather extensively in commercial buildings. However, it seems to us that the number of reported cases, involving personal injuries from bodily contact with transparent glass doors and walls is some indication that with the advantages that may be derived from such construction are concomitant risks which the proprietor must assume. Of course, whether the proprietor is responsible to a patron who comes in contact with a glass door or wall and sustains injuries, depends on the facts and circumstances surrounding the incident judged in light of the controlling legal standards. . . . The jury was not required to speculate as to the dangerous and unsafe condition created by the glass front. There was evidence to that effect. A former employee of Jiffy testified that during a period of eight months he observed four or five persons come in contact with the glass front and "bounce off." A safety engineer testified it was a hazardous arrangement, and detailed the methods that could have been employed to correct the lack of visibility of the glass.

Without further discussion, we conclude and hold that there was substantial evidence from which the jury could find: (1) that the glass front constituted a dangerous and unsafe condition; (2) that Vogel was exercising ordinary care for his own safety; (3) that there was a duty on the part of Jiffy to warn its patrons of the condition and (4) that Jiffy breached its duty. . . .

Roberts v. American Brewed Coffee

319 N.E.2d 212 (Ct. App. Ohio 1973)

Suit by Roberts, mother of Cheryl Roberts, age 4, (plaintiff) against American Brewed Coffee (defendant) for injuries sustained by Cheryl. Roberts appealed from a dismissal of her suit. Reversed.

A "Mister Softee" ice cream truck operated by American played music and stopped on a busy street in order to attract customers. Where the truck stopped there was no intersection or crosswalk. Cheryl ran across the street and was struck by a car.

VICTOR, JUDGE. As pointed out in *Thomas v. Goodies Ice Cream Co.:*

> The operation of such a vending business upon the public streets depends upon the customer, frequently a child, coming to the vendor's vehicle at the place it is stopped in the roadway.

Many of the customers cross the road or enter the paved portion of the street in coming to the vendor or in being served or in leaving. Crossing any traveled street presents hazards. For children to cross without direct supervision is fraught with danger. . . . In our opinion, the risk to a child is obvious and substantial. The defendants owed a duty to exercise reasonable care to protect the child customer from that obvious hazard.

We agree with that statement of the law.

We hold that street vendors (modern Pied Pipers), selling ice cream (a product tastefully delectable to young children), from a vehicle temporarily parked on a busy street, thereby requiring some children to cross the street to make a purchase, and who play recorded music to attract children to their place of business, owe a duty to such invitees to exercise ordinary care for their safety, and to protect them from the hazards of moving traffic while they are crossing the street.

The fact that the driver of another car actually struck Cheryl, does not, as a matter of law establish a lack of proximate cause as to the defendants.

Scott v. John H. Hampshire, Inc.

227 A.2d 751 (Ct. App. Md. 1967)

This was an action brought by Scott (plaintiff) against John H. Hampshire, Inc. (defendant) for injuries sustained when Scott was hit by a chain. Judgment for Hampshire Company and Scott appealed. Reversed and remanded.

On the date of the accident, Scott was working for a contractor in the construction of a regional library. He noticed that a piece of chain attached to a steel cable for the purpose of lengthening it was being used as a choker in the unloading of steel from a truck with a crane. Concerned about what he had observed, Scott came down from the building to warn nearby workmen of the dangerous situation. When the supervisor was informed that the use of the chain to unload steel was dangerous and that someone was likely to get hurt, the supervisor and crew ignored the warning. As the steel was moved ahead, the chain broke and struck Scott on his head and about his body while he was standing about 20 feet away. Hampshire, which was the roofing contractor, was the owner of the steel.

When Hampshire Company moved for a directed verdict at the close of the case for Scott, the trial judge, assuming the existence of primary negligence, ruled that Scott had assumed the risk and was therefore guilty of contributing to the accident.

HORREN, Judge. There is a difference between an assumed risk and contributory negligence in that an assumed risk implies an intentional exposure to a known danger whereas contributory negligence is the doing or failure to do something which directly contributes to the injury sustained. The distinction between the two is often difficult to draw and, as is the case here, is often without importance. So regardless of whether the defense was contributory negligence or assumption of risk, neither defense is applicable in this case where the conduct of Hampshire Company appears to have created such a situation as to justify if not to compel Scott to undergo the risk of being injured in order to warn others and avert their harm.

This court, in recognizing the principle that it is commendable to save life, has consistently held that a person who endeavors to avert the consequences of the negligence of another person, by an act which is dangerous but not reckless, is not precluded from recovering damages for injury suffered as a consequence of having interposed. In *Marney* it was said that the "law had so high a regard for human life that it will not impute negligence to an effort to preserve it, unless made under such circumstances as to constitute rashness."

Trout v. Bank of Belleville

343 N.E.2d 261 (Ct. App. Ill. 1976)

Etta Trout (plaintiff) as administratrix of the estate of her deceased son, Gilbert Trout, brought an action against the Bank of Belleville (defendant) for the wrongful death of her son. The trial court granted the bank's motion for a directed verdict and granted judgment against the administratrix who appeals. Affirmed.

Gilbert Trout's death occurred when he drove his motorcycle into a chain which was strung across the parking lot of the bank. The decedent and several of his friends were riding their motorcycles through town at approximately 2:00 A.M., and decided to take a shortcut through an alley. Trout was the only rider who cut through the bank's lot. The parking lot was well lighted and several signs were posted on the chain although no signs were in the vicinity of the area in which Trout crashed.

JONES, JUSTICE. Under Illinois law the duty of a landowner with respect to a person who comes upon the premises varies according to the status of the person. It has long been settled that a landowner has a duty to exercise reasonable care for the safety of an invitee. To a trespasser or a licensee, however, the landowner only owes the duty not to wilfully and wantonly injure him and to use ordinary care to avoid injuring him once his presence is known in a place of danger.[2]

An invitee is a person who goes upon the premises of another by an express or implied invitation to transact business in which he and the owner have a

---

[2] Under the majority rule the landlord also owes a licensee the duty to warn the licensee of hidden defects known to the landlord.

mutual interest or to promote some real or fancied material, financial or economic interest of the owner. A licensee is a person who goes upon the premises of another with the express or implied consent of the owner, to satisfy his own purposes rather than for the mutual benefit of himself and the owner or a purpose connected with the business in which the owner is engaged or permits to be carried on upon the premises. A trespasser is one who enters the premises of another without permission, invitation, or other right, and intrudes for some purpose of his own, or at his convenience, or merely as an idler.

As to what will constitute wilfull and wanton conduct, Illinois and other jurisdictions have recognized that where a well-defined path or roadway has developed through continuance use or where a private path or roadway has been continuously used by the public through the tolerance of the landowner, an affirmative act of the landowner making the path or roadway more dangerous will, unless the landowner gives sufficient notice thereof to the public, constitute wilfull and wanton conduct sufficient for recovery by any person injured thereby.

On the night of this occurrence, Gilbert Trout was not an invitee of the defendant. There was no evidence that he was a customer of the bank or that he was on the bank lot by express or implied invitation to transact any business or to promote any interest of the bank. Similarly, there was no evidence that the defendant had any knowledge that Trout or anyone else used the lot at night or that defendant continuously acquiesced in such use. The fact that the chain had been in use for eight to twelve months would seem to negate any inference of acquiescence by defendant. Since Trout was on the bank lot without the consent, express or implied, of the defendant, he was present as a trespasser, not a licensee nor invitee. The standard of care required of defendant with respect to Gilbert Trout as a trespasser was to refrain from wilful or wanton conduct that would cause an injury. We are of the opinion that the defendant's conduct was not wilful or wanton.

Bias v. Montgomery Elevator Co. of Kansas, Inc.

532 P.2d 1053 (Sup. Ct. Kan. 1975)

Suit by Bias (plaintiff) against Montgomery Elevator Co. (defendant) for personal injuries. Bias appealed from an adverse decision. Affirmed.

Bias was seriously injured when an elevator in a hospital fell while he was a passenger. Montgomery was under contract with the hospital to keep the elevator in repair. Bias sued under the doctrine *res ipsa loquitur.*

OWSLEY, JUSTICE. Essential to the application of the doctrine in any given case are three conditions. First, it must be shown that the thing or instrumentality causing the injury or damage was within the exclusive control of the defendant. Second, the occurrence must be of such kind or nature as ordinarily does not occur in the absence of someone's negligence. Third, the occurrence must not have been due to the contributory negligence of the plaintiff.

We agree with Bias that an elevator would not ordinarily fall unless someone was negligent; however, Bias has the burden of showing that the negligence can reasonably be attributed to Montgomery. This can be accomplished by showing that it had exclusive control of the instrumentality.

As to the nature of the requisite control, it has been held that the word "exclusive" does not connote that such control must be individual and the defendant singular. In fact, it is well settled in this state that the doctrine of *res ipsa loquitur* is applicable to multiple defendants.

According to Prosser, *Torts,* 4th Ed., § 39, p. 211, in order to establish exclusive control it is not necessary for the plaintiff to eliminate all other possible causes of the accident. All that is required is that the plaintiff produce sufficient evidence from which a reasonable man could say that on the whole it was more likely than not there was negligence on the part of the defendant. If the evidence establishes that it was at least equally probable the negligence was that of another, the court should refuse to submit to the jury the negligence of the defendant on the theory of *res ipsa loquitur.*

A leading case in this state illustrating the control requirement and containing an exhaustive analysis of *res ipsa loquitur,* is *Mayes v. Kansas City Power & Light Co.* That case arose from an injury to Mayes when he was struck on the head by a falling street light globe. Suit was brought against the defendant light company which had manufactured, installed, and maintained the instrumentality causing the injury.

In discussing the doctrine of *res ipsa loquitur,* the court said:

> . . . The lamp and fixtures were such that ordinarily no injury would be expected from their use if carefully constructed and maintained. Although defendant was not an insurer of the safety of those who use the streets, the duty of carefully constructing and maintaining the lamp, so that it would not be likely to cause injury to those who rightfully used the street, was upon the defendant, under its contract with, and the ordinances of, the city, and the injury happened without any voluntary action of plaintiff.

While other jurisdictions have considered the applicability of *res ipsa loquitur* to an elevator maintenance company, no clear principle of law has developed.

In the instant case the evidence discloses there were other equally possible causes of the accident in addition to the possibility of Montgomery's negligence. The operation of the automatic elevator in this case involved highly complex electrical and mechanical equipment which was designed, manufactured and installed by a company other than Montgomery. The responsibility of a maintenance company does not extend to manufacturing defects, but is limited to liability for negligence in the performance of its duties. Montgomery had no control over any design defects, mistakes in installation, or any possible faulty construction of the elevator shaft. These are all possible causes of the accident which would not have been subject to the control of defendant. Bias has introduced no evidence which would indicate it is probable the accident was caused by negligent servicing rather than by negligent manufacturing or installation.

Kelley v. Kokua Sales and Supply, Ltd.

532 F.2d 673 (Sup. Ct. Hawaii 1975)

Tekare was driving a truck and trailer toward Honolulu when the truck experienced a brake failure and Tekare was unable to halt the speeding vehicle, which collided with a car occupied by Thomas and her two children. Tekare, an employee of Kokua Sales and Supply (defendant), and Thomas were killed. When Thomas' father, Kelley, was informed of the accident through a long-distance telephone call to California, he suffered a fatal heart attack. His estate (plaintiff) brought an action against Kokua for negligent infliction of serious mental distress upon Kelley. Judgment for Kokua and Kelley's estate appealed. Affirmed.

JUSTICE KOBAYASHI. Without a reasonable and proper limitation of the scope of the duty of care owed by Kokua, Kokua would be confronted with an unmanageable, unbearable and totally unpredictable liability.

As stated in W. Prosser, *Law of Torts* § 54 at 334 (4th ed. 1971):

> It would be an entirely unreasonable burden on all human activity if the defendant who has endangered one man were to be compelled to pay for the lacerated feelings of every other person disturbed by reason of it, including every bystander shocked at an accident, and every distant relative of the person injured, as well as his friends.

Thus, notwithstanding our sympathies for the plaintiffs for their loss and for the suffering of and death of Mr. Kelley, a reevaluation of the various considerations pertinent to the question of an untrammeled liability of Kokua leads this court to conclude, as a matter of law, that Kokua did not owe a duty to refrain (duty of care) from the negligent infliction of serious mental distress upon Mr. Kelley.

Stated in a different terminology but reaching the same conclusion as above, we hold that Kokua could not reasonably foresee the consequences to Mr. Kelley. Clearly, Mr. Kelley's location from the scene of the accident was too remote.

Strict Liability

Nature of Strict Liability. Under some circumstances one is held liable for the results of one's acts without reference to the question of negligence. In such a situation the actor is an "insurer" of those who may be injured by such acts. These cases involve a situation in which the undertaking is hazardous and harm is foreseeable even though the greatest of precaution is taken, yet the undertaking is of sufficient social benefit that it will be permitted. The actor is permitted to proceed but is required to assume all the risks of the undertaking. The keeping of wild or vicious animals, spraying crops from aircraft, blasting, and trespassing of domestic animals are examples of situations in which strict liability has been imposed. In addition, many legal authorities have noted a trend in the cases to expand the application of the doctrine of strict liability.[3] In recent years, for example, strict liability has become the majority rule concerning sales of defective products where such defects expose purchasers to unreasonable risks. In a growing number of jurisdictions various forms of strict liability are being applied to the leasing of goods, to sales of services, and even to the sale of new houses.

Conduct in violation of a statute can amount to negligence *per se* which resembles strict liability in that no actual negligence needs to be proved.[4] The injured person can recover under this doctrine only if such person is a member of the class that the legislation seeks to protect; and, the type of harm suffered is the type contemplated in the statute.

Defenses to Strict Liability. A growing number of states hold that contributory negligence is not a defense where there is negligence *per se* by statute. It should be noted that contributory negligence is not a defense to an action based on strict liability although some forms of assumption of risk may provide a defense. For example, the user or consumer of a product who voluntarily and unreasonably proceeds to use it in the face of danger which he knows or should know exists cannot recover. The expansion of strict liability in the product liability area is covered in detail in Chapter 37.

SUMMARY

Cases of strict liability may involve situations in which the undertaking is hazardous and harm is foreseeable yet the undertaking is of sufficient social benefit so as to make outright prohibition of such conduct not feasible. The full risk of injury is placed upon the person engaged in this type of conduct. The modern trend is to expand strict liability on the basis of social policy criteria. Negligence *per se* may be created by statute. Contributory negligence is not a defense to actions based on strict liability. Strict liability appears to be spreading into many new areas of the law.

---

[3] In 1914 Roscoe Pound wrote: "There is a strong and growing tendency, where there is blame on neither side, to ask, in view of the exigencies of social justice, who can best bear the loss and hence to shift the loss by creating liability where there has been no fault." "The End of Law as Developed in Legal Rules and Doctrines," 27 *Harv. L. Rev.*, 195 (1914).

[4] Statutory liability similar to tort liability is being imposed in other areas of law. For example, Section 1983 (1970) imposes liability for damages for conduct infringing upon constitutional rights. See Chapter 48.

Martin v. Ryder Truck Rental

353 A.2d 581 (S. Ct. Del. 1976)

Mr. and Mrs. Martin (plaintiffs) were injured when a truck leased by Gagliardi Brothers, Inc. from Ryder (defendant) collided with their automobile in an intersection. The truck failed to stop because of a brake failure. The Martins sued Ryder in strict tort liability. The lower court ruled in favor of Ryder. Reversed.

CHIEF JUSTICE HERRMANN. The present-day magnitude of the motor vehicle rental business, and the trade practices which have developed therein require maximum protection for the victims of defective rentals. This translates into the imposition of strict tort liability upon the lessor. The public policy considerations which appeared in the development of the doctrine during the past decade, are especially relevant where, as in the instant case, the bailor-lessor retains exclusive control and supervision over the maintenance and repair of the motor vehicle it places in circulation upon the highways. All of the societal policy reasons leading to the expansion of strict tort liability in sales cases are equally applicable in this motor vehicle rental case: (1) the concept that the cost of compensating for injuries and damages arising from the use of a defective motor vehicle should be borne by the party who placed it in circulation, who is best able to prevent distribution of a defective product, and who can spread the cost as a risk and expense of the business enterprise; (2) the concept that the defective motor vehicle was placed on the highways in violation of a representation of fitness by the lessor implied by law from the circumstances and trade practices of the business; and (3) the concept that the imposition upon the lessor of liability without fault will result in general risk-reduction by arousing in the lessor an additional impetus to furnish safer vehicles.

Bystander recovery is the prevailing rule in the application of the doctrine of strict tort liability by the overwhelming weight of authority. Fairness and logic, as well as the philosophy underlying the doctrine require that an injured bystander be covered in its application.

Borel v. Fibreboard Paper Products Corp.

493 F.2d 1076 (5th Cir. 1973)

Action by Borel (plaintiff) against Fibreboard Paper Products Corp. (defendant), and other asbestos products manufacturers. Fibreboard appealed from a verdict for Borel based upon strict liability. Affirmed.

Borel began working as an industrial insulation worker in 1936 and worked numerous places until disabled by the disease of asbestosis in 1969. Part of his employment was a regular exposure to heavy concentrations of asbestos dust caused by insulation materials.

Borel brought an action against various manufacturers of insulation materials containing asbestos to recover damages for injuries caused by defendants' alleged breach of duty in failing to warn Borel of the dangers involved in handling asbestos. Borel's allegations concerned the full thirty-three year period he had worked in the industry.

CIRCUIT JUDGE WISDOM. Asbestosis has been recognized as a disease for well over 50 years. In the United States, the first official claim for compensation associated with asbestos was in 1927. By the mid-1930s, the hazard of asbestosis as a pneumoconiotic dust was universally accepted.

Here, Borel alleged that the manufacturers' product was unreasonably dangerous because of the failure to give adequate warnings of the known or knowable dangers involved. . . . As explained in *Comment k* to *section 402A* of the *Restatement of Torts,* "unavoidably unsafe products" are those which, in the present state of human knowledge, are incapable of being made safe for their ordinary and intended use. Strict liability may not always be appropriate in such cases because of the important benefits derived from the use of the product. This is especially so with respect to new drugs that are essential in treating disease but involve a high degree of risk. It may also be so with respect to other commercial products possessing both unparalleled utility and unquestioned danger. As a practical matter, the decision to market such a product requires a balancing of the product's utility against its known or foreseeable danger. But, as comment k makes clear, even when such balancing leads to the conclusion that marketing is justified, the seller still has a responsibility to inform the user or consumer of the risk of harm. The failure to give adequate warnings in these circumstances renders the product unreasonably dangerous.

So it is with the case at bar. The utility of an insulation product containing asbestos may outweigh the known or foreseeable risk to the insulation workers and thus justify its marketing. The product could still be unreasonably dangerous, however, if unaccompanied by adequate warnings. An insulation worker, no less than any other product user, has a right to decide whether to expose himself to the risk.

Brockett v. Kitchen Boyd Motor Co.

100 Cal. Rpt. 752 (Cal. Ct. App. 1972)

The Brocketts (plaintiffs) brought this action against Kitchen Boyd Motor Company (defendant) after having an automobile collision with Jimmie Huff, an intoxicated minor who was an employee of Boyd's. The Brocketts appealed from a trial court adverse decision. Reversed.

The Brocketts were injured when the automobile in which they were riding was struck by a Thunderbird driven by Jimmie Huff, an intoxicated minor of the age of 19, who was an employee of Boyd Motor Company. Huff became intoxicated at his employer's Christmas party where he was served copious amounts of liquor, and placed in his automobile and directed to drive home. Section 25658 of a state statute made it a misdemeanor to sell, furnish, or give alcoholic beverages to a minor.

GARGANO, ASSOCIATE JUDGE. The common-law rule, immunizing the furnisher of liquor from civil liability, has been picturesquely described as a "back-eddy running counter to the mainstream of modern tort doctrine." In some states the rule has been partially eliminated by statutes, known as "Dram Shop Acts"; these statutes impose liability on vendors of intoxicating beverages for injuries caused by the intoxication of persons to whom the beverages are sold. In other states, the specious reasoning of the common law has been modified by judicial fiat; liability is imposed when, in contravention of a statute, liquor is sold to intoxicated persons or to a minor.

In June 1971, the California Supreme Court unmasked the common law fiction; it declared that the real question to be decided in each case is one not of proximate cause but rather whether the defendant is guilty of a breach of duty to the injured party. The high court, in *Vesley v. Sager,* said:

> A duty of care, and the attendant standard of conduct required of a reasonable man, may of course be found in a legislative enactment which does not provide for civil liability. In this state a presumption of negligence arises from the violation of a statute which was enacted to protect a class of persons of which the plaintiff is a member against the type of harm which the plaintiff suffered as a result of the violation of the statute. The Legislature has recently codified this presumption with the adoption of Evidence Code Section 669: "The failure of a person to exercise due care is presumed if: (1) He violated a statute, ordinance, or regulation of a public entity; (2) The violation proximately caused death or injury to person or property; (3) The death or injury resulted from an occurrence of the nature which the statute, ordinance, or regulation was designed to prevent; and (4) The person suffering the death or the injury to this person or property was one of the class of persons for whose protection the statute, ordinance, or regulation was adopted."
>
> In the instant case a duty of care is imposed upon defendant Sager by Business and Professions Code Section 25602, which provides: "Every person who sells, furnishes, gives, or causes to be sold, furnished, or given away, any alcoholic beverage to any habitual or common drunkard or to any obviously intoxicated person is guilty of a misdemeanor." This provision was enacted as part of the Alcoholic Beverage Control Act of 1935 and was adopted for the purpose of protecting members of the general public from injuries to person and damage to property resulting from the excessive use of intoxicating liquor.

Boyd Co. points out that the Supreme Court narrowed the perimeter of the *Vesely* decision to commercial vendors; the court did not "decide whether a noncommercial furnisher of alcoholic beverages may be subject to civil liability under Section 25602 or whether a person who is served alcoholic beverages in violation of the statute may recover for injuries suffered as a result of that violation." Nevertheless, the rationale of the *Vesely* decision charts the course to be followed in this state. We consider the problem presented in this appeal with this premise in mind.

Boyd Co. suggests that if we lift the common law immunity of noncommercial suppliers of alcohol, we will subject every social host to civil liability for injuries caused by intoxicated guests and will soon flood the courts with a myriad of perplexing problems. Following are a few examples: How is an unsophisticated social host to determine when a guest has reached his alcoholic tolerance; to what extent is a host to supervise social activities; is a host required to ignore social convention by refusing to serve a guest a drink because he merely suspects the guest may be intoxicated?

We do not reach the broad question as to whether a host at a social gathering is subject to liability under Section 25602 for injuries caused by intoxicated guests. Section 25658 is directed to a special class; it pertains to young people who because of their tender years and inexperience are unable to cope with the imbibing of alcoholic beverages. Under this section a person's duty is unequivocal; it requires no expertise to perform; it involves no exercise of judgment, nor is one faced with undue difficulties because of traditional niceties or convention or compulsion.

It is suggested that the extension of the *Vesely* rationale to furnishers of alcoholic beverages to minors imposes almost absolute liability on vendors and on every parent who keeps intoxicating liquor in the home. As we have stated, the scope of this decision is limited to the facts as alleged in Brockett's complaint, that the minor's intoxication was induced by his employer as the result of a Christmas party where the employer did *knowingly make available* to the minor copious amounts of intoxicating beverage with knowledge that the minor was going to drive a vehicle upon the public highways.

Problem Cases

1. On November 23, Mrs. Enos and her daughter and daughter-in-law were shopping in Grant's department store. The store was more crowded than usual and the patrons included both adults and children. While ascending the stairway leading from the basement to the ground floor, Mrs. Enos was bumped by a 10 to 12 year old girl who was running up the stairs. As a result she lost her balance and fell to the floor. Mrs. Enos sued Grant. What result?

2. Franc was crossing a railroad bridge on foot when she fell through a hole in the floor of the bridge due to a missing plank and sustained serious personal injuries. The gap was covered by snow and had been in the bridge for three weeks. Although the bridge was the private property of the Pennsylvania Railroad, the public had used the bridge for many years with the knowledge of the defendant. The railroad had in the past maintained the bridge, but argued that Franc was a trespasser, and as such could not recover damages. Is the railroad liable to Franc for the injuries she sustained by her fall?

3. Linda Sorensen is an unemancipated minor who was injured in an automobile accident allegedly caused by the negligence of her father. Linda sues her father, asserting that the tort doctrine of parental immunity should not apply to the present case because her father's insurer is the real party in interest and that the doctrine no longer reflects

the policies of modern life. Will the court abrogate the doctrine of parental immunity and allow recovery?

4. Quinlivan parked his car in a parking lot of a supermarket intending to make purchases in the store. The parking lot was snow-covered and icy, although snow had not fallen for several days. Quinlivan fell due to these conditions, suffering physical and mental disablement. Quinlivan alleges that the supermarket was negligent in permitting a dangerous icy condition to exist in the parking lot area. The supermarket responded by alleging no duty is owed Quinlivan, an invitee, with respect to hazards arising from natural accumulations of ice and snow. Who will prevail?
5. Miles and his wife were watching Ace Van Lines move their furniture out. The first of two tables was removed by a process of lowering it, with the use of a rope, over the railing of the second story porch to the ground below. This was accomplished without participation or comment by Miles. As the second table was being lowered, Miles, without comment or invitation, leaned out over the railing to help free the table from an obstacle, and fell to the ground when the railing broke. The trial court jury found that both Miles and Ace Van Lines had been negligent, but that only the negligence of Ace Van Lines was the cause of Miles' injuries. Should this case be reversed?
6. Cox's husband was a passenger on a DC-7 aircraft which crashed into the Pacific Ocean. Although wreckage identified from the aircraft was recovered, no bodies of either the passengers or the crew was found. There was no evidence as to the cause of the aircraft's crash into the ocean. Mrs. Cox now sues the airline company for the death of her husband. The airline company urges that it has demonstrated due care by use of its maintenance and pilot competency records and thus no inference of negligence can be demonstrated by Mrs. Cox. Mrs. Cox relies upon the doctrine of *res ipsa loquitur* to demonstrate negligence on the part of the airline company. Does she have a good cause of action?
7. Mrs. Howard gave birth to a daughter who was afflicted with Tay-Sachs disease. There are tests available to determine whether the parents are carriers of the disease and whether the fetus is afflicted with the disease; but Lecher, her doctor, did not run these tests. The Howards now sue Lecher for the negligent infliction of mental and emotional distress. Is this a compensable injury?
8. Cities Service Company operates a phosphate rock mine in Florida. On December 3, 1971, a break in a dam restraining a settling pond occurred, allowing approximately one billion gallons of phosphate slimes to enter Peace River, causing a gigantic fish kill and other substantial damage. The State sues to enjoin Cities Service's activities and for compensatory damages. Cities Service defends against strict liability on the basis that this use is the natural method of mining phosphate rock, and hence not ultrahazardous activity. Will this defense prevail?
9. Dolinski suffered physical and mental distress when he partially consumed the contents of a bottle of "Squirt" containing a decomposed mouse. As a consequence, he filed an action for damages against Shoshone Coca-Cola Bottling Company, the manufacturer and distributor of "Squirt." Dolinski relied solely upon the theory of strict tort liability. Is Shoshone liable to Dolinski?
10. The Becks purchased a lot of ground at the bottom of a canyon in a hillside area in California being developed by Bel Air Properties and built a house upon it. During the development of the area, Bel Air cut and leveled the hill surrounding the Becks' property and constructed two soil and rock fills at the rear of the Becks' property. Heavy winter rainfalls there caused soil and rocks to flow in large quantities over the Becks' land. The Becks' sued Bel Air and their contractors on a theory of strict liability in tort. The

law of strict liability in tort in California is that strict liability applies to certain activities which are "obviously and plainly" ultrahazardous. An activity is ultrahazardous if it (1) necessarily involves a risk of serious harm to the person, land, or chattels of others which cannot be eliminated by the utmost care and (2) is not a matter of common usage. The trial court applied the theory of strict liability to the case and the jury awarded the Becks $30,000. Will the case be reversed on appeal?

PART III

Contracts

6

Introduction

History and Nature of Contracts

Evolution of the Contract. The courts and law writers have given us many definitions of a contract, all of which recognize the promise, or the agreement which is the result of promises, as an element. A generally accepted definition is: "A contract is a promise or a set of promises for the breach of which the law gives a remedy or the performance of which the law in some way recognizes as a duty."[1] The contract has been accepted as the basis of commercial transactions from the earliest times. It was known to and enforced by the Egyptians and Mesopotamians 3,000 or 4,000 years before Christ. By 1603 the common law courts of England recognized the enforceability of the simple contract, that is, a promise not under seal.

Basic Requirements. The common law requirements for a valid contract are (1) an offer, (2) an acceptance of the offer, (3) supported by consideration (with some exceptions), (4) by parties having capacity to contract, and (5) the objective of the contract must be legal. In all cases the promise or promises (offer and acceptance) which are the basis of the contract must be made voluntarily. In addition, in some cases an otherwise valid contract is not enforceable unless it has been reduced to writing. Each of these elements will be discussed in subsequent chapters along with how the Uniform Commercial Code has modified contract law involving the sale of goods.

Changing Role of Contracts

Role at Turn of Century. The laissez-faire economic theories espoused by 18th and 19th century classical and neoclassical economists had an impor-

---

[1] American Law Institute, *Restatement of the Law of Contracts* (Ten. Draft 1973) Section 1.

tant influence on the evolution of Anglo-American contract law in the 19th and the first half of the 20th centuries. Under these theories the private contract was to be the major mechanism by which economic plans were to be effectuated. Neither the legislative branches of government nor the courts should "tamper" with business contracts because they represented the voluntary choices of the parties in an economy stressing individualism and free choice. Free contracting was viewed as an essential ingredient of the decentralized economic planning that was supposed to take place in a laissez-faire market controlled economy.[2]

The high pedestal this "free contract" concept occupied in law was summarized in 1875 in the frequently quoted words of Sir George Jessel:

> If there is one thing more than any other which public policy requires, it is that men of full age and competent understanding shall have the utmost liberty of contracting, and that contracts when entered into freely and voluntarily, shall be held good and shall be enforced by courts of justice.[3]

These strict hands-off policies of the courts meant businessmen had an ideal legal mechanism for effectuating economic plans which were enforceable in the courts. These policies also provided businessmen with a means, within broad limits, for shifting or limiting many of their economic risks. During this period the courts, except in extreme circumstances, would not consider claims or defenses to contract litigation based on alleged "inequality" of bargaining power of "unfairness" in the terms of contracts.

Contracts after 1900. The first basic change has been the widespread adoption of form contracting by business. Llewelyn recognized and summarized the reasons for this development in 1931 when he wrote:

> Standardized contracts in and of themselves partake of the general nature of machine-production. They materially ease and cheapen selling and distribution. They are easy to make, file, check and fill. To a regime of fungible goods is added one of fungible transaction—fungible not merely by virtue of simplicity (the over-the-counter sale of a loaf of bread) but despite complexity. Dealings with fungible transactions are cheaper, easier. One interpretation of a doubtful point in court or out gives clear light on a thousand further transactions. Finally, from the angle of the individual enterprise, they make the experience and planning power of the high executive available to cheaper help, and available forth with, without waiting through a painful training period.[4]

---

[2] This was noted by Justice Frankfurter in *AFL v. American Sash & Door Co.,* 335 U.S. 538, 540 (1949): ". . . (In the 19th century) Adam Smith was treated as though his generalizations had been imparted to him on Sinai and not as a thinker who addressed himself to the elimination of restrictions which had become fetters upon initiative and enterprise in his day. Basic human rights expressed by the constitutional conception of liberty were equated with theories of laissez-faire. The result was that economic views of confined validity were treated by lawyers and judges as though the framers had enshrined them in the constitution. . . ."

[3] *Printing and Numerical Registering Co. v. Sampson,* 19 L.R. *Eq.* 462, 465 (1875).

[4] Karl N. Llewelyn, "*What Price Contract—An Essay in Perspective,*" 40 *Yale L. J.* 704, 731 (1931).

Concurrently with the development of form contracting the Industrial Revolution was changing the entire nature and institutional structure of our economy. New theories of "imperfect" and "monopolistic" competition challenged the validity of utilizing laissez-faire economic theories as a basis for public policy in a modern industrial-urban society. The courts began to be persuaded by arguments that inequalities in bargaining power had developed which justified the "intervention" of public agencies into various economic relationships including many types of contracting relationships. In addition, many important contract relationships traditionally left to bargaining between the parties began to be substantially or fully controlled by legislation.[5]

The Uniform Commercial Code (discussed later) contains a provision (2–302) which makes "unconscionability" a defense in all legal and equitable sale of goods actions based on contracts. In a recent law review note discussing the Code, the writer states:

> Form contracts generally reflect complete control of negotiations by the party drafting the instrument and almost total lack of bargaining power in the other party. Section 2–302 is designed to avoid exploitation of such situations by limiting the stronger party's ability to enforce the terms he dictates, thus forcing him to exercise restraint in drafting.[6]

Today a growing number of courts may refuse to enforce; or even may rewrite terms in private contracts if this is deemed necessary to protect the real or presumed victims of one-sided or unfair contracts. For example, disclaimer of liability clauses found in many form sales contracts or so-called warranties given with the sale of goods, now are strictly construed against sellers so as to afford maximum protection to consumers. In an increasing number of circumstances, disclaimers and other "boiler-plate" terms are found to be against public policy and hence invalid. Despite these modern trends the agreement reached by the parties still provides the fundamental basis for the enforcement of private contracts.

Classification of Contracts

To aid in the analysis of contractual problems contracts have been classified according to their various characteristics. These classifications are not all-

---

[5] As an example, consider all of the federal and state laws that now establish or condition the terms of an ordinary employment relationship entered into by a corporation engaged in interstate commerce. Not only are there laws prohibiting various forms of discrimination and establishing safety standards; there also are laws influencing or controlling the level of compensation. The employee rights established include those related to minimum pay, maximum hours, job injuries, and unemployment and retirement benefits. The trend has been for "legislated" rights and duties to replace, or modify, rights and duties created by private contract in an increasing number of important areas.

[6] Note 63 *Yale L. J.* 560, 562 (1954).

inclusive or all-exclusive and the same contract may be classified under more than one category.

Formal and Informal or Simple. Contracts under seal, negotiable instruments, and recognizances are classified as formal contracts. All other contracts, whether oral or written, are classed as informal or simple contracts.

Unilateral and Bilateral. As the terms indicate, a *unilateral contract* is one in which only one of the parties makes a promise, whereas in a *bilateral contract,* both of the contracting parties make promises. A unilateral contract may be a promise for an act or an act for a promise. For example, a promise to pay a reward for the return of lost property is a promise for an act. The person offering the reward makes a promise and the person returning such property performs the requested act. And a promise to repay money loaned is an act for a promise. The lender performs the act of paying the borrower who in return promises to repay the money. A promise to sell and deliver goods given in exchange for a promise to pay the agreed purchase price at some future date is a bilateral contract or a promise for a promise.

Valid, Unenforceable, Voidable, Void. A valid contract is one which fulfills all the legal requirements for a contract. A court will lend its aid to the enforcement of a valid contract.

An unenforceable contract is one which satisfies the basic requirements for a valid contract, but which the courts deny enforcement becaue of some statutory requirement or some rule of law. Such a contract may create, in an indirect way, a duty of performance. An oral contract required by statute to be in writing, is an example of an unenforceable contract. Under some circumstances, such a contract, although not enforceable, may give rise to rights on which a cause of action may be based.

A voidable contract is one which binds one of the parties to the contract, but gives to the other party the right, at his election, to withdraw from the contract. For example, a person who has been induced by fraudulent representation to make a promise is given the right to elect not to be bound by his promise. If he elects to perform his promise, however, he can hold the other party to the performance of his duties under the contract.

The term *void* is applied to a contract which is a nullity due to the lack of some essential element of a contract, that is, it has no legal force or effect. In some respects, it is inaccurate to call such a promise a contract. A promise to murder a person given in exchange for a promise to pay an agreed sum would be termed a void contract.

Executed and Executory. A contract becomes executed when all the parties to the contract have fulfiled all their legal obligations created by the contract. Until all such legal obligations have been fulfilled, the contract is executory. If one of the parties has partially fulfilled his obligations under the contract, the contract is often referred to as a partially executed contract.

The contract might be executed as to one of the parties to the contract and executory as to the other party.

Express and Implied. An express contract is one in which the promise or promises are stated or declared in direct terms, that is, set forth in words. They may be stated orally or put in writing. An implied contract is one in which the promise or promises are not stated in direct words but are gathered by necessary implication or deduction from the circumstances, the general language, or the conduct of the parties. For example, suppose you go to the dentist and request to have a tooth filled for you, and say nothing at the time about payment. You would, under the circumstances, have impliedly promised to pay the standard fee for such services. You would be bound by a contract implied in fact.

SUMMARY

The basis of a contract is a promise but all promises do not give rise to contractual obligations. The modern concept of a contract was developed in the English law after the 15th century and the simple contract did not attain its present characteristics until the 19th century. The role of contracts changed as our society changed from an agrarian to an industrial-urban society. The courts now are more inclined to review and even modify contract terms—particularly where form contracts are utilized.

Contracts are divided into classes in order to aid in analysis of contractual problems. The recognized classifications are formal and informal or simple; unilateral and bilateral; valid, unenforceable, voidable and void; executed and executory; and express and implied.

Quasi Contracts

Historical Development. During the early formative period of the common law, the courts tended to stress stability and continuity in the principles of law being developed. It will be recalled that the inflexibility of common law rules was a principal factor behind the development of courts of equity. Even after courts of equity developed, however, there were special fact situations not adequately covered by existing rules.

For example, if Able through an honest mistake conferred a benefit on Baker under circumstances where Baker knowingly received the benefit, Able had no remedy in either contract or tort law. To preserve the general consistency of the existing rules and yet to avoid the resulting injustice, the common law judges resorted to a fiction: they held that a promise had been made or was implied in law. These obligations based on promises implied in law are known as "quasi contracts." The basis for a recovery in an action in quasi contract is the unjust enrichment of one party at the expense of another. In most cases the remedy is a money judgment for the amount of the unjust enrichment.

Measure of Damages. The measure of damages for the breach of a contract is, as a general rule, the sum of money which is necessary to place the injured party in substantially the same position he would have occupied had the contract been performed. In quasi contract the court, as a general rule, awards a judgment for an amount equivalent to the unjust enrichment of the party defendant. Some courts allow the plaintiff to recover for the reasonable value of detriment incurred even where no benefit is conferred on the defendant.

Basis for Recovery. The cases which come under the heading of quasi contracts are of infinite variety, and it is impossible to list the situations that may arise which will jutify a recovery in quasi contract. In any situation in which a party is justified in believing that a contract exists and the party performs under such belief, thereby benefiting the other party, recovery may be possible in a suit in quasi contract. If the parties have entered into a valid contract, the courts will not add to or alter the terms of the contract or allow additional recovery by the application of the principles of quasi contract. Recovery in quasi contract is limited to the reasonable value of benefits conferred.

One cannot recover in quasi contract for benefits voluntarily conferred on another without his knowledge or consent, or under circumstances which justify him in accepting the benefits believing them to be a gift. Suppose Parks paints Oren's house when Oren is away on his vacation. Parks cannot recover for the benefits conferred on Oren in a suit in quasi contract. One cannot force benefits on another without the knowledge and consent of the other person and then force him to pay for the benefits.

SUMMARY

The purpose of granting a remedy in quasi contract is to prevent unjust enrichment of one party at the expense of another. The amount of the recovery is based on the amount of the unjust enrichment. Quasi contract cannot be brought where there is an express or implied valid contract covering the subject matter.

County of Champaign v. Hanks
353 N.E.2d 405 (App. Ct. Ill. 4th Dis. 1976)

Suit by state's attorney (plaintiff) to recover for free public defender legal services provided to Hanks (defendant) in a prior criminal trial in which

Hanks had been charged with burglary. Hanks appealed from a judgment in favor of the plaintiff in the amount of $2,000. Affirmed.

Hanks was charged with a burglary and filed a false affidavit claiming that he was indigent. When it was discovered that Hanks had over $28,000 in assets the state's attorney brought suit in quasi contract on behalf of the county to recover the reasonable value of services rendered.

STENGEL, JUSTICE. A quasi contract, or contract implied in law, is one which reason and justice dictate and is founded on the equitable doctrine of unjust enrichment. A contract implied in law does not depend on the intention of the parties, but exists where there is a plain duty and a consideration. The essential element is the receipt of a benefit by one party under circumstances where it would be inequitable to retain that benefit without compensation.

The county does not officiously confer the benefits of free legal representation, but furnishes legal services to those criminal defendants who qualify by virtue of their indigency. The undisputed facts reveal that defendant received free legal representation when he clearly was not entitled to such representation and that defendant failed to disclose his assets. Under these circumstances the law will imply a promise by defendant to compensate the county and, accordingly, we find that summary judgment was properly granted.

The Uniform Commercial Code[7]

Purpose of the Code. The aim of the Uniform Commercial Code is to estabish a coordinated code covering most of commercial law and to establish a means of continuing revision to improve it and keep it up to date. The Uniform Commercial Code is the product of the combined efforts of the American Law Institute and the National Conference of Commissioners on Uniform State Laws. By 1975 the Code had been adopted in all of the states. In addition, it had been adopted in the District of Columbia and in the Virgin Islands.

Scope of the Code. The scope of the Code is stated in the comment to the title of the Code (p. 3, *1962 Official Text* with comments) as follows: "This Act purports to deal with all the phases which may ordinarily arise in handling a commercial transaction, from start to finish."

The Code is divided into ten articles:

Article 1, General Provisions
Article 2, Sales
Article 3, Commercial Paper

[7] Selected sections of the Code are printed in the Appendixes.

Article 4, Bank Deposits and Collections
Article 5, Letters of Credit
Article 6, Bulk Transfers
Article 7, Warehouse Receipts, Bills of Lading and Other Documents of Title
Article 8, Investment Securities
Article 9, Secured Transactions, Sales of Accounts, Contract Rights and Chattel Paper
Article 10, Effective Date and Repealer

Although the Code does not purport to affect any areas of the law other than those specifically stated, its adoption brings about some changes in other areas of law. The Code requires a higher standard of conduct for merchants by imposing a duty to act in "good faith." The duty to act in "good faith" is defined as honesty in fact including the observance of reasonable commercial standards of fair dealing in the trade. The duty to act in "good faith" is imposed on every contract or duty falling within the Code.

The Code recognizes that most contracting today is done by means of forms usually prepared by one of the parties. In some situations the terms may be one-sided or oppressive. The Code stipulates that the courts may find that such terms are "unconscionable" and deny enforcement. The Code further provides that the obligations of good faith and reasonableness may not be disclaimed by contract.

There are other sections of the Code which restrict the right of one or both parties as to the use of specific types of contract terms. In the case of certain types of terms the party signing a form must initial particular terms separately or he will not be bound. In other cases disclaimer of liability terms must be in "conspicuous" print and specific words must be used or the disclaimer terms will not be effective. These latter requirements reduce the possibility that a person will bind himself inadvertently in the signing of these form contracts.

Application of the Code. It should be kept in mind that although the general provisions of the Code have application to most business transactions, some important business transactions are not covered by the Code. For example, neither contracts to sell real estate nor contracts to provide services are covered under Article 2 (Sales) of the Code because the application of Article 2 is limited to contracts for the sale of goods.

In addition, many provisions of the Code provide one set of rules for merchants selling or buying goods and a different set of rules where one or both parties to the sales agreement are not merchants. Even a merchant may not be subject to the rules provided for merchants unless in the particular transaction, the goods he is selling are those which he customarily sells as a merchant.

Finally, even though the Code may not apply to some types of business transactions, a number of courts have applied various parts of the Code by analogy to transactions not covered by the Code. Because of these complexities it is essential that each part of the Code be studied carefully to determine its possible application to each area of law under study.

SUMMARY

The Uniform Commercial Code sets out the law for a major part of all business transactions. Topics covered are: sales; commercial paper; bank deposits and collections; letters of credit; bulk transfers; warehouse receipts and other documents of title; investment securities; secured transactions; sale of accounts, contract rights, and chattel paper; and some general provisions. The sales provisions of the Code do not apply to contracts for the sale of real estate or the sale of services. Special rules apply to sales by merchants.

Questions and Problem Cases

1. Define a contract.
2. From the standpoint of a business manager, what are some of the advantages and disadvantages associated with the use of form contracts?
3. What is the difference between an unilateral and a bilateral contract?
4. What is the difference between an unenforceable contract and a voidable contract?
5. Gebhardt entered a subcontract with Semrow, a general contractor, whereby Gebhardt was to supply fill for construction work to be done by Semrow on Brimmel's land. The prime contract between Semrow and Brimmel included the cost of this fill work. Semrow failed to pay Gebhardt for the fill delivered and Gebhardt sued Brimmel. The lower court ruled that Brimmel was liable in quasi contract for the reasonable value of the fill since Brimmel had benefited by the work done by Gebhardt. Is this a correct ruling?
6. What are some of the factors which might explain the increasing adoption of uniform laws in the United States?

7

Offer

Introduction

The significant changes in the law of offer as applied to sale of goods contracts subject to the Code will be discussed at the end of this chapter.

Nature of Offer. Before parties enter into a contractual relationship they usually engage in informal negotiations. Whether these informal negotiations result in the creation of a contractual relationship will depend on whether the parties reach a mutual agreement and on the presence of other essential elements.[1] Although these informal negotiations may not be a part of the final agreement, they do indicate the intent of the parties.

To have an agreement, two or more persons must arrive at a mutual understanding with one another. Generally, this is accomplished by the making of a proposition by one party and the acceptance of that proposition by the other. A proposal or offer looks to the future and is an expression of what the party making the offer—the offeror—promises shall be done or happen or shall not be done or happen, provided the party to whom the offer is made—the offeree—complies with stated conditions.

Form of Offer. The expression by the offeror may be made in any form which will serve to communicate his proposition to the offeree. It may be made by acts, by spoken words, by written words, or by any combination of these. All that is necessary is that the one making the offer communicate his proposition, by some means, to the offeree.

Business firms frequently use a standard form of purchase order in making an offer to buy. Such forms usually include a statement of the terms of the offer to purchase. Purchase order forms prepared by sellers frequently contain a term stating the order is taken "subject to approval home office of seller."

[1] Consideration, parties having capacity to contract, and a legal objective.

The general effect of this provision is to limit the authority of the salesperson representing such sellers to merely soliciting orders (offers) from buyers.

Intent. Since a contract is based on an obligation voluntarily assumed, the offeror must make any proposition with the intent to contract, thus making "intent" an essential element of an offer. In the law, intent is always tested by an objective standard. In determining the presence of intent, the circumstances surrounding the parties, their acts, their words, and any other facts which may aid the courts in reconstructing the situation are offered in evidence, and from this reconstruction of the entire happening, the court decides whether a reasonable man familiar with the business being transacted would be justified in believing that an offer had been made.

It is not essential that the party be conscious of the legal effect of his words and acts. It is essential, however, that the acts manifesting the making of the offer be done intentionally, and that they be done voluntarily.

Certainty of Terms and Omissions. An offer, the terms of which are incomplete or vague, cannot serve as the basis for a contract. Judges frequently make the statement that if the parties have not made a contract, the courts will not make one for them. The offeror need not state the terms of his offer with absolute certainty. However, they must be sufficiently definite to enable the court to determine the intention of the parties and to fix the legal rights and duties arising therefrom. An offer need not state time, price, quantity, or other terms with mathematical exactness, but it must state a formula or basis whereby such matters can be determined with reasonable certainty.

If the contracting parties omit from their agreement material terms or leave material terms for future agreement, the court will hold that because of uncertainty of terms, no contract results. The omission of minor or immaterial terms will not affect the validity of an offer; and under some circumstances, what appears to be an omitted term may be supplied by usage of trade.

These common law requirements that the parties to contracts must have manifested their intent with a reasonable degree of certainty and without any omissions of material terms have been relaxed to a considerable extent for sale of goods contracts subject to the Code.[2]

Usage of Trade. Usage of trade is defined in the Uniform Commercial Code (1–205 [2]) as follows: "A usage of trade is any practice or method of dealing having such regularity of observance in a place, vocation or trade as to justify an expectation that it will be observed with respect to the transaction in question.[3] The existence and scope of such a usage are to be proved as fact." When a contract is negotiated the presumption is that the parties intend any usage of trade to be a part of the contract. If the parties do not

---

[2] This matter is explored subsequently.

[3] The numbers in parentheses refer to the sections of the Uniform Commercial Code.

wish to be bound by an established usage of trade they must make it clear by their words or acts that they do not wish to be so bound.

Preliminary Negotiations. There are times when one may wish to enter into a contract with another person but, instead of making an offer, will try to induce the other party to make the offer. To accomplish this, one will extend an invitation to negotiate.

In the negotiation of a sale, it is a common practice for the seller to make statements of what he thinks he should receive for the property, and for the buyer in turn to make statements as to his idea of the value of the property, without either party making a clear-cut proposition which would be interpreted as an offer. This is what is known as "dickering," and the courts have recognized that in the transaction of business it is often to the advantage of the parties to dicker.

Advertisements. As a general rule the courts have held that an advertisement of goods for sale at a stated price is not an offer to sell the goods at that price, that it is merely an invitation to negotiate for the sale of the goods. Likewise, they have held that the distribution of a price list, either through the mails or by general advertisement, or a mere quotation of a price is not an offer to sell the goods at the listed price. However, if an advertisement contains a positive promise and a positive statement of what the advertiser demands in return, the courts will generally hold that it is an offer.

Rewards. Advertisements of rewards for the return of lost property or for the capture of criminals are common examples of offers made through advertising. Such offers are offers for unilateral contracts. The offer is accepted by the performance of the requested act—the return of the lost property or the capture of the criminal.

Bids. When one advertises for bids on construction work, the advertisement is an invitation to make offers. One may expressly state in the advertisement for bids that the job will be let to the lowest responsible bidder without reservation. In such a situation as this, the advertisement is an offer to let the job to the lowest bidder unless the party advertising for bids can prove lack of responsibility on the part of the low bidder.

As a general rule the advertising for bids and the letting of contracts by governmental units are controlled by statute, and general contract law does not apply. Such statutes usually set out the method of advertising to be used and the form to be followed in making the bid, and provide that the contract is to be let to the lowest responsible bidder.

Auctions. Unless, in the terms governing the auction, language is used which clearly expresses the intention to sell without reservation to the highest bidder or to the lowest bidder, as the case may be, the bidder will be the offeror, and the seller will be free to accept or reject bids, as the case may be. In the ordinary auction, no contract is made until the auctioneer strikes the goods off to the highest bidder. In Section 2–328 of the Uniform Commercial Code the rules of law which apply to an auction of goods are set out.

SUMMARY

The offer must state (1) what the offeror promises, and (2) what demand is made in return. It may be made in any manner whereby the offeror can communicate such proposition to the offeree. It must be made with "intent" to contract, and its terms must be reasonably certain. General business practices and common usages play an important role in determining whether an offer has been made. Since dickering is common in the transaction of business, an indication of a willingness to negotiate will not be interpreted as an offer; and as a general rule, advertisement of goods for sale are not offers.

An advertisement offering to pay a reward is usually an offer. An advertisement for bids is, as a general rule, a solicitation of offers, and substantially the same rule applies to sales at auction. Whether or not an offer is made by an advertisement will depend on its wording.

Barnes v. Treece

549 Pac. 2d 1152 (Ct. App. Wash. 1976)

Suit by Barnes (plaintiff) against Treece (defendant) for a $100,000 payment due under an alleged contract. Treece appealed from a decision against him for $100,000. Affirmed.

Treece was a vice president of Vend-A-Win, Inc., a manufacturer of punchboards. Treece gave testimony before the Washington State Game Commission in which he said: "I'll put up $100,000 to anyone to find a crooked board. If they find it, I'll pay it."

The statement evoked laughter from the audience. The next morning Barnes heard the statement by Treece repeated on a TV newscast and then read a report of the hearings. A few years earlier Barnes, while a bartender, had purchased two fraudulent punchboards which he then located. He called Treece and asked him if his statement was made seriously. Treece assured him that the statement was "firm" and the $100,000 was "in escrow." Treece denied participating in this conversation.

Barnes later traveled to Seattle, met Treece and Vend-A-Win's secretary-treasurer in Vend-A-Win's offices, produced one punchboard, and received a receipt for presentation of the board written on Vend-A-Win stationery, signed by Treece and witnessed by Vend-A-Win's secretary-treasurer.

Both Treece and Vend-A-Win refused to pay Barnes $100,000.

CALLOW, JUDGE. When expressions are intended as a joke and are understood or would be understood by a reasonable person as being so intended, they cannot be construed as an offer and accepted to form a contract. However, if the jest is not apparent and a reasonable hearer would believe that an offer was being made, then the speaker risks the formation of a contract which was not intended. It is the objective manifestations of the offeror that count and not secret, unexpressed intentions.

If a party's words or acts, judged by a reasonable standard, manifest an intention to agree in regard to the matter in question, that agreement is established, and it is immaterial what may be the real but expressed state of the party's mind on the subject.

Although the original statement of Treece drew laughter from the audience, the subsequent statements, conduct, and the circumstances show an intent to lead any hearer to believe the statements were made seriously.

In present day society it is known that gambling generates a great deal of income and that large sums are spent on its advertising and promotion. In that prevailing atmosphere, it was a credible statement that $100,000 would be paid to promote punchboards.

The trial court properly categorized Treece's promise of $100,000 as a valid offer for a unilateral contract. The offer made promised that a contract would result upon performance of the act requested. Performance of the act with the intent to accept the offer constituted acceptance.

O'Keefe v. Lee Calan Imports, Inc.

262 N.E.2d 758 (Ct. App. Ill. 1970)

O'Keefe (plaintiff) brought this action as administrator of the estate of O'Brien against Lee Calan Imports, Inc. (defendant). Judgment for defendant and O'Keefe appealed. Affirmed.

On July 31, 1966, Calan Imports advertised a 1964 Volvo station wagon for sale in the *Chicago Sun-Times.* Calan had instructed the newspaper to advertise the price of the automobile at $1,795. However, through an error of the newspaper and without fault on part of Calan, the newspaper inserted a price of $1,095 for the automobile in the advertisement. O'Brien visited Calan's place of business, examined the automobile and stated that he wished to purchase it for $1,095. One of Calan's salesmen at first agreed, but then refused to sell the car for the erroneous price listed in the advertisement. O'Brien brought suit against Calan for an alleged breach of contract. O'Brien died subsequent to the filing of the lawsuit, and the administrator of his estate was substituted in his stead.

MCNAMARA, JUSTICE. It is elementary that in order to form a contract there must be an offer and an acceptance. A contract requires the mutual assent of the parties.

The precise issue of whether a newspaper advertisement constitutes an offer which can be accepted to form a contract or whether such an advertisement is merely an invitation to make an offer, has not been determined by the Illinois courts. Most jurisdictions which have dealt with the issue have considered such an advertisement as a mere invitation to make an offer, unless the circumstances indicate otherwise. As was stated in *Corbin on Contracts* § 25 (1963):

It is quite possible to make a definite and operative offer to buy or to sell goods by advertisement, in a newspaper, by a handbill, or on a placard in a store window. It is not customary to do this, however; and the presumption is the other way. Neither the advertiser nor the reader of his notice understands that the latter is empowered to close the deal without further expression by the former. Such advertisements are understood to be mere requests to consider and examine and negotiate; and no one can reasonably regard them otherwise unless the circumstances are exceptional and the words used are very plain and clear.

In *Craft v. Elder & Johnston Co.*, defendant advertised in a local newspaper that a sewing machine was for sale at a stated price. Plaintiff visited the store, attempted to purchase the sewing machine at that price, but defendant refused. In holding that the newspaper advertisement did not constitute a binding offer, the court held that an ordinary newspaper advertisement was merely an offer to negotiate. In *Ehrlich v. Willis Music Co.*, defendant advertised in a newspaper that a television set was for sale at a mistaken price. The actual price was ten times the advertised price. The court found that no offer had been made, but rather an invitation to patronize defendant's store. The court also held that defendant should have known that the price was a mistake. In *Lovett v. Frederick Loeser & Co.*, a newspaper advertisement offering radios for sale at 25 percent to 50 percent reductions was held to be an invitation to make an offer.

We find that in the absence of special circumstances, a newspaper advertisement which contains an erroneous purchase price through no fault of the defendant advertiser and which contains no other terms, is not an offer which can be accepted so as to form a contract. We hold that such an advertisement amounts only to an invitation to make an offer. It seems apparent to us in the instant case, that there was no meeting of the minds nor the required mutual assent by the two parties to a precise proposition. There was no reference to several material matters relating to the purchase of an automobile, such as equipment to be furnished or warranties to be offered by defendant. Indeed the terms were so incomplete and so indefinite that they could not be regarded as a valid offer.

In *Johnson v. Capital City Ford Co.*, defendant advertised that anyone who purchased a 1954 automobile could exchange it for a 1955 model at no additional cost. Plaintiff purchased a 1954 automobile and subsequently attempted to exchange it for a 1955 model, but was refused by defendant. The court held that the advertisement was an offer, the acceptance of which created a contract. However, in that case, the advertisement required the performance of an act by plaintiff, and in purchasing the 1954 automobile, plaintiff performed that act. In the case at bar, the advertisement did not call for any performance by plaintiff, and we conclude that it did not amount to an offer. . . .

Savoca Masonry Co., Inc. v. Homes & Son Const. Co., Inc.

542 P.2d 817 (Sup. Ct. Ariz. 1975)

Savoca Masonry Co. (plaintiff) brought this action for breach of contract against Homes and Son Construction Co. (defendant). Judgment for Homes appealed. Affirmed.

Savoca submitted an oral bid to Homes, the general contractor, as the masonry subcontractor for a construction project. Savoca's bid was accepted by Homes; but three days later Homes entered into a contract with a third party for the masonry work to comply with the architect's desire to save money on the masonry work. Holmes informed Savoca that Savoca had no binding contract because the oral bid did not cover all of the essential elements involved in the project.

STRUCKMEYER, JUDGE. Homes argues that there is such a lack of specified material terms that the parties cannot be said to have shown a mutual assent to incur contractual obligations and cites *Plumbing Shop, Inc. v. Pitts* (1965). There, a subcontractor submitted an oral bid to a general contractor who was bidding on a government construction project. The general contractor was awarded the contract and informed the subcontractor of that fact. Discussions were had with the subcontractor on procedures for completing the work and, among other things, the subcontractor submitted a cost breakdown for the work proposed. The general contractor, however, refused to enter into written contract with the subcontractor. On appeal after suit, the Washington court said:

> More importantly, the record before us is devoid of any evidence of agreement, express or otherwise, to any term of the alleged contract other than the price. Such essentials, as manner of payment, time for completion of the mechanical portion of the work, penalty provisions, bonding, etc., are normally critical to any construction contract. The plaintiff argues that substantial agreement had been reached on the essential terms, and with respect to such "housekeeping" items, as time of performance, the law will imply a reasonable time. . . . But our role is not that of contract maker; we merely give legal effect to bargained-for contractual relations. Any prudent general contractor, with the attendant responsibility for coordinating all aspects of a project in order to meet the quality and time requirements of the general contract, probably would require a substantial degree of specificity with respect to time of completion of various portions of the mechanical work in order to insure the overall progress of the project.

This is precisely the case here. Only the price and work involved were agreed upon; other provisions which might in the end have proven critical were not. We think important mutual obligations of the parties were still to be agreed upon at the time of the asserted oral acceptance.

Communicating an Offer and Its Terms

The offer does not take legal effect until it is communicated to offeree by the offeror or by the duly authorized agent of the offeror. An offer has not been communicated until the offeree has knowledge of the proposition. The writing and mailing of a letter stating the offeror's proposition is not effective as an offer until it is received by the intended offeree or his agent. If one writes a letter in which one makes an offer but the letter is lost and never delivered, no offer has been made.

A more difficult situation arises when the offeror prints a proposition on a tag attached to goods shipped, on a ticket delivered to the purchaser of a service, on an invoice sent for goods shipped, or on a folder delivered with monthly bills or distributed as handbills. When has a proposition made in some such manner been communicated to the offeree? No clear-cut rules can be extracted from the decided cases, but the courts have developed standards which aid in solving the problem. If the offeree actually reads the terms, or if he does not read them but under the circumstances should know as a reasonable person that the tag, ticket, invoice, or handbill contains the terms of the offeror's proposition, the proposition has been communicated to him. However, if the offeree has no reason to know that the printed matter on the tag, ticket, invoice, or handbill contains a proposition and he does not read it, there has been no communication. There is presumption against the inclusion in contracts of terms located in unusual places or printed in microscopic print.

SUMMARY

An offer must be communicated to be effective. Only the offeree has the right to accept an offer. Whether a proposition printed on a tag, ticket, invoice, or handbill has been communicated depends on the facts and circumstances of each individual case, but the test is what a reasonable person would have intended.

Termination of Offer

Duration of Offer. When an offeror makes an offer, he thereby confers on the offeree the power to create a contract by the acceptance of the offer;

but for practical as well as legal reasons, such a power cannot exist for an indefinite period. The power to convert an offer into a contract may be terminated in the following ways: (1) by provisions in the contract, (2) by lapse of time, (3) by revocation, (4) by rejection of the offer, (5) by death or insanity of the offeror or offeree, (6) by destruction of the subject matter of the proposed contract, or (7) by the performance of the proposed contract becoming illegal.

Provisions in Offer. When the offeror states in his offer that the offer must be accepted within a designated time, the offeree does not have the privilege of accepting after the expiration of the designated time. After the stated time has elapsed, it is impossible for the offeree to comply with all the terms of the original offer. Often, in limiting the time for acceptance, the offeror will use such expressions as "by return mail," "for immediate acceptance," and "prompt wire acceptance." "By return mail" does not of necessity require the acceptance to go out by the next mail, especially in large cities where mails are leaving hourly; but it does require an answer the same day the offer is received unless received too late to be answered that day, and in that event the acceptance must be dispatched on the opening for business the succeeding day. "Immediate acceptance" and "prompt wire acceptance" give the offeree a shorter time than "by return mail." The time would depend to some extent on the nature of the transaction; in any event, a few hours at the longest would be the limit of time allowed in which to accept.

An offeror may state that the offer must be accepted within a specified number of days without expressly stating the date from which the time shall start to run. For example, an offer may contain a provision that the offer must be accepted or rejected within ten days. This creates an ambiguity, and the courts have not been in accord in their holdings. One view is that the offer is not communicated until it is received and therefore the time does not start to run until the offer is received. The opposing view is that the offeror is imposing the time limit for his own benefit and that the time should begin to run from the date of the offer.

An attempt to accept an offer after it has terminated due to the lapse of the time stated therein is, in legal effect, an offer to contract on the terms of the original offer. If the original offeror is still willing to contract on the terms of his original offer and indicates his willingness to the original offeree, a contract will result.

Lapse of Time. If no time for acceptance is stated in the offer, the offer terminates on the lapse of a reasonable time. This rule of law has been developed by the courts and is based on practical grounds. In effect, it writes into an offer which contains no provision for its termination a provision that the offer must be accepted within a reasonable time. The length of time which is reasonable must depend on the circumstances of the case. Each case will have to be decided as a separate proposition, and general rules will be of little help.

If the parties are trading on the floor of the stock or commodity exchanges, any offer made will have to be accepted immediately. Under such circumstances, trading is very rapid, and anyone trading on the exchange knows that offers made are not intended to be held open for more than a very short time. If the offer is made relative to the sale of real estate, a reasonable time for acceptance might well be counted in days. But if the offer is made relative to the sale of a commodity for which there is an established market, the court will hold that the offeree has waited an unreasonable time if he delays his acceptance until he can determine the price trends in the market.

If an offer is made when the parties are negotiating face to face, the time for acceptance will not extend beyond the period of the negotiations unless special words or circumstances clearly indicate that the offeror intends to hold his offer open after they part.

In cases of offers of reward for the capture of criminals, the offer may be open for acceptance for a very long time. In one case in which there was an offer to pay a reward for the capture of the person who had committed a particular crime, the court held that the offer would not lapse until the running of the statute of limitations on the crime.

Revocation. As a general rule the offeror may revoke his offer at any time before acceptance. This rule applies even though the offer states that it will remain open or the offeror promises to hold it open for a stated period of time. However, if the offeror contracts to hold the offer open for a stated period of time, that is, promises for a consideration to hold it open, the offer is irrevocable for the agreed period. This is known as an option. Also, in those states which enforce contracts under seal, a promise under seal to hold an offer open for a stated period is irrevocable for the stated period. An increasing number of courts have held that if an offer is made under such circumstances that the offeror knows or should know that the offeree will change his position in reliance on the offer and he does change his position in justifiable reliance on the offer, the offeror will be estopped from withdrawing his offer for a reasonable time. This exception is usually treated under the doctrine of promissory estoppel.[4]

Communication of Revocation. If the offeror wishes to revoke his offer, he must communicate his revocation to the offeree. The rules which apply to the communication of an offer also apply to the communication of a revocation. In all but a few states, a letter, telegram, or message of revocation is not effective until it is received by the offeree. In a few states a revocation is effective when dispatched.

If the offeror has offered to sell designated property to the offeree and thereafter, but before the offer has terminated, the offeror sells the property to another and this is known to the offeree, the courts have held that the

---

[4] For additional discussion of this important doctrine see Chapter 10.

offeree cannot, by giving notice of acceptance, create a contract. The knowledge on the part of the offeree that the offeror has changed his position in such a manner that he can no longer perform the promise in his offer has been held as equivalent to notice of revocation.

Revocation of Offer to Public. An offer to the general public is communicated by making a general announcement of the offer. This announcement may be made through the newspapers, magazines, posters, handbills, radio, or any other means suitable to the purpose of the offeror. If the offeror, after having made the offer, wishes to withdraw it, he must announce his withdrawal in substantially the same manner as that used in announcing the offer. The fact that one read or heard the offer but did not read or hear the withdrawal is of no moment. If the same publicity has been given to the revocation as was given to the offer, the offer is revoked as to the entire public, and an attempt to accept after the publication of the withdrawal is ineffective.

Revocation of Offer for Unilateral Contracts. The general rule that an offer may be revoked at any time before acceptance applies to some types of offers for unilateral contracts, but there is some question whether the courts will apply the rule in all cases. If an offer for a reward is made and the offeror revokes the offer before the reward is claimed, the revocation will be effective.

If the act requested is of such a nature that an appreciable period of time is required for its performance, should the offeror be permitted to revoke the offer an instant before the act is performed and the offer accepted? If the nature of the act is such the offeror receives benefits from the performance, a recovery for the benefits conferred will be allowed in a suit in quasi contract. If the act is such that, although the performance is detrimental to the offeree, it is not beneficial to the offeror, no recovery can be had in quasi contract. Justice would dictate in such a case that the offer should be held to be irrevocable until the offeree, having started performance, would have a reasonable time to complete the performance.

Cases involvng the revocation of offers for unilateral contracts are not very common. Business contracts are generally bilateral; and the courts, if the facts permit, will interpret a contract to be bilateral rather than unilateral.

Rejection. When the offeree rejects an offer, it is terminated, and any subsequent attempt to accept it is inoperative. The offeree may reject the offer by expressly stating that he will not accept it, or he may indicate his rejection by acts or words or by conduct which will justify the offeror in believing that the offeree does not intend to accept the offer.

If the offeree replies to the offeror by making a counteroffer or a conditional acceptance, the offer is terminated. A counteroffer is a statement by the offeree that he will enter into the transaction only on the terms stated by him in his counteroffer. A conditional acceptance is a statement by the offeree that he will accept the offer only if certain changes are made in the terms of the offer. Both, by implication, are rejections of the original offer.

Inquiry Regarding Terms. An inquiry by the offeree regarding the terms of the offer is neither a counteroffer nor a conditional acceptance, and it will not terminate the offer. An unequivocal acceptance of an offer accompanied by statements that the terms of the offer are harsh or unreasonable or that better terms should be granted (a grumbling acceptance) is not a counteroffer or a conditional acceptance. Whether the offeree has made an inquiry as to the terms of an offer, a counteroffer, a conditional acceptance, or an unequivocal acceptance accompanied by statements regarding the terms of the offer is a matter of interpretation to be decided according to the facts of each case.

If an offeror makes an offer to be accepted within a certain time and then further states that he will consider counteroffers made within the time limit without such counteroffers terminating the offer, a counteroffer will not be a rejection if it comes within the terms of the offer.

Death or Insanity. There are some situations over which the parties have no control which will terminate an offer. It is a well-established rule that the death or insanity of either party will terminate the offer. This rule was developed in the English courts at the time that a "meeting of the minds" of the parties was the test of the existence of a contract. After death there is no mind; and at that time the courts held that an insane person had no mind. Consequently, if one of the parties died or became insane, it was impossible to have the essential "meeting of minds."

In the case of death the courts have held that the notice of the death is not necessary to terminate the offer. This rule is not in full accord with the general rules governing the termination of offers and sometimes results in injustice, but it is so well established that it will no doubt require legislative action to change it.

Destruction of Subject Matter. If the subject matter of a proposed contract or subject matter essential to the performance of a proposed contract is destroyed without the knowledge or fault of either party, after the making of an offer but before its acceptance, the offer is terminated. For example, suppose Ames has a stack of hay on his farm which he offers to sell to Ball and, without the knowledge or fault of either party, the stack of hay is destroyed by fire before Ball has accepted the offer. The courts will hold that when the stack of hay burned, the offer terminated.

Keep in mind that while destruction of essential subject matter may terminate offers, such destruction does not necessarily terminate liability on contracts. The effect of such events on contracts is discussed in subsequent chapters.

Intervening Illegality. If the performance of a proposed contract becomes illegal after the making of the offer but before the acceptance, the offer is terminated. For example, suppose Ames offers to kill and sell to Ball 60 wild rabbits each week during the month of December, and before Ball accepts the offer the state legislature enacts a statute making the sale of wild rabbits illegal. The courts will hold that when the state made the sale illegal, the offer was terminated.

SUMMARY

An offer confers on the offeree the power to create a contract by acceptance of the offer. The duration of an offer is limited. It may be terminated by the terms of the offer. If the offer contains no stated time for acceptance, it terminates on the lapse of a reasonable time. Unless the offer is under seal, or unless there is a valid contract to hold the offer open for a stated period, the offeror may revoke the offer at any time before acceptance. With few exceptions a revocation is not effective until communicated to the offeree. An offer is terminated if rejected by the offeree. A counteroffer or conditioned acceptance terminates an offer, but an inquiry does not. Death or insanity of either the offeror or the offeree, destruction of the subject matter of the proposed contract, or intervening illegality terminates an offer; but different rules apply if the same events take place after completion of a contract.

Davis v. Satterfield Construction Co., Inc.
210 S.E.2d 596 (S.C. Sup. Ct. 1974)

This was an action brought by Davis (plaintiff), a landowner, against Satterfield Construction Co. (defendant), a highway builder, for breach of contract. The trial court granted Davis' motion for summary judgment against Satterfield, and Satterfield appealed. Affirmed.

Satterfield Construction Co. had a contract, File No. 31.317, with the South Carolina State Highway Department for the construction of a section of interstate highway. In connection with this highway construction, it was necessary for Satterfield to have "borrow pits" from which earth could be taken for use in making embankment and fills for the road. On January 27, 1970, Satterfield executed a written instrument with Davis concerning the use of materials from her lands. The instrument, entitled "Option to Purchase," provided that Davis agreed "to sell" to Satterfield materials from her land at a price of $300 per acre "until completion of File No. 31.317." Satterfield never used any materials from Davis' land and Davis filed suit against Satterfield for breach of a contract. Satterfield in answering Davis' complaint, alleged that the instrument executed on January 27, 1970, was merely an option to purchase which was never exercised.

MOSS, CHIEF JUSTICE. *In Hutto v. Wiggins,* in considering whether a written instrument is an option to sell or is a contract of sale and purchase, we said:

> . . . the chief difference between a contract to sell and purchase real property, and an option to purchase said property lies in the fact that, while the former creates a mutual obligation on the part of one party to sell and the other to purchase, the option merely gives the right to purchase, at a fixed price, within a fixed time, without imposing any obligation to do so.

It is the contention of Satterfield that the designation at the head of the instrument "Option to Purchase" determines the nature of the instrument. We think not.

The nature of a contract as an option or obligation to purchase is to be determined not by the name which the parties have given it, but by the nature of the obligations which it imposes, because the law regards substance and not form.

In the instrument in the case at bar, Davis agreed to sell to Satterfield borrow pit material from seven acres of land owned by her. Satterfield agreed to use this material and to pay her $300 per acre until the completion of File No. 31.317. The instrument in question is a contract of purchase and sale and not an option. The provisions of the contract "until completion of File No. 31.317" is not a time limitation within which Satterfield was to exercise the so-called option, but was clearly the time within which it had to remove the borrow pit material under the terms of the contract.

Changes under the Uniform Commercial Code

The Offer. Under the provisions of the Code an offer or a contract for the sale of goods does not fail for indefiniteness of terms even though one or more terms are left open if the parties have intended to make a contract and there is a reasonably certain basis for giving an appropriate remedy. (2–204 [3].) As under the general rules of contract law, the contract may be made in any manner sufficient to show agreement, including conduct of both parties which recognizes the existence of such contract.

The Comment of the American Law Institute and the National Conference of Commissioners on Uniform Law states:

> Subsection (3) states the principle as to "open terms" underlying later sections of the Article. If the parties intend to enter into a binding agreement, this subsection recognizes that agreement as valid in law, despite missing terms, if there is any reasonably certain basis for granting a remedy. The test is not certainty as to what the parties were to do nor as to the exact amount of damages due the plaintiff. Nor is the fact that one or more terms are left to be agreed

upon enough of itself to defeat an otherwise adequate agreement. Rather, commercial standards on the point of "indefiniteness" are intended to be applied, this Act making provision elsewhere for missing terms needed for performance, open price, remedies and the like.

The more terms the parties leave open, the less likely it is that they have intended to conclude a binding agreement, but their actions may be frequently conclusive on the matter despite the omissions.

As was previously stated, a promise to hold an offer open which is not supported by consideration is unenforceable under the common law. Merchants in their dealings commonly rely on such a promise. In recognition of this, it is provided in the Code that an offer by a merchant to buy or sell goods in a signed writing which by its terms gives assurance that it will be held open is not revocable for lack of consideration during the time stated, or if no time is stated, for a reasonable time, but in no event may such period of irrevocability exceed three months. (2–205.) To assure that a promise to hold an offer open is consciously and intentionally made, the Code further provides that if the promise is included in a form supplied by the offeree it must be separately signed by the offeror.

E. A. Coronis Assocs. v. M. Gordon Constr. Co.

216 A.2d 246 (Sup. Ct. N.J. 1966)

M. Gordon Construction Company (plaintiff on counterclaim) sought damages for breach of contract from E. A. Coronis Associates (defendant on counterclaim). A summary judgment was entered in favor of E. A. Coronis Associates (Coronis) and M. Gordon Construction Co. (Gordon) appealed. Reversed.

Gordon is a general contractor. In anticipation of making a bid to construct two buildings for Port Authority, Gordon sought bids from subcontractors. Coronis sent the following letter to Gordon:

April 22, 1963

Dear Mr. Ben Zvi:

We regret very much that this estimate was so delayed. Be assured that the time consumed was due to routing of the plans through our regular sources of fabrication.

We are pleased to offer:

All structural steel including steel girts and purlins
Both Buildings delivered and erected $155,413.50
All structural steel equipped with slips for wood girts & purlins
Both Buildings delivered and erected 98,937.50
NOTE:
This price is predicated on an erected price of .1175 per Lb. of steel and we would expect to adjust the price on this basis to conform to actual tonnage of steel used in the project.

Thank you very much for this opportunity to quote.

Very truly yours,
E. A. CORONIS ASSOCIATES
/s/ Arthur C. Pease

Gordon contends that at some date prior to April 22 the parties reached an oral agreement and that the above letter was sent in confirmation.

Bids were opened by the Port Authority on April 19, 1963, and Gordon's bid was the lowest. He alleges that Coronis was informed the same day. The Port Authority contract was officially awarded to Gordon on May 27, 1963, and executed about two weeks later. During this period Gordon never accepted the alleged offer of Coronis. Meanwhile, on June 1, 1963, Coronis sent a telegram, in pertinent part reading:

> Due to conditions beyond our control, we must withdraw our proposal of April 22nd 1963 for structural steel Dor Buildings 131 and 132 at the Elizabeth-Port Piers at the earliest possible we will resubmit our proposal.

Two days later, on June 3, 1963, Gordon replied by telegram as follows:

> Ref your tel. 6–3 and for the record be advised that we are holding you to your bid of April 22, 1963 for the structural steel of cargo bldgs 131 and 132.

Coronis never performed. Gordon employed the Elizabeth Iron Works to perform the work and claims as damages the difference between Coronis' proposal of $155,413.50 and Elizabeth Iron Works' charge of $208,000.

COLLESTER, J. A. D. Gordon contends that the April 22 letter was an offer and that Coronis had no right to withdraw it. Two grounds are advanced in support. First, Gordon contends that the Uniform Commercial Code firm offer section precludes withdrawal and, second, it contends that withdrawal is prevented by the doctrine of promissory estoppel.

Prior to the enactment of the Uniform Commercial Code an offer not supported by consideration could be revoked at any time prior to acceptance. The drafters of the Code recognized that the common law rule was contrary to modern business practice and possessed the capability to produce unjust results. The response was section 2–205 which reverses the common law rule and states:

> An offer by a merchant to buy or sell goods in a *signed writing which by its terms gives assurance that it will be held open* is not revocable, for lack of consideration, during the time stated or if no time is stated for a reasonable time. . . . [Emphasis added.]

Coronis' letter contains no terms giving assurance it will be held open. We recognize that just as an offeree runs a risk in acting on an offer before accepting it, the offeror runs a risk if his offer is considered irrevocable. In their comments to section 2–205 of the Code the drafters anticipated these risks and stated:

> However, despite settled courses of dealing or usages of the trade whereby firm offers are made by oral communication and relied upon without more evidence, such offers remain revocable under this Article since authentication by a writing is the essence of this section. Uniform Commercial Code, comment, par. 2.

We think it clear that Coronis' writing does not come within the provision of section 2–205 of a "signed writing which by its terms gives assurance that it will be held open."

Having so concluded, we need not consider the question of whether the Coronis letter was an offer or whether the letter dealt with "goods." We note in this connection that Coronis quoted the price for structural steel delivered and erected.

Gordon also argues that even if Coronis' writing of April 22 is not a firm offer within the meaning of section 2–205, justice requires that we apply the doctrine of promissory estoppel to preclude its revocation. *Restatement, Contracts,* § 90 provides:

> A promise which the promisor should reasonably expect to induce action or forbearance of a definite and substantial character on the part of the promisee and which does induce such action or forbearance is binding if injustice can be avoided only by enforcement of the promise.

Gordon argues that it relied on Coronis' bid in making its own bid and that injustice would result if Coronis could now revoke. Thus, Gordon contends that Coronis' bid is made irrevocable by application of the doctrine of promissory estoppel.

The authorities are not uniform in applying the doctrine of promissory estoppel to situations comparable to that before us. We believe the better line of authority applies the doctrine.

The *Drennan* case involved an oral bid by a subcontractor for paving work at a school project on which plaintiff general contractor was about to bid. Defendant's paving bid was the lowest, and the general contractor computed his own bid accordingly. Plaintiff was the successful bidder but the following day was informed by defendant it would not do the work at its bid price. The California Supreme Court, per Justice Traynor, applied the doctrine of promissory estoppel to prevent defendant's revocation of its bid, stating:

> When plaintiff used defendant's offer in computing his own bid, he bound himself to perform in reliance on defendant's terms. Though defendant did not bargain for this use of its bid neither did the defendant make it idly, indifferent to whether it would be used or not. On the contrary, it is reasonable to suppose that defendant submitted its bid to obtain the subcontract. It was bound to realize the substantial possibility that its bid would be the lowest, and that it would be included by plaintiff in his bid. It was to its own interest that the contractor be awarded the general contract; the lower the subcontract bid, the lower the general contractor's bid was likely to be and the greater chance of acceptance and hence the greater defendant's chance of getting the paving subcontract. Defendant had reason not only to expect plaintiff to rely on his bid but to want him to. Clearly defendant had a stake in plaintiff's reliance on its bid. Given this interest and the fact that plaintiff is bound by his own bid, it is only fair that plaintiff should have at least an opportunity to accept defendant's bid after the general contract has been awarded to him.

To successfully establish a cause of action based on promissory estoppel Gordon must prove that (1) it received a clear and definite offer from Coronis;

(2) Coronis could expect reliance of a substantial nature; (3) actual reasonable reliance on Gordon's part, and (4) detriment. *Restatement, Contracts,* § 90.

The Law Division did not think promissory estoppel would apply in the situation *sub judice.* Therefore we reverse.

Problem Cases

1. John Woods, son of Susan Woods, several years before the death of his mother called on her regularly, giving her personal attention and aiding her in the managing of her property, which consisted of securities of the value of about $80,000. On several occasions during this period the mother told John that he would be paid for his trouble, and she also told several of her friends that "her son, John, was taking care of her business and that he would be paid for his services." During this period John never asked for pay for his services and was never paid. After the death of his mother John filed a claim in her estate for pay for services rendered and the executor refused to pay the claim. John Woods brought suit to enforce the claim. Susan Woods had willed one half of her estate to John and one half to a daughter. Is John entitled to pay for his services to his mother?

2. On December 15th, Patrick wrote Kleine concerning a lot owned by her: "If you have not sold, I, of course, am the logical purchaser, as it is worth more to me than anybody else. . . . I hope I shall have the pleasure of hearing from you shortly."

   On the 16th day of December, Kleine acknowledged Patrick's letter and wrote: "If you should be interested in this (my lot) would be glad to hear from you. Size of lot 20 X 100, Price $1,000 (one-thousand dollars)."

   The next day, the following letter was written Kleine by Patrick: "Enclosed you will find contracts in the usual form and also my check for $100 as an evidence of good faith, and will you please sign and return one copy to me, so that the title company can institute search?"

   On the 23rd day of December Kleine returned the contract and check and advised Patrick that the lot had been sold. Patrick sued for specific performance. Can Patrick get the property?

3. On Thursday, Surplus Store published the following advertisement in the newspaper: "Saturday 9 A.M. Sharp—3 Brand New Fur Coats—Worth to $100—First Come First Served—$1 Each." The following Thursday, Surplus Store again published an advertisement in the same paper as follows: "Saturday 9 A.M.—2 Brand New Pastel Mink 3-Skin Scarfs—Selling for $89.90—Out they go—Saturday Each . . . $1—1 Black Lapin Stole—Beautiful, worth $139.50 . . . $1—First Come First Served." On each Saturday following publication Lefkowitz was the first one to present himself at Surplus Store and each time demanded the coat and stole so advertised, offering the $1. On both occasions, Surplus refused to sell, stating on the first occasion that by a "house rule" the offer was intended for women only, and on the second that Lefkowitz knew Surplus's house rules. Lefkowitz sued Surplus for breach of contract and won a judgment. Can Surplus win a reversal on appeal?

4. Deere advertised a repossessed tractor for sale at auction, stating that the tractor would be sold to the highest bidder at the sale. At the sale Drew bid $1,500 but the auctioneer did not accept the bid; instead he announced that Deere had itself bid $1,600 and accordingly struck down the tractor to Deere. Drew sued Deere for breach of contract claiming that Deere was disqualified to bid because it had not announced intention to bid in

advance and, in effect, resting his case on the theory that the auction was "without reserve," where the owner may not withdraw the property after commencement of the bidding. Should Drew succeed?

5. Morton engaged the architect Eisenstadt to draw up plans for a new luxurious home he wanted constructed. Included in the contract was a provision for landscaping:

   "Landscape planting plans showing location, size, and description of all planting material to be installed will be completed by February 10. Cost will be $3,000 plus travel expenses and a supervision fee of 10 percent of the total amount spent for landscaping."

   When landscaping began, Morton's contractor was confused about Eisenstadt's planting plans, but Eisenstadt seldom appeared on the job site to explain his landscape plan. Eisenstadt explained that it was his policy to leave many details to the discretion of the contractor. After the construction was finished, Morton offered to pay only Eisenstadt's travel expenses to and from the job site. Eisenstadt sued to recover damages allegedly due under the contract, and Morton defended by claiming that there was never a meeting of the minds over the specific meaning of "planting plans" and "supervision." Can Eisenstadt recover?

6. The School District mailed an employment contract and a calendar of the school year to Adamick, a teacher. At the time the contract was mailed, the district was having severe financial difficulties and depended on the voters to pass a new tax rate to prevent schedule disruption. School did not start as scheduled and the district issued a revised calendar. Adamick seeks to prevent the school district from holding make-up classes on days not specified in the original school calendar. Adamick claims that the calendar became part of his contract and cannot be changed without his consent. Can the School District change the school calendar without Adamick's consent?

7. Glenn owned and operated a bus company. The buses were purchased with money borrowed from the First National Bank, which held a mortgage on the buses. Glenn made an agreement with Stoberl to have all of Glenn's buses repaired and fueled at Stoberl's gas station in return for parking facilities for the buses. Glenn became sick and failed to make the mortgage payments to the bank. The buses remained stored at Stoberl's gas station. Upon being informed of the location of the buses, the First National Bank asked Stoberl to prepare the vehicles for winter and to continue to provide storage. First National Bank paid Stoberl $200 for the work done in preparing the buses for winter, but was unable to reach agreement with him as to a reasonable rental for storage. Negotiations deteriorated and the bank sued Stoberl for possession of the buses. Can Stoberl get compensation for storing the buses, despite the lack of a formal agreement?

8. Wescoat, for a valuable consideration, gave Ryder an option to purchase a 120-acre farm upon which Wescoat had an option. Ryder's option was to expire on September 1; but on August 20, Ryder told Wescoat that he (Ryder) was going to "pass" on the option. Wescoat then talked to a bank about financing so that he could exercise his option. Wescoat also talked to a bulldozer operator about doing some work on the farm and investigated the possibility of getting some liming done. On August 30 Ryder offered Wescoat a signed agreement picking up Ryder's option along with the down payment as originally agreed. Wescoat refused to sign the agreement or accept the money. Can Ryder pick up the option after once passing it?

9. On February 16, 1966, Burgess signed a document which purported to grant to State University a 60-day option to purchase Burgess' home. That document, drafted by State University's agent, acknowledged the receipt by Burgess of "One and no/100 ($1.00)

Dollars and other valuable consideration." Neither the one dollar nor any other consideration was ever tendered or paid to Burgess. Hours after the purported option was executed, Burgess called State University and told them she was revoking the offer. On April 14, 1966, State University delivered to Burgess a written notice of its intention to exercise the option. On the closing date, Burgess rejected State University's tender of the purchase price. State University now sues for specific performance of the purported option. Burgess claims that the purchase option was void for want of consideration and that she effectively revoked the option by telephone. Was the document signed by Burgess on February 16, 1966, a valid option?

10. Apex Parts Company sent its salesperson Nelson to solicit parts orders from Green Distributing Company. Green placed an order for $5,000 and signed the order form provided by Nelson. The order form contained many terms but one term stated, "All orders are subject to approval by home office and buyer agrees this order will remain firm for 30 days from date placed." Green signed the form at the bottom. Ten days later Green wrote Apex asking that the order be cancelled. Apex immediately notified Green that the parts were being shipped. Green refused to accept delivery and Apex sued for breach of contract contending Green had made a firm offer. Is Apex right?

8

Acceptance

The Acceptance

The significant changes in the law of acceptance as applied to sale of goods contracts subject to the Code will be discussed at the end of this chapter.

Requirements for Acceptance. The basis of a contract is the mutual consent of the parties to the contract. This consent is manifested by one party—the offeror—making an offer to another party—the offeree—and by the offeree indicating, either expressly or by implication, a willingness to be bound on the terms stated in the offer. The offeree has no legal right to insist that the proposition made be reasonable, practical, or sensible. The proposition is that of the offeror, and if the offeree wishes to accept it, the offeree must agree to all of its terms. Any attempt on the part of the offeree, in the acceptance, to alter the terms of the offeror's proposition will terminate the offer.

The common law rule is that the offeree's acceptance must correspond in all respects with the offer. This does not mean that the offeree must, in accepting an offer, repeat the words of the offer; but it does mean that the offeree must, by words or acts, clearly manifest an intent to comply in all aspects with the terms which the offeror has stipulated.

Offer in Unilateral Contract. An offer in a unilateral contract is, as a general rule, a promise for an act. To accept such an offer, the offeree must perform the act as requested. Any material variance between the requested act and the tendered performance will result in no acceptance. If the nature of the requested act is such that it will take a substantial period of time for its completion, there will have been no acceptance of the offer until the act has been completed. Under some circumstances, if the offeree has started performance of the requested act, the offer may be irrevocable until he or she has had a reasonable opportunity to complete the performance. If the offeree has started performance and the offeror revokes his offer before performance is completed, the offeree can recover in a suit in quasi contract for benefits conferred.

Offer in Bilateral Contract. An offer for a bilateral contract states or implies the promise which the offeror requests the offeree to make if he wishes to accept the offer. Except for the provisions of the Code stated below relative to offers for contracts for the sale of goods, if the offeree wishes to accept the offer he must make the promise requested, as requested. No other or different promise than that stated in the offer will suffice as an acceptance. If the offeree, in attempting to accept the offer, makes a promise which adds to, subtracts from, or alters the terms of the promise requested, it is a counter-offer or conditional acceptance, and no contract results.

When a Writing Is Anticipated. Frequently, the parties negotiating a contract will have a written draft of the agreement drawn and signed. Whether a binding contract is entered into by the parties before they sign the written draft or at the time they sign, depends entirely on the intentions of the parties. Their intention will be determined by the application of the objective standard of what a reasonable person familiar with the facts and circumstances would be justified in believing the parties intended.

Usually, where the parties have completed their negotiations and have reached an agreement on all the material provisions of their transaction, the courts have held that a binding contract results. A decision to have a written draft of the agreement drawn and signed by the parties will not affect the time at which the binding contract came into existence. If the parties do not agree on the terms of the written draft, their disagreement will not discharge them from their liability on the contract into which they have already entered. If they agree on the terms of the written draft and sign it, the writing will be accepted in court as the best evidence of the terms of their contract.

Where the parties are negotiating a complicated agreement and make rough drafts of the agreement for the purpose of correcting mistakes and making alterations, the courts usually will hold that a binding contract does not result until the final written draft is approved by the parties. Such final approval is usually indicated by the signing of the written draft.

Silence as Acceptance. The legal principle that one cannot impose a contractual obligation on another without the consent of that person, either expressed or implied, is well established. The application of this legal principle prevents the offeror from so wording his offer that the offeree will be forced to act or be bound by a contract. Mere silence on the part of the offeree, as a general rule, is not acceptance.

The relation of the parties, the course of dealing, usage of trade, a prior agreement, or other special circumstances may impose on the offeree a duty to reject an offer or be bound by it. If this is true, the offeree's silence will amount to an acceptance, and a contract will result.

Intention to Accept. In order to have a valid acceptance of an offer, the offeree must have performed the act or made the promise requested in the offer with the intention of accepting the offer. The same standards are applied in determining the intentions of the offeree as are applied in determining the intentions of the offeror. The objective test of what a reasonably prudent person would be justified in believing under the circumstances is the test applied.

SUMMARY

An offeree, in order to accept an offer, must perform the requested act as requested or make the requested promise with the intent to accept the offer. In the case of a unilateral contract the offeree must perform the requested act, and in the case of a bilateral contract the offeree must make the requested promise. If a written draft of the agreement is anticipated, whether the parties are bound before the signing of the written draft or at the time of the signing will depend on the intention of the parties. As a general rule, silence on the part of the offeree is not an acceptance. However, by the agreement of the parties, by usage of trade, or by course of dealing, the offeree may owe a duty to reject an offer, in which case his failure to give notice of rejection will amount to an acceptance. In order to have an acceptance of an offer, the offeree must have performed the requested act or made the requested promise with the intention of accepting the offer. In determining intention, one must apply the objective test of what a reasonably prudent person would be justified in believing the offeree intended.

Corbin-Dykes Electric Co. v. Burr

500 P.2d 632 (Ct. App. Ariz. 1972)

This is an action by Corbin-Dykes Electric Company (plaintiff) against Burr (defendant) for failure to give them a subcontract. Judgment for Burr and Corbin-Dykes appealed. Affirmed.

General Motors Corporation requested bids from general contractors to construct the central air-conditioning plant at its Mesa plant. Burr, a general contractor, was interested in obtaining the contract and as a result received bids for the electrical subcontract. One of the bids received by Burr was from Corbin-Dykes.

Burr incorporated Corbin-Dykes' subcontract bid, which was the low bid, into this general contract bid and submitted it to General Motors Corporation. All bids were rejected by General Motors because they exceeded the cost estimate; and the project was rebid. The second bid submitted by Burr also included the Corbin-Dykes subcontract bid; however, prior to submitting the second bid, Burr had received another bid from Sands. This bid matched the Corbin-Dykes bid but also provided that, in the event Sand could work the proposed project in conjunction with its current project at the plant, they would reduce their subcontract bid by $4,000. When the second round of bids was opened, Burr was awarded the general contract, and since Sands' other project at the plant was not yet completed, Burr accepted Sands' bid for the electric subcontract as the low bid.

Corbin-Dykes objected to this selection of Sands as the subcontractor and sued Burr for breach of their alleged subcontract.

EUBANK, JUDGE. In Arizona the law is clear that Corbin-Dykes' bid to Burr was nothing more than an offer to perform the subcontract under specified terms, and that it did not ripen into a contract until it was voluntarily accepted by Burr. The law and its related problems are well stated in the 53 *Virginia L. Rev.* 1720 (1967).

From the time a general contractor (general) receives bids from subcontractors (subs) until he formally accepts one of those bids, the parties are not adequately protected by the common law. Although they are forced by the commercial context to rely upon each other during this period, at common law their relationship cannot be contractual until the general responds with the requisite promise of acceptance. To some extent the promissory estoppel doctrine has alleviated the general's problems by binding the sub to perform according to the terms of his bid. But this protection is one-sided, and despite the view of some courts that promissory estoppel is a panacea, it appears that in confining the scope of protection to the general, the doctrine in fact raises serious problems.

Corbin-Dykes relies on no evidence of the acceptance of their offer by Burr except . . . custom and usage. As we have seen, a "voluntary acceptance" is required to bind Burr. It is also clear from the cited case law that such custom and usage evidence cannot be used to initially establish acceptance or the manifestation of mutual assent.

In our opinion the record shows no evidence of a voluntary acceptance of the offer involved, since the inclusion of Corbin-Dykes' subcontract bid as a part of the general contract bid did not constitute such an acceptance, and the offer never was accepted by Burr in any other manner.

Crouch v. Marrs

430 P.2d 204 (Sup. Ct. Kan. 1967)

This was a suit by Crouch (plaintiff) against Marrs, Purex Corporation and others (defendants) to establish Crouch's rights in regard to a certain building. From a judgment for the defendants; Crouch appealed. Reversed.

On February 26, 1964, Crouch wrote to the Purex Corporation asking for their lowest price if they were interested in selling an old plant building and its contents located in Meade, Kansas. The letter read in part:

I would be interested in buying the old building that housed the plant and what other items that are still left. The items that are still left are: two crushers, furnace and the elevator is about all that is left.

On March 4, 1964, Crouch received a letter of reply from Purex Corporation signed by Frank Knox which stated:

We will sell this building and equipment in and about the building for a total of $500.

On March 19, 1964, Crouch wrote to Frank Knox, Purex Corporation, stating that the building was in "pretty bad condition" and asking, "Would you consider taking $300 for what is left?" This letter was not answered. On April 16, 1964, Crouch addressed another letter to Knox, Purex Corporation, which read:

I guess we will buy the building for the amount you quoted, $500.

I am sending you a personal check for this amount.

It will be two or three weeks before we can get started; and I presume that we will be allowed all the time that we need to remove the material.

On April 17, 1964, the Purex Corporation, through Knox, wrote a letter to another potential buyer, Asche, which stated:

In answer to your inquiry about our property approximately six miles north of Meade, Kansas. We will sell for $500 the mine building and whatever machinery and equipment which remains in or about that building. A condition of sale will require that the property purchased be removed from the premises within 45 days.

If this price is acceptable we will be pleased to receive a cashier's check to cover.

On April 23, Knox, on behalf of Purex Corporation, endorsed and cashed the check which Crouch had mailed on April 16.

On April 24, 1964, Asche wrote a letter accepting the offer of April 17, which read:

We are enclosing a cashier's check for $500 and the bill of sale of mine buildings with the agreement of option to purchase property.

If the corporation has any other property and machinery in this area for sale, we would be pleased to deal with the corporation. It was our pleasure to deal with the Purex Corporation.

On April 27, 1964, Knox sent Crouch the following telegram:

Your counter offer received April 23 is unacceptable. Your check mistakenly deposited by Purex will be recovered and returned to you or Purex check will be issued to you if your check cannot be located.

There followed a letter dated May 16, 1964, which read:

This is a follow-up to our telegram to you of April 27, advising you that your check which we received on April 23 was not acceptable, but that it had been deposited by mistake. Since we were unable to recover your check, we herewith enclose our check for $500 to reimburse you.

We wish to explain, that the reason we could not accept your counter-offer of $500 for the mine building and machinery at Meade, Kansas was because we had received and accepted an offer from another party prior to receipt of yours on April 23.

In the meantime Asche had entered into a contract to sell the building to Roy Marrs who owned the land surrounding the building site for $500 and had entered into a contract to sell the equipment to the C. & D. Used Truck Parts for $800.

Crouch started to salvage the building but Roy Marrs put a lock on the gate and would not allow Crouch to enter.

Crouch then brought an action to enjoin Marrs from interfering with his salvage operations.

HATCHER, COMMISSIONER. Marrs contends that Crouch's check was cashed through inadvertence or an error in office procedure and under such circumstances the cashing of the check did not constitute an acceptance of Crouch's offer. The difficulty with this contention is that there was no evidence of any character as to why the check was cashed. Neither would the error void the contract unless mutual mistake was pleaded.

Crouch suggests that the statement in the letter of May 6, 1964, to the effect "we have received and accepted an offer from another party prior to receipt of yours" was a "falsehood" as Asche's acceptance was dated one day after Crouch's check was in the Los Angeles Clearing House. We need not speculate as to the binding effect of Purex Corporation's offer to Asche. The question is whether the endorsing and depositing of Crouch's check constituted an acceptance of his offer to buy. We think it did.

The endorsing and depositing of a check constitutes an acceptance of the offer to buy which accompanies it because the act itself indicates acceptance. An offer may be accepted by performing a specified act as well as by an affirmative answer. Also, where the offeree exercised dominion over the thing offered him—in this instance the check—such exercise constitutes an acceptance of the offer.

Johnson v. Star Iron and Steel Co.

511 P.2d 1370 (Ct. App. Wash. 1973)

Johnson (plaintiff) sued Star Iron and Steel Company (defendant) for compensation under an alleged contract whereby Johnson was to help Star Iron procure some loan funds. Judgment for Star Iron and Johnson appealed. Affirmed.

In a letter dated September 29, 1969, Johnson offered to arrange loan funds for Star Iron in the amount of $500,000. Paragraph 3 stipulated that the funds were to be in the form of "bank book deposits in a local bank of our choice." In a letter dated October 3, Star Iron accepted on condition that "in a local bank of our choice" be changed to read "Bank of Tacoma." On October 8, Star Iron notified Johnson that Star Iron was withdrawing its conditional acceptance. By a letter dated October 8 and mailed October 9, Johnson notified Star Iron that he agreed to the paragraph 3 change included in Star Iron's letter of October 3. Johnson sued when Star Iron refused to proceed with the transaction.

PEARSON, CHIEF JUDGE. It is axiomatic that an expression of assent that changes the terms of an offer in any material respect may operate as a counteroffer, but is not an acceptance. The issue then raised is whether the exceptions noted above were *material* modifications of the offer.

In *Northwest Properties Agency, Inc. v. McGhee,* this court held that if a "condition *added* by the intended acceptance can be implied in the original offer then it does not constitute a material variance so as to make the acceptance ineffective." [Italics ours.] Otherwise, the condition is a material variance. In our view, this principle applies equally to variances in the acceptance that would change terms of the offer. Using this test, the change in paragraph 3 was clearly material.

The modification of paragraph 3 meant that Johnson's performance would be entirely dependent on the willingness of the Bank of Tacoma to extend credit on the basis of a plan which had been worked out in the Bank's absence. The original offer gave Johnson the option of completing his performance through any local bank. The limitation on the scope of performance effected by the alteration of paragraph 3 in the purported acceptance does not even remotely resemble the scope of performance afforded by the terms of the original offer. Consequently, the paragraph 3 revision must be characterized as a material variance.

Communication of Acceptance

Requirements for Communication. The acceptance of a unilateral contract, as a general rule, requires the doing of an act, although under some circumstances it may require the making of a promise. The acceptance of a bilateral contract requires the making of the requested promise. The law does not recognize as valid an uncommunicated promise; consequently, if the acceptance of an offer requires the making of a promise, the acceptance is not effective until the promise is communicated to the offeror. If the offeror, in the offer, stipulates the time, place, or method of communicating the acceptance, the offeree must comply fully with these terms if the offeree wishes to accept. An attempt to accept at a time or place, or in a manner other than that stipulated, would be, in legal effect, a counteroffer.

If a method or place of communication is merely suggested and not stipulated, acceptance may be communicated by a different method or at a different place, provided it is delivered to the offeror before the offer terminates.

If the offer is silent as to the time, place, or method of communicating the acceptance, the offeree may accept within a reasonable time, at any place, and by any recognized method of communication, provided the acceptance is received by the offeror before the offer terminates.

When Acceptance Is Communicated. Under some circumstances, it becomes important to determine the place and exact time at which a contract comes into existence. A contract comes into existence at the time the offer is accepted and at the place in which the last act is performed which creates the contract. This raises the question of when an acceptance is communicated.

If the parties are dealing face to face, the contract comes into existence at the time the words or acts of acceptance are spoken or performed and at the location of the two parties at this time. If the parties are negotiating over the telephone, the contract comes into existence at the time the offeree speaks the words of acceptance into the telephone and at the location of the offeree at this time.

If the parties are using some agency of communication such as the mails or telegraph, there will be a time lag between the dispatching and the receipt of the acceptance. There will also be a risk that the message of acceptance will never reach its destination—the offeror. Since the offeror is in a position to include any provisions in his offer he wishes, he may so word the offer that the acceptance is not operative until it is actually received.

Authorized Means of Communication. An acceptance is effective and a contract arises when the acceptance is dispatched, provided the offeree uses the means of communication authorized by the offeror. If the offer states no agency of communication, the means of communication used by the offeror to communicate the offer is the authorized means of communication. That is, if the offer is sent by mail, the offeree is authorized to use the mail to communicate acceptance, and a contract arises at the time the letter of acceptance is dropped into an official depository for mail. Likewise, if the offeror in his offer expressly authorizes the offeree to send his acceptance by a designated means of communication, an acceptance sent by the designated means of communication is effective, and a contract arises at the time the acceptance is dispatched.

The courts have distinguished between a stipulated means of communication and an authorized means of communication. Whether a means of communication mentioned in an offer is stipulated or authorized will depend on the language of the offer interpreted in relation to trade usage and the surrounding circumstances. If the offeror has, in effect, stated "*you must*" use this means of communication, the means of communication is stipulated; but if the offeror has stated "*you may*" use this means of communication, the means of communication is authorized. In all events the acceptance must be communicated before the offer terminates.

When Acceptance Is by a Means Not Authorized. If an acceptance is sent by a means of communication other than that authorized by the offeror, the acceptance is not effective until it is received and then only if it is received by the offeror within the time the acceptance would have been received had the authorized agency of communication been used. By using a means of communication not authorized by the offeror, the offeree assumes all the risks of the means selected.

SUMMARY

An acceptance is not effective until communicated to the offeror. If, as a part of an offer, the time, place, and method of communication of the acceptance are stipulated, such stipulation must be complied with by the offeree in accepting the offer. If the offer is silent in respect to time, place, and method of communication of the acceptance, the offeree may communicate acceptance to the offeror at any reasonable time, to any reasonable place, by a method of communication.

If a means of communication is used by the offeror to communicate an offer, by implication, the offeror authorizes the offeree to use the same means of communication to communicate the acceptance; and if the offeree uses such means of communication, the acceptance is effective, and a contract results when the acceptance is delivered to the means of communication. The offeror, in the offer, may expressly authorize the offeree to use a particular means of communication to communicate an acceptance, or a means of communication may be authorized by usage of trade. If the offeree uses the authorized means of communication to communicate the acceptance, the acceptance is effective, and a contract results when the acceptance is delivered to such means of communication. The offeror accepts all the risks of the means of communication.

If the offeree uses an unauthorized means of communication he or she assumes all the risk of the communication of the acceptance. The acceptance is not effective until it is received, and then only provided it is received within the time an acceptance by the authorized means would have been received had it been delivered in the ordinary course.

Morello v. Growers Grape Products Assoc.

186 P.2d 463 (Ct. App. Cal. 1947)

This was an action by Morello (plaintiff) against Growers Grape Products Association and others (defendants) to recover damages for the breach of an alleged contract to sell brandy. Judgment on a directed verdict for Growers Grape Products Association, and Morello appealed. Judgment reversed.

Morello and Growers Grape Products Association (Association) entered into a contract under which Morello processed brandy for Association. This contract provided that Association would give Morello an opportunity to purchase the brandy which he processed. By the terms of this contract Association was to notify Morello when they had decided to sell the brandy and the price at which they were selling, and Morello was to have five days in which to accept the offer. On November 9, 1942, Association wrote Morello as follows: "The unsold brandy of your distillation remaining in the pool, according to our records, amounts to approximately 23,902—46 original proof gallons. This amount, which is subject to our final verification, or any quantity thereof, is offered to you at $1.25 cash, per original proof gallon, f.o.b. the storage racks within the Internal Revenue Service Bonded Warehouse where it is now held, provided: "1. That you accept this offer in writing or by telegraphic notification delivered within five days from the date of this letter."

On November 13, 1942, Morello called Association by telephone and attempted to accept the offer but Association told Morello that his acceptance must be in writing or by telegraphic notification. On November 13, 1942, Morello mailed his acceptance at Fresno, California. Association claims that it did not receive the letter of acceptance until Monday, November 16, 1942. The offices of Association are in San Francisco and they were closed on Sunday, November 15. Association claims that no contract resulted because Morello did not accept its offer in writing within five days.

GOODELL, JUSTICE. Morello testified that he telephoned his acceptance to Association on the 13th and was told that he must put it in writing. The offer called for either written or telegraphic notification, so the telephonic "acceptance" has to be disregarded. However, if Morello's letter dated the 13th was mailed even as late as the 14th—the fifth day—it was within time, although not *received* in San Francisco until Monday, the 16th. Neither paragraph 13 nor the offer itself specifies that the acceptance must be *received* within five days; they call for an acceptance *delivered* within five days.

It is elementary that a contract is complete when the letter of acceptance is posted. The word "delivered" in the offer creates only an apparent, not a real difficulty, because under the law dealing with the formation of contract *delivery of an acceptance to the post office operates as delivery to the person addressed,* except in unusual cases.

There are many cases holding substantially that the deposit by one party in the mails of an instrument properly addressed to the other party, with postage thereon prepaid, constitutes a *delivery* to the other party, *at the place where* and the *time when it is so deposited.*

The post office was clearly the agent of the offeror, for the offer was itself sent by mail and it called for an acceptance in writing and thereby invited the use of the same medium as that chosen for the offer.

Changes under the U.C.C.

The Code attempts to make the enforceability of business contracts depend more on the intent of the parties and less upon technical rules and legal formalities. A contract for the sale of goods may be made in any manner sufficient to show agreement even though the moment of its making cannot be determined. A contract may exist even though many terms are left open. (2–308—2–311.)[1] The only requirement is that there must be a "reasonably certain basis" for giving an "appropriate" remedy. (2–204.)

The fact that the price is left unsettled, is later to be agreed upon, or is to be set by one of the parties does not defeat the contract. (2–305.) Output, requirements, and exclusive dealing contracts are rendered more enforceable. (2–305.) In all of these "loose" or informal contractual situations the basic duty to act in good faith and in accordance with standards of commercial reasonableness helps to define the obligations of the parties.

The mercantile practice of using forms in the buying and selling of goods has created some problems. For example, A may use a form in offering to buy goods from B, and B may use a form in accepting the offer, and the terms of acceptance may differ in some respects from those of the offer. Under the common law no contract resulted. However, with some exceptions, merchants were inclined to ignore these differences and proceed to perform.

The Code has been drafted on the assumption that agreements should be enforced if they have been consummated by commercial understanding. To implement this view the Code provides: A definite and seasonable expression of acceptance or a written confirmation which is sent within a reasonable time operates as an acceptance even though it states terms additional to or different from those offered or agreed upon, unless acceptance is expressly made conditional on assent to the additional or different terms. (2–207 [1].) Under this provision, if the offeree expressly states that his different or additional terms must be agreed to by the offeror, such an attempt to accept would be a counteroffer and would terminate the original offer.

If the negotiating parties are merchants and the acceptance includes additional or different terms, such terms will be treated as proposals for additions to the contract, and the offeror will be bound by such terms unless one of three circumstances occur. The offer must either expressly limit acceptance to the terms of the offer, or the proposed additional of different terms must materially alter the terms of the offer, or the offeror must give reasonable notification of his objection to the changed terms. (2–207 [2].) If the parties, by their conduct, recognize the existence of a contract when their writings do not otherwise establish one, the terms of the particular contract consist of those terms on which the writing of the parties agree, together with any supplementary terms incorporated under any other provision of the Code. (2–207 [3].)

The rules relative to the means used to communicate an acceptance have

[1] The numbers in parentheses refer to the sections of the Uniform Commercial Code, 1962.

been relaxed under the provisions of the Code. Unless the offeror expressly stipulates that a designated agency of communication must be used, the offeree may accept in any manner or by any medium reasonable under the circumstances. (2–206.) If an offer is made by mail and the acceptance is made by telegram, the acceptance would be effective and the contract would be consummated when the telegram was dispatched, provided a telegraphic acceptance was reasonable under the circumstances.

If a buyer orders goods for prompt shipment, his or her offer can be accepted either by a prompt promise to ship or by the shipment of conforming goods. The failure of the seller to either promptly notify or to promptly ship causes the offer to lapse. A shipment of nonconforming goods is not an acceptance if the seller notifies the buyer that he or she is shipping nonconforming goods as an accommodation. (2–206–1 [b].) If a seller receives an order or offer to purchase goods for prompt shipment and the seller ships nonconforming goods without giving the buyer the required notice, the shipment of the goods is an acceptance and since the seller has shipped nonconforming goods, the seller will be liable for breach of the contract.

SUMMARY

The Code gives greater weight to the intentions of the parties and less weight to technical form requirements. The "matching terms" concept is replaced by (2–207) which permits a contract to exist even though no full agreement exists. Acceptance may be by any reasonable means and orders for immediate shipment must be handled promptly either by notice or by shipment. If a seller ships nonconforming goods in response to an order for immediate shipment, the seller will be deemed to have accepted the buyer's original order unless he or she notifies the buyer that the nonconforming goods are being shipped for the buyer's accommodation.

Southwest Engineering Co. v. Martin Tractor Co.

473 P.2d 18 (Sup. Ct. Kan. 1970)

This is an action by Southwest Engineering Company (plaintiff) against Martin Tractor Company (defendant) to recover damages for breach of contract. Judgment for Southwest and Martin appealed. Affirmed.

In April, 1966, Southwest was interested in submitting a bid to the Corps of Engineers for the construction of certain runway lighting facilities at an Air Force Base at Wichita. However, before submitting a bid, and on April 11, 1966, Southwest's construction superintendent, Cloepfil, called the manager of Martin's engine department, Hurt, asking for a price on a standby generator and accessory equipment. Hurt replied that he would phone him back which he did quoting a price of $18,500. This quotation was reconfirmed by Hurt over the phone on April 13.

Southwest submitted its bid on April 14, 1966, using Hurt's figure of $18,500 for the generating equipment, and its bid was accepted. On April 20, Southwest notified Martin that the bid had been accepted. Hurt and Cloepfil thereafter agreed over the phone to meet in Springfield on April 28.

At the Springfield meeting it developed that Martin had upped its price for the generator and accessory equipment from $18,500 to $21,500. Despite this change of position by Martin, the two men continued their conversation and, according to Cloepfil, they arrived at an agreement for the sale of a D353 generator and accessories for the sum of $21,500. In addition it was agreed that if the Corps of Engineers would accept a less expensive generator, a D343, the aggregate price to Southwest would be $15,000.

A memorandum with these terms was drawn at that time but there was no definite agreement concerning the exact time and method for payment. Hurt later refused to deliver a D353 generator as requested by Southwest, and Southwest had to procure one from another source. Southwest secured the generator equipment from Foley Tractor Co. at a price of $27,541 and then filed suit seeking damages of $6,041 for breach of the contract.

Fontron, Justice. It is quite true, as the trial court found, that terms of payment were not agreed upon at the Springfield meeting. Hurt testified that as the memorandum was being made out, he said they wanted 10 percent with the order, 50 percent on delivery and the balance on acceptance, but he did not recall Cloepfil's response. Cloepfil's version was somewhat different. He stated that after the two had shaken hands in the lobby preparing to leave, Hurt said their terms usually were 20 percent down and the balance on delivery; while he (Cloepfil) said the way they generally paid was 90 percent on the tenth of the month following delivery and the balance on final acceptance. It is obvious the parties reached no agreement on this point.

However, a failure on the part of . . . Hurt and Cloepfil to agree on terms of payment would not, of itself, defeat an otherwise valid agreement reached by them. K.S.A. 84–2–204(3) reads:

> Even though one or more terms are left open a contract for sale does not fail for indefiniteness if the parties have intended to make a contract and there is a reasonably certain basis for giving an appropriate remedy.

So far as the present case is concerned, K.S.A. 84–2–310 supplies the omitted term. This statute provides in pertinent part:

> Unless otherwise agreed.
> (*a*) payment is due at the time and place at which the buyer is to receive the goods even though the place of shipment is the place of delivery . . .

In our view, the language of the two Code provisions is clear and positive. Considered together, we take the two sections to mean that where parties have reached an enforceable agreement for the sale of goods, but omit therefrom the terms of payment, the law will imply, as part of the agreement, that payment is to be made at time of delivery. In this respect the law does not greatly differ from the rule this court laid down years ago.

We do not mean to imply that terms of payment are not of importance under many circumstances, or that parties may not condition an agreement on their being included.

Air Products and Chemical Inc. v. Fairbanks Morse, Inc.

206 N.W.2d 414 (Wis. Sup. Ct. 1973)

Air Products (plaintiff) sued Fairbanks Morse (defendant) for damages due to defective motors delivered under an alleged contract between Air Products and Fairbanks. The lower court ruled for Fairbanks and Air Products appealed. Reversed.

Air Products sent a purchase order for motors containing many terms but no express provision making assent to different or additional terms conditional upon Air Products' assent to them. Fairbanks signed the purchase order and sent it back with an acknowledgment form which had printed on it in reasonably bold type:

> WE THANK YOU FOR YOUR ORDER AS COPIED HEREON, WHICH WILL RECEIVE PROMPT ATTENTION AND SHALL BE GOVERNED BY THE PROVISIONS ON THE REVERSE SIDE HEREOF UNLESS YOU NOTIFY US TO THE CONTRARY WITHIN TEN DAYS OR BEFORE SHIPMENT WHICHEVER IS EARLIER.

On the reverse side of the "acknowledgment of order" there are printed six separate provisions which are appropriately numbered and at the very beginning it is stated that:

> The following provisions form part of the order acknowledged and accepted on the face hereof, as express agreements between Fairbanks, Morse & Co. ('Company") and the Buyer governing the terms and conditions of the sale, subject to modification only in writing signed by the local manager or an executive officer of the Company:"

Provision no. 6 which is the subject of the dispute between the parties provided that:

> 6. The Company nowise assumes any responsibility or liability with respect to use, purpose, or suitability, and shall not be liable for damages of any character, whether direct of consequential, for defect, delay, or otherwise, its sole liability and obligation being confined to the replacement in the manner aforesaid of defectively manufactured guaranteed parts failing within the time stated.

HANLEY, JUSTICE. Fairbanks contends that provision no. 6 contained on the reverse side of their "acknowledgment of order" became part of the contract between it and Air Products while Air Products contends that its right to rely on the implied warranty of merchantability (U.C.C. 2–314) fitness for particular purposes (U.C.C. 2–315) and consequential damages (U.C.C. 2–714) has in no way been limited by provision no. 6, since it never was assented to by it, and, therefore, it never became part of the contract.

[U]nder subsection (1), 2–207, there are two instances in which a contract may not have been formed. First, if the offeror could not reasonably treat the response of the offeree as an acceptance there is no contract. Second, if the offeree's acceptance is made expressly conditional on the offeror's assent to variant provisions, the offeree has made a counteroffer. However, under section 2–207(3) either situation may result in contract formation by subsequent conduct of the parties.

Because the reverse side of Fairbanks' Acknowledgment of Order states that the provisions contained there ". . . form part of the order acknowledged and accepted on the face hereof . . ." it would seem that Air Products could have "reasonably" assumed that the parties "had a deal."

Since there is no express provision in the purchase orders making assent to different or additional terms conditional upon Air Products' assent to them, the second requirement of coming under U.C.C. 2–207 is also met.

At this point a contract does in fact exist between the parties under (1). Subsection (2) must now be resorted to see which of the "variant" terms will actually become part of the contract.

We think Fairbanks was aware of the particular needs of Air Products. A reading of section 2–714 and 2–715 indicates that a potential recovery for consequential loss is implicit in the contract.

Air Products next contends that if the added terms of the "acknowledgment of order" were "additional" terms they still do not become part of the contract because the prerequisite to their becoming a part of the contract which are contained in subsection (2) were not satisfied. Section 2–207(2) required that:

> The additional terms are to be construed as proposals for addition to the contract. Between merchants such terms become part of the contract unless:
> (a) the offer expressly limits acceptance to the terms of the offer;
> (b) they materially alter it; or
> (c) notification of objection to them has already been given or is given within a reasonable time after notice of them is received.

The language employed by Air Products in its "terms and conditions" was not express enough to bring into play the provisions of either subsection 2–207(a) or (c). The ultimate question to be determined, therefore, is whether the disclaimer contained in Fairbanks' "acknowledgment of order" materially altered the agreement between the parties pursuant to section 2–207 (2)(b). If they materially alter what would otherwise be firmed by the acceptance of an offer, they will not become terms unless the buyer expressly agrees thereto. "If, however, they are terms which would not so change the bargain they will be incorporated unless notice of objection to them has already been given or is given within a reasonable time."

We conclude that the disclaimer for consequential loss was sufficiently material to require express conversation between the parties over its inclusion or exclusion in the contract.

Problem Cases

1. Chalkley Metals Company had contracted to supply the U.S. Navy with 500,000 pounds of copper ingot. Because the Navy needed more copper, Hoover, a Navy procurement officer, telephoned Chalkley and inquired whether Chalkley could supply another 600,000 pounds of copper. Hoover and Chalkley discussed the terms of the new agreement, and Hoover said, "It's practically in the bag, but I'll need formal approval from the top brass. I seldom get turned down on contracts like this." Chalkley purchased 600,000 pounds of copper from primary sources and then learned that Hoover's agreement had been unacceptable to the Navy. After the new copper was sold at less than the Hoover agreement anticipated, Chalkley sued for breach of contract to recover the balance. The Navy claimed that there was no new contract. Is the Navy correct?

2. The Rio Grande Pickle Co. offered Fujimoto an employment contract whereby, if he assented to it, he would receive a bonus of 10 percent of the company's profits for each fiscal year. The written offer was made in order to prevent Fujimoto from terminating his employment with the company. Fujimoto signed the contract and continued to work for the Company for another 14 months, but he failed to return the contract to the Company. The Company argued that by his failure to return the contract, Fujimoto had failed to accept the offer. Can Fujimoto bind the Company to the terms of the contract?

3. Dohman offered his residence for sale. Sullivan was interested and offered to buy the property for $10,250 cash. Dohman was in Florida and negotiations were carried on by letter and telegrams. When negotiations were completed, Dohman sent his broker a contract embodying the terms agreed upon. Sullivan signed the contract and it was returned to Dohman for his signature. Dohman refused to sign and refused to convey the residence to Sullivan. Sullivan brought suit asking specific performance of the contract. Dohman set up a defense that he had not signed the formal contract. Is the defense good?

4. Mr. and Mrs. Colburn brought an action against Mid-States Homes, Inc. to restrain a foreclosure sale. Mid-State was the assignee of Jim Walter Corporation, mortgagee of the property in dispute. Plaintiffs alleged that the facially valid mortgage document was "null, void, and of no effect." The basis for the charge was that plaintiffs never realized at the time of signing that they were signing a mortgage document. The signatures were properly notarized. No fraud was alleged. Assuming the plaintiffs' ignorance about the mortgage was correct, does Mid-State hold a valid mortgage assignment?

5. Swingle was vice president of a Tucson Savings and Loan Association. Myerson, while lunching with Swingle, remarked that it was too bad that Swingle's firm was not interested in buying another savings and loan company that he knew was available for acquisition. Swingle then told Myerson that although his firm would not be interested, he was. Later, he told Myerson that he would consider purchasing the stock of the other savings and loan company if a Tucson branch could be established and if he could own 51 percent of its stock. Myerson then put Swingle in contact with the savings and loan company and mentioned that he expected to be compensated for his efforts if the transaction was

effected. Swingle bought the company, but refused to pay Myerson. May Myerson recover a "finders' fee" against Swingle?

6. Seigel entered a Giant Food supermarket to purchase groceries. While he was removing a six-pack carton of Coca-Cola from the display bin to a shopping cart, four of the bottles exploded spraying Coca-Cola on the floor and causing him to lose his footing and fall. There was no evidence of mishandling or improper stacking of the bottles. In a suit against Giant to recover damages for his personal injuries, Seigel relied upon a breach of implied warranty of merchantability. Giant denied that such a warranty existed under these circumstances because no contract existed until the items were checked out. Is this a valid defense?
7. In 1970, the University of Wisconsin invited bids from contractors for the construction of water transmission lines. Janke, intending to bid on the job, obtained price quotations from several suppliers. One such supplier, Vulcan, submitted a quotation to Janke over the phone. As this quotation was the lowest, Janke used it in his bid; subsequently Janke was awarded the contract. Later on, a dispute arose over the type of pipe to be used in the project and Vulcan ultimately refused to furnish the type of pipe requested by Janke. Janke sued Vulcan for breach of contract contending that a valid offer and acceptance occurred when he used Vulcan's price quotation in his bid. Is Janke correct?
8. Swisshelm offered to sell 1,500 bushels of corn to Ohio Grain Co. at $2.45 per bushel. Ohio Grain Co.'s agent orally accepted the offer and later the same day sent a written confirmation and details to Swisshelm, providing that its retention by seller was an acceptance of the contract. Swisshelm made no response, but later sold the corn in the market at $2.70 per bushel. Can Ohio Grain Co. collect damages against Swisshelm for breach of contract?
9. McAfee sent a letter to Brewer offering to sell items of furniture at specified prices, $3,000 due upon acceptance, and $2,635 within 120 days. The first clause read: "If the above is satisfactory, please sign and return one copy with the first payment."

   Brewer answered: "Exams were horrible but Florida was great! Enclosing a $3,000 check. I've misplaced the contracts. Can secretary sent another set? Please include red secretary on the contract for entrance foyer."

   A disagreement arose as to just what Brewer had purchased, with McAfee believing all the furniture had been sold. Brewer argued that the $3,000 check covered only certain items totalling $3,000. Can McAfee recover the additional $2,635?
10. Doughboy, Inc., sent a purchase order for film to Pantasote Co. Pantasote immediately mailed back an acknowledgment form, and subsequently delivered the film. The acknowledgment form conflicted with Doughboy's purchase form; it contained a general arbitration clause for disputes, while the Doughboy purchase form did not; it provided that a failure to object in writing to the acknowledgment was acceptance of all its terms, Doughboy's purchase form said that no term could be changed without its written approval. Doughboy never objected to the terms of the Pantasote acknowledgment. A dispute has arisen which Pantasote wishes to settle by arbitration, Doughboy wants court litigation. Pantasote sues to require that Doughboy submit to arbitration. Must Doughboy arbitrate?
11. N&D Fashions sent a purchase order to DHJ Industries, agreeing to purchase some fabric from DHJ. DHJ, in turn, sent to N&D an acknowledgment of this purchase order. On the front side of this acknowledgment contract was a statement which said that the contract was "subject to all the terms and conditions printed on the reverse side." On the reverse side, DHJ had inserted an arbitration clause which materially altered the terms of the agreement between N&D and DHJ. N&D, upon receiving this acknowl-

edgment contract from DHJ, signed and returned it to DHJ. N&D now claims that since it failed to read the acknowledgment contract and the word "arbitration" did not appear on the front of the contract to indicate the presence of an arbitration clause on the reverse side, this arbitration clause must, therefore, not be included in the final sales agreement between the parties. Is N&D correct?

9

Reality of Consent

Introduction

Nature of Real Consent. One of the fundamental requirements for holding a person liable for the nonperformance of a contractual promise is that the promise must have been made voluntarily. Honesty and fair dealing are essential to the success of a private enterprise economy. Under our contract law a person receives protection against sharp dealing in contracts by the law dealing with misrepresentation, fraud, duress, or undue influence. In negotiating contracts the promisor will be required to exercise reasonable caution and judgment, and he will seldom be permitted to escape from promises carelessly made. Standards have been developed by the courts which are used as the basis for determining whether or not the promisor should be held to his promise.

Closely related to a promise induced by misrepresentation, fraud, duress, or undue influence is the promise based on a mistake of fact. If both parties to an agreement have acted in the erroneous assumption as to the existence or nonexistence of a material fact relating to their agreement, the courts have, as a general rule, granted relief.

Misrepresentation and Fraud

Misrepresentation. If one person, by words or acts or by any other conduct, has created in the mind of another an impression which is not in accordance with the facts, such person is guilty of misrepresentation. Misrepresentation of a material fact justifiably relied on is grounds for holding a contractual promise voidable. Knowledge of the falsity on the part of the person making the misrepresentation is not essential. The misrepresentation may be the result of either a honest mistake or negligence on the part of the misrepresenting party.

The misrepresentation must be of a material fact. To be material, the fact need not be the sole fact which induced the injured party to make the contractual promise, nor need it be the major inducement. It must be a contributing factor, however, and the circumstances must be such that it is reasonable to presume that the party would not have made the contractual promise had he known the true facts.

The misrepresentation must be of an existing or past fact. An expression of future happenings is prospective and is not a statement of fact. Likewise, arguments intended to convince a party that the transaction is a "good deal" are not statements of fact. In general, a "factual" representation is one concerning a matter that is reasonably subject to exact knowledge. A representation concerning a used car asserting, "This is the finest used car in town," is obviously not reasonably subject to exact knowledge, and hence is a statement of mere opinion. A representation, "The motor of this car has been rebuilt" is a statement of fact.

A party, in order to be entitled to a remedy, must have justifiably relied on the misrepresentations. If the party knows that the statements are erroneous, or if the facts and circumstances are such that, in the exercise of reasonable prudence, he or she should have investigated and discovered the falsity of the statements, he or she is not justified in relying on the statements.

As a general rule, if both parties have equal knowledge and equal opportunity to learn the true facts, neither party can safely assume that the law will provide any protection in the event of fraud by the other party. But if the party making the misrepresentations has superior knowledge or is in a better position to know the facts, the other party may, as a general rule, be justified on relying in the statements.

The remedy available to a party who is induced by misrepresentation to make a contractual promise is rescission—that is, the injured party may return what he has received and recover what he has given in performance of the contract, or its value. If no performance has been rendered, the injured party may give notice that he disaffirms the contract; and if suit is brought against him for breach of contract, he may set up the misrepresentation as a defense.

In all cases of misrepresentation the injured party must act seasonably. Failure to rescind or disaffirm within a reasonable time after the injured party learns of the misrepresentation amounts to waiver of the right to rescind or disaffirm.

Fraud. Fraud is an intentional misrepresentation of a material fact made for the purpose of inducing another, in reliance upon it, to part with some valuable thing belonging to him, or to surrender a legal right. If one party, through misrepresentations knowingly made, creates a mistaken belief as to the existence or nonexistence of a fact material to a transaction and thereby influences the action of the party to whom the representation is made, the party making the misrepresentation is guilty of fraudulent conduct.

The method used to create the mistaken belief is immaterial. It may be by words, acts, concealment, or any other method. The result is important, not the method whereby the result is attained. The terms *misrepresentation* and *fraud* are frequently used synonymously; however, misrepresentation, as used in law, signifies innocent misrepresentation, whereas fraud signifies intentional misrepresentation.

If a person is induced to make a contractual promise by fraudulent representations, he or she may rescind the contract, since the right to rescind is based on misrepresentation. However, if the elements of an actionable deceit are present—(1) misrepresentation of a material fact, (2) knowingly made, (3) with intent to defraud, (4) justifiably relied on, (5) with resulting injury—the injured party has an election of remedies. He may rescind the contract, or he may affirm the contract and bring an action in tort to recover damages for the deceit.[1] Damages for deceit include compensation for all injury resulting directly from the deceit and may include punitive damages. As in misrepresentation, the injured person must act seasonably, and his failure to give notice within a reasonable time after he learns of the deceit will amount to a waiver of his rights.

SUMMARY

A contract induced by innocent misrepresentations or by fraud does not bind the party induced to enter the contract by such means.

The remedy for misrepresentation is rescission. At common law persons guilty of deceit were subject to an election of remedies on the part of the party defrauded.

Sharp v. Idaho Investment Corp.

504 P.2d 386 (Sup. Ct. Idaho 1972)

Dr. Sharp (plaintiff) brought this action for damages for alleged fraudulent misrepresentations by Idaho Investment Corporation (defendant) in selling certain stock to Dr. Sharp. The trial court found for Dr. Sharp and Idaho Investment appealed. Reversed.

---

[1] The modern trend is to allow the defrauded party to pursue these remedies in sequence. Thus, if an action in deceit results in an unsatisfied judgment, the defrauded may then seek rescission unless, of course, the rights of innocent third parties have intervened.

McFadden, Justice. Although the district court found that misrepresentations had been made in the "pitch kit," prospectus, sales material, bulletins and "other written material," there is no indication which statements in particular were false. In reviewing the numerous exhibits we conclude that there are no misrepresentations. True enough, optimism and enthusiasm pervade the sales material. However, Dr. Sharp has not carried his burden of producing clear and convincing evidence of the falsity of any statement in the written material he supposedly relied on.

As a final basis for imposing liability on Idaho Investment . . . we must consider the omission of facts material to the transaction which deprived Dr. Sharp of exercising his business investment judgment. The district court found that Idaho Investment . . . "omitted certain facts" which deprived Dr. Sharp of a "fair and honest" opportunity to evaluate the stock. First, we are unable to determine whether such omissions were intentional or negligent. Second, we are unable to discover the extent or exact nature of the omissions. Third, there is no evidence showing that such omissions, if there were any, were material. . . . Furthermore, Dr. Sharp did not read the prospectus or offering circular until after he had purchased the stock. Thus, any omission in the prospectus was not material to his decision to purchase.

Reliance is a fundamental element of fraud which must be proven by clear and convincing evidence. On direct examination Dr. Sharp was asked: "Doctor, would you tell me why you purchased stock in the Idaho Investment?" Dr. Sharp replied, "Because I believed Mr. Neilson. I was acquainted with Mr. Frazier and other officers of Sierra Life. I knew the officers and expected it to be a profitable venture." From Dr. Sharp's own testimony it is evident that rather than relying on representations or misstatements by Idaho Investment and its agents he relied on expectations based on his experience with another corporation.

Midwest Supply, Inc. v. Waters

510 P.2d 876 (Sup. Ct. Nev. 1973)

Action for damages caused Waters (plaintiff) due to alleged false and fraudulent representations by Midwest Supply, Inc. (defendant). Judgment for Waters for actual damages plus $100,000 in punitive damages. Midwest Supply appealed. Affirmed.

Midwest Supply was in the business of preparing income tax returns. Waters, induced by public advertisements, contacted Midwest Supply about the possibility of filing amended tax returns for several years in order to obtain refunds. Midwest Supply caused Waters to apply for and receive improper refunds, causing an Internal Revenue Service audit which resulted in the assessment of greater tax liability for the previous years. Waters was caused severe hardship by the Internal Revenue Service's collection procedures, which included the filing of tax liens and levies on wages and bank accounts.

GUNDERSON, JUSTICE. Midwest Supply contends the trial court erred in instructing the jury as to fraud because there was no evidence that Midwest intentionally misled Plaintiffs when undertaking to prepare their tax returns. We disagree. The record contains evidence of willful and wanton misrepresentations, in Midwest's advertising and in their internal business practices, specifically aimed at deceiving the members of the public who might rely on Midwest for tax expertise.

In their public advertising, Midwest "guaranteed accurate tax preparation," stating that they would prepare "complete returns—$5 up." Thereby, Midwest suggested their employees' expertise in preparing all types of tax returns. Despite this, they made no effort to hire employees with even rudimentary skill in accounting or in the preparation of tax returns. The temporary employee who prepared plaintiff's tax returns had been employed in construction work for several years prior to his employment with defendants, and had received no formal training in the preparation of tax returns, either prior to or during his employment with Midwest.

Midwest's manual instructed their office managers to counter inquiries concerning the qualifications of employees by saying that "[the company] has been preparing taxes for 20 years." The manual further instructed office managers not to refer to an employee as a "specialist or tax expert," but never to correct news reporters or commentators if they referred to employees in this manner. In our view, such evidence supports a determination of fraud.

Finally, Midwest contends the jury's award of $100,000 punitive damages was actuated by passion and prejudice. Our law authorizes punitive damages in proper cases to punish and deter culpable conduct. At trial, Midwest's net worth was established at $6 million. The jury was properly instructed, and under the circumstances of this case we do not find the jury's award of punitive damages excessive.

Griffith v. Byers Construction Co. of Kansas, Inc.

510 P.2d 198 (Sup. Ct. Kan. 1973)

Mr. and Mrs. Griffith (plaintiffs) sued Byers Construction Company (defendant) for damages for fraud. Plaintiffs appealed from adverse judgment. Reversed.

Byers Construction Company developed land and then sold lots to home building contractors. These home building contractors built houses on the lots and then sold the houses and lots to home buyers. Mr. and Mrs. Griffith purchased a house and lot from one of the building contractors and then sued Byers (the developer) when they discovered that the soil was defective.

FROMME, JUSTICE. This court has held that the purchaser may recover on the theory of fraud from a vendor-builder for nondisclosure of defects. In *Jenkins v. McCormick,* it is stated:

Where a vendor has knowledge of a defect in property which is not within the fair and reasonable reach of the vendee and which he could not discover by the exercise of reasonable diligence, the silence and failure of the vendor to disclose the defect in the property constitutes actionable fraudulent concealment.

We see no reason why the rule in *Jenkins* should not be extended in the present case to a developer of residential lots.

Defendant Byers next contends, without agency, there can be no privity and without privity there can be no duty to disclose. Here, of course, the plaintiffs never dealt with . . . Byers. The duty to disclose the saline nature of the soil must extend to the plaintiffs if their fraud claims are to be upheld. However, the doctrine of privity provides no defense to . . . Byers if the plaintiffs were within a class of persons Byers intended to reach. Liability for misrepresentation is not necessarily limited to the person with whom the misrepresenter deals. The rule is embodied in *Restatement, Second, Torts,* § 531:

One who makes a fraudulent misrepresentation is subject to liability for pecuniary loss

(*a*) To the persons or class of persons whom he intends or has reason to expect to act or to refrain from action in reliance upon the misrepresentation; and

(*b*) For pecuniary loss suffered by them through their reliance in the type of transaction in which he intends or has reason to expect their conduct to be influenced.

Under the alleged facts of our present case, . . . we must assume . . . Byers had knowledge of the saline content of the soil of the lots it placed on the market. After the grading and development of the area this material defect in the lots was not within the fair and reasonable reach of the vendees, as they could not discover this latent defect by the exercise of reasonable care. The silence of . . . Byers, and its failure to disclose this defect in the soil condition to the purchasers could constitute actionable fraudulent concealment.

Strong v. Retail Credit Co.

552 P.2d 1025 (Ct. App. Col. 1976)

Suit for damages for fraud and gross negligence brought by Strong (plaintiff) against Retail Credit Co. (defendant). Strong appealed from a judgment dismissing her complaint. Affirmed.

On August 1, 1968, Fidelity Mutual Life Insurance Co. hired Retail Credit to prepare a "Special Narrative Agent's Report" on Canino. Fidelity was considering employing Canino as an agent. The report prepared by Retail Credit stated that Canino had had no "past or present financial difficulty" and had no "adverse" personal traits. In fact, Canino had been convicted of writing bad checks in 1961 and larceny in 1962 and 1965. Fidelity hired Canino and as a result of this employment Canino became acquainted with

Strong. Strong claims that she had confidence in Fidelity Co. and its employment policies and she therefore entrusted $115,000 to Canino on August 1, 1969. Canino misappropriated all but $13,000 of this money.

RUTLAND, JUDGE. Generally, one may not claim to have relied upon misrepresentations contained in a report when he was not aware of the existence of the report at the time he suffered injury. However, Strong argues that she indirectly relied upon the report and that indirect reliance is sufficient. This argument is predicated upon her allegations that obtaining the report was one of the more important and indispensable procedures employed by Fidelity in determining Canino's fitness for employment, and that Canino's employment by Fidelity clothed him with the appearance of honesty, and, as a result thereof, Strong entrusted him with the misappropriated funds.

Even assuming that these allegations established reliance upon the report as a matter of fact, such reliance is not sufficient to impose liability upon Retail Credit under the circumstances of this case. One who makes a misrepresentation is not liable to those persons whom he has no purpose to reach or influence and when there is no special reason to expect that the misrepresentation will influence such persons. While this rule has been based upon concepts of duty, foreseeability, and even intent, the result is the same.

Duress and Undue Influence

General Nature. Duress is unlawful coercion exercised upon a person to do some act that he or she otherwise would not have done. Undue influence is closely related to duress. It exists where one party is under the domination of another and is induced, by the unfair persuasion of the dominant party, to follow a course of action which he would not have followed of his own free will.

A contractual promise made under duress or undue influence is voidable. The reason for this is that since the party making the promise has been deprived of his ability to exercise a free choice, he should not be bound by his promise. In both duress and undue influence the parties are not bargaining on an equal basis. As a general rule the equality of the bargaining power of the parties to a contract is immaterial. The parties are presumed to be capable of protecting their own interests, and the courts will not assume the role of arbiters of the equality of bargaining powers in the everyday give-and-take of the marketplace. However, when the situation is such that the inequality cannot, in fairness and good conscience, be ignored, the courts will grant relief by declaring voidable the contractual promise made under the pressure of duress or induced by undue influence.

Duress. Duress had its origin in the law of crimes and torts. In the early stages of its development the test of duress was the threat of physical injury sufficient to overcome the will of a constant man of ordinary courage made by one having the power to execute the threat. The modern cases have not developed a clear rule or test for the existence of duress.

As a general rule the courts have stated that the means used must be wrongful. An analysis of the cases reveals that the word *wrongful* is not confined to criminal or tortious acts but may also include unconscionable conduct. In applying this test, the court must determine, in the exercise of its judicial discretion, where the line shall be drawn. Each case is treated as presenting a separate problem. If the act is wrongful, and if it deprives the coerced person of his ability to make a free choice, the courts will, as a general rule, grant relief.

Threats of criminal prosecution made to coerce a person into making payment of a claimed defalcation or to compensate for claimed unlawful gains have been held to be duress if the person making the threat gains thereby advantages to which he is not lawfully entitled.

The courts have generally held that the threat of a civil suit does not constitute duress. However, if the bringing of a civil suit is clearly an abuse of civil process, it may amount to duress. The threat to bring suit on an unfounded claim, when the person threatening suit knows that the financial situation of the person threatened is such that a suit would bring financial ruin to him, would be held by some courts to amount to duress.

The unjustified witholding of a person's goods for the purpose of forcing him to pay an unreasonable charge is generally held to be duress. The person paying the excessive charges to obtain possession of the goods is permitted to recover the amount of the overcharge.

Undue Influence. The objective of the defense of undue influence is to protect the aged, the timid, and the physically or mentally weak from the unscrupulous who succeed in gaining their confidence and take advantage of them. There is no precise definition of undue influence. It is a form of coercion. Before the courts will grant relief on the ground of undue influence, there must be a difference in the bargaining ability of the parties. The victim of undue influence must have the mental capacity to contract but at the same time not have the ability to protect himself or herself against unscrupulous persons who gain his or her confidence.

Most of the cases involving undue influence involve a close relative or long-time friend who takes advantage of or induces an old or sick victim to make a gift or property transfer for wholly inadequate consideration. The principal test is whether the confidential relationship was used to divert property from its normal course, in view of all the circumstances, to the person exercising the undue influence.

SUMMARY

Duress is the obtaining of an advantage over a person by means of coercion brought to bear which deprives that person of the ability to make a free choice. A contractual promise obtained by duress is voidable. In contract law, if the means of executing the pressure is wrongful and the contractual promise is unjust or unconscionable, the courts will grant relief. The relief granted may be rescission of the contract or the granting of a judgment for any sum obtained over and above that to which the coercing party was, in fairness and honesty, entitled. Tort damages are not recoverable for duress.

Undue influence is based on a confidential relationship wherein one party dominates the other and wherein the dominant party owes a duty to look for the interests of the servient party. If such a relationship exists and the dominant party, in breach of his duty, uses his position to benefit himself at the expense of the servient party, the courts will hold the transaction voidable on the ground of undue influence.

In both duress and undue influence, the party with superior bargaining power takes advantage of the situation and gains an economic advantage which is so unequal and unfair that it is, as the courts frequently state, shocking to the conscience of man. The modern trend is for the courts to expand duress to include many of the more subtle forms of coercion not recognized at common law.

Laemmar v. J. Walter Thompson Co.

435 F.2d 680 (7th Cir. 1970)

Suit by Laemmar and others (plaintiffs) against J. Walter Thompson (defendant) seeking rescission of an agreement to sell stock. Judgment for Thompson and Laemmar appealed. Reversed.

Laemmar and others were employees-at-will of (defendant) Thompson for many years. For several years the plaintiffs purchased shares of Class B common stock of Thompson. It is undisputed that all of such stock purchases were subject to an option retained by Thompson to repurchase the stock if the plaintiffs' employment were terminated for any reason.

In 1965 various officers of Thompson solicited plaintiffs to resell their stock either to Thompson or to certain officers of Thompson. Plaintiffs rejected this solicitation and were told, "expressly and by innuendo," that they would be discharged from their employment unless they executed the sale in accordance with an offer then outstanding. Plaintiffs unwillingly sold the stock to Thompson in March of 1965 because of the threat of losing their employment, receiving therefore corporate notes payable over three years at six and one-half percent interest for the purchase price offered by Thompson.

Plaintiffs remained in Thompson's employ until, after having notified

Thompson on May 8, 1969, of their desire to rescind the resale together with a tender of the purchase price (including interest) and having been refused the return of the stock, they filed a lawsuit in state court seeking rescission and were then discharged by Thompson upon its receipt of a summons.

SWYGERT, CHIEF JUDGE. In sum, it is the theory of the plaintiffs that the agreement to sell their stock may be rescinded because they were under duress at the time of the making of the agreement. They postulate that the threatened termination of their employment so deprived them of the exercise of free will that the contract to sell the stock is rendered voidable.

As the Illinois Supreme Court has observed, adopting the general theory of duress argued by plaintiffs herein:

> Under modern views and developments . . . duress is no longer confined to situations involving threats of personal injury or imprisonment, and the standard of whether a man of ordinary courage would yield to the threat has been supplanted by a test which inquires *whether the threat has left the individual bereft of the quality of mind essential to the making of a contract.* (*Kaplan v. Kaplan.*)

Applying the *Kaplan* test to the facts pleaded in the verified complaint, we hold that plaintiffs' allegations of duress by means of threatened discharge from employment are legally sufficient to withstand defendant's motion for judgment on the pleadings. Whether duress actually existed in this instance must be determined by the trier of fact, however, for "the issue of duress generally is one of fact, to be judged in light of all the circumstances surrounding a given transaction."

Austin Instrument, Inc. v. Loral Corporation

272 N.E.2d 533 (Ct. App. N.Y. 1971)

Action by Austin Instrument, Inc. (plaintiff) to recover the balance due for goods delivered to Loral Corp. (defendant). Loral counter-claimed seeking damages for price increases paid to Austin due to alleged duress. Judgment for Austin appealed. Reversed.

In July, 1965, Loral was awarded a $6 million government contract to produce radar sets. This contract contained a schedule of deliveries, a liquidated damages clause for late deliveries and a cancellation clause in the event of Loral's default. Loral solicited bids for the production of 40 precision gears necessary for production and Austin's bids were accepted for 23 of these gears.

In May, 1966, Loral was awarded a second similar contract. Austin bid on all 40 gears but was accepted only for those on which it was the low bidder. Austin refused to accept an order for less than all 40 gears and told Loral it would breach the first contract if it was not granted the second subcontract for all 40 gears and if prices were not raised on the first contract.

Loral made extensive efforts to secure the needed gears elsewhere, but could not fill the contracts in time, whereupon Loral accepted Austin's conditions

FULD, CHIEF JUDGE. A contract is voidable on the ground of duress when it is established that the party making the claim was forced to agree to it by means of a wrongful threat precluding the exercise of his free will. The existence of economic duress or business compulsion is demonstrated by proof that "immediate possession of needful goods is threatened" or, more particularly, in cases such as the one before us, by proof that one party to a contract has threatened to breach the agreement by withholding goods unless the other party agrees to some further demand. However, a mere threat by one party to breach the contract by not delivering the required items, though wrongful, does not in itself constitute economic duress. It must also appear that the threatened party could not obtain the goods from another source of supply and that the ordinary remedy of an action for breach of contract would not be adequate.

Loral had the burden of demonstrating that it could not obtain the parts elsewhere within a reasonable time, and there can be no doubt that it met this burden. The 10 manufacturers whom Loral contacted comprised its entire list of "approved vendors" for precision gears, and none was able to commence delivery soon enough.

It is hardly necessary to add that Loral's normal legal remedy of accepting Austin's breach of the contract and then suing for damages would have been inadequate under the circumstances, as Loral would still have had to obtain the gears elsewhere. . . . In other words, Loral actually had no choice, when the prices were raised by Austin, except to take the gears at the "coerced" prices and then sue to get the excess back.

Mistake

Nature of Mistake. Mistake applies only to those situations where the contracting party or parties believe that a present or past fact which is material to their transaction exists when it does not, or believe that it does not exist when it does. Mistake must not be confused with ignorance, inability, or poor judgment.

Likewise, if a person makes a contractual promise to perform a service or bring about a designated result but finds that he is mistaken as to his capacity and that he is unable to perform the service or accomplish the promised result, the court will not relieve him from his obligation on the ground of mistake. This is not mistake but only inability.

When a person has entered into a transaction which is less beneficial than expected or which proves detrimental, the courts will not relieve the party from his or her obligations on the ground of mistake. This may be a mistake of judgment, but the courts do not relieve from mistakes of judgment.

Two closely related yet distinguishable situations have been recognized as justifying relief on the ground of mistake. One is a mistake resulting from ambiguity in the negotiation of the transaction. The other is a mistake as to a material fact which induced the making of the contractual promise.

Mistake Resulting from Ambiguity. In negotiating a contract, it may happen that the parties will use language which is susceptible equally to two interpretations. In such a situation, if one party honestly places one interpretation on the language and the other party, with equal honesty, places the other interpretation on it, the courts will generally hold that the parties did not, in fact, reach a mutual agreement, and as a result there was no contract.

Mistake as to Material Fact. A mistake as to a material fact is fundamentally a matter of the mind. A person may believe that a fact exists which does not, or he or she may believe that a fact does not exist when it does. To justify the courts in granting relief, the fact must be material, and, as in fraud cases, it must be as to a present or past fact. A mistake as to the happening of future events is never ground for relief from the obligations of a contractual promise.

Mutual Mistake. Mutual mistake of material fact is ground for granting relief both in law and in equity. To come within this rule, both of the parties must have contracted in the mistaken belief that certain material facts existed. A court might grant relief if the mistake was as to future happenings; but as a general rule, it is presumed that the contracting parties assume the risks of future events.

Unilateral Mistake. Whether or not the court will grant relief when only one of the contracting parties is in error as to the existence or nonexistence of a material fact depends on the surrounding circumstances. If one of the parties knows or should know that the other party is mistaken in his belief that certain facts exist and enters into the contract for the apparent purpose of taking advantage of the situation, the courts will grant relief. As a general rule, if the mistake is the result of the negligence of the party in error, the courts will not grant relief. However, even though the mistake is the result of slight negligence, if relief can be granted to the party in error without imposing material loss on the other party, the courts will grant relief, especially if the enforcement of the contract would impose unwarranted hardship on the party in error. As in fraud cases, if a party wishes to be relieved of the burden of a mistake, he or she must act as soon as he or she discovers the mistake. An unreasonable delay in asking relief will amount to a waiver of the right to rescind the contract.

Mistakes in Drafting Writing. Courts will grant relief in those cases in which a mistake has been made in drafting a written contract, deed, or other document. Suppose Arnold bargains to sell Barber a vacant lot which adjoins Arnold's home. The vacant lot is "Lot 3, block 1"; Arnold's house is on

"Lot 2, block 1." In drawing the contract the stenographer strikes the wrong key, and the contract reads "Lot 2, block 1." Neither Arnold nor Barber notices this error when they read and sign the contract. A court will reform the contract. Usually, no relief will be granted if one of the parties is mistaken as to the meaning of the language used in a contract; however, if the language is ambiguous, or both parties are mistaken as to the meaning and it does not express the intentions of the parties, no contract is formed.

Mistakes of Law. Mistake as to one's legal rights under a contract is not generally accepted as sufficient justification for granting relief. If the mistake of law is coupled with mistake of fact, relief may be granted. Some courts have attempted to distinguish between mistake of law—error of judgment as to legal rights—and ignorance of law—lack of knowledge of the existence of the law. Such a distinction is difficult to apply and has no secure foundation, because one's error in judgment as to legal rights usually is the result of some degree of ignorance of the law.

SUMMARY

Under some circumstances the courts will relieve a party of a contractual obligation on the ground of mistake. Mistake as to the subject matter of a contract is generally accepted as ground for holding that no contract came into existence, since the parties, as the result of the mistake, never reached an agreement. Mistake of fact is fundamentally a matter of mind. Relief will be granted only if the facts and circumstances make the enforcement of the contract unjust and if the parties can be restored to their original positions without injury to innocent third persons.

As a general rule the courts will grant either the remedy of rescission or the remedy of reformation of a contract entered into under a mutual mistake of a material fact. If the mistake is unilateral, that is, only one of the parties is negotiating under a mistaken conception of fact, the courts will grant no relief. However, the courts grant relief if the circumstances are such that justice and fair dealing demand it.

If one party is mistaken as to a material fact and the other party knows or should know of the mistake, that party will not be permitted to take advantage of it. If the mistaken party has proceeded with reasonable care and the mistake is the result of a clerical error and not an error in judgment, relief will be granted if necessary to avoid grave injustice.

Mistakes made in drafting will be corrected through the remedy of reformation. Before a writing will be reformed to correct a claimed mistake, there must be clear and convincing evidence that it was a mistake in drafting the instrument and not merely a lack of understanding of the language used. The statement frequently made that the courts will not relieve from mistakes of law is the generally accepted rule. However, the rule is subject to some exceptions, and relief may be granted if necessary to avoid serious injustice.

Interstate Indus. Uniform Rental Serv., Inc. v. Couri Pontiac, Inc.
355 A.2d 913 (Sup. Ct. Maine 1976)

This action was commenced by Interstate Uniform Rental (plaintiff), a business engaged in renting costumes and uniforms to others, against Couri Pontiac (defendant) for alleged breach of contract between the parties. The trial court found mutual mistake in the formation of the contract and held this prevented formation of a legally binding contract. Interstate appealed from this judgment. Reversed.

Couri Pontiac had been acquired by John Wiley in early 1970. Couri Pontiac and Interstate later executed a Uniform Rental Agreement; but before the agreement was executed, Wiley's secretary made a rough search to determine whether the car dealership had any other uniform rental agreements. The search revealed nothing, although Couri Pontiac in fact was under a long-term contract to another uniform rental agency. At the time of the contract between Couri Pontiac and Interstate, both parties knew that Couri Pontiac was then being serviced by the other uniform rental agency although neither was aware of the long-term contract. Upon discovery later that he had a prior contract for the same services, Wiley announced that he would do business with the rental agency that would agree to indemnify him in the event of a law suit by the other. Interstate refused to agree to these terms and brought this suit for breach of its contract.

WEATHERBEE, JUSTICE. The principle that a contract is not legally binding if both parties had entered into it under an actual and good faith mutual misunderstanding is well established in this jurisdiction. A mistake of fact occurs if the parties entertain a conception of the facts which differs from the facts as they really exist. The mistake must be mutual, that is, the minds of the parties must fall prey to the same misconception with respect to the bargain. The doctrine of mutual mistake requires that the mistake touch the subject matter of the bargain, and not merely be collateral to it. In other words, the mutual mistake must so vitally affect the facts upon the basis of which the bargain was struck that the written contract does not express the intent of the parties. The parties must have, in fact, agreed to something other than that established by the writing.

In the present case we believe that if any mutual mistake occurred, it related solely to a collateral issue involving the propriety or wisdom of entering into the contract and does not, therefore, render the contract unenforceable. The basic subject matter of the contract between the plaintiff and defendant is unaffected by their misconceptions although the defendant, had he been aware of the true facts, would doubtlessly have perceived the need for the contract differently. The defendant could legally have executed a score of agreements with different uniform rental companies and each contract would express the correct respective intent of the parties to supply and receive rented uniforms. The contract adequately expresses the bargain agreed to by both parties and we believe that the Justice below erred in rescinding the contract.

Clover Park School Dist. v. Consolidated Diary Products Co.

500 P.2d 47 (Ct. App. Wash. 1976)

Suit by Clover Park (plaintiff) against Consolidated Dairy, operating as Darigold (defendant) for damages for breach of contract to supply milk. Darigold appealed from a decision for Clover Park. Affirmed.

School District invited bids on 1,490,118 half pints of milk, the invitation providing "no bidder may withdraw his bid after opening time." A secretary at Darigold saw penciled figures on the bid form and typed in the price of $0.0713 per half pint. In reality, the figure she typed was the previous year's price rather than the intended bid price of $0.079 per half pint.

Darigold's area manager was at the opening on May 24, and he immediately recognized the error, requesting that the bid be rejected. Clover Park later accepted the bid at a meeting on May 30.

On June 14, Darigold contacted Clover Park stating that Foremost Dairies was willing to supply the milk "at the lower price." Foremost changed its mind and Darigold arranged for Sanitary Dairy to supply the milk. In October Sanitary ceased operations due to insolvency.

Darigold then offered to supply the milk "until something could be arranged" at the "correct price of $0.079." On December 6, Darigold informed Clover Park that no milk would be delivered after the end of December. The extra cost of obtaining the milk to Clover Park was $11,466 over Darigold's bid price.

REED, JUDGE. We begin with the premise that a bid is no more than an offer to contract. Clover Park's advertisement for bids provided that no bid could be withdrawn after the time for opening. Once the bid was submitted, its acceptance by the school district formed a contract. However, the general rule is that communication of the error in computation by Darigold before Clover Park could change its position in reliance on the bid, rendered the contract voidable by rescission.

In *Puget Sound, Painters, Inc. v. State* (1954), the court set forth guidelines . . . under which relief will be decreed:

(*a*) if the bidder acted in good faith, and (*b*) without gross negligence, (*c*) if he was reasonably prompt in giving notice of the error in the bid to the other party, (*d*) if the bidder will suffer substantial detriment by forfeiture, and (*e*) if the other party's status has not greatly changed, and relief from forfeiture will work no substantial hardship on him.

We are convinced the criteria justifying rescission were initially met in this case, for Darigold acted in apparent good faith and without gross negligence; it promptly gave notice of the error; it stood to suffer substantial detriment by virtue of the error; and Clover Park had not irrevocably acted in reliance when notice was given; that is, the bid could have been awarded to someone else, at relatively low additional cost. Ordinarily, the offeree who has reason to know of a unilateral mistake will not be permitted to "snap up" such an offer and profit thereby.

However, rescission of an agreement once made must be prompt upon discovery of the facts warranting such an action. When a party fails to take steps to rescind within a reasonable time and instead follows a course of conduct inconsistent therewith, the conclusion follows that he has waived his right of rescission and chosen to continue the contract.

Problem Cases

1. Bezner agreed to purchase a dry cleaning business from Continental Dry Cleaners, Inc. The president of Continental repeatedly informed Bezner that the business was grossing about $1,000 per week, when, in fact, the business was actually grossing between $400 and $500 per week. During the negotiations for purchase, Bezner requested to see the company's records. Continental replied that its manager had been stealing and that therefore it did not have accurate records. Relying upon these statements, Bezner agreed to purchase the dry cleaning business.

   Upon operation, Bezner found the weekly receipts to be between $400 and $500. Believing this amount to be the result of a change in ownership and her lack of business knowledge, Bezner continued operations. After nine months Bezner found accounting records indicating that Continental had lied to her concerning the amount of gross receipts. Bezner sues Continental to rescind the purchase agreement and to get her money back. Is Continental liable to Bezner?
2. The Klotts signed an agreement to purchase a house owned by the Stewarts. The day after the Klotts moved into the house they became aware of a malfunctioning water well in need of major repairs. During the negotiations for the sale of the house, no mention was ever made about the water supply. The Klotts did not ask for any information; they had assumed the water came from the city well. Nor did the Stewarts volunteer any information. The Klotts sue the Stewarts for damages, claiming that there was a fraudulent nondisclosure and concealment of the faulty well. Assuming the Stewarts were aware of the faulty condition of the well at the time of the sale, are they liable for damages for not disclosing this information?
3. Kennedy contracted to sell his business for 4,000 shares of Flo-Tronics stock having a market value of $8.50 per share. Under the contract, Kennedy was obliged to retire the $17,500 in debts he then owed. Kennedy claimed that he was induced to enter the contract by the assurance of Flo-Tronics that their stock would rise to $25 a share within a year. The stock increased to $17 within three months, but under SEC regulation Kennedy was required to hold the stock for six months. The stock subsequently dropped to $3 a

share causing severe financial problems for Kennedy. Is he entitled to rescission on the grounds of misrepresentation?

4. Sunderhaus brought a diamond ring from Perel and Lowenstein for $699.25. At the time she purchased the ring, the salesperson in Perel's store told her that the ring was worth $699.25. Sunderhaus later had the ring appraised by two other jewelers. One jeweler appraised the ring as having a value of $300 and the other appraised it at a value of $350. Sunderhaus brought an action against Perel for fraud and deceit. Perel defends on the ground that misrepresentations of value are merely matters of opinion and cannot be justifiably relied upon. Is this a good defense?

5. Franklin, an oil supply company, entered into an agreement with Servicios, a Venezuela corporation, to purchase all of the capital stock of Peticon, another Venezuela corporation. It was agreed that Franklin would assume control on May 1, 1971, and that the purchase price of the stock would be the book value of the stock as of April 30, 1971. The parties agreed to employ Peat, Marwick, Mitchell and Co. (P.M.M.), Servicios' auditors, to perform the audit. On May 1, Franklin paid $50,000 in cash and gave Peticon guaranteed notes for $1,000,000—a total book value of $1,050,000, as reported by P.M.M. In January 1972, Franklin dishonored the first note and in July filed suit to rescind the Peticon transaction, asserting overvaluation of inventory. Franklin also alleged that P.M.M. did not perform an independent audit because the audit was in charge of one Southerland, who was both an employee of P.M.M. and an alternate director of Servicios and who had formerly been a director of Peticon. Because of this and the failure of P.M.M. to formally disclose these facts, P.M.M. was charged with having acted in violation of a fiduciary relationship and in violation of an implied duty of independence. Should the transaction be set aside on the ground of constructive fraud?

6. In 1965 Business Incentives entered into a contract with Sony, whereby it agreed to interest business firms in the use of Sony products for employee awards. This agreement was to give Business Incentives the lucrative New York territory. Several amendments were subsequently made to the agreement, including changing the territory serviced by Business Incentives from New York to New Jersey, and lowering its commission. All contracts had a termination clause, empowering either party to terminate the agreement on 15 days notice. Sony terminated the agreement, pursuant to this clause, effective December 31, 1973. Business Incentives seeks to recover for the wrongful termination, claiming that Sony's superior bargaining power forced it to accept the contractual clause allowing termination at will. Is this a valid claim?

7. ISL Corporation had been experiencing operating losses for some time and was unable to raise new funds by issuing new debt or equity. Plessey Corporation agreed to purchase ISL's assets in a sales contract which provided in part that Plessey could assume full management control of ISL within three months if ISL's profits did not exceed $15,000 per month as reflected in their financial statements. Prior to the closing date of the contract of sale, Plessey learned of inaccuracies in ISL's financial statements, resulting in an amendment to the sales contract so that Plessey could assume full management control of ISL within two months if profits did not exceed $15,000 per month. Two months after the closing date, profits did not exceed the required amount and Plessey assumed full management control of ISL. ISL now claims that the contract amendment was invalid due to economic duress. Should ISL prevail?

8. The Basset Construction Company was awarded a contract to construct a building in Colorado. Prior to being awarded the contract, the Basset Company advertised for various subcontracting bids, with books detailing the specifications required by Basset being availa-

ble in several places for potential subcontractors to read. Schmitz Painting gave the Basset Company a bid for the painting subcontract that was approximately 50 percent lower than any other bid submitted. Basset questioned the bid, but Schmitz reaffirmed it, and subsequently, the parties signed a contract for the amount bid. Schmitz Painting worked on the project for two days, but then refused to continue, claiming that adequate preparations for painting had not been made. The Basset Company referred Schmitz to the specifications book which indicated that such preparations were to be performed by the painting subcontractor. Schmitz again refused to perform, and Basset hired another subcontractor to finish the job. Basset sues Schmitz Painting to recover the increased cost of employing the second subcontractor. Schmitz defends on the ground that there was a mistake; that there was never a "meeting of the minds" as to what the subcontractor was required to do. Is Schmitz liable to Basset for the increased cost of employing a second contractor?

9. Gerber visited Slenderella Systems, Inc. to receive a complementary weight reduction treatment. Slenderella's treatment method consisted of using vibratory and oscillatory machinery to massage the body, including the back. Gerber mentioned a chronic back problem to Slenderella's manager, who stated that his methods would probably help her back. After receiving the free treatment, Gerber signed a $300 contract to continue the massages. Soon after, Gerber's back condition worsened due to her first treatment and she refused to make any payments under the contract. Slenderella sued to recover $300, and Gerber defended on the grounds of mutual mistake. Is this a good defense?
10. Monarch sued Reed to recover the price of 4 million labels allegedly ordered by Reed and shipped to Reed by Monarch. Reed's order specified shipment of "4MM" labels from Monarch, M being the roman numeral designation for 1,000 and understood as such in the label industry. Monarch knew that Reed had never ordered any quantity remotely near 4 million labels in prior dealings with Monarch over a period of many years and that Reed had never ordered over 4,000 labels at any one time of any item. Reed now wants to rescind the contract on the basis of unilateral mistake. May it do so?

10

Consideration

History and Function of Consideration

Historical Development. The idea evolved in Anglo-American law that purely gratuitous promises should not be enforceable in the courts as a general rule. This idea led to the development of the so-called "bargain theory of consideration." Under this theory no promisee can hold a promisor to a promise unless the promisee has in effect promised or given something in exchange or as the "price" of the promise. Stated in legalistic terms, the general test for consideration applied by the courts is whether or not detriment to the promisee or benefit to the promisor has been bargained for and given in exchange for the promise.

Detriment or Benefit

Legal Detriment. Legal detriment is the surrendering of a legal right or the assuming of a legal burden. In our society each individual has the right to do or not to do many things. When a person surrenders one of these rights or obligates himself to do something which he has a legal right not to do, he has suffered a legal detriment. In the transaction of business the parties to a deal are exchanging legal rights. In the ordinary business contract each party suffers a legal detriment, and each party enjoys a legal benefit. For example, suppose a customer buys a radio from a merchant for $50. The customer suffers a legal detriment—surrenders his right to keep the $50. The merchant also suffers a legal detriment—he surrenders his right to keep the radio. Each gains a benefit—the customer gains the right to the radio, and the merchant gains the right to the $50.

Legal Benefit. In the majority of situations, if the promisee has suffered a legal detriment, the promisor has enjoyed a corresponding legal benefit. Detriment to the promisee, without a corresponding benefit to the promisor, also can be sufficient as consideration.

For example, Able owes Baker $500 and Baker threatens a suit to collect the debt. Carl, a friend of Able, offers to pay Able's debt within 30 days if Baker will refrain from bringing suit. If Baker accepts Carl's offer, Baker is suffering a legal detriment which is consideration for Carl's promise to pay the debt. Observe that Carl, the promisee of Baker's promise to refrain from suit, receives no benefit from the performance of Baker's promise. Thus consideration need not involve an exchange of things having economic value, and need not confer a benefit on the promisee.

SUMMARY

Consideration under the bargain theory may be defined as "detriment to the promisee or benefit to the promisor, bargained for and given in exchange for a promise." Detriment, as used in this definition, is the surrendering of a legal right or the assumption of a legal obligation. As a general rule, when the promisee has suffered a detriment, the promisor has enjoyed a corresponding benefit. Detriment to the promisee, standing alone, is sufficient consideration.

Investment Properties of Asheville, Inc. v. Norburn

188 S.E.2d 342 (Sup. Ct. N.C. 1972)

Action by Investment Properties of Asheville, Inc. (plaintiff) against Norburn (defendant) to recover on a written promise of guaranty made by the latter. Investment appealed from a judgment for Norburn. Reversed and remanded.

On May 10, 1965, Allen, sister of Norburn, leased a tract of land to Investment. The lease provided that the lessee should have complete control in grading, reshaping, and developing the land, as well as full responsibility for listing and paying taxes. Investment attempted to obtain financing for the construction of a motel on this property, but found that the lease was not in the proper form to permit such financing. On June 17, 1965, Investment met with Norburn, who was acting as agent for his sister, and informed Norburn that the grading of the property had reached such a point that the machinery might have to be removed if a revised and satisfactory lease could not be obtained. To avert this circumstance Norburn signed the following paper:

> This is to certify that I will stand personally liable for the Conduit grading and necessary expenses (at actual cost) for the land preparation of the Action property now owned by my sister, in case the lease is not continued after June 1, 1966.
>
> Charles S. Norburn

Investment continued work on the tract spending a total of $19,456.88 on the grading work. Investment was unable to obtain a new lease and in October 1967 the Allen tract was leased to another development company. Investment sued Norburn on his guaranty, and the trial court jury found that Norburn had received no consideration for his promise to pay.

MOORE, JUSTICE. The determinative issue then is: Did defendant Norburn receive valuable consideration from Investment for the execution and delivery of this guaranty agreement?

It is well-settled law in this State that in order for a contract to be enforceable it must be supported by consideration. A mere promise, without more, is unenforceable. . . . As a general rule, consideration consists of some benefit or advantage to the promisor or some loss or detriment to the promisee. However, as stated by Chief Justice Stacy in *Stonestreet v. Southern Oil Co.:* "It has been held that "there is a consideration if the promisee, in return for the promise, does anything legal which he is not bound to do, or refrains from doing anything which he has a right to do, whether there is any actual loss or detriment to him or actual benefit to the promisor or not."

It is not necessary that the promisor receive consideration or something of value himself in order to provide the legal consideration sufficient to support a contract. Forbearance to exercise legal rights is sufficient consideration for a promise given to secure such forbearance even though the forbearance is for a third person rather than that of the promisor. In a guaranty contract, a consideration moving directly to the guarantor is not essential. The promise is enforceable if a benefit to the principal debtor is shown or if detriment or inconvenience to the promisee is disclosed.

The court in the charge to the jury in this case correctly stated: "There must be a sufficient consideration in order to support a contract or legal agreement. Any benefit, right or interest accruing to the one who makes the promise or guaranty, or any forbearance, detriment or loss suffered or undertaken by one to whom the promise for guaranty is made is a sufficient consideration to support such guaranty or contract."

The jury should also have been instructed that if, by reason of the guaranty signed by defendant Norburn, Allen received benefits from Investment by their furnishing additional work on her property, including fertilizing, seeding, and additional leveling, or if Investment, at the request of plaintiffs, did additional work upon the Allen property and thereby incurred added expense by reason of this guaranty, either would be sufficient legal consideration to support such guaranty.

Preexisting Obligation

Nature of Preexisting Obligation. A preexisting obligation, as used in the law of consideration, is an obligation which the promisor already owes at the time he makes a promise to assume such obligation. When a party promises to do or does that which he is already legally obligated to do, or promises to refrain or does refrain from doing that which he has no right to do, he is suffering no detriment, and his promise or act is not sufficient consideration to support a promise.

The question of a preexisting obligation may arise in an infinite variety of situations, but four important areas involving preexisting obligation are: (1) acts which are criminal or tortious; (2) acts which the holder of an office is under a duty to perform; (3) acts which the promisee has already obligated himself by contract to perform, but the performance of which, owing to unforeseen and unforeseeable factors, is more burdensome than either of the contracting parties contemplated; and (4) substitution of an existing contract.

Criminal and Tortious Acts. Since each individual in our society is under a duty to refrain from the commission of a crime or tort, a promise to refrain or a refraining from the commission of such an act cannot be sufficient consideration to support a promise. The commission of a criminal or tortious act or the promise to commit such an act cannot, for obvious social reasons, be considered sufficient consideration to support a promise. A contract to commit a crime or tort is void.

Public Officers. A person, by accepting a public office, obligates himself to perform those official acts which are incidental to the office. The performance of an act which the holder of a public office is obligated to perform is universally held not to be legal detriment and not sufficient consideration to support a promise. This position is supported by both logic and public policy.

Unforeseen Difficulties. If a person is under a legal duty created by contract to perform an act, and the person to whom the duty is owed promises to pay additional compensation for the performance of that act, such promised performance is not a legal detriment. Promising to do that which a person is already legally bound to do is not sufficient consideration to support a promise.

There are exceptional circumstances, however, under which the courts have enforced such promises. Suppose, for example, the parties enter into a contract on the assumption that certain conditions exist but, after performance is started, one of the contracting parties encounters substantial unforeseen and unforeseeable difficulties. If the other party makes a new promise to pay additional compensation for the completion of the contract despite these difficulties, the courts will, as a general rule, enforce the new promise. Strikes, bad weather, an inflation in raw material prices, and various production bottlenecks are normally classed as foreseeable occurrences and hence would not justify application of the exception rule. An unprecedented flood or a rare or unusual circumstance, such as running into a large amount of sub-surface quicksand on an excavation job in an Arizona desert, probably would justify enforcing a promise to pay additional compensation under the unforeseeable difficulties exception rule.

Substitution of a Contract. The parties to a contract may, by mutual agreement, terminate a contract and enter into a new one whereby the obligations of one party are the same as under the terminated contract but the obligations of the other are greater. In such a situation the courts require clear and convincing evidence that the old contract was terminated by mutual agreement of the parties and that the entire transaction was free from fraud, duress, or undue influence.

SUMMARY

The doing of an act which a person is already under a legal obligation to do is not sufficient consideration to support a promise. On the grounds of logic and public policy the courts have held that the performance of an act which is a part of the official duties of the holder of a public office is not sufficient consideration to support a promise. Likewise, the performance of contractual obligations by one of the parties to a contract is not sufficient consideration to support a promise on the part of the other party to pay additional compensation. The courts have recognized exceptions to this latter statement. If unforeseen and unforeseeable conditions are encountered in the performance of a contract and the promisor promises to pay additional compensation to offset the additional burden of performance resulting from such conditions, the courts will enforce the promise if justice and fair dealing demand that it be enforced. The parties may terminate a contract by mutual agreement and thereafter enter into a new contract covering the same subject matter as that covered by the terminated contract.

Robert Chuckrow Construction Co. v. Gough

159 S.E.2d 469 (Ct. App. Ga. 1968)

This was an action by Ralph Gough (plaintiff) against Robert Chuckrow Construction Company (defendant) to collect for work done on trusses. Judgment for Gough and Construction Company appealed. Reversed.

Gough was a subcontractor of Construction Co. on a construction job known as the Kinney Shoe Store, having agreed with Construction Co. in a written contract dated April 30, 1965, to perform carpentry work required by the drawings and specification for that building. By the express provisions of the written contract, Gough undertook to "provide all labor and materials, scaffolding, tools, equipment and all other things necessary for the prosecution and completion of the work in strict accordance with the drawings and specification and job control chart." Gough's employees had erected approximately 38 trusses on May 15, 1965, when 32 of them fell off the building. On the following Monday, Gough was told by Construction Co. representative to remove the fallen trusses from the building, disassemble, inspect, rebuild, and re-erect them and to submit an additional bill for this work. Gough proceeded to do so. He also erected the balance of the trusses required to complete the roof truss structure and completed the carpentry work on the project. He was paid by Construction Co. all sums owed under the written contract but given nothing for the costs incurred by him in connection with the fallen trusses.

QUILLAN, JUDGE. The pivotal question on which the decision of the present case turns is whether the evidence adduced upon the trial showed the parol contract sued upon to be an enforceable agreement. Assent of the parties to the terms of the contract and a consideration for the performance of the same are essential requisites to its validity. Where either of these elements is lacking the contract is not binding or enforceable.

Gough, under the terms of the parol agreement, assumed no obligation or duty that he was not bound to perform under the written contract he had previously entered into with the defendant. Under both the written contract and the oral agreement Gough assumed the obligation to erect and properly place the same number of trusses to support the decking for the roof of the building.

The Supreme Court held in *Johnson v. Hinson,* "An agreement on the part of one to do what he is already legally bound to do is not a sufficient consideration for the promise of another."

It should be noted that the cause of the trusses' falling was unexplained and there was no evidence that their collapse was due to Construction Co.'s fault or any deficiency in the specifications as to how the trusses were to be erected.

Debt, Compromise, and Composition

Liquidated Debt. The courts have consistently held that a promise to discharge a liquidated debt on payment of part of the debt at the place where the debt is payable and at or after the time the debt is due is not enforceable because of lack of consideration. This rule is the result of following to its logical conclusion the rule that the performance of an act which one is already bound to perform is not sufficient consideration to support a promise. The courts have expressed dissatisfaction with the rule on the ground that it is contrary to general business practices; yet the rule is so firmly established that the courts hesitate to overrule it.

This rule applies only if all the following requirements are satisfied.

1. The debt must be liquidated; that is, the parties must be in complete agreement as to the amount. For example, suppose you receive a bill for $50 from your doctor for services she has rendered you while you were ill. You feel that the doctor has charged too much and tell her so. After some time, you and the doctor agree on $40 as the amount of the bill. The debt, which up to the time of the agreement was unliquidated, now becomes liquidated—the amount is certain and undisputed.
2. Payment must be made at or after the due date. If the debtor pays any part of the debt before the due date in exchange for the creditor's promise to accept a lesser sum in full payment, the debtor has done something he or she is not legally obligated to do—pay before due date—and this is sufficient consideration to support the promise of the creditor to accept a lesser sum.[1]
3. Payment must be made at the place where the debt is payable. Payment at any other place, if made in exchange for a promise by the creditor to accept a lesser sum, is sufficient to support such promise.
4. Payment must be made in the same medium of exchange as that provided for in the contract. Payment in any other medium, if done in exchange for a promise to accept such payment in discharge of the debt, is sufficient consideration to support such promise.

In those cases in which a creditor has promised (without new consideration) to extend the due date of an obligation, the courts have held that since the debtor (promisee) has suffered no detriment, the promise is unenforceable for lack of consideration. The rule has been applied only to contracts requiring the payment of money or the delivery of fungible goods—goods of which any unit is from its nature or by mercantile usage treated as the equivalent of any other unit.

Compromise (Accord and Satisfaction). A compromise is the settlement of a disputed claim by the mutual agreement of the parties. In legal terminology an agreement to settle a disputed claim is an "accord," and the fulfillment of the agreement is a "satisfaction." A compromise is referred to as an "accord and satisfaction."

If there is an honest dispute as to the amount of a debt or as to the existence of a debt, the debt is unliquidated. In such a case the parties have the right to submit the dispute to the courts for adjudication. But if the parties arrive at a mutual agreement of settlement without court action, each has suffered

[1] In some states payment must have been requested by the creditor.

a legal detriment since each has surrendered his or her right to have the claim submitted to the courts for adjudication, and the surrender of this right is legal detriment and is sufficient consideration to support the mutual promises to pay and accept the agreed sum in full satisfaction of the disputed claim. Therefore a promise to pay an agreed sum in discharge of an unliquidated debt is supported by consideration and is enforceable by court action.

Composition. A composition is an agreement between a debtor and two or more of his other creditors whereby the debtor agrees to pay each creditor who is a party to the agreement a pro rata portion of his claim, and the creditors agree to accept the amount in full satisfaction of their claims. Under such an agreement the debtor has discharged liquidated claims by the payment of a lesser sum at or after the due date. Some courts have held that the consideration to support the agreement is found in the mutual promises of the several creditors to accept the lesser sum. Under this reasoning the legal detriment is found in the surrendering of a portion of a creditor's claim, and this is accepted as consideration to support the promises of the other creditors who are parties to the agreement to surrender a like portion of their claims. Other courts have enforced composition agreements as exceptions to the general rule based on a public policy of encouraging such out of court settlements. A composition agreement which is free from misrepresentation and fraud will be enforced by court action.

SUMMARY

A promise to discharge a liquidated debt on the payment of a lesser sum on the due date and at the place where the debt is payable is not supported by sufficient consideration and, consequently, is not enforceable by court action. An agreement to settle a disputed claim—an unliquidated debt—is supported by consideration and therefore is enforceable by court action. A composition agreement between a debtor and two or more creditors, if free of misrepresentation, fraud, duress, or undue influence, in enforceable by court action.

Clark Leasing Corp. v. White Sands Forest Prod., Inc.

535 P.2d 1077 (Sup. Ct. N.M. 1975)

Suit by Clark Leasing Corp. (plaintiff) against White Sands Forest Products (defendant) to recover deficiency judgment on resale of repossessed logging equipment. Clark appealed from an adverse decision. Reversed.

White Sands had purchased the equipment under an installment contract that gave Clark the right to repossess and resell the equipment in the event of default. White Sands defaulted and agreed to turn over the equipment to

Clark provided Clark would accept the equipment in full settlement of the indebtedness. Clark accepted delivery and resold the equipment, but the resale did not bring in enough to cover the balance due. Clark then brought suit for the deficiency and White Sands sets up accord and satisfaction as a defense.

STEPHENSON, JUSTICE. An accord is nothing more nor less than a contract and must be supported by a new consideration. In the case of a liquidated claim or demand, some consideration for the asserted release of the unpaid balance, apart from the payment of a lesser sum, must be found to support an alleged accord. For that reason, our precedents hold that one of the prerequisites of a valid accord is that the claim or demand involved must be unliquidated, at least in the absence of a new and independent consideration.

White Sands asserts that Clark was allowed to repossess the equipment with the understanding it would be in full settlement of the existing indebtedness under the contract and that this was sufficient new consideration. We are not persuaded, for the alleged understanding

. . . shows nothing more than the attempted unilateral imposition without consideration of a condition contrary to the terms of the original contract recognizing the immediate right of repossession upon default. The defendant had already legally obligated himself to surrender possession upon default, and he agreed to do nothing more at the time of repossession. "An agreement on the part of one to do what he is already legally bound to do is not a sufficient consideration for the promise of another." *Barnes v. Reliable Tractor Company* (1968).

Forbearance to Sue

Right to Bring Suit. Every member of our society has the legal right to bring to the courts for enforcement any claim which one may have against other members of society. If a person has a claim which he or she reasonably and honestly believes is valid, that person has a right to bring suit to enforce the claim, and the postponing of or refraining from bringing suit is sufficient consideration to support a promise.

Valid Claims and Reasonable Claims. Forbearance to bring suit on a wholly spurious claim is not sufficient consideration to support a promise. The promisee must honestly believe that the claim is valid, and the circumstances must be such that a reasonable person in the same position would be justified in believing the claim to be valid. The fact that the claim may be doubtful does not prevent forbearance to sue from being sufficient consideration to support a promise.

SUMMARY

Forbearance to bring suit on a claim which the promisee is justified in believing is a valid claim is legal detriment and is sufficient consideration to support a promise. A promise made by a third party may be supported by the promisee's forbearance to sue.

Frasier v. Carter

437 P.2d 32 (Sup. Ct. Idaho 1968)

This was an action by Lena Frasier (plaintiff) against D. L. Carter (defendant) for damages for breach of contract. Judgment for the plaintiff and the defendant appealed. Affirmed.

Lena Frasier brought this action against Carter, a practicing attorney, upon the following letter agreement:

D. L. Carter
Lawyer
May 12, 1962

Dear Lena

This is to advise and confirm our agreement—that in the event the J. W. Frasier estate case now on appeal is not terminated so that you will receive settlement equal to your share of the estate as you would have done if your waiver had been filed in the estate in proper time, that I will make up any balance to you in payments as suits my convenience and will pay interest on your loss at 6 percent.

Sincerely
/s/D. L. Carter

By his will, her husband has devised and bequeathed all of the separate and community property to Lena and the three children. The specific devises and bequests to Lena were more valuable than her interest in the community property. However, the specific devises and bequests were conditioned upon a waiver by Lena of her interest in the community property, and the will provided that if she failed to waive her community property rights then she would receive her interest in the community property and nothing more.

No such waiver was executed by Lena and under the decree, distribution was made to Lena of her half share of the community property in lieu of the specific devises and bequests provided for by the will.

TAYLOR, JUSTICE. The principal ground urged for reversal is that the promise of Mr. Carter to pay to Mrs. Frasier any loss she sustained by reason of failure to waive her community interest in the Frasier estate, was without consideration. We think consideration was sufficiently established. The promise was in writing, which is presumptive evidence of consideration, and the burden of showing want of consideration sufficient to support the written promise was upon Carter.

Mrs. Frasier contends that Carter's promise to pay was supported by her forbearance from prosecuting an action against him for his negligence in failing to advise her properly respecting her interest in the Frasier estate. Waiver of, or forbearance to exercise, a right which is not utterly groundless is sufficient consideration to support a contract made in reliance thereon.

Consideration, Present and Past

The Bargain. Whether or not a detriment or benefit has been bargained for will depend on the intent of the parties. Nothing will be held to be consideration unless the parties intend it to be such. In determining intent, that is, in determining whether the promise or act has been bargained for and given in exchange for the promise, the same standards are applied as would be applied in determining the intent to make or accept an offer.

Adequacy of Consideration. The statement that the courts will not inquire into the adequacy of the consideration is frequently made. However, this statement cannot be accepted as a rule of law which will be followed under all circumstances. It is true that if the parties are dealing on an equal basis and the transaction is free from misrepresentation, fraud, duress, undue influence, or mistake, the courts will not refuse to enforce the contract solely on the ground that a burdensome duty was assumed in exchange for a relatively small consideration. This is especially true if the exchange does not involve items of a readily determinable economic value. In general, each party to a contract has the right to judge the value of the exchange according to personal standards, and the court will not substitute its judgment of values for that of the parties to the contract.

Writings which recite $1 or other small sums as the consideration have given rise to many conflicting decisions by the courts. For example, in a written agreement the consideration for a promise made may be recited as "one dollar in hand paid, receipt of which is hereby acknowledged." If it is reasonably certain from the relation of the parties and the surrounding circumstances that the "one dollar" was actually bargained for and given in exchange for the promise, the courts are uniform in holding that the consideration is adequate. On the other hand, if it is reasonably clear that the recitation of consideration was included in the writing to give it the appearance of validity, and the consideration was not bargained for and given in exchange for the promise, a majority of the courts hold that the promise is not supported by sufficient consideration and that it is not enforceable by court action.

Past Consideration. The term *past consideration* is applied to a situation in which the parties attempt to support a present promise on a benefit conferred at some time in the past. This involves a consideration of terms, because, as a matter of fact, past consideration is not sufficient consideration. At the time the promise is made, the promisee is under no obligation to the promisor and suffers no legal detriment in exchange for the promise. The parties attempt to support a present promise on a legal detriment which was suffered at some time past.

Implied Promises to Compensate. Past consideration cases must be distinguished from those cases in which a promise is made to pay a sum certain in discharge of an existing but unliquidated obligation. Such a promise is supported by sufficient consideration. It differs from an "accord and satisfaction" only in one respect: the claim is not a disputed claim. The promise merely makes definite the unliquidated obligation.

SUMMARY

If the parties do not intend as consideration the legal detriment given in exchange for a promise but intend it as a gratuity, it will not be sufficient consideration to support the promise. The courts will not inquire into the adequacy of the consideration so long as a sufficient consideration is given; but if in addition to the gross inequality of the exchange there is evidence of unfair dealing, the court will refuse to enforce the promise on the ground of misrepresentation, fraud, duress, or undue influence.

Past consideration is an attempt to support a present promise on a benefit conferred in the past. Past consideration will not support a present promise. Past consideration cases should not be confused with those cases in which a promise is made to pay a sum certain in discharge of an existing but unliquidated obligation. Such promises are supported by sufficient consideration and are enforceable.

Consideration in Bilateral Contracts

Mutual Obligation. The parties to a bilateral contract exchange promises, each is promisor and each is promisee. The test of consideration is not merely one of determining whether there has been an exchange of promises but whether the promises exchanged have created a binding obligation the performance of which will be a detriment to the promisee or a benefit to the promisor. If the obligation created by the promise is one which the promisor is already legally bound to perform, the promise cannot be sufficient consideration to support an exchange promise.

Illusory Promise. An illusory promise is one which is so worded that the fulfillment of the promise is left to the election of the promisor. It is not sufficient consideration to support a bilateral contract. Since the promisor may or may not fulfill the promise, depending on one's own desires and wishes, one has not made a binding promise. Unless the contract provides for adequate consideration on both sides it is said to be lacking in mutuality and, in general, is thereby rendered unenforceable as an executory agreement.

Right to Cancel Contract. If one or both parties to a contract reserve the right to cancel it at will, the contract is not a binding contract, since, by canceling the contract, one or both of the parties may avoid the binding effect of any promises made. If the contract provides that it will remain in force for a stipulated period of time after notice of cancellation is given, the promises are mutual, since both parties are bound for at least the time that elapses from the making of the contract until the notice of cancellation becomes effective. If one of the parties is given the right to cancel the contract on the happening of a stated event, such a provision does not give the promisor the right to cancel at will, and promisor's promise is sufficient consideration to support the promise given in exchange.[2]

SUMMARY

If a bilateral contract is to be valid, both contracting parties must make legally binding promises. If one of the parties is not bound, the other is not bound. If the promise of one of the parties to a bilateral contract is so worded that the performance of the promise depends on that party's will, wish, or desire, the promise is not a legally binding promise and cannot be sufficient consideration to support a bilateral contract. If the right to cancel a contract at will is reserved by either or both of the parties, the contract is void for lack of consideration.

Streich v. General Motors Corp.

126 N.E.2d 389 (App. Ct. Ill. 1955)

Streich (plaintiff) brought this action for damages for breach of contract against General Motors (defendant). Judgment for General Motors and Streich appealed. Affirmed.

G.M. placed an order for air magnet valves with Streich. The order provided as follows:

> Deliveries are to be made both in quantities and at times specified in schedules furnished by Buyer. Buyer will have no liability for payment for material or items delivered to Buyer which are in excess of quantities specified in the delivery schedules. Buyer may from time to time change delivery schedules or direct temporary suspension of scheduled shipments.
>
> Buyer reserves the right to cancel all or any of the undelivered portion of this order if Seller does not make deliveries as specified in the schedules, or if Seller breaches any of the terms hereof including the warranties of Seller.

On April 19, 1949, the order was cancelled by General Motors.

McCormick, Presiding Judge. There is no question but that under the law a contract properly entered into whereby the buyer agrees to buy all its

---

[2] For a discussion of cancellation clauses in franchises and franchises in general, see Chapter 16, p. 271.

requirements of a commodity for a certain period, and the seller agrees to sell the same as ordered, is a valid and enforceable contract and is not void for uncertainty and want of mutuality.

The contract in the instant case is not such a contract. The result is an agreement on the part of the seller to sell a certain identified valve at a certain fixed price in such quantities as the buyer may designate, when and if it issues a purchase order for the same. The word "release" as used throughout these documents is treated by both parties as equivalent to "order."

In *Corbin on Contracts,* Vol. 1, Sec. 157, the author says:

> In what purports to be a bilateral contract, one party sometimes promises to supply another, on specified terms with all the goods or services that the other may order from time to time within a stated period. A mere statement by the other party that he assents to this, or "accepts" it, is not a promise to order any goods or to pay anything. There is no consideration of any sort for the seller's promise; and he is not bound by it. This remains true, even though the parties think that a contract has been made and expressly label their agreement a " contract." In cases like this, there may be no good reason for implying any kind of promise by the offeree.

Here, the buyer proffers purchase order 11925, with its 25 or more clauses, to the seller for acceptance. In the instrument it makes no promise to do anything. On the surface it appears to be an attempt to initiate a valid bilateral contract. The seller accepts, and as by a flash of legerdemain the positions of the buyer and the seller shift. The buyer now becomes the promisee and the seller the promisor. The promise of the seller to furnish identified items at a stated price is merely an offer and cannot become a contract until the buyer issues a release or order for a designated number of items. Until this action is taken the buyer has made no promise to do anything, and either party may withdraw. The promise is illusory, and the chimerical contract vanishes. "An agreement to sell to another such of the seller's goods, wares, and merchandise as the other might from time to time desire to purchase is lacking in mutuality because it does not bind the buyer to purchase any of the goods of the seller, as such matter is left wholly at the option or pleasure of the buyer."

Professor Fuller, in a note to *Alexander Hamilton Institute v. Jones,* . . . says:

> One often has the impression of a kind of running battle between draftsmen and the courts, with much shifting of ground on the part of both.
>
> Back of this development lies a problem that touches the basic philosophy of contract law. The law of contracts is founded generally on the principle that it is the business of the courts to interpret and enforce the agreements that the parties have negotiated. This theory confronts the social reality that in many cases no real negotiations take place, and the terms of the contract are in fact set by the will of one party alone. This situation may arise where one party is indifferent or ignorant, or it may result from a superiority of bargaining power on one side. In such situations, there seems to be emerging a principle of law not yet frankly acknowledged which might be phrased something as follows: where one party to a contract has the power to dictate its terms, the terms of the contract are subject to judicial review,

and may be modified by the court if they are unduly harsh. Fuller, *Basic Contract Law*, p. 260.

The agreement was artfully prepared. It contains, in print so fine as to be scarcely legible, more than twenty-three clauses, most of which are applicable to bilateral contracts. It has all the indicia of a binding and enforceable contract, but it was not a binding and enforceable contract because the promise was defective. Behind the glittering facade is a void. This agreement was made in the higher echelons of business, overshadowed by the aura of business ethics. To say the least, the agreement was deceptive.

Nevertheless, as the law is today, on the pleadings in the instant case, the trial court could do nothing but sustain the motion to dismiss the complaint.[3]

Laclede Gas Co. v. Amoco Oil Co.

522 F.2d 33 (8th Cir. 1975)

Laclede (plaintiff) brought this action against Amoco (defendant) for breach of contract. Judgment for Amoco and Laclede appeals. Reversed.

Laclede and Amoco entered into a written agreement wherein Amoco was to supply Laclede with propane gas for the latter's customers in new residential development areas. Since the parties contemplated that the propane systems would eventually be converted into natural gas systems, the agreement gave Laclede the right to cancel the agreement upon thirty days written notice; there was no provision under which Amoco could cancel the agreement. Subsequently, Amoco "terminated" the contract, claiming it had a right to do this because the agreement lacks mutuality.

ROSS, JUDGE. A bilateral contract is not rendered invalid and unenforceable merely because one party has the right to cancellation while the other does not. There is no necessity that for each stipulation in a contract binding the one party there must be a corresponding stipulation binding the other. The important question in the instant case is whether Laclede's right of cancellation rendered all its other promises in the agreement illusory so that there was a complete failure of consideration. This would be the result had Laclede retained the right of immediate cancellation at any time for any reason.

Professor Williston notes:

> Since the courts do not favor arbitrary cancellation clauses, the tendency is to interpret even a slight restriction on the exercise of the right of cancellation as constituting such legal detriment

[3] This case represents the traditional strict interpretation approach still followed in many states. A growing number of states might find for the plaintiff under promissory estoppel, unconscionability, or good faith doctrines. See cases pp. 170 and 273.

as will satisfy the requirement of sufficient consideration; for example, where the reservation of right to cancel is for cause, or by written notice, or after a definite period of notice, or upon the occurrence of some extrinsic event, or is based on some other objective standard.

Here Laclede's right to terminate was limited by the agreement in three ways: (1) Laclede could not cancel the contract for one year; (2) any cancellation could be effective only on the anniversary date of the first delivery under the agreement; Laclede had to give Amoco thirty days written notice. Thus the restrictions on Laclede's right to cancel clearly bring this case within the rule.

When Consideration Is Unnecessary

Promissory Estoppel. Where a promisor makes a promise which the promisor, as a reasonable person, should expect would induce the promisee, in justifiable reliance thereon, to take some action or forbearance of a definite and substantial character, the courts will enforce the promise although it is not supported by consideration. The enforcement of such promises is based on doctrine of promissory estoppel which is discussed and applied in the case that follows. This doctrine is being applied in a growing number of business situations where its application will promote fair dealing or help to avoid an injustice.

Charitable Subscriptions. A charitable subscription is a promise to make a gift for a charitable, educational, or eleemosynary purpose. In England, such promises are held to be unenforceable; but in the United States, such promises are enforced provided the institution to which the promise is made has incurred obligations in reliance on the promise. Until obligations are incurred in reliance on the promise, the promisor may withdraw his promise without liability. The holdings of the courts are justified on the basis of either promissory estoppel or as an exception to the bargain theory based upon public policy.

Debts Barred by Statute of Limitations. The states are not in accord in their holdings relative to the enforceability of an unconditional promise to pay a debt barred by the statute of limitations. In general, such a promise is enforceable although the promise is not supported by consideration. In some, but not all, states a voluntary payment on the debt or a securing of the debt will be held to be an unconditional promise to pay the debt, and such new promise will be enforceable by court action until the statute of limitations has run against it for a second time.

Debts Discharged in Bankruptcy. If a debtor makes an unconditional promise to pay a debt or some portion thereof after he or she has been adjudged a bankrupt or after the debt has been discharged in bankruptcy, such a promise will be binding only as to that debt. A few states require that such a promise, if it is to be enforceable, need be in writing. A promise to pay a debt discharged in a composition agreement is not enforceable unless it is supported by a new consideration.

Promise to Perform a Conditional Duty. If the happening of a condition or event is made a condition precedent to the promisor's duty to conform and the condition is not fulfilled and thereafter a promise is made by the promisor to perform, such promise will be enforced, and no new consideration will be required.

SUMMARY

To avoid injustice, certain promises not supported by consideration are enforced. Promises justifiably relied on by the promisee, which induce substantial action on his or her part, will be enforced if a refusal to enforce would result in substantial injustice. In the United States charitable subscriptions are enforced provided the beneficiary of the promise has changed his or her position in reliance thereon. Promises made in business transactions are not usually enforced unless supported by sufficient bargain theory consideration.

Promises to pay debts barred by the statute of limitations or discharged in bankruptcy are enforced. A promise to pay a debt discharged in a composition agreement will not be enforced unless supported by a new consideration.

Hoffman v. Red Owl Stores, Inc.

133 N.W.2d 267 (Sup. Ct. Wis. 1965)

Hoffman (plaintiff) sued Red Owl Stores, Inc. (defendant) for breach of contract. Red Owl appealed from a judgment for Hoffman. Affirmed.

Lukowitz, an agent for Red Owl, represented to Hoffman that Red Owl would build a store building in Chilton and stock it with merchandise for Hoffman to operate in return for which Hoffman was to invest a total sum of $18,000. In reliance upon these representations Hoffman sold his grocery store and purchased the building site in Chilton and rented a residence for himself and his family in Chilton.

After Hoffman had sold his grocery store and paid the $1,000 on the Chilton lot, the $18,000 figure was changed to $24,100. Then in November, 1961, Hoffman was assured that if the $24,100 figure were increased by $2,000 the deal would go through. Hoffman was induced to sell his grocery store fixtures and inventory in June 1961, on the promise that he would be in his new store by fall. In November, Hoffman sold his bakery building on the urging of defendants and on the assurance that this was the last step necessary to have the deal go through.

CURRIE, CHIEF JUSTICE. Originally the doctrine of promissory estoppel was invoked as a substitute for consideration rendering a gratuitous promise enforceable as a contract. In other words, the acts of reliance by the promisee to his detriment provided a substitute for consideration. If promissory estoppel were to be limited to only those situations where the promise giving rise to the cause of action must be so definite with respect to all details that a contract would result were the promise supported by consideration, then the defendants' instant promises to Hoffman would not meet this test. However, sec. 90 of *Restatement, 1 Contracts,* does not impose the requirement that the promise giving rise to the cause of action must be so comprehensive in scope as to meet the requirements of an offer that would ripen into a contract if accepted by the promisee. Rather the conditions imposed are:

(1) Was the promise one which the promisor should reasonably expect to induce action or forbearance of a definite and substantial character on the part of the promisee?
(2) Did the promise induce such action or forbearance?
(3) Can injustice be avoided only by enforcement of the promise?

We deem it would be a mistake to regard an action grounded on promissory estoppel as the equivalent of a breach of contract action. As Dean Boyer points out, it is desirable that fluidity in the application of the concept be maintained. While the first two of the above listed three requirements of promissory estoppel present issues of fact which ordinarily will be resolved by a jury, the third requirement, that the remedy can only be invoked where necessary to avoid injustice, is one that involves a policy decision by the court. Such a policy decision necessarily embraces an element of discretion.

We conclude that injustice would result here if plaintiffs were not granted some relief because of the failure of defendants to keep their promises which induced plaintiffs to act to their detriment.

Consideration under the Uniform Commercial Code

In General. It will be recalled that a promise in writing to hold open an offer made between merchants is enforceable even though it is not supported by consideration. (2–205.) And likewise an agreement modifying a contract to sell goods needs no consideration to be binding. (2–209.) The Code introduces additional uncertainties into the law with (2–204) as the *Warrick* case which follows demonstrates. A franchise transaction involving sale of goods may create legally enforceable obligations even though the court finds the franchise agreement itself was lacking in mutuality and unenforceable.

Warrick Beverage Corp. v. Miller Brewing Co.
352 N.E.2d 496 (Ct. App. Ind. 1976)

Suit by Warrick Beverage Corporation (plaintiff) against Miller Brewing Co. (defendant) asking that Miller be enjoined from appointing an additional distributor in Posey County, Indiana where Warrick claimed it has an exclusive distributorship with Miller. Miller appealed from a decision by the trial court holding that the parties had a binding contract. Affirmed as to existence of contract but reversed on other grounds.

Miller purchased control of Meister Brau, Inc. and sent the following letter to all Meister Brau distributors including Warrick:

> While we have not assumed any of Meister Brau's rights or obligations under any agreement or arrangement you might have had with Meister Brau, Inc., we, as seller, hereby makes sales to you, as buyer, or its Buckeye Division, with the understanding that you bear the responsibility actively and aggressively to market and distribute such brands of beer to retailers and other persons to whom you are legally authorized to sell beer in the Area of Responsibility previously set forth for you by Meister Brau, Inc., or its Buckeye Division.
>
> With regard to your Area of Responsibility, Miller does not restrict you as to where or to whom you may resell beer. State laws (such as Illinois) may do so. Our relationship is that of seller and buyer and in no other respect is any relationship established between us. You are not required to place orders, nor are we required to accept orders for beer. As is the custom in our industry, these sales are made on a shipment-to-shipment basis only, and either of us can terminate this relationship at any time without incurring liability to the other. You are and shall remain an independent business and neither of us is in any sense to be regarded as the principal or agent or employee of the other.
>
> We are sending this letter to you in duplicate with the understanding that the terms hereof do not become effective until one copy, signed by you in the space below, has been returned to us within fifteen days of your receipt of this letter.

Following the return of the signed copy of this letter to Miller, Warrick began purchasing and distributing the new Miller beer. In the latter part of 1974 Miller concluded that it was not economically feasible to continue to distribute its new Lite beer exclusively through the twenty-two Meister Brau distributors in Indiana.

To realize its goal of maximum market saturation for its new product Miller entered into a distributorship agreement with Central which allowed it to distribute Miller's new Lite beer in Posey County.

LOWDERMILK, JUDGE. The Michigan District Court had occasion to construe the very letter we now have before us in the case of *Oak Distributing Co., et al. v. Miller Brewing Company* (1973). The court stated therein at page 906:

> Under the rationale of the aforementioned decision, it is beyond doubt that the letters of agreement in question are unenforceable for lack of mutuality. Either party, Miller or plaintiffs,

> could terminate said letter agreements at will without cause. Furthermore, said agreements neither obligated Miller to sell, nor plaintiffs to buy, the beer products involved herein.
>
> This conclusion, however, is merely a restatement of the obvious. It is the clear intent of the agreement to obviate any obligation of future performance with respect to both parties. The absence of mutuality is not the result of mistake or machination, nor is it concealed in clever or cunning language; it is the clear intent of the agreement and, presumably, that of the signators thereto.
>
> Moreover, it is not accurate to say that such an agreement is null or void. It is merely prospectively unenforceable. With regard to past or present activities, it is clear that the agreement is viable, and provides a basis upon which the parties may deal with each other if they so desire . . . The agreement is, therefore, valid to the extent that it describes the relationship of the parties as they perceived it and desired it to be.

Although not bound by Oak Distributing Co., *supra,* we agree that since either Warrick or Miller could have terminated their duties of performance at will without cause the letter agreement executed between them lacked mutuality and was unenforceable as respects their future performance.

[However] any contract entered into by the parties for the purchase and sale of beer products would be governed by the provisions of the Indiana Uniform Commercial Code. Sec. 2–204 provides:

> (1) A contract for sale of goods may be made in any manner sufficient to show agreement, including conduct by both parties which recognizes the existence of such a contract.
>
> (2) An agreement sufficient to constitute a contract for sale may be found even though the moment of its making is undetermined.
>
> (3) Even though one or more terms are left open a contract for sale does not fail for indefiniteness if the parties have intended to make a contract and there is a reasonably certain basis for giving an appropriate remedy.

The record discloses that Warrick, subsequent to being notified by Miller that Central would in the future be handling Miller's new Lite beer, continued to place orders for the new beer product. In fact, the record discloses that during the first eight months of 1975, Warrick was sold and received for purposes of resale more Lite beer than Central. Therefore, the trial court could have found that the letter agreement executed between Warrick and Miller, coupled with their conduct after the execution of the letter, recognized the existence of a binding contract.

We therefore hold that the trial court committed no reversible error in finding that a binding contract did exist between the parties herein at the time Warrick sought to obtain a preliminary injunction against Miller.

Cambern v. Hubbling

238 N.W.2d 622 (Sup. Ct. Minn. 1976)

Action by Cambern (plaintiff) against Hubbling (defendant) for damages based on allegations Hubbling had sold Cambern some diseased calves. Hubbling appealed from a decision for Cambern. Affirmed.

In August, 1973, Cambern entered an oral agreement with Hubbling to purchase 179 calves at $214 a head. When the calves were delivered, Cambern signed a receipt containing the following clause:

> IMPORTANT—The undersigned hereby acknowledges receipt of cattle purchased from Quality Dairy Cattle, Hardwick, Minnesota to be in good condition and further agrees that as far as health, shipping fever or death of any cattle which may hereafter occur that Quality Dairy Cattle will in no way be held liable for any loss. The purchaser of livestock listed above agrees that the title of said livestock shall be retained by Quality Dairy Cattle until check or draft is paid.

Cambern signed the receipt on the hood of his truck without reading the words. The words were not in conspicuous print nor did Hubbling call his attention to the wording.

PER CURIAM. The district court initially excluded the disclaimer clause from evidence on the ground that it was unconscionable, but by memorandum accompanying its order denying defendant's post-trial motions the court added as a reason that there had been no agreement between the parties to include the clause in their contract for sale. We hold that the latter, rather than the former is the more sound reason for its exclusion.

The testimony of the parties fully supports the conclusion that an oral contract for sale, without disclaimer of warranty, was made prior to the delivery of the calves. Although [under U.C.C. 2–209] parties may expressly modify a contract without a new consideration, it must be established that such an agreement was in fact made. From plaintiffs' offer of proof, it is evident that there was no assent by plaintiffs to a subsequent modification of the contract for sale.

Problem Cases

1. Baehr owned a gas station, which he leased to Kemp. Kemp had severe financial problems and was heavily indebted to Penn-O-Tex Oil corporation. Subsequently, Kemp transferred his rights to receive payments on all his claims to Penn-O-Tex. Kemp eventually defaulted in his rent payments to Baehr. Baehr, knowledgeable of the Kemp-Penn-O-Tex transfer agreement, complained to the corporation. Penn-O-Tex gave Baehr its unqualified assurance that the overdue rent would be paid. The rent was not paid, and Baehr sues Penn-O-Tex. Is Penn-O-Tex liable on its promise to pay Baehr the rent?

2. Graham entered into a written agreement with Jonnell to equip a dormitory with electrical wiring for which Graham would be paid approximately $70,000. At the time they made the agreement, Graham thought that the wiring was to be performed on only one wing of the dormitory, but, after a few days' work, Graham discovered there was a second wing which needed to be wired. Graham refused to include the wiring of the second wing for the $70,000, and entered into a new oral agreement with Jonnell to wire both wings for $65,000, but not requiring Graham to provide entrances and a heating system as he was required in the first agreement. Jonnell claims that this second agreement,

amending original written agreement, is void because no consideration was given for the amendment. Is Jonnell correct?

3. Hunter had been working for the telephone company when Hayes and the Winslow Construction Co. promised her a job as a flag girl on a construction job. Hunter was told to quit her present job, which she did. Hayes and the Winslow Construction Co. did not fulfill their promise to employ Hunter, and she sues to recover lost wages during her period of unemployment. Are Hayes and Winslow Construction Co. liable on their promise?
4. Signs was employed by Insurance Company as a selling agent. The contract of employment set out in detail the commisions to be paid to Signs on business produced by him, and it provided that the stipulated commissions were "full and complete compensation" for all business produced. In December, Insurance Company put out a bulletin stating that the company would distribute $1 million to deserving agents, and that agents selling $20,000 worth of life insurance during the month of December would receive $10,000. Signs sold in excess of $20,000 during the month of December but the company refused to pay him a bonus. Signs brought suit against Insurance Company to recover a judgment for $10,000. Insurance Company set up lack of consideration as a defense. Is the defense good?
5. On September 1, 1967, Monroe entered into a written contract to sell a house and lot to Bixby for $4,000. A payment of $60 was made at the time the contract was signed and the balance, with interest at the rate of 6 percent per annum, was to be paid in monthly installments of $30 or more per month the first year and $35 or more each month thereafter until the contract price was paid in full.

   Sometime later Bixby asked to have the monthly payments reduced, and Monroe drew up a purported agreement as follows:

   Agreement

   First party, Anna V. Wiley Monroe; Second party, Hazel May Bixby;

   First party agrees to accept 6% interest on contract. The first party agrees to accept Thirty ($30.00) Dollars a month payment instead of Thirty-five ($35.00) Dollars a month. The first party agrees to give the second party a deed when the first party has received Twenty-five Hundred ($2,500.00) Dollars from September 1, 1969.

   The second party is not to transfer the contract unless the first party agrees to the transfer.

   (S) Mrs. Anna V. Wiley Monroe"

   This paper was signed by Monroe but not by Bixby.

   Bixby made payments until January 25, 1970, when she refused to make further payments on the ground that she had paid $2,500 and was entitled to a deed, and that she was under no obligations to pay the balance of the $4,000. Monroe claims that there is an unpaid balance of $1,178.08 due on the original contract. Is Monroe right?
6. Mangeon, age 87, conveyed 960 acres to his son. In return, his son promised to pay him $1,800 annually for life. The property had a fair market value of $40,000. An heir, who would have received the 960 acres if it had been in the estate, seeks the return of the property. He argues inadequacy of consideration. Can the heir recover?
7. Hardy, an attorney, was employed by Murphy, president of CPC Corporation, to draft several documents relating to Gregory becoming the major shareholder and chief executive officer of CPC Corporation. Murphy was the present chief executive officer of CPC and was relinquishing control to Gregory upon Gregory's arranging for a loan for CPC. Hardy drew up the required documents for Murphy and then later requested payment

for his services from Gregory, who had then become the chief executive officer for CPC. Gregory promised Hardy that he would be paid for his services. Subsequently, Hardy sent a bill for his services to CPC and was denied payment by Gregory. Gregory maintained that the work performed by Hardy was for Murphy, the former chief executive of CPC, and so his oral promise to pay Murphy's debt was without consideration. Is Gregory correct?

8. Dr. Browning contracted to purchase the equipment and the practice of Dr. Johnson. Shortly thereafter, Browning decided not to buy and wanted to be released from the contract, but Johnson refused to cancel unless Browning paid him $40,000. Browning agreed. When payment became due, Browning refused to tender Johnson the $40,000. Johnson sues. Browning contends that there was a lack of consideration on his part to pay Johnson $40,000. Can Johnson recover?
9. Kincaid Carolina Corporation purchased some lumber from the Baillie Co. on credit. Five months later Baillie received a letter from Kincaid's attorneys informing them that Kincaid was insolvent and offering a 35 percent compromise settlement. Baillie said it would accept the 35 percent offer if payment was made within 25 days. A check arrived from Kincaid six months later. Baillie endorsed the check "with reservation of all our rights." Baillie decides to sue Kincaid for the remaining 65 percent of the debt. Kincaid contends that its check discharged the agreed settlement. Can Baillie recover?
10. National Chemsearch Corporation of New York, Inc. (Chemsearch), employed Bogatin as a salesperson. Prior to employing Bogatin, Chemsearch gave him one week's training. After the contract of employment was executed Chemsearch gave Bogatin the customer list and other sales aids. The contract included a restrictive covenant which provided that Bogatin would not give the customer list to a competitor or use it for his own benefit, would not reveal secret information, and would not solicit for a competitor in the territory assigned to him for a period of one year after termination of his employment. The employment was terminable at will by either party. Bogatin, in breach of his contract, accepted employment with a competitor of Chemsearch and gave it the customer list and certain secret information. Bogatin contends that since the contract is terminable at will by either party it is void for lack of consideration. Is this contention correct?

11

Capacity of Parties

Introduction

Capacity. The term "capacity" as used in the law denotes the ability to perform legally valid acts, that is, the ability to incur legal liability or to acquire legal rights. Where suit is brought to enforce a contractual promise, the plaintiff need not allege and prove that the parties to the contract have capacity to contract, since lack of capacity to contract is the exception rather than the rule. Any party seeking to base a claim or a defense on incapacity has the burden of alleging and proving the incapacity. The principal classes of persons afforded some degree of special protection on their contracts include (1) minors, (2) insane persons, and (3) drunken persons.

Minors' Contracts

Theory of Minors' Incapacity. Since the courts have recognized from an early date that a person of immature years does not have the capacity to compete on an equal basis with mature persons, they have granted to a minor the privilege of disaffirming his or her contracts. The minor contract is voidable only at the option of the minor. Any adult contracting with a minor finds himself or herself in the precarious legal position of being bound on the contract unless it is to the advantage of the minor to disaffirm the contract.

Period of Minority. At common law the age of minor was fixed at 21 years for both men and women. In counting time, the law generally disregards parts of days. Under this rule a minor becomes of age at the first moment of the day before the 21st anniversary of his or her birth. In a few states a minor becomes of age on his or her birthday.

At least 23 states have reduced the age of majority below 21 for males while 34 have reduced it below 21 for females. The trend seems to be towards establishing 18 years as the age for reaching majority. The impetus for many of these changes came from the passage in 1971 of federal legislation giving 18-year-olds the right to vote.

Emancipation. As a general rule the father of a minor has the right to the minor's services and can collect the minor's wages. If the father is dead, the widowed mother succeeds to the father's rights in this respect. A person who employs a minor is not discharged of liability to the parent by payment of wages to the minor unless the minor is emancipated. When a parent emancipates a child, he or she surrenders the right to the child's wages. There are no formal requirements for emancipation. All that is necessary is that the parent expressly or impliedly consent to the minor's entering into a contract of employment. If a minor has been emancipated, he or she can recover, either on the contract or on the basis of quasi contract, for services rendered. Emancipation does not enlarge the minor's capacity to contract.

General Rule. A minor contract binds both the minor and the adult unless the minor exercises the right to elect to disaffirm the contract; consequently, minor contracts are voidable, not void. If the minor elects to be bound by the contract, the relation existing between the minor and the other contracting party is the same as that existing between contracting parties who have full capacity to contract. If a minor, on reaching his or her majority, elects to ratify a contract entered into while a minor, no new promises are involved, and no new consideration need be given. The minor, by ratifying the contract, has exercised the privilege of election, and thereafter both parties are bound by the contract.

Business Contracts. As a general rule a minor is not liable on business contracts, even though the minor may be dependent on the income from the business for his or her living. In some cases the courts have held minors liable for equipment which has been purchased for the purpose of aiding in earning a living, such as machinery necessary to operate a farm or a truck to be used in trucking operations, but these cases are clearly exceptions to the general rule. The courts have usually held minors liable for the reasonable value of tools of a trade which have been purchased for the purpose of following a trade. Contracts for such equipment have been classed as contracts for necessaries and not as business contracts.

Minor Partner. A minor may become a member of a partnership, or a partnership may be composed of members all of whom are minors, and it will in no way affect the validity of partnership contracts. A minor partner may withdraw from the partnership without liability to a copartner or copartners for damages for breach of the contract of partnership. However, the minor partner cannot withdraw his or her original investment in the partnership capital if such withdrawal will injure partnership creditors. If a minor purchases the capital stock of a corporation, he or she has the right to disaffirm the purchase, return the stock, and recover the amount paid for it even though the capital of the corporation has been impaired in the interim.

SUMMARY

A minor has the privilege of disaffirming his or her contracts. The period of minority was 21 years at common law but there is a strong trend reducing the minority age period to 18 years.

A parent is entitled to the services of a minor child unless he emancipated the child—that is, unless he gives his consent to permit the child to enter into employment contracts and to collect his own wages. Emancipation does not enlarge a minor's capacity to contract.

A minor's contracts are voidable, not void, and they are held to be valid until the minor has exercised the privilege and disaffirmed the contract. The adult party to a contract is bound by the contract until the minor disaffirms it. As a general rule a minor may disaffirm business contracts, even though engaged in a business as a means of support. Many states by statute have altered, in some respects, a minor's capacity to contract. These statutes are not uniform in their terms or coverage.

A minor may become a member of a partnership. A minor partner may disaffirm the partnership agreement without liability to his partners for breach of such agreement, and may disaffirm personal liability to partnership creditors, but the minor may not withdraw his or her capital investment to the injury of such creditors.

Necessaries

Liability for Necessaries. A minor is liable for the reasonable value of necessaries furnished him, but his or her liability is quasi contractual in nature. If a minor contracts for necessaries and the contract price is greater than the reasonable value of necessaries furnished, the minor is liable only for their reasonable value. Liability is not based on a contractual promise.

Nature of Necessaries. Necessaries are confined to those things which are personal to the minor, that is, things which are essential to the minor's continued existence and general welfare. Generally, necessaries are food, clothing, shelter, and medical care, suitable to the infant's station in life, and a basic education or vocational training and the tools of his or her trade.

A minor's liability for necessaries is limited to the reasonable value of necessaries actually furnished to the minor. For example, if a minor contracts to rent a room for one year and occupies it for only three months, the minor's liability would be the reasonable rent for the room for the three months he or she occupied it. Also, if a minor is furnished with adequate necessaries by a parent or guardian, the minor will not be liable for necessaries furnished him or her by other persons. Since the minor's needs are already supplied by a parent or guardian, any items for which the minor contracts, even though they might fall into the classification of necessaries, will be held not to be necessaries.

Gastonia Personnel Corp. v. Rogers

172 S.E.2d 19 (Sup. Ct. N.C. 1970)

Suit by Gastonia Personnel Corporation (plaintiff) against Rogers (defendant). Gastonia appealed from a judgment for Rogers. Reversed.

Rogers, age 19, was emancipated and married. For assistance in obtaining suitable employment, Rogers went to the office of Gastonia, an employment agency, on May 29, 1968, where he signed a contract containing the following:

> If I ACCEPT employment offered me by an employer as a result of a lead (verbal or otherwise) from you within twelve (12) months of such lead even though it may not be the position originally discussed with you, I will be obligated to pay you as per the terms of the contract.

Under the contract, Rogers was free to continue his own quest for employment. He was to become obligated to Gastonia only if he accepted employment from an employer to whom he was referred by Gastonia.

Gastonia referred Rogers to an employer and Rogers accepted the job offered. Rogers then refused to pay Gastonia the agreed fee of $295.

BOBBITT, CHIEF JUSTICE. In general, our prior decisions are to the effect that the "necessaries" of an infant, his wife and child, include only such necessities of life as food, clothing, shelter, medical attention, etc. In our view, the concept of "necessaries" should be enlarged to include such articles of property and such services as are reasonably necessary to enable the infant to earn the money required to provide the necessities of life for himself and those who are legally dependent upon him.

To establish liability, plaintiff must satisfy the jury by the greater weight of the evidence that defendant's contract with plaintiff was an appropriate and reasonable means for defendant to obtain suitable employment. If this issue is answered in plaintiff's favor, plaintiff must then establish by the greater weight of the evidence the reasonable value of the services received by defendant pursuant to the contract. Thus, plaintiff's recovery, if any, cannot exceed the reasonable value of its services to defendant.

Disaffirmance of Contract

Right to Disaffirm. A minor's right to disaffirm his or her contracts is absolute and is personal to the minor. As a general rule, the minor's right to disaffirm his contracts is not conditioned on the minor's ability to return the consideration received or on the ability to fulfill other conditions. The minor or his or her personal representative (administrator of a deceased minor or a guardian) are the only ones who can exercise the right to disaffirm.

Time of Disaffirmance. The minor may exercise a right to disaffirm all executed contracts, except contracts affecting title to real estate, at any time from the time the minor enters into the contract until a reasonable time after reaching majority. The minor cannot disaffirm a contract affecting title to real estate until reaching majority. In some states a minor may repossess real estate which the minor has sold and conveyed to another, but cannot disaffirm the conveyance during minority. If the minor, after reaching majority, disaffirms a sale of real estate, the adult must account to the minor for the rents and profits during the period the adult was in possession.

If the minor does not disaffirm within a reasonable time after he or she reaches majority, he or she will be bound. The contracts of a minor are valid until he or she exercises his or her right to disaffirm, and if the minor does not exercise this right seasonably he or she thereby waives the right. What is a reasonable time for disaffirmance is a question of fact, and the time allowed the minor to disaffirm will depend on the facts and circumstances of each case. No general rule can be stated.

Return of Consideration. The objective of the law in giving a minor the right to disaffirm his or her contracts is the protection of the minor's estate from dissipation during minority, but the courts will not permit the minor to use this right to defraud adults. There is considerable diversity in the decisions as to the relative rights of the parties if the minor disaffirms his or her contract. The trend appears to be in the direction of holding the minor liable for the reasonable value of any benefits he or she has received where the consideration cannot be returned.

If the disaffirmed contract is wholly executory, the disaffirmance cancels all the legal obligations brought into existence by the contract. If the minor has received consideration, he or she will be required, on disaffirmance of the contract, to return any of the consideration or the benefits from such consideration which the minor still has in his possession at the time of disaffirmance of the contract. However, as a general rule, the right to disaffirm does not depend on the ability to return the consideration he has received.

Rights on Disaffirmance. At common law, when a minor disaffirmed a contract, the minor had the right to recover from the adult any consideration which the minor had given or its value. This right was not conditioned on the minor's returning the consideration received or on his or her placing the adult *in statu quo.* However, if the minor had in possession at the time of disaffirmance any of the consideration the minor had received, or if the minor's estate had been enhanced by the transaction, the minor would not be permitted to retain the benefits and at the same time recover the consideration given. The courts in some states and the statutes of other states require the minor on disaffirmance to pay for the benefits received or to place the adult *in statu quo.* This duty is limited under some circumstances.

If a minor disaffirms, the minor can recover what he or she has parted with, even though it has been transferred to an innocent third-party purchaser. This rule, however, does not apply to goods sold by a minor if the sale is subject to the Uniform Commercial Code. Under the Code, a good-faith purchaser for value from a seller having a voidable title acquires good title.[1]

Misrepresentation of Age. The misrepresentation of age by the minor does not, as a general rule, estop the minor from exercising the right to disaffirm the contract induced by the fraud. In some cases the courts have held that a minor who by misrepresentation of age has induced the adult to enter into the contract, will not be granted remedy on disaffirmance of the contract.

Some courts will permit a minor who, by misrepresenting his or her age, has induced the adult to enter into a contract, to disaffirm the contract and recover what he or she has given without requiring the minor to account for benefits received. But the majority of the courts now require the minor to restore the consideration received and to account for its use and its depreciation in value.

SUMMARY

A minor has the right to disaffirm contracts, except those affecting title to real estate. The minor may exercise this right from the time the minor enters into the contract until a reasonable time after reaching majority. A minor will not be permitted to use minority as a means of enhancing his or her estate; consequently, on disaffirmance, the minor must return to the adult any consideration received which he or she still has or any amount by which his or her estate has been enhanced. However, the minor's right to disaffirm is not conditioned on putting the adult *in statu quo.* If the minor has dissipated the consideration received, he or she can, under the majority rule, recover the consideration parted with without reimbursing the adult. The courts have held, with few exceptions, that misrepresentation of age does not estop a

[1] U.C.C. Sec. 2–403.

minor from disaffirming the contract induced by the misrepresentation. However, a majority of the courts will require the minor on disaffirmance, to return the consideration received and to account for its depreciation and for the value of its use.

Kiefer v. Fred Howe Motors, Inc.

158 N.W.2d 288 (Sup. Ct. Wisc. 1968)

This was an action brought by an infant, Steven Kiefer (plaintiff), against Fred Howe Motors, Inc. (defendant), to recover payments made on the purchase of an automobile. Judgment for Kiefer and Howe Motors appealed. Affirmed.

WILKIE, JUSTICE. Three issues are presented on this appeal. They are:

1. Should an emancipated minor over the age of 18 be legally responsible for his contracts?
2. Was the contract effectively disaffirmed?
3. Is Kiefer liable in tort for misrepresentation?

The law governing agreements made during infancy reaches back over many centuries. The general rule is that ". . . the contract of a minor, other than for necessaries, is either void or voidable at his option." The only other exceptions to the rule permitting disaffirmance are statutory or involve contracts which deal with duties imposed by law such as a contract of marriage or an agreement to support an illegitimate child. The general rule is not affected by the minor's status as emancipated or unemancipated.

Howe Motors does not advance any argument that would put this case within one of the exceptions to the general rule, but rather urges that this court, as a matter of public policy, adopt a rule that an emancipated minor over 18 years of age be made legally responsible for his contracts.

The underpinnings of the general rule allowing the minor to disaffirm his contracts were undoubtedly the protection of the minor. It was thought that the minor was immature in both mind and experience and that, therefore, he should be protected from his own bad judgments as well as from adults who would take advantage of him. The doctrine of the voidability of minors' contracts often seems commendable and just. . . . However, in today's modern and sophisticated society the "infancy doctrine" seems to lose some of its gloss.

Paradoxically, we declare the infant mature enough to shoulder arms in the military, but not mature enough to vote; mature enough to marry and be responsible for his torts and crimes, but not mature enough to assume the burden of his own contractual indiscretions. In Wisconsin, the infant is deemed mature enough to use a dangerous instrumentality—a motor vehicle—

at 16, but not mature enough to purchase it without protection until he is 21.

No one really questions that a line as to age must be drawn somewhere below which a legally defined minor must be able to disaffirm his contracts for nonnecessities. The law over the centuries has considered this age to be twenty-one. Legislatures in other states have lowered the age. We suggest that Howe Motors might better seek the change it proposes in the legislative halls rather than this court. A recent law review article in the *Indiana Law Journal* explores the problem of contractual disabilities of minors and points to three different legislative solutions leading to greater freedom to contract. The first approach is one gleaned from the statutes of California and New York, which would allow parties to submit a proposed contract to a court which would remove the infant's right to disaffirmance upon a finding that the particular contract is fair. This suggested approach appears to be extremely impractical in light of the expense and delay that would necessarily accompany the procedure. A second approach would be to establish a rebuttable presumption of incapacity to replace the strict rule. This alternative would be an open invitation to litigation. The third suggestion is a statutory procedure that would allow a minor to petition a court for the removal of disabilities. Under this procedure a minor would only have to go to court once, rather than once for each contract as in the first suggestion.

Undoubtedly, the infancy doctrine is an obstacle when a major purchase is involved. However, we believe that the reasons for allowing that obstacle to remain viable at this point outweight those for casting it aside. Minors require some protection from the pitfalls of the marketplace. Reasonable minds will always differ on the extent of the protection that should be afforded. For this court to adopt a rule that the defendant suggests and remove the contractual disabilities from a minor simply because he becomes emancipated, which in most cases would be the result of marriage, would be to suggest that the married minor is somehow vested with more wisdom and maturity than his single counterpart. However, logic would not seem to dictate this result especially when today a youthful marriage is oftentimes indicative of a lack of wisdom and maturity.

Howe Motors questions whether there has been an effective disaffirmance of the contract in this case

Williston, while discussing how a minor may disaffirm a contract, states:

> Any act which clearly shows an intent to disaffirm a contract or sale is sufficient for the purpose. Thus a notice by the infant of his purpose to disaffirm . . . a tender or even an offer to return the consideration or its proceeds to the vendor, . . . is sufficient.

The 19th-century view was that a minor's lying about his age was inconsequential because a fraudulent representation of capacity was not the equivalent of actual capacity. This rule has been altered by time. There appear to be two possible methods that now can be employed to bind the defrauding minor: He may be estopped from denying his alleged majority, in which case the contract will be enforced or contract damages will be allowed; or he may be allowed to disaffirm his contract but be liable in tort for damages. Wisconsin follows the latter approach.

The trial produced conflicting testimony regarding whether Kiefer had been asked his age or had replied that he was "21." Kiefer and his wife, Jacqueline, said "No," and Frank McHalsky, Howe Motors' salesman, said "Yes." Confronted with this conflict, the question of creditability was for the trial court to decide, which it did by holding that Kiefer did not orally represent that he was "21."

Ratification

Nature of Ratification. A minor cannot ratify a contract until he or she reaches majority. During minority the minor is incapable of making a binding contractual promise. If permitted to ratify contracts during the period of minority the minor would be able to remove his or her disability by his or her own act. This the courts will not permit.

Requirements for Ratification. There are no formal requirements for the ratification of a minor's contract. The minor's ratification, on reaching majority, may be either expressed or implied. Any words or act on the part of the minor after reaching majority, which indicate with reasonable clarity the minor's intent to be bound by the contract, are sufficient.

If the contract is executed, the retaining of the consideration by the minor for an unreasonable time after reaching majority amounts to a ratification. If a minor accepts benefits of tendered performance, or if he or she performs his or her part of the contract after reaching majority, it will be evidence of intention to ratify, although either one standing alone would not necessarily be conclusive. The courts have generally held that if a minor, after reaching majority, indicates an intent to ratify a contract, the minor cannot escape the effects of ratification by showing that he or she did not know that he or she had a right to disaffirm. In this situation the courts have usually applied the rule that ignorance of the law is no excuse.

If the contract is executory, some courts have held that mere inaction on the part of the minor after reaching majority does not amount to a ratification. Other courts have held that since a minor's contract is valid until it is disaffirmed, failure to disaffirm within a reasonable time amounts to a waiver of the right to disaffirm and is a ratification.

Effect of Ratification. A ratification makes the contract valid from its inception. When the minor ratifies a contract after reaching majority, the minor thereby exercises his or her right to elect whether or not he or she wishes to be bound by the contract. Having exercised the right to elect and having elected to be bound, the minor cannot thereafter disaffirm.

SUMMARY

A minor cannot ratify a contract until the minor reaches majority. All that is necessary for ratification is an indication of an intention to be bound. If the contract is executed, inaction for an unreasonable time will, as a general rule, amount to a ratification. If the contract is executory, some courts have held that mere inaction will not amount to a ratification. Ratification makes the contract valid from its inception.

Robertson v. Robertson

229 So.2d 642 (Ct. App. Fla. 1969)

A suit by father (plaintiff) against son (defendant) on son's agreement to repay father for college expense. Judgment for father and son appealed. Affirmed.

During the son's last year of high school, at age 18, the subject of the son's future education was seriously discussed between the parties. At the conclusion of this discussion, the father agreed to lend his son enough money to finance the son through college.

To adequately meet the expenses of his son's premedical and postgraduate education, the father whose employment was that of a salesman, mortgaged his home and took out loans against existing life insurance policies.

The son graduated from dental school in 1962. The father did not attempt to demand repayment of the monies he had expended for the son's education until June 1964, at which time he wrote to his son a letter which recited his appraisal of the circumstances surrounding their mutual obligations, and concluded by requesting that the son begin repaying to him the sum of $30,000. Repayment was requested by installments in the amount of $400 per month.

After the son received the letter, he and his father had telephone conversations. On June 28, 1964, the son wrote to his father a letter in which he agreed to repay a total debt of $24,000 at the rate of $100 per month. The letter read in pertinent part:

> Four hundred dollars is a lot of money to write a check for each month. According to my memory I offered to pay $100 per month to help re-pay some of the expenses of my college education. We will be happy to pay $100 each month to you, as I had originally promised. However we cannot afford to pay any more than this.

Accordingly, the son paid the sum of $100 per month for the next three years until September 1967, at which time he stopped after he had paid a total sum of 3,846.00.

HENDRY, JUDGE. As to the issue of whether an infant's [minor's] contract is void or voidable, see the case of *Lee v. Thompson,* Therein the court stated:

Since the contracts of an infant are voidable, . . . subject to the possibility of disaffirmance, it follows that when the infant attains his majority and ratifies a contract made in infancy its infirmity is removed and it will be treated as valid from inception and the optional right to disaffirm abandoned. Ratification does not now require a new consideration to make it binding.

Thus, our attention is next focused on the issue of whether or not the father proved that the son, having attained majority, thereafter ratified the contractual agreement to repay his father for the amounts expended for education. The jury had before it evidence that the son had received and accepted the benefits of his father's contractual agreement, i.e., to pay for educational and related expenses, for a period of four years after obtaining his majority; evidence of oral affirmances by the son that the agreement he made during his infancy was valid and binding, such affirmances having been made after he attained majority; the hand-written letter . . . which affirmed the agreement and the obligation therein; and evidence showing monthly payments over a period of three years, specifically noted as "college payment," and "education refund." It appears that the trial court was eminently correct in submitting the case to the jury on the issue of whether or not the son had ratified the act committed during infancy, after he had attained majority. The jury determined that he had so ratified, and its finding should stand.

Minors' Tort Liability

Nature of Liability. A minor is liable for torts and crimes. The general rule applied in determining a minor's liability for tort, including negligence, is whether or not he or she used that degree of care ordinarily exercised by children of like age, mental capacity, and experience. This is usually a question of fact for the jury. In determining a minor's criminal liability, the statutes of the state in which the crime is committed must be consulted.

Insane and Drunken Persons

Nature of Liability. The basic theory of the liability of insane persons is the same as that of minors; that is, it is presumed that the insane person, like the minor, does not have the capacity to protect his or her interests in the give-and-take of a market economy. As a general rule, the drunken person is dealt with in the same manner as though he were insane, but before he will be considered drunk, he must be intoxicated to such an extent that he does not have the mental capacity to comprehend the business at hand. Some states do not follow the general rule, and in such states the fact that one of the parties to the contract was drunk at the time he or she entered into the contract is not ground for the disaffirmance of the contract.

Test of Insanity. The courts recognize that persons have varying degrees of mental capacity and that no simple rule whereby mental capacity may be tested can be formulated. The test usually applied is whether or not the contracting party had, at the time the contract was entered into, sufficient mental capacity to comprehend the business involved. The same test is applied in determining the contractual capacity of drunken persons.

The nature of the mental weakness of the contracting party is immaterial. The incapacity may result from lunacy, idiocy, senility, or other defects or diseases of the mind. A person may have periods of insanity and be lucid at all other times. A contract made during a lucid interval is binding. A person may be laboring under insane delusions, but his or her contracts will be binding unless the insane delusions are so connected with the subject matter of the contract as to render him or her incapable of comprehending its nature.

Effect of Adjudication of Insanity. In most states the contracts of a person who has been adjudged insane are void. The statutes of some states expressly provide that the contracts of a person who has been adjudged insane are void, and in others the same result has been reached by judicial decision. This rule applies only where there has been a regular hearing before a court having jurisdiction over such cases, and where, after due investigation, the court has adjudged the person to be of unsound mind and incapable of managing his or her estate and has appointed a guardian or conservator of the estate. If a person is sued on a contract and sets up as a defense insanity at the time he or she entered into the contract, a finding that the person was insane at the time he or she entered into the contract would not be an adjudication of insanity. Such a finding is binding only as to the case being tried. The contracts made by persons later found to have been insane at the time of contract as generally treated *voidable* rather than *void* contracts.

Necessaries. An insane person is liable for the reasonable value of necessaries furnished him. The rules relative to what are necessaries and the liability for necessaries generally are the same as those applying to minors.

Disaffirmance of Contract. If a person contracts with an insane person and does not know or does not have reasonable cause to know of the person's insanity, and if the contract is fair and entered into in good faith, the insane party cannot disaffirm the contract unless he or she can put the sane party *in statu quo.*

If the sane party knows or, in the exercise of reasonable care, should know, of the insanity of the other party, the insane party can disaffirm the contract without putting the sane party *in statu quo.* However, he or she must return to the sane person any portion of the consideration which he or she still has. The rule in such cases is the same as the rule governing minors' contracts.

Ratification of Contract. A contract entered into by a person while insane may be ratified by that person if and when he or she regains his sanity, or it may be ratified by one's personal representative in the event the insane person is adjudged insane or dies. The ratification of an insane person's contract has the same effect on the rights of the parties to the contract as has the ratification of a minor's contract. The contract will be considered as valid from its inception.

SUMMARY

The contracts of an insane person entered into while insane are voidable unless the party has been adjudged insane by a court having jurisdiction of the case, in which event the majority of jurisdictions hold that the contract is void.

An insane person cannot disaffirm a fair contract entered into with a person ignorant of the insanity unless he or she puts the party *in statu quo.* Knowledge of the insanity on the part of the sane person gives the insane party the same rights to disaffirm a contract as an infant.

Cundick v. Broadbent

383 F.2d 157 (10th Cir. 1967)

This was an action brought by Irma Cundick (plaintiff), guardian *ad litem* for her husband, Darwin Cundick, to set aside an agreement for the sale of (1) livestock and equipment; (2) shares of stock in a development company; and (3) base range land in Wyoming to J. R. Broadbent (defendant). The alleged grounds for nullification were that at the time of the transaction Cundick was mentally incompetent to execute the agreement. Judgment for Broadbent and Cundick appealed. Affirmed.

MURRAH, CHIEF JUDGE. The modern rule, and the weight of authority, seems to be as stated in 2 Jaeger's *Williston on Contracts,* 3d ed., § 251, ". . . the contractual act by one claiming to be mentally deficient, but not under guardianship, absent fraud, or knowledge of such asserted incapacity by the other contracting party, is not a void act but at most only voidable at the instance of the deficient party; and then only in accordance with certain equitable principles."

In recognition of different degrees of mental competency the weight of authority seems to hold that mental capacity to contract depends upon whether the allegedly disabled person possessed sufficient reason to enable him to understand the nature and effect of the act in issue. Even average intelligence is not essential to a valid bargain. In amplification of this principle, it has been said that if a maker of a contract ". . . has sufficient mental capacity to retain in his memory without prompting the extent and condition of his property and to comprehend how he is disposing of it and to whom and upon what consideration, then he possesses sufficient mental capacity to execute such instrument." The Wyoming court adheres to the general principle that "mere weakness of body or mind, or of both, do not constitute what the law regards as mental incompetency sufficient to render a contract voidable. . . . A condition which may be described by a physician as *senile dementia* may not be insanity in a legal sense."

Against the background of medical and lay evidence tending to show Cundick's incompetency on the crucial date, there is positive evidence to the effect that at the time in question he was 59 years old, married and operating a sheep ranch in Wyoming; that in previous years he had sold his lamb crop to Broadbent and on a date prior to this transaction the parties met at a midway point for the purpose of selling the current lamb crop. Although there is innuendo concerning what transpired at the meeting, neither party testified and no one else was present. We do know that the meeting resulted in a one page contract signed by both parties in which Cundick agreed to sell all of his ranching properties to Broadbent. It is undisputed that Cundick and his wife thereafter took this one-page contract to their lawyer in Salt Lake City who refined and amplified it into an 11-page contract providing in detail the terms by which the sale was to be consummated. The contract was signed in the lawyer's office by Cundick and Broadbent in the presence of Cundick's wife and the lawyer. The lawyer testified that the contract had been explained in detail and that all parties apparently understood it.

The narrated facts of this case amply support the trial court's finding to the effect that Broadbent did not deceive or overreach Cundick. In the absence of any evidence that Broadbent knew of Cundick's mental deficiency, the only evidence from which it can be said that Broadbent took advantage or overreached him is the proof concerning the value of the property sold under the contract. As to that, there is positive evidence that the property was worth very much more than what Broadbent paid for it. But as we have noted, there was evidence to the effect that after the original contract was signed and some complaint made about the purchase price, the parties agreed to raise the price and the contract was so modified.

Problem Cases

1. Kabler, a minor, was killed while driving a Simco, Inc.'s, truck under a lease agreement whereby Kabler used the truck to sell ice cream products supplied to him by Simco, Inc. Suit was brought by Byrne, administratrix of Kabler's estate. Byrne charged Simco, Inc., with failure to maintain the truck in safe operating condition.

   Simco, Inc., set up as a defense the written contract between it and Kabler, in which Kabler agreed to hold Simco, Inc., harmless for any injury suffered by him arising from the use of the truck.

   Byrne contends that since Kabler was a minor the contract was not binding and that Simco, Inc.'s, defense is not valid. Is the provision in the contract binding on Kabler or his estate?

2. Bell, a minor, went to work as an employee of the Pankas Beauty Parlor. As a condition of employment, Bell agreed that if he left the employ of Pankas, he would not work in or run a beauty parlor business within a ten-mile radius of downtown Pittsburgh for a two-year period. Bell eventually quit the Pankas Beauty parlor and immediately opened a shop of his own three blocks away from Pankas, violating his agreement not to compete. Pankas sues to enforce the noncompetition agreement. Bell claims that as a minor he is not bound by the terms of the covenant. Can Pankas prevent Bell from competing?

3. Rose, a minor under the age of 21, purchased an automobile from a Buick dealer. Seven months later, Rose declared the contract invalid since, as a minor, he wasn't permitted by law to make a contract for the purchase of an automobile. Rose demanded: (1) that the contract be declared invalid and (2) that the entire purchase price of the automobile be refunded to him. Will his demands be honored?

4. Heiman had been actively involved in various and numerous business enterprises since his 17th birthday. While still a minor, Heiman issued several personal checks to Eastern Airlines in payment for airline tickets in 1963 and through February 1964. On April 21, 1964, Heiman reached the age of majority. Over five months later, on September 26, 1964, he wrote Eastern Airlines a letter disaffirming these personal checks. Heiman is now sued by Eastern Airlines and he sets up his minority and letter of disaffirmance as a defense. Is this a good defense?

5. Hurley and his grandmother, Price, inherited as co-owners 575 shares of the common stock of Edison Company. At the time of inheritance, Hurley was a minor of the age of 20 years and lived with his grandmother. On December 11, 1955, the grandmother requested Hurley to sign a dividend order authorizing Edison Co. to pay all dividends due on the shares of stock to Price. Hurley signed the dividend orders without receiving any consideration therefor and without knowing the nature of the document being signed. Price died December 27, 1970, and it was not until March 18, 1971, that Hurley first learned that he was co-owner of the stock. On March 20, 1971, Hurley gave notice to Edison Co. that he disaffirmed the dividend order which he had signed earlier and demanded that the Edison Co. pay his one half of all dividends paid on the stock since he became co-owner thereof. The Edison Co. refused to pay and Hurley brought suit. Edison Co. contends that Hurley did not disaffirm within a reasonable time after he became of age. Does Hurley have the right to disaffirm the contract?

6. Krasner and Berk, doctors, shared a suite of medical offices, splitting the rent and applicable taxes. In 1969 the parties renewed the agreement for three years in writing. Performance was demanded even if one of the parties became disabled. Professional testimony indicated that Berk began suffering from premature senility in 1967. Prior to the signing of the agreement, Berk's wife spoke with Krasner about her husband's medical condition. Two weeks after signing the agreement, Berk consulted a brain surgeon; within six months Berk followed his doctor's advice and gave up his practice. Krasner sues alleging breach of contract. Berk defends claiming mental incapacity. Can Krasner recover?

7. Rotondo, on August 8, 1953, purchased a diamond ring from Kay Jewelry Company (Kay) informing the latter that he was a minor 19 years of age and that he was buying it as an engagement ring. Rotondo made a part payment of $94.49 on the ring. On that same day he presented the ring to his fiancée.

   On April 10, 1954, the engagement was terminated but the ring was not returned. Rotondo testified that he asked Kay to repossess the ring shortly after the engagement was broken, but there was no evidence that the ring was repossessed.

On July 6, 1954, Rotondo, while still a minor, brought this suit to recover the payment made on the ring. Can Rotondo recover his payments?

8. Earlier in a criminal proceeding Davis had been found not guilty on the grounds of insanity. He was committed to a hospital for the criminally insane but in a mental health proceeding was not declared to be insane. He escaped from the hospital about five years before the bringing of this suit. During that time he had married and had established a trucking business. In connection with the trucking business he had bought equipment from the Colorado Kenworth Corporation (Kenworth) as follows: Kenworth tractor $15,000—paid on purchase price $9,058.90; trailer—paid $8,693.74; refrigerator unit, purchase price $17,450; tires $1,125, paid $242.50. Davis sold his business, including this equipment for $1,600, the value of his equity in the equipment. Notice of disaffirmance was given but no offer was made to place the parties *in statu quo.* Davis contends that since he was found to be insane in the criminal proceedings all his contracts are void. Is Davis right?

12

Illegality

Introduction

Nature of Illegality. A bargain is illegal if either its formation or its performance is detrimental to the general public interest. The courts recognize and protect the individual's right to bargain, but public welfare is paramount to individual rights, and whenever the bargain of individuals, either in its formation or in its performance, is criminal, tortious, or contrary to accepted standards of morality, it will be declared to be illegal and will not be enforced by court action. In general, illegal bargains are void; however, there are exceptions to the rule. (Note: In legal treatises and judges' opinions, the term "illegal contract" is commonly used. The term "bargain" is used in preference to "contract" because "bargain" is a neutral word. "Illegal contract" is a contradiction of terms, and its use tends to be confusing.)

Classification. There are an infinite number of situations which give rise to illegal bargains. However, for the purpose of discussion, illegal bargains may be roughly classified into the following categories: (1) bargains in violation of positive law,[1] (2) bargains made void by statute, and (3) bargains contrary to public policy.

Presumption. In determining the legality of a bargain, the courts will presume that the parties intended a legal result and will interpret the bargain so as to hold it legal, unless it is clear that the parties intended an illegal bargain. All doubts are resolved in favor of the legality of the bargain.

[1] Law actually and specifically enacted or adopted by proper authority for the government of an organized jural society. *Black's Law Dictionary,* 4th ed. (St. Paul, Minn.: West Publishing Co., 1951), p. 1,324.

Allen v. Jordanos' Inc.

125 Cal. Rptr. 31 (Cal. App. 1975)

Action commenced by Allen (plaintiff), a former employee of Jordanos' Inc. (defendant), for breach of contract. Judgment entered for Jordanos on the breach of contract issue and Allen appealed. Affirmed.

During 1972, Allen was an employee of Jordanos. Jordanos had insufficient evidence to prove that Allen was guilty of theft and dishonesty within the course and scope of his employment there. Allen, due to his membership in a local union, was entitled to have a fair and impartial arbitration to prove Jordanos' charges of theft and dishonesty. The union negotiated with Jordanos and an oral agreement was reached whereby Allen agreed to accept a permanent layoff from Jordanos, and Jordanos agreed to permit Allen to obtain unemployment and union benefits and to not communicate to any third persons that Allen had been laid off under suspicions of theft and dishonesty. Jordanos subsequently informed the state unemployment bureau of Allen's voluntary layoff and the reasons therefor. Allen was later denied unemployment benefits.

HANSON, ASSOCIATE JUSTICE. It is readily seen that the reason for the part of the oral contract that Jordanos would inform no one of the reasons for Allen's voluntary layoff was to insure Allen that Jordanos would not inform the state unemployment bureau of those reasons. Section 1256 of the Unemployment Insurance Code states in pertinent part:

> An individual is disqualified for unemployment compensation benefits if the director finds that he left his most recent work voluntarily without good cause or that he has been discharged for misconduct connected with his most recent work.

Section 2107 of the Unemployment Insurance Code states:

> It is a misdemeanor for any employing unit or any officer or agent of an employing unit or any individual to connive or conspire to aid such individual to obtain benefits to which he is not entitled by the wilful withholding of information or by the wilful failure to report any relevant information.

Thus Allen was bargaining for an act that was illegal by definition—to withhold information from or give false information to the state bureau.

The nondisclosure was not a minor or indirect part of the contract, but a major and substantial consideration of the agreement. A bargain which includes as part of its consideration nondisclosure of discreditable facts is illegal. It has long been the law that consideration which is void for illegality is no consideration at all. The action for breach of contract was properly dismissed in Jordanos' favor at the trial court.

Bargains in Violation of Positive Law

Bargain to Commit a Crime. It is axiomatic that a bargain which requires the commission of a crime is illegal. Also, a bargain which does not require the commission of a crime, but which is of such a nature that it tends to induce the commission of a crime, is illegal. The fact that a party to a bargain might benefit from the bargain if he or she commits a crime will not, as a general rule, make the bargain illegal, but if the inducement is strong enough to endanger the welfare of society, the bargain is illegal.

The nature of the bargain may be such that its formation is a crime. Connivance is a crime; and a bargain whereby one party, for a consideration, agrees to "look the other way" while the other party commits a crime is an illegal bargain. Also, if parties enter into a series of bargains, each innocent in itself but each a part of a plan to accomplish a criminal result, all of the bargains are illegal. For example, suppose the creation of a monopoly is made a crime under the statutes of the state. Arthur, Burton, Clayton, and Dyer own all the theaters in the area. They enter into a bargain to form a partnership to operate their theaters. The purpose of the partnership is to obtain a monopoly of the theater business in the area so that they can charge higher prices. The bargain is illegal, although a bargain to form a partnership to operate a theater is, standing by itself, legal, and the bargains to convey the theaters owned by the parties are, standing by themselves, legal. All of the bargains taken together are illegal, since the objective of the series of bargains is to create a monopoly in violation of positive law.

Bargain to Commit a Tort. The commission of a tort is clearly detrimental to the general public welfare; consequently, a bargain which cannot be performed without the commission of a tort is illegal. The fact that a tort may be committed during the performance of the bargain does not make it illegal. For example, suppose Adams contracts to build a large office building. During the course of the construction of the building an employee of Adams may negligently injure a pedestrian who is passing the building. The fact that such a tort may be committed in the performance of the construction contract does not make the contract illegal.

SUMMARY

If the formation or the performance of a bargain requires a violation of positive law, it is illegal. The commission of a crime or a tort is a violation of positive law. If the formation or the performance of a bargain requires the commission of a crime or will induce the commission of a crime, the bargain is illegal. If a bargain cannot be performed without the commission of a tort, it is illegal. The fact that a tort may be committed in the performance of a contract does not render the contract illegal.

Bargains Made Illegal by Statutes

Types of Statutes. The statutes affecting the legality of bargains may be divided into three classes: (1) criminal statutes, (2) statutes expressly declaring contracts void, and (3) regulatory statutes. All of these statutes are, as a general rule, so drafted that a penalty is imposed for the violation of the statute; consequently, they are basically criminal in nature. This classification considers as criminal statutes only those statutes the violation of which involves moral turpitude.

Wagering Statutes. All states have enacted statutes prohibiting or regulating wagering. Such statutes are of special significance in the law of contracts. There is a thin line of distinction between wagering, risk shifting, and speculative bargaining. Risk shifting and speculative bargaining are legal; wagering is illegal. When the parties create a risk, which has no prior existence, for the purpose of bearing it, such a bargain is a wager or bet and is usually prohibited by wagering statutes.

A bargain for insurance is a typical example of a risk-shifting bargain and is, of course, legal. If the insured does not have an insurable interest in the insured property, then the bargain to insure is a wagering bargain and is illegal. In the case of property insurance the insured's relation to the property insured must be such that he or she will suffer pecuniary loss on the happening of the event against which the property is insured. The recovery of the insured is based on the principle of indemnity; and, as a general rule, recovery cannot be greater than the pecuniary loss suffered. The pecuniary interest is not important in life insurance. In life insurance the relationship between the insured and the person obtaining the insurance must be such as to negate the existence of an intent to speculate in human life.

Stock and Commodity Market Transactions. A good faith transaction on the stock or commodity market is not illegal. It may be a speculative bargain, but it is not a wager. A wager based on the fluctuation in the price of a stock or commodity is illegal. The primary difference between the two is that in the valid stock or commodity market transaction, the stock or commodity is purchased, and the seller is bound to deliver the shares of stock or quantity of commodity bargained for, and the buyer is obligated to accept delivery and pay the agreed price; whereas in the wager transaction, no stock or commodity is purchased. It is merely a bargain to pay an amount based on the fluctuation in the price of a stock or commodity.

The fact that the purchaser may intend never to accept delivery of the stock or commodity does not affect the validity of the transaction. However, if there is an understanding between the broker and the purchaser to the effect that the purchaser will not be obligated to accept delivery of the stock or commodity, the transaction will be interpreted as a wager and will be illegal.

Statutes Declaring Bargains Void. State legislatures have enacted statutes which declare certain defined classes of bargains, or bargains made under certain circumstances, to be void. In some instances, it is clear from the wording of the statute and the surrounding circumstances that the legislative intent is to declare the bargain to be voidable, not void. There is little uniformity in the provisions of such statutes or in the subject matter included. In general, there is no moral turpitude involved in the violation of such statutes, and, with some exceptions, no penalty is imposed for their violation.

Usury laws and Sunday laws are examples of such statutes. Both have been generally adopted. The usury laws provide that if a charge for the use of money is made which is in excess of a stated amount, the lender will be subject to a penalty. The penalty imposed ranges from forfeiture of principal and interest to forfeiture of any amount of interest charged in excess of the legal rate of interest. In several states the usury laws do not apply to loans to corporations, and many states hold that a higher price may be charged for a credit sale than for a cash sale without the difference in price being treated as interest.

The Sunday laws prohibit the performance of certain labors and the transaction of business on Sunday. These statutes are not uniform in their provisions. The commoner forms of Sunday statutes prohibit all contracts and sales not of necessity or charity.

Regulatory Statutes. A variety of statutes have been passed by Congress and the state legislatures regulating the dealings in a particular article of commerce. These statutes are not uniform either in their wording or in their scope, but certain types of statutes predominate. The commonest type of regulatory statute requires the obtaining of a license before a person, partnership, or corporation engages in the regulated activity. The purpose of such statutes is to protect the public against dishonest and unskilled persons. Lawyers, doctors, dentists, and other professionals are required to pass examinations before they are granted a license to practice their profession. In most states, real estate brokers, stock brokers, insurance agents, and others who are engaged in performing special services for the public are required to prove that they are of good character, and they may also be required to pass some type of examination or test of skill before they are granted a license.

Barbers, beauty parlor operators, building contractors, electricians, plumbers, and others performing skilled services may be required to obtain a license before they engage in their trade. In addition, some business persons, such as pawnbrokers, retailers and wholesalers of liquor and tobacco, and sellers of other special commodities, are required to obtain a license before they engage in the regulated business. If a person bargains to perform services or engages in a regulated business without first having obtained a license, the bargain is illegal.

Revenue-Raising Statutes. Some licensing statutes have as their objective the raising of revenue. Whether a statute requiring the obtaining of a license is a regulatory statute or a revenue-raising statute depends on the intention of the legislature. Some statutes are so worded that the intent of the legislature is not clearly expressed. However, if the statute requires proof of character and skill and imposes a penalty on a person who engages in the regulated activity before he or she first obtains a license, the statute, as a general rule, will be interpreted as a regulatory statute. But if the statute imposes a substantial license fee and provides that a license shall be issued to anyone paying the fee, and if the penalty imposed is a percentage of the fee or an interest charge based on the fee, the statute, as a general rule, will be interpreted as a revenue-raising statute. The failure to obtain a license required by the provisions of a revenue-raising statute in no way affects the validity of the bargains of the unlicensed person.

SUMMARY

There are three classes of statutes which affect the legality of bargains: (1) criminal statutes, (2) statutes expressly declaring the bargain to be void, and (3) regulatory statutes.

Wagering bargains are illegal. A wager is the creation of a risk for the purpose of bearing it. Risk-shifting bargains are not illegal. Stock market and commodity market transactions entered into in good faith are not illegal; and likewise, margin transactions entered into in good faith are not illegal. However, if the principal purpose of a bargain is to wager on the fluctuation in the market price of a stock or commodity, it is illegal.

A wide variety of bargains and especially those involving certain subject matter are made void by state statute. If a person bargains to perform any of the skilled services which require a license without first obtaining a license, his or her bargains are illegal. However, if the licensing statute is a revenue-raising statute instead of a regulatory statute, the bargains of the unlicensed person are not illegal.

Wilson v. Kealakekua Ranch, Ltd.

551 P.2d 525 (Sup. Ct. Hawaii 1976)

Wilson (plaintiff), an architect, sued Kealakekua Ranch (defendant) for $33,900 for architectural services performed. Wilson appealed from a decision for the defendant. Reversed.

Wilson was a licensed architect but had failed to pay the annual registration fee of $15 as required by the licensing statute at the time he did the work for the defendant.

RICHARDSON, CHIEF JUSTICE. Where, as here, the statute provides a criminal sanction but is silent as to whether its violation will deprive the parties of their right to sue on the contract, the courts have distinguished between statutes for revenue and statutes for protection of the public against incompetence and fraud. If the purpose of the statute is for collection of revenue, the express statutory penalties are held to be exclusive and contracts made without a license are not thereby rendered unenforceable. On the other hand, if the purpose is to protect the public, the statute breaker will be denied the enforcement of his bargain. However, as Corbin points out:

> [E]ven in these cases enforcement of the wrongdoer's bargains is not always denied him. The statute may be clearly for protection against fraud and incompetence; but in very many cases the statute breaker is neither fraudulent nor incompetent. He may have rendered excellent service or delivered goods of the highest quality, his non-compliance with the statute seems nearly harmless, and the real defrauder seems to be the defendant who is enriching himself at the plaintiff's expense. Although many courts yearn for a mechanically applicable rule, they have not made one in the present instance. Justice requires that the penalty should fit the crime; and justice and sound policy do not always require the enforcement of licensing statutes by large forfeitures going not to the state but to repudiating defendants.
>
> It must be remembered that in most cases the statute itself does not require these forfeitures. It fixes its own penalties, usually fine or imprisonment of minor character with a degree of discretion in the court. The added penalty of non-enforceability of bargains is a judicial creation. In most cases, it is wise to apply it; but when it causes great and disproportionate hardship its application may be avoided . . . 6A *Corbin* on *Contracts* § 1512, pp. 712–714 (1962).

Furthermore, we see no relationship between the payment of annual fees and the competence or character of an architect. The failure to remit such fees does not indicate deterioration of the competence or integrity required to qualify for registration as an architect. We conclude, therefore, that the provision requiring renewal by way of payment of a $15.00 fee was not for public protection, but for revenue.[2]

Public Policy

General Concept. Public policy is one of those broad concepts which gives flexibility to the law where flexibility is needed. In many respects, it is comparable to the concept of the general public welfare. Public policy changes from time to time along with social and economic development. Conduct which may be acceptable in one era may not be acceptable in a later era, and vice

[2] The court noted that Wilson already was subject to a $500 fine plus imprisonment up to one year and saw no reason to make Wilson forfeit his fee of $34,000 which he had earned.

versa. Also, the public policy of one state may differ in some degree from that of another.

Our concept of public policy goes beyond that of tortious or criminal conduct. A bargain, the performance of which would require the doing of an immoral or unethical act, would be illegal. There is no simple standard or rule which the court can use as the basis for determining whether or not a bargain is against public policy and illegal. Each case is treated as a separate problem, and the presiding judge has broad discretionary powers in determining the legality of the bargain. The public policy of a nation or state is reflected in its laws and judicial decisions.

Bargains Injurious to Public Service. Any bargain is illegal if it tends to induce a public servant to deviate in any degree from the duty owed the public. A bargain is illegal if it is a bargain to pay additional compensation to a public servant or if it is a bargain to pay an amount less than the salary provided by law for the performance of the duties of a public office. Any bargain is illegal if it is a bargain by a public officer whereby personal interests conflict with duty to the public. Persons may make their desires regarding legislation known to a member of Congress or a state legislature, but it is illegal to offer an elected official presents or personal favors to influence any decision on legislative matters. Obviously, a bargain to pay a public servant a bribe is illegal.

Bargains to Influence Fiduciaries. Any bargain is illegal if it tends to induce a fiduciary—trustee, administrator, agent, or partner—to breach fiduciary duties to the beneficiary or principal. Such a bargain is basically a fraud on the beneficiary or principal. In general, a fiduciary is not permitted to enter into any transactions whereby personal interests will conflict with fiduciary duties, unless the fiduciary makes full disclosure of the conflicting interests and the beneficiary or principal effectively consents.

Bargains Relieving from Liability for Negligence. The legality of a bargain relieving a person from the consequences of his or her own negligence depends on the relation of the parties and the nature of the duties owed. As a general rule a bargain whereby one of the parties attempts to provide against liability for willful negligence or for fraud is illegal. Also, as a general rule a bargain relieving a person from the consequences of negligence in the performance of a duty owed to the public is illegal. For example, if a common carrier bargains to relieve himself from liability for damage to property while in transit, where such damage results from the negligence of his agents or servants, the bargain is illegal. However, the common carrier may bargain to limit, to a reasonable degree, the amount of damages recoverable for injury to property in transit, where the injury is not due to the willful negligence of the carrier's agents or servants, and such a bargain will not be illegal.

If no duty is owned to the public and the parties are bargaining on a fair and equal basis, free from duress and undue influence, a bargain relieving one of the parties from nonwillful negligence is legal. Property damage and public liability insurance contracts are legal. The objective of such contracts is to protect the insured against liability for negligent acts.

Bargains in Restraint of Trade. Bargains in direct restraint of trade are illegal. Any bargain whereby a person, for consideration, agrees not to compete in trade with another is illegal. If people could enforce bargains not to compete, free competition could be destroyed.

Bargains are permitted which restrain trade if the restraint is reasonable and if valid interests are protected by the restraint. For example, if a contract for the sale of a business or for employment contains a provision which provides that the seller or employee will not compete with the buyer or employer, such provision is legal, provided the restraint is reasonable. A bargain in restraint of trade, if it is to be legal, must be a part of a contract—that is, ancillary to the contract—must be for the purpose of protecting interests created by the contract, and must be no greater than is reasonable to protect those interests. If the contract is an employment contract, the restraint must be limited as to both space and time. As a general rule the restraint in a contract for the sale of a business or other property must be limited as to space but need not be limited as to time. However, under some circumstances the limitation must be as to both space and time.

The courts are not in complete accord as to the rights of the parties to a contract which includes a restraint provision which imposes a greater restraint on a party than is reasonably necessary to protect the interests created by the contract. If the restraint provision is divisible, the courts have, as a general rule, enforced that part of the restraint which is reasonable and refused to enforce that part which is unreasonable. In such cases the controversy is usually whether or not the restraint provision is divisible.

If the restraint provision is indivisible and is greater than is reasonably necessary to protect the interests created by the contract, a majority of the courts hold that the provision is illegal and void in its entirety and that it affords the party no protection. A minority of the courts hold that, even though indivisible in terms, the restraint provision is enforceable for as much of the restraint as would be reasonable.

Bargains to create monopolies and bargains which prevent the free alienation of property are in restraint of trade and are illegal. For example, suppose Arnold sells his farm, Willow Brook, to Bates, and Bates, as a part of the contract of sale, promises never to sell or mortgage Willow Brook. This promise is illegal and void.

Miscellaneous Illegal Bargains. It is impossible to list and discuss all types of bargains which are against public policy and are illegal. Such bargains are limited only by the limitations of the ingenuity of people. Bargains to commit immoral acts, bargains which tend to interfere with marital relations or parental relations, collusive bargains to obtain a divorce, bargains to defraud, bargains which induce the breach of other contracts, and a variety of other bargains, the formation or performance of which would be detrimental to the general welfare, are illegal.

SUMMARY

Bargains opposed to public policy vary so greatly that it is impossible to list them. The public policy of a state or nation is reflected in its constitution, laws, and judicial decisions. In general, any bargain is illegal if its formation or performance will be detrimental to the general welfare. Each case must be decided according to the facts of the case. Bargains are illegal if they tend to induce persons who owe a duty to serve the public to breach their duty. Bargains are illegal if they tend to induce a fiduciary to breach his or her fiduciary duty to a beneficiary or principal. Bargains relieving a person from liability for nonwillfull negligence are legal, unless the duty of due care is owed to the public and unless the negligence will result in injury to the public.

From an early period, bargains in restraint of trade have been held to be illegal. However, a bargain in restraint of trade is legal if the restraint is ancillary and is no greater than is reasonably necessary to protect the interests created by the principal contract.

Troutman v. Southern Railway Co.
441 F.2d 586 (5th Cir. 1971)

Troutman, an attorney, (plaintiff) brought this action against the Southern Railway Company (defendant) to recover $200,000 as the reasonable value of legal services rendered. Judgment in the amount of $175,000 for Troutman and Southern appealed. Affirmed.

In 1963 the Interstate Commerce Commission issued an order directing Southern to increase certain rates on grain shipments from the Midwest to the Southeast by approximately 16 percent. The order created a difficult situation for Southern: if allowed to stand, the order, according to Southern, would result in its losing a $13,000,000 investment in "Big John" railroad cars plus a "tremendous" loss of revenue in the future. Wilbanks, a vice president and assistant to the president of Southern, turned for help to Troutman, who had only recently come to Southern's aid in the Central of Georgia case. Troutman, an Atlanta attorney, had no experience in I.C.C. matters, but he was known to Wilbanks as a personal friend and political ally of President John F. Kennedy. Wilbanks told Troutman that Southern was filing suit in a federal district court in Ohio to enjoin the order of the I.C.C. He asked Troutman to persuade the President and the Department of Justice, then headed by the President's brother, Robert F. Kennedy, to "ditch" the I.C.C. and enter the case on the side of Southern. Troutman's efforts were successful: the Department of Justice filed an answer in the Ohio lawsuit opposing the I.C.C. and supporting Southern's position. As a result of the Ohio litigation (in which Troutman played no further part), the I.C.C. order was struck down. Troutman demanded compensation for his services in the grain rate case and when Southern refused to pay, Troutman filed suit.

WISDOM, CIRCUIT JUDGE. Southern's first contention is that the district court erred in refusing to grant Southern's motion for judgment notwithstanding the verdict because the evidence conclusively establishes that the contract upon which Troutman sued was "to exert his personal and political influence upon the President of the United States." Southern argues that such a contract is in violation of public policy and unenforceable; therefore, the court erred as a matter of law in failing to render judgment for Southern. We cannot agree.

It is of course true that a contract to influence a public official in the exercise of his duties is illegal and unenforceable when that contract contemplates the use of personal or political influence rather than an appeal to the judgment of the official on the merits of the case. Nevertheless, all citizens possess the right to petition the government for redress of their grievances. (United States Constitution, Amendment I.) To that end, one may employ an agent or attorney to use his influence to gain access to a public official. Moreover, once having obtained an audience, the attorney may fairly present to the official the merits of his client's case and urge the official's support for that position. As the district court well stated in its opinion overruling Southern's motion for summary judgment, it is "only the elements of 'personal influence' and 'sinister means' that will void the contract and deny its enforcement."

Moreover, the illegal or sinister nature of a contract for professional services will not be presumed; the burden of proving the illegality of the contract is clearly upon the party asserting it.

It necessarily follows then that the decision whether to enforce a claim for compensation for these kinds of legal services will depend largely upon the facts of each case. Whether the parties in fact entered into a contract calling for the improper exercise of personal influence upon a public official is therefore a question for the jury, guided of course by proper instructions. In this case the jury concluded that Troutman had agreed with Southern to use his influence merely to gain access to the President and present to him the merits of Southern's case; therefore, the contract was valid and enforceable.

Hy-Grade Oil Co. v. New Jersey Bank

350 A.2d 279 (Super. Ct. N.J., 1975)

Hy-Grade Oil Co. (plaintiff) brought action against New Jersey Bank (defendant) which refused to credit the customer's account with an amount assertedly deposited in the bank's night depository box. The trial court granted the bank's motion to dismiss the complaint, and the customer appealed. Judgment reversed.

BISCHOFF, J.A.D. The resolution of this appeal requires us to determine whether a clause in a "night depository agreement" between a bank and a customer, providing that "the use of the night depository facilities shall be at the sole risk of the" customer, is valid and enforceable.

In February, 1974, in order to protect the increasing cash supply generated by operations of its fuel business, plaintiff's manager, Flaster, signed a night depository agreement with defendant bank. This agreement (in printed form and apparently used by other banks in the area) contained the following provision:

> . . . it is hereby expressly understood and agreed that the use of the night depository facilities is a gratuitous privilege extended by the bank to the undersigned for the convenience of the undersigned, and the use of the night depository facilities shall be at the sole risk of the undersigned.

It is clear that where a party to the agreement is under a public duty entailing the exercise of care he may not relieve himself of liability for negligence, and unequal bargaining power or the existence of a public interest may call for the rejection of such clauses.

The Uniform Commercial Code, "Bank Deposits and Collections," contains many provisions protecting banks in their daily operations. We find it significant that the Legislature provided in the same statute, that a bank may not, by agreement, disclaim responsibility for "its own lack of good faith or failure to exercise ordinary care" in the discharge of the duty imposed upon it by that statute.

A review of the cases in other states considering the validity of similar exculpatory clauses in night depository contracts indicates that the majority rule is to give full force and effect to the clauses.

The basic theory underlying these and other similar cases is that the absence of an agent of the bank when the night depository facilities are used creates the possibility of dishonest claims being presented by customers. In New Jersey we have rejected such a thesis in other situations and have held that the possibility of fraudulent or collusive litigation does not justify immunity from liability for negligence.

Other courts have refused to recognize the validity of such clauses. In holding such a clause inimical to the public interest, the court in *Phillips Home Furnishings, Inc. v. Continental Bank* (1974) said:

We find the public need for professional and competent banking services too great and the legitimate and justifiable reliance upon the integrity and safety of financial institutions too strong to permit a bank to contract away its liability for its failure to provide the service and protections its customers justifiably expect, that is, for its failure to exercise due care and good faith. . . .

We therefore hold that a bank cannot, by contract, exculpate itself from liability or responsibility for negligence in the performance of its functions as they concern the night depository service.

Central Credit Collection Control Corp. v. Grayson

499 P.2d 57 (Ct. App. Wash. 1972)

Central Credit (plaintiff) brought an action against a former employee, Grayson (defendant), to enforce a restrictive covenant contained in an employment contract. Judgment for Central and Grayson appealed. Affirmed.

Central was engaged in the debt collection business in Pierce County and its surrounding counties. In May, 1964, Central entered into a six-year employment contract with Grayson which contained this restrictive covenant:

The employee will not, in Pierce County, Washington, or in any county bordering on Pierce County within the State of Washington, directly or indirectly engage in the same or similar line of business as that now carried on by the employer or in which the employer becomes engaged during the term of this contract for a period of two years from and after termination of employment under this contract. [Section 6.]

Another clause of the contract stated the reason that a restrictive covenant was incorporated into the agreement:

The employee agrees that it would be impossible, after having received training afforded by the employer, to work for any other collection agency or credit company without using some or all of the trade secrets and information imparted to the employee by the employer or without disclosing some of the employer's trade practices, secrets, methods of operation and information. It is for this reason that the employee has agreed to not become directly or indirectly engaged in such business for a period of two years after the termination of his employment with the employer named in this contract. [Section 10.]

Employment under the contract terminated in May, 1970, but Grayson continued in Central's employment until October 30, 1970. In July or August of that year, Grayson commenced discussions with others concerning the opening of a competing collection business in Pierce County.

In November, 1970, Grayson organized a collection agency corporation and located its principal office some 73 yards from Central's business location. Subsequently, he commenced handling a number of accounts formerly serviced by Central. In December the total accounts in Grayson's new corporation amounted to $26,000, and by February, 1971 had risen to approximately $44,000. Collections on accounts were averaging $5,000 to $7,000 per month.

PEARSON, JUDGE. It is well settled that covenants not to compete upon termination of employment are valid, but should not be greater than reasonably necessary to protect the business or good will of the employer.

The contract recited that the employer had expended considerable sums of money in developing business in Pierce, King, Kitsap, Thurston, Mason, Grays Harbor, and Lewis counties. This recitation was not challenged by any testimony to the contrary which might raise a factual issue that the area was broader than necessary to protect Central's business interests.

We think the trial court was warranted in concluding that as a matter of law the act of Grayson in locating his competing business within 73 yards of Central's business was violative of a reasonable area restriction. See *Wood v. May,* where it was held that a court of equity may enforce a covenant not to compete to a reasonable area, even though it was factually demonstrated that the area restriction was unreasonable.

The same rationale applies to the time restriction, which becomes crucial only if an injunction is granted for the full time limit. Where the undisputed evidence presented to the trial court showed that Grayson opened the competing business within one month of the termination of his employment, the trial court was warranted in determining as a matter of law, that for the purposes of granting damages a reasonable time restriction covenant was breached.

Geldermann & Co., Inc. v. Lane Processing, Inc.

527 F.2d 571 (8th Cir. 1975)

Geldermann and Company, Inc. (plaintiff), a commodities broker, sued Lane Processing, Inc. (defendant) for balance due after liquidation of a short position. Lane counterclaimed for breach of contract and conversion. Lane appealed from an adverse judgment. Affirmed.

Lane Processing, a sophisticated trader on the commodities market, was playing the market short during the onset of the bizarre commodity market of 1972–73 when extreme and adverse climatic conditions, combined with the Russian wheat deal of the summer of 1972, skyrocketed commodity prices to historic highs.

Lane Processing, by signing a commodity signature card when it commenced futures trading in 1969, agreed to properly margin the account. With the advancing market Geldermann was forced to make a number of margin calls on Lane Processing's account. After repeated delays by Lane in meeting margin posting demands, Geldermann sold Lane's account at a $1 million loss.

Lane contends that the basic terms of the commodity signature card and the provisions of Rule 209 of the Chicago Board of Trade, incorporated in the signature card agreement, were unconscionable and hence unenforceable, and that the liquidation of its short position constituted both a breach of contract and a conversion of its property interest in the short trading position.

The commodities signature card signed by Lane provided:

> I further agree that I will at all times without notice or demand from you maintain and keep my account fully margined and protected in accordance with your requirements and that you will be kept secure by me against fluctuations of the market price of the commodities in my account.
>
> In case of my failure to maintain with you at all times such margin as you may deem adequate for your protection, you may, without prior demand or notice to me, Sell and/or Purchase such commodities as you may consider necessary to fully protect my account.

GIBSON, CHIEF JUDGE. The doctrine of unconscionability inherent in equitable matters also finds acceptance in the law. In 1889 the United States Supreme Court approved the definition of an unconscionable contract as one which " 'no man in his senses and not under delusion would make on the one hand, and . . . no honest and fair man would accept on the other. . . .' " *Hume v. United States* (1889). The doctrine has been in a state of constant evolution and is now codified in § 2–302 of the Uniform Commercial Code. In assessing whether a particular contract or provision is unconscionable, the courts should review the totality of the circumstances surrounding the negotiation and execution of the contract. Two important considerations are whether there is a gross inequality of bargaining power between the parties to the contract and whether the aggrieved party was made aware of and comprehended the provision in question.

Ordinarily, one who signs an agreement without full knowledge of its terms might be held to assume the risk that he has entered a one-sided bargain. But when a party of little bargaining power, and hence little real choice, signs a commercially unreasonable contract with little or no knowledge of its terms, it is hardly likely that his consent, or even an objective manifestation of his consent, was ever given to all the terms.

An equally important factor that must be balanced in making this determination is whether the provision is commercially reasonable "according to the mores and business practices of the time and place." Based on the commercial environment which engendered the provision under attack, the party purporting to uphold the provision must show that the provision bears some reasonable relationship to the risks and needs of the business. The fact that the provision is part of a printed "form" contract does not render it automatically unenforceable, particularly when all parties have knowingly assented to the inclusion of the provision. It is not the province of the courts to scrutinize all contracts with a paternalistic attitude and summarily conclude that they are partially or totally unenforceable merely because an aggrieved party believes that the contract has subsequently proved to be unfair or less beneficial than anticipated.

Applying these standards to the circumstances surrounding the signing of the commodities signature card, we conclude that the liquidation provision in the card is not unconscionable. Clift Lane, whose net worth approximated $4,598,000 in fiscal year 1972 and $7 million in 1973, was a sophisticated investor and entrepreneur.

Furthermore, Lane read the signature card before signing it and apparently understood the summary liquidation provision. The record supports the conclusion that Lane was not victimized by an overreaching party to the contract. He was aware of his obligations as stated in the signature card and voluntarily assumed the risks inherent in futures trading. Lane was also cognizant of the consequences if he failed to meet the margin calls.

The liquidation provision in the signature card was eminently reasonable in light of the commercial background of futures trading.

Unenforceable Contracts and the Uniform Commercial Code

Unconscionability. The court may refuse to enforce an unconscionable contract or an unconscionable clause in a contract for the sale of goods. The Code (2–302) provides:

(1) If the court as a matter of law finds the contract or any clause of the contract to have been unconscionable at the time it was made the court may refuse to enforce the contract, or it may enforce the remainder of the contract without the unconscionable clause, or it may so limit the application of the unconscionable clause as to avoid any unconscionable result.

(2) When it is claimed or appears to the court that the contract or any clause thereof may be unconscionable the parties shall be afforded a reasonable opportunity to present evidence as to its commercial setting, purpose and effect to aid the court in making the determination.

An unconscionable contract is one in which one of the parties being in a strategic position takes advantage of the situation and drives a bargain which is unfair and commercially unreasonable. In the past this concept has been applied in equity in that a court will not grant specific performance of an unconscionable contract. The expanded concept does not require that the situation involve fraud, duress, or undue influence although elements of fraud and duress frequently are present. The following illustrate some of the situations where various courts have applied Section 2–302 as a basis for denying enforcement of certain contract provisions.

1. Small print on the back of signature cards prepared by banks which waived the depositor's right to a jury trial in the event of litigation.[3]
2. A clause in a home improvement contract between a Maine corporation and a Massachusetts citizen which stipulated the New York law would apply.[4]
3. A clause disclaiming all liability on warranties where the goods were found to be worthless.[5]
4. Excessively high prices or excessive credit charges.[6]

[3] *David v. Manufacturers Hanover Trust Co.,* 4 U.C.C. Rep. 1145 (N.Y. Civ. Ct. 1968).

[4] *Paragon Homes, Inc. v. Carter,* 4 U.C.C. Rep. 1144 (N.Y. Sup. Ct. 1968).

[5] *Vlases v. Montgomery Ward & Co., Inc.,* 377 F.2d 846 (3rd Cir. 1967).

[6] *Central Budget Corp. v. Sanchez,* 279 N.Y.2d 391 (N.Y. Civ. Ct. 1967).

Additional examples of the application of the "unconscionable" concept are discussed in the case which follows.

SUMMARY

The court may find that a contract or any part of it to be unconscionable and unenforceable as a matter of law. To be unconscionable a clause must be unfair and commercially unreasonable at the time of making of the contract. The principle is prevention of oppression and unfair surprise. The court may enforce the contract in part or limit the application of any unconscionable clause so as to avoid an unconscionable result.

Singer Co. v. Gardner

323 A.2d 457 (Sup. Ct. N.J. 1974)

Singer Co. (plaintiff) sued Gardner (defendant) and appealed from an adverse judgment. Reversed for Singer.

Gardner purchased, in order, a sewing machine and three vacuum cleaners from the Singer Co., using Singer's "1 to 36 month plan." The sales price of the sewing machine was $400, and each vacuum cleaner cost approximately $70. After paying $200 on account, Gardner defaulted, and Singer instituted an action to recover all Gardner's purchases along with, as damages, the balance allegedly remaining unpaid.

Gardner claimed that the credit sales contract was unconscionable because Singer retained cross-collateral in all goods until the whole balance was paid off.

CLIFFORD, JUSTICE. We are of the view that the court below was in error in holding that the credit plan here under consideration was unconscionable. By classifying the arrangment as a cross-collateral security agreement, the trial court sought to justify a finding of unconscionability under the rationale of *Williams v. Walker Thomas Furniture Co.*

Examining such a clause, the *Williams* court remanded the case for findings on the unconscionability issue, strongly intimating that it believed the clause in question to be unconscionable. In so holding, the court relied heavily on the peculiar circumstances of the case. There, a welfare recipient had paid $1,400 over a period of several years, reducing her balance to $164. Then she bought a stereo set on which she defaulted, and all items were reclaimed by the seller. Of particular interest to the *Williams* court was the disparity of bargaining power between the parties and the lack of understanding of the contract terms by the purchaser.

Except for the trial court's decision in this case, no court since *Williams* has held cross-collateral security agreements unconscionable. Nor does the opinion below suggest circumstances which would bring this case under the *Williams* rationale.

But even if it were correct to assume unconscionability from the lone fact of retained cross-collateral by the seller, the factual basis for the conclusion is absent from the case. The agreement did not create such collateral. Singer claims that each payment was applied against the cost of the items in the order purchased. In the instant case all items were replevied[7] only because the first, being the most expensive, had not yet been paid off. Therefore, there is no basis for a finding of unconscionability on this record.

Effect of Illegality

General Rule. As a general rule a court will not enforce an illegal bargain but will leave the parties where it finds them. They cannot recover damages for breach of the illegal promises, cannot recover consideration from which they have parted, and cannot recover in quasi contract for benefits conferred. The courts do not follow this rule as a means of punishing one of the parties, but for the reason that the results obtained thereby best serve the interests of the public. If the facts and circumstances are such that the interests of the public are best served by allowing a recovery, such recovery will be granted.

Ignorance of Fact or Special Regulation. Even though ignorance is no excuse, the courts have in exceptional cases granted recovery to a party to an illegal bargain if the party has been ignorant of the facts which made the bargain illegal, provided the other party had knowledge of the illegality and provided the illegality does not involve moral turpitude. If both parties are ignorant of the facts which make the bargain illegal, the courts have permitted the parties to recover for performance rendered before they learned of the illegal nature of the bargain. In no case will the courts allow recovery for performance rendered after knowledge of the illegality.

In cases in which one of the parties is ignorant of a special statutory regulation of the other's business and of the violation thereof, the courts will allow recovery for performance rendered by the innocent party before he or she learns of the illegality. For example, suppose Alberts, an actor, contracts to perform for Bates, the operator of a theater. Bates has not obtained a license to operate the theater as required by a penal regulatory statute. Alberts, in ignorance of the violation of the statute by Bates, performs his part of the bargain. Alberts can recover the compensation promised by Bates.

Rights of Protected Parties. Most regulatory statutes have as their objective the protection of the public. As a general rule, if a bargain is entered into by a person who is guilty of the violation of a regulatory statute with

[7] A legal action brought to obtain possession of goods.

another for whose protection the statute was adopted, such bargain will be declared void as to the party violating the statute but enforceable by the protected party. For example, suppose a foreign corporation does intrastate business in a state without obtaining a license, and the laws of the state expressly provide that the contracts of an unlicensed foreign corporation doing intrastate business in the state shall be void. The corporation, in such a case, cannot enforce a contract made by it while unlicensed, but the other party to the contract can enforce it against the corporation.

If the parties to an illegal bargain are not equally guilty but one of the parties has been induced to enter into the bargain by the other party, the courts will grant recovery to the less guilty person. For example, suppose a confidence man induces his victim to enter into a bargain which is illegal as a means of defrauding him. The victim can recover what he has parted with, unless the illegal act involved moral turpitude.

Knowledge of Illegal Use. Knowledge that an article sold will be used for an illegal purpose will not make the sale illegal, unless the use to be made of the article is a serious crime. If an article is sold or money is loaned for the purpose of aiding in the commission of a crime, the sale or the loan is illegal, and the party making the sale or the loan cannot recover the sale price of the article or the money loaned. For example, if Alberts loans Bates $50 knowing that Bates intends to play cards for money that evening, Alberts can recover a judgment for the $50 loaned. However, if Bates is at the card table gambling and Alberts loans Bates $50 to enable Bates to continue his gambling, the loan is illegal, and Alberts cannot recover a judgment for the $50 loaned.

Divisible Contracts. If part of a bargain is legal and part is illegal, the courts will enforce the legal part if the legal can be separated from the illegal. But if the bargain is an indivisible bargain and part of it is illegal, the illegal part will taint the entire bargain, and the whole will be void.

A contract is divisible when it consists of several promises or acts on the part of one party and each promise or act is matched by a corresponding promise or act on the part of the other party so that there is a separate consideration for each promise or act.

If a provision in a contract is illegal but the illegal provision does not affect the principal purpose of the contract, the principal portion will be enforced but the illegal provision will not. For example, suppose Alberts sells his barber shop to Bates. The contract of sale provides that Alberts will not engage in barbering during the remainder of his life. The restraint provision is illegal, but the sales contract, except the restraint provision, will be enforced.

Rescission before Performance of Illegal Act. If one of the parties to an illegal contract rescinds the contract before the performance of the illegal act, he or she may recover a part or all of any consideration given as an exception to the general rule. This exception is based on a policy of encouraging parties to illegal bargains to back out before the transactions are executed. If a party to a bet gives notice of withdrawal and demands the return of his money before the stakeholder has paid it over, he can recover his money. However, if a stakeholder refuses to pay to the winner the money which has been bet, the winner can recover the money. The statutes of some states provide that one who has lost money gambling can recover it.

SUMMARY

As a general rule, if parties have entered into an illegal bargain, neither can recover a judgment if the other party fails to fulfill his or her promises. No recovery is granted in quasi contract for the benefits conferred in the fulfillment of an illegal bargain. If the parties are not equally at fault, the courts may, if the circumstances demand it, grant one party relief.

If one party is justifiably ignorant of the facts which make the bargain illegal or is ignorant of a special regulation, that party may recover for consideration given. Also, the party protected by a regulatory statute may recover for breach of a contract entered into with a person who has not complied with the provisions of the statute.

As a general rule, knowledge that an article sold will be used illegally does not make the sale illegal, but if the use intended is the commission of a serious crime, the sale is illegal. Also, if the sale is for the purpose of aiding in the commission of a crime, it is illegal.

If a bargain is divisible and part is legal and part is illegal, the courts will enforce the legal parts and not the illegal parts, unless the illegal parts go to the principal objective of the contract. If the bargain is indivisible and part is illegal, the entire bargain is void. A party may rescind an executory illegal bargain before the performance of the illegal act and recover any consideration given.

Lawn v. Camino Heights, Inc.

93 Cal. Rptr. 631 (Ct. App. Cal. 1971)

Action by Lawn (plaintiff) against Camino Heights, Inc. (defendant) for compensation due under a contract. Lawn appealed from an adverse judgment. Reversed in part. Harold Brock and Eleanor Brock were husband and wife and the owners of about 325 acres of agricultural land ("Camino Heights Orchards"). They were in serious financial straits and Mr. Brock decided to subdivide the ranch. He consulted the plaintiff who suggested that a subdivision development corporation be formed to which the Brocks would convey their ranch in exchange for shares of stock. Lawn prepared the articles of incorporation which were filed on November 27, 1961.

On December 18, 1961, Lawn and Camino Heights, Inc., (through Mr. Brock, as its president), entered into the following written agreement:

Camino Heights, Inc. proposes to employ you in the capacity of consultant . . . for a period of two years at $8,400 per year effective immediately and payable in stock of the corporation at the end of each year of employment.

We further agree that when residential lots are developed we will convey to you or your nominee five (5) such lots free and clear provided that you or your nominee agree to start construction within six months of such conveyance. After dwellings have been completed on the above five lots, we will make available to you or your nominee additional residential lots at the regular sales price but on a subordinated basis.

The purpose of the contract was to compensate Lawn for his services in developing the subdivision as neither the Brocks nor the corporation had any money. Lawn never received any of the consideration promised by the corporation in the contract of December 18, 1961.

JANES, ASSOCIATE JUSTICE. Since no permit had been obtained from the Commissioner of Corporations at the time the agreement for such payment was made, defendant corporation's promise to compensate Lawn in stock was illegal and unenforceable even though the parties may have intended to obtain a permit before the stock was issued.

Lawn contends that Camino's further promise to convey five residential lots was severable from its agreement to pay him in stock.

[T]he rule relating to severability of partially illegal contracts is that a contract is severable if the court can, consistent with the intent of the parties, reasonably relate the illegal consideration on one side to some specified or determinable portion of the consideration on the other side. . . .

If any part . . . of several considerations for a single object, is unlawful, the entire contract is void.

Nothing in the written agreement of December 18, 1961, nor in the other evidence before the court, suggested that any *part* of Lawn's services had been promised in exchange for the illegal promise to pay stock, or that the parties had allocated the rest of Lawn's services as consideration for the legal promise to convey lots. Camino's two promises were consideration for a single object—namely, Lawn's promise to serve as a consultant. Therefore, the promise to convey lots was not severable from the illegal promise, and cannot provide the basis for a recovery of damages under the written contract.

Lawn further contends that he was entitled to recover the reasonable value of his services under the common count even though the aforesaid illegality and inseverability of consideration preclude relief under his cause of action for breach of the express contract. His contention must be sustained.

The proper rule, amply supported by authority, is thus stated in 27 *Cal.Jur.* p. 210, § 17:

The law does not imply a promise to pay for services illegally rendered under a contract expressly prohibited by statute. But if the services rendered under a void contract by one party thereto were not intrinsically illegal and the other party fails voluntarily to perform on his part, the former may recover as upon a quantum meruit for what the latter actually received in value, though no recovery can be had upon the contract.

Camino's will be unjustly enriched at Lawn's expense if he cannot recover from it the reasonable value of his services.

Problem Cases

1. Tovar, a Kansas physician, sought employment in an Illinois hospital as a resident physician. Terms of employment were agreed upon and Tovar signed a contract. After two weeks of employment with the Illinois hospital, Tovar was summarily dismissed on the grounds that he did not have a valid Illinois medical license. Tovar sues the hospital for wrongful termination of his employment contract, despite acknowledging that he did not have an Illinois license. Tovar claims that the license is not necessary to the fulfillment of the terms of the contract. Is the hospital liable on the contract?
2. Kennedy brought an action against Smith for damages for personal injuries consisting of burns on her neck, head, and back suffered while she was receiving a permanent wave. Kennedy had signed a "hold harmless agreement" with the Student Operator Beauty School operated by Smith purporting to absolve the school of any liability for negligence. The student operator misjudged the amount of solution necessary for a permanent, and Kennedy suffered second-degree chemical burns when the chemicals ran down her neck. Is Smith liable to Kennedy?
3. Beavers borrowed $5,000 from Taylor, executing a note payable to Taylor, and made an agreement with Taylor to pay her monthly dividends of: 1) 1 percent of first $10,000 gross sales per month of Beavers' business; 2) .75 percent of the next $15,000 gross sales; 3) .5 percent of the gross sales over $25,000 per month until the principal was fully paid. Beavers paid $12,495 to Taylor over the period from February 3, 1958 through 1967. This amounted to 20 percent of the $5,000 note annually and Beavers claims that this constituted *usurious* interest. Is Beavers correct?
4. Aztec, Inc. borrowed $50,000 from Union Planters Bank, executing in return a promissory note and agreeing to repay the principal "in constant United States Dollars adjusted for inflation (deflation)," and the stated interest which was set at the maximum legal rate. The adjusted principal was to be calculated by dividing the consumer price index at maturity by the consumer price index at the date of borrowing. Aztec seeks to avoid the payment of the adjustment on the basis that the payment of such additional money would be contrary to the usury law. Will Aztec prevail?
5. Helfenbein borrowed $500,000 for commercial use from Barnes, not a regular lender. The loan was secured by a mortgage on land which was not used for homesteading or agricultural purposes. After the defendant defaulted on repayment, Barnes instituted a foreclosure action. Helfenbein's defense was that the 38 percent interest rate constituted usury. State law, very similar to the Uniform Commercial Credit Code, imposed a 10 percent maximum rate of interest on "consumer loans." All other loans had a maximum interest rate of 45 percent. Was the loan usurious?
6. An unwed pregnant women agreed to release the putative father from liability in a pending paternity action. The father acknowledged paternity and agreed to pay the mother $500 for dropping the paternity suit. After the birth of the child the mother reinstituted paternity proceedings. The father raises the defense of release. Is this a good defense?
7. Baker purchased Seline's majority stock interest in Meet Houston, Inc., a corporation that provided convention arrangements and tour services. As part of the sale, Seline also agreed not to compete within 300 miles of the headquarters of her former corporation

for three years. The agreement prohibited direct and indirect competition. The corporation expands its business under Baker's guidance. Because of business expansion by Baker, Seline is now indirectly competing with Meet Houston. Baker sues to enforce the noncompetition agreement. Can she stop Seline from competing with her?

8. Kaye signed a 20-year consulting agreement with Orkin in 1964, the terms of which contained the following restrictions against competition: ". . . consultant covenants and agrees with the Company, its successors and assigns, until August 31, 1984, whether such consultative services shall cease by reason of the expiration of the term of this contract or by the discharge of consultant by the Company, with or without cause, that he shall not, . . . engage . . . in any business which is at the time competitive with the business or activities conducted by Company or Predecessor on the date of this contract of consultation hereunder in any area in which the Company or Predecessor shall operate on such date." In 1965 Orkin wrote Kaye that the "agreement was terminated." Is Kaye bound by the no-competition clause?

9. Bridgeman took part in a prison riot and escape attempt, during which time several hostages, including Corrections Director Hardy, were assaulted and brutalized. Bridgeman pleads immunity from criminal charges based on an oral contract he claims he entered with Hardy during the riot. Hardy promised Bridgeman immunity from prosecution if he would stop all acts of violence. Is this a valid defense?

10. Weaver Aircraft, Inc., a large charter service, purchased a helicopter from B. L. Isbrandtsen Corp., a manufacturer of helicopters. The contract contained the following language: "The B. L. Isbrandtsen Corp. disclaims any liability in connection with this sale. This sale is unconditional, and no warranties are expressed or implied."

    After only 20 hours of flight the helicopter crashed and was severely damaged. Weaver brought suit for breach of an implied warranty of merchantibility, claiming that it was against public policy for a helicopter manufacturer to disclaim liability for any aircraft. Can Weaver recover?

11. International Dairy Queen negotiated an irrevocable letter of credit with the Bank of Wadley that was in excess of 20 percent of the bank's capital. The Bank refused to perform on the contract and defended against the action brought by Dairy Queen on the basis that such a contract was void and unenforceable as a violation of statute. The statute stated "no bank shall lend to any one corporation more than 20 percent of its capital. . . ." Is this a good defense?

13

Writing

Statute of Frauds

It is widely believed that contracts are not binding until reduced to writing and signed. Although there are some circumstances where the belief is justified, as a general proposition oral contracts are binding and enforceable in the courts. In addition, as was noted earlier, where parties negotiating a contract reach full agreement on all of the terms, a binding oral contract may be created despite the fact that the parties later intend to put their agreement into written and signed form.[1]

At one extreme the courts could enforce all contracts whether oral or written. The advantages of this policy would include a reduction in the time and expense of entering transactions since oral agreements could be used. Oral contract terms, however, are more easily misunderstood or forgotten with passing time. In addition, complicated transactions usually necessitate writing and oral agreements are more susceptible to the perpetration of frauds. At the other extreme the law could require that all contracts be written in order to be enforceable. Advantages of clarity and less misunderstandings would be offset by the time and expense required by such a policy.

The statutes of frauds, now adopted in all states, are patterned after a similar group of statutes first adopted in England in 1677. These statutes embody a compromise approach between the two extremes. First, only certain specific types of transactions are selected and made subject to the writing requirements imposed in the statutes. Second, even where the statutes apply, full written contracts are not necessary—only a limited form of written evidence of the agreement is required. Lastly, several of the statutes provide circumstances where oral agreements subject to the statutes are enforceable

[1] See Chapter 8.

even in the absence of written evidence. It usually is good business policy, of course, to reduce all important and complicated business transactions to writing where practicable to do so.

Provisions of Statute of Frauds. Considered here are only those provisions of the statute of frauds which define certain classes of contracts and declare such to be unenforceable unless evidenced by a writing. The following are the classes of contracts generally included in the statute of frauds: (1) contracts by an executor or administrator to be answerable from his or her own estate for a duty of the decedent's estate; (2) contracts with an obligee to answer for the debt, default, or miscarriage of the obligor; (3) the contracts in which the consideration is marriage or a promise to marry, except contracts consisting only of mutual promises by two persons to marry each other; (4) contracts for sale of an interest in land; (5) bilateral contracts, so long as they are not fully performed by either party, which are not capable of performance within a year from the time of their formation; and (6) contracts for the sale of goods or choses in action of a value above an amount fixed by state statutes.

In addition to these classes of contracts, the statutes of a substantial number of states require (1) a promise to pay a debt barred by the statute of limitations or by a discharge in bankruptcy and (2) a contract to pay a commission for the sale of real estate to be evidenced by a note or memorandum in writing and signed by the party.

Scope of the Statute of Frauds. The statute of frauds applies only to informal contracts. Consequently, before any question of its application can apply, there must be a valid contract. The statute of frauds does not make illegal a contract falling within the scope of its provisions; it merely makes it unenforceable. If one of the parties to the oral contract has performed, thereby conferring benefits on the other contracting party, and the right of action is barred by the statute, the person can recover in quasi contract for the benefits conferred. Under special circumstances a court will hold that part performance will justify the court in ordering performance of the contract.

The statute of frauds of some states provides that the contract, unless evidenced by the required writing, is void. In most cases, however, the courts have interpreted the statute to mean that the contract will be unenforceable, not void.

SUMMARY

The English Parliament, in 1677, enacted a "Statute for the Prevention of Frauds and Perjuries," which provided that no action could be brought to enforce defined classes of informal contracts unless they were evidenced by a note or memorandum in writing signed by the party to be bound. The several states have enacted statutes which follow the general pattern of the English statute, but they are not uniform in their provisions.

The courts have given a strict interpretation to these statutes. The parties must have entered into a valid contract before the statute of frauds applies. The statute makes an oral contract which falls within one of the defined classes unenforceable, not illegal.

Collateral Contracts of Guaranty

Nature of Collateral Contracts. A collateral or secondary contract is one made with an obligee (promisee) in which a third person promises to pay the debt, default, or miscarriage of the obligor (promisor) in the event the obligor fails to perform that duty. Since a contract by an executor or administrator to be answerable from his or her own estate for a duty of the decedent's estate is, under most circumstances, a collateral contract, such contracts will not be discussed as a separate class.

Whether a contract is an original or a collateral contract is primarily a question of the intention of the parties. One must analyze the transaction and from the language used, the relation of the parties, and all the surrounding circumstances determine whether the obligor has contracted to perform in all events or only in the event that some other person fails to perform the duty owed to the obligee. If an oral contract is in fact collateral (or secondary) in character, it is unenforceable if the statute of frauds is used as a defense. If, however, the oral contract is classed as "original," the oral contract is enforceable despite the defense of the statute of fraud.

Original Contracts. Often a three-party transaction may appear to include a collateral contract—that is, a contract to answer for the debt, default, or miscarriage of another—when, in fact, it will include only an original contract. The following are examples of some such transactions:

1. Clark orders from Able flowers to be sent to Brown, Clark promising to pay Able for the flowers. The contract between Clark and Able is an original contract. The fact that Brown receives the consideration given in no way affects the character of the contract.
2. Brown purchases an automobile from Able on a title-retaining contract by the terms of which Brown agrees to pay Able $100 per month until a $1,000 balance is paid in full. After paying $200 of the indebtedness, Brown sells the automobile to Clark, who contracts with Brown to pay to Able the unpaid balance of $800. The contract between Brown and Clark, whereby Clark promises to pay Able $800, is an original contract.

Clark is obligated to pay Able in all events. Able is a third-party creditor beneficiary of the contract.

3. Able owes Brown $100, and Brown owes Clark $100. Able, Brown, and Clark enter into an agreement whereby Able agrees to pay Clark $100; Able thereby discharges his $100 debt to Brown, and Brown discharges his $100 debt to Clark. The resulting Able-Clark contract is an original contract. Able is obligated to pay Clark $100 in all events. This type of transaction is termed a "novation."
4. Clark owns shares of the capital stock in the Brown Corporation. He sells the stock to Able and contracts to guarantee the payment, by Brown Corporation, of an annual dividend of not less than 5 percent. Clark's guarantee contract is an original contract. A corporation owes no obligation to its stockholders to pay a dividend; consequently, Clark's guarantee is not a contract to answer for the debt, default, or miscarriage of another. Instead, it is more in the nature of a warranty of the quality of goods sold.

Suppose, however, that Clark owns 5 percent corporate bonds issued by the Brown Corporation and he sells the bonds to Able and contracts to pay the 5 percent annual interest payment if Brown Corporation defaults. The Clark-Able contract is a collateral contract and is unenforceable unless evidenced by a note or memorandum in writing signed by Clark or his duly authorized agent. Brown Corporation is obligated to pay the interest on the bonds, and Clark's contract to pay in the event Brown Corporation defaults is a contract to answer for the debt, default, or miscarriage of another—in this case, Brown Corporation.

There are other transactions of this same general type which occur less frequently than those described. For example, if Clark contracts to pay Able a debt owed to Able by Brown in consideration of Able discharging Brown, such a contract is an original contract, or if Clark purchases from Able a debt owed to Able by Brown, the contract is an original contract.

SUMMARY

A collateral contract is one made with an obligee to pay the debt, default, or miscarriage of the obligor in the event he or she fails to perform that duty. Whether a contract is original or collateral will depend primarily on the intention of the parties to the contract.

An original contract is one in which a promisor obligates himself or herself to perform in all events. Often a contract in which three persons are involved may appear to include a collateral contract, but an analysis of such a transaction will reveal that only an original contract is involved.

Pravel, Wilson & Matthews v. Voss

471 F.2d 1186 (5th Cir. 1973)

Action by Pravel, Wilson & Matthews (plaintiffs), a law firm, against Voss (defendant) for legal fees. Judgment for plaintiff firm and Voss appealed. Affirmed.

The plaintiff's law firm sued to recover the reasonable value of services rendered in connection with an unsuccessful patent infringement suit filed by V&S Ice Machine Company, a shell corporation organized solely to hold the patent on an "ice blade" and to conduct patent infringement litigation.

Matthews, a member of the plaintiff firm, was hired to represent V&S but upon learning that V&S was a mere shell, Matthews sought assurances from Voss that the firm would be paid for their services.

Matthews told Voss that the case was in "bad shape" and that the firm's fee for handling the case through trial would be between $10,000 and $20,000. Voss told Matthews to "go for broke," and agreed to have a second partner work on the case. Voss attended several sessions of the trial, and indicated to Matthews that he was pleased with its progress. During the trial, Voss told Wilson, the other partner, that he viewed the litigation like any other investment, and that he was willing to spend as much as $25,000 in attorneys' fees because he expected that the litigation would yield a "return" of several hundred thousand dollars to him. He told Wilson that he would "take care" of the fee, and that if the lawyers were successful, they would be rewarded by a trip to Las Vegas which Voss said he had used as an incentive in some of his other business dealings.

V&S lost the patent infringement suit. The law firm withdrew from the case, and sent several bills for approximately $14,000 in attorneys' fees to Voss at both his home and business addresses. After the bill had gone unpaid for several months, Wilson telephoned Voss and told him that the firm was looking to him personally for payment. Voss did not dispute his personal liability, but said that the bill was larger than he had expected it to be. He later refused to pay anything.

THORNBERRY, CIRCUIT JUDGE. Voss's statute of frauds argument is untenable, for several reasons. First, there is nothing in the record or in the trial court's findings to support Voss's claim that he promised to answer for a debt owed by the corporation. Voss clearly and repeatedly promised the lawyers that he personally would pay their fee. Thus, the statute of frauds is simply inapplicable to this case on its facts.

But even if the record did disclose evidence that Voss promised to answer for a corporate debt, the law firm would nevertheless be entitled to a recovery. In the first place, the courts afford recovery in quantum meruit as an alternative remedy for breach of promises rendered unenforceable by the statute of frauds.

Secondly, even if Voss did promise to answer for a debt of the corporation, his " leading object" in making the promise was to secure a direct, personal benefit (i.e., to protect his share of the contemplated recovery), and the promise was enforceable notwithstanding the statute of frauds.

Some cases have refused to apply the "leading object" exception when the promisor was a shareholder in the corporation whose debt he guaranteed and the only benefit accruing to him by reason of his promise was the prospect of continued corporate prosperity, which benefitted all stockholders alike.

The promisor's purpose, however, is a question of fact and the courts have not hesitated to apply the leading object exception in cases involving stockholders where, as here, the record compels the conclusion that the promisor could have been acting only to protect his personal interests.

Interest in Land

Scope of Provision. One of the provisions of the statute of frauds requires contracts for the sale of an interest in land to be evidenced by a memorandum in writing and signed by the party to be bound thereby or his or her duly authorized agent. Although the statute of frauds is worded "interest in land," the courts have interpreted land to mean real estate, and any contract, the performance of which will affect the ownership rights in real estate, comes within the statute of frauds. Contracts to sell, to mortgage, to permit the mining and removal of minerals on the land, and to give easements fall within this class. Leases fall within this class, but in most states, leases are provided for by a special provision of the statute. Contracts to insure buildings, to erect buildings, to organize a partnership to deal in real property, and similar contracts are not within this class because they do not affect an interest in the real property.

SUMMARY

If the performance of the contract will require the transfer of any interest in real property, it comes within the provisions of the statute and is not enforceable unless it is evidenced by a writing. The distinction between real property and personal property is a part of the law of property and is discussed in Chapter 32.

Gene Hancock Construction Co. v. Kempton & Snedigar Dairy
510 P.2d 752 (Ct. App. Ariz. 1973)

Suit by Hancock Construction Co. (plaintiff) against Kempton & Snedigar Dairy (defendants) on an oral contract for the sale of realty and on an oral authorization to sell realty. The plaintiffs appealed from an adverse judgment. Affirmed.

Hancock Construction Co. alleged that Dairy acting through its authorized agent Snedigar, entered into an oral contract for the sale of certain real property, and Hancock specifically asked Snedigar whether the contract was considered to be binding and one upon which Hancock could rely. Snedigar answered in the affirmative and shook hands on it. In reliance on this oral contract Hancock immediately had engineering studies of the property made and made arrangements to obtain a loan of $292,830. Dairy refused to go through with the deal and when sued set up the defense of the statute of frauds. Hancock argued that part performance had removed the statute of frauds defense.

HATHAWAY, CHIEF JUDGE. Part performance necessary to take an oral contract out of the statute of frauds must be unequivocably referable to the contract. Unless the acts of part performance are exclusively referable to the contract, there is nothing to show that the party seeking to enforce it relied on the contract or changed his position to his prejudice so as to give rise to an estoppel. In this jurisdiction, *Restatement of Contracts* § 197, has been cited with approval. This section states:

> Where, acting under an oral contract for the transfer of an interest in land, the purchaser with the assent of the vendor (*a*) makes valuable improvements on the land, or (*b*) takes possession thereof or retains a possession thereof existing at the time of the bargain, and also pays a portion or all of the purchase price, the purchaser or the vendor may specifically enforce the contract.

Adverting to the allegations of the complaint, the "part performance" relied upon by Hancock, was obtaining financing and having engineering studies made of the subject property. The sufficiency of the particular acts to constitute part performance can be decided as a matter of law. An act which admits of explanation without reference to the alleged oral contract does not constitute part performance. We believe Hancock's acts are not unequivocally referable to the oral contract and therefore the trial court did not err in ruling, as a matter of law, that the doctrine of part performance did not preclude the defense of the statute of frauds. Since the contract was unenforceable, not only did Hancock's claim for specific performance fail, but likewise its claim for damages.

Hancock refers to the allegation in its complaint that Snedigar offered to have his attorney prepare the necessary documents to memorialize the contract. Even if this allegation can be construed as a promise to make a memorandum that would satisfy the statute of frauds, an agreement to reduce to writing a contract within the statute of frauds must itself be in writing to be enforceable.

Not to Be Performed within One Year

Scope of Provision. This provision applies only to executory bilateral contracts. If Allen loans Bates $100 and Bates orally promises to repay the loan in two years, the contract is a unilateral contract and need not be evidenced by a writing. Likewise, if a bilateral contract has been fully performed, the fact that the contract was oral and could not be performed within a year of the making thereof would in no way affect the rights acquired by the parties to the performed contract. Since the statute is worded in the negative, "*not* to be performed within one year," the courts have held that if, under the terms of the contract, it is possible to perform the contract within a year of the making thereof, it need not be evidenced by a writing to be enforceable. The fact that it is highly improbable that performance will be completed or that performance was not completed within one year is not controlling.

The one-year period is computed from the time the contract comes into existence, not from the time performance is to begin. For example, a contract entered into on July 1, 1972, whereby the promisor agrees to work for the promisee for one year, work to begin on July 3, 1973, cannot be performed within one year from the making thereof and, if it is to be enforceable, would have to be evidenced by a memorandum in writing signed by the party to be bound or his duly authorized agent.

Computing Time. In computing time, as a general rule, parts of days are not counted. A contract entered into today to work for one year, work to begin tomorrow, can be performed within one year under the rule generally followed. However, if such a contract were entered into on Saturday, work to begin the following Monday, it could not be performed within one year from the making thereof. In a few states the day the contract is entered into is counted. In these states if a contract to work for one year is entered into today, work to begin tomorrow, it cannot be performed within one year from the making thereof.

Contracts to Extend Time of Performance. In determining whether or not a contract to extend the time for the performance of an existing contract can be performed within one year, time is computed from the day the contract to extend the time of performance is entered into until the time the performance under the extended time contract will be completed. For example, on July 1, 1970, Able contracts to work for Brown for six months beginning on July 2, 1970. On September 1, 1970, Able and Brown enter into a contract whereby Able agrees to work for Brown for an additional 11 months after the performance of the existing contract. The contract for the extension of time cannot be performed within one year from the making thereof.

An Indefinite Time Stated. When the time of performance of the contract is stated in indefinite terms, such as "for life" or "as long as needed," and under existing conditions it is possible to perform the contract within one year, it need not be evidenced by a writing to be enforceable, even though the actual time of performance is more than one year.

The courts are not in accord in their interpretation of contracts to support someone and contracts to refrain from action. All courts hold that a contract whereby Ames contracts to support Barnes for life need not be in writing. They reason that the contract will be fully performed on the death of Barnes and this may occur within a year.

A majority of the courts hold that a contract whereby Ames contracts not to compete with Barnes for a period of five years must be evidenced by a writing to be enforceable whereas a few courts hold that the contract will be completely performed on the death of Ames and that this may occur within a year and that no writing is required.

SUMMARY

The provision of the statute of frauds which requires that a contract must be in writing if it cannot be performed within one year from the making thereof applies only to bilateral contracts. Since it is worded in the negative, "not fully performed," no writing is required if it is possible, under the terms of the contract, to complete performance within one year. Time is computed from the time of the formation of the contract, not from the time the promisor is to begin performance. A contract to extend the time of performance of an existing contract must be evidenced by a writing if the time from the formation of the contract to extend time of performance until the time of complete performance of the contract, under the terms of the contract, exceeds one year. If the time for performance is stated in indefinite terms, such as "for life" or "for long as needed," the courts hold, in the absence of a special statute, that no writing is required.

Lucas v. Whittaker Corp.

470 F.2d 326 (10th Cir. 1972)

Lucas (plaintiff) sued Whittaker (defendant) to recover the balance due him on an alleged two-year oral employment contract. Whittaker denied the existence of the contract and also relied on the statute of frauds as a defense, claiming it was an agreement not to be performed within a year. The trial court held that under the circumstances the doctrine of equitable estoppel prevented Whittaker from asserting the statute as a defense. Whittaker appealed. Affirmed.

PICKETT, CIRCUIT JUDGE. The contract having been consummated in California, Colorado law requires the application of California law in determining its validity. In California the doctrine of estoppel to assert the statute of frauds is applied to prevent fraud that would result from a refusal to enforce an oral contract. It is said that such fraud may inhere in the unconscionable injury that would result from denying enforcement of the contract after one party has been induced by the other seriously to change his position in reliance on the contract.

The nub of Whittaker's argument is that Lucas gave up no more than any person who leaves his present employment for what he thinks is a better job. The trial court held that Lucas' detrimental reliance on the two-year contract in moving to Colorado was more than that suffered in the ordinary change of jobs.

Lucas, in accepting the offered employment by Whittaker, resigned from what appeared to be a secure job with a company for whom he had worked for nine years, including incidents of that employment—medical and life insurance benefits, stock options, accrued vacation time and a college tuition supplement for eligible dependents. He sold a custom-built house in which he and his family lived for only eight months. He gave up business and social contacts. All of this obviously was lost because of Lucas' reliance on the oral agreement. The trial court's fact finding of unconscionable injury is not clearly erroneous. That Lucas earned more during his 13 months with Whittaker than he would have earned in two years at his old job is irrelevant in determining unconscionable injury.

Whittaker also contends that Lucas failed to meet his burden of proof in showing that Whittaker breached the employment contract and that the trial judge erred in not instructing the jury on whether Lucas was discharged for cause. Although it is generally held that an employee claiming breach of an employment contract has the burden of proving the employer's breach . . . when the employee establishes the breach, the burden is on the employer to show justification.

The evidence establishes that Whittaker discharged Lucas before the expiration of the period of employment. Whittaker offered no evidence to show that Lucas' discharge was for cause and no issue was present for the jury. . . .

The Writing

Nature of Writing Required. The statutes of fraud of the several states are not uniform in their provisions for writing. In most of the states the statutes require "a memorandum," or "a note of memorandum," but in some of the states the statutes require "a contract in writing."

If a memorandum is required, it may be made at any time up to the time suit is filed. If it has been signed but has been lost, its loss and its content may be proven by parol evidence. It may be in any form, such as a formal contract, letters, telegrams, receipts, or any other writing accurately stating the material provisions of the contract.

The memorandum may consist of several documents, in which case the documents must show, either by attachment physically or by the content or references in the documents themselves, that they all refer to the same transaction. If a contract in writing is required, it must include all the material provisions of the agreement, and must be made with the intent to bind the party signing it. The memorandum need not be made with the intent that it be binding.

Content of the Memorandum. The memorandum must state the names of the parties, or designate them so that they can be identified from the content of the writing, must describe the subject matter of the contract with reasonable certainty (a more detailed description of real property than of personal property is required), must state the price to be paid (with some exceptions), and must state credit terms, if credit is extended, and all other terms that are material. The statutes of frauds of some states expressly provide that the consideration need not be stated in the memorandum; however, if price is a material term, it must be stated.

It is immaterial in what order the terms are stated or how the parties are indicated. The parties may be indicated by their signatures on the memorandum, by the appearance of their names in the heading of the memorandum, by an address on an envelope in which the memorandum is mailed, or by a statement in the memorandum expressly setting out the names of the parties.

Under the provisions of the Uniform Commercial Code (discussed later), the requirements for the memorandum of a contract to sell goods[2] are not as strict as are those required in general.

The Signing. The statute of frauds in force in most of the states provides that the memorandum must be signed by the *party* to be bound or a duly authorized agent. Since the statute is worded in the singular, the memorandum need not be signed by both parties but must be signed by the party who is being sued or by an agent. Unless the statute expressly provides that the memorandum or contract must be signed at the end thereof, the signature may appear any place on the memorandum.

In a sale at auction the auctioneer is impliedly authorized to sign the note or memorandum as agent for both the buyer and the seller. However, this implied authority continues only during the auction sale.

Oral Variation of Contract. By the great weight of authority, an oral variation of a contract, for which contract a sufficient note or memorandum exists, is not enforceable. The contract may be enforced as originally negotiated, but the variation is not enforceable. However, a mutual oral agreement to cancel a contract, for which a sufficient memorandum exists, is effective.

SUMMARY

A note or memorandum in writing is generally a sufficient writing to satisfy the statute of frauds. It may be made at any time prior to the bringing of

---

[2] Uniform Commercial Code, § 2–201 (1) and (2).

suit to enforce the contract and need not be in any particular form. If several documents are relied on, they must be physically attached together, or it must be clearly indicated from their contents that they refer to the same transaction. The memorandum must include the names of the parties and describe the subject matter of the contract with reasonable certainty and in addition must contain all the material provisions of the contract.

The memorandum must be signed by the party to be charged or a duly authorized agent; that is, it must be signed by the party who sets up the statute of frauds as a defense. No particular place or mode of signing is stipulated by the statute. An agent may sign in the principal's name or in his or her own name. An auctioneer has implied authority to sign for both the buyer and the seller. An oral variation of a contract, where such contract is evidenced by a sufficient memorandum, is not enforceable.

Babdo Sales v. Miller-Wohl Co.

440 F.2d 962 (2nd Cir. 1971)

In an action brought to determine whether Babdo Sales (plaintiff) was entitled to continued use and occupancy of certain departments of Miller-Wohl Co.'s (defendant) stores under contracts entered into by the two parties, the court granted judgment in favor of Babdo Sales and Miller-Wohl appealed. Affirmed.

Babdo Sales is a corporation engaged in retail sale of records, novelties, and other merchandise which obtains licenses or leases from department stores to conduct business on their premises in return for a percentage of its gross sales. For some years Babdo had concededly valid written agreements with Miller-Wohl and occupied space in a number of Miller-Wohl stores throughout the country. In 1968 the parties entered into negotiations as to a lease in Miller-Wohl's new store soon to be opened in Springfield, Ohio. Agreement was reached as to the terms of this new lease, and at the same time the parties agreed to a renewal of the previously existing leases in eleven other stores until February 28, 1975, in consideration of an increase in rentals based on the terms of the Springfield negotiations.

On February 12, 1969, Fortgang, a vice president of Miller-Wohl sent an unsigned internal memorandum to the company's assistant comptroller informing him as to the terms of the new agreements which would become effective on March 1, 1969. Sometime thereafter in March or April Miller-Wohl sent to Babdo ten separate formal agreements and requested that they be signed and returned. These were dated February 28, 1969. On April 7, 1969, Miller-Wohl's assistant comptroller sent Babdo a letter entitled "Final Accounting under Existing Leases" setting forth the balance due to Babdo under the terms of the previously existing leases which had been terminated as of March 1, 1969, and referring to "our agreement . . . to initiate the new leases."

In the meantime new management had taken over control of Miller-Wohl and decided that in the future Miller-Wohl would operate its own departments rather than license others, and the executives of Miller-Wohl were instructed as to this policy in a memorandum dated May 5, 1969. Miller-Wohl never executed the ten letter agreements which had been signed by Babdo and returned. Instead Miller-Wohl informed Babdo that it regarded the renewals as ineffective and that the existing licensing agreements would not be renewed upon their expiration. Babdo contends that binding agreements had been entered into and seeks a declaratory judgment to this effect.

SMITH, CIRCUIT JUDGE. Once two parties have reached agreement on the material terms of a contract, it may or may not become binding at that point depending solely on the intention of the parties. Professor Corbin has noted:

> One of the most common illustrations of preliminary negotiation that is totally inoperative is one where the parties consider the details of a proposed agreement, perhaps settling them one by one, with the understanding during this process that the agreement is to be embodied in a formal written document and that neither party is to be bound until he executes this document. Often it is a difficult question of fact whether the parties have this understanding; and there are very many decisions holding both ways.

In the present case the evidence strongly suggests that both parties considered the new leases binding and in force as of March 1, 1969. Thus the Fortgang memorandum of February 12, 1969, states: "We have today negotiated a new license agreement . . . the above agreement will be effective as of March 1, 1969." Likewise the April 7, 1969 letter of Miller-Wohl's assistant comptroller to Babdo begins: "In accordance with our agreement, we are terminating your existing leases in the Welles Stores as of February 28, 1969 in order to initiate the new leases as of March 1, 1969."

Assuming that a binding oral agreement is found to exist, the next question . . . is whether the agreement is nevertheless void under the statute of frauds.

Babdo and the court below relied on the . . . decision in *Crabtree v. Elizabeth Arden Sales Corp.,* which stated:

> The statute of frauds does not require the "memorandum . . . to be in one document. It may be pieced together out of separate writings, connected with one another either expressly or by the internal evidence of subject-matter and occasion.

None of the terms of the contract are supplied by parol. All of them must be set out in the various writings presented to the court, and at least one writing, the one establishing a contractual relationship between the parties, must bear the signature of the party to be charged, while the unsigned document must on its face refer to the same transaction as that set forth in the one that was signed. Parol evidence—to portray the circumstances surrounding the making of the memorandum—serves only to connect the separate documents and to show that there was assent, by the party to be charged, to the contents of the one unsigned.

The lower court correctly found that the signed letter of Miller-Wohl's assistant comptroller dated April 7, 1969, which included the reference to "our agreement . . . to initiate the new leases" was sufficient to come within the *Crabtree* requirement that the signed document "establish a contractual relationship between the parties" and that the unsigned documents of February 12 and the agreements dated February 28, 1969, set forth all the material terms of the contract. . . .

Effect of Failure to Comply

General Effect. The statute of frauds does not, as a general rule, declare an oral contract which comes within the scope of the statute's provisions void or voidable if it does not comply with the requirements of the statute; it declares such a contract unenforceable. If suit is brought to enforce an oral contract which comes within the provisions of the statute of frauds and the defendant does not plead noncompliance with the statute as a defense, he or she thereby waives the defense, and the court will proceed in the same manner as though the plaintiff were in compliance with the statute of frauds.

Rights of Parties to Oral Contract. If the parties have entered into an oral contract which comes within the provisions of the statute of frauds and one party has performed, thereby conferring benefits on the other party, he or she can recover for the benefits conferred in an action in quasi contract.

Part performance will take the contract out of the statute of frauds in cases involving the purchase of real property where the purchaser has been given possession of the property and has made extensive improvements to it. Part performance may limit the statute of frauds defense in some cases involving sale of goods (discussed next) to the extent that there is either part payment or part delivery. Absent special facts, part performance does not remove the statute of frauds defense where either the "one year" or "promises to answer" statutes are involved.

If an oral contract which comes within the statute of frauds has been fully performed, neither party will be permitted to rescind the contract and recover the consideration given. Once the contract has been performed, the transaction is a closed deal and cannot be reopened on the ground of noncompliance with the provisions of the statute of frauds.

SUMMARY

An oral contract which comes within the provisions of the statute of frauds is unenforceable, not void or voidable. If one of the parties to an oral contract which is within the statute of frauds performs, thereby conferring benefits on the other party, the party who has performed can recover in quasi contract for the benefits conferred. In transactions concerning real estate, if there has been part performance of an oral contract, the court may grant specific performance if the circumstances are such that specific performance is necessary to avoid an unjust result. If the parties have performed an oral contract which comes within the provisions of the statute of frauds, neither party can rescind the contract on the ground of noncompliance with the statute of frauds.

Sale of Goods and the Code

The Memorandum. The statute of frauds in the Code which applies to the sale of goods in the amount of $500 or more is Section 2–201. Such an oral contract is not enforceable by way of action or defense unless the requirements of the statute of frauds are complied with. These requirements can be met by the execution of a memorandum signed by the party against whom enforcement is sought or by an authorized agent or broker. The memorandum satisfies the requirements of the statute of frauds if it is "some writing sufficient to indicate that a contract of sale has been entered into between the parties." It is not insufficient because it omits or incorrectly states a term agreed upon. A sales contract is not enforceable beyond the quantity of goods stated in the memorandum. (2–201 [1].)[3]

As between merchants, if an oral contract has been negotiated and one of the parties, within a reasonable time thereafter, sends a written confirmation, sufficient to bind him or her to the other party, such writing is sufficient to bind the receiver. Even if the receiver does not sign it, if he or she has reason to know its contents, the receiver loses the defense of the statute unless written notice of objection to its contents is given within ten days after it is received. (2–201 [2].)

Part Payment or Part Delivery. Under the Code, part payment or delivery of part of the goods satisfies the statute of frauds but only "with respect to goods for which payment has been made and accepted or which have been received and accepted." (2–201 [3] [*c*].) This provision of the statute makes the oral contract of the parties enforceable only to the extent that payment has been made and accepted or that the goods have been received and accepted; it does not make the oral contract enforceable in its entirety.

Admissions in Pleadings or Court. Although a sufficient writing has not been executed and no part payment or part delivery has been made, if the party being sued admits in pleadings or in court that an oral sales contract was entered into, he or she can be held liable. The oral contract is not enforceable, however, beyond the quantity of goods admitted. (2–201 [3] [*b*].)

[3] The numbers in the parentheses refer to the sections of the Uniform Commercial Code, 1962.

Specially Manufactured Goods. Oral contracts for goods to be specially manufactured are enforceable (1) if the goods are not suitable for sale in the ordinary course of the seller's business, and (2) if the seller, before notice of repudiation is received and under circumstances which reasonably indicate that the goods are for the buyer, has made a substantial beginning of their manufacture or commitment for their procurement. (2–201 [3] [*a*].) Under this section of the statute of frauds a wholly executory oral contract for goods to be specially manufactured is unenforceable.

Effect of Noncompliance. The statute of frauds does not declare oral contracts which come within its scope void or voidable if they do not comply with the requirements of the statute, but it does declare such contracts unenforceable. If suit is brought to enforce an oral contract for the sale of goods for the price of $500 or more, the party sued, if he wishes to avail himself of the protection of the statute, must plead it specially in the trial court. If the contract has been completely performed, neither party will be permitted to rescind the contract and recover the consideration given.

SUMMARY

An oral contract for the sale of goods for the price of $500 or more is unenforceable unless evidenced by a writing signed by the party against whom enforcement is sought. The writing need not set out all the terms of the agreement but must be sufficient to indicate that a contract was entered into. It is not enforceable beyond the quantity stated. It may be satisfied by part payment or part delivery or by admission in the pleadings or in court but not for a quantity beyond payment made, goods received and accepted, or admitted. A written confirmation sufficient to bind the sender will bind the receiver unless he or she objects to its terms within ten days of its receipt. The statute of frauds declares the contract coming within its provisions unenforceable and the defendant must plead the statute as a matter of defense in the trial court if he or she wishes its protection.

Reich v. Helen Harper, Inc.

3 U.C.C. Rep. 1048 (Civ. Ct. N.Y. 1966)

This was an action brought by Reich (plaintiff) against Kaplan (defendant) for the breach of an oral contract to purchase 11,500 yards of India madras for 75 cents per yard. Held: Kaplan's motion to dismiss on grounds of the statute of frauds denied.

A document entitled "Rate Confirmation" was sent by Amtec to both Kaplan and Reich. It described the goods, stated the quantity, the price per yard, and that Amtec was acting as sales agent for Ricky Fabrics (a designee of Reich), and that the goods were being sold to Kaplan. On January 9, 1966, Reich sent Kaplan a bill for 11,528 yards of madras at 75 cents a yard on the printed bill form of Brian Mills, a name under which Reich does business. On February 18, 1966, Kaplan sent a letter to Brian Mills, attention of Mr. Reich, reading as follows:

> Brian Mills, 152 W. 27th St., New York, N.Y.
> Att: Mr. Elliott Reich
> Gentlemen:
> Replying to your letter of the 18th, please be advised that we examined a few pieces of merchandise that were billed to us against your invoice No. 10203, and found that it was not up to our standard.
> We are, therefore, unable to accept this shipment, and we also wish to advise that the few pieces that we examined are also being held for return to you.
> Very truly yours,
> /s/ Isidor Kaplan

GOLD, JUDGE. The Code makes it necessary for a merchant buyer or merchant seller to watch his mail and to act promptly if he is not to be bound by a contract for sale with respect to which he has signed no writing. It deprives the party who fails to answer the confirmation, by rejecting it, of the defense of the statute of frauds. The burden of persuading the trier of the facts that a contract was in truth made orally prior to the written confirmation is unaffected.

In *Harry Rubin & Sons, Inc. v. Consolidated Pipe Co.*, the Supreme Court of Pennsylvania stated:

> As between merchants, the present statute of frauds provision (i.e., under § 2–201 [2]) significantly changes the former law by obviating the necessity of having a memorandum signed by the party sought to be charged. The present statutory requirements are: (1) that, within a reasonable time, there be a writing in confirmation of the oral contract; (2) that the writing be sufficient to bind the sender; (3) that such writing be received; (4) that no reply thereto has been made although the recipient had reason to know of its contents. Section 2–201 [2] penalizes a party who fails to "answer a written confirmation of a contract within ten days" of the receipt of the writing by depriving such party of the defense of the statute of frauds.

It becomes necessary now to determine whether the document sent by Amtec is "sufficient against the sender." In short, would it bind Reich so that he, Reich, would be deprived of the statute of frauds as a defense were Kaplan the party suing herein? The court finds that the document would in and of itself so bind Reich to the transaction. Moreover, this commitment would be reinforced by Reich's invoice to Kaplan.

Whether examined together with Reich's invoice or standing alone, the sales confirmation would also bind Kaplan so as to deprive him of the defense of the statute of frauds in light of Kaplan's failure to give written notice of objection to its contents within ten days from the receipt thereof. The invoice rendered by Reich to Kaplan promptly after the sending of the sales confirmation would leave not the slightest doubt that the written confirmation was complete and that Kaplan would in effect forfeit the right to utilize the statute of frauds if he failed to make timely written objection to its contents.

The contention of Kaplan that the sales confirmation is not "signed" and is therefore not binding upon the sender and therefore cannot be binding upon the recipient is without basis in law. The authorities clearly hold to the contrary.

The term "signed," used in U.C.C. § 2–201, is defined in U.C.C., § 1–201 (39) in part as follows:

" 'Signed' includes any symbol executed or adopted by a party with present intention to authenticate a writing. . . ."

The question remaining then is whether the sale confirmation sent to Kaplan was "signed." In the context of the facts here present, the question may also be posed in the following manner: Was there an intent to authenticate the writing? This court believes so.

In the instant transaction not only was there the printed name of the agent, "Amtec," but in addition the name of the seller's principal was hand-lettered thereon.

The court is likewise of the opinion that the statute of frauds is not available to Kaplan for the further reason that Kaplan's letter, written some 45 days after the receipt of the sale confirmation and some 40 days after receipt of Reich's bill, may in and of itself constitute a sufficient memorandum to satisfy § 2–201 of the Uniform Commercial Code.

It has long been held that a memorandum sufficient to satisfy the statute of frauds need not be contained in one document but "It may be pieced together out of separate writings, connected with one another either expressly or by the internal evidence of subject matter and occasion." If the writings so conjoined meet the three requirements of the code, that a contract is evidenced, it is signed and the quantity of goods is specified, then the agreement is enforceable.

In re Augustin Bros. Co.

460 F.2d 376 (8th Cir. 1972)

This is an action by Wright (plaintiff) against Augustin Bros. Co. (defendant) to recover damages for an alleged breach of oral contract. Judgment for Augustin and Wright appealed. Affirmed.

Wright operates a grain elevator, its principal business being the storage, processing, and sale of corn for use as cattle feed. Wright filed suit against Augustin, alleging in substance that Augustin had incurred liability to it in the amount of $64,187.95 due to its breach of an oral contract to purchase corn for cattle feed.

In April, 1967, Wright and Augustin entered into an oral arrangement by which it was agreed that Wright would acquire any corn available on the market and thereafter Augustin would buy it at Wright's cost plus four cents per bushel for handling.

During the next four months, Wright increased its stored corn inventory substantially. In August the market price fell sharply. Shortly before October, however, due to financial difficulties, Augustin declined to honor the oral commitment to purchase the corn held in inventory although at that time Augustin had made a prepayment in the amount of $27,882.24. Wright was forced to liquidate its corn inventory at a lower market price. It sustained a substantial loss both as compared to the oral contract price it would have received and as compared to its acquisition cost.

BRIGHT, CIRCUIT JUDGE. The Statute of Frauds bars enforcement of the overall oral contract between the parties which called for Augustin to purchase all of Wright's inventory of corn. The Statute of Frauds does, however, permit partial enforcement of this contract under the doctrine of part performance.

The statute U.C.C. § 2–201, as is here pertinent, provides:

(1) Except as otherwise provided in this section a contract for the sale of goods for the price of five hundred dollars ($500) or more is not enforceable by way of action or defense unless there is some writing sufficient to indicate that a contract for sale has been made between the parties and signed by the party against whom enforcement is sought or by his authorized agent or broker.

* * * * *

A contract which does not satisfy the requirements of subsection (1) but which is valid in other respects is enforceable . . . (c) *with respect to goods for which payment has been made and accepted or which have been received and accepted* . . . [Emphasis supplied].

"Partial performance" as a substitute for the required memorandum can validate the contract only for the goods which have been accepted or for which payment has been made and accepted.

Receipt and acceptance either of goods or of the price constitutes an unambiguous overt admission by both parties that a contract actually exists.

We agree with the conclusion of the district court that enforcement of an oral contract for goods in which an advance payment has been made by the buyer is limited to that quantity of goods which the advance payment would buy at the market price.

We therefore conclude that Augustin by making a part payment, and Wright by accepting that part payment, made an enforceable contract only as to that quantity of goods that could have been purchased by that part payment.

Lewis v. Hughes

346 A.2d 231 (Ct. App. Md. 1975)

Lewis (plaintiff) brought this action to enforce an oral contract for sale of a mobile home against Hughes (defendant). Judgment for Hughes and Lewis appeals. Reversed.

DIGGES, JUDGE. We conclude that the Statute of Frauds has been satisfied per 2–201(3) which states in part:

A contract which does not satisfy the requirements of [2–201(1)] but which is valid in other respects is enforceable . . . (b) If the party against whom enforcement is sought admits in his pleading, testimony or otherwise in court that a contract for sale was made, but the contract is not enforceable under this provision beyond the quantity of goods admitted.

Hughes repeatedly acknowledged the existence of the contract in his testimony. If a party admits an oral contract, he should be bound to his bargain. The Statute of Frauds were not designed to protect a party who made an oral contract, but rather to aid a party who did not make a contract, though one is claimed to have been made orally with him. The fact that the admission by Hughes be voluntary or involuntary is of no consequence under the Uniform Commercial Code, as even involuntary admissions can be used to satisfy the Statute of Frauds under 2–201(3) (b). We hold that the Statute of Frauds does not bar enforcement of the contract for the sale of the mobile home involved in this case.

Interpretation

Necessity for Interpretation. Interpretation of a contract is the process of discovering and explaining the meaning of words and other manifestations used by the parties to the contract. If suit is brought to enforce a right claimed under a written contract, the court must interpret the meaning of the writing in order to determine the existence of a contract and the rights and duties of the parties to the contract.

Basic Standards of Interpretation. The courts have adopted broad, basic standards of interpretation which they follow in determining the meaning of contracts and agreements which are expressed in writing. They will, as a general rule, give the writing the meaning that the contracting parties would be expected to give it under the circumstances surrounding the making of the contract. And they will give to the words and phrases used the meaning usually given to them by the business, trade, or profession in which the parties are engaged.

Rules of Interpretation. If the language used in a contract is clear and definite, the interpretation of the writing is a matter for the judge; but if the writing is uncertain and ambiguous, and parol evidence is introduced in aid of its interpretation, the question of its meaning should be left to a jury.

When the court is asked to interpret a writing which is being litigated it will attempt first to determine, by reading the writing in its entirety, the principal objective of the parties. Ordinary words will be given their usual meaning and technical words will be given their technical meaning unless it clearly appears that a different meaning was intended. Each clause and provision will be interpreted with regard to its relation to the principal objective of the contract.

If the parties have used general terms followed by special terms, the court will assume that the special terms qualify the general terms. If the parties have used a form contract, or a contract which is partly printed and partly written, and there is a conflict between the printed and the written terms, the written terms will control. If there is an ambiguity in a contract and one of the parties has drawn the contract, the contract will be construed more strongly against the party who has drawn it.

Usage. Usage is a uniform practice or course of conduct which is followed in a line of business or profession or in a locality and which is either known to the parties or so well established that the parties must be presumed to have acted with reference thereto.

Usage may give to certain words a meaning different from the general meaning of the words. It may add to a written contract provisions not actually written into the writing. The courts have generally held in such cases that there is a presumption that the parties did not intend to reduce the entire agreement to writing but intended to contract with reference to those known usages. If both contracting parties live in the same community or are members of the same trade or association, the presumption is that they contract with reference to the usage of the community or trade and that they are both familiar with such usages. If the parties do not wish so to contract, they should express an intention not to be bound by such usages. Where the parties are not residents of the same community or members of the same trade group, the presumption is that they contract in regard to general usages and not in respect to local or special usages. It may be shown, however, that the local or special usages were known to both parties and that they contracted in reference to them. Where different usages prevail in different sections, the presumption is that the parties contracted in reference to the usage prevailing at the place where the contract was made and was to be performed.

SUMMARY

Interpretation of a contract is the process of determining the meaning of words and other manifestations used by the parties to the contract. If an action is based on a writing, the writing must be interpreted in order to determine the rights and duties of the parties thereto. As guides to the court in the interpretation of written instruments, general standards and rules of interpretation have been adopted. Usage plays an important role in the interpretation of contracts. Usage is a uniform practice or course of conduct followed in a business or profession or in a locality, and may give to the language used a special meaning, or it may add terms to the contract.

Stender v. Twin City Foods, Inc.

510 P.2d 221 (Sup. Ct. Wash. 1973)

Action by Stender (plaintiff), a grower, against Twin City Foods (defendant), a food processor, for damages for breach of contract. Twin City appealed from an adverse decision made by the Court of Appeals. Reversed and the trial court judgment for Twin Foods affirmed.

The contract required Twin Foods to harvest and vine the peas at proper maturity and pay a stipulated price but gave the processor option to divert, at a substantially lower price, such portion of the grower's acreage for seed or feed purposes as quality ". . . of salvage might dictate in the event of *adverse weather conditions that might delay harvest of pea crop beyond optimum maturity for processing.*" The weather resulted in an unexpected maturation of the entire crop. Twin Foods claimed the right to divert Stender's crop under the "adverse weather" clause.

WRIGHT, JUSTICE. Determination of the intent of the contracting parties is to be accomplished by viewing the contract as a whole, the subject matter and objective of the contract, all the circumstances surrounding the making of the contract, the subsequent acts and conduct of the parties to the contract, and the reasonableness of respective interpretations advocated by the parties.

Both Stender and Twin City were heavily involved in the Washington pea industry, Stender as a grower with 8 years of experience and Twin City as a large processor. This fact would indicate that the contract should be construed in light of the usages of the pea industry existing at the time the contract was executed.

As the trial court indicated, it was the well-established plan of all the pea processors in the Skagit County area to plant the peas in a staggered manner in order to avoid the entire crop maturing at once. This system was in wide use and known by all the individual growers. In fact, Stender testified as to his knowledge of the custom of staggered planting and the planning and calculation of harvest scheduling. Thus, Stender must be held to have had knowledge of the existence of other pea contracts with Twin City Foods, the staggered planting schedule and the reasons therefor.

The record supports the trail court's conclusion that the reason that Twin City bypassed Stender's crop is that the weather conditions increased the size of the crops ready for processing beyond any reasonable expectations.

The definition of adverse weather conditions must be determined in light of reasonable industry custom and usage. Once a contract is established, usage and custom are admissible into evidence to explain the terms of the contract. And, parol evidence is admissible to establish a trade usage even though words in their ordinary or legal meaning are unambiguous. In view of custom and usage of the pea industry, it can be most reasonably stated that the term "adverse weather conditions" includes unusual temperature fluctuations resulting in an unexpected maturation of an entire pea crop which has been systematically planted with the objective of partial maturation over a period of time to allow for orderly harvesting. This construction of the term in question is especially valid when both parties to the contract were well aware that the purpose of scheduling crops was to avoid maturity of all the contract crops at once and to provide for systematic harvesting.[4]

Parol Evidence

Scope and Purpose of Parol Evidence Rule. Under the parol evidence rule, oral or extrinsic evidence is not admissible to add to, alter, or vary the terms of a written contract. The purpose of the parol evidence rule is to lend stability to written agreements by excluding from consideration any evidence of facts tending to show that the parties intended something different from that set out in the written contract. When the parties have expressed their contract or agreement in a writing free from ambiguity, such writing is the best evidence of their intent; all preliminary negotiations are merged in the writing.

The parol evidence rule has been made a part of the law of sales in the Uniform Commercial Code. (2–202.)

Admissible Parol Evidence. Parol evidence is admissible if it is offered to prove that the writing is not a valid contract because it was induced by misrepresentation, fraud, duress, or undue influence, or to prove that the contract is illegal. In all such instances, oral evidence is offered to prove that the contract is voidable or is based on an illegal bargain, and not to add to, alter, or vary the terms of the contract. Parol evidence is also admissible to prove that a writing was executed on the condition that it was not to be operative unless or until an agreed, uncertain future event happened.

Subsequent Contracts. An oral contract, entered into subsequent to the making of the written contract, may be proved by oral evidence even though the terms of the oral contract are such that they cancel, subtract from, or add to the obligations of the prior written contract. Such parol evidence is not offered to alter, vary, or add to the written contract but is offered to prove the existence of a valid oral contract entered into subsequent to the making of the written contract.

Partial Writings. If a writing is incomplete and such fact is apparent from a reading of the writing in the light of the relation of the parties, the subject matter of the contract, and the surrounding circumstances, parol evi-

[4] Three judges dissented. The case demonstrates the importance of having unambiguous language in contracts.

dence is admissible to fill in the gaps. However, the parol evidence admitted must not tend to alter, vary, or contradict the written terms of the contract.

As to sales contracts the U.C.C. rejects the assumption that because a writing has been set out which is final as to some, or even as to most terms, it is to be taken as including *all* matters agreed upon. Under the U.C.C. 2–202 (*b*) the court must find that the *parties intended* the writing to be the *complete and exclusive* statement of the terms of the agreement before the writing can operate to exclude parol evidence of additional terms consistent with those written.

Ambiguous Contracts. Parol evidence is admissible to clear up ambiguities in a written contract or agreement. Such evidence is limited to testimony of facts and circumstances surrounding the making of a contract which will aid the court in interpreting the contract. Likewise, if there is nothing in the writing which indicates that the parties did not intend to contract in accordance with an existing usage, oral evidence of a business usage is admissible.

SUMMARY

The parol evidence rule is a rule of substantive law. Under the parol evidence rule, oral evidence is not admissible to add to, alter, or vary the terms of a written contract. Oral evidence is admissible to prove the writing is voidable or illegal; to prove that at the time it was executed it was agreed that it would not be operative unless a specified future, uncertain event happened; to prove a subsequent contract; or to clear up an ambiguity in the contract.

From a practical standpoint a person should read a proposed writing carefully and be certain that all the terms of the agreement are expressed in clear, concise language. If there are any provisions or words in the writing which a person does not understand, an explanation should be demanded concerning their meaning before signing.

Under the U.C.C. the court must find that the parties intended no additions to the written sales contract before the parol evidence rule will be used to exclude additional terms.

Preferred Risk Mutual Ins. Co. v. Jones

211 S.E.2d 720 (Sup. Ct. Ga. 1975)

Action to enforce covenant not to compete brought by Preferred Risk Mutual Insurance Co. (plaintiff) against Jones (defendant). Dismissal of case appealed by plaintiff. Reversed.

Jones entered into a contract of employment with Preferred to serve as an insurance agent. The contract provided that Jones would not compete within a 25 mile radius of "the city __________ to which he is assigned under the contract for a period of *one* year following the termination of the contract." The space in the contract for the name of the city was left blank. Preferred asserts that Jones was assigned to the City of Carrollton and requests that he be enjoined from soliciting in that area pursuant to the contract. The trail judge ruled that the parole evidence rule prevented proof of the name of the city.

PER CURIAM. The general rule is that parol evidence is inadmissible to add to, take from, vary or contradict the terms of a written instrument. However, "if there is an ambiguity, latent or patent, it may be explained; so if a part of a contract only is reduced to writing (such as a note given in pursuance of a contract), and it is manifest that the writing was not intended to speak the whole contract, then parol evidence is admissible." If the writing appears on its face to be an incomplete contract and if the parol evidence offered is consistent with and not contradictory of the terms of the written instrument, then the parol evidence is admissible to complete the agreement between the parties. A party is entitled to prove "the existence of any separate oral agreement as to any matter on which a document is silent, and which is not inconsistent with its terms, if from the circumstances of the case the court infers that the parties did not intend the document to be a complete and final statement of the whole of the transactions between them."

The blank that was left in the contract for the city or territory designation raised an ambiguity on the face of the contract as to which city or territory Jones was assigned and as to whether the territorial designation was omitted inadvertently or omitted deliberately to show a failure to agree as to the designation. Accordingly, parol evidence would be admissible to prove the city or territory, if any, to which Jones was assigned.

Problem Cases

1. Weitnauer agreed to act as a purchasing agent for Annis and to guaranty to creditors the payment of Annis' orders. This agreement provided that Annis was to be personally liable to Weitnauer for the amount of the orders up to $100,000. Subsequently, orders from Annis exceeded $100,000 and Weitnauer requested an additional $50,000 personal guaranty from Annis to cover these increases, which Annis promised to do, orally. Annis later sent several signed letters to Weitnauer in which he admitted entering the new guaranty agreement. Eventually Weitnauer had to pay creditors on these accounts and sued Annis to collect on these personal guaranties. Annis set up the statute of frauds as his defense. Will Annis prevail?
2. Colonial Distributors, a sundries business, attempted to establish a credit account with Star Sales, a wholesaler, in 1958. Star was unwilling to grant credit to Colonial but was satisfied with the financial responsibility of Arnoult, one of the partners, and agreed to bill Arnoult personally for goods purchased by Colonial. All invoices were thereafter billed in Arnoult's name. Colonial was soon after incorporated with Arnoult with the

other partners becoming stockholders. Payments on the account were made by Colonial before and after incorporation and the checks were co-signed by Arnoult until 1960 when Arnoult withdrew from the company. Thereafter, although Arnoult did not sign any checks, no change in the billing of the account was made. Late in 1960, Star discontinued the account because of delinquency accruing after Arnoult's departure. Shortly thereafter Colonial notified Star that they were going into bankruptcy, whereupon Star reclaimed merchandise equivalent to 40 percent of the debt. Star sued Arnoult for the deficiency and Arnoult set up the statute of frauds as a defense. Should Arnoult be held liable for the balance?

3. Hartford issued a three-year term fire insurance policy to Gillespie Co. through its agent, Frontier. The policy contained a provision that it could be cancelled at any time at the request of Gillespie. Later, Gillespie expanded to a second location and Frontier orally contracted with Hartford to modify the original contract to provide coverage at the new location. A fire occurred at the new location, resulting in a loss of $107,000. Hartford refuses to pay the claim saying that the oral contract was unenforceable under the statute of frauds since it was a contract not to be performed within one year. Is this a valid defense?

4. On October 20, 1973, Uscian and Blacconeri entered into a written contract for the sale of a certain parcel of land owned by Uscian. The contract was expressly contingent upon Uscian obtaining approval from the city to subdivide the property. Uscian's application for subdivision was denied by the city. Thereafter, in December of 1973, the parties orally agreed to sell the property without first obtaining a subdivision. Later Uscian backed out of the deal. Blacconeri now sues for specific performance of the written contract. Uscian sets up the statute of frauds as his defense. Is this a good defense?

5. Powless responded over the telephone to an advertisement offering employment. Pawtucket Screw Company's plant manager allegedly made an oral wage offer that was higher than Powless subsequently received for working. Powless continued to work for five years but there was no specified length of time for Powless to remain employed discussed in the telephone conversation. Powless sued for back pay due under the oral agreement. Is Powless' claim barred by the statute of frauds?

6. Tradeways, Inc. brought an action for breach of contract against Chrysler Corporation. Tradeways offered to conduct an advertising campaign for Chrysler, payment to be made in one of two alternative ways. First, Chrysler would pay $130,000 cash or second, each Chrysler dealer could be assessed $180. The services would be rendered over a two-year period. Chrysler stated that it wanted the offer reduced to writing, and a representative of Chrysler, Blount, telephoned Tradeways that it had been "selected" by Chrysler. Chrysler later refused to go ahead with the deal. Can Tradeways collect damages?

7. Owens successfully bid on a job of installing a plastic water pipe system for a small Alabama community. Clow Corporation orally agreed to supply pipe as needed by Owens and sent Owens an invoice describing the amount of pipe and prices for the pipe. Neither the proposal nor invoice prescribed times for delivery, although Clow orally agreed to attempt to supply a truckload of pipe per day. After satisfactorily delivering pipe for three days, Clow fell behind in delivery, and Owens was forced to buy from an alternative supplier at a higher price. Can Owens recover damages from Clow if Clow can prove that the agreed price exceeded $500 and raises the defense of the statute of frauds?

8. In April, 1973, Lyle orally offered to sell Farmers Elevator 20,000 bushels of corn for $1.22 per bushel for May delivery. Farmers Elevator accepted the offer and entered a note to this effect in the company ledger and then in line with customary trade practice

began to sell various amounts of corn to buyers for future delivery. When Lyle refused to deliver his corn in May, Farmers Elevator had to cover the deficiency in its inventory by buying elsewhere at prices averaging about $1.80 per bushel. When sued, Lyle set up the statute of frauds as a defense. Will Lyle prevail?

9. Delta Dynamics, developer of a safety lock for firearms, gave its distribution rights to the Pixey Distributing Company. Pixey agreed to sell a minimum number of the devices per year and if it failed, the contract stated, ". . . this agreement shall be subject to termination by Delta on thirty days' notice." Pixey failed to sell the minimum number of devices in the first year, and Delta sued for damages. Pixey claims that Delta's only remedy under the contract is termination, and at trial, Pixey attempts to offer the testimony of a Pixey official to explain that termination was the sole intended remedy at the time the contract between Delta and Pixey was signed. Delta objected to this testimony on the grounds that it called for the admission or parol evidence. Is Delta Right?
10. Ranch, Inc. contracted in writing with Washington Tent & Awning Co. to manufacture and install a canopy in front of Ranch's restaurant. It was understood that Ranch needed the permission of its landlord for the installation of the canopy. The canopy was installed and Ranch now refuses to pay for it, contending it never received the landlord's permission. Washington argues that the admission of the evidence concerning the landlord's refusal to give permission was barred by the Parol Evidence Rule. Will the court permit Ranch to prove that the written agreement was conditioned on the approval being given by the landlord?

14

Rights of Third Parties

Assignment of Contracts

Introduction. In many early systems of the law the obligation of a debtor was personal in a literal sense, in that the body of the debtor could be taken by his creditors. In England, a debtor who did not fulfill obligations could be imprisoned for debt. The accepted attitude toward one who did not pay honest debts was that he was in effect a thief. This general attitude, together with the right of a creditor to have his debtor imprisoned if he failed to pay the debt, emphasized the personal nature of debt. At this time the courts held that a contract was personal to the parties and that neither party could assign rights under the contract to a third person.

With the development of trade and the attainment of higher standards of commercial morality, the practice of extending credit, especially in the area of commercial transactions, became common. The needs of merchants demanded procedural reforms in the courts in relation to commercial cases. The courts began to recognize the right to assign contract rights, yet any suit on the contract had to be brought in the name of the party to the contract and not in the name of the assignee. By gradual development the rules of law regarding the assignment of contracts became more liberal, and now the assignability of contracts which are not personal to the parties are recognized.

Contracts Not Assignable. An assignment is a transfer, to the assignee, of the rights which the assignor has under a contract. The assignee has the right to have the performance of the contract rendered to him or her. From the beginning of the law of contracts, we have recognized that the promisee cannot demand of the promisor a performance which differs in any material respects from that promised; consequently, if the duties of the promisor will be altered in any material respect by the assignment of the contract, the contract is not assignable.

Any contract which is personal in nature cannot be assigned, since the nature of the contract is limited by the personality of the original promisee, and the substitution of the assignee changes the nature of the performance required by the promisor.

Any contract the performance of which involves personal skill, judgment, or character is not assignable. A contract to support for life cannot be assigned. A property insurance policy cannot be assigned before the loss of the material insured because such policies are based in part on the character of the insured. A sharecrop lease is not assignable, since the rent received depends directly on the skill, ability, and honesty of the tenant.

If a contract contains a provision expressly prohibiting the assignment of the contract, the courts will hold that the contract is not assignable. The modification of this rule under the U.C.C. is discussed subsequently.

Contracts Which Are Assignable. The typical example of an assignable contract is one in which a promisor is obligated to pay money to a promisee. In such a contract the promisor's duty to pay is fixed, the burden of performance is not increased by requiring payment to the assignee instead of to the promisee, and a minimum of personal relationship is involved. As a general rule a contract to sell and deliver goods or to sell land is assignable. However, if the contract to sell goods is what is known as a "needs" or "output" contract, such a contract is, as a general rule, not assignable, since the assignee's "needs" or ability to produce may vary materially from that of the promisee.

Contracts not to compete with the buyer of a business or with an employer have been held by the majority of the courts to be assignable. The purpose of such a restraint clause is to protect the goodwill of a business. The goodwill is an asset which may be sold with the business; consequently, the courts have held that a contract not to compete can be assigned as an incident of the sale of the business to be protected.

The Delegation of Duties. The courts have held that the duties under a contract cannot be assigned but, in the absence of special circumstances, may be delegated. For instance, the courts have recognized the validity of the delegation of the duty to do building or engineering work, if the work is of such a nature that it may be performed by many persons, and if its performance does not depend on the skill, training, or character of an individual or group of individuals. The promisor cannot, however, be relieved of an obligation under a contract by delegating duties to some third party. The promisor can still be held liable for breach of the contract if the party to whom the duties are delegated fails to perform.

The right to delegate the duties created by a contract to sell goods is expanded by Section 2–210 of the Code.

SUMMARY

In the early period of the development of our law, if a debt was not paid, the debtor could be imprisoned. Under the law the contractual relation was held to be highly personal, and no contract was assignable. As the country developed and trade expanded, the extension of credit became a common practice, especially in connection with commercial transactions. By gradual development the right to assign contracts was recognized, and today a contract is assignable if it does not involve the performance of personal services or the skill or character of the promisor, and if the duties of the promisor will not be materially altered by the assignment. A contract to receive money is a typical example of an assignable contract. Duties under a contract cannot be assigned, but they can be delegated if they are wholly impersonal in character. The promisor cannot be relieved from an obligation under a contract by the delegation of duties.

Although the basic principles of law relative to the assignment of contracts are not changed under the provisions of the Code, some aspects of the law are simplified and made more flexible and more practical.

Munchak Corp. v. Cunningham

457 F.2d 721 (4th Cir. 1972)

In a suit of Munchak Corp. (plaintiff), owner of a professional basketball club, to enjoin Cunningham (defendant) from performing services as a player for any other basketball club, the lower court denied relief and plaintiffs appealed. Reversed.

For the first year of the contract Cunningham was to receive a salary of $100,000, for the second year $110,000, and for the third year $120,000. Additionally, Cunningham was to receive $125,000 as a bonus for signing the contract. Cunningham refused to play for the Cougars contending that his contract was assigned illegally to Munchak Corporation, the new owner of the Cougars.

WINTER, CIRCUIT JUDGE. Cunningham's contention that his contract was not assignable and that by reason of a purported assignment he is excused from performance arises from these facts. Cunningham's contracts with the Cougars were made at a time when Southern Sports Corp., owned and operated primarily by James C. Gardner, was the owner of the Cougars' franchise. His contract with Southern Sports Corporation prohibited its assignment to another "*club*" without his consent, but it contained no prohibition against its assignment to another owner of the same club. In 1971, Southern Sports Corp. assigned its franchise and Cunningham's contracts to Munchak. Cunningham was not asked to consent, nor has he consented, to this assignment. While Cunningham's contracts require him to perform personal services, the services were to the club.

We recognize that under North Carolina law the right to performance of a personal service contract requiring special skills and based upon the personal relationship between the parties cannot be assigned without the consent of the party rendering those services.

But, some of such contracts may be assigned when the character of the performance and the obligation will not be changed. To us it is inconceivable that the rendition of services by a professional basketball player to a professional basketball club could be affected by the personalities of successive corporate owners. Indeed, Cunningham had met only Gardner of Southern Sports Club, and had not met, nor did he know, the other stockholders. If Gardner had sold all or part of his stock to another person, Cunningham could not seriously contend that his consent would be required.

The policy against assignability of certain personal service contracts is to prohibit an assignment of a contract in which the obligor undertakes to serve only the original obligee. This contract is not of that type, since Cunningham was not obligated to perform differently for plaintiffs than he was obligated to perform for Southern Sports Club. We, therefore, see no reason to hold that the contract was not assignable under the facts here. . . .

Rose v. Vulcan Materials Co.

194 S.E.2d 521 (Sup. Ct. N.C. 1973)

In an action for breach of contract to supply stone at a specified price, the court entered judgment in favor of Vulcan Materials Co. (defendant) and Rose (plaintiff) appealed. Reversed.

Rose owned and operated a stone quarry and ready-mix cement business in Yadkin County, North Carolina. He used stone from his quarry in his cement business. Dooley was also in the rockcrushing business in Yadkin County in competition with Rose. Late in 1956 Dooley contracted to buy Rose's rockcrushing business and to lease his quarry for ten years. The purchase contract obligated Dooley to provide Rose with enough stone to meet his business requirements for ten years at favorable listed prices. Sometime prior to 12 April 1960, Dooley advised Rose that he had an offer from Vulcan Materials Co. to purchase his quarry operations and requested Rose to release him from the contract so he could consummate the sale. Rose declined to do so and advised Dooley he would not release him unless Vulcan Materials Co. would agree in writing to comply with all of Dooley's obligations.

In April, 1960, Vulcan purchased the quarry operations and all of the assets and obligations of Dooley. Vulcan then sent Rose a letter which stated that they intended to carry out Dooley's obligations. In 1961, however, Vulcan notified Rose that all prices for stone sold to Rose would have to be increased above the prices listed in the Rose-Dooley contract. Rose paid the higher prices under protest and then sued Vulcan for breach of contract.

HUSKINS, JUSTICE. In most states, the assignee of an executory bilateral contract is not liable to anyone for the nonperformance of the assignor's duties thereunder unless he expressly promises his assignor or the other contracting party to perform, or "assume," such duties. . . . These states refuse to *imply* a promise to perform the duties, but if the assignee expressly promises his assignor to perform, he is liable to the other contracting party on a third-party beneficiary theory.

And, if the assignee makes such a promise directly to the other contracting party upon a consideration, of course he is liable to him thereon.

A minority of states holds that the assignee of an executory bilateral contract under a general assignment becomes not only assignee of the rights of the assignor but also delegatee of his duties; and that, absent a showing of contrary intent, the assignee *impliedly* promises the assignor that he will perform the duties so delegated. This court has never expressly adopted the Restatement Rule (§ 164) in North Carolina. However . . . [we] apparently recognized the rule of implied assumption that later became the Restatement Rule.

This rule is regarded as the more reasonable view by legal scholars and textwriters.

In addition, with respect to transactions governed by the Uniform Commercial Code, an assignment of a contract in general terms is a delegation of performance of the duties of the assignor, and its acceptance by the assignee constitutes a promise by assignee to perform those duties. Our holding in this case maintains a desirable uniformity in the field of contract liability.

We further hold that the other party to the original contract may sue the assignee as a third-party beneficiary of his promise of performance which he impliedly makes to his assignor, under the rule above laid down, by accepting the general assignment. . . . When Vulcan accepted such assignment it thereby became delegatee of its assignor's duties under the contract and impliedly promised to perform such duties.

Rights Acquired by Assignee

General Rule. An assignment of a contract is in legal effect a sale to an assignee of an assignor's rights under a contract. The assignee takes the place of the assignor and is entitled to all the rights of the assignor. The assignee can, however, acquire no greater rights than the assignor has at the time of the assignment, and takes the contract subject to all the defenses that the promisor has to the contract.

Notice of Assignment. If the assignee wishes to protect the rights acquired by the assignment, the assignee, or someone acting in his behalf, must give the promisor notice of the assignment. If the promisor is not given notice of the assignment and renders performance to the original promisee, the promisor will have discharged his duty and will not be liable to the assignee under the contract.

Successive Assignments. If an assignor assigns rights to one assignee and at a later date wrongfully assigns the same rights to a second assignee, who takes for value and without notice or knowledge of the prior assignment, the question then arises as to which of the respective assignees has the better right. There are two views on this point.

Under the rule known as the "American rule," the courts have held that the first assignee has the better right. This view is based on the rule of property law that a person cannot transfer greater rights in property than are owned. Under the rule known as the "English rule," the assignee who first gives notice of the assignment of the contract has the greater right. Under this rule, the giving of notice is considered equivalent to the taking of possession of tangible property. Under the Code, if the same item of property is sold to two different innocent purchasers for value, the first to take possession has the better right.

Assignment of Wages. Under the common law an assignment of future wages was void unless the assignor had a contract of employment. This rule has been relaxed, and now, as a general rule, if the assignor is regularly employed, the courts will enforce an assignment of the future wages of such employee.

However, substantially all the states have enacted statutes regulating the assignment of future wages. These statutes range from those which make all assignments of future wages void to those which place various limitations on such assignments.

SUMMARY

The assignee of a contract can acquire by the assignment no greater rights than those had by the assignor at the time of the assignment. If the assignee wishes to protect the rights acquired notice of the assignment must be given to the promisor. The rights acquired by the assignment will be such rights as the assignor had against the promisor at the time notice of the assignment was given to the promisor. In most states the assignment of future wages is regulated by statute.

General Factors, Inc. v. Beck

409 P.2d 40 (Sup. Ct. Ariz. 1965)

This action was brought by General Factors (plaintiffs) as assignees of a claim for construction materials sold by Tempe Gravel Co. to A. Deal Beck (defendant). Judgment for Beck and General Factors appealed. Reversed.

In early October, Beck purchased from Tempe Company certain materials for use by Beck in his construction business. Invoices representing these purchases were then sent to General Factors, Inc., under an alleged assignment and factoring account. General Factors paid for these invoices, between the 10th and 31st of October, and mailed these invoices to Beck at his place of business.

The invoices bearing the name of Tempe had at the bottom the following statement: "Accounts due and payable 15th of month following purchase."

General Factors affixed a sticker to each invoice which read as follows: "Pay only to General Factors, Inc., 3500 North Central Avenue, Phoenix, Arizona. This account and the merchandise covered hereby is assigned and payable only to said corporation, to which notice must be given of any merchandise returns or claims of any kind."

And also stamped to the invoice was the following: "To facilitate our accounts receivable bookkeeping, this invoice has been factored with General Factors, Inc., 3500 North Central Building, Suite 332 in Phoenix, Arizona. Make payment directly to factor."

Invoices were received by Beck's bookkeeper and the bookkeeper merely opened the letters and checked the amounts on the invoices to determine any set-offs or "charge-backs." The bookkeeper did not have the authority to draw checks for payment of the invoices or any other accounts. These invoices were not handed to Beck until sometime between the 7th and 15th of November, 1960.

In the meantime, Tempe was experiencing financial difficulties and Beck paid off this account with Tempe.

VOALL, JUSTICE. Thus, the primary issue in this case concerns the question of notice of an assignment under the statutes and laws of the State of Arizona. The pertinent Arizona statute provides as follows:

> If a debtor, *without actual notice* that an assignment of his account has been made, makes full or partial payment of his debt to the assignor, his debt shall thereby be extinguished or reduced. [Emphasis supplied]

The requirement of actual notice in the above statute would seem to import that the notice actually reach the debtor. Otherwise, where the debtor has paid his creditor prior to actual notice, his debt is extinguished or reduced according to the amount paid.

General Factors gave written notice addressed to Beck personally that the account was being factored with them. The invoices were received at Beck's usual place of business by an employee who opened the letters, checked the amount due, and presented at a later date the invoices to Beck for payment.

There is support for the proposition that an agent or clerk ostensibly in charge of the place where the principal's business is carried on has apparent authority to accept notification in relation to the business.

It has been held that an employee in charge of the receipt of mail may accept written notification. The cases split as to the effect of notification served upon bookkeepers.

If the law is to be practical, it must recognize other channels through which notice may be served. The phrase "actual notice" is properly distinguishable from "actual knowledge" and includes notice to an authorized agent as well as generally the communication of any information enabling the recipient to acquire therefrom, by the exercise of reasonable diligence, actual knowledge.

We therefore hold there was actual notice to the debtor under the facts of this case by the notification received by the employee.

Assignor's Liability to Assignee

Implied Warranties. When an assignor assigns a contractual claim for value to an assignee, the assignor impliedly warrants that the claim is a valid claim, that is, that the parties have capacity to contract, that the claim is not void for illegality, and that it has not been discharged prior to the assignment or rendered unenforceable for any reasons known to the assignor. The assignor also impliedly warrants good title to the claim.

If the claim is represented by a written instrument, the assignor impliedly warrants the the instrument is genuine. The assignor also impliedly agrees to do nothing which will defeat or impair the value of the assignment. The assignment does not warrant the solvency of the promisor. These implied warranties may be limited or enlarged by the express agreement of the parties.

General Liability. If, after the assignment of a contract, payment is made to and received by the assignor, he or she holds the money as trustee for the assignee and is liable to the assignee for the money collected. If the assignor makes successive assignments of the same claim to two or more assignees, the assignor is liable to those who acquire no right against the promisor.

SUMMARY

An assignor impliedly warrants that the claim is a valid, subsisting claim and that he will do nothing to defeat or impair the value of the assignment. The assignor does not warrant the solvency of the promisor.

If the assignor collects the assigned claim, he is liable to the assignee for all moneys collected. If the assignor makes successive assignments of the same claim, he is liable to the defrauded assignees.

Third-Party Beneficiary

Classes of Third-Party Beneficiary Contracts. Where the performance of the promise in a contract will benefit some person other than the promisee, the party benefited is a third-party beneficiary. As a general rule a person who is not a party to a contract has no rights in the contract, even though he or she may derive some advantage from its performance. However, if the parties to the contract enter into the contract with the intent of benefiting a third party, the beneficiary under the contract may enforce it by court action. Third-party beneficiaries have been divided into three classes: (1) donee beneficiaries, (2) creditor beneficiaries, and (3) incidental beneficiaries.

Donee Beneficiaries. If the primary purpose of the promisee, in contracting for performance to be rendered to the third person, is to make a gift of the performance to the third person, the third person is a donee beneficiary. If the promisor does not perform the promise, both the promisee and the beneficiary have a cause of action against him. The beneficiary can recover a judgment for the value of the promised performance. The promisee can recover a judgment for any damage suffered as a result of the promisor's failure to render performance to the beneficiary. As a general rule the promisee can recover only nominal damages.

A life insurance contract whereby the insurance company, in consideration of premiums paid, contracts to pay to the named beneficiary the amount of the policy on the happening of a stipulated event, usually the death of the insured, is a common form of the donee beneficiary contract. If the insurance company does not pay on the happening of the contingency, the beneficiary can bring suit and recover a judgment.

Creditor Beneficiaries. A person is a creditor beneficiary if the performance of the promise will satisfy an actual or supposed legal duty of the promisee to the beneficiary. The primary distinction between a donee beneficiary and a creditor beneficiary is that the benefits conferred on the donee beneficiary, are a gift, whereas the performance of the promise in the case of the creditor beneficiary is intended to discharge a duty or supposed duty by the promisee. The duty need not be the payment of money but may be any type of obligation.

For example, Anson buys a car on an installment contract from Sharp Motor Company. Anson then sells the car to Baker and Baker agrees to assume Anson's indebtedness to Sharp as a part of the purchase price. Sharp is a creditor beneficiary of the Baker-Anson agreement and may hold either one or both of them liable on the installment contract. Sharp, of course, can collect no more than the full amount owing on the debt.

Incidental Beneficiaries. An incidental beneficiary is one who will benefit in some way from the performance of a contract which has been entered into by the promisee without any intent of benefiting a third person. The purpose of the contract is to obtain the benefits for the promisee, not for a third person. An incidental beneficiary has no rights in the contract and cannot recover damages in a suit for breach of contract.

For example, suppose Adams contracts with Ball to dig a ditch which will drain a low place on Adams' farm. The low place extends over onto Clark's farm, and the drainage ditch will be of benefit to Clark also.

If Ball then breaches his contract with Adams and does not dig the ditch, Clark will not be allowed to recover damages in an action against Ball for breach of the contract. Although Clark would have benefited from the performance of the contract, he was not a party to the contract, nor was the contract entered into with the intent of benefiting Clark. Clark is an incidental beneficiary and has no rights under the contract.

Municipal or Governmental Contracts. As a general rule the members of the public are incidental beneficiaries of contracts entered into in the regular course of the carrying-on of the functions of the municipality or governmental unit. A member of the public cannot recover a judgment in a suit against the promisor, even though as a taxpayer he or she will suffer some injury from nonperformance. However, a municipality or governmental unit may enter into contracts which have as their objective the protection of the individual members of the public. A member of the public who is injured by breach of such a contract can recover damages.

SUMMARY

A contract may expressly provide that performance shall be rendered to a named third person who is not a party to the contract, or a third person who is not a party to the contract may be benefited by the performance of the contract without being named. Such persons fall into three groups: (1) donee beneficiary, (2) creditor beneficiary, and (3) incidental beneficiary.

If the purpose of the promisee is to make a gift to a named third person of part or all of the performance of the promisor, such third person is a donee beneficiary. If the purpose of the promisee is to impose on the promisor an obligation to pay a debt owed to a third person by the promisee, such third person is a creditor beneficiary. Both donee beneficiary and creditor beneficiary have the right to bring suit on the contract. If a third person will benefit from the performance of the contract without any intent on the part of the promisee to confer such benefits, such person is an incidental beneficiary and has no rights in the contract.

United States v. State Farm Mutual Automobile Ins. Co.

455 F.2d 789 (10th Cir. 1972)

Action by U.S. (plaintiff) against State Farm (defendant). U.S. appealed from trial court judgment for State Farm. Reversed.

On November 24, 1969, Mack was injured in a car accident near Fort Sill, Oklahoma. Mack then owned a State Farm automobile liability insurance policy. He was treated free of any personal cost or expense at Government medical facilities. Such free hospital and medical services for servicemen are prescribed in 10 U.S.C.A. § 1074. The medical expenses incurred by the United States for Sergeant Mack were $1,855.00.

The United States sued State Farm claiming that it is entitled to collect as a third party beneficiary under Mack's State Farm Policy.

The pertinent provisions of the policy are as follows:

COVERAGE C—MEDICAL PAYMENTS

To pay reasonable medical expenses incurred for services furnished within one year from the date of the accident:

Division 1. to *or for* the first *person* named in the declarations . . . who sustains *bodily injury,* caused by accident, while *occupying* the owned motor vehicle. . . .

POLICY CONDITIONS

7. Payment of Claim; Autopsy-Coverages C, M, S, T, and U. Under coverages C and M *the company may pay the injured person or any person or organization rendering the services* and such payment shall reduce the amount payable hereunder. Any payment shall not constitute admission of liability of the insured or, except hereunder, of the company. [Emphasis ours.]

BARRETT, CIRCUIT JUDGE. It is a general rule that where the third-party beneficiaries are so described as to be ascertainable, it is not necessary that they be specifically named in the contract in order to recover thereon and it is not necessary that they are identifiable at the time the contract is made.

In *United States v. United Services Automobile Association,* the minor son of an Air Force officer was injured by a car and was treated free of cost at Government facilities. The United States and the officer sued the officer's insurance company under the medical payments provision of the policy. The policy required the insurance company to pay all reasonable medical expenses incurred within a year of any accident to or for the named insured. It also provided, as in the State Farm policy, that the Company may pay any person or organization rendering the services for the insured. The Court found that the United States was entitled to sue and recover as a third-party beneficiary.

We hold that the United States qualifies as a third-party beneficiary under the policy in that it is an "organization rendering the services."

"Organization" is defined as a corporation, government or governmental subdivision or agency. Where a contract creates a right or imposes a duty in favor of a third party, the law presumes that the parties intended to confer a benefit on the party and allows the party a remedy.

The United States is entitled to recover from State Farm for the reasonable value of those medical services it rendered to Sergeant Mack. To hold otherwise we must ignore the clear language of the policy, thus granting State Farm a windfall represented by that portion of Sergeant Mack's premium payments for coverage which, under the facts of this case, State Farm, in effect, contends he really did not need. . . .

Assignment under the Uniform Commercial Code

Main Provisions. The main provisions relative to the assignment of contracts for the sale of goods are to be found in Section 2–210 of the Code. This section provides that duties may be delegated unless the other party has a "substantial interest" in having the original party perform or control the acts required in the sales contract. All rights are assignable except where the assignment would "materially" change the duties of the obligor or "materially" increase risks. A right to damages for breach of a sales contract may be assigned despite an agreement prohibiting any assignment. Unless the circumstances indicate a contrary intent, a clause prohibiting assignment of a contract will be construed as barring only the delegation of duties. An assignment of "all of my rights" normally will operate as a delegation of duties. The other party may treat any assignment which also delegates duties as grounds for demanding assurances from the assignor. Until the assurances of due performance are made the other party may, if commercially reasonable, suspend any performance for which he has not received the agreed return.

SUMMARY

In general, contract rights are assignable under the U.C.C. A right to damages for breach of a sales contract may be assigned despite terms in the contract prohibiting any assignment. Rights cannot be assigned where such assignment materially changes the duties of the obligor or materially increases risks. Duties may be delegated in some contracts but the person delegating the duties remains liable.

First National Bank of Elgin v. Husted

205 N.E.2d 780 (Ct. App. Ill. 1965)

This was an action brought by First National Bank (plaintiff) against Husted (defendant) to recover payments due on a car purchase installment contract which Husted had entered with Reed Motors. Reed Motors assigned the contract to First National Bank.

The contract provided: "Buyer agrees to settle all claims against Seller directly with Seller and will not set up any such claims against Seller as defense, counterclaim, set off, cross-complaint or otherwise in any action for the purchase price or possession brought by any assignee of this contract."

DAVIS, JUSTICE. The Uniform Commercial Code provides:

(1) Subject to any statute or decision which establishes a different rule for buyers of consumer goods, an agreement by a buyer that he will not assert against an assignee any claim or defense which he may have against the seller is enforceable by an assignee who takes his assignment for value, in good faith and without notice of a claim or defense, except as to defenses of a type which may be asserted against a holder in due course of a negotiable instrument under the Article on Commercial Paper. (Article 3). A buyer who as part of one transaction signs both a negotiable instrument and a security agreement makes such an agreement.

The first sentence of this subsection permits a contractual waiver of certain defenses by the buyer, and it is in accord with prior Illinois case law. While this section provides that either the legislature or the courts may establish a different rule, we view this as a legislative function, the exercise of will rather than judgment, and we are reluctant to change the prior decisional law.

The defenses which may be asserted against a holder in due course are:

a. infancy, to the extent that it is a defense to a simple contract; and
b. such other incapacity, or duress, or illegality of the transaction, as renders the obligation of the party a nullity; and
c. such misrepresentation as has induced the party to sign the instrument with neither knowledge nor reasonable knowledge nor reasonable opportunity to obtain knowledge of its character or its essential terms; and
d. discharge in insolvency proceedings; and
e. any other discharge of which the holder has notice when he takes the instrument (3–305[2]).

Thus, a buyer may contractually waive, as against an assignee, any defenses except those enumerated in articles [Sections] 3–305(2) and 9–206(2). In absence of allegation in Husted's affidavit that First National Bank did not take the assignment for value, in good faith, and without notice of claim or defense, and in view of the date of the contract and assignment, we believe that First National Bank is an assignee for value, in good faith, and without notice of claim or defense.

The buyers' defenses of failure of consideration, and subsequent promise and failure to repair the car were waived, as against First National Bank.

Problem Cases

1. Davis owned a tract of land which contained mineral deposits which he sold to Basalt Rock Co. As part of the consideration for the conveyance of the land to it, Basalt Rock Co. agreed that over a period of 60 years it would sell to Davis "as he may require, such amount of basalt of any size for plastering purposes" at an agreed price. The contract further provided that "the price is based on a blend of basalt in accordance with the formula attached." The contract gave Davis the right to change the formula and provided for price adjustments to compensate for the changes. Davis assigned the contract to Soule and Basalt Rock Co. refused to recognize the assignment and refused to make deliveries to Soule. Soule sued Basalt Rock Co. for damages for breach of contract and Basalt Rock

Co. set up as a defense that the contract was not an assignable contract. Is the contract assignable?

2. Newman contracted to sell all of the eggs produced to Sunrise Eggs Co. Newman then gave Crosby a written assignment of the proceeds of this contract. Sunrise knew of this assignment, but ignored it and made payments to Crosby only when Newman told Sunrise to do so, making all other payments directly to Newman. Newman failed to pay $17,000 of the assigned proceeds delivered by Sunrise. Crosby sued Sunrise for this amount. Can Crosby collect?

3. Smith, owner of an apartment complex, sold individual units. Each purchaser was required to pay an extra $15 per month for utilities, taxes, and insurance. Smith sold these interests to Roberts and conveyed the entire contracts by way of assignment. Roberts failed to pay the applicable property tax. Radley, a purchasing tenant, sues Roberts to compel the payment of the property tax. Roberts claims that in purchasing Smith's interests, all that was bought was the right to collect the payments made by tenants; Roberts had no intention of assuming the burdens. Is Roberts liable for the property tax?

4. Murray contracted with the McDonald Construction Co. to build an addition to his building. The contract required McDonald Construction to build the addition within 75 days. It took 239 days to finish the project. Queen Ann News, Inc., the would-be tenant in the new addition, sued McDonald for damages resulting from the delay. Assuming that McDonald was aware that Queen Ann News was going to be the tenant in the addition at the time the contract was signed, should it be liable for damages to Queen Ann News?

5. Wiscombe Painting and Sandblasting Co. was a member of the Decorating Association of America, which had signed a collective bargaining agreement with the Decorators and Paperhangers of America, Local 77. Wiscombe was bound by Section V of the contract to make contributions to an apprenticeship trust fund on behalf of its employees. Section I of the agreement provided:

   > The Association recognizes the Union as the bargaining representative of all the employees employed by its contractor members wherever such employees are performing work covered by this agreement.

   Wiscombe contributed to the trust on behalf of only its employees who belonged to Local 77. To force Wiscombe to contribute to the trust for its nonunion employees also, the trustee of the fund brought suit against Wiscombe claiming a breach of Sections I and V of the contract. Wiscombe's defense is that only Local 77, not the trustee, can attempt to enforce the contract. Is Wiscombe correct?

6. Bilich, a contractor, entered into a contract with Reliable Trucking Co., whereby Bilich agreed to install designated sewer lines for Reliable Trucking Co. and Reliable Trucking Co. agreed that they would have Barnett prepare survey lines and grade sheets covering the work that was to be done by Bilich for Reliable Trucking Co. Barnett prepared survey lines and grade sheets and submitted them to Bilich. The grade sheets were negligently prepared and were an inaccurate representation of the grade lines on the property. Bilich relied on the grade sheets and discovered, on the completion of the grading, that the excavation was not as it should have been according to plans and specifications. As a result of the errors, Bilich was required to fill in part of the excavation and incur additional expenditures of $382. Bilich sued Barnett to recover a judgment of $382 on the theory that Bilich was a third-party beneficiary of the contract between Reliable Trucking Co. and Barnett. Is Bilich a third-party beneficiary of the contract?

7. Clancy owned a building which he leased to ABC Corp. ABC was in reality owned and its stock controlled by Arnold Corp. Rental payments were made to Clancy by ABC, and Clancy was not aware of the ABC-Arnold relationship. Clancy did not keep the building in proper repair as required by the lease agreement. Arnold Corp. sued Clancy for damages, on the theory that Arnold Corp. was a third-party beneficiary to the lease agreement. May Arnold Corp. maintain the action?
8. Auto-Lite Co. entered into a collective bargaining agreement with Metal Polishers Union. According to this agreement: (1) 8 consecutive hours except for lunch constituted a "normal" work day and 40 hours of five consecutive days (Monday-Friday) constituted a "normal" work week; (2) when a reduction in the work force becomes necessary, probationary employees were to be laid off first followed by others according to seniority to maintain "normal" work days and weeks.

   Auto-Lite's chief customer cut its orders severely; and, as a result, the company decided to cut production to a four-day week without a reduction in work force. Wesley, third man in seniority in the Union was laid off for seven consecutive Fridays as was the rest of the work force. Wesley sued for wages lost in violation of the bargaining agreements. Can Wesley collect?

15

Performance and Remedies

Conditions

Nature of Conditions. As a general rule the duty of performance arises at the time the contract is entered into although the time of the performance of the duty does not arise until some future date. The parties may provide in their contract that no duty to perform shall arise until the happening of some future, uncertain event. Such a provision is a condition precedent. Likewise, the parties may provide in their contract that on the happening of some future, uncertain event the party on whom is imposed the duty of performance will be relieved of that duty. Such a provision is a condition subsequent.

In some contracts the terms of the contract and the accompanying circumstances are such that the courts will imply a provision that the parties will perform simultaneously. Such an implied provision is a concurrent condition.

Creation of Conditions. A condition in a contract is, as a general rule, created by an express provision in the contract. Although no particular language need be used to create a condition, a conditional clause will, as a general rule, be introduced by words such as "provided that," "on condition that," "if," "when," "while," "after," or "as soon as."

Conditions may also be implied from the nature of the performance promised. If a person contracts to unload the cargo of a ship which is at sea, there is an implied condition that the ship will arrive in port.

Concurrent conditions are usually implied by law. In a contract to sell for cash, the law implies concurrent conditions, that is, the seller's duty to deliver the goods is conditioned on the buyer's tender of the purchase price, and the buyer's duty to pay the purchase price is conditioned on the seller's tendering delivery of the goods. If neither party makes a tender within a reasonable time, both are discharged from their duty under the contract.

Independent Promises. In many contracts the promises are independent;

the duty of one of the parties to perform is not conditioned on the happening of any event or on the other party's tender of performance. In all contract situations, if one of the parties is guilty of a material breach of the contract, the injured party will be discharged from the duty to perform. The effect of a breach of contract will be discussed later in this chapter under "Performance and Breach."

SUMMARY

A condition in a contract is a stipulation that on the happening of some future, uncertain event the promisor will owe a duty of performance—a condition precedent—or will be relieved from an existing duty—a condition subsequent. A concurrent condition requires simultaneous performance by the parties. Conditions may be created by express promises or by implication, or may be implied by law.

Clarkson v. Wirth

481 P.2d 920 (Ct. App. Wash. 1971)

Action by Clarkson (plaintiff), a real estate broker, against Wirth (defendant) to recover a commission. Clarkson appealed from an adverse judgment. Affirmed.

Wirth signed an exclusive listing contract which gave Clarkson the right to sell certain real estate for a period of 30 days. Clarkson asked for and received a verbal extension of this listing and finally on July 20, 1965, arranged to have Grimnes and Wirth sign an earnest money agreement which contained the following provision:

> This offer to purchase is made subject to purchasers disposing of certain properties upon which deals are now pending and said deals to be closed prior to the closing of this deal. Legal description of these properties will be furnished sellers upon request. Sale to be closed not later than October 1st, 1965.

All parties to the contract understood the down payment of $30,000 would have to come from the proceeds of those properties owned by the purchasers, upon which deals were then pending. Clarkson agreed to aid the Grimnes brothers in selling their property. He attempted to do so by advertising their property to other brokers but was unable to generate a sale by October 1, 1965.

In April, 1966, the Grimnes brother, learning that the Wirth property had not yet been sold, and still being interested, joined with two other men in an offer to purchase the Wirth property. The parties negotiated the sale without the benefit of Clarkson's services, and the sale was closed on August 26, 1966.

Upon learning of this sale Clarkson brought suit for a commission.

EVANS, JUDGE. Clarkson is not entitled to any commission from Wirth in that the earnest money agreement entered into between Clarkson and Grimnes is unenforceable for two reasons: (*a*) The offer to purchase was made subject to the purchasers disposing of certain properties on which deals were then pending with said deals to be closed prior to the closing of the transaction contained in the earnest money agreement, said transactions never being closed; and (*b*) The offer to sell and the offer to purchase were clearly made subject to the condition that the sale was to have been closed not later than October 1, 1965.

Any words which express, when properly interpreted, the idea that the performance of a promise is dependent on some other event will create a condition. Phrases and words such as "on condition," "provided that," "so that," "when," "while," "after," or "as soon as" are often used.

It is clear from the evidence that it was the understanding of Grimnes as purchaser, and Wirth as seller, that performance by the purchasers was conditioned upon the sale of the Grimnes property by October 1, 1965.

Clarkson contends, however, that he obtained the Grimnes . . . as purchaser, and his offer was accepted by Wirth, and even though the Grimnes . . . was unable to obtain adequate financing to purchase before October 1, 1965, Clarkson was still entitled to his commission upon execution of the earnest money agreement. Clarkson bases this contention upon the holding in *Dryden v. Vincent D. Miller, Inc.*, where the court stated:

> We have held that, when a real-estate broker has procured a prospective purchaser who is accepted by the seller, and the seller promises to pay the broker a certain commission for services rendered, the broker has earned the commission, and the promise to pay it may be enforced.

In *White & Bollard, Inc. v. Goodenow,* the court made the following observation concerning the above stated rule in *Dryden:*

> Implicit in this rule is the requirement that the purchaser be willing to purchase, and that in contracting with the seller, he has agreed to purchase the property. Here we do not have such an unqualified promise, but rather a conditional promise, and the respondent's right to collect his fee was also made conditional upon the purchaser's obtaining satisfactory financing. *The securing of such financing was a condition precedent. Until it has occurred, the respondent was not obliged to sell, and the purchaser was not obliged to buy the property, and the appellant was not entitled to its fee.*

Architects' and Engineers' Certificates

Requirement of Certificate. The building or construction contracts in common use usually contain a clause making the payments provided for in the contract conditional on the production of the certificate of a named architect or engineer. The courts enforce such a provision and will deny the contractor the right to recover in a suit on the contract unless he produces the certificate or can excuse his failure to produce it.

When Failure to Produce Certificate Is Excused. Failure to produce the certificate is excused by showing that the named architect or engineer is dead, insane, or otherwise incapacitated and cannot issue the certificate, or that the certificate is fraudulently, collusively, or arbitrarily withheld; and in some instances the courts have excused the production of the certificate if it can be shown that the withholding is unreasonable. As a general rule, if the architect or engineer is acting honestly and has some reason for withholding the certificate, the courts will not allow a recovery unless it is produced. The parties have contracted for the expert judgment of the named architect or engineer, and if he has exercised that judgment honestly, the courts will not substitute their judgment for that of the architect or engineer and hold that the architect or engineer is mistaken or that his decision is incorrect. If a mistake has been made in computation, the courts will correct it.

SUMMARY

When a contract makes the production of an architect's or engineer's certificate a condition precedent to payment, the certificate must be produced before a duty of immediate payment arises. However, the death or incapacitating illness of a named architect or the fraudulent or unjustified withholding of the certificate will excuse the failure to produce the certificate.

Performance and Breach

Duty of Performance. A promisor is obligated to perform as promised. In attempting to solve the problems relative to the performance of contractual obligations, the courts have attempted to set up practical, workable standards. As a general rule, they recognize three degrees of performance: (1) complete or satisfactory performance, (2) substantial performance, and (3) material breach.

Complete or Satisfactory Performance. Some types of contractual obligations can be completely performed; others cannot. Such obligations as the payment of money, delivery of a deed, and, in some instances, the delivery of goods can be performed either exactly or to a high degree of perfection, whereas such obligations as the erection of a building, the construction of a road, the cultivation of a crop, and many similar obligations cannot be performed without some slight deviation from perfection, due to the limitations of human ability.

Substantial Performance. Substantial performance is a degree of perfection of performance which is slightly below that of complete or satisfactory performance. If the promisor has made an honest effort to perform but, due to lack of ability or other reasons beyond promisor's control, has deviated in some slight degree from accepted standards, and if, in addition, the consideration given to the promisee is such that it cannot be returned to the promisor, the courts will hold that the promisor has substantially performed the contract. The promisor will, as a general rule, be entitled to the contract price less any damage the promisee has suffered as a result of the defective performance. Each case involving substantial performance must be decided on the basis of the facts of that individual case.

Material Breach. The promisor will be guilty of a material breach of contract if performance or tendered performance fails to reach that degree of perfection which the promisee is justified in expecting under the circumstances. If the promisor has materially breached the contract, the promisor has no right of action on the contract, unless the promisee has accepted the defective performance without objection.

If one party notifies the other in advance that he has no intention of carrying out his part of the contract, the party so notified may take such party at his word and look elsewhere so as to protect himself. Under this "anticipatory breach" doctrine the party notifying of his intention to breach will remain liable for damages suffered by the other party.

Prevention of Performance. The promisee owes a duty to cooperate with the promisor in the performance of the contract. The extent of the promisee's duty to cooperate will depend on the subject matter of the contract and the surrounding circumstances. If the promisee fails to cooperate or if the promisee is guilty of affirmative acts which materially hinder or delay performance, the promisee will be guilty of a material breach of the contract, and the promisor will be relieved of a duty of further performance.

Time Is of the Essence. The time in which the promisor is to complete performance may not be expressly stated in the contract. If no time for performance is expressly stated or implied, the courts will hold that performance must be completed within a reasonable time. What is a reasonable time is a question of fact and must be determined from all the surrounding circumstances. If the time for performance is stated or implied in the contract, the promisor's failure to perform within the allotted time is a breach of the contract.

Under some circumstances a failure to perform on time will be held to be a material breach on the part of the promisor, and such breach will relieve the promisee of the duty of reciprocal performance. If failure to perform on time is a material breach of the contract, then "time is of the essence" of the contract. The contract may expressly stipulate that time is of the essence of the contract, in which case the courts will enforce the provision, unless enforcement would impose on the promisor an unjust and burdensome penalty. If the circumstances are such that the promisee will derive little or no benefit from late performance, the courts will hold that time is of the essence of the contract even though the contract does not expressly so provide.

If time is not of the essence of the contract, the promisee will be required to accept late performance, provided performance is completed within a reasonable time after that stipulated in the contract. If the promisee has suffered an injury as the result of a delay in performance, promisee is entitled to set off against the contract price the loss suffered.

Performance to Personal Satisfaction. The promisor may obligate oneself to perform to the personal satisfaction of the promisee. Such contracts fall into two categories: (1) those situations in which personal taste and comfort are involved, and (2) those situations in which mechanical fitness or suitability for a particular purpose is involved.

If personal taste and comfort are involved, the promisee has the right to reject the performance without liability to the promisor, if the promisee is honestly dissatisfied with the performance rendered or tendered.

If mechanical fitness or suitability is involved, the court will apply the "reasonable man" test; and if the court holds that a reasonable person would be satisfied with the performance rendered or tendered, the promisee must accept the performance and pay the contract price.

Good Faith Performance under the U.C.C. The Code (1–203) provides that every contract or duty within its provisions imposes an obligation of *good faith* in its performance or enforcement. One legal scholar defines this obligation of good faith as:

> . . . an implied term of the contract requiring cooperation on the part of one party to the contract so that another party will not be deprived of his reasonable expectations.[1]

At common law buyers and sellers dealt at "arms' length." Just how great a departure from the common law this adoption of "good faith" duties represents, is yet to be determined by the courts.

SUMMARY

A promisor is obligated to perform as promised. Since performance may range from perfection to no performance at all, the courts recognize three stages of perfection of performance: (1) complete or satisfactory performance, (2) substantial performance, and (3) material breach. Complete or satisfactory

[1] Farnsworth, "Good Faith Performance and Commercial Reasonableness under the Uniform Commercial Code," 30 *Chicago L. R.* 666, 669 (1963).

performance is performance up to accepted standards; substantial performance falls short of complete performance only in minor respects, and the promisee is not deprived of a material part of the consideration bargained for. The promisor is guilty of material breach if his or her performance is defective in some major respect.

If the performance is complete or satisfactory, the promisor is entitled to the contract price; if substantial, the promisor is entitled to the contract price less damage resulting from defects. If guilty of a material breach, the promisor cannot recover on the contract but may be entitled to some recovery in a suit in quasi contract.

The promisor may be relieved from duty of performance by an implied condition precedent, by impossibility, or by interference on the part of the promisee.

If time is of the essence of a contract, failure to perform within the permitted time is a material breach of the contract, and such breach will relieve the promisee from obligations under the contract. If time is not of the essence, the promisee must accept late performance, if completed within a reasonable time. The promisee, however, is entitled to compensation for injury suffered because of the delay.

If personal taste and comfort of the promisee are involved, the promisee need not accept performance if honestly dissatisfied. If fitness or utility is involved, the "reasonable man" test is applied. The Code imposes a broad obligation to perform in "good faith" on all contracts and duties within the Code.

Kole v. Parker Yale Development Co.

536 P.2d 848 (Col. Ct. App. 1975)

Kole (plaintiff) sued to have a contract to purchase a condominium unit to be built by Parker Yale (defendant) rescinded. Judgment for Kole and Parker Yale appealed. Reversed and remanded.

Kole entered into a contract with Parker Yale for the construction and sale of a condominium unit. The contract provided for completion of the unit within 180 days. The contract also provided that Kole could make written changes in the plans and specifications during construction of the unit. The construction was not completed within the 180-day period, and Kole then sent a letter to Parker Yale rescinding the contract prior to the completion of the unit. No certificate of occupancy had been issued on the date of the attempted rescission.

KELLY, JUDGE. Rescission may be granted where the facts show, among other things, that there was a substantial breach, or that the injury caused by the breach is irreparable, or that damages would be inadequate, difficult, or impossible to assess. However, it is not a proper remedy for a mere variance from the terms of the contract.

There is no evidence that the parties intended the 180-day completion clause to be a time of the essence clause in the contract, and except for the completion clause itself, the contract is silent on the subject. Time is not of the essence of a contract unless it is made so by express provisions in the contract or by the facts of the case. A completion requirement in a building contract is ordinarily construed as providing the buyer with a remedy in damages for breach of contract in lieu of strict performance. In the contract at issue, the very presence of provisions in the contract authorizing the buyer to make changes in the plans during the progress of the work supports the interpretation that the parties did not intend time to be of the essence, and this is so, whether or not the buyer exercises the right.

Here there was neither evidence of a substantial breach, nor evidence of any injury or damages caused by the delay, and the trial court made no such findings. The attempted rescission was legally ineffective.

Impossibility of Performance

Nature of Impossibility. The common law legal concept of impossibility is narrower than the popular concept. Impossibility means: "It cannot be done," not "I cannot do it." If a person contracts to perform an obligation, inability to perform or intervening hardship will not discharge the obligation. The promisor who fails to perform will be liable to the promisee for any injury resulting from such failure.

Traditionally, the courts have recognized three situations in which the promisor will be discharged from failure to perform on the ground of impossibility: (1) incapacitating illness or death of the promisor, (2) intervening illegality, and (3) destruction of the subject matter essential to performance. In addition, some courts have recognized a fourth ground for discharging the promisor from the obligation: commercial impracticality—often referred to as the doctrine of *commercial frustration.* This impracticality standard has been adopted for sale of goods contracts under the U.C.C.

Types of Impossibility

Traditional Types. Death terminates a contract for personal service but usually does not affect other types of contracts. Whether illness will justify termination of the contract will depend on the nature of the work, the term of the employment, the seriousness of the illness, and the duration or probable duration of the illness.

Before a statute or governmental regulation can be used to excuse nonperformance, it must be such that the performance of the contract will be illegal. A statute or governmental regulation which makes performance more difficult or less profitable will not excuse the promisor from performance on the ground of impossibility.

Destruction of the subject matter which is essential to the performance of the contract will excuse the promisor from performance. Destruction of subject matter which the promisor expects to make use of in the performance of the contract but which is not essential to the performance of the contract will not be an excuse for nonperformance.

Commercial Impracticality. Some courts have extended the scope of impossibility to include those cases in which performance by the promisor would be impractical due to unforeseen developments having made performance of no value to the promisee. Other courts have included in the scope of impossibility cases in which the cost of performance to the promisor would be great, due to some extreme or unreasonable difficulty, expense, injury, or loss, and the benefits to the promisee would be of little or no value. The trend appears to be in the direction of relaxing the strict common law stance in regard to excuses for nonperformance.

The Uniform Commercial Code (2–615) adopts less rigorous standards for excusing nonperformance of sales of goods contracts. Nonperformance is excused if the performance as agreed has been made "impracticable by the occurrence of a contingency the nonoccurrence of which was a basic assumption on which the contract was made or by compliance in good faith with any applicable foreign or domestic governmental regulation or order." The Code further provides, however, that if the contingency affects only a part of the seller's capacity to perform, the seller must allocate production and deliveries among customers in a "fair and reasonable" manner.[2] The seller is also required to give buyers reasonable notice of any delay and of any limited allocation of the goods.

SUMMARY

Impossibility of performance should be distinguished from inability to perform. The impossibility must arise after the contract is entered into, and it must be due to the nature of the thing to be done. Impossibility of performance arises in three situations: (1) incapacitating illness or death of promisor if contract requires performance of personal service, (2) intervening statutes or governmental regulation making performance illegal, and (3) destruction

[2] See Chapter 38 for additional treatment of this area.

of subject matter essential to the performance of the contract without fault of either party.

Courts also excuse performance under the doctrine of commercial frustration. The U.C.C. adopts less rigorous standards for excusing nonperformance of sale of goods contracts.

La Gasse Pool Const. Co. v. City of Fort Lauderdale

288 So.2d 273 (Dis. Ct. App. Fla. 1974)

Suit by La Gasse (plaintiff) against Fort Lauderdale (defendant) for costs in redoing part of pool. La Gasse appealed from a judgment for the city. Affirmed.

La Gasse contracted to repair and renovate a city swimming pool and had completed most of the work when vandals damaged the pool so badly one night that a large part of the work had to be completely redone. La Gasse sued for compensation for the extra work.

DOWNEY, JUDGE. The general rule is that under an indivisible contract to build an entire structure, loss or damage thereto during construction falls upon the contractor, the theory being that the contractor obligated himself to build an entire structure and absent a delivery thereof he has not performed his contract. If his work is damaged or destroyed during construction he is still able to perform by rebuilding the damaged or destroyed part; in other words, doing the work over again.

In the case of contracts to repair, renovate, or perform work on existing structures, the general rule is that total destruction of the subject matter of the contract, without fault of either the contractor or owner, excuses performance by the contractor and entitles him to recover for the value of the work done. The rationale of this rule is that the contract has an implied condition that the structure will remain in existence so the contractor can render performance. Destruction of the structure makes performance impossible and thereby excuses the contractor's nonperformance. But where the building or structure to be repaired is not destroyed, but the contractor's work is damaged so that it must be redone, performance is still possible, and it is the contractor's responsibility to redo the work so as to complete his undertaking. In other words, absent impossibility of performance or some other reason for lawful nonperformance, the contractor must perform his contract. Any loss or damage to his work during the process of repairs which can be rectified is his responsibility. The reason for allowing recovery without full performance in the case of total destruction (i.e., impossibility of performance) is absent where the structure remains and simply requires duplicating the work.

Parker v. Arthur Murray, Inc.

295 N.E.2d 487 (Ct. App. Ill. 1973)

Parker (plaintiff) sued to have dancing lesson contracts he had signed with Arthur Murray, Inc. (defendant) rescinded. Judgment for Parker and Arthur Murray appealed. Affirmed.

In November, 1959, Parker went to the Arthur Murray Studio in Oak Park to redeem a certificate entitling him to three free dancing lessons. At that time he was a 37-year-old college-educated bachelor who lived alone in a one-room attic apartment in Berwyn, Illinois. During the free lessons the instructor told Parker he had "exceptional potential to be a fine and accomplished dancer" and generally encouraged further participation. Parker thereupon signed a contract for 75 hours of lessons at a cost of $1,000. At the bottom of the contract were the bold-type words, **"Non-cancellable Negotiable Contract."** This initial encounter set the pattern for the future relationship between the parties. Parker attended lessons regularly. He was praised and encouraged regularly by the instructors, despite his lack of progress. Contract extensions and new contracts for additional instructional hours were executed. Each contained the bold-type words, **"Non-cancellable Contract."** Some of the agreements also contained the bold-type statement, **"I Understand that no Refunds Will be Made under the Terms of this Contract."**

On September 24, 1961, Parker was severely injured in an automobile collision, rendering him incapable of continuing his dancing lessons. At that time he had contracted for a total of 2,734 hours of lessons, for which he had paid $24,812.80.

STAMOS, PRESIDING JUDGE. Parker was granted rescission on the ground of impossibility of performance. The applicable legal doctrine is expressed in the *Restatement Contracts,* §§ 459, as follows:

> A duty that requires for its performance action that can be rendered only by the promisor or some other particular person is discharged by his death or by such illness as makes the necessary action by him impossible or seriously injurious to his health, unless the contract indicates a contrary intention or there is contributing fault on the part of the person subject to the duty.

In Illinois impossibility of performance was recognized as a ground for rescission in *Davies v. Arthur Murray,* wherein the court nonetheless found for the defendant because of the plaintiff's failure adequately to prove the existence of an incapacitating disability.

Authur Murray does not deny that the doctrine of impossibility of performance is generally applicable to the case at bar. Rather they assert that certain contract provisions bring this case within the *Restatement's* limitation that the doctrine is inapplicable if "the contract indicates a contrary intention." It is contended that such bold type phrases as **"Non-cancellable Contract,"**

"Non-cancellable Negotiable Contract" and **"I Understand that No Refunds Will Be Made under the Terms of this Contract"** manifested the parties mutual intent to waive their respective rights to invoke the doctrine of impossibility. This is a construction which we find unacceptable. Courts engage in the construction and interpretation of contracts with the sole aim of determining the intention of the parties. We need rely on no construction aids to conclude that plaintiff never contemplated that by signing a contract with such terms as **"Non-cancellable"** and **"No Refunds"** he was waiving a remedy expressly recognized by Illinois courts. Were we also to refer to established tenets of contractual construction, this conclusion would be equally compelled. An ambiguous contract will be construed most strongly against the party who drafted it. Exceptions or reservations in a contract will, in case of doubt or ambiguity, be construed least favorably to the party claiming the benefit of the exceptions or reservations. Although neither party to a contract should be relieved from performance on the ground that good business judgment was lacking, a court will not place upon language a ridiculous construction. We conclude that Parker did not waive his right to assert the doctrine of impossibility.

Discharge

Nature of Discharge. A contract is discharged where the parties to the contract are released from all obligations of the contract, and in the majority of contractual transactions this is brought about by complete performance by the parties to the contract.

Earlier in this chapter, the discharge of a contract by the occurrence or nonoccurrence of a condition precedent or subsequent, by material breach, and by impossibility of performance was discussed. A contract may also be discharged by agreement. The agreement may be in the form of a mutual agreement to cancel, a rescission, an agreement to forego rights, a substitute contract, a novation, or a waiver. Under some circumstances a contract may be discharged or the right of action to enforce the contract may be barred by operation of law.

Discharge by Agreement A contract is created by the mutual agreement of the parties, and it may be discharged in like manner, unless rights of third parties will be involved. Any agreement to discharge a party to a contract from obligations under the contract must be supported by consideration if such agreement is to effect a discharge. Mutual promises to rescind an executory contract will make the rescission valid since such an agreement is supported by consideration, in that both parties surrender their rights under the contract.

Waiver. A party to a contract may voluntarily relinquish a right which the party has under the contract. Such a relinquishment is known as a "waiver." If one party tenders an incomplete performance and the other party accepts such defective performance without objection, knowing that the defects will not be remedied, the accepting party will have waived the right to strict performance. The party who wishes to insist on strict performance should object to the incomplete or defective performance. In any instance in which performance is defective, notice should be given within a reasonable time that the defects must be remedied or damages will be claimed. If failure to give notice will justify a belief that strict performance will not be claimed, failure to give notice will amount to a waiver.

Discharge by Alteration. If a party to a written instrument intentionally alters it in any material respect, the other party to the instrument is discharged from all duties. If the instrument is altered by one not a party to it and without the knowledge and consent of either of the contracting parties, the alteration does not affect the rights of the parties. If an alteration is made by one of the contracting parties with the consent of the other contracting party, or if the other contracting party consents to the alteration after she learns of it, the party consenting to the alteration is not discharged from her duties.

Discharge by Statute of Limitations. From the earliest times the courts have refused to grant a remedy to one who has delayed an unreasonable time in bringing suit. In modern times the various states have by statute declared that an action must be brought within a stated time after the action accrues. Such statutes are known as "statutes of limitations."

The time limit for bringing suit for breach of contracts differs in the various states, and in many states the statutes distinguish between oral contracts and written contracts; for example, in Indiana the time limit for bringing suit on an oral contract is six years, whereas on a contract in writing it is ten years. In Illinois the time limit is five years on oral contracts and ten on written contracts. The time is computed from the time the cause of action accrues.

If one is incapacitated or beyond the jurisdiction of the court, the time during which the incapacity continues, or the time during which one is beyond the jurisdiction of the court is not, by the terms of many statutes, counted in computing the statutory time for bringing suit.

Uniform Commercial Code. The Code provides "any claim or right arising out of an alleged breach can be discharged in whole or in part without consideration by a written waiver or renunciation signed and delivered by the aggrieved party." (Section 1–107.)

Sections 2–309 (2) (3) are the only parts of the Code which specifically treat termination rights and liabilities. Subsection (2) states that where a contract "provides for successive performances but is indefinite in duration it is valid for a reasonable time but unless otherwise agreed may be terminated at any time by either party." Subsection (3) "provides termination of a contract by one party except on the happening of an agreed event requires that reasonable notification be received by the other party and any agreement dispensing with notification is invalid if its operation would be unconscionable."

Comment 7 to Subsection (2) by the editorial board which drafted the Code states that when an arrangement has been carried on over many years the reasonable time "can continue indefinitely and the contract will not terminate until notice." Comment 8 to Subsection (3) states that this subsection:

> . . . recognizes that the application of principles of good faith and sound commercial practice normally call for such notification of the termination of a going contract relationship as will give the other party reasonable time to seek a substitute arrangement. An agreement dispensing with notification or limiting the time for the seeking of a substitute arrangement is, of course, valid under this subsection unless the results of putting it into operation would be the creation of an unconscionable state of affairs.

Comment 10 states: ". . . The requirement of notification is dispensed with where the contract provides for termination on the happening of an 'agreed event.' 'Event' is a term chosen here to contrast with 'option' or the like."

The Code (2–725) stipulates a four-year statute of limitations for contracts involving the sale of goods.

SUMMARY

A contract is discharged when the parties to a contract are released from their obligations under the contract. A contract is generally discharged by performance. The promisor is generally discharged from his or her duty to perform by a material breach of the contract, by the failure of the event to occur, which event has been stipulated in a condition precedent, by the occurrence of the event stipulated in a condition subsequent, or by impossibility. A contract may be discharged by mutual agreement, rescission, substitute contract, novation, or waiver. Under some circumstances a contract may be discharged by operation of law.

The Code requires that reasonable notification be given where sales of goods contracts provide for successive performances but are of indefinite duration. Any agreement dispensing with notification is invalid if its operation would be unconscionable.

Franchises

Termination of Franchises. A franchise system has been defined in marketing-management terms as an organization composed of distributive units established and administered by a supplier as a medium for expanding and controlling the marketing of its products. It is an integrated business system. Franchised dealers are legally independent but economically dependent units of the system.

The franchise approach offers a supplier a highly effective means of gaining rapid market expansion with minimum capital outlay. The growth rate and profitability of many franchise systems has been fantastic. Since most franchised dealers have the major investment in their outlets strong profit and loss incentives are present.

The franchise method of distribution first gained national recognition and success in the automobile industry. The standard form of franchise contract formerly used by automobile manufacturers did not require the dealer to whom the franchise was given to represent the manufacturer for any specified period of time nor did it provide that the dealer would purchase any automobiles. These franchises provided that either party could cancel on relatively short notice "with or without cause" or on causes left to the sole judgment of the franchisor. Many franchises currently used in other industries were modeled after automobile dealer franchises.

Until recent times the courts, with few exceptions, ruled that such franchises were not enforceable as contracts.[3] This strict-enforcement-of-contracts approach allows franchisors to exercise a maximum of control over their franchisees with a minimum of legal risks. Franchisees failing to follow policies can be canceled or threatened with cancellation, and those with highly specialized investments in particular franchises can ill-afford to have their franchise canceled.

After extensive hearings concerning the one-sided nature of automobile dealer franchises, Congress in 1956 enacted legislation imposing liability on manufacturers of automobiles if they exercise coercion against a dealer to the damage of the dealer.[4] The U.C.C. (1–203) requires the exercise of "good faith" in franchise relationships involving the sale of goods. In addition, Section 2–309 of the Code requires the giving of reasonable notice of termination of a sales contract which provides for successive performances but is indefinite as to duration. An agreement dispensing with notice will not be enforced if it is unconscionable.

The trend in contract law, particularly in franchise relationships, appears to be away from the strict and technical application of the rules of contract law relative to consideration and requirements of definiteness. Rights may be granted even though, from a technical standpoint, the contract or franchise may be indefinite or lacking in consideration, or may have been canceled or not renewed.[5]

---

[3] See the classic case, *Ford Motor Co. v. Kirkmyer Motor Co., Inc.*, 65 F.2d 1001 (1933).

[4] United States Code, Annotated, Title 15, §§ 1,221–25.

[5] See the *Warrick* case, p. 172.

SUMMARY

Many franchises have been held to be unenforceable as contracts because of indefiniteness and lack of consideration. The Code tends to make more of these loose informal arrangements enforceable as contracts. Franchisors with one-sided contracts may encounter cancellation or termination difficulties under the Code provisions dealing with good faith, unconscionability, and reasonable notice requirements.

Shell Oil Co. v. Marinello

307 A.2d 598 (Sup. Ct. N.J. 1973)

This was an action by Marinello (plaintiff) to enjoin Shell Oil Co. (defendant) from terminating his service station lease and product franchise. Judgment for Marinello and Shell appealed. Affirmed.

In 1959, Shell leased a station to Marinello, and at the same time entered into a written dealer-franchise agreement with the lessee. The original lease was for a one-year term and was regularly renewed in writing for fixed terms. The last lease between Shell and Marinello was dated April 28, 1969, and ran for a three-year term ending May 31, 1972, and from year-to-year thereafter, but was subject to termination by Marinello at any time by giving at least 90 days' notice and by Shell at the end of the primary period or of any subsequent year by giving at least 30 days' notice. The last dealer agreement was also dated April 28, 1969, and was for a three-year term ending May 31, 1972, and from year-to-year thereafter, but was subject to termination at any time by giving at least ten days notice.

By letter dated April 14, 1972, Shell notified Marinello that it was terminating the lease and the dealer agreement pursuant to the provisions in each agreement effective May 31, 1972. Marinello immediately filed suit seeking to have Shell enjoined from taking this proposed action. Shell then filed a summary dispossess complaint for possession of the service station premises.

SULLIVAN, JUDGE. We are in full agreement with the basic determination of the trial court that Shell had no legal right to terminate its relationship with Marinello except for good cause, i.e., the failure of Marinello to substantially comply with his obligations under the lease and dealer agreement.

Marinello testified that when the station was offered to him in 1959, he was told by the Shell representative that the station was run down, but that a good operator could make money and that if he built up the business his future would be in the station. Shell's own witnesses admitted that it was Shell's policy not to terminate its relationship with a lessee-dealer except for good cause, which was described as not running the station in a good and businesslike manner.

Viewing the combined lease and franchise against the foregoing background, it becomes apparent that Shell is the dominant party and that the relationship lacks equality in the respective bargaining positions of the parties. For all practical purposes Shell can dictate its own terms. The dealer, particularly if he has been operating the station for a period of years and built up its business and clientele, when the time for renewal of the lease and dealer agreement comes around, cannot afford to risk confrontation with the oil company. He just signs on the dotted line.

Where there is grossly disproportionate bargaining power, the principle of freedom to contract is nonexistent and unilateral terms results. In such a situation courts will not hestitate to declare void as against public policy grossly unfair contractual provisions which clearly tend to the injury of the public in some way.

. . . It is clear that the provisions of the lease and dealer agreement giving Shell the right to terminate its business relationship with Marinello, almost at will, are the result of Shell's disproportionate bargaining position and are grossly unfair.

It is a fallacy to state that the right of termination is bilateral. The oil company can always get another person to operate the station. It is the incumbent dealer who has everything to lose since, even if he had another location to go to, the going business and trade he built up would remain with the old station.

We hold (1) that the lease and dealer agreement herein are integral parts of a single business relationship, basically that of a franchise, (2) that the provision giving Shell the absolute right to terminate on ten days' notice is void as against the public policy of this State, (3) that said public policy requires that there be read into the existing lease and dealer agreement, and all future lease and dealer agreements which may be negotiated in good faith between the parties, the restriction that Shell not have the unilateral right to terminate, cancel or fail to renew the franchise, including the lease, in absence of a showing that Marinello has failed to substantially perform his obligations under the lease and dealer agreement, i.e., for good cause, and (4) that good cause for termination has not been show in this case.

(Authors' Note) The U.S. Supreme Court refused to review Shell's appeal from the New Jersey Supreme Court's decision. More than 20 states now have laws attempting to protect franchisees from "bad faith" or arbitrary termination of their franchises. An increasing number of courts are finding "good faith" obligations in franchise relationships by using the U.C.C.[6]

Nature of Remedies

Objective in Granting Remedy. When a party has failed to perform obligations under a contract and the other party to the contract has suffered a

[6] See *Ashland Oil v. Donahue*, 223 S.E.2d 433 (1976).

resulting injury, the injured party is entitled to be put, as nearly as is practicable, in the same position as if the contract had been performed. If the injured party is granted a money judgement for the value of the thing contracted or for the profit realized had the contract been performed, the injured party will be in substantially the same position. Consequently, the remedy usually granted is the legal remedy of damages.

If the circumstances are such that the legal remedy of damages is inadequate, the court may grant the injured party an appropriate equitable remedy. The equitable remedy of specific performance of the contract is the one most frequently granted for breach of a contract.

Enforcement of Remedy. When a money judgment has been granted, the creditor is entitled to the aid of the court in the enforcement of the judgment if the debtor does not pay it. In the enforcement of the judgment the clerk of the court will issue either a writ of execution or a writ of garnishment.

A writ of execution directs the sheriff to take possession and sell so much of the judgment debtor's property that is not exempt from execution as is necessary to satisfy the judgment. All states have exemption laws, although they vary widely, which provide that certain property or property of a stated value shall be exempt from levy of execution.

Garnishment is also statutory and is supplemental to the execution. In general, it is used to reach property or credits of the judgment debtor which are in the hands of a third person, and the procedure varies. As a general rule, garnishments are used to reach bank accounts, wages due, or accounts receivable; however, under some statutes, one can reach goods in storage, the redemption value of pawned goods, and other similar assets.

Under some circumstances the plaintiff may have the sheriff seize property of the defendant at the time suit is started. This procedure is called an "attachment." The grounds for attachment are generally set out by statute and are not uniform throughout the United States.

SUMMARY

The remedy usually granted for breach of contract is a judgment for damages, but if the remedy at law is inadequate, an equitable remedy may be granted. A judgment is enforced by levy of execution, garnishment, or attachment.

Damages

Classification. The different classes of damages awarded by the court as a remedy for injury resulting from breach of contract are known as (1) compensatory, (2) consequential or special, (3) liquidated, (4) nominal, and (5) punitive damages, which a growing number of courts now allow where special facts justify it.

Compensatory damages are damages which can be compensated for by the payment of a sum of money which will make good or replace the loss caused by the wrong or injury. They are the damages which would normally and usually result from the breach of a contract such as that into which the parties have entered.

Consequential or special damages are those damages which do not flow directly or immediately from the breach of the contract but only from some of the special or unusual circumstances of the particular contractual relation of the parties.

Liquidated damages is the term applicable when a specific sum of money has been expressly stipulated by the parties as the amount of damages to be recovered by the injured party in the event the contract is breached.

Nominal damages are those damages awarded to the injured party where there is a technical breach of the contract but still no actual loss suffered as a result of the breach.

Punitive damages are allowed for breach of contract by some courts where extreme circumstances justify penalizing the defendant.

Mitigation of Damages. If the defendant has breached the contract, the plaintiff owes a duty to the defendant to make a reasonable effort to avoid damages. If the plaintiff can avoid or minimize the damages he will suffer as a result of the defendant's breach without undue risk, expense, or humiliation, the plaintiff owes a duty to the defendant to avoid the damage.

In employment contracts, if the employer wrongfully discharges an employee before the end of the term of the employment, the employee is entitled to recover his or her wages for the remainder of the term. However, the employee owes a duty to make a reasonable effort to obtain similar employment elsewhere and minimize the damages. If the employee is employed as a skilled plumber, the employee would not be expected or required to accept employment such as digging sewers to minimize the damages; but he would be required to make a reasonable effort to obtain other employment as a skilled plumber in the same locality.

Liquidated Damages. The courts will not enforce a provision in a contract for liquidated damages unless (1) the damages to be anticipated are uncertain in amount or difficult to prove, (2) the parties intended to liquidate the damages in advance, and (3) the amount stipulated is a reasonable one, that is, not greatly disproportionate to the presumable loss or injury. If the amount stipulated to be paid in the event of the breach of a contract is disproportionate to the loss or injury suffered, the courts will declare it to be a penalty and refuse to enforce it.

If a liquidated damage provision in a contract is declared to be a provision for a penalty or a forfeiture and therefore unenforceable, the injured party will be granted compensatory damages, provided the person can prove that he or she suffered a loss as the direct result of the breach of the contract and can prove with reasonable certainty the amount of the resulting loss.

Damages are awarded on the basis of the reasonable contemplation of the parties at the time the contract is entered into. The measure of compensatory damages is the value of the unfulfilled promise less the cost to the injured party of fulfilling the promise. The measure of consequential (special) damages is the loss suffered as the direct result of the default. Loss of profit may be allowable as an element of damages if such loss can be established with reasonable certainty. In all instances the injured party owes a duty to make a reasonable effort to minimize the damages. The measure of liquidated damages is the amount stipulated by the parties, and they are allowed by the court unless the amount stipulated is unreasonable, that is, it amounts to a penalty. Nominal damages is a token amount awarded for the breach of contract in those cases when the injured party establishes the breach of the contract but cannot prove with reasonable certainty that he or she suffered a loss as the direct result of the breach.

SUMMARY

Damages awarded for the breach of a contract may be (1) compensatory, (2) consequential (special), (3) liquidated, or (4) nominal. Damages are awarded on the basis of the reasonable contemplation of the parties at the time the contract is entered into. The measure of compensatory damages is the value of the unfulfilled promise less the cost to the injured party of fulfilling the promise. The measure of consequential (special) damages is the loss suffered by the injured party as the direct result of the default. Loss of profit may be allowable as an element of damages if such loss can be established with reasonable certainty. In all instances the injured party owes a duty to make a reasonable effort to minimize the damages suffered by reason of a default. The measure of liquidated damages is the amount stipulated by the parties, and they are allowed by the court unless the amount stipulated is unreasonable, that is, it amounts to a penalty. Nominal damages is a token amount awarded for the breach of a contract in those cases when the injured party establishes the breach of the contract but cannot prove with reasonable certainty that he or she suffered a loss as the direct result of the breach. Some courts now allow punitive damages for breach of contract.

Parker v. Twentieth Century-Fox Film Corp.

474 P.2d 689 (Sup. Ct. Cal. 1970)

Shirley MacLaine Parker (plaintiff) brought this action against Twentieth Century-Fox (defendant) to recover her agreed compensation under a contract for her services in a motion picture. Fox Film appealed from an adverse judgment. Affirmed.

BURKE, JUSTICE. Under the contract, dated August 6, 1965, Parker was to play the female lead in Fox Film's contemplated production of a motion picture entitled "Bloomer Girl." The contract provided that Fox Film would pay Parker a minimum "guaranteed compensation" of $53,571.42 per week for 14 weeks commencing May 23, 1966, for a total of $750,000. Prior to May, 1966, Fox Film decided not to produce the picture and by a letter dated April 4, 1966, it notified Parker of that decision and that it would not "comply with our obligations to you under" the written contract.

By the same letter and with the professed purpose "to avoid any damage to you" Fox Film instead offered to employ Parker as the leading actress in another film tentatively entitled "Big Country, Big Man" (hereinafter, "Big Country"). The compensation offered was identical, as were 31 of the 34 numbered provisions or articles of the original contract. Unlike "Bloomer Girl," however, which was to have been a musical production, "Big Country" was a dramatic "western type" movie. "Bloomer Girl" was to have been filmed in California; "Big Country" was to be produced in Australia. Also, certain terms in the proffered contract varied from those of the original. Parker was given one week within which to accept; she did not and the offer lapsed. Parked then commenced this action seeking recovery of the agreed guaranteed compensation.

As stated, Fox Film's sole defense to this action which resulted from its deliberate breach of contract is that in rejecting its substitute offer of employment Parker unreasonably refused to mitigate damages.

The general rule is that the measure of recovery by a wrongfully discharged employee is the amount of salary agreed upon for the period of service, less the amount which the employer affirmatively proves the employee has earned or with reasonable effort might have earned from other employment.

However, before projected earnings from other employment opportunities not sought or accepted by the discharged employee can be applied in mitigation, the employer must show that the other employment was comparable, or substantially similar, to that of which the employee has been deprived; the employee's rejection of or failure to seek other available employment of a different or inferior kind may not be resorted to in order to mitigate damages.

In the present case Fox Film has raised no issue of *reasonableness of efforts* by Parker to obtain other employment; the sole issue is whether Parker's refusal of defendant's substitute offer of "Big Country" may be used in mitigation. Nor, if the "Big Country" offer was of employment different or inferior when compared with the original "Bloomer Girl" employment, is there an issue as to whether or not Parker acted reasonably in refusing the substitute offer. Despite Fox Film's arguments to the contrary, no case cited or which our research has discovered holds or suggests that reasonableness is an element of a wrongfully discharged employee's option to reject, or fail to seek, different or inferior employment lest the possible earnings therefrom be charged against him in mitigation of damages.

. . . It is clear that the trial court correctly ruled that Parker's failure to accept Fox Film's tendered substitute employment could not be applied in mitigation of damages because the offer of the "Big Country" lead was of employment both different and inferior, and that no factual dispute was presented on that issue. The mere circumstance that "Bloomer Girl" was to be a musical review calling upon Parker's talents as a dancer as well as an actress, and was to be produced in the City of Los Angeles, whereas "Big Country" was a straight dramatic role in a "Western Type" story taking place in an opal mine in Australia, demonstrates the difference in kind between the two employments; the female lead as a dramatic actress in a western style motion picture can by no stretch of imagination be considered the equivalent of or substantially similar to the lead in a song-and-dance production.

Additionally, the substitute "Big Country" offer proposed to eliminate or impair the director and screenplay approvals accorded to Parker under the original "Bloomer Girl" contract . . . and thus constituted an offer of inferior employment. Judgment for plaintiff in the amount of $750,000 plus interest and costs affirmed.

Vernon Fire and Casualty Insurance Co. v. Sharp

349 N.E.2d 173 (Sup. Ct. Ind. 1976)

Sharp (plaintiff) carried corporate fire insurance with the Vernon Insurance Co. (defendant). A fire destroyed Sharp's corporation, and Sharp subsequently filed a claim for the proceeds. A disagreement ensued over the exact amount of the Vernon's liability, but at trial it conceded its minimum liability was more than $23,000. Vernon never offered to pay Sharp any sum of money prior to the trial, although it knew that Sharp was in desperate need of funds in order to rebuild.

A separate lawsuit, brought by a third party, resulted from the same fire that gutted Sharp's corporation. Vernon was arguably liable to this third party and it sought to require that Sharp settle this lawsuit, and it refused to pay until Sharp did so. Under the terms of the insurance policy, Sharp was not required to settle such a lawsuit. The trial court awarded Sharp actual damages and $17,000 punitive damages. Vernon appealed the award for punitive damages. Affirmed.

HUNTER, JUSTICE. Vernon maintains that their conduct in dealing with their insured reflects nothing more than a legitimate exercise of an insurer's "right to disagree" as to the amount of recovery . . . the insurer is permitted to dispute its liability in good faith because of the prohibitive social costs of a rule which would make claims nondisputable. Insurance companies burdened with such liability would either close their doors or increase premium rates to the point where only the rich could afford insurance.

Sharp charged that Vernon acted in an intentional and wanton manner in refusing to pay Sharp the proceeds of the policies. From the evidence herein the jury could reasonably conclude that Vernon acted in an "intentional and wanton" manner in dealing with Sharp in regard to securing a settlement of (the third party's) claim, and since this conduct did not relate solely to Vernon's actions in paying the legal proceeds, it was not privileged. . . . Sharp's evidence showed that the insurers dealt with his claim with an "interested motive" and wrongfully attempted by virtue of their superior position to exact additional consideration from Sharp before performing their obligations under the contract. This evidence was sufficient to establish a serious intentional wrong.

As noted above, punitive damages "do not rest upon any ground of abstract or theoretical justice but upon the basis of an established public policy which seeks to promote the public safety."

Vernon's actions in demanding noncontractual settlement service from their insured as a pre-condition to paying the loss they were already obligated to pay under the contract offend the statutes governing the rate-making process. If Vernon's demands had been met, it is clear that it would have reaped an unbargained-for benefit from the insured, which would have operated to increase the value of the premium paid by the insured. This type of behavior ignores the rights of the individual insured and undercuts the rights of insurers who abide by the rate-making laws.

We conclude that the public policy of this state permits the recovery of punitive damages under the circumstances of this case.

Equitable Remedies

Specific Performance. The granting of the equitable remedy of specific performance rests in the sound discretion of the court. The court will not grant specific performance of a contract if a money judgment, the remedy at law, is adequate. Since the remedy is equitable, the court has the power to withhold it when the ends of the law will thus be best served.

Injunction. The injunction is an equitable remedy designed to protect property or other rights from irreparable injury by commanding acts to be done or prohibiting their commission. It is used in a multitude of situations and affords the court of equity a flexible remedy. For example, if one having exceptional skills contracts to employ those skills exclusively for a party and then threatens, in violation of the contract, to employ those skills for others, the court may enjoin the use of such skills for anyone except the one with whom he or she contracted.

Problem Cases

1. Johnsrud contracted with Lind to sell Lind "approximately 600 steers at 41¢ per pound and approximately 300 heifers at 39¢ per pound." Johnsrud actually delivered 398 steers and 351 heifers, but Lind refused to pay until more steers were delivered by Johnsrud. Johnsrud sued to collect the purchase price of the cattle, and Lind counter-claimed for breach of contract, offering to return all the cattle if Johnsrud could not deliver more steers. Is Lind right?

2. On October 30, 1966, Wasserman Theatrical Enterprises, Inc. (Wasserman), entered into a contract with Jed Harris whereby Harris agreed to present Walter Huston in a theatrical performance entitled *The Apple of His Eye* at Worcester, Massachusetts, on the night of December 16, 1966. On December 12, 1966, Harris canceled the performance due to Huston's illness. Prior to that time Wasserman had spent considerable money in advertising the performance and in preparing the theater for the performance. Wasserman brought this suit to recover for money expended in preparation for the show and for loss of profits. Harris set up as a defense that Huston was the chief artist and essential performer in the production, and that by reason of his illness performance of the contract on December 16, 1966, was rendered impossible. Is Harris liable for breach of contract?

3. Commercial Contractors was hired to demolish a building. Robinson contracted with Commercial to purchase the bricks from the demolished building for $4,000. The contract did not mention the time limit Robinson had to remove the bricks. Commercial was under pressure from the landowner to fill the excavation and, after allowing Robinson 60 days to remove the bricks, began filling in the excavation with most of the bricks Robinson had purchased. Robinson sued for breach of contract. Upon what issue does this recovery depend?

4. Kennedy entered into a contract with Reese whereby Kennedy was to drill a 12-inch well to an estimated depth of 400 feet and case it with 6-inch casing, with the bottom half perforated and gravel packed. Kennedy selected the site on Reese's land and drilled to a depth of 130 feet where he struck rock. Reese obtained permission for Kennedy to drill on neighboring land at a site selected by Kennedy. Kennedy drilled to a depth of 270 feet and again struck rock whereupon he abandoned without the permission of Reese. Evidence was offered at the trial of the case to the effect that the rock encountered was brittle and that it could be drilled through. Kennedy sued to recover for labor performed and set up impossibility as a defense to the counterclaim filed by Reese. Is this a good defense to the counterclaim?

5. Bunge Corporation contracted to buy 10,000 bushels of soybeans from a grower named Recker. There was no delivery of soybeans under the contract, which did not specifially identify any of the beans. Severe weather, which had struck Recker's area of the country, made it impossible for him to harvest 865 acres. Recker's defense to Bunge's action for breach of contract was impossibility because of an act of God. Is this a good defense?

6. Vector, Inc. contracted with the Department of Housing and Urban Development (HUD) to construct low-cost housing in Puerto Rico. The agreement specified that Vector should construct 396 dwelling units which it would sell to HUD for $7 million. No guaranteed profitability clause appeared in the written contract. When subcontracting major portions of the project, Vector learned that because of increased costs the expenditures it would have to make were in excess of $8 million. Vector sought to renegotiate the contract with HUD, but HUD refused. Vector then refused to proceed with construction. In a

suit by HUD for specific performance of the contract, Vector claims that to perform would entail a loss of at least $500,000. Must Vector perform the contract?

7. Lowenschuss tendered 2,000 shares of A&P Tea Company stock to Gulf and Western pursuant to a tender offer to purchase "up to 3,750,000 shares" of A&P stock. The tendering of the shares created an enforceable contract between Lowenschuss and Gulf and Western. A&P later challenged the tender offer on the basis that the merger would be a probable antitrust violation. A preliminary injunction was issued to bar the tender offer. Does the issuance of the preliminary injunction give Gulf and Western a complete defense under the impossibility doctrine?
8. Cramer contracted to remodel a house for Essivein. In performing the contract, Cramer installed only seven radiators instead of eight as specified in the contract, leaving the bathroom without a radiator. He failed again to carry out the terms of the contract when he installed in the bathroom a used bathtub and a used washbasin, whereas the contract provided that both be new. Essivein refused to pay Cramer, and Cramer brought suit on the contract to recover the contract price for work and material. Is Cramer entitled to a judgment under the doctrine of substantial performance?
9. Bailey entered into a contract with the Martins whereby he agreed to furnish all the materials and perform all the work for the construction of a residence on property owned by the Martins, such work to be done in accordance with certain drawings and specifications. The total cost was $11,927.62. The contract provided that no deviation from the drawings and specifications or changes or substitution of material, "shall be made without prior written approval of the owner (the Martins)."

   During the course of the construction of the residence, the Martins orally ordered several additions and changes, and Bailey carried out these orders. The costs required in making the additions and changes was $751.77. The Martins refused to pay for these extras and when sued set up that since they were not ordered in writing as stipulated in the contract they were not liable. Bailey claimed that the original contract was altered by mutual agreement. Had the original contract been altered?
10. Otinger contracted with City Water Board to construct a pump and water station on Catona Creek. Due in part to flood conditions on the Catona, Otinger went over the time specified for completion. The contract contained a provision stating that time was of the essence and authorizing the City to withhold $50 per day for every day, including Sundays and holidays, which the work remained uncompleted beyond the date specified. The $50 was stated to represent not liquidated but actual stipulated damage which the City would have sustained. The total amount of the contract was $120,000. Otinger maintained that the City waived the time limit when, in reply to his letter requesting an extension, they instructed him to "proceed with the unfinished work with reasonable and continual progress until completion" and stated that upon completion they "would gladly have you appear for a review of the delay and assure you of full consideration of the circumstances." Otinger sued for a balance due on the contract and the City counterclaimed for overpayment because the amount of the stipulated damages had exceeded this balance. Who should prevail?

PART IV

Agency and Employment Law

16

Creation of Agency Relation and Authority

Introduction

Background. Agency law grew out of the desire of people to extend their activities beyond the physical limits of their own bodies. In simple societies this desire was primarily for additional labor—through slaves or servants, but leaders also deputized others to transact business for them. As commerce grew in importance, merchants and traders also began to transact business through others. Brokers and factors began to play a prominent role in business in England by the latter part of the 17th century. Such persons are now typical examples of agents but were originally treated by the English courts as servants. It was not until the 19th century that the law began to distinguish between servants and agents.

Nature of Relation. An agency relationship is based upon the mutual consent of the two parties. Once the relationship is found to exist, the law defines the rights and liabilities of the parties with respect to each other and to third persons. The fact that the agent is acting without compensation and there is no enforceable contract of agency does not substantially affect those rights and duties nor the validity of contracts negotiated by the agent in the name of the principal.

Creation and Termination. The agency relationship arises when two people consent that one shall act for the benefit of the other and under the latter's direction. Whether an agency exists is a question of fact. If from all of the circumstances it appears that one person is acting for the benefit and under the control of another, courts will hold that an agency relationship exists. The legal relationship of agency may be created without either party being aware of its existence and even though the parties have expressly stated that they do not intend to create it.

No formality is required except in a few instances. For example, in many states authority given to an agent to sell or otherwise act for the principal in transactions involving real estate must be in writing. However, it is desirable in order to avoid later disputes that an express agency agreement be entered into and that it be reduced to writing.

Although termination of an agency may involve a breach of contract, generally either party has the power to terminate it at will. Unless notice is given to third parties who have dealt with the agent, liability of the principal for the agent's acts may continue, on the ground of apparent agency, after termination of the agency.

Scope. The legal problems to which agency law is addressed include questions such as the following: When is the dominant person (principal or master or employer) liable on contracts made by the subordinate person (agent or servant or employee)? When is the dominant person liable for the torts of the subordinate person? What duties does each person in the relationship owe to the other? Differences in the nature of the services rendered and the degree of control that the dominant person in the relationship is entitled to exercise have led to classifications of parties that are sometimes confusing.

Master and Servant. The term "principal and agent" is often used in the law to include both the relationship of principal and agent and that of master and servant. It has been common to distinguish agents from servants (employees) according to the nature of the services rendered: agents are empowered to change the legal relationships of the principal (e.g. when they buy or sell for the principal), while servants perform physical acts such as operating a machine or using a tool. However, this distinction tends to lead to confusion in considering when the dominant person is liable for the torts committed by the subordinate person. For this purpose, the important determination is whether the dominant person has the right to control the subordinate's physical activities. If so, the latter is a *servant* in legal terminology, even though he or she may be president of a corporation, and his or her employer (the corporation) will be liable for the person's torts. Because the legal term *servant* connotes servility in common speech, the terms *employee* and *employer* are tending to replace *master* and *servant* even in the law. Therefore, this text will generally use the terms *employee* and *employer.*

It is not uncommon for an employee to be directed to do work for another employer, with the original employer being paid for the services of the employee. The question arises as to which employer (master) is liable for a tort committed by an employee (servant) in this situation. The inference is that the *"borrowed servant"* remains the employee of the original employer, who will be liable to the employee for his or her pay and will remain the employer under most statutes, such as social security and unemployment and workmen's compensation. However, if the primary right of control is shifted to the special employer, under the "borrowed servant doctrine," the special employer becomes liable for the employee's torts. Which employer has the right of control is frequently a difficult question of fact.

Principal and Agent. As indicated above, the term *agent* may, in its broadest legal sense, include an employee who does nothing but manual labor. However, it is usually applied to one who conducts business transactions for his or her *principal.* Such an agent may be one who is an employee of a corporation or a person who is an independent business person, perhaps employing other people. Agents of the latter type are sometimes called *professional agents.* Manufacturers' representatives, realtors, stockbrokers, auctioneers, and attorneys fall into this category. With respect to these agents the principal's control is limited to determining the objectives and limitations of the agent's authority in the business the agent is transacting for the principal, and the principal has no right to control the agent's physical acts. Whether the agent travels by automobile or airplane or takes three hours for lunch is not within the realm of control by the principal.

General and Special Agents. Agents are often further classified as general or special agents. A *general agent* is a person who acts for the principal in a number of transactions over a period of time. This person may be given authority to act for the principal in a rather wide range of matters, such as the manager of a business, or may be authorized to handle all transactions of a certain class for the principal, such as a general purchasing agent. A *special agent,* on the other hand, is one who is authorized to act either in a single transaction or a limited series of transactions.

Franchising and Other Relationships. The terms *agent* and *agency* are sometimes used to refer to relationships which do not come within the law of agency. For example, a merchant who has a franchise to sell the products of the Ford Motor Company is often referred to as a Ford agent, and the business is referred to as a Ford agency; but the merchant is not an agent of the Ford Motor Company, and the relationship between the Ford Motor Company and the merchant is not that of agency. The franchisee is an independent contractor dealing in the franchisor's (Ford Motor Company) products.

Independent Contractor. The term *independent contractor* is used in contrast to that of employee (or servant). An independent contractor includes an individual, or a partnership or corporation, who contracts to do something for another but who is not an employee. The distinction between employee and independent contractor is based upon the degree of control over the physical conduct of the one performing the service, and the principal is generally not liable for the torts of an independent contractor. The relationship is especially common in the building trades.

Whether a person is acting as an independent contractor is often a difficult question of fact.[1] If Archer needs a new machine, he may build it in his own shop, in which case those persons who build the machine will be Archer's employees. Archer may submit the specifications for the machine to Burch, who will contract to build the machine according to the specifications and for an agreed price. In this case, Burch will not be an employee of Archer, since Burch has contracted to produce a result and is free to proceed by whatever method he may wish in producing that result. Burch's physical conduct is not under the control of Archer. Burch is an independent contractor. The employee is subject to the direction of his or her employer; the independent contractor is obligated to produce a result and is free to pursue self-chosen methods in the performance of the work.

SUMMARY

Agency law grew out of the desire of people to extend their activities, both in performing labor and in transacting business, beyond the physical limits of their own bodies. Agency is a relationship which exists when two parties agree that one shall act for the benefit and under the control of the other. The law of agency governs the relationship of the parties to each other and to third persons. The fact that the agent is not paid does not substantially change those rights and duties. Generally, an agency may be terminated at will even if termination involves a breach of contract. For purposes of determining tort liability it is important to distinguish between agents who are and those who are not employees. An independent contractor is not an employee because the dominant person does not control the means used to perform the assigned task.

Massey v. Tube Art Display, Inc.

551 P.2d 1387 (Ct. App. Wash. 1976)

Massey (plaintiff), a tenant in a building damaged by fire, brought an action against Tube Art Display (defendant) for damages resulting from the negligence of a backhoe operator who hit a gas pipeline while digging a hole for the erection of a sign owned by Tube Art. Judgment for Massey for $143,000 appealed by Tube Art. Affirmed.

Redford had been a backhoe operator for five years. Although he worked for other sign companies, he had spent 90 percent of his time for the past

[1] See the criteria applied by the court in *Massey v. Tube Art Display Inc., infra.*

three years working for Tube Art. He had no employees, was not registered as a contractor or subcontractor, was not bonded, and did not obtain the permits required for the jobs he did. He dug holes exactly as directed by the sign company employing him. He did, however, pay his own business taxes and did not participate in any of the fringe benefits available to other Tube Art employees.

Tube Art obtained a permit from the City of Seattle to install a sign in the parking lot of a combination commercial and apartment building in which Massey carried on a business. Tube Art's service manager laid out the exact location of a 4 X 4 foot square on the asphalt surface with yellow paint and in the same manner directed that the hole was to be six feet deep. Redford started work that evening. At 9:30 P.M. he struck a small natural gas pipeline with the backhoe. He examined the pipe and, finding no indication of a leak or break, he concluded the line was not in use and left the worksite. About 2 A.M. an explosion and fire occurred in the building serviced by the line. Two people were killed and most of the contents were destroyed.

Massey sued for the destruction of his business and inventory. He alleged Redford was negligent in not making an inspection before digging and for not notifying the gas company that he had struck the line and, further, that he was operating under the control of Tube Art as its employee. The court in its jury instructions declared that Redford was the agent of Tube Art and that if he was found negligent Tube Art would be liable. Tube Art alleged this was error.

SWANSON, JUDGE. Traditionally, servants and non-servant agents have been looked upon as persons employed to perform services in the affairs of others under an express or implied agreement, and who, with respect to physical conduct in the performance of those services, is subject to the other's control or right of control.

An independent contractor, on the other hand, is generally defined as one who contracts to perform services for another, but who is not controlled by the other nor subject to the other's right to control with respect to his physical conduct in performing the services.

In determining whether one acting for another is a servant or independent contractor, several factors must be taken into consideration. These are listed in Restatement (Second) of *Agency* § 220(2) (1958), as follows:

a. the extent of control which, by the agreement, the master may exercise over the details of the work;

b. whether or not the one employed is engaged in a distinct occupation or business;

c. the kind of occupation, with reference to whether, in the locality, the work is usually done under the direction of the employer or by a specialist without supervision;

d. the skill required in the particular occupation;

e. whether the employer or the workman supplies the instrumentalities, tools, and the place of work for the person doing the work;

f. the length of time for which the person is employed;

g. the method of payment, whether by the time or by the job;

h. whether or not the work is a part of the regular business of the employer;
i. whether or not the parties believe they are creating the relation of master and servant; and
j. whether the principal is or is not in business.

All of these factors are of varying importance in determining the type of relationship involved and, with the exception of the element of control, not all the elements need be present. It is the right to control another's physical conduct that is the essential and oftentimes decisive factor in establishing vicarious liability whether the person controlled is a servant or a non-servant agent.

We . . . find no disputed evidence of the essential factor—the right to control, nor is there any dispute that control was exercised over the most significant decisions—the size and location of the hole. Consequently, only one conclusion could reasonably be drawn from the facts presented. In such a circumstance, the nature of the relationship becomes a question of law. [Therefore, the jury instructions were proper.]

Kuchta v. Allied Builders Corp.

98 Cal. Rptr. 588 (Ct. App. Cal. 1971)

This was a suit by Joseph G. Kuchta and his wife (plaintiffs) against Allied Builders Corporation and its franchisee, Raphael Weiner, (defendants) for fraud and breach of a building contract. Allied's primary defense was that Weiner was an independent contractor. Judgment was granted the Kuchtas on jury verdicts for $5,585 in general damages against Allied and Weiner jointly and $3,750 punitive damages against each of them individually. Judgment affirmed.

Mr. and Mrs. Kuchta saw a sign on the lawn of a neighbor's home indicating that Allied had just constructed an outdoor living area attached to the neighbor's house. Desiring a similar facility and not finding an Allied listing in Orange County, they phoned Allied in Los Angeles. They were told by the vice president of Allied that they should contact Allied's branch in Anaheim, and he gave them Weiner's phone number. Weiner appeared two days after they phoned the Anaheim office. He represented that he was from Allied Builders, and a few days later the Kuchtas entered into a written contract with Allied Builders System. It provided that the franchisee, as contractor, would furnish all labor and materials for $5,671, that construction would conform to local and state codes and that Allied would obtain necessary building permits.

The plans were submitted by Weiner to the building department of Orange County but were not approved because the planned structure would extend to the property line while the applicable zoning restrictions prohibited building within five feet of the lot line except for a fence. Without the knowledge of the Kuchtas, a second set of plans was submitted by Weiner to the building department. They omitted the roof and side supports provided for in the contract and called for only a slab. Nevertheless, the construction followed the original plan. About five months later the Kuchtas received notice of violation of the building code and were required to demolish the addition and to restore the property to its original condition.

KERRIGAN, ACTING PRESIDING JUSTICE. The law is clear that a franchisee may be deemed to be the agent of the franchisor. In the field of franchise agreements, the question of whether the franchisee is an independent contractor or an agent is ordinarily one of fact, depending on whether the franchisor exercises complete or substantial control over the franchisee

In the case under review, there was evidence that Allied Builders exercised strong control over Weiner. The franchise agreement itself gave Allied Builders the right to control the location of the franchisee's place of business, to prescribe minimum display equipment, to regulate the quality of the goods used or sold, to control the standards of construction, to approve the design and utility of all construction, and to assign persons to see that the franchisee performed according to the franchisor's standards. Additionally, Allied enjoyed the right of inspection over the franchisee's plans and specifications, the franchisee's work in progress, and finished jobs, as well as the right to train Weiner's salesmen. Moreover, Allied Builders was entitled to share in the profits of the franchisee and to audit Weiner's books. These elements of control were sufficient to support an implied finding of agency.

The trial court also properly instructed the jury on the doctrine of ostensible agency. An agency is ostensible when the principal intentionally, or by want of ordinary care, causes a third person to believe another to be his agent who is really not employed by him. Ostensible authority is such as a principal, intentionally or by want of ordinary care, causes or allows a third person to believe the agent to possess.

There was formidable evidence establishing Weiner's ostensible authority. When the plaintiffs first contacted Allied Builder's vice president in Los Angeles, they were referred to Allied's "branch office" in Anaheim. The vice president characterized the Los Angeles office as the "main office." Both the main office and the branch office answered their phone in the same manner, to wit, "Allied Builders." Both the franchisor and the franchisee did business under the same name at that time, to wit, Allied Builders System. The contract listed "Allied Builders System" as the contractor. Both offices employed common advertising in newspapers and in the yellow pages of the telephone book. Calls to the main office brought swift and certain reaction from the franchisee. Weiner represented to the Kuchtas that the firm had been in business for over 50 years, which covered the entire span of Allied's experience in the building business. The plaintiffs' check for payment on the contract price was endorsed and deposited to the account of "Allied Builders System." Consequently, there was ample evidence that Allied Builders either intentionally, or by want of ordinary care, led third persons, including plaintiffs, to believe that the franchisee and Allied Builders were part of the same business operation.

While Allied Builders argues that no agency relationship existed by virtue of the franchise agreement, in that the agreement itself stated that no such agency relationship was created, the declarations of the parties in the agreement respecting the nature of the relationship are not controlling.

Allied also takes the position that the plaintiffs elected to hold Weiner alone responsible in that they contracted solely with him and, therefore, are estopped from holding the principal liable. There is authority that if, at the time the contract is made in the name of the agent, the third party has knowledge of the identity of the principal and nevertheless proceeds to contract with the agent, there is no "undisclosed" principal, and this has sometimes been considered as an election to hold the agent alone. However, it is equally well settled that knowledge of the identity of the principal is not conclusive, and the election to hold the agent must be established by other evidence of actual intent. The evidence herein reflects that both the franchisor and the franchisee held themselves out to the public as one construction firm and that the plaintiffs contracted with Allied on that basis. Consequently, the trial court was correct in not requiring the plaintiffs to make an election.

Butler v. Colorado International Pancakes, Inc.

510 P.2d 443 (Colo. App. 1973)

Ruth Butler (plaintiff) brought this action for breach of contract against Colorado International Pancakes, Inc. (CIPI) and International Pancakes (International) (defendants). Appeal by International from a default judgment against CIPI and a judgment against International for $30,165 on a jury verdict for Butler. Affirmed.

International is a franchisor of restaurants operating under the name of The International House of Pancakes. In 1961 International granted an area franchise to William Brown who incorporated CIPI to exercise the rights under the franchise. Brown also incorporated South-Gate Pancake House, Inc. to construct and operate a restaurant in Colorado Springs. Ruth Butler and her husband bought all of the stock of South-Gate from CIPI in 1964 shortly after the restaurant opened, and they operated it together. The Butlers were divorced in 1965, and she acquired all of the stock. She continued to operate the restaurant until August 1966 when she sold all of the assets of South-Gate back to CIPI. Under the terms of the sale there was $30,165 due Mrs. Butler. After a year's operation by CIPI the restaurant came under the control of International through foreclosure of a security interest. The amount due Butler from CIPI still being unpaid, she then sued International as well as CIPI.

ENOCH, JUDGE. Mrs. Butler claims that CIPI was the agent of International and that International is liable to Mrs. Butler for the $30,164.56. In support of this position, Mrs. Butler asserts that the written franchise agreement between International and CIPI did in fact and law create a principal-agent relationship between these companies. Mrs. Butler further contends that the circumstances under which CIPI repurchased the business from her were such that International cannot escape liability. We agree with Mrs. Butler's latter contention which is dispositive of this case.

Mrs. Butler's unrebutted evidence discloses that International did not want a woman holding a franchise and that International directed CIPI to repurchase the business from Mrs. Butler. International instructed CIPI that, in order to induce Mrs. Butler to sell out, CIPI should inspect her premises and operation daily, if necessary, and send her "seven-day termination letters," as provided for in the franchise agreement, to the point that she would become so harassed that she would be willing to sell out. CIPI, through its officers, followed these directions and as a result repurchased the business from Mrs. Butler. She was not advised at the time of the repurchase agreement that CIPI was in bad financial circumstances.

An agent is one who acts for or in place of another by authority from him. The evidence is quite clear that International wanted the franchise repurchased from Mrs. Butler for its own benefit. International not only specifically instructed CIPI to "buy back" her subfranchise but also instructed CIPI as to the method for accomplishing that objective. That method consisted of sustained harrassment until she was willing to acquiesce in despair. CIPI carried out International's plan while CIPI itself obviously was in no financial position to pay Mrs. Butler. International was the only party between the two that was in a position to benefit from the transaction. International, by its involvement in this repurchase transaction, clearly demonstrated the existence of an agency relationship irrespective of any franchise agreement. Agency may be established by the conduct of the principal and the agent.

Capacity of Parties

Capacity to Act as Principal. A person of limited legal capacity, such as a minor or insane person, cannot enlarge his or her legal powers by acting through an agent. The minor or insane person who authorizes an agent to act for him is bound only to the extent he or she would have been bound by taking the action in person. Business organizations such as corporations and partnerships may appoint agents, and, of course, a corporation can act only through an agent. In a partnership each partner acts as the agent of all copartners in transacting partnership business.

Unincorporated Associations as Principals. Under the common-law rule, an unincorporated association is not recognized as an entity having legal capacity. It cannot, as a general rule, sue, be sued, own property, or enter into a contract. Under special statutes, however, such associations generally have been made subject to suit and their assets are subject to execution. This is especially true of labor unions. If an unincorporated association is not liable to suit under the provisions of a statute, its members who have legal capacity may be held liable.

Capacity to Act as Agent. A person may have capacity to act as an agent even though he or she does not have the capacity to contract. In the transaction of business through an agent, the principal is the party obligated to perform, not the agent. The agent's capacity is immaterial so long as the agent has sufficient ability to carry out the principal's instructions. Both corporations and partnerships can act as agents. A husband or wife may act as the agent of the spouse, but there is no agency merely by virtue of the marital relationship. The liability of a husband for the necessities purchased by his wife is an aspect of the marital relationship itself and does not constitute the wife an agent for her husband. The same would apply to the wife's liability under statutes imposing liability on her for family expenses.

SUMMARY

A minor or insane person may appoint agents, but they cannot enlarge their legal capacity by acting through agents. At common law an unincorporated association had no capacity to contract and could not appoint an agent. This has generally been changed by statute.

Authority to Bind Principal

Authorization. An agent is authorized to act for a principal when the principal's representations or conduct make it manifest to the agent that the principal intends the agent to act for the principal. The extent of the authority of the agent to bind the principal is also based upon the representations and conduct of the principal. In general, the authority to act on the account of the principal may be conferred on the agent by written or spoken words or by other conduct of the principal which, reasonably interpreted, causes the agent to believe that the principal intends the agent so to act on the principal's account.

In analyzing the power of an agent to bind the principal, the courts and writers have not been consistent in the terms used. This analysis shall follow a three-part classification: (1) express authority, (2) implied authority (also referred to as incidental authority), and (3) apparent authority (also referred to as ostensible authority and similar to "authority by estoppel").

Express Authority. Express authority is that authority which is explicitly conferred on the agent by the principal. It may be conferred either orally or in writing, but in either event the principal must express to the agent the acts the agent is to perform. For example, if the principal instructs the agent, either orally or in writing, to draw a check payable to Tucker for a stated sum and to sign the check in the principal's name and deliver it to Tucker, the agent will have express authority to draw, sign, and deliver the check.

Implied Authority. Unless the principal limits the authority of the agent by express instructions or by clear implication, the authority to negotiate a transaction includes the authority to do those acts that are usually or customarily done in conducting transactions such as the agent is authorized to transact or to do those acts that are reasonably necessary to accomplish the objective of the agency. This authority is in addition to whatever authority is expressly granted. Such authority is generally termed "implied authority" or "incidental authority."

If the agent is a special agent, the express authority may include the majority of acts the agent is authorized to perform. If the agent is a general agent, the express authority, even though carefully worded to cover the agent's duties in detail, cannot include more than the major acts the agent is to perform. In carrying out the objective of the agency, the agent will have implied authority to do many acts not detailed in the express authority, whether or not the principal actually would have given such authority if he had thought about it.

In determining the scope of the agent's implied authority, the measure used is the justified belief of the agent. The same principles apply to the interpretation of an agent's authority as apply in interpreting an offer to contract. The nature of the agency, whether special or general, usages of trade, prior relations between the principal and agent, and such other facts and circumstances as are material in the particular case are weighed in determining what authority the agent is justified in believing the principal intended to confer on him or her.

Apparent Authority. While the scope of an agent's express or implied authority is determined by analyzing the relation between the principal and the agent, an agent's apparent authority is determined by analyzing the relation between the principal and a third person. An agent's apparent authority may be less than, coextensive with, or greater than, his or her express or implied authority. An agent's apparent authority, sometimes termed ostensible authority, is the authority which the principal by representations or conduct has led the third person, acting as a reasonable and prudent person, justifiably to believe has been conferred on the agent by the principal.

Apparent authority is created by the same method as that by which express or implied authority is created except that the manifestations of the principal are made to the third person or to the community rather than to the agent. In holding the principal liable on the ground of the apparent authority of the agent, the third person must prove that the principal was responsible for the information which justified the third person in believing that the agent was authorized to so act and that the third person relied upon it. The information on which the third person justifies his or her belief may come not only directly from the words or conduct of the principal, but it may be based on standard practices of trade; or it may result from the principal entrusting certain documents to the agent; or from the appointment of the agent to a position that carries with it the implication of authority. Apparent authority also may be established by showing that the agent has been conducting similar transactions or doing similar acts to the knowledge of and without objection by the principal.

SUMMARY

The authority of an agent to act for a principal is based on a manifestation of the principal. Authority may be conferred by written or spoken words, or by other conduct of the principal. The authority of the agent may be express, implied, or apparent. The agent has the express authority explicitly conferred upon him or her by the principal. The agent has, in addition, the implied authority which he or she, as a reasonable person familiar with the business to be transacted, is justified in believing the principal intended to confer. This would include authority to do those acts that are reasonably necessary to accomplish the objectives of the agency. The agent has such apparent authority as the principal, by conduct, has led a third person, acting as a reasonable person familiar with the business to be transacted, justifiably to believe has been conferred on the agent.

Dudley v. Dumont

526 S.W.2d 839 (Ct. App. Mo. 1975)

Dudley (plaintiff) brought an action for fraud against Dumont (defendant) for misrepresenting the effective date of coverage of an automobile liability insurance policy. Appeal from judgment awarding Dudley $1,080 actual and $4,500 punitive damages. Reversed.

On December 20, Dudley and his son went to a State Farm Insurance office to obtain liability insurance on an automobile. The State Farm agent, Gainey, filled out blanks on a printed form which contained the words, "John T. Dumont, Jr., Insurance," and a handwritten signature which Dumont testified was not his. The instrument stated it was a receipt for $131.50 from Carl F. Dudley "for liab 10/20/5 on '56 Ply.—Effective date 12/20/65." There was evidence at the trial that Gainey made a telephone call prior to preparing the receipt but none as to the subject of or other party to the call. Dumont testified that he had not received any call concerning Dudley on that day and had not heard of Dudley before December 27. The Dudley check and an application for insurance on a State Farm form was received by Dumont's office on December 27. The information on the application was transcribed to a Prudence Mutual Insurance form, the check indorsed to that company, and both were forwarded to Prudence. The Prudence policy, bearing date of issuance of December 27, was sent to Dumont's office, and on January 7 it was mailed to Dudley with an invoice bearing that date showing payment in full for "liability $10/20/5,000" coverage on a "1956 Plymouth 4 door" issued "12/20/65" to expire "6/20/66."

Gainey had sent the application to Dumont as he had done over a number of years with other "high risk" applications which State Farm would not accept.

Dudley's son was involved in an automobile accident on December 23, and Dudley reported this by phone on December 26 to Dumont's office and requested claim forms. A search of office files at that time turned up no information about insurance for Dudley, and no claim forms were sent. Dudley was threatened with suit as a result of the accident and settled the claim for $300 plus $100 for his attorney and $75 for a security deposit with the Missouri Department of Revenue. Dudley demanded and received a return of the premium he had paid. Dudley sued Dumont alleging that Gainey was Dumont's agent and had made an intentional misrepresentation in telling Dudley when he applied that the insurance would be effective on December 20.

RENDLEN, JUDGE. Dumont correctly states the relationship of principal and agent cannot be presumed but must be proved by the party asserting the existence of that relationship. Similarly, the existence and scope of agency cannot be established by declarations of the alleged agent. Having carefully examined the record, we find Dudley failed to prove that Gainey was acting as agent of Dumont. The facts and inferences therefrom, taken in a light most favorable to Dudley, would permit the conclusion that Dumont gave Ken Gainey certain receipt forms imprinted with Dumont's name for the purpose of enabling Gainey to refer insurance clients to Dumont and that such referrals occurred frequently over a period of years. It could be found that Dumont knew or should have known that Gainey would execute receipts given to him by Dumont. The facts permit the inference that Gainey, on December 20, 1965, represented to Dudley he would receive automobile insurance effective that date through the efforts of Dumont. However, there was no evidence nor supportable inference that Gainey or Dudley communicated with Dumont on December 20. The mere fact that Gainey placed a telephone call on December 20 of an undisclosed nature to an unidentified third party is no proof of agency.

Dudley argues that Gainey's agency for Dumont is established by one or more theories: Express agency, implied agency, apparent authority, agency by estoppel, [or] agency by ratification. The argument portion of Dudley's brief does not nicely separate these theories; we nevertheless examine them individually.

Express agency is not a viable issue since there is no evidence of a specific agreement between Gainey and Dumont authorizing the one to act for and under the control of the other.

Implied or inferred agency is actual authority given implicitly by the principal to his agent, ". . . circumstantially proved, or evidenced by conduct, or inferred from a course of dealing between the alleged principal and the agent." Since implied authority is based on an inferred agreement between the purported principal and agent, it is possible to circumstantially prove the relationship by means of course of conduct between the two. Dudley argues implied agency is established by the fact that transactions between Gainey and Dumont during the 13 or 14 prior years "were of like character to the controversy here." This, however, assumes Gainey had acted as Dumont's agent during those prior years though the evidence discloses only that Gainey referred business to Dumont; there is no evidence that Gainey acted in a representative capacity with the knowledge or acquiescence of Dumont.

Next Dudley contends Gainey had apparent authority to act for Dumont. To find apparent agency the appearance of authority must have been created by the principal. The only indication that Gainey might be an agent of Dumont was his possession of Dumont's receipt forms; however, as pointed out above, mere possession of billheads is insufficient to establish agency. Possession of receipt forms may indicate authority to take orders without implying authority to execute a final contract. The evidence suggests Gainey acted more as broker for Dudley than as sales or soliciting agent for Dumont. A person dealing with a supposed agent under these circumstances has the duty of ascertaining the extent of the agent's authority. The fact that Dumont sent Dudley an invoice dated January 7, 1966, containing terms similar to the representations made by Gainey to Dudley on December 20, 1965, is of no assistance to establish apparent authority since apparent authority can only be predicated on facts or appearances shown at the time of the transaction; knowledge subsequently acquired is irrelevant.

Agency by estoppel is similar to apparent authority except it requires that the person dealing with the purported agent change his position in reasonable reliance upon a manifestation of authority by the purported principal. If the manifestation of authority to the third person is by some formality, there may be apparent authority, if by parol the principle of estoppel applies. As noted, there is no credible evidence Dumont held out Gainey as having any authority other than to submit applications for insurance to him. Even if we assume the signature on the receipt was that of Dumont, placed there at some prior time, these requirements are not met since Gainey filled in the receipt in Dudley's presence who thus had notice the form was not completed by Dumont. Dudley could not reasonably believe such blank receipt form, though it may have borne Dumont's signature, would authorize Gainey to do more than take orders and give receipts for money paid. Dudley's reliance on estoppel to establish agency is misplaced.

Dudley next relies on a theory of ratification to hold Dumont liable for Gainey's misrepresentation of immediate insurance coverage. The basis of this argument is the January 7 invoice executed by Dumont showing the same terms as Gainey's receipt of December 20. We do not agree. It is well established in our law that there must be scienter, either actual or constructive, to support an action at law for fraud and deceit. Scienter implies guilty knowledge by the tortfeasor or a guilty lack of knowledge; the former is charged here.

If Dumont were truly aware of Gainey's misrepresentation to the effect that coverage was already afforded and if he also knew that this application was from a person who had already experienced an accident, he would not have acted as he did. We consider the fact that on January 7, 1966, the invoice was sent (after the policy had been issued showing its effective date December 27) erroneously stating the date of issuance as December 20, 1965. If Dumont had guilty knowledge and had been intending to defraud Dudley on December 27 and likewise on January 7, he would have made certain the invoice of January 7 showed December 27 (the actual date of issuance) as the "Date Issued" instead of the erroneous date of December 20. These acts bespeak an administrative or clerical mistake by Dumont's employee who copied the date of December 20 from the application over to the invoice, as she so testified, rather than intentional ratification of fraud.

Ratification

Nature of Ratification. Ratification in the law of agency is the subsequent adoption and affirmance by one person of an act which another, without authority, has previously assumed to do for the first while purporting to act as the other's agent. Ratification is equivalent to a previous authorization and relates back to the time when the act ratified was done, except where intervening rights of third parties are concerned. Any act which the principal could have authorized at the time the act was done may be ratified.

Requirements for Ratification. To have a valid ratification, the following conditions must be satisfied: (1) The person ratifying must have had the present capacity to do the act personally or authorize it to be done, (2) the person for whom the act was done must have been identified or the circumstances must have been such that he or she was capable of identification, (3) the person acting must have acted as agent of the principal or the person represented to be the principal, (4) the principal or person represented to be the principal must have been in existence at the time the act was done and must have been competent to do or authorize the act done, (5) the principal or person represented to be the principal must have had knowledge of all the material facts at the time he or she ratified, (6) the third party must not have canceled the transaction, and (7) the circumstances must have been such that the intervening rights of third persons were not cut off by the ratification.

There are no formal requirements for ratification. It may be expressed or implied from the acts of the principal. Usually, acceptance of benefits or failure to repudiate within a reasonable time will be convincing evidence of intent to ratify, provided the principal, at the time, has knowledge of all the material facts.

What Acts May Be Ratified. As a general rule, any act of the agent which at that time could have been done or authorized by the principal may later be ratified by the principal. This includes illegal acts. If the act ratified is both a tort and a crime, ratification by the principal will make the principal liable for the tort, but it will not alone make the principal liable for the crime, since the principal had no criminal intent at the time the act was committed. Ratification by the principal of an agent's illegal act will not relieve the agent from individual tort or criminal liability.

Since ratification relates back to the time the act was done, and since the principal must have been in existence at that time, it naturally follows that a proposed but nonexistent corporation, when it comes into existence (receives its charter), cannot ratify the acts done by the promoters in the name of the proposed but nonexistent corporation. It may, however, as discussed in Chapter 26, adopt such acts when it comes into existence.

Effect of Ratification. When a principal ratifies the unauthorized acts of his or her agent, the principal then accepts and receives all responsibility for such acts from the time they were done. When the principal has effectively ratified the acts of the agent, the principal cannot at a later time repudiate the ratification.

Ratification releases the agent from liability to both the principal and third persons for having exceeded authority. It also gives the agent the same rights against the principal as to compensation that the agent would have been given had the acts been previously authorized. In return the principal is entitled to receive from the agent everything to which the principal would have been entitled had the act been originally authorized.

Under the rule generally followed in the United States, the third person has the right to cancel or withdraw from the unauthorized transaction at any time before the principal ratifies it, but not afterward.

Ratification Must Be Entire. If the principal wishes to ratify, the entire transaction must be ratified. The principal cannot ratify those portions of the contract which are beneficial and repudiate those parts which are detrimental.[2] On ratification the principal will be bound in the same manner and to the same extent as he or she would have been if the agent had had full authority in the first instance.

SUMMARY

Ratification is the subsequent adoption of an act which was unauthorized originally. In order to make the ratification valid, the existing and identifiable principal, with knowledge of the material facts, must indicate an intention to be bound by the agent's unauthorized acts done for the principal. All that is necessary for ratification is for the principal, either expressly or impliedly, to indicate an intention to be bound by the originally unauthorized act of the agent. Any act which could have been done or authorized by the principal may be ratified. The principal must have been in existence at the time the act was done.

A ratification is retroactive and supplies the authority lacking at the time of the commission of the act. Unless third parties have acquired rights which would be cut off by ratification, the effect of ratification is to place all involved parties in the position they would have held had the act been authorized at the time it was done. If the principal wishes to ratify, the transaction must be ratified in its entirety.

Problem Cases

1. McIlroy, a forest ranger, engaged Humphreys to clean out a well being used by the U.S. Forest Service. Humphreys was given complete charge of cleaning out the well, was hired for that specific job alone, and did not normally work for the Forest Service. The government supplied him with a rope and pulley, and Humphreys was to obtain any other equipment he needed on his own. In cleaning out the well, Humphreys was asphyxiated by poisonous gas. Humphreys' wife sues for wrongful death under the Federal Tort Claims Act. The act provides for recovery by employees of the government but not by independent contractors. Can Humphreys' wife recover for his death?

2. Dodson purchased a policy of health insurance on his wife, Maria, from Mutual of Omaha Insurance Company through Edwards, a salesperson. Edwards' duties were to solicit applications for insurance and submit them to Mutual of Omaha's local office. Edwards told Dodson that although the policy did not cover normal pregnancy that if something "should go wrong" with the first-born baby after birth, the policy would cover the illness of the child. The terms of the policy, which had been read by Dodson, provided as to newborn children, "Any child of the Insured born while the policy is in force and while

[2] See *Navrides v. Zurich Insurance Co.*, p. 314.

at least one dependent is covered under the policy shall be automatically covered under this policy until the first day of the second month following birth." The policy also declared, "This policy constitutes the entire contract of insurance. No change in this policy shall be valid until approved by an executive officer of the Company and unless such approval be endorsed hereon or attached hereto. No agent has authority to change this policy or to waive any of its provisions."

The policy was issued in September and the Dodson's first child was born in November. It required extensive medical and surgical care and died in December. Dodson paid the bills, and when Mutual of Omaha refused to reimburse on the ground that the baby was not covered under the policy because there was no other dependent of the insured covered by the policy, Dodson sued. Will he recover?

3. Phillips Petroleum Company contracted with Boman-Chase, a construction company, to dismantle a cooling tower at its refinery and with Robinson to furnish a truck and driver to haul the dismantled materials away. Wigert, a Boman-Chase employee, was killed while helping to unload a welding shed from the Robinson truck. Wigert and Britain, the Robinson driver, had agreed that the method to be used was to "shake off" the shed. This involved unwinding the cable on the truck's winch two or three feet, backing the truck, then braking quickly so that momentum caused the shed to slide backwards a little each time. Boman-Chase employees had indicated where the shed was to be placed and had given hand signals to Britain during the operation. The shed fell on Wigert when Britain left some slack on the winch line. The jury found Britain to be negligent and that he was not a borrowed servant of Bowman-Chase, and judgment was entered against Robinson. Was Britain a borrowed servant of Boman-Chase?

4. Mr. and Mrs. Mills borrowed $5,580 secured by a second mortgage on their home. An employee of a mortgage broker, learning of the loan, suggested that it could refinance the loan on better terms. The Mills signed an agreement with the broker authorizing negotiation of a loan of up to $5,800 that provided that the broker would be entitled to a $700 commission if the negotiations were successful, even if the Mills failed to complete such a loan. State National Bank made the loan and the $700 commission to the broker was shown as a "service charge" in the bank's financing charge disclosure required by the Federal Truth-in-Lending Act. This amounted to an annual percentage rate of 19.75 percent. The broker obtained the relevant data concerning the Mills' home and prepared for the bank all of the papers involved in the loan. The broker had also published a circular advertising a $16 million loan program by certain banks in connection with which the broker would provide services as the banks' agent.

The Mills sought to void the loan as violating the Illinois usury statute on the ground that the broker was acting as the bank's agent so his commission should be computed in determining the interest rate for the usury statute purposes. Was the broker acting as the bank's agent?

5. Lang leased a cotton farm from Parker. He financed his operations through Independent Gin Company, and at the conclusion of the 1964 crop year he was in debt in the amount of $190,000 to Gin. At the beginning of the 1965 season, Gin insisted upon certain restrictions to the effect that Lang would be allowed $500 per month for living expenses but all bills were to be presented to Gin for payment. After the 1965 cotton crop was planted, Lang informed Gin he was unwilling to continue under the agreement and that he was abandoning farming. Gin requested Lang to permit it to carry on the farming operation. He then signed documents appointing Gin as his agent and giving its manager power of attorney to act for him.

Gin operated the farm until 1969, negotiated an amendment to the farm lease, and Lang received no money or participated in any way. In the summer of 1969 Lang attempted to revoke the powers given Gin so that he could collect the subsidy payment on the 1969 crop. Gin then brought an action to prevent the subsidy being paid to Lang, and this was settled out of court. When the lease expired in 1969, Parker sued Gin for the $8,443 past-due rent. Gin's defense was that it was merely an agent of Lang and neither a party to nor assignee of the lease. Is this a good defense?

6. On August 4, Mrs. Dickerson ordered $2,380 worth of carpeting to be installed in the Dickerson residence from Brenner Company. After a credit check, an account was opened in Mr. Dickerson's name, and this purchase was charged to it and paid by him on September 23. Other transactions entered into by Mrs. Dickerson, charged to the account and paid for by Mr. Dickerson included delivery of $370 worth of furniture on September 17 and drapes at $1,133 ordered on October 14. On October 10, Mrs. Dickerson ordered custom-made draperies and bedspreads amounting to $3,352 and work began October 16. In November the game room was completely redecorated. Mr. Dickerson was dissatisfied and the furniture was returned for full credit. He wrote Brenner saying, "In the future, please do not work at my house unless you have my written approval."

   Brenner advised Mrs. Dickerson on December 15 that the bedspreads and drapes ordered on October 10 were ready. She twice asked postponement of delivery. They were finally installed on February 3. On January 29 Mr. Dickerson sent a check completing payment on all purchases except the bedspread and drapes order and asked that his account be closed. On March 2 he wrote another letter again requesting that his account be closed and stating that he would not be responsible for any purchase made and charged to him after February 27. A bill for $3,353 for the bedspreads and drapes was sent to him on February 27. On May 18 he wrote Brenner saying he had no knowledge of this purchase by his wife and did not intend to pay. The Dickersons had separated by this time.

   Can Brenner recover the $3,353 from Mr. Dickerson on the ground that Mrs. Dickerson was acting as his agent in making the purchase?

7. Studley, a real estate broker, was asked by Burkhiser, manager of the building services department of Gulf Oil, to prepare a report on office space in New York City which might meet Gulf's needs. Burkhiser had been instructed by Gulf's president to review Gulf's New York office situation. Studley was told that the matter was confidential and should not be disclosed to Gulf's employees in New York. Studley showed Burkhiser the Sperry Rand and other buildings, and there were subsequent phone calls and letters between Studley and Burkhiser. When Cadman, the senior executive of Gulf in New York, learned of plans to consolidate several scattered offices in New York into one in a different building than the one in which he had been located, he contacted Cushman & Wakefield and was shown several buildings, including Sperry Rand. Cadman later notified Burkhiser that all future negotiations regarding the Sperry Rand building were to be conducted by Cushman & Wakefield. Gulf leased the Sperry Rand space and Rock-Uris, the owner of the building, paid a commission to Cushman & Wakefield who Cadman advised was Gulf's broker. Studley admits he had no agreement with Gulf that Gulf would pay him a commission. However, he claims that there was an agreement that if he found a suitable lease Gulf would enter into it and that he would be the broker in the transaction and entitled to the owner's commission. Can Studley recover a commission from Gulf?

8. The Wichita State University athletic director signed for the university an agreement with Golden Eagle Aviation, Inc., to provide an airplane and crew to transport the universi-

ty's football team and other personnel to games at other universities. Under the agreement the university undertook to provide the passenger liability insurance required of air taxi operators by the CAB. A plane carrying the football team and some faculty and alumni crashed in the mountains west of Denver. After the crash it was determined that the plane had taken off 2,900 pounds overweight by FAA specifications and that the university had failed to take out passenger liability insurance.

When actions for injuries and death were brought against the university, it moved for summary judgment, arguing that the athletic director had no authority to bind it on the contract. It alleged that such contracts were to be entered into by Physical Education Corporation (PEC), a nonprofit corporation formed to conduct the transactions of the intercollegiate athletic programs of the university, of which the athletic director was an authorized agent. The university declared that it was only through mutual mistake that the contract with Golden Eagle had named the university, rather than PEC, as a contracting party. All members of the board of directors of PEC were appointed by the president of the university, and he had given instructions for the operation of PEC.

Did the athletic director bind the university?

9. Bruton loaned his D-8 Cat bulldozer to Ekvall to clear some of his land. By their oral agreement Ekvall was to provide an operator, pay for the fuel used, and perform routine maintenance. Nothing was said about major repairs or overhauls. When mechanical problems appeared, Ekvall phoned AWS. It made field repairs but these proved only temporarily effective, and Ekvall authorized AWS to remove the machine to its shop. There major repairs were made to the extent of $2,340.89. When they essentially were completed, Bruton went to the AWS shop on other business and recognized his machine. He learned of the scope of the repairs, but their cost or who was to pay it was not discussed. He then authorized additional work in the amount of $387.80. When the repairs were completed AWS returned the machine to Ekvall and billed Bruton for all of the repairs. Unable to get any portion of the bill paid, AWS brought suit against both Bruton and Ekvall. Is Bruton liable for more than $387.80?

10. In August 1967, Theis opened a commodities trading account with duPont, Glore, Forgan, Inc., a brokerage house, and traded in "pork bellies" futures. The account executive, Benjamin, entered into transactions for Theis' account without authorization almost from the beginning, and Theis reprimanded him several times. On March 11, 1968, he wrote Benjamin insisting that he stop this practice, but it continued. In April he ordered Benjamin to stay "short" but this instruction was disregarded. Theis learned of this and in May repeated it and said it was his final warning. Benjamin made two more "long trades," and on May 24, after Theis told Benjamin to hold his short position as the market fell rapidly, Benjamin bought in the contracts. As soon as Theis learned of this he phoned the duPont cashier and demanded that his account be closed immediately. If Benjamin had followed Theis' orders on May 24, Theis could have closed out his account on June 3—the day he finally received a check for the balance in his account—with $11,100 more profit.

    Theis brought an action for $80,000 damages for all unauthorized trading. The trial court awarded judgment for the $11,100 lost profit opportunity on the May 24 transaction. DuPont appealed, arguing that Theis had ratified that transaction along with all the preceding ones. Is this good grounds for reversal?

17

Relation of Principal and Third Person

Disclosed or Partially Disclosed Principal

Liability of Agent of Disclosed Principal. A principal is disclosed when both the existence of the agency and the identity of the principal are known to the third person. If the agent is acting for a disclosed principal, the third person will, as a general rule, intend to contract with the principal, not the agent. For that reason the principal is bound by all contracts which are negotiated by the agent in the name of the principal, provided the agent has acted within the scope of his or her authority, express, implied, or apparent, or if the principal has ratified the acts of the agent. The third person does not intend to contract with the agent, and the agent is not bound by such a contract.

An agent may make a contract in his or her own name, in which event the agent is one of the contracting parties and is liable on the contract; the agent may join the principal as joint obligor in the making of the contract, in which case the agent is jointly liable with the principal; or the agent may guarantee the performance of the contract by the principal, in which event the agent is liable as surety. The mere fact that an agent, in negotiating a contract, uses such expressions as "I will sell" or "I will build," when it is clearly understood that he or she is acting for and in the name of the principal, will not make the agent a party to the contract or a surety for the principal.

Liability of Agent of Partially Disclosed Principal. A principal is partially disclosed when the existence of the agency is known to the third person but the identity of the principal is not known. The agent for the partially disclosed principal will, in the usual situation, be a party to the transaction he or she is negotiating. Since the identity of the principal is unknown to the third person, such third person will not, as a general rule, be willing to rely wholly on the credit and integrity of an unknown party. The third party will desire the promise of the agent either as a guarantor or as a copromisor. In such a situation, both the principal and the agent will be liable to the third person. The agreement may, however, expressly state that the agent is not liable and that the third person will look solely to the principal for performance.

Execution of Writings. An agent for a disclosed or partially disclosed principal need not sign an informal writing in any particular manner in order to make the writing binding on the principal. In the event the writing is drafted and signed in such a manner that it is not clear who the parties to the contract are, the courts will admit parol evidence to clear up the ambiguity. Good business practices, however, dictate that the principal should be named in the body of the writing as the party to be bound by the writing, and the agent should sign it in such a way as clearly to indicate that he or she is executing the writing for the principal in a representative capacity. For example, the following would clearly indicate the relations of the parties.

I, Peters, hereby * * *.
(Signed) Peters
By Archer, his agent

As explained in Chapter 42, only persons whose names appear on negotiable instruments can be held as parties to them. Therefore, the principal who is not disclosed on the instrument will not be liable on it.

SUMMARY

A principal is disclosed when the existence of the agency and the identity of the principal are known to the third person; a principal is partially disclosed when the existence of the agency is known to the third person, but not the identity of the principal. In the usual situation the agent of a disclosed principal will not be a party to the transaction, provided the agent is acting within the scope of his or her authority, expressed, implied, or apparent. The agent may, by express agreement, make himself or herself a party to a transaction being negotiated for the principal. The agent of the partially disclosed principal is, together with the principal, a party to the transaction being negotiated unless it is understood that the agent is not to be liable.

To avoid doubt, the agent should sign clearly as the agent.

Undisclosed Principal

Nature of Relation and Liability. A principal is undisclosed if both the existence of the agency and the identity of the principal are unknown to the third person. Under the law of agency, the undisclosed principal is held liable as if a party to the contract, provided the agent intends, in negotiating the transaction, to act for the undisclosed principal and has acted within the scope of his or her powers. The liability of the undisclosed principal is imposed by operation of law.

Rights of the Third Person. Since, in the case of an undisclosed principal, the agent is the contracting party, he or she is liable on the contract. If the third person discovers that an agency exists and learns the identity of the principal, the third person has the right to recognize the agency and hold the principal liable or to pursue his or her rights on the contract against the agent. The third person must make an election to hold either the principal or the agent liable; they are not both liable.

Just when the third person has made an election as to whether to pursue his or her rights under the contract and hold the agent liable or recognize the agency and hold the undisclosed principal liable will depend, primarily, on the circumstances of each case. Obviously, the third person cannot make an election until he or she learns of the existence of the agency and knows the identity of the principal.

Scope of Liability of Undisclosed Principal. The liability of an undisclosed principal for the authorized transactions of the agent is the same as that of a disclosed principal. However, an undisclosed principal runs a greater risk that the agent will bind him or her on transactions exceeding the agent's authority because the principal is unable to put a third person on notice of limitations on the authority of the agent. If the agent is a general agent, the undisclosed principal is liable for acts done on his account if usual or necessary in conducting the business entrusted to the agent even if the acts are forbidden by the principal. For example, if Prindle does not wish to be disclosed and appoints Adams to manage a retail food business, Adams will bind Prindle on groceries purchased on credit from Terman even though Prindle instructed Adams to buy only for cash and specifically not to buy from Terman.

Rights of Undisclosed Principal. The undisclosed principal is given substantially the same rights in a transaction negotiated by an agent as is given an assignee or beneficiary of a contract. The undisclosed principal takes such rights subject to all the outstanding equities as they exist at the time the third person learns of the existence of the agency and the identity of the principal. That is, he takes the transaction subject to all defenses, such as setoff, counterclaims, and payment, which the third person would have against the agent had the agent brought suit on the contract at the time the third person learned of the agency and the identity of the principal.

SUMMARY

A principal is undisclosed if both the existence of the agency and the identity of the principal are unknown to the third person. When the third person who has entered a transaction with the agent of an undisclosed principal discovers the existence of the agency and identifies the principal he or she may elect to hold either the agent or the principal.

An undisclosed principal may be liable for unauthorized, as well as authorized, acts of the agent provided such unauthorized acts are done for the account of the principal and are usual or necessary for carrying out the transaction entrusted to the agent.

Lagniappe of New Orleans, Ltd. v. Denmark

330 So.2d 626 (Ct. App. La. 1976)

This was an action by Laniappe of New Orleans, Ltd. (plaintiff), against Herbert and Elma Denmark (defendants), d/b/a Courtyard Curio Shoppe, to recover on open account for goods sold. The Denmarks' defense was that the business was a corporation and they were only its agents. Appeal from a judgment holding the defendants personally liable. Affirmed.

Mr. and Mrs. Denmark operated the Courtyard Curio Shoppe as a partnership for several years. The business was incorporated as Courtyard Curio Shoppe, Inc., on March 20, 1974. In June a representative of Lagniappe called on Mrs. Denmark, who placed an order. The representative continued to deal with Mrs. Denmark until the final order was placed on November 5, 1974. The sales representative testified that she had not been informed and was unaware of the incorporation. All invoices sent to the Denmarks were addressed to "Courtyard Curio Shoppe." The sign outside the business had not been changed and still read "Courtyard Curio Shoppe" when the business closed.

MORIAL, JUDGE. The jurisprudence of this state is clear to the effect that if an agent acting on behalf of a corporation wishes to avoid personal liability, he must disclose his status as agent and identify his principal. It is also well established that the one asserting the agency relationship bears the burden of proving disclosure.

Defendants assert that plaintiff was or should have been aware of the corporate status due to its receipt of a check dated October 28, 1974, bearing the word "Inc." after the name Courtyard Curio Shoppe. We consider this to be of little significance in light of the fact that this was the first payment ever received from defendants and that it was dated only seven days before plaintiff's final business transaction with defendants. Furthermore, it has been held that mere acceptance of a corporate check is not sufficient to put one on notice that one is dealing with a corporation rather than with an individual.

From our consideration of the facts before us, we conclude that it was reasonable for plaintiff to believe that it was transacting business with an unincorporated entity. Defendants made no attempt to disclose their corporate status and thus have clearly failed to sustain their burden of proof.

Liability on Special Transactions

Basis of Liability. In transactions negotiated by an agent, the basis of the principal's liability is the authority of the agent. It is sometimes difficult to determine the scope of this authority, even though it is set out in writing. The nature of the business entrusted to the agent, standard practices in business, and the circumstances surrounding the transaction will be considered in determining the scope of an agent's authority, both implied and apparent. The third person is bound by notice or knowledge of limitations on the agent's authority and has the burden of proving that the agent had authority to bind the principal.

Presumptions as to an agent's authority or lack of authority in relation to certain common types of transactions have been developed by the courts. Such presumptions apply only in the absence of credible evidence as to the agent's actual authority or lack of authority.

Liability for Agent's Representations. In the ordinary course of transacting business, statements and representations relative to the business at hand will be made by the negotiators. An agent has implied authority to make such statements and representations as are reasonably necessary to accomplish the objective of the agency, and has apparent authority to make such statements and representations as are usual and customary in the transaction of the business entrusted to the agent. The principal may be liable on representations by the agent even after instructing the agent not to make certain statements or informing the agent of defects in goods. However, liability would be imposed only if the third person has no notice or knowledge of the limitations on the agent's authority or of the violation by the agent of the instructions.

A third person has the right to rescind a contract into which he or she has entered in reliance on false representations made by the agent. According to the better view, this is true despite the use of what is sometimes referred to as an "exculpatory clause" in the contract. Many businesspersons, in seeking to avoid liability for misrepresentations of salespeople (as well as to control the contract price), adopt the practice of limiting their salespeople to soliciting only written offers from their customers on preprinted forms which must be accepted by them as principal in order to complete the sales contract. The offer form includes a clause which specifically states that the salesperson has no authority to make oral representations and that only such representations as appear on the offer form in writing will be binding.

Courts have tended to take the view that even though the seller has done all he or she reasonably can in such a case to give notice to the customer of the limitation on the agent's authority, it would be unjust to permit the principal to enjoy the benefit of a misrepresentation and yet disclaim responsibility for it. A few recent cases have even permitted the buyer to recover damages for fraudulent misrepresentations of the agent despite such an exculpatory clause.[1]

Liability for Agent's Warranties. A principal is liable for warranties made by his or her agent in a sale of goods if such a warranty is customarily made on such goods in the market in which the goods are sold. The principal is also liable on warranties made by the agent which are no more extensive than those implied by law. The principal is not liable on an unauthorized warranty which is unusual or extraordinary in nature. The third person is bound by any limitations or instructions given the agent of which the third person has knowledge or notice.

Liability for Payment to Agent. The fact that an agent has negotiated a transaction does not, as a matter of law, confer on the agent the authority to collect. Such authority arises when it is the usual and reasonable incident of the business to be transacted. As in other cases, it may be shown that the agent has express, implied, or apparent authority to collect; but as a general rule, authority to sell does not confer on the agent authority to receive payment. A sales agent who has authority to solicit orders for future delivery does not thereby have the authority to collect the purchase price of the goods. However, it is generally held that if the selling agent has possession of the goods, he has implied authority to collect the purchase price of goods sold. Also, it is generally held that an agent making over-the-counter sales has authority to collect. Usage of trade, course of dealing, or the acts of the principal may confer on the agent authority to collect.

Possession of an instrument evidencing the debt is strong, yet not conclusive, evidence of authority to collect. If the agent has negotiated a loan, sold property, or transacted other similar business for the principal and has received from the third person a negotiable instrument payable to the principal, the agent has apparent authority to receive payment and discharge the instrument if the principal permits the agent to retain possession of the instrument. However, in several cases the courts have held that payment to the agent before the due date does not discharge the debt. If the agent has not been permitted to retain the instrument evidencing an indebtedness, the third person is put on notice that the agent does not have authority to collect.

Liability for Credit Contracted by Agent. The agent, in the absence of express authority, will not have authority to purchase on the principal's credit. This rule is not absolute. If the agency is general, and if, in order to carry

[1] See, for example, *Brunswick Corp. v. Sittason,* 167 So.2d 126 (Ala. 1964).

out the purpose of the agency, it becomes necessary for the agent to borrow money or purchase goods on the principal's credit, the principal will be bound. Also, if the principal has held the agent out as having authority to borrow money or purchase goods on his or her credit or has knowingly permitted the agent to borrow money or purchase goods on his or her credit, the principal will be bound.

If the agent is given money by the principal to purchase goods and the third person accepts the agent's personal check without knowledge that the principal has furnished funds to pay for the goods, the third person cannot recover from the principal if the check is not honored. If the agent is authorized to purchase the goods but is not furnished the money with which to pay for the goods, the agent will have implied authority to purchase on the credit of the principal.

Liability on Negotiable Instruments. The negotiable instrument is given a separate and distinct place in the business world. The nature of the negotiable instrument and the liability of the parties to it are such that the authority to sign, or to indorse and negotiate, or to cash such instruments is sparingly conferred on an agent.

Express authority to sign or indorse negotiable instruments is strictly construed and will not be enlarged by interpretation. The authority to sign or indorse negotiable instruments will not be implied unless the nature of the business entrusted to the agent is such that it cannot be effectively carried on without the signing or indorsing of negotiable instruments. An authorization "to transact any and all business" does not expressly or impliedly authorize the agent to sign or indorse negotiable instruments unless such acts are essential to the carrying-on of the business entrusted to him or her.

Only in exceptional cases will the courts hold that an agent has apparent authority to sign or indorse negotiable instruments. The fact that an agent is given a special title, such as president, secretary, treasurer, general manager, or cashier of a corporation, does not as a general rule give him or her apparent authority to sign or indorse negotiable instruments in the name of the corporation. A member of a partnership has the authority, under partnership law, to sign or indorse negotiable instruments in the partnership name, unless such authority is withheld by the terms of the partnership agreement.

SUMMARY

Where the scope of the agent's authority is not specified or is ambiguous, the law makes certain presumptions: generally the principal is liable for representations of his or her agent which are reasonably necessary to accomplish the objective of the agency or are customary in the transaction of such business, provided they are relied upon by the third person. The third person has the right to rescind a transaction where misrepresentations are made even if they were unauthorized or expressly forbidden by the principal.

The principal is bound by the warranties made by a selling agent, provided they are of the nature usually made in the trade, but the principal is not liable for unusual warranties made by the agent.

Authority to sell does not confer on the agent authority to collect the purchase price. Authority to make a loan does not imply authority to accept payment and discharge the debt when the loan falls due. If negotiable paper is left in the hands of the agent, it is evidence of authority to accept payment on the due date, but it is not evidence of authority to accept payment before the due date.

As a general rule an agent does not have authority to pledge the principal's credit. Such authority is not implied unless there is a clear necessity for such action. Nor does the agent have authority to sign or indorse negotiable instruments in the principal's name unless the authority is express or unless the nature of the business entrusted to the agent is such that it is necessary to sign or indorse negotiable instruments in order to transact the business. A strong case is necessary to establish apparent authority to sign or indorse negotiable instruments.

Taco Bell of California v. Zappone

324 So.2d. 121 (Ct. App. Fla. 1976)

This was an action by Ralph Zappone (plaintiff) against Taco Bell of California (defendant) for misrepresentation through its franchise salesman. The jury returned a verdict for Zappone of $41,250 in compensatory damages and $68,750 in punitive damages. Taco Bell appealed. Reversed.

Taco Bell was a California corporation operating restaurants in Florida and elsewhere. Zappone operated a restaurant in California that was netting him approximately $1,000 per month. Interested in associating himself with a company that might enable him to operate more than one restaurant, Zappone contacted Taco Bell about franchises. Taco Bell referred him to one of its franchise salesmen in California, William Radford. Radford presented Zappone with a document entitled "Initial Deposit Receipt and Agreement to Pay." Radford had signed it and there was another place for "Home Office Approval by Taco Bell." Zappone never signed but arrangements were made for him to operate the Taco Bell restaurant in Lakeland, Florida.

After he had operated the Lakeland restaurant for two and one-half months, Zappone signed a license agreement and sublease agreement with Taco Bell without reading them. The license agreement contained a disclaimer by Taco Bell as to any representations of profits that might be derived from the business. After another month and a half Zappone discontinued the relationship. He brought an action for economic losses and for mental distress as a result of the move with his family from California. He testified that Radford had represented to him during negotiations that the restaurant had a volume of $8,000 per month in sales, that the operator would net $1,600 per month, and that Zappone could become the exclusive franchise operator in the Orlando area for at least two Taco Bell restaurants if he later moved there. He also testified that his sales volume and net were much less than had been represented, that there was already a Taco Bell restaurant in Orlando, and that he had learned that Taco Bell had no intention of opening others there.

The trial court instructed the jury that Radford was Taco Bell's agent, "and as such, his acts were the acts of the defendant." Taco Bell appealed, alleging this instruction was error.

SCHEB, JUDGE. It is undisputed that Radford was a franchise salesman and thereby an agent for Taco Bell. In an action for misrepresentation, a principal is liable for the fraud of his agent while acting in the scope of his authority, and this principle of law is fully applicable to corporations. But, to bind his principal, an agent's actions must be within the scope of his express or implied, i.e., his "actual or real" authority, or be of such a nature as third parties would be entitled to rely upon as being within his "apparent" authority. This issue of apparent authority often presents a mixed question of law and fact, and is one which should be submitted to the jury under appropriate instructions.

There was no evidence that Radford had actual authority to make the representations in question. Taco Bell's chairman of the board and its vice president both testified that they were never informed of the representations attributed to Radford by Zappone. Significantly, the testimony elicited from the officers of Taco Bell did not elaborate the scope of Radford's authority beyond decribing him as a "franchised salesman." Any liability of Taco Bell must therefore be based upon Radford's apparent authority.

Apparent or ostensible authority arises where a principal allows or causes others to believe the agent possesses such authority, as where the principal knowingly permits the agent to assume such authority or where the principal by his actions or words holds the agent out as possessing it. The doctrine rests on the premises that one who allows another to serve as his agent must bear the loss which results to a third party from that party's dealings in reliance on that agent's supposed authority. But as Mechem points out, the doctrine rests on appearances created by the principal and not by agents who often ingeniously create an appearance of authority by their own acts.

If the actions of Radford were not within the scope of his actual or apparent authority, and not specifically authorized or ratified by Taco Bell, then there would be no liability to Taco Bell as a principal. And where, as here, the evidence showed that Radford was an agent with certain actual authority, but the scope of his apparent authority was in dispute, it was critical for the trier of fact to have the opportunity to make its own finding on this point. The exculpatory language in the "Initial Deposit Receipt and Agreement to Pay" signed by Radford and exhibited to, but not signed by, Zappone clearly was evidence tending to negate Radford's apparent authority to promise an exclusive franchise in the Orlando area. This document could have, and arguably should have, suggested to Zappone that only a corporate officer could make such a representation binding on Taco Bell.

Navrides v. Zurich Insurance Co.
488 P.2d 637 (Sup. Ct. Cal. 1971)

This was an action by Audrey Navrides (plaintiff) against Zurich Insurance Company (defendant) to recover the proceeds of a check in settlement of her tort claim which had been paid to her attorney. Judgment for Navrides and the insurer appealed. Judgment reversed.

Navrides had been injured on the premises of Crancer, who was insured by the Zurich Insurance Company. She employed an attorney, Robert S. Forsyth, who filed an action for damages on her behalf. Forsyth negotiated with Zurich a compromise settlement of the claim. Navrides rejected the settlement of $9,000 but Forsyth represented to Zurich that she had approved it. Zurich then submitted to Forsyth for signature a release of all claims, a request for the dismissal of the pending action, and a draft for $9,000 payable to Navrides and Forsyth. Forsyth retained the draft and returned the release, purportedly signed by Navrides, together with the request for dismissal. The latter document was then filed and the action dismissed. Three days later the settlement draft, bearing the purported endorsements of Navrides and Forsyth, was cashed and in due course charged to Zurich's bank account in Chicago.

Miss Navrides' signature on the draft and on the release were forgeries by Forsyth, and she received none of the settlement money. About a year later she discovered that her personal injury action had been dismissed and the draft had been delivered to her attorney. She was unable to recover from him and then filed an action against Zurich.

SULLIVAN, JUSTICE. The trial court's conclusion that Navrides' signature on the draft was a forgery is amply supported by the findings and the evidence. Unfortunately, however, the court nowhere indicates any legal theory explaining its leap from its findings and first conclusion of law to its second conclusion that Zurich owed Navrides $9,000 plus interest. It is a fair assumption that the trial judge, relying on former Civil Code section 3104, concluded that the forged endorsement was wholly inoperative and that as a consequence Zurich still owed Navrides $9,000.

Although Forsyth clearly had no authority, express or implied, to compromise Navrides' claim, the record before us establishes as a matter of law that Navrides, by bringing the instant action against Zurich for the $9,000, ratified the settlement. . . .

It is well settled that a client may ratify the unauthorized actions of his attorney (citations); that a principal may ratify the forgery of his signature by his agent (citations); and that a principal may ratify the unauthorized act of an agent by bringing suit based thereon (citation).

By virtue of such ratification, there then existed between Navrides and Zurich a *valid* compromise agreement which was fully performed on the part of Navrides by Forsyth's delivery of the release and dismissal to Zurich. The true and indeed only tenable theory of Navrides' action thus emerges: that Zurich owes her $9,000 under the settlement agreement and that she had not been paid. . . . However, inherent in the ratification of the settlement is ratification of Forsyth's authority to settle the claim, which, as we explain, *infra,* necessarily includes authority to receive and collect the payment of the settlement on behalf of Navrides.

Unfortunately for Navrides, she cannot stop at this point. She must reckon with the elementary rule of agency law that a principal is not allowed to ratify the unauthorized acts of an agent to the extent that they are beneficial, and disavow them to the extent that they are damaging. If a principal ratifies part of a transaction, he is deemed to ratify the whole of it (citations). The reason for the rule is obvious. Ratification is approval of a transaction that has already taken place. Accordingly the principal has the power to approve the transaction only as it in fact occurred, not to reconstruct it to suit his present needs.

The foregoing authorities support the now-settled rule that where an agent authorized to collect a debt owing his principal accepts in lieu of cash a valid check *payable to the agent,* the debtor is discharged upon payment of the check, although the agent absconds with the proceeds, since payment to the agent is equivalent to payment to the principal. . . .

The crucial question presented to us in the instant case is whether the above rule applies where the attorney receives a check payable to the *client* or to the *client* and the *attorney together.*

Zurich argues, a proper correlation of these competing principles is found in section 178 of the *Restatement Second of Agency* the effect of which is to relieve the maker where the payee's endorsement has been forged by his agent authorized to receive the check.

The twofold justification for this rule, which amply demonstrates its wisdom, is best articulated in two similar cases. In *Burstein v. Sullivan* (1909), one Melle, the general manager of a garage, had authority to render bills and receive payments, but not to sign checks. He presented a bill to defendant, who delivered to the manager a check payable to the garage for the amount of the bill. Melle endorsed the check by using a rubber stamp of the firm's name in connection with which he signed his name as manager. The court said: "A payment to Melle in cash would have been a payment to the plaintiff's though he had stolen the money; and the defendant should not be compelled to pay twice, or subjected to the hazards of a lawsuit with the bank, for having taken the precaution to protect the plaintiffs by making a check payable to their order. . . ."

In *McFadden v. Follrath* (1911) the court explained the justification for this rule in terms of business practice and its need for negotiable paper. "It would be a novel burden if the drawer of a check given in the usual course of business, to the authorized agent of the payee, upon such check being indorsed by such agent, was charged with the duty of determining that the indorsement on the check was authorized."

The rule articulated by the line of authority of which the foregoing decisions are a part has been expressly adopted in the *Restatement Second of Agency.* Section 178(2) thereof provides: "If an agent who is authorized to receive a check payable to the principal as conditional payment forges the principal's endorsement to such a check, the maker is relieved of liability to the principal if the drawee bank pays the check and charges the amount to the maker."

Notice to or Knowledge of Agent

Effect of Notice to Agent. Generally, notice to the agent is notice to the principal if the information acquired by the agent relates to the business that the agent is transacting for the principal. The duty to communicate to the principal with respect to matters coming to the agent's notice that are within the scope of the agency and material to the principal for protection or guidance is imposed on the agent by law for reasons of public policy. If the agent fails to perform duties, the principal rather than the innocent third person should bear any resulting loss because the principal selected the method of doing business and the agent. The agent is not required to communicate to the principle every rumor or detailed fact which comes to the agent's notice, regardless of the reliability of the source. Notice to the agent of matters not within the scope of the agency is not binding on the principal unless the agent does in fact communicate it to the principal.

Knowledge of Agent. Knowledge of the agent includes knowledge gained in transactions for the principal and knowledge which, by the exercise of reasonable prudence, the agent should have obtained. Knowledge of facts material to the agency gained during the transaction of business unrelated to the agency may be imputed to the principal if it was present in the mind of the agent and used to the advantage of the principal during the agency. Of course, the agent has no duty to disclose confidential information obtained while serving another principal. Knowledge gained by the agent after the termination of the agency is not binding on the principal unless the agency is a continuing one. In such a case the principal will be bound by notice given to the agent by a third person who has dealt with the agent during the agency and at the time the third person gave the notice was unaware of the termination of the agency.

Limitations on the Rule. The rule does not apply in those situations in which it is clear that the agent would not communicate the knowledge to the principal. The courts have held that if the agent's interests conflict with the interests of the principal and the agent's interests will be furthered by not communicating a fact to the principal, the principal will not be bound by the knowledge of the agent. If, however, an innocent third person will be injured if the principal is not bound by the uncommunicated knowledge of the agent, the courts will hold that the principal is bound. If the agent and the third person collusively or fraudulently withhold knowledge from the principal, the principal will not be bound.

Under this rule the knowledge of the agent is imputed to the principal; hence the principal's knowledge is constructive, not actual. Therefore, the principal will not be held liable for a crime for which actual knowledge is an essential element.

SUMMARY

Notice of facts given to the agent regarding business being transacted by the agent for the principal is binding on the principal. Notice of facts given to the agent regarding matters unconnected with the business entrusted to the agent is not binding on the principal unless communicated to him or her. Knowledge of the agent, at the time the agent is transacting business for the principal, will be imputed to the principal.

If the agent's personal interests conflict with the duties owed to the principal, of if the agent and third person are in collusion to defraud the principal, the knowledge of the agent will not be imputed to the principal.

A principal cannot be held criminally liable for an act of an agent if knowledge is an essential element of the crime, even though the agent has knowledge but has not actually communicated that knowledge to the principal.

Peoria & Eastern Ry. Co. v. Kenworthy

287 N.E.2d 543 (App. Ct. Ill. 1972)

This was an action by Peoria & Eastern Railway Company (plaintiff) against Glenn Kenworthy and Vaughn McDowell (defendants) seeking indemnity. Appeal from a directed verdict for Kenworthy and McDowell. Reversed and remanded.

McDowell owned land in the town of Leroy, Illinois, adjacent to the railroad's tracks. McDowell permitted Kenworthy to park a truck trailer on his property that extended into the railroad right of way approximately four feet. This obstructed the view from a nearby road crossing, and because of this a motorist was struck by a Peoria & Eastern locomotive. Since a statute required the railroad to keep its right of way clear, it made a settlement of $25,000 with the motorist for his damages and then sought indemnity from McDowell and Kenworthy. They defended on the ground, among others, that a conductor, two brakemen, and two engineers employed by the railroad had seen the trailer or others parked in the same or similar locations from time to time for varying periods. Each of these men further testified that he had not reported this to his railroad superiors and that he did not know where the boundaries of the right of way of the railroad were. The railroad argued that the knowledge of these employees should not be imputed to it because such knowledge did not fall within the scope of their authority as agents of the railroad.

TRAPP, PRESIDING JUSTICE. Restatement of the law of Agency, Vol. 1, p. 505, par. 228, states that the conduct or duties which the employee is employed to perform determines the scope of employment. Par. 229 provides that to be within the scope of employment, the conduct must be of the same general nature as that authorized by the employer, or for which the employee is employed. The rule that notice to the agent or employee is notice to the principal or employer is not applicable unless the notice has reference to business in which the employee is engaged and pertains to matters coming with that employment.

In *United Disposal & Recovery Co. v. Indus. Com.*, a timekeeper learned that certain employees were using motor trucks in deviation from the authorized and instructed route. It was contended that acquiescence in the deviation should be imputed to the employer. The court determined that the timekeeper had no authority over the use of the trucks and that knowledge would not be imputed to the employer. In *C.,B.&Q.R.R. Co. v. Hammond* it was held that a landowner's advice of his claim of right-of-way made to a section foreman would not be notice imputed to the railroad.

In this record the available evidence is that the trainmen did not know the boundaries of the property owned by the railroad. An inference may be drawn that the conditions upon such property were not a part of the work they were employed to perform, or over which they possessed any authority.

Liability for Acts of Subagents

Appointment of Subagents. The liability of a principal for the torts or contracts of a subagent or subemployee will depend upon the relation between the appointing agent and the principal. The agent may have express, implied, or apparent authority to appoint agents or employees for the principal, either to perform tasks delegated by the agent or to do other tasks for the principal.

In such cases, the agent or employee is the agent or employee of the principal. This is, of course, the only way agents and employees of corporations are appointed. A professional agent such as a stock broker may have authority from the principal to appoint subagents who are employees of the agent, not employees of the principal, but who will have authority to bind the principal on certain kinds of contracts.

Liability of Principal for Acts of Subagents. If an agent has acted within the scope of his or her authority in appointing an agent or employee of the principal, the principal is liable for the contracts made or torts committed by such persons to the same extent as if the principal had made the appointment. The appointing agent would not be liable for the acts of such an agent or employee. However, the appointing agent might be held liable for failure to exercise reasonable care and skill in choosing the agent or employee.

The circumstances may be such that the agent will be authorized to select agents and employees and to delegate certain acts required in the performance of agent's duties to the principal. Such appointees are the agents and employees of the original agent and as such are under his control, and he is liable for their acts. However, the original principal is liable indirectly for their acts which are done at the direction of or are delegated to them by the original agent, provided such acts are within the scope of the authority of the original agent. For example, suppose Albert is the agent of Perfect Insurance Company and he appoints Bates as his agent, authorizing him to prepare and execute insurance policies of Perfect Insurance Company in fulfillment of applications for insurance which Albert has approved. If Bates prepares and delivers a policy of insurance in the name of Perfect Insurance Company which is issued within the scope of Albert's authority, Perfect Insurance Company will be liable on the policy. But suppose Bates, when on his way to deliver the policy, operates his automobile in a negligent manner and injures a pedestrian. Perfect Insurance Company will not be liable to the injured pedestrian, since Bates is not an employee of Perfect Insurance Company.

If the principal, in appointing an agent, makes the appointment in reliance on the discretion, judgment, skill, or character of the appointee, such agent cannot delegate his or her authority to a third person and any attempt to delegate such authority is a nullity. Acts that involve no discretion but which are ministerial in nature may, as a general rule, be delegated.

SUMMARY

The authority to appoint subagents and employees will depend on the circumstances of the particular case. The agent may be authorized to make appointments in behalf of the principal, in which event such appointees will be under the control of the principal and will be his or her agents or employees.

The agent may be authorized to perform portions of his or her duties to the principal by delegating certain functions to others. In such a situation the appointees will be the agents and employees of the original agent, and the original principal will be liable indirectly for the acts of such appointees only to the extent that they are performing delegated acts that the original agent is authorized to delegate. An agent cannot delegate authority if the principal has selected the agent on the basis of judgment, discretion, skill, or character. As a general rule, ministerial acts may be delegated.

Liability for Torts and Crimes

Agents Who Are Employees. Today, most agents are employees, and thus the principal (employer), as well as the employee, is liable for the employee's torts committed within the scope of the employment under the doctrine of *respondeat superior.* The meaning of this very old legal doctrine is "let the master answer," and it imposes liability on the employer without fault on his part. The employer cannot escape liability by proving that he exercised the greatest of care in the selection of the employee, that the employer trained the employee in safety measures or that the employer gave the employee specific instructions not to do the act or to make the representation that was tortious. Since the employer's liability is derivative, if the employee is not liable neither is the employer.

Scope of Employment. Whether or not a tort committed by an employee was committed within the scope of the employment is frequently a difficult question of fact. Several factors are examined in making the determination. One factor is whether the tort was committed within the time and space limits of the employment. A second factor is whether the employee was actuated, in part at least, by the purpose of serving the employer. A third is whether the act is of the same general nature as or incidental to the authorized conduct.

As a general rule, an employer is not liable for the torts committed by an employee who has abandoned his or her employment temporarily. The courts have distinguished between degrees of digression from the employment. The employer remains liable for torts committed during a mere deviation from the employment. For example, if a truck driver while making deliveries takes a one- or two-block detour and stops only briefly at the home of a friend, the employer would be liable for damages due to injuries suffered by a pedestrian resulting from negligent driving of the truck just before the trucker reaches the friend's house. However, if after the trucker arrives at the friend's house they decide to go fishing and they have started off in the employer's truck in a new direction toward a lake at the time the pedestrian is struck, the employer would not be liable.

There is considerable diversity in the decisions as to when the employee has returned to his employment after a temporary abandonment. In the fishing trip example, some courts would hold that the driver had returned to his employment as soon as he started toward his next delivery. Others would hold that he had not returned until he was at or near a point on his original route.

Liability for Torts of Professional Agent. A professional agent, such as a manufacturer's representative or stockbroker, is not an employee of the person for whom he or she conducts transactions, but is like an independent contractor. A professional agent is an agent with respect to those transactions for which he is employed by his principal. The principal is not liable for the torts of the professional agent which result from misconduct in respect to physical acts, such as negligence in driving his or her automobile, but the principal may be liable for other torts committed in the course of the negotiation of the principal's business.

Liability for Deceit of Agent. The trend of court decisions has been toward holding the principal liable for fraudulent representations when it is usual in that trade for agents to make representations or when the agent commits the deceit while apparently acting within his or her authority unless the reliance upon the representation by the third party was unreasonable. A number of cases have held banks liable for fraudulent schemes of their officers, such as the sale of stolen negotiable bonds, perpetrated on customers of the bank even though the bank had no material connection with the scheme except for the position of the officer and the wrongful use of its name. There is, of course, no doubt that the principal is liable for any deceit which he or she directs, causes, or participates in. Likewise, if the principal ratifies an unauthorized transaction in which a tortious act occurred, the principal is liable for the tort (assuming the principal has knowledge of the tort).

Intentional Torts. In the past, the employer was generally held not liable for an intentional physical act of an employee which was tortious, such as striking or shooting a third person, unless the employer authorized the act. However, courts today are much more likely than earlier to find an employer liable for an intentional tort. If use of force is foreseeable by the employer, this is generally sufficient for liability, and some courts let the question of scope of employment go to the jury without regard to foreseeability.

Tort Liability Is Joint and Several. The principal or employer and the agent or employee are jointly and severally liable for the torts of the agent or employee. That is, the principal and agent or employee may be joined in the same action, or they may each be sued in separate actions. However, the injured party is entitled to only one satisfaction. When the injured party has been compensated for injuries, whether recovery is made from the principal or from the agent or employee, there is no further right of action.

Crimes. The older view was that an employer could not be liable for crimes committed by an employee unless the employer directed or participated in the crime at least to the extent of being an accessory. Recently updated criminal codes and some recent court decisions have held the employer guilty of crimes requiring intent where the person who did have the requisite intent was a decision-making managerial employee. Where no intent is required, and particularly in the case of crimes defined by statute such as in the antitrust laws, the statutory penalties may be imposed on the principal for the criminal act of the employee or agent.

SUMMARY

The employer (as well as the employee) is liable without fault on his or her part for the torts of employees if the tort is committed within the scope of the employment. If the tortious act is committed by the employee while the employee is engaged in the performance of his or her duties and the act is viewed as aiding in some way or is incidental to the task assigned by the employer, the employer is likely to be held liable.

The principal is not liable for tortious physical acts of a professional agent but is liable for fraudulent representations if it is customary in the trade for agents to make representations or if the agent is acting within his apparent authority. Although generally employers have not been held liable for crimes of employees where intent is required, the trend is toward liability if the crime is committed by a high managerial employee.

The liability of the principal or employer for the torts of an agent or employee is joint and several.

Lange v. National Biscuit Co.

211 N.W.2d 783 (Sup. Ct. Minn. 1973)

This was an action by Lange (plaintiff) against National Biscuit Company (defendant) for damages resulting from an assault upon him by an employee of Nabisco. Appeal from a decision granting judgment for Nabisco notwithstanding a jury verdict for Lange. Reversed.

Lange was the manager of a small grocery store. Lynch was hired by Nabisco as a cookie salesman-trainee in October 1968, and in March 1969 was assigned his own territory which included Lange's store. Between March 1 and May 1 Nabisco received numerous complaints from grocers served by Lynch that Lynch was overly aggressive and that he was taking shelf space reserved for competing cookie companies.

On May 1 while Lynch was stocking Lange's shelves with Nabisco products an argument developed between them over Lynch's activities in the store. Lynch became very angry and started swearing. Lange told Lynch either to stop swearing or leave the store, as children were present. Lynch then became uncontrollably angry, saying, "I ought to break your neck." He went behind the counter and dared Lange to fight. Lange refused, whereupon Lynch proceeded to assault him viciously. Upon completion of the assault, Lynch proceeded to throw merchandise around the store and then left.

TODD, JUSTICE. There is no dispute with the general principle that in order to impose liability on the employer under the doctrine of respondeat superior it is necessary to show that the employee was acting within the scope of his employment. Unfortunately, there is a wide disparity in the case law in the application of the "scope of employment" test to those factual situations involving intentional torts. The majority rule as set out in *Annotation,* 34 A.L.R. 2d 372, 402, includes a twofold test: (a) Whether the assault was motivated by business or personal considerations; or (b) whether the assault was contemplated by the employer or incident to the employment.

Under the present Minnesota rule, liability is imposed where it is shown that the employee's acts were motivated by a desire to further the employer's business. Therefore, a master could only be held liable for an employee's assault in those rare instances where the master actually requested the servant to so perform, or the servant's duties were such that that motivation was implied in law.

Respondeat superior or vicarious liability is a principle whereby responsibility is imposed on the master who is not directly at fault. Its derivation lies in the public policy to satisfy an instinctive sense of justice. It has been explained most frequently under the "entrepreneur theory." This justification holds that an employer, knowing that he is liable for the torts of his servants, can and should consider this liability as a cost of his business. He may then avoid the cost by insuring against such contingencies, or by adjusting his prices so that his patrons must bear part, if not all, of the burden of insurance. In this way, losses are spread and the shock of the accident is dispersed. A secondary consideration lies in the fact that an employer, knowing that he is responsible, will be alert to prevent the occurrence of such injuries.

In developing a test for the application of respondeat superior when an employee assaults a third person, we believe that the focus should be on the basis of the assault rather than the motivation of the employee. We reject as the basis for imposing liability the arbitrary determination of when, and at what point, the argument and assault leave the sphere of the employer's business and become motivated by personal animosity. Rather, we believe the better approach is to view both the argument and assault as an indistinguishable event for purposes of vicarious liability. . . .

Attempts, in cases where altercations arise, to distinguish the doctrine of respondeat superior on the theory that at some point the argument becomes personal and not related to the scope of employment are unduly restrictive and attribute to the employee, enraged by reason of his employment, a rational decision, that he is crossing some imaginary line to pursue personal business. Whether the nature and character of the dispute change from a work-related incident to a personal assault, and, if so, when they do, is not dispositive of the issue.

We hold that an employer is liable for an assault by his employee when the source of the attack is related to the duties of the employee and the assault occurs within work-related limits of time and place. The assault in this case obviously occurred within work-related limits of time and place, since it took place on authorized premises during working hours. The precipitating cause of the initial argument concerned the employee's conduct of his work. In addition, the employee originally was motivated to become argumentative in furtherance of his employer's business. Consequently, under the facts of this case we hold as a matter of law that the employee was acting within the scope of employment at the time of the aggression and that Lange's post-trial motion for judgment notwithstanding the verdict on that ground should have been granted under the rule we herein adopt. To the extent that our former decisions are inconsistent with the rule now adopted, they are overruled.

Among other states which have abandoned the "motivation test" and allow recovery for assaults arising out of or ancillary to the work being done by the employee are Mississippi, California, Kentucky, Illinois, Alabama, Connecticut, and Montana.

Problem Cases

1. In January 1971, Darrel Ireland purchased a business in Colorado Springs known as "George Pet Supply Shop." He continued the business under that trade name with George Hall employed as general manager. Hall purchased merchandise for the shop on open account from Feed Company under authority from Ireland. In June 1972 Hall and his wife purchased the business from Ireland and assumed all existing liabilities, including an account with Feed. The Halls continued to make purchases on account from Feed. No notice of the change in ownership was given and Feed continued the account as before, the payments being made by "George Pet Supply Shop." The Halls were not successful in the business and filed in bankruptcy in August 1973. Is Ireland liable for feed bought after he sold the business?

2. Davis entered into a contract with Moore, vice president of Fletcher Emerson Management Company, to landscape a new building, Emerson Center in Atlanta. The contract contained a provision "Ship to Fletcher Emerson Management Co. . . . TO BE USED FOR EMERSON CENTER." After the work had been done but while $11,795 was still due of the total of $37,683 on the contract, Davis received a notice from Fletcher Emerson declaring that it would not be responsible for any further purchases for Emerson Center and that future invoices should be sent to Atlanta Venture No. 1.

When sued for the balance due, Fletcher Emerson argued that it was only an agent for Atlanta Venture No. 1 and that its trade name made it clear that it was only an agent. It produced an affidavit of Moore declaring that it was his practice to inform all with whom he did business that it was acting only as an agent for the owners of Emerson Center, that he had no recollection of departing from this practice, and that he would recall any such departure. Davis filed affidavits denying knowledge that Fletcher Emerson was acting as an agent and moved for summary judgment. Should the motion be granted?

3. Buford and Mr. and Mrs. Epstein executed a document titled a "Lease and Purchase and Sale Agreement." It was essentially a sale of real estate to Buford, but initially the property was leased to Buford for up to 36 months at a fixed monthly rental plus real estate taxes and insurance plus a $1,000 deposit. It was agreed that upon the cancellation of an identified encumbrance the lease would terminate and the rental payments and deposit would be credited toward the $18,000 purchase price. The agreement included a nonassignment clause as follows:

    > That he (Buford) will not transfer nor assign this agreement, nor let nor sublet the whole or any part of said premises without written consent of Landlord first had and obtained such consent shall not be unreasonably withheld.

    Monthly payments were timely made from September through February but the March payment was two weeks late and then the check was returned for insufficient funds. The April payment was also late and the Epsteins notified Buford on April 6 that they were cancelling the contract for nonpayment. In May the described encumbrance was removed. Subsequently Buford learned that the property had been sold to the District of Columbia Redevelopment Land Agency for $27,000. Thereafter, Buford died, and Cooper brought an action against the Epsteins on the contract entered into with Buford, claiming to be Buford's undisclosed principal.

    Does the nonassignment clause bar his claim as an undisclosed principal as a matter of law?

4. Stewart, a salesperson for Harring, sold Skaggs a safe and warranted it to be fire- and burglarproof. Burglars stole money and other valuables from the safe. The locks on the safe were found to be inadequate, and the safe could be burglarized with little difficulty. Skaggs sued Harring to recover damages for breach of warranty. Harring set up as a defense that Stewart had no authority to warrant the safe. Is Harring liable?

5. Coats entered into a conditional sale contract for the purchase of a power shovel from Harnischfeger Sales Corporation (Harnischfeger). The contract was negotiated by an agent of Harnischfeger and contained the following provision: "This agreement shall not be considered as executed, and shall not become effective until accepted by the vendee, and executed and approved by the president, or vice president, or secretary of the vendor, and it is hereby further declared, agreed and understood that there are no prior writings, verbal negotiations, understandings, representations or agreements between the parties, not herein expressed." Coats, when sued, set up that the agent induced him to execute the contract by making fraudulent representations, and he counterclaimed for tort damages for the fraud. Is Coats liable on the contract?

6. Exxon and Johnson and Johnson entered into license agreements with duPont for the right to use certain processes in return for the payment of certain royalties. The licensees had been directed by a certain duPont employee to send the royalty payments quarterly to its Elastomer Chemicals Dept., "Attention: C.H.D., Control Division." The employee developed a pattern of fraudulently indorsing and depositing the checks to his personal account while covering his defalcations by making false records. In this way he converted

approximately $135,000 from 1962 to 1969 until a routine audit brought to light a questionable indorsement on one of the checks. duPont and its bonding company then brought suit to recover the amounts paid but not received by duPont, claiming that Exxon and Johnson and Johnson should have noticed the fraudulent indorsements and that C.H.D. had never been authorized to direct the payments to himself or to indorse the checks. Did C.H.D. have authority to receive the payments on behalf of duPont?

7. A life insurance policy was issued on the life of Roney D. Boykin without medical examination. In the application, materially false statements regarding the health of Boykin were made. Boykin died three months later, the insurance company refused to pay the amount of the policy, and suit was brought. The insurance company set up the misrepresentation as a defense. The beneficiary proved that the insured gave the correct information regarding his health to the agent of the insurance company, but the agent filled in incorrect answers. The insured signed the application and knew what answers had been filled in. The beneficiary contends that since the agent of the insurance company knew the true state of the insured's health, such knowledge would be imputed to the insurance company, and the defense of misrepresentation is not available to it. Is the insurance company liable on the policy?

8. The Coast Guard vessel *Tamaroa* was being overhauled in Bushey & Sons' floating drydock when a drunken sailor, returning to the ship from shore leave, opened the valves that controlled the flooding of the tanks on one side of the drydock. The ship soon lifted and slid off the blocks which held it up to permit repairs to be made to its drive shaft and hull. It then fell against the drydock, part of which sank. One of the provisions in the contract for repair of the ship declared:

   > . . . The work shall, whenever practical, be performed in such manner as not to interfere with the berthing and messing of personnel attached to the vessel undergoing repair, and provision shall be made so that personnel assigned shall have access to the vessel at all times, it being understood that such personnel will not interfere with the work or the contractor's workmen.

   Bushey and Sons sued the United States for the damages suffered. The defense raised was that the sailor was not acting within the scope of his employment. Is this a good defense?

9. A barbershop singing quartet calling themselves the "Discords" were auditioned by WMMN, a radio station. It agreed to permit them to make tape recordings in its studio at mutually convenient times to be broadcast, solely at WMMN's discretion, at a specified time each week. No remuneration was paid the Discords but the arrangement continued for about a year. Immediately after making a tape, one of the quartet, McKinney, who weighed 328 pounds, used a WMMN restroom. In raising himself from the toilet seat, McKinney rested his weight on the washbasin, pulling it from the wall and breaking the water pipe. The water damaged Levin's premises below and he sued WMMN for his loss. The jury found McKinney was an employee of WMMN and that he was acting within the scope of his employment. Should these findings be overruled?

10. Lathrop was employed by Torens as a trainee in his photography studio. Lathrop was on the way home late at night, after taking photographs for Torens at a wedding and reception, when due to his negligence, his automobile collided with another, and Bajdek was killed. Bajdek's administrator joined Torens as a defendant in his suit. Torens argued that Lathrop was not in the course of his employment since he was not required to return the camera equipment that night. The administrator argued that he was in the

course of his employment because he was required to safeguard the equipment and film. Can Torens be held liable?

11. Heritage Land Sales, Inc., was incorporated in 1964 to act as a broker, promoter, and agent for the sale of real estate in the Bahamas. Most of its stock was owned by Bert Dubbin, a nephew of the president of Freeport Ridge Estates, Ltd., a developer of a large tract of land on Grand Bahama Island. Over a two and one-half year period Freeport advanced Heritage more than $600,000 for working capital and in early 1967 the president of Freeport insisted that all Heritage checks be cosigned by his secretary as a means of ascertaining that all funds were properly disbursed.

    In 1966 Reckner was hired by Heritage, in a meeting involving both Bert Dubbin and his uncle, to provide plane service to fly prospective buyers to view the lots Freeport was selling on Grand Bahama. His schedules were worked out with Freeport officials, and he served as private pilot for the uncle, Daniel Dubbin. The flights ceased in 1967 with $39,600 owing to Reckner unpaid. Because of the poor financial condition of Heritage, Reckner agreed to purchase certain Freeport lots upon which Heritage was paid a commission of $25,600. It then gave Reckner a check for that amount. Reckner was unable to sell the lots and defaulted on the purchase money mortgages.

    Reckner then sued Freeport for the full $39,600, alleging that he was a subagent for Freeport. Was Reckner Freeport's subagent?

12. Davis, a cattle buyer for Prairie Livestock Company, went to a public livestock auction to purchase cattle and entered the stands surrounding the arena. Believing there to be a vacant seat on the far side of Crenshaw, an acquaintance who was also a cattle buyer, he entered that row. When he got to where Crenshaw was seated he observed that no space was available. He then jokingly requested Crenshaw to give him his seat and playfully sat down on Crenshaw's lap. Just as he did this, Mitchell, another cattle buyer who was sitting behind Crenshaw, "goosed" Crenshaw. This caused Crenshaw to jump up violently, hurling Davis down the aisle steps onto Chandler who was several rows below.

    Chandler sued only Prairie for his injuries. Its defense was that Davis was not acting within the scope of his employment. The jury verdict was for $10,000 against Prairie, and Prairie appealed. Should the judgment be reversed?

18

Relation of Agent to Third Person

Liability on Authorized Contracts

Disclosed Principal. An agent who is acting for a disclosed principal and who acts within the scope of his or her authority and in the name of the principal is ordinarily not liable on the contract he or she makes. If the agent expressly or impliedly makes himself a party thereto or contracts to act as surety for the principal, the agent becomes liable on the contract. As indicated in Chapter 16, the fact that the agent, in the negotiation of the contract, uses such expressions as "I will sell" or "We will buy" in negotiating a contract for the principal will not make the agent a party to the contract.

Partially Disclosed or Undisclosed Principal. The agent is a party to the contract and liable on it if the principal is partially disclosed—that is, the existence of an agency is known to the third person but the identity of the principal is unknown. However, the third person and the agent may overcome this rule by agreement—for example, that the agent is to remain liable only until he reveals the principal.

If the principal is undisclosed, the contract is between the agent and the third person. Since the third person does not know of the existence of the agency, it is clear that the third person intended to contract with the agent, and the agent is liable on the contract. On the discovery of the existence of the agency and the identity of the principal, the third person may elect to hold the principal, as discussed in Chapter 17.

SUMMARY

The agent of a disclosed principal is not liable to the third person unless otherwise agreed. An agent is a party to a contract negotiated for an undisclosed principal, and, generally, the agent is a party to the contract if he or she is acting for a partially disclosed principal.

Agent's Liability on Unauthorized Contracts

General Rule. When a third person is negotiating with an agent of a disclosed principal, a third person expects and is entitled to an obligation binding on the principal. If the agent exceeds his or her authority, or if no agency exists, the principal will not be bound, in which event the third person will be injured to the extent that his expectation is not realized. If the third person has acted in good faith, without notice or knowledge of the lack of authority and in justifiable reliance on the misrepresentation of authority, and if the principal has not ratified the transaction, the agent will be liable for any resulting loss.

Remedies against the Agent. If the person purporting to be acting as an agent knowingly and intentionally misrepresents his or her authority, a third person justifiably relying on the misrepresentation may recover for any resulting injury under the tort law of deceit. If the person purporting to be acting as an agent acts honestly in the mistaken belief that he has been authorized or justifiably believes the principal will ratify his acts, then a third person relying upon the misrepresentation may recover from the agent on an implied warranty of authority if the principal refuses to ratify. There is no implied warranty of authority if the parties have so agreed or if the third party knows that the agent's acts are not authorized.

If an agent who is uncertain as to the scope of his authority makes a full disclosure to the third person, the agent escapes liability. For example, if the agent shows his contract of employment or power of attorney to the third person, and the third person decides that the agent has authority to bind the principal, the agent is not liable to the third person even if, in fact, the agent does not have such authority. There is neither a misrepresentation nor a warranty as to the scope of the agent's authority.

Ratification or Knowledge of Third Person. Since ratification by the principal relates back to the time the transaction was negotiated, the relation of the parties after ratification is the same as it would have been had the agent had full authority to bind the principal at the time the transaction was negotiated. Since the principal is bound, the agent is not liable to the third person either for misrepresentation or on the theory of implied warranty.

The agent's liability to the third person is based on misrepresentation of authority by the agent, justifiably relied on by the third person. If the third person knows or, in the exercise of ordinary prudence, should know that the agent is not authorized to negotiate the transaction in behalf of the principal, the agent will not be liable to the third person, since such third person is not justified in relying on the agent's misrepresentation.

SUMMARY

If a person purports to act as agent for a party when that person has no power to bind such party, the agent will become liable on the contract to the third person upon an implied warranty of authority. If the agent intentionally misrepresents the existence of the agency or the scope of his authority, he will be liable in tort for the deceit.

If the third person knows that the agent does not have authority, or if the agent informs the third person that he is uncertain as to the scope of his authority or reveals the facts and circumstances of the agent's authorization, the agent will not be liable to the third person for misrepresentation of the authority nor for breach of implied warranty of authority.

Killinger v. Iest

428 P.2d 490 (Sup. Ct. Idaho 1967)

Action by Gale Killinger (plaintiff) against Case Iest and A. W. Tadlock (defendants) to recover for furnishing and installing an irrigation pump. Motion for dismissal granted and Killinger appealed. Affirmed as to Iest, reversed and remanded as to Tadlock.

Iest owned a farm near Twin Falls, Idaho, and Tadlock was his tenant under an oral lease. Tadlock telephoned Killinger, who operated an electric appliance repair shop, to repair a malfunctioning irrigation pump used on the farm. The pump was taken to his shop by Killinger. The next day Tadlock went to inspect the pump which needed extensive repairs. Believing that it would take a long time to repair the pump, he decided that a new, more efficient pump should be installed immediately. At this time he informed Killinger that he was Iest's tenant but asserted that he had authority to repair the pump or to purchase a pump and that Iest would pay the agreed price.

A few days later Killinger installed a new pump and sent the bill for $2,048 to Iest. This was Iest's first knowledge of the new pump. He refused to pay and denied that Tadlock had authority to bind him on the purchase. A major expenditure for a concrete pipeline earlier installed and paid for by Iest had been ordered personally by Iest. Tadlock once had a broken shaft repaired on Iest's tractor, but Tadlock himself paid the bill without consulting Iest.

SMITH, JUSTICE. Killinger first contends that the trial court erroneously ruled that Tadlock's declarations as to the existence and scope of his authority would not be binding on Iest, the alleged principal. That ruling was proper. The declarations of an alleged agent, standing alone, are insufficient to prove the grant of power exercised by him and to bind his principal to third parties.

The statements by the alleged agent, as to the scope of his authority, are admissible if, at the time the statements are offered in evidence, the existence of the agency has been proven by independent evidence.

Killinger adopted the position at trial that, even if Tadlock originally lacked authority to act as Iest's agent in purchasing the pump, Iest subsequently ratified the transaction by accepting and retaining benefits resulting from Tadlock's use of the pump. Killinger established that Tadlock irrigated the 1963 crops with the new pump, but Killinger nevertheless failed to prove that Iest in any way benefited from Tadlock's use of the pump. The benefits must accrue directly to the principal as the proximate result of the unauthorized transaction in order to constitute ratification by the principal.

Although the dismissal of Killinger's action against Iest was proper, the dismissal of the action against Tadlock stands upon different grounds. Killinger's evidence, particularly his own testimony, established that Tadlock had represented he had authority as Iest's agent "to make this extensive repair and improvement," "to repair the pump or purchase a pump," and to bind Iest for the agreed purchase price. The testimony of Ralph Taylor, Killinger's assistant, corroborated Killinger's testimony, and this evidence remained uncontradicted through the examination of Iest and Tadlock.

A party entering into a contract in his self-assumed capacity as agent, with no actual authority from the purported principal, or in excess of an existing authority, is personally liable to the other contracting party who acted in good faith and in reliance on the false representations. The liability terminates only if the purported principal is estopped to deny the authority or subsequently ratifies the transaction.

Lack or Limitation of Capacity of Principal

Nonexistent Principal. If an agent purports to act for a legally nonexistent principal, such as an unincorporated association, the agent will be personally liable as a party to the contract unless the parties expressly agree that the agent does not warrant his or her authority or the existence of the principal. In that event, there is no binding contract due to lack of mutuality. A common example of an agent acting for a nonexistent principal is afforded in the case of a promoter of a corporation contracting in the name of the corporation prior to the time it receives its charter. As a general rule the promoter is personally liable on such contracts. The liability of a promoter is discussed in detail in Chapter 26.

Principal Lacking in Capacity. An agent who purports to act for a person who is wholly incompetent, such as a person who has been officially adjudged insane, is liable as a party to the contract. However, an agent acting for a person who does not have capacity to contract, as in the case of a minor, is not liable to the third person on the contract unless the agent misrepresents or conceals the status of his or her principal's capacity. If the agent knows that the third person is unaware of the principal's lack of capacity, the agent's failure to inform the third person may amount to concealment.

Defenses Available to Agent. An agent who is a party to a contract has all the defenses that arise out of the transaction itself, such as fraud, misrepresentation, nonperformance, payment, accord and satisfaction, infancy, and setoff, together with illegality if the third person is a party to a collusive agreement or other plan which requires or permits the agent to violate his or her fiduciary duty to the principal. In addition, the agent will have the defenses that are personal in nature and that exist between the agent and the third person.

SUMMARY

A person who purports to act for a nonexistent or wholly incompetent principal is personally liable to the third person in a transaction involving such principal unless it is the understanding of the parties that the agent is not to be held liable.

If the principal lacks capacity to contract, the agent is not liable on the contract he or she negotiates for the principal and is not liable to the third person on the contract unless the agent misrepresents the capacity of the principal or conceals the fact that the principal does not have full capacity.

As a general rule, all defenses which arise out of a transaction and all defenses, personal in nature, which exist between the agent and third person are available to the agent when sued on the contract.

Dixie Drive It Yourself System v. Lewis

50 S.E.2d 843 (Ct. App. Ga. 1948)

This was an action by Dixie Drive It Yourself System (plaintiff) against John G. Lewis (defendant) to recover a judgment for the damage to a rented station wagon. Judgment for Lewis and Dixie Drive It Yourself System appealed. Judgment reversed.

John G. Lewis, principal of Hapeville High School, rented two station wagons from Dixie Drive It Yourself System to be used in transporting students engaged in athletic activities. The rental contract was signed, "Hapeville High School, John G. Lewis, Principal." One of the terms of the contract was that the customer would pay for any damage which might occur to the vehicle while in his possession. During the rental of these two station wagons, a wreck occurred and damaged one of them to the extent of $400. Dixie Drive It Yourself System sued Lewis and he set up as a defense that he signed the contract as agent for Hapeville High School. The trial court held that Lewis was not liable and Dixie Drive It Yourself appealed.

GARDNER, JUDGE. The only question presented here for decision is whether the contract in question is the individual undertaking of Lewis. It is clear that both parties to the contract knew that the Hapeville High School had no legal entity. It could not sue or be sued. So neither Dixie Drive It Yourself System nor Lewis were misled. They were both bound by this knowledge. This is true, even though the Hapeville High School is a unit of the Fulton County school system. Therefore, as a legal entity the Hapeville High School was nonexistent. The question before us was discussed at length in *Hagan v. Asa G. Candler, Inc.* The court in that case said: "One who professes to contract as agent for another, when his purported principal is actually nonexistent, may be held personally liable on the contract, unless the other contracting party agrees to look to some other person for performance." In a similar case, *Wells v. Fay & Egan Co.,* the Supreme Court said: "If one contracts as agent, when in fact he has no principal, he will be personally liable." This court, in *Harris v. Stribling,* said: "The note sued on is signed 'Harris-Stribling Sales Company, L.S., by J. D. Stribling, L.S.' It is alleged that at the time of the execution of the note there was no such person, corporation, or other legal entity as 'Harris-Stribling Sales Company,' and that J. D. Stribling is personally liable on the note. The note, on its face, purports to have been signed by J. D. Stribling. He signed it 'Harris-Stribling Sales Company,' by himself, 'J. D. Stribling.' If 'Harris-Stribling Sales Company' is not a person or corporation or other legal entity, it is a purely fictitious name, and the note being signed by J. D. Stribling as such constitutes his individual obligation." We do not think that the decision sustains the contentions of Lewis. Upon reading the other cases relied on by Lewis, it will be found that in each of those cases there was an existing principal and legal entity. Not so in the instant case. That is the distinction. A nonexistent legal entity can have no agent. This principle was ruled very clearly in *Hagan v. Asa G. Candler, Inc.,* where the Supreme Court said: "At the time the contract was executed and at the time the suit was filed, no such corporation as Food Shops, Inc. was in existence, but this fact was unknown to the plaintiff. By reason of these facts, the contract was one between Asa G. Candler, Inc. and H. G. Hagan, individually." In that case H. G. Hagan represented that the Food Shops, Inc. was a corporation and that he had a right to sign the contract "Food Shops, Inc., by H. G. Hagan." Under those circumstances, this court held that this was an individual undertaking of H. G. Hagan, and on *certiorari* the Supreme Court affirmed the judgment of the Court of Appeals. In view of the authorities cited and the record in the instant case, the contract was the individual undertaking of Lewis.

Agent's Liability for Torts and Crimes

General Rule. As a general rule the fact that an agent is acting within the scope of his or her authority or at the direction of the principal does not relieve the agent from personal liability for tortious or criminal acts. An agent may escape tort liability when exercising a privilege of the principal or a privilege held by the agent for the protection of the principal. For example, if the principal has an easement of right-of-way over the land of another, the agent would not be liable to the owner of the land if the agent uses the right-of-way in carrying on the business of the principal, provided the agent does not exceed, in using the right-of-way, the principal's rights under it. The tort liability of a principal and an agent is joint and several. The injured party can recover from either but, of course, is not entitled to more than one satisfaction.

Liability for Deceit and Duress. An agent is liable to an injured third person if the agent knowingly makes misrepresentations in the transaction of the principal's business or knowingly assists the principal or other agents of the principal in defrauding the third person. However, if the agent is innocent and does not know, and in the exercise of reasonable prudence would not know, that the representations he or she makes are false, the agent is not personally liable. For example, suppose Parker authorizes Arnold to sell his house. He tells Arnold that the house is fully insulated with rock wool when it is not. Arnold does not know that the house is not insulated, and he would not discover such fact on an ordinary inspection. If Arnold, in making a sale of the house to Thomas, tells Thomas that the house is fully insulated with rock wool, only Parker and not Arnold will be liable to Thomas in an action for deceit.

In making a sale, an agent may use sales talk and puff his principal's goods in the same manner and to the same extent as may the principal, in which case the agent is not liable to the third person for deceit.

The same general rules that apply regarding an agent's liability for deceit apply in determining the agent's liability for duress.

Liability for Conversion. An agent is personally liable for the conversion of another's goods, and this is true even though at the time the agent takes possession of the goods he or she has reason to believe that the principal is entitled to the possession of the goods. For example, suppose Parker has loaned his plow to Thomas, and Parker tells Arnold, his employee, to get the plow. Arnold goes to Thomas' tool shed and gets a plow which he believes is Parker's plow but which really belongs to Thomas. Arnold is liable to Thomas for the conversion of the plow.

An agent is not liable to the third person for conversion if he has acted under direction of the principal and has either returned the goods to the principal or delivered them to another at the direction of the principal. However, the agent would be liable for conversion if, after receiving notice of the third person's right to the goods, the agent delivers them either to the principal or another.

Liability for Negligence. An agent is liable to a third person for any injury the third person may suffer as a result of the negligence of the agent. If the principal furnishes the agent a defective instrument and the agent does not know and by the exercise of reasonable care would not know of the defects in the instrument, and owes no duty to third persons to discover such defects, the agent will not be liable to third persons for injuries resulting from the defects in the instrument.

Liability to Third Persons for Breach of Duty to Principal. Although courts have not been in full agreement, the trend of decisions has been to hold that agents who fail to perform their duties to their principal and thereby cause physical harm to third persons or their property are liable to them if they have relied upon the performance owed the principal. For example, a consulting engineer, employed by the owner to inspect a building, who negligently fails to find structural defects is liable to a tenant who is injured due to its collapse. Generally, courts have not held an agent liable for economic harm to others caused by a failure to perform duties owed to the principal.

A number of cases have involved accountants engaged to audit the books of a business. If the accountant is negligent in making the audit, those relying upon the audited financial statements may suffer a loss. The question is whether third parties can hold the accountant liable for their losses resulting from the accountant's errors and omissions. Earlier cases had found no liability. Later, liability was imposed if the accountant had been grossly negligent on the theory of constructive fraud. More recently a few courts have gone further and have held the professional agent liable for his or her negligence to anyone relying on the agent's work who is in the class of persons or is the person for whose benefit or guidance the work was prepared. Accountants may also be held liable to third parties for failure to disclose information under the federal securities laws.[1]

Liability for Crimes. A person who commits a crime under instructions from his or her principal or employer is liable. This is true whether the crime is one deriving from the common law, such as murder, assault and battery, or larceny, or a crime defined under a regulatory statute, such as price fixing under the Sherman Act. The agent or employee's duty to society overrides his duty to follow the instruction of the principal or employer. As discussed in Chapter 17, the principal directing the commission of a crime would also be liable.

[1] See Chapter 29.

SUMMARY

An agent is liable to third persons for his or her torts, and the fact that the principal may also be liable does not relieve the agent.

The agent is liable for deceit for false representations knowingly made even though the agent does not profit personally therefrom. The agent is not personally liable for making statements which he has no reason to know are false and which are based on information given by the principal. An agent is liable for conversion even if he or she is following the instructions of the principal in the taking of the goods and is not aware that the act is wrongful. An agent is liable for injury resulting from his own negligent conduct but not from the negligence of the principal.

An agent, as a general rule, is not liable to a third person for injury resulting from the agent's failure to perform a duty owed to the principal. However, professional agents such as accountants have in some instances been held liable to third persons who might be expected to and do rely on their work.

An agent is liable for his or her crimes even when they are committed under direction of the principal.

Musser v. Libertyville Realty Assoc., Inc.

358 N.E. 2d 39 (App. Ct. Ill. 1976)

Robert Musser (plaintiff) brought an action against Libertyville Realty Assoc., Inc., and Schwandt Realty (defendants) for injuries occurring while he was viewing office space as a prospective tenant. Appeal by Musser from a summary judgment for Schwandt Realty. Affirmed.

Musser was looking for office space and went to see a property with James Bales, an agent of Libertyville Realty. Schwandt Realty, the rental agent for the property, had given Bales the key to permit him to show it to Musser. An inner room was windowless and was dark. Bales crossed the room to turn on the light, which he correctly believed to be next to a door outlined by light behind it. At the same time Musser walked toward the center of the room, tripped over a roll of carpeting and fell down a flight of stairs just as Bales found the light switch. The trap door that covered the stairs had been propped open. Schwandt Realty did not manage the property.

O'CONNOR, JUSTICE. Schwandt Realty had no authority to make or to order repairs. Its authority was strictly limited to showing the premises to prospective tenants, either directly or through other brokers. If it found a tenant, it would receive a full broker's commission or would split the commission with the broker who had secured the tenant. It would receive nothing more. At the time of the injury to plaintiff, it was not even showing the premises; it had merely given the key to Libertyville Realty so that it might show them. The rolls of carpeting over which the plaintiff tripped were not placed there by Schwandt Realty. The record does not show that Schwandt Realty had any knowledge when the trap door was opened, who opened it, or for what purpose; nor does it show that Schwandt Realty had any knowledge of how many hours or days the rolls of carpeting were there, nor where exactly they came from, although there is an inference that they belonged to the former tenant. Schwandt Realty's connection with them is too remote to impose a duty on it.

Third Person's Liability to Agent

Agent's Right of Action on Contract. An agent who is acting for a disclosed principal and who has negotiated a contract within the scope of his authority and in the name of the principal has no right to bring an action to enforce the contract. However, the principal may assign a contract, negotiate commercial paper, or assign a right of action to the agent. Then, of course, the agent may sue in his or her own name.

An agent acting for an undisclosed or partially disclosed principal will be a party to the contract and may bring an action on the contract in the agent's own name. However, if the undisclosed or partially disclosed principal wishes to bring the action in his or her name instead of the agent's, the principal has the right to do so.

Exceptional Situations. If the agent is also a party to the contract, other than as a surety for the principal, the agent will be a party in interest and as such may bring an action in his or her own name to recover for a breach of the contract.

An auctioneer or commission merchant (factor) who has sold goods for the principal may, by custom, bring suit in his or her own name to collect the purchase price of the goods.

An agent who is entrusted with goods by his or her principal and whose possession is tortiously interferred with by a third person may bring an action in his or her own name for the unlawful interference with his possession. Likewise, if a third person has the possession of goods owned by the principal when the agent is entitled to their possession, the agent has the right to bring an action in his own name to recover possession of the goods. In both of these situations the agent is basing the action on his personal right to possession.

SUMMARY

An agent acting within the scope of his or her authority and contracting in the name of the principal cannot bring an action in his own name to recover against the third party for the breach of the contract. An agent who is acting for an undisclosed or partially disclosed principal, or who is acting for a disclosed principal but at the same time is a party to the contract other than as surety for the principal, may bring an action in his own name for breach of the contract. An agent may bring an action in his own name against a person who has interfered with his possession of the principal's goods or who has wrongfully injured the agent.

Problem Cases

1. All-Pro Reps, Inc., in the business of representing professional athletes in making contracts for their services and in providing them with financial management services, was retained by Nate Archibald, a basketball player. It made a contract with Kenneth Jones for Archibald to appear for the day of August 15, 1973, at Jones' boys basketball camp, and it was paid the fee on Archibald's behalf. On the night of August 9, Archibald notified All-Pro that circumstances would prevent his appearance. On August 10, All-Pro notified Jones and sent a check to refund the fee. Jones received the letter on August 14. Jones then sued All-Pro for $200,000 damages and $100,000 punitive damages claiming that Archibald willfully breached the contract and that All-Pro's method of communication did not allow Jones time to find a replacement. Should All-Pro be held liable?
2. Oxford Building Services, Inc., contracted with William Gresham, d/b/a/ Gresham Realty, to clean certain commercial buildings. Oxford performed under the contract for two years. The bills were sent to Gresham, and he paid them for a time. However, he later was $7,000 in arrears in the payments, and Oxford filed suit. Gresham's defense was that he was not the owner of the buildings but acting only as an agent. Gresham had not previously disclosed this fact to Oxford. Is Gresham liable?
3. Bowman, a broker, negotiated the sale of the fixtures and equipment of a restaurant as agent for Macris. The purchaser, Priolette, gave Bowman a $1,000 down payment, which Bowman turned over to Macris. Macris refused to perform the contract, and Priolette sued Macris and Bowman to recover the $1,000 down payment and damages for breach of the contract. Is Bowman liable?
4. Konodi hired Stockholm to make certain repairs on the S.S. *Providencia,* an Italian ship docked at Albany, N.Y. Konodi was on board the ship and gave instructions to Stockholm's workers. Konodi was acting merely as an agent for the owner of the ship in ordering the repairs. Earlier Stockholm had worked on the same ship and had been paid by Konodi's own check. Stockholm again billed Konodi and brought suit when he refused to pay. Konodi's defense was that he was only an agent. Is he liable?
5. Anderson, assuming to act for the owner of real estate, listed it for sale with Brawley, who found a buyer ready, willing, and able to buy the property at the price fixed by Anderson. Anderson was not authorized to act for the owner of the property and instead of submitting the purchaser's offer to the owner of the property returned it to Brawley. Brawley sued Anderson to recover the commission he would have earned had Anderson been authorized to list the property. Will he recover?
6. Zuspan owned a farm which she rented to Byers. Her son, Newell Zuspan, negotiated with Byers for the sale of the farm to him, representing that he was his mother's agent. An agreement was reached to sell the farm to Byers. In reliance on the agreement, Byers made improvements on the farm. Later Newell Zuspan told Byers that his mother would not sell the farm and that he had no authority to sell it. There was no writing executed

by Zuspan which would satisfy the statute of frauds. Byers sued Newell Zuspan to recover damages for his failure to get the farm. Will he recover?

7. Graham, the head of an unincorporated association, engaged Comfort as attorney to represent the interests of the association. The association did not pay Comfort for his services, and Comfort sued Graham on the contract of employment to recover a judgment for the amount due him for services rendered to the association. Is Graham liable on the contract of employment?

8. Mid-South Machinery Company, a distributor of Norge coin-operated laundry equipment, advertised a laundromat for sale in a newspaper in Anderson, South Carolina. In response to the ad, James Gilbert contacted Mid-South's president, Thomas Coker. He was inexperienced in the laundromat business, and Coker represented himself as an expert. Coker told him that the business, which Mid-South had purchased from its former owner, would net $1,000 per month. Gilbert several times asked Coker if there were records of the operation by the former owners that he could examine and was told there were none. Gilbert assumed the lease of the laundry equipment, which had a balance due of more than $32,000, paid $7,000 to Mid-South and agreed to pay an additional $5,000 with interest in annual payments over the next five years. Gilbert made payments on the lease for four months although sustaining monthly losses. A judgment was then entered against Gilbert for the balance due on the lease.

   Gilbert sued Mid-South and Coker for deceit. Testimony was presented that complete records of prior operation had been in existence and that the laundromat had never made a profit. The jury awarded Gilbert $45,000 actual and $5,000 punitive damages against both Mid-South and Coker. Is Coker as well as Mid-South liable for the tort?

9. The president of Shatterproof Glass Corporation contacted Buddy Paschal, owner of four corporations known as Paschal Enterprises, to become a distributor for Shatterproof. Paschal employed the CPA firm of James, Guinn and Head to prepare additional information for Shatterproof concerning the financial condition of Paschal Enterprises and to release to them statements earlier prepared for a bank. Shatterproof advised the CPAs that it acted as "bankers" for its distributors, and, in fact, did advance $425,000 to Paschal Enterprises on the strength of the CPA audit reports. The audit showed that Paschal Enterprises had a net worth of $173,000, while in reality liabilities exceeded assets by $150,000. The loan was not repaid, and Shatterproof sued the accountants, proving a number of acts of negligence. Did the trial court properly direct a verdict for the accountants?

10. Glenn stole some cattle from Caviness and sold them to Preston. Preston delivered the cattle to Walker, a livestock commission merchant, who sold the cattle and paid the proceeds of the sale to Preston. Caviness sued Preston and Walker in tort to recover a judgment for the conversion of the cattle. Walker set up as a defense that he sold the cattle as agent for Preston and therefore was not liable. Is Walker liable for the conversion of the cattle?

11. Scott, as agent for Coal Company, contracted in the name of her principal to sell Railroad Company 34,500 tons of coal. The contract with Coal was in writing, and was drawn and signed in the name of Coal by Scott, its agent. Under Coal's contract with Scott, it was obligated to pay Scott a commission of ten cents a ton for all coal sold by her, provided the buyer accepted delivery and paid for the coal ordered. Railroad refused to accept and pay for 22,210 tons of the coal contracted for. Scott sued Railroad to recover a judgment for the commission she would have received had Railroad accepted and paid for the coal in fulfillment of the contract. Is Scott entitled to a judgment against Railroad for the claimed commissions?

19

Relation of Principal and Agent

Duties of Agent in General

Sources of Duties. Most agency relationships are created by contract. In addition to the duties imposed by the contract, the agent, as a fiduciary, has a duty of loyalty to the principal. The agent also has the duty of obedience, which is derived from the nature of the relationship, and the duties of care and diligence in carrying out the principal's instructions. The terms of the contract may relieve the agent of some of the duties he or she might otherwise, by the law of agency, owe the principal. However, courts are reluctant to interpret contractual provisions as eliminating or even substantially diminishing the agent's fiduciary duties.

Gratuitous Agent. The fiduciary duties of a gratuitous agent are basically the same as a paid agent, and a gratuitous agent has the same power to bind the principal and may exercise the same rights as a paid agent. The difference is that the gratuitous agent has no obligation to act for the principal unless the agent causes the principal reasonably to rely upon him or her to perform certain acts. For example, suppose Astor agrees as an accommodation to his friend Pogue to submit a written bid for a certain parcel of real estate in Pogue's behalf at an auction. Astor fails to do so and the bid would have been successful. If Pogue does not learn of the failure to act until too late to submit another bid, Astor is liable for Pogue's damages on account of his failure to act. The standard of care imposed upon a gratuitous agent may be somewhat less than that imposed upon an agent who is paid.

SUMMARY

In addition to contractual duties, an agent owes the principal the fiduciary duty of loyalty and also the duty to follow directions and the duties of exercising care and diligence. These duties may be modified by contract, except that courts are likely to hold that a duty of loyalty still remains. A gratuitous agent does not escape the duties of loyalty and obedience, but ordinarily such an agent has no obligation to act for the principal.

Agent's Duty of Loyalty

Conflicts of Interest. The agent's duty of loyalty requires him or her to exercise scrupulous honesty in dealings with the principal, to use his best efforts to further the principal's interests, and to avoid getting into a position where the agent's own interests are in conflict with those of the principal. The taking of a "gift," bribe or "kickback" from a third party, would, of course, be a breach of this duty.

An agent who is authorized to buy or sell property for the principal will not be permitted to buy from or sell to himself or herself unless the agent makes a full disclosure of all the material facts to the principal and the principal consents to the transaction. Contracts which put the agent, directly or indirectly, in the position of buying from or selling to the principal without the assent of the principal are voidable at the election of the principal, unless a custom in the trade of which the principal is aware permits such action. For example, if an agent has sold to a corporation of which he is a substantial shareholder or to a relative or someone who has agreed to sell the property to the agent at a later date, the principal may get the transaction set aside when he learns of it. This right is not affected by the fact that the price was the best obtainable.

Even if the principal acquiesces in the agent's acting on his own account in dealing with the principal, the agent has the duty to deal fairly with the principal and to disclose to him or her all facts which might have a bearing on the desirability to the principal of the transactions.

Unless there is agreement by the principal, the agent may not compete with the principal with respect to the subject matter of the agency. If employed to purchase certain property, the agent may not buy it himself nor may the agent, while still employed, solicit the principal's customers while making plans to enter a competing business for himself.

Duty to Act for Only One Party to Transaction. As a general rule an agent will not be permitted to act as an agent for both parties to a transaction without first disclosing the agent's double role and obtaining the consent of both parties. An exception is where the agent is merely acting as a middleman to bring the parties together so that they may negotiate their own contract.

Confidential Information. The agent has a duty not to disclose to others or use for his or her own benefit confidential information acquired by him as an agent. Although in the absence of a restrictive agreement, the agent is free to compete with the principal after termination of the agency, the agent may not use or disclose confidential information. Such information includes trade secrets such as mechanisms, formulae, and processes and may include customer lists or special knowledge about customers. However, an agent may use, in competition with his former principal, the skills and general knowledge of a line of business the agent has learned while working for the principal.

Agent's Right to Compensation and Profits. If the agent is acting for both parties without the knowledge and consent of both, the agent is not entitled to compensation. If only one of the parties knows of and consents to the agent's acting for both parties to the transaction, the party having knowledge and giving his or her consent is bound, but the other party may elect to have the transaction set aside. In such a situation the agent is not entitled to compensation from either party. The agent has breached his duty to the party not consenting, and the agreement between the agent and the party consenting is a fraud on the other party, is against public policy, and is illegal.

A similar situation arises if a third person agrees to pay an agent a secret commission, make him or her a gift, or compensate an agent in any way. A promise on the part of a third person to benefit an agent in any respect is a fraud on the principal and is illegal. Any benefits given the agent by the third person may be claimed by the principal, whether the benefits are in the form of a secret commission or a gift.

SUMMARY

The agent's duty of loyalty to the principal requires the agent to be honest, to use his best efforts to further the principal's interests, and to avoid conflicts between the agent's own interests and the principal's. The agent may not buy from or sell to the principal directly or indirectly without the assent of the principal after full disclosure. Without such disclosure such contracts are voidable by the principal.

Generally the agent may not act as agent for both parties to a transaction unless both parties agree after full disclosure, although the agent may serve as a middleman. The agent who acts for both parties without the consent of both is not entitled to compensation from either. The principal is entitled to any gift or compensation paid the agent by a third person who is dealing with or wishes to deal with the principal.

The agent may not use for his or her own benefit or disclose to others confidential information acquired in the agency relationship even after termination of the agency. Nor may the agent compete with the principal during the existence of the relationship.

Wormhoudt Lumber Co. v. Cloyd

219 N.W.2d 543 (Sup. Ct. Ia. 1974)

Wormhoudt Lumber Company (plaintiff) brought this suit for an accounting for secret profits against Jon Cloyd (defendant), a former employee. Wormhoudt appealed from a judgment dismissing the suit. Reversed and remanded.

Cloyd was employed by Wormhoudt Lumber Company to find construction jobs that would use his employer's materials by finding property owners seeking to build and bringing them together with contractors. He computed costs for materials and labor, including a profit for the contractor, and if the contractor and owner were satisfied, they would make a contract between themselves. If the contractor paid Wormhoudt for the materials used within 30 days of the billing, he would be entitled to a 10 percent discount. Cloyd persuaded several contractors to split the 10 percent discount with him in return for being recommended by him. Later he got some contractors to commit themselves to a price for the labor on a job, to which he added the materials at retail plus a profit for the contractor and then he split both the profit and the discount with the contractor.

Shortly after Cloyd left his employment with Wormhoudt, one of the contractors reported to Wormhoudt what had been going on, and two contractors started suit against Cloyd but they were dismissed because of their own complicity.

UHLENHOPP, JUSTICE. The general principle is stated thus in § 387 of the Restatement of Agency 2d:

> Unless otherwise agreed, an agent is subject to a duty to his principal to act solely for the benefit of the principal in all matters connected with his agency.

And § 388 states with respect to profits:

> Unless otherwise agreed, an agent who makes a profit in connection with transactions conducted by him on behalf of the principal is under a duty to give such profit to the principal.

Cloyd's argument in this appeal is that the company is not the real party in interest; the contractors are the ones who are out half of the discounts and profits. But Cloyd apparently misses the point of the agent's duty to pass back to the principal any gains that are made in the course of the employment. As the authorities state, it matters not that the principal actually sustains no loss; he is entitled to the gain. If the agent is able to get third persons to accept less or to pay more, and the agent can thus increase the profit, that profit belongs to the principal.

Cloyd further argues that the company, if successful in the present suit, intends to distribute the recovery it obtains among the contractors from whom Cloyd extracted the payments. But that is none of Cloyd's affair. The company can keep the money or distribute it among the contractors or give it to charity; the company is nonetheless the real party in interest in this accounting suit against the disloyal agent.

We therefore direct the district court to conduct an accounting and then render final decree for the balance found due, together with interest and costs.

Desfosses v. Notis

333 A.2d 83 (Sup. Ct. Me. 1975).

Desfosses (plaintiff), a mobile home park developer, brought this action against Notis (defendant), an employee who was a real estate broker, to recover the difference between the amount given to the broker to purchase land and the actual amount paid for it by the broker. Judgment for Desfosses, and both parties appealed. Affirmed for Desfosses.

Desfosses hired Notis to assist him generally in his business with the special assignment of acquiring land for development of mobile home parks and paid Notis $125 per week from May through August 1969. Notis informed Desfosses of the availability of a suitable tract of land at a cost of $32,400. Notis was directed to purchase the land as a "straw man" and then to convey it to Desfosses, and he was given the $32,400 for this purpose. After the transfer to him was completed, Desfosses learned that the actual price of the land had been $15,474.62 and that prior to the employment Notis had entered into a purchase agreement for the land in question and had made a deposit of $1,000. Notis, in his defense, argued that rescission was the only appropriate remedy. Because of his prior ownership interest, Notis declared, Desfosses as principal could not compel him as agent to refund the amount above his cost if the principal chose to keep the property.

DELAHANTY, JUSTICE. No principle of law is better settled than that which requires the agent in all his dealings concerning the matter of his agency to act with utmost faith and loyalty and disclose all facts within his knowledge which bear materially upon his principal's interest. An agent acting for the purchaser, whether by appointment or as a volunteer, must see that he meets fairly and squarely the responsibility of his position and does not take any advantage, either for his own gain or to the injury of the person whom he represents. The agent's fiduciary duties to his principal may be broadly phrased as duties of service and obedience, and duties of loyalty. Here, Desfosses has satisfactorily established numerous breaches by Notis of his fiduciary duties, to wit: failure to fully disclose material facts; misrepresentations of matters within the scope of the agency; false inducements to obtain money from the principal; and misuse and wrongful retention of funds peculated by defendant from his principal. A fiduciary who commits a breach of his duty as fiduciary is guilty of tortious conduct and the beneficiary can obtain redress either at law or in equity for the harm done.

Notis urges that although he did not disclose his antecedent, independent interest in the land, Desfosses is without remedy unless he wants to rescind the sale altogether. The shortcoming of Notis' argument is that it fails to consider an additional aspect of his wrongful conduct, that Notis used Desfosses' money to complete Notis' own purchase of the property under the bond for a deed. Whatever the nature of Notis' antecedent interest in the property, his acquisition of the property was an indubitable incident of the agency. An agent who, in violation of his duty to his principal, uses for his own purposes or those of a third person assets of the principal's business is subject to liability to the principal for the value of the use. If an agent has received a benefit as a result of violating his duty of loyalty, the principal is entitled to recover from him what he has so received, its value, or its proceeds, and also the amount of damage thereby caused.

The fact that Notis may have parted with these funds, or paid some of them over to the erstwhile partner in the bond for a deed arrangement, of course does not erase or reduce Notis' liability. Notis may not avoid a just accounting by inculpating an evanescent co-venturer with whom he may have shared his booty. Notis owed plaintiff a fiduciary obligation; Notis bought the land in his own name under a contract for $15,474.62; he conveyed the land to his principal, who had given him $32,400.00 to make the purchase. Notis must now answer for the $16,925.38, together with interest and costs.

Agent's Duty to Obey Instructions and to Use Care and Skill

Duty to Obey Instructions. The agent owes a duty to follow faithfully all lawful and reasonable instructions given to the agent by the principal. The agent is engaged to transact business or perform services for his or her principal, and the principal has the right, within the limits of legality, to have the business transacted or the services performed as he or she wishes. If the agent, even though it be a gratuitous agency, fails or refuses to follow the legitimate instructions of the principal, the agent will be liable to the principal for any damages suffered by the principal as the result of the agent's failure to act as instructed. In addition, the agent's failure or refusal to follow instructions will, as a general rule, justify the principal's termination of the agency.

There are some situations in which the agent may be justified in not following instructions. If an emergency arises and the agent cannot consult with the principal, the agent may be justified in using his or her own judgment, especially if following instructions would clearly result in injury to the principal; but if no emergency has arisen, the agent must follow instructions, even though the agent deems the course of action designated by the principal to be clearly injurious to the principal. If the principal instructs the agent to do an illegal or criminal act, the agent is not bound to follow instructions. If the agency is general in its nature and the principal has not given the agent detailed instructions, the agent must use his or her own judgment in following that course of action which will best further the principal's interests.

Standard of Care and Skill. In the absence of an agreement imposing on the agent a duty of a greater or lesser degree, the agent owes a duty to act with standard care and skill. That is, the agent must possess and exercise the care and skill which is standard in the locality for the kind of work he or she is employed to perform. If the agent is acting gratuitously, this fact may be taken into consideration in determining whether the agent has acted with reasonable care and skill. In all instances the paid agent owes a duty to exercise at least the skill that the agent represents himself as having. The agent may warrant that his undertakings will be successful or that his performance will be satisfactory to the principal, but in the absence of such a warranty, the agent does not assume the risk of the success or satisfaction of his or her performance.

Duty to Communicate Notice or Knowledge. The principal is bound by notice given to the agent or knowledge acquired by the agent during the transaction of the principal's business. Therefore, the agent owes a duty to communicate promptly to the principal all notice which is given to him or her in the course of the transaction of the principal's business and to disclose all facts within his knowledge which are material to the matters entrusted to the agent by the principal and which do not violate a confidence. Failure to communicate notice or to disclose knowledge is a breach of duty and will render the agent liable to the principal for any resulting injury.

Duties of Agents in Certain Transactions. Agents employed to buy or sell have a duty to obtain terms which are most advantageous to the principal even when the principal has fixed a price, unless the agent is directed to adhere to the price fixed. An agent making collections has a duty to exercise reasonable diligence and to accept payment only in the medium customary. This will usually be money or the debtor's check, but the situation may require a certified check. An agent making collections or receiving goods for the principal has the duty to use care to keep them safely and to remit or deliver them in accordance with the principal's instructions. An agent making loans is not an insurer of the loans made but must use care in investigating the credit standing of the borrower and, if customary to require security, to investigate its adequacy.

SUMMARY

An agent owes a duty to follow and obey the instructions of his or her principal, provided the principal does not instruct the agent to do a criminal or illegal act. In an emergency, when the agent cannot communicate with the principal, an agent may be justified in not following instructions if doing so would result in injury to the principal.

The standard of care and skill required of the agent is that which is standard in the locality for the work to be performed or at least the skill the agent represents himself or herself as having. In the absence of a warranty, the agent does not assume the risk of the success of his performance.

An agent owes a duty to communicate to the principal all notices received in the course of the transaction of the principal's business. The agent also owes a duty to disclose all facts material to the purpose of the agency which come to the agent's knowledge during the performance of his duties.

Nash v. Sears, Roebuck and Co.

174 N.W.2d 818 (Sup. Ct. Mich. 1970)

Mary Nash (plaintiff) brought an action against Sears, Roebuck and Company, Heidt's Protective Service, Inc., and Art Keolian (defendants) for false arrest and assault and battery on a customer. Judgment for Mrs. Nash against all three defendants and against Sears on its cross claim against Heidt's. Sears appealed. Reversed and remanded with respect to the judgment on the cross claim.

Keolian was an employee of Heidt's Protective Service serving as a uniformed security guard in a Sears' store. Both Heidt's and Sears gave Keolian detailed instructions and both retained the right to supervise and direct him and to discharge him from further work for Sears. Keolian had been instructed not to arrest unless he himself witnessed a shoplifting incident but was expected to respond to information received from Sears' employees.

Based upon information from a Sears' salesperson who allegedly witnessed a woman, identified by her as Mary Nash, shoplifting, Keolian confronted Mrs. Nash and requested her to accompany him back to the store. She refused and started to walk away. Keolian shoved her to the ground, straddled her body, and pinned her arms above her head. Police arrived and took both Keolian and Mrs. Nash to the police station. A subsequent investigation proved the shoplifting charge to be without foundation. Sears filed a cross claim against Heidt's for reimbursement for any liability it was found to have. Sears alleged that the contract with Heidt's required Heidt's to furnish a qualified guard and that Keolian was not qualified and had not performed his work properly. The trial judge submitted to the jury the question whether there had been an agreement between Sears and Heidt's that a qualified guard was to be sent over. Sears appealed urging this as error.

KAVANAGH, JUSTICE. Every contract of employment includes an obligation, whether express or implied, to perform in a diligent and reasonably skillful workmanlike manner. The general rule is fully stated in Am. Jur.2d as follows:

> As a general rule, there is implied in every contract for work or services a duty to perform it skillfully, carefully, diligently, and in a workmanlike manner. Moreover, a contracting party may be bound by the terms of the contract to perform it in a good and workmanlike manner.
>
> With respect to the skill required of a person who is to render services, it is a well-settled rule that the standard of comparison or test of efficiency is that degree of skill, efficiency, and knowledge which is possessed by those of ordinary skill, competency, and standing in the particular trade or business for which he is employed. Where the contract does not provide for a degree of skill higher than this, none can be required. Where skill as well as care is required in performing the undertaking, and where the party purports to have skill in the business and he undertakes for hire, he is bound to exercise due and ordinary skill or, in other words, to perform in a workmanlike manner. In cases of this sort he must be understood to have engaged to use a degree of diligence and attention and skill adequate to the performance of his undertaking. It seems, however, that he is not liable for an error due to an honest mistake of judgment, and not to [sic] gross ignorance. Nor, in the absence of an express provision to that effect, does he become a guarantor of the results.
>
> Failure to comply with the implied duty to perform in a skillful and workmanlike manner may not only defeat recovery but may entitle the other party to damages resulting from the unskillful and unworkmanlike performance.

An independent contractor, undertaking to discharge a contractual duty to his or her employer, is bound to proceed with skill, diligence, and in a workmanlike manner, as is any employee under the common-law rule above quoted. This necessary implication of any contract of employment, if not expressly provided for by the parties, will be supplied in law by construction.

We hold that the trial judge committed reversible error when he instructed the jury that they were to determine whether Heidt's obligated itself to send over a qualified guard.

Agent's Duty to Account

Duty to Account for Money and Property. Both the agent's duty of loyalty and the agent's duty of exercising care require him or her to account to the principal for any money or property coming into his or her possession in the course of the agent's transaction of the principal's business, including any "kickbacks" paid to him by a third party. The principal may demand an accounting at any time he or she wishes, and the agent owes a duty to make such an accounting. If the nature of the business entrusted to the agent involves collections, receipts, expenditures, and similar transactions, the agent owes a duty to keep accurate accounts and to render such accounts to his or her principal.

Duty to Keep Principal's Property Separate. An agent owes a duty not to commingle the property of the principal with the agent's own property, and if the agent does, he or she will be liable to the principal for any resulting loss. If the commingled property—grain or money, for example—cannot be separated, the agent must satisfy the legitimate claim of the principal even if this results in the principal taking the entire mass of commingled property.

An agent also owes a duty not to deposit the principal's money in the agent's own name or in his or her own personal bank account. The agent should either use the principal's name or the form, "Ames, in trust for Peters."

Liability for Use of Principal's Property. If an agent uses the principal's property with the intent of depriving the principal of it, the agent will be guilty of the crime of embezzlement. If the agent has used the principal's property or failed to keep it separate, the principal may claim his or her property if the principal can identify it, or the principal may hold the agent liable for the value of the property in the tort action of conversion.

If the agent has used the principal's money for his or her own purposes, the principal is entitled to a judgment against the agent for the amount of the money used, or if the agent has purchased property with the principal's money, the principal may, at his or her election, claim such property, even though it has increased in value since the agent acquired it. For example, suppose Alden, acting as agent for Pape, collects $5,000 for Pape and, instead of remitting the money to him, purchases corporate stock with it. Pape, if he can prove that Alden purchased the stock with his money, may claim the stock even though it has increased in value since Alden purchased it, or he may hold Alden accountable for the money collected.

SUMMARY

An agent owes a duty to keep a true and accurate account of all property and money of the principal coming into his or her possession. The agent owes a duty not to commingle the principal's property or money with the agent's own. If the agent commingles the principal's property with his own, deposits the principal's money in the agent's own name, or uses the principal's money or property for the agent's own use and benefit, the agent is liable for any and all resulting loss.

Bain v. Pulley

111 S.E.2d 287 (Sup. Ct. Va. 1959)

This was an action by Marion T. Bain and Harry L. Bain (plaintiffs) against Douglas H. Pulley (defendant) asking for an accounting. Judgment for Pulley and the Bains appealed. Judgment reversed and remanded.

The Bains were trustees of the Thomas L. Bain, deceased, estate, which was composed of a business and farms. The Bains as trustees employed Pulley as agent to operate and manage the business and farms. Pulley continued in the employ of the Bains from June 1936 to January 1, 1956. During this time Pulley kept and maintained books and records pertaining to the estate business and properties. The books and records were kept entirely in Pulley's handwriting. Over the years, substantial profits from the operation were paid to the beneficiaries of the estate.

From January 1952, and continuing through January 1956, Pulley rendered an annual income report. These reports were not verified or checked with the records by the accountants or the trustees or the beneficiaries. No audit of Pulley's accounts was made between 1943 and 1956, when Pulley resigned as agent and manager of the estate. This action was brought asking for an accounting. Pulley contended that since he had rendered an annual report the Bains were not entitled to an accounting.

EGGLESTON, CHIEF JUSTICE. The general duty of an agent who is required to handle money is thus laid down in *Restatement of the Law of Agency,* 2d, Vol. 2, § 382, p. 185:

> Unless otherwise agreed, an agent is subject to a duty to keep, and render to his principal, an account of money or other things which he has received or paid out on behalf of the principal.
>
> Where such fiduciary relation exists the principal may invoke the aid of a court of equity in requiring an accounting by his agent.
>
> In an action for an accounting, the agent has the burden of proving that he paid to the principal or otherwise properly disposed of the money or other thing which he is proved to have received from the principal.

We do not agree that the acceptance by the beneficiaries of the income reports for the years 1951 to 1955, both inclusive, was a valid and sufficient reason for denying the prayer for an accounting. Clearly, these reports did not constitute an annual accounting between the parties and a settlement of their transactions. As has been said, the reports merely showed a list of items of income and disbursements and the amount of cash in bank for the respective years. There was no showing that the stated amount of cash had been reconciled with the records of the estate or those of the bank. Nor was there any evidence that the trustees, beneficiaries, and Pulley agreed or considered that they were final accountings for the respective years.

But even if the furnishing and acceptance of these reports be considered an account stated for the respective years, it does not constitute an estoppel but is subject to impeachment for mistake or error clearly proved.

Neither do we agree with the trial court's holding that since the beneficiaries knew of and acquiesced in Pulley's "method of bookkeeping and the method in which the business was conducted," they are estopped to demand an accounting of him. There is no showing that his method of keeping his books and conducting the business were improper. Indeed, he insists in his brief that these were proper and that his records correctly show his transactions. Nor is there any evidence that the beneficiaries had actual or implied knowledge of, or acquiesced in, the discrepancies disclosed by the evidence, or the lack of records and vouchers which might have explained and accounted for such discrepancies. Not until they received the auditors' preliminary report in August 1956, did the beneficiaries know of these alleged discrepancies and lack of adequate records. Within a few months thereafter the present suit was brought. Hence, there is no showing that the beneficiaries were guilty of laches which would preclude their right to require an accounting of Pulley for the recent period in controversy, from 1951 to 1955, both inclusive.

Principal's Duties to Agent

Duty to Compensate Agent. Many agency relations are created by contract and there is agreement upon the compensation the agent is to receive. Controversies as to the amount of compensation due are then settled by applying rules of law for contract interpretation. Where the agency agreement is implied or the contract omits reference to compensation, whether the agent is to be compensated is determined from the relation of the parties and the surrounding circumstances. In such cases the rate of compensation would be the reasonable value of the services.

The courts have held that the agent is not entitled to compensation (1) if the agent is also representing interests adverse to those of the principal without the knowledge or consent of the principal, (2) if the agent is guilty of fraud or misrepresentation, (3) if the agent is negligent in the performance of his or her duties and the agent's negligence results in material injury to the principal, or (4) if the agent is transacting business which is illegal.[1]

Contingent Compensation. Frequently, the agent's compensation is contingent on his or her accomplishment of a stipulated result. In such cases, the agent is not entitled to compensation until he or she has accomplished the result, regardless of how much effort and money the agent expends in attempting to do so. If the agent is to be paid on a contingent basis, the principal must cooperate with the agent in the accomplishment of the result and must not do anything which will prevent the agent from earning the agreed upon compensation. If the principal by his or her acts prevents the agent from accomplishing the stipulated result, the agent will be entitled to the designated compensation.

When the agent has accomplished the stipulated result, the agent is entitled to his or her compensation even though the principal is not benefited by the agent's performance. For example, suppose a salesperson is to be paid a

[1] See the earlier discussion in this chapter under Agent's Duty of Loyalty.

commission on all orders accepted and approved by the principal. The principal has accepted and approved orders taken by the salesperson but, as the result of a shortage of materials, is unable to produce and ship the goods. The principal must pay the agent the agreed commission on the orders taken and approved. On the other hand, no matter how hard the salesperson works, if no orders are obtained, he or she is entitled to no compensation.

Compensating Professional Agents. The basis of compensation for professional agents varies according to custom for different types of agents in different geographical areas. Statutes in some states require that contracts of employment of certain types of professional agents, for example real estate brokers, must be in writing or the agent is not entitled to compensation.

The courts have decided many controversies over the compensation, if any, due real estate brokers and other agents who are employed on a contingent basis. Certain general rules have evolved which are subject to variation according to jurisdiction and, of course, subject to express contract agreement. Only a few of these rules are stated here.

Where the principal gives the broker what purports to be his or her complete terms and the broker finds a buyer (or seller) "ready, willing and able" to buy (or sell) on those terms, the broker is entitled to the commission, even if the principal refuses to contract with the third party, provided that the broker is the "effective cause" of accomplishing the result. If the principal provides the broker with only incomplete terms, the principal may terminate negotiations without liability for the commission if no agreement is reached with the third party on additional terms, unless the principal acts in bad faith. Unless the contract with the agent provides otherwise, the agent is entitled to his or her commission even if the third party defaults in carrying out a promise to buy or sell. A provision stating that the principal is to receive a certain net price is usually interpreted as imposing not only the condition that the offer from the broker's customer provide that sum to the principal but also that the sum be paid before the agent is entitled to the commission.

Reimbursement and Indemnity. If the agent has made advancements in behalf of the principal in the transaction of the principal's business and within the scope of the agent's authority, the agent is entitled to reimbursement for all such advancements. Also, if the agent has suffered losses in the conduct of the principal's business, the principal is legally bound to indemnify the agent for such losses, provided the agent has acted within the scope of his or her authority.

SUMMARY

The principal owes a duty to pay the agent any compensation due him or her by the terms of the contract of employment. If there is no agreement as to the compensation to be paid to the agent and it is clear that the agency is not gratuitous, the principal must pay the reasonable value of the agent's services.

If the agent's compensation is made contingent on accomplishing a stipulated result, the principal must cooperate with the agent in its accomplishment.

There are certain rules adopted by the courts to interpret contracts with real estate brokers and other agents employed on a contingent basis that do not clearly specify under what circumstances the agent has earned his or her commission.

The principal must reimburse the agent for all money advanced and expenditures made in the course of the performance of the agent's duties, if the advances or expenditures are expressly or impliedly authorized.

Floyd v. Morristown European Motors, Inc.

351 A.2d 791 (Super. Ct., N.J. 1976)

Michael Floyd (plaintiff) brought an action against Morristown European Motors, Inc. (defendant) for commissions he claimed due. Motors appealed from a judgment for Floyd. Affirmed.

Floyd was employed on an oral contract to sell foreign automobiles. He was to be entitled to a "draw" of $100 per week against commissions, use of an automobile, and commissions of 25 percent of the net profit to Motors. Nothing was said as to when the commissions would become earned.

Between January 8 and February 13, at a time when the new models were not in stock and prices had not been set on them, Floyd took signed orders for three automobiles and the buyers paid 10 percent of the expected purchase price. The deposits were said to be "refundable." Floyd took a leave of absence in March and was gone when the cars arrived and the buyers took delivery. Motors refused to pay Floyd the $721.25 he claimed as commissions on the sales, taking the position that at the time the cars were shown, the balance due paid, and the cars registered and turned over to the customers, Floyd was not an employee.

FRITZ, PRESIDING JUDGE. The underlying issue in this case is at what point an automobile salesman's right to his commission vests when the employment contract is silent in this regard. We have been cited to no previous dispositive decision in this State nor have we found any.

Considerations of equity and justice cause us to reject defendant's suggestion that the absence of the salesman from the scene at the time of "consummation" of the sale should, of itself, preclude his commission. That which is said to be "the general rule recognized in this and other jurisdictions" not only does not require the presence of the salesman, but protects his commission "notwithstanding the fact that the sale was consummated by the principal personally or through another agent," so long as the salesman is the "procuring cause of [the] sale."

We share this view that the matter should be decided by a determination of whether the salesman seeking the commission was, in fact, the effective cause of accomplishing the sale. *Restatement, Agency* 2d, § 448 at 355 (1958). If, factually, a salesman effectively produces a sale which ultimately occurs, then he should be paid his commission, and this irrespective of whether the written memorandum or order, if any, was "enforceable" or whether he was in fact present when the delivery took place.

It is apparent here, as is implicit if not express in the findings of the trial judge, that plaintiff was in fact the effective cause of the sales of the three cars in question. He should not be deprived of his commissions.

Termination of Agent's Powers

Termination by Will of Parties. Since an agent's authority is derived from the will of the principal, such authority terminates when the agent knows, or the circumstances are such that the agent should know, that the principal does not wish the agent to continue to exercise the authority previously granted. No formalities are necessary for such termination. All that is needed is that the principal indicate that he or she does not wish the agent to represent the principal or that the agent indicate that he does not intend to represent the principal. While either party has the *power* to terminate, there may be no *right* to do so. If the termination constitutes a breach of the contract of employment, the terminating party is liable in damages to the injured party.

Termination of Contract Provisions. A contract of agency will terminate at the time or upon the happening of an event stated in the contract, and if no time or event is stipulated, it terminates after a reasonable time. An agency created to accomplish a specified result terminates when that result is accomplished.

Termination by Change of Circumstances. Certain occurrences may cause the termination of the agency. The courts have held that, as a general rule, the agency is terminated by (1) the death of either the principal or the agent, (2) the insanity of the principal (to continue for at least the period of insanity), (3) the bankruptcy of the principal (as to matters affected by the bankruptcy), (4) the bankruptcy of the agent (under limited circumstances), (5) the objective of the agency becoming illegal, (6) impossibility of performance, (7) the disqualification of principal or agent (e.g. loss of license when license is required), (8) loss or destruction of subject matter of agency, or (9) changes in values or in business conditions.

In general, the basis for holding that the agency is terminated on the happening of the events listed above is that it is reasonable to believe that the principal, if he or she knew the circumstances, would not wish the agent to act further, or that the event is such that the accomplishment of the objective is rendered impossible or illegal. In most of the situations mentioned, there may be circumstances which justify the courts in holding that the general rule does not apply.

Termination of Powers Given as Security. An agency power given as a security, sometimes called an agency coupled with an interest (sometimes referred to as an irrevocable agency), cannot be terminated without the consent of the agent. The commonest example of such an agency is a secured transaction in which the secured party or some person acting for his or her protection is authorized to sell the property pledged as security in the event of default. For instance, suppose Allen loans Peters $1,000, and Peters pledges his diamond ring as security for the repayment of the loan. Such a pledge agreement usually authorizes Allen to act as Peters' agent to sell the ring at public or private sale in the event that Peters fails to repay the loan. In such a case Allen is said to have "a power given as security," and the power to sell is irrevocable by Peters and is not terminated by the death or loss of capacity of either Peters or Allen. Of course, the power to sell is terminated when the loan is repaid. It may also be terminated by the agent, Allen (or if three parties are involved, by either the agent or the beneficiary) if he voluntarily surrenders his power.

A situation where a power is given as security must be distinguished from one where the agent has only an expectation of profits to be realized. An agent promised a commission cannot prevent the termination of the agency merely because this will bar the agent from earning the commission.

Notice to Third Persons. An agent may have apparent authority to bind the principal after the termination of the agency. If the agency is general, third persons who have transacted business with the principal through the agent are justified in believing that the agent still has authority to represent the principal unless they have notice or knowledge of the termination of the agency. If the principal wishes to be protected against the results of the acts of a former agent, he or she should give third persons who have dealt with him through the agent personal notice of the termination of the agency. As to all other persons, notice by publication is usually sufficient.

If the agency is terminated by operation of law, such as by illegality or the death of the principal, any act of the agent after the termination will not bind the principal or his or her estate. This rule places a heavy burden on innocent agents and third persons who act without notice or knowledge of the termination. In some states the rule as to death has been relaxed by statute. In general, the rule is not applied to banks that pay checks that have been issued prior to the drawer's death but presented for payment after his or her death and before the bank has notice of the death, or to checks which are in the process of being collected at the time of the drawer's death. (U.C.C. 4–405.)

SUMMARY

The relationship of principal and agent may be terminated at the will of either the principal or the agent. If the termination of the agency is a breach of the contract of employment, the injured party is entitled to a judgment for the resulting damage. The agency may be terminated by the terms of the appointment, the accomplishment of its objective, the death of the principal or agent, the illegality of the objective, the loss or destruction of the subject matter of the agency, or the happening of events which would make it reasonably clear that the principal would not wish the authority of the agent to continue.

A power given as security is created when the power is granted for the protection of the power holder or third person. It is not revocable by the grantor of the power nor is it usually affected by death or incapacity.

If notice of the termination of the agency is not given to third persons who have been dealing with the agent, and they have no actual or constructive knowledge of the termination, the principal will be bound by the acts of the agent. At common law, this rule did not apply if the agency was terminated by the operation of law. The common law rule applies today with some exceptions, especially as to the payment of checks after the death of the principal.

Problem Cases

1. Rushing was a sewer contractor with a fifth-grade education. He wanted to borrow $1,800 for use in his business, and he and his wife went to Stephanus, a mortgage loan broker. Stephanus indicated that he could secure a first mortgage loan for them at 8 percent interest which would refinance the preexisting $3,200 mortgage on their home and provide $1,800 in cash. He asked Rushing and his wife to sign a stack of papers, representing that the loan application, which was on top, was in several copies. In this manner the Rushings signed blank forms not only for a loan application but a note, a mortgage and a hold harmless agreement. Stephanus filled in the application to show the loan amount as $6,600.

   Although the proposed loan was marketable, Stephanus did not place it promptly. After a month, the Rushings expressed concern and were told that there was a problem with the title to the home, and Stephanus suggested an interim loan of $1,000. The Rushings again signed another stack of papers in blank. On this loan Stephanus received a commission of $160. Finally, a month later a savings and loan association accepted the original loan. Stephanus advised the association prior to the closing that he held a recorded mortgage on the premises (one of the papers the Rushings signed) which had an unpaid balance of $660. This was actually his $660 commission, and it was paid in the closing transactions. By the use of this device, Stephanus' commissions were not noticed by the Rushings.

When he learned the facts, Rushing sued Stephanus for the total of $820 in commissions plus $565 in expenses he had paid to obtain the loans. Can he recover?

2. Becker, a physician without experience in real estate investment, entered into an agreement with Capwell, a realtor, to advise him concerning investment in land. Capwell told him the Lancaster property was for sale and made a favorable analysis of its investment possibilities. Becker purchased the property and later learned that the actual seller had been Capwell, who had purchased it before entering into the relationship with Becker for substantially less than the sales price to Becker. Becker sued to recover the "secret profit." The trial court granted Capwell's motion for nonsuit on the ground that Becker had failed to prove the value of the property at the time he bought it. Is Becker entitled to the difference between Capwell's purchase cost and the sales price to Becker?

3. Opal Conklin was employed by the Hofgesang Sand Company in a sand and gravel pit and landfill operation. She dispatched the trucks removing top soil, sand, and dirt from the pit and bringing trash and garbage. She also weighed the trucks and prepared weight tickets for each truck, and she prepared bills and invoices for credit customers and deposited cash receipts in the bank. Without the company's knowledge she had an arrangement with Corum (and other truckers, it was alleged) to pay her one cent (later two cents) per load of sand hauled out of the pit. Her tax return for 1970 showed $351 from this arrangement, $1,228 in 1971, and $3,758 for 1972, the year she resigned. She was being paid $140 per week and working six days and up to 60 hours per week.

   After her resignation she filed a complaint under the Fair Labor Standards Act alleging that she was entitled to $9,840 as minimum wages and overtime due her. Sand sought to establish as a defense and counterclaim for $150,000 the fact that she had embezzled or was reckless in handling its property and money. Is this a good defense, and is Sand entitled to recover the money it can be proved she obtained from truckers through her position?

4. Merkley employed MacPherson, a realtor, to find a buyer for Merkley's apartments. MacPherson located a buyer and presented a purchase agreement to Merkley, which Merkley signed. The agreement stated that MacPherson had received from the buyers and was holding earnest money in the form of a demand note for $2,700, and it provided that upon forfeiture by the buyers the earnest money should be divided equally between Merkley and MacPherson. The buyers refused to complete the sale, forfeiting the earnest money under the agreement. However, MacPherson was unable to produce the note upon demand of Merkley, having negligently failed to procure it from the buyers. Merkley sues MacPherson for the amount of the note. Is he entitled to all or any part of this amount?

5. Jarrell furnished McQueen certain appliances to be built into a new house McQueen was constructing for sale. Dallas Title Company was financing the project, and its authorized agent promised Jarrell that Dallas Title would withhold and pay over to Jarrell, when the house was sold, the amount due Jarrell for the appliances furnished by him for the house. The house was sold, but Dallas Title did not withhold and pay to Jarrell the amount of his claim. Jarrell was unable to collect for the appliances and sued Dallas Title to recover the amount of his loss. Dallas Title set up as a defense that its promise to collect was a promise to act as a gratuitous agent and that it was not liable for the loss. Is Dallas Title liable to Jarrell for the loss?

6. Thomas Vatterott purchased two trucks in Nebraska, financing the purchase through General Motors Acceptance Corporation. He failed to keep up the payments and GMAC threatened foreclosure. Thomas' father, Joseph Vatterott, obtained a loan, paid off GMAC, received the certificates of title, and assumed ownership. He tried to sell them without

success. He then made an arrangement with Gryder Motors, Inc., to sell them. Gryder sold the first on the basis of receiving as its commission the amount by which the price exceeded $18,000. Joseph agreed that upon the sale of the second any money received above $17,500 would be Gryder's. Gryder sold the truck for $20,500 and gave possession. However, because of irregularities in applying for a Missouri title that were not the fault of Joseph, Gryder refused to forward the $17,500. Is Joseph entitled to the $17,500?

7. In March 1973 John Swan entered into a written franchise agreement with Oregon Modular Designed, Inc., for an exclusive franchise to sell in the Willamette Valley homes manufactured by Modular. In April Mr. and Mrs. Christenson visited Modular's plant, and shortly thereafter Swan was directed by Modular to visit the Christensons. They entered a written contract of purchase for a modular home and made a down payment. Swan placed the order with Modular. During June, Swan's franchise was terminated by Modular, and later Modular refused to honor the contract with the Christensons, and insisted they enter a new one with it.

   The Christensons finally sued for the return of their down payment and won. Swan then sued Modular for his anticipated commission, which would be $2,804. Is he entitled to it?

8. Want was employed by Century Supply Co. as a salesperson to solicit Want's former customers for Century. The arrangement was that Want could have "whatever time was necessary" to develop this business and would be paid a 5 percent commission on all of it. Want was to pay his own expenses. After Want had been employed for seven months and had brought Century an average of $10,000 of business per month and had incurred expenses of $3,600, Century terminated Want. Want then sued for an accounting to recover the share of his expenses that was connected with soliciting business not yet credited to his commission account. Does Want have a right to recover such expenses?

9. Collection Agency entered into an agreement with Wanamaker whereby Wanamaker submitted its delinquent accounts to Agency for collection. The agreement provided that Agency would be paid a fee for collection based and contingent upon the accounts it successfully collected. The arrangement continued with Agency being paid for the accounts it collected until Wanamaker notified Agency that its services were no longer desired. Agency then sued Wanamaker alleging that it was entitled to a fee based on all the accounts referred to it, both collected and uncollected, because Wanamaker had not shown "just cause" in terminating Agency relationship. Must Wanamaker pay for the uncollected accounts?

20

Employment Law

Collective Bargaining and Union Activities

Introduction. The Industrial Revolution brought about profound changes in the employer-employee relationship. Goods that previously were hand produced in small shops were now produced by operators of high-speed machines in larger and larger factories. Few transferable skills were developed, the workplace was crowded, and working conditions were often unpleasant and unsafe.

Master-servant law (agency law) had developed prior to that period when production of goods and services and commerce were largely carried on by families and organizations that were little more than extended families. The law gave the master (employer) complete freedom in the hiring and firing of servants (employees), and, short of directing illegal acts, complete control over the employee's activities on the job. Where interests of employer and employee were in conflict, the law tended to support the new class of entrepreneurs who were rapidly adding to the prosperity of the society as well as their own wealth.

The early labor unions, beginning about 180 years ago, were weak and no match for the rapidly growing industrial firms, in part because the common law considered any collective action by employees to raise wages to be a criminal conspiracy. Nevertheless, unions struggled to alter the overwhelming power of the employer not only through collective bargaining but also through statutory enactment. However, it was not unusual for unions prior to the twentieth century to oppose workmen's compensation and other protective legislation for fear that if enacted the appeal of unions to workers might be reduced.

The Norris-LaGuardia Act. The first general legislation specifically designed to strengthen unions in dealing with management was the Norris-La-

Guardia Act of 1932. This Act greatly limited the circumstances in which federal courts could enjoin strikes and picketing in labor disputes, which had been a very effective anti-union weapon used by employers. It also prohibited federal courts from enforcing "yellow dog" contracts. These were agreements, frequently required by employers of prospective employees, by which the employee agreed not to join a labor union.

The National Labor Relations Act. In the midst of the Great Depression, Congress sought to equalize the disparity in bargaining power between employers and employees by passage of the National Labor Relations (Wagner) Act of 1935. It gave covered employees the right to organize and to bargain collectively. It also prohibited certain employer practices believed to discourage collective bargaining and declared these to be unfair labor practices.

The Act was amended by the Taft-Hartley Act in 1947. The amended statute is known as the Labor Management Relations Act (LMRA). It declared certain acts by labor unions to be unfair labor practices. It also provided for an 80-day "cooling off" period in strikes which the President might find likely to endanger national safety or health, and it created a Federal Mediation and Conciliation Service to assist employers and unions in settling labor disputes.

The LMRA was further amended by the Labor Management Reporting and Disclosure (Landrum-Griffin) Act of 1959. It established a "bill of rights" for union members as well as requiring reports from unions to the Secretary of Labor. The general purpose of this statute is to promote democracy and honesty in the control of union affairs. It also added to the list of unfair labor practices by unions.

Rights of Employees. The rights of employees are set forth primarily in Section 7 of the Act, which provides that employees shall have the right to form, join, and assist labor organizations, to bargain collectively through representatives of their own choosing, and to engage in other concerted activities for the purpose of collective bargaining. Section 7 also provides that employees shall have the right to refrain from any or all such activities.

The definition of an "employee" is extremely broad. The largest group of employees not covered by the Act are federal, state, and local government employees. Agricultural laborers and domestic servants are also excluded. Many states have enacted statutes regulating collective bargaining activities of state and local employees. Most federal employees are covered by various Executive Orders.

The NLRB. To ensure that employees would, in fact, have the right to form, join, and assist labor organizations, Congress created the National Labor Relations Board (NLRB) to administer the Act. It consists of a five-member panel appointed by the President, with the advice and consent of the Senate. The Board's main function is to process two categories of cases, representation cases and unfair labor practice cases. Representation cases involve the process whereby employees located in an appropriate unit select a labor organization for purposes of collective bargaining. Under the Act, a petition for an election may be filed by a group of employees, a labor organization, or an employer. After a petition is filed, the Board will usually conduct an election provided that the parties have complied with the requirements of the statute and the rules and regulations of the NLRB. If a labor union receives a majority of the votes, the Board will certify it as the exclusive bargaining representative for all the employees in the unit, not just those who voted for the union.

Unfair Labor Practices. The major task of the Board involves reviewing unfair labor practice complaints after they are first heard by an Administrative Law Judge. Various unfair labor practices are designated by the statute and classified into employer and union unfair labor practices. Practices by employers declared to be unfair include the following:

1. Restraining employees in the exercise of their right to form a labor union;
2. establishing or dominating a labor union;
3. discriminating with respect to hire or tenure of employment for reasons of union affiliation;
4. discriminating against employees because they have filed charges with the NLRB;
5. refusing to bargain collectively with the duly designated representative of the employees.

Union unfair labor practices include the following:

1. Restraining or coercing an employee in the exercise of the right to refrain from joining a labor union and also restraining or coercing an employer in the selection of representatives for purposes of collective bargaining;
2. causing or attempting to cause an employer to discriminate against an employee who is not a union member, unless he or she is not a member for failure to pay union dues;
3. refusing to bargain collectively with the employer;
4. conducting a secondary boycott or strike for an illegal purpose (another provision of the statute prohibits "hot cargo" agreements—requiring the employer to refrain from dealing in products of another employer considered to be unfair to the union);
5. imposing excessive initiation fees under a union shop agreement;
6. featherbedding (forcing an employer to pay for work not performed);
7. picketing for purposes of collective bargaining where the picketing union is not certified as the bargaining representative of the employees.

Judicial Review. Either the NLRB or an employer or union that has been found by the Board to have committed an unfair labor practice may appeal to the appropriate circuit court of appeals for enforcement or review of a Board decision. Generally there is no court review of representation proceedings.

SUMMARY

The common law on employer-employee (master-servant) relations failed to give employees needed protection after the Industrial Revolution. Modern labor unions arose to offset the overwhelming power of the employer over the worker. Unions supported the passage of the National Labor Relations (Wagner) Act which gave employees the legal right to organize and bargain collectively. After unions had become powerful, the Taft-Hartley and Landrum-Griffin Acts were passed by Congress to amend the Wagner Act to deal with certain practices of some unions. Now the LMRA prohibits what it defines as unfair labor practices both by employers and unions. The National Labor Relations Board was established to administer the Act, including the conduct of representation elections and adjudication of charges of unfair labor practices.

J. I. Case Co. v. NLRB

321 U.S. 332 (U.S. Sup. Ct. 1944)

J. I. Case Co. (plaintiff) petitioned for review of an order against it by the National Labor Relations Board (defendant). The court of appeals granted an order of enforcement. Affirmed.

Beginning in 1937, Case at its Rock Island, Illinois, plant offered each employee an individual one year contract of employment. About 75 percent of the employees worked under these contracts. While they were in effect in 1941 a CIO-affiliated union petitioned the NLRB for certification as the exclusive bargaining agent of the employees. Subsequently the union was certified but Case refused to bargain in any manner that would affect the rights and obligations under the individual contracts until their expiration. It did offer to negotiate on other matters. The Board then ordered the company to bargain and to cease and desist giving effect to the individual contracts.

MR. JUSTICE JACKSON. Collective bargaining between employer and the representatives of a unit, usually a union, results in an accord as to terms which will govern hiring and work and pay in that unit. The result is not, however, a contract of employment except in rare cases; no one has a job by reason of it and no obligation to any individual ordinarily comes into existence from it alone. The negotiations between union and management result in what often has been called a trade agreement rather than in a contract of employment. Without pushing the analogy too far, the agreement may be likened to the tariffs established by a carrier, to standard provisions prescribed by supervising authorities for insurance policies, or to utility schedules of rates and rules for service, which do not of themselves establish any relationships but which do govern the terms of the shipper or insurer or customer relationship whenever and with whomever it may be established.

After the collective trade agreement is made, the individuals who shall benefit by it are identified by individual hirings.

But, however engaged, an employee becomes entitled by virtue of the Labor Relations Act somewhat as a third-party beneficiary to all benefits of the collective trade agreement, even if on his own he would yield to less favorable terms. The individual hiring contract is subsidiary to the terms of the trade agreement and may not waive any of its benefits, any more than a shipper can contract away the benefit of filed tariffs, the insurer the benefit of standard provisions, or the utility customer the benefit of legally established rates.

Individual contracts, no matter what the circumstances that justify their execution or what their terms, may not be availed of to defeat or delay the procedures prescribed by the National Labor Relations Act looking to collective bargaining, nor to exclude the contracting employee from a duly ascertained bargaining unit; nor may they be used to forestall bargaining or to limit or condition the terms of the collective agreement.

But it is urged that some employees may lose by the collective agreement, that an individual workman may sometimes have, or be capable of getting, better terms than those obtainable by the group and that his freedom of contract must be respected on that account. We are not called upon to say that under no circumstances can an individual enforce an agreement more advantageous than a collective agreement, but we find the mere possibility that such agreements might be made no ground for holding generally that individual contracts may survive or surmount collective ones.

H. K. Porter Co. v. NLRB

397 U.S. 99 (U.S. Sup. Ct. 1970)

H. K. Porter Co. (plaintiff) brought an action to review an order of the National Labor Relations Board (defendant) requiring Porter to "check off" union dues for the United Steelworkers of America. After the order was affirmed by the court of appeals, the Supreme Court granted certiorari. Reversed.

The NLRB certified the United Steelworkers as bargaining agent for certain employees at Porter's plant in Danville, Virginia, in 1961. Negotiations for a contract continued for the next eight years, with the checkoff demand of the union the primary issue. The company did make payroll deductions for insurance, taxes, and contributions to charities, but it refused deduction of union dues saying it was "not going to aid and comfort the union." The

Board ordered Porter to cease and desist from refusing to bargain. When this was reviewed by the court of appeals it intimated that the Board might have required Porter to agree to the checkoff provision as a remedy to prior bad faith bargaining. The Board then so ordered.

MR. JUSTICE BLACK. It is implicit in the entire structure of the Act that the Board acts to oversee and referee the process of collective bargaining, leaving the results of the contest to the bargaining strengths of the parties. It would be anomalous indeed to hold that while § 8(d) prohibits the Board from relying on a refusal to agree as the sole evidence of bad-faith bargaining, the Act permits the Board to compel agreement in that same dispute. The Board's remedial powers under § 10 of the Act are broad, but they are limited to carrying out the policies of the Act itself. One of these fundamental policies is freedom of contract. While the parties' freedom of contract is not absolute under the Act, allowing the Board to compel agreement when the parties themselves are unable to agree would violate the fundamental premise on which the Act is based—private bargaining under governmental supervision of the procedure alone without any official compulsion over the actual terms of the contract.

Advance Industries Div. v. NLRB

540 F.2d 878 (7th Cir. 1976)

Advance Industries Division of Overhead Door Corporation (plaintiff) petitioned for review of an order of the NLRB (defendant), which cross petitioned for enforcement of its order to reinstate certain employees discharged during a strike. The Administrative Law Judge (ALJ) had found that the picket line conduct of three employees was not serious enough to warrant discharge and, therefore, the company had committed an unfair labor practice, and the NLRB agreed. As to five other employees the ALJ also found no violation of the NLRA but the Board disagreed. Reversed in part and affirmed in part.

About 80 out of 150 employees participated in a strike to attempt to force Advance Industries to bargain with the United Brotherhood of Carpenters. The strike was unsuccessful, and the company refused reemployment to a number of employees who were involved in misconduct during and immediately after the strike.

Darlene Romenesko was discharged for firing a gun at a light in the Company parking lot. The ALJ found that although the Company proved that she had drawn a handgun from under her coat and aimed it at the light, testimony did not support a finding that the weapon was actually fired or that it was the cause of the light breakage.

Vicki Marheine and Betty Koester were discharged for throwing gravel at a security guard and also Koester had rocked, although not damaged, a post in a plant driveway as well as pounding on a non-striker's car with her hand. The ALJ found proof of the gravel throwing unpersuasive and the other conduct not serious enough to warrant termination.

Five other employees who were discharged had been working on the second shift on the day after the strike ended. Although normally working until midnight, they were told that work would end at 10 P.M. that night when they would complete 40 hours for the week. After discussing the matter with two supervisory employees, they called the union business agent who advised them to "stay working even though they turn the lights off." When the five refused to leave at 10 P.M. despite further conversations with plant supervisors, their time cards were punched out and police were called. After trying to persuade the employees to leave, the police arrested them and removed them from the plant. They were then discharged. Although the ALJ upheld the discharge, the NLRB ordered their reinstatement.

PELL, CIRCUIT JUDGE.

I. Discharges for Picket Line Events.

An employer may not refuse to reinstate strikers unless he can show that his action is due to legitimate and substantial business justifications. Picket line misconduct may be sufficient to warrant termination. Trivial rough incidents or moments of animal exuberance must be distinguished from misconduct so violent or of such a serious character as to render the employee unfit for further service.

Romenesko's misconduct was sufficiently serious to justify the Company in denying reinstatement to her. We need not decide whether some particular circumstances might warrant a striking employee displaying a handgun on or near a picket line. We find no such justifying circumstances claimed or existing here. Romenesko did not inadvertently bring the gun to the picketing scene. It was brought as a concealed weapon and then brought out into the open upon which [*sic*] she went into a crouching position and aimed the gun at Company property for a minute or two. Her actions could not have failed to direct attention to her and to what she was doing. The actions were openly performed in the picketing area of a plant which was not shut down but which was attempting to continue its operation with non-strikers. Word that strikers were armed could have a strong coercive effect on non-strikers; a striker's apparent willingness to use a weapon makes the effect even stronger. That this effect was not demonstrated to the ALJ is not relevant; the misconduct still occurred. We deny enforcement of the Board's order to the extent it applies to Romenesko.

The alleged misconduct of Koester and Marheine was not sufficient justification for the Company to deny them reinstatement. The ALJ's finding that the Company did not show either engaged in serious misconduct is supported by substantial evidence. The rocking of the post and a single incident of pounding on a car by Koester were not egregious incidents; or at least, the Board was acting within its authority in so finding, and it is the primary responsibility of the Board, not the courts, to strike the proper balance between asserted business justifications and employee rights.

II. Discharges for Events in the Plant.

[E]mployees' rights under the Act must be accommodated with private property rights with as little destruction of one as is consistent with the maintenance of the other. The locus of that accommodation may fall at different points along the spectrum depending on the nature and strength of the rights asserted in a particular context. The primary responsibility for making this accommodation rests with the Board.

Employees have the right to make limited use of their employer's property in the exercise of their rights. In the absence of established grievance procedures, they may stop work and approach their employer's representatives to present grievances. They may walk out even if they do not articulate their grievance if the company has reasonable grounds for knowing the basis of their action.

A more complex problem is presented when employees stop work but refuse to leave the premises when requested to do so by their employer. *NLRB v. Fansteel Metalurgical Corp.* presents an extreme example of employee abuse of an employer's property rights. In Fansteel employees seized two of their employer's key buildings and occupied them for nine days. They were only evicted at that time by force.

Cone Mills Corp. presents facts closer to the present case. In *Cone Mills* the employees stopped work in protest over the discharge of another employee. When told to return to work or leave the plant, they refused to do either until they were arrested or escorted from the premises. When one employee was told to leave, he stated that he was staying until the regular quitting time. In deciding that the employer did not violate the Act by discharging the employees, the court placed heavy emphasis on the failure of the employees to utilize an established grievance procedure. In *NLRB v. Pepsi Cola Bottling Co.* the court found that the employer violated the Act by discharging employees who ceased working, went to the plant manager to protest the dicharge or six other employees, and upon the plant manager's refusal to reinstate the six, sat down and refused either to return to work or to leave the plant. Before the end of the shift, the employer called the police; and upon request by the police, the employees left the plant and began picketing outside. The court found that the facts did not tend to show that the employees were holding the plant in defiance of the owner's right to possession, noting that the sitdown did not carry over into the next shift and that the employees left immediately when requested by the police. The court indicated that the employees' refusal to obey the employer's order to leave the plant was not dispositive because it served no immediate employer interest and unduly restricted the employees' right to present their grievances. The court distinguished Cone Mills on the ground that the employer interest in maintaining an established grievance procedure was not present in the case before it because there was no such procedure.

[We] hold that the Board abused its discretion in applying the law to these facts to hold that the Company violated the Act by discharging the five who refused to leave the plant at the end of their shift. In contrast to the facts in Pepsi-Cola and in the other cases relied on by the Board, the employees presented no grievance to company representatives; they refused to leave after the end of their shift when ordered to do so by management representatives and the police, thereby preventing the employer from closing the plant for the night; and they had available an established grievance procedure through which they could have presented their complaints.

The Fair Labor Standards Act

Minimum Wages and Overtime. The Fair Labor Standards Act (FLSA) of 1938 requires covered employers to pay their employees a minimum hourly wage and to pay time and one-half for hours worked in excess of 40 in one week. The minimum wage has been adjusted upward from time to time and became $2.65 in January 1978. Coverage under the Act has also been expanded a number of times and in 1977 included both employers engaged in interstate commerce and those with a gross volume of sales exceeding $250,000 per year whose business affects interstate commerce in any way. Covered employers are required to keep certain records to aid in the enforcement of the Act and to comply with specified child labor standards. The Act is administered by the Wage and Hour Division of the U.S. Department of Labor.

Discrimination in Employment

Title VII, The Civil Rights Act of 1964. This Act, as amended in 1972, explicitly prohibits discrimination in employment as to hiring, firing, compensation, terms, conditions, or privileges of employment on the basis of race, color, religion, sex, or national origin. Since 1972 the Act has applied to employers engaged in interstate commerce who have 15 or more employees on each working day in each of 20 or more calendar weeks in the current or preceeding calendar year. It also applies to employment agencies procuring employees for such an employer and to almost all labor organizations. The 1972 amendments also extended coverage to all state and local governments, government agencies, political subdivisions, and the District of Columbia department and agencies.

The Equal Opportunity Commission (EEOC) was established to administer the Act. Initially the EEOC was limited to investigation, mediation, and conciliation. The 1972 amendments gave the EEOC power to initiate a civil action in federal court against any person where reasonable cause exists to believe that such person has committed an unlawful employment practice and attempts at conciliation have failed.

The reach of Title VII's prohibitions against employment discrimination has been expanded by the courts. An employment practice or procedure, such as barring employment of those with arrest records, that has the effect of operating in favor of an identifiable group of employees over a protected class is prohibited unless it can be demonstrated as a business necessity.

Discrimination based on religion, sex, or national origin is regulated by a different statutory standard from that applied to race and color. Employment discrimination with respect to religion, sex, or national origin is permitted where one of those characteristics is a bona fide occupational qualification (BFOQ) reasonably necessary to the normal operation of a particular business. The BFOQ exception is not available with respect to discrimination based on race or color. There has been much litigation under Title VII involving the BFOQ exception and, in general, the courts have construed the exception narrowly in favor of minorities. An example of a BFOQ might be a policy of a French restaurant to hire only natives of France as waiters.

The Equal Pay Act of 1963. This Act was passed to prohibit discrimination on account of sex in the payment of wages. Since the equal-pay standard is an amendment to the Fair Labor Standards Act, coverage is the same, and administration and enforcement of the Act is entrusted to the Wage and Hour Division of the Department of Labor. Under the statute, any person who knows of a violation of the equal-pay standard may notify the Wage and Hour Division of an alleged violation.

The Equal Pay Act essentially makes it unlawful for an employer covered under the statute to pay wages "at a rate less than the rate at which he pays wages to employees of the opposite sex in such establishment for equal work on jobs the performance of which requires equal skill, effort, and responsibility, and which are performed under similar working conditions. . . ." Hence, the equal-pay standard only focuses on wage differentials based on sex. Differentials based on race, color, religion, and national origin, although perhaps prohibited under other civil rights legislation, are not subject to claims under the Equal Pay Act. In addition, wage differentials paid pursuant to a seniority or merit system, or differentials paid pursuant to a system that measures earnings by quantity or quality of production (piece rate) are exempted from the standard.

Most of the litigation in the equal-pay area has involved questions of ascertaining whether wage differentials are in fact reflective of differences in the job performed. In general, the courts have uniformly held that Congress, in referring to "equal" work, did not require that jobs be identical, but only that they must be substantially equal.

Age Discrimination Act. This Act was adopted by Congress in 1967. Similar to the Equal Pay Act, the statute is administered by the U.S. Department of Labor's Wage and Hour Division.

Essentially the law protects persons 40 through 64 years of age[1] from discrimination in employment by employers, employment agencies, and labor organizations. The stated purpose of the Act is "to promote the employment of older workers based on ability rather than age, to prohibit arbitrary age discrimination in employment, and to help employers and employees to find ways to meet problems arising from the impact of age on employment."

Under the statute it is unlawful for a covered employer to fail or refuse to hire, discharge, or otherwise discriminate against any individual with respect to his or her compensation, terms, conditions, or privileges of employment because of age. In addition, employers are prohibited from reducing the wage rate of any worker in order to comply with the Act.

Labor organizations subject to the Act are prohibited from excluding or expelling from its membership, or otherwise discriminating against, any individual because of age. Causing or attempting to cause an employer to discriminate against an individual because of age is also prohibited.

Employment agencies serving employers covered by the Act are prohibited from failing or refusing to refer for employment, or in any other way discriminating against an individual, because of age.

Exempt from the Act are jobs where age is a bona fide occupation qualification reasonably necessary to the normal operations of a particular business. For example, an employer may indicate preference for a young person to play the part of a teenager in a stage production and not violate the statute.

SUMMARY

Title VII prohibits discrimination on the basis of race, color, religion, sex or national origin in hiring, firing, compensation, and in the conditions or privileges of employment. It applies to most private employers except those with few employees. The EEOC administers the Act and has the power to bring enforcement actions in federal court. A bona fide occupational qualification (BFOQ) such as age or sex is permitted where reasonably necessary to the operation of the business, but this does not apply to race and color.

The Equal Pay Act prohibits wage differentials based on sex. The Age Discrimination Act prohibits discrimination in employment against people aged 40–64.

[1] At press time HR 8353, which would raise the age to 69 years, was in conference committee after being passed by both houses but with different exemptions.

Griggs v. Duke Power Co.

401 U.S. 424 (U.S. Sup. Ct. 1971)

Griggs and others who were black employees (plaintiffs) brought an action against Duke Power Co. (defendant) alleging discrimination on the basis of race in violation of Title VII of the Civil Rights Act of 1964. The employees petitioned for a writ of certiorari after the district and circuit courts denied their claims. Reversed.

Prior to 1965 Duke Power Co. had openly discriminated against blacks in hiring and assigning employees at its Dan River plant, restricting blacks to the Labor and Coal Handling Departments. In 1955 it had instituted a policy of requiring a high school education for an initial assignment to its three "inside" departments—Operations, Maintenance, and Laboratory. Early in 1965 it made a high school education a requirement for transfer from Labor or Coal Handling to any other department. After Title VII became effective on July 2, 1965, Duke began requiring satisfactory scores (approximately the national median for high school) on the Wonderlick Personnel Test, which purported to measure general intelligence, and the Bennett Mechanical Aptitude Test for placement in or transfer to the "inside" departments. To assist undereducated employees of all races, Duke financed two thirds of the cost of tuition for high school training.

MR. CHIEF JUSTICE BURGER. The objective of Congress in the enactment of Title VII is plain from the language of the statute. It was to achieve equality of employment opportunities and remove barriers that have operated in the past to favor an identifiable group of white employees over other employees. Under the Act, practices, procedures, or tests neutral on their face, and even neutral in terms of intent, cannot be maintained if they operate to "freeze" the status quo of prior discriminatory employment practices.

. . . Congress did not intend by Title VII, however, to guarantee a job to every person regardless of qualifications. In short, the Act does not command that any person be hired simply because he was formerly the subject of discrimination, or because he is a member of a minority group. Discriminatory preference for any group, minority or majority, is precisely and only what Congress has proscribed. What is required by Congress is the removal of artificial, arbitrary, and unnecessary barriers to employment when the barriers operate invidiously to discriminate on the basis of racial or other impermissible classification.

. . . The Act proscribes not only overt discrimination but also practices that are fair in form, but discriminatory in operation. The touchstone is business necessity. If an employment practice which operates to exclude Negroes cannot be shown to be related to job performance, the practice is prohibited.

On the record before us, neither the high school completion requirement nor the general intelligence test is shown to bear a demonstrable relationship to successful performance of the jobs for which it was used. Both were adopted, as the Court of Appeals noted, without meaningful study of their relationship to job-performance ability. Rather, a vice president of the Company testified, the requirements were instituted on the Company's judgment that they generally would improve the overall quality of the work force.

The evidence, however, shows that employees who have not completed high school or taken the tests have continued to perform satisfactorily and make progress in departments for which the high school and test criteria are now used. The promotion record of present employees who would not be able to meet the new criteria thus suggests the possibility that the requirements may not be needed even for the limited purpose of preserving the avowed policy of advancement within the Company. In the context of this case, it is unnecessary to reach the question whether testing requirements that take into account capability for the next succeeding position or related future promotion might be utilized upon a showing that such long range requirements fulfill a genuine business need. In the present case the Company has made no such showing.

The Company contends that its general intelligence tests are specifically permitted by § 703(h) of the Act. That section authorizes the use of "any professionally developed ability test" that is not "designed, intended, *or used* to discriminate because of race . . . [Emphasis added.]."

The Equal Employment Opportunity Commission, having enforcement responsibility, has issued guidelines interpreting § 703(h) to permit only the use of job-related tests. The administrative interpretation of the Act by the enforcing agency is entitled to great deference. Since the Act and its legislative history support the Commission's construction, this affords good reason to treat the Guidelines as expressing the will of Congress.

Nothing in the Act precludes the use of testing or measuring procedures; obviously they are useful. What Congress has forbidden is giving these devices and mechanisms controlling force unless they are demonstrably a reasonable measure of job performance. Congress has not commanded that the less qualified be preferred over the better qualified simply because of minority origins. Far from disparaging job qualifications as such, Congress has made such qualifications the controlling factor, so that race, religion, nationality, and sex become irrelevant. What Congress has commanded is that any test used must measure the person for the job and not the person in the abstract.

Corning Glass Works v. Brennan

417 U.S. 188 (U.S. Sup. Ct. 1974)

Brennan, Secretary of Labor (plaintiff) brought this case against Corning Glass Works (defendant) to enjoin Corning from violating the Equal Pay Act and to collect back wages for women inspectors. The Supreme Court granted certiorari because the Second Circuit Court of Appeals found a violation while the Third Circuit found no violation in a similar case involving a different plant of Corning. Second Circuit decision affirmed, Third Circuit's reversed.

Corning had used female inspectors prior to the introduction of a night shift before 1930. At that time, since it was illegal to employ women at night, it was necessary to employ men as inspectors. However, because the men transferred to the night shift as inspectors insisted on higher pay, they were paid more than the women inspectors working days. Other men working at night received the same rates as the day workers. After the start of collective bargaining in 1944 a night shift differential was established, but it was imposed upon the existing differential between male night inspectors and female day inspectors.

After the effective day of the Equal Pay Act (and elimination of the state prohibition against women working at night) Corning opened the night shift jobs to bidding by women and consolidated the male and female seniority lists. In 1969 a new union agreement abolished for the future the separate base wages for day and night shift inspectors and established a new rate higher than the previous night shift rate. It further provided for a higher "red circle" rate for employees hired prior to that date when working as night shift inspectors. The effect was to perpetuate a differential between day and night shift inspectors, most of the latter being men.

MR. JUSTICE MARSHALL. Congress' purpose in enacting the Equal Pay Act was to remedy what was perceived to be a serious and endemic problem of employment discrimination in private industry—the fact that the wage structure of "many segments of American industry has been based on an ancient but outmoded belief that a man, because of his role in society, should be paid more than a woman, even though his duties are the same." The solution adopted was quite simple in principle: to require that "equal work be rewarded by equal wages."

The Act's basic structure and operation are similarly straightforward. In order to make out a case under the Act, the Secretary must show that an employer pays different wages to employees of opposite sexes "for equal work on jobs the performance of which requires equal skill, effort, and responsibility, and which are performed under similar working conditions." Although the Act is silent on this point, its legislative history makes plain that the Secretary has the burden of proof on this issue, as both of the courts below recognized.

The Act also establishes four exceptions—three specific and one a general catch-all provision—where different payment to employees of opposite sexes "is made pursuant to (*i*) a seniority system; (*ii*) a merit system; (*iii*) a system which measures earnings by quantity or quality of production; or (*iv*) a differential based on any other factor other than sex." Again, while the Act is silent on this question, its structure and history also suggest that once the Secretary has carried his burden of showing that the employer pays workers of one sex more than workers of the opposite sex for equal work, the burden shifts to the employer to show that the differential is justified under one of the Act's four exceptions. All of the many lower courts that have considered this question have so held, and this view is consistent with the general rule that the application of an exemption under the Fair Labor Standards Act is a matter of affirmative defense on which the employer has the burden of proof.

The contentions of the parties in this case reflect the Act's underlying framework. Corning argues that the Secretary had failed to prove that Corning ever violated the Act because day shift work is not "performed under similar working conditions" as night shift work. The Secretary maintains that day shift and night shift work are performed under "similar working conditions" within the meaning of the Act. Although the Secretary recognizes that higher wages may be paid for night shift work, the Secretary contends that such a shift differential would be based upon a "factor other than sex" within the catch-all exception to the Act and that Corning has failed to carry its burden of proof that its higher base wage for male night inspectors was in fact based on any factor other than sex.

While a layman might well assume that time of day worked reflects one aspect of a job's "working conditions" the term has a different and much more specific meaning in the language of industrial relations. As Corning's own representative testified at the hearings [on the bill], the element of working conditions encompasses two subfactors: "surroundings" and "hazards." "Surroundings" measure the elements, such as toxic chemicals or fumes, regularly encountered by a worker, their intensity, and their frequency."Hazards" take into account the physical hazards regularly encountered, their frequency, and the severity of injury they can cause.

Nowhere in any of these definitions is time of day worked mentioned as a relevant criterion. The fact of the matter is that the concept of "working conditions," as used in the specialized language of job evaluation systems, simply does not encompass shift differentials.

This does not mean, of course, that there is no room in the Equal Pay Act for nondiscriminatory shift differentials. Work on a steady night shift no doubt has psychological and physiological impacts making it less attractive than work on a day shift. The Act contemplates that a male night worker may receive a higher wage than a female day worker, just as it contemplates that a male employee with 20 years seniority can receive a higher wage than a woman with 2 years seniority. Factors such as these play a role under the Act's four exceptions—the seniority differential under the specific seniority exception, the shift differential under the catch-all exception for differentials "based on any other factor other than sex."

The question remains, however, whether Corning carried its burden of proving that the higher rate paid for night inspection work, until 1966 performed solely by men, was in fact intended to serve compensation for night work, or rather constituted an added payment based upon sex. We agree that the record amply supported the District Court's conclusion that Corning had not sustained its burden of proof.

Injury Compensation and Safety Legislation

Workmen's Compensation. Prior to the enactment of workmen's compensation legislation, the employee who lost an arm or leg while on the job faced numerous barriers to recovering damages from the employer. Besides the normal problems of attorney fees and court delays associated with a lawsuit, the injured employee would have to prove that the injury was due to the employer's negligence. Furthermore, even if negligence could be proved, the employer could avail himself of the common-law defenses of assumption of risk, contributory negligence, and the fellow servant rule (negligence caused by a fellow worker) to defeat any recovery by the injured employee. It is not surprising that employees who were injured in industrial accidents usually received little or no compensation.

In an attempt to eliminate the uncertainities of getting damages for injuries based on a negligence theory and to place the costs of industrial injuries on the employer, all states have enacted some form of workmen's compensation which provide benefits regardless of fault. That is, all that the employee need prove is that he or she is disabled and that the injury or disease was incurred on the job.

Most of the states enacted laws between 1911 and 1925 but the last state did not until 1948. Generally, the statutes require the employer to provide medical treatment, including rehabilitation services, to provide a prescribed level of income during disability (most commonly two thirds of wages but frequently with quite low maximums), and to pay scheduled amounts for death or loss of limb or other permanent disability. In return for the liability without fault imposed on the employer, the worker is normally precluded from bringing an action at law against the employer. However, actions by injured employees against suppliers of machinery and other third parties have sometimes been successful.

Statutes frequently permit employers to elect whether to (1) self-insure, (2) buy insurance, or (3) participate in a state fund and relate payments into the fund to claims experience so as to encourage safety promotion by employers.

There is no federal workmen's compensation statute applicable to private employers generally, although the establishment of mandatory federal standards has often been proposed. Many laws exempt employers with few employees—three for example—and in certain classes of employment such as those in agriculture, domestic service, and charitable organizations. Disability caused by certain diseases is not covered by some states, and the amount of disability pay for one with the same earnings or same disability may vary substantially from state to state.

Health and Safety Legislation. The rise of factories resulted in greatly increased exposure of workers to on-the-job injuries and disease. States enacted legislation seeking to force employers to reduce work-place hazards during the same period as workmen's compensation laws were passed.

Although there had been federal safety legislation applicable to mining, atomic energy plants, and other especially hazardous industries, there was no federal statute of general application until passage of the Occupational Safety and Health Act (OSHA) of 1970. All businesses affecting commerce, including those with only one employee are covered. It requires an employer to conform to detailed health and safety standards promulgated by the Secretary of Labor. Where no standards are provided it imposes a general duty on covered employers to furnish employment that is free from recognized hazards that may cause death or serious physical harm. Reports of fatalities and accidents requiring hospitalization of five or more employees must be made to the Secretary of Labor within 48 hours. Employers with more than ten employees are subject to record keeping requirements include a log kept for five years of all work-related deaths, injuries and illness.

Responsibility for enforcing the Act is placed in the Department of Labor's OSHA division. OSHA is empowered to make inspections (it usually makes them without giving prior notice)[2] and to issue citations for violations. A labor representative is entitled to be present during the inspection. Workers are protected if they notify OSHA of alleged violations.

Penalties of up to $1,000 per violation may be imposed for nonwillful violations. A willful violation resulting in death can lead to a fine of up to $10,000 and/or imprisonment for up to 6 months. The courts have ruled that no private action by employees is created by the Act.

An Occupational Safety and Health Review Commission was established by the Act to rule on citations contested by employers. Cases are first heard by a Review Commission Judge. If the employer is dissatisfied he may take the case to a panel of the Commission itself. Judicial review by the U.S. Court of Appeals may follow exhaustion of the administrative remedies.

States are permitted to develop and enforce their own employee health and safety programs so long as they provide protection at least as great as that provided in OSHA. More than 20 states have programs approved by OSHA.

---

[2] A three judge federal district court has held inspection provisions of OSHA violative of the Fourth Amendment because they do not require a warrant based upon probable cause. *Barlow's Inc. v. Usery,* 424 F.Supp. 437 (D. Idaho 1976). The Supreme Court has noted probable jurisdiction *sub nom. Marshall v. Barlow's Inc.*

SUMMARY

In order to provide employees with a better remedy than a negligence action for obtaining damages for work-related injuries, all states have workmen's compensation statutes. These statutes make the employer liable without fault.

OSHA is a federal statute under which the Secretary of Labor promulgates detailed safety standards applicable to almost all employers. It also imposes a general duty on employers to provide safe working conditions where detailed standards are not applicable.

Electro-Voice, Inc. v. O'Dell

519 S.W.2d 395 (Sup. Ct. Tenn. 1975)

Gladys O'Dell (plaintiff) filed a petition under the Tennessee Workmen's Compensation Act against Electro-Voice, Inc. (defendant), seeking an adjudication that she was totally and permanently disabled as a result of a bee sting. The trial court awarded temporary total disability from the date of injury to the date of trial and Electro-Voice appealed, claiming that the injury did not arise out of and in the course of employment. Affirmed (modified as to length of disability).

O'Dell was stung by a bee while at work. She had a violent allergic reaction and suffered swelling all over her body. She was hospitalized for treatment for a week. After the swelling subsided she continued to complain of stiffness, swelling, and numbness, especially in her legs.

COOPER, JUSTICE. An injury by accident to an employee is "in the course of employment" if it happened while he was doing a duty he was employed to do. It is an injury "arising out of" employment if caused by a hazard incident to such employment.

There is no question but that O'Dell suffered a bee sting while performing a work task assigned to her. The issue is: Was the bee sting a hazard incident to her employment?

In *Carmichael v. J. C. Mahan Motor Co.* an employee working at his assigned task was struck by a pellet accidentally fired from an air rifle by children who, by previous conduct, had shown themselves to be a hazard to employees in that they had shot and thrown missiles at employees. This court found that the injury arose out of the employment, saying:

> It is said that an injury arises out of the employment when it is apparent to the rational mind, upon consideration of all the circumstances, a causal connection between the conditions under which the work is required to be performed and the resulting injury.

On considering these circumstances, we are forced to the conclusion that the bees in the plant were part of the environment of working on the assembly line and consequently, were a risk or hazard of O'Dell's employment.

National Realty and Constr. Co. v. Occupational Safety and Health Rev. Comm.

489 F.2d 1257 (D.C. Cir. 1973)

Proceeding to review order of OSHRC which found National Realty had violated the general duty clause of the Occupational Safety and Health Act. Order against National Realty set aside.

WRIGHT, CIRCUIT JUDGE. An employer's duties under the Act flow from two sources. First, he must conform to the detailed health and safety standards promulgated by the Secretary of Labor. Second, where no promulgated standards apply, he is subject to the general duty to

> furnish to each of his employees employment and a place of employment which are free from recognized hazards that are causing or are likely to cause death or serious physical harm to his employees.

On September 24, 1971 the Secretary cited National Realty for serious breach of its general duty

> in that an employee was permitted to stand as a passenger on the running board of an Allis Chalmers 645 Front end loader while the loader was in motion.

This charge was doubly unfortunate. Permission usually connotes knowing consent, which is not a necessary element of a general duty violation. Second, the charge overemphasized a single incident rather than directly indicting the adequacy of National Realty's safety precautions regarding equipment riding. Nevertheless, the pleadings were not so misleading as to foreclose the Secretary from litigating the statutory sufficiency of National Realty's safety program.

Under the clause, the Secretary must prove (1) that the employer failed to render its workplace "free" of a hazard which was (2) "recognized" and (3) "causing or likely to cause death or serious physical harm." The hazard here was the dangerous activity of riding heavy equipment. The record clearly contains substantial evidence to support the Commission's finding that this hazard was "recognized" and "likely to cause death or serious physical harm." The question then is whether National Realty rendered its construction site "free" of the hazard.

Construing the term in the present context presents a dilemma. On the one hand, the adjective is unqualified and absolute: A workplace cannot be just "reasonably free" of a hazard or merely as free as the average workplace in the industry. On the other hand, Congress quite clearly did not intend the general duty clause to impose strict liability: the duty was to be an achievable one. Congress' language is consonant with its intent only where the "recognized" hazard in question can be totally eliminated from a workplace. A hazard consisting of conduct by employees, such as equipment riding, cannot, however, be totally eliminated. A demented, suicidal, or willfully reckless employee may on occasion circumvent the best conceived and most vigorously enforced safety regime. This seeming dilemma is, however, soluble within the literal structure of the general duty clause. Congress intended to require elimination only of preventable hazards.

The hearing record shows several incidents of equipment riding, including the Smith episode where a foreman broke a safety policy he was charged with enforcing. It seems quite unlikely that these were unpreventable instances of hazardous conduct. But the hearing record is barren of evidence describing, and demonstrating the feasibility and likely utility of, the particular measures which National Realty should have taken to improve its safety policy. Having the burden of proof, the Secretary must be charged with these evidentiary deficiencies.

To assure that citations issue only upon careful deliberation, the Secretary must be constrained to specify the particular steps a cited employer should have taken to avoid citation, and to demonstrate the feasibility and likely utility of those measures.

REA Express, Inc. v. Brennan

495 F.2d 822 (D.C. Cir. 1974)

REA Express, Inc. (plaintiff), petitioned for a review of a final order made by Occupational Safety and Health Review Commission holding REA liable for $1,000 for violation of the general duty clause of OSHA. Petition denied.

The feeder for a conveyor belt in an REA shipping terminal failed to operate because of a short circuit in the underground cable. REA's local manager called Traugott, president of a licensed electrical contractor. When Traugott arrived he found Coy, REA's maintenance supervisor, in the circuit breaker room with Soccio, an REA maintenance employee. The concrete floor was wet, and an attempt was being made to soak the water up with sawdust. Coy directed Soccio to cut three cables while the switch was out, and then Coy reenergized the cables. Traugott, believing that they carried only 600 volts rather than 15,000, then tested for voltage. When he did this a blinding flash occurred which electrocuted Coy, who was standing on the damp floor four or five feet from the cut live wires. Traugott, who was standing on a wooden platform about two feet from the wires, was knocked unconscious and burned on his hands and arms.

WRIGHT, CIRCUIT JUDGE. REA argues that since the circuit room was off limits to its employees generally, it could not be considered a "place of employment." However, the statute requires the employer to furnish "each employee" a place of employment free from recognized hazards.

REA also contends that the Act does not make the employer an insurer of the safety of the places of work he furnishes; it suggests that the employee must exercise reasonable care for his own safety and urges that the ultimate risk creation and the responsibility here was that of the independent contractor,

Mr. Traugott. This argumentation might well be relevant if this were a common law action brought against REA seeking a damage recovery for the death of Coy or the injuries of Traugott. However, that is not the issue here. The question before us involves the liability of the employer under the Act for the asserted failure to afford each of his employees a safe place to work. This question is wholly separate and apart from the employer's liability for damages in a personal injury action. The statute may well be violated even though no accident or injury occurs.

In view of the clear purpose of the statute to set new standards of industrial safety, we cannot accept the proposition that common law defenses such as assumption of the risk or contributory negligence will exculpate the employer who is charged with violating the Act. Nor are we persuaded that because he summoned an independent contractor for advice, his statutory obligation to provide his employees with a safe place to work is somehow excused. At the same time, we do not consider that the Act imposes an absolute liability upon the employer. The congressional declaration of purpose and policy states that the Act is designed "to assure so far as possible every working man and woman in the Nation safe and healthful working conditions. . . ." It may well be that some hazards are unpreventable, particularly if an employee's conduct is willfully reckless or so unusual that the employer could not reasonably prevent the existence of the hazard which his behavior creates.

Employment Retirement and Income Security Act

ERISA. Responding to complaints of underfunding, loss of right to benefits of long-service employees who are terminated or change employers, dishonest or careless management of pension funds, and other problems, including those caused by employers going out of business, Congress passed the Employment Retirement and Income Security Act of 1974 (ERISA). Like most other recent federal labor legislation, it covers all employers engaged in commerce or activities affecting commerce. It also covers pension plans established by unions and other employee organizations. Plans established by governmental bodies, although frequently more seriously underfunded than private plans, are excluded.

Although the law does not require an employer to establish a pension plan, and in fact quite a few were terminated under the law because its provisions and reporting requirements were believed to be too onerous, existing or new plans must meet certain minimum standards to qualify for tax deductions for the employer. These standards cover six basic areas: (1) fiduciary standards, imposing heavy responsibilities upon pension fund managers and others who make decisions about the investments and operation of the funds; (2) reporting and disclosure, requiring reports giving certain information to the Secretary of Labor and to covered employees; (3) eligibility to participate, prohibiting delay in participation for more than one year after hiring or age 25, whichever is later, unless 100 percent immediate vesting[3] is granted; (4) vesting, requiring the plan to give the employee a right to the employer contributions to the fund for his benefit according to a schedule that begins no later than ten years and provides full vesting in no more than 15 years after employment; (5) funding, requiring full funding of credits for current services and amortization of the present value of any past service credit granted over a period of 30–40 years; and (6) plan termination insurance, to cover the contingency that the plan's total assets are insufficient to pay promised benefits. The Pension Benefit Guaranty Corporation, established within the Labor Department, is the insurance agency set up by the Act.

The Department of Labor and the Internal Revenue Service share in the administration of the Act. Civil and criminal penalties are provided for violations.

SUMMARY

The purpose of ERISA is to protect the interests of employees and their beneficiaries of pension plans by making sure that benefits will in fact be paid in accordance with their terms and conditions. It does not require an employer to establish a plan. Insurance benefits are provided for through the Pension Benefit Guaranty Corporation. The Act establishes fiduciary standards for fund managers, requires reports to the Department of Labor, and disclosure to beneficiaries. It also establishes standards for eligibility of employees for the vesting of benefits, and for funding obligations of the plan.

Problem Cases

1. The Budd Manufacturing Company in 1933 formed the Budd Employee Representation Association. Weigand was a representative of the Association. He was frequently under the influence of liquor while at the plant. He came to work pretty much when he chose and left his shift and the plant when he pleased. His supervisors frequently demanded that he be discharged. However, each time higher officials intervened, and he was given pay increases four different times in addition to one general pay increase. In July 1941, there were rumors, denied by Weigand, that he had joined the United Auto Workers. On July 22, however, he admitted this to other members of the Association and was seen with other Association representatives talking to an Auto Workers' organizer. The following day Weigand was discharged, allegedly because of the cumulative complaints about his conduct.

   The NLRB ordered that Weigand should be reinstated because the company had

[3] Vesting occurs when the employer's contributions become irrevocably credited to the employee even though the employee may later quit.

committed an unfair labor practice in discharging him for his union activities. Should this order be enforced?

2. The Otsego Ski Club operated a resort hotel and restaurant. The company's employees went on strike. Seven of the striking employees were discharged for misconduct during the strike. The NLRB ordered the reinstatement of four of these. One was discharged for spreading nails on the main driveway into the resort and two others were discharged for serving as lookouts while the nails were being spread and for harassing a nonstriker by "tailgating" him for several days. The Board held that their misconduct was not sufficiently serious to warrant discharge.

   A fourth employee was discharged for throwing an egg at the windshield of the auto of a nonstriker while occupied by him and two daughters who were not employees. The Administrative Law Judge had credited the noncorraborated testimony of this employee denying the egg throwing but two Pinkerton security guards had testified they had observed her activity.

   Did the discharge constitute unfair labor practices by the employer?

3. Gregory applied for employment with Litton Systems, Inc., as a sheet metal mechanic. After verifying his references, Litton offered employment beginning March 18 and Gregory accepted. As part of the employment process Litton required new employees to complete a form called "Preliminary Security Information." It required a listing of all arrests other than for minor traffic offenses. Gregory had 14 such arrests, none resulting in a conviction, only one of them within the last nine years. Under Litton's policy, which was objectively applied without regard to race but which was not required by any national security regulation, Litton then withdrew its employment offer. Evidence brought out at the trial included the fact that although blacks comprise 11 percent of the population they account for 27 percent of the arrests and 45 percent of all arrests reported as "suspicion arrests." There was also evidence that employees who had been arrested but not convicted were no less efficient or honest, as a group, than other employees.

   Gregory brought an action under Title VII. Is the Litton policy as applied a violation?

4. Mr. Diaz applied for a job as flight cabin attendant with Pan American Airlines. Pan Am had a policy restricting its hiring for that position to females, and Diaz was rejected. Pan Am testified that, on the basis of long experience with both male and female flight attendants, it had found that the average performance of females was superior to males in providing reassurance to anxious passengers and giving courteous personalized service and that they were overwhelmingly preferred by passengers. A psychologist testified that an airplane cabin is a unique environment requiring the carrier to take account of the special psychological needs of the passengers and that these are better attended to by females.

   Is being female a bona fide occupational qualification (BFOQ) for flight attendants?

5. General Electric had a disability plan for employees that paid disabled employees 60 percent of their normal wages. It excluded coverage of certain disabilities including pregnancy. Several women employees who had been unable to work for several weeks due to pregnancy brought an action under Title VII of the Civil Rights Act of 1964 alleging the failure to cover pregnancy was unlawful sex discrimination. Will they win?

6. Boyd applied to Ozark Air Lines for a position as pilot. She was then working as Chief Flight Instructor at St. Charles Flying Service. She met all the preemployment criteria for the position except for height. She was less than 5 feet 2 inches tall, and Ozark's criteria were from 5 feet 7 inches to 6 feet 2 inches.

   Boyd brought an action under Title VII alleging discrimination based on sex. Among the general population in the age range of those employed as pilots the 5 feet 7 inches minimum height requirement excluded approximately 26 percent of males and 93 percent of females. Among active fliers of all ages 11 percent of males and 74 percent of females would be excluded. Cockpit instruments and the windshield are designed around a reference point. A pilot sitting below this reference point would find landing difficult because of distortion of view. When seated in either of Ozark's two models of airplane Boyd could not safely handle the controls of the plane.

Should Ozark be ordered to employ her as a pilot?

7. Moses had served as secretary to Griesedieck, an officer of Falstaff Brewing Corporation, for 22 years. When he retired as Chairman of the Board, Moses was discharged and told the position as secretary to Griesedieck was being eliminated. She was then 48 years old. Falstaff's policy was for secretaries of executive officers to remain secretary for the individual as he or she changed positions within the Falstaff organization and to eliminate the position when the officer left the company.

   She filed an action under the Age Discrimination in Employment Act. Other older women remained at work, and no pattern or practice of age discrimination was shown. Is her discharge a violation of Title VII?

8. Schillinger was a purchasing agent for Swiss Colony, Inc. Within about ten years the gross mail order sales of Swiss Colony, for which Schillinger was responsible, grew from $2 million to $13 million a year. Although she had three employees working under her, this did not reduce the pressures and strains on Schillinger which accompanied such a growth in business. In addition, Schillinger's immediate supervisor was negative, brusque, and belittling to her on all possible occasions. The result of these factors produced severe physical and mental problems for Schillinger requiring periodic hospitalization and eventually a demotion for her. Schillinger now applies for workmen's compensation due to the mental injury arising out of her employment at Swiss Colony. Is she entitled to it?

9. Shimp, a nonsmoking employee of New Jersey Bell Telephone Company is severely allergic to cigarette smoke. Shimp brought an action under state law to require that Bell prohibit smoking in the area where she is employed. She alleges that Bell is causing her to work in unsafe conditions. Can Shimp require that Bell prohibit smoking in her work area?

10. Southern Contractors was engaged in disassembling the structural steel members of a missile launching tower at Cape Kennedy. An employee fell to his death from an exposed beam, which brought an investigation by OSHA. OSHA had issued the following regulation:

    > A safety net should be provided when workplaces are more than 25 feet above [the surface] where the use of ladders, scaffolds . . . or safety belts is impractical.

    The OSHA district director issued a citation because no safety device was in use. This was contested by Southern. A safety specialist testified that only a safety belt with a lanyard would provide the worker with enough mobility. The law judge ruled that because a safety net was impractical there was no violation.

    Did Southern violate OSHA?

PART V

Partnerships

21

Creation of Partnership

Introduction

Nature of Partnership. "A partnership is an association of two or more persons to carry on as co-owners a business for profit." This definition from the Uniform Partnership Act is similar to the concept recognized in the Code of Hammurabi—2300 B.C., so conducting business through a partnership is an ancient concept. Perhaps the most important feature of a partnership is the unlimited liability of the individual partners for debts of the firm.

There has long been contention between two theories of partnership. Businesspersons and their accountants have tended to view the partnership as an entity—a body distinct from its members. This is the view of the law in France and other civil-law countries. However, the English common-law courts tended to treat the partnership as an aggregate of the individuals composing it. Under this view partners hold property in joint or common tenancy and are joint obligors on their contracts. American courts, although generally following the common-law view, occasionally gave recognition to the entity theory. This confusion stimulated the development of the Uniform Partnership Act (UPA) by the Commissioners on Uniform State Laws as one of their earliest efforts.

The original draft of the UPA clearly adopted the entity theory, but the final form, completed in 1914, is more of a hybrid. Although it does not provide for suits in the firm name, it does permit ownership of property in the firm name, accounting is between the firm and the partners rather than merely between partners, and creditors of the firm are given priority in partnership assets over creditors of the individual partners. In addition, the firm is permitted to continue to operate in situations where the aggregate theory would suggest immediate dissolution and discontinance.

The UPA and the Uniform Limited Partnership Act (UPLA) have been adopted by all the states except Louisiana, with the exception that Georgia has not adopted the UPA. Louisiana, following the civil-law tradition, follows the entity theory, and Nebraska has modified the UPA to define a partnership as an entity. Several states by separate statutes permit suits by and against partnerships in the firm name.

SUMMARY

The partnership was known from early recorded history. There has been inconsistency in both the English and American law because of conflicting concepts of a partnership—between the entity theory that the firm is separate from its members and the aggregate theory or the view that it is merely an aggregation of its members. The Uniform Partnership Act, which has been adopted by almost all states, does not adopt the entity theory in all particulars but several of its provisions appear to treat the partnership as something different from its members.

Creation of Partnership

Tests of Existence of Partnership. No formalities, such as registration with the state or even a written agreement between the partners, are required to form a partnership. However, under UPA (7[4]),[1] receipt by a person of a share of the profits of a business is prima facie evidence he or she is a partner in the business. This presumption may be rebutted by showing that a share of the profits was received (1) as payment on a debt, (2) as wages or as rent, (3) as an annuity to a widow or representative of a deceased partner, (4) as interest on a loan, or (5) as consideration for the sale of the goodwill of a business.

Following is a discussion of the characteristics of a partnership. However, the most critical factor is whether the parties are sharing in profits and the management of a business. If they are, they are almost certain to be held to be partners.

Intent. Partnership is a voluntary relationship. It cannot be imposed, as for instance by the inheritance of property. Frequently it is said by courts that there must be intent to form a partnership. However, the subjective intent of the parties is immaterial. Intent is determined by the words and acts of the parties interpreted in the light of surrounding circumstances. Therefore, even an explicit, written statement that the parties do not intend to form a partnership is not exclusive.

[1] The numbers in the parentheses refer to the sections of the Uniform Partnership Act (UPA), which is reprinted in the Appendix.

Carrying on a Business. The carrying on of a business is usually considered to require a series of transactions directed toward a definite end and conducted over a period of time. This requirement is referred to by the drafters of the UPA in their commentary. At least one court has held that engaging in a single venture, such as constructing buildings on several lots of land, is not carrying on a business even though the venture involves several transactions.[2] However, frequently if a short-term venture is before a court, it will be treated as a joint venture and partnership law will be applied, as discussed later in this chapter.

Any trade, occupation, or profession is treated as a business for the purpose of partnership determination. For example, ownership of unimproved land as an investment would not ordinarily be carrying on a business but the operation of an apartment house would probably be so treated. If a group of farmers joined together to buy supplies in order to get lower prices this would probably not be viewed as carrying on a business. However, if they bought harvesting equipment with which they performed custom harvesting for others for a fee, this would probably be considered a business.

Even if the endeavor might otherwise be treated as a business, if it is carried on by a charitable or nonprofit association, those participating in it will not be considered to be partners since their objective is not profit.

Co-ownership. The ownership must be of the business as such. There is no requirement that there be co-ownership of the capital or other property, real or personal, used in the business. A distinction is made between the partners' separate property used in the business and "partnership property." "Community of interest" may be a more descriptive term for the requirement than "co-ownership." In a partnership there is a community of interest in both the profits of the business and in the control of the business. However, a partnership may be found even if one (or a group) of the partners is by agreement given the management of the business.

A voice in management standing alone is not conclusive proof of the existence of a partnership. For example, a creditor may be granted considerable control in a business, such as a veto power and the right of consultation, without becoming a partner.

A clearly expressed intent not to share losses is evidence inconsistent with the partnership relation but is not conclusive. A failure to make provision for sharing losses is of no effect since the possibility of loss is seldom in the contemplation of the parties as they undertake to form a business.

Persons may be simply co-owners of property and not be partners. For example, assume that Allen and Beech inherit a commercial building and own it as tenants in common. If they merely rent the building to a tenant and share income and expenses, it is not likely they would be held to be

---

[2] *Walker, Mosby & Calvert, Inc. v. Burgess,* 151 S.E. 165 (Va. 1930).

partners since the partnership relation is consensual and cannot be imposed by another. However, if they then go on to buy other buildings and one or both of them become active in seeking out tenants, they would probably be held to be partners since it appears they are in the business of providing commercial space rather than just holding a building as an investment.

As a general rule, an owner of a farm and his or her tenant who own livestock and equipment together and who divide income and expenses are not deemed to be partners, since this is a very common method of farm tenancy. However, if the farm owner participates regularly in determining crops to be planted or when the livestock is to be sold, the farm owner may be held to be a partner and bound by acts of the tenant such as purchases made.

Where there is a clear agreement to be partners, partnership liability is found even though the business itself never gets underway. A partnership and partnership liability may also be found if associates operate a business without carrying out an intention to incorporate it.

SUMMARY

There is no simple test for the existence of a partnership. The major requirements of a partnership are: intent, co-ownership of the business, and carrying on the business for a profit. No formalities are required to create a partnership.

The intent required is not the intent to form a partnership but the intent to perform acts which are viewed as constituting the establishment of a partnership. Sharing in profits is prima facie evidence of the existence of a partnership although this presumption may be rebutted. The co-ownership requirement applies to the business. It is not necesary that there be co-ownership of the property used in the business. Co-ownership implies a voice in management but partners may agree to appoint a managing partner or partners. Conducting a trade, occupation, or profession is considered to be carrying on a business. There is no partnership if the activities are conducted by a nonprofit group.

As a general rule, the sharing of profits together with having a voice in the management of a business are sufficient evidence of the existence of a partnership.

Stuart v. Overland Medical Center

510 S.W.2d 494 (Ct. App. Mo. 1974)

Wallace Stuart (plaintiff) brought this action against Overland Medical Center and certain physicians alleged to be partners (defendants) seeking the value of Stuart's interest in the alleged partnership and certain accounts receivable. Judgment for Stuart appealed by defendents. Affirmed.

Dr. Stuart, a dermatologist, began practicing at the Overland Medical Center in 1963. Shortly thereafter Dr. Yanow, the medical administrator of the Center, approached Stuart about the possibility of purchasing the department of dermatology of the Center. Stuart accepted the offer, which established the consideration to be 10 percent of Dr. Stuart's gross receipts for a five-year period from the beginning of his practice at the Center plus 8 percent of his outstanding accounts receivable at the end of the five-year period, none to be more than one year old. This amounted to $17,182, of which $11,297 had been paid by Dr. Stuart at the time of trial.

Dr. Stuart conveyed by letter to Dr. Yanow his decision to terminate his association with the Center effective July 31, 1971, and prior to that date he notified his patients of his new location. The Center sent his patients a notice that another dermatologist would be available to treat them at the Center beginning August 1. There was a dispute over the amount due Dr. Stuart from the Center, and he filed an action claiming that it had been agreed that the formula used to establish the purchase price would also be used to establish the value of his interest if he withdrew. Use of this formula would yield $30,350 for the five years preceding his termination plus $28,200 for his accounts receivable. The Medical Center argued that there was no partnership but only an agreement to share expenses in proportion to the billings of the various physicians. Therefore, Dr. Stuart would be entitled only to his accounts receivable less his share of expenses.

WEIER, JUDGE. Under the Uniform Partnership Law . . . a partnership is defined as "an association of two or more persons to carry on as co-owners a business for profit." A partnership is defined judicially as a "contract of two or more competent persons to place their money, effects, labor and skill, or some or all of them, in lawful commerce or business and to divide the profits and bear the loss in certain proportions." The contract creating the partnership need not be written, but may be expressed orally or implied from the acts and conduct of the parties. The primary consideration in determining the existence of a partnership is whether the parties intended to carry on as co-owners a business for profit.

The evidence proved that Stuart was practicing his profession with the other doctors in the Center as a co-owner of the Center's facilities for a profit. While co-ownership and the sharing of profits by those engaged in business are not factors which conclusively establish the parties' relationship as that of partnership, they are prima facie evidence of partnership. As such, the presumption of partnership prevails unless evidence sufficient to rebut the presumption is brought forward. In this case, the Center physicians presented no evidence which would lead to the conclusion that the relationship between Stuart and them was anything other than a partnership. Indeed, their evidence actually aids the conclusion that the relationship was a partnership. By 1970 Stuart was listed in a financial statement of the Overland Medical Center for the years 1969 through 1971, one of their exhibits, as a partner with an equity interest in the Center of four percent. . . . [A] "Partnership Agreement" was entered into on January 1, 1954, by the three physicians who started the Overland Medical Center. While Stuart never signed this agreement, the agreement was evidence that the physicians who founded the Center intended to and actually did practice medicine as partners in a partnership from its inception.

Under these facts and circumstances, combined with the defendants' failure to prove that no partnership relation was intended, the trial court did not err in concluding that the professional arrangement between Stuart and defendants was a partnership.

Rosenberger v. Herbst

232 A.2d 634 (Sup. Ct. Pa. 1967)

This was an action by Rosenberger d/b/a Clover Leaf Mill (plaintiff) against Herbst (defendant) on account for grain, feed and fertilizer. Judgment for Clover Leaf Mill and Herbst appealed. Reversed.

Clover Leaf Mill had sold farm supplies to Parzych who operated a farm owned by Herbst. Parzych operated the farm under an agreement which gave him use and occupancy of the farm and acknowledged his indebtedness to Herbst in the amount of $6,000, repayable with 5 percent interest per annum. Herbst and Parzych were to equally share net profits and losses and the actual farming operation was to be "under the full control of Parzych." The agreement further recited that "the parties do not intend by this agreement to establish a partnership of any kind or type, but rather (a relation) of Debtor and Creditor and Landlord and Tenant." Parzych failed to pay for farm supplies purchased from Clover Leaf and Clover Leaf demanded payment for these debts from Herbst.

HOFFMAN, JUDGE. The Uniform Partnership Act, § 12(4), specifically provides:

> The receipt by a person of a share of the profits of a business is prima facie evidence that he is a partner in the business, *but no such inference shall be drawn if such profits were received in payment:* (a) As a debt by installments or otherwise, (b) As . . . rent to a landlord . . . (d) As interest on a loan, though the amount of payment vary with the profits of the business. . . . [Emphasis supplied.]

As previously noted, Parzych's indebtedness to Herbst was to be repaid from the proceeds of the farming operation. Furthermore, the agreement specifically provided that Herbst's remuneration was to be considered rental payments. Accordingly, no inference of partnership may be drawn from Herbst's receipt of a fractional share of the proceeds of the farming operation.

The construction of this contract must, ultimately, be determined by reference to the intent of the parties. Our Supreme Court has held: "[W]here [the parties] expressly declare that they are not partners this settles the question, for, whatever their obligations may be as to third persons, the law permits them to agree upon their legal status and relations [as between themselves]." In light of the parties' express statement of intention, coupled with the inconclusive nature of the remainder of the agreement, we hold that defendant Herbst and Eugene Parzych were not partners *inter se.*

There is testimony in the record that Parzych represented himself as Herbst's partner to Clover Leaf, at some unspecified date, and that Clover Leaf allegedly relied on Herbst's credit, for some unspecified period of time. There is nothing in the record, however, to suggest that Herbst, himself, by words spoken or written or by conduct, ever made or consented to such a representation. Parzych's unauthorized statement, without more, cannot give rise to an estoppel against Herbst.

Capacity to Be a Partner

Minors and Insane Persons. A minor may become a member of a partnership, but since a minor's contracts are voidable, a minor has a right to disaffirm the contract and withdraw at any time. The courts are divided as to whether the minor, upon disaffirmance, can recover from his or her adult partners the full amount of his investment or must bear a proportionate share of losses up to, but not exceeding the amount of the minor's investment. There is agreement that the minor is not permitted to recover his capital contributions unless creditors' claims can be satisfied. The fact that a member of a partnership is a minor does not permit disaffirmance of the contracts of the partnership.

The UPA (32) provides that upon the application of or for any partner, dissolution of a partnership shall be decreed if a partner has been adjudged insane. However, until there is dissolution by court action or by withdrawal of a partner, an insane person probably is in the same position in a partnership as is a minor.

Corporations. The UPA (2 and 6 [1]) includes corporations as persons who may form partnerships. The Delaware statute, the Model Business Corporation Act, and other modern corporation statutes explicitly empower corporations to join partnerships.

SUMMARY

A minor may become a member of a partnership, but he or she may disaffirm the contract of partnership and withdraw. Courts differ as to whether a minor must bear losses beyond his investment. If a partner is adjudged insane, this is a basis for dissolution by court action. Under modern corporation statutes a corporation can become a member of a partnership.

Persons Represented to Be Partners

Effect of Holding Out as Partner. Some of the earlier cases held that a person could become a member of a partnership by being held out as a partner, even though he or she never consented to becoming a partner and never actually participated in the affairs of the partnership. This theory of ostensible partnership has been abandoned. The UPA (7 [1]) provides: "(1) . . . persons who are not partners as to each other are not partners as to third persons." However, a person not a partner may, by holding himself or herself out or permitting himself or herself to be held out as a partner, incur liability to a third person who has dealt with the partnership in reliance on such holding out. The liability is based on the theory of estoppel, not on the theory that the party is a member of the partnership. In order to recover against a party as if he or she were a partner, a person must prove (1) that the party held himself out or permitted himself to be held out as a partner, (2) that the person dealt with the partnership in justifiable reliance on the holding out, and (3) to the person's injury. The only person who can hold a party liable as a partner is one who knows of the holding out and in justifiable reliance thereon has dealt with the partnership to his injury.

Holding Out or Consenting to Holding Out. The cases are not in accord as to what acts on the part of a person who has been held out to be a partner will amount to permission. Some of the earlier cases have held that if one is held out to be a partner and is aware of that fact, and yet does not take affirmative action to stop it, and also takes no action to notify the public that he or she is not a partner, this amounts to permitting oneself to be held out as a partner. The later cases and the UPA take the view that to be held liable as a partner, one must consent to the holding out. Under this view, knowledge that one is being held out as a partner, without other facts, will not amount to consent.

SUMMARY

Persons who are not partners as to each other are not partners as to third persons. However, if a person holds himself or herself out as a partner, that person will be liable to a party who in justifiable reliance on the holding out has dealt with the partnership to his or her injury.

Unless the party being held out as a partner acquiesces in the holding out, thereby contributing to the creation of the appearance that he or she is a partner, that party cannot be held liable as a partner.

Cox Enterprises, Inc. v. Filip

538 S.W.2d 836 (Ct. Civ. App. Tex. 1976)

Cox Enterprises, Inc. (plaintiff) bought an action against Filip and Elliott (defendants) as partners d/b/a/ Trans Texas Properties to recover on account for newspaper advertising. Appeal by Cox Enterprises from judgment in favor of Elliott. Affirmed.

Filip was the owner of Trans Texas Properties. One of his employees, Tracey Peoples, in placing advertising in the Austin American-Statesman, owned by Cox Enterprises, stated on a credit application that Elliott was a partner with Filip in Trans Texas Properties. Peoples testified that Elliott was aware that his name was on the credit application. Elliott testified that he did not authorize Peoples to make the representation and was unaware of it.

SHANNON, JUSTICE. In the proper exercise of its function, the court considered the testimony and refused to believe the testimony of Tracey Peoples, and obviously relied upon the testimony of Elliott. The court's finding was not so contrary to the great weight and preponderance of the evidence so as to be manifestly unjust.

Cox Enterprises' other point of error is that the court erred in not entering judgment for it predicated upon the court's finding of Elliott's failure to exercise ordinary care to discover that he had been held out to Cox Enterprises as an owner of Trans Texas Properties.

The argument is bottomed upon the Texas Uniform Partnership Act. Section 16(1) provides as follows:

> Sec. 16. (1) When a person, by words spoken or written or by conduct, represents himself, or consents to another representing him to any one, as a partner in an existing partnership or with one or more persons not actual partners, he is liable to any such person to whom such representation has been made, who has, on the faith of such representation, given credit to the actual or apparent partnership, and if he has made such representation or consented to its being made in a public manner he is liable to such person, whether the representation has or has not been made or communicated to such person so giving credit by or with the knowledge of the apparent partner making the representation or consenting to its being made. . . .

Prior to the enactment of the Texas Uniform Partnership Act, the rule in Texas was that for liability to be based upon partnership by estoppel, it must be established that the person held out as a partner knew of, and consented in fact to the holding out.

Section 16(1) codifies and enlarges upon the common law of partnership by estoppel. That section imposes a duty on a person to deny that he is a partner once he knows that third persons are relying on representations that he is a partner. We do not read section 16(1) as creating an affirmative duty upon one to seek out all those who may represent to others that he is a partner.

Limited Partnership and Related Forms

Nature of Limited Partnership. A limited partnership is composed of one or more general partners and one or more limited partners. It can only be created by complying with the filing requirements of the applicable statute (ULPA except in Louisiana). The management of the firm is in the hands of the general partners, and they have the unlimited personal liability for partnership debts that is characteristic of an ordinary or general partnership. A limited partner is merely an investor. He or she may share in the profits and losses of the partnership but liability is limited to the limited partner's contribution of capital to the partnership. General partnership law applies to limited partnerships except as changed by the applicable statute. The ULPA does not require that a limited partnership so designate itself in its name or otherwise in its dealings. The surnames of limited partners may not be used in the firm name.

The investor partner's limited liability is conditional upon avoidance of participation in the management of the business. Unfortunately, court decisions under the ULPA do not make it very clear as to how far a limited partner can go in giving advice or in reviewing management decisions without losing the exemption, but he or she can be an employee of the partnership. Since limited liability is more surely attained by incorporation, limited partnerships are used primarily where being taxed as a partnership (an aggregate) is advantageous. The limited partnership has been used extensively for "tax shelter" enterprises.

A revised Uniform Limited Partnership Act was approved by the National Conference of Commissioners on Uniform State Laws in 1976, but had not yet been adopted in any state at this writing. It constitutes a substantial revision. It provides for a name reservation system similar to and coordinated with that for corporations and requires that the name include the words "limited partnership." It makes the function of the certificate of limited partnership mainly the giving of notice to creditors and others and assumes that the partnership agreement is the basic constitutional document. Furthermore, it seeks to clarify the activities in which a limited partner may participate without becoming liable as a general partner.

Nature of Joint Venture. Courts frequently distinguish joint ventures (sometimes called joint adventures, joint enterprises, or syndicates) from partnerships. A joint venture may be found where a court is reluctant to call an arrangement a partnership because the purpose is not to establish an ongoing business involving many transactions but is limited to a single project. For example, an agreement to buy and resell for profit a particular piece of real estate, perhaps after development, is likely to be viewed as a joint venture rather than a partnership. Corporate promoters transacting business prior to incorporation may be treated as joint venturers, although some courts call them partners. Like a partnership, there must be a business (profit-seeking) purpose. However, a "joint enterprise" is sometimes found in vehicle tort cases where profit is not an objective.

The legal implications of the distinction between a partnership and a joint venture are not entirely clear either. Generally, partnership law applies. For example, all participants in the venture are personally liable for debts, and the same fiduciary duties as are imposed on partners are owed by joint venturers to each other. Distinctions have been made in the power of the individual members to bind other joint venturers, there appearing to be greater reluctance by courts to find apparent authority. This is related to the tendency of courts to put less emphasis upon common control of the enterprise than in the case of partnerships. Although less likely to be treated as entities, joint ventures are treated as partnerships for income tax purposes. A joint venturer, like a partner, is entitled to an accounting in equity.

Two or more corporations frequently join together to form a corporation to conduct some business in which both are interested. These are frequently referred to as joint ventures, but since incorporated they fall under the rules of corporation rather than partnership law.

Mining Partnership. A mining partnership, as recognized in some states, is a distinct relationship somewhat similar to a joint venture. In these states when co-owners share expenses and the proceeds of operation of mining property, a mining partnership is formed. A partner in a mining partnership can charge the other partners with necessary expenses but his or her agency powers are less than in an ordinary partnership. Unlike an ordinary partnership, bankruptcy or death of a partner does not work a dissolution, and membership is freely transferable by assignment.

SUMMARY

A limited partnership is a statutory form of business organization composed of one or more general partners and one or more limited partners. Limited partners are not liable for partnership debts in excess of their capital contribution unless statutory formalities are not followed in formation or they participate in the management of the business.

A joint venture is similar to a partnership but tends to be limited to a single project rather than an ongoing business. In some states the development and operation of a mine by co-owners of the property constitutes a mining partnership. Participants in joint ventures and mining partnerships have rights and duties similar to partners but they differ principally in the power of one party to bind his or her associates.

Delaney v. Fidelity Lease Limited

526 S.W.2d 543 (Sup. Ct. Tex. 1975)

Delaney (plaintiff) brought suit against Fidelity Lease Limited (Fidelity), Interlease Corp., and 22 individuals (defendants) for breach of a lease contract. The claims against three of the individuals—Crombie, Sanders, and Kahn—were severed from the rest, and the trial court granted them summary judgment, which was affirmed by the Court of Appeals. Modified and remanded.

Fidelity was a limited partnership of which the sole general partner was Interlease Corp. Crombie was president, Sanders vice president, and Kahn treasurer of Interlease Corp. Twenty-two individuals, including Crombie, Sanders, and Kahn, were limited partners in Fidelity. Fidelity entered into a lease with Delaney for a fast food service restaurant to be operated by the partnership. When the structure was completed, Fidelity failed to take possession and paid none of the rental due. Delaney sought to hold Crombie, Sanders, and Kahn individually liable under the lease on the theory that they had become general partners of Fidelity, the leasee, because they had participated in the management and control of the partnership by virtue of being the active officers of the corporation that was the general partner.

DANIEL, JUSTICE. Pertinent portions of the Texas Uniform Limited Partnership Act provide:

> Sec. 8. A limited partner shall not become liable as a general partner unless, in addition to the exercise of his rights and powers as a limited partner, he *takes part in the control of the business.*
>
> Sec. 13. (a) A person may be a general partner and a limited partner in the same partnership at the same time; (b) A person who is a general, and also at the same time a limited partner, shall have all the rights and powers and be subject to all the restrictions of a general partner; except that, in respect to his contribution, he shall have the rights against the other members which he would have had if he were not also a general partner. (Emphasis added.)

. . . [W]e hold that the personal liability, which attaches to a limited partner when "he takes part in the control and management of the business," cannot be evaded merely by action through a corporation.

The defendant limited partners also contend that the "control" test enumerated in Section 8 [of the ULPA] for the purpose of inflicting personal liability should be coupled with a determination of whether Delaney relied upon the limited partners as holding themselves out as general partners. Thus they argue that, before personal liability attaches to limited partners, two elements must coincide: (1) the limited partner must take part in the control of the business, and (2) the limited partner must have held himself out as being a general partner having personal liability to an extent that the third party, or plaintiff, relied upon the limited partners' personal liability. They observe that there is no question in this case but that Delaney was in no way misled into believing that these three limited partners were personally liable on the lease, because the lease provided that Delaney was entering into the lease with "Fidelity Lease, Ltd., a limited partnership acting by and through Interlease Corporation, General Partner."

We disagree with this contention. Section 8 simply provides that a limited partner who takes part in the control of the business subjects himself to personal liability as a general partner. The statute makes no mention of any requirement of reliance on the part of the party attempting to hold the limited partner personally liable.

Crombie, Kahn, and Sanders argue that, since their only control of Fidelity's business was as officers of the alleged corporate general partner, they are insulated from personal liability arising from their activities or those of the corporation. This is a general rule of corporate law, but one of several exceptions in which the courts will disregard the corporate fiction is where it is used to circumvent a statute. That is precisely the result here, for it is undisputed that the corporation was organized to manage and control the limited partnership. Strict compliance with the statute is required if a limited partner is to avoid liability as a general partner. It is quite clear that there can be more than one general partner. Assuming that Interlease Corporation was a legal general partner, a question which is not before us and which we do not decide, this would not prevent Crombie, Kahn, and Sanders from taking part in the control of the business in their individual capacities as well as in their corporate capacities. In no event should they be permitted to escape the statutory liability which would have devolved upon them if there had been no attempted interposition of the corporate shield against personal liability. Otherwise, the statutory requirement of at least one general partner with general liability in a limited partnership can be circumvented or vitiated by limited partners operating the partnership through a corporation with minimum capitalization and therefore minimum liability.

Misco-United Supply, Inc. v. Petroleum Corp.

462 F.2d 75 (5th Cir. 1972)

Action by Misco-United Supply, Inc. (plaintiff), a seller of oil-well construction supplies, against Petroleum Corporation (Petco), C. J. Pinner, and others alleged to be joint venturers (defendants) for the purchase price of supplies furnished. Appeal from judgment against Pinner but in favor of the other defendants. Affirmed.

Pinner and Petco agreed to drill a test well—the Persons well—and a development well—the Youngblood well—on two parcels of ground under lease to Pinner. In connection with the drilling, which was to be conducted by him, Pinner ordered supplies in the amount of $141,716.61 on his account. The account was not paid and learning later of Petco's participation, Misco sued Petco and others who had agreed to participate in the well drilling.

The agreement between Pinner and Petco involved two written contracts that appeared to be inconsistent in part. The agreement required Pinner to give 60 days' notice and evidence of marketable title before drilling the Youngblood well. This was not done. The agreement also provided that Petco could elect not to participate further in drilling at the Persons site after expending $82,200, its share of the cost of drilling to an agreed upon depth. This depth was reached on February 24, 1969, and the following day Petco elected not to participate further. No supplies were delivered by Misco to the Persons well until after that date.

Bell, Circuit Judge. If a joint venture exists under Texas law, one joint venturer has the authority to bind other joint venturers by contracts made in furtherance of the joint enterprise. Misco's case is dependent on the establishment of a joint venture among Pinner and the defendants or some of them. If the joint venture is established, the venturers would then be jointly liable for the cost of the goods sold to Pinner. If the defendants were merely owners of an interest in realty, or owners who have contracted for the operation of a lease by another, they would not be liable for the contracts of the operator or drilling contractor. A joint venture or mining partnership would not be created. The nonoperators would have only a contractual liability to the operator predicated upon the terms of the operating agreement, and not to third persons. Furthermore, and as Misco concedes, whether a particular agreement constitutes a joint venture depends upon the intentions of the parties thereto.

The matter of disagreement, however, is whether in the present case the question of intent should have been presented to the jury.

Opposing inferences from contractual provisions as to the intentions of the parties regarding the creation of a joint venture will ordinarily give rise to a question of fact. Whether such opposing inferences exist in the first place is a question of law. Here the contracts were of great length and were complex. Conflicting descriptions and definitions were used to describe the relationship of the parties. The language defining the liabilities of the parties and the conditions precedent to liability were open to more than one interpretation. Which parts of the agreement were to be in effect at a given time is not by any means clear. The conflicting inferences are apparent with respect to the joint venture liability asserted against the defendants. The district court did not err in allowing evidence as to the intention of the parties.

With respect to Petco, there was ample evidence of record to support the submission to the jury of the question of intent to enter into a joint venture with Pinner in the Youngblood well and to support the jury's finding. For example, we have previously noted the evidence which supports the position that Petco's obligations as to the Youngblood well were contingent upon Pinner's performance with respect to notice and title. Contrary to Misco's argument, it is a matter of substantive law in Texas that conditions precedent had to be met before a joint venture was created. "(Where) an agreement is made for a future partnership, but the partnership is to go into effect only after stipulated things are done, no partnership exists until the conditions are fulfilled." *Shell Petroleum Corp. v. Caudle* (1933).

As to Petco's participation in the Persons well, the matter is posed in a different context. The jury found that Petco did intend to participate in this well as a joint venturer. However, the jury also found that Misco delivered no equipment prior to noon, February 25, 1969. Upon consideration of Petco's letter to Pinner, delivered prior to noon, February 25, 1969, by which Petco declined to participate further in the Persons well, the court entered judgment for Petco.

Misco challenges the effectiveness of Petco's withdrawal, contending that its liability could not be limited without first giving notice to third parties. While we agree with the proposition that a private agreement between partners will not limit their liability to third parties, we deem this rule to be inapposite on the present facts. Petco's right to withdraw from further participation in the Persons well was specifically provided for in the written agreement of the parties. Reliance by a third party, the *sine quo non* of the rule, is totally absent here. Misco never, in any way prior to delivering the supplies, had knowledge of the participation in the well of any person other than Pinner. Under these circumstances, the district court was correct in giving effect to Petco's withdrawal.

Problem Cases

1. Elwood Grissum died in 1970 holding title to 1,104 acres of farmland valued at $220,902 and personal property—largely farm equipment, livestock, and feed—valued at $65,504. His sister, Nora, had lived with him on the farm for more than 30 years. She served as housekeeper, kept the farm accounts, fed and sorted livestock, and did some of the heavy farm labor. She was regularly consulted by her brother concerning the purchase and sale of livestock and land, and she usually accompanied him on trips for the purchase and sale of livestock. There was a sign that Elwood had placed over the harness shed and visible to anyone approaching the house from the highway that said, "Elwood & Nora Grissum—Boonville, Mo." A similar legend appeared on the farm truck. Elwood had told a number of people both in and out of Nora's presence that they were partners on a 50–50 basis. The farm insurance was applied for and issued in both names. However, Elwood filed individual income tax returns and alone signed all notes for borrowed money. He also maintained an individual bank account until 1967 when it was changed to a joint account. Neither party used any funds for other than living expenses, and all profits went into expansion of the enterprise by the purchase of land, livestock, and equipment.

Nora Grissum brings suit for her share of all of the property, claiming to be a 50–50 partner. Is this correct?

2. Charlie Borum left his home to his wife for life, remainder to his four children. After the death of the wife the children continued to occupy the residence as their home. They shared equally the expenses of the home—taxes, insurance, repairs, and improvements—and also their living expenses such as food, but not clothing.

   H. B. Deese, claiming to have contributed $1,200 more than the others toward these purposes, brought this action asking that the property be sold and that out of the proceeds he be reimbursed for the $1,200 and that the balance be divided among the parties. V. B. Borum defended on the ground that the parties were partners and that the proper action was dissolution and winding-up of the partnership. Was the arrangement a partnership?

3. Pete Pallesen owned over 1,000 acres in Kansas, and he and his son James operated a beef feeding and farming operation. Pete furnished the land and machinery and James did most of the work, each paying half of the expenses and sharing equally the gross income. They also operated a grain elevator. They reported income from the farming operation as individuals but filed a partnership return with respect to the grain elevator.

   Dwane Grimm was married to Pete's daughter. He approached Pete and James seeking to engage in farming with them. They decided that, in order to support three families, they would start a dairy herd. Grimm sold his home and his interest in a barber shop and moved his family to the farm in October 1970. He put $10,000 into a "Pallesen Dairy" account. Over the winter this account was used to erect a dairy barn on the Pallesen land. When it was gone Pete added $4,000 to it in April, $10,000 in May, and another $10,000 in June. The three men searched for suitable dairy cows and when found each withdrew $2,400 from the account and individually borrowed the balance to purchase cows for the herd. Grimm and James began milking in June.

   There was no discussion of the nature of the business relationship between the parties until an accountant was employed to set up the books in March 1971. At that time Pete flatly rejected a partnership and it was agreed that James and Grimm would share gross receipts and costs on a 50–50 basis. Soon friction developed between Grimm and the two Pallesens, and Pete told Grimm he would have to leave, which he did in October 1971. Settlement negotiations failed, Grimm's cattle were repossessed by the bank, and Grimm brought suit against Pete and James claiming one-third ownership of the land, machinery, crops, and cattle as a partner. Were these partnership property?

4. Johnson and McNaughton jointly leased a parcel of ground on which Johnson erected a store building at his own expense. McNaughton operated a package liquor store in the building under an agreement whereby McNaughton was to receive $60 per week in salary and was to pay 50 percent of the balance of the net profits to Johnson. Johnson loaned McNaughton the funds used for stocking the store but this was repaid. McNaughton carried on the business in his own name and performed all financial and management functions. The business ran into financial difficulty, and Escoe, alleging a partnership, sued Johnson as well as McNaughton to recover on dishonored checks. Did a partnership exist?

5. The seven children of C. H. Sternberg inherited his farm. They entered into a detailed agreement making William, one of the heirs, manager of the farm with broad authority. He was paid an agreed compensation and was to distribute profits to the heirs when he deemed it advisable and could call on the heirs pro rata for money to operate the farm. He contracted with Sternberg Dredging Company for dredging to be done on the farm and gave a promissory note signed by William as agent for the heirs. The note was not

paid and at his death was filed as a claim against William's estate. His executor argues that the note is a partnership obligation, and the heirs deny the existence of a partnership. Was there a partnership?

6. Scott Muse entered into an agreement with Western Marketing Co. to plant and harvest 66 acres of popcorn. In September 1969, Bernard Baker wrote for Western to Muse advising him to store the popcorn after harvest for which he would be paid one cent per bushel per month. Later, because he had rented his farm, Muse contacted Baker to ask Western to take delivery and pay him. Baker then informed him that the business was operating under the name of Baker and Company. In the following June, at Baker's direction, the popcorn was picked up and transported to Texas for processing. Muse demanded payment for the corn from Baker. Baker declared that he had been only an employee of W. R. Whitely, sole owner of Western and, after Western suffered financial reverses, of Baker and Company. He claimed he had only begun doing business on his own account as Baker Popcorn Company in October 1970.

   Is Baker liable for the contract price of the popcorn as either a partner or sole proprieter of Baker and Company.

7. Albina supplied scaffolding and cables to Safway under a contract which named Safway as "agent and representative" of Albina for sale, rental, and servicing of the equipment under terms, conditions, and prices prescribed by Albina. Title to all rental equipment remained in Albina, and Albina was entitled to 50 percent of its "suggested rental schedule" on all rentals of its equipment, regardless of the rental Safway actually received. Safway used its own rental forms, assumed all credit risks, and serviced all equipment. Abel was injured when a scaffold collapsed as a result of Safway's failure to repair damaged cables. Able sues Albina and Safway as joint adventurers. Albina claims Safway was an independent contractor with reference to the equipment rental. Should Albina be held liable as a joint adventurer in the rental enterprise?

8. Blomquist Electric Company operated under a "Certificate of Formation of Limited Partnership" which designated Blomquist and Preston as general partners and Lowe as a limited partner. Preston left the partnership early in 1962. Blomquist and Lowe operated the business on this basis until September 3, 1963, when they filed a new partnership agreement which made no mention of Lowe remaining a limited partner.

   Sometime after Preston's withdrawal, Power and Light extended credit to Blomquist Electric. In a suit to collect money due on that account, Preston claimed that he made a valid withdrawal prior to the extension of credit and Lowe maintained that the limited partnership certificate protected him from liability on the partnership debt. Can either Preston or Lowe be held liable on the partnership debt?

9. Robert and James Davis were engaged in a trucking business. They had signed a certificate of limited partnership but did not file this certificate with the county clerk as required by statute. Throughout the years, Robert and James had assumed equal liability on debts of the partnership and had shared equally in the profits of the growing firm. During the last two years, Robert devoted more time to the actual running of the business than did James; however, during the middle period of the business relationship both partners had devoted equal time to its affairs. James elected to terminate the partnership and insisted that Robert was only a limited partner and entitled only to return of his original investment and his undistributed share of partnership profits. Robert claimed to be a general partner and sued for dissolution and an equal distribution of the partnership assets. Will he succeed?

10. Holvey and his wife, builders of apartments, and Stewart, a general insurance broker, entered into an agreement in December 1968 stating that Stewart would pay $1,500 then and another $1,500 in 60 days and would acquire "50 percent of all units in La Grande." Only $1,000 of the second $1,500 was actually paid. An additional $6,300 was paid to the Holveys in August and September 1969, for a total of $8,800 and a 17-unit apartment building was completed about this time. A certificate of limited partnership dated in August was filed with the state in November which recited that Stewart had paid $3,000. In October the Holveys formed Bomar, a corporation, to construct an eight-unit building. Expected financing did not materialize, and the Hoveys, Bomar, and Stewart entered into an agreement reciting that Stewart had deposited $20,000 as security with the lender who would then lend another $20,000 to Bomar and that Stewart would receive a half-interest in the eight-unit apartment. Stewart's collateral was returned to him when later the Holveys built a four-unit apartment.

    The Holveys put the $8,800 contributed by Stewart in their personal bank account and paid construction costs for all three buildings from it. Following completion of the buildings no accounting was made to Stewart. Mrs. Holvey had kept the books, which showed no payments from Stewart. Stewart sued for an accounting, dissolution of the partnership, and one half the partnership assets, claiming a half interest in the construction of all three buildings. Was the trial court correct in finding a partnership only on the eight-unit building?

11. Trans-Am Builders, Inc. was a contractor and a creditor of Wood Mill, Ltd., a limited partnership that was developing an apartment complex. Wood Mill got into financial difficulties, whereupon the limited partners held two meetings to discuss the problems with the general partner, a corporation. They participated in the raising of additional money. One of the limited partners went to the project and went over it with Trans-Am's superintendent and complained about the way the work was being done. However, at least one of the limited partners attended no meeting and did not visit the work site. When Wood Mill could not pay Trans-Am, it sued the limited partners for the debt, alleging that they had participated in control of Wood Mill. Are the limited partners entitled to a judgment in their favor?

12. LNP was a limited partnership involved in development, engineering, and technical advice relating to the use of liquified natural gas. It had ten limited partners who were furnished periodic reports concerning the partnership by the general partner, Petsinger. Some of them attended meetings of the partnership where additional reports on the business were made and personal meetings between Petsinger and certain of the employees for the purpose of raising additional capital. Two of the limited partners, Garwin and Apt, were employed by the partnership, and they carried the title of Project Managers. They each served as consultants with respect to certain LNP projects. The limited partnership agreement provided that management and control of the partnership's day-to-day operation would rest exclusively with the general partner. Gast, an employee of the partnership, sued the limited partners as well as Petsinger, the general partner, for unpaid salary, alleging that all of the limited partners had participated in control.

    Should a court find the limited partners free of liability?

22

Relation of Partners between Themselves

Relation between Partners

Nature of Duty. Most partnerships arise from an oral or written agreement to form a partnership, although courts occasionally find the relationship between associates to be a partnership despite their lack of such a purpose or even the contrary subjective intent. The duties the partners owe to each other are subject to the contract between them. They may, for example, provide by agreement for unequal sharing of profits and losses, for the payment of salary or interest or some minimum compensation to some of the partners, and for unequal shares in management decision-making. Different classes of partners (such as junior and senior partners) may be established.

However, agency law provides a body of rules that will determine the relations between the partners if their agreement does not. Furthermore, partnership law—like agency law—imposes fiduciary duties which arise from the relationship itself and need not be specified in the agreement. They can be modified to some extent by the agreement but they cannot be eliminated.

Articles of Partnership. Although not required for the existence of a partnership, written articles of partnership are highly desirable for the same reasons written contracts are generally to be preferred. The process of preparing the agreement, if done properly, requires the parties to consider and provide for contingencies, such as the possibility of losses and the death of one or more partners, for which they might not otherwise plan. A written partnership agreement also tends to eliminate disagreements arising from misunderstanding and failure of memory. Many lawsuits involving partnerships could have been avoided if the partners had followed this practice. However, even in the most carefully drawn articles of partnership it is impossible to anticipate all of the contingencies which may arise in conducting the business. As to these, general partnership law will apply.

Articles of partnership usually include provisions covering at least the following matters: name of the firm, business to be carried on, place at which the business is to be conducted, term of the partnership, capital investment of each partner, how the profits and losses will be shared, how the business will be managed, how the books will be kept, salary and drawing accounts, definition of authority of the partners to bind the firm, provisions for withdrawal of partners and for dissolution and winding up of the business and, frequently, for continuing the business after the death or withdrawal of one of the partners.

Unless another rule is provided by the agreement, a partnership agreement can be modified only by the unanimous consent of the partners.

SUMMARY

Partners may, by agreement, define their relationship to each other within certain limits, and it is desirable to have written articles of partnership. They cannot, however, relieve themselves of the fiduciary duties they owe each other. Partnership law determines their relations in situations not covered by a provision in the partnership agreement.

Partnership Property

What Is Partnership Property? Most partnerships need to use property in the conduct of the business, whether they are engaged in manufacturing, in trade, or in providing a service. Usually, a partnership commences with capital, either in cash or other property, contributed by the partners. However, the partnership, as such, may own no property other than the business, and all the other tangible and intangible property used by the partnership may be individually or jointly owned by one or more of the members of the partnership or rented from third parties by the partnership. To determine what is partnership property becomes essential not only when the partnership is dissolved and the assets are being distributed but also when both the partnership and one or more of the partners are insolvent, since partnership creditors have first claim on partnership property and individual creditors have first claim on individual property.

The Uniform Partnership Act (UPA) (8) [1] provides that "(1) all property

[1] The numbers in the parentheses refer to the sections of the Uniform Partnership Act (UPA), which is reprinted in the Appendix.

originally brought into the partnership stock or subsequently acquired by purchase or otherwise, on account of the partnership, is partnership property, and (2) unless the contrary intention appears, property acquired with partnership funds is partnership property."

Application of this rule is not always easy. Fundamentally, intent of the partners controls. To provide a record of that intent with respect to the original property used by the partnership is one of the major advantages of having a written partnership agreement. A well-kept set of books for the partnership will show the partnership assets, and those assets appearing there will be presumed to belong to the partnership. It is also presumed that money used by a partnership as working capital is partnership property in the absence of clear evidence that it was intended to be merely a loan. The presumption is very strong that property purchased with partnership funds and used in the partnership is partnership property. In contrary decisions it usually appears that the court was strongly influenced by the rights of nonpartners. The presumption applies even when the property is not necessary to the partnership business or where partnership property rather than cash is exchanged for the asset.

Title to Partnership Property. The task of determining ownership is made especially difficult because under common law the firm had no existence separate from its members. Therefore, title to real estate could not be carried in the firm name. Despite the contrary provision of the UPA (8[3]), it is not uncommon for individual partners to take or retain title in partnership property because they believe this to be more convenient.

If title is taken in the partnership name it will be presumed that the property is partnership property. However, because of the common law rule, the presumption is not as strong that property held in the name of a partner is individual property.

Other Indicia. The mere fact that property is used by the partnership creates no presumption that it is partnership property. This applies equally to personal as well as real property. The payment of taxes, or insurance, or the making of repairs by the partnership, and deduction of these expenses on the partnership income tax return will be used as indications of the intent of the parties with respect to property not held in the name of the partnership. Of similar effect is the making of improvements on such property or mortgaging of crops or rentals by the partnership. Listing the property on a partnership financial statement given to a prospective lender may be treated as an admission of the partners. Frequently such indicia are in conflict, complicating a determination of ownership.

Ownership and Possession of Partnership Property. The partnership owns the partnership property as a unit; the partners as individuals do not own proportionate interests in separate items of partnership property. The UPA

(25) states that this form of ownership makes the partners "tenants in partnership."

Each partner has the right of possession of partnership property for partnership purposes. If a partner takes possession of partnership property for his or her own purposes without the consent of the other partners and to their exclusion, the partner will have violated his duties as a partner, and the wrongful acts may be ground for the dissolution of the partnership. Although a partner has wrongfully deprived the partnership and his or her partners of the possession of partnership property, the other partners cannot maintain a possessory action, such as replevin, against the wrongdoing partner, since the only remedy available to partners for breach of partnership duties is the remedy of dissolution and accounting.

Creditors of Individual Partner. A partner cannot assign any interest in separate items of partnership property, nor are they subject to levy of execution or attachment by the creditors of an individual partner. Prior to the general adoption of the UPA the courts of different jurisdictions disagreed on how a creditor of an individual partner might reach his or her interest. Section 27 provides that a partner may assign his interest but that this does not dissolve the partnership nor terminate the assignor's participation in it. It entitles the assignee to receive the assigning partner's share of the profits and does not even give him a right to inspect the books or to information about its affairs.

Section 28 authorizes a court granting a creditor a judgment against a partner to enter a "charging order," charging that partner's interest in the partnership with payment of the unsatisfied amount of the judgment. The court may also and frequently does appoint a receiver to receive the profits for the creditor and to look after the creditor's interest. If the profits are insufficient, the court may order foreclosure and sell the partner's interest to satisfy the charging order. Again such a sale does not automatically dissolve the partnership but would entitle the purchaser to dissolve a partnership that is at will. Provision is also made for the payment of the judgment by other members of the partnership so that it can be relieved of the charging order.

SUMMARY

Whether property used by the partnership or purchased with partnership funds is partnership property is fundamentally a question of the intent of the parties. A partnership may operate with all its tangible and intangible property except the business itself owned individually by its partners or others. There is a very strong presumption that property purchased with partnership funds and used in the partnership is partnership property. If title is taken in the partnership name, it is presumed that it is partnership property.

Each partner has the right to possess partnership property for partnership purposes, but a partner has no right to use it for his or her own purposes without the consent of the other partners. Partnership property is owned by the partners as tenants in partnership.

Neither the assignment of the interest of a partner in the partnership nor the imposition of a charging order on that interest by a court dissolves the partnership. An assignee during the existence of the partnership is entitled only to the profits which would otherwise be due the assigning partner. A court may decree foreclosure, and if it is a partnership at will the purchaser will then have the right to dissolve the partnership.

In re Estate of Schaefer

241 N.W.2d 607 (Sup. Ct. Wis. 1976)

Marilynn Schaefer (petitioner) sought a determination that certain property claimed by Arthur Schaefer (defendant) to be partnership property was held by her deceased husband as a tenant in common. Appeal from denial of the petition. Affirmed.

Ben and Arthur Schaefer went into partnership in an auto dealership in 1933. It was later incorporated. Between 1944 and 1967 they acquired considerable real estate. Their real estate business was kept separate from the auto dealership, and all payments for real estate purchased, proceeds from real estate sold, income from leases, and expenses were paid from or deposited in a checking account titled "Ben G. Schaefer and Arthur E. Schaefer, Real Estate Trust Account, Partnership." When purchasing 13 parcels of real estate, the Schaefers took nine deeds in which the grantees appeared merely as the two Schaefers, three deeds indicated they were tenants in common, and one deed referred to them as partners. Some leases were signed by one partner alone, some signed by both, and some by both men and their wives. Some deeds on realty sold were signed by all four. Tax returns were uniformly filed on a partnership form.

DAY, JUSTICE. The evidence overwhelmingly supports the trial court's finding that a partnership did exist. In *Skaar v. Dept of Revenue* this court expressed the requirements for proof of a partnership:

> Since Wisconsin has adopted the Uniform Partnership Act, we must initially look there for guidance. [It] defines a partnership as an 'association of 2 or more persons to carry on as co-owners a business for profit.' More specifically, it is recognized that four elements need be met so as to qualify as a partnership. Initially, the contracting parties must intend to form a bona fide partnership and accept the legal requirements and duties emanating therefrom. Secondly, there must exist a community of interest in the capital employed. Thirdly, there must be an equal voice in the management of the partnership. Finally, there must be a sharing and distribution of profits and losses.

The essentially uncontradicted evidence in this case establishes each of the four elements. Marilynn Schaefer's argument that a "community of interest" was not shown, because of a lack of evidence that each partner could dispose of the property, overlooks the leases introduced in evidence which were signed by Arthur E. Schaefer alone.

Once the existence of a partnership is established, there is a statutory presumption that property purchased with partnership funds belongs to the partnership unless a "contrary intent" is shown. The evidence in this case is plainly insufficient to establish a "contrary intent." The only evidence of intent not to operate as a partnership are the references to "tenants in common" on three of the thirteen deeds conveying the lands in question to Ben and Arthur, and the inclusion of the Schaefers' spouses as grantors on the two conveyances introduced. Even if this would be sufficient to overcome the statutory presumption, it must be weighed against the overwhelming mass of evidence showing that the lands were purchased with partnership funds, managed as a partnership activity, and sold for partnership benefit.

Management of Business and Compensation

Voice in Management. In the absence of an agreement to the contrary, each partner has an equal voice in the management of the business (UPA 18[e]). The vote of the majority of the partners controls in making decisions related to the normal business of the partnership. However, by agreement the partners may grant authority to manage the business to one or more partners, or they may set up an organization in which the authority to manage certain defined activities of the business is given to one or more of the partners.

Even if the management is in the hands of less than all the partners, any major change in the nature of the business of the partnership or its location which would materially alter the risks of the business must be approved by all the partners.

Right to Compensation. In the absence of a contrary agreement, each partner owes a duty to devote his or her entire time and energy to the partnership business. This does not mean that a partner cannot have outside interests, but it does mean that the partner must not engage in outside activities which will interfere with the performance of the duties he or she owes to the other partner or partners. A partner must not engage in activities which are in competition with the partnership business or which will be injurious to it.

A partner is not ordinarily entitled to salary or wages, even if quite disproportionate amounts of time are spent by certain partners in conducting the business of the partnership. Unless there is a contrary agreement, actual or implied, a partner's compensation is presumed to be his or her share in the profits of the business. The same principle applies to rent for the use by the partnership of property belonging to one of the partners. A surviving partner, however, is entitled to reasonable compensation for winding up partnership affairs UPA (18[f]).

If a partner does not perform his or her duty to serve, he may be charged with the cost of hiring an employee to perform his expected services or the other partners may be allowed compensation. A partner's breach of duty may also be ground for dissolution.

Profits and Losses. In the absence of an agreement defining the partner's rights in the profits of the partnership business, profits are distributed equally, irrespective of the capital contributions of the partners. Likewise, each partner is liable for an equal share of any losses suffered by the partnership.

If the partnership agreement sets out the proportions by which the profits of the business will be divided among the partners but is silent as to the way the liability for losses will be divided, each partner will be liable for losses according to the proportion in which he or she shares in the profits.

SUMMARY

In the absence of a contrary agreement, each partner has an equal voice in the management of the business. A majority of the partners have the right to make decisions regarding the everyday operation of the business. However, all partners must consent to the making of fundamental changes.

A partner is not entitled to wages for services rendered to the partnership or rent for property used by the partnership except by agreement. A partner's share of the profits is presumed to be his or her only compensation. In the absence of agreement profits and losses are distributed equally. If there is an agreement only with respect to profits, losses will be shared in the same proportion.

Rosen Trust v. Rosen

386 N.Y.S.2d 491 (Sup. Ct. N.Y. App. Div. 1976)

The estate of Harold Rosen (plaintiff) brought an action against Herbert and Maurice Rosen (defendants) to dissolve a partnership and for an accounting. Appeal from judgment holding that Maurice Rosen was not entitled to management fees and leasing commissions paid or accrued after the death of Harold Rosen (and other issues not here covered). Modified.

Three brothers formed a partnership for dealing in real estate in 1958. Harold and Herbert were executives of Helene Curtis Cosmetic Co. They were to contribute most of the operating funds. Maurice was a licensed real estate broker, and he was to manage the partnership. The partnership agreement provided that profits and losses would be divided equally and that no partner would receive a salary for services to the partnership. It provided that upon the death of a partner the business would be continued and the deceased's representative would participate in the profits or could, with notice, withdraw. If the later option were chosen the surviving partners were required either to purchase the deceased partner's interest or to terminate the business with reasonable promptness. The agreement provided that no compensation would be paid the surviving partners for their services in liquidating the partnership.

Harold Rosen died in August 1964, and his estate notified the surviving partners that it wished to withdraw as of December 31. The survivors did not exercise their option to purchase the estate's share, nor did they begin liquidation. In October 1967, the estate filed an action claiming breach of fiduciary duties in failing to liquidate and distribute the partnership assets and in paying Maurice management fees and leasing commissions in violation of the partnership agreement.

MOULE, JUSTICE. In spite of the express language to the contrary in the partnership agreement, Maurice and Herbert attempt to justify the payment of the fees and commissions on three alternative grounds: First, that they were extraordinary services rendered in the continuation of an ongoing business; second, that they were properly compensable services in liquidation of the partnership; and, third, they were compensable under the terms of an oral agreement which effectively modified the provisions of the partnership agreement.

Generally, the services of one partner are rendered for the common benefit of all and, absent some specific provision in the partnership agreement, the partner so rendering these services is not entitled to special compensation. It is accepted that the subsequent division of profits constitutes the only reward for such services. This is true even in those situations where the parties at the time the partnership was begun clearly did not contemplate that such services would eventually be required. Thus, the mere fact that such services were extraordinary, in that they were above and beyond any service envisioned by the parties, does not automatically justify compensation.

However, an exception to this rule has been recognized where the services are rendered after technical dissolution but while the partnership is continued as an ongoing business. Thus it has been held that "where the surviving partner has in good faith and with consent of the heirs and next of kin of the deceased partner continued the business with profit, the latter were given the option of either sharing in the profits or requiring him to account for their decedent's share in the profits; and where they elected to share in the profits, an equitable allowance was made to the surviving partner for his services. The grant of this compensation is based solely upon the equities of the situation and is usually premised upon some express consent or tacit acquiescence on the part of the deceased partner's estate in the activities of the survivors.

The record in the instant case establishes that, despite their duty to liquidate the partnership with reasonable promptness, the surviving brothers carried on the business and operated it in essentially the same manner as they had prior to Harold Rosen's death. Thus it cannot be reasonably argued that Maurice Rosen's post 1964 management and leasing activities were performed in the liquidation of a dissolved partnership. However, it also cannot be seriously questioned that the continuation of the business was undertaken without the estate's consent and in direct defiance of its demands for dissolution and liquidation. Thus, despite the fact that the estate has elected to share in the post-dissolution profits, under these circumstances the application of the exception to the general rule of denying compensation would be inequitable.

In light of our conclusion that the partnership has been conducted as an ongoing business since 1964 the services of Maurice Rosen are not alternately compensable as being rendered in liquidation of the partnership. Even if we did hold that the partnership was in the process of liquidation, Maurice Rosen would still not be entitled to compensation. UPA Section 40 provides that, absent any agreement to the contrary, "a surviving partner is entitled to reasonable compensation for his services in winding up the partnership affairs." Since paragraph 11 of the partnership agreement in this case specifically provides that "[n]o compensation shall be paid to the surviving partners for their services in liquidation," that provision would supersede the statute.

We do, however, find that Maurice and Herbert have properly established that the partnership provision relating to the payment of compensation for services rendered in the course of the business was effectively modified by an agreement between the partners and, based upon this modification, Maurice Rosen is entitled to management fees from 1964 to 1971.

At the original trial of this action, Herbert Rosen testified that there was an oral agreement among all three brothers that, in spite of the language of the partnership agreement, appropriate management fees and leasing comissions would be paid to Maurice. This testimony was corroborated by that of Maurice Rosen. He did not, however, regard these payments as compensation since they did not, in fact, cover the actual operating expenses of his company in providing management, janitorial and maintenance services on the partnership properties.

It is well established that where the intention of the parties to a partnership agreement is expressed plainly in the language of the agreement, such intention is not open to speculation, and parol evidence cannot be admitted to vary or change the language of the agreement. However, it is equally true that any written agreement, even one which provides that it cannot be modified except by a writing signed by the parties, can be effectively modified by a course of actual performance.

In the instant case, the partnership books indicate that Maurice Rosen was paid management fees during the years 1958 to 1964. Since the annual financial statements encompassing these payments were sent to all the partners and since no objections were raised concerning these payments prior to Harold's death, it is clear that the parties altered the terms of the partnership agreement by their acceptance of this compensation as a legitimate expense. In such a situation, it was error for the courts to refuse compensation for management services from 1964 to 1971. These fees, totaling $95,544 should be paid to Maurice Rosen and charged off against income in computing the profits for those years.

We do not, however, reach the same conclusion with respect to the leasing commissions. The partnership books show that the first entry of this expense was not made until after Harold Rosen's death.

Fiduciary Duties

Loyalty and Good Faith. Since each partner is an agent of the partnership and the partnership relation is one of trust and confidence, partners owe to each other the highest degree of loyalty and good faith in all partnership matters. This is a duty imposed by law and need not be provided for in the partnership agreement. Nor can a partner be relieved of this duty by contract.

A partner may deal with the firm or the individual members of the firm provided he or she deals in good faith and makes a full disclosure of all matters which affect the transaction and which a partner should know are not known to the other party. A partner must return to the partnership any profit made in a transaction with the partnership where he or she has used misrepresentation or concealment. If a partner, in contemplation of the organization of the partnership, acquires property which will be needed by the partnership when organized, he will not be permitted to sell the property to the partnership at a profit.

A partner is liable to his or her copartners if he uses partnership property for his individual purposes, misappropriates partnership funds, makes a secret profit out of the transaction of partnership business, engages in a competing business without the knowledge and consent of the copartners, accepts a secret commission on partnership business, or uses information gained as a partner to the detriment of the partnership.

Duty in Transacting Partnership Business. In transacting partnership business, each partner owes a duty to use reasonable care and skill and not to exceed the authority granted him or her by the partnership agreement. A partner is not liable to his partner or partners for losses resulting from honest errors in judgment, but a partner is liable for losses resulting from his negligence or lack of care and skill in the transaction of partnership business, and for losses resulting from unauthorized transactions negotiated in the name of the partnership. For example, suppose Arnold, Bond, and Cline are partners and the partnership agreement provides that no partner shall accept in the partnership name any draft for the accommodation of a third person. Suppose Arnold then accepts a draft in the name of the partnership for the accommodation of Thomas and the partnership has to pay the draft, thereby suffering a loss. Arnold will have to bear the loss because of breach of the partnership agreement.

Books of Partnership. The UPA (19) provides for the keeping of partnership books, and further provides that such books shall be kept at the principal place of business and that "every partner shall at all times have access to and may inspect and copy them." The books to be kept are determined by the agreement of the partners. Each partner owes a duty to keep a reasonable record of all business transacted by him or her for the partnership and to make such records available to the person keeping the partnership books. Under some circumstances a partner may be entitled to a formal accounting.

Knowledge and Notice. Each partner owes a duty to disclose to the other partner or partners all information material to the partnership business. He or she owes a duty to inform the partner or partners of notices he has received which affect the rights of the partnership. Partners are presumed to have knowledge of matters appearing on the books of the partnership, and failure to inform a partner of such matters is not a breach of duty.

If one partner is selling his or her interest in the partnership to a copartner, he owes a duty to disclose to the buying partner all the facts having a bearing on the value of the interest in the partnership which are not open to the buying partner. Likewise, the buying partner owes the same duty of full disclosure to the selling partner. Neither the buying nor the selling partner owes a duty to disclose facts appearing on the books or in the records of the partnership.

Duty to Account. Partners have a right to be reimbursed for expenditures they properly make on behalf of the partnership from personal funds. They also have a duty to account for their expenditures of partnership funds and their use or disposal of partnership property, as well as for any benefit or profit derived by them without the consent of the other partners UPA (21).

In addition to a right to inspect the books of the partnership, a partner has a right to a formal account ("or an accounting") as to partnership affairs. Under the UPA (22) this right arises when a partner is excluded from the partnership business or possession of its property, when the right arises under the terms of an agreement, when there have been benefits or profits received by a partner without the consent of the other partners, and whenever other circumstances make it just and reasonable. If a partner asks his or her copartners for an accounting and they refuse or he is dissatisfied with it, a partner may bring an action for an accounting.

Actions by the partnership against a partner for breaches of duty to the partnership are not permitted except through an accounting. The same applies to actions by a partner against the partnership.

SUMMARY

Each partner owes to the partnership loyalty and good faith, a duty to use due care and a duty to account. These fundamental duties cannot be eliminated by contract. A partner cannot make a secret profit in engaging in the business of the partnership or in dealing with it. A partner is liable for losses to the partnership resulting from his or her negligence or from making unauthorized transactions.

Each partner is entitled to free access to all the books and records of the partnership. A partner owes a duty to disclose to the other partner or partners all matters affecting the partnership business which are not disclosed by the books and records of the partnership. A partner also has a right to a formal accounting under certain circumstances and may ask the court to order and supervise the accounting.

Auld v. Estridge

382 N.Y.S.2d 897 (Sup. Ct. N.Y. 1976)

Auld (plaintiff) brought a suit against Estridge (defendant) charging fraud in the distribution of partnership assets. Judgment for Auld.

Auld, Stark, and Estridge (the sole owner of Kenway Metals Corp. and a non-practicing lawyer) entered into a joint venture to conduct a woodworking business. Auld, who had long lived in Haiti, was to provide the woodworking skill and production in Haiti, Stark would provide salesmanship, and Kenway would provide the necessary financing. All the business assets were in Kenway. The venture was unsuccessful and Estridge took it upon himself to find a buyer for the business. On June 7, 1968, he exchanged the woodworking business for 60,000 shares of unregistered stock in Allen Electronic Industries, Inc., an unrelated company. One week later he received as a spinoff on the Allen stock 60,000 shares of freely tradable stock in Calculator Computer Leasing Corp.

On July 25, Estridge met in New York with Auld, who was not represented by counsel. Estridge told Auld that he had made a good deal and that Auld would receive 5,000 shares of Allen, worth $25,000, and that he would get the money for him. Auld signed a general release as requested by Estridge and met him the next day to get the money. Estridge said he couldn't get it until the stock could be sold. Auld said he had to have the money to return to Haiti. Finally Estridge guaranteed a loan of $10,000 to Auld by Estridge's bank that was backed by the stock as collateral. Auld repaid only $2,000 and Estridge took over the 5,000 shares of Allen stock.

In December Auld learned that Estridge had received 60,000 shares each in Allen and Calculator. He brought suit for breach of fiduciary duty against Estridge, demanding the one third of the liquidation proceeds to which he was entitled under the joint venture agreement. Estridge argued that Auld must first sue for a partnership accounting, joining Stark. Further, he claimed that because Kenway had made advances to the venture, Auld was entitled to nothing after their repayment and that the 5,000 shares was merely a gratuity to Auld.

HARNETT, JUSTICE. The apparent rule which Estridge seeks to invoke is that where one partner wishes to sue another for acts within the partnership context, there must first be a full partnership accounting with all partners joined. This is so that a net balance of all net assets and outstanding partnership claims are dealt with, and no premature awards are made which require later adjustment. Moreover, the litigative presence of all partners will preclude the risks inherent in multiple litigation of similar issues.

Estridge, however, misconceives the cast of this case. The partnership is over here; it was sold in its entirety and a fund of stock realized in its stead. There are no practical questions of its accounts.

The Court finds Estridge breached his fiduciary duty to his partner Auld.

The Court has no doubt Auld knew or should have known Estridge was dealing to dispose of the business. While he may not have known specifications, he entrusted Estridge with those affairs. The gist of Auld's complaint is in what he got out of the deal, not in the deal itself.

Auld feels betrayed by his partner Estridge. A partner has a special obligation of undivided loyalty to his partners—quite different from an obligation owed to strangers. For Estridge, who alone was managing the sale of the business, this burden was particularly great. He was under a duty to disclose to his partners information uniquely his, which was fundamental to their enterprise. In the end, nothing was more fundamental or basic to Auld's interest in the business than the price for which it was sold. Yet, Estridge was misleadingly silent here.

The classic statement of Judge Cardozo in *Meinhard v. Salmon,* rings sonorously through the archives of this case, where he proclaimed that nonfraudulent conduct alone is not sufficient between partners, not the morals of the marketplace, "[n]ot honesty alone, but the punctilio of an honor the most sensitive, is then the standard of behavior."

Estridge fell far short of this standard. His concealment of the total Allen share payment and the 60,000 share Computer Calculator Leasing dividend was inexcusable. In view of their relationship and the existing circumstances, Auld had the right to rely on Estridge's assurance that he was getting his share. Estridge, on the other hand, had the duty to disclose fully to Auld, including the valuations and the amount of the setoff advance he was using.

Problem Cases

1. Gloria Harestad, a licensed real estate broker, and Victor Weitzel, a licensed real estate salesperson, made an oral agreement in September 1970 to become partners in a real estate and building business and opened an office with a sign reading, "Harestad & Co.—Realty—Builders—Residential—Commercial—Acreage." Each contributed $1,250 and they opened a bank account under the name, "Harestad & Co. Realty." In October Weitzel purchased a five acre parcel of land in his own name and with his own funds and arranged for financing and for architects and contractors for the construction of an apartment complex based upon his own financial statement. Harestad was involved in meetings with city officials, consultations with the architects, selection of carpeting and appliances, etc., for the project. Many of the payments to subcontractors and checks for other expenses in connection with the apartment project were drawn on the partnership account. Also certain payments received were deposited in the account, including the down payment for its sale in July 1971 for $629,332. At that time both Harestad and Weitzel drew checks to themselves on the account for $7,500, Weitzel explaining that this was a "commission," while Harestad denied any discussion of a commission. Articles of partnership describing the business as "real estate and building" were signed by the parties in August 1971.

   The tax returns for the partnership in 1971 made no reference to the apartment project. However, both Harestad and Weitzel included deductions indicating a 50 percent interest in it on their individual returns. The 1972 partnership tax return showed as an account receivable the balance due on the sale of the apartments but was signed only by Harestad. The partnership was terminated in November 1972, at which time there was a disagreement as to whether Harestad had an interest in the apartment project.

   Is Harestad entitled to a 50 percent share of the profit on the apartments?

2. Gates Rubber Company obtained a court judgment against Deese for $3,987. Deese was a member of a partnership at will, and Gates gained a charging order against Deese's interest in the partnership. Upon execution, Gates purchased the interest at public auction for $500. It then brought an action against the partners seeking dissolution of the partnership, an accounting, and distribution of the net assets. The partners appeared at the hearing in the case involving the charging order but filed nothing in opposition to that petition. However, they strongly opposed the later petition for dissolution and liquidation, and they claimed Deese's interest had been acquired by one of the other partners. Does Gates have a right to dissolution and liquidation?

3. Dean and Clemmer, partners in the operation of a restaurant, wanted new quarters for the restaurant. Dean conveyed to Clemmer an undivided half interest in a lot he owned. A building for the restaurant was constructed on the lot and used by the partnership. The cost of erecting the building, the taxes and insurance for the building were paid out of partnership funds. Rents from a part of the building not used by the partnership were paid to and used by the partnership. Upon Dean's death the lot and building were sold as partnership property. Rockingham Bank, a creditor of Dean, seeks to have the sale set aside and the property declared to be held by Dean and Clemmer as tenants in common. Is this contention correct?

4. Four brothers owned and operated a dairy farm under the firm name of Bender Bros. Two of the brothers had mortgaged specific items of partnership property to Klein as security for the repayment of money loaned to the two brothers as individuals. Windom Bank obtained a judgment against the two brothers and, in conformity with the provisions of the Uniform Partnership Act, had a receiver appointed over the interest of the brothers

in the partnership. Windom Bank contends that the mortgage given to Klein is void. Is the mortgage given to Klein void?

5. Hargett procured an option on a piece of property upon which he desired to erect a motel. He cleaned off the property and poured the footings for the building, but being financially unable to exercise the option or erect the building, he formed a partnership with Miller. Bank financing was arranged and Miller agreed to pay $825 monthly on the indebtedness until the motel was in operation and funds available to make the payments. Hargett was to manage the motel and reimburse Miller from partnership profits. The motel was unsuccessful and was sold. A balance remained after payment of partnership obligations (including Miller's reimbursement). Hargett contends that prior to division of surplus he is entitled to reimbursement for his expenditures prior to formation of the partnership. Should Hargett recover?

6. Koenig and Huber entered into a written partnership agreement to operate a plumbing and heating business. The agreement declared that the partners would "at all times diligently employ themselves in the business," that one half the capital was contributed by Huber in the form of plumbing tools and the building, equipment, and inventory of the business and one half by Koenig in the form of digging machinery and equipment, and that profits and losses would be shared equally. Few records were kept by the partners. When Koenig petitioned a court for dissolution and an accounting, a CPA was appointed by the court, and his written accounting was adopted by the court. He found an excess of partnership assets over liabilities of $24,017 but that Koenig had withdrawn $6,528 more than Huber in cash during the operation of the partnership so that Huber was now entitled to this much more than Koenig.

   Koenig argued that since Huber had operated an oil station for more than a year and had served as a deputy sheriff for almost a year out of the 6½ years the partnership existed, the extra drawing by Koenig should be treated as compensation for his "extra time" in the business. Is Koenig correct?

7. Kovacik, a building contractor, and Reed, a job superintendent and estimator, entered into a joint venture for kitchen remodeling work in the San Francisco area. Kovacik agreed to invest $10,000 in the venture if Reed would supervise and estimate the jobs. Profits were to be shared on a 50-50 basis. Reed's only contribution was his own labor and Kovacik provided all financing throughout the venture. After about nine months, Kovacik determined that the venture was unprofitable, terminated the venture, and demanded that Reed share the loss estimated at $8,680. Reed refused to contribute or pay any loss. Can Kovacik recover 50 percent of the loss from Reed?

8. Two brothers were partners in two businesses operated on adjoining city lots, sharing profits equally. They agreed to dissolve the partnership, with Ralph Styron taking the service station business and Roma Styron the plumbing business. Ralph drafted the termination agreement which both signed. It provided with respect to the plumbing business that Roma "will pay all accounts payable before 5 P.M. August 7 and collect all accounts receivable before 5 P.M. August 7. After all accounts payable are paid, then Roma Styron and Ralph Styron will divide equally the balance of the accounts receivable and Roma will collect his and Ralph will collect his."

   The accounts payable, it turned out, were substantially in excess of the accounts receivable, and upon a suit by the major creditor against the two brothers, Ralph sought indemnity from Roma based upon the quoted provision of their termination agreement. Is Ralph liable to the creditors of the plumbing business?

9. Dewees, Duley, and two others formed a joint venture to own and develop a 14.6-acre parcel of land on which Dewees and Herring owned a restaurant business. Duley died holding a 25 percent interest in the venture. Dewees and Herring persuaded Offutt to buy a share in the venture, representing that a 24.5-percent interest could be purchased for $25,000. Offutt agreed to buy a 10-percent interest for $10,000. Dewees and Herring then bought Duley's 25-percent interest for $14,000, reselling two fifths of it to Offutt. Five years later Offutt learned the true facts and sued Dewees and Herring for breach of fiduciary duty as partners because of the secret profit. Should Offutt recover?
10. Lavin, Dillworth, and Ehrlich entered a partnership to operate a tax preparing business. Ehrlich managed the business and the other two were essentially investors. Ehrlich wrote his partners a letter announcing his immediate withdrawal from and the dissolution of the partnership. Later the same month he contracted to buy the storefront property from the landlord. He refused to negotiate with his partners for a new lease. He also kept the customers' tax records. Lavin and Dillworth bring suit seeking to impress a constructive trust on the building for the partnership, claiming a breach of fiduciary duty by Ehrlich. Will they succeed?
11. Sims and Alexander had been partners in the retail jewelry business. Sims became ill and underwent surgery. The operation disclosed cancer in an advanced stage, but this was not made known to Sims. Learning of Sims's condition, Alexander had a new partnership agreement prepared which provided that upon the death of one partner all of the partnership assets should become the sole property of the surviving partner. Sims signed the agreement while in the hospital. The following day Sims learned of her condition. A few months later she asked for a copy of the partnership agreement and then executed a will in which she expressly bequeathed her interest in the partnership to her parents. After Sims's death her executor brought an action to recover the value of her interest in the partnership. Did Sims's interest in the partnership pass to Alexander upon her death?
12. Lichtman and Sasson were partners in the operation of a business. Lichtman presented false invoices and, on the basis of the false invoices, withdrew funds from the partnership. When Sasson discovered that Lichtman had fraudulently withdrawn funds from the partnership, Sasson brought an action at law to recover a judgment against Lichtman for the amount fraudulently withdrawn. Is Sasson entitled to a judgment against Lichtman?
13. Hensley was one of eight partners in the firm of Mary Gail Coal Company. The partnership operated a coal mine and had a fleet of 30 or more trucks which were regularly serviced at a filling station owned and operated by the company. Hensley personally owned one truck which was "hired" by the company to haul coal. On June 10, 1958, this truck was destroyed as a result of a fire at the company gasoline station. Hensley sued the partnership and the individual partners (including himself) claiming that negligence of partnership employees in permitting spilled gasoline to remain exposed on the ground caused the fire. Can such a suit be maintained?

23

Relation of Partners to Third Persons

Partner as Agent of Partnership

General Powers of Partner. The relations of the partnership to third persons, and the power of a partner to bind the partnership and his or her copartners, are set out in Sections 9–14 of the Uniform Partnership Act (UPA). In the absence of agreement between the partners, every partner is an agent of the partnership for the purpose of conducting the partnership business. However, even where there is such an agreement limiting the power of one or all of the partners to bind the partnership (for example an agreement that partners may not make purchases on behalf of the partnership above some specific sum of money without the concurrence of a majority of the partners) the limitation is not binding on third parties conducting normal transactions with the partnership unless they are aware of the limitation.

There are three kinds of evidence of authority which will give a partner power to bind the partnership: (1) specific agreement between the partners, whether or not contained in the articles of partnership; (2) the course of business of the partnership (that is the way the business has, in fact, been conducted); and, (3) the course of business of similar partnerships in the locality. Therefore, if the partnership is not to be bound by acts of partners which have been customary in the past or which are usual in partnerships of that type in the locality, those doing business with the partnership must be informed of the limitations. In the words of the UPA (9)[1] this general authority includes "the execution in the partnership name of any instrument,

[1] The numbers in the parentheses refer to sections of the Uniform Partnership Act (UPA), which appears in the Appendix.

for apparently carrying on in the usual way the business of the partnership."

The partnership is bound by admissions or representations made by a partner concerning partnership affairs which are within the scope of his or her authority. Likewise, notice to or the knowledge of a partner relating to partnership affairs is binding on the partnership.

Partner's Power to Convey Partnership Real Property. Since each state, by statute, requires certain formalities for the conveyance of real property located within its borders, the power of a partner to convey partnership real property and the manner in which the instrument of conveyance must be signed will be affected by such statutory requirements. To bind the partnership, the conveyance must be made in the regular course of the partnership business. Under the UPA (10) if the real property has been conveyed to the partnership in the partnership name, it may be conveyed by an authorized conveyance executed in the name of the partnership by a partner. If title to the real property is in the name of the partnership, a conveyance signed by a partner in his or her name will pass the equitable interest of the partnership in the property. If title to the real property is in the name of one or more but not all of the partners and the record does not disclose the partnership's rights in the property, a conveyance signed by the partners in whose name the property stands will pass good title to an innocent purchaser for value. If the purchaser, however, has notice or knowledge of the partnership's interest in the property, the purchaser will take subject to such interest. If the title to the real property is held in the name of all the partners and the conveyance is executed by all the partners, the conveyance passes all their rights in such property.

Limitations on a Partner's Power. Certain actions are specifically stated by the UPA (9[3]) not to be binding on the partnership unless all of the partners have authorized them. They include an assignment for the benefit of creditors, disposal of the goodwill of the business, an act which would make it impossible to carry on the partnership business in the usual way (such as the sale of the entire stock of goods of a retailing partnership), confession of a judgment, and (although it now appears quaint)[2] submission of a claim to arbitration. Other acts which would not ordinarily bind a partnership unless authorized by all of the partners because they would not be "apparently for the carrying on of the business of the partnership in the usual way," UPA (9[2]), would be an agreement of suretyship or a guarantee of the debt of another, paying or assuming an individual debt of a partner or, at least under old precedents, making charitable gifts or subscriptions or providing gratuitous services.

---

[2] Courts no longer have the antipathy for arbitration they did when the act was drafted in the early part of this century.

SUMMARY

In the absence of an agreement limiting the authority of a partner, each partner has the power to bind the partnership by acts which are ordinarily done in the carrying on of a business such as that in which the partnership is engaged, but this may be limited by agreement of the partners. In general, agency rules apply to admissions, to representations of a partner, and to notice to or knowledge of a partner. Title to real property which is in the partnership name may be conveyed by a conveyance executed by an authorized partner in the name of the partnership.

As a general rule, a partner does not have the authority to do acts which will defeat the purposes of the partnership or impose unreasonable burdens on the partnership, such as selling all the partnership assets, obligating the partnership as surety or guarantor for third persons, or paying or assuming an individual debt of a partner.

Borrowing on Partnership's Credit

Trading and Nontrading Partnerships. The extent of the implied and apparent authority of a partner to bind the partnership depends upon the nature of the business being carried on by the partnership. Although the UPA does not recognize the distinction, a number of courts have distinguished between trading and nontrading partnerships. A trading partnership is engaged in buying and selling for profit, such as retailing, wholesaling, importing, or exporting. A nontrading partnership is engaged in providing a service, such as the practice of law, medicine, the carrying on of a real estate brokerage or insurance business. Businesses such as general contracting, manufacturing, or operating a commercial farm, where working capital is necessary, are treated as trading partnerships.

Partner's Power to Borrow Money. The distinction between trading and nontrading partnerships is most frequently made in connection with cases involving the borrowing of money or the execution of a negotiable instrument where a partner's act is, in fact, unauthorized by the other partners. Courts making the distinction hold trading partnerships liable for money borrowed in the name of the partnership. Of course, a nontrading partnership may also be held liable if borrowing has been customary by that firm or by similar firms in the locality or appears necessary in the light of the nature of the business. The power to borrow money on the firm's credit will ordinarily carry with it the power to pledge firm assets to secure the repayment of the borrowed money.

If a partner having the power to borrow money does so and then converts it to his or her own use, the partnership will be liable. If, however, money is borrowed in a partner's own name, the fact that it is used for partnership purposes does not create partnership liability to the third party.

Partner's Power to Bind Firm on Negotiable Instruments. Negotiable instruments play such an important role in the carrying on of a business that a partnership will, regardless of the nature of its business, use negotiable instruments to some extent. If the partnership has a commercial account with a bank, a partner will have the power to indorse for deposit in the partnership bank account checks drawn payable to the partnership. As a general rule, a partner will have the power to indorse and cash checks drawn payable to the order of the partnership, and will likewise have the power to indorse drafts and notes payable to the order of the partnership and to discount them.

If the partnership has a checking account, a partner whose name is not on the signature card filed with the bank may bind the partnership on a check signed in the partnership name if such check is issued to a third person who has no knowledge of the limitations of the partner's authority. If, as is normal, a partner has the power to borrow money on the firm's credit, a partner has the incidental power to give a promissory note for that purpose, and if for such a loan it is customary to give security, he or she has the power to pledge the firm's assets.

SUMMARY

A partner's power to borrow money on the firm's credit will depend primarily on the nature of the partnership's business and whether or not it is standard practice in such business to use borrowed money to aid in financing its operation. The nature of the business is sometimes categorized as a trading or nontrading partnership, and an unauthorized partner will be held to have the power to bind a trading partnership.

Ordinarily a partner has the power to indorse for deposit or for discount negotiable instruments drawn payable to the order of the partnership. A partner's power to issue negotiable instruments in the name of the partnership is closely related to a partner's power to borrow money on the firm's credit.

Holloway v. Smith

88 S.E.2d 909 (Sup. Ct. Va. 1955)

Holloway (plaintiff) brought an action on a note against Milton Smith, Maude Smith, and Warren Ten Brook (defendants) as partners d/b/a Greenwood Sales & Service. The trial court rendered judgment only against Ten Brook and Holloway appealed. Reversed with judgment against all partners.

Ten Brook had been an employee of a proprietorship engaged in selling new and used cars and the operation of a service station under the name Greenwood Sales & Service. He was offered a chance to purchase the business but did not have sufficient funds. Milton Smith and his wife, Maude, agreed to join him in a partnership to purchase the business, each acquiring a one-third interest. The price was $22,894 and the Smiths paid the whole amount. The partnership agreement stated that the initial capital would be $25,800 to be contributed equally ($8,600) by the partners and reciting that the Smiths would advance $2,600 to Ten Brook and that Ten Brook would pay his portion of the capital from his share of the profits of the business. It also provided that Ten Brook would devote his entire time to the business as general manager but that either Maude or Milton Smith would sign all checks. Mrs. Smith kept the books and handled the money of the partnership.

The business was short of operating funds and had to sell some used cars at a loss in order to continue operations. An acquaintance of Ten Brook agreed to loan the business $6,000, giving him her check made out to Greenwood Sales & Service. This was deposited by one of the Smiths in the partnership bank account and withdrawn for use in buying and selling automobiles. Ten Brook gave her a note paying interest at 5 percent, which he signed for the partnership.

The Smith's argued that the loan was made to Ten Brook personally rather than to the partnership and that the amount when added to the amount of their loan to him constituted his capital contribution to the partnership.

SPRATLEY, JUSTICE. *Hobbs v. Virginia National Bank* . . . set out the principles which apply for ascertaining the liability of partners in a trading or commercial partnership with respect to a third person for the acts of a partner. In that case, the court approved the following instructions:

> The jury are instructed that, under the law, each member of a partnership is the agent of the other members, and that, when created, each partner has full power and authority to bind all the partners by his acts or contracts in relation to the business of the partnership, including the borrowing of money and the making and delivery of the notes of the partnership therefor; and as between the firm, and third persons dealing with them in good faith, it is of no consequence whether the partner is acting in good faith with his copartners or not, provided the act done is within the scope of the partnership business and professedly for the firm.

The Smiths selected Ten Brook as their partner. The partnership was a going concern when the $6,000 note was executed. In the absence of a restriction on his authority, known to Mrs. Holloway, Ten Brook had the same power to bind the partnership as his copartners had. Ten Brook, as the agent of the partnership, solicited the loan professedly for the firm and executed the note evidencing it, for "apparently carrying on in the usual way the business of the partnership" of which he was a member. [UPA Section 9]

Enforcement of Partnership Rights and Liabilities

Suits by and against Partnerships. Since partnerships were not considered a legal entity at common law, a partnership could neither sue nor be sued in its own name, but rather all partners had to be joined. Furthermore, since partners are jointly liable on partnership contracts, it was necessary to get personal service on each of the joint obligors. The difficulty this creates when partnerships conduct business in and are formed by people from different jurisdictions has resulted in remedial statutes in most states. Some statutes make all joint obligations joint and several, that is, suit may be brought against the partners jointly or against each individual partner. Common-name statutes permit the complainant to proceed to judgment if he or she serves one or more of the partners even though service is not gained over all. The judgment, when obtained, is enforceable against the joint assets of the partnership and against the individual assets of those parties served with process.

Partnership Liability for Torts and Crimes. The standards and principles of agency law are applied in determining the liability of the partnership and of the other partners for the wrongful acts of a partner. If the wrongful act is committed within the scope and in the course of the transaction of partnership business or is a breach of trust, the UPA (14 & 15) provides that the partnership and the partners will be jointly and severally liable. Whether or not the tort was within the scope and was committed in the course of the transaction of partnership business is a question of fact. Under the UPA a partnership is not liable in tort to any of the partners (13), but this does not affect the liability of the tortfeasor to his or her partner.

If a partner commits a crime in the course of the transaction of partnership business, his or her partners are not criminally liable unless they have participated in the criminal act. The partnership itself, since it is not a legal entity, cannot be held to be criminally liable for the crimes of its partners.

SUMMARY

Partners are jointly liable on contracts of the partnership and jointly and severally liable for torts chargeable to the partnership. At common law all partners had to be served in a suit against the partnership on joint obligations. Most states have changed this by statute to make it possible to reach partnership property if any individual partner can be served and to reach the individual property of all partners personally served with process.

The rules of agency law are applied in determining when the tort of a partner becomes the act of the partnership. A partnership is not liable for the crimes of the partners.

Vrabel v. Acri

103 N.E.2d 564 (Sup. Ct. Ohio 1952)

This was an action by Vrabel (plaintiff) against Acri (defendant) to recover damages for personal injuries. Judgment for Vrabel, and Acri appealed. Judgment reversed and judgment entered for Acri.

Florence and Michael Acri owned and operated a cafe as partners. They had had domestic difficulties and Florence had sued Michael for divorce. At times Florence had helped in the cafe, but following their domestic troubles, Michael was in complete control of the management of the cafe.

On February 17, 1947, Vrabel and a companion went into the cafe to buy alcoholic drinks. While Vrabel and his companion were sitting at the bar drinking, Michael, without provocation, shot and killed Vrabel's companion and assaulted and seriously injured Vrabel. Michael was convicted of murder and sentenced to life in the state prison.

Vrabel brought suit against Florence Acri to recover damages for his injuries on the ground that Florence, as a partner of Michael, was liable for the tort of Michael.

ZIMMERMAN, JUDGE. The authorities are in agreement that whether a tort is committed by a partner or a joint adventurer, the principles of law governing the situation are the same. So, where a partnership or a joint enterprise is shown to exist, each member of such project acts both as principal and agent of the others as to those things done within the apparent scope of the business of the project and for its benefit.

The Uniform Partnership Act provides: "Where, by any wrongful act or omission of any partner acting in the ordinary course of the business of the partnership or with the authority of his copartners, loss or injury is caused to any person, not being a partner in the partnership, or any penalty is incurred, the partnership is liable therefor to the same extent as the partner so acting or omitting to act."

Such section, although enacted after the cause of action in the instant case arose, corresponds with the general law on the subject.

However, it is equally true that where one member of a partnership or joint enterprise commits a wrongful and malicious tort not within the actual or apparent scope of the agency or the common business of the particular venture, to which the other members have not assented, and which has not been concurred in or ratified by them, they are not liable for the harm thereby caused.

We cannot escape the conclusion, therefore, that the above rules, relating to the nonliability of a partner or joint adventurer for wrongful and malicious torts committed by an associate outside the purpose and scope of the business, must be applied in the instant case. The willful and malicious attack by Michael Acri upon Vrabel in the Acri Cafe cannot reasonably be said to have come within the scope of the business of operating the cafe, so as to have rendered the absent defendant accountable.

Since the liability of one partner or of one engaged in a joint enterprise for the acts of his associates is founded upon the principles of agency, the statement is in point that an intentional and willful attack committed by an agent or employee, to vent his own spleen or malevolence against the injured person, is a clear departure from his employment and his principal or employer is not responsible therefor.

Horn's Crane Service v. Prior

152 N.W.2d 421 (Sup. Ct. Neb. 1967)

This was an action by Horn's Crane Service (plaintiff) against Wendell Prior and Orie Cook (defendants) to recover sums due under a written contract and for supplies and services furnished a partnership comprised of Prior, Cook, and Piper. Piper was not joined in the action. Dismissed for failure to state a cause of action and Horn's Crane Service appealed. Affirmed.

The substance of Horn's theory of recovery was that Prior and Cook were members of a partnership and on that basis individually and jointly liable for the partnership debts. Horn's did not bring suit against the partnership itself and did not allege that the partnership property was insufficient to satisfy the debt.

WHITE, CHIEF JUSTICE. In an action seeking a personal judgment against the individual members of a partnership or a joint adventure the petition does not state a cause of action if it fails to state that there is no partnership property or that it is insufficient to satisfy the debts of the partnership or joint adventure. There are several reasons for the rule. One of the most obvious is that credit having been extended to the partnership or firm, the members ought to have a right to insist that the partnership property be exhausted first. And to permit a firm creditor to by-pass the partnership property and exhaust the assets of an individual member leaving the partnership property extant, would be an obvious injustice, permit the other partners to profit at his expense, and place him in an adverse position with relation to his copartners.

Problem Cases

1. Petrikis and Ellis owned and operated the Chariot Bar as partners. Petrikis and Ellis signed the following agreement: "We hereby agree to sell our interest in the Chariot Bar. If and when the sale takes place and after all bills are accounted for, the remainder of the money is to be divided according to the share each partner now attains in the said business." Thereafter, Petrikis negotiated a sale of the business to Hanges. Hanges' attorney

drew up a contract of sale, and Hanges deposited with the attorney in escrow a cashier's check for $17,500—the agreed sale price of the business. Hanges took immediate possession of the Chariot Bar, and the stock was inventoried. Petrikis and Hanges signed the contract of sale, Petrikis signing in the name of the partnership and in his own name. When the contract of sale was presented to Ellis for his signature, Ellis objected to certain restrictive clauses in the contract. Two days later and before Ellis had signed the contract, Hanges gave notice of the withdrawal of his offer to purchase the business and returned the possession of the Chariot Bar back to Petrikis and Ellis. Petrikis and Ellis contend that the "contract of purchase" signed by Petrikis in the partnership name and by Hanges was a binding contract, and they brought suit to recover damages for breach of the contract. Is Hanges liable for breach of the contract?

2. Wheeler & Company was a partnership engaged in the plumbing contract business. It did not maintain a retail store but purchased from jobbers and manufacturers plumbing supplies used in the fulfillment of its contracts, and it also hired laborers to do the work necessary in performing the contracts. Marsh, a partner, executed in the partnership name and issued certain promissory notes. The notes were not paid, and suit was brought against the partnership on the notes. The partnership set up the defense that Marsh had no authority to issue the notes. Is the defense good?
3. Brewer, who had been known to the president of Big Lake State Bank for 30 years, brought Freeman, who had previously had no dealings with the bank, into the bank and introduced him as Brewer's partner in B&F Construction Company. Brewer advised the bank loan officer that the partnership might need credit and to take care of its needs. He said that Freeman would handle the business of the partnership. While Brewer was present an account in the name of the partnership was opened with Freeman's name only appearing on the signature care, and a $10,000 line of credit was established. Loans were made to Freeman in the name of the partnership, and when they were in default, the bank sued Brewer. Brewer's defense was that he was not, in fact, a partner and that he had not signed the notes. Is Brewer liable?
4. Mr. and Mrs. Kaback, both principals in the New York City school system, had been quite successful in securities investments. Through an acquaintance they became interested in investing in Schweickart & Company, a limited partnership that was a member of the New York Stock Exchange. They agreed to loan the securities in their investment portfolio, which were worth more than $200,000, to the partnership for a return of 6 percent on their market value. This was to be in addition to their right to the dividends on the securities. Because of NYSE rules it was decided that the loan of the securities should be made to Mr. Schweickart, one of the partners, who in turn would loan the securities to the partnership. The agreement between Mr. Schweickart and the Kabacks clearly stated that it was a loan to Schweickart personally. The loan was renewed annually. Interest checks were paid from a Schweickart & Company account but were debited to Mr. Schweickart's capital account. Schweickart & Company failed while the loan was outstanding.

   The Kabacks seek to hold the partnership, and hence the other general partners, liable for the loaned securities. Will they succeed?
5. Dr. and Mrs Pearson were partners operating under the name of Casa Blanca. They exchanged properties with the Nortons. Dr. Pearson died and Mrs. Pearson brought an action seeking damages for deceit against the Nortons. The Nortons then filed a cross-complaint against Pearson and the partnership for deceit in the same transaction. Judgment was given the Nortons by the trial court. Pearson appeals claiming that, since she was not a party to the deceit, it was error to grant a judgment against her individually. Is she correct?

6. Carl and Mary Yeoham and David Markowitz were in partnership as owners and operators of Sunnyside Tavern. The Yeohams were in active charge of the tavern, and Markowitz took no part in day-to-day operations. On July 21 at 1:30 A.M., Mr. and Mrs. Yeoham closed the tavern and started home in their automobile with the day's receipts, consisting of checks and cash. When they arrived in front of their house, a stranger approached the car and opened the door. Carl picked up the revolver he had on the seat and shot the stranger, seriously wounding him. It turned out that the stranger, Martin, thought the Yeohams were coming to a party to be held nearby, and he had no criminal intent. Martin sued Markowitz as well as the Yeohams for his injuries. At the trial Carl testified that he shot the weapon to defend his wife and himself. Markowitz testified that he did not know that Carl carried a gun. If it is determined that Carl Yeoham committed a tort and partnership assets are insufficient to pay the judgment, is Markowitz liable?
7. Wosek and his wife were partners owning the Wosek Delivery Service, which despite its name merely owned a delivery truck. It leased the truck to Love Brothers, Inc. Richard Wosek was an employee of Love Brothers making deliveries in the leased truck. While another Love Brothers' employee and Wosek were driving in Wosek's automobile on business for Love Brothers, an accident occurred due to Wosek's negligence. Mathews sued Wosek Delivery Service for his injuries. Under the Workmen's Compensation Act, Mathews could not recover from Richard Wosek because of the "fellow servant rule." Can Mathews recover from the partnership?
8. Gran-Wood Company, a partnership, joined Gaither & Boe, also a partnership, in acquiring and developing certain real estate. The agreement between them had the effect of establishing a partnership. One of its provisions declared, "Neither of the contracting parties herein shall be liable to any third person, firm, or corporation for the debt, default or undertaking, contract or tort of the other contracting party, but shall be answerable only for its own acts or omissions." Construction was undertaken on several dwellings but was halted due to defective foundations and walls. A number of subcontractors and suppliers filed mechanics' liens against the property and claimed that both Gaither & Boe and Gran-Wood were individually liable. Can Gran-Wood escape liability on the basis of the above-quoted contract provision?
9. The Government brought an action under Section 1 of the Sherman Act against the West Coast Linoleum and Carpet Company, a partnership, and several corporations. West Coast moved to dismiss the case against it on the ground that partnerships, as such, are not subject to criminal prosecution. Section 1 provides that "every person" who shall make any contract or engaged in any combination or conspiracy in restraint of trade shall be guilty of a violation. Section 7 of the Act provides that the word "person" in the Act "shall be deemed to include corporations and associations." Does the Sherman Act apply to partnerships?

24

Dissolution and Winding Up

Dissolution

Effect of Dissolution. Dissolution is defined in the Uniform Partnership Act (UPA) (29)[1] as "the change in the relation of the partners caused by any partner ceasing to be associated in the carrying on as distinguished from the winding up of the business. Dissolution does not automatically terminate the business; indeed, the business may be carried on without any interruption by the remaining partners, by one of the partners as a sole proprietorship, by a purchaser, or by a corporation formed by all or some of the partners. However, dissolution may have a very significant effect on the business and the value of the partnership interests because under the UPA, in the absence of an agreement to the contrary, a partner may insist upon liquidation of the partnership assets after dissolution, except when dissolution is caused by a violation of the partnership agreement (38[1]). The value of partnership assets for purposes of liquidation seldom equals the value of the partnership as a going business. The process of liquidation is called "winding up," and usually this involves continuing to operate the business for some period of time. "Termination" does not occur until liquidation is complete.

A partnership may be dissolved without any violation of the partnership agreement; it may be dissolved in violation of the partnership agreement; or it may be dissolved by operation of law.

Dissolution without Violation of Agreement. A partnership dissolves at the end of the term—if one was agreed upon—for which the partnership was created or when its objectives have been accomplished. If no period of time or specific undertaking was agreed upon by the partners, any partner may dissolve the partnership at any time by so notifying his or her copartners.

[1] The numbers in the parentheses refer to sections of the Uniform Partnership Act (UPA), which appears in the Appendix.

Of course, the partners may, despite earlier agreement on the term of the partnership or on a specific undertaking, dissolve the partnership at any time by unanimous agreement. Such an agreement may be made at the time the partnership is formed, as in a buy-out agreement, permitting a partner to retire or withdraw and establishing a method of determining the amount to be paid a partner for his or her share by the other partners continuing the business.

Dissolution in Violation of Agreement. Under the UPA (31[2]) a partner has the "power," in contrast to a "right," to dissolve the partnership at any time. If such dissolution is contrary to the partnership agreement, he or she will be liable in damages for its breach to the copartners who are injured thereby. In this event the UPA (38[2]) gives the innocent partners the right to continue the business themselves or with new partners. The partner wrongfully causing dissolution must, nevertheless, be paid the value of his or her interest less damages, or the payment must be secured by a bond and he or she must be indemnified against partnership liabilities. However, the goodwill of the business is not to be taken into account in determining the value of the wrongdoing partner's interest. Courts have tended to treat any dissolution which is "wrongful," as where a partner refuses to carry out his or her financial or service obligations to the partnership, as a dissolution "in contravention" of the agreement so as to give the innocent partners the rights just described.

Dissolution by Operation of Law or Court Decree. Under the UPA (31 [4] and [5]) the death or bankruptcy of any partner automatically dissolves the partnership. The UPA (32) also sets out several grounds for dissolution by judicial decree: insanity of a partner, other incapacity to perform according to the partnership contract, persistence in conduct which is prejudicial to the carrying on of the business, willful or persistent breach of the partnership agreement, and when the business can be conducted only at a loss.

Dissolution after Assignment. An assignment of a partner's interest does not itself dissolve the partnership nor permit the assignee to participate in management or to look at the books. It only entitles the assignee to the assignor's share of the profits (27). However, the assignment of the assignee's interest by a partner or the imposition of a charging order by a creditor permits the partners whose interests have not been assigned or charged to dissolve the partnership by agreement among themselves (31[1]c).

SUMMARY

Any change in the membership of a partnership causes its dissolution. Dissolution, which usually does not involve an interruption in the firm's business, should be distinguished from the winding up and termination of the partnership.

Dissolution without violation of the partnership agreement may be caused by the expiration of the term or by the accomplishment of the objective of the partnership, or if no term or objective is stated, at the will of any partner, or by the mutual agreement of the partners. A partner can withdraw and dissolve the partnership even if it amounts to a breach of the partnership agreement, but he or she is then subject to liability to the other partners for damages.

A partnership is automatically dissolved by the death or bankruptcy of a partner, or it may be dissolved by court decree on a number of grounds stated in the UPA. An assignment of a partner's interest does not automatically dissolve the partnership.

Lebanon Trotting Ass'n. v. Battista

306 N.E.2d 769 (Ct. App. Ohio 1972)

This was an action for a declaratory judgment by Lebanon Trotting Association (plaintiff), a limited partnership, against Peter Battista (defendant), one of its limited partners, seeking to liquidate the partnership property. Battista appealed from a ruling for the Association. Reversed.

The partnership agreement of the Trotting Association established it for a term of 20 years from January 1, 1952. Its purpose was to engage in the business of harness racing. The main asset of the partnership was a lease for a fairgrounds racetrack owned by the Warren County Agricultural Society. The lease extended beyond December 31, 1971, and contained an option to renew as well as a prohibition of assignment without the lessor's consent.

WHITESIDE, JUDGE. The lease, including the option to renew, appears to be the most valuable asset of the partnership.

While a sale of the leasehold interest, if feasible and possible, would be one method of winding up partnership affairs, this is not the only method of winding up partnership affairs and completing transactions begun but not yet finished. After dissolution, the partnership continues for the purpose of doing all acts necessary to complete partnership contracts previously entered into. The lease is such a contract.

Accordingly, if a purchaser of the leasehold interest could not be found, or if the consent of the Warren County Agricultural Society to an assignment or sale of the lease could not be obtained, then, in winding up the affairs of the partnership, it would be necessary, in order to preserve the rights under this valuable asset, to continue to operate under the lease as a transaction begun but not yet completed at the time of dissolution. The taking of such steps as are necessary for the reasonable preservation of the partnership assets, or in procuring a favorable market for the disposal, constitute proper action in connection with winding up the affairs of a partnership after dissolution.

The limited continuation of the business of the partnership, even for a period of years, may be warranted in connection with the winding up of the affairs of the partnership, if such continuation of the business is necessary for the partners to realize the advantages of a valuable contract or lease entered into prior to dissolution.

The dissolution of a partnership operates only with respect to future new transactions, but as to everything past, including the performance of existing contracts, the partnership continues until all preexisting matters are terminated.

Cooper v. Isaacs

448 F.2d 1202 (D.C. Cir. 1971)

This was a suit by Cooper (plaintiff) against Isaacs (defendant) seeking dissolution of their partnership. The District Court appointed a receiver to supervise partnership business pending determination on the merits. Affirmed.

Cooper and Isaacs were partners in the sale of janitorial supplies, doing business as Lesco Associates. In 1965, after three years of operations, they entered into a written partnership agreement. The agreement provided that the partnership would continue "until terminated as herein provided." Then followed specific provisions regarding termination by sale of interests, mutual consent, retirement of a partner, death of a partner, or incompetency of a partner.

In 1970 Cooper brought suit under section 32 of the Uniform Partnership Act seeking dissolution of the partnership because of irreconcilable differences between the partners on matters of policy and requesting the appointment of a receiver *pendente lite* and permanently until the business was wound up. Isaacs filed a counterclaim charging that Cooper's filing of his complaint constituted a wrongful dissolution in contravention of the partnership agreement under section 31. Isaacs claimed that under section 38 he was entitled to continue the business in the name of the partnership and sought damages and both a *pendente lite* and a permanent injunction prohibiting Cooper from interfering with the business or engaging in a competing business within a 25-mile radius of the District of Columbia. Then both the partners moved for the *pendente lite* relief they had requested. The District Court granted Cooper's motion and denied Isaacs.

TAMM, CIRCUIT JUDGE. In determining whether the District Judge's appointment of a receiver *pendente lite* was a permissible exercise of his authority, we must first decide whether appellee Cooper's filing of his complaint requesting dissolution of the partnership on the ground of irreconcilable differences regarding business policy was itself a wrongful dissolution of the partnership in contravention of the partnership agreement. If it was, then appellant Isaacs was entitled to relief under section 38, and the appointment of the receiver was improper as a matter of law.

Section 31 of the Uniform Partnership Act provides:

Dissolution is caused:

* * * * *

by *decree of court* under section 32 (emphasis added)

Turning to section 32, we find the following provisions:

(1) On application by or for a partner the court shall decree a dissolution whenever—

* * * * *

(*c*) a partner has been guilty of such conduct as tends to affect prejudicially the carrying on of the business;

(*d*) a partner willfully or persistently commits a breach of the partnership agreement, or otherwise so conducts himself in matters relating to the partnership business that it is not reasonably practicable to carry on the business in partnership with him.

* * * * *

(*f*) other circumstances render a dissolution equitable.

Courts interpreting these provisions have consistently held that serious and irreconcilable differences between the parties are proper grounds for dissolution by decree of court. Since the Act provides for dissolution for cause by decree of court and Cooper has alleged facts which would entitle him to a dissolution of this ground if proven, his filing of his complaint cannot be said to effect a dissolution, wrongful or otherwise, under the Act; dissolution would occur only when decreed by the court or brought about by other actions.

A partnership agreement can presumably change this result, but the terms of the agreement must be quite specific to effect such a change. . . .

We do not believe it can be said at this time, with the case in its present posture, that the partnership agreement involved here was clearly meant to exclude the possibility of dissolution of the partnership by decree of court under section 32. True, the partnership agreement does discuss certain ways by which the partnership can be terminated and states that the partnership "shall continue until terminated as herein provided." However, it may well be that the parties did not consider the possibility that serious disagreements would arise at the time they made the agreement; the language limiting the methods of terminating the partnership may have been intended only to prevent a partner from dissolving the partnership voluntarily and without good cause. We thus conclude that without further inquiry into the partnership agreement and the claims made by the parties, it is impossible to say that the mere filing of the complaint by Cooper constituted a wrongful dissolution.

Having concluded that the appointment of the receiver *pendente lite* was not invalid as a matter of law, we must now decide whether the District Judge abused his discretion in making the appointment. Although there is some conflict in the opinions as to when it is permissible to appoint a receiver in a case involving the proposed dissolution of a partnership, we believe the action taken here was clearly a proper exercise of judicial discretion. There appears to be no question that very serious disagreements have frequently occurred between the parties to this case. The parties are in conflict as to whether these disagreements threaten the continued success of the business, but considering their apparent seriousness and frequency, the District Judge's conclusion that they do is certainly a reasonable one.

Winding Up Partnership Business

The Process. If a partnership business is to be terminated, the next step after the dissolution is the winding up of the partnership business. This involves the orderly liquidation of the assets of the business. The partnership continues to exist until the liquidation is completed and the proceeds are distributed. During this period the partners continue to owe a fiduciary duty to each other, especially in negotiating sales or making distribution of partnership assets to members of the partnership. However, the powers of a partner to bind the partnership are limited to those acts which are reasonably necessary to the winding up of the partnership affairs.

Who Winds Up Business? Under the provisions of the UPA (37), if the dissolution of a partnership is brought about amicably and during the lifetime of the partners, they have the right to wind up the business. If the dissolution is due to the death or bankruptcy of a partner, the surviving partners, or partners not bankrupt, have the right to wind up the business. If the dissolution is by court decree, a receiver is usually appointed to wind up the business. A partner winding up the business is generally entitled to compensation beyond his or her share in the profits only by agreement, unless a partner is the survivor after dissolution by death.

Partner's Power in Winding Up. The partner or partners who have charge of winding up the partnership business have the power to bind the partnership in any transaction necessary to the liquidation of the assets. They may collect on negotiable paper held by the partnership, collect moneys due, sell partnership property, sue to enforce partnership rights, and do such other acts as the nature of the business and the circumstances dictate. As a general rule, a partner who is winding up a partnership business cannot borrow money in the name of the partnership. However, if by borrowing money and using it to pay partnership obligations a partner can preserve the assets of the partnership or enhance them for sale, he or she will make, renew, or indorse negotiable instruments.

A partner's power to bind the partnership on contracts will depend on the nature of the contract. If the contract is in furtherance of the orderly liquidation of the assets, he or she can bind the partnership; but if it is "new business," the partnership will not be bound.

In addition, a partner who has the right to wind up the business has apparent authority to bind the partnership by any act which would have bound the partnership prior to dissolution unless the other party had knowledge of the dissolution or specified steps to notify him or her had been taken (35). If the other party had been a creditor of the partnership prior to dissolution, that other party must be directly informed of the dissolution or a written notice of the dissolution must be delivered to him or her or to a proper person at his or her residence or place of business. If the other party were merely aware of the earlier partnership, newspaper notice to him or her is sufficient to protect the partnership from liability.

At the death of a partner, right to all partnership property vests in the surviving partner or partners. He or she or they may pass title to real estate held in the partnership name without joinder of the decedent's representatives. In the absence of agreement, the survivors have only the right to wind up the business.

SUMMARY

If the partnership business is to be terminated after dissolution, the partnership relation will continue to exist until the assets of the partnership are liquidated, the partnership creditors are paid, and the remaining assets are distributed to the partners.

In the event the dissolution is caused by the death or bankruptcy of a partner, the surviving partners or those not bankrupt have the right to wind up the business. If the partners cannot agree, a receiver may be appointed for this purpose. After dissolution the partner or partners who are winding up the partnership business have the authority to do those acts which are reasonably necessary to wind up the business, but they do not have authority to engage in new business.

In addition, one winding up the business has broad apparent authority which will bind the partnership to those who may do business with the firm unless they are notified in accordance with the provisions of the UPA.

State v. Ed Cox and Son

132 N.W.2d 282 (Sup. Ct. S.D. 1965)

This was an action by the State of South Dakota for the benefit of Farmers State Bank (plaintiff) against Ed Cox and Son and William B. Cox (defendants) to recover a judgment for money loaned. Judgment for Farmers State Bank; and Tennefos Construction Company and United Pacific Insurance Company, surety, and Ed Cox and Son appealed. Judgment affirmed.

Ed Cox and Son, a partnership consisting of Ed Cox and William B. Cox, entered into a contract with the State of South Dakota for the construction of a section of highway. Ed Cox and Son executed a performance bond with United Pacific Insurance Company (Pacific) as surety. Tennefos Construction Company was co-contractor with Ed Cox and Son. Ed Cox and Son, prior to June 1, 1956, borrowed money from Farmers State Bank (Bank). Between June 1, 1956, and August 16, 1956, Ed Cox borrowed from Bank further sums and after August 16, 1956, William B. Cox, as surviving partner (Ed Cox died on August 16, 1956), borrowed further sums. Ed Cox and Son owed Bank $108,492.42 at the time of suit. On June 1, 1956, Ed Cox and William B. Cox dissolved the partnership of Ed Cox and Son but Bank was not given notice of dissolution and had no knowledge of it. The money borrowed from Bank by William B. Cox as surviving partner was used to pay for labor and materials necessary to complete the construction contract. Pacific contends that it is not liable for moneys loaned to Ed Cox and Son by Bank after June 1, 1956.

RENTTO, JUDGE. The death of Ed Cox dissolved the partnership, but it did not terminate it. As declared in SDC 49.0602 the partnership continued until the winding up of its affairs was completed. The dissolution resulting from the death of Ed Cox terminated the authority of William Cox to act for the partnership "Except so far as may be necessary to wind up partnership affairs or to complete transactions begun but not then finished." This is reiterated in SDC 49.0607 wherein it is provided that "After dissolution a partner can bind the partnership . . . (a) By any act appropriate for winding up partnership affairs or completing transactions unfinished at dissolution; . . .". Transactions unfinished at dissolution have been held to include road and other construction contracts. Funds advanced or furnished to the surviving partner for such purpose are legitimate expenses for which the partnership is liable.

Under SDC 49.0609 William Cox as a surviving partner had the right to wind up the affairs of the partnership. In fact it was his duty. He was so engaged when the notes in question were executed. In our view they are proper obligations of the partnership. Ed Cox and Pacific argue that because of the dissolution agreement of June 1st he was not a surviving partner when his father died. This dissolution was secret as far as the bank was concerned and the subsequent conduct of William Cox in his dealings with it was consistent with the partnership's continuation. As to the bank the partnership continued until the death of Ed Cox.

When the Business Is Continued

Advantage of Continuing. When a partner dies or if he or she desires to or is forced to withdraw from the partnership, all parties involved usually find it advantageous to continue the business because its going concern value is normally greater than its liquidated value. Certainly, for large partnerships (some have more than 100 partners) the necessity of going through a winding up process whenever a partner dies or retires would make this form of organization completely impracticable. The advantage of avoiding liquidation at the demand of any partner or his or her legal representative is so great that a prior agreement for continuing the business is advisable. Frequently, the plan specified in the agreement involves the use of life insurance on the lives of the partners to facilitate a transfer of a deceased partner's interest to the surviving partner or partners, and payment to the estate or heirs.

It is this "going concern" value which accounts for the UPA giving the other partners the right, discussed above, to continue after a partner has dissolved the partnership wrongfully.

Although it is arguable that there is technically a dissolution, many partnerships provide in the original partnership agreement that death or withdrawal of individual partners and the admission of new partners will not dissolve the partnership. The agreement then outlines a plan whereby the financial interests of partners leaving and entering the partnership are protected. Tax consequences to the various parties differ under different arrangements and the needs of the various parties and the business itself also vary so that drafting either a general plan in advance or a continuation agreement for a specific situation is often difficult and must be done with great care.

Liability for Obligations Incurred Prior to Dissolution. Dissolution itself has no effect upon existing liabilities of the partnership or of the partners. Contracts, unless calling for services in which a personal factor is crucial, are ordinarily not affected, and obligations under them must be completed or settled by negotiation during the winding up process.

If the business is to be continued rather than terminated, the original partners or their estate remain liable for obligations incurred prior to dissolution unless there is agreement with the creditor to the contrary. When the business is continued after one or more partners withdraw and assign their rights to others, or when a partner dies or is expelled, creditors of the old partnership are creditors of the person or partnership continuing the business. This gives them equal status with creditors of the new sole proprietorship, corporation, or partnership (41). Creditors of the original partnership are further protected by the UPA (41[8]) by being given priority over separate creditors of a retiring or deceased partner with respect to the consideration due or paid to the former partner or his or her representative.

Usually when the business is being continued the continuing or new partners specifically agree to relieve the withdrawing partner from the obligations of the preceding partnership, the settlement between the original partners taking this into account. Courts have occasionally found an implied agreement to this effect where the assets are retained in the continuing business. Nevertheless, even an express agreement to hold the withdrawing partner harmless is not binding on creditors unless they join in it so as to constitute a novation. However, the withdrawing partner or deceased partner's estate is only secondarily liable as a surety. Mere receipt by a creditor of partial payment or a negotiable instrument from a continuing partner does not release the withdrawing partner, but an agreement by a creditor to hold only the person or partnership continuing the business may be inferred from his or her dealings with the continuing business if he or she has knowledge of the change of membership in the partnership. Acceptance of a negotiable instrument in full settlement of a claim has been held to be an implied novation.

A person joining an existing partnership becomes liable for all previous obligations of the partnership as if he or she had been a partner except that this liability is limited to the partnership assets (17).

Liability for Obligations Incurred after Dissolution. Former partners or their estates may be liable for obligations incurred by the partnership continuing the business unless the prescribed notice discussed above is given (35) or the new creditor has knowledge of the change. The UPA does not exclude dissolution by death or bankruptcy of a partner from these notice provisions.

Rights of Noncontinuing Partner. If after dissolution the partnership affairs are wound up and its assets liquidated, the normal sharing of profits and losses continues among the partners. However, when the business is continued, whether by right, agreement, or acquiescence, the noncontinuing partner becomes a creditor of the new partnership (subordinate to other creditors), and his or her interest in the partnership assets is determined at the time of the dissolution. If dissolution results from death or retirement, the noncontinuing partner then has an election, which doesn't need to be made until there is an accounting. The noncontinuing partner can determine which of two positions is more favorable: (1) taking the value of his partnership interest at dissolution plus interest or (2) that dissolution value plus a share of subsequent profits based upon the proportion of that value to the total value of the partnership at the time of dissolution (42). This option, of course, provides some incentive for the continuing partners to settle with the noncontinuing partner promptly.

Goodwill. When a partnership business is continued after dissolution, it is frequently difficult to determine the value of the goodwill of the partnership that is transferred to the continuing partners. In service partnerships the goodwill may be so closely tied to the individual partners that none carries over with the business. Because of these difficulties and uncertainties, it is usually advisable to include an agreement on this matter in the original articles of partnership. Too frequently courts conclude that goodwill should be ignored unless there is such an agreement or (in the unusual case) goodwill appears in the partnership accounts. The UPA specifically excludes goodwill in providing for valuation of a partner's interest who has wrongfully caused dissolution (38[2]*c* II).

SUMMARY

The business of financially successful partnerships is usually continued after the death or withdrawal of a partner because it is worth more as a going concern. This makes it wise to have in advance a well-drafted agreement for continuing the business and buying the interest of the partner or partners not continuing.

Dissolution normally does not affect obligations incurred by the partnership, and they must be satisfied. If the business is continued, the original partners or their legal representatives remain liable unless they are released by a novation, which requires the assent of the creditors. Also, unless there is a contrary agreement, the creditors of the previous partnership remain creditors of the continuing business. A person joining an existing partnership assumes liability for its previous obligations but only to the extent of the partnership assets.

If the business is continued after dissolution, the noncontinuing partner becomes a creditor of the new partnership. If the noncontinuing partner retires or dies, that partner or partner's representative has an election whether to be paid interest on the value of the partnership interest or to share in the profits from operations after dissolution.

Smith v. Kennebeck

502 S.W.2d 290 (Sup. Ct. Mo. 1973)

This was an action by Charles Smith (plaintiff) against Kennebeck and Thomas Smith, Jr. (defendants), seeking a winding up, an accounting, and a determination of the value of Charles Smith's interest in a partnership. The trial court accepted the valuations of the partners' interests established by the accountants for the former partnership, and Charles Smith appealed. Reversed and remanded.

Charles and his brother Thomas Smith entered into a partnership with Kennebeck in October 1963. On November 10, 1964, Thomas Smith and Kennebeck informed Charles Smith by letter that they were dissolving the partnership and were forming a corporation to operate the business. He was offered the same 25 percent share in the corporation that he had in the partnership. Charles Smith did not accept the offer, and the other two partners continued the business as partners, completing work in process for previous orders, until the corporation was chartered on December 24.

The assets of the partnership then passed to the corporation. The continuing partners had Bo-Tax Co., the accountants for the former partnership, determine the value of the partnership and each partner's interest. Although revised articles of partnership dated February 1964 stated Charles' interest as $5,000, Bo-Tax's figures showed the value at $1,901. No share of the profit (estimated to be $18,000) from the orders that were completed later was included.

HYDE, SPECIAL COMMISSIONER. (adopted per curiam by the court) "Winding up" means the administration of the assets for the purpose of terminating the business and discharging the obligations of the partnership to its members. In this case instead of administration of the partnership assets, it appears the two remaining partners kept all the partnership assets and continued the business, only making plaintiff an offer for his share which appears to be based on an inadequate estimate of the value of his interest.

The Bo-Tax Co. computation does not appear to be a proper basis for determining plaintiff's interest. The Bo-Tax agent who made it was not a certified public accountant. It was reviewed by Ernst & Ernst, who did not examine the books of the partnership, and their report shows the Bo-Tax accountant had not seen a copy of the partnership agreement which stated the value of plaintiff's capital interest as $5,000. Moreover, it states profits only through November 10, 1964, and does not consider profits on uncompleted work on contracts on hand at that time or all profits on completed contracts. The court apparently considered the Bo-Tax statement to be a "winding up" account as it found plaintiff only "entitled to the value of his share as computed on November 10, 1964." We cannot hold that was a valid "winding up" of the partnership [and] that plaintiff was only entitled to the amount shown by it. It is insufficient not only because it did not take into consideration the work on then existing contracts but also because the individual defendants continued the business as partners until its incorporation and then had the corporation continue it without any other offers or effort to settle plaintiff's claim for his interest.

Since our view is that the evidence fails to show there ever was a valid winding up of the partnership but instead shows a continuation of the business without plaintiff's consent, plaintiff's rights were as stated in Crane and Bromber, Law of Partnership § 86: "The situation changes if the business is not wound up, but continued, whether with or without agreement. In either case, the noncontinuing partner (or his representative) has a first election between two basic alternatives, either of which can be enforced in an action for an accounting. He can force a liquidation, taking his part of the proceeds and thus sharing in profits and losses after dissolution. Alternatively, he can permit the business to continue (or accept the fact that it has continued) and claim as a creditor (though subordinate to outside creditors) the value of his interest at dissolution. This gives him a participation in all values at dissolution, including asset appreciation and good will, and means he is unaffected by later changes in those values. If he takes the latter route, he has a second election to receive in addition either interest (presumably at the local legal rate) or profits from date of dissolution."

Distribution of Assets

Order of Distribution. The order of distribution of the assets of a partnership is set out in the UPA (40) as follows:

I. Those owing to creditors other than partners,
II. Those owing to partners other than for capital and profits,
III. Those owing to partners in respect of capital,
IV. Those owing to partners in respect of profits.

If the partnership has been operated without losses which impair the capital, few problems are presented in the distribution of the assets. Everyone having an interest in the partnership will be paid in full. If there is a disagreement as to the amount due any party in interest, the dispute will usually be resolved by an accounting that will be ordered by the court and which will, as a general rule, settle the fact question of the amount due.

Distribution of Assets of Insolvent Partnership. If the partnership has suffered losses, the order of distribution set out above will be followed, but additional problems will be encountered. For example, the relative rights of partnership creditors and individual creditors, and the distribution of losses will be involved. In adjusting the rights of partnership creditors and individual creditors, the rule that partnership creditors have first claim on partnership assets and individual creditors have first claim on individual assets is usually followed.

If a partner has, in addition to contributing capital, loaned money to the partnership, no distinction will be made, on dissolution, between the capital contributed and the money loaned as far as the rights of the partnership creditors are concerned. The only difference which might arise would be in adjusting the rights of the partners. After payment of creditors, a partner, under some circumstances, will be allowed interest on a loan, whereas no interest is allowed on capital contributed.

As an example of distribution of the assets of an insolvent partnership, suppose Alden, Bass, and Casey organize a partnership. Alden contributes $25,000, Bass contributes $15,000, and Casey contributes $10,000. After operating for several years, the firm suffers losses and is insolvent. The assets of the partnership, when liquidated, total $30,000. The partnership owes to partnership creditors $40,000. The accounts of the individual partners are as follows:

	Contributed to Capital of Partnership	Individual Assets	Individual Liabilities
Alden	$25,000	$75,000	$5,000
Bass	15,000	10,000	2,000
Casey	10,000	2,000	6,000

The $30,000 will be distributed to partnership creditors pro rata, leaving $10,000 of partnership debts unpaid. Alden's individual creditors will be paid in full, leaving a $70,000 balance in Alden's individual estate. Bass's individual creditors will be paid in full, leaving an $8,000 balance in Bass's individual estate. Casey is insolvent; his creditors will receive 33⅓ percent of their claims.

The losses of the partnership total $60,000 (capital investment, $50,000, plus unpaid debts after distribution of assets, $10,000). In the absence of a provision in the partnership agreement as to distribution of profits and losses, they are distributed equally. Each partner would be liable for $20,000, one third of the loss.

	Capital	Loss	
Alden	$25,000	$20,000	+$ 5,000
Bass	15,000	20,000	− 5,000
Casey	10,000	20,000	− 10,000

In this case, Bass is legally liable to contribute $5,000 and Casey, $10,000. This sum would be distributed $10,000 to partnership creditors and $5,000 to Alden. In our illustration, Casey is insolvent and can contribute nothing; consequently, his share of losses over and above his capital investment will be redistributed between the solvent partners. However, Bass had only $3,000 in his estate, and the final result will be that Bass will pay $3,000 of his loss and Alden will pay $7,000. Bass will have a claim against Casey for the $3,000 he pays, and Alden will have a claim against Casey for $7,000. If one of the partners is a minor, that fact will alter the distribution of the assets accordingly.

SUMMARY

If a partnership has been operated without a loss, the order of distribution of assets is unimportant, since everyone will be paid in full.

If the partnership has suffered losses, the order of distribution is important. Partnership creditors have first claim on partnership assets, and individual creditors have first claim on the individual assets of their debtor. The order of distribution is set out in UPA (40).

Mahan v. Mahan

489 P.2d 1197 (Sup. Ct. Ariz. 1971)

Helen Mahan (plaintiff) brought this action against T. Gordon Mahan (defendant) for an accounting and division of partnership property. Helen Mahan appealed from a judgment for T. Gordon Mahan. Reversed and remanded.

Helen Mahan's deceased husband, Terrell Mahan, and his brother T. Gordon Mahan, were partners in an agricultural and construction partnership. In 1964 the partnership traded one of the partnership properties for a home into which Terrell and Helen moved, and Terrell's capital account was reduced by $23,000, leaving a balance of $4,005.45 which was one eighth of the total capital account of $21,308.06. Soon thereafter the partnership became inactive and remained so until Terrell's death in 1966 and the bringing of this suit in 1969.

There was disagreement at the trial as to the market value of the partnership assets, which were carried on the books as follows:

Red Lake Ranch	$15,622.61*
Investments	9,150.00†
Oil Lease	4,000.00‡
Miscellaneous	4,502.00§
	$33,274.61

* Sold in 1961 for $284,200 but sale not completed; appraised for $43,868.44 in 1963; the $15,622.61 was a figure allowed by the I.R.S. for tax purposes after the aborted sale.

† Represents 7,500 shares of Unita Finance Company, which the plaintiff's (and partnership's) accountant testified was worthless, and 180 shares of Arizona Livestock Production Credit Association, which the accountant testified was worth $5.00 per share or $900.

‡ Valueless, according to the accountant.

§ Subject to extreme disagreement on several items.

Gordon claimed Helen was entitled to one eighth of the partnership assets of $33,274.61, or $4,159.29.

CAMERON, JUSTICE. Helen contends that after payment of the partnership debts, she should share with Gordon on a 50–50 basis. We agree with Helen as long as it is understood that the capital account, as used by the bookkeeper in this case, represents a debt of the partnership.

Upon liquidation, the rules of payment are governed by [UPA 40], which decrees that the liabilities of the partnership shall rank in the following order of payment:

a. Those owing to creditors other than partners.
b. Those owing to partners other than for capital and profits.
c. Those owing to partners in respect of capital.
d. Those owing to partners in respect of profits.

"The capital of the partnership is the amount specified in the agreement of the partners, which is to be contributed by the partners for the purpose of initiating and operating the partnership business." Thus, ordinarily we would look to the initial contributions for a determination of the amounts "owing to partners in respect of capital." While the general rule is that the amount of capital may not be changed absent consent of all the partners, the partners in this case have apparently conceded to adjustments in their capital accounts. Thus, we accept, for purposes of this case, adjustments in plaintiff's and defendant's capital accounts to $4,005.45 and $27,302.61 respectively.

Therefore, whether the money left after satisfaction of creditor's claims and recoupment of partnership capital is termed profits or surplus, the clear mandate of the authorities is that, absent agreement to the contrary, it is divided equally as profits.

Gordon has placed reliance on [UPA 42], relating to continuation of the business when a partner dies. In the instant case, the business was not continued by the surviving partner. Quite the contrary. The partnership remained dormant and nothing was done until suit was brought by the plaintiff to compel an accounting. Where the efforts of one partner in the production of profits in an active partnership cease, it is apparent that he no longer bears full entitlement to his respective share of the profits. In this case, however, where the partnership has been and continues to be inactive, any appreciation of worth is due to the nature of the partnership property rather than the effort of the surviving partner. Thus, we hold that any profit or surplus resulting shall be shared equally.

This conclusion is buttressed by the situation confronting Helen and her husband Terrell when they gave up $23,000 of their capital account for a $23,000 home. They knew that the partnership had few or no debts and owned a piece of property that had sold for $284,200 a few years previous. If the value of the land had stayed reasonably constant in the interim, the partnership would have been worth over $300,000. It is highly unlikely that the plaintiff and her husband intended, when they gave up $23,000 of their capital account for a $23,000 house, that they were actually giving up not $23,000 but well over $100,000.

The answer to the question of whether the court erred in accepting the book value of the assets can be answered by looking at the figures we have reconstructed. Every single component of the $33,274.61 book value has been strongly contested. The Red Lake Ranch, for example, was sold in 1961 for over $280,000, but has an arbitrary book value of $15,622.61. An "investment" valued at $9,150 is made of two investments, one worthless and the other worth only $900. In short, the book values are completely arbitrary and should not have been used.

Our determination that the trial court erred in accepting book value is in accord not only with the Arizona case of *Hurst v. Hurst,* supra, but with general principles of partnership accounting. The normal rule is that book value is only used in ascertaining the respective share when there is an explicit contractual provision to that effect, and even then is not used where the facts of the case make it inequitable to do so. Here there was no contractual provision mandating the use of book value, and even if there were, the facts show book value in this case to be so disproportionate to possible real values that it would be inequitable for it to be used anyway.

Having decided that book value should not be used in valuing the partnership assets, we are forced to conclude that the trial court should have granted plaintiff's wish to have the assets liquidated.

We hold that the partnership assets must be liquidated, and that the general creditors be paid first. If the assets are insufficient for this purpose, the estate and Gordon should be charged equally for the losses. If the assets are more than sufficient, then the surviving partner should be paid first up to the amount of $23,297.16 to set off the withdrawal from the capital account by Terrell. Any amount left over should be equally divided between Terrell's estate and the surviving partner, Gordon Mahan.

Dissolution in Limited Partnerships

Differences from Ordinary Partnerships. Limited partners must obtain a court decree to bring about dissolution other than by expiration of its term or undertaking. Death or bankruptcy of a limited partner does not bring about dissolution. In distribution after dissolution of a limited partnership, the limited partners are prior to general partners but follow creditors. However, subject to partnership agreement, profits are paid to limited partners prior to capital contributions. A limited partner who is a creditor of the firm is treated the same as outside creditors with respect to money loaned to rather than invested in the firm. The limited partner is not liable beyond his capital contribution for debts of the firm unless he has lost his status as a limited partner.

Problem Cases

1. Drs. Langdon, Hurdle, and Hoffman established a partnership for the practice of medicine, and the survivers continued as partners when Langdon died four years later. However, disagreements arose, and after a year they ceased practice as partners. Hurdle sought an accounting and claimed he was entitled to damages against Hoffman for leaving the partnership and setting up a separate practice. The partnership agreement contained no provision as to the length of time the partnership was to continue. Is Hurdle entitled to damages?
2. Sjo and Cooper entered into an oral partnership agreement in 1960 to build and operate a restaurant and to share equally the profits and losses. Sjo supplied the labor and materials to fill and grade the land for the restaurant, and a mortgage loan signed by both partners was used to finance the rest of the construction. The partnership operated the restaurant under a Dog 'N' Suds franchise from 1961 to 1965.

   In the spring of 1968 the partnership sold the restaurant equipment on credit and leased the building for five years, but the new operator defaulted after the first summer. All payments on the lease and equipment purchase contracts were made to Cooper, and Cooper met all partnership expenses.

   Cooper and Sjo got into a disagreement in 1969 over Cooper's demand that Sjo contribute to the expenses and Sjo's demand that Cooper account for payments made to him by the lessee in 1968, which Cooper claimed he did. In June 1970 Cooper executed a 20-

year lease on the restaurant and informed Sjo that due to his failure to contribute for 18 months that Sjo had no interest in the lease.

Cooper then filed suit for an accounting. Was the partnership dissolved by Sjo's failure to contribute funds?

3. Dr. Cox and Dr. Jones were partners in a medical practice. The written partnership agreement provided that a withdrawing partner's capital investment would be purchased by the remaining partner at book value and that, for six months following withdrawal, all accounts receivable collections would be divided per the existing percentage formula. At the end of this period, all accounts receivable were to become the property of the remaining partner. Following a series of disagreements, Dr. Jones orally informed Dr. Cox that he was leaving as of October 1, 1963. Dr. Cox thereafter sought another doctor to join the practice, but prior to October 1, Dr. Jones gave notice that he had changed his mind and was not leaving. Dr. Jones refused to set a definite termination date, and on November 9, 1963, Dr. Cox wrote to Dr. Jones requesting his withdrawal as of December 31, 1963. The letter stated that if Dr. Jones refused to withdraw, Dr. Cox would withdraw as of February 15, 1964. Dr. Jones took no further action, and on February 15, Dr. Cox left the practice. Dr. Cox claimed that the was entitled to the accounts receivable as the remaining partner by reason of Dr. Jones's oral notice of withdrawal as of October 1, 1963. Is this correct?

4. A newspaper was operated as a partnership by Lyman Stoddard, his wife, Alda, and their son, Lyman, Jr. Alda died in 1963 and Lyman a year later. No winding up of the partnership took place before Lyman's death and operations were continued by Lyman, Jr., following his father's death. Another son, John, was executor of both estates, and he urged his brother to wind up the business. He then made some unsuccessful efforts to sell the business himself. Finally, he sued Lyman to force an accounting and liquidation. This was resolved by an agreement by Lyman to assume all debts arising after the father's death and this was approved by the probate court. Continuation of the business was unsuccessful and it was eventually discontinued.

   King and White had been the accountants for the newspaper for a number of years, and they continued to serve following Alda's and Lyman's deaths. Being unpaid, they sued the estates of Alda and Lyman for all work done for a five year period after Alda's death. Are the estates liable?

5. Davis and Shipman formed a partnership to operate a lumber business. About a year and a half later a notice of dissolution was published in a newspaper of general circulation in the county where the business was conducted but no actual notice of dissolution was given to the firms which had extended credit to the partnership at the time of dissolution.

   Under the terms of the dissolution agreement Shipman was to continue the business and was to assume and pay all partnership debts. After the dissolution several firms which had previously extended credit to the partnership continued to extend credit to the continued business. Their claims were not paid, and suit was brought against Davis. Is Davis liable?

6. On September 1, 1953, Mousseau and John and James Walker commenced a partnership business under the name of "Sanitation Service." Mousseau conducted the business personally for almost seven months until the Walkers came to work full time. Several disagreements arose as to the division of responsibilities between the partners and in December 1954, the Walkers forcibly ejected Mousseau from the premises and declared the partnership at an end. Mousseau had no desire to sell his interest and after dissolution the Walkers used his assets to continue the business. In 1956, Mousseau filed suit to dissolve the partnership and for an accounting, including his share of the 1955 net profits. The Walkers admit a net profit of $8,387 during 1955, but claim that this amount is subject to deduction

for wages for themselves in the amount of $6,240. Were the Walkers entitled to compensation for their services following Mousseau's departure from the business?

7. Ingrao and Karsten operated, as partners, the Venetian Dining Room. On January 3, 1947, the partnership was dissolved, but no notice of the dissolution was given, either actual or by advertising. On January 25, 1957, Karsten borrowed $2,400 from Falzone, and executed and delivered to Falzone a promissory note payable to Falzone and signed in the name of the partnership by Karsten. The note was negotiated to Vogler. The note was not paid when due, and Vogler sued Ingrao and Karsten. Ingrao set up as a defense the dissolution of the partnership prior to the giving of the note. Vogler claims that the defense is not valid because of failure to give notice of dissolution. Is Ingrao liable on the note?
8. Settle, a radiology specialist, had engaged in practice since 1946. In 1958, he entered into a partnership agreement with Berg, who had been employed as an assistant, whereby Berg agreed to purchase a 45 percent interest in the business for $40,500. Thus for the purpose of this agreement the business was valued at $90,000. In 1960, pursuant to the entry of a third partner into the practice, a valuation formula was derived whereby the total partnership business was valued at $100,000. This transaction was never carried to completion. In 1962, Berg withdrew from the partnership and Settle continued operation of the business. Berg sues for an accounting to determine his rightful share upon dissolution. Is Berg entitled to a proportionate share based on a fair market value of approximately $100,000 or to a much smaller share based on the book value of $40,000?

PART VI

Corporations

25

Nature of Corporation and Incorporation

Historical Background and Principal Characteristics

Early History. The general idea is very old that a corporation is a fictitious legal person distinct from the actual persons who compose it. The Romans recognized the corporation, and in England the corporate form was used extensively even before A.D. 1600, although most early corporate charters were granted to municipalities or to ecclesiastical, educational, or charitable bodies. For example, the church used the "corporation sole" as a device for holding the title to land. If the title were in "the Bishop of Exeter," a corporation, rather than in Bishop John Fitzwilliam, then the complications which would arise in regard to the descent of the land upon the death of an individual person as title holder could be avoided, since the corporation's existence would be perpetual.

The famous British trading companies, such as the Hudson's Bay Company, which was chartered as a corporation by the king in 1670 and still operates in Canada, were the forerunners of the modern corporation. They were given monopolistic privileges in trade and even granted governmental powers in the areas they colonized.

Beginning about 1780 the corporate form of organization began to be used in the United States. The early corporations were chartered by the state legislatures, most of them to operate businesses of a public nature such as toll roads, toll bridges, and water systems. In 1811 New York State enacted the first general corporation-for-profit statute. Under this statute any group of persons who complied with the procedures established in the statute would be granted a corporate charter. However, incorporation tended still to be viewed as a privilege and many restrictions were placed upon corporations.

Incorporation was permitted for only relatively short periods of time, maximum limits on capitalization were relatively low, the purpose of the business had to be specifically and narrowly defined, and limits on land and personal property holding were often restrictive. Today these restrictive provisions have disappeared in most states and the incorporation statutes are mostly enabling, permitting the controlling persons very great flexibility in establishing, financing, and operating the corporation. However, state incorporation statutes vary greatly.

Principal Characteristics. The essential nature of the corporate form of organization has not, however, changed very much from the description in Blackstone's *Commentaries,* which was written before 1765. They are: (1) existence independent of its members and unaffected by their death; (2) right to sue and be sued in the corporate name; (3) right to acquire, hold, and convey property for corporate purposes in the corporate name; (4) right to have a seal; and (5) right to make bylaws. However, the principal reason for incorporation today is that shareholders are not ordinarily held liable for the debts of the corporation. Their loss is limited to their investment.

Classifications. Historically corporations have been of three classes: (1) corporations for profit, (2) corporations not for profit, and (3) governmental corporations. Ordinarily, separate statutes establish procedures for incorporating each class of corporation and for their operation. There is a large body of common law which applies equally to the first two classes and to a lesser extent to governmental corporations.

A corporation for profit is a corporation operated for the purpose of making a profit that may be distributed in dividends to the stockholders. Generally, corporations for profit which operate a business affecting the public interest, such as railroads, banks, insurance companies, building and loan associations, and farm marketing cooperatives, are incorporated under special statutes which impose on them different regulations than are imposed by the general corporation-for-profit statutes.

Hospitals, schools, churches, lodges, and fraternities are frequently incorporated as not-for-profit. A not-for-profit corporation cannot distribute any surplus it may have to its members or shareholders. Most of these are chartered by states but a few such as the American Red Cross have federal charters.

Municipalities are one form of governmental corporation. Others are formed to furnish more specific services. Examples would be school corporations, sewage districts, and irrigation districts. Others, such as the Tennessee Valley Authority and the Federal Home Loan Bank have no taxing powers and operate much like for-profit corporations except that at least some of their directors are appointed by governmental officials and frequently they are financed in part or totally by government. The two examples given are chartered by Congress, but states sometimes establish this hybrid kind of corporation also.

Corporations for profit are frequently divided into publicly held and close (privately held) corporations. The distinction is not clear cut but a close corporation is one where most of the stock is held by and the corporation is managed by a family or a small group of people who are personally known to each other (for example, a family-owned retail business). In contrast, a publicly held corporation (for example, General Motors) is owned by a large number of people who do not know each other and are frequently widely scattered. The close corporation in practice is often operated more like a partnership than a corporation. A few states recognize this in specific statutory provisions covering close corporations.

A Subchapter S corporation is a corporation for profit whose shareholders elect, under a provision in the Internal Revenue Code, to be taxed as a partnership. The principal limitation is that the corporation must have no more than ten shareholders who are individuals or estates.

Distinction between Corporation and Shareholder. As an artificial legal entity, a corporation has an existence separate from its shareholders. The shareholders normally have no individual liability for the debts of the corporation. Their liability for loss is limited to their investment in their shares. However, the separateness between corporation and shareholder may be disregarded if the corporate form is adopted to promote fraud, to evade the law, or to accomplish purposes detrimental to society. This problem arises most frequently in the close corporation. If the shareholders' personal transactions are intermingled with those of the corporation and corporate formalities, such as holding shareholder and director meetings, are not observed, if the corporation is established with so little capital as to be unable to meet normal business obligations, or if the corporation is otherwise formed to defraud or to evade existing obligations, courts will disregard the corporate entity or, as it is often phrased, will "pierce the corporate veil." They will hold the shareholders liable on the same basis as if no effort had been made to incorporate. Generally, this means the active shareholders will be held liable as if they were general partners.

Similar principles are followed by the courts in dealing with suits brought against corporations which operate a segment of their business through a subsidiary corporation whose stock is controlled or fully owned by the parent corporation. If, in fact, the two corporations have no separateness except their individual charters or the subsidiary is formed as a shield for a "shady" purpose, the parent corporation will be held responsible for the acts and debts of its subsidiary.

Other Aspects of the Distinction. The corporation has its own domicile separate from its shareholders, which is in the state in which it is incorporated and the place in that state where it has its registered office. Where it is a different place, the site of its principal office is sometimes said to be its "commercial domicile."

Generally, there is no fiduciary duty between the shareholders and the artificial person which is the corporation.[1] The shareholders may deal with the corporation in the same manner and to the same extent as would any other person. The shareholder is not an agent or representative of the corporation by virtue of his or her stock ownership. The courts recognize the separateness of the corporation and its shareholders even though all the shares of the corporation are owned by one person.

Corporations are treated as persons and have the legal rights of natural persons in most instances. However, decisions recognizing these rights are becoming more controversial when applied to huge corporations, which may resemble states more than individual proprietors of a business.[2]

SUMMARY

Early corporations were chartered by the Crown in England and by special enactment of state legislatures in the United States. Today incorporators need only to conform to the procedures established in a general statute, and these impose few limitations in organizing, financing, and operating the corporation.

A corporation is a legal entity separate and distinct from its shareholders and is usually treated by the law as a person. A corporation can hold property and sue and be sued in its own name. The members of a corporation are not personaaly liable for its debts and its existence is not affected by the death of its members.

Shareholders normally have no individual liability for the debts of the corporation, so their risk of loss is limited to their investment. However, courts may "pierce the corporate veil" where incorporation is for the purpose of promoting fraud, or to evade the law, or where the business affairs of a close corporation or corporate subsidiary and its shareowners are intermingled.

The corporation has its own domicile and shareholders ordinarily have no fiduciary duties to the corporation.

Old Town Development Co. v. Langford

349 N.E.2d 744 (Ct. App. Ind. 1976)

Langford (plaintiff) sued Old Town Development Co., a partnership owning an apartment house, and Ogle, a heating contractor (defendants), for the death of his wife and two children in a fire in their apartment alleged to

[1] However, controlling shareholders may owe fiduciary duties, at least when selling control of the corporation, *Perlman v. Feldman* 219 F.2d 173 (2d Cir. 1955); *cf. Essex Universal Corp. v. Yates,* 305 F.2d 572 (2d Cir. 1962). See also *Jones v. H. F. Ahmanson & Co.,* 460 P.2d 464 (Cal. 1969) and the discussion at the end of Chapter 28.

[2] *cf. GM Leasing Corp. v. U.S.,* 429 *U.S.* 338 (1977) and *U.S. v. Security National Bank,* 546 F.2d 492 (2d. Cir. 1976).

have been caused by a defective heating system. Old Town appealed from a judgment of $505,500 on several grounds, one of which was that the jury found Old Town liable because of constructive knowledge of latent defects in the heating system. Affirmed.

Old Town acquired a parcel of land, which it conveyed without payment to Mey, Inc., an Indiana corporation of which the four partners of Old Town were the officers and directors. Mey, Inc., then contracted with Town Construction Corp., another Indiana corporation with the same four individuals as its officers and directors and which had been incorporated on the same date, to construct an apartment complex on the unimproved acreage. The address given for the Principal Office of both corporations was that of the law office of three of the partners of Old Town. Mitchell, the incorporator and Resident Agent for both corporations, was a partner in the law firm as well as of Old Town and an officer-director of the corporations. Town Construction subcontracted the heating installation to Ogle. Mitchell was the individual who at all times dealt with Ogle. After construction, the real estate was reconveyed to Old Town Development Co. without money changing hands.

Mey, Inc.'s charter was shortly thereafter revoked by the state for failure to file annual reports. Nelson, one of the partners in Old Town and an officer-director of both corporations testified that he knew nothing of the operations of either corporation. Although stipulating that it was owner of the apartment at the time it was leased to Langford, Old Town argued that Mey, Inc. and Town Construction were separate entities and it [Old Town] could not be held to have constructive knowledge of the defective heating system in the apartment necessary to hold it liable in Indiana as landlord for breach of an implied warranty of habitability. The jury found liability under court instructions that it could hold Old Town liable if Mey, Inc., and Town Construction were merely instrumentalities of or the alter egos of the partners in Old Town.

BUCHANAN, PRESIDING JUDGE. The legal basis for casting Old Town in the role of a builder-owner (it having already stipulated to the role of landlord-owner at the lease's inception) is that separate corporate existence will be ignored on equitable grounds in some circumstances.

Indiana, like other jurisdictions, has recognized: "[T]hat there are cases where, to prevent fraud or injustice, it is necessary to disregard the fiction of distinct corporate existence, and to hold as a matter of equity that such separate legal entity does not exist."

"Piercing the corporate veil" can be traced back to 1809. *Bank of United States v. DeVeaux.* Unfortunately, use of this metaphor through the years has become inextricably intertwined with other words and phrases more or less descriptive of circumstances in which separate corporate existence is ignored, e.g., "instrumentality," "agency," "alter ego," "identity," and "adjunct."

Various standards have been proposed from time to time to escape the resulting confusion, but we need only be concerned with Indiana Law. We note that no general formula such as "alter ego" or "instrumentality" can satisfy all cases. Rather, the only realistic approach is to deal with each case on its own merits.

The instrumentality rule is a triad, liability being predicated upon the presence of:

> . . . control by the parent to such a degree that the subsidiary has become a mere instrumentality [having no separate mind, will or existence of its own]; fraud or wrong by the parent through its subsidiary, e.g., torts, violation of a statute or stripping the subsidiary of its assets; and unjust loss or injury to the claimant, such as insolvency of the subsidiary.

To establish the requisite degree of control, courts consider numerous factors. To name a few—ownership of the subsidiary's capital stock, common directors or officers, financial support of the subsidiary's operation by the parent, the subsidiary being without substantial business contacts except for the parent, the subsidiary's acts referred to or treated as those of the parent, use of the subsidiary's property by the parent as its own, directors or executives of the subsidiary not acting independently, and failure of the subsidiary to observe formal legal requirements, such as keeping separate records and filing needed reports.

The instrumentality rule is generally stated in terms of related corporations, but it need not necessarily be so.

We are aware of no reason why a partnership manipulating corporations for its own purposes should be any less subject to the instrumentality rule than a parent corporation. Most of the factors necessary to satisfy the element of control ". . . to such a degree that the subsidiary has become a mere instrumentality . . ." are present in this case.

In view of the degree of control exerted by the partners at each stage of the development of the Old Town Apartment complex the jury could conclude these two corporations were business conduits or instrumentalities conveniently utilized for the purpose of avoiding personal liability.

As to the second and third elements of the instrumentality rule, there was evidence from which the jury could conclude (1) that the parent (Old Town) through Town Construction Corp. committed a wrong against Langford by failing to inspect and construct the apartment in compliance with the building code and then renting the apartment with a concealed dangerous condition unknown to Langford; and (2) that an unjust injury to Langford would result if Old Town was allowed to maintain its corporate facade . . . a facade which Old Town allowed to crumble by failing to file annual corporate reports before Langford filed his complaints.

Krivo Indus. Supply Co. v. National Dist. & Chem. Corp.

483 F.2d 1098 (5th Cir. 1973)

Krivo Industrial Supply Co. and nine others (plaintiffs) brought this action against National Distillers and Chemical Corporation (defendant) to recover on accounts owed them as creditors of Brad's Machine Products, Inc., which had failed financially while being assisted by National Distillers, its major supplier and major creditor. They alleged that National Distillers was liable because it had dominated Brad's to such an extent that it was a "mere instrumentality" of National Distillers. The district court directed a verdict for National Distillers. Affirmed.

John Bradford, a country-western singer, operated a small machine shop in California. With the help of a person experienced in government contracting, Bradford obtained in 1966 a $2.7 million contract to produce M-125 fuses using a unique and very efficient method of manufacturing the fuse bodies which Bradford had developed. He then moved the operation to Gadsden, Alabama, where he employed approximately 500 persons. The operation appeared to prosper but Bradford had many other investments that became a financial drain on Brad's. In early 1969, Bridgeport Brass, a subsidiary of National Distillers, was shipping $400,000 to $500,000 worth of brass rod to Brad's each month, and in March Brad's owed $1 million to Bridgeport. At Brad's request the delinquent payments were converted to a promissory note with scaled down payments and a "balloon" at the end of the payment schedule, and Brad's promised to keep payments for future shipments current. However, by July Brad's was again in arrears and the federal government was threatening cancellation of the current fuse contract. Bradford then requested National Distillers to intervene with the Government and offered to put up all of his assets as collateral for required current operating funds. A new agreement was then entered into whereby National Distillers deferred the current arrearage of $630,000, loaned Brad's $600,000 in cash and agreed to help Bradford and Brad's liquidate unprofitable investments to create more working capital and to furnish an employee to assist Brad's in developing financial management controls. Under this agreement one of National Distillers' internal auditors, Rudd, was sent in as a full-time advisor, and a vice president of Bridgeport visited Brad's nearly once a week. Rudd's signature was required on all Brad's checks, and purchase orders were sent to him for approval before going out. However, despite these controls and further loans of cash by National Distillers and another deferral of payments to Bridgeport totalling more than $836,000, Brad's ceased operations in December 1970, leaving the debts to Krivo and the other plaintiffs unpaid.

RONEY, CIRCUIT JUDGE. Basic to the theory of corporation law is the concept that a corporation is a separate entity, a legal being having an existence separate and distinct from that of its owners. This attribute of the separate corporate personality enables the corporation's stockholders to limit their personal liability to the extent of their investment. But the corporate device cannot in all cases insulate the owners from personal liability.

[A] corporation may be held liable for the debts of another corporation when it misuses that corporation by treating it, and by using it, as a mere business conduit for the purposes of the dominant corporation. The rationale for holding the dominant corporation liable for the subservient corporation's debts is that, since the dominant corporation has misused the subservient corporation's corporate form by using it for the dominant corporation's own purposes, the debts of the subservient corporation are in reality the obligations of the dominant corporation. In these cases, "the courts will look through the forms to the realities of the relation between the companies as if the corporate agency did not exist and will deal with them as the justice of the case may require." Here, then, the corporate form of the subservient corporation is disregarded so as to affix liability where it justly belongs. Krivo's claim in this case is based on this second theory of liability.

Although the Alabama courts have yet to delineate a more precise test, the parties in the case at bar agree, and we agree, that two elements are essential for liability under the "instrumentality" doctrine. First, the dominant corporation must have controlled the subservient corporation, and second, the dominant corporation must have proximately caused plaintiff harm through misuse of this control.

In considering the first element, that of control, the courts have struggled to delineate the kind of control necessary to establish liability under the "instrumentality" rule. Two problem areas have persistently troubled the process of ascertaining the extent of control. First, to what extent is stock ownership critical, and second, how much weight should be given to the existence of a creditor-debtor relationship in those cases where the debtor corporation is alleged to be the "instrumentality" of its creditor?

As to the effect of stock ownership, an examination of the case law in this area indicates that the fact that the allegedly dominant corporation held an ownership interest in another, allegedly subservient, corporation does not, per se, resolve the question of control.

On the other hand, the fact that the allegedly dominant corporation held no stock ownership interest in the allegedly subservient corporation has not precluded application of the "instrumentality" rule where actual and total control has been otherwise established.

As with stock ownership, a creditor-debtor relationship also does not per se constitute control under the "instrumentality" theory. The general rule is that the mere loan of money by one corporation to another does not automatically make the lender liable for the acts and omissions of the borrower. The logic of this rule is apparent, for otherwise no lender would be willing to extend credit. The risks and liabilities would simply be too great. Nevertheless, lenders are not automatically exempt from liability under the "instrumentality" rule. If a lender becomes so involved with its debtor that it is in fact actively managing the debtor's affairs, then the quantum of control necessary to support liability under the "instrumentality" theory may be achieved.

An examination of "instrumentality" cases involving creditor-debtor relationships demonstrates that courts require a strong showing that the creditor assumed actual, participatory, total control of the debtor. Merely taking an active part in the management of the debtor corporation does not automatically constitute control, as used in the "instrumentality" doctrine, by the creditor corporation.

Rudd's activities while at Brad's simply do not amount to active domination of the corporation. His job was to provide internal financial management assistance and all that he did was in keeping with this mission. Although he kept a fairly tight rein on disbursements, the evidence shows that his role was that of providing a centralized control over purchases and disbursements. His job was two-fold: (1) to eliminate costly duplication, e.g., multiple orders of the same supply, and (2) to eliminate all disbursements not directly and immediately related to the machine shop business. These controls were strong, and Rudd was not afraid to exercise his power, but we cannot conclude from the evidence before us that his activities could justify a jury verdict that found control. Rudd limited the scope of his position to overseeing the finances of Brad's. Neither he nor anyone else from National Distillers or from Bridgeport Brass had much, if any, influence, let alone control, over other key areas of managerial decision-making at Brad's.

Although National Distillers' position as a major creditor undoubtedly vested it with the capacity to exert great pressure and influence, we agree with the District Court that such a power is inherent in any creditor-debtor relationship and that the existence and exercise of such a power, alone, does not constitute control for the purposes of the "instrumentality" rule.

Regulation and Termination of Corporations

State Regulation of Corporations. The framers of the Constitution decided not to provide for the chartering of business corporations by Congress. Therefore, they have been chartered by the individual states. However, under the Constitution one state cannot grant to its citizens privileges which are to be exercised in another state. Therefore, if a "foreign corporation" (a corporation chartered either by another state or a foreign country) wishes to transact intrastate business, it must first obtain a license permitting it to do business within the state as a foreign corporation. Since interstate commerce is regulated by the federal government, corporations have the right to transact interstate commerce in any state. This distinction and the rights and liabilities of foreign corporations are discussed in Chapter 30.

The right to charter corporations carries with it the right to regulate them. This is done today in every state through a general incorporation law for profit-making corporations. These set up requirements for incorporation, provide for the payment of certain fees and taxes and the filing of annual reports, grant certain powers to the directors in managing the corporation, and establish certain rights and liabilities of shareholders. In part because there is competition among states to become the legal domicile of the larger corporations doing an interstate and perhaps international business, the general corporation statutes of most states have tended to be liberal enabling acts rather than regulatory devices. Delaware has been the leader in this movement over the past 60 years. Effective state regulation tends to be limited to regulation of the activities of corporations, within the state, both domestic and foreign, rather than through limitations placed in charters.

Federal Regulation of Corporations. Critics of business, most recently Ralph Nader, have from time to time proposed federal chartering or licensing of the largest corporations so that it might be easier to require them to operate in the public interest. However, the proposal has dropped from public view each time when a federal regulatory statute was passed dealing with the primary concern of that period. These include the Interstate Commerce Act, the Sherman Act, the Clayton Act, the Federal Trade Commission Act, the Securities Act of 1933, and the Securities Exchange Act of 1934.[3] Whether dealing with problems posed by large business through a federal chartering or licensing statute, coupled with a super agency to administer it, would be more successful than a patchwork of statutes and a number of administrative agencies appears problematical at this time. However, the huge size of some corporations and their importance to the livelihood and well-being of the citizenry, and the fact that a few individuals through the proxy machinery can control management are reasons the proposal is currently being supported by some influential people.

Termination. Being a creature of the state, a corporation cannot be unilaterally dissolved; it must have the consent of the state. Today the corporation statutes establish procedures for dissolution, and consent is given in advance if those procedures are followed. For example, the Model Business Corporation Act, which is discussed in some detail later in this chapter, provides five methods of dissolution. They are: by a majority of the incorporators if the corporation has not commenced business (82)[4]; by written consent of all of its shareholders (83); by act of the corporation, which requires a vote of a majority of the shareholders after proper notice of a meeting to be held for that purpose (84); by act of the attorney general for failure by the corporation to file an annual report or pay its franchise tax, for abuse of its corporate authority, or failure to appoint or maintain a registered agent in the state (94); or by a court upon petition of a shareholder or creditor (97). The end of the term of a corporation chartered for a specific period of time will, of course, also dissolve the corporation. A new charter may be obtained, however, and the business may be continued without interruption.

---

[3] See Chapter 50 for a discussion of the Sherman Act, Chapter 51 for the Clayton Act, Chapter 53 for the Federal Trade Commission Act and Chapter 29 for the securities acts.

[4] The numbers in the parentheses refer to the sections of the Model Business Corporation Act, which appears in the Appendix.

Bases for dissolution upon petition of a shareholder include deadlock of directors which cannot be broken by the shareholders and irreparable injury is threatened, illegal or oppressive acts by by the directors, failure to elect directors for a period including two consecutive annual-meeting dates because of shareholder deadlock and, finally, misapplication or waste of corporate assets. In a few states, courts have dissolved corporations upon petition of a shareholder where it appeared that the main purpose of the corporation was no longer attainable. However, courts tend to be reluctant to order an involuntary dissolution.

If a corporation merges into another under statutory authority, the former corporation is dissolved. If two corporations consolidate into a new corporation, both of the original corporations are dissolved.

Under the Model Act a creditor may get a court to dissolve the corporation if the corporation is insolvent and execution on a judgment is unsatisfied or the corporation admits in writing that the creditor's claim is due and owing.[5] In addition, a court is given jurisdiction to liquidate the corporation when the state's attorney general files an action to dissolve.

SUMMARY

The right to charter a corporation for profit is vested in the states. This carries with it the right to regulate the corporation.

Despite numerous proposals there is no law requiring large corporations doing an interstate business to be chartered by or licensed by the federal government. Instead, statutes establishing a regulatory framework and an administering agency for each of several major types of problems between corporations and society have been enacted.

The existence of a corporation may be terminated by: (1) voluntary dissolution, (2) forfeiture of its charter, (3) expiration of its charter, (4) merger or consolidation, and sometimes by suit of (5) minority shareholders (6) creditors, or (7) the attorney general.

Incorporation

Where to Incorporate? If the business of such corporation is to be primarily intrastate, it will ordinarily be most advantageous to incorporate in the state where the principal office is located. If the business is to be primarily interstate, the promoters of the corporation will usually wish to incorporate in the state that has corporate statutes that best serve the purpose of the proposed corporation.

---

[5] See Chapter 47 for discussion of the Federal Bankruptcy Act.

Comparative taxes are, of course, an important factor. There is a considerable range among states with respect to the imposition of or amount of organization taxes, annual taxes such as franchise and income taxes, and taxes on the issuance and transfer of shares in the corporation. A few states impose a "cessation" or dissolution tax. Of equal or greater concern may be the limitations placed upon the operation of the corporation. The statutes, as interpreted by courts of some states, especially Delaware, give promoters and management much greater freedom than do some other states. Such liberality, however, may not always be in the interest of minority shareholders.

Model Business Corporation Act. In 1946 the Committee on Corporate Laws, a part of the American Bar Association's Corporation, Banking and Business Law Section drafted the Model Business Corporation Act. The Committee was composed of leading corporate lawyers and scholars. The Model Act served both as a stimulus and as a guide to the many states which had not substantially revised their general corporation statutes in the light of current business practices and the changes in incorporation statutes made by the more progressive states. It has been used as a basis, though not followed in every detail, for the statues of 28 states and has substantially influenced ten others.[6] Several others have used the Model Act as a guide in amending parts of their statute. However, the most popular domicile for large corporations, Delaware (39 percent of the corporations listed on the New York Stock Exchange are incorporated there),[7] does not follow the act; nor do several other major commercial and industrial states, such as New York, Massachusetts, and California.

Since the Model Business Corporation Act comes closest to being a common denominator between the corporation statutes of the various jurisdictions, it will be used as the primary basis for this discussion. However, the discussion will call attention to the Delaware Act where it is substantially different. The Delaware Act differs in some respects merely because it covers nonprofit corporations as well as corporations for profit.

The Model Business Corporation Act follows the policy of granting broad discretion to the incorporators. It is drafted so as to permit them, by adoption of appropriate articles and bylaws, to adapt the corporation to their interests whether the corporation be a close corporation or a large publicly held corporation. For example, although Section 32 provides that normally a quorum for taking action at a meeting of shareholders shall be a majority of the shares, it permits the corporation in its articles to set the quorum as low as one third of the shares or as high as 100 percent. Section 143 permits the

---

[6] The Model Act was extensively revised in 1969 and to a lesser extent more recently. Many of the adopting states have not amended their statutes to conform to the changes.

[7] As of January 1973. As of January 1965, 35 percent were Delaware corporations, but the percentage appears to have stabilized.

corporation to establish a requirement of a higher proportion of shares voting in favor of any corporate action than provided for in the act by so declaring in its articles.

Who May Incorporate? Many states require that three natural adult persons serve as incorporators, as did the Model Act prior to amendment in 1962. It now specifies that the incorporators may be "one or more persons, or a domestic or foreign corporation." (53). Most states specifically permit a partnership or an association to be an incorporator.

Steps in Incorporation. The steps prescribed by the incorporation statutes of the different states vary but they generally include the following, which appear in the Model Act: (1) preparation of articles of incorporation and signing and authenticating the articles by one or more persons or a domestic or foreign corporation; (2) filing of the articles, accompanied by the specified fees, with the Secretary of State; (3) issuance of a certificate of incorporation by the Secretary; and (4) holding an organization meeting of the board of directors named in the articles for the purpose of adopting bylaws, electing officers, and transacting other business. Many states require the payment of some minimum capital (typically $1,000) before the transaction of business.

In addition, in many states, including Delaware, copies of the articles must be filed with a county official in the county where the registered office of the corporation is located and in some states the articles must be published in a newspaper. Furthermore, qualification or registration of the corporation's stock may be required under either the federal or state securities laws or both.[8]

Articles of Incorporation. The statutes of various states also vary somewhat with respect to what must be included in the articles of incorporation, but in general, the requirements are similar to the following which appear in the Model Act (54): (1) name of the corporation; (2) its duration; (3) its purpose; (4) number and classes of shares; (5) if appropriate, designation of classes and relative rights; (6) if appropriate, designation of relative rights between series; (7) if desired, a provision limiting or denying preemptive rights; (8) any additional provisions desired, not inconsistent with law, for the regulation of the internal affairs of the corporation, including any restrictions on the transferability of shares; (9) registered office and registered agent; (10) number of and names and addresses of initial directors; and (11) the name and address of each incorporator.

Name and Seal. The incorporators must give the corporation a name, and it is customary, but not required, that it adopt a seal. Under the Model Act (8) the name must contain the word "corporation," "incorporated," or "limited," or an abbreviation of one of these words. It may not be the same as or deceptively similar to the name of any other corporation incorporated

[8] See Chapter 29.

in or authorized to transact business in the state. The Model Act also prohibits the use of a word in the name which indicates that the corporation is organized for any purpose other than those stated in its articles. A number of corporation statutes specifically prohibit the use of a word denoting an activity, such as "bank," "trust," or "insurance," which would indicate that it has been incorporated under a special, more restrictive statute rather than the general corporation statute.

To facilitate the selection of a name unlike those of preexisting corporations, the Model Act (9) provides for advance application to the secretary of state for a desired name. If the name is available, it may be reserved for a period of 120 days while the corporation is being formed.

Many states require the signing on behalf of the corporation of documents pertaining to real estate, such as deeds and mortgages, to be authenticated by a "seal." If the corporation does not adopt a seal, it may be asked to furnish a certificate to that effect when executing such documents. Therefore, it is advisable to adopt a simple seal, which is customarily held in the custody of the corporate secretary and affixed to documents by him or her.

Duration and Purposes. Most statutes permit corporations to have perpetual existence.[9] If desired, the articles of incorporation may provide for a shorter period even when the applicable statute permits perpetual life.

All jurisdictions require that the corporate purpose or purposes be set forth in the articles. Under the Model Act and the Delaware statute, it is sufficient to state, alone or together with specific purposes, that the corporation may engage in "any lawful activity." Other statutes require corporations to list specific purposes or limit a corporation to a single purpose. Most general corporation statutes, including the Model Act (3), exclude types of activity which require incorporation under special statutes. Otherwise, the limitations as to scope of business placed upon the corporation are self-imposed, and they are stated in the articles for the protection of stockholders.

Financial Structure. Modern statutes, including that of Delaware and the Model Act, give wide latitude to the incorporators in establishing the capital structure of the corporation. Various classes of shares may be established with or without par value and with or without voting rights (except in the case of certain extraordinary transactions). Certain classes may be subject to redemption by the corporation or may be given convertibility at the option of the holder into a different class of share. Under the Model Act the board of directors may be given authority by the articles to divide the classes of shares into series and establish the different rights and preferences for the various series. Some state statutes are more restrictive and a few do not permit a corporation to limit voting rights of common shares or do not allow no par or convertible shares or liquidation preferences for shares desig-

[9] Exceptions are Kansas, 100; Mississippi, 99; and Oklahoma, 50 years.

nated as common stock. Some states require that shares designated as preferred stock have some preferential features.

Management. Revised Section 35 of the Model Act states ". . . the business and affairs of a corporation shall be managed under the direction of a board of directors except as may otherwise be provided in . . . the articles of incorporation." Many states require a minimum of three directors but Delaware and the 1969 revision of the Model Act (36) permit a corporation to have a single director. They do not require that the directors be shareholders of the corporation, adults, residents of the state of incorporation, or even United States citizens. The articles need only state the number of initial directors and their names and addresses. These directors hold office until the first annual meeting of shareholders. Subsequently, the number is to be specified in the bylaws and may be increased or decreased by amendment of the bylaws. Some statutes reserve the power to change the number of directors to the shareholders. Directors must be elected at each annual shareholders' meeting, but the Model Act permits dividing the directors into two or three classes when they number nine or more. When classes are established, one class is to be elected at each annual meeting.

The bylaws are, in effect, private legislation for the structuring and operation of the corporation. Under the Model Act (27) the initial bylaws are to be adopted by the board of directors, and the power to alter them or to adopt new bylaws is vested in the board unless reserved to the shareholders by the articles of incorporation. Delaware vests bylaw-making authority in the shareholders unless given to the directors in the articles. Bylaws, of course, must be consistent with law and the articles of incorporation.

Regulation of the calling of, conduct of, and voting at shareholders' and directors' meetings is also generally specified in the bylaws. Most state corporation laws contain provisions in this respect designed to ensure minimum standards of fairness. The Model Act (50) specifies that there "shall be a president, one or more vice presidents as may be prescribed in the bylaws, a secretary, and a treasurer." It provides that the board of directors may elect or appoint such other officers and assistant officers and agents as may be prescribed in the bylaws and that their duties shall be provided in the bylaws or by resolution of the board of directors. The Model Act (50) permits the same person to hold any two or more offices except those of the president and secretary. Delaware does not specify titles for officers and declares that any number of offices may be held by the same person.

SUMMARY

The incorporators of a business must first decide in which state they wish to incorporate. Since the corporation laws of the states are not uniform, there may be advantages to be gained by incorporating under the laws of a particular state. A majority of the states, but excluding some of those in which the largest number of businesses have incorporated, have adopted all or substantially all of the Model Business Corporation Act, which follows the policy of granting broad discretion to the incorporator or incorporators. A number of states require three natural persons as incorporators.

The corporation statutes will set out the framework within which the business may be incorporated and the steps to be followed. The articles of incorporation and the bylaws define the basic structure of the corporation and, in very general terms, the procedures for its management.

The purpose or purposes of the corporation must be stated in the articles of incorporation but most states permit this to be very general. It is necessary in most states to incorporate under special statutes to conduct special types of businesses, such as banking, railroading, insurance, and building and loan associations.

Corporations de Jure *and* de Facto

The *de Facto* Doctrine. Since the process of incorporation involves a series of steps, courts have frequently been faced with the question of how to classify a business association which holds itself out to be a corporation but which has not completed all of the formalities required by statute. The question usually is whether the persons involved are to be given the limited liability of owners of corporate shares or to be treated as partners.

Over the years the courts developed a tripartite classification system: (1) *de jure* corporation, (2) *de facto* corporation, and (3) no corporation.

If the incorporators essentially comply with all of the mandatory provisions of the corporation statute and fulfill in a substantial manner all the required prerequisites for the organization of the corporation, they will create a *de jure* corporation. The validity of a *de jure* corporation is not subject to attack even in a direct action brought by the state despite the fact its organization may not be perfect. Failure to comply with statutory provisions which are considered only directive, not mandatory, will not prevent the organization of a *de jure* corporation.

***De Facto* Corporation.** If the incorporators fail in some material respect to comply with the mandatory provisions of the corporate statutes, they will not have organized a *de jure* corporation. The courts have held, on the basis of public policy, that a *de facto* corporation is formed when: (1) there is a valid statute under which the corporation could be organized, (2) the parties have made an honest effort to organize under the statute, and (3) they have done business as a corporation. The corporate existence of a *de facto* corporation cannot be collaterally attacked. That is, in a suit by or against the corporation, neither the corporation nor the other party to the suit will be permitted to defend on the ground of the defects in the corporation's organization. However, the state may attack its claim of corporate status in a direct action brought for that purpose (*quo warranto*). A corporation whose charter has expired is usually treated as a *de facto* corporation during the interval before it is renewed.

Estoppel to Deny Corporate Existence. If persons hold themselves out as doing business as a corporation and induce third persons to deal with them as such, they will not be permitted to set up their lack of incorporation as a defense against the third persons. Likewise, if a third person has dealt with an association of persons as a corporation, such third person will not be permitted to escape liability by setting up the lack of corporate existence as a defense. Having dealt with the persons as a corporation, the third person has impliedly agreed that his or her rights and liabilities will be determined on the basis that such persons are transacting business as a corporation.

This theory of estoppel to deny corporate existence is an extension of the theory of *de facto* corporate existence. However, the theory of estoppel to deny corporate existence applies only in determining the rights and liabilities of the parties in particular transactions, whereas the *de facto* corporation is recognized as having a corporate existence for all corporate purposes.

Statutory Effect on *de Facto* Doctrine. The Model Act (56) states that issuance of a certificate of incorporation by the secretary of state is conclusive evidence of incorporation except against the state, which is permitted to bring an action challenging corporate status. Since it is unlikely that failure to complete steps in the procedure short of the issuance of the certificate would be held to constitute the enterprise a *de facto* corporation, this would appear to eliminate the distinction between a *de facto* and a *de jure* corporation. The Delaware statute does not specifically give the issuance of the certificate this effect.

Liability on Failure to Organize Corporation. If persons attempt to organize a corporation but their efforts are so defective that not even a *de facto* corporation comes into existence, or if they carry on a business for profit representing that they have incorporated the business when they have made no effort to do so, the courts have generally held such persons to be partners and liable as such.

The courts are not in accord as to the liability of a person who purchases stock in a corporation which is so defectively organized that it does not have even the status of a *de facto* corporation. Some courts have held that such a person is a co-owner of the business and as such is liable as a partner. Other courts have held that one who justifiably believes that he or she is purchasing stock in a validly organized corporation will not be held liable as a partner. These courts impose the unlimited liability of a partner on only those stockholders who are actively engaged in the management of the business or who are at fault for the defects in the organization of the corporation.

A third person may be estopped from denying the existence of the corporation and may be denied the right to recover from the stockholders as partners.

SUMMARY

If the organizers of a corporation have substantially complied with the mandatory provisions of the corporation statutes and have fulfilled all the required prerequisites for incorporation, they will have organized a *de jure* corporation. The organization of a *de jure* corporation is not subject even to direct attack by the state.

If a statute exists under which a corporation may be incorporated and persons make an honest effort to incorporate under the statute and do business as a corporation but do not comply with all the mandatory provisions, a *de facto* corporation will have been created. Any attack on a *de facto* corporation must be made by the state in a direct proceeding brought for that purpose.

If persons have held themselves out as doing business as a corporation but either have made no attempt to comply with the corporation statutes or have complied so defectively that they have not formed even a *de facto* corporation, they will be estopped, under some circumstances, from denying their existence as a corporation. Likewise, a third person dealing with such an association of persons will be denied the right to escape liability by setting up the lack of corporate existence of the association.

As a general rule, persons purporting to carry on a business for profit as a corporation but who have made no attempt to incorporate or have made an attempt which was so defective that even a *de facto* corporation was not brought into existence, will be liable as partners.

By statute in many states the distinction between *de jure* and *de facto* corporations has been eliminated.

Terrel v. Industrial Commission

508 P.2d 355 (Ct. App. Ariz. 1973)

Petition by Terrel (plaintiff) for a writ of certiorari seeking review of an award by the Industrial Commission of Arizona (defendant) which denied the liability of the major shareholder of an uninsured corporation. Affirmed.

Terrel was injured on February 25, 1969, while employed by AC&C Wreckers, Inc., which was engaged in the business of building demolition. Because it employed three or more persons AC&C was subject to the Arizona workmen's compensation laws, but it had not complied with them. AC&C had filed its articles of incorporation on August 30, 1968, but had neglected to file a certified copy with the county recorder and to publish them in a newspaper as required by statute. AC&C conducted its business as a corporation, kept corporate minutes, and had assets of its own.

Collins, a lawyer who was not in charge of the corporation's business, was the major shareholder. Terrel sought to hold him personally liable because of failure to complete required steps in incorporation.

HAIRE, JUDGE. There is a substantial agreement among the authorities that a *de facto* corporation can result even in the absence of compliance with all of the technical statutory incorporation provisions. The reason generally given for holding such a corporation to have achieved a *de facto* existence is that if rights and franchises have been usurped, they are the rights and franchises of the state, which alone can object.

The authorities are also in agreement that once it has been determined that *de facto* existence has been achieved, then the stockholders cannot be held liable to third persons who deal with the corporation merely on account of the technical defect in the formation of the corporation. The three prerequisites to the creation of a *de facto* corporation are:

1. The existence of a charter or law under which a corporation with the powers which it undertakes to exercise may lawfully exist.
2. An effort in good faith to incorporate thereunder.
3. An actual use or exercise of corporate powers.

The disagreement and the apparent conflict in the decisions arise from the application of the second element to different fact situations to determine just how far the statute must be followed to demonstrate a "good faith effort to incorporate" under the applicable statutory law. Many decisions differentiate between statutory conditions precedent to the actual existence of the corporation as opposed to conditions precedent to its right to commence or do business. Failure to comply with the latter type of condition precedent does not preclude a finding of *de facto* existence.

It is petitioner's contention that AC&C's failure to file a certified copy of its articles of incorporation with the county recorder precludes *de facto* corporate existence. A review of the pertinent Arizona constitutional and statutory provisions discloses the following:

> No domestic . . . corporation shall do any business in this State without having filed its articles of incorporation or a certified copy thereof with the Corporation Commission, and without having one or more known places of business and an authorized agent, or agents, in he State upon whom process may be served.

AC&C fully complied with these constitutional filing requirements. A.R.S. § 10–123, set forth in footnote 2, *supra,* adds another filing requirement—the filing of a certified copy of the articles with the county recorder "before doing business." As previously stated, AC&C did not comply with this filing requirement. While it is generally held that there can be no *de facto* corporation where there has been a complete failure to file in any office, it is also generally held that the failure to file in one of two required offices does not preclude *de facto* existence.

Here, petitioner places great reliance upon the language requiring the omitted filing "before doing business." Similar language has been considered by many courts and held not to preclude *de facto* existence.

Robertson v. Levy

197 A.2d 443 (Ct. App. D.C. 1964)

This was an action by Martin G. Robertson (plaintiff) against Eugene M. Levy (defendant) to recover the balance due on a note signed by Levy as president of Penn Ave. Record Shack, Inc., which had not been incorporated at the time the note was executed. Judgment for Levy and Robertson appealed. Judgment reversed.

Levy agreed with Robertson to form a corporation to purchase Robertson's record store business. An agreement assigning Robertson's lease was made to Penn Ave. Record Shack, Inc., and signed by Levy as president on December 22, 1961. Levy submitted articles of incorporation to the Superintendent of Corporations on December 27. On January 2, 1962, Levy began to operate the business as Penn Ave. Record Shack, Inc. On this same day he received notification that his articles of incorporation were rejected. On January 8, Robertson executed a bill of sale of his assets to the "corporation" and received a note signed in the name of the corporation by Levy as president. A certificate of incorporation of Penn Ave. Record Shack, Inc., was issued on January 17. One payment was made on the note. In June 1962, the corporation ceased doing business and no assets remained.

HOOD, CHIEF JUDGE. One of the reasons for enacting modern corporation statutes was to eliminate problems inherent in the *de jure, de facto,* and estoppel concepts. Thus sections 29–921c and 950 were enacted as follows:

> § 29–921c. (§ 56 of Model Act) Effect of issuance on incorporation.
>
> Upon the issuance of the certificate of incorporation, the corporate existence shall begin, and such certificate of incorporation shall be conclusive evidence that all conditions precedent required to be performed by the incorporators have been complied with and that the corporation has been incorporated under this chapter, except as against the District of Columbia in a proceeding to cancel or revoke the certificate of incorporation.
>
> § 29–950. (§ 146 of Model Act) Unauthorized assumption of corporate powers.
>
> All persons who assume to act as a corporation without authority so to do shall be jointly and severally liable for all debts and liabilities incurred or arising as a result thereof.

The authorities which have considered the problem are unanimous in their belief that section 29–921c and section 29–950 have put to rest *de facto* corporations and corporations by estoppel. Thus the Comment to section 50 (56 of 1969 revision) of the Model Act, after noting that *de jure* incorporation is complete when the certificate is issued, states that: "Since it is unlikely that any steps short of securing a certificate of incorporation would be held to constitute apparent compliance, the possibility that a *de facto* corporation could exist under such a provision is remote."

The portion of § 29–921c which states that the certificate of incorporation will be "conclusive evidence" that all conditions precedent have been performed eliminates the problems of estoppel and *de facto* corporations once the certificate has been issued. The existence of the corporation is conclusive evidence against all who deal with it. Under § 29–950, if an individual or group of individuals assumes to act as a corporation before the certificate of incorporation has been issued, joint and several liability attaches. We hold, therefore, that the impact of these sections, when considered together, is to eliminate the concepts of estoppel and *de facto* corporateness under the Business Corporation Act of the District of Columbia. It is immaterial whether the third person believed he was dealing with a corporation or whether he intended to deal with a corporation. The certificate of incorporation provides the cutoff point; before it is issued, the individuals, and not the corporation, are liable.

Turning to the facts of this case, Penn Ave. Record Shack, Inc., was not a corporation when the original agreement was entered into, when the lease was assigned, when Levy took over Robertson's business, when operations began under the Penn Ave. Record Shack, Inc., name, or when the bill of sale was executed. Only on January 17 did Penn Ave. Record Shack, Inc., become a corporation. Levy is subject to personal liability because, before this date, he assumed to act as a corporation without any authority so to do. Nor is Robertson estopped from denying the existence of the corporation because after the certificate was issued he accepted one payment on the note. An individual who incurs statutory liability on an obligation under section 29–950 because he has acted without authority, is not relieved of that liability where, at a later time, the corporation does come into existence by complying with section 29–921c. Subsequent partial payment by the corporation does not remove this liability.

Problem Cases

1. Tri-State Building Corporation was organized in 1962 with a capital of $5,000. William Folsom owned 40 percent of the stock, his wife 20 percent, and two others owned 20 percent each. Folsom was president and chief executive. No minutes of corporate activities, stockholders' or directors' meetings were made, and Folsom handled all business without direction from the other shareholders. No financial records were kept by Tri-State separate

from Folsom's personal records. Folsom drew no salary from Tri-State and no dividends were paid to the other shareholders.

Folsom arranged with Moore-Handley, Inc., a building supply company, to furnish materials to Tri-State for building residences in a subdivision on lots he said were owned by Tri-State. In fact, the lots were owned by Folsom and his wife. Later he sold the newly-constructed residences executing affadavits declaring that he was the owner and builder. Moore-Handley was not paid for the materials and sued Folsom personally, Tri-State being inactive and having no assets. Is Folsom individually liable for the materials sold to Tri-State?

2. Long Island Reo Company, Inc., was a dealer of trucks manufactured by White Motor Corporation. It financed its purchases of new and used trucks through Universal CIT with those obligations guaranteed by White, which agreed to take over all of the dealer's paper on demand if it should default. In November 1966 CIT determined that L.I. Reo was "out of trust," having sold trucks without paying to CIT the indebtedness on them out of the proceeds from their sale. CIT called on White to honor its guarantee, and White complied, at which time L.I. Reo's debt to White had reached $200,000. White and L.I. Reo then executed a financing agreement signed by Thomas Vincel as president of L.I. Reo and also by Vincel and other shareholders of L.I. Reo. It gave White a security interest in all new or used trucks then or subsequently owned by the dealer and put all of the shares in a voting trust, naming the treasurer of White as trustee and empowering him to appoint a general manager of L.I. Reo.

   By mid-1967 L.I. Reo had defaulted on the agreement by selling trucks without forwarding the proceeds to White, and White brought an action against Vincel and L.I. Reo for breach of the agreement and conversion of the trucks. White obtained an order of attachment and repossessed all of the dealer's vehicles subject to its security interest, and it terminated the voting trust. A few months later L.I. Reo filed for bankruptcy. White filed claims as a creditor amounting to $323,600 and the trustee in bankruptcy filed counterclaims of $3,000,000 alleging among other matters that White had driven L.I. Reo out of business.

   With the approval of the bankruptcy referee and over the objection of Vincel and the other shareholders, White and the bankruptcy trustee compromised all claims with White paying L.I. Reo $100,000, specifically agreeing that White's claims against Vincel and Vincel's defenses and counterclaims would not be affected. In 1969 Vincel and the other shareholders then sued White in federal court making several claims, including breach of the financing contract, breach of fiduciary duties, and conspiring to drive L.I. Reo out of business. White's defense was that these claims are claims of the corporation which were settled in the agreement with the trustee in bankruptcy. Is this a good defense?

3. Fagan was the majority shareholder in Cooper Petroleum Company, and all of the rest of Cooper's stock was owned by a son and two sons-in-law. The four constituted Cooper's officers and directors. Fagan also controlled IMI, another company in the oil business. IMI was heavily indebted to La Gloria Oil Company for the purchase of petroleum products, and Cooper had guaranteed the debt. Although Cooper was insolvent (had its assets and liabilities been properly stated) it paid its officers large profit-sharing bonuses even though no profits were earned. It transferred the bulk of its physical assets, mostly service stations, to another Fagan family corporation, and it assigned all of its accounts receivable to two of the officers. Debts owed to the Fagans and to outsiders that had been guaranteed by the Fagans were paid.

   IMI went into bankruptcy. La Gloria got a judgment against Cooper as guarantor of the account owed it by IMI. However, it was unable to recover. It then sued Fagan and the other officers, seeking to hold them personally liable. Their defense was that only the corporation or a shareholder acting for the corporation could prosecute an action for breach of a fiduciary duty by officers or directors of a corporation. Can they be held liable to La Gloria?

4. Carlton organized and was a principal shareholder in ten corporations each owning and operating two taxicabs in New York City. Each corporation carried a $10,000 liability insurance policy, the minimum required by state statute. The vehicles, the only assets of each corporation, were mortgaged. The ten corporations were operated more or less as a unit with respect to supplies, repairs, employees, etc. Walkovszky was severely injured when run down by one of the taxicabs and sues Carlton personally, alleging that the multiple corporate structure amounts to fraud upon those who might be injured by the taxicabs.

   Should the court "pierce the corporate veil" to reach Carlton individually?

5. The personal property tax statute of Illinois exempted from tax personal property owned by individuals and taxed that owned by corporations and other "non-individuals." Lake Shore Auto Parts brought a class action on behalf of itself and all other "non-individuals," alleging violation of the Equal Protection Clause of the 14th Amendment because corporations are not treated the same as individuals. Should the circuit court opinion holding the statute unconstitutional with respect to corporations be upheld?

6. The State Liquor Commission issued off-sale permits to several corporations which were owned by the same small group of shareholders. The state law provided, "No person shall directly or indirectly hold more than two off-sale permits at one time." The Wholesale Beverage Association seeks to have the permits revoked, and the Commission defends on the grounds that a corporation is a "person." Was the Commission action justified?

7. Hearth Corporation sued C-B-R Development Company to enforce a contract. C-B-R contended that Hearth Corporation's certificate of incorporation had been cancelled by the issuing state prior to the date upon which the contract was made and had not been reinstated until several months later. The pertinent statute declared, "The cancellation of the certificate of incorporation shall not take away or impair any remedy available to or against such corporation, its directors, officers or shareholders for any right or claim existing or any liability incurred prior to such cancellation, but no action or proceeding thereon may be prosecuted by such corporation until it shall have been reinstated."

   The trial court sustained the motion, and upon appeal Hearth argued that corporate existence may be attacked only by the state in a *quo warranto* action. What should the court decide?

8. Couhig's Pestaway Company, Inc., was given a charter by Louisiana in 1967, and engaged in the termite and pest control business for residences and commercial establishments in 11 parishes. In its advertising it emphasized the word "Pestaway." Pestaway, Inc., was incorporated in Louisiana in 1971 and engaged in a similar business but entirely within Lafayette Parish. In its advertising it also emphasized "Pestaway." Couhig's learned of the incorporation and activities of Pestaway, Inc. It then sought an injunction against the use of "Pestaway" in Pestaway, Inc.'s corporate name, declaring that although the two firms were not then in direct competition, Couhig's was growing rapidly and had recently terminated negotiations to purchase a competing pest control firm in Lafayette because of the similarity of names. Should the injunction be granted?

9. Norman R. Harris, a carpenter, decided to get into the building business. He obtained a business license in the name of Bessemer Building & Improvement, Inc., opened a bank account, leased office space, and received telephone service in that name. He arranged

to buy building materials on credit from Stephens Wholesale Bldg. Supply Company. The name of the account on the credit application was Bessemer Building & Improvement, and Harris did not sign in a representative capacity. Nothing was said to the contrary and Stephens Supply treated the account as dealing with Harris as a sole proprietor. A certificate of incorporation was issued for Bessemer Building & Improvement, Inc., about two months after the credit application was signed. Checks paying Stephens Supply were drawn on the account of the corporation. The business failed about four years later, and Stephens Supply sued Harris for the amount outstanding—$3,248.89.

Harris admitted that the corporation owed the money, but denied that he did. Is Harris liable personally?

10. George Love acquired certain lands near Valdez, Alaska, under a war veteran's homestead statute prior to 1906. In 1906 Love and three others executed articles of incorporation for the North Valdez Land Company in which Love was a shareholder and an initial director. In 1907 he conveyed his interest in the real estate to the corporation. The necessary steps for incorporation were not completed until March 1908, and at the time of the conveyance to the corporation no attempt to file the articles with the appropriate authority had been made. In 1975 Love's heirs brought suit to quiet title to the land in themselves, claiming that the corporation was not in existence when the deed to it was given.

    Should the heirs be able to recover the land?

26

Organizing and Financing the Corporation's Business

Promoters

Function of Promoters. The function of a promoter is to bring about the incorporation and organization of a corporation. It is a most vital activity in a free enterprise system, and it is unfortunate that a few unscrupulous individuals have given the term a stigma. The promoter initiates the business; finds persons who are willing to finance the project; negotiates all contracts, leases, purchases, and so forth, necessary for the initial operation of the proposed venture; incorporates the business; and gets it started as a going concern.

In its broadest sense the term "promoter" applies to anyone who assumes the task of organizing and starting a corporation. If a member of a going partnership is instrumental in forming a corporation to which the assets of the partnership are transferred in exchange for stock in the corporation, such a person would be a promoter. However, the term is generally applied to one who causes the formation of a corporation for the purpose of carrying on a new business.

Relation of Promoter and Corporation. The relation of a promoter to the corporation and the persons whom he or she interests in the venture is unique. The promoter is not an agent, since he or she is self-appointed. Technically, the promoter cannot be the agent of the proposed corporation, since it is not in existence. The promoter is not the agent of the persons interested in the venture, since they did not appoint him or her and the promoter is not subject to their direction and control in regard to the promotion of the proposed corporation. A few courts have attempted to draw an analogy between the relation of a promoter and the corporation and that of a trustee and the beneficiary, but important elements of a common law trust are missing.

The promoter owes the duty of a fiduciary to the corporation he or she is promoting and to the persons interested in it. In a promoter's dealings he or she owes a duty of perfect candor, full disclosure, the utmost of good faith, and absolute honesty. It would be a breach of this duty to divert money received on stock subscriptions to the payment of promotional expenses, unless agreed to in the subscription contract, or to take a secret profit at the expense of the subscribers or the corporation. Those injured by the breach of duty, including the corporation, if formed, may recover from the promoter.

For example, if the promoter takes an option on property or purchases property in contemplation of selling it to the corporation after its incorporation and he or she misrepresents to the corporation the option or purchase price of the property, thereby making a secret profit, the corporation may recover a judgment against the promoter for the secret profit. However, if the promoter makes a full disclosure to an independent board of directors who purchase at the increased price, the corporation would have no right of action against the promoter. If the board of directors is under the control of and is manipulated by the promoter, the corporation may rescind the transaction or recover damages because assent has not been freely given.

If the misrepresentations are made to the persons interested in the corporation and they, in behalf of the corporation, take up the option or purchase the property, paying the promoter a secret profit, a majority of the courts have permitted the corporation, when it is incorporated, to bring an action to rescind or recover damages. A few courts have held that only the persons who purchased from the promoter have a right of action.

A more confused situation is one in which property is conveyed to the corporation at a greatly inflated value in payment for shares of stock of the corporation, with the knowledge and consent of all persons interested in the corporation, and then the issued stock is sold to the public at a price substantially in excess of its true value. The federal courts have held that in such a situation the corporation has no right of action against the promoters of the corporation who have engineered the deal because the corporation had full knowledge when it adopted the contract.[1] However, in a case on similar facts, a Massachussetts court held that the corporation could recover.[2] The Massachusetts court reasoned that the stock was issued with the intent to bring in new shareholders and that bringing in these new shareholders was the equivalent of creating a new corporation with the same rights as if the promoters had made a secret profit in selling to the corporation. In a later U.S. Supreme Court case bonds were issued in payment for property purchased

---

[1] *Old Dominion Copper Mining & Smelting Co. v. Lewisohn,* 210 U.S. 206 (1908).

[2] *Old Dominion Copper Mining & Smelting Co. v. Biglow,* 203 Mass. 159, 89 N.E. 193 (1909); *aff'd,* 225 U.S. 111 (1912).

at a greatly inflated value, thereby rendering the corporation insolvent from its inception. The court permitted the receiver of the corporation to recover, for the benefit of creditors, a judgment against the promoters for the secret profit.[3] The preponderance of states have followed the Massachusetts rule permitting recovery by the corporation. The opportunities for illegal manipulation by promoters have been greatly lessened by the adoption of the Securities Act of 1933 and by the Securities Exchange Act of 1934, as well as state securities laws.

Corporation's Liability on Promoter's Contracts. The corporation, when it comes into existence, does not automatically become liable on contracts made in its behalf by the promoter. It cannot be held liable as principal since it was not in existence when the contracts were made. Except for Massachusetts, American courts have held that a contract made by a promoter in behalf of a corporation to be formed can become binding between the corporation and the second party. They have used various theories to reach this result. All require some action by the corporation after it is formed, if only acceptance of the benefits of the contract. The most common ones are: (1) adoption, (2) ratification, (3) novation, and (4) continuing offer. The adoption and novation theories both appear to depend upon the fourth, that is, that the third party with whom the promoter dealt impliedly made a continuing offer to the corporation to adopt the contract, or in the case of novation, for the corporation to be substituted for the promoter. The ratification theory is based upon the agency concept permitting a principal to ratify the unauthorized acts of the agent, although it is a dubious extension because no principal was in existence when the act was done. Massachusetts, like England, does not accept any of these theories, including implied novation, and requires an express agreement between the three parties after the corporation is formed.[4]

Regardless of which one of these theories the state follows as the basis for finding the corporation liable on promoter's contracts, the corporation will not be held liable if the promoter's contract is illegal, fraudulent, not supported by consideration or is beyond the powers of the corporation. For the corporation to adopt or ratify a promoter's contract, the contract must be a valid, subsisting contract which is within the powers of the corporation. The corporation must accept the contract in its entirety, and the officers or agents who purport to adopt or ratify the promoter's contract must have authority to bind the corporation to such a contract.

Liability of Promoter. Contracts made by promoters on behalf of proposed corporations have generally been held to bind the promoters. If the corporation is not formed or fails to adopt or ratify the agreement, the promoter remains

---

[3] *McCandless v. Furlaud*, 296 U.S. 140 (1935).

[4] *Abbott v. Hapgood*, 22 N.E. 907 (1889); *Henshaw v. McBride*, 2 N.E.2d 445 (1936).

liable on it. Obviously, the promoter alone is liable if the contract is made by him or her without reference to a proposed corporation but with the intent to assign it to the corporation later.

The effect on the liability of the promoter differs under the adoption and ratification theories. Under the adoption theory the promoter remains liable. The promoter would not under the ratification theory. No agreement between the corporation and the promoter will relieve the promoter of liability unless the third party consents to it, thus establishing a novation. Courts have held in a few cases that neither the third party nor the promoter intended to bind the promoter. Such an arrangement would be only a "gentleman's agreement" rather than a contract and would not bind the third party either.

SUMMARY

The function of a promoter is to bring about the incorporation and organization of the corporation and to do those things necessary to get it operating as a going business.

The relation of the promoter to the corporation is unique. The promoter is neither agent nor trustee, yet he or she owes a fiduciary duty to the corporation and the persons interested in the venture. The promoter will not be permitted to make a secret profit at the expense of the corporation or of the persons interested in the venture. The courts are not in accord as to a corporation's rights against the promoter who conveys property to the corporation at an inflated value when all the parties interested in the corporation have full knowledge of the transaction. If there is intent to sell the issued stock to the public at a price greatly in excess of its true value, most states permit the corporation to recover.

The corporation is not liable on the promoter's contracts, but it may, by its actions, make itself liable. Ratification, adoption, continuing offer, and novation are theories used to support liability.

The promoter normally continues liable on preincorporation contracts unless there is a novation. The promoter is not relieved from the liability by the adoption of the contract by the corporation.

Whaler Motor Inn, Inc. v. Parsons

339 N.E.2d 197 (App. Ct. Mass. 1975)

This was an action by Whaler Motor Inn, Inc., (plaintiff) against Parsons and three others who acted as promoters of the corporation (defendants) for return and cancellation of capital stock issued without payment and for

Parson's profit in a sale of land to the corporation. Appeal from judgment for Whaler. Reversed and remanded for a determination of the value of the services of each promoter that should be credited towards purchase of the stock.

Parsons, Lipton and Mr. & Mrs. Freedman agreed early in 1966 to explore the feasibility of building a motel in the New Bedford, Massachusetts, area. They visited existing motels, considered sites, made several out-of-state trips to investigate franchising opportunities, engaged engineers, architects, lawyers, consultants for feasibility studies, and others in planning and preliminary development work on the project. Parsons made expenditures of $18,453 and Lipton of $31,433, but no evidence was introduced as to expenditures by the Freedmans.

The corporation was formed early in 1967 and the four promoters and another person became the directors. Each of the promoters offered to buy $108,000 worth of stock and the directors voted to accept the offers and to issue the stock on receipt of the purchase price. The stock was issued, however, without payment by the promoters. The minutes of the board of directors were silent as to the consideration given for the shares. Parsons conveyed two parcels of land and assigned an option on an adjoining parcel to the corporation for $75,000. Payment by the corporation was made by issuing unissued shares in the corporation to Parsons' uncle and a sister, with their payments going directly to Parsons. The land became the site of the motel. Parsons had paid a total of $37,000 for the land about three years earlier with the intent of building a motel there. He had persuaded the city to close a street through the property and had granted an easement for the utility services he had arranged. The estimated value of the property at the time of the conveyance to the corporation was $150,000.

The motel was constructed and opened in 1968. The following year Parsons was replaced as president. He offered to sell his stock to the corporation or individual board members at $108,000. There was no response to this offer but later his offer to sell for $100,000 was accepted by the corporation and he resigned as director. Later in the same year Lipton became involved in financial problems and assigned his shares to trustees for the benefit of creditors. It was at this time that outside investors and the new president, who had also purchased shares, learned that none of the promoters had paid cash for their stock.

HALE, CHIEF JUSTICE. The master found that Parsons' fellow promoters were aware of the price he had paid for the parcels and the option but that none of the outside investors was informed or was aware that the property had been acquired at that price. As a promoter, Parsons was a fiduciary in his dealings with the corporation and as such he would be liable for profits improperly made.

The corporation argues that the proper measure of damages is, as the court ruled, the difference between the sales price and Parsons' cost. We think that, on the facts of this case, the use of that method of computing damages was incorrect.

We are of the opinion that the proper measure of damages here is the difference between the price paid by the corporation and the fair market value of the property at the time of the sale. The property had been acquired by Parsons prior to the formation of the corporation and prior to its selection by the promoters as the site for the motel. It appears that the combined lots in their condition at the times of Parsons' acquisitions were unsuitable for the purposes of a motel. It was not until he, by his own efforts, had among other things, obtained the discontinuance of a public way which ran through the property and secured extensions of water and sewer mains to service the property that the site was rendered suitable for such purpose.

While we do not approve of the slipshod way in which the transaction was handled with respect to corporate votes concerning the acquisition of the property and the means by which Parsons received payment, it is nevertheless clear that the corporation received more than full value in return for the price it paid. While the outside investors were not informed of the details of the transaction, the master did not find, as the corporation contends, that Parsons actively misled the outside stockholders as to his cost or as to the sales price of the land to the corporation.

The defendants do not contend that $108,000 in cash was paid for each block of 130 shares, nor do they make any contention that the master did not properly determine the amount of the expenses incurred by each of the promoters. Their position is that the entrepreneurial services and the expenses of each promoter were the equivalent in value of that amount.

The master made no finding that there was any intention on the part of the promoters to deceive or defraud the outside investors, and we infer that there was none. Nonetheless, it was the duty of the promoters either to inform the investors that the stock had been issued for services and expenses and not for cash, or to obtain the ratification of such issuance at a later time upon a complete revelation of the facts to the outside stockholders or to an independent board of directors. Having failed to do either, they are accountable to the corporation for the profits realized.

The offers which were accepted by the corporation spoke of payment in terms of cash, not in terms of services and expenses. However, we are of the opinion that to limit credit on the stock subscriptions to cash payments would amount to a rank injustice to the promoters. All of the extensive efforts of the promoters, which culminated in the issuance of a motel franchise and the transfer of the product of their labors to the corporation, accrued to the benefit of the corporation. All of those efforts were undertaken prior to the actual issuance of stock to the promoters. Depriving the promoters of credit for their contribution to the value of the corporation through services and expenses would preclude them from any participation in the corporation and would unjustly enrich the equity of the outside investors.

The evidence to be taken on rehearing is to be limited to the determination of the value of the services of the several promoters. As those are matters of affirmative defense, the burden is upon each promoter to prove the amount of credit to which he may be entitled.

KEVILLE, JUSTICE (dissenting). Not only did the promoters have a contractual obligation by virtue of their subscription agreements to pay cash for their stock, but more importantly, they stood in a fiduciary relation to those persons who were to invest in the enterprise as future stockholders. In the absence of full disclosure that they were claiming remuneration for promoters' services, they could not honestly make such a claim without the approval of the outside stockholders.

Since it would have been improper in the first instance for the promoters to have made payment for their stock in the form of organizational services without full disclosure, I find no basis for the validity of their claim of credit for those services made only after the outside stockholders had learned of their misrepresentations that they had paid cash for their stock.

Much of the same reasoning is applicable to the issue whether Parsons may rightly retain his profit from the sale of his real estate to the corporation. With respect to that transaction, he and his fellow promoters stood in a fiduciary relation to the corporation and future stockholders. In the absence of full disclosure, he was not entitled to retain his secret profit.

Parsons seeks to justify the transaction by reliance upon the master's finding that the real estate was worth approximately $150,000. In my view that consideration is irrelevant. It is no defense against a claim by the corporation for secret profits realized by a promoter in the sale of property to the corporation that the property was worth as much as or more than the corporation paid for it.

Completing Corporate Organization

Organization Meeting. As noted in Chapter 25, after the charter has been granted, the Model Act (57)[5] requires an organization meeting of the board of directors, which is to be named in the articles. Many statutes specify that the organization meeting shall be held by the incorporators. Delaware provides that the organization meeting will be held by the incorporators unless the articles specify the initial board of directors instead. Even where the statute does not specifically require one, it is customary to hold an organization meeting although the incorporators, or even, in some cases, the directors, are "dummies" who are associates and employees of the lawyer handling the incorporation. The use of dummies may facilitate completion of the routine business of incorporation, the substitutes then resigning in favor of the operat-

[5] The numbers in the parentheses refer to the sections of the Model Business Corporation Act, which appears in the Appendix.

ing directors. The organization meeting requires a proper notice. The Model Act requires a call by the majority of the directors named in the articles and the giving of three days' notice by mail to the directors.

Business of Organization Meeting. The business to be transacted at an organization meeting will depend on the nature of the business to be carried on by the corporation, on the laws of the state of incorporation, and on the provisions of the articles of incorporation. The Model Act specifies only that bylaws shall be adopted and officers elected. Where the meeting is held by the incorporators, election of directors would be necessary unless they are named in the articles. Other matters usually included would be adoption of a corporate seal, approval of the form of stock certificates, acceptance of stock subscriptions, authorization of issue of stock, adoption of promoters' contracts, authorization of payment of or reimbursement for incorporation expenses, and fixing the salaries of officers. Action on other matters which are appropriate to get the corporation into operation may also be taken at this time.

Bylaws of Corporation. Shareholders have an inherent right to make bylaws (the internal governing rules of the corporation). However, the Model Act (27) gives the power to adopt the initial bylaws to the initial directors. Some statutes give it to the incorporators or initial shareholders. The Model Act and most statutes give the power of amendment and repeal of bylaws to the directors unless this power is reserved to the shareholders by the articles of incorporation.

Although normally the procedures outlined in the bylaws for their amendment must be adhered to, if a different practice is customarily followed with the implied consent of those who could amend it, the courts will treat the bylaw as amended or repealed "by custom and usage."

To be valid, bylaws must be consistent with state law and with the articles of incorporation. They must also be "reasonable" and related to a corporate purpose. Since under most statutes a bare majority may make and amend bylaws, the latter requirement provides the minority with some protection against oppression by the majority.

Persons Bound by Bylaws. Officers, directors, and shareholders of the corporation are bound by bylaws properly adopted. Corporate employees, however, have been held not to be bound unless they have notice or knowledge of them, and the same is true of third persons.

Provisions of Bylaws. The purpose of the bylaws is to regulate the conduct and define the duties of the members toward the corporation and among themselves. They usually include provisions setting out the authority of the officers and directors, the time and place at which the annual shareholders' meetings shall be held, how special meetings of shareholders may be called, defining a quorum, stating how shareholders' meetings shall be organized, and regulating how the voting shall be carried on and how elections shall be conducted. They will also provide for the organization of the board of directors and the conduct of its meetings, state the officers to be elected or appointed and the duties of the officers, and also state who shall be authorized to sign various kinds of contracts in behalf of the corporation. The bylaws may make provision for special committees, defining the scope of their activities and the membership of such committees. They will set up the machinery for the transfer of shares of stock, for the keeping of stock records, and will also make provision for the declaring and the paying of dividends.

SUMMARY

An organization meeting is held after the corporation has been granted its charter. Under the Model Act the initial board of directors are the participants in this meeting. Some statutes specify that the incorporators conduct the meeting. The business to be transacted at the meeting depends upon the laws of the state of incorporation and also the nature of the business and the provisions of its articles of incorporation.

Shareholders have the power to make bylaws. However, under the Model Act the initial bylaws and later changes are adopted by the board of directors unless the articles of incorporation give the power of amendment and repeal to the shareholders. Some statutes specify that the incorporators will adopt initial bylaws.

The bylaws usually include provisions regarding annual meetings of shareholders, meetings of the directors, and the duties of the officers of the corporation. They will set up the machinery for the transfer of stock and such other details as the nature of the corporate business warrants.

To be valid bylaws must be consistent with the state law and the articles of incorporation. They are binding on officers, directors and shareholders of the corporation. Third persons, as a general rule, are not bound by any provision of the bylaws of the corporation unless they have notice or knowledge of it.

Financing the Corporation

Sources of Funds. The initial funds and property for a corporation may come from the promoters or from other investors. They furnish money and property or settle claims for services rendered in exchange for securities of the corporation, which may be one or more types of stock and possibly bonds as well. However, sometimes a potentially large supplier or customer or a bank may provide money on notes of the corporation, perhaps cosigned by the promoters or shareholders.

Once the corporation is operating profitably, it may rely heavily on retained earnings for increasing the funds available to the business. In addition, it may use accounts receivable financing, inventory financing, and other means for increasing its available funds. Dollars charged off to depreciation which are not actually spent for replacement, renewal, or additions to plant and equipment also become additional available funds.

There are two main types of securities: equity securities and debt securities. Each type has many variants, and there have been some securities which are hybrids.

Equity Securities. Every business corporation must issue some stock or equity securities. Traditionally, shareholders were viewed as having a threefold proportionate interest in the corporation: in its earnings, in its control, and in its net assets upon liquidation. However, modern statutes permit corporations to issue more than one class of stock and to vary the preferences, limitations, and rights of the various classes. Most statutes even permit voting rights to be restricted or denied. The Model Act (60) provides, however, that the articles cannot eliminate the right to vote of any class of stock on certain amendments to the articles of incorporation. The shareholder's contract is determined by the articles of incorporation and the bylaws as well as by what may be printed on the certificate.

The equity securities constitute the "capital stock" of the corporation and the value received for these shares appears in the capital accounts in the shareholders' investment section of the corporation's balance sheet. Because of much confusion in terminology and definition with respect to "capital" and "stock," the Model Act uses the term "stated capital." Whatever the term, the value of the capital stock, which may be divided into two or more classes of differing amounts and stated values, is fixed at the time the stock is issued. That value will be the par value or, in case of stock without par value, the value determined by the directors to be the stated value (18 and 21). If the stock is sold for more than the par or stated value, the excess will become capital surplus. The value of the capital stock on the books of the corporation will not be affected by changes in the value of the corporation's assets or the market price of its stock. It can be changed only by amending the articles of incorporation.

Stock may be issued for money, for property—tangible or intangible—or for labor actually performed or services rendered to the corporation under the Model Act (19), but not for promissory notes nor future services. Delaware does not foreclose the use of promissory notes but does by court decision prohibit issuing stock for services to be performed in the future. Subscriptions for shares may be paid by installments so long as the calls are uniform as to all shares of a particular class. However, under the Model Act (23), certificates may not be issued until the shares are fully paid.

In order to cope with the problem of "watered" stock (shares issued for an inadequate consideration), it was common in the past to require some public record of the valuation placed upon property exchanged for shares. These requirements have tended to disappear, and the state and federal securities laws are relied upon to deal with the problem. See Chapter 29.

Stock Certificates. Certificates are issued to represent the shares of stock, but they are not the stock. There have been recent proposals to eliminate stock certificates due to the burden on brokerage houses in handling a very large quantity of such documents. However, presently under the Uniform Commercial Code (8–105 [1]) all types of corporate securities, including stocks, stock warrants, and bonds are declared to be negotiable instruments, but Article 8 rather than Article 3 of the Code applies.

Debt Securities. A corporation has the power to borrow money for the purpose of carrying on its operations. Long-term debt securities of corporations are usually called "bonds." However, short-term debt securities may be designated "notes," and evidences of debt that is unsecured may be called "debentures." Debenture and note holders participate on a pro rata basis with general creditors in the event of insolvency while the holder of a mortgage bond will have priority over general creditors as to the assets covered by the mortgage. The possible variations in the terms of bonds are endless. The rights of the bondholder depends upon the provisions of the contract which constitutes the bond.

Neither the Model Act nor most statutes require authority of the shareholders to issue corporate bonds. Several statutes appear to require shareholder approval if a mortgage of all or substantially all of the assets of the corporation is to be given as security. However, this is not required by the Model Act (78) nor by the Delaware statute.

By the terms of the contract for the bond or debenture issue, called an indenture, the corporation may be obligated to pay a fixed rate of interest or it may be obligated to pay interest only in case the corporate income is sufficient to cover the interest on the bonds or debentures. Instead of being entitled to a fixed rate of interest, the investors may be paid a proportional percentage of the net profits of the corporation. Bondholders, as a general rule, do not have voting rights but may be given them if the interest on the bonds is not paid. Also, a bond or debenture may be convertible, that is, the holder may be given the right to take common or preferred stock in exchange, according to the indenture. A sinking fund may be provided. Bonds or debentures may be issued for a special purpose such as the purchase of certain equipment. In such a case it may be provided that interest is to be paid only out of the proceeds from the use of the equipment.

SUMMARY

The initial funds and property for the corporation usually come from the promoters and from investors in exchange for securities. There are two major types of securities: equity securities (stock) and debt securities (called bonds if secured and debentures if unsecured).

Every business corporation must issue some equity securities or stock and may issue two or more classes and vary their preferences, limitations, and rights so that shareholders do not have their traditional threefold proportionate interest in the corporation: in its earnings, in its net assets, and in its control. Stock certificates are issued to represent the shares but they are not the stock itself.

Bonds and debentures represent debts of the corporations, and their holders are creditors of the corporation. In the event of the insolvency of the corporation, bondholders have priority over general creditors as to the assets pledged as security. Interest may be a fixed obligation, or it may be payable out of profits. In general, debtholders have priority over all classes of stockholders.

Eastern Oklahoma Television Co. v. Ameco, Inc.

437 F.2d 138 (10th Cir. 1971)

In an action for damages brought by Eastern Oklahoma Television Company (plaintiff) against Ameco, Inc. (defendant), in which certain promoters and original subscribers of Eastern Oklahoma Television Co. (KTEN) became third party defendants, the basic issue was whether corporate stock allotted to the promoters in consideration of services rendered and property furnished had been validly issued. There was an appeal from the ruling that the stock was valid. Affirmed.

C. C. Morris, Brown Morris, and Bill Hoover were owners and operators of two radio stations in Ada, Oklahoma. In 1953, they organized KTEN to operate a TV station in Ada. They obtained a channel from the Federal Communications Commission, pledging all of the assets of the radio stations to "undergird" the venture, personally guaranteed payment to Radio Corporation of America in the amount of $240,000 for equipment, designed the facilities, planned the operations and hired and trained personnel. The articles of incorporation authorized 650 shares of Class A voting stock and 650 shares of Class B nonvoting stock, both classes having a par value of $500 per share.

The Class B Stock was sold to the public at par by the promoters, who were also the directors. Each subscriber was told of the necessary organizational services which had been or were to be performed by the directors and that the Class A stock would be alloted to them. The subscriptions and payments on the Class B stock were to be held in escrow in a local bank until the construction permit from the FCC was received. The Class A stock was issued by a resolution of the directors which recited that the consideration was their experience in broadcasting, their standing with the FCC and their personal guarantee of the debt to RCA for equipment.

The early years of operation of KTEN were plagued with financial difficulties. The promoters not only returned 250 shares of Class A stock to the treasury to be sold for working capital but also made personal loans to the corporation. $170,000 worth of preferred stock was also issued. One of the original shareholders contests the validity of the stock issued to Bill Hoover, one of the two major Class A shareholders.

PICKETT, CIRCUIT JUDGE. It is first argued that the directors in the meeting of January 22, 1954, did not have a quorum and could not vote the issuance of shares to themselves as such action was in contravention of their fiduciary responsibility to the corporation, since at that moment they had a personal interest in the resolution and were hence disqualified as interested directors. A contract between a corporation and an interested director, which in essence is what the stock issuance in the instant case presents, does not render the contract void per se but at most merely voidable at the option of the corporation. . . . It is obvious that the directors and Class A shareholders were completely informed of and had consented to the resolution since they were one and the same as the interested directors who had passed the resolution. Likewise, it was found by the trial court . . . that the Class B shareholders were informed prior to their subscription for shares that the Class A shares were to be issued to the directors for their organizational services and property received by the corporation, all of which was of considerable value to the corporation. Under such circumstances we conclude that the shares were issued with the full knowledge and consent of all parties at the time and the resolution had at least been ratified by the acquiescence of the Class B shareholders.

It is further urged that the issuance of the stock to the directors was in violation of the Oklahoma Constitution and statutes as having been made without adequate consideration. The record clearly discloses that the stock transfer was for property, goodwill, extensive valuable services rendered, and the personal guaranty given by the directors for the RCA note. That the corporation received valuable services and property from the organizers cannot be doubted. Apparently from the beginning they contributed their time and abilities, together with the risk of all their personal assets for the corporate success. The goodwill, which included Hoover's experience, expertise, and favorable broadcasting record with the FCC was extremely valuable in the acquisition of FCC permits by KTEN and in the actual construction of the station, including the design and construction of a signal relay system from Oklahoma City. Where goodwill constitutes property and if actually existent and of value at the time, it may be included in determining a valid consideration for the issuance of stock. . . .

In objecting to the personal guaranty upon the RCA note as part of the consideration for the issuance of shares, appellants rely on the rule in Oklahoma that a promissory note or other obligation of the subscriber is not valid consideration for such purposes. But here, the guaranty was for an obligation of the corporation. Absent the guaranty, the essential equipment for the operation of a television station could not have been obtained. The organizers personally furnished the security for the purchase of this property. Without it the cost to the corporation would have been substantial if it had been possible to obtain the security by other means. The record clearly indicates that the result of this security was the completion of the station, which eventually led to a successful corporate operation. The guaranty was valuable property or services within the meaning of the Oklahoma Constitution.

Kinds of Equity Securities

Par and No Par. Most statutes permit corporations to issue either par or no-par stock.[6] If a par value is established, it is done so in the articles. However, par is not always the price at which the corporation will sell par value shares. The Model Act (18) provides that the price of par value stock is to be established from time to time by the directors, but it cannot be less than the value stated in the articles of incorporation except for treasury stock.[7] If sold for more than par, the overage becomes "capital surplus." A few states permit corporations to issue stock for less than par value in certain circumstances.

The Model Act (18) and the Delaware Act both give to the directors the right to establish the issue price of no-par stock, but this right can be given to the shareholders by an appropriate provision in the articles. Under the Model Act (21) the directors may allocate some proportion of the sales price of no-par stock to capital surplus; otherwise it is all allocated to stated capital.

Common Stock. If a corporation has only one class of stock, it is common stock. When there is more than one class of stock, the common shareholders generally bear the major risks of the venture and stand to profit most if it is successful. Therefore, ordinarily no special contract rights or preferences are granted to common shareholders. They receive what is left over after the preferences of other classes have been satisfied, both with respect to net earnings payable in dividends and net assets upon liquidation. To balance this, they generally have control or the predominant voice in management.

However, there is under the Model Act and most statutes no limit on the ingenuity of promoters and their financial advisors in apportioning prefer-

---

[6] Nebraska prohibits no-par stock.

[7] Delaware allows directors to set a lower price after a good faith determination that par value cannot be obtained.

ences, rights, and limitations to suit their interests and those of prospective buyers of the securities. As a result, the distinction between common and preferred stock is frequently blurred. It is not unusual to have one class of common shares with voting rights, perhaps designated "Class A," and another without voting rights except in case of certain extraordinary transactions which might be referred to as "Class B" shares.

Preferred Stock. Classes of stock that have rights or preferences over other classes of stock are called preferred stock. Preferred shareholders are customarily given preference as to dividends and in the distribution of assets on the dissolution of the corporation. In regard to dividends the preferences granted may vary greatly. The stock may be cumulative or noncumulative, and participating or nonparticipating. Dividends on cumulative preferred, if not paid in any year, will be payable later if funds are available for payment of dividends, whereas dividends on noncumulative preferred not earned and paid in any one year are not payable at a later date. Participating preferred has priority as to a stated amount or percentage of the dividends, and after a prescribed dividend is paid to common shareholders, the preferred shareholders participate with the common shareholders in additional dividends paid. Various combinations, such as cumulative participating or noncumulative participating, may be issued. If funds are not available for the payment of dividends, no dividends will be paid on preferred stock regardless of the type of stock. Under the Model Act (45) and the laws of substantially all states, it is unlawful to pay dividends out of capital.

Preferred stock may be made redeemable, and provision may be made for the setting up of a sinking fund for the redemption of such stock. It may be convertible, in which case provision will be made whereby it may be converted into common stock or into other securities of the corporation. Preferred stock may be given voting rights, usually in the event of default in the payment of dividends.

The preferences granted will usually be set out in the articles of incorporation. The Model Act (15 and 16) provides that the preferences of the various classes, if more than one, must be stated in the articles of incorporation but permits the articles to authorize the directors to issue any preferred class of stock in series and to establish variations between the different series with respect to: (1) the rate of dividend; (2) whether the stock may be redeemed, and if so, the price and terms of redemption; (3) the amount payable upon the stock in liquidation; (4) sinking-fund provisions, if any, for redemption of the stock; and (5) the terms and conditions, if any, on which the stock may be converted.

Warrants, Rights, and Options. The Delaware Act and the Model Act (20), as well as other statutes, specifically permit the directors to issue options or rights to purchase shares of the corporation, whether or not in connection with the sale of its other securities. If they are to be issued to directors, officers, or employees, shareholder approval must be secured under the Model Act. In the absence of fraud the judgment of the directors as to the adequacy of the consideration received is conclusive.

Options to purchase stock of a corporation which are evidenced by a certificate are known as warrants. They give the holder the right to buy a specified number of shares of the stock (usually common) at a specified price and they generally have a termination date. Although customarily issued in combination with another security, warrants may be bought and sold alone and may be listed on the American Stock Exchange. Although out of favor for a period after the 1920s, warrants have been used rather extensively in recent years both as a "sweetener" in public- and private-debt placement and as a separate security usually issued as part of a "package" in connection with a merger or acquisition offer.

The term "rights" is usually applied to short-term and often nonnegotiable options. They usually are a device used to give a present security holder the right to subscribe to some proportional quantity of the same or a different security in his corporation, often pursuant to preemptive right requirements.

SUMMARY

Under most statutes corporations may issue common or preferred stock as par or no par shares. If there is more than one class of stock, the common shareholders generally bear the major risks of the venture, stand to gain the most, and have control of the corporation. If there is only one class, it will be common. Usually the common shareholders' claim to both income and assets come after other investors, but they are generally given the predominant or sole right to select the management.

Preferred shareholders are usually given preferences over one or more other classes of stock as to dividends and distribution of assets in case of liquidation. The shares may be cumulative or noncumulative as to dividends. Preferred stock may be redeemable either with or without a sinking fund.

Warrants and rights are options to purchase shares.

Stock Subscriptions, Issuance, Transfer, and Redemption

Nature of Stock Subscription. In the absence of statutes most courts have held that preincorporation subscriptions to stock are merely offers which continue open until the corporation is chartered and that subscribers may revoke their offers at any time before the occurrence of that event. Other courts have held that the subscription is a mutual agreement between the subscribers and enforceable unless all subscribers agree to release each other. The Model Act (17) and the statutes of Delaware and many other states make such subscriptions irrevocable for a period of six months in the absence of a contrary provision in the subscription. Several states provide either that the filing of articles of incorporation or the issuance of the certificate constitute acceptance of the subscriptions. Delaware and several other states require all stock subscriptions to be in writing, but the Model Act does not.[8]

If a subscription is made for the unissued shares of stock of an existing corporation, the generally accepted view is that the subscription is an offer to purchase which ripens into a contract on acceptance by the corporation. On acceptance the subscriber immediately becomes a stockholder, even though the delivery of the stock certificates is postponed until the purchase price of the stock is paid. An existing corporation may, in soliciting subscriptions for its unissued stock, so word its subscription agreement that it amounts to an offer to sell which is accepted when the subscriber agrees to purchase.

The subscription may provide for payment of the price of the stock on a specified day or in installments or it may be payable upon call of the board of directors. The Model Act (17) requires that calls for payment must be uniform as to all shares of the same class or series.

Issuing Shares of Stock. When a person has subscribed for stock in a proposed or existing corporation and the subscription has been accepted, the making of the contract between the subscriber and the corporation is generally termed "issuing stock," and thereafter the subscriber is a shareholder. If the subscription agreement is a preincorporation agreement and more stock is subscribed than the corporation is authorized to issue, the corporation will, as a general rule, issue stock to the subscribers on a pro rata basis. Under the general rule, stock subscribed for by preincorporation agreement is issued when the corporation is chartered.

Although one can be a shareholder without having been issued a stock certificate and before fully paying for the shares, the Model Act (23) provides that no certificate shall be issued until the shares are fully paid. It also provides (25) that an assignee or transferee of shares or a subscriber in good faith and without notice will not be personally liable to the corporation or its creditors for any unpaid portion of the consideration for the shares.

Liability of Issuer under U.C.C. A corporation has a duty not to issue more than the shares authorized by its articles and often employs a bank or trust company as a registrar to prevent overissue through error in the issuance or transfer of its stock. Overissued shares are void. However, the Uniform Commercial Code (8–104) requires the issuer to obtain identical stock, if

---

[8] Shares of stock are not considered goods. Therefore, a preincorporation subscription is not covered by the statute of frauds and need not be in writing.

reasonably available, and to deliver it to the holder or, if unavailable, to reimburse holder for the value paid plus interest.

Transfer of Corporate Stock. Stock certificates have the effect of making the stock registered investment securities under Article 8, since they specifically name the owner or owners. Most stock certificates have an assignment form printed on the back, and this is indorsed by the registered owner to effect a transfer. However, a separate document, often referred to as a "stock power," may be used for assignment. If an assignment of a stock certificate is made without naming a transferee, it becomes transferable by delivery and is called a "street certificate."

Bonds, debentures, and notes, are also covered by Article 8 as investment securities. A registered bond is transferred in the same manner as a stock certificate while a bearer bond is transferred by delivery. Interest is paid on the latter upon the presentation to the issuer or its agent of an interest coupon attached to the bond which is due and payable.

Restrictions on Transfer. In the absence of a valid restriction, investment securities are freely transferable. In close corporations the shareholders often wish not only to select carefully their original business associates but to control the future disposition of the stock so that they can choose competent and compatible associates or keep control in the remaining members. However, any restriction that would in effect make the stock nontransferable would be against public policy and void. Therefore, the validity of a restriction will turn on whether it is reasonable in objective and degree. Keeping outsiders from becoming shareholders and maintaining the proportionate interests between shareholders are usually held to be proper objectives. The most common restriction requires the shareholder to offer his or her stock to the corporation and/or proportionately to other shareholders before transferring it to an outsider. The restriction may be imposed in the bylaws or by agreement between the shareholder and the corporation, but it appears from the cases that where there is doubt the restriction is more likely to be enforced if it is stated in the articles of incorporation. To be effective against anyone not having actual knowledge of it, the restriction must be noted conspicuously on the certificate (U.C.C. 8–204).

Corporation's Duty to Transfer. A corporation owes a duty to register the transfer of any registered security presented to it for registration, provided the security has been properly endorsed and other legal formalities have been complied with. (8–401.) If the corporation refuses to make the transfer, it is liable to the transferee. The nature of the corporation's liability will depend on the laws of the state having jurisdiction of the case and the surrounding circumstances. In some cases the transferee has been able to recover the value of the stock in a suit in conversion, and in other cases the transferee has been granted the remedy of specific performance by a court of equity.

The corporation has the right to make reasonable inquiry and investigation before it transfers stock or registered bonds. It will not be liable for any delay which is reasonably necessary to make whatever investigation the circumstances of the case warrant. If the corporation has a lien on the stock for an obligation owed to the corporation by the shareholder, it has the right to refuse to register a transfer until the obligation is satisfied. However, any lien in favor of the corporation, if it is to be valid against a purchaser of the security, must be noted conspicuously on the security. (8–103.)

If the owner of corporate stock or bonds dies, the ownership of such security passes to his or her estate, and the administrator or executor has the right to transfer the security. The procedure followed will depend on the probate laws of the state of domicile. If the corporate security is held by one acting as trustee, the trustee is the legal owner of the stock, but such trustee may not have the authority to sell. The procedure to be followed in obtaining a new registered security or the transfer of a lost, destroyed, or stolen security is set out in Section 8–405.

Redemption and Purchase of Stock by Corporation. It is quite common for corporations to issue preferred stock subject to call or redemption. Redemption is an involuntary sale by the shareholder at a fixed price. Under the Model Act (15) the right of the corporation to redeem a preferred stock issue and the redemption price must be stated in the articles of incorporation. Redemption is not permitted when the corporation is or would become insolvent or when the prior claim of other shareholders upon its assets would be impaired (66). It has been held that preferred shares may be redeemed in the absence of statute if the articles so provide.

A corporation may purchase from any willing seller any of its securities without specific authorization in its articles. In the Model Act (6) and most other statutes the restrictions safeguarding creditors and other shareholders are more confining than in the case of redemption. The Model Act permits such purchases only out of unrestricted earned surplus or, upon a majority vote of shareholders, unrestricted capital surplus may be used. When redeemable shares are reacquired by the corporation, the Model Act (67) requires their cancellation but purchased shares may be held as treasury shares and resold, or they may be canceled (5).

SUMMARY

A stock subscription is an agreement to purchase a stated number of shares of stock when issued. Generally a preincorporation subscription agreement is treated as an offer which is accepted when the corporation is chartered. A subscription to purchase the unissued stock of an existing corporation is an offer to buy stock, and a contract is completed when the corporation accepts the offer. Immediately on acceptance the subscriber becomes a stockholder, irrespective of when the stock certificate evidencing the shares of stock is executed and delivered.

Stock is issued when the contract to purchase it is completed.

The Uniform Commercial Code in Article 8 sets forth the duties and liabilities of the corporation as issuer of stocks and bonds, which are referred to as investment securities and are given characteristics of negotiable instruments.

A corporation may usually redeem preferred stock if such a power is reserved in its articles. Generally it may purchase any outstanding securities without a provision in the articles.

B&H Warehouse, Inc. v. Atlas Van Lines, Inc.

490 F.2d 818 (5th Cir. 1974)

This was a shareholder action by B&H Warehouse, Inc. (plaintiff) against Atlas Van Lines, Inc. (defendant), seeking damages for conversion of its stock in Atlas because of a restriction upon its alienability or, alternatively, for a declaratory judgment that the restriction is invalid. Appeal by B&H from a judgment upholding the validity of the restriction. Reversed and remanded.

Atlas is a Delaware corporation engaged in the interstate transportation of household goods with its shares held by local truckers participating in its operations. B&H purchased 30 shares of Atlas stock in 1949, the year after Atlas was incorporated. At that time there were no restrictions on the stockholders' right to sell their shares. However, in 1950 B&H put its shares in a voting trust which prohibited sale without first giving Atlas an opportunity to purchase them at book value. The trust was terminated in 1961. In 1966 the Atlas articles of incorporation were amended to provide that alienation could be accomplished only after offering the shares to the corporation at $100 per share over book value. 1970 amendments required the offer to the corporation to be at book value. A 1967 amendment to the Delaware corporation law provided that restrictions on transferability of securities would not be binding as to those issued prior to the adoption of the restriction unless the holders are parties to an agreement or voted in favor of the restriction. Paragraph 14 of the Atlas articles provides that all rights conferred upon stockholders are subject to amendment or repeal.

B&H alleged that the market value of its shares was $60,000 greater than book value, which is the price at which the 1970 restriction requires offering them to the corporation before sale to others.

MORGAN, CIRCUIT JUDGE. [T]he Delaware courts, while following the general rule that any amendment is permissible if it is authorized by the articles of incorporation (and, by implication, the corporation law), have at times vacillated from that position and read into the unrestricted constitutional provisions certain limitations.

The *Lawson* line of cases demonstrates that if the restriction being contested had been included in the original articles of incorporation, or had been a part of the by-laws when B&H acquired its stock, there would be no question that the restriction would be valid. Alternatively, if B&H had specifically agreed to the possibility that its shares might at some future time be encumbered with such a restriction, we would have no trouble in upholding the restriction.

But neither situation confronts us here. In this case, all B&H agreed to was the very general right to amend which is included in virtually every corporate charter and in the Delaware corporation law. What we must decide is whether these provisions provided B&H with sufficient notice that it can be held to have assented to such a change.

After a careful consideration of all of the factors in this area of the law, we conclude that the courts of Delaware would rule that the restriction is invalid. Although the restriction would have been valid had it been in effect when B&H obtained its stock, to add it afterwards contravenes two important policy considerations prevalent in the law of Delaware. The first is the rule that restraints on alienation are disfavored generally. We interpret this rule of law to mean that whenever there is ambiguity or uncertainty, the restraint ought not to be enforced. The second is that restrictions on alienation are to be allowed only so long as they reasonably relate to a valid corporate purpose. There is a valid purpose involved in this case. That is, Atlas is organized as a cooperative association of transport companies, that and the restriction was [sic] obviously intended to retain control of Atlas among its associated moving companies. Nevertheless, we find that the restraint being challenged is too restrictive to be sustained by reference to this purpose. The interest of Atlas in restricting ownership to associated movers could have been accomplished, at least with respect to those obtaining stock before the amendment took effect, by providing that the corporation would have its right of first refusal based on the market price of the shares. We would then have a situation like the one in *Tu-Vu,* in which only the choice of buyer and not the amount of money to be received for the stock would have been restricted. Such a mechanism would have been much more closely related to the valid corporate purpose. But in forcing shareholders to offer their shares to the corporation at book value, Atlas has imposed a restriction significantly broader than necessary to effectuate its purpose. When this occurs, it cannot be said that the general grant of the power to amend contained in the fourteenth paragraph of the articles of incorporation suffices to validate the amendment. B&H can be held to have assented only to amendments reasonably related to a valid corporate purpose, not to any and all amendments which a majority of shareholders agree upon, regardless of their content. We are unwilling to hold that B&H consented to being bound by the contested restrictions because of the very vague language of the fourteenth paragraph.

Ling and Co. v. Trinity Savings and Loan Ass'n

482 S.W.2d 841 (Sup. Ct. Tex. 1972)

Action by Trinity Savings and Loan Association (plaintiff) against Bruce Bowman and Ling and Company, Inc. (defendants), to recover balance due on a note and to foreclose on Bowman's collateral, which consisted of 1500 shares of Ling and Co. class A common stock. Summary judgment for Trinity affirmed by Court of Appeals. Reversed and remanded.

Ling contended that its articles restricted transferability of the shares. It argued that Bowman's assignment to Trinity violated this restriction and therefore Trinity was not entitled to the shares.

On the front side of the stock certificates in small print, it was stated that the shares were subject to the provisions of the articles of incorporation, that a copy could be obtained from the secretary of the corporation or the secretary of state and that specific references to provisions setting forth preferences, limitations, and restrictions were on the back of the certificate. On the back, also in small type, the reference to the articles was repeated and specific reference was made to article four. It referred to a number of rights and limitations contained in article four, including those which:

> Restrict the transfer, sale, assignment, pledge, hypothecation, or encumbrance of any of the shares represented hereby under certain conditions, and which under certain conditions require the holder thereof to grant options to purchase the shares represented hereby first to the Corporation and then pro rata to the other holders of the Class A common stock.

REAVLEY, JUSTICE. The court of civil appeals struck down the restrictions for three reasons: the lack of conspicuous notice thereof on the stock certificate, the unreasonableness of the restrictions, and statutory prohibition against an option in favor of other stockholders whenever they number more than 20. [Discussion of the third reason is omitted here.]

CONSPICUOUSNESS

The Texas Business Corporation Act as amended in 1957, provides that a corporation may impose restrictions on the transfer of its stock if they are "expressly set forth in the articles of incorporation . . . and . . . copied at length or in summary form on the face or so copied on the back and referred to on the face of each certificate. . . ." The Legislature at the same time, permitted the incorporation by reference on the face or back of the certificate of the provision of the articles of incorporation which restricts the transfer of the stock. The court of civil appeals objected to the general reference to the articles of incorporation and the failure to print the full conditions imposed upon the transfer of the shares. However, reference is made on the face of the certificate to the restrictions described on the reverse side; the notice on the reverse side refers to the particular article of the articles of incorporation as restricting the transfer or encumbrance and requiring "the holder hereof to grant options to purchase the shares represented hereby first to the Corporation and then pro rata to the other holders of the class A Common Stock. . . ." We hold that the content of the certificate complies with the requirements of the Texas Business Corporation Act.

There remains the requirement of the Texas Business and Commerce Code that the restriction or reference thereto on the certificate must be conspicuous. [UCC 8–204] requires that a restriction on transferability be "noted conspicuously on the security." [UCC 1–201(10)] defines "conspicuous" and makes the determination a question of law for the court to decide. It is provided that a conspicuous term is so written as to be noticed by a reasonable person. Examples of conspicuous matter are given there as a "printed heading in capitals . . . [or] larger or other contrasting type or color." This means that something must appear on the face of the certificate to attract the attention of a reasonable person when he looks at it.

Our holding that the restriction is not noted conspicuously on the certificate does not entitle Trinity Savings and Loan to a summary judgment under this record. The restriction is effective against a person with actual knowledge of it. The record does not establish conclusively that Trinity Savings and Loan lacked knowledge of the restriction on January 28, 1969, the date the record indicates when Bowman executed an assignment of this stock to Trinity Savings and Loan.

REASONABLENESS

A corporation may impose restrictions on disposition of its stock if the restrictions "do not unreasonably restrain or prohibit transferability." The court of civil appeals has held that the restrictions on the transferability of this stock are unreasonable for two reasons: because of the required approval of the New York Stock Exchange and because of successive options to purchase given the corporation and the other holders of the same class of stock.

Ling & Company in its brief states that it was a brokerage house member of the New York Stock Exchange at an earlier time and that Rule 315 of the Exchange required approval of any sale or pledge of the stock. Under these circumstances we must disagree with the court of civil appeals holding that this provision of article 4D of the articles of incorporation is "arbitrary, capricious, and unreasonable." Nothing appears in the summary judgment proof on this matter, and the mere provision in the article is no cause for vitiating the restrictions as a matter of law.

It was also held by the intermediate court that it is unreasonable to require a shareholder to notify all other record holders of Class A Common Stock of his intent to sell and to give the other holders a ten day option to buy. The record does not reveal the number of holders of this class of stock; we only know that there are more than twenty. We find nothing unusual or oppressive in these first option provisions. Conceivably the number of stockholders might be so great as to make the burden too heavy upon the stockholder who wishes to sell and, at the same time, dispel any justification for contending that there exists a reasonable corporate purpose in restricting the ownership. But there is no showing of that nature in this summary judgment record.

Problem Cases

1. Mr. and Mrs. McDaniel owned an 800-acre farm in Maryland and operated a restaurant in New Jersey. Through the efforts of Zimmerman, president of AG Industries, a corporation engaged in management of cattle raising and feeding, they became interested in participating in an investment group that would lease their farm and conduct there a substantial cattle feeding and perhaps breeding operation. Several meetings of the McDaniels with representatives of AG Industries and with two other prospective investors, Vogel and Mumma, were held and they proposed to form a corporation. On May 15, AG's farm manager advised the group that planting must be started immediately or the proposed operations would have to be postponed for a year. Zimmerman called Vogel for authority to plant, and Vogel instructed him to call the McDaniels, who granted permission to plant the first 200 acres. AG's farm manager purchased seed, fertilizer, and herbicide from Service Feed and Supply, Inc. in the name of the proposed corporation. However, Vogel and Mumma disagreed on financing at a meeting held in early June between the McDaniels, Vogel, and Mumma, and the contract to form the corporation was not signed and no lease of the farm was executed.

   Service Feed and Supply's bill for $16,053 remained unpaid, and it sued the McDaniels on the ground they were promoters of the aborted corporation. The trial court found the McDaniels liable, and Mrs. McDaniel appealed. Is she liable?

2. Watchie, a Seattle real estate broker, finder, and developer, became interested in several tracts of real estate near Portland, Oregon. He made an extensive study of population trends, availability of utilities, and acquired other data likely to affect the success of a proposed development. After acquiring options to purchase 965 acres at a total of $729,000, he interested a syndicate composed of Seattle investors to put up the money. The arrangement was that he would take title to the land as trustee and it would be held until it could be resold at double the purchase price.

   Two years later he decided to form a publicly owned corporation, Park City Corporation, to acquire that land at $1,458,000 and an additional 1,600 acres adjacent to it. He prepared a stock subscription agreement setting forth the development plans in detail which stated that the property would be acquired by Park City at cost plus a commission to Watchie. The venture was financially unsuccessful, and Watchie resigned as president. New directors and officers were elected, and they caused the corporation to file suit against Watchie for recovery of secret profits because he had sold the 965 acres to the corporation at twice its cost to him without disclosing the profit to subsequent subscribers.

   For how much, if any, is Watchie liable to the Corporation?

3. Richard L. Chartrand and Barney E. O'Malia agreed to form a corporation. The agreement provided that they would contribute $80,000 each to a proposed corporation, Barney's Club, Inc., and both would receive 255 shares or 25½ percent of the outstanding stock. The corporation was formed with O'Malia acting as president and director. The other two directors of Barney's Club, Inc., were O'Malia's wife and son, so for all intents and purposes O'Malia ran the corporation. After incorporation and acceptance by the corporation of Chartrand's $80,000, the board of directors issued 240 shares to Chartrand,

240 shares to O'Malia, 15 shares to O'Malia's son, and 15 shares to O'Malia's wife. Chartrand sues to compel the corporation to issue him 15 additional shares of stock. Can the corporation be compelled to issue the stock even though Chartrand and O'Malia's agreement was entered into before incorporation?

4. Mr. and Mrs. Dooley owned real estate which they leased to the Akel Corporation. At the time the lease was entered into the Akel Corporation had not been incorporated, although incorporation was completed prior to the start of the leasehold term. Can the Dooleys hold Mr. and Mrs. Akel, owners and officers of the corporation who executed the lease, personally liable on it if the Dooleys were unaware at the time of executing the lease that the corporation was nonexistent?

5. Quaker Hill negotiated with Parr and Presba, principal officers of Denver Memorial Gardens, a corporation which had recently been formed to operate a cemetery, for the sale of a large quantity of nursery stock. Quaker Hill suggested that a separate corporation be formed to consummate the order. An agreement providing for a down payment of $1,000 with the balance, $13,500, due one year later and guaranteeing replacement of stock that might die was signed, "Denver Memorial Nursery, Inc., E. D. Parr, Pres., James P. Presba, Sec'y.-Treas."

   Because of name confusion, Denver Memorial Nursery was never formed, but articles for Mountain View Nurseries, Inc., were properly filed about a week after the purchase was made. Then, at the suggestion of Quaker Hill, a new contract in the name of Mountain View Nurseries was prepared and signed by the same individuals. Neither Denver Memorial nor Mountain View ever functioned as a going concern nor had any assets. The nursery stock died prior to the due date of the balance. Can Quaker Hill hold Parr and Presba personally for the balance?

6. Van Noy and Gibbs formed a corporation to operate an amusement center. Shortly thereafter they got into a dispute over management of the business and each offered to buy the other out. At that time they both believed the corporation owned a lease valued at $3,100 on the premises occupied by the amusement center. Other assets of the corporation had a value of $6,900. The dispute was resolved by Van Noys assigning his shares to Gibbs for $2,000, of which Gibbs paid $750 down. Gibbs refused to pay any more when it was discovered that the lease was not valid, and Van Noys sued.

   Is Gibbs entitled to recision of the contract because of mutual mistake?

7. Stetenfeld and two others organized Area, Inc., in 1970 to engage in the real estate business. Each of the firm's three founders was issued 2,500 shares. The other two paid $2,500 cash but Stetenfeld gave his unsecured promissory note. The note was paid prior to February 25, 1972. In March 1972 Stetenfeld resigned as general manager at the request of the board of directors because of disagreement over his management practices. In connection with the resignation, a settlement of all outstanding accounts between Stetenfeld and the corporation was made. Under this agreement, Stetenfeld sold his 2,500 shares back to the corporation for $44,000 ($17.60 per share, which was the computed book value) and was paid $5,241 in separation pay.

   Stetenfeld, who was not an accountant, had kept the books. After his departure an audit was conducted by a CPA. The auditor, primarily as a result of making an allowance for tax liability on deferred commissions consistent with generally accepted accounting practice (even though no actual tax liability was expected), computed book value at $12.48 per share. He also pointed out that the original issue of stock to Stetenfeld had been improper. The board then discontinued its monthly payments to Stetenfeld under the repurchase agreement.

   Is Area, Inc., entitled to rescission of the stock repurchase agreement under a statute that provided: "A promissory note or future service does not constitute payment or part payment for shares of a corporation?"

8. The Chicago Stadium Corp. and the Chicago Blackhawk Hockey Team, Inc. owned 52 percent of the stock of Medicor, which operated an ice show business. Thomas Scallen, its president, owned 16 percent. The remaining 32 percent of the shares were publicly held. Scallen had control of the board of directors. Management of the two corporate shareholders decided in mid-1975 that Scallen should be removed as president of Medicor. On October 10, after considerable pressure from the dissatisfied corporate shareholders, Medicor mailed notice of a special shareholders' meeting for the election of directors on November 1. Prior to that meeting, on October 17, the board of directors met and authorized issuance of 623,710 shares to Scallen in exchange for the cancellation of an alleged debt of $311,859 of Scallen to Medicor. The effect was to give Scallen 46 percent, the corporate shareholders only 34 percent, and to leave 20 percent of the shares held publicly.

   The alleged indebtedness had been outstanding for several years and included notes payable to Scallen and a claim for accrued salary while Scallen was out of the United States for an extended period of time. The corporate shareholders contest the validity of both alleged debts and also claim that the shares were substantially undervalued. The board issued the shares despite the opinion of counsel that there was substantial doubt as to the validity of such action. Medicor admitted that the purpose of issuing the shares was to perpetuate Scallen's control because the directors thought "a change in management would not be in the best interests of the corporation at a critical point in its business cycle."

   Should the trial court grant a temporary injunction against issuance of the shares to Scallen and prohibit Scallen and Medicor from cancelling or delaying the shareholders' meeting?

9. Mr. Steak issued 2,400 shares of stock to Price, its employee. The stock was issued for investment purposes only and not for redistribution. This was known to Price. However the stock certificate had no notation of any restrictive legend. Price pledged these shares as security for a loan from Edina State Bank. The bank asked Price if there was any restriction on the stock and Price said no. Later the bank, in an attempt to secure its position offered 1,000 shares for sale. These were sold; however, the transfer agent refused to register the transfer on advice from Mr. Steak that the shares were restricted. Edina sued Mr. Steak as issuer of the stock for refusal to register the transfer of the pledged shares.

   Should Edina recover for its loss?

10. Theodore Sette and L. M. Stenehjem and their wives together purchased a majority of the shares in the State Bank of Burleigh County, North Dakota, in 1961. The shareholders entered into an agreement that before any shares would be sold they would be offered to the spouse and then next to the other couple at the then book value plus the same ratio over book value paid when the majority interest was purchased. Nothing as to the agreement was added to the stock certificates. Sette assumed the presidency and the bank was moved to Bismarck, where he lived. Stenehjem continued to manage another bank in Watford City.

   In October 1970 Sette suffered a stroke, and his son James gradually assumed some of the father's duties. Disagreements then arose between the Settes and Stenehjems, one of them over the Sette's desire to make James president. In January 1972, without the knowledge of the Settes, Stenehjem entered into an agreement with the Wildfang heirs to vote their shares, which with Stenehjem's then constituted a majority, as a bloc to make Stenehjem chief executive. The two Sette's resigned later in 1972, at which time Settes offered to sell their stock to Stenehjem. He declined.

In September 1973, unknown to Stenehjem, Uttke of Baker, Montana, paid $40,000 to the Settes for an option until December to purchase their stock for cash, and the Wildfang heirs gave a similar option. Uttke, without disclosing his option, asked Stenehjem if he would sell. He was told that Stenehjem would not and that it was probable that no other block was for sale. Uttke was not told of the 1961 agreement restricting sale of the stock, and he found no restriction on the Sette stock certificates he had examined. Between 1961 and 1973 there had been a number of transfers of stock to Sette and Stenehjem relatives and to several business people in Bismarck without regard to the 1961 agreement. Uttke resigned the presidency of a bank and moved to Bismarck.

Stenehjem then brought an action against the Settes and Uttke to enforce the 1961 agreement by requiring the Settes to sell their stock to the Stenehjems. The trial court held that since no statute was applicable, both the Stenehjems and the Settes had waived the restrictions on transfer by their previous actions in disregarding the 1961 agreement and that Uttke's attempted purchase is valid. Should this be affirmed?

27

Operating the Corporate Business

Corporate Powers

Sources of Powers. A corporation obtains its powers from the state, and it cannot have powers that exceed those conferred by the constitution and statutes of the state of its incorporation and its articles of incorporation. The articles of incorporation may also limit the powers of the corporation, most frequently by the manner in which its purpose or scope of business is described.

A few states limit or prohibit the acquisition of agricultural land by corporations, including trust departments of banks. Corporations have, in the recent past, been denied altogether the privilege of engaging in some of the professions such as, for instance, that of law, medicine, or dentistry. However, a number of states have recently enacted statutes that permit physicians and other professionals to incorporate as "Professional Associations" or "P.A.s" in order to take advantage of federal tax laws encouraging establishment of retirement plans by corporations. Some of these statutes expressly provide that individual liability is not limited.

The powers outlined by Blackstone that were referred to in Chapter 25 have long been considered inherent in the corporate form of organization. The trend in this century has been to increase the powers of business corporation by court decision as well as statute. Section 4 of the Model Act sets out the general powers of corporations to be chartered under it. A number of these and the powers added in Sections 5 and 6 are inserted specifically because earlier decisions had denied or raised a doubt about such a power. Examples of provisions to remove doubt include: to make gifts for charitable and educational purposes (4m),[1] to enter a partnership (4p), to indemnify the corporation's officers and directors who are defendants in suits growing out of their performance of corporate duties (5), and to purchase and dispose of its own shares (6). Also the 1969 revision (4n) states that the corporation may "transact any lawful business which the board of directors shall find will be in aid of governmental policy." This was inserted to clarify an earlier provision authorizing the corporation to aid the United States government in time of war. In an era of undeclared wars this provision was too narrow. The revised clause is intended to cover other governmental programs such as the elimination of poverty.

Limitations in Articles of Incorporation. Under both the Model Act (54) and the Delaware statute it is unnecessary to enumerate in the articles the powers set out in the incorporation statute. It is, however, required to state the corporate purposes. The purposes can be phrased in the broadest and most general terms or "for any lawful purpose." However, the incorporators may desire to use the statement of purpose as a self-imposed limitation. The statement becomes then a promise on the part of the corporation to its shareholders that it will confine the business risks taken by the corporation to those normally incident to the operation of a business such as that defined in the purpose section of the articles of incorporation.

The *Ultra Vires* Doctrine. The original conception of the corporation was that it was an artificial person created by and given limited powers by the state. It was deduced from this view that any act of the corporation that is beyond the authority given it by the state is void as being *ultra vires.* Therefore, any act not permitted by the statute under which it is incorporated or by its articles of incorporation that are consistent with that statute is void for want of capacity. The lack of capacity or power in the corporation could be urged either by the corporation or the other party as a defense to a suit on a contract alleged to be *ultra vires.* Oftentimes it was merely a convenient justification for reneging on an agreement no longer considered desirable.

The Model Business Corporation Act (7) and the Delaware statute have eliminated such collateral attacks on the capacity of the corporation. The trend in business corporation statutes toward granting corporations very broad powers and for drafters of articles of incorporation to use very broad statements of purpose have also diminished the vitality of the *ultra vires* doctrine in the states which have not abolished it.

Under Section 7 direct attacks upon *ultra vires* actions are still permitted. A shareholder may seek an injunction to restrain the corporation from carrying out a proposed action which is beyond its powers, thus seeking to prevent a

[1] The numbers in the parentheses refer to the sections of the Model Business Corporation Act, which appears in the Appendix.

breach of his or her membership contract with the corporation. The corporation itself, or through a legal representative such as a receiver or shareholder in a representative suit, may bring an action against its officers or directors for damages resulting from *ultra vires* action taken by them. Also under Section 7, the state's attorney general may enjoin the corporation from transacting unauthorized business or bring an action to dissolve the corporation as is set out in greater detail in Section 94.

Liability under the Doctrine. One reason for the strong trend toward abolishing the doctrine is that there had been much confusion and uncertainty in the holdings of the courts in regard to *ultra vires* contracts. Courts have generally refused to enforce contracts that are wholly executory but have been unwilling to strike down contracts that are fully executed by both parties even when viewed as being beyond the corporate capacity. The partially executed contracts have been the source of confusion and disagreement. The older rule was that a partially executed contract would not be enforced, although a quasi-contractual remedy might be appropriate. A majority of courts have held that such a contract is enforceable if one of the parties has received a benefit.

SUMMARY

The powers of a corporation are limited to those conferred by the constitution and statutes of the state of its incorporation, although certain traditional powers are considered inherent in the corporate form of organization. The trend of modern corporation statutes, including the Model Act, is to broaden the powers of general business corporations.

The articles of incorporation are required to set forth the purpose(s) of the corporation, which may be as broad as permitted by the statute. However, a more restricted statement of purpose acts as a self-imposed limitation for the benefit of the shareholders. Some statutes, including the Model Act, do not require a specific statement of corporate powers in the articles, and the corporation will then have all those powers granted by the statute under which it is formed.

Under the *ultra vires* doctrine any act of a corporation that is beyond the powers given to it by the state or its articles of incorporation is void, and either the corporation or the other party to a contract may allege as a defense that the making of the contract is beyond the powers of the corporation. The Model Act and some other modern statutes have eliminated this defense, but they permit shareholders or the state attorney general to enjoin an *ultra vires* act, and the corporation may bring an action against its officers or directors for damages resulting from their breach of duty in taking actions beyond the corporation's power.

Marsili v. Pacific Gas and Electric Co.

124 Cal. Rptr. 313 (Ct. App. Cal. 1975)

This was a derivative action by Mr. and Mrs. Marsili and other shareholders (plaintiffs) against Pacific Gas and Electric Co. (PG&E) and its directors as individuals (defendants) challenging the propriety of a contribution to help defeat a proposition to be voted on in a political election. Appeal from a summary judgment for PG&E. Affirmed.

On the ballot in the city election in San Francisco in 1971 was Proposition T, which would prohibit construction of any building more than 72 feet high unless the proposed building was approved in advance by the voters. A group called Citizens for San Francisco opposed Proposition T and asked PG&E to contribute $10,000 to its campaign. PG&E management reviewed the potential effect of Proposition T on the corporation. It concluded that it would raise its property taxes in San Francisco by an estimated $380,000 the first year and as much as $1,135,000 per year in ten years, and that it would also require redesigning and additional land for an already planned substation. The executive committee of the board of directors approved the contribution, it was reported to the California Public Utilities Commission and not treated as an operating expense for rate making purposes or claimed as an income tax deduction.

KANE, ASSOCIATE JUSTICE. The shareholders contend that the contribution in question was ultra vires "because neither PG&E's articles of incorporation nor the laws of this state permits PG&E to make political donations. . . ." We disagree.

By definition adopted by the shareholders themselves, "ultra vires" refers to an act which is beyond the powers conferred upon a corporation by its charter or by the laws of the state of incorporation.

The parties are in agreement that the powers conferred upon a corporation include both express powers, granted by charter or statute, and implied powers to do acts reasonably necessary to carry out the express powers. In California, the express powers which a corporation enjoys include the power to "do any acts incidental to the transaction of its business . . . or expedient for the attainment of its corporate purposes."

In addition to the exercise of such express powers, the generally recognized rule is that the management of a corporation, "in the absence of express restrictions, has discretionary authority to enter into contracts and transactions which may be deemed reasonably incidental to its business purposes."

No restriction appears in the articles of PG&E which would limit the authority of its board of directors to act upon initiative or referendum proposals affecting the affairs of the company or to engage in activities related to any other legislative or political matter in which the corporation has a legitimate concern. Furthermore, there are no statutory prohibitions in California which preclude a corporation from participating in any type of political activity. In these circumstances, the contribution by PG&E to Citizens for San Francisco was proper if it can fairly be said to fall within the express or implied powers of the corporation.

The crux of the controversy at bench, therefore, is whether a contribution toward the defeat of a local ballot proposition can ever be said to be convenient or expedient to the achievement of legitimate corporate purposes. The shareholders take the flat position that in the absence of express statutory authority corporate political contributions are illegal. This contention cannot be sustained. We believe that where, as here, the board of directors reasonably concludes that the adoption of a ballot proposition would have a direct, adverse effect upon the business of the corporation, the board of directors has abundant statutory and charter authority to oppose it.

Management of the Corporation

Authority. The shareholders are the owners of the corporation and have the ultimate power to determine the course of the business through their power to elect directors and to amend the articles. However, unlike partners they do not have, by virtue of ownership, the right and duty of management. The law gives these to the directors, who are elected by the shareholders. Shareholders' approval is required for certain extraordinary corporate matters (as discussed in Chapter 28) such as changes in the articles of incorporation, sale of assets not in the regular course of business, merger, and dissolution. The power to make other major decisions for the corporation is given to the directors, who also elect the officers and delegate to them the authority to manage the everyday operations of the business.

This right and duty of the directors to manage the corporation exists under the corporation statutes of all states, even when one person owns all of the stock of the corporation and holds the office of president and chief executive or general manager (the latter is an older term which today is used more frequently by small than large corporations). As has been frequently pointed out by students and critics of corporations, even in large, publicly held corporations the chief executive may choose the board members and/or make all policy decisions for the corporation with the board of directors acting merely as a rubber stamp. Even what may be the directors' most important duty, to choose the chief executive's successor, may effectively have been usurped by the training opportunities given to possible candidates within the organization. However, in the long run, acceptance of a rubber stamp role by the board may lead to corporate stagnation and decay and even to personal liability for the board members.

Directors

Duties and Powers of Directors. Most state statutes use wording similar to that of Section 35 before its recent amendment. It then said, "The business and affairs of a corporation shall be managed by a board of directors." This, of course, was impossible for the board as such except in quite small businesses. In 1974 the American Bar Association committee responsible for the Model Act revised this section to read, "All corporate powers shall be exercised by or under authority of, and the business and affairs of a corporation shall be managed under the direction of, a board of directors." Delaware has made a similar change in its statute. Under either version the board has the power, although normally delegated, to make all decisions for the corporation except those reserved by statute to the shareholders.

Corporate actions that can be taken only by authorization of the board under the Model Act include: authorizing a change in the registered office or registered agent of the corporation (13); establishing the time of payment of stock subscriptions (17); establishing the price for sale by the corporation of shares of stock, except when the power to establish the price of no-par stock is reserved in the articles to the shareholders (18); establishing the value of noncash consideration received for shares (19); increasing stated capital by transfer of surplus (21); adopting initial bylaws and, unless this power is reserved to the shareholders in the articles, amendment or repeal of bylaws (27); establishing record dates for dividend and shareholder meeting purposes (30); filling a vacancy on the board of directors (38); declaring dividends (45); electing officers and assigning duties to them not inconsistent with the bylaws (50); removing officers (51); and selling, leasing, or mortgaging assets of the corporation in the normal course of its business (78).

Directors are required under the Model Act to initiate and propose to the shareholders certain major changes affecting the corporation which can be accomplished only with approval of the shareholders. These include: amendments to or restatements of the articles of incorporation (59 and 62); reduction in stated capital (69); merger or consolidation (71 and 72); a sale, lease, or mortgage of substantially all assets of the corporation other than in the normal course of business (79); and a voluntary dissolution of the corporation (85).

Practices of Boards of Directors. A number of studies have been made as to what boards of the larger corporations do. The Conference Board has made periodic surveys. Although it has found wide variations in the functions of directors, seven were found to have general acceptance in its 1967 study. They were: (1) to establish the basic objectives and broad policies of the corporation; (2) to elect the corporate officers, advise them, approve their actions, and audit their performance; (3) to safeguard, and approve changes in, the corporate assets; (4) to approve important financial decisions and actions and to see that proper reports are made to shareholders; (5) to delegate special powers to officers and employees to sign contracts, open bank accounts, sign checks, borrow money, and perform other such activities; (6) to maintain, revise, and enforce the corporate articles and bylaws; and (7) to assure maintenance of a sound board through selection of the management slate at regular elections and filling interim vacancies.[2]

In a study published in 1975, The Conference Board identified four broad, overriding duties of boards as follows:

1. To protect the assets and other interests of the owners of the corporation.
2. To ensure the continuity of the corporation by enforcing the charter and bylaws and seeing that a sound board is maintained.
3. To see that the company is well managed.
4. To make certain decisions, such as the payment of dividends, that are not delegable.[3]

Some boards undertake to approve broad corporate policies in certain areas such as defining the business of the corporation in terms of products and markets and establishing guidelines for product pricing, labor relations, and so forth. However, one recent study declared that the generally accepted idea that the board selects top executives, determines policy, measures results, and asks discerning questions which uncover weaknesses or stimulate desirable executive action is a myth. The author concluded that what boards do is to advise management (rather than making business decisions), to provide some sort of discipline for management through the necessity of making reports to the board, and to act in emergencies to replace the chief executive when he or she dies or is incapacitated unexpectedly or when the chief executive's performance or the corporation's fortunes are perceived as unusually bad.[4] More recently, under prodding from the SEC and because of an increase in suits against directors, boards of publicly-held corporations seem to be more active and self-assertive.

Powers and Rights of Director as Individual. An individual director has no management function or power except as he or she may be appointed an agent of the corporation. A director does, however, have the right to inspect corporate books and records, since information concerning the corporation

---

[2] Conference Board, *Corporate Directorship Practices,* Studies in Business Policy No. 125 (New York, 1967), pp. 93–94.

[3] Jeremy Bacon and James K. Brown, *Corporate Directorship Practices: Role, Selection and Legal Status of the Board,* The Conference Board, 1975, p. 13.

[4] Miles L. Mace, "The President and the Board of Directors," *Harvard Business Review* (March–April 1972), p. 37.

and its affairs is essential for carrying out the duties of a director. Although often said to be an absolute right, in contrast to the qualified right of a shareholder, the director's right of inspection may be denied in cases where the director has an interest adverse to the corporation.

Number and Qualifications of Directors. Some states require a minimum of three directors. The Model Act (36), Delaware, and a number of other states, require only one director. This recognizes the reality that in close corporations it is not unusual for one person to own all or substantially all of the stock and that additional board members are superfluous. Most statutes, including the Model Act, provide that the number of directors may be fixed by either the articles or the bylaws. A few states require directors to be shareholders, and some require that a certain percentage be citizens of the state of incorporation and/or the United States. The Model Act makes no such requirement but permits qualifications to be specified in the articles of incorporation (35).

Most publicly held corporations and not a few close corporations have both "inside" and "outside" directors. The term "inside" director is applied to one who is an officer of the corporation or an affiliated corporation and devotes substantially his or her full time to it. The term is also often applied to controlling shareholders who are not officers and to former officers of the firm. There has been a trend toward having more "outside" members on corporate boards. Outside directors constitute the majority on the boards of more than two thirds of the 1,000 largest industrial firms.[5]

Election of Directors. Directors are elected by the shareholders at their annual meeting and normally hold office until the succeeding annual meeting or until a successor has been elected and qualified. However, most statutes, including the Model Act, permit a corporation to provide in its articles for staggered terms for directors. Under the Model Act a corporation having a board of nine or more members may establish either two or three approximately equal classes of directors with only one class of directors coming up for election at each annual meeting. Staggered terms are usually adopted to make a corporate takeover by outsiders more difficult.

Vacancies occurring on the board of directors can be filled only by the shareholders, absent a provision in the statute, articles or bylaws. Most statutes permit the directors to fill vacancies at least until the next shareholders' meeting. The Model Act (38) provides that a majority vote of the remaining directors, even though less than a quorum, is sufficient to elect persons to serve out unexpired terms. It also explicitly deals with the troublesome question whether if directors have the power to increase the size of board, they may,

[5] *The Changing Board* (New York: Heidrick and Struggles, Inc., 1977), p. 6.

without a vote by the shareholders, also fill the "vacancy" created. It provides that such "vacancy" may be filled by the directors only until the next election of directors by the shareholders.

Removal of Directors. Unless there is authorization for such shareholder action in the statute or in articles or bylaws adopted prior to his election, a director may not be removed without cause, that is without misconduct or action contrary to the interests of the corporation. Shareholders, but not directors, have inherent power to remove directors for cause and may do so even if the articles or bylaws give this power to the directors and despite a shareholder agreement. Bylaw provisions establishing the proportion of vote required are upheld, however. A shareholder agreement to elect and maintain in office certain persons as directors would prevent removal without cause by such shareholders. Before removal for cause, the director must be given adequate notice and an opportunity for a hearing.

The Model Act (39) permits shareholders at a meeting expressly called for the purpose to remove directors with or without cause by a majority of the shares entitled to vote. The rationale of this section is that as owners the shareholders should have the power to judge the fitness of directors at any time. If less than the entire board is to be removed and cumulative voting[6] is in effect, then a removal action fails if the votes cast against the removal of a director would have been sufficient to have elected him or her initially.

Directors' Meetings. Board meetings need not be held within the state of incorporation. Traditionally, directors can act only when properly convened as a board and cannot vote by proxy or informally, as by a telephone poll. This rule is based upon belief in the value of consultation and collective judgment. Obviously, agreement with a proposal by the chairperson is more likely if each director is approached individually and there is no opportunity to consider the doubts or opposition expressed by a potential dissenter. However, where the statute is silent some courts have upheld action in casual meetings not properly called but attended by all directors and also action taken which has been consented to by all directors without a meeting.

Today the corporation laws of a majority of states, including Delaware, and the Model Act (44) specifically permit action by the directors without a meeting if all directors consent in writing. Although subject to possible abuse, such authorization is useful for routine matters or when formal action is required by a third party and the underlying policy decision has been previously made after full discussion. Close corporations are likely to take advantage of such a method of action more than large public corporations holding monthly meetings of the board.

Reasonable notice, including the purpose, is required of special but not

---

[6] For discussion of cumulative voting, see Chapter 28.

of regular meetings. Actual attendance at a meeting by all directors, unless for the limited purpose of raising an objection to the lack of notice, is generally held to cure defects in the notice. Also, directors may waive notice, and it is normal practice for corporate secretaries to obtain signed waivers when notice is defective. To be effective under common law, a waiver of notice must be signed by all directors either before or during the meeting. However, the Model Act (144) makes waivers of notice signed after the meeting equally effective.

Directors each have one vote regardless of their stock holdings. In order for the directors to act, a quorum must be present. The Model Act (40) provides that a quorum shall be a majority of the number of directors fixed by the bylaws. If none is so fixed, then a majority of the number stated in the articles constitutes a quorum. If there is a quorum, the act of the majority of directors present is the act of the board. However, the Model Act permits the corporation to require a greater number for a quorum by a provision in the articles or bylaws.

Committees of the Board. The bylaws of most large corporations establish an executive committee of the board which is given full authority to act for the board when the entire board is not in session, although this is frequently limited to matters not already acted upon by the board. The executive committee is usually composed of inside directors or board members who can easily be summoned to a meeting on short notice. Thus, the executive committee is available to give a timely formal authorization such as approval of a routine sale of property or a bank transaction. It may also serve as a screening committee for preliminary consideration of complicated or weighty matters prior to presentation to the full board. Other common board committees are salary, audit, finance, and bonus and stock option committees. The New York Stock Exchange now requires its listed firms, and the SEC strongly encourages all publicly held firms, to establish an audit committee composed of outside directors.

The Model Act (42) provides that the directors may by resolution establish an executive committee and other committees which may exercise all the authority of the board within the limits established in the resolution or in the articles or bylaws, except that committees shall not have authority to act in connection with extraordinary corporate matters such as amendment of articles, merger, disposition of substantially all of the assets not in the normal course of business or a voluntary dissolution.

Compensation of Directors. The traditional view was that directors are presumed to perform their ordinary duties as director without compensation and that they have no power to fix their own salaries. The Model Act (35) and other modern statutes permit the directors to fix their compensation unless forbidden by the articles. Outside directors of most large publicly held firms are compensated by an annual retainer plus a fee for board and committee meetings attended. A 1976 study showed that total annual compensation rarely estimated $15,000.[7] Among the Fortune 1,000 firms, two thirds of those with sales under $150 million paid outside directors less than $6,000.

SUMMARY

Since corporation statutes generally provide that directors have the duty of "management of the corporation" they have the power to make all decisions for the corporation not reserved to the shareholders. The statutes specifically require directors to authorize certain actions. However, generally most other management decisions are delegated to the officers or employees. An individual director as such has no management function or power, although a director may be appointed an agent of the corporation.

Although a director is said to have an absolute right of inspection of corporate books and records, inspection may be denied where the director clearly has an interest adverse to the corporation.

Some states require a minimum of three directors but the Model Act and Delaware require only one. A few states have other requirements, for example, that they be shareholders in the corporation or citizens of the state or the United States.

Directors are normally elected by the shareholders at their annual meeting and hold office until the next annual meeting. Most statutes and the Model Act permit staggered terms. Vacancies are filled by shareholders unless, as is usually the case, the statute, articles, or bylaws give this power to the directors to fill the vacancy until the next shareholders' meeting.

Shareholders have inherent power to remove a director for cause but not without cause unless this power is specifically given in the statute, articles, or bylaws prior to his election.

Generally, directors take action only in a properly convened meeting, but many statutes today specifically permit action without a meeting if all directors consent in writing. Reasonable notice is required for a special meeting but not for a regular meeting of the directors. A majority of the board is usually required to constitute a quorum but many statutes permit the articles or bylaws to establish a higher number for a quorum.

Although traditionally directors serve without compensation, modern statutes permit directors to fix their own compensation. Most outside directors are today paid for their service as a director.

---

[7] *The Changing Board* (New York: Heidrick and Struggles, Inc., 1977), p. 13.

Grossman v. Liberty Leasing Co., Inc.
295 A.2d 749 (Del. Ch. 1972)

Howard Grossman and Maurice Gross and other shareholders (plaintiffs) sought a declaration that the election of certain persons to the board of directors of Liberty Leasing Co., Inc., (defendant) was void and for an injunction to prohibit the management from soliciting proxies. Election held valid and injunction denied.

Liberty is a diversified corporation incorporated in Delaware but based in Chicago. Grossman and Gross and members of their families owned approximately 20 percent of the common stock of Liberty, a publicly held company. They had been directors for about ten years and Grossman had been president and treasurer and Gross executive vice president and secretary. Liberty's bylaws called for five directors, but between April 14, 1970, and December 29, 1971, there were only four. At the annual shareholder meetings in 1970 and 1971 management had recommended that only four directors be elected and that was done. In the fall of 1971 there was discussion of adding a fifth director but the four directors could not agree on a nominee. They finally agreed on December 29, 1971, to amend the bylaws to increase the number of directors to seven and Haas, Malkin, and Roland were elected by the board to fill the vacancy and the new positions. The next day Grossman and Gross wanted to rescind the action but Sachnoff, one of the continuing directors and an attorney, told them this could not be done.

At a board meeting attended by both the old and the newly elected directors on February 21, 1972, all the directors except Grossman and Gross voted to liquidate immediately the equipment leasing division of the company. There was also consideration given to removing Grossman and Gross as executives, but this was deferred. On March 3 the three new directors and Sachnoff voted to oust Grossman and Gross. Haas was then elected chairman of the board, Malkin was made president, and Roland was chosen as executive vice president. Both factions then began soliciting shareholder proxies for the annual meeting of shareholders scheduled for May 23.

DUFFY, CHANCELLOR. At the December 29 meeting two new directorships were created. Grossman and Gross concede that such action was within the power of the board under Liberty's bylaws and 8 Del. C. § 223 which provides in part:

> Unless otherwise provided in the certificate of incorporation or bylaws, vacancies and newly created directorships resulting from any increase in the authorized number of directors may be filled by a majority of the directors then in office, although less than a quorum, or by a sole remaining director. . . .

But, they argue, a "vacancy" within the contemplation of § 223 requires a previous incumbency. They say at the time of the December 29 meeting there was not such a vacancy and, therefore, the board, as a matter of law, did not have the power to fill the office.

Grossman and Gross rely upon the Supreme Court decision in *Automatic Steel Products, Inc. v. Johnston. . . .*

In Johnston the directors created new directorships and then filled them. The Court viewed the statute as a limitation on the power of directors and held that they could not do what they did. At that time, when "vacancies" were defined in terms of prior incumbency, directors did not have the power to elect or appoint directors; all such power was reserved to stockholders with only one exception: directors in office could choose a director when a vacancy occurred in their number.

. . . However, what was once regarded as the prerogative solely of stockholders is now permissible action under § 223.

Under § 223 directors in office now may fill vacancies in their membership if stockholders do not do so and if other requirements of the statute are met; a prior incumbency is not a condition precedent to such action. In so stating I do not consider any question of fraud upon the stockholders, or an estoppel upon directors to fill a vacancy in their membership, or circumstances amounting to a change by stockholders in the authorized number of directors.

I conclude that Liberty's directors had the power to fill the fifth directorship, and it therefore follows that Malkin, Haas, and Roland were validly elected to the Board.

Grossman and Gross argue also that Liberty's bylaws provide for the filling of vacancies and newly created directorships "at a special meeting called for that purpose" and, they say, the December 29 meeting was not called for either of those purposes. They argue that the actions taken were therefore invalid.

Such bylaw provisions do, of course, serve a useful purpose and they are enforceable. But both the Delaware Corporation Law and the bylaws of Liberty permit waiver of these requirements. . . . And the bylaws provide that any director may waive notice of any meeting, and that attendance of a director at any meeting constitutes a "waiver of notice of such meeting" except when he attends for the express purpose of objecting to the transaction of business because the meeting is not lawfully convened. Since the statute is applicable to "any meeting," it follows that it is applicable to a special meeting.

It is undisputed that Grossman and Gross, together with the other directors, attended the December 29 meeting, voted for the action taken and signed the minutes. Under these circumstances I conclude that they waived any defect with respect to notice of the meeting.

Officers and Employees

Officers of the Corporation. The Model Act (50) provides that the officers of a corporation shall be the president, one or more vice presidents, a secretary, and a treasurer. Some statutes require fewer officers and most allow more if desired. It is increasingly common for a corporation to establish the office of chairman of the board. Under the Model Act any two or more offices may be held by the same person except the offices of president and secretary. This permits dual signatures on corporate documents.

The officers are agents of the corporation, and as such, they will have the express authority which is conferred upon them in the bylaws or by the board of directors. In addition, they will have implied authority to do those things reasonably necessary to accomplish the functions delegated to them. Like any agent they may be held accountable by the corporation for exceeding such actual authority. However, like any agent they also may bind the corporation on the basis of apparent authority, when acting beyond their actual authority.

In addition, courts have held that certain officers may have authority by virtue of their office. The cases are difficult to reconcile, but such *ex officio* powers are much more restricted than laymen are likely to expect. Even the president traditionally had no power to bind the corporation by virtue of the office held, but merely served as presiding officer in shareholder and director meetings. However, if an executive acts as general manager or chief executive— that is, he or she is given general supervision and control of the business—the executive is vested with broad implied authority to make such contracts and do such other acts as are appropriate in the ordinary business of the corporation.

A vice president has no authority by virtue of that office. However, an executive who is vice president of sales or some other department of the business will have the authority of a manager of the specified department to transact the normal business of the corporation which falls within the function of that department.

The secretary, or clerk as he or she is called in some states, usually keeps the minutes of director and shareholder meetings and other corporate records and has custody of the corporate seal. The secretary has no authority to bind the corporation by virtue of that office but there is a presumption that a document to which he or she affixes the seal has been duly authorized.

The treasurer has custody of the funds of the corporation and is the proper officer to receive payments to the corporation and to disburse corporate funds for authorized purposes. A treasurer binds the corporation by his or her receipts, checks, and indorsements but does not by virtue of the office alone have authority to borrow money or issue negotiable instruments.

Like any principal, the corporation may ratify the unauthorized acts of its officers. This may be accomplished through a resolution of the board of directors or of the shareholders.

Statutory Liabilities of Officers. The Model Act (136) imposes criminal liability on corporate officers (and directors as well) who sign a report or application filed with the secretary of state which is known by the officer to be false or who refuses to answer truthfully and fully questions asked by the secretary in accordance with his or her duties under the act. Provisions are found in several state statutes which impose either civil or criminal liability upon officers for failure to perform other statutory duties, such as filing proper annual reports for the corporation or denying access to shareholders to the corporate books and records. Similar liabilities exist under federal statutes requiring corporate reports.

Employees of the Corporation. Employees of the corporation who are not officers may also be delegated to act as agents for the corporation and the usual rules of agency will apply both to their relationship to the corporation and to third parties. Both officers and other agents can best protect themselves from personal liability by having their authority for conducting out-of-the-ordinary transactions for the corporation stated in writing, either in a bylaw or a specific resolution of the board of directors. Also, they should make it clear in signing as agent for the corporation that they do not intend to contract in their individual capacity (see Chapter 17).

SUMMARY

The Model Act specifies that the officers of a corporation shall be the president, one or more vice presidents, a secretary, and a treasurer and that two or more offices may be held by one person, except the offices of president and secretary. Officers are agents of the corporation and have express, implied, and apparent authority like any agent.

Ex officio powers are limited even for the president. Only if the president acts as general manager does he or she have broad implied authority to make contracts and conduct the ordinary business of the corporation. A vice president has only such authority as he or she may be given as manager of some division of the corporation's business. The secretary's function is to keep minutes and other records, and the secretary has no implied authority except to affix the corporate seal. The treasurer can bind the corporation by receipts, checks, and indorsements but does not, by virtue of that office, have authority to borrow money.

Employees of the corporation other than officers may be delegated to act as agents for the corporation. Statutory criminal or civil liability may be imposed upon officers for failure to perform certain statutory duties such as filing the corporation's annual report with the secretary of state or for making reports known to be false.

Duties of Directors and Officers to the Corporation

General. Directors as such are not agents of the corporation but hold a position which is *sui generis.* Nevertheless, they and corporate officers are treated as having fiduciary, or at least quasi-fiduciary, duties to the corporation that are essentially similar to the duties any agent owes his or her principal. They may generally be stated as (1) to act within one's authority and within the powers given to the corporation, (2) to act diligently and with due care in conducting the affairs of the corporation, and (3) to act in loyalty and good faith for the benefit of the corporation.

The trend of statutory and case law, and especially of the regulatory activity of the Securities and Exchange Commission, has been to raise the standard of conduct required of directors and officers and to extend some of the prohibitions to employees who are not officers and to controlling shareholders. There also appears to be a trend toward more suits by shareholders against directors for breach of their duties to the corporation.[8]

Acting within Authority. Like any agent, officers have a duty to act within the authority conferred upon them by the articles and bylaws of the corporation and by the directors. Directors must act within authority given to the corporation and to them by statute and by the articles and bylaws, as discussed above in the section on *ultra vires.* Either an officer or director may be liable to the corporation if it is damaged by an act exceeding the person's or the corporation's authority.

If directors honestly believe that a transaction approved by them is within the scope of the corporate business, and they are justified in that belief, they will not be held personally liable for injury to the corporation resulting from the transaction, even if the transaction is held to be *ultra vires.* Also, if the transaction is not illegal and is later ratified by the shareholders, the directors will be relieved of personal liability to the corporation.

Due Care and Diligence. Directors and officers are liable for losses to the corporation resulting from their negligence or lack of attention to their responsibilities. The New York statute defines the standard of care in a manner similar to that declared by some courts. It states: "Directors and officers shall discharge the duties of their respective positions in good faith and with that degree of diligence, care, and skill which ordinarily prudent men would exercise under similar circumstances in like positions."[9] Revised Section 35 of the Model Act has what appears to be a less onerous and, at least in a large corporation, a more practicable standard. It says a director shall perform

---

[8] Class suits against directors brought under the federal securities laws are treated in Chapter 29. Derivative actions by shareholder are discussed in Chapter 28.

[9] McKinney, *N.Y. Bus. Corp. Law* 717.

his duties "in good faith, in a manner he reasonably believes to be in the best interests of the corporation, and with such care as an ordinarily prudent person in a like position would use under similar circumstances." It specifically states that the director may rely upon data, opinions, and reports prepared by the officers and consultants whom he reasonably believes to be competent and reliable, as well as upon board committees on which he does not serve as to matters within their designated authority.

The cases are in conflict as to whether a person's lack of capacity as a director will prevent liability. Certainly the failure to attend directors' meetings or the fact that a director receives no compensation does not permit him or her to escape liability. However, if a director receives no compensation, is engaged full time in another business, and lives at a distance from the corporation, these are circumstances that would affect the degree of care and diligence expected.

The Business Judgment Rule. Directors and officers are not liable for mere errors of judgment if they act with care, diligence, and in good faith. This rule is known as the "business judgment rule." The courts will not exercise hindsight to second-guess decisions made in good faith. However, directors are liable for negligence both in taking action and in failing to take appropriate action. This would include liability for negligence in the selection and supervision of officers and employees of the corporation.

Loyalty and Good Faith. Cardozo in a much quoted opinion well stated the duty to act in loyalty and good faith. He declared that a director:

> owes loyalty and allegiance to the corporation—a loyalty that is undivided and an allegiance that is influenced by no consideration other than the welfare of the corporation. Any adverse interest of a director will be subjected to a scrutiny rigid and uncompromising. He may not profit at the expense of his corporation and in conflict with its rights; he may not for personal gain divert unto himself the opportunities which in equity and fairness belong to his corporation. He is required to use his independent judgment. . . . He must, of course, act honestly and in good faith. . . .[10]

The requirement of loyalty and good faith is general and is as broad as the inventiveness of avaricious humans to which it is addressed. Only four kinds of situations where questions of the good faith of directors or officers have been adjudicated will be discussed. They are: (1) transactions with the corporation, (2) usurpation of a corporate opportunity, (3) transactions in the corporation's stock, and (4) oppression of minority shareholders.

Transactions with the Corporation. Fiduciaries are generally not permitted any type of self-dealing, and earlier decisions held that any transaction with the corporation in which a director was involved directly or indirectly was voidable at the discretion of the corporation. However, transactions in which

[10] *Meinhard v. Salmon,* 164 N.E. 545, 546 (1928).

a director or officer (or another business organization in which he or she has an interest) supplies facilities, products, or services to or is served by the corporation may clearly benefit the corporation. So more recently the majority of courts have held that such a transaction is voidable only if unfair to the corporation. If the director or officer represents both the corporation and himself or herself in the transaction, or if the director's presence is necessary for a quorum, or his vote is essential for the approval of the transaction, then a court is less likely to enforce the contract. A failure to disclose fully an interest in the transaction is more important and may be fatal to the director's attempt to enforce the contract even if its terms are fair to the corporation.

The Model Act provides (41), and Delaware is similar, that transactions between the corporation and a director (or between it and a corporation in which a director is interested) are not automatically void or voidable under any one of three conditions. These are: (1) with knowledge or after disclosure of the conflicting interest, the board, without counting the vote of interested directors, approves or ratifies; (2) with knowledge or after disclosure the shareholders approve or ratify; or (3) the transaction is fair to the corporation. Section 35 authorizes the directors to fix their own compensation—a situation where there is an inherent conflict of interest.

Usurpation of a Corporate Opportunity. Directors and officers may not take for themselves business opportunities which come to them in their corporate capacity and which fall within the normal scope of the corporation's business and which it is able to undertake. They may not, for example, buy up land that the corporation could use and then resell it to the corporation at a profit nor may they personally buy the rights to manufacture a product which would fit into the corporation's line. If the corporation is unable to finance the opportunity or accepting it would be *ultra vires* or a noninterested majority of directors vote against accepting it, then a director or officer is free to exploit it personally unless it would result in harmful competition to the corporation.

Transactions in the Corporation's Stock. Directors and officers have access to information affecting the value of the corporation's securities unavailable to other securities holders. Are they entitled to make a profit from that knowledge by buying and selling the corporation's stock or other securities without disclosing this information to the other party in the transaction? In the early cases courts concluded that directors and officers had no fiduciary duty to existing or potential shareholders but only to the corporation. Therefore, they are accountable for their trading profits neither to the corporation, which suffered no loss, nor to the individuals from whom they bought or to whom they sold stock. However, in this century there has been a trend in the court decisions toward finding a duty on the part of the director or officer, and even an employee or controlling shareholder, to disclose inside knowledge as a condition to his or her right to buy or sell. Under this view the other party to the transaction may recover the difference between the stock's value had the information been known and the actual trading price. As will be discussed in Chapter 29, this is already the law under the Securities and Exchange Act, but it remains only a minority rule in suits not brought under that Act.

Some relatively recent decisions have held that controlling shareholders are liable to their fellow shareholders for breach of a duty to exercise due care to guard their interests against potential looters of the corporate assets and also have permitted shareholders to recover the premium over and above the inherent value of the stock paid the controlling shareholders for sale of control of the corporation.

Oppression of Minority Shareholders. Directors and officers owe a duty to the corporation to exercise their management functions in the best interests of the corporation as a whole. Although this duty is generally recognized, so also is the right of the majority to manage the corporation with considerable discretion through the "business judgment" rule. Courts are frequently faced with suits, usually involving close corporations, that allege oppression of minority shareholders or attempts to "freeze" them out of the corporation which require balancing these two principles. The means of oppression complained of are many. They include dividend withholding, siphoning off profits in high salaries to controlling shareholders in management, mergers or reorganizations or merely charter amendments that alter the rights and preferences of a certain class or classes of stock and sale or lease of major corporate assets to or from controlling shareholders for an unfair consideration. Generally minority shareholders have been successful in obtaining an injunction or recovering damages only where the acts of directors have been clearly in bad faith, arbitrary, or clearly abuse the discretion allowed them under the "business judgment" rule.

Federal Securities Laws. The federal securities laws have imposed new duties on directors and officers and Rule 10b–5 of the Securities and Exchange Commission has been said to be the basis of a new federal corporation law. These laws and their effect on the duties of directors, officers, and others who are considered "insiders" are discussed in Chapter 29.

Other Statutory Liabilities of Directors. The Model Corporation Act (48) imposes personal civil liability to the corporation upon directors for certain acts taken in conducting the internal affairs of the corporation. These acts include: (1) assent to the payment of a dividend or a distribution of assets in violation of the statute or the articles; (2) assent to an improper purchase of its own shares by the corporation, and (3) assent to the distribution of assets during liquidation without providing for the payment of all known debts. For protection, a director who attends a board meeting at which any of these illegal actions is taken must have his or her dissent recorded in the minutes. If the director voted in opposition to the motion, immunity from liability may be gained by filing a written dissent with the secretary of the corporation immediately after adjournment of the meeting.

SUMMARY

Although directors are not agents of the corporation, they and corporate officers are treated as having fiduciary duties to the corporation. The trend of the law is toward raising the standard of conduct required of directors and officers and there appears to be an increase in suits brought against them, usually by stockholders, for breach of their duties to the corporation.

Directors and officers must act within their authority and within the powers given to the corporation. They are liable to the corporation for losses due to their negligence or lack of attention to their responsibilities but not for mere errors in judgment. They also owe a duty of loyalty and good faith to the corporation and must put its welfare above their own.

A director or officer may transact business with the corporation but he or she should disclose to the corporation any conflict of interest. The corporation may usually avoid a contract which is unfair to the corporation. A director or officer may not usurp a corporate opportunity by taking for personal advantage some opportunity coming to him or her in his corporate capacity or which may have the effect of putting the director or officer in competition with the corporation.

There is a trend in the case law towards holding that directors and officers may not use information not generally available to the investing public to personally buy and sell the corporation's shares. This is now clearly the law under the Securities Exchange Act.

The duty of good faith is to act for the best interests of the corporation as a whole and if the actions of the directors or officers are taken primarily for the purpose of oppressing minority shareholders or "freezing" them out of the corporation, the minority may be able to obtain injunctive relief or damages.

Patient Care Services, S.C. v. Segal

337 N.E.2d 471 (App. Ct. Ill. 1975)

Patient Care Services, S.C. (plaintiff), brought an action against Dr. Segal and Medical Services, S.C. (defendants), to recover for breach of fiduciary duty in setting up a competing corporation and in seizing Patient Care's assets. The trial court entered judgment for the defendants and Patient Care appealed. Reversed and remanded.

Drs. Martinez and Segal formed Patient Care Services as a professional service corporation [S.C.] with each owning 50 percent of the shares and both serving as officers and directors. It made an oral contract with a hospital to furnish doctors to staff the emergency room and out-patient clinic of the hospital, and to provide health care planning. A written contract was contemplated but never executed due to failure to reach agreement on several of the draft provisions. Martinez and Segal agreed upon the salaries they would draw and their own compensation from the corporation while working in the emergency room.

The arrangement with the hospital began on July 1, and a couple of months later Martinez went to Harvard for a Ph.D. Later Segal became unhappy because he was bearing most of the administrative burden of operating Patient Care, and he alleged that Martinez failed to live up to their oral agreements, including a promise to commute weekly from Boston to assist in conducting corporate business. He communicated this to Martinez, and an adjustment was made in the salaries drawn by the two officer-directors. On February 21, Segal wrote Martinez that he had concluded that their association had reached an impasse requiring its termination and that the corporation's arrangement with the hospital would be concluded at the end of June. He declared that if Martinez would not sell his interest to him, Segal would take steps to dissolve the corporation. Various communications among the officer-directors, their attorneys, and the hospital followed. Segal individually then negotiated a contract with the hospital to take over on the following July 1, on a month-to-month basis, the services that had been provided by Patient Care. He then formed Medical Services, S.C., another professional service corporation for this purpose.

McNamara, Justice. The duties that an officer or director owe to his corporation are so well established as to need no citation of authority to support them. They include the requirement of undivided, unselfish, and unqualified loyalty, of unceasing effort never to profit personally at corporate expense, of unbending disavowal of any opportunity which would permit the fiduciary's private interests to clash with those of his corporation. These duties are rooted not only in elementary rules of equity but also in business morality and public policy. It therefore follows that an officer or director who strays from faithful adherence to these precepts and actively engages in a rival or competing business to the detriment of his corporation must answer to the corporation for the injury sustained.

It must first be recognized that at least initially the finalization of a written contract to cover the first year of its operation of services at the hospital as well as the preparation and execution of a new one to embrace succeeding years constituted a corporate opportunity for Patient Care. Patient Care was organized for the purpose of providing comprehensive health services to a hospital. For the first year of its incorporation it was engaged in furnishing those services to the hospital, and the hospital was satisfied with those services. Obviously, the very nature of its business necessitated a continuation and development of this relationship. When such a corporate opportunity exists, it is inherent in an officer's or director's fiduciary obligations to refrain from purchasing property for himself in which the corporation has an interest, actual or expectant, or which may hinder or defeat the plans and purposes of the corporation in the carrying on or development of the legitimate business for which it was created.

Viewed in this light, this court finds it indisputable that Segal blatantly violated those duties of loyalty and trust which he owed to Patient Care. While an officer and director of that corporation, he helped set up and subsequently took over control of a different corporation organized to perform the very similar, if not identical, services Patient Care was organized to perform. . . . At the time Segal knew that Patient Care's contract with the hospital was the corporation's sole asset. When the first year of Patient Care's contract with the hospital concluded, Segal's new corporation, Medical Services, took over on a month-to-month basis. At the time of trial, almost a year after Medical Services had begun work at the hospital, Segal remained an officer and director of Patient Care.

The recital of these facts, all admitted by Segal, reveal a violation of his duties and loyalty to Patient Care. They not only signify a course of conduct bent on seizing his corporation's business but also evidence a willingness to destroy his corporation in the process.

Segal's response is to point out alleged breaches of contract by Martinez and to argue that any continuation of his relationship with Martinez would have resulted in his peonage to Patient Care. The disagreements with Martinez would still not condone the actions taken by Segal vis-a-vis Patient Care. If Segal felt undercompensated or taken advantage of, he could have resigned from Patient Care. If he felt Martinez breached any contract with him and/or Patient Care, the proper recourse was, and is, for Segal to sue in the courts for breach of contract.

Guth v. Loft, Inc.

5 A.2d 503 (Sup. Ct. Del. 1939)

This was a bill in Chancery by Loft, Inc. (plaintiff), against Charles G. Guth, Grace Company and Pepsi-Cola Company (defendants) seeking to impress a trust in favor of Loft upon all of the capital stock of Pepsi-Cola. The Chancellor found for Loft. Affirmed.

Loft manufactured and sold candies, syrups, beverages, and foodstuffs in 115 retail stores on the Middle Atlantic seaboard and its wholesale activities amounted to sales of $800,000. It dispensed Coca-Cola at all of its stores. Guth, a man of long experience in the candy and soft drink business, joined

Loft in 1929 and became president and general manager in 1930. In 1931 he tried to persuade Coca-Cola to give Loft a jobber's discount in view of its very large purchases. Coca-Cola refused and Guth learned that Pepsi-Cola syrup could be purchased for about two thirds the price of Coca-Cola. While this was under consideration, the corporation owning the secret formula and trademark for Pepsi-Cola was adjudicated a bankrupt and the man controlling it sought Guth's help in forming a new corporation. This was done with approximately half of the stock going to Grace, a corporation owned by Guth's family which made syrups for soft drinks and which sold one of its syrups to Loft. Most of the rest of the stock came to be owned by Guth through subsequent transactions with the man previously controlling Pepsi-Cola. During this period Guth was very heavily indebted to Loft, Guth was in serious financial straits, and Grace was insolvent.

Guth used Loft's working capital, its credit, its plant and equipment, and its executives and employees in producing Pepsi-Cola, although Loft was subsequently reimbursed for wages paid to workers. Loft was Pepsi-Cola's chief customer. It suffered diminution of profits in its retail stores estimated at $300,000 due to discarding Coca-Cola, despite advertising expenditures of $20,000 to promote Pepsi-Cola, which was relatively unknown.

Guth claimed he offered the Loft directors the opportunity to take over Pepsi-Cola but they declined because they did not wish to compete with Coca-Cola, that it was not in line with Loft's business, and that it involved too great a financial risk. However, he also claimed that later the directors authorized the use of Loft facilities and resources upon Guth's guarantee of all advances. No record of either action appeared in the corporate minutes of Loft, and the Chancellor found that the directors were without knowledge of the use of Loft's money, credit, facilities, and personnel in furthering the Pepsi-Cola venture.

LAYTON, CHIEF JUSTICE. Corporate officers and directors are not permitted to use their position of trust and confidence to further their private interests. While technically not trustees, they stand in fiduciary relation to the corporation and its stockholders. A public policy, existing through the years, and derived from a profound knowledge of human characteristics and motives, has established a rule that demands of a corporate officer or director, peremptorily and inexorably, the most scrupulous observance of his duty, not only affirmatively to protect the interests of the corporation committed to his charge, but also to refrain from doing anything that would work injury to the corporation, or to deprive it of profit or advantage which his skill and ability might properly bring to it, or to enable it to make in the reasonable and lawful exercise of its powers. The rule that requires an undivided and unselfish loyalty to the corporation demands that there shall be no conflict between duty and self-interest. The occasions for the determination of honesty, good faith, and loyal conduct are many and varied, and no hard and fast rule can be formulated. The standard of loyalty is measured by no fixed scale.

If an officer or director of a corporation, in violation of his duty as such, acquires gain or advantage for himself, the law charges the interest so acquired with a trust for the benefit of the corporation, at its election, while it denies to the betrayer all benefit and profit. The rule, inveterate and uncompromising in its rigidity, does not rest upon the narrow ground of injury or damage to the corporation resulting from a betrayal of confidence, but upon a broader foundation of a wise public policy that, for the purpose of removing all temptation, extinguishes all possibility of profit flowing from a breach of the confidence imposed by the fiduciary relation. Given the relation between the parties, a certain result follows; and a constructive trust is the remedial device through which precedence of self is compelled to give way to the stern demands of loyalty.

The rule, referred to briefly as the rule of corporate opportunity, is merely one of the manifestations of the general rule that demands of an officer or director the utmost good faith in his relation to the corporation which he represents.

It is true that when a business opportunity comes to a corporate officer or director in his individual capacity rather than in his official capacity, and the opportunity is one which, because of the nature of the enterprise, is not essential to his corporation, and is one in which it has no interest or expectancy, the officer or director is entitled to treat the opportunity as his own, and the corporation has no interest in it, if, of course, the officer or director has not wrongfully embarked the corporation's resources therein.

Although the facts and circumstances disclosed by the voluminous record clearly show gross violations of legal and moral duties by Guth in his dealings with Loft, Guth makes bold to say that no duty was cast upon him, hence he was guilty of no disloyalty. The fiduciary relation demands something more than the morals of the marketplace. Guth's abstractions of Loft's money and materials are complacently referred to as borrowings. Whether his acts are to be deemed properly cognizable in a civil court at all, we need not inquire, but certain it is that borrowing is not descriptive of them. A borrower presumes a lender acting freely. Guth took without limit or stint from a helpless corporation, in violation of a statute enacted for the protection of corporations against such abuses, and without the knowledge or authority of the corporation's Board of Directors. Cunning and craft supplanted sincerity. Frankness gave way to concealment. He did not offer the Pepsi-Cola opportunity to Loft, but captured it for himself. He invested little or no money of his own in the venture, but commandeered for his own benefit and advantage the money, resources and facilities of his corporation and the services of his officials. He thrust upon Loft the hazard, while he reaped the benefit. His time was paid for by Loft. The use of the Grace plant was not essential to the enterprise. In such manner he acquired for himself and Grace ninety-one percent of the capital stock of Pepsi-Cola, now worth many millions. A genius in his line he may be, but the law makes no distinction between the wrongdoing genius and the one less endowed.

Gimbel v. Signal Companies, Inc.

316 A.2d 599 (Del. Ch. 1974)

This was a shareholder suit by Louis S. Gimbel III (plaintiff) against Signal Companies, Inc. (Signal) (defendant), to enjoin the sale of its stock in a subsidiary. The court granted a preliminary injunction conditioned upon posting a bond of $25 million.

The action was by Gimbel as a representative of a group holding 12 percent of the shares of Signal on December 24, 1973, to prevent the consummation of a sale by Signal to Burmah Oil Incorporated (Burmah) of all of the capital stock of Signal Oil and Gas Co. (Oil Co.), a wholly owned subsidiary of Signal. The sale had been approved by Signal's board of directors on December 21, 1973, and the price was approximately $480 million, $420 million in cash.

Signal was originally in the oil business but had diversified. At the time of the suit Oil Co. represented 26 percent of the total assets of Signal and 41 percent of its net worth, but it produced only about 15 percent of Signal's earnings. The book value of Oil Co.'s assets was approximately $376 million.

A proposed merger between Signal and United Aircraft had fallen through in September 1973. In connection with that transaction a valuation of Oil Co.'s reserves was made by prominent oil geologists who valued all of Oil Co.'s properties at $350 million. Other reports were prepared by Price Waterhouse. On October 17 representatives of Burmah approached the president of Oil Co. to discuss acquiring some or all of its properties. They were referred to the president of Signal, who said that any offer in excess of $400 million would be submitted to Signal's board of directors. The valuation reports of the outside experts and other confidential information were given Burmah, and the attorneys of Burmah and Signal engaged in several drafting sessions. A Burmah representative addressed a meeting of Oil Co.'s board of directors to discuss Burmah's history, business, and operating policies. By early December a press release announcing the transaction had been drafted. However, Signal's board of directors was advised at its November 27 meeting only that management had inquiries from others with possible interest in Signal subsidiaries since the United Aircraft transaction was terminated.

On December 3 an attorney for the minority group of shareholders wrote a letter to Signal declaring opposition to the rumored sale of oil and gas properties, indicating that shareholder approval would be required, and requesting consultation. Burmah's formal offer was presented to Signal on December 18 and required acceptance on or before December 21.

A special meeting of the Signal board of directors was called for Friday, December 21, without notice of its purpose. Three of the four outside directors were unaware of the proposed sale prior to the meeting. The meeting lasted about two hours. A handwritten outline of the transaction was handed to the directors and an oral presentation was made supporting it. The tax consequences of the sale and the use of the proceeds were discussed, especially the advantage of prepaying certain indebtedness and the needs of other subsidiaries. The general financial status of Oil Co., including its sales, income, cash flow, balance sheet, projected capital expenditures, and risks in its North Sea investment were discussed. The current situation in the oil industry, including contemplation of price increases, was also reviewed. The advisability of waiting for a better offer was also considered.

QUILLEN, CHANCELLOR. Gimbel attacks the proposed transaction on the grounds that the $480 million sale price is wholly inadequate compensation for the assets of Oil Co. In evaluating the merits of this allegation, precedent requires the Court to start from the normal presumption that Signal's Board of Directors acted in good faith in approving the sale of Oil Co. to Burmah.

This presumption, an important aspect of what has generally come to be known as the "business judgment rule," has been consistently reaffirmed and broadened with respect to the sale of corporate assets over the past several decades. Application of the rule, of necessity, depends upon a showing that informed directors did, in fact, make a business judgment authorizing the transaction under review.

In challenging the sale of Oil Co. to Burmah, Gimbel here does not seriously charge that the proposed transaction constitutes fraudulent self-dealing on the part of Signal's Board of Directors. Indeed, only one member of the Board, Willis H. Thompson, Jr., is expected to have any relationship with Burmah after the sale. Thompson is President and Chief Executive Officer of Oil Co. He plans to continue in that position if Oil Co. is sold to Burmah. Other than that, the only benefit any members of the Board would receive from the sale is that which would accrue to any ordinary shareholder according to his holdings in Signal. It is usually assumed that such individual benefit also works for the benefit of the corporation.

Actual fraud, whether resulting from self-dealing or otherwise, is not necessary to challenge a sale of assets. And, although the language of "constructive fraud" or "badge of fraud" has frequently and almost traditionally been used, such language is not very helpful when fraud admittedly has not been established. There are limits on the business judgment rule which fall short of intentional or inferred fraudulent misconduct and which are based simply on gross inadequacy of price. This is clear even if language of fraud is used.

Factually, to support his claim of recklessness, Gimbel basically relies on three related factors: the alleged gross inadequacy of price; the failure of the Board of Directors to act on such an important matter with informed reasonable deliberation; and specifically the failure of the Board of Directors to obtain an updated appraisal of Oil Co.'s properties before agreeing to accept Burmah's offer. Except for the key question of value, there is not significant dispute over the factual chronology.

(I)t is apparent that the Board was aware that Signal had cash needs and was naturally reluctant to do anything that might upset a sale which would bring to the Board $420 million cash and which was for a total consideration that exceeded by approximately $75 million the market value of the total number of Signal shares currently outstanding. They were understandably fearful of challenging the time factor imposed by Burmah's offer of December 18.

But having given full weight to the legitimate considerations of the Board, it is necessary, at the risk of repetition, to pinpoint elements which suggest imprudence. The circumstances are such as to raise the question as to whether the Signal Board, when the sale of Oil Co.'s stock was presented, were able to perform their fiduciary obligation as directors to make an informed judgment of approving the transaction. In particular, it is difficult to ignore the following facts.

The transaction had been in progress since October. I am satisfied that management decided early in the game, and probably in October, that the offer, when made, would be recommended to the Board. Certainly by early December the only reasonable assumption was that management would recommend the transaction to the Board.

To highlight the fact that management did not bring the proposed transaction to the attention of the Signal Board, it should be noted that in early December management did bring the transaction to the attention of the Oil Co. Board, evidently because personnel at Oil Co. were somewhat restless about the investigation being conducted by the Burmah people. But the point is management was ready to go out of its way of relieving anxiety in the subsidiary that was being transferred and yet made no advance effort to educate the directors whose responsibility it was to approve the transaction. The point is aggravated by the fact that there was a regular board meeting with one hundred percent attendance on November 27, 1973.

Even granting that management had prior legal difficulties with the minority group of which Gimbel is a member, it is hard to overlook the fact the minority interest wrote to each board member, expressed opposition to the sale of the oil and gas interest, further stated its belief that any such transaction required shareholders' approval and further requested to be consulted. Except for obtaining an opinion of counsel to counter the legal position on the requirement of shareholder action, this request was totally ignored by management and by the Board. Such lack of consideration for a minority viewpoint of the substantial block of stock, and perhaps the largest single block of stock, gives rise to the allegation, which probably cannot be established as motivation, that management was trying to effectively freeze out a minority interest.

The decision to call a special meeting of the Board on approximately two days' notice highlights the failure of management to advise the Board in their capacity as Board members of this very important transaction. Not only was the call short but management failed to give any notice of the subject matter in advance. The question is not one of legality. The question is one of permitting the Board the opportunity to make a reasonable and reasoned decision.

There is no question that the energy crisis has created a drastic change in the value of oil and gas properties. Even granting that there may be wide divergence in expert viewpoint, the situation made desirable an updated evaluation. Indeed, Signal's own expert in this proceeding, while he values Oil Co. at less than the sale price, also values Oil Co. at $60 million more on December 21 than he did on September 30.

Thus, the ultimate question is not one of method but one of value. The method does not appear so bad on its face as to alter the normal legal principles which control. But a hasty method which produces a dollar result which appears perhaps to be shocking is significant. On the basis of affidavits relating to value, the Court has the tentative belief that Gimbel would have a reasonable prospect of success on the merits since limited record [sic] indicates a gross disparity between the fair market value of Oil Co. on December 21, 1973, and what the Board of Directors were willing to sell the company for, namely, $480 million. To the extent the scale tips, on the present record, the nod is to Gimbel. But I hasten to add that an extremely high security consistent with the figures being discussed, should be required.

Donahue v. Rodd Electrotype Co.

328 N.E.2d 505 (Sup. Jud. Ct. Mass. 1975)

Donahue (plaintiff), a minority shareholder in Rodd Electrotype Co. (defendant), a close corporation, brought suit against the corporation, the directors, and the controlling shareholder seeking to rescind the corporation's purchase of shares from the former controlling shareholder. The appellate court affirmed the trial court's judgment for the defendants and Donahue appealed. Reversed and remanded.

Harry C. Rodd had been an employee of and then general manager of a predecessor of Rodd Electrotype Co. He acquired a minority interest in the company and persuaded Joseph Donahue, plant superintendent, to buy shares also. He was then able, by loaning money to the corporation that he had borrowed by mortgaging his home, to arrange for the corporation to purchase the majority of the shares and to hold these as treasury shares. This left him holding 80 percent of the shares and Donahue 20 percent. The name of the corporation was then changed to Rodd Electrotype Co.

Thereafter, Rodd made gifts of some of his shares to his two sons who were employed in the business and to his daughter. In 1965 Charles Rodd succeeded his father as president, and about that time Frederick Rodd succeeded Joseph Donahue as plant superintendent. In 1970 the two sons urged Harry, who was then 77 years old and in poor health, to retire. In July 1970, after a number of conferences and a meeting of the board of directors, Harry disposed of his remaining shares by "giving" each child 10 shares and selling them each 2 shares at $800 per share and selling 45 shares to the corporation at $800 per share. This left each of the Rodd children holding

51 shares and Donahue holding 50. Frederick replaced his father on the board of directors.

At the next annual meeting of shareholders Donahue and his wife learned of the stock transactions, and a few weeks after the meeting they offered their shares to the corporation at the same price. They were informed that the corporation was not in a financial position to buy them. Suit was then filed alleging that the purchase of Harry Rodd's shares was an unlawful distribution of corporate assets to the controlling shareholder and a breach of fiduciary duty of the controlling shareholder to a minority shareholder.

TAURO, CHIEF JUSTICE. In previous opinions, we have alluded to the distinctive nature of the close corporation, but have never defined precisely what is meant by a close corporation. There is no single, generally accepted definition. We deem a close corporation to be typified by: (1) a small number of stockholders; (2) no ready market for the corporate stock; and (3) substantial majority stockholder participation in the management, direction and operations of the corporation.

As thus defined, the close corporation bears striking resemblance to a partnership. Commentators and courts have noted that the close corporation is often little more than an "incorporated" or "chartered" partnership. The stockholders "clothe" their partnership "with the benefits peculiar to a corporation, limited liability, perpetuity and the like." In essence, though, the enterprise remains one in which ownership is limited to the original parties or transferees of their stock to whom the other stockholders have agreed, in which ownership and management are in the same hands, and in which the owners are quite dependent on one another for the success of the enterprise. Just as in a partnership, the relationship among the stockholders must be one of trust, confidence and absolute loyalty if the enterprise is to succeed. Close corporations with substantial assets and with more numerous stockholders are no different from smaller close corporations in this regard. All participants rely on the fidelity and abilities of those stockholders who hold office. Disloyalty and self-seeking conduct on the part of any stockholder will engender bickering, corporate stalemates, and, perhaps, efforts to achieve dissolution.

Although the corporate form provides the above-mentioned advantages for the stockholders (limited liability, perpetuity, and so forth), it also supplies an opportunity for the majority stockholders to oppress or disadvantage minority stockholders. The minority is vulnerable to a variety of oppressive devices, termed "freeze-outs," which the majority may employ.

The minority can, of course, initiate suit against the majority and their directors. Self-serving conduct by directors is proscribed by the director's fiduciary obligation to the corporation. However, in practice, the plaintiff will find difficulty in challenging dividend or employment policies. Such policies are considered to be within the judgment of the directors. [G]enerally, plaintiffs who seek judicial assistance against corporate dividend or employment policies do not prevail.

Thus, when these types of "freeze-outs" are attempted by the majority stockholders, the minority stockholders, cut off from all corporation-related revenues, must either suffer their losses or seek a buyer for their shares. Many minority stockholders will be unwilling or unable to wait for an alteration in majority policy. Typically, the minority stockholder in a close corporation has a substantial percentage of his personal assets invested in the corporation. The stockholder may have anticipated that his salary from his position with the corporation would be his livelihood. Thus, he cannot afford to wait passively. He must liquidate his investment in the close corporation in order to reinvest the funds in income-producing enterprises.

At this point, the true plight of the minority stockholder in a close corporation becomes manifest. He cannot easily reclaim his capital. . . . In a partnership, a partner who feels abused by his fellow partners may cause dissolution by his "express will . . . at any time" and recover his share of partnership assets and accumulated profits. By contrast, the stockholder in the close corporation or "incorporated partnership" may achieve dissolution and recovery of his share of the enterprise assets only by compliance with the rigorous terms of the applicable chapter of the General Laws. To secure dissolution of the ordinary close corporation, the stockholder, in the absence of corporate deadlock, must own at least fifty percent of the shares or have the advantage of a favorable provision in the articles of organization.

Under settled Massachusetts law, a domestic corporation, unless forbidden by statute, has the power to purchase its own shares. When the corporation reacquiring its own stock is a close corporation, the purchase is subject to the additional requirement, in the light of our holding in this opinion, that the stockholders, who, as directors or controlling stockholders, caused the corporation to enter into the stock purchase agreement, must have acted with the utmost good faith and loyalty to the other stockholders.

To meet this test, if the stockholder whose shares were purchased was a member of the controlling group, the controlling stockholders must cause the corporation to offer each stockholder an equal opportunity to sell a ratable number of his shares to the corporation at an identical price.

Liability for Torts and Crimes

Torts. The view in the early cases was that torts committed by a corporation's employees were *ultra vires* and, therefore, the corporation was not responsible. Today, as is clear from the cases in Chapters 3 and 4, the rule of *respondeat superior* applies to corporations, and the only issue is whether the employee was acting within the scope of his or her authority. The corporation may be liable even though it had expressly instructed its employees to avoid the act. Where the employee's acts are willful, wanton, or malicious and punitive damages would be appropriate, however, there is a split of authority as to whether the corporation will be held liable for punitive damages in the absence of authorization or ratification.

Since neither the directors nor the officers are the principal, they are not personally liable unless they have authorized or participated in the tort.

Crimes. The traditional view of the law was that a corporation could not be guilty of a crime involving intent. Today a number of courts find little difficulty in holding them guilty, particularly where the offense is requested by, authorized by, or performed by the board of directors or an officer or other person having responsibility for formulating company policy or by a high-level administrator having supervisory responsibility over the subject matter of the offense and acting within the scope of his or her employment. The Model Penal Code, for example, distinguishes between an agent and a "high managerial agent" of a corporation and attributes the felonies of only the latter to the corporation.

A number of statutes specifically defines crimes that are most likely to be committed by corporations. Examples include the Sherman Act, the Securities Act of 1934, and the Sunday closing laws of a number of states. Others impose penalties for failing to file or filing false reports with taxing or regulatory authorities.

Directors and officers may be held individually guilty if they request, authorize, conspire, or aid and abet the commission of a crime by an employee, even if the corporation is acquitted, because they have acted outside the scope of their authority. Likewise, of course, an employee committing an unauthorized crime is individually guilty even though his or her only motive was to benefit the corporation. However, the trend is away from finding lack of authority.

Penalties imposed by courts upon "white collar" criminals, especially corporate executives, have in the past been little more than "slaps on the wrist." This appears to be changing in response to recent publicity of widespread corporate payoffs, often covered up by false accounting entries, and public awareness of past judicial leniency.

SUMMARY

The general agency rules concerning torts and crimes apply to corporations. A corporation is liable for the torts of its employees done within the scope and in the course of the employment, even when it expressly instructs the employee to avoid the act. Corporations may also be found guilty of crimes, including those requiring intent, if the offense is authorized or performed by policy-making managers or high-level administrators acting within the scope and in the course of employment. Directors and officers may be held criminally liable although the corporation is acquitted because they have acted beyond their authority.

U.S. v. Park

421 U.S. 658 (U.S. Sup. Ct. 1975)

Acme Markets, Inc., and its president, John R. Park, (defendants) were charged by the U.S. with violating the Federal Food, Drug, and Cosmetic Act. Acme pleaded guilty but Park did not. Park, after objecting to the court's instructions, was convicted, and the Court of Appeals reversed. Reversed and conviction sustained.

Acme Markets, Inc., is a national retail food chain with headquarters in Philadelphia. It employs approximately 36,000 employees and operates 16 warehouses. The Government charged that Acme received food in interstate commerce that was contaminated by rodents while stored in Acme's Baltimore warehouse and thus became adulterated in violation of the Act.

In 1970 Park had received a letter from the Food and Drug Administration (FDA) setting forth in detail unsanitary conditions, including rodent infestation, found in Acme's Philadelphia warehouse. In December 1971 FDA found similar conditions in the Baltimore warehouse during a 12-day inspection. In January 1972 the Chief of Compliance of FDA's Baltimore office wrote Parks concerning the findings. The letter included the following statements:

> We note with much concern that the old and new warehouse areas used for food storage were actively and extensively inhabited by live rodents. Of even more concern was the observation that such reprehensible conditions obviously existed for a prolonged period of time without any detection, or were completely ignored. . . .
>
> We trust this letter will serve to direct your attention to the seriousness of the problem and formally advise you of the urgent need to initiate whatever measures are necessary to prevent recurrence and ensure compliance with the law.

Following receipt of the January 1972 letter, Park conferred with Acme's vice president for legal affairs, who informed him that the Baltimore division vice president "was investigating the situation immediately and would be taking corrective action." Except for the division vice president the same persons had supervisory responsibility for sanitation in both the Philadelphia and Baltimore warehouses.

In March 1972 FDA reinspected the Baltimore warehouse, finding an improvement in sanitation but still some rodent-contaminated food.

Park objected to portions of the trial judge's instructions to the jury, including the following:

> The individual is or could be liable under the statute, even if he did not consciously do wrong. However, the fact that the Defendant is president and is a chief executive officer of the Acme Markets does not require a finding of guilt. Though he need not have personally participated in the situation, he must have had a responsible relationship to the issue. The issue is, in this case, whether the Defendant, John R. Park, by virtue of his position in the company, had a position of authority and responsibility in the situation out of which these charges arose.

The statute provides a penalty for individuals of imprisonment for not more than one year and/or a fine of $1,000. The jury found Park guilty, and he was sentenced to pay a fine of $50.

Burger, Chief Justice. Central to the Court's conclusion [In *U.S. v. Dotterweich*] that individuals other than proprietors are subject to the criminal provisions of the Act was the reality that "the only way in which a corporation can act is through the individuals who act on its behalf."

At the same time, however, the Court was aware of the concern . . . that literal enforcement "might operate too harshly by sweeping within its condemnation any person however remotely entangled in the proscribed shipment." A limiting principle, in the form of "settled doctrines of criminal law" defining those who "are responsible for the commission of a misdemeanor," was available. In this context, the Court concluded, those doctrines dictated that the offense was committed "by all who have . . . a responsible share in the furtherance of the transaction which the statute outlaws."

The Act does not, as we observed in *Dotterweich,* make criminal liability turn on "awareness of some wrongdoing" or "conscious fraud." The duty imposed by Congress on responsible corporate agents is, we emphasize, one that requires the highest standard of foresight and vigilance, but the Act, in its criminal aspect, does not require that which is objectively impossible. The theory upon which responsible corporate agents are held criminally accountable for "causing" violations of the Act permits a claim that a defendant was "powerless" to prevent or correct the violation to "be raised defensively at a trial on the merits." *U.S. v. Wiesenfeld Warehouse Co.* If such a claim is made, the defendant has the burden of coming forward with evidence, but this does not alter the Government's ultimate burden of proving beyond a reasonable doubt the defendant's guilt, including his power, in light of the duty imposed by the Act, to prevent or correct the prohibited condition.

Turning to the jury charge in this case, it is of course arguable that isolated parts can be read as intimating that a finding of guilt could be predicated solely on respondent's corporate position. . . . Viewed as a whole, the charge did not permit the jury to find guilt solely on the basis of respondent's position in the corporation; rather, it fairly advised the jury that to find guilt it must find respondent "had a responsible relation to the situation," and "by virtue of his position . . . had authority and responsibility" to deal with the situation. The situation referred to could only be "food . . . held in unsanitary conditions in a warehouse with the result that it consisted, in part, of filth or . . . may have been contaminated with filth."

Park testified in his defense that he had employed a system in which he relied upon his subordinates, and that he was ultimately responsible for this system. He testified further that he had found these subordinates to be "dependable" and had "great confidence" in them. . . .

[The rebuttal] evidence was not offered to show that respondent had a propensity to commit criminal acts, that the crime charged had been committed; its purpose was to demonstrate that respondent was on notice that he could not rely on his system of delegation to subordinates to prevent or correct insanitary conditions at Acme's warehouses, and that he must have been aware of the deficiencies of this system before the Baltimore violations were discovered. The evidence was therefore relevant since it served to rebut Park's defense that he had justifiably relied upon subordinates to handle sanitation matters.

Problem Cases

1. Rio Refrigeration Company and Coastal Refrigeration Service, were competitors in the refrigeration and air-conditioning business. Rio purchased the business, parts, and assets of Coastal and, as part of the transaction, contracted to pay the account owed by Coastal to Thermal Supply of Harlingen, Inc., in the amount of $2,161.35. Rio then refused to pay Thermal Supply, and it brought suit.

   Rio set up as a defense that the contract was a guaranty of debt of a third person and was *ultra vires* and did not bind it. Is this a good defense?

2. The W. E. Belcher Lumber Company was a family-owned business. Brady Belcher, son of the founder, was president and had slightly more shares than the families of his four brothers and sisters. Some of the shares had been distributed to the third generation. Without discussing it with the board of directors or stockholders except for members of the family directly involved in operating the business, Brady Belcher organized a subsidiary corporation to exploit a timber contract to log certain public lands in Costa Rica. This involved an investment in road building and other development of approximately $400,000 plus an annual capital investment after allowance for depreciation of $200,000 per year for ten years.

   A member of the family who was the beneficiary of a trust holding shares in Belcher Lumber sued the trustee, a bank, which in turn sued Brady Belcher seeking an accounting for misuse of corporate funds through actions taken in excess of his authority. Is Brady personally liable for indemnifying the corporation for losses suffered?

3. At a special shareholder meeting of Scott County Tobacco Warehouses, Inc., a resolution to remove all 16 directors and to replace them with a new board of three named persons was passed by 1,419 shares in favor and 1,215 opposed with three shares not voting. James E. Cozart was the only former director among the three on the new board. Cozart owned 1,419 shares out of a total of 2,794 shares outstanding. R. J. and J. T. Harris, two of the former directors who were not named to the new board, together with their attorney, participated in the meeting and objected to some of the proceedings. Later they brought an action claiming that the new board was illegally elected because the effect of the resolution was to shorten the term of 15 of the 16 incumbent directors in violation of a provision of the corporation statute of Virginia declaring: "No decrease in number [of directors] shall have the effect of shortening the term of any incumbent director." This was part of a section of the statute dealing with the power of the directors to amend or repeal bylaws in the absence of a reservation of this power to shareholders. Unlike the Model Business Corporation Act, which the Virginia statutes closely followed, there was no express provision that the shareholders could simultaneously remove all members of the board of directors.

   Was the new board validly elected?

4. A rock music group known as Rare Earth incorporated under Michigan law in 1970. Some of the original members of the group departed and transferred their stock back to the corporation. In 1974 two of the original members, Hoorelbeke and Bridges, together with Guzman, who had joined earlier as a sixth member, continued playing as the Rare Earth group with three replacement performers. Hoorelbeke was president of the corporation. In July of 1974 they split into two factions. One faction, Bridges and Guzman, heard through the musical "grapevine" that Hoorelbeke had resigned as a band member and officer and director of the corporation. A director's meeting was convened in Los Angeles on July 12. Hoorelbeke was not given notice of the meeting and did not attend. Bridges was elected president to replace Hoorelbeke and authority was given Bridges to undertake a lawsuit to establish in the corporation the exclusive right to use the trademark, Rare Earth. Hoorelbeke filed a counterclaim alleging that he has been wrongfully deprived of the presidency and that his faction controls the majority of the shares of the corporation.

   Were the actions taken at the July 12 meeting, including the election of Bridges as president, proper?

5. Thompson was the executive director of Covington Housing Development Corporation. City officials of Covington were successful in halting federal funds to a project which CHDC was developing. Thompson brought suit against the city for damages in the name of the corporation. City of Covington's defense was that Thompson lacked the capacity to sue in the name of CHDC. Corporate bylaws provide that the executive director shall have all the general powers and duties which are usually vested in the office of the chief executive officer of the corporation. Is Covington's defense good?

6. Todd was employed by Gehrig, president of Ennis Business Forms, Inc., to serve the company as an accountant. Todd had been self-employed and was 65 years old at the time. Four years later, a young accountant was employed by the firm at a higher salary than Todd was receiving. He told Gehrig he was going to retire. To induce him to remain, Gehrig promised him an additional $200 per month to be paid upon retirement for every month he continued working. Todd retired 28 months after this agreement, and the corporation refused to pay the deferred compensation, claiming that Gehrig, who himself had by then retired, had no authority to make such a promise because it was unusual and extraordinary.

   The corporate bylaws provided that the president "shall be the chief administrative officer of the corporation" and "shall have the power and authority to execute bonds, mortgages, and other contracts of the corporation in the ordinary course of the business of the company." Gehrig's duties had included hiring the nonofficer employees of the company, setting their salaries, and granting them raises. The corporation had agreed to and paid deferred compensation to several other employees but they had been officers and the agreements had been approved by the board of directors.

   Is the corporation liable to Todd for the deferred compensation?

7. Majors owned one fifth of the shares of Tek Annex Company and of Tekseed Company, which were located at Tekemah, Nebraska. Tekseed was producing and selling hybrid seed corn. Tek Annex was an inactive corporation which had been partially liquidated, and Major sold her shares back to that corporation in 1967. On July 1, 1968, Tek Annex was merged into Tekseed. After consulting with their accountant who had been performing accounting work for Tekseed for 20 years, the directors established the basis for the exchange of shares in the merger solely upon the book values: $106.02 for Tek Annex shares and $73.22 for Tekseed shares. They gave no weight to potential earnings of goodwill of Tekseed because they thought its plant and equipment were obsolete, the plant's location was poor, and it was anticipated that the business manager would leave shortly and no

qualified replacement appeared to be available. Majors sued the Tekseed directors to recover damages on grounds of negligent misrepresentation at the time of the sale. Does the business judgment rule protect the directors from liability for the manner in which they established the exchange ratios and in advising Major?

8. Engdahl was a stockholder in J. H. Cox Manufacturing Co., a wholesale supplier of drapery material located in Indianapolis, and an administrative assistant to Mr. Cox. He was also a 10 percent shareholder, a director, and treasurer of Aero Drapery of Kentucky, a retailer of custom-made draperies in Louisville. Cox was the controlling shareholder of both corporations. Engdahl lived in Indianapolis but he spent two days a month at Aero in his capacity as treasurer and reported to Cox on the status of accounts receivable, employee morale, and other Aero business information.

   On one of his trips Engdahl learned that Bland, Aero's office manager, was dissatisfied with his job with Aero. Engdahl suggested that they meet after work. Out of this grew plans for a competing business to be participated in as well by Brown, Aero's workroom manager, and Underwood, a top salesperson for Aero. Space was rented, goods purchased, a listing in the yellow pages taken out, and other arrangements completed and the other three resigned from Aero without notice (none had contracts) after Engdahl had given notice and sold his stock back to Cox.

   Aero Drapery and Cox Manufacturing then brought action against Engdahl, Bland, Brown, and Underwood. Should any of them be held liable?

9. Joseph and Jennie Miller founded a scrap business in Winona, Minnesota, in 1890 which was later incorporated as Miller Waste Mills, Inc. Their eight children all worked in the business at times, and Rudolph and Benjamin continued in it, and in a reorganization in 1940 they gained a majority of the shares and assumed the management from the parents. It became the largest producer of packing and wiping waste in the United States. Because of production problems in the plant, Unit Manufacturing Co. was formed in 1943 by the wives of Rudolph and Benjamin to conduct a waste packaging business to take over a government contract obtained for Miller Waste, with Miller Waste furnishing raw materials to Unit.

   Unit later expanded into producing filters using Miller's waste. Rudolph, under an agreement reached with the other shareholders in 1940, continued development of a lubricator for railroad freight cars, and these were manufactured by his corporation, Filter Supply, and marketed by Miller Lubricator Co., owned by Rudolph and Benjamin. The filter was in direct competition with the packing waste sold by Miller Waste, but its demand for waste from Miller Waste tended to offset decreased sales to railroads as the lubricator took a substantial share of the market. Miller Waste sold and leased real estate to these and other corporations controlled by Rudolph and Benjamin and furnished maintenance, labor, and accounting services to them. The rentals and the sales of products and services furnished by Miller Waste to the various corporations were made at prices equal to or higher than to nonrelated customers. Sales of real estate were made at prices based upon independent appraisals by professional appraisers.

   Oscar Miller, a minority shareholder, brought a derivative suit on behalf of Miller Waste seeking to recover assets and profits of the other corporations operated by his brothers Rudolph and Benjamin and their families. Will he win?

10. MAI was in the business of financing computer installations through sale and leaseback arrangements with commercial and industrial users. Under the leases, MAI was required to maintain and repair the computers. Since it lacked the capacity to do this itself, it contracted with International Business Machines, the manufacturer of its machines, to service them. As a result of a sharp increase by IBM in its charges for such services,

MAI's expenses for August 1966 rose considerably and its net earnings declined approximately 75 percent from $262,253 in July to $66,233 in August.

This information was not released to the public until October, but before this time Oreamuno, chairman of the board of directors, and Gonzalez, president of MAI, sold 56,500 shares of their MAI stock at the then current market price of $28 per share. When the information concerning the reduction in earnings became known to the public, the price of the stock immediately dropped to $11.

Diamond, a shareholder, brought a derivative action charging that Oreamuno and Gonzalez had used inside information for their personal advantage and asked that they account to the corporation for the $800,000 difference between the selling price and $11 per share. Should a motion to dismiss the complaint because the corporation suffered no damage be sustained?

11. Lincoln Land Company was a Georgia corporation engaged in real estate development. One of its subdivisions was Oak Hills Estates in Hall county, Georgia. Palfrey and others bought lots in Oak Hills Estates upon representations made in corporate advertising material and by employees of the corporation that there would be an abundant supply of water. These representations were continued to buyers after it became clear in 1966 that the water was insufficient even for the 50 percent of the lots already sold and that the sale of additional lots would aggravate the problem and no new source of water was at hand. Blades, Habit, and Goodwin were the officers, directors, and owners of all of the stock of Lincoln Land Co. They were aware of the representations being made.

    Are the officer-directors individually liable in deceit to purchasers of the lots relying upon the representations who are unable to build upon or sell their lots because of the lack of water?

12. Ebasco Corporation was charged with criminally negligent homicide for its role in the death of two workers on a construction project which Ebasco was supervising. The relevant statute read "A person is guilty of criminally negligent homicide when, with criminal negligence, he causes the death of another." Ebasco's defense is that as a corporation it cannot be indicted for such a crime. Is this a good defense?

28

Shareholders' Rights and Liabilities

Shareholders' Meetings

Exercise of Shareholder Functions. Shareholders of a corporation ordinarily have few functions. Functions which generally are required to be performed by shareholders include: the annual election (36)[1] and the removal of directors (39); the adoption, amendment, and repeal of bylaws under a few statutes but not the Model Act (27); approval of extraordinary corporate matters such as merger or consolidation (73), sale of assets not in the normal course of business (79), reduction of stated capital (69), voluntary dissolution (84), and amendment of corporate articles (59); and under the Model Act (47) approval of loans to officers and approval of stock option plans (20). As will be discussed later in this chapter, certain classes of shares may be denied all voting rights except in specific extraordinary corporate transactions.

The shareholders' functions can generally be exercised only by voting in shareholders' meetings. However, the Model Act (145) and the statutes of many states permit shareholders to act without a meeting if consent to the action in writing is signed by all shareholders. Delaware requires written consent only by the holders of the number of shares required for approval.

Unless a higher proportion is required by the statute, articles, or bylaws, a majority of the shares represented at the meeting will decide issues put to a vote. The Model Act (33) permits including a provision in the articles to give the shareholders of any class more or less than one vote per share.

Annual Meetings. The general corporation statutes of most states and the Model Act (28) provide that an annual meeting of shareholders shall be

[1] The numbers in parentheses refer to the sections of the Model Business Corporation Act, which appears in the Appendix.

held at the time specified in the bylaws. Delaware, however, no longer requires an annual meeting. The Model Act specifies that any shareholder may petition a court to order a meeting if none is held for 13 months.

Usually, the most important business at the annual shareholders' meeting is the election of directors. Other matters which may be voted on include amendments to the articles of incorporation, approval of the firm's auditors, approval of a stock-option plan for executives and such resolutions as management or shareholders may propose. It is also customary for one or more members of the top management to give reports with regard to the operation and prospects of the corporation.

Only a few states require that shareholders' meetings be held within the state of incorporation. Some publicly held corporations hold their meetings in their state of incorporation even though few shareholders live nearby and they are not required to do so. Others seek to encourage shareholder attendance by hiring large halls in convenient locations. A few rotate their meetings between the major cities of the country for the convenience of their shareholders.

Special Meetings. Special shareholders' meetings may be held whenever corporate matters arise that require shareholders' action. Under the Model Act (28) a special shareholders' meeting may be called by the president, the board of directors or the holders of not less than one tenth of the shares entitled to vote at the meeting. It permits the corporation, in its articles of incorporation or bylaws, to specify that other officers or persons may call a special meeting.

Notice of Meetings. The Model Act (29) and the statutes of most states set forth the requirements for notice of annual and special meetings of shareholders. The Model Act states that written notice giving the place, day, and hour of the meeting and, for special meetings, the purpose(s) of the meeting must be delivered not less than 10 nor more than 50 days before the date of the meeting to all shareholders entitled to vote at the meeting. For extraordinary changes such as merger, dissolution, or sale or mortgage of assets out of the regular course of business, specific notice of the proposal must be given all shareholders (73, 79, 84). Specific notice must be also given shareholders entitled to vote thereon when a reduction in stated capital (69) is proposed. Those entitled to notice are the shareholders of the class or classes of shares entitled to vote who are "of record," that is, those whose names appear on the stock-transfer book of the corporation.

If the prescribed notice is not given, any action taken at the meeting is a nullity, unless notice is waived in writing before, during, or after the meeting (144) or the action taken is later ratified in a properly called meeting. Actual attendance at a meeting, unless merely to object to the transaction of business, constitutes a waiver. Waiver is effective only if all shareholders either attend or waive in writing. Some statutes require written waiver by all shareholders.

Quorum. In order to be able to conduct business at a meeting, a certain number of shares (a quorum) must be represented in person or by proxy. In the absence of a statute those shares represented, even though a minority, constitute a quorum. However, most statutes and the Model Act (32) define a quorum as the majority of shares outstanding but permit a different requirement to be established in the articles and bylaws. Statutes usually establish one third of the shares as a minimum for a quorum. In large corporations most of the shares are represented by proxy and only a very small proportion of shareholders actually attend. Delaware establishes no minimum but leaves it to the corporation. Once a quorum is present, a later withdrawal of shareholders will not affect the validity of action taken by those remaining.

Conduct of the Meeting. The articles or bylaws generally state who shall preside at shareholders' meetings, and this is usually the chairman of the board, if there is such an office, or the president. If there is no such provision, then any shareholder may call the meeting to order and preside while a meeting chairman is elected. In publicly held corporations it is customary to provide inspectors of election whose responsibility it is to determine whether or not a person claiming to be a shareholder is entitled to vote. A few states have statutory provisions dealing with inspectors of election. It is customary and desirable, though not required by statute in most states, to keep minutes of shareholders' meetings, and they are usually recorded and kept by the secretary of the corporation.

Shareholder Proposals and Right to Speak. Among the rights of shareholders is full participation in shareholders' meetings. This includes the right to offer resolutions,[2] to speak for or against such resolutions as are proposed, and to ask questions of the officers of the corporation. In recent years these rights have been rather systematically pursued by certain shareholders who might be said to fall into two classes. One might be typified by Lewis D. Gilbert, who has made an occupation of attending the shareholder meetings of large corporations and proposing resolutions that are aimed at protecting or enhancing the interests of small shareholders. The proposals include amending the corporate articles to permit cumulative voting for directors, setting ceilings on top-executive pay and limiting charitable contributions by the corporation. More recently, groups seeking social or political changes, such as elimination of the use of napalm in Vietnam, provision of greater opportunities for minority groups, environmental protection, and the elimination of apartheid in South Africa, have introduced or sought to introduce resolutions at shareholders' meetings that would limit certain corporate activity or require publication of certain information. They have also questioned and criticized manage-

---

[2] See Chapter 29 for a discussion of SEC rules on such proposals.

ment in regard to these issues. None of the proposals has drawn more than a few percent of shareholders' votes, and in most cases it appears that calling attention to the issue was the primary motivation of those making them.

SUMMARY

Shareholders generally have few functions. They elect and remove directors and vote on extraordinary corporate transactions such as merger and sale of assets. Under most statutes authority to amend the articles of incorporation is reserved to them.

Annual meetings of shareholders are held at a time specified in the bylaws. All shareholders "of record" of classes entitled to vote are entitled to notice of special meetings and also of regular meetings if the specific time and place is not established in the bylaws.

Most statutes establish a majority of the shares as the quorum for a meeting but permit the number to be established by the corporation as low as one third. Who is to preside at the meeting is usually established by the bylaws.

Shareholders have the right to offer resolutions and to comment and ask questions at shareholders' meetings. Resolutions offered by small shareholders in large corporations generally get few votes.

Darvin v. Belmont Industries, Inc.

199 N.W.2nd 542 (Ct. App. Mich. 1972)

Action by Frank Darvin (plaintiff) for writ of mandamus to set aside actions taken at shareholders' meetings of both Belmont Industries, Inc., and V&F Investment Company (V&F) (defendants). Judgment for Belmont and V&F and Darvin appealed. Reversed and remanded.

Frank Darvin owned 170 out of 700 shares of the stock in Belmont. There were four other shareholders. Underwood, Sychta, and Punturiere each also owned 170 shares and the fifth shareholder owned 20 shares. Underwood, Sychta, Punturiere, and Darvin each owned 3,200 shares out of a total of 12,800 shares outstanding in V&F. The four men comprised the boards of directors of both corporations, and they were officers and employees of both corporations.

A dispute over corporate management arose between Darvin and Underwood, the president. The other three directors concluded they no longer wanted Darvin in the two companies. Accordingly, special shareholders' meetings and boards of directors' meeting of both corporations were scheduled for September 12, 1969. Darvin received notice of the meetings on September 11.

Darvin and his attorney attended the shareholders' meetings of both corporations, and at the beginning of each meeting they objected to the lack of notice. At the meetings the board of directors of each company was reduced to three, and Underwood, Sychta, and Punturiere were elected. The directors then held a meeting and Darvin was eliminated as an officer of each company. He was later terminated as an employee.

The bylaws of each corporation provide that shareholders shall receive notice "at least ten days prior to any meeting." Darvin claims that the actions taken at the shareholders' and directors' meetings are ineffective not only because of the fact he was given notice only one day in advance but also because the Michigan corporation statute requires that the notice give the purpose for a special shareholders' meeting.

LESINSKI, CHIEF JUDGE. The question that we address, then, is whether plaintiff Darvin's attendance at the meetings, his objections to the lack of notice, and his responses that he did not wish to vote his shares when so asked at the meetings, as testified to by Directors Underwood, Punturiere, and Sychta, constituted a waiver of the notice defects.

A purpose of the time-notice requirement is, of course, to allow a shareholder sufficient time to arrange to attend the meeting. If the shareholder did, in fact, attend the meeting, despite a failure by the corporation to comply with the time-notice requirement, courts have reasoned that he has suffered no harm because he was still able to be present. The purpose-notice requirement serves another function, however. It provides a shareholder with sufficient opportunity to study contemplated action at the meeting and the legality thereof. When the shareholder possesses knowledge of the purpose of a special meeting, he can study the proposal, arrive at a position, and either oppose it or support it. One commentator has even suggested that notice be given of any extraordinary matter that is to be considered at a regular meeting:

> With such notice, the shareholder has the opportunity to think upon, and discuss with other shareholders, the matter and be prepared to vote intelligently upon it. Lattin on *Corporations.*

We find the language of two Michigan Supreme Court cases, although they concern the problem of notice at directors' meetings and not shareholders' meetings, to be relevant to the issue which confronts us here. In *Zachary v. Millin* . . . the Court held that the members of the board not only had to be present, but also had to participate, before a defect in notice would be deemed waived.

The case of *Bourne v. Muskegon Circuit Judge* concerned a purpose-notice requirement at a directors' meeting. Notice of the special directors' meeting was sent out with several purposes enumerated, but no mention was made of the fact that dissolution or receivership proceedings were contemplated by the corporation. The Court held that such omission was fatal to the validity of the notice and pointed out that the situation "was not a dire emergency requiring individual action." That notice of a special shareholders' meeting must include the purpose of the proceeding has long been the law in Michigan. . . .

Courts in other jurisdictions have ruled specifically on the issue at hand, holding that attendance at a meeting, without participation, does not constitute waiver of defective notice.

Although the notice given to plaintiff Darvin in the instant case was sufficient to obtain his physical presence at the meeting, it is plain that it was not sufficient to allow him to ascertain what action was to be taken at the special meeting of defendant corporations, and to determine what steps could be taken to protect his position. The weight of the evidence at trial, although it was contradicted, revealed that Darvin had not voted his shares at the meeting. He specifically refused the opportunity to do so. If he had voted his shares he could have made use of the protection afforded him by [the statute relative to cumulative voting] which governs reduction of members of the board of directors in this State. With sufficient notice, plaintiff Darvin and his attorney could have had the opportunity to apprise themselves of the existence of this provision which has been recognized as supplying special protection to the minority shareholder in the close corporation.

Accordingly, we hold that plaintiff Darvin's mere attendance at the meeting coupled with the nonvoting of his shares was not sufficient participation to waive the notice requirement under the facts of this case.

Voting Rights

Shareholders Entitled to Vote. Whether a shareholder is entitled to vote at a shareholders' meeting depends upon statutory provisions and the articles and bylaws of the corporation. The Model Act (15, 33) permits the issuance of a class or classes of nonvoting stock if so provided in the articles. However, such nonvoting classes are entitled to vote on extraordinary corporate transactions (60, 73, 74, 84). The person who has legal title to the stock is the one generally entitled to vote, but it is common in publicly held corporations for the directors to establish a "record date." Those entitled to vote will be those appearing on a voting list prepared as of that date. A title owner who is not the owner of record may obtain a proxy from the record holder. The Model Act (30) also provides that if none is established, the record date shall be the date of mailing of notice of the meeting.

Neither the corporation nor its subsidiary may vote treasury shares (those once issued and then reacquired) if any, and, of course, unissued stock has no vote.

The fact that a shareholder has a personal interest in the matter being voted will not disqualify him or her from voting or affect the validity of the action taken, since ordinarily shareholders have no fiduciary duty to the corporation. However, controlling shareholders will not be permitted to manipulate the corporate affairs in fraud of the rights of the other shareholders.

Cumulative Voting. Although most corporations conduct the election of directors on the basis that each share is entitled to one vote for each vacancy, many corporations give shareholders the option to cumulate their votes by giving one candidate as many votes as the number of directors to be elected multiplied by the shareholder's number of shares. The option to cumulate votes is given to all shareholders by constitutional provisions or statute in almost half of the states. Most of the rest of them permit corporations to provide for cumulative voting in their articles. A few statutes are silent, in which case some courts have permitted cumulative voting if so provided in articles or bylaws.

The purpose of cumulative voting is to give minority shareholders an opportunity to be represented on the board of directors. Whether this is desirable is a highly controversial issue. Its opponents argue that representatives of minority interests tend to be devisive. Few large publicly held corporations are domiciled in states with mandatory cumulative voting, and promoters tend to avoid incorporation in these states.

The formula for determining the minimum number of shares required to elect one director under cumulative voting is:

$$X = \frac{S}{D+1} + 1$$

where S is the number of shares voting and D is the total number of directors to be elected. Obviously, the fewer the number of directors to be elected the larger the minority interest must be to enable a shareholder to elect a director. One device for reducing the effect of cumulative voting is to provide for electing directors by classes, each class to remain in office for three years, the maximum permitted by the Model Act (37).

Proxy Voting. All state statutes permit shareholders to appoint an agent, known as a proxy, to vote for them. The Model Act (33) requires that the authority to vote as a proxy must be given in writing, but some states permit oral proxies. Both the writing and the person designated to vote for the shareholder are called a proxy. Usually proxies are general, permitting the agent to vote on all matters properly coming before a shareholders' meeting, but they may be limited to a particular matter. Most states put a limit on the duration of a proxy. The Model Act limits it to 11 months from the date of execution unless the writing itself provides otherwise. Generally, proxies are revocable at any time by the shareholder. Exceptions are those "coupled with an interest," such as where the proxy is given to a pledgee of the shares or to a purchaser of the shares under an executory contract. Otherwise, irrevocability is considered against public policy. A proxy is automatically revoked when another proxy is given subsequently. The Securities and Exchange Commission is given rule-making power over solicitation of proxies by the Securities Exchange Act of 1934. It limits a proxy to a single meeting plus any adjournment.

Voting Trust. The Model Act (34) and most state statutes permit shareholders to establish voting trusts. The purpose of a voting trust is to concentrate shareholder power in one or a few persons who can control the corporation through the election of directors. One frequent use of the device is to give control of the corporation to creditors during corporate reorganization after bankruptcy.[3] Although courts earlier tended to hold voting trusts illegal as against public policy, the modern cases tend to uphold them even in the absence of statute, unless the purpose for which the voting trust is formed is illegal, such as to gain a monopoly as in the case of the Standard Oil trust and others near the end of the 19th century, or to defraud minority shareholders.

The Model Act (34) and a number of state statutes require that a voting trust be established by an agreement in writing among the participating shareholders and that it be filed with the corporation. They also establish a maximum life, usually ten years, for the agreement. It is common for voting trust certificates to be given the shareholder in exchange for the shares in the corporation, and they entitle the holder to a ratable share of dividends and distributions paid by the corporation.

SUMMARY

The voting rights of the shareholder are based on the statutes of the state of incorporation and on the articles and bylaws of the corporation. Nonvoting classes of stock are entitled to vote on certain extraordinary corporate transactions. Shareholders listed on the books of the company on the record date are those who are entitled to vote.

A corporation cannot vote unissued or treasury stock. The personal interest of a shareholder in a matter being voted on does not disqualify the shareholder from voting.

Many states require corporations formed under their statutes to grant cumulative voting and most of the rest permit this system of voting, which is designed to give representation to minority shareholders, if provided for in the articles. Proxy voting is generally permitted and the SEC has rule-making power over the solicitation of proxies. Voting trusts are permitted if they have a legitimate purpose and a reasonable length of life.

---

[3] The most notable recent voting trust was established in 1960 at the insistence of Trans World Arilines' creditors to vote the 78 percent of TWA shares owned by Hughes Tool Co.

Levin v. Metro-Goldwyn-Mayer, Inc.

264 F.Supp. 797 (S.D. N.Y. 1967)

This was an action by Levin and other shareholders (plaintiffs) against Metro-Goldwyn-Mayer, Inc., and certain of its directors (defendants) seeking to enjoin methods used by management is soliciting proxies. Injunction denied.

Levin, a director of MGM, and his associates in this action owned 11 percent of the outstanding shares of MGM and were seeking to gain control of the corporation through a proxy contest. They charged the MGM management with wrongfully committing the corporation to pay for the services of attorneys, a public relations firm, and a proxy soliciting organization to secure support from shareholders for the current management. They further claimed that the use of MGM employees and business contacts was improper. No charge was made that any false or fraudulent statements had been made by the management group in connection with proxy solicitation.

RYAN, DISTRICT JUDGE. It is quite plain that the differences between "the O'Brien [management] group" and "the Levin group" are much more than mere personality conflicts. These might readily be resolved by reasoning and hard-headed, profit-minded businessmen. There are definite business policies advocated by each group, so divergent that reconciliation does not seem possible. They appear so evident from the papers before us that detailed analysis would be a waste of time. However, in such a situation the right of an independent stockholder to be fully informed is of supreme importance. The controlling question presented on this application is whether illegal or unfair means of communication, such as demand judicial intervention, are being employed by the present management. We find that they are not and conclude that the injunctive relief now sought should be denied.

. . . Contrary to the shareholders' unsupported statement that 9,000 MGM employees are at work soliciting proxies, MGM has stated that the total number of employees who on their own time have consented to telephone shareholders to vote is less than 150. We do not find this an unreasonable situation under the circumstances. . . .

The employment of two proxy solicitation firms and the fees agreed to be paid to them were fully disclosed in the MGM proxy statement. Georgeson & Co. is in charge of solicitation of proxies from stockholders directly; the Kissel-Blake Organization is directing its efforts to brokerage solicitation. Here again, MGM states without contradiction that "in every year since 1956, MGM has employed the firms of Georgeson & Co. and the Kissel-Blake Organization, Inc., to solicit proxies for its stockholders' meetings." We do not find basis for injunctive relief in their employment, nor in the employment of Dudley King & Co., as a consultant in connection with corporate matters and stockholder relations. . . .

There have been set forth in paid advertisements statements by actors, directors, writers, and exhibitors supporting and expressing confidence in the present management. MGM states these expressions have been unsolicited and spontaneous and have been published by these persons [and] . . . paid for completely out of their own pockets without any direct or indirect promise of repayment by MGM. There is no proof to challenge this. Certainly, MGM should not be expected to deny or contradict what they regard as well-deserved compliments graciously paid to them. Nor do we find the publication of such unsolicited individual advertisements a violation of the Act of 1934.

. . . MGM engaged the services of Thomas J. Deegan Co., Inc. Deegan is a recognized and reputable public relations firm. The engagement was long before the present proxy contest. The employment is neither unusual nor unreasonable. It does not afford ground for injunctive relief.

Dividends

Introduction. The law assumes that the purpose of a business corporation is to make a profit. Shareholders usually invest in a corporation primarily to share in the expected profit through dividends, although it is not unusual for corporations to retain all earnings over long periods of time and to reinvest them in the business. Such a policy may be attractive to shareholders in the higher income tax brackets if the result is appreciation of the market value of their shares so that they can enjoy capital gains. Dividends must be paid ratably on the shares of any class or series within a class.

Types of Dividends. Dividends are usually paid in cash but assets of the corporation, such as shares in another corporation, may be distributed as a dividend. Such dividends are referred to as "property dividends" or "dividends-in-kind." Distribution of assets, including cash, which amount to a partial liquidation are not included within the meaning of the term dividend as used in the Model Act. "Stock dividends" are distributions of shares in the corporation itself and are discussed later in this chapter. An "extra dividend" is not a special kind of dividend but is usually so designated by the directors to indicate that it is given in addition to what they consider to be the normal or regular dividend that they expect to be able to maintain.

Funds Available for Dividends. The corporation statutes of all states specify the sources from which dividends may be paid. The common-law rule was that payment of a dividend was illegal if it resulted in the impairment of the capital of the corporation. The ingenuity of corporate promoters and managers in designing various types of shares and methods of establishing their value has made it difficult for the courts and legislatures to accomplish their objective of maintaining the original capital of the corporation as a "trust fund" for the protection of creditors and to help assure stockholders that the corporation may be able to carry out its purposes.

Tests of Validity of Dividend Payments. There are three principal tests of the validity of dividend payments. They are: (1) the noninsolvency test, (2) the surplus test, based upon the balance sheet, and (3) the current earnings test, based upon the income statement. Some statutes include more than one. For example, the Model Act (45) forbids a dividend that would render a corporation insolvent, that is unable to pay its debts as they fall due, as well as limiting dividends to "earned surplus" (although it has an alternative provision that would permit dividends to be paid out of unreserved and unrestricted net earnings of the current and next preceding fiscal years even if there is no earned surplus.) A dividend that would make the corporation insolvent is probably illegal as an invasion of creditors' rights without a statutory provision.

The Model Act (45a) limits dividends to "earned surplus," and it is available for dividends in all states. A number of states permit the use of surplus arising from other sources, a few limiting such dividend payments to preferred shareholders. A corporation has a surplus when its assets exceed its liabilities plus its stated capital. A surplus may arise from several kinds of corporate transactions. "Earned surplus" arises from net profits made in the operation of the business. "Paid-in surplus" arises out of the difference between the par value (or stated value in case of no-par shares) and the price the corporation receives when it sells the shares to investors. "Revaluation surplus" is created by an upward revaluation of assets of the corporation. "Reduction surplus" is created by reducing stated capital.

Delaware permits the payment of a dividend out of current net profits regardless of a negative surplus, but only if the capital equals the liquidation preferences. A few statutes specifically forbid payment out of unrealized appreciation or require assets to be reduced by unrealized depreciation in computing the source of dividends.

Directors' Discretion in Payment of Dividends. Declaration of dividends is the responsibility of the directors under the Model Act and most statutes, although under some statutes the shareholders may retain this power by an appropriate provision in the articles. Declaration of dividends is discretionary and within the business judgment of the directors. This discretion applies even to shares with a dividend preference, although a clearly worded provision in the articles may make the payment of a dividend mandatory if one can legally be paid. However, dividends are not gratuities handed out to shareholders by a benevolent board of directors; they are the expected returns on capital investment. Although the burden of proof is on the complaining shareholder and courts are hesitant to substitute their judgment for that of the directors, shareholders have occasionally been able to get a court to decree the payment of a dividend when the directors have refused to do so through a flagrant abuse of their discretion.

The federal government imposes heavy punitive taxes upon improper accumulation of corporate earnings, which also limits the discretion of directors. On the other hand, it is very common for lenders to prohibit the payment of dividends or to limit them to funds defined more narrowly than the legal prohibitions.

Dividend Payment on Preferred Stock. The preferred shareholder's right to dividends is based upon his or her shareholder contract, subject to the availability of funds from which dividends can be paid. Considerable confusion exists as to the dividend rights of preferred shareholders under varying conditions, and great care in drafting the contract is essential. Unless the contract is interpreted as making the declaration of a dividend upon a preferred class of shares mandatory, the directors may refuse to declare and pay a dividend even though funds are available from which a dividend could legally be paid if, in their honest judgment, the payment of the dividend would be detrimental to the corporation.

Four types of contractual provisions are found in preferred stock: (1) a mandatory dividend preference entitles the holder to the contractual dividend if payment is legally permissible, leaving no discretion to the directors (such contracts are very rare; in case of ambiguity courts avoid interpreting preferences as mandatory, and at least one court has held such a contract unenforceable[4]); (2) a cumulative dividend preference entitles the shareholder to unpaid dividends for all prior periods before any dividend or distribution may be paid upon shares that are subordinate with respect to dividend rights; (3) a cumulative-to-the-extent-earned preference entitles the shareholder to unpaid dividends for all prior periods in which there were funds legally available for such dividends before subordinate shareholders may receive dividends or distributions; (4) a noncumulative preference gives the shareholder the right to dividends in a fiscal period before dividends or distributions are paid to other shareholders.

There is a divergence of authority as to whether the preference on noncumulative shares extends beyond the current fiscal year. Most jurisdictions hold that even though earnings are legally sufficient for a dividend on the preferred shares, directors may retain them for reinvestment in the business. Whether holders of cumulative preferred shares are entitled to the arrearages in case of liquidation of the corporation depends upon the interpretation of the shareholders' contract. Most courts hold that arrearages must be paid upon liquidation, if assets are sufficient, even though there were insufficient earnings to pay them when due.

Stock Dividends and Stock Splits. A stock dividend is a distribution to shareholders of additional shares in the corporation and is, in effect, a capitali-

[4] *Lindgrove v. Schulter & Co.*, 176 N.E. 832 (Ct. App. N.Y. 1931).

zation of surplus. The shares distributed may be either of the same class as those held or of a different class or series. Under the Model Act (45e) no dividend payable in shares shall be paid to holders of shares of any other class unless the articles of incorporation so provide or such payment is authorized by a majority of the outstanding shares of the class in which payment is to be made. This limitation, of course, is for the protection of the holders of the class of shares being distributed, since such a distribution would dilute their shares. A dividend payable in the same class of shares has no effect on the equity of the shareholders since their interest in the corporation remains proportionately the same. Nevertheless, the total market value of the shareholder's interest frequently increases and shareholders seem to value the additional piece of paper. If the dividend rate remains the same on a per share basis, of course, the effect will be to increase the dividend received by the shareholder.

The difference between a stock dividend and a stock split is that in the former case the par or stated value of the shares distributed must be transferred from the surplus to the capital account (unless treasury shares are distributed) while in the case of a stock split there is no change in the total capital account but only in the par value or stated value of the shares. Payment of a stock dividend in the same class of shares requires only director approval while approval of shareholders is required for the amendment of the articles of incorporation necessary to make a stock split (58i, 60f). A reverse stock split is a decrease in the number of shares of a class such that, for example, two shares become one share. The most common purpose of a stock split is to adjust the market price to fall within the popular $20 to $40 range. It may also mask rapid changes in earnings per share.

Distributions from Surplus. The Model Act (46) distinguishes a dividend from what it designates as a distribution from capital surplus. Such distribution may be made from capital surplus as distinguished from earned surplus. However, distributions may not be made when the corporation is insolvent, and unless the articles provide for such a distribution, a majority of the shares of each class of shares, whether regularly entitled to voting rights or not, must vote in favor of the distribution. If it is a distribution from capital surplus, that fact must be disclosed to the shareholders when it is received. Other limitiations include a provision that no distribution may be made when cumulative dividends have accrued or when the remaining net assets of the corporation would be insufficient to pay off preferential shares in a voluntary liquidation. In addition, this section of the Model Act permits, without a shareholder vote or authorization in the articles, distributions from capital surplus to discharge cumulative dividend rights of preferred shareholders so long as insolvency is avoided.

A partial liquidation of the capital of a corporation, either in money or property, is also called a distribution. However, if the in-kind dispersion is charged to surplus, it should be called a dividend.

Dividend Declaration. A dividend is declared by formal action of the board of directors. Once declared, a lawful cash dividend becomes a debt owing to the shareholders, although a Massachusetts case has held that the directors may rescind their action prior to the time the declaration has become known to shareholders.[5] Thereafter, should the corporation become insolvent, the shareholders may share in the assets with other creditors to the extent of the dividend. However, stock dividend declarations, since they do not actually change the shareholders' interest in the corporation, are held to be revocable. Dividends other than stock dividends may be paid in cash or property of the corporation, such as stock in another corporation.

Effect of Transfer on Right to Dividend. As between the corporation and the shareholder, the corporation may treat the shareholder of record as the person entitled to receive the dividend. For this purpose a record date is established by the directors. As between the transferor and transferee, the right to the dividend will depend on the agreement between the parties. In the absence of agreement the transferor is entitled to the dividend if the sale was made after the record date. If the sale is made on a stock exchange, the transferee is entitled to the dividends unless he or she buys the stock after it is declared "ex dividend," which is five business days before the record date for the dividend.

SUMMARY

Shareholders usually expect to share in the profits of a corporation through dividends. These are normally paid in cash but may be paid in property, such as shares in another corporation.

Corporation statutes usually specify the sources from which dividends may be paid. Earned surplus is available for dividends in all states but a dividend may not be paid if the result would be to make the corporation insolvent. Three principal tests of the validity of dividends are used: (1) the noninsolvency test, (2) the surplus test, and (3) the current earnings test.

Declaration of dividends is the responsibility of the directors and is subject to their business judgment even with respect to shares with a dividend preference, except in the rare case of a mandatory dividend. Three other types of dividend preferences are: cumulative, cumulative-to-the-extent-earned, and noncumulative.

A stock dividend is a distribution of additional shares in the corporation

---

[5] *Ford v. Easthampton Rubber Thread Co.*, 32 N.E. 1036 (Mass. 1893); cf. *Brown v. Luce Mfg. Co.*, 96 S.W.2d 1098 (K.C. Ct. App. Mo. 1936).

and is, in effect, a capitalization of surplus. A stock split does not change the total capital account but only the par or stated value of the shares.

Under the Model Act a distribution is distinguished from a dividend and may be made from capital surplus while a dividend must be charged against earned surplus. Distributions may be used to discharge cumulative dividend rights.

Once declared a cash dividend becomes a debt but a stock dividend declaration may be rescinded.

The corporation may treat the stockholder of record as entitled to the dividend. In the absence of an agreement the transferee of shares bought on a stock exchange is entitled to the dividend unless he buys after it is declared "ex-dividend."

Dodge v. Ford Motor Co.

170 N.W. 668 (Sup. Ct. Mich. 1919)

This was an action by John F. Dodge and Horace E. Dodge (plaintiffs) against Ford Motor Company and others (defendants) to force the directors of Ford Motor Company to pay a special dividend. Judgment for the Dodges, and Ford Motor Company appealed. Judgment affirmed in part and reversed in part.

Dodge *et al.* were stockholders in the Ford Motor Company. From the beginning in 1903 to July 31, 1916, the corporate business had been profitable. The capital stock had been increased from $150,000 in 1903 to $2 million in 1908. A regular dividend of 5 percent per month on its capital stock of $2 million had been paid since 1911, and in addition thereto special dividends had been paid which ranged from $1 million to $10 million per year and which totaled $41 million for the years 1911 to 1915 inclusive. In 1916 the directors decided to continue to pay the regular dividend of 5 percent per month on the corporation's capital stock of $2 million but to discontinue all special dividends. At this time the corporation had a surplus of $112 million; its yearly profits were $60 million; its total liabilities including capital stock were less than $20 million; it had cash on hand of $54 million; and all planned improvements would cost approximately $24 million. This action was brought to force the directors to pay a special dividend.

OSTRANDER, CHIEF JUSTICE. The rule which will govern courts in deciding these questions is not in dispute. It is, of course, differently phrased by judges and by authors; and, as the phrasing in a particular instance may seem to lean for or against the exercise of the right of judicial interference with the actions of corporate directors, the context, or the facts before the court, must be considered. This court, in *Hunter v. Roberts, Throp & Co.,* recognized the rule in the following language:

It is a well-recognized principle of law that the directors of a corporation, and they alone, have the power to declare a dividend of the earnings of the corporation, and to determine its amount. Courts of equity will not interfere in the management of the directors unless it is clearly made to appear that they are guilty of fraud or misappropriation of the corporate funds, or refuse to declare a dividend when the corporation has a surplus of net profits which it can, without detriment to the business, divide among its stockholders, and when a refusal to do so would amount to such an abuse of discretion as would constitute a fraud, or breach of that good faith which they are bound to exercise towards the stockholders.

The record, and especially the testimony of Mr. Ford, convinces that he has to some extent the attitude towards shareholders of one who has dispensed and distributed to them large gains and that they should be content to take what he chooses to give. His testimony creates the impression, also, that he thinks the Ford Motor Company has made too much money, has had too large profits, and that, although large profits might be still earned, a sharing of them with the public, by reducing the price of the output of the company, ought to be undertaken. We have no doubt that certain sentiments, philanthropic and altruistic, creditable to Mr. Ford, had large influence in determining the policy to be pursued by the Ford Motor Company—the policy which has been herein referred to.

In discussing this proposition, counsel have referred to certain decisions. These cases, after all, like all others in which the subject is treated, turn finally upon the point, the question whether it appears that the directors were not acting for the best interests of the corporation. We do not draw in question, nor do counsel for the Dodges do so, the validity of the general proposition stated by counsel nor the soundness of the opinions delivered in the cases cited. The case presented here is not like any of them. The difference between an incidental humanitarian expenditure of corporate funds for the benefit of the employees, like the building of a hospital for their use and the employment of agencies for the betterment of their condition, and a general purpose and plan to benefit mankind at the expense of others, is obvious. There should be no confusion (of which there is evidence) of the duties which Mr. Ford conceives that he and the stockholders owe to the general public and the duties which in law he and his co-directors owe to protesting, minority stockholders. A business corporation is organized and carried on primarily for the profit of the stockholders. The powers of the directors are to be employed for that end. The discretion of directors is to be exercised, in the choice of means to attain that end and does not extend to a change in the end itself, to the reduction of profits or to the nondistribution of profits among stockholders in order to devote them to other purposes.

There is committed to the discretion of directors, a discretion to be exercised in good faith, the infinite details of business, including the wages which shall be paid to employees, the numbers of hours they shall work, the conditions under which labor shall be carried on, and the price for which products shall be offered to the public.

It is said by Ford Motor Company that the motives of the board members are not material and will not be inquired into by the court so long as their acts are within their lawful powers. As we have pointed out, and the proposition does not require argument to sustain it, it is not within the lawful powers of a board of directors to shape and conduct the affairs of a corporation for the merely incidental benefit of shareholders and for the primary purpose of benefiting others, and no one will contend that, if the avowed purpose of the directors was to sacrifice the interests of shareholders, it would not be the duty of the courts to interfere.

The directors of Ford Motor Company say, and it is true, that a considerable cash balance must be at all times carried by such a concern. But, as has been stated, there was a large daily, weekly, monthly receipt of cash. The output was practically continuous and was continuously, and within a few days, turned into cash. Moreover, the contemplated expenditures were not to be immediately made. The large sum appropriated for the smelter plant was payable over a considerable period of time. So that, without going further, it would appear that, accepting and approving the plan of the directors, it was their duty to distribute on or near the 1st of August, 1916, a very large sum of money to stockholders.

Inspection of Books and Records

Common-Law Right to Inspect. Disputes are frequent between corporations and shareholders who seek to examine records of the corporation. These may arise when a challenge to management through a proxy campaign is suspected, when management fears a use of the information which may be harmful to the corporation or sometimes just because of a general desire for secrecy.

At common law, shareholders have the right to inspect corporate books and records, including shareholders' lists, books of account, minute books, and the properties of the corporation, so long as it is exercised for a proper purpose. However, even if his or her purpose were proper, the shareholder might suffer much delay and find it very expensive to obtain a remedy, which is usually a writ of mandamus.

The line between proper and improper purposes is not always clear, and in the earlier cases the courts put the heavy burden of proving a proper purpose upon the shareholder. Requests to inspect the books of account to determine the value of shares or the propriety of dividends and to inspect the stock ledger to identify fellow shareholders in order to communicate with them concerning corporate affairs—including an effort to replace management—are clearly proper purposes. On the other hand, to learn business secrets, to aid a competitor, to get the names of shareholders for a "sucker list," or to obtain prospects for a personal business would clearly be improper purposes. Bare ownership of stock in a competing corporation would not, in itself, however, be sufficient grounds for denying access to the records. Mere curiosity or even a desire to be informed about corporate affairs has been held an insufficient purpose, especially where other means of gaining information, such as attendance at shareholders' meetings, have not been fully utilized.

Statutory Inspection Rights. Statutes giving inspection rights usually aim to make it more difficult for a corporation to resist or delay proper requests by shareholders. The shareholder may employ a lawyer or accountant to exercise his right. Some statutes give shareholders an absolute right of inspection, particularly with respect to the stock ledger or shareholder list.

The Model Act (31) gives an absolute right of inspection of a complete record of shareholders entitled to vote at a meeting and their shareholdings. This must be made available at the meeting. The act (52) also provides that the corporation's books of account, minutes of shareholders' and directors' meetings, and a shareholder list must be kept available at its registered office. Upon a written demand stating his or her purpose, any shareholder of record for the preceding six months or who holds 5 percent of the outstanding shares may examine for any proper purpose any of these records that are relevant. Under the Model Act but not all statutes, any official who denies a proper demand may be liable for a penalty of 10 percent of the value of the stockholder's shares plus damages unless the requesting shareholder has made an improper use of information gained from a similar request within the past two years.

SUMMARY

At common law shareholders have the right to inspect corporate books and records and properties of the corporation so long as it is for a proper purpose. Statutes usually seek to make it more difficult for a corporation to resist or delay proper requests by shareholders and often give an absolute right to inspect the voting list of shareholders. The Model Act imposes penalties in addition to provable damages on corporate officers or agents who refuse proper requests.

State ex rel. Pillsbury v. Honeywell, Inc.

191 N.W.2d 406 (Sup. Ct. Minn. 1971)

Mandamus action on behalf of Charles Pillsbury (petitioner) to compel Honeywell, Inc., (respondent) to produce its original shareholder ledger, current shareholder ledger, and all corporate records dealing with weapons and munitions manufacture. Relief denied and Pillsbury appealed. Affirmed.

Pillsbury attended a meeting on July 3, 1969, of a group opposed to American involvement in Vietnam who believed that a substantial part of Honeywell production consisted of munitions used in that war. Pillsbury had long opposed the Vietnam involvement, but it was at this meeting that he first learned of Honeywell's production of antipersonnel fragmentation bombs. He was upset to learn that such bombs were produced in his own community by a company he had known and respected. On July 14 he purchased 100 shares of Honeywell stock for the sole purpose of gaining a voice to persuade Honeywell to cease producing munitions. Later he learned that he was beneficiary of a trust with an interest in 242 shares of Honeywell.

He then made two formal demands on the corporation for shareholder records and all corporate records dealing with weapon and munitions manufacture. Honeywell refused and this petition resulted.

KELLY, JUSTICE. The trial court ordered judgment for Honeywell, ruling that Pillsbury had not demonstrated a proper purpose germane to his interest as a stockholder. Pillsbury contends that a stockholder who disagrees with management has an absolute right to inspect corporate records for purposes of soliciting proxies. He would have this court rule that such solicitation is per se a "proper purpose." Honeywell argues that a "proper purpose" contemplates concern with investment return. We agree with Honeywell.

. . . But for his opposition to Honeywell's policy, Pillsbury probably would not have bought Honeywell stock, would not be interested in Honeywell's profits, and would not desire to communicate with Honeywell's shareholders. His avowed purpose in buying Honeywell stock was to place himself in a position to try to impress his opinions favoring a reordering of priorities upon Honeywell management and its other shareholders. Such a motivation can hardly be deemed a proper purpose germane to his economic interest as a shareholder.

The fact that Pillsbury alleged a proper purpose in his petition will not necessarily compel a right to inspection. . . . Neither is inspection mandated by the recitation of proper purpose in his testimony. Conversely, a company cannot defeat inspection by merely alleging an improper purpose. From the deposition, the trial court concluded that Pillsbury had already formed strong opinions on the immorality and the social and economic wastefulness of war long before he bought stock in Honeywell. His sole motivation was to change Honeywell's course of business because that course was incompatible with his political views. If unsuccessful, Pillsbury indicated that he would sell the Honeywell stock.

We do not mean to imply that a shareholder with a bona fide investment interest could not bring this suit if motivated by concern with the long- or short-term economic effects on Honeywell resulting from the production of war munitions. Similarly, this suit might be appropriate when a shareholder has a bona fide concern about the adverse effects of abstention from profitable war contracts on his investment in Honeywell.

In the instant case, however, the trial court, in effect, has found from all the facts that Pillsbury was not interested in even the long-term well-being of Honeywell or the enhancement of the value of his shares. His sole purpose was to persuade the company to adopt his social and political concerns, irrespective of any economic benefit to himself or Honeywell. This purpose on the part of one buying into the corporation does not entitle Pillsbury to inspect Honeywell's books and records.

Pillsbury argues that he wishes to inspect the stockholder ledger in order that he may correspond with other shareholders with the hope of electing to the board one or more directors who represent his particular viewpoint. . . .

While a plan to elect one or more directors is specific and the election of directors normally would be a proper purpose, here the purpose was not germane to Pillsbury's or Honeywell's economic interest. Instead, the plan was designed to further his political and social beliefs. Since the requisite propriety of purpose germane to his or Honeywell's economic interest is not present, the allegation that Pillsbury seeks to elect a new board of directors is insufficient to compel inspection.

Preemptive Rights

General. The shareholders' proportionate interests with respect to dividends, control, and assets are adversely affected by the nonproportionate issue of additional shares. A sale of additional shares at a price lower than book value would reduce the book value of existing shares and even a sale above book value may not necessarily result in earnings per share equal to the rate previously enjoyed. If there is but one class of shares these problems can be minimized if existing shareholders are given an opportunity to add proportionately to their holdings whenever new shares are to be sold by the corporation. The preemptive rights doctrine was evolved by the courts to accomplish this purpose, and many of the corporation statutes have codified the principal. Briefly stated, the doctrine gives the shareholder an option to subscribe to a new allotment of shares in proportion to the shareholder's present interest in the corporation prior to an offering of the shares to the public.

Application of Preemptive Rights. Generally, courts have held that preemptive rights do not apply to treasury shares, shares issued in connection with a merger or consolidation or issued for a noncash consideration. There is a conflict of authority with respect to shares that are unissued but which were authorized when the corporation was chartered. The rationale of courts holding that preemptive rights do not apply is that there was an implied agreement with original subscribers that these shares would be sold to raise capital for the business. If the sale of these shares is long postponed, the rationale breaks down and they are probably subject to preemptive rights. A common device used to give effect to preemptive rights is the issuance of short-term warrants or stock rights which entitle the holder to purchase a specified number of shares at a price fixed somewhat below the anticipated market price. The warrants are transferable and permit the shareholder to sell them if he or she does not wish to purchase the additional shares.

Many states permit but do not require corporations to grant preemptive rights. Even when shareholders are not entited to preemptive rights by statute or the corporation's articles, courts will grant relief necessary to hold directors and majority shareholders to a high standard of reasonableness and fairness in issuing new shares. They will not be permitted to issue additional shares to themselves or to some favored group in order to gain an advantage over other shareholders.

SUMMARY

A shareholder's preemptive right is the option of subscribing to a new allotment of shares, in proportion to his or her holding of outstanding shares. Preemptive rights have generally been held not to apply to treasury shares, shares issued in connection with a merger or issued for a noncash consideration. There is a conflict of authority with respect to shares that are unissued but which were authorized when the corporation was chartered.

Many statutes permit a corporation to avoid preemptive rights.

Extraordinary Corporate Transactions

Introduction. At common law the corporate charter was considered as a contract between the state and the corporation, between the corporation and the shareholders and among the shareholders, and it could not be changed without the consent of all the parties, including unanimous consent of the shareholders. Modern corporation statutes [Model Act (149)] reserve the right to the legislature to change the statutes and regulations, thus changing the corporate charter, and to permit the corporation itself to change its articles and to make substantial changes in the nature of its business and the rights of its shareholders with approval of less than all of the shareholders. Thus the "vested rights" doctrine no longer is a bar to extraordinary corporate transactions, including amendment of articles, merger and consolidation, sale or mortgage of assets, and dissolution.

Procedure for Amending Articles. To amend the articles of incorporation, the procedure set out by the statutes of the state of incorporation must be complied with. The Model Act (59, 60) requires that a written notice setting forth the proposed amendment or a summary of the changes to be affected by it must be given to all shareholders entitled to vote and that the amendment be approved by a majority of the shares. The Act (60) further provides that the holders of any class of shares are entitled to vote as a class on certain amendments which would affect the value or rights of that class of shares. Such changes include changing the number of authorized shares of the class, changing the par value of those shares, changing the preferences or rights of the shares of the class, changing the shares into a different number of shares or a different class, creating a new class with preferences superior to an existing class, limiting or denying existing preemptive rights or canceling accrued dividends of that class of shares. Such amendments, however, require only a majority vote under the act unless greater voting requirements are established in the articles (143).

Other Extraordinary Transactions. The statute of the state of incorporation must also be complied with in other extraordinary corporate transactions. The Model Act establishes similar procedures to effect a merger or consolidation (71–73), a sale of substantially all of the assets other than in the regular course of business (79), or a voluntary dissolution of the corporation (84). The procedure includes approval of the board of directors, notice to all shareholders whether or not entitled to vote, and a majority vote of shareholders entitled under the articles or bylaws to vote on the proposal. A higher percentage of favorable votes may be required by the articles or bylaws.

In case of merger or consolidation, shareholders are entitled to vote as a class, whether or not otherwise entitled to vote, if their shares would be affected in a manner similar to one of the amendments to the articles of incorporation specified in Section 60. However, under Section 75 a merger between a parent and subsidiary at least 90 percent of whose shares are owned by the parent may be accomplished by the directors without a vote of the shareholders of either corporation. This is known as a "short form" merger.

Appraisal Rights. Most state corporation statutes, including Delaware, as well as the Model Act, give shareholders who disapprove of certain extraordinary transactions the right to demand payment of the value of their shares. The Model Act (80, 81) gives this right in connection with a merger or consolidation or a sale of substantially all of the corporate assets other than in the normal course of business. However, this right does not apply to a short-form merger, nor does it apply when the corporation's shares are registered on a national securities exchange. A few states give appraisal rights in case of certain amendments to the articles of incorporation, such as change in corporate purposes, change in the rights of shares, and extension of corporate life.

There has been litigation in a few states on the question whether an acquisition by one corporation of all the assets of another, together with assumption of the second corporation's liabilities, in exchange for the stock of the first corporation, is a de facto merger such that appraisal rights apply. The Delaware court has held that there is no merger and no right of appraisal,[6] but other courts have taken the opposite view.

The Model Act requires a dissenting shareholder to file a written objection with the corporation prior to voting against the proposed transaction. If the proposal is approved, the corporation must so advise the dissenting shareholders and give them an offer for their shares at what it considers to be their fair value. If any dissenting shareholder is unwilling to accept the offer, he or she may petition a court in the county where the corporation's registered office is located to determine the fair value of the shares. All dissenting shareholders, wherever they live, must be made parties to the suit and will be bound by the judgment. Costs of the action may be assessed against any or all dissenting shareholders if the corporation made an offer and the refusal was arbitrary or vexatious. However, if the corporation made no offer or one which was materially less than the judgment, the court is authorized to require it to pay the reasonable compensation of any expert or attorney employed by the dissenters in the proceedings. The Act (5) exempts the purchase of shares from dissenters from the requirement that purchase of its own shares may be made only from unrestricted earned surplus.

SUMMARY

The fundamental structure and purpose of the corporation may not be changed without the shareholders' consent. Corporation statutes today provide for amendment of the articles of incorporation with the approval of the owners of some proportion of the voting shares, usually two thirds, but a majority under the Model Act. If the proposed amendment substantially affects the rights of a nonvoting class of shares, most states give that class a vote. Approval of voting shares is also usually required for extraordinary transactions such as merger, consolidation, sale of assets not in the normal course of business and for voluntary liquidation.

Dissenting shareholders are entitled to payment for the value of their shares in some of these situations. The Model Act gives the right of appraisal in case of merger or consolidation and in case of a sale of assets.

Santee Oil Co., Inc. v. Cox

217 S.E.2d 789 (Sup. Ct. S.C. 1975)

Santee Oil Co., Inc. (plaintiff), brought suit under the South Carolina appraisal statute seeking a determination of the "fair value" of Cox's (defendant's) shares in the corporation. Cox appealed the valuation. Affirmed.

---

[6] *Harton v. Arco Electronics, Inc.*, 182 A.2d 22(1962), *aff'd* 188 A.2d 123 (1963); *cf. Rath v. Rath Packing Co.*, 136 N.W.2d 410 (Iowa 1965).

Cox owned 37.5% of the stock in Santee, a closely held family corporation operating an oil jobbership in several South Carolina counties. Cox had duly objected to a statutory merger of Services, Inc., another South Carolina corporation in which Cox had a similar minority interest, into Santee. The trial court had established the value of both corporations to be $1,032,214 and Cox's stock interest to have a fair value of $387,080.

BUSSEY, JUSTICE. The act's explicit reference to value of shares indicates that fair value means "intrinsic value." But "fair value" does not restrict the appraising court to the use of any one method of valuation. "Market value undoubtedly is a pertinent consideration. So is net asset value. Neither, however, deserves necessarily to be accepted as exclusive." . . . In essence the trial court must undertake to compute the fair value by establishing "the fair market value of the corporate property as an established and going business." . . . Under the weight of authority the three major factors to be considered are: (1) net asset value; (2) market value; and (3) the earnings or investment value of the dissenting stock.

The circuit court found the net asset value of the corporation to be $1,032,214. The book value thereof was the sum of $635,516. Such is here quite relevant because of the testimony of one of the appraisers, uncontradicted, that two somewhat similar Shell jobberships in South Carolina had been up for sale for over two years and that to his knowledge no offer in excess of the book value of the jobberships had been made to the controlling stockholders.

While there were appraisals of portions of the assets by other appraisers, who testified, only three appraisers undertook to appraise the net value of all of the corporate assets. The high appraisal was in the amount of $1,375,000, but errors therein, developed on cross-examination, reduced it to $1,304,000. The next highest appraisal was in the amount of $1,169,000, and the low appraisal was in the amount of $895,000. The lowest appraiser took into consideration a number of factors, recognized as appropriate in other jurisdictions, in addition to asset value, in arriving at his appraisal. The high appraisal was predicated strictly on asset value without taking into consideration other factors having a bearing upon a fair value of the stock. The average of the three appraisals was the sum of $1,122,666.

Dividends paid by the corporation for the years 1969 through 1971 yielded on the basis of a valuation of $1 million, a return of 2.25, 2.75, and 2.25 percent. Of course, the higher the valuation the lower the percentage yield. The average earnings of the corporation for these three years amounted to $53,748 per annum. An accepted method for determining the capitalization, or stock value, of a corporation is to multiply its earnings by an appropriate multiplier (price/earnings ratio). The evidence is uncontradicted that during the pertinent period of time oil stocks generally were selling at a price/earnings ratio lower than 12 to 1. Thus, in the light most favorable to Cox we use 12 as a multiplier with the following result: 12 × $53,748 = $644,976, average capitalized earnings of the corporation over the three year period.

Approximately nine months prior to the merger there was a willing buyer and purchaser sale of 10 percent of the shares in both corporations, and on the basis of this sale, all the stock in both corporations was worth $931,603. In brief summary the principal factors involved in determining the "fair value" of appellant's shares are as follows:

Average appraisal of net assets	$1,122,666
Market value of stock	931,603
Capitalized earnings	644,976

Of these factors we are inclined to the view that, under the evidence, greater weight should be given to the net asset value factor than any other factor, but that the other factors have a real impact upon what in truth was the fair value of Cox's shares of stock. We need not determine whether the following relative weights of the different factors is precisely correct, but such are sufficient to demonstrate that the lower court's findings of fact as to the valuation of Cox's shares of stock was not against the clear weight and preponderance of the evidence.

Value factor		*Weight*	
Net asset value	$1,122,666	70%	$ 785,866
Market value	931,603	15	139,740
Capitalization earnings	644,976	15	96,746
Total value of corporation stock			$1,022,352

The foregoing is the methodology which is almost universally followed and applied in other jurisdictions in arriving at the fair value of stock in cases such as this. The relative weight to be given to the different factors, of course, varies in the light of the evidence. . . . The valuation of the stock of the corporation found by the lower court was some $10,000 in excess of our calculation above. While our calculation may not be entirely accurate, such is certainly not unreasonable in light of the evidence and is sufficient to show that the result reached by the lower court was not opposed to the clear weight and preponderance of the evidence.

Shareholders' Actions

Shareholders' Individual Actions. As a general rule a shareholder has no right to bring an action in his or her own name to recover a judgment for the impairment of the shareholder investment where such impairment resulted from a wrong to the corporation. In such a case the person wronged is the corporation and it has the cause of action. If individual shareholders were permitted to sue for their proportional share of a wrong to the corporation, there could be a multiplicity of suits and the shareholders might benefit to the detriment of corporate creditors.

The courts have, however, recognized the shareholder's right to sue in his or her own name under some circumstances in which, although the wrong is based on corporate rights, the injury is primarily to the shareholder and rights of the creditors are not affected. For instance, where all but a small number of shareholders have participated in a misappropriation of funds, the nonparticipating shareholders have been allowed to recover a judgment sufficient to place them on a par with the participating shareholders.

The shareholder has the right to bring an action in his or her own name to prevent or redress a breach of the shareholder contract. For example, a shareholder may sue to enforce his right to inspect the books, to recover dividends paid but not declared, to enjoin the corporation from committing an *ultra vires* act, and to enforce his preemptive rights.

Shareholder Class Action Suits. As indicated in Chapter 2, when a number of people have a right or claim against the same defendants growing out of substantially the same event, one or a few may bring the action for the benefit of all. Any recovery is proportionalized to all members of the class. Most shareholder class actions have been brought under the federal securities laws, which are discussed in the next chapter. An example of an appropriate class action under state corporation law would be a preferred shareholder bringing an action for all preferred shareholders seeking the payment of a dividend.

Shareholders' Derivative Actions. One or more shareholders are also permitted under certain circumstances to bring an action for the benefit of the corporation when the directors have failed to pursue a corporate cause of action. For example, if the corporation has a claim against its chief executive for wrongfully diverting corporate assets to personal use but because the chief executive controls the board of directors the corporation is unlikely to bring an action, a shareholder may bring a derivative action. A derivative action may also be used to bring a corporate claim against an outsider. If a judgment is obtained, it ordinarily goes to the corporate treasury for the benefit of the corporation and the creditors as well as all shareholders.

Although the possibility of a derivative action may be a major deterrent to wrongdoing on the part of officers and directors, it is also susceptible to abuse. "Strike suits" brought to gain an out-of-court settlement for the complaining shareholder personally or to earn large attorney's fees rather than a recovery for the corporation have not been uncommon. The U.S. Supreme Court long ago established several requirements for actions brought in federal courts to discourage abuse.[7] Under these rules the shareholder bringing the action must be a present owner who held his or her shares or acquired them by operation of law (such as inheritance) from someone who held them at the time the alleged wrong was committed. The shareholder must also show that intracorporate remedies have been exhausted by a prior demand upon the directors and, if appropriate, a demand on the shareholders. By statute or court rules many of the states have adopted these and additional safeguards.

---

[7] *Hawes v. Oakland,* 104 U.S. 450 (1882).

The Model Act (49) also provides that the corporation may require the plaintiff(s) to post security for reasonable expenses and attorneys' fees which may be incurred by it and other defendants unless the plaintiff(s) own 5 percent of the outstanding shares or their shares have a market value in excess of $25,000. It also authorizes the court to assess against the plaintiff the defendants' expenses and attorneys' fees if it finds that the action was brought without reasonable cause. To prevent benefit only to the shareholder bringing the action, statutes in a number of states and the federal court rules require approval of the court of any settlement as well as notice to all shareholders.

Occasionally, the officers or managers will refuse to defend a suit brought against a corporation. If a shareholder shows that the corporation has a good defense to the suit and that the refusal or failure of the directors or managers to defend is a breach of their fiduciary duty to the corporation, the courts will permit a shareholder to defend for the benefit of the corporation, its shareholders, and its creditors.

Reimbursement in Class and Derivative Actions. A plaintiff in a class action or derivative action who gets a judgment or who gains a benefit for the class or the corporation is entitled to be reimbursed by the corporation for reasonable expenses, including attorneys' fees. Otherwise, a shareholder could hardly afford to sue, since ordinarily the cost of the suit will far exceed the benefit to the shares alone. The result often is that the attorneys' fees and expenses of both plaintiffs and defendants are paid out of corporate funds should the suit be successful, and if the court thinks the suit is unreasonably brought, it may under Section 43a and similar statutes assess the costs of both parties to the unsuccessful shareholder complainant.

Minority Shareholder Suits. The right to control the affairs of a corporation is vested in the holders of a majority of the shares, subject to the requirements of some statutes or the articles of incorporation for approval of a higher proportion of shares or even unanimous approval for certain corporate actions. However, if the majority of shareholders pursue a course which will operate to deprive minority shareholders of their rights in the corporation, a court of equity will, on suit by minority shareholders, grant whatever relief the circumstances of the case demand. The courts are reluctant to interfere in the internal affairs of a corporation, and they will grant relief to minority shareholders only when the conduct of the majority shareholders amounts to a fraud on the minority shareholders.

Dissolution at Suit of a Minority Shareholder. In a number of cases, although there is authority to the contrary, courts have appointed a receiver for the corporation upon the petition of a minority shareholder. In a few cases courts have decreed dissolution of the corporation without specific statutory authority. These cases have included situations where: (1) those in control of the corporation are benefiting themselves at the expense of the other shareholders in a cavalier manner or actually defrauding them; (2) corporate functions have been abandoned or the corporation has been inactive since organization; (3) the main purpose of the corporation can no longer be carried on without utter ruin or because the business has become illegal; and (4) there has been such a deadlock among directors and shareholders that corporate functions cannot be carried on. The Model Act (94, 97) gives statutory authorization for liquidation and dissolution in all of these situations but the second. However, the power given is discretionary and would be exercised only if the court were convinced that liquidation and dissolution would benefit the shareholders as a whole.

SUMMARY

As a general rule a shareholder has no right to bring a suit in his or her own name to recover damages for the impairment of his investment resulting from a wrong to the corporation. A shareholder may bring an action in his or her own name to redress or prevent a breach of the membership contract, or under certain conditions one shareholder may bring a class action representing himself and a large group similarly harmed.

A shareholder may bring a derivative suit for the benefit of the corporation, its stockholders, and creditors if the directors and managers of the corporation have, in breach of their fiduciary duty, refused or failed to bring suit, and if their failure to bring suit will result in injury to the corporation.

Although courts are reluctant to interfere in the internal affairs of a corporation, they will grant relief to minority shareholders if the conduct of the majority amounts to a fraud upon them. In a number of cases, courts have appointed a receiver and have sometimes decreed the dissolution of a corporation upon the suit of a minority shareholder. Some statutes specifically authorize dissolution in certain circumstances.

Shareholder Liability

Shareholder Liability on Shares. A shareholder is liable to the corporation on his or her share subscription contract, and a receiver or trustee of an insolvent corporation may recover the unpaid balance for the benefit of creditors. However, a shareholder who has paid a lawful agreed price for nonassessable shares is not liable for creditors' claims. The Model Act (25) makes all paid up shares nonassessable, that is not subject to further call for contribution, but at one time it was common for bank shares to be assessable. If the stock is "watered," that is, less than par value was given for it, then the shareholder is likely to be held liable either to the corporation or to creditors for the difference between the amount paid and what would constitute lawful payment. In the absence of statute, courts apply several different theories which result in different conclusions in some situations.

Statutes also vary. The Model Act (19) recognizes neither promissory notes nor future services as payment for shares, but property and services actually performed are valid consideration. It makes the judgment of directors or shareholders as to the value of property or services received for shares conclusive in the absence of fraud.

The record holder of the shares is usually the one subject to shareholder liabilities. However, a transferee who in good faith believes that full consideration has been paid is not liable to the corporation or its creditors for any unpaid portion of the consideration (25).

Shareholder Liability on Illegal Dividends and Distributions. Dividends received by a shareholder with knowledge of their illegality may be recovered on behalf of the corporation even though he or she had no part in their declaration. However, despite lack of knowledge of the illegality, a shareholder is liable for a dividend received if the corporation were insolvent at the time the dividend was declared. Under the Model Act (48) primary liability is placed upon the directors who declared the dividend. However, any director against whom a claim is asserted for the wrongful payment of a dividend or distribution of assets of the corporation is entitled to contribution from shareholders who received a dividend or distribution knowing it was illegally declared.

Shareholder Liability for Corporate Debts. A number of states at one time imposed personal liability on shareholders for wages due to corporate employees, even though their shares were fully paid for and nonassessable. New York and Wisconsin still impose this liability. In several states shareholders may be held liable for corporate debts if business is commenced before the required capital is paid in or the certificate of incorporation filed.

Duties of Controlling Shareholders. A question which has been extensively discussed by legal scholars is whether controlling shareholders have any obligation to other shareholders when selling control of the corporation. They have been held liable where control was sold to persons they should have known would not act in the best interests of the corporation,[8] and in another case the controlling shareholders were held liable to other shareholders for the premium paid for control.[9] Also controlling shareholders have been held liable

---

[8] *Gerdes v. Reynolds,* 28 N.Y.S.2d 622 (NY Co. Sup. Ct. 1941).

[9] *Perlman v. Feldman,* 219 F.2d 173 (2d Cir. 1955).

for not giving other shareholders an opportunity to participate in recapitalization which resulted in large profits to the controlling shareholders.[10]

SUMMARY

The shareholder remains liable to the corporation on any unpaid portion of his or her subscription and may become liable on "watered" stock. Creditors may enforce the right of the corporation.

Dividends received by a shareholder knowing of their illegality may be recovered on behalf of the corporation. Shareholders may be held liable for corporate debts if business is commenced before certain requirements for incorporation are met. A few states still impose personal liability on shareholders for wages due to corporate employees. The extent of liability of controlling shareholders to other shareholders in selling control is the subject of dispute.

Jones v. H. F. Ahmanson & Co.[10]

460 P.2d 464 (Sup. Ct. Cal. 1969)

Class action by June Jones (plaintiff), a minority shareholder in the United Savings and Loan Association of California, against H. F. Ahmanson & Company, United Financial Corporation of California, and others (defendants) seeking to recover for economic injuries suffered by minority shareholders. Judgment for defendants on demurrer. Reversed.

United Savings and Loan Association of California (the Association) converted from a mutual to a stockholder owned savings institution in 1956. Of the 6,568 shares issued, 987 (14.8 percent) were purchased by depositors, including June Jones, through warrants issued in proportion to the amount of their deposits at that time. The shares allocated to unexercised warrants were sold to the then chairman of the board who resold them to H. F. Ahmanson & Co., which became the controlling shareholder, and to others. The Association retained most of its earnings in reserves so that book value of the shares increased to several times their 1956 value. Because of high book value and the fact the shares were closely held there was little buying and selling of shares, and these sales were mostly among existing shareholders.

Savings and loan stocks which were publicly traded were enjoying a steady increase in market price in 1958, but not those of the Association. To take advantage of this opportunity for profit H. F. Ahmanson & Co. and a few other shareholders of the Association incorporated United Financial Corporation of California (United) in 1959 and exchanged their Association shares

[10] *Jones v. H. F. Ahmanson Co.,* 460 P.2d 464 (Cal. 1969). This case does not presently represent the majority view.

for shares in United. United then owned more than 85 percent of the shares of the Association. The minority shareholders, including June Jones, were not given an opportunity to exchange their shares.

United then made a public offering of its stock in 1960, and the following year the original shareholders in United made a secondary public offering of a block of their shares. However, Ahmanson remained in control. By mid-1961 trading in United shares was very active while sales of Association shares decreased to half of its formerly low level. In 1960 United offered to purchase Association stock for $1,100 per share while those who had exchanged their shares for United stock had shares worth $3,700 for each share originally held in the Association. In 1959 and in 1960 the Association had paid extra dividends of $75 and $57 per share but after 350 shares were purchased by United pursuant to its offer, United caused the Association president to announce to the minority shareholders that in the near future only the $4.00 regular dividend would be paid. In 1961 United proposed to exchange United stock showing a book value of $210 and earnings at the rate of $134 per year for the Association stock of the minority shareholders which then had a book value of $1,700 per share and annual earnings at the rate of $615 per share. At this time the United shares of the former majority shareholders in the Association had a market value of $8,800.

TRAYNOR, CHIEF JUSTICE. Defendants take the position that as shareholders they owe no fiduciary obligation to other shareholders, absent reliance on inside information, use of corporate assets, or fraud. This view has long been repudiated in California. The Courts of Appeal have often recognized that majority shareholders, either singly or acting in concert to accomplish a joint purpose, have a fiduciary responsibility to the minority and to the corporation to use their ability to control the corporation in a fair, just, and equitable manner. Majority shareholders may not use their power to control corporate activities to benefit themselves alone or in a manner detrimental to the minority. Any use to which they put the corporation or their power to control the corporation must benefit all shareholders proportionately and must not conflict with the proper conduct of the corporation's business.

The rule that has developed in California is a comprehensive rule of "inherent fairness from the viewpoint of the corporation and those interested therein." The rule applies alike to officers, directors, and controlling shareholders in the exercise of powers that are theirs by virtue of their position and to transactions wherein controlling shareholders seek to gain an advantage in the sale or transfer or use of their controlling block of shares. Thus we held in *In re Security Finance,* that majority shareholders do not have an absolute right to dissolve a corporation, although ostensibly permitted to do so by Corporations Code, section 4600, because their statutory power is subject to equitable limitations in favor of the minority. We recognized that the majority had the right to dissolve the corporation to protect their investment *if* no alternative means were available *and* no advantage was secured over other shareholders, and noted that "there is nothing sacred in the life of a corporation that transcends the interests of its shareholders, but because dissolution falls with such finality on those interests, above all corporate powers it is subject to equitable limitations."

. . . Had defendants afforded the minority an opportunity to exchange their stock on the same basis or offered to purchase them [*sic*] at a price arrived at by independent appraisal, their burden of establishing good faith and inherent fairness would have been much less. At the trial they may present evidence tending to show such good faith or compelling business purpose that would render their action fair under the circumstance. On appeal from the judgment of dismissal after the defendants' demurrer was sustained we decide only that the complaint states a cause of action entitling Jones to relief.

In so holding we do not suggest that the duties of corporate fiduciaries include in all cases an obligation to make a market for and to facilitate public trading in the stock of the corporation. But when, as here, no market exists, the controlling shareholders may not use their power to control the corporation for the purpose of promoting a marketing scheme that benefits themselves alone to the detriment of the minority. Nor do we suggest that a control block of shares may not be sold or transferred to a holding company. We decide only that the circumstances of any transfer of controlling shares will be subject to judicial scrutiny when it appears that the controlling shareholders may have breached their fiduciary obligation to the corporation or the remaining shareholders.

Newmark v. RKO General, Inc.

332 F. Supp. 161 (S.D.N.Y. 1971)

Proceeding on petition of attorneys for Margot Newmark (plaintiff) to recover from RKO General, Inc. (defendant), attorneys' fees and costs after recovering judgment for Newmark in behalf of Frontier Airlines. Attorneys' fees and disbursements of $750,000 awarded to the law firm of Kaufman, Taylor, Kimmel and Miller.

Margot Newmark, a securities holder in Frontier Airlines, Inc., brought a derivative action under Section 16(b) of the Securities Exchange Act of 1934 to recover short-swing profits made by RKO General, Inc., at the time of the merger of Central Airlines, Inc., into Frontier. She recovered a judgment of over $7,920,000 plus interest of more than $553,000 on behalf of Frontier.

BONSAL, DISTRICT JUDGE. Frontier and RKO also suggest that since RKO owns 56 percent of Frontier, the benefit of the judgment to Frontier's public stockholders is limited to 44 percent thereof, and that the Kaufman attorneys' fee should be based on the recovery attributable to Frontier's public stockholders. However, the court holds that Kaufman's fee should be based on Frontier's recovery, exclusive of postjudgment interest.

Kaufman contends that the amount sought of $2.5 million in legal fees and $16,000 in disbursements is fair and reasonable in view of the successful outcome of this litigation. Frontier contends that a generous fee should not exceed $575,000, and RKO contends that the fee should not exceed $300,000. Some of the letters from Frontier stockholders which were filed in this proceeding suggest a fee of 10 percent of the amount recovered.

The court invited the Securities and Exchange Commission to file a brief *amicus curiae* on the amount of the fee. On April 6, 1971, the Commission filed a memorandum in which it stated, ". . . the Commission believes that an allowance of $2.5 million in counsel fees, as requested by plaintiff's attorneys, would be excessive."

It is true that there have been a number of Section 16(b) cases in this court in which the plaintiff's attorney have been awarded fees ranging from 20 percent to 50 percent of the amount recovered, where the amounts recovered ranged from $70,000 to $190,000. However, as pointed out by the Securities and Exchange Commission in its memorandum *amicus,*

> . . . there comes a point where, as in the present case, the judgment is so large that a fee based primarily on a percentage of recovery exceeds the limits of reasonable compensation for the attorneys' efforts.

In determining a reasonable fee for Kaufman, the court has considered the following factors: (1) the amount of the recovery; (2) the novelty and complexity of the legal issues; (3) the skill with which the services were performed, and the standing of Kaufman; (4) the benefits to Frontier; (5) the contingent nature of Kaufman's employment; (6) the hours reasonably expended by Kaufman.

Problem Cases

1. Manufacturing Corporation had 4,000 shares of common stock outstanding. Washington Industries, Inc., owned 2,711 shares and Merchants Warehouse Company owned 869 shares. The remaining 420 shares were held by six individuals. Five of the seven directors of Manufacturing also comprised five of the seven directors of each of the parent corporations. At an annual shareholders meeting of Manufacturing, the right of Washington Industries to vote its stock in an election of directors was challenged on the basis of a provision of the state incorporation statute that provided:

   > A corporation for profit may not vote at any meeting any treasury shares or any other of its shares which it owns or controls, directly or indirectly, and no such shares shall be counted in determining the total number of the outstanding shares of the corporation at any given time.

   It was argued that because a majority of the directors of Manufacturing are the same as those who are voting for Washington Industries, that they are in effect voting their own shares in their own election, permitting them to perpetuate their control of the two corporations.

Should the trial court refuse to enjoin the directors of Washington Industries from voting its Manufacturing shares in the election?

2. Erdman and three other persons formed a corporation to carry on a hairdressing business, each owning a 25 percent interest and working in the business. During 18 years of operation no dividend had been declared but the owners increased and decreased their salaries in accordance with the amount of cash on hand. Erdman terminated his employment with the corporation in October 1970 but retained his ownership interest. Soon thereafter the three other owners cashed in life insurance policies on Erdman's life for $1,600 and sold investment properties held by the corporation for $38,852. Over Erdman's objection they then voted themselves a substantial increase in salary as well as each a $5,000 bonus, although income of the corporation was reduced because of Erdman's departure.

   Erdman sued the other three owners alleging wrongful depletion of corporate assets. He was awarded the full cash value of the life insurance and 25 percent of the corporate assets sold after he left employment with the corporation on the grounds that the payments to the three owners amounted to a dividend rather than salary. The three owners appealed, alleging the court erred in granting individual relief rather than awarding a money judgment in favor of the corporation. Should the award be affirmed?

3. Gay's Super Markets, Inc., was a corporation in which 51 percent of the common stock was owned by Hannaford Brothers Company, a food wholesaler, and the remaining shares were held equally by Lawrence Gay and his brother, Carroll Gay. Carroll Gay was president and general manager and one of three directors. Lawrence was manager of one of the corporation's retail stores.

   In July 1971 Lawrence was dismissed as manager of the Machias, Maine, store. Despite the fact that the corporation had approximately $125,000 in cash toward the end of 1971, no dividend was declared that year. Lawrence Gay then brought an action to compel the payment of a reasonable dividend, alleging that the board of directors abused its discretion by withholding the dividend as a means of forcing him to sell his interest in the corporation. The defense of Carroll Gay, the other directors, and the corporation was that because of new competition in Machias, it was necessary to improve and expand the store there and that the corporation was planning to open a new store in Calais. Anticipated start-up costs would result in losses for a year or two in the new stores, Carroll testified. The minutes of the board meeting showed that the matter of a dividend was discussed but not declared because of "the anticipated needs of the corporation, particularly in Calais."

   Should an injunction be issued directing the payment of a dividend?

4. Campbell was a mechanical engineer for and shareholder in Ford Industries, Inc. He was discharged shortly after he requested certain information from the corporation in order to determine the value of his stock and whether the officers of the corporation "were engaged in any corporate misdealing." He alleged that his discharge was intended to deter other employee-shareholders from requesting corporate information and that he was entitled to the requested information under the Oregon corporation statute.

   How should the court rule?

5. Miles, who was dissatisfied with the management of the Bank of Heflin, wrote to the bank requesting that the bank permit his accountant to review the books and records of the bank "to ascertain whether any action had been taken contrary to the best interests of the stockholders, such as misuse of corporate funds; abuse of corporate office; diversion of corporate assets to the personal benefit of any officer, director, employee, or stockholder;

misapplication of corporate assets, or favoring of certain customers of the Bank because of personal connections with officers or directors of the Bank." The Bank refused and Miles brought suit. Should the court direct the Bank to permit the inspection?

6. Fuller and Krogh were, except for one share owned by Fuller's wife, the sole shareholders in Cormier Corporation. The corporation was formed to furnish a building for a manufacturing corporation owned by the two men. Cormier was undercapitalized and the contractor quit because it was unable to pay him the monthly progress payments. Krogh took over the responsibility for completing the building in 1954. Prior to this time each of the parties had invested equal amounts and had been issued 218 shares of stock. Thereafter, Fuller was financially unable to pay his half of the costs incurred on the building and Krogh accepted additional shares in lieu of cash payments for the materials, labor and supervision he furnished the corporation. As president of the corporation, Fuller signed the certificates issued to Krogh. By July, 1955, Fuller owned 244 shares and Krogh 527 shares. Fuller claims a preemptive right to purchase enough shares to equalize ownership. Is Fuller entitled to do so?

7. A family-owned retail department store business came under the control of DieMax Corporation when holders of 80 percent of the shares sold out at $600 per share. Approximately 21 months later it was merged into a wholy owned subsidiary. Two of the Stewarts who held on to their 10 percent interest objected to the merger and sought their statutory remedy—the "fair value of their shares." The surviving corporation, D. J. Stewart & Company, offered $105 per share. A witness for the dissenters who was a CPA estimated the fair value at $750 per share after applying a formula based upon increases in sales, net operating profit, net income before taxes, and book value to adjust the price of $600 established in the original arm's length transaction. A witness for DieMax who was an economist gave an estimate of $105, considering adjusted earnings over five years and applying price-earnings ratios of companies in the same business that were listed on stock exchanges. The values of these stocks had gone down between the date of the DieMax purchase and the date of trial. He gave a weight to the book value—which had increased from $800 to $830 per share after the DieMax purchase—of only 10 percent and the same to the DieMax acquisition figure of $600.

   The trial judge found the fair value to be $660 per share. Should this be reversed upon appeal for giving too much weight to book value and the prior purchase figure?

8. Dr. Horne was one of 12 physicians who formed Radiological Health Services (RHS) as a professional corporation to take over the radiology practice they had developed as a partnership. Each shareholder signed an agreement as an employee of the corporation not to compete for two years in case of withdrawal or termination. The 12 shareholders were divided into three groups, each covering a geographical area of the practice. Because the western area was unprofitable the shareholders discussed the possibility of dissolving the corporation. Dr. Horne made it known that in that event he would not join in a partnership with Dr. Fiore, who was a younger physician working with him in the eastern area.

   The proposed dissolution was cancelled because of portability problems with the employee's pension rights but the shareholders approved severing the western group of radiologists and waived as to them enforcement of the covenant not to compete. At that meeting Dr. Horne cast the only negative vote and resigned as an employee, having previously written a letter to the board of directors alleging that the separation agreement was illegal but demanding that he be permitted to resign on the same terms. He then sought to make a separate contract with the Southhampton Hospital but it terminated negotiations when notified by RHS of the covenant not to compete in Dr. Horne's contract with it.

Horne then brought an action to dissolve RHS on the ground that it was paralyzed by dissension and was being held together solely for the purposes of forcing an unwanted associate upon him. Would a court dissolve the corporation?

9. Cinnoca died as a result of the failure of a heart valve prosthesis manufactured and sold by Surgitool, Inc. After the sale of the prosthesis but before Cinnoca's death, Travenol Laboratories, Inc., acquired all or substantially all of Surgitool's assets under an agreement which explicitly stated that it was intended to comply with a provision of the Internal Revenue Code giving an exchange of assets for stock a tax free status if effected as part of a "Plan of Reorganization." Travenol Laboratories continued the business of Surgitool.

   Cinnoca's widow brought a product liability suit against Travenol Laboratories and it moved for summary judgment on the ground that it had merely purchased Surgitool's assets rather than merging that corporation with itself. Cinnoca argued that the transaction was in effect a merger, which would make Travenol Laboratories liable. The Internal Revenue Service regulations stated, "The term [Plan of Reorganization] does not embrace the mere purchase by one corporation of the properties of another, for it imports a continuity of interest on the part of the transferor or its shareholders in the properties transferred."

   How should the court rule?

10. Harf and others were owners of convertible subordinated debentures of Metro-Goldwyn-Mayer (MGM). They brought a derivative action against Kerkorian, a director and the controlling shareholder in MGM, after the board of directors had declared and paid a cash dividend of $1.75 per share in the fall of 1973, the first to be paid by MGM since 1969. The debenture holders alleged that it damaged MGM by depleting its capital and, although not resulting in insolvency, this endangered MGM's future prospects and impaired the value of the conversion feature of the debentures.

    Is Kerkorian correct in his defense that only shareholders have standing to bring a derivative action and that the debenture holders are merely creditors until such time as they exercise their conversion privilege?

29

Securities Regulation

Introduction

Background and Objectives. The major federal laws dealing with securities were passed in response to studies of the stock market crash of 1929, which ended a period of extravagant speculation in corporate securities by a rather broad segment of the American population. The purposes of this legislation were to provide investors with more information to help them make buy-sell decisions and to prohibit some of the unfair, deceptive, and manipulative practices which had resulted in substantial losses to the less-informed and less-powerful investors during the stock market debacle at the end of the 1920s.

The two principal statutes are the Securities Act of 1933 and the Securities Exchange Act of 1934.[1] They impose duties and liabilities upon certain corporations and their directors, officers, and controlling shareholders as well as upon certain persons involved in issuing and distributing securities to the public, such as underwriters, stockbrokers, accountants, and lawyers. The Securities and Exchange Commission (SEC) was established by the 1934 Act to administer the 1933 and 1934 Acts, and it has subsequently been given the administration of other related statutes. The SEC was granted and has exercised rather broad rule-making power under these statutes. The discussion of these acts will emphasize their impact upon corporations and upon their officers and directors rather than upon those engaged in the marketing and trading of securities.

---

[1] Other federal statutes applying to securities and security issuers, such as the Public Utility Holding Company Act of 1935 and the Investment Company Act of 1940, will not be discussed here because they apply only to certain kinds of businesses. Nor will the Securities Investor Protection Act of 1970, which was passed to protect investors from financial failure of brokerage firms, be discussed.

The securities legislation and the body of rules and practices developed by the SEC constitute a very complex body of law. Indeed, it is so complex that most of the law practiced in this area, both in advising clients and in registering securities, is handled by a relatively small number of specialists, most of whom are located in large financial centers. All the business student or businessperson who is not directly involved in the securities industry can expect is to obtain sufficient information to understand some of the terminology and to become generally familiar with the requirements the statutes impose upon corporations and their officers and directors.

What Is a Security? Although corporate stocks and bonds are the most common types of securities, they are not the only kinds of contract covered by the securities regulation statutes. The 1933 Securities Act (2[1]) defines a security in broad language in part as follows:

> . . . any . . . note, stock . . . evidence of indebtedness, certificate of interest or participation in any profit-sharing agreement, . . . investment contract, . . . voting trust certificate, . . . fractional undivided interest in . . . mineral rights, or in general, any interest or instrument commonly known as a "security," . . .

The 1934 Act definition is similar. Many of the state statutes are equally broad. Under such definitions contracts not generally thought of as securities have been held subject to regulation. Sales of limited partnerships, of live animals with contracts to care for them, of restaurant properties and citrus groves with management contracts and sales of franchises have all been held to constitute investment contracts subject to the Federal securities law. In 1977 an employee's interest in a union-sponsored pension plan was held to be a security for the purpose of fraud recovery.[2] If an investment involves participation with others in an enterprise in which the investor is led to expect profits solely from the efforts of the promoter or some third person rather than his or her own efforts, the arrangement falls within the United States Supreme Court's definition of an investment contract.[3] The fact that there is no certificate or that what is being offered for sale purports to the tangible property is immaterial. Of course, all offers or sales of such contracts do not come under the securities laws because certain exemptions may apply.

Exemptions. There are a number of exemptions from the requirements of the Securities Act of 1933 for the filing with the SEC of a registration statement and furnishing investors with a prospectus. The exemptions are of two types: one exempts certain kinds of securities; the other exempts certain transactions in securities. Examples of the first include exemptions of securities that are part of an exclusively intrastate issue and small offerings where the

---

[2] *Daniel v. International Brotherhood of Teamsters,* 46 LW 2119 (7th Cir. 1977); *rev'd* 47 LW 4135 (U.S. Sup. Ct. 1979).

[3] *SEC v. W. J. Howey Co.,* 328 U.S. 293, 298–99 (1946).

aggregate offering price does not exceed $1,500,000, although in the latter case the SEC prescribes certain conditions. The commercial paper exemption applies to instruments that are of prime quality, are of the type discounted by banks, the proceeds of which are to be used for current business transactions, and are not issued to the general public. Among numerous other exemptions are securities issued by non-profit institutions such as schools and churches and those which are exchanged by the issuer exclusively with its existing shareholders where no commissions are paid for soliciting the exchange.

The SEC has stated conditions for the application of the intrastate exemption in Rule 147. No part of the issue may be offered to or sold to nonresidents of the state within nine months after the original distribution. The issuer, if a corporation, must be incorporated and doing business in the same state as the residence of all of the offerees. To be considered as doing business within the state 80 percent of the assets must be located in and 80 percent of the gross business of the issuer and it subsidiaries must be from operations within the state. If only one of the offerees is a resident of another state or intends to resell the security to a nonresident, the exemption is lost. Issuers intending to rely on this exemption usually require an "investment letter" from each purchaser. In such a letter the investor declares that he or she is purchasing the securities for investment and not for resale.

Most *transactions* in securities are exempt from registration requirements since generally individual investors are exempt. However, issuers, underwriters, and dealers are not exempt. Also, those in control of the issuer may not be able to sell their securities without registration. Also exempt are "transactions by an issuer not involving any public offering"—the so-called private offering.

Although the SEC has tried to make it easier for issuers and security holders to stay within the exemptions by issuing rules that provide more specific guidelines than the statutes and court decisions, this remains a quite complicated and technical area of the law.

Private Offerings. An issuer may avoid the rather considerable difficulty and expense as well as the need to make the public disclosures required in a registration statement if the offering of a security is limited to a "private offering." Rule 146 establishes guidelines for this exemption. They include: no offer can be made to the public; there can be no more than 35 purchasers; offerees must be limited to knowledgeable and experienced investors who are able to assume the economic risk; information similar to that included in a registration statement is available to them (perhaps through their relationship to the issuer—such as being an officer); and the seller must exercise reasonable care to avoid sales to people who might resell rather than hold for investment. Such care would involve: requiring a statement from a purchaser that the purchase is made only for investment (an "investment letter"); placing a legend on the certificate indicating that it is restricted stock; and arranging to stop transfer of the securities except where the requirements of Rule 144 on resale are met.

SEC Rule 144 permits resale by holders of "restricted" or nonregistered securities obtained through private placement, including corporate profit sharing plans. Requirements include: holding for a period of two years; the availability of adequate public information about the issuer; limited volume of sale within any six month period (the lesser of 1 percent of shares outstanding or the average weekly volume of trading); sale through broker; and notice to the SEC.

SUMMARY

The purposes of the Securities Act of 1933 and the Securities Exchange Act of 1934 are to provide investors with adequate information and to prohibit unfair, deceptive, and manipulative practices which had caused losses to ordinary investors. The securities laws and rules of the SEC constitute a complex body of law which tends to be the province of legal specialists.

The law applies a broad definition of "security." It includes any sort of investment which involves participation with others in an enterprise holding out the expectation of profit from the efforts of the promoter or others rather than the investor's own efforts.

There are two types of exemptions from the registration and other requirements of the 1933 Act. One exempts certain types of securities such as those sold only intrastate, those of nonprofit institutions, and those which are offered in exchange for those held by existing shareholders. The other exempts certain transactions, including "private offerings" and sales by individual investors rather than distributions by underwriters and dealers. The criteria for meeting several of the exemptions are set out in frequently quoted SEC rules. They include Rule 147 for the intrastate exemption, Rule 146 for the private placement exemption, and Rule 144, which sets forth the conditions under which restricted securities purchased in a private offering my be resold.

SEC v. Koscot Interplanetary, Inc.

497 F.2d 473 (5th Cir. 1974)

The Securities and Exchange Commission (plaintiff) brought action against Koscot Interplanetary, Inc. (defendant), to enjoin violation of the federal securities laws by selling unregistered securities and using methods that contravened the anti-fraud provisions. Appeal from denaial of the injunction. Reversed and remanded.

Koscot was a subsidiary of Glen W. Turner Enterprises. Its business involved a multi-level network of distributors purportedly engaged in selling a line of cosmetics. At the lowest level was a "beauty advisor" whose income was solely derived from retail sales of Koscot cosmetics, normally made available to the "advisor" at a 45 percent discount. For $1,000 one could become a supervisor or retail manager. The supervisor typically purchased cosmetics at a 55 percent discount to be sold directly to the public or to beauty advisors. A supervisor who introduced to Koscot a prospect who became a supervisor received $600 of the $1,000 paid Koscot. A distributorship cost $5,000 and entitled one to a 65 percent discount, to $600 for the fruitful sponsorship of a supervisor, and $3,000 if a sponsored person became a distributor.

The investors (supervisors and distributors) brought their prospects to Opportunity Meetings. The Koscot manual instructed them not to mention to prospects details of the business in advance of the meetings but rather to arouse their curiosity. It said, "Tell him you have discovered a wonderful financial opportunity that will fit him like a glove! Or, tell him you have seen a money tree and would like for him to take a look at it." The illusion of affluence was carefully fostered at the meetings. Koscot employees and investors were instructed to drive expensive cars, to dress expensively, and to flaunt large sums of money. They were instructed to follow the Koscot script verbatim and they were told that those who didn't would be replaced.

The trial court denied the injunction. It held that the scheme did not involve the sale of a security under the federal securities laws because the profit to be expected would not come solely from the efforts of individuals other than the investors.

GEWIN, CIRCUIT JUDGE. The district court correctly cited the following language from *SEC v. W. J. Howey Co.*, as the standard controlling its disposition of the case.

> [A]n investment contract for purposes of the Securities Act means a contract, transaction or scheme whereby a person invests his money in a common enterprise and is led to expect profits solely from the efforts of the promoter or a third party. . . .

This test subsumes within it three elements: first, that there is an investment of money; second, that the scheme in which an investment is made functions as a common enterprise; and third, that under the scheme, profits are derived solely from the efforts of individuals other than the investors. The district court [passed over] a consideration of the first two elements in finding that the third component of the test was not satisfied because Koscot investors expended effort in soliciting recruits to meetings, in participating in the conduct of meetings, and in attempting to consummate the sale of distributorships and subdistributorships.

Since it cannot be disputed that purchasers of supervisorships and distributorships made an investment of money, our initial concern is whether the Koscot scheme functions as a common enterprise. As defined by the Ninth Circuit, "[a] common enterprise is one in which the fortunes of the investor are interwoven with and dependent upon the efforts and success of those seeking the investment or of third parties."

The critical factor is not the similitude or coincidence of investor input, but rather the uniformity of impact of the promoter's efforts.

Similarly, here, the fact that an investor's return is independent of that of other investors in the scheme is not decisive. Rather, the requisite commonality is evidenced by the fact that the fortunes of all investors are inextricably tied to the efficacy of the Koscot meetings and guidelines on recruiting prospects and consummating a sale.

[T]he critical issue in this case is whether a literal or functional approach to the "solely from the efforts of others" test should be adopted, i.e., whether the exertion of some effort by an investor is inimical to the holding that a promotional scheme falls within the definition of an investment contract. We measure the viability of the SEC's advocacy of a functional approach by its compatibility with the remedial purposes of the federal securities acts. . . .

[W]e hold that the proper standard in determining whether a scheme constitutes an investment contract is that explicated by the Ninth Circuit in *SEC v. Glen W. Turner Enterprises, Inc.* In that case, the court announced that the critical inquiry is "whether the efforts made by those other than the investor are the undeniably significant ones, those essential managerial efforts which affect the failure or success of the enterprise."

Since Koscot's Opportunity Meetings are run according to preordained script, the deviation from which would occasion disapprobation or perhaps exclusion from the meetings, the role of investors at these meetings can be characterized as little more than a perfunctory one. . . . The act of consummating a sale is essentially a ministerial not managerial one, one which does not alter the fact that the critical determinant of the success of the Koscot Enterprise lies with the luring effect of the opportunity meetings. . . . Once attendance is secured, the sales format devised by Koscot is thrust upon the prospect. An investor's sole contribution in following the script is a nominal one. Without the scenario created by the Opportunity Meetings and Go-Tours, an investor would invariably be powerless to realize any return on his investment.

We confine our holding to those schemes in which promoters retain immediate control over the essential managerial conduct of an enterprise and where the investor's realization of profits is inextricably tied to the success of the promotional scheme. Thus, we acknowledge that a conventional franchise arrangement, wherein the promoter exercises merely remote control over an enterprise and the investor operates largely unfettered by promoter mandates presents a different question than the one posed herein. But the Koscot scheme does not qualify as a conventional franchising arrangement.

Doran v. Petroleum Management Corp.

545 F.2d 893 (5th Cir. 1977)

William Doran (plaintiff) brought this action against Petroleum Management Corp. (PMC) (defendant) to rescind the purchase of a limited partnership interest in an oil drilling venture on grounds of violation of the Securities Acts of 1933 and 1934. Judgment for PMC and Doran appealed. Reversed and remanded.

PMC organized a California limited partnership for the purpose of drilling and operating four wells in Wyoming. The agreement provided both for "participants" and "special participants." PMC and another corporation were the "participants." Doran was approached by phone by a California securities broker to become a "special participant." Offers were made to only four other persons and they declined.

PMC then sent Doran the drilling logs and technical maps of the proposed drilling area. PMC informed Doran that two of the proposed four wells had already been completed. Doran agreed to become a "special participant" in the Wyoming drilling program. In consideration for his partnership share, Doran agreed to contribute $125,000 toward the partnership. He was to discharge this obligation by paying PMC $25,000 down and in addition assuming responsibility for the payment of a $113,643 note owed by PMC to Mid-Continent Supply Co. Doran's share in the production payments from the wells was to be used to make the installment payments on the Mid-Continent note.

During 1970 and 1971 PMC periodically sent Doran production information on the completed wells of the limited partnership. Throughout this period, however, the wells were deliberately overproduced in violation of the production allowances established by the Wyoming Oil and Gas Conservation Commission.

In November 1971 the Commission ordered the wells sealed for 338 days, and when they were reopened their flow was reduced. As a result the note went into default and a judgment in state court against Doran and PMC was granted to Mid-Continent. Doran then sought rescission of his limited partnership agreement. The trial court found that the offer was a private offering because Doran was a sophisticated investor and that PMC had not made any misrepresentations of material facts.

GOLDBERG, CIRCUIT JUDGE. This court has in the past identified four factors relevant to whether an offering qualifies for the [private placement] exemption. The relevant factors include the number of offerees and their relationship to each other and the issuer, the number of units offered, the size of the offering, and the manner of the offering. Consideration of these factors need not exhaust the inquiry, nor is one factor's weighing heavily in favor of the private status of the offering sufficient to ensure the availability of the exemption. Rather, these factors serve as guideposts to the court in attempting to determine whether subjecting the offering to registration requirements would further the purposes of the 1933 Act.

The number of offerees, not number of purchasers, is the relevant figure in considering the number of persons involved in an offering. A private placement claimant's failure to adduce any evidence regarding the number of offerees will be fatal to the claim. The number of offerees is not itself a decisive factor in determining the availability of the private offering exemption. Just as an offering to few may be public, so an offering to many may be private. *SEC v. Ralston Purina Co.*

In considering the number of offerees solely as indicative of the magnitude or scope of an offering, the difference between one and eight offerees is relatively unimportant. Rejecting the argument that Doran was the sole offeree is significant, however, because it means that in considering the need of the offerees for the protection that registration would have afforded we must look beyond Doran's interests to those of all his fellow offerees. Even the offeree-plaintiff's 20–20 vision with respect to the facts underlying the security would not save the exemption if any one of his fellow offerees was in a blind.

Since *SEC v. Ralston* courts have sought to determine the need of offerees for the protections afforded by registration by focusing on the relationship between offerees and issuer and more particularly on the information available to the offerees by virtue of that relationship.

The lower court's finding that Doran was a sophisticated investor is amply supported by the record, as is the sophistication of the other offerees. Doran holds a petroleum engineering degree from Texas A&M University. His net worth is in excess of $1 million. His holdings of approximately twenty-six oil and gas properties are valued at $850,000.

Nevertheless, evidence of a high degree of business or legal sophistication on the part of all offerees does not suffice to bring the offering within the private placement exemption. We clearly established that proposition in *Hill York Corp. v. American International Franchises, Inc.* We reasoned that "if the plaintiffs did not possess the information requisite for a registration statement, they could not bring their sophisticated knowledge of business affairs to bear in deciding whether or not to invest. . . ." Sophistication is not a substitute for access to the information that registration would disclose.

More specifically, we shall require on remand that PMC demonstrate that all offerees, whatever their expertise, had available the information a registration statement would have afforded a prospective investor in a public offering. Such a showing is not independently sufficient to establish that the offering qualified for the private placement exemption, but it is necessary to gain the exemption and is to be weighed along with the sophistication and number of the offerees, the number of units offered, and the size and manner of the offering. Because in this case these latter factors weigh heavily in favor of the private offering exemption, satisfaction of the necessary condition regarding the availability of relevant information to the offerees would compel the conclusion that this offering fell within the exemption.

In determining on remand the extent of the information available to the offerees, the district court must keep in mind that the "availability" of information means either disclosure of or effective access to the relevant information. The relationship between issuer and offeree is most critical when the issuer relies on the latter route.

To begin with, if PMC could prove that all offerees were actually furnished the information a registration statement would have provided, whether the offerees occupied a position of access pre-existing such disclosure would not be dispositive of the status of the offering. If disclosure were proved and if, as here, the remaining factors such as the manner of the offering and the investment sophistication of the offerees weigh heavily in favor of the private status of the offering, the absence of a privileged relationship between offeree and issuer would not preclude a finding that the offering was private. Any other conclusion would tear out of context this court's earlier discussion of the § 4(2) exemption and would conflict with the policies of the exemption.

Alternatively it might be shown that the offeree had access to the files and record of the company that contained the relevant information. Such access might be afforded merely by the position of the offeree or by the issuer's promise to open appropriate files and records to the offeree as well as to answer inquiries regarding material information. In either case, the relationship between offeree and issuer now becomes critical, for it must be shown that the offeree could realistically have been expected to take advantage of his access to ascertain the relevant information. Similarly the investment sophistication of the offeree assumes added importance, for it is important that he could have been expected to ask the right questions and seek out the relevant information.

Requirements of Issuers

Registration under the 1933 Act. The 1933 Act requires the registration of any issue of securities (subject to exemptions discussed above) with the SEC prior to offering that issue for sale. A very large amount of historical and current data about the issuing company and its business (including certified financial statements) must be filed along with full details about the securities being offered, how the proceeds of the issue are to be used (if a new issue), agreements between the parties involved in the distribution of the securities and copies of important contracts to which the issuer is a party which were not made in the usual course of business. Most of this must be included in the prospectus that is required to be given to those to whom the securities are offered for sale. The registration statement must be signed by the issuing company, its principal executive officer, its principal financial officer, its principal accounting officer, and by at least a majority of its board of directors. In addition, any expert named in the registration statement as having prepared or certified information must sign a consent. Such experts would include the accountant who has given his opinion on the financial statements or a specialist who has estimated mineral reserves or the value of other assets.

The statute provides that the registration becomes effective on the 20th day after filing, but the SEC may advance the date or require an amendment which will start the 20-day period running again. The effective date normally is later than 20 days after filing. Since the offering price and the "spread" or commission for the underwriters and dealers usually aren't finally determined until just before the securities are to go on sale, the issuer almost always files at least one amendment so as to insert or update the price. However, it is ordinarily possible to schedule the date of issue so that SEC approval is secured promptly upon the filing of this final amendment.

The review by the SEC only involves the completeness of the registration statement and prospectus. It does not indicate any opinion about the worth of the securities or even whether the statements in the filed documents are accurate, although if the staff doubts their accuracy the SEC will usually delay approval and ask for more information.

Registration under the 1934 Act. Under an amendment to the 1934 Act (12g), corporations having total assets exceeding $1 million and a class of equity securities held by 500 or more shareholders must register that security under the act even if it is not traded on a public stock exchange. Registration under the 1933 Act is essentially a registration of a transaction. It covers a particular issue at a particular time, and later sale by the corporation of another issue of the same class of securities would require a new registration. In contrast, registration under the 1934 Act provides registered status for the entire class of securities until action is taken to deregister it.

The information required in the registration statement is similar to that required under the 1933 Act. Companies registered under the 1934 Act become subject to certain further requirements that will be discussed later in this chapter, such as the rules pertaining to the solicitation of proxies and the filing of certain periodic reports. The 1934 Act also subjects directors and officers to the recapture of "short-swing profits" (as defined later in this chapter) and requires them to report monthly any transactions in the stock of the company.

The Prospectus. The instrument by which investors are to be given the information required by the 1933 Act is the prospectus. It must be furnished to every purchaser of the security being registered for distribution through underwriters and brokers prior to or concurrently with the transmission of the security to him. During the waiting period before the registration statement becomes effective, a preliminary or "red herring" prospectus may be used. The term is applied because a legend on the cover of the preliminary prospectus (which ordinarily will contain blanks instead of the offering price and the "spread" or commission going to those in the channels of distribution) is required to be printed in red ink. It warns that the document is incomplete and that securities may not be sold until the registration becomes effective. If 90 days have elapsed and the distribution of the issue is complete, a prospectus is no longer required for sales of the security by a dealer.

"Prospectus" is defined in the 1933 Act as being any notice, circular advertisement, letter, or radio or TV statement which offers a security for sale. The use of a "prospectus" thus defined is prohibited except when such information is given to one to whom a proper written document, confusingly also known as a prospectus, has been given. The purpose is to prevent a company planning to issue stock from "conditioning the market" by publicizing favorable news. Therefore, a prospective issuer and its directors and officers acting as individuals must be careful to avoid publicity about the company before the distribution of a new issue is completed. While the registration and distribution processes are under way, press releases, brochures, advertisements, speeches, and press conferences that have any relation to the issue or the prospects for the company may be dangerous and, if used, should be carefully prepared under expert legal guidance. An announcement called a "tombstone advertisement" is permitted during distribution. These are commonly seen in financial periodicals and merely give the name of the issuer, the type of security and its price, and tell from whom a proper prospectus can be obtained.

Periodic Reports. The Securities Exchange Act of 1934 (15d) requires registrants under the 1933 Act to file periodic reports with the SEC. Firms meeting certain criteria specified in Section 12 of the 1934 Act (presently total assets exceeding $1,000,000 and a class of equity securities held by 500 shareholders or a listing of securities on a national stock exchange) must file such reports even if they have no securities registered under the 1933 Act. These reports include: an annual report (form 10–K), a quarterly report (form 10–Q) and, when applicable, a current report (form 8–K).

Under SEC rules the 10–K report must include audited financial statements for the fiscal year plus current information about the conduct of the business and the management and the status of its securities. In effect, the 10–K report is intended to bring up to date the information required in the registration statement. The quarterly report, 10–Q, requires only a summarized and unaudited operating statement and unaudited figures on capitalization and shareholders' equity. The 8–K report is required within ten days of the end of any month in which any of certain specified events occur, such as changes in the amount of securities, a default under the terms of an issue of securities, acquisition or disposition of assets, changes in control of the company, revaluations of assets, or "any materially important event."

Proxy Statements and Annual Reports. SEC rules require that a corporation registered under the 1934 Act furnish a proxy statement containing certain information with the proxy if it solicits proxies for a shareholders' meeting. If directors are to be elected, any employment contract with the nominee, salary, pension benefits, and any options to purchase the corporation's shares held by him or her must be disclosed in the proxy statement as well as any material transaction between the corporation and any officer, director, nominee or holder of 10 percent or more of any class of shares of the company. The proxy form itself must give the shareholder a "yes" or "no" choice on matters to be voted upon and a place to insert the date.

If the corporation does not solicit proxies, it must send all shareholders entitled to vote at the meeting an "Information Statement," which contains substantially the same information. A preliminary form of the proxy statement or information statement must be filed with the SEC at least ten days before mailing to shareholders. If the proxy or information statement is issued in connection with an annual meeting of shareholders at which directors are to be elected, it must be preceded by a mailing of an annual report containing audited figures including a balance sheet and comparative operating statement of the current and immediately preceding fiscal years.

If misleading statements or omissions are made in the proxy solicitation, a court may enjoin the holding of the meeting or void the action taken. This statutory remedy is in addition to the common law remedy for breach of fiduciary duty to shareholders.

The corporation must furnish a shareholder who wishes to solicit proxies in competition with the management either a shareholder list or send his proxy material to the shareholders for him or her. It must also include in its own proxy a proposed resolution submitted by a shareholder. If the management opposes the proposal, it may include in its proxy statement a comment by the shareholder of not more than 200 words supporting the proposal. Management may omit proposals relating to personal claims or grievances, proposals that are beyond the power of the corporation to effectuate, proposals that are not proper subjects for action by shareholders under the laws of the corporation's domicile, and proposals for action with respect to matters relating to the conduct of the ordinary business of the firm. A proposal that has been included in the proxy within the last three calendar years may also be omitted unless it has received 3 percent or more of the vote. If it has been voted upon twice within the last five years, it must be included in the proxy only if it received 6 percent of the vote the last time it was submitted. If the proposal has been voted on twice within five years, it must be included on the proxy only if 10 percent of the shares favored it when last presented.

SUMMARY

The Securities Act of 1933 requires corporations preparing to issue securities to provide the SEC and prospective investors with a great deal of information through a registration statement, as well as a prospectus, which must be furnished to every purchaser prior to or concurrently with the transmission of the security to him or her. Securities cannot be sold until the registration statement is in effect after being filed with the SEC. The SEC approves the registration statement and prospectus only in the sense of determining that they are complete.

Registration under the 1934 Act is a registration of a class of securities rather than of a particular transaction or issue, as is the case under the 1933 Act. Companies of a certain size must register even though their securities are not traded on an exchange. Registration requirements are similar to the 1933 Act. In addition, requirements as to proxy solicitation and periodic reporting to the SEC are imposed.

Rather elaborate rules have been issued by the SEC with respect to the solicitation of proxies for voting at shareholders' meetings, and the proxy statement must be filed in advance with the SEC.

Escott v. BarChris Construction Corp.

283 F. Supp. 643 (S.D.N.Y. 1968)

An action by Escott and other investors (plaintiffs) against BarChris Construction Corporation, the corporate directors—including its legal counsel, certain officers, the underwriters and its public auditors (defendants). Recovery was sought for losses suffered due to allegedly false statements and omissions in a prospectus that would constitute a violation of Section 11 of the Securities Act of 1933. Held for investors, with additional issues not here pertinent being reserved for later decision. [Note: The excerpts from the opinion deal only with those defendants indicated in the subheads.]

BarChris was in the business of constructing bowling centers. With the introduction of automatic pin-setting machines in 1952 there was a rapid growth in the popularity of bowling, and BarChris's sales had increased from $800,000 in 1956 to over $9 million in 1960. By 1960 it was building about 3 percent of the lanes constructed while Brunswick Corporation and AMF were building 97 percent. Unlike its larger competitors, BarChris did not manufacture bowling equipment. Its method of operation was to contract with a customer for the construction and equipping of a bowling alley, requiring a relatively small down payment in cash and taking the balance, after the work was completed, in notes which it discounted with a factor. The factor held back part of the face value of the notes as a reserve and could call on BarChris to repurchase the notes if the debtors were in default. In 1960 it began to offer an alternative method of financing which involved selling the equipment to a factor, James Talcott, Inc., which would then lease it back either to BarChris's customer or to a subsidiary of BarChris which would then sublease to the customer. Under either financing method BarChris made substantial expenditures before receiving reimbursement and was, therefore, in constant need of cash, which grew as operations expanded.

In December 1959, BarChris sold additional common stock, but by early 1961 it needed more working capital. It determined to offer debentures, and part of the proceeds of the debentures was to be devoted to this purpose. The preliminary registration statement was filed with the SEC in March, it became effective on May 16, and the closing was held on May 24, 1961. By that time BarChris was experiencing difficulties in collecting amounts due it from some of its customers, and others were in arrears on their payments to the factors. Due to overexpansion in the number of bowling alleys, many operators failed. The result was that on October 29, 1962, BarChris itself filed a petition under the Bankruptcy Act and defaulted on the payment of interest on the debentures.

The court found that BarChris had in the prospectus overstated sales and earnings and also its current assets in its 1960 financial statements. It also understated, the court found, its contingent liabilities by $375,795 as of December 31, 1960, and by $618,853 as of March 31, 1961. First quarter 1961 earnings were overstated by $230,755 (92%) and the March 31, 1969, backlog was overstated by $4,490,000 (185 percent) the court held. It also found that the prospectus was in error in stating that prior loans from officers had been paid off, finding loans outstanding of $386,615. Further, the court held that: $1,160,000 of the proceeds of the debentures were used to pay off old debts and this was not disclosed in the prospectus; BarChris had a potential liability to factors due to customer delinquencies of $1,350,000 which it did not disclose; and it misrepresented the nature of its business by failing to disclose that it was already engaged and was about to become more heavily engaged in the operation of bowling alleys to try to minimize its losses from customer defaults.

Each of the defendants had either signed the registration statement or had consented to being named in it as an "expert." Each except BarChris asserted in his defense that he had acted with due diligence as defined in Section 11b (3).

McLean, District Judge. I turn now to the question of whether defendants have proved their due diligence defenses. The position of each defendant will be separately considered:

TRILLING

[Trilling] was BarChris's controller. He signed the registration statement in that capacity, although he was not a director. Trilling entered BarChris's employ in October 1960. He was Kircher's (BarChris's treasurer) subordinate. When Kircher asked him for information, he furnished it.

Trilling was not a member of the executive committee. He was a comparatively minor figure in BarChris. The description of BarChris's "management" on page 9 of the prospectus does not mention him. He was not considered to be an executive officer.

Trilling may well have been unaware of several of the inaccuracies in the prospectus. But he must have known of some of them. As a financial officer, he was familar with BarChris's finances and with its books of account. He knew that part of the cash on deposit on December 31, 1960, had been procured temporarily by Russo for window-dressing purposes. He knew that BarChris was operating Capitol Lanes in 1960. He should have known, although perhaps through carelessness he did not know at the time, that BarChris's contingent liability on Type B lease transactions was greater than the prospectus stated. In the light of these facts, I cannot find that Trilling believed the entire prospectus to be true.

But even if he did, he still did not establish his due diligence defenses. He did not prove that as to the parts of the prospectus expertised by Peat, Marwick he had no reasonable ground to believe that it was untrue. He also failed to prove, as to the parts of the prospectus not expertised by Peat, Marwick, that he made a reasonable investigation which afforded him a reasonable ground to believe that it was true. As far as appears, he made no investigation. He did what was asked of him and assumed that others would properly take care of supplying accurate data as to the other aspects of the company's business. This would have been well enough but for the fact that he signed the registration statement. As a signer, he could not avoid responsibility by leaving it up to others to make it accurate. Trilling did not sustain the burden of proving his due diligence defenses.

AUSLANDER

Auslander was an "outside" director, i.e., one who was not an officer of BarChris. He was chairman of the board of Valley Stream National Bank in Valley Stream, Long Island. In February 1961, Vitolo [president] asked him to become a director of BarChris. Vitolo gave him an enthusiastic account of BarChris's progress and prospects.

In February and early March 1961, before accepting Vitolo's invitation, Auslander made some investigation of BarChris. He obtained Dun & Bradstreet reports which contained sales and earnings figures for periods earlier than December 31, 1960. He caused inquiry to be made of certain of BarChris's banks and was advised that they regarded BarChris favorably. He was informed that inquiry of Talcott had also produced a favorable response.

On March 3, 1961, Auslander indicated his willingness to accept a place on the board. Shortly thereafter, on March 14, Kircher sent him a copy of BarChris's annual report for 1960. Auslander observed that BarChris's auditors were Peat, Marwick. They were also the auditors for the Valley Stream National Bank. He thought well of them.

Auslander was elected a director on April 17, 1961. The registration statement in its original form had already been filed, of course without his signature. On May 10, 1961, he signed a signature page for the first amendment to the registration statement which was filed on May 11, 1961. This was a separate sheet without any document attached. Auslander did not know that it was a signature page for a registration statement. He vaguely understood that it was something "for the SEC."

At the May 15 directors' meeting, however, Auslander did realize that what he was signing was a signature sheet to a registration statement. This was the first time that he had appreciated the fact. A copy of the registration statement in its earlier form as amended on May 11, 1961, was passed around at the meeting. Auslander glanced at it briefly. He did not read it thoroughly.

At the May 15 meeting, Russo and Vitolo stated that everything was in order and that the prospectus was correct. Auslander believed this statement. . . . Auslander knew that Peat, Marwick had audited the 1960 figures. He believed them to be correct because he had confidence in Peat, Marwick. He had no reasonable ground to believe otherwise.

As to the [remainder of the prospectus], however, Auslander is in a different position. He seems to have been under the impression that Peat, Marwick was responsible for all the figures. This impression was not correct, as he would have realized if he had read the prospectus carefully. Auslander made no investigation of the accuracy of the prospectus. He relied on the assurance of Vitolo and Russo, and upon the information he had received in answer to his inquiries back in February and early March. These inquiries were general ones, in the nature of a credit check. The information which he received in answer to them was also general, without specific reference to the statements in the prospectus, which was not prepared until some time thereafter.

It is true that Auslander became a director on the eve of the financing. He had little opportunity to familiarize himself with the company's affairs. The question is whether, under such circumstances, Auslander did enough to establish his due diligence.

Section 11 imposes liability in the first instance upon a director, no matter how new he is. He is presumed to know his responsibility when he becomes a director. He can escape liability only by using that reasonable care to investigate the facts which a prudent man would employ in the management of his own property. In my opinion, a prudent man would not act in an important matter without any knowledge of the relevant facts, in sole reliance upon general information which does not purport to cover the particular case. To say that such minimal conduct measures up to the statutory standard would, to all intents and purposes, absolve new directors from responsibility merely because they are new. This is not a sensible construction of Section 11, when one bears in mind its fundamental purpose of requiring full and truthful disclosure for the protection of investors.

PEAT, MARWICK

The part of the registration statement purporting to be made upon the authority of Peat, Marwick as an expert was, as we have seen, the 1960 figures. But because the statute requires the court to determine Peat, Marwick's belief, and the grounds thereof, "at the time such part of the registration statement became effective," for the purposes of this affirmative defense, the matter must be viewed as of May 16, 1961, and the question is whether at that time Peat, Marwick, after reasonable investigation, had reasonable ground to believe and did believe that the 1960 figures were true and that no material fact had been omitted from the registration statement which should have been included in order to make the 1960 figures not misleading. In deciding this issue, the court must consider not only what Peat, Marwick did in its 1960 audit, but also what it did in its subsequent "S–1 review." The proper scope of that review must also be determined.

Peat, Marwick's work was in general charge of a member of the firm, Cummings, and more immediately in charge of Peat, Marwick's manager, Logan. Most of the actual work was performed by a senior accountant, Berardi, who had junior assistants, one of whom was Kennedy.

Berardi was then about 30 years old. He was not yet a CPA. He had had no previous experience with the bowling industry. This was his first job as a senior accountant. He could hardly have been given a more difficult assignment.

It is unnecessary to recount everything that Berardi did in the course of the audit. We are concerned only with the evidence relating to what Berardi did or did not do with respect to those items which I have found to have been incorrectly reported in the 1960 figures in the prospectus. More narrowly, we are directly concerned only with such of those items as I have found to be material.

First and foremost is Berardi's failure to discover that Capital Lanes had not been sold. This error affected both the sales figure and the liability side of the balance sheet. Fundamentally, the error stemmed from the fact that Berardi never realized that Heavenly Lanes and Capitol were two different names for the same alley. . . . Berardi assumed that Heavenly was to be treated like any other completed job.

Berardi testified that he inquired of Russo about Capitol Lanes and that Russo told him that Capitol Lanes, Inc., was going to operate an alley some day but as yet it had no alley. Berardi testified that he understood that the alley had not been built and that he believed that the rental payments were on vacant land.

I am not satisfied with this testimony. If Berardi did hold this belief he should not have held it. The entries as to insurance and as to "operation of alley" should have alerted him to the fact that an alley existed. He should have made further inquiry on the subject. It is apparent that Berardi did not understand this transaction.

The burden of proof on this issue is on Peat, Marwick. Although the question is a rather close one, I find that Peat, Marwick has not sustained that burden. Peat, Marwick has not proved that Berardi made a reasonable investigation as far as Capitol Lanes was concerned and that his ignorance of the true facts was justified.

The purpose of reviewing events subsequent to the date of a certified balance sheet (referred to as an S–1 review when made with reference to a registration statement) is to ascertain whether any material change has occurred in the company's financial position which should be disclosed in order to prevent the balance sheet figures from being misleading. The scope of such a review, under generally accepted auditing standards is limited. It does not amount to a complete audit.

Berardi made the S–1 review in May 1961. He devoted a little over two days to it, a total of 20½ hours. He did not discover any of the errors or omissions pertaining to the state of affairs in 1961 which I have previously discussed at length, all of which were material. The question is whether, despite his failure to find out anything, his investigation was reasonable within the meaning of the statute.

What Berardi did was to look at a consolidating trial balance as of March 31, 1961, which had been prepared by BarChris, compare it with the audited December 31, 1960, figures, discuss with Trilling certain unfavorable developments which the comparison disclosed, and read certain minutes. He did not examine any "important financial records" other than the trial balance.

In substance, what Berardi did is similar to what . . . Ballard did. He asked questions, he got answers which he considered satisfactory, and he did nothing to verify them. . . .

Berardi had no conception of how tight the cash position was. He did not discover that BarChris was holding up checks in substantial amounts because there was no money in the bank to cover them. He did not know of the loan from Manufacturers Trust Company or of the officers' loans. Since he never read the prospectus, he was not even aware that there had ever been any problem about loans from officers.

During the 1960 audit, Berardi had obtained some information from factors, not sufficiently detailed even then, as to delinquent notes. He made no inquiry of factors about this in his S–1 review. Since he knew nothing about Kircher's notes of the executive committee meetings, he did not learn that the delinquency situation had grown worse. He was content with Trilling's assurance that no liability theretofore contingent had become direct.

There had been a material change for the worse in BarChris's financial position. That change was sufficiently serious so that the failure to disclose it made the 1960 figures misleading. Berardi did not discover it. As far as results were concerned, his S–1 review was useless.

Accountants should not be held to a standard higher than that recognized in their profession. I do not do so here. Berardi's review did not come up to that standard. He did not take some of the steps which Peat, Marwick's written program prescribed. He did not spend an adequate amount of time on a task of this magnitude. Most important of all, he was too easily satisfied with glib answers to his inquiries.

This is not to say that he should have made a complete audit. But there were enough danger signals in the materials which he did examine to require some further investigation on his part. Generally accepted accounting standards required such further investigation under these circumstances. It is not always sufficient merely to ask questions.

Here again, the burden of proof is on Peat, Marwick. I find that burden has not been satisfied. I conclude that Peat, Marwick has not established its due diligence defense.

Requirements of Directors, Officers, and Others

Reports of Stock Transactions. Section 16a of the 1934 Act requires that the directors and officers of a corporation registered under the Act and beneficial owners of 10 percent or more of any class of its equity securities file individually a statement disclosing the amount of such holdings. Thereafter, they must report any transactions in such securities within ten days following the end of the month in which the transaction occurs. Purchases and sales made before or after one becomes obligated to report transactions must also be reported if they are made within six months of transactions made while an officer, director or 10 percent shareholder. Those required to report are also prohibited from making short sales of the securities (sales of shares not owned at the time of sale).

"Short-Swing Profits." Section 16b of the 1934 Act provides that any profit made by anyone required to report their transactions in the stock belongs to the company if it resulted from the purchase and sale or sale and purchase of its securities within less than a six-month period. Either the corporation itself or a holder of its securities may file a suit to recapture the profit for the corporation. This provision was designed to remove temptation from insiders to make short-term profits in the corporation's securities by buying and then selling, or the reverse, in order to take advantage of short-term price swings resulting from events concerning which they have advance information. However, the application of the provision is without regard to intent. In a number of cases courts have held inadvertent or otherwise innocent sales and sales made without the benefit of inside knowledge, to be subject to the provision, although recently the United States Supreme Court appeared to give the section a somewhat narrower interpretation.[4]

Tender Offers. After a wave of corporate acquisitions through tender offers, the Williams Act amendments to the 1934 Act were passed in 1968 to provide investors with more information in these situations. Under these amendments anyone—which, of course, includes corporations—seeking to gain ownership of more than 5 percent of a class of equity securities registered under the 1934 Act must file with the SEC and provide shareholders of the "target company" certain information. This includes information about the offeror and his or her background, shares held by the offeror and his associates, agreements made to gain support for the tender offer, sources of funds, the

[4] *Foremost-McKesson, Inc. v. Provident Securities Co.*, 423 U.S. 232 (1976) and *Kern County Land Co. v. Occidental Petroleum Corp.*, 411 U.S. 582 (1973).

purpose in making the offer, and, if the purpose is control, specific plans for liquidation or merger of the "target company." The amendments also give the shareholder an opportunity to withdraw the tender of his or her shares within certain time limits. They also require the offeror to accept shares tendered during the first ten days of the offer on a pro rata basis and to extend any increased offering price to tenders made earlier. If the target company management wishes to make a recommendation on the offer to its shareholders, it must make a filing with the SEC. An antifraud provision specifically applying to tender offers was added.

SUMMARY

Directors, officers, and holders of 10 percent or more of any class of equity securities of a corporation must file reports of their shareholdings and transactions in the stock with the SEC, and they are prohibited from making "short sales." "Short-swing profits," or those made from buying and selling within a six months' period by such "insiders," may be recovered by the corporation. The Williams Act amendments impose numerous requirements upon those making tender offers for shares of a corporation and upon management of the "target company."

Antifraud Provisions

Introduction. To accomplish its objective of preventing fraud, unfair, deceptive, and manipulative practices and providing remedies to the victims of such practices, Congress included a number of provisions in the securities acts. These provisions are not all mutually exclusive in their application. Rule 10b–5 has come to be used by plaintiffs more than any other provision.

Antifraud Provisions of 1933 Act. Section 11a of the 1933 Act provides civil liabilities for damages resulting to an investor who finds, after acquiring a security, that the registration statement for the security contained an untrue statement or an omission of a material fact. Those potentially liable for such misleading or false information in the registration statement are all who signed it, all directors (whether or not they signed), every "expert" who gave consent to be named in the registration statement as having prepared or certified part of it and the underwriters of the distribution of the security. Among the defenses permitted is what has come to be known as the "due diligence defense." If a defendant can show that after making a reasonable investigation he has reasonable grounds to believe that the statements in it were true and there was no omission of a material fact, he will not be held liable.

Section 12(2) prohibits making untrue or misleading statements in a prospectus or in oral communication in connection with the offering or sale of a security. This is not limited to securities which are required to be registered and it applies to anything which is held under the Act to be a prospectus, not just the formal document usually so named. Section 17a broadly prohibits the use, in connection with an offer or sale of any security (again whether or not required to be registered), of any device or scheme to defraud or the use of any untrue or misleading statement. Section 17b is designed to deal with the evils of the "tipster" sheet. It requires anyone who publicizes, for a consideration, a security in a newspaper or other publication, to disclose that fact and give the amount of pay he is receiving.

All of these provisions apply to the use of the mails or anything "touching" interstate commerce. This has been interpreted to include the use of the telephone even when both buyer and seller are in the same city.[5]

Antifraud Provisions of 1934 Act. Section 9 specifically prohibits a number of deceptive practices that had previously been used to cause security prices to rise or fall by stimulating market activity. Prohibited practices include sales involving no change in beneficial ownership and certain other actions seeking to affect the price of a security. Section 10b is an extremely broad provision prohibiting the use of any manipulative or deceptive device in contravention of any rules the SEC may prescribe as necessary or appropriate in the public interest.

Rule 10b–5. This rule was adopted under Section 10b of the 1934 Act. It couples the broad language of Section 10b with the somewhat more detailed language of Section 17a of the 1933 Act so as to make the prohibitions of 17a apply to purchasers as well as sellers. The rule speaks in very general terms as follows:

> It shall be unlawful for any person, directly or indirectly, by use of any means or instrumentality of interstate commerce or of the mails, or of any facility of any national securities exchange, (*a*) to employ any device, scheme, or artifice to defraud, (*b*) to make any untrue statement of a material fact or to omit to state a material fact necessary in order to make the statements made, in the light of the circumstances under which they were made, not misleading, or (*c*) to engage in any act, practice, or course of business which operates or would operate as a fraud or deceit upon any person, in connection with the purchase or sale of any security.

Its sweeping language and the recognition in 1946[6] of an implied right of an injured party to recover under it have encouraged imaginative counsel for private plaintiffs as well as the SEC and sympathetic courts to expand the scope of its applicability so wide that the case law interpreting the rule is frequently described as a federal law of corporations. It is applicable to

---

[5] *Myzel v. Fields,* 386 F.2d 718 (8th Cir. 1967).

[6] *Kardon v. National Gypsum Co.*, 73 F.Supp. 798 (E.D. Pa. 1946), *modified* 83 F.Supp. 613 (E.D. Pa. 1947).

all securities transactions. Therefore, it concerns nonregistered securities, those not listed on an exchange, and face-to-face transactions, as well as those transactions completed on an exchange. In 1976 the Supreme Court held that a right to private damages under Rule 10b–5 is confined to actual purchasers or sellers of securities.[7]

The boundaries of its applicability remain rather uncertain, and the decisions under it are not easy to reconcile—a not unusual situation in new and rapidly growing areas of the law. Also, lack of precision is, of course, a continuing and necessary characteristic of the related tort law of fraud, due to the unlimited ingenuity of those who would deceive.

Section 10b–5 has been used to deal with both of the evils to which the securities laws are principally addressed—deceptive practices and lack of sufficient information for the ordinary investor. In applying the rule to deceptive practices, courts have interpreted the prohibitions to be much broader than common law fraud.

A number of the cases brought under 10b–5 allege conduct that would amount to fraud. For example, a manager of a business which had been unprofitable induced shareholders to sell their stock to him by representing that the business would continue to decline although he knew that it had become potentially profitable, and in fact he sold the business at a very large profit to himself.[8] Other false statements or misleading statements, such as those published by a company to promote its product just prior to going public, may be violations of 10b–5 even though not common-law fraud.[9]

Efforts to manipulate stock prices which do not involve false statements, such as reducing dividends for the purpose of depressing stock prices,[10] are also violations. Action by company executives to manipulate the price of the company's stock by transactions on behalf of an employee stock-bonus trust for which they were trustees has also been declared a violation.[11]

Although an early case held that there was no right of action under Rule 10b–5 against directors for mismanagement, some breaches of fiduciary duty by company insiders have been successfully attacked under 10b–5. One such case involved issuance of shares by directors to themselves at a price below the fair value, but the *Sante Fe Industries* case below suggests that the present Supreme Court is not sympathetic to this kind of application of Rule 10b–5.[12]

---

[7] *Blue Chip Stamps v. Manor Drug Stores,* 421 U.S. 723 (1975).

[8] *Janigan v. Taylor,* 344 F.2d 781 (1st Cir., 1965).

[9] *SEC v. Electrogen Industries, Inc.,* CCH ¶92,156 (1967–69 Transfer Binder) (E.D.N.Y. 1968).

[10] *Cochran v. Channing Corp.,* 211 F.Supp. 239 (S.D.N.Y. 1962).

[11] *SEC v. Georgia–Pacific Corp.,* CCH ¶91,692 (1964–66 Transfer Binder) (S.D.N.Y. 1966).

[12] *Sante Fe Industries, Inc. v. Green,* 430 U.S. 462 (1977). *Cf., Weitzen & Epstein v. Kearns,* 271 F.Supp. 616 (S.D.N.Y. 1967).

Failure to meet requirements of other sections of the securities laws have been held to violate Rule 10b–5. In one case, for example, failure to file required information on form 10–K, the annual report, was so treated although company officials did not trade in the stock at that time.[13]

Many cases involve concealment or failure to disclose information known to an insider. Some of these involve face-to-face transactions between an insider and another shareholder, as where two directors acquired all of the outstanding stock of the corporation without disclosing the existence of a written agreement with a third party to sell the company's assets at a much higher value.[14] Others, such as the famous *SEC v. Texas Gulf Sulphur Co.* case, below, involve trading on a stock exchange by persons in possession of information that has not been disclosed generally.

The *Texas Gulf Sulphur* case clearly holds that it is a violation to buy or sell either on an exchange or in a direct transaction when one is privy to "material" information which is not generally available to the investing public. This applies to almost anyone, not just those usually viewed as insiders, such as directors, officers, and those who own a major interest in the company. It would include secretaries, employees such as researchers or geologists and their supervisors. Included also are outside consultants, lawyers, engineers, financial and public relations advisors, and others given "inside" information for special purposes, such as news reporters and personnel of government agencies. Furthermore, "tippees" (those who are given or acquire the information without a need to know) such as stockbrokers or financial analysts and even relatives or friends of those acquiring the information for a corporate purpose are forbidden to trade and are subject to recovery of their profits if they do. Although stock exchanges have rules as to when issuers must release "material" information, the cases so far merely hold that the securities laws forbid trading while in possession of unreleased information which is material.

The test for materiality of corporate information has been variously stated but in essence it is any information that is likely to have an impact upon the price of a security in the market. The SEC has said that a fact is material if its disclosure would reasonably be expected to affect the market price of the stock or would materially affect the decision of a prospective buyer or seller whether to buy, sell, or delay. Certainly such matters as proposed mergers, tender offers for the corporation's stock, plans to introduce an important new product or indications of an abrupt change in the profit expectations of the company are examples of what would be considered material facts. A more difficult question, which troubled the courts in the *Texas Gulf Sulphur* case, is when information with some element of uncertainty about it becomes

[13] *Heit v. Weitzen,* 402 F.2d 909 (2d Cir. 1968).

[14] *Kardon v. National Gypsum Co.,* 73 F.Supp. 798 (E.D. Pa. 1947).

material or how early in the development of a plan or trend a disclosure or abstention from buying or selling is required.

SUMMARY

Both the 1933 and 1934 acts include antifraud provisions. The most used is Section 10b of the 1934 Act, under which Rule 10b–5 of the SEC has been issued. It has been used extensively both to impose liabilities for failure to provide an investor with adequate information and for the use of deceptive practices. Practices which would not allow recovery for common law fraud are covered by this section.

SEC v. Texas Gulf Sulphur Co.

401 F.2d 833 (2d Cir. 1968)

This was an action by the Securities and Exchange Commission (plaintiff) against the Texas Gulf Sulphur Company (TGS) and thirteen of its officers, directors, and employees (defendants) alleging violations of Section 10b of the Securities Exchange Act of 1934. The District Court found that two of the individuals, Clayton and Crawford, had violated the act but otherwise dismissed the complaint. On appeal the judgment was affirmed as to Clayton and Crawford and reversed as to all other parties but one, Murray, who was held not to have committed a violation. The case was remanded to determine whether TGS had violated the Act and to determine remedies.

TGS had for several years made aerial geophysical surveys in eastern Canada followed by drilling exploratory cores into geological formations that looked promising. On November 12, 1963, the core from the first drilling on a parcel of land near Timmins, Ontario, was fabulously high in copper content as well as in zinc and silver. Diversionary holes were then drilled elsewhere until the balance of the land covered by the formation could be acquired by TGS. The land-acquisition program had progressed far enough for TGS to resume drilling in the area on March 31, 1964. The next two cores also showed substantial quantities of the same minerals and additional rigs were put to work drilling more holes beginning on April 8. Meanwhile, rumors of a major ore strike were circulating in Canada and on Saturday, April 11, two major New York papers printed reports of TGS activity and appeared to infer a rich strike from the fact that the drill cores were being flown to the United States.

Following this publication on Saturday, Stephens, the president of TGS, and Fogarty, the executive vice president, were concerned by the publicized rumors and talked with Mollison, the TGS vice president who was in charge of the operations near Timmins. He had left the drilling on Friday and was at his home near New York City for the weekend. As a result on Sunday a news release was distributed for use on Monday, April 13. The release stated that most of the drilling in eastern Canada had shown nothing of value with a few holes indicating small or marginal ore bodies. It said that shipment of the cores to the United States was routine. It then added:

> Recent drilling on one property near Timmins has led to preliminary indications that more drilling would be required for proper evaluation of this prospect. The drilling done to date has not been conclusive, but the statements made by many outside quarters are unreliable and include information and figures that are not available to TGS.
>
> The work done to date has not been sufficient to reach definite conclusions and any statement as to size and grade of ore would be premature and possibly misleading. When we have progressed to the point where reasonable and logical conclusions can be made, TGS will issue a definitive statement to its stockholders and to the public in order to clarify the Timmins project.

On April 16 at 10:00 A.M. TGS held a conference for the financial press and disclosed that the ore body would run to at least 25 million tons of ore. This information was published on the Dow-Jones tape at 10:54 A.M.

Some of the individual defendants had purchased stock or calls upon stock in TGS between the time the results were known to them of the first core drilled on the site and the appearance of the second release on the Dow-Jones tape. Others, including Stephens and Fogarty, had accepted options to buy TGS stock from the stock-option committee of the board of directors which was unaware of the find. The market price of TGS stock rose from approximately $18 per share on November 12, 1963, to $58 on May 15, 1964. In addition to alleging a violation of the Securities Exchange Act by the individuals, the SEC claimed that the first press release of TGS, issued April 12, was deceptive and misleading in violation of the Act.

WATERMAN, CIRCUIT JUDGE. . . . The essence of the Rule is that anyone who, trading for his own account in the securities of a corporation has "access, directly or indirectly, to information intended to be available only for a corporate purpose and not for the personal benefit of anyone" may not take "advantage of such information knowing it is unavailable to those with whom he is dealing," that is, the investing public.

Insiders, as directors or management officers are, of course, by this Rule, precluded from so unfairly dealing, but the Rule is also applicable to one possessing that information who may not be strictly termed an "insider" within the meaning of Sec. 16(b) of the Act.

Thus, anyone in possession of material inside information must either disclose it to the investing public, or if he is disabled from disclosing it in order to protect a corporate confidence, or he chooses not to do so, must abstain from trading in or recommending the securities concerned while such inside information remains undisclosed. So, it is here no justification for insider activity that disclosure was forbidden by the legitimate corporate objective of acquiring options to purchase the land surrounding the exploration site: if the information was, as the SEC contends, material, its possessors should have kept out of the market until disclosure was accomplished. . . . Material facts include not only information disclosing the earnings and distributions of a company, but also those facts which affect the desire of investors to buy, sell, or hold the company's securities.

In each case, then, whether facts are material within Rule 10b–5 when the facts relate to a particular event and are undisclosed by those persons who are knowledgeable thereof will depend at any given time upon a balancing of both the indicated probability that the event will occur and the anticipated magnitude of the event in light of the totality of the company activity.

Here, notwithstanding the trial court's conclusion that the results of the first drill core, were "too 'remote' . . . to have had any significant impact on the market, that is, to be deemed material," knowledge of the possibility, which surely was more than marginal, of the existence of a mine of the vast magnitude indicated by the remarkably rich drill core located rather close to the surface (suggesting mineability by the less expensive open-pit method) within the confines of a large anomaly (suggesting an extensive region of mineralization) might well have affected the price of TGS stock and would certainly have been an important fact to a reasonable, if speculative, investor in deciding whether he should buy, sell or hold.

We hold, therefore, that all transactions in TGS stock or calls by individuals apprised of the drilling results were made in violation of Rule 10b–5.

Appellant Crawford, who ordered the purchase of TGS stock shortly before the TGS April 16 official announcement, and defendant Coates, who placed orders with and communicated the news to his broker immediately after the official announcement was read at the TGS-called press conference, concede that they were in possession of material information. They contend, however, that their purchases were not proscribed purchases for the news had already been effectively disclosed. We disagree. . . . Before insiders may act upon material information, such information must have been effectively disclosed in a manner sufficient to insure its availability to the investing public. Particularly here, where a formal announcement to the entire financial news media has been promised in a prior official release known to the media, all insider activity must await dissemination of the promised official announcement.

Assuming that the contents of the official release could instantaneously be acted upon, at the minimum Coates should have waited until the news could reasonably have been expected to appear over the media of widest circulation, the Dow-Jones broadtape, rather than hastening to insure an advantage to himself and his broker son-in-law.

Contrary to the belief of the trial court that Kline had no duty to disclose his knowledge of the Kidd project before accepting the stock option offered him, we believe that he, a vice president, who had become the general counsel of TGS in January 1964, but who had been secretary of the corporation since January 1961, and was present in that capacity when the options were granted, and who was in charge of the mechanics of issuance and acceptance of the options, was a member of top management and under a duty before accepting his option to disclose any material information he may have possessed, and, as he did not disclose such information to the Option Committee we direct rescission of the option he received.

II. The Corporate Defendant

[I]t seems clear from the broad legislative purpose Congress expressed in the Act, and the legislative history of Section 10b that Congress when it used the phrase "in connection with the purchase or sale of any security" intended only that the device employed, whatever it might be, be of a sort that would cause reasonable investors to rely thereon, and, in connection therewith, so relying, cause them to purchase or sell a corporation's securities. There is no indication that Congress intended that the corporations or persons responsible for the issuance of a misleading statement would not violate the section unless they engaged in related securities transactions or otherwise acted with wrongful motives; indeed, the obvious purposes of the Act to protect the investing public and to secure fair dealing in the securities markets would be seriously undermined by applying such a gloss onto the legislative language.

Absent a securities transaction by an insider it is almost impossible to prove that a wrongful purpose motivated the issuance of the misleading statement. The mere fact that an insider did not engage in securities transactions does not negate the possibility of wrongful purpose; perhaps the market did not react to the misleading statement as much as was anticipated or perhaps the wrongful purpose was something other than the desire to buy at a low price or sell at a high price. Of even greater relevance to the Congressional purpose of investor protection is the fact that the investing public may be injured as much by one's misleading statement containing inaccuracies caused by negligence as by a misleading statement published intentionally to further a wrongful purpose.

To render the Congressional purpose ineffective by inserting into the statutory words the need of proving, not only that the public may have been misled by the release, but also that those responsible were actuated by a wrongful purpose when they issued the release, is to handicap unreasonably the Commission in its work.

. . . [T]he investing public is hurt by exposure to false or deceptive statements irrespective of the purpose underlying their issuance. It does not appear to be unfair to impose upon corporate management a duty to ascertain the truth of any statements the corporation releases to its shareholders or to the investing public at large.

Accordingly, we hold that Rule 10b–5 is violated whenever assertions are made, as here, in a manner reasonably calculated to influence the investing public, for example, by means of the financial media, if such assertions are false or misleading or are so incomplete as to mislead irrespective of whether the issuance of the release was motivated by corporate officials for ulterior purposes. It seems clear, however, that if corporate management demonstrates that it was diligent in ascertaining that the information it published was the whole truth and that such diligently obtained information was disseminated in good faith, Rule 10b–5 would not have been violated.

In the event that it is found that the statement was misleading to the reasonable investor it will then become necessary to determine whether its issuance resulted from a lack of due diligence. The only remedy the Commission seeks against the corporation is an injunction, and therefore we do not find it necessary to decide whether a lack of due diligence on the part of TGS alone, absent a showing of bad faith, would subject the corporation to any liability for damages. . . .

We hold only that, in an action for injunctive relief, the district court has the discretionary power under Rule 10b–5 and Section 10(b) to issue an injunction, if the misleading statement resulted from a lack of due diligence on the part of TGS. The trial court did not find it necessary to decide whether TGS exercised such diligence and has not yet attempted to resolve this issue.

It is not altogether certain from the present record that the draftsmen could, as the SEC suggests, have readily obtained current reports of the drilling progress over the weekend of April 10–12, but they certainly should have obtained them if at all possible for them to do so.

However, even if it were not possible to evaluate and transmit current data in time to prepare the release on April 12, it would seem that TGS could have delayed the preparation a bit until an accurate report of a rapidly changing situation was possible.

At the very least, if TGS felt compelled to respond to the spreading rumors of a spectacular discovery, it would have been more accurate to have stated that the situation was in flux and that the release was prepared as of April 10 information rather than purporting to report the progress "to date." Moreover, it would have obviously been better to have specifically described the known drilling progress as of April 10 by stating the basic facts. Such an explicit disclosure would have permitted the investing public to evaluate the "prospect" of a mine at Timmins without having to read between the lines to understand that preliminary indications were favorable—in itself an understatement.

The choice of an ambiguous general statement rather than a summary of the specific facts cannot reasonably be justified by any claimed urgency. The avoidance of liability for misrepresentation in the event that the Timmins project failed, a highly unlikely event as of April 12 or April 13, did not forbid the accurate and truthful divulgence of detailed results which need not, of course, have been accompanied by conclusory assertions of success.

We conclude, then, that having established that the release was issued in a manner reasonably calculated to affect the market price of TGS stock and to influence the investing public, we must remand to the district court to decide whether the release was misleading to the reasonable investor and if found to be misleading, whether the court in its discretion should issue the injunction the SEC seeks.

Ernst & Ernst v. Hochfelder

425 U.S. 185 (U.S. Sup. Ct. 1976)

Hochfelder and others (plaintiffs) filed an action for damages against Ernst & Ernst (defendant), a public accounting firm, under Rule 10b–5 of the Securities and Exchange Commission, alleging that Ernst & Ernst had aided and abetted the carrying out of securities fraud by the president of First Securities Company of Chicago. The district court dismissed the action on motion for summary judgment. The Court of Appeals for the Seventh Circuit reversed and remanded, finding that there were genuine issues of fact as to whether Ernst & Ernst had breached its duties of inquiry and disclosure in conducting its audits. The Supreme Court reversed, holding for Ernst & Ernst.

Hochfelder had invested in a fraudulent securities scheme perpetrated by Leston B. Nay, who owned 92 percent of the stock of First Securities. Hochfelder had invested from 1942 to 1966 in "escrow accounts" that yielded a high rate of return. In fact, Nay converted the funds to his own use immediately upon receipt, and no such escrow accounts were reflected on the records of First Securities nor included in First Securities' filings with the SEC or the Midwest Stock Exchange. The fraud came to light in 1968 when Nay committed suicide, leaving a note describing First Securities as bankrupt and the escrow accounts as "spurious."

The basis of the action was the allegation that Ernst & Ernst had failed to utilize proper auditing procedures in auditing First Securities. Hochfelder relied particularly upon Ernst & Ernst's failure to discover that Nay had a rule that only he could open mail addressed to him at First Securities or addressed to First Securities to his attention, even if it arrived in his absence. Had it discovered this irregular procedure, Hochfelder argued, Ernst & Ernst should then have investigated and this would have revealed the fraudulent scheme.

MR. JUSTICE POWELL. We granted certiorari to resolve the question whether a private cause of action for damages will lie under § 10(b) and Rule 10b–5 in the absence of any allegation of "scienter"—intent to deceive, manipulate, or defraud. We conclude that it will not and therefore we reverse.

Although the extensive legislative history of the 1934 Act is bereft of any explicit explanation of Congress' intent, we think the relevant portions of that history support our conclusion that § 10(b) was addressed to practices that involve some element of scienter and cannot be read to impose liability for negligent conduct alone.

The most relevant exposition of the provision that was to become § 10(b) was by Thomas G. Corcoran, a spokesman for the drafters. Corcoran indicated:

> Subsection (c) § 9(c) of H.R. 7852—later § 10(b) says, "Thou shalt not devise any other cunning devices" . . . Of course subsection (c) is a catch-all clause to prevent manipulative devices. I do not think there is any objection to that kind of clause. The Commission should have the authority to deal with new manipulative devices.

This brief explanation of § 10(b) by a spokesman for its drafters is significant. The section was described rightly as a "catch-all" clause to enable the Commission "to deal with new manipulative (or cunning) devices." It is difficult to believe that any lawyer, legislative draftsman, or legislator would use these words if the intent was to create liability for merely negligent acts or omissions. Neither the legislative history nor the briefs supporting Hochfelder identify any usage or authority for construing "manipulative (or cunning) devices" to include negligence.

We also consider it significant that each of the express civil remedies in the 1933 Act allowing recovery for negligent conduct is subject to significant procedural restrictions not applicable under § 10(b). Section 11(c) of the 1933 Act, for example, authorizes the court to require a plaintiff bringing a suit under § 11, § 12(2), or § 15 thereof to post a bond for costs, including attorneys' fees and in specified circumstances to assess costs at the conclusion of the litigation. Section 13 specifies a statute of limitations of one year from the time the violation was or should have been discovered, in no event to exceed three years from the time of offer or sale, applicable to actions brought under § 11, § 12(2), or § 15. These restrictions, significantly, were imposed by amendments to the 1933 Act adopted as part of the 1934 Act.

The Commission contends, however, that subsections (2) and (3) of Rule 10b–5 are cast in language which—if standing alone—could encompass both intentional and negligent behavior.

We note first that such a reading cannot be harmonized with the administrative history of the rule, a history making clear that when the Commission adopted the rule it was intended to apply only to activities that involved scienter. More importantly, Rule 10b–5 was adopted pursuant to authority granted the Commission under § 10(b).

Its scope cannot exceed the power granted the Commission by Congress under § 10(b).

Myzel v. Fields

386 F.2d 718 (8th Cir. 1967)

Separate actions by Harry Fields, Samuel King, Rita Vertelney, and Gordon Cohen (plaintiffs) seeking damages for violation of Section 10b of the Securities Exchange Act of 1934 against Benn Myzel, the Levines, and others (defendants) were consolidated for trial before a jury. Verdicts totalling $411,000 were returned in favor of Fields, King, Vertelney and Cohen. Affirmed.

Fields and King each purchased 30 shares at $50 per share in Lakeside Plastics and Engraving Co. (LPE), a close corporation, of Duluth, Minnesota, when it was founded in 1946. Vertelney purchased 100 shares and Cohen 40 shares. They had made the investment upon the advice of their close friend, Benn Myzel, who was also a relative of Zelman Levine, one of the founders of the company. Myzel was an early director of the company, going off the board in 1949 but returning to it in 1954. At all times relevant to the case he served the corporation as a financial advisor. The company made advertising signs, and from 1946 to 1951 it struggled for sales, made little profit and paid the shareholders nothing on their investment. The shareholders were discouraged and in the 1949 shareholders' meeting Fields made a motion for dissolution. In 1952 sales increased substantially but not to a record level and a profit of $7,500 was made, after which the company still showed a $43,000 deficit. The company secured a large contract with Blatz Brewing Company and in the first four months of 1953 the company earned a profit of $30,000 but this interim financial statement was not disclosed at the June shareholders' meeting.

Myzel and his brother, who acted as his undisclosed agent, using the telephone and personal solicitation, bought the shares of Fields, King, Vertelney and Cohen toward the end of 1953 and in early 1954 at prices from $6.67 to $45.00 per share. In each instance the Myzels made representations that the stock was not worth anything, that the company was not making money and that Benn Myzel was "going to get out of the company" or suggested that the company was on the verge of bankruptcy.

Myzel later sold the shares at a substantial profit to the Levines who came to own all of the shares of the company. In addition, he received other substantial amounts from the Levines for his service in buying the stock. After 1953 the sales of LPE increased very greatly and large profits came shortly thereafter.

Lay, Circuit Judge. Both Section 10 of the Act and Rule 10b–5 require as a jurisdictional basis "the use of *any means or instrumentality of interstate commerce or of the mails,* or any facility of any national securities exchange." The evidence is undisputed that the telephone was used only on an intrastate basis in the solicitation or purchase of (the) stock. . . . We hold . . . that intrastate use of the telephone comes within prohibition of the Act.

Proof of affirmative misrepresentation, generally an essential element of commonlaw fraud, is not required in actions brought under Rule 10b–5, since the rule expressly prohibits material omissions as well. Several undisclosed facts in the present case assume relevance when coupled with the factual statements and reckless opinions offered by the Myzels. Among facts the jury could find not disclosed in the purchases were (1) the increased sales in 1953, (2) the April 1953 interim financial statements showing the successful Blatz contract and $30,000 profit, (3) the potential of 1954 sales or at least Zelman Levine's (President of LPE) optimism over prospects for the future, and (4) the identity of the controlling purchasers.

These nondisclosures assume materiality when considered in the context of the affirmative representations made severally to Fields, King, Vertelney, and Cohen. Phil Myzel's statement to Vertelney that Benn was "going to get out" of the company could be considered actionable as a misstatement of another's intent or state of mind. Benn's statements to King that he himself had sold his stock, that it was worthless and that the company wasn't making any money were misleading. Phil's statements to Fields that the company was on the "verge of bankruptcy" or "in bad shape" were material in view of the nondisclosures. And Benn's statements to Cohen that "he was not getting any money from the company" become significant with the discovery of Benn's commissions commencing in August 1953.

Under the circumstances we conclude, although not without great difficulty, that all of the appellees presented sufficient proof of an "assortment" of nondisclosures and positive misrepresentations to carry their respective cases to the jury.

Sante Fe Industries, Inc. v. Green

430 U.S. 462 (U.S. Sup. Ct. 1977)

Green and others (plaintiffs) brought this action under Section 10b of the Securities Exchange Act of 1934 against Sante Fe Industries, Inc., (defendant) asking that a merger between Sante Fe and Kirby Lumber Corporation be set aside or that they be paid the fair value of their shares in Kirby. The trial court's decision for Sante Fe was reversed by the court of appeals. The Supreme Court reversed, holding for Sante Fe.

Sante Fe owned 95 percent of the shares of Kirby, a Delaware corporation. Sante Fe wished to acquire 100 percent of the stock. Under Delaware's "short form" merger statute a parent corporation owning at least 90 percent of the stock of a subsidiary can merge with the subsidiary by merely obtaining the approval of the board of directors of the parent and making a cash payment for the stock of the minority shareholders. Any minority shareholder who is dissatisfied with the price established for the shares by the parent may ask the Delaware court to determine the fair value of the shares. Sante Fe fully complied with the statute in effecting the merger.

Green and the other plaintiffs, who were minority shareholders in Kirby, did not pursue the remedy provided by the statute but brought suit in the federal district court.

MR. JUSTICE WHITE. The language of §10(b) gives no indication that Congress meant to prohibit any conduct not involving manipulation or deception. Nor have we been cited to any evidence in the legislative history that would support a departure from the language of the statute. "When a statute speaks so specifically in terms of manipulation and deception, . . . and when its history reflects no more expansive intent, we are quite unwilling to extend the scope of the state. . . ." Thus the claim of fraud and fiduciary breach in this complaint states a cause of action under any part of Rule 10b–5 only if the conduct alleged can be fairly viewed as "manipulative or deceptive" within the meaning of the statute.

It is our judgment that the transaction, if carried out as alleged in the complaint, was neither deceptive nor manipulative and therefore did not violate either §10(b) of the Act or Rule 10b–5.

As we have indicated, the case comes to us on the premise that the complaint failed to allege a material misrepresentation or material failure to disclose. The finding of the District Court, undisturbed by the Court of Appeals, was that there was no "omission" or "misstatement" in the Information Statement accompanying the notice of merger. On the basis of the information provided, minority shareholders could either accept the price offered or reject it and seek an appraisal in the Delaware Court of Chancery. Their choice was fairly presented, and they were furnished with all relevant information on which to base their decision.

It is also readily apparent that the conduct alleged in the complaint was not "manipulative" within the meaning of the statute. Manipulation is "virtually a term of art when used in connection with securities markets." *Ernst & Ernst.* The term refers generally to practices, such as wash sales, matched orders, or rigged prices, that are intended to mislead investors by artificially affecting market activity. . . . No doubt Congress meant to prohibit the full range of ingenious devices that might be used to manipulate securities prices. But we do not think it would have chosen this "term of art" if it had meant to bring within the scope of §10(b) instances of corporate mismanagement such as this, in which the essence of the complaint is that shareholders were treated unfairly by a fiduciary.

The language of the statute is, we think, "sufficiently clear in its context" to be dispositive here; but even if it were not, there are additional considerations that weigh heavily against permitting a cause of action for violations of §10(b). Although we have recognized an implied cause of action under that section in some circumstances, we have also recognized that a private cause of action under the antifraud provisions of the Securities Exchange Act should not be implied where it is "unnecessary to ensure the fulfillment of Congress' purposes" in adopting the Act. The Court repeatedly has described the "fundamental purpose" of the Act as implementing a "philosophy of full disclosure"; once full and fair disclosure has occurred, the fairness of the terms of the transaction is at most a tangential concern of the statute.

A second factor in determining whether Congress intended to create a federal cause of action in these circumstances is "whether 'the cause [is] one traditionally relegated to state law. . . .' " *Piper v. Chris-Craft Industries, Inc.* The Delaware Legislature has supplied minority shareholders with a cause of action in the Delaware Court of Chancery to recover the fair value of shares allegedly undervalued in a short-form merger. Of course, the existence of a particular state law remedy is not dispositive of the question whether Congress meant to provide a similar federal remedy, but as in *Piper* and *Cort,* we conclude that "it is entirely appropriate in this instance to relegate respondent and others in his situation to whatever remedy is created by state law."

It is difficult to imagine how a court could distinguish, for the purposes of Rule 10b-5 fraud, between a majority stockholder's use of a short-form merger to eliminate the minority at an unfair price and the use of some other device, such as a long-form merger, tender offer, or liquidation, to achieve the same result; or indeed how a court could distinguish the alleged abuses of these going private transactions from other types of fiduciary self-dealing involving transactions in securities. The result would be to bring within the Rule a wide variety of corporate conduct traditionally left to state regulation. In addition to posing a "danger of vexatious litigation which could result from a widely expanded class of plaintiffs under Rule 10b-5," *Blue Chip Stamps v. Manor Drug Stores,* this extension of the federal securities laws would overlap and quite possibly interfere with state corporate law. Absent a clear indication of congressional intent, we are reluctant to federalize the substantial portion of the law of corporations that deals with transactions in securities, particularly where established state policies of corporate regulation would be overridden.

We thus adhere to the position that "Congress by §10(b) did not seek to regulate transactions which constitute no more than internal corporate mismanagement." *Superintendent of Insurance v. Bankers Life & Casualty Co.* There may well be a need for uniform federal fiduciary standards to govern merger such as that challenged in this complaint. But those standards should not be supplied by judicial extension of §10(b) and Rule 10b-5 to "cover the corporate universe."

Liabilities and Penalties

Civil Liabilities. The SEC enforces both the 1933 and 1934 Acts by seeking injunctions against violators so that they will be subject to contempt of court proceedings for future violations. Section 12 of the 1933 Act imposes civil liability upon persons selling securities that are required to be but have not been registered or who use untrue or misleading statement in any filing under the 1933 Act. In addition, an implied right of action for damages has been found as stated above, for violation of rules such as 10b–5 or sections of the statute such as 14a[15] that do not include explicit penalties.

Criminal Sanctions. Criminal penalties are also provided. In 1975 penalties under both Acts were increased. A fine of up to $10,000 and/or not more than five years in prison may be imposed for willful violations of either Act. The same penalties apply to violations of rules issued by the SEC under the acts.

---

[15] *J. I. Case Co. v. Borak,* 377 U.S. 426 (1964).

United States v. Natelli

527 F.2d 311 (2d Cir. 1975)

The United States (plaintiff) won a conviction of Anthony Natelli and Joseph Scansaroli (defendants) for violation of Section 32(a) of the Securities Exchange Act of 1934 for willfully and knowingly making false and misleading statements in a proxy statement. They appealed. Affirmed as to Natelli; reversed as to Scansaroli.

Natelli was the partner in charge of the Washington, D.C., office of Peat, Marwick, Mitchell & Co., a large CPA firm, and the engagement partner with respect to the audit of National Student Marketing Corporation. Scansaroli was Peat, Marwick's audit supervisor on that engagement. Student Marketing issued a proxy statement in September 1969 in connection with a shareholder meeting to consider merging six companies into Student Marketing.

Student Marketing was formed in 1966. Peat, Marwick became its public auditors in August 1968 after determining from previous auditors that there had been no professional disagreement with the company. In its financial statements for the nine months ended May 31, 1968, Student Marketing had counted as income the fee agreed upon with customers for what it designated as its "fixed-fee marketing programs" although the programs would extend over a substantial period of time. In making the year-end audit Natelli concluded that he would use a percentage-of-completion approach on these commitments. The auditors immediately encountered the difficulty that the commitments were not in writing and had not been booked during the fiscal year ended August 31. A refusal to recognize these oral "commitments" would result in showing a large loss—$232,000—for the fiscal year at a time when the stock was selling for $80, an increase of $74 in the five months since Student Marketing had "gone public."

Natelli directed Scansaroli to try to verify the "commitments" by telephoning the customers but not to seek written verification. Scansaroli accepted a schedule prepared by Student Marketing showing the account executives' estimate of the percentage of completion and the amount of each account's commitment for each customer. This resulted in an adjustment after the close of the fiscal year of $1.7 million for "unbilled accounts receivable," and it turned a loss for the year into a profit twice that of the year before. Natelli informed Student Marketing that Peat, Marwick thereafter would allow income to be recorded only on written commitments supported by contemporaneous logs kept by account executives.

By May 1969 a total of $1 million of the "commitments" had been written off, three quarters of it attributable to "sales" purportedly made by an account executive who was fired for taking kickbacks. The effect was to reduce 1968 income by $209,750 but Scansaroli, with Natelli's approval, offset this by reversing a deferred tax item of approximately the same amount. In the proxy statement the footnote purporting to reconcile Student Marketing's prior reported net sales and earnings for 1968 with restated amounts resulting from pooling the figures from companies acquired after fiscal 1968 did not show any retroactive adjustment for Student Marketing's own fiscal 1968 figures.

The proxy statement required an unaudited statement of nine months earnings through May 31, 1969. This was prepared by the company with the assistance of Peat, Marwick. A commitment for $1.2 million from the Pontiac Division of GM was produced two months after the end of the fiscal period but it was dated April 28, 1969. At 3 A.M. on the day the proxy statement was to be printed Natelli informed Randall, the chief executive and founder of Student Marketing, that this could not be included because it was not a legally binding contract. Randall responded at once that he had a "a commitment from Eastern Airlines" in a somewhat comparable amount attributable to the same period. Such a letter was produced at the printing plant a few hours later, and the Eastern commitment was substituted for the Pontiac "sale" in the proxy. Shortly thereafter, another Peat, Marwick accountant, Oberlander, discovered $177,547 in "bad" commitments from 1968. These were known to Scansaroli in May 1969 as being doubtful but had not been written off. Oberlander suggested to the company that these, plus others for a total of $320,000, be written off but Scansaroli, after consulting with Natelli, decided against the suggested writeoff.

There was no disclosure in the proxy statement that Student Marketing had written off $1 million (20 percent) of its 1968 sales and over $2 million of the $3.3 million of unbilled sales booked in 1968 and 1969. A true disclosure would have resulted in Student Marketing showing no profit for the first nine months of 1969.

GURFEIN, CIRCUIT JUDGE. It is hard to probe the intent of a defendant. Circumstantial evidence, particularly with proof of motive, where available, is often sufficient to convince a reasonable man of criminal intent beyond a reasonable doubt. When we deal with a defendant who is a professional accountant, it is even harder, at times, to distinguish between simple errors of judgment and errors made with sufficient criminal intent to support a conviction, especially when there is no financial gain to the accountant other than his legitimate fee.

Natelli argues that there is insufficient evidence to establish that he knowingly assisted in filing a proxy statement which was materially false. After searching consideration, we are constrained to find that there was sufficient evidence for his conviction.

The original action of Natelli in permitting the booking of unbilled sales after the close of the fiscal period in an amount sufficient to convert a loss into a profit was contrary to sound accounting practice, particularly when the cost of sales based on time spent by account executives in the fiscal period was a mere guess. When the uncollectibility, and indeed, the non-existence of these large receivables was established in 1969, the revelation stood to cause Natelli severe criticism and possible liability. He had a motive, therefore, intentionally to conceal the write-offs that had to be made.

Whether or not the deferred tax item was properly converted to a tax credit, the jury had a right to infer that "netting" the extraordinary item against ordinary earnings on the books in a special journal entry was, in the circumstances, motivated by a desire to conceal.

With this background of motive, the jury could assess what Natelli did with regard to (1) the footnote and (2) the Eastern commitment and the Oberlander "bad" contracts.

Honesty should have impelled Natelli and Scansaroli to disclose in the footnote which annotated their own audited statement for fiscal 1968 that substantial writeoffs had been taken, after year end, to reflect a loss for the year. A simple desire to right the wrong that had been perpetrated on the stockholders and others by the false audited financial statement should have dictated that course.

. . . The accountant owes a duty to the public not to assert a privilege of silence until the next audited annual statement comes around in due time. Since companies were being acquired by Marketing for its shares in this period, Natelli had to know that the 1968 audited statement was being used continuously.

The argument that the disclosure was not material is weak, since applying write-offs only against pooled earnings, without further explanation, conceals the effect of the write-offs on the prior reported earnings of the principal company. It is the disclosure of the true operating results of Marketing for 1968, now come to light, that was material.

Natelli contends that he had no duty to verify the Eastern "commitment" because the earnings statement within which it was included was "unaudited."

This raises the issue of the duty of the CPA in relation to an unaudited financial statement contained within a proxy statement where the figures are reviewed and to some extent supplied by the auditors. It is common ground that the auditors were "associated" with the statement and were required to object to anything they actually "knew" to be materially false. In the ordinary case involving an unaudited statement, the auditor would not be chargeable simply because he failed to discover the invalidity of booked accounts receivable, inasmuch as he had not undertaken an audit with verification. In this case, however, Natelli "knew" the history of post-period bookings and the dismal consequences later discovered.

We do not think this means, in terms of professional standards, that the accountant may shut his eyes in reckless disregard of his knowledge that highly suspicious figures, known to him to be suspicious, were being included in the unaudited earnings figures with which he was "associated" in the proxy statement.

There is some merit to Scansaroli's point that he was simply carrying out the judgments of his superior Natelli. The defense of obedience to higher authority has always been troublesome. There is no sure yardstick to measure criminal responsibility except by measurement of the degree of awareness on the part of a defendant that he is participating in a criminal act, in the absence of physical coercion such as a soldier might face. Here the motivation to conceal undermines Scansaroli's argument that he was merely implementing Natelli's instructions, at least with respect to concealment of matters that were within his own ken.

We think the jury could properly have found him guilty on the specification relating to the footnote. Scansaroli himself wrote the journal entry in Marketing's books which improperly netted the tax credit with earnings, the true effect never being pointed out in the financial statement. This, with the background of Scansaroli's implication in preparation of the 1968 statement, could be found to have been motivated by intent to conceal the 1968 overstatement of earnings.

With respect to . . . the Eastern commitment, we think Scansaroli stands in a position different from that of Natelli. Natelli was his superior. He was the man to make the judgment whether or not to object to the last-minute inclusion of a new "commitment" in nine-months statement. There is insufficient evidence that Scansaroli engaged in any conversations about the Eastern commitment at the Pandick Press or that he was a participant with Natelli in any check on its authenticity. Since in the hierarchy of the accounting firm it was not his responsibility to decide whether to book the Eastern contract, his mere adjustment of the figures to reflect it under orders was not a matter for his discretion.

State Securities Legislation

Purpose and History. State securities laws are frequently referred to as "blue-sky" laws, since the early statutes were designed to protect investors from promoters and security salespersons who offered stock in companies organized to pursue visionary schemes or to exploit uncertain resources. However, even legitimate ventures typically provided the investor with little hard information and most investors are not educated in the intricacies of corporate organization and finance. The first state to enact such a law was Kansas in 1919. All states presently have such legislation.

Types of Statutes. There are three basic types of state statutes. Some combine two or more of these approaches. Those which might be called the "fraud type" provide penalties for fraudulent sales and injunctive proceedings to protect investors from further or anticipated fraudulent acts. Many do not rely upon full disclosure but give the administrator power to deny registration on the "merits" of the security. Some state official, usually the attorney general, is given broad investigative powers and criminal penalties are provided for selling fraudulent securities and conducting fraudulent transactions. The second type of law regulates the seller. It provides licensing of security salespersons and requires proof of financial responsibility of dealers. It puts a duty upon dealers to disclose pertinent facts about the securities they are selling and to avoid sales of fraudulent securities. The third type controls the issuer. It requires the filing by the issuer of certain information with the state regulatory agency and prohibits sales without such filings. The Uniform Securities Act, which has been adopted in whole or in part by 25 states, combines all three types. It contains antifraud provisions, requires broker-dealer registration, and also requires the registration of securities.

The Securities Act of 1933 specifically permits concurrent jurisdiction by state agencies. However, a number of states with registration of securities (issuer control) provisions exempt securities which have been registered with the SEC under the 1933 Act.

Anti-Takeover Statutes. Twenty-three states have statutes aimed at discouraging unfriendly takeovers of domestic corporations and those with their principal place of business or substantial assets in the state. These require the filing of information with the state securities department and impose a waiting period. Some allow for a hearing on the merits of the proposal. The result is to delay action as well as to eliminate secrecy. There is considerable doubt as to their constitutionality as applied to those businesses not incorporated by the state.[16]

SUMMARY

Securities regulation statutes, commonly called blue-sky laws, were passed by a number of states before the federal legislation. Three basic types of regulation are used: (1) prohibition of fraud and misrepresentation, (2) licensing of securities sellers, and (3) requiring of issuers the disclosure of information relevant to the security. The Uniform Securities Act, adopted in whole or in part by 25 states, includes all three types of regulation.

Problem Cases

1. Shirley Woolf, a lawyer and businessperson, and Robert Milberg, a securities broker, purchased $10,000 subordinated convertible debentures in Fiberglass Resources Corporation through S. D. Cohn, a securities broker-dealer. Fiberglass was to be formed by taking over a plant and a line of business that had been owned by Koppers Company. Cohn's plan of financing involved an issue of $600,000 in debentures through a private offering. Woolf and Milberg had been involved in previous business relations with Cohn. All contact had been by phone.

   Fiberglass was unsuccessful and Woolf and Milberg sued Cohn to recover their losses,

[16] *Great Western United Corp. v. Kidwell,* 577 F. 2d 1256 (5th Cir. 1978) held that the Idaho statute was preempted by the William's Act. Cert. granted U.S. Sup. Ct.

alleging certain misrepresentations and that the issue did not qualify as a private offering. Cohn testified that he had sold the debentures to only ten investors. He also defended on the ground that Woolf and Milberg were equally at fault because they signed a statement that they were buying the securities for investment and that no other person had a beneficial interest although they were representing five other investors besides themselves.

Was the trial court correct in holding that the offer was a private offering and that in any case Woolf and Milberg could not win because of the misrepresentation?

2. Parvin designed and furnished new officers for Davis Oil Company in Denver and later developed social relations with the Davis family. In February 1968, one of the Davises phoned Parvin, who lived in Loss Angeles, and invited him to participate in an oil and gas drilling venture. Parvin, who had substantial experience as an investor in oil and gas properties, mailed a $15,000 check. In July and August Parvin joined in two other Davis ventures in which he would have a fractional interest in oil and gas leases. Parvin requested and the Davises provided very little information concerning the venture. Under the agreements Parvin and the other investors could decide whether drilling should continue beyond a certain point but the Davises selected the leases and determined whether to drill and directed the drilling.

   The ventures were unsuccessful and Parvin brought an action for violation of the federal securities acts. The district court dismissed the action on the grounds that the transactions did not involve securities and that, in any case, the private offering exemption would apply. Was the district court correct?

3. C.N.S. Enterprises, Inc., purchased the fixtures, merchandise, and good will of the "Village Well," a coin-operated laundry and dry cleaning business in Justice, Illinois, from G&G Enterprises. The purchaser assumed a chattel mortgage on the fixtures held by a bank, borrowed an additional $20,000 from the bank, and paid a portion of the purchase price in cash to G&G. The notes involved had terms exceeding nine months. The buyer operated the business for four months, spending substantial sums in promotion, and then sent G&G a notice of rescission. C.N.S. alleged that the purchase had been made upon representations as to monthly sales that were false. It brought an action in federal court under Section 10b of the 1934 Act and Rule 10b–5 seeking rescission of the transaction. G&G moved to dismiss the action because a security was not involved. The Act provides:

   "(10) The term 'security' means any note . . . but shall not include any note . . . which has a maturity at time of issuance of not exceeding nine months . . ."

   Is this a good defense?

4. Chris-Craft Industries began in early 1969 to acquire Piper Aircraft shares in the open market and later made several public tender offers for Piper stock in exchange for Chris-Craft securities. The Piper family, which owned 31 percent of the shares, advised other shareholders that the tender offer by Chris-Craft was inadequate and they considered it to be a corporate raider. On May 8 the Piper family agreed to exchange its shares for specified Bangor Punta Corporation securities and to support a public exchange offer by Bangor Punta. Bangor Punta then issued a press release that, among other things, stated that its tender offer was of a value of $80 or more per written opinion of The First Boston Corporation.

   Rule 135 exempted from the definition of an "offer to sell" certain disclosures of forthcoming issues. Expressly exempted was a notice to present shareholders that the issuer "proposes to offer its securities to them in exchange for other securities." The Rule declared that the notice should state that the offering will be made only by a prospectus and shall give "no more than the following additional information." It then listed six items including "the basis upon which the exchange is proposed to be made and the period during which the exchange may be made." The value of the exchange was not included among the items listed in the rule.

Was this press release "an offer to sell" in violation of Section 5c of the 1934 Act because no registration statement had been filed with the SEC?

5. LaForce, Inc., was a Vermont corporation involved in the invention and marketing of an improved engine and carburetor. Webster, who had formerly worked in a stock brokerage office, was an "assistant to the president" of LaForce, who was based in Washington, D.C. During the spring and summer of 1961, Webster sold some 25,000 shares in LaForce to approximately 80 persons at $5 per share. Shimer invested $11,500, others invested as little as $500. They were told that because of some difficulty with the SEC they would receive the certificates in January 1962 when the stock was registered. However, no effort was made to have the stock registered. After numerous phone calls and a formal demand for shares, the shares were delivered to Shimer and others in December 1964, but they were informed that the stock was not registered. By this time it was worthless.

   Shimer brought an action against Webster to rescind the contract to purchase the stock, alleging a violation of the 1934 Act. Is Webster's defense that the transaction was exempt from registration requirements as a private offering good?

6. Whiting was a director of Dow Chemical Co. His wife was a granddaughter of the company's founder. During September and November 1973 she sold 29,770 shares of Dow stock at an average price of $55–$56. In December 1973 Whiting exercised an option to purchase 21,420 shares of Dow at a price of $24.3125. He borrowed the funds for the purchase from his wife, who used part of the proceeds of her sale for this purpose.

   These transactions were part of a long-range investment plan arranged by the Whitings with their financial advisor. It was designed to diversify the holdings of the family and to obtain tax benefits. The Whitings maintained separate investment accounts but the income of both was used for family expenses. Mrs. Whiting paid for the education of their children, the maintenance of a vacation home, real estate taxes, medical expenses, etc.

   Whiting sought a declaratory judgment that he was not liable to the corporation for profits on the sale and purchase under Section 16b of the 1934 Act, and Dow counterclaimed for recovery of shortswing profits. The trial court held for Dow, treating Whiting as the beneficial owner of his wife's shares. Should this judgment be affirmed?

7. Douglas Aircraft Company shareholders were told at the annual meeting in April 1966 that earnings for the 1966 fiscal year ending December 1 would exceed the $3.15 per share for 1965. Toward the end of May the president became concerned about profits because of slow deliveries to Douglas of certain subassemblies and other problems. After working over the Memorial Day weekend, Douglas financial officers reported to him that earnings for the year would be approximately $2. The following day, June 1, Douglas announced only that delays in deliveries of aircraft sold would have an adverse effect on 1966 earnings. On June 14 the chief financial officer of Douglas learned that May figures would probably show a very large loss, much larger than anticipated. Outside auditors were called in to determine whether an inventory write-down would be required. They decided it would and this increased the loss. On June 20 an estimate of earnings for the first six months of 49 cents per share was made but the auditors and company financial people continued their study and on the evening of June 23 arrived at the figure of 12 cents per share. This figure was announced publicly the next day.

   Financial Industrial Fund, a mutual fund, decided on June 21 to purchase 100,000 shares of Douglas common over a short period of time. It bought 80,000 in the next two days. Market price of the stock was approximately $90 on June 22 and dropped to under $77 by Friday, June 24, after the special six months earnings announcement was made. It then dropped to under $64 during the following week. The Fund sold its shares at a substantial loss and brought an action against Douglas for violation of Rule 10b–5 on grounds that the special earnings report should have been made earlier.

Will the fund win?

8. Douglas Aircraft filed a registration statement for a $75 million issue of debentures with the SEC on June 7, 1966. Merrill Lynch was the managing underwriter. On June 7 Douglas had released an earnings statement showing 85 cents per share for the first five months of its fiscal year. Later in June certain Merrill Lynch personnel learned, because of the underwriting relationship, that Douglas would report substantially less earnings for six than for the five months.

   Within a few days and before any public announcement, Merrill Lynch personnel disclosed this information to several Merrill Lynch customers who were institutional investors and who knew the May loss had not been announced. These investors sold 166,000 shares of Douglas common on the New York Stock Exchange before and during a rapid drop in its price.

   Several individual investors who were unaware of the unfavorable information bought shares on NYSE during this period. They brought an action under Rule 10b–5 against Merrill Lynch and their customers who received the "tip" and sold Douglas stock. Is the position of the defendants sound that the *Texas Gulf* case does not apply because damages rather than an injunction is sought and because the purchasers could not prove that the shares they bought had been sold by the defendants?

9. Anaconda Lead & Silver Company was a Nevada corporation with its office in Denver, Colorado. It had not been in operation nor had it realized any income for several years when Scott Taylor & Company (Stevens) and Theodore Landau, a large shareholder, began to offer its shares to residents of various states. Stevens told customers that the company was backed by Anaconda (a well known copper company), although he knew this to be untrue. Landau placed bids to purchase Anaconda Lead at prices from $4.00 to $4.25 on every business day but one from April to August in the National Daily Quotation sheets. The bids were based on an order for the account of Scott Taylor. More than 30,000 shares were sold at from $4.25 to $4.75 per share.

   Prior to the sales effort by Stevens and Landau, the president, who was a large shareholder of Anaconda Lead, had advised Stevens that some stock had sold at 40 cents per share and that for trading purposes its value was from 25 cents to 40 cents per share.

   The SEC brought a suit to enjoin Landau and Stevens from violating Section 17a of the 1933 Act and also 10b of the 1934 Act. Were the untrue statements with respect to the association between Anaconda Lead and the Anaconda Co. a violation of 17a and the bids by Landau "manipulative and deceptive" devices prohibited by Section 10b?

10. Harold Roth controlled both Continental Vending Machine Corporation and Valley Commercial Corporation. Valley loaned money to Continental and others in the vending machine business. Continental also loaned money to Valley, which in turn loaned it to Roth to finance his personal transactions in the stock market. At the insistence of Simon, partner of Lybrand, Ross Bros. & Montgomery in charge of auditing Continental, the loans to Valley were secured by stock owned by Roth. Simon, for Lybrand, certified Continental's 1962 financial statement. It showed an operating loss of $867,000 plus writeoffs of $3 million. A footnote stated that as of February 15, 1963, the equity in the stock put up as collateral exceeded the receivable from Valley, which was $3.5 million,

but it did not state that 80 percent of the collateral was in Continental securities. The financial statements were mailed on February 20, and by that time the price of Continental's stock (and hence the collateral) was dropping rapidly. On February 24 the American Stock Exchange suspended trading in Continental's stock and bankruptcy of Continental came shortly thereafter.

Simon was prosecuted under Section 32 of the 1934 Act for certifying a false and misleading financial statement because the footnote did not state that the loan to Valley was uncollectible because Valley had loaned approximately the same amount to Roth who was unable to pay and that this was known to Simon. Is Simon's conviction under the criminal provision of the 1934 Act proper?

30

Foreign Corporations

Rights of Foreign Corporations

Introduction. A corporation is a "domestic corporation" in the state or country which has granted it its charter and is a "foreign corporation" in all other states, territories, countries, or subdivisions of countries.

A corporation has no right to transact business except in interstate commerce in a state other than the one granting its charter. However, all states permit foreign corporations to become "domesticated" (licensed or qualified) to do intrastate business within the state upon compliance with general statutes. They may impose in such statutes any reasonable condition upon foreign corporations seeking the privilege to do intrastate business. Some require certain kinds of corporations providing important public services, such as railroads, to incorporate a subsidiary within the state. The term "domesticate" is sometimes used in this limited sense.

Under the Commerce Clause of the U.S. Constitution the power to regulate interstate commerce is given to the federal government, and states have no power to exclude or to discriminate against foreign corporations which are engaged solely in interstate commerce.[1] Nor can a state deny a foreign corporation due process of law or equal protection of the laws if it is admitted to do intrastate business. However, even if it is engaged only in interstate commerce, a foreign corporation is subject to nondiscriminatory regulations of business activities such as sanitary standards for food products, regulations on truck size and usury laws, and under recent Supreme Court decisions, it is subject to a suit in the state growing out of its activities and to taxation.

The Model Act. The provisions which apply to foreign corporations in the Model Business Corporation Act are set out in sections 106 to 124. Similar

[1] See Chapter 48 for related discussion.

to most such statutes, Section 110 requires the foreign corporation to apply for a certificate of authority from the secretary of state, giving information similar to that required from a domestic corporation in an application for a charter and to file a copy of its articles.

The foreign corporation must maintain a registered office and a registered agent in the state upon whom service of process upon the corporation may be served. The registered agent may be and frequently is a corporation which makes a business of providing such representation. The foreign corporation must also make an annual report.

A license fee, based upon the number of authorized shares of stock of the corporation apportioned according to the relative value of its property located in the state and outside and its gross income inside and outside of the state, must be paid at the time of filing for certificate of authority to do business in the state. An additional license fee is required when the articles are amended to authorize additional shares. In addition, a franchise tax is payable annually based upon the proportion of its property in and business done within the state.

If the taxes are not paid, if the reports are not submitted, or if other requirements are not met, the secretary of state, under the Model Act and most state statutes, may revoke the certificate of authority of the foreign corporation to do intrastate business in the state. The penalties for failing to obtain a certificate of authority when required are discussed later in the chapter.

SUMMARY

A corporation is a domestic corporation in the state which grants it its charter and a foreign corporation elsewhere. A corporation has a right to engage in intrastate business only in the state granting its charter, but generally it has a right under the Commerce Clause to conduct interstate business throughout the country.

To qualify to do intrastate business a foreign corporation must apply for a certificate of authority giving information similar to that required of a domestic corporation seeking a charter and must maintain a registered agent within the state. License and franchise fees must be paid to the states in which it is qualified.

"Doing Business"

Introduction. The courts recognize three general types of "doing business" by foreign corporations. They are: (1) that which subjects the foreign corporation to suit in the state courts, (2) that which subjects the foreign corporation to taxation by the state, and (3) that which requires that the foreign corporation comply with statutes granting it permission to do intrastate business in the state. More business activity within a state is required to subject a corporation to admission (or qualification or license) as a foreign corporation than for either service of process or taxation, but it is difficult to say today that more activities are necessary to subject the foreign corporation to taxation than to subject it to service of process. Although there have been literally thousands of cases, clear standards have not been arrived at by the courts in any one of the three categories. What is "doing business" is a question of fact determined by all the circumstances in a particular case and apparently inconsistent decisions by the same court are not infrequent. The trend has been to require fewer local activities for any of the three types than in earlier times.

Subjecting Foreign Corporations to Suit. The leading case on the issue whether a foreign corporation can be hailed into court in the state is *International Shoe Company v. State of Washington,* which follows. There the court rejected the traditional "doing business" test and held that an unlicensed foreign corporation could be subjected to suit if to do so would not offend traditional notions of fair play and substantial justice. Jurisdiction of the state court depends, under this decision, as much upon matters of convenience to the parties, location of witnesses and the expense of producing them within the state, and the place where the events leading up to the suit took place as upon the extent of business activities with the state. Some local activity, or "minimum contacts" with the state, by the corporation are necessary, however, to give the state courts jurisdiction and then only with respect to a suit based upon or resulting from those contacts.

As a result of this decision, most states have passed so-called "long-arm" statutes to take advantage of the broadened jurisdictional power permitted in the *International Shoe* case. These statutes frequently specify several kinds of corporate activities which make the foreign corporation subject to suit within the state, such as the commission of a tort, the making of a contract or the ownership of property. Most of the statutes grant jurisdiction with respect to causes of action growing out of any doing of business or any transaction within the state, and some grant jurisdiction in product liability cases if the foreign corporation should have expected use of the product in the state. Many have a "catchall" provision that indicates the legislature's attempt to assert the full extent of jurisdiction granted by the constitution as interpreted by the *International Shoe* case. It subjects any nonresident to jurisdiction who has "the necessary minimum contacts with the state." Such a statute turns each case into an exercise in interpretation of the Due Process Clause of the Fourteenth Amendment, each being decided upon its particular facts.

Taxing Foreign Corporations. A foreign corporation which is not required to apply for a certificate of authority to do business within the state may be subject to taxation by that state. There has never been any doubt that the property of the corporation stored in or otherwise located in the state is subject to taxation even though it is used in carrying on the corporation's interstate business.

More troublesome for the courts have been attempts by states to impose income taxes upon foreign corporations conducting only an interstate business and, therefore, not required to obtain a certificate of authority. The Supreme Court had tended toward permitting taxation with fewer and fewer activities within the state until its decision in *Northwestern States Portland Cement Co. v. Minnesota.* In that case the court upheld the imposition by Minnesota of an apportioned, nondiscriminatory net income tax on a corporation engaged solely in interstate commerce in Minnesota and which had not qualified in Minnesota as a foreign corporation.

As a result of what it appeared to think was a too liberal decision by the court, Congress enacted the Federal Interstate Income Law in 1959. It prohibits taxing bodies, state or local, from imposing net income taxes on income which is derived from interstate commerce in which the only activity in the taxing jurisdiction is the solicitation of orders to be accepted and shipped from another state. Also under the act a foreign corporation may employ an independent contractor who represents more than one principal as sales agent, even if he has an office in the state, without becoming subject to taxation.

Admission of a Foreign Corporation. Subjection of the foreign corporation to the necessity of becoming domesticated (being admitted or qualifying) is dependent upon the wording of the statute, but so long as it limits its activities in the state to interstate commerce, a corporation is protected by the Constitution from the necessity of obtaining a certificate of admission. The Supreme Court, of course, has the final determination of what constitutes interstate commerce.

The Model Act (106)[2] provides that "no foreign corporation shall have the right to transact business in this State until it shall have procured authority to do so. . . ." It then lists a number of activities that the foreign corporation may carry on which will not be considered transacting business for the purposes of the Act. These activities include: bringing or defending suit, holding corporate meetings, maintaining bank accounts, soliciting sales through independent contractors, soliciting orders by mail or agents if the orders require acceptance outside of the state, collecting debts, conducting isolated transactions completed within 30 days if they are not in the course of a number of repeated transactions of like nature, as well as transacting business in interstate commerce.

[2] The numbers in parentheses refer to the sections of the Model Business Corporation Act, which appears in the Appendix.

It is difficult to state a general rule as to what activities constitute intrastate commerce. The following frequently quoted rule hardly seems to clarify the matter: "A foreign corporation is doing, transacting, carrying on, or engaging in business within a state when it transacts some substantial part of its ordinary business therein."[3] Generally, the maintenance of a stock of goods within a state even though the orders filled from the stock are accepted outside the state is treated as doing business. Even peddling goods from a truck sent in from outside the state or mere ownership of real estate have been held to require qualification. Statutory definitions such as Section 106 of the Model Act may not reach as far in requiring qualification as the Constitution has been interpreted to permit.

Penalty for Failure to Obtain Permission. Generally, the states impose by statute a penalty on foreign corporations which do intrastate business without first obtaining permission. The statutory penalties usually include one or more of the following: a fine imposed upon the corporation, its agent in the state or its officers; denial to the corporation of the right to bring suit in the state courts; and holding officers, directors, or agents personally liable on contracts made within the state. In addition, a few states declare contracts made within the state to be void. Nevada denies even the right to defend a suit brought against the corporation in the state.[4] The Model Act (124) denies the right to bring an action in the state courts plus the penalty for failure to pay fees and franchise taxes. Generally, if a corporation complies with the statute of the state after having transacted intrastate business without obtaining permission, such compliance will be retroactive and will cure the defect in such prior transactions.

Under the majority rule, if the intrastate contracts of a foreign corporation doing business in a state without having qualified are declared to be void by the state statute, such contracts are not enforceable by the corporation but may be enforced against it. These statutes are for the protection of the public; if the corporation were permitted to set up illegality as a defense to such contracts, it would be taking advantage of its own wrong.

SUMMARY

The courts recognize three general types of "doing business" by foreign corporations: (1) that which subjects the foreign corporation to suit in the state courts, (2) that which subjects the foreign corporation to taxation by the state, and (3) that which requires qualification by the foreign corporation.

---

[3] *Royal Insurance Co. v. All States Theatres,* 6 So.2d 494 (Ala. 1942).

[4] Nevada Rev. Stat., 80.210(1).

More business activity is necessary to require the corporation to qualify to do intrastate business than for either service of process in a lawsuit or for taxation. There are no clear standards in any of the three situations but the trend has been toward requiring fewer local activities.

Under the most recent decisions of the U.S. Supreme Court, whether a foreign corporation can be subjected to suit within a state depends as much on matters of convenience to the parties as on the extent of the defendant corporation's business activities within the state. A single contract entered into within the state or a single tort committed within the course of the corporation's business within the state, even if the business is essentially interstate, will give jurisdiction to local courts.

The right of a state to tax property of a foreign corporation located in the state even though used solely in carrying on its interstate business has long been upheld. Recent decisions, however, have permitted states to impose income taxes on foreign corporations doing only interstate business, although limitations on such taxation have been established by Congress.

States cannot require qualification by a foreign corporation which does only an interstate business in the state as defined by the Supreme Court in interpreting the Commerce Clause. States frequently penalize foreign corporations which fail to qualify when necessary by denying them the right to bring suit in state courts and/or by fines.

International Shoe Co. v. State of Washington

326 U.S. 310 (U.S. Sup. Ct. 1945)

This was an action by the Office of Unemployment Compensation and Placement of the State of Washington (plaintiff) against International Shoe Company (defendant) to recover money alleged due as contributions under the Unemployment Compensation Act. Shoe Company appealed from a decision of the Washington Supreme Court affirming judgment for the State. Affirmed.

Shoe Company maintained neither an office nor a stock of goods in Washington, and it made no deliveries in intrastate commerce there. During the years in question it employed eleven to thirteen salesmen in Washington who were under the direct supervision of sales managers located in its headquarters office in St. Louis. The salesmen occasionally rented rooms in hotels or other buildings in which they displayed samples of Shoe Company's merchandise. They solicited orders on terms fixed in St. Louis for acceptance or rejection there. When accepted the merchandise was shipped f.o.b. to the Washington customers from points outside Washington. The salesmen had no authority to make collections and merchandise was invoiced at the place of shipment.

Shoe Company argued that its activities within the state were not sufficient to manifest its "presence" there and that in its absence the state courts were without jurisdiction, and, therefore, it was a denial of due process for the state to subject it to suit.

MR. CHIEF JUSTICE STONE. Due process requires only that in order to subject a defendant to a judgment *in personam,* if he be not present within the territory of the forum, he have certain minimum contacts with it such that the maintenance of the suit does not offend "traditional notions of fair play and substantial justice."

Since the corporate personality is a fiction, although a fiction intended to be acted upon as though it were a fact, it is clear that unlike an individual, its "presence" without, as well as within, the state of its origin can be manifested only by activities carried on in its behalf by those who are authorized to act for it. To say that the corporation is so far "present" there as to satisfy due process requirements, for purposes of taxation or the maintenance of suits against it in the courts of the state, is to beg the question to be decided. For the terms "present" or "presence" are used merely to symbolize those activities of the corporation's agent within the state which courts will deem to be sufficient to satisfy the demands of due process. Those demands may be met by such contacts of the corporation with the state of the forum as to make it reasonable, in the context of our federal system of government, to require the corporation to defend the particular suit which is brought there. An "estimate of the inconveniences" which would result to the corporation from a trial away from its "home" or principal place of business is relevant in this connection.

Finally, although the commission of some single or occasional acts of the corporate agent in a state sufficient to impose an obligation or liability on the corporation has not been thought to confer upon the state authority to enforce it, other such acts, because of their nature and quality and the circumstances of their commission, may be deemed sufficient to render the corporation liable to suit.

Applying these standards, the activities carried on in behalf of International Shoe in the State of Washington were neither irregular nor casual. They were systematic and continuous throughout the years in question. They resulted in a large volume of interstate business, in the course of which International Shoe received the benefits and protection of the laws of the state, including the right to resort to the courts for the enforcement of its rights. The obligation which is here sued upon arose out of those very activities. It is evident that these operations establish sufficient contacts or ties with the state of the forum to make it reasonable and just according to our traditional conception of fair play and substantial justice to permit the state to enforce the obligations which International Shoe has incurred there. Hence we cannot say that the maintenance of the present suit in the State of Washington involves an unreasonable or undue procedure.

Inpaco, Inc. v. McDonald's Corp.

413 F.Supp. 415 (E.D.Pa. 1976)

Action by Inpaco, Inc. (plaintiff), for breach of contract against McDonald's Corporation (defendant). Motion to dismiss by McDonald's. Denied.

Inpaco, Inc., entered into a contract with McDonald's to develop and manufacture a system for dispensing food sauces that would be suitable for use by McDonald's, a fast food restaurant chain. The work, other than on-site testing, was to be done in Inpaco's plant in Allentown, Pennsylvania. On at least two occasions a representative of McDonald's met with Inpaco representatives in Allentown. Other McDonald's representatives made business trips to Pennsylvania that had no connection with the Inpaco contract, including visits to a Philadelphia meat supplier.

McDonald's is a Delaware corporation not licensed to do business in Pennsylvania with its principal place of business in Oak Brook, Illinois. It conducted its business in Pennsylvania through two wholly-owned subsidiaries, McDonald's Systems, Inc., and Franchise Realty Inter-State Corp. When Inpaco brought suit against McDonald's in Pennsylvania for alleged breach of the contract under the Pennsylvania "long arm" statute, McDonald's moved to dismiss, alleging that the statute did not give the federal court seated in Pennsylvania jurisdiction over it.

DITTER, DISTRICT JUDGE. Rather than "doing it all for you," McDonald's Corporation claims in a motion now before the court that it does nothing for anybody in Pennsylvania. Believing its ad men have assessed the situation more accurately than its lawyers, I deny McDonald's motion to dismiss this diversity action for lack of jurisdiction.

Section 8302 provides that a nonqualifying foreign corporation which does any business in Pennsylvania is conclusively presumed to have designated the Department of State as its agent for accepting service of process in any action arising in this Commonwealth. For a definition of the conduct which constitutes doing business under § 8302 reference must be made to § 8309. The latter section, in pertinent part, provides:

§ 8309. Acts affecting jurisdiction

(a) *General rule.*—Any of the following shall constitute "doing business" for the purposes of this chapter:

(1) The doing by any person in this Commonwealth of a series of similar acts for the purpose of thereby realizing pecuniary benefit or otherwise accomplishing an object.

(2) The doing of a single act in this Commonwealth for the purpose of thereby realizing pecuniary benefit or otherwise accomplishing an object with the intention of initiating a series of such acts.

(3) The shipping of merchandise directly or indirectly into or through this Commonwealth.

(4) The engaging in any business or profession within this Commonwealth, whether or not such business requires license or approval by the Commonwealth or any of its agencies.

(5) The ownership, use or possession of any real property situate within this Commonwealth.

(b) *Exercise of full constitutional power over foreign corporations.*—In addition to the provisions of subsection (a) of this section the jurisdiction and venue of courts of the Commonwealth shall extend to all foreign corporations and the powers exercised by them to the fullest extent allowed under the Constitution of the United States.

I am satisfied that defendant's contacts with Pennsylvania are sufficient to satisfy the requirements of Pennsylvania's long-arm statute. In *Proctor & Schwartz, Inc. v. Cleveland Lumber Co.* it was held that § 8309(b) gave Pennsylvania courts jurisdiction over a Georgia corporation whose sole contact with the Commonwealth was a contract that it had made with a Pennsylvania corporation.

In *Proctor,* Judge Jacobs identified three relevant guidelines which aid in making the factual evaluation of each case., First is the requirement of *Hanson v. Denckla* that the defendant have "purposefully avail[ed] itself of the privilege of conducting activities within the forum State, thus invoking the benefits and protections of its laws." The contract between Inpaco and McDonald's was to be performed almost entirely in Pennsylvania and thus there can be no question that the defendant could reasonably have foreseen that it would have a "realistic economic impact on the commerce of this Commonwealth." While there is no indication that the contract in this case was "made" in Pennsylvania or that it was to be governed by Pennsylvania law, I do not believe that these represent significant differences in terms of the economic reality rationale adopted by the *Proctor* court, in view of the fact that substantial performance of the contract was to take place in Pennsylvania.

The second *Proctor* guideline requires that the cause of action arise from the defendant's activities within the forum state. This requirement is also satisfied in the instant case. Here, among other things, the activity which satisfies the "purposefully availed" test is, as in *Proctor,* the entering into contractual obligations. And, also as in *Proctor,* the cause of action here arises from the breach of those same obligations.

The final and most important guideline of *Proctor* requires a determination as to whether the exercise of jurisdiction over the defendant under the circumstances of the particular case is fair and reasonable. This determination should be made objectively, but with reference to the particular defendant involved in the case. The court cited *In-Flight Devices Corp. v. Van Dusen Air, Inc.,* for the proposition that:

To the extent the buyer vigorously negotiates, perhaps dictates, contract terms . . . and otherwise departs from the passive buyer role it would seem that any unfairness which would normally be associated with the exercise of long-arm jurisdiction over [it] disappears.

Here, the complaint and the uncontroverted affidavit of Mr. Christine indicate that the contract resulted from active arms-length bargaining between the parties. Moreover, considering economic realities, it seems unlikely that a corporation the size of McDonald's could be dictated to at the bargaining table. This is especially true where, as here, the contract involves the development of a system to meet the particular requirements of the defendant. Furthermore, far from being "essentially localized," the business of McDonald's Corporation is nationwide in scope.

Bearing in mind that "the due process clause defines a rather low threshold of state interest sufficient to justify exercise of the state's sovereign decisional authority with respect to a given transaction," I have no difficulty in holding that subjecting defendant to in personam jurisdiction in Pennsylvania is fully consistent with due process requirements.

Complete Auto Transit, Inc. v. Brady

430 U.S. 274 (U.S. Sup. Ct. 1977)

Complete Auto Transit, Inc. (plaintiff), a trucker engaged solely in interstate commerce, paid taxes to the State of Mississippi (defendant) under protest, and then brought suit for refund. The Chancery Court sustained the assessment, and the Mississippi Supreme Court affirmed. The U.S. Supreme Court affirmed.

Auto Transit was a Michigan corporation engaged in transporting motor vehicles in Mississippi under contract with General Motors. The vehicles were manufactured outside the state and shipped by rail to Jackson, Mississippi. Auto Transit usually picked them up within 48 hours and delivered them to GM dealers throughout Mississippi. The state assessed taxes and interest of $165,000 for a four-year period under Mississippi's statutes which imposed on transportation companies a 5 percent gross income tax on "the privilege of engaging or continuing in business or doing business within this state." Auto Transit had considerable property and a substantial number of employees in Mississippi.

Auto Transit sought to recover the taxes paid, claiming that its services were part of an interstate movement of goods and under *Spector Motor Service v. O'Connor* and other decisions the imposition of the tax on purely interstate transportation was unconstitutional.

MR. JUSTICE BLACKMUN. Auto Transit's attack is based solely on decisions of this Court holding that a tax on the "privilege" of engaging in an activity in the State may not be applied to an activity that is part of interstate commerce. This rule looks only to the fact that the incidence of the tax is the "privilege of doing business"; it deems irrelevant any consideration of the practical effect of the tax. The rule reflects an underlying philosophy that interstate commerce should enjoy a sort of "free trade" immunity from state taxation.

Mississippi, in its turn, relies on decisions of this Court stating that "[i]t was not the purpose of the commerce clause to relieve those engaged in interstate commerce from their just share of state tax burden even though it increases the cost of doing the business." These decisions have considered not the formal language of the tax statute, but rather its practical effect, and have sustained a tax against Commerce Clause challenge when the tax is applied to an activity with a substantial nexus with the taxing state, is fairly apportioned, does not discriminate against interstate commerce, and is fairly related to the services provided by the State.

The Court recognized [in *Spector Motor Service v. O'Connor*] that "where a taxpayer is engaged both in intrastate and interstate commerce, a state may tax the privilege of carrying on intrastate business and, within reasonable limits, may compute the amount of the charge by applying the tax rate to a fair proportion of the taxpayer's business done within the state, including both interstate and intrastate." It held, nevertheless, that a tax on the "privilege" of doing business is unconstitutional if applied against what is exclusively interstate commerce.

The view of the Commerce Clause that gave rise to the rule of *Spector* perhaps was not without some substance. Nonetheless, the possibility of defending it in the abstract does not alter the fact that the Court has rejected the provision that interstate commerce is immune from state taxation.

Not only has the philosophy underlying the rule been rejected, but the rule itself has been stripped of any practical significance. If Mississippi had called its tax one on "net income" or on the "going concern value" of Auto Transit's business, the *Spector* rule could not invalidate it. There is no economic consequence that follows necessarily from the use of the particular words "privilege of doing business," and a focus on that formalism merely obscures the question whether the tax produces a forbidden effect. Simply put, the *Spector* rule does not address the problems with which the Commerce Clause is concerned. Accordingly, we now reject the rule of *Spector Motor Service Inc. v. O'Connor* that a state tax on the "privilege of doing business" is *per se* unconstitutional when it is applied to interstate commerce, and that case is overruled.

Problem Cases

1. Mr. and Mrs. Gullett, residents of Nashville, Tennessee, purchased tickets for a flight to Australia from a Nashville travel agency. The tickets were issued by American Airlines. The flight to Australia was on Quantas Airways. Mr. Gullett's mother died in Nashville while they were stopping in Nandi, Fiji Islands, and a relative phoned Quantas there requesting them to notify the Gulletts of the event. A message was not delivered until just after the Quantas plane had taken off for Australia, a five and one-half hour flight, and then it only stated, without more, that the Gulletts faced a grave emergency. They had to wait 22 hours in Sydney before they could start their return trip.

   The Gulletts brought an action against Quantas in Nashville for $75,000 for their extra expenses and for emotional distress on account of Quantas' failure to convey a proper message in Nandi. Quantas appeared specially to move dismissal on the grounds that the claim arose outside of Tennessee and Quantas was not amenable to process in Tennessee because it did not do business there. It had no flights to and no personnel nor office in

Tennessee. It does have a listing of a toll-free number in both Knoxville and Memphis, and magazines such as *Time, National Geographic,* and *Sports Illustrated* carrying its advertisements are distributed in Tennessee. It supplies travel agents there with brochures, and its employees occasionally visit the travel agents.

Is Quantas subject to suit in Tennessee?

2. Graham Engineering Corporation brought an action against Kemp Productions Limited (KPL), a Canadian corporation, for inducing another defendant, Carlisle, to violate a patent owned by Graham. KPL had entered into a licensing agreement with Carlisle, an Ohio corporation, for the production of plastic milk bottles. The agreement provided that KPL would supply "technical information and confidential knowhow" to Carlisle and gave KPL a right to inspect Carlisle's books to ascertain the correctness of the royalty computations. KPL did not, however, actually provide technical assistance under the licensing agreement. KPL had no other contacts with Ohio.

   Is KPL subject to suit under Ohio's "long-arm" statute?

3. Standard Pressed Steel Company manufactured industrial and aerospace fasteners in Pennsylvania and California. In the state of Washington it sold its products primarily to Boeing Aircraft. Martinson, an engineer, was Standard's only employee in the state and he maintained no office outside his home. The State Board of Tax Appeals ruled that Standard was subject to a state tax on fasteners sold to Boeing through Martinson's contacts with Boeing engineers. Standard argued that the imposition of the tax in the amount of $33,500 violated the Due Process Clause of the Constitution because its in-state activities were so small and inconsequential that there was no relation between the tax and the protection and benefits conferred on Standard by the State of Washington.

   Is imposition of the tax on such interstate commerce unconstitutional?

4. Cement Company was an Iowa corporation that regularly solicited orders in Minnesota for its products, each order being subject to acceptance by and delivery from its plant in Iowa, and this business constituted 48 percent of its total sales. It owned no real estate, warehoused no merchandise, and kept no bank account in Minnesota, but it did maintain an office occupied by four employees. Two additional salespersons were supervised from this office. It had not qualified to do business in Minnesota. Minnesota imposed a net income tax upon corporations, including those whose business consisted "exclusively of foreign commerce." The statute imposed a tax apportioned on the basis of the ratio of the sales, property, and payroll in Minnesota to the total for the corporation.

   When Minnesota sued to collect the tax, Cement argued that a tax on only interstate commerce violated the Commerce and Due Process Clauses of the Constitution. Is this a good defense?

5. Miles Laboratories, Inc., an Indiana corporation, operated a warehouse in Oregon from which it shipped merchandise to fill orders for its goods from Washington as well as Oregon customers. It had 12 salespersons who were also responsible for placing product displays in retail outlets. They each maintained a stock of samples for display to prospective customers and also exchanged them with customers for small quantities of damaged merchandise. Miles is qualified to do business in Washington.

   Under Oregon's income tax Miles could apportion its income attributable to sales in Washington delivered from the Oregon warehouse if Washington could have taxed income from those sales, whether or not in fact Washington did tax it. Under the Federal Interstate Income Tax Law, Washington could impose such a tax, even though the sales were in interstate commerce, if Miles activities in Washington amounted to more than "solicitation of orders." Is Miles entitled to apportionment?

6. Mountain States Advertising, Inc., is a Colorado corporation qualified to do business in New Mexico. It constructs and maintains outdoor advertising signs for national accounts in eight states in the Rocky Mountain region, including New Mexico. All employees reside in Colorado. It has no office, warehouse, salespersons, construction facilities, nor telephone listings in New Mexico, and it signs no contracts and neither bills nor receives money in New Mexico. Ten percent of its cost of doing business is in placing the advertising material on the signs and otherwise maintaining the signs. The rest is for activities carried on outside of New Mexico.

   New Mexico seeks to impose its gross receipts tax against all revenue derived from Mountain States signs located in New Mexico. Mountain States argues that it should pay no more than 10 percent of the assessed tax, if any. Should the tax be apportioned?

7. Delta Molded Products, Inc., an Alabama corporation, purchased several plastic molding machines and auxiliary equipment from IMPCO on an installment purchase contract executed in Alabama. The contract provided for installation services by IMPCO. Delta went into bankruptcy, and IMPCO sought to repossess the machines, which had not been fully paid for. Other creditors alleged that IMPCO was doing business in Alabama without having qualified to do so and, therefore, under an Alabama statute could not bring suit.

   IMPCO argued that it was merely seeking to recover possession of machinery wrongly held by the Bankruptcy Trustee and that for this it was entitled to pursue its action. Is this argument sound?

8. James Barbee was a franchisee of United Dollar Stores. United operated a chain of franchised retail stores, including several in Mississippi. Its franchise agreement with Barbee was lengthy. It gave United sole control over the design and decor of the store, fixtures, signs and record keeping and operating practices. All merchandise had to be purchased from United or approved suppliers. Barbee was required to take out certain insurance naming United as an additional insured as well as to conduct certain advertising and public relations programs. Reports of operations were to be submitted to United by the tenth of the following month. There was also an arrangement for the exchange of goods between Barbee's and other United stores.

   United, an Arkansas corporation not qualified to do business in Mississippi, brought an action against Barbee in Mississippi to recover the price of merchandise sold and for royalty payments due on gross receipts of Barbee's store. Barbee brought a counter-claim for damages due to the delivery of defective and inferior merchandise and the return of his $1,500 franchise fee. Mississippi has a statute barring a corporation doing business within the state without a certificate from maintaining any action in Mississippi courts. United claimed that it was doing only an interstate business and that, in any case, Barbee was estopped from pleading the statute as a defense because of his counterclaim. Is United entitled to maintain its suit in Mississippi?

PART VII

Property

31

Personal Property

Nature and Classification

Nature of Property. Property or ownership may be defined as the right to possess, enjoy, and dispose of objects or rights having economic value. Property, in its legal sense, has a variety of meanings. It may refer to an object having a physical existence; it may refer to legal rights connected with and growing out of an object having physical existence; or it may refer to legal rights which are of economic value but not connected with a physical object.

A tract of land is property. If the owner leases the land, the lease is also property. The lease grants to the lessee the right to use the land, a right connected with and growing out of the physical object of land. A patent right is property; yet the patent right does not refer to or grow out of a physical object.

In the United States the legal concept of property is synonymous with ownership. To have property in the legal sense, it is necessary to have an organized society which has developed some concepts and some laws relative to property and ownership. A careful analysis of our concepts of property and ownership reveals that property or ownership is based on a bundle of legal rights recognized and enforced by society. People commonly refer to the physical object or to the specific right as the property, but from a legal sense, property is the right to the physical object or the right to enjoy the benefits flowing from the exercise of the specific right.

For example, people say that the house is John's property. From a legal standpoint the physical object is not property. The property is really the legal right which John has to use, enjoy, sell, mortgage, or rent the physical object, the house. Likewise, people say the patent is John's property. A patent has no physical existence. It is a bundle of rights which protects one in the enjoyment of the benefits flowing from the exclusive right to reproduce the patented object. The owner of the patent may sell the patent, may license others to produce the patented article, or may produce it personally. The total of these rights is the patent.

Under our free competitive society, private ownership of property is of primary importance. This concept is written into the Constitution of the United States. The Fourteenth Amendment provides that no state shall "deprive any person of life, liberty, or property without due process of law." This concept recognizes and protects the individual's right to acquire, enjoy, and dispose of property; yet the concept does not grant anyone unlimited property rights. Under the philosophy of a free competitive society the individual is encouraged to use one's efforts to produce; and our laws are framed to secure the fruits of one's labors to one who has produced something beneficial to society. It is also recognized that if each individual is to reap the greatest reward for his or her efforts, restrictions are necessary; consequently, one must pursue a course which does not deprive other individuals in society of their right of freedom of action. Our property laws have developed out of this philosophy of a free competitive society.

Possession. The importance of possession in the law of property is indicated in the old saying, "Possession is nine points of the law." In any primitive society, possession is the equivalent of ownership. In the early development of our law the courts held that in a case of violation of property rights, the right violated was the right of peaceful possession.

In our modern society, possession is used with such a variety of meanings that it is futile to attempt to define it in precise terms. In its simplest sense, possession signifies that a person has manual control over a physical object; however, in law this simple concept is inadequate. In connection with possession of personal property, two elements are of general importance: (1) manual control and (2) intent to claim property rights. The courts recognize legal possession, which is the legal right to control the physical object; manual control is not an essential element of legal possession. If a person is wearing his watch, she has both legal and manual control of the watch. She has possession of the watch in the popular sense of the word, and she also has legal possession. If she leaves her watch in her house while she is on vacation, she does not have manual control of the watch but does have legal control. She has legal possession, and anyone taking the watch from her house without her consent has invaded her right of possession.

A servant or an agent may have manual control of his or her employer's or principal's property yet not have legal possession of the property. The servant or agent has only custody of the property; the employer or principal has legal possession. For example, if a storekeeper gives a clerk the day's receipts to count in the storekeeper's presence, the clerk has custody of the receipts, but the storekeeper has legal possession.

The term "possession," when used in the abstract, includes such a multiplicity of situations that it loses its significance. Possession may indicate one factual and legal situation when one says that "to have a valid levy of execution, the sheriff must take possession of the property," another when one says that "to create a bailment of property, possession must be delivered to the bailee," and still another when one says that "the crime of larceny involves the felonious taking possession and carrying away of another's property."

Real and Personal Property. Because of the breadth of the subject of property and the varied incidents of ownership, property has been divided into various classes. These classes are not mutually exclusive; the same piece of property may, owing to its various characteristics, fall into more than one classification.

The most important classification is that of "real" and "personal" property. The earth's crust and all things firmly attached to it are real property, while all other objects and rights capable of ownership are personal property.

Although the distinction as stated is simple, the problems arising are frequently complex because that which is real property can be converted into personal property by severance and that which is personal property can be converted into real property by attachment. Stone in the ground is real property, but when quarried, it becomes personal property and if it is used in the construction of a building, it will again become real property. Perennial products, such as trees, grass, and fruit trees which need not be seeded each year, are, as a general rule, treated as part of the land. Crops resulting from annual labor, such as potatoes, corn, and oats are in many cases treated as personal property, although generally they pass with the land when the land is sold. If perennial products are severed from the land, they become personal property.

Tangible and Intangible Property. Property may be classed as "tangible" or "intangible." The basis for classifying property as tangible or intangible is the physical nature of the property. Property which has a physical existence, such as land, buildings, and furniture is tangible; and property which has no physical existence, such as patent rights, easements, and bonds, is intangible. This distinction is important in determining the right to tax, in the probating of estates, and in similar situations. As a general rule, tangible property is subject to taxation by the state in which it is located, whereas intangible property is taxable at the domicile (home) of the owner.

Public and Private Property. Property is also classed as "public" or "private." The classification of property into public and private is based on the ownership of the property. If the property is owned by the government or a government unit, it is classed as public property; but if the property is owned by an individual, a group of individuals, a corporation, or some other business organization, it is classed as private property.

SUMMARY

Property, or more specifically, ownership, is the exclusive right to possess, enjoy, and dispose of objects or rights having economic value. In law, property is a bundle of legal rights to things having economic value, which rights are recognized and protected by society.

The concept of possession is of outstanding importance in our society; however, possession is used with such a variety of meanings that it is futile to attempt to define it in precise terms. Basically, it is the right to control things having physical existence.

Property is classified according to its various characteristics. The earth's crust and all things firmly attached to it are classed as real property; all other objects and rights subject to ownership are classed as personal property.

Those things which have a physical existence are classed as tangible property. Rights which have economic value but which are not related to things having a physical existence and rest solely in contemplation of law are classed as intangible property.

Property owned by the government or a government unit is classed as public property, whereas property owned by any person or association, even though used exclusively for public purposes, is classed as private property.

Acquisition of Personal Property

Production or Purchase. A person owns the product of his or her own labors unless he or she has agreed to perform labor for another, in which event the employer is the owner of the product of the labors. This rule of law is so well-established and so generally accepted in the United States that it is almost never the subject of litigation.

The most common means of acquiring ownership of personal property, other than by production, is by purchase. A special body of law regarding the purchase and sale of personal property has been developed which is treated in the section of this textbook entitled "Sales."

Taking Possession. Ownership of personal property was acquired, in the very early times, by taking possession of property which was unowned. This right to acquire ownership of unowned property by taking possession thereof is recognized today; however, it is of relatively little importance in modern society. Wildlife and abandoned property are classed as unowned property, and the first person to take possession of such property becomes the owner.

To acquire ownership of a wild animal by taking possession of it, a person must attain such a degree of control over it as will deprive it of its freedom. Manual control is not necessary. A mortally wounded animal becomes the property of the person wounding it, even though he has not as yet obtained manual control of it. Animals in a trap or fish in a net have been held to be the property of the person who set the trap or net. However, if a captured animal escapes and is again caught by another person, that person becomes the owner unless he or she knows that the animal is an escaped animal and that the prior owner is pursuing it with the intent of recapturing it.

If property is abandoned by the owner, it then becomes unowned property, and the first person who takes possession of it with the intention of claiming ownership becomes the owner of it.

Gift. A gift is a voluntary transfer of property by one person to another without any consideration being given for the transfer. To make a valid gift, the donor must deliver the property to the donee or to some third person, who holds the property for the donee, and this delivery must be unconditional and must be made with the intent of vesting ownership in the donee. Delivery is the transfer of possession from one person to another, and, as a general rule, there can be no gift without delivery. If the delivery is to a third person, who holds for the donee, the delivery must be made with the intent of divesting the donor of all rights in the property. After the delivery the third person must hold the property as trustee for the donee. If the donor reserves rights in the property, the third person will be held to hold as agent for the donor, and a valid gift will not result.

If the donee is already in possession of the property, a clear declaration by the donor that he or she gives the property to the donee is sufficient to make the gift valid. In some instances the courts have recognized symbolic delivery. For example, the delivery of the keys to a strongbox is symbolic delivery of the contents of the strongbox.

A gift of intangible property requires the execution and delivery of a certificate of gift. If the intangible property is evidenced by a stock certificate or a negotiable instrument, the delivery of the stock certificate or the negotiable instrument properly endorsed, if endorsement is required, is sufficient delivery.

In determining whether a gift has actually been made, the law places great importance on "delivery." Surrender of possession through delivery to the donee or a third person should make clear to the donor the significance of the act, that the donor is giving up ownership of that property without obtaining anything in return. Basic contract law requires "consideration" in order to make a promise enforceable. Gift law compliments contract law by refusing to acknowledge a mere promise to make a gift and insisting on completion of the gift through delivery before recognizing the validity of the gift.

Two types of gifts are recognized: gifts *inter vivos,* and gifts *causa mortis.* A gift *inter vivos* is a gift between living persons; a gift *causa mortis* is a gift in contemplation of death. A gift *causa mortis* has some of the elements of a testamentary disposition of property.

If a gift *causa mortis* is to be valid, the donor must make the gift in contemplation of death in the immediate future, and the donor must comply with all the requirements for a valid *inter vivos* gift. However, the gift *causa mortis* is a conditional gift and is subject to three conditions implied by law, the occurrence of any one of which will defeat the gift: (1) recovery of the donor from the peril or sickness under fear of which the gift was made, (2) revocation of the gift by the donor before his or her death, and (3) death of the donee before the donor. When one of these events takes place, title and the right to possession are immediately revested in the donor.

Lost Property. Lost property becomes the property of the finder as against all persons except the original owner. If Abbott loses his ring and Birge finds it, and later Birge loses the ring and Crum finds it, Birge may claim the ring from Crum; but Abbott, the original owner, has the superior right to the ring and may claim it from either Birge or Crum.

The finder of lost property who knows the identity of the person who lost it yet appropriates it to his own use, is guilty of larceny. If he does not know the identity of the owner and does not have reasonable means of discovering his identity and appropriates the property to his own use, he will be liable to the owner in conversion for the value of the property if he later learns who the true owner is and refuses to return it. Some states have enacted statutes which permit the finder of lost property to clear his or her title by complying with the statutory procedure; this procedure commonly includes the giving of public notice, for example, by publication in a newspaper. In addition the states have statutes of limitations which provide that the true owner of personal property must bring an action to recover the possession of it from someone else within a certain number of years or he will lose the right to do so. Thus a person who possesses lost or unclaimed property for the statutory period will become the owner of it.

The courts have made a distinction between lost property and mislaid property. If Abbott, while in Birge's store, drops his wallet in the aisle, the wallet will generally be classed as lost property; but if he lays it on the counter and, forgetting it, leaves the store, it will be classed as mislaid property. If the wallet is mislaid, Birge will become the bailee of it. If Crum finds the wallet in the aisle, he will have the right to take possession of it; but if Crum discovers the wallet on the counter, Birge will have the right to take possession of it. The distinction between lost and mislaid property was developed to increase the chance the property would be returned to its real owner where owner knowingly placed it down but had forgotten to pick it up and might well be expected to remember later where he or she had left it and return for it. It is very difficult to distinguish between lost property and misplaced property; consequently, the decisions of the courts on the subject are not consistent.

Confusion. Title to personal property may be acquired by confusion or by accession. Confusion of goods is the inseparable intermixture of goods belonging to different owners. For example, suppose crude oil belonging to several persons is mixed in one tank. If the mixing is by common consent or inevitable accident, each party will be deemed the ower of a proportionate part of the mass. If the mixing is by willful, tortious act, the innocent party will be protected, and the entire mass will become the property of the innocent party if such action is necessary to protect his or her interest. In case of accidential confusion, if one of the owners is guilty of negligence, he or she will have to bear any loss resulting from the confusion.

Accession. Literally, "accession" means that something has been added, and as applied to property, it means that new value has been added to existing property by labor or by the addition of other property or by a combination of both. As a general rule, the owner of the original property will become the owner of the improvements. If Birge repairs Abbott's automobile by adding some new parts, Abbott will be the owner of the automobile when repaired and will also be the owner of the new parts which Birge has added.

Difficulty arises where one person improves the property of another by labor or by the addition of materials, or both, when the owner has not contracted for or consented to the improvement. The decisions of the courts in regard to the rights of the parties in such a situation are not in accord, and in many respects they are confusing. As a general rule, if one person has tortiously taken property of another and, by his labor or the addition of his materials, improved the property, the owner of the original property may recover it in its improved state and will not be obligated to compensate the tortfeasor for labor or materials.

If the person making the improvement honestly but mistakenly believes that he is the owner of the property at the time he makes the improvement, the courts will, as a general rule, permit recovery for the benefits conferred on the true owner of the property as a result of the improvement. If the owner of the property wishes, he may sue the wrongdoer in tort for conversion of his property and recover a judgment for the value of the unimproved property. Whether the property itself can be recovered, after payment of due compensation to the improver for his improvements, will depend on: (1) the relative increase in value, (2) whether the form or identity of the property has been changed, and (3) whether the improvements can be separated from the original property.

SUMMARY

Ownership of personal property may be acquired by (1) production, (2) purchase, (3) taking possession, (4) gift, (5) finding, (6) confusion, and (7) accession.

A person owns property produced by his own labor or by the labor of persons whom he hires to work for him.

The owner of personal property may sell or barter his or her property to another, and the purchaser then becomes the owner of the property.

The person who first reduces unowned property—wildlife or abandoned property—to possession with the intent of claiming ownership of the property acquires ownership.

A gift is the transfer of the ownership of property from the donor to the donee without any consideration being given by the donee. To have a valid gift, the donor must deliver the possession of the property to the donee or to some third person with the intent of vesting ownership in the donee.

The finder of lost property acquires ownership of the property against everyone except the original owner. A distinction, which is not clear cut, is made between lost property and mislaid property.

If a person confuses his or her property with that of another, the other party may acquire ownership of the entire mass.

If property is improved by the labor and addition of materials by another without the owner's consent, the owner of the original property becomes the owner of the property in its improved state.

Lieber v. Mohawk Arms, Inc.

314 N.Y.S.2d 510 (Sup. Ct. N.Y. 1970)

This was an action by Lieber (plaintiff) against Mohawk Arms, Inc., (defendant) to recover possession of several items of personal property. Mohawk Arms moved for summary judgment. The motion was denied and the court granted summary judgment to Lieber.

The facts are given in the opinion.

LYNCH, JUDGE. In 1945 Lieber, then in the United States Army, was among the first soldiers to occupy Munich, Germany. There he and some companions entered Adolph Hitler's apartment and removed various items of his personal belongings. Lieber brought his share home to Louisiana. It included Hitler's uniform jacket and cap and some of his decorations and personal jewelry.

Lieber's possession of these articles was publicly known. Louisiana newspapers published stories and pictures about Lieber's collection, and he was the subject of a feature story in the *Louisiana State University Alumni News* of

October, 1945. There is some indication that the articles were occasionally displayed to the public.

In 1968 the collection was stolen by Lieber's chauffeur who sold it to a New York dealer in historical Americana. The dealer sold it to Mohawk Arms who purchased in good faith. Through collectors' circles Lieber soon discovered the whereabouts of his stolen property, made a demand for its return that was refused, and commenced this action seeking the return.

Mohawk Arms resists and asks summary judgment on the ground that Lieber cannot succeed in the suit since he "never obtained good and legal title to this collection," and "the collection properly belongs to the occupational Military authority and/or the Bavarian Government."

This defense, title in a third party, was at one time effective. . . . But it did not survive the enactment of the Civil Practice Law and Rules, Section 7101 of which provides for the recovery of a chattel by one who has the superior right to possession. In proposing the elimination of this defense the draughtsmen of the CPLR sought to prevent the very thing being attempted by Mohawk Arms here.

> The present law thus allows a defendant who has a lesser right to possession than the plaintiff to keep the property and withstand a replevy by asserting the superior right of a third person, even though there is no assurance that he will turn over the property to the third person. There is no good reason to perpetuate this situation, for if the holder of a chattel is genuinely concerned about the rights of the true owner, he may employ the modern procedural device of interpleader to protect them, or may merely notify the person who claims to be the true owner and the latter may intervene. (Fourth Preliminary Report of the Advisory Committee on Practice and Procedure, Legislative Document No. 20, p. 254.)

The question presented by an action to recover a chattel is "whether or not a plaintiff has such a title in the cause of action so that a recovery or satisfaction by it will protect the defendant from the claims of third parties. . . ." Applying this test we find that Lieber must recover possession of the chattels. Mohawk Arms, despite its good faith, has no title since its possession is derived from a thief (Uniform Commercial Code, § 2–403). Lieber's possession prior to the theft and since 1945 is unquestioned. He further benefits from Article 3509 of the Louisiana Civil Code which provides that when "the possessor of any movable whatever has possessed it for ten years without interruption, he shall acquire the ownership of it without being obliged to produce a title or to prove that he did not act in bad faith."

Dolitsky v. Dollar Savings Bank

118 N.Y.S.2d 65 (City of N.Y. Mun. Ct. 1952)

This was an action by Betty Dolitsky (plaintiff) against Dollar Savings Bank (defendant) to recover $100 allegedly found by Dolitsky. Judgment for Dollar Savings Bank.

Betty Dolitsky rented a safe-deposit box from Dollar Savings Bank. The safe-deposit vault of the bank is in the basement, and the vault area is walled off from all other parts of the bank. Only box renters and officers and employees of the bank are admitted to this area. To gain access to the area a box renter must obtain an admission slip, fill in his box number and sign the slip, have the box number and signature checked by an employee against the records of the bank, and then present the slip to a guard who admits the renter to the safe-deposit vault area.

On November 7, 1951, Dolitsky requested access to her box and the procedure as outlined was followed. While Dolitsky was in the booth she was looking through an advertising folder which had been placed there by the bank and found a $100 bill which she turned over to the attendant. Dolitsky waited one year and during that time the rightful owner of the $100 bill made no claim for it. Dolitsky then demanded that the bank surrender the bill to her claiming that she was entitled to the bill as finder. The bank claims the bill is mislaid property and that they owe a duty to keep the bill for the rightful owner.

TRIMARCO, JUSTICE. At common law property was lost when possession had been casually and involuntarily parted with, so that the mind had no impress of and could have no knowledge of the parting. Mislaid property was that which the owner had voluntarily and intentionally placed and then forgotten.

Property in someone's possession cannot *be found in the sense of common-law lost property.* If the article is in the custody of the owner of the place when it is discovered it is not lost in the legal sense; instead it is mislaid. Thus, if a chattel is discovered anywhere in a private place where only a limited class of people have a right to be and they are customers of the owner of the premises, who has the duty of preserving the property of his customers, it is in the possession of the owner of the premises.

In the case of mislaid property discovered on the premises of another, the common-law rule is that the proprietor of the premises is held to have the better right to hold the same for the owner, or the proprietor has custody for the benefit of the owner, or the proprietor is the gratuitous bailee of the owner. The effect of the cases, despite their different description of the relationship, is that the proprietor is the bailee of the owner. Thus, the discoverer of mislaid property has the duty to leave it with the proprietor of the premises, and the latter has the duty to hold it for the owner. New York statutory requirements do not change this rule.

The bank is a gratuitous bailee of mislaid property once it has knowledge of the property. As such the bank has the duty to exercise ordinary care in the custody of the articles with a duty to redeliver to the owner.

The recent case of *Manufacturers Savings Deposit Co. v. Cohen,* which held that property found on the floor of a booth located in an outer room used by a safe-deposit company in conjunction with a bank, access thereto not being limited to box holders or officials of the safe-deposit company, was lost property and as such should have been turned over to the property clerk of the Police Department, can be distinguished from the present case. In the *Cohen* case the court found that the booth on the floor of which the money was found was not located within the safe-deposit vault but rather in an outer room adjoining said vault and in a part of the bank which was accessible to the ordinary customer of the bank for the purchase of bonds and the opening of new accounts; as such the court considers the room in which the booth was located a public place which was not restricted to safe-deposit officials and persons having safe-deposit boxes in the vault. The case is further distinguished from the present case since its facts disclose that the money was found on the floor of the booth which indicated to the court that the money was not mislaid. The court points out that the testimony shows the money to have been found on the floor of the booth and not on any table or other normal resting place.

Nature and Creation of Bailment

Essential Elements. Normally, in a bailment the title of personal property is in one person, the bailor, and the right of possession is in another person, the bailee. Not all transactions in which there is a division of title and possession are bailments. These essential elements must be present in order to have a bailment: (1) the title of the property or a superior right to possession must be in the bailor, (2) the bailee must have lawful possession without title, and (3) the bailee must owe a duty to return the property to the bailor or dispose of it as directed by him or her. The bailment is a common transaction, and frequently a bailment exists when the parties to the transaction are not aware of its existence. For instance, if you loan your lawn mower to your neighbor, a bailment arises.

Creation of Relation. As a general rule a bailment is created by a contract. Whether or not a bailment exists must be determined from all the facts and circumstances of the case. The test generally applied is whether possession has been delivered and whether the person into whose possession the article has been delivered intended to assume custody and control over the object and has expressly or impliedly promised to return the article to the owner or to dispose of it as directed by the owner. Usually, if one goes into a restaurant or barber shop or like place and hangs his hat and coat on a rack provided for that purpose, no bailment will arise; but if the circumstances are such that it can be established that the owner of the establishment either expressly or impliedly assumes control over the hat and coat, the existence of a bailment may be established. If a checkroom is provided and the hat and coat are checked with the attendant in charge, a bailment will arise.

The courts have held that if a person parks an automobile in a parking lot, retaining the keys to the automobile and having the privilege of retrieving it at will, the transaction is a lease of space and not a bailment. However, if a person takes an automobile to a parking garage and surrenders it to an attendant who parks it and returns it to the owner when the owner calls for it, a bailment is created.

Custody of Servant or Agent. The distinction between custody and possession of personal property is technical and is based on the law of master and servant. If a master (employer) entrusts his or her property to a servant, the master technically retains the legal possession of the property and the servant has the custody. For instance, a clerk working in a store has custody of the goods entrusted to her for sale, but the master has possession of the goods. In such a situation, no bailment exists since, in contemplation of law, there is no surrender of the possession of the goods.

SUMMARY

A bailment is created when the owner of personal property, the bailor, delivers the possession of the property to another, the bailee, who is obligated to return the property to the bailor or to dispose of it as directed by the bailor.

A bailment is created by contract, expressed or implied. Whether or not a bailment is created will depend on the facts and circumstances of the case.

Delivery of goods by a master to his or her servant does not, as a general rule, create a bailment. The servant has custody of the goods, not possession.

Kuchinsky v. Empire Lounge, Inc.

134 N.W.2d 436 (Sup. Ct. Wis. 1965)

This was an action by Kuchinsky (plaintiff) against Empire Lounge (defendant) to recover for the loss of Kuchinsky's coat. The trial court dismissed the complaint and Kuchinsky appealed. Affirmed.

Kuchinsky entered the Empire Lounge as a customer and hung his coat on a clothes tree near his table. His coat was stolen while he ate.

CURRIE, CIRCUIT JUDGE. A case very much in point is *Montgomery v. Ladjing.* There the plaintiff entered the restaurant kept by the defendant with a party of friends; he removed his overcoat and hung it on a hook affixed to a post near the table at which he seated himself; the attention of neither the defendant nor of any of his employees was called to the coat in any way; and fifteen minutes later the coat was missing. The court held that the plaintiff had wholly failed to show failure on the part of the defendant to exercise ordinary care, and declared:

The rule to be deduced from all these cases therefore is that, before a restaurant keeper will be held liable for the loss of an overcoat of a customer while such customer takes a meal or refreshments, it must appear either that the overcoat was placed in the physical custody of the keeper of the restaurant or his servants, in which cases there is an actual bailment, or that the overcoat was necessarily laid aside under circumstances showing, at least, notice of the fact and of such necessity to the keeper of the restaurant, or his servants, in which case there is an implied bailment or constructive custody, that the loss occurred by reason of the insufficiency of the general supervision exercised by the keeper of the restaurant for the protection of the property of customers temporarily laid aside.

In *National Fire Insurance Co. v. Commodore Hotel,* the plaintiff was a guest at a luncheon held at the defendant's hotel. She hung her mink jacket in an unattended cloakroom on the main floor across from the lobby desk. After the luncheon and ensuing party the plaintiff went to the cloakroom to retrieve her jacket and discovered it was gone. The court held that no negligence had been established against the defendant and stated:

In any event, we do not feel that it is incumbent upon a hotel or restaurant owner to keep an attendant in charge of a free cloakroom for luncheon or dinner guests or otherwise face liability for loss of articles placed therein. The maintenance of such rooms without attendants is a common practice, and where the proprietor had not accepted control and custody of articles placed therein, no duty rests upon him to exercise any special degree of care with respect thereto.

Likewise, failure to post a warning disclaiming responsibility would not seem to constitute negligence when, as here, a guest is aware that a cloakroom is unattended, adjacent to the lobby, and accessible to anyone; and has used it under similar circumstances on many prior occasions. The absence of such warning signs does not appear to have been material in a number of decisions absolving proprietors from liability although when posted they appear to be regarded as an added factor in establishing such nonliability.

Weinberg v. Wayco Petroleum Co.

402 S.W.2d 597 (Ct. App. Mo. 1966)

This was an action by Weinberg (plaintiff) against Wayco Petroleum Company (defendant) for the theft of personal property which occurred while Weinberg's car was parked in Wayco's parking garage. The circuit court awarded Weinberg a $500 judgment. Reversed.

Weinberg was the holder of a "Parkard" issued by Wayco for which he paid $10.50 per month and which entitled him to park his automobile at Wayco's garage located in St. Louis. This garage had five stories and entrance was gained by inserting the "Parkard" into a slot causing the entrance gate to open. This was a so-called self-park garage and there were no attendants on duty at the time. Weinberg parked his automobile at about 11:30 P.M. on September 25, 1962. After securing admission to the garage with the Parkard, Weinberg parked his own car, locked it, and took the keys with him. When he returned to his automobile in the evening of September 27th, he found it had been broken into and certain personal property stolen from it. The automobile had not been moved.

The "Parkard" stated: "This card licenses the holder to park one automobile in this area at holder's risk. Lock your car. Licensor hereby declares himself not responsible for fire, theft, or damage to or loss of such automobile or any article left therein. Only a license is granted hereby, and no bailment is created." Weinberg testified that prior to this occurrence he had read this language on the card and knew what it said.

BRADY, COMMISSIONER. With respect to cases involving automobiles and the contents thereof when loss occurs after the automobile is left in a parking lot, the relationship between the parties is usually one of bailment or license, and whether it is one or the other depends upon the circumstances of the particular case and especially upon the manner in which the parking lot in question is being operated and with whom control of the allegedly bailed article or articles is vested.

A "bailment" in its ordinary legal sense imports the delivery of personal property by the bailor to the bailee who keeps the property in trust for a specific purpose, with a contract, express or implied, that the trust shall be faithfully executed, and the property returned or duly accounted for when the special purpose is accomplished or that the property shall be kept until the bailor reclaims it. This court has said that ". . . the term 'bailment' . . . signifies a contract resulting from the delivery of goods by bailor to bailee on condition that they be restored to the bailor, according to his directions, so soon as the purposes for which they were bailed are answered."

It is obvious from the facts in the instant case that there was no delivery to Wayco sufficient to create the relationship of bailee and bailor between the parties here involved. Cases of the nature here involved are to be distinguished from those where the parking operation is such that the attendants collect a fee and assume authority or control of the automobile by parking it and/or retaining the keys so that the car can be moved about to permit the entrance or exit of other automobiles and where the tickets that are given to the owner of the automobile are issued for the purpose of identifying the automobile for redelivery. In such instances a bailment relationship is almost invariably held to exist. In the instant case Wayco never secured control or authority over Weinberg's automobile. No agent or employee of Wayco parked it or kept the keys to it or issued any ticket whereby the automobile could be identified by comparison of a portion of the ticket left with the automobile when it was parked. Weinberg parked his own automobile, locked it, and took the keys with him. Certainly Wayco, the alleged bailee, did not have the right under these circumstances to exclude the purposes of the owner or even of anyone else who might have had the keys. In the instant case Weinberg never made a delivery, actual or constructive, of the automobile to Wayco under circumstances leading to the creation of a bailee-bailor relationship between them.

Rights and Liabilities of Parties

Bailee's Duty of Care. In determining the liability of the bailee for damage to or loss of the bailed property, bailments have been divided into three classes: (1) mutual benefit bailments, (2) bailments for the sole benefit of the bailor, and (3) bailments for the sole benefit of the bailee.

All commercial bailments are mutual-benefit bailments, that is, both the bailee and the bailor receive benefits from the relation. For example, if goods are stored in a warehouse, the warehouseman (the bailee) is compensated for his services, and the owner of the goods (the bailor) has his or her goods cared for during the period of storage. The mutual benefit bailee owes a duty of ordinary care and is liable for damage to or loss of the goods only if such damage or loss is the result of his negligence. Ordinary care has been defined as that care which a person of ordinary prudence would take of his or her goods of like nature under the same or similar circumstances.

A bailment for the sole benefit of the bailor is one in which the bailee renders some service in respect to the bailed property without receiving a return benefit. For instance, if you permit your neighbor to put his automobile in your garage while he is away on a trip, and he pays you nothing for the privilege, the bailment is for the sole benefit of the bailor. In such a bailment the bailee owes a duty of slight care. The bailee will be liable for damage to or loss of the bailed goods only if he does little or nothing to protect them when it is apparent that they will be damaged or lost and when the bailee could prevent the damage or loss without any substantial cost or sacrifice on his part.

A bailment for the sole benefit of the bailee arises when the owner of goods permits another to use those goods free of charge. For instance, if you loan your lawn mower to your neighbor, the bailment is for the sole benefit of the bailee. In such a bailment, the bailee owes a duty of great care. If the bailee is negligent in any respect in his or her use or care of the bailed goods, and as the result of such negligence the goods are damaged or lost, the bailee is liable.

Some courts have moved away from the three classes of bailments with their distinctions as to degree of care which sound fine in theory but are often difficult to apply in practice. Instead, these courts require a reasonable amount of care on the part of all bailees. What is reasonable care in any given situation depends on: (1) the nature and value of the bailed property, (2) who the bailee is—for example, whether one is a professional bailee, and (3) whether the bailment was paid for or whether it was gratuitous.

Alteration of Liability by Contract. The liability of the bailee may be either increased or decreased by the contract of the parties. An attempt by a bailee to relieve himself of liability for intentional or reckless wrongdoing is against public policy, and the extent to which a bailee may relieve himself from his liability for his own negligence is limited. Under the law of contracts, a contract whereby a person relieves himself of liability for his own negligence may be against public policy and void. The courts have, as a general rule, enforced provisions in contracts of bailment whereby the bailee is relieved from specific perils; but the courts have been reluctant to enforce provisions in such contracts whereby the bailee is relieved from all liability for his negligent acts.

The effect of the posting of notices, the printing of terms on a check or receipt given to the bailor, or the doing of other similar acts by the bailee in an attempt to limit his liability was discussed in Chapter 6, "Offer." The question is primarily one of communication of the terms of the contract. The knowledge of the bailor of the facilities of the bailee or of his method of doing business or the nature of prior dealings may give rise to an implied agreement as to the duties of the bailee. The bailee may, if he wishes, assume all the risks incident to the bailment and contract to return the bailed property undamaged or to pay any damage to or loss of the property.

Bailee's Duty to Return Property. On the termination of the bailment, the bailee owes a duty to return the bailed property in an undamaged condition to the bailor or to dispose of it as directed by the bailor. If the bailee cannot return the property to the bailor in an undamaged condition, he may excuse his failure by showing that the goods were damaged or destroyed without negligence on his part. If the bailed property is taken from the bailee by legal process, the bailee should notify the bailor and must take whatever action is necessary to protect the bailor's interest.

If a third person claims to have, in the bailed property, rights which are superior to the rights of the bailor and demands possession of the bailed property, the bailee is in a dilemma. If the bailee refuses to deliver the bailed property to the third-person claimant and the third-person claimant is entitled to the possession of it, the bailee will be liable to such claimant. If the bailee delivers the bailed property to the third-person claimant and the third-person claimant is not entitled to possession, the bailee is liable to the bailor. The circumstances may be such that the conflicting claims of the bailor and the third-person claimant can be determined only by judicial decision. In some cases the bailee may protect himself by bringing a bill of interpleader, but this remedy is not available in all cases. The bailee cannot set up a claim to the bailed property which is adverse to the rights of the bailor if the claim is based on right which existed at the time the property was bailed. By accepting the property as bailee, the bailee is estopped from denying the bailor's title to the bailed property.

Bailee's Right to Compensation. The bailee's right to compensation will depend entirely on the agreement or understanding of the parties. If the bailment is a gratuitous bailment, the bailee will be entitled to no compensation even though the bailment is for the sole benefit of the bailor. If the bailment is created by the rental of personal property, the bailee will be obligated to pay the agreed rent. If the bailment is for the storage or repair of property, the bailee will be entitled to the contract price for his or her services. If there is no agreement as to compensation, the bailee will be entitled to recover the reasonable value of the services rendered. In many situations the bailee, if entitled to compensation, will have a lien on the bailed property for the reasonable value of his or her services.

Bailor's Liability for Defects in Bailed Property. If personal property is rented or loaned to a bailee, the bailor impliedly warrants that there are no defects in the property which will make it unsafe for use.

If the bailment is a mutual-benefit bailment, that is, if the property is rented to the bailee, the bailor must use reasonable care in inspecting the property and in seeing that it is in a safe condition for the purpose for which it is rented. The bailor is liable to the bailee or an employee of the bailee for damages resulting from the use of the defective property if the bailee should have, in the exercise of due care, discovered the defect.

If the bailment is for the sole benefit of the bailee, as is the case when the bailor loans property to the bailee, the bailor is liable for injuries resulting from defects in the bailed property only if the bailor has knowledge of the defects and fails to give the bailee notice of the defects.

SUMMARY

The bailee owes a duty of due care to prevent loss of or damage to the bailed property. In determining whether or not due care has been exercised by the bailee, the nature of the bailment is of considerable importance.

The parties within the limits of the legality of their contract, may, by agreement, increase or decrease the scope of the liability of the bailee.

On the termination of the bailment the bailee must return the bailed property to the bailor or dispose of it according to the direction of the bailor. If a third person having a right of possession superior to that of the bailor demands the surrender of the property to him or her, the bailee is obligated to deliver the property to such third person.

The bailee is entitled to reasonable compensation for services rendered in the care of the property. If the contract of bailment stipulates the compensation, the bailee is entitled to the stipulated compensation.

If the bailor rents property to the bailee, the bailor owes a duty to inspect the property to see that it is free from dangerous defects. If the bailor loans the property to the bailee, he or she owes a duty to warn the bailee of any known dangerous defects in the property.

Hy-Grade Oil Co. v. New Jersey Bank

18 UCC Rep. 729 (Sup. Ct. App. Div., N.J. 1975)

This was an action brought by the Hy-Grade Oil Company (plaintiff) against the New Jersey Bank (defendant) to recover for a deposit Hy-Grade placed in the Bank's night depository box which it claimed was negligently handled by the Bank and never credited to Hy-Grade's account. The trial court dismissed the complaint and Hy-Grade appealed. Reversed.

Hy-Grade Oil Company was a regular customer of New Jersey Bank. In February 1974, in order to protect the increasing cash supply generated by operations of its fuel business, Hy-Grade's manager Ronald Flaster signed a night depository agreement with the Bank. This agreement (in printed form and apparently used by other banks in the area) contained the following two provisions:

3(a)—The bank shall not be responsible for the loss or destruction of the pouch or its contents, in whole or in part, either before or after its being placed in the night depository, resulting directly or indirectly from (1) defects in the pouch or its lock; (2) defects in or failure of the night depository entrance chute or safe; (3) theft, burglary or embezzlement. The finding of the bank as to the presence or absence of the pouch in the night depository, and as to the contents thereof shall be conclusive and binding upon the undersigned.
(b)—It is hereby expressly understood and agreed that the use of the night depository facilities is a gratuitous privilege extended by the bank to the undersigned for the convenience of the undersigned, and the use of the night depository facilities shall be at the sole risk of the undersigned.

Flaster claimed that these provisions were neither pointed out nor explained to him. At the time of signing the agreement, Flaster received a leather bag with a zipper and lock on top, together with a key to the lock.

On February 18, 1974, Flaster deposited $1,585 into the night depository box. On February 20, 1974, he called the bank to verify the amount in Hy-Grade's account and learned that the amount placed in the night depository on February 18 had not been credited to Hy-Grade's account. Flaster went to the bank and made inquiry and was shown the top portion of the bag still locked with the lower portion torn away. He was informed that when the bank opened on February 19 and the collection bin opened, the portion of the bag exhibited was found but no money was located and the balance of the bag was missing. When the bank refused to credit Hy-Grade's account with the amount Flaster contended was deposited in the chute, Hy-Grade instituted an action contending the Bank (1) wrongfully refused to credit its account with the amount deposited and (2) negligently handled the contents of the night depository.

BISCHOFF, JUDGE. It is essential to the creation of a bailment that the property be turned over to the possession and control of the bailee, for where the reputed bailee does not know of the article or that it has been delivered to him, there cannot be a bailment.

Our review of the record satisfies us that the testimony as to delivery, or placement of the alleged deposit into the night depository, is not at all clear and is subject to divergent inferences and conclusions. The trial judge made no findings of fact on that basic issue and the matter must be remanded for a further consideration thereof.

If the trial judge concludes there was no delivery of funds to the bank that will, of course, be the end of the matter. If, on the other hand, he concludes that the testimony discloses delivery, then our following observations on the validity of the exculpatory clauses included in the night depository agreement will become relevant.

"Where they do not adversely affect the public interest, exculpatory clauses in private agreements are generally sustained."

It is clear that where a party to the agreement is under a public duty entailing the exercise of care he may not relieve himself of liability for negligence, and unequal bargaining power or the existence of a public interest may call for the rejection of such clauses.

Turning to the factual situation before us, it involves the relationship between a national bank and a depositor. We have held that a "bank has been entrusted with an important franchise to serve the public and has from time to time received broad legislative protection."

The Uniform Commercial Code—Bank Deposits and Collections—contains many provisions protecting banks in their daily operations. We find it significant that the Legislature provided in the same statute, 4–103, that a bank may not, by agreement, disclaim responsibility for "its own lack of good faith or failure to exercise ordinary care" in the discharge of the duty imposed upon it by that statute.

A review of the cases in other states considering the validity of similar exculpatory clauses in night depository contracts indicates that the majority rule is to give full force and effect to the clauses.

The basic theory underlying these and other similar cases is that the absence of an agent of the bank when the night depository facilities are used creates the possibility of dishonest claims being presented by customers. In New Jersey we have rejected such a thesis in other situations and have held that the possibility of fraudulent or collusive litigation does not justify immunity from liability for negligence.

Other courts have refused to recognize the validity of such clauses. In holding such a clause inimical to the public interest, the court in the case of *Phillips Home Furnishings Inc. v. Continental Bank,* said:

> We find the public need for professional and competent banking services too great and the legitimate and justifiable reliance upon the integrity and safety of financial institutions too strong to permit a bank to contract away its liability for its failure to provide the service and protections its customers justifiably expect, that is, for its failure to exercise due care and good faith. . . .

Banks perform an important and necessary public service. It cannot be seriously argued that they are not affected with a public interest. That this is so is obvious from only a cursory examination of the extensive statutory regulations covering every phase of the banking business, including organization, merger, establishment of branches, investments, insurance of deposits, and others, appearing in the Banking Act of 1948, and the Uniform Commercial Code, Bank Deposits and Collection.

We, therefore, hold that a bank cannot, by contract, exculpate itself from liability or responsibility for negligence in the performance of its functions as they concern the night depository service.

It is immaterial whether the purported exculpation is based on the device of placing the sole risk of loss on the depositor, as appears in clause 3(b) of the agreement in question, or by the device of making "the finding of the bank as to the presence or absence of the pouch in the night depository and as to the contents thereof . . . conclusive and binding . . ." as appears in clause 3(a).

We should not be understood by implying that a bank and a customer may not, by negotiation and agreement, determine the standards by which the responsibility of the bank is to be governed so long as those standards are not unreasonable. The burden of proof of a violation of such a standard and proximate causation would remain on the depositor. However, an agreement such as the one now before us, which exculpates the bank from all responsibility without reference to any standard of care, we hold to be contrary to public policy and invalid.

It follows from what we have said that Hy-Grade's right to recover herein is based on the usual principles of negligence and proximate cause as they are applied between bailor and bailee.

Karmely v. Alitalia—Linee Aeree

18 UCC Rep. 479 (Sup. Ct. N.Y. 1975)

This was an action brought by Karmely (plaintiff) against Alitalia—Linee Aeree (defendant) to recover damages for loss of 22 rubies which had been bailed to Alitalia. Judgment for Karmely.

Karmely traveled from Milan, Italy to J.F.K. International Airport via Alitalia Airlines on July 27, 1969. He declared 22 precious rubies of varying sizes and cuts with the U.S. Customs. Customs thereafter put a cord and seal on the package and turned it over to Alitalia pending appraisal. Alitalia, by one of its employees, took the package from a U.S. Customs official, signed for the package on the declaration and turned the package over to another employee of Alitalia for storage of the package in Alitalia's valuable room located in a warehouse in Hollis, Queens. The package, unopened, was placed in the warehouse's valuable room on July 27, 1969, and was thereafter called for by a brokerage agent on behalf of Karmely on or about August 6, 1969. It was then discovered to be missing. Karmely then brought suit against

Alitalia, seeking $65,500 for his damages, plus interest, as the value of the rubies as of July 27, 1969.

ASCH, JUDGE. The transaction involved in this case is a classic illustration of the bailment principle. It is clear that the carrier is under an obligation to act as a warehouse for holding goods for customs pending appraisal. In any event, it undertook that responsibility. Alitalia's warehouse manager testified that he never turned down any merchandise sent from customs. A U.S. Customs officer, Alitalia's witness, testified that customs turned over such merchandise awaiting appraisal to the carrier who had transported the passenger and the merchandise into the country.

Moreover, 19 U.S.C § 1448(a) sets up the procedure for customs to follow in cases such as the one at bar, as well as the obligation of carriers to hold and be responsible for goods subject to appraisal and duty while awaiting entry into the country. If Alitalia wished to operate as an international carrier within the United States, it was required to have procedures set up and available to customs for the keeping and storage of commercial merchandise imported into the United States for sale.

The Court of Appeals of New York has ruled: "If he (bailor) proves the demand upon the warehouseman and his refusal to deliver, these facts unexplained are treated by the courts as prima facie evidence of negligence." The bailee has the burden of explaining the loss or disappearance of the property bailed. In this case, Alitalia has come forward with an excuse for its failure to return the rubies to Karmely. Alitalia claims that the valuable gems, left in Alitalia's warehouse, were stolen. Although the bailor must prove the negligence of a bailee who accounts for his failure to deliver the goods by showing a loss from theft, the burden still remains on the warehouseman to explain the circumstances of the loss. When there is a theft, the bailee is required, in order to evade liability, to show that the loss was caused by occurrences beyond his control, giving proof of the circumstances of the loss and at least prima facie evidence of due care on his part. Alitalia here has offered not one single word of explanation for the disappearance of Karmely's rubies beyond a categorial statement that they were stolen.

The Uniform Commercial Code in § 7–204 provides:

> (1) A warehouseman is liable for damages for loss of or injury to the goods caused by his failure to exercise such care in regard to them as a reasonably careful man would exercise under like circumstances.

In determining what constitutes such care, the nature and value of the property, the means of protection possessed by the bailee and the relation of the parties and other circumstances must be considered. In general, the bailee is required to guard against a reasonably foreseeable loss to the owner of the bailed goods. In the case at bar, Alitalia has failed to live up to the standard of care enunciated by the UCC and judicial mandate.

Once in the storeroom, the rubies were allegedly safe. Only the personnel who had responsibility for a special key could have access, or give access to others. The key, Mr. Lavin, Alitalia's manager, testified was one which had written upon it "do not duplicate." When asked if that would stop it from being duplicated, he said he did not know. When asked if he knew if any of the many people who were entrusted with the key had ever duplicated it, he said he did not know. He was further asked about where the records of the Alitalia with respect to the package were kept. He replied that the documentation was kept in the warehouse offices in full view and accessible to any Alitalia employees who were in the warehouse. There was no evidence of the door to the room being "jimmied" or tampered with in any way. The steel bars over the chimney in the room were intact. There was no testimony of burglary or robbery or evidence to show how the package came to be missing. There was not even any testimony as to when the package was no longer in the room; and, further, no way of knowing when it was stolen as no inventory log was kept on a shift basis to be passed on from one duty cargo manager to the next duty cargo manager when a changing of the guard took place.

Moore v. Ellis

385 S.W.2d 261 (Ct. Civ. App. Tex. 1964)

This was an action by Harold Ellis (plaintiff) against John J. Moore and H. R. Wardlaw (defendants) to recover a judgment for personal injuries. Judgment for Ellis, and Moore and Wardlaw appealed. Judgment reversed and judgment entered for Moore and Wardlaw.

Moore and Wardlaw furnished a tractor and disk to Harper for use in disking land. The hydraulic cylinder lift used to raise and lower the disk was not operating properly. The disk could be raised by the three-point hitch lift. However, if the disk was overloaded with dirt when lifted with the three-point lift, it would cause the front end of the tractor to raise up. Upon disengaging the clutch or releasing the gas throttle, the front of the tractor would then come down. Moore informed Harper that the hydraulic cylinder lift was inoperative. Harper hired Harold Ellis to operate the tractor and disk. The ground being disked at the time was wet and this wet condition was causing the disk to become overloaded. Twice on the day before the accident the front of the tractor reared up. Ellis was told by McCrary, an employee of Moore and Wardlaw, and he knew that the hydraulic cylinder lift (which was safe to use if in working order) was defective and would not work. The fourth time the tractor reared up when Ellis lifted the disk it flipped over, pinning Ellis underneath and injuring him seriously.

DUNAGAN, CHIEF JUSTICE. In the case of *Nesmith v. Magnolia Petroleum Co.*, the court said:

> One who supplies directly or through a third person a chattel for another to use, is subject to liability to those whom the supplier should expect to use the chattel with the consent of the other or to be in the vicinity of its probable use, for bodily harm caused by the use of the chattel in the manner for which and by a person for whose use it is supplied, if the supplier (a) knows, or from facts known to him should realize, that the chattel is or is likely to be dangerous for the use for which it is supplied; (b) and has no reason to believe that those for whose use the chattel is supplied will realize its dangerous condition; and (c) fails to exercise reasonable care to *inform* them of its dangerous condition or of the facts which make it likely to be so. These general principles apply alike to donors, lenders, and lessors of chattels.

Therefore, all three of the above elements must exist concurrently before liability can be assessed against Moore and Wardlaw.

In the case at bar it is undisputed that Harold Ellis knew of the inoperable cylinder lift, and it is further undisputed that McCrary told Harold Ellis about the inoperable cylinder lift. Furthermore, the jury found that at the time and on the occasion in question, Harold Ellis knew that the cylinder lift was not in operating condition. Therefore, elements (b) and (c) did not exist, but, rather, the evidence showed that the duty imposed was fulfilled and not breached.

Special Bailment Situations

Bailment of Fungible Goods. As a general rule the bailee is required to return to the bailor the identical goods he or she deposited. If the parties enter into a contract whereby the party to whom the goods are delivered has the right to surrender other goods, though of the same kind and value, the transaction is a sale, not a bailment. This rule has not been applied to the storage of grain and other fungible goods. The courts hold that if grain of several persons is stored in a common mass in an elevator and the operator of the elevator contracts to return to the depositor an equal quantity of grain of the same kind and quality, the transaction is a bailment.

The courts are not in complete accord as to the nature of the transaction if the storage contract permits the payment of the purchase price of the grain in lieu of delivery. They are in accord in holding that the transaction is a bailment if the depositor has the absolute right to demand the return of grain of the same kind and quality or to demand the payment of the market price at the time he or she makes his or her demand in lieu of accepting delivery of the grain. But most of the courts hold that the transaction is a sale if the depositary (the elevator) has the right, at the time the demand is made, to pay the market price of the grain in lieu of delivery of the grain. Some courts hold that if the depositary is given an option to purchase at the market price at the time the depositor returns his or her receipt and demands delivery, the transaction is a bailment until such time as a demand is made and the option to purchase is exercised, at which time it becomes a sale.

Safe-Deposit Boxes. In the operation of a safe-deposit box, the box and the property in the box are in the manual possession of the bank. However, neither the bank nor the renter can gain access to the contents of the box without the consent and cooperation of the other. To open the box, two keys are used. One of the keys is kept by the bank and the other by the renter. The bank need have no knowledge of the nature, amount, or value of the property in the safe-deposit box. Although there is some diversity of opinion as to the nature of the relationship, some courts have held that the renter is a bailor and the bank is a bailee.

Involuntary Bailments. Sometimes a person finds himself in possession of the personal property of another without having consented to accept such possession. For instance, the personal property of one person may be deposited on the premises of another by storm or flood, or the animals of one person may stray onto the premises of another. In such cases a few courts have held that no bailment arises, whereas other courts have held that an involuntary bailment arises.

There are no well-established rules as to the rights and duties of the involuntary bailee. He or she does not have a right to destroy the property willfully, convert it to his or her own use, or refuse to redeliver it to the owner. The affirmative duties of the involuntary bailee are uncertain and, in many instances, do not require him or her to assume control over the goods. Under the circumstances of some cases the duties imposed are those of the bailee in a bailment for the sole benefit of the bailor. Each case must be decided according to the facts of the case.

Common Carrier. A person is a common carrier if he holds himself out to carry, for hire, the property of any person who chooses to employ him. A person is a private carrier if he carries the property only for those whom he selects. Both common carriers and private carriers are bailees. The common carrier is held to a standard of responsibility higher than of the private carrier. This distinction is historical and is based on the social conditions which existed in England during an early period. To prevent collusion between the carrier and highwaymen, the carrier was held to be the insurer of the property he carried. This imposed an absolute liability on the carrier for the damage or loss of property he carried.

This rule is in force in the United States today; however, there are several exceptions to the general rule. The common carrier is not liable if the damage or loss is the result of an act of God, an act of the public enemy, an act of the state, or an act of the shipper, or if the damage or loss is caused by the nature of the goods.

Innkeepers. The hotel owner or innkeeper is one who holds himself out to provide food and/or lodging to transients. He is obligated to serve the public, and like the common carrier, is held to a responsibility greater than that of the ordinary bailee. The hotel owner or innkeeper is not a bailee in the strict sense of the word, since the guest does not surrender the exclusive possession of his or her property to the hotel owner or innkeeper; but the hotel owner or innkeeper is the insurer of the guest's property. Losses resulting from acts of God or acts of public enemies, and losses suffered by guests resulting from the acts of members of their own parties, are exceptions to this strict liability. Many states have enacted statutes which relieve the hotel owner or innkeeper from this strict liability or, in other words, limit his or her liability. Commonly, they require the hotel owner to post a notice advising guests that any valuables should be checked into the hotel vault and limit the hotel owner's liability for any valuables which are not deposited with owner.

SUMMARY

The courts have held a transaction to be a bailment if fungible goods of several persons are stored in a common mass and the depositary is to return an equal quantity of goods of the same kind and quality. Most courts have held the transaction to be a sale if the depositary has the right, at the time demand for return of the goods is made, to pay the market price in lieu of returning the goods.

The courts are not in accord as to the relation between the bank and the renter of a safe-deposit box. Some courts have held the relation to be that of bailor and bailee.

A person may become an involuntary bailee if the goods of another are deposited on his land by storm or flood or by the acts of third persons, or if the domestic animals of another stray onto his or her land. Such a bailee owes a minimum of duty. He cannot willfully destroy the property or convert it to his own use.

A common carrier is the insurer of the goods he carries against loss or damage unless such loss or damage is caused by an act of God, an act of the public enemy, an act of the state, or an act of the shipper, or by the nature of the goods.

An innkeeper is an insurer of the goods of his or her guests. Many states have statutes permitting innkeepers to limit their liability.

Problem Cases

1. Henry Blandy desired to make some provisions for the maintenance and support of his daughter, Amanda Flanders. He purchased and set apart as a "gift" to her $2,000 worth of U.S. bonds. The bonds were never delivered to Amanda who lived some distance away

and she never had manual possession of them. Rather, by her request and assent they were left under the dominion and control of her father for safekeeping. Each year he collected and sent to her the interest that had accrued on the bonds. Blandy became interested in the cashmere goat business and decided that such an investment would be more profitable to his daughter. So he sold the bonds and invested the money in that business. He then wrote Amanda, telling her if she did not accept the new investment, he would pay to her, in place of the bonds, $2,000 plus interest. Blandy dies and Amanda claims she is entitled to $2,000 because her father had made a valid gift to her of the bonds. Did he make a valid gift?

2. While the Olympia, a passenger ship, was moored at a pier in New York City and receiving passengers for an imminent sailing, Kalyvakis, who was a steward on the ship, found $2,010 in U.S. currency on the floor of a public men's room on the upper deck. The room was accessible to all passengers, their guests and the ship's personnel; the money was found shortly before visitors and guests were required to leave the ship. Kalyvakis deposited the money with the chief steward to be held for the true owner should he make any claim for it. No claim has been made for the money for three years, and Kalyvakis asks that the money be returned to him. His employer contends the money belongs to it, the owner of the ship. Who is entitled to the money?

3. Faulke, a passenger on Railroad Company's train, saw on the seat opposite him a package which had been left by a passenger who had alighted. Faulke picked up the package, examined it, found no name or mark on it, and took the package with him when he disembarked. Was the package lost property?

4. Roberts employed Danielson to clean the rubbish out of an old hen house. While so engaged, Danielson dug out of the rubbish a can of gold coins. The premises had been owned by several persons, and no one knew who had placed the can of gold coins in the hen house. Who has the best right to the gold coins, Roberts or Danielson?

5. Pond owned and operated a parking lot. Rehling parked his automobile on Pond's lot, which was near Crosley Field, and proceeded with others to a night baseball game. Rehling paid $1 to the parking lot attendant, for which he received a "claim check." Before leaving his automobile, Rehling turned the ignition switch to off, rolled up the windows, locked the doors, and took the keys with him. When he returned after the ball game to get his automobile, it was gone. The parking lot attendants testified that at about the third inning of the ball game, they saw a person walk directly to Rehling's automobile, get in, back up, and drive away. There was no showing that the claim check was ever used for anything but identification in case a patron was unable to find his automobile on the lot. Is Pond liable as bailee for the loss of the automobile?

6. Alderman delivered his automobile containing some personal property to Welding Shop to have it equipped with a hitch and agreed to pay Welding Shop for its work. When the automobile was returned, it was in a damaged condition, and the personal property which was in the automobile when it was delivered to the shop was missing. Alderman sued Welding Shop to recover damages, stating in his complaint only the facts relative to the delivery of the automobile and personal property, and the damage and loss. Welding Shop made no defense but claimed that since Alderman did not allege acts of neligence on its part resulting in the damage and loss, it was not liable. Is Welding Shop's contention correct?

7. Wells rented a trailer from Brown and agreed to return the trailer clean and in the same condition as when rented. The trailer was damaged when a tree was blown across it during a violent windstorm. The damage was caused solely by the volence of the storm and

without any negligence of fault on the part of Wells. Brown sues Wells to recover for the damage done to the trailer. Can he recover?

8. The American Numismatic Association (ANA) held its annual convention at a hotel in Washington and arranged for the display and selling of coins, medals and paper money during the convention. The ANA entered into a contract with Searcher's Detective Agency under which it would provide protection at the convention and security room for safekeeping of the displays when not on exhibit. Picker, a professional coin dealer, applied for display space at the convention and his application was accepted. One day he placed his collection valued at $135,000 in two attache cases and checked them at a security room provided by ANA. When he went to pick it up the next morning the cases had disappeared. Employees of both ANA and Searcher's were in attendance at the security room. At the time he checked the attache cases, Picker signed a three-part check, the middle portion of which read as follows:

   In consideration for permitting me to use without charge the Security Room at the 19— ANA Convention, I hereby agree that the liability of American Numismatic Association . . . and all officers, board members and other representatives of each of them shall be limited to the aggregate sum of $25 for loss, theft, damage and/or destruction (through negligence or otherwise) of all property held for me in said Security Room; provided, however, that the foregoing provision shall not limit the liability of any individual who may be personally guilty of theft, willful damage or destruction of my property.

   Picker was given one part of the check which contained nothing but a number and place for signature; the third portion of the check was placed on the attache cases. Picker claimed that when he checked his cases the security room was very busy, that he did not read the limitation of liability clause, was not asked to read it, and was not aware of its terms. Picker brought suit against ANA and Searcher's. They defended on the grounds their liability was limited to $25 per item. Can Picker recover?

32

Real Property

Fixtures

Nature of Fixture. A fixture is personal property which is so attached to or used with real estate that it is considered to be a part of that real estate. The term *fixture* is also used to designate personal property, such as, for instance, a store fixture, which may appear to be a part of the real estate but is not attached to it and is removable. A wide variety of fact situations have been before the courts in controversies which arise when one person claims that an article of personal property has become a fixture and another claims that the article continues as personal property. The courts have developed standards for determining issues regarding fixtures.

In the modern cases the courts apply the reasonable-man standard, which is: Would a reasonable man familiar with the community and with the facts and circumstances of the case be justified in assuming that the person attaching or using the personal property with the real estate intended it to become a fixture? The intention of the parties, determined by the application of this objective test, is usually controlling. In applying this standard, all the facts of the case, such as the time, place, usage, relation of the parties, mode of attachment, and adaptability for use with the particular premises, must be considered, and the case must be decided by a common-sense application of this accepted standard.

Express Agreement. Since intention of the parties is controlling, if the parties have, by express agreement, indicated their intention as to whether or not an article of personal property shall or shall not become a fixture, the courts will, within limits, enforce the agreement of the parties. Parties cannot, however, by their agreement convert into personal property such property as a city lot or a farm, nor can they convert into a fixture an article which is no way attached to or used with real property.

Mode of Attachment or Annexation. In some of the early cases the courts held that "attachment" or "annexation" was the sole test for determining whether or not an article of personal property had become a fixture. Today, attachment is of outstanding importance, but it is not conclusive in determining the intention of the parties.

As already noted, if an article of personal property is built into a building so that it becomes an integral part of the building, it loses its character as personal property and becomes real property, irrespective of any declared intention of the parties. If an article of personal property is firmly attached to the real property in such a manner that its removal will substantially destroy the article and will also injure the real property to which it is attached, the court will consider such attachment as very strong evidence that the parties intended the article to become a fixture. If attachment is slight and the article can be removed without injury to the article, such attachment is of little importance as evidence.

An article which is attached to the land only by gravity may become a fixture. For example, a building set on blocks on top of the ground and a statue weighing several tons set on a cement foundation, but not attached to the foundation, have been held to be fixtures.

Use with Real Property. The appropriateness of the use of the article of personal property with the real property is important as evidence of the intention of the parties. As a general rule, some degree of attachment is considered as necessary to indicate an intention that an article is to become a fixture, but the courts have held certain articles to be fixtures, even though the articles are not attached to the real property, if such articles would be of little or no value except as used with that particular property. Such articles as keys to doors, storm windows, and screens for windows have been held to be fixtures although not attached to the real property.

In one case, in-a-door beds, refrigerators, stoves, cabinets, and similar items, installed in an apartment house, were held to be fixtures even though they were so attached to the real property that they could be easily removed. In such a case the appropriateness of the use of the article with the real property is given great weight in determining the intentions of the parties.

Additions by Owner. The relation of the parties is also of outstanding importance. If the owner of real property improves it by the addition of personal property, there is an all but conclusive presumption that the owner intended the improvement to become a part of the real property; and if he or she sells or mortgages the real property without reservation, the courts have held that the additions are fixtures and pass as real property to the purchaser or mortgagee.

When the owner of real estate purchases personal property, the seller may retain a security interest in such property as security for the payment of the purchase price. If the purchasor then attaches the personal property to his or her real estate, the seller's security interest in the attached property will, under the Uniform Commercial Code, have priority over all persons having an interest in the real estate, provided the seller's security interest has been "perfected" by filing in the local real estate records prior to attachment to the property. On default, the seller may remove the personal property but he or she will be liable to third parties, such as prior real estate mortgagors, for damage to the real estate caused by its removal.[1]

Additions by Tenants. As between landlord and tenant, the earliest cases held that any improvement made by a tenant became a part of real property; but the courts soon began to make a distinction between attachments made by tenants of business property for trade purposes and those made by tenants of other kinds of real property. This distinction is important today. The courts have generally held that personal property brought onto premises leased for business purposes, for use in the carrying on of the business for which the premises are leased, remains personal property irrespective of the mode of attachment. Such property is known as trade fixtures. However, if the personal property is so built into the real property that its removal will weaken the structure, the courts have held that it becomes a part of the real property.

In cases involving domestic and agricultural tenancies, the general rule of intention has been applied. However, the presumption that the property which is attached to the real property is to remain personal property is usually not so strong in the case of domestic and agricultural tenancies as in the case of business tenancies.

In all cases in which a tenant has added trade, domestic, or agricultural fixtures, if the tenancy is for a definite period, the tenant must remove the article before the expiration of his or her term, and if he or she does not, the article becomes the property of the landlord. This rule had its origin in the early English land law and has been recognized by the courts ever since. Two reasons for the rule have been given: (1) that the failure to remove is conclusive indication of an intention to abandon the article, and (2) that after the expiration of the term the tenant would be a trespasser if he or she entered the land to remove the article.

If the tenancy is for an indefinite period, such as a tenancy for life or a tenancy at will, the tenant will have a reasonable time after the termination of the tenancy to remove such property. The courts have held that if there is an express agreement that articles attached by the tenant shall remain personal property and may be removed by him, he will have a reasonable time after the expiration of his term in which to remove the articles.

---

[1] Uniform Commercial Code, Article 9, Section 9–313.

SUMMARY

A fixture is personal property which by attachment to or association in use with land is regarded as real property. The reasonable-person standard is applied by the courts in determining whether or not an article of personal property has become a fixture. The objective intent of the parties is the basic test.

Within reasonable limits the courts enforce the agreement of the parties relative to whether an article of personal property shall or shall not become a fixture.

Mode of attachment is important as evidence to be considered in determining the intention of the parties. If there is no attachment, that fact is prima facie evidence that the article of personal property is not a fixture.

The appropriateness of use with the real property is a fact which is always considered in determining the intention of the parties. In exceptional cases, appropriateness of use with the real property, without attachment, may be sufficient to justify holding that the article is a fixture.

The relation of the parties is also of importance. If an owner attaches his own personal property to his real property for the purpose of improving the real property, the article becomes a fixture.

Under the Unform Commercial Code if one sells personal property to be attached to real estate, retaining a security interest in such property, the seller's lien will have priority over rights of third persons provided it is perfected.

Tenants who have added to the leased premises articles of personal property which are classed as trade, domestic, or agricultural fixtures may remove the articles on the termination of the lease. If the lease is for a definite term, the articles must be removed before the expiration of the term; if the lease is for an indefinite term, the articles must be removed within a reasonable time after the expiration of the lease.

Sigrol Realty Corp. v. Valcich

212 N.Y.S.2d 224 (App. Div. N.Y. 1961), *aff'd mem.,* 225 N.Y.S.2d 748 (1962)

This was an action brought by Sigrol Realty Co. (plaintiff) against Valcich and six others (defendants) to enjoin the removal of seven frame bungalows from land recently purchased by Sigrol Realty. The trial court granted the injunction. Reversed on appeal.

In 1891, six members of the Wilmore family acquired a tract of waterfront land on Staten Island, known as "Robinson's Beach." During the Wilmore ownership seven frame bungalows were placed on the land by various tenants who rented the land space from the landowners for that purpose. The tenants paid rent for the use of the land; they paid for the maintenance and insurance of the bungalows; and from time to time they repaired, altered and sold the bungalows without approval or hindrance from the landowners. The tenants occupied the bungalows during the summer months only. The bungalows rested on cinder blocks which were not sunk into the ground; the bungalows were not bolted to the ground; and they had no basements. The bungalows were so constructed that upon severance of the water and electrical connections they could be removed without injury either to them or to the land. Some of the tenants who originally erected the bungalows sold them without requesting or obtaining permission from the Wilmores.

On April 9, 1959, the Wilmores for the sum of $12,250, contracted to sell to Sigrol Realty the land acquired by them in 1891, with the buildings and improvements thereon, "*subject to the rights of tenants, if any.*" The contract contained the printed provision that fixtures and articles of personal property attached or appurtenant to the premises "are represented to be owned by the seller, free from all liens and encumbrances." This provision was amended, however, to read that the seller merely represented that all such fixtures and articles of personal property "which are owned by the seller, are free from all liens and encumbrances." On June 11, 1959, the Wilmores executed and delivered a deed in accordance with the contract.

When the original tenants or their assignees were ordered to leave the property, they asserted their ownership of the bungalows and their right to remove them. Sigrol Realty, as buyer, sought a court order, declaring it owned the bungalows and restraining the tenants from removing them.

BELDOCK, JUDGE. For the purpose of determining whether chattels annexed to realty remain personalty or become realty, chattels are divided into three classes: (1) some chattels, such as gas ranges, because of their character as movables, remain personalty even after their annexation, regardless of any agreement between the chattel owner and the landowner; (2) other chattels, such as brick, stone and plaster placed in the walls of a building, become realty after annexation, regardless of any agreement to the contrary between the chattel owner and the landowner; such personal property does not retain its character as such if it be annexed to the realty in such manner as to become an integral part of the realty and be immovable without practically destroying the personal property, or if all or part of it be essential to the support of the structure to which it is attached; and (3) still other chattels, after attachment, continue to be personalty or become realty, in accordance with the agreement between the chattel owner and the landowner.

In my opinion, these bungalows were in the third class, i.e., they were movables which continued to be personalty or become realty, depending on the agreement between the bungalow owners and the landowners, the Wilmores. There is no contention by Sigrol Realty that the Wilmores ever claimed ownership of the bungalows during their long ownership of the land after the bungalows were placed thereon. The bungalows were erected by defendants or by their predecessors in title without any intention of making them permanent accessions to the realty. The manner of their annexation was such as to make them easily removable without injury either to them or to the land. Defendants and their predecessors in title were tenants of land space only. They repaired, maintained, insured, altered, and sold the bungalows without the consent or interference by the Wilmores.

The fair inference to be drawn from the evidence is that the agreement between the Wilmores and the original owners and the latters' vendees, was that the bungalows were to remain personalty; that the lessees of the land space, at the expiration of the term, would have the right to remove the bungalows as their own personal property; and that the landowner would have no right to prevent them from making such removal.

Sigrol Realty is not a purchaser for value without notice. It does not claim that the Wilmores ever represented to it, either orally or in writing, that they owned the seven bungalows in question. Only the fixtures and articles of personalty owned by the Wilmores were sold. The contract of sale expressly negated any representation by the Wilmores that they did own the fixtures and articles of personalty. Under the contract the Wilmores sold and Sigrol Realty purchased the land subject to the rights of the tenants.

Rights and Interests in Real Property

Fee Simple. The basic land ownership interest in the United States is the fee simple which entitles the owner to the entire property for an unlimited duration of time with the unconditional power to dispose of it during his life or upon his death, and which will descend to his heirs if he dies without making a will. The holder of a fee simple may grant many rights to others without changing the nature of his interest. For example, Archer, who owns land in fee simple, may give Burch a mortgage on the land, grant Clark an easement of right-of-way over the land, and lease the land to Fox for a period of years. Archer has granted rights to Burch, Clark, and Fox; but Archer still owns the land in fee simple. On the termination of the rights of Burch, Clark, and Fox, such rights revert to the owner of the fee and merge into the fee, and may again be granted by the owner.

Life Estate. A life estate is an interest in land which is limited in time to the life or lives of persons in being. A life estate may be for the life of the holder or for the life or lives of another or others. The life tenant has the right to use the property, but he or she does not have a right to do acts which will result in permanent injury to the property.

Leasehold. A leasehold gives the lessee the right to occupy and possess a given piece of real property. This right may be for a fixed period of time, such as a month or a year, in which case it is known as a "periodic tenancy," or for what is known as a "tenancy at will" where the time period is not fixed in advance and either the lessor or the lessee can terminate the leasehold after giving notice to the other party of his intention to do so.

Easements. An easement is the nonpossessory right to use or enjoy the land of another person. It may be an "easement appurtenant" or an "easement in gross." An easement appurtenant is the right which the owner of a particular parcel of land has, by reason of such ownership, to use the land of another for a specific purpose. The land benefited by the easement is known as the "dominant tenement," and the land subject to the easement is known as the "servient tenement." For instance, if the owner or occupier of land, tract A, has an easement of right-of-way over the land, tract B, tract A is the dominant tenement, and tract B is the servient tenement.

An easement may be created which is not tied to adjoining land. Such an easement is known as an "easement in gross." If the easement in gross is granted to an individual, it will, as a general rule, be held to be personal to that individual and not assignable, transferable, or inheritable. In a few cases such an easement has been held to be transferable. Easements to utility companies are usually easements in gross.

An easement may be an affirmative or a negative easement. An affirmative easement is the right to make certain uses of the land of another. The right to drive across, to run a sewer across, or to drill for gas and oil on the land of another are affirmative easements. A negative easement is the right to have an adjoining landowner refrain from making certain uses of his or her land. The right to have an adjoining landowner refrain from erecting a structure on his or her premises which would cut off light and air from your buildings is a negative easement.

In recent years increased use has been made of easements to help preserve values considered socially desirable. For example, the owner of a historic building might grant the local historical society a "historic easement" agreeing not to change its facade, or an environmental group or the state might obtain a scenic" easement or a "conservation" easement whereby the owner agrees to leave his property, or a portion of it, in an undeveloped state.

Easements may be acquired in a number of different ways:

1. *By grant.* For example, the owner of Blackacre may sell or give the owner of the adjoining property, Whiteacre, the right to cross Blackacre to get to an alley behind Blackacre.

2. *By reservation.* For example, the owner of Blackacre sells the property to Alice, reserving the mineral rights to the property and also reserving an easement to cross Blackacre to remove the minerals.

3. *By implication or implied grant.* For example, the owner of a store building used a narrow strip of land for access to the building. He sold the store to Arthur and later sold the passage land to Blanche. The court held that by selling the store to Arthur, the owner had conveyed by implication an easement

over the passageway. An implied easement is based on some degree of prior use.

4. *By necessity.* An easement of necessity is created when the existence of the easement is necessary for the beneficial use of land sold or retained, regardless of the existence of such prior use. For example, A owns 80 acres fronting on a road and bounded on the other three sides by a limited access highway. If A sells the back 40 acres to B, B has an easement of necessity across A's remaining property because that is B's only means of access to his property.

5. *By estoppel.* A person who sells land may be estopped to prevent the use of the land by the buyer for a purpose that was disclosed at the time of the sale. For example, A owned a large tract of land adjacent to a lake. A sold part of the land fronting on the lake to a city for use as a municipal water source. A was then estopped to use the lake for resort purposes in a way that would contaminate the lake and make it unsuitable for the city's use.

6. *By prescription.* An easement may be created pursuant to the doctrine of "adverse possession" when one person makes an adverse (nonpermissive), open and notorious use of another's property continuously and exclusively for the statutory period. The property owner should thus be on notice that someone else is acting as if he has certain rights to use the property—and if the true owner does not move to assert his rights during the statutory period, he may lose his right to stop that other person from making that use of his property. The doctrine of adverse possession is discussed in more detail later in this chapter.

Because an easement is an interest in land, it is within the purview of the statute of frauds and usually must be in a writing if it is to be enforceable. Under the statutes of most states, the grant of an easement must be executed with the same formalities as is the grant of a fee simple in real property. However, nonexpressly-granted easements such as those by implication, necessity, estoppel, or prescription are enforceable even though they are not in writing.

Licenses. A license is similar in some respects to an easement; however, it is not an interest in land and may be created orally and, unless coupled with an interest in land, may be revoked at the will of the licensor. Permission to cross the land of another or to hunt or fish on the other's land is a license. A person entering on the land of another for the purpose of transacting business is a licensee. If a person purchases from another trees which are to be cut and hauled away, the purchaser would have an irrevocable license to go onto the land for the purpose of cutting and hauling the logs. There are innumerable situations in which one person has a license to go onto the land of another. A license, as a general rule, creates a temporary right to use another's land in a limited and specific manner.

SUMMARY

Ownership in fee simple is the highest estate a person can hold in land. It is the original source of all rights in land and is not limited in time.

A life estate is an estate for the life or lives of persons in being.

A leasehold is the right to occupy and possess real property and is limited in time.

An easement is a nonpossessory right to use the land of another. An easement in gross is an easement which is not tied to adjoining land and an easement appurtenant is tied to adjoining land. An affirmative easement gives the owner of the easement the right to make certain uses of another's property, and a negative easement gives the owner of the easement the right to have another refrain from making a certain use of the other's land.

An easement may be acquired by an express grant, by a reservation in a grant, by implication, by estoppel, by necessity, or by prescription. It is an interest in land, and to be enforceable, it usually must be in writing.

A license creates a temporary privilege to make some specific use of another's land, and it is not an interest in land.

Helton v. Jones

402 S.W.2d 694 (Ct. App. Ky. 1966)

This was an action by Jones (plaintiff) to enjoin Helton (defendant) from interfering with a passway easement Jones claimed to have over Helton's land. Judgment for Jones. Affirmed.

Prior to 1929 Tom Noe owned a single tract of ground bounded on two sides by parallel highways. Across Noe's land was a roadway approximately 125 feet in length connecting the two highways and which for more than fifty years had been used for access to the principal parallel highway. In 1929 Noe died and his land was divided into two tracts. Since that time the owners and occupants of the tract now owned by Jones have continued to use the roadway over the other tract now owned by Helton. Prior to the time Jones acquired the property in 1943, a gate was put up across the road. Sometimes this gate was locked by Helton but Jones was given a key to it. Then in 1964 Helton put a new lock on the gate and did not give Jones a key. Jones sued Helton to enjoin him from blocking the road.

CLAY, COMMISSIONER. Helton's contention is that the use of this passway (for a period of fifty years) has always been *permissive* and therefore the use of it never ripened into an easement. Jones contends that when the lands were originally divided an easement was created, but in any event, the long-continued use matured into an absolute right.

The facts in this case are almost identical with those in *Delong v. Cline.*

It was therein held that upon a division of a tract of land under the same circumstances we have here, an easement will pass by implication "as if he had a deed thereto" to the party who acquired the parcel whose enjoyment required the use of a preexisting passway over another parcel.

This principle amply supports the Chancellor's finding of the existence of an easement although his finding appears to have been based on his conclusion that Jones had acquired his rights by prescription or adverse possession. Such alternate ground of the the decision is also amply supported by the record. The circumstances would justify no other conclusion but that Jones had a permanent easement as a matter of right. The existence of the gate may have restricted the scope of the easement but certainly did not destroy it.

Co-Ownership of Real Property

Nature of Co-Ownership. Co-ownership of real property exists when two or more persons own an undivided interest in such property. The co-owners do not have separate rights in any portion of the real property; each has a share in the whole property.

There are seven kinds of co-ownership of real property recognized in the United States today: (1) tenancy in common, (2) joint tenancy, (3) tenancy by the entirety, (4) community property, (5) tenancy in partnership, (6) condominiums, and (7) cooperatives.

Tenancy in Common. A tenancy in common is created when real property is deeded to two or more persons as tenants in common or when two or more persons inherit real property. In most states, if real property is conveyed to two or more persons and the instrument of conveyance does not state how they shall hold the property, they will hold as tenants in common.

The interest which the tenants in common hold in the property is known as an estate of inheritance, that is, each tenant holds an interest as individual property, and on that tenant's death the interest will descend to tenant's heirs or devisees. Each tenant may sell or encumber his interest in the property, and it is subject to levy of execution by a judgment creditor. The shares of tenants in common need not be equal, that is, one tenant may own a two-thirds interest in the property and his or her cotenant may own the remaining one-third.

The only common right of tenants in common is the right of possession. Each tenant has the right to possess and use the common property, but he has no right to exclude his cotenants from equal rights of possession and use. If the property is rented, the cotenants share ratably in the income from the property and must make a ratable contribution to the taxes, the repairs, and the upkeep.

A tenant in common may petition the court to divide the property. In such an action the property will be physically divided if it is practical, and each tenant will receive his or her proportionate share in kind. If this is not practical, however, the court will order the property sold, and the proceeds from the sale will be divided according to the share of each tenant. The tenants may divide the property by mutual agreement.

Joint Tenancy. A joint tenancy is created when equal interests in real property are conveyed to two or more persons by one instrument which expressly states that the persons take as joint tenants. The outstanding characteristic of the joint tenancy is the right of survivorship; that is, on the death of one of the joint tenants, his or her interest passes to the surviving joint tenant or tenants. The interest of a joint tenant cannot be devised by will.

The interest of a joint tenant is subject to levy by his or her creditors, and the jointure may be destroyed by a conveyance by one of the joint tenants. If a joint tenant conveys his or her interest, the person to whom the interest is conveyed holds as a tenant in common with the other joint tenant or tenants.

The right of use, possession, contribution, and partition of joint tenants is the same as that of tenants in common.

The joint tenancy with right of survivorship has been abolished in some states and is not generally favored by the law. It is thought that on the death of an owner his or her interest in property should pass to his or her estate and not to a joint tenant. Moreover, in many cases where people acquire property as concurrent owners, they are not fully aware of the right of survivorship.

Tenancy by the Entirety. Tenants by the entirety must be husband and wife. This is fundamentally a joint tenancy with rights of survivorship. It can be created only by a conveyance to persons who are husband and wife at the time of the conveyance. A tenancy by the entirety cannot be destroyed by the acts of one of the parties. Real property owned by the entirety cannot be sold under execution issued on a judgment rendered against either the husband or the wife individually, but it may be sold on execution issued on a judgment rendered against them on a joint obligation. Neither can convey the real property by deed unless the other joins, and neither can dispose of the property by will. Tenancies by the entirety are not recognized in all states.

Community Property. In some states, the system of "community property" prevails. The principal characteristic of the system is that whatever property is acquired by the efforts of either the husband or the wife during marriage becomes a common fund or, as it is called, "community property." Either the husband or the wife may own, in addition to his or her interest in the community property, "separate property." Generally, separate property includes that property owned prior to marriage or acquired after marriage by gift, devise, or descent, or in exchange for property owned as separate property.

The details of the system are set out by the statutes of each of the community property states.

Tenancy in Partnership. Tenancy in partnership was discussed in Chapter 22. The incidents of the tenancy in partnership are set out in Section 25 of the Uniform Partnership Act.

Condominium Ownership. In resort and urban areas the form of ownership known as condominium has come into extensive use. In a condominium, the purchaser gets title to the apartment or townhouse unit he or she occupies and also becomes a tenant in common of the facilities shared in common with the other owners such as hallways, elevator and utility shafts, swimming pools, and parking areas. The condominium owner pays property taxes on his individual unit, he can take out a mortgage on his unit, and he is generally free to sell the unit without having the prospective buyer approved by the other owners. He also makes a monthly payment to cover the maintenance of the common areas. For federal income tax purposes he is treated like the owner of a single-family home and is allowed to deduct his property taxes and mortgage interest expenses.

Cooperative Ownership. In a cooperative, the entire building is owned by a group of people or by a corporation. Usually the buyer of a unit buys stock in the corporation and holds his apartment under a long-term lease which he can renew. Frequently the cooperative owner must obtain the approval of the other owners in order to sell or sublease his or her unit.

SUMMARY

Seven types of co-ownership of real property are recognized: (1) tenancy in common, (2) joint tenancy, (3) tenancy by the entirety, (4) community property, (5) tenancy in partnership, (6) condominiums, and (7) cooperatives.

Tenants in common need not hold equal shares. On the death of a tenant in common, if he dies intestate, his or her interest passes to his heirs. A tenant in common may devise his interest by will. Tenants in common have the right to possess and use the property, and each is entitled to his proportionate share of the income. Each must contribute to taxes, repairs, and upkeep in proportion to his or her share or interest.

Joint tenants hold equal interests which must be created by the same instrument at the same time. They have the right of survivorship. In other respects, their rights are substantially the same as the rights of tenants in common.

Tenants by the entirety must be husband and wife. On the death of either, his or her interest passes by the right of survivorship to the other. Neither party can destroy the tenancy by his or her individual acts, and the property is not subject to the individual debts of either.

Community property is a type of ownership by husband and wife. The rights are created by statute, and the details of the system are set out by the statutes of the state.

Condominiums and cooperatives are forms of joint ownership developed relatively recently to allow apartment dwellers many of the advantages of individual home ownership.

Acquisition of Real Property

Origin of Title to Real Property. Original title to land in the United States was acquired either by grant from the federal government or by grant from a country which held the land prior to its acquisition by the United States. The land which was within the boundaries of the original 13 states was land which had, for the most part, been granted by the king of England to the colonies or to certain individuals. The Northwest Territory was ceded by the states to the federal government. Original title to this land was a patent from the federal government signed by the President. Most of the land in Florida and sections of land in the Southwest were held by Spain, and the ownership of this land is based on Spanish grants.

Acquisition by Purchase. One of the rights of ownership is the right to sell (the right of alienation). Under our law any agreement or restriction which deprives the owner of land of his right to alienate his land is against public policy and is void. Most persons who own real property today have acquired their title by purchasing the property from a prior owner. Each state has the right to regulate the formal requirements for the transfer of the ownership of the lands within the state.

Acquisition by Gift. Ownership in real property may be acquired by gift. The donor of such property must deliver to the donee, or to some third person for the benefit of the donee, a deed which complies with all the statutory requirements of the state in which the property is located. It is not necessary for the donee, or some third person acting for the donee, to take actual physical possession of the property. The essential element of the gift is the delivery of the deed. If the donor makes deeds to real property and leaves them in a safe-deposit box to be delivered to the named donee after the death of the donor, the gift will fail for lack of delivery.

Acquisition by Adverse Possession. Title to real property may be acquired by adverse possession. The statutory law of the states provides that no action shall be brought for the recovery of the possession of land after a stated number of years, which varies from 5 to 20 years. A person who holds land by open, continuous, and adverse possession for the statutory period can acquire title to the land by complying with certain statutory requirements. In order to acquire title by adverse possession, there must be (1) actual occupancy,

(2) which is hostile to the owner's title, (3) with open claim to title, (4) continuously for the statutory period. In some states the claimant must, in addition to the four requisites set out above, pay the taxes. The same person need not occupy the land for the entire period, but the adverse possession must be continuous. Suppose, for instance, Bixby takes possession of land owned by Altman and claims title to the land and remains in possession for four years, at which time Bixby sells his interest to Clay, who immediately takes possession and remains in possession for six years. If the statutory period is ten years, Clay can acquire title to the land at the end of his six-year occupancy. He acquired Bixby's rights which, added to his rights, satisfy the statutory requirement. It is Altman's responsibility to take legal action to remove the trespasser from his property prior to the expiration of the statutory period; his failure to act as the owner and to remove the trespasser means that the law will recognize as the true owner of the property the person who acts like an owner for the statutory period.

Acquisition by Tax Sale. If the taxes assessed on real property are not paid, they become a lien which is prior to the claims of all persons having an interest in the property. After a stated period of time, if the taxes remain unpaid, the state will sell the property at a tax sale, and the purchaser at such sale will acquire title to the property. The entire procedure is statutory, and there is no uniformity in the tax laws of the several states.

Acquisition by Will or Descent. The owner of real property has the right, subject to some restrictions which are discussed in Chapter 33, to dispose of his or her real property by will. The will, to be effective, must be drawn and executed in accordance with the statutory requirements of the state in which the real property is located. If the owner of real property dies without having made a will, the land will descend to his or her heirs according to the laws of the state in which the real property is located.

SUMMARY

Original title to all lands in the United States was acquired either by grant from the federal government or by grant from a government which held the land prior to its acquisition by the United States.

Real property is usually acquired by purchase. The formal requirements for the transfer of real property are determined by the statutes of the state in which it is located.

Real property may be acquired by gift. To have a valid gift, the donor must deliver to the donee, or to some third person for the benefit of the donee, a deed which complies with the statutory requirements of the state in which the property is located.

To acquire ownership of real property by adverse possession, the claimant must have had open, adverse, and continuous possession of the property for the statutory period.

If the taxes on real property are not paid, the property, under the laws of most states, will be sold for taxes, and the purchaser at the tax sale will be given a tax deed which, if valid, cuts off prior claims to the real property.

The owner of real property may dispose of such property on his or her death by will. If the owner leaves no will, the ownership descends according to the statutes of the state in which it is located.

Converse v. Kenyon

132 N.W.2d 334 (Sup. Ct. Neb. 1965)

This was an action by George N. Converse and others (plaintiff) against Guy E. Kenyon and others (defendants) to establish the boundaries of land. Kenyon claimed that he had acquired title to approximately twenty acres of the land by adverse possession. Judgment for Kenyon and Converse appealed. Affirmed.

Kenyon and Converse owned adjoining tracts of land. Kenyon owned the east half of the section of land and Converse owned the west half. Converse claimed that the line fence dividing their land had been moved to the west of the actual boundary and that the true line should be established, whereas Kenyon claimed that the fence had been in the same location for over 21 years and claimed the land east of the fence by adverse possession. Converse claimed that he had paid the taxes on the entire southwest quarter of the section, which included the land in dispute. In 1962 Kenyon wrote Converse that he would move the fence but that he did not know when he could get it done.

Kenyon had farmed the east half of the section including the disputed tract from 1934 until 1956 when he leased the land to his son who has farmed it since that date.

BROWER, JUSTICE. "What is sufficient to meet the requirements for actual possession depends upon the character of the land and all of the circumstances of the case.

Acts of dominion over land must, to be effective against a true owner, be so open, notorious, and hostile as to put an ordinarily prudent person on notice of the fact that his lands are in the adverse possession of another.

Where one, by mistake as to the boundary line, constructs upon and takes possession of land of another, claiming it as his own to a definite and certain boundary by an actual, open, exclusive, and continuous possession thereof under such claim for ten years or more, he acquires title thereto by adverse possession.

The fact that one claiming title by adverse possession never intended to claim more land than is called for in his deed is not a controlling factor. It is the intent with which possession is held, rather than the intention to hold in accordance with the deed, that is controlling. The claim of adverse possession is founded upon the intent with which the occupant has held possession, and this intent is ordinarily determined by what he has done in respect thereto.

In 3 Am. Jur. 2d, Adverse Possession, § 240, p. 339, it is said:

After the running of the statute, the adverse possessor has an indefeasible title which can only be divested by his conveyance of the land to another, or by a subsequent disseisin for the statutory limitation period. It cannot be lost by a mere abandonment, or by a cessation of occupancy, or by an expression of willingness to vacate the land, or by the acknowledgement or recognition of title in another, or by subsequent legislation, or by survey.

In *Martin v. Martin,* this court held: "One who has acquired absolute title to land by adverse possession for the statutory period does not impair his title by thereafter paying rent to the owner of the paper title." In the opinion of the cited case it was stated: "The law is well settled that recognition of title in the former owner by one claiming adversely after he has acquired a perfect title by adverse possession will not divest him of title."

Transfer by Sale

Steps in a Sale. The major steps normally involved in the sale and purchase of real property are: (1) contracting with a real estate broker to sell the property or to locate suitable property for sale; (2) negotiating and signing a contract to sell the property; (3) arranging for the financing of the purchase and satisfaction of other contingencies such as a survey or acquisition of title insurance; and (4) closing the sale, at which time the purchase price is paid and the deed is signed, delivered, and recorded.

Real Estate Brokers. Although it is not necessary to engage a broker, commonly a prospective seller of real estate will enter into a listing agreement with a real estate broker. The broker's job is to locate a buyer ready, willing, and able to buy the property on the seller's terms and to work out the details of the transfer of the property. The listing agreement should be in writing, specify the length of the listing period, and provide for the amount or percentage of the commission. Generally a seller must pay the commission regardless of who actually sells the house, so long as the broker produces a ready, willing, and able buyer, even if the seller decides not to go through with the sale. However, a few courts have held that the commission was not due where the sale was not consumated.

Contract for Sale. The agreement between the seller and the buyer to purchase real property should be in writing to be enforceable under the statute of frauds. The agreement commonly spells out such things as the purchase price, the type of deed the purchaser will get, and what items of personal property such as appliances and carpets are included. It may also make the "closing" of the sale contingent on the buyer's finding financing at a specified rate of interest and the seller's procurement of a survey, title insurance, and termite insurance.

Financing the Purchase. The various arrangements for financing the purchase of real property such as mortgages, land contracts and deeds of trust are discussed in Chapter 46.

Federal Disclosure Laws. The federal Real Estate Settlement Procedures Act (RESPA) requires that a buyer receive advance disclosure of the settlement costs that will be incurred in settlement, and that a record be kept of the actual settlement charges, in all real estate transactions involving federally related loans, such as VA and FHA loans. The required Settlement/Disclosure Statement itemizes each settlement cost charged to the buyer and each charged to the seller. These settlement charges commonly include: (1) real estate broker's commissions; (2) loan origination fees; (3) loan discount points; (4) appraisal fees; (5) credit report fees; (6) lender's inspection fees; (7) insurance premiums; (8) settlement closing/escrow fees; (9) prepaid interest and taxes; (10) title search fees; (11) notary and/or attorney fees; (12) survey fees; (13) title insurance premiums; and (14) transfer and recording fees.

Among the purposes of the Settlement Statement are to give the buyer notice of the cash he will need to have at settlement and to give the buyer an opportunity to engage in "comparison shopping" of settlement terms so that he can arrange the most favorable terms.

RESPA prohibits a number of practices including kickbacks or payments for referral of business to title companies. It also prohibits any requirement by the seller that title insurance be purchased from any particular company.

In response to fraud and misrepresentations made by some sellers of land, particularly retirement and vacation properties, Congress enacted the Interstate Land Sales Full Disclosure Act.[2] The Act generally applies to developers who subdivide into 50 or more lots and who use interstate means, such as the mail and telephone, to sell the property. The Act requires that a "property report" be prepared disclosing certain kinds of information about the property and the developer's plans regarding it. The report is filed with the U.S. Department of Housing and Urban Development and must be made available to prospective buyers. Civil and criminal penalties can be imposed for violations of the Act.

Transfer by Deed. Since the states have the power to regulate the conveyance of land within their borders, each state has enacted statutes which set out the formalities with which the parties should comply in such conveyance. As a general rule the conveyance of land is accomplished by the execution and delivery of a deed; and in the law of real property a deed is an instrument

[2] 17 U.S.C.A. Section 1701 *et seq.*

in writing whereby the owner of land (the grantor) conveys to another (the grantee) some right, title, or interest in real property.

Quitclaim and Warranty Deeds. Two types of deeds are in general use in the United States: the quitclaim and the warranty deed. When the grantor conveys by a quitclaim deed, he conveys to the grantee whatever title he has at the time he executes the deed, but he does not, by the form of the deed, claim to have good title or, in fact, any title; and if the title proves to be defective, or if the grantor has no title, the grantee has no action against him or her under the deed. Quitclaim deeds are frequently used to cure a technical defect in the chain of title to property. In such a case the grantor may claim no right, title, or interest in the property.

A warranty deed may be a deed of general warranty or of special warranty. A warranty deed contains covenants of warranty; that is, the grantor, in addition to conveying title to the property, binds himself or herself to make good any defects in the title he or she has conveyed. In a general warranty deed the grantor warrants against all defects in the title and all encumbrances, whereas in a special warranty deed the grantor warrants against only those defects in the title or those encumbrances which arose after he or she acquired the property. If the property conveyed is mortgaged or subject to some other encumbrance, such as an easement or long-term lease, it is a common practice to give a general warranty deed which contains a provision excepting specific encumbrances from the warranty.

Form and Execution of Deed. Some states have enacted statutes setting out the form of deed which may be used in that state. These statutes have been held to be directive, not mandatory; that is, a deed may be valid even though it does not follow the statutory form. The statutory requirements of the different states for the execution of deeds are not uniform, but they do follow a similar pattern. As a general rule a deed states the name of the grantee, contains a recitation of consideration and a description of the property conveyed, and is executed by the grantor. In most states the deed, to be eligible for recording, must be acknowledged by the grantor before a notary public or other officer authorized to take acknowledgment.

No technical words of conveyance are necessary; any language is sufficient which indicates with reasonable certainty an intent to transfer the ownership of the property. The phrase "give, grant, bargain, and sell" and the phrase "convey and warrant" are in common use.

A consideration is recited in a deed for historical reasons. At an early time in England, if the deed did not recite a consideration, the presumption was that the grantee held the land in trust for the heirs of the grantor, and for that reason it became standard practice to recite a consideration in the deed. The consideration recited is not necessarily the purchase price of the real property; it may be "one dollar and other valuable consideration."

The property conveyed must be described in such a manner that it can be identified. In urban areas, descriptions are as a general rule by lot, block, and plat. In rural areas the land, if it has been surveyed by the government, is usually described by reference to the government survey; otherwise, it is described by metes and bounds.

Delivery is essential to the validity of a deed. Whether or not a deed has been delivered is, in cases of dispute, a question of fact. If a person executes deeds to his or her real property and puts them in his or her safe-deposit box together with a note directing that the deeds be delivered to named persons after his or her death, the deeds are inoperative and pass no title by delivery after the death of the grantor. A deed, to be valid, must be delivered in the lifetime of the grantor.

Recording Deeds. The states have recording statutes which establish a system for the recording of all transactions affecting the ownership of real property. The statutes are not uniform in their provisions; but in general, they provide for the recording of all deeds, mortgages, and other such documents, and further provide an unrecorded transfer is void as against an innocent purchaser or mortgagee for value. Under this system, it is customary in some states for the seller to give the buyer an abstract of title certified to date. The abstract is a history of the title of the real property according to the records and is not a guarantee of title. The buyer, for his or her own protection, should have the abstract examined by a competent attorney who will render an opinion as to the title held by the grantor. The opinion will state whether or not the grantor has a merchantable title to the property; and if the title is defective, the nature of the defects will be stated. In many states the buyer obtains this protection by acquiring title insurance; in many cases where the purchase of the property is being financed by a third party, the lender will require a policy of title insurance for the lender's protection.

Several of the states have adopted the "Torrens system." Under this system the person who owns the land in fee will obtain, through the procedure set up by the statute, a certificate of title from the designated official; and when the real property is sold, the grantor will deliver a deed and his or her certificate of title to the grantee, who delivers the deed and certificate of title to the designated official and receives a new certificate of title. All liens and encumbrances against the property will be noted on the certificate of title, and the purchaser is assured that his or her title is good except as to liens and encumbrances noted on it. In some states, some encumbrances, such as liens for taxes, short-term leases, and highway rights, are good against the purchaser even though they do not appear on the certificate.

Warranties in the Sale of a House. Traditionally, unless there was an express warranty of the habitibility or condition of a house, or unless there was some fraud or misrepresentation involved, the purchaser of a house was subject to the doctrine of *caveat emptor.* This was based on the fact that buyer and seller dealt at arm's length and the buyer had the opportunity to acquaint himself with the condition and quality of the property he or she was acquiring. Thus, the buyer either had to obtain an express warranty as to quality, or he or she took at his or her own risk.

Recently, several courts have abandoned the *caveat emptor* doctrine in the sale of new homes by builder-sellers as far as latent defects are concerned and have adopted the doctrine of *caveat venditor.* This tends to put the buyer of a new home in roughly the same position the buyer of goods is in: the buyer gets an implied warranty of merchantable fitness or habitibility. The court decisions to date have not dealt with the quality of the reality itself, but rather they have separated out the new home and treated it like any other manufactured product.

Other courts have imposed a duty on sellers of property to disclose any known defects in the premises which are not discoverable by reasonable inspection by the buyer. If the seller does not make such disclosure, such silence may be held to constitute misrepresentation.

SUMMARY

Any agreement affecting an interest in land and a conveyance of real property is required to be in writing.

Two forms of deed are in general use in the United States: the quitclaim deed and the warranty deed. In a quitclaim deed the grantor conveys his or her interest, whatever it may be. In a warranty deed the grantor conveys his or her interest and, in addition, warrants the title to be free from all defects except those stated in the deed.

A deed, to be valid, must comply with certain formal requirements. These requirements are not uniform, but as a general rule the deed must name the grantee, contain words of conveyance, recite a consideration, describe the property, and be executed by the grantor. It will usually be acknowledged, may be sealed and witnessed, and must be delivered.

Tristram's Landing, Inc. v. Wait

327 N.E.2d 727 (Sup. Jud. Ct. Mass. 1975)

This was an action brought by Tristram's Landing, Inc. (plaintiff) against Wait (defendant) to recover a real estate brokerage commission alleged to be due. Judgment for Tristram's Landing. Reversed on appeal.

Tristram's Landing is a real estate broker doing business in Nantucket. Wait owned real estate on the island which she desired to sell. In the past

Tristram acted as broker for Wait when she rented the same premises. Tristram heard that Wait's property was for sale and in the spring of 1972 an agent for Tristram telephoned Wait and asked for authority to show it. Wait agreed that Tristram could act as broker, although not as exclusive broker, and told the agent that the price for the property was $110,000. At no time during the conversation or during any of the dealings between Tristram and Wait was there any mention of a commission. Tristram knew that the normal brokerage commission in Nantucket was five percent of the sale price.

Tristram produced a Mrs. Cushman who entered a purchase agreement with Wait to buy Wait's property for $105,000 and a closing date of October 1 was set. The agreement contained a clause that provided: "It is understood that a broker's commission of five (5) percent on the said sale is to be paid to the broker by the said seller." Cushman did not show up for the closing and refused to go through with the sale. Tristram presented Wait with a bill for commission in the amount of $5,250 which Wait refused to pay.

TAURO, CHIEF JUDGE. The general rule regarding whether a broker is entitled to a commission from one attempting to sell real estate is that, absent special circumstances, the broker "is entitled to a commission if he produces a customer, ready, able, and willing to buy upon the terms and for the price given the broker by the owner." In the past this rule has been construed to mean that once a customer is produced by the broker and accepted by the seller, the commission is earned, whether or not the sale is actually consummated. Furthermore, execution of a purchase and sale agreement is usually seen as conclusive evidence of seller's acceptance of the buyer. We believe, however, that it is both appropriate and necessary at this time to clarify the law, and we now join the growing minority of States who have adopted the rule of *Ellsworth Dobbs, Inc. v. Johnson.*

In the *Ellsworth* case, the New Jersey court faced the task of clarifying the law regarding the legal relationships between sellers and brokers in real estate transactions. In order to formulate a just and proper rule, the court examined the realities of such transactions. The court noted that "ordinarily when an owner of property lists it with a broker for sale, his expectation is that the money for the payment of commission will come out of the proceeds of the sale." It quoted with approval from the opinion of Lord Justice Denning, in *Dennis Read, Ltd. v. Goody,* where he stated: "When a house owner puts his house into the hands of an estate agent, the ordinary understanding is that the agent is only to receive a commission if he succeeds in effecting a sale. . . . The common understanding of men is . . . that the agent's commission is payable out of the purchase price. . . . The house-owner wants to find a man who will actually buy his house and pay for it. He does not want a man who will only make an offer or sign a contract. He wants a purchaser 'able to purchase and able to complete as well.' "

The court went on to say that the principle binding "the seller to pay commission if he signs a contract of sale with the broker's customer, regardless of the customer's financial ability, puts the burden on the wrong shoulders. Since the broker's duty to the owner is to produce a prospective buyer who is financially able to pay the purchase price and take title, a right in the owner to assume such capacity when the broker presents his purchaser ought to be recognized." Reason and justice dictate that it should be the broker who bears the burden of producing a purchaser who is not only ready, willing and able at the time of the negotiations, but who also consummates the sale at the time of closing.

Thus, we adopt the following rules: "When a broker is engaged by an owner of property to find a purchaser for it, the broker earns his commission when (*a*) he produces a purchaser ready, willing and able to buy on the terms fixed by the owner, (*b*) the purchaser enters into a binding contract with the owner to do so, and (*c*) the purchaser completes the transaction by closing the title in accordance with the provisions of the contract. If the contract is not consummated because of lack of financial ability of the buyer to perform or because of any other default of his . . . there is no right to commission against the seller. On the other hand, if the failure of completion of the contract results from the wrongful act or interference of the seller, the broker's claim is valid and must be paid."

Accordingly, we hold that a real estate broker, under a brokerage agreement hereafter made, is entitled to a commission from the seller only if the requirements stated above are met. This rule provides necessary protection for the seller and places the burden with the broker, where it belongs.

We recognize that this rule could be easily circumvented by language to the contrary in purchase and sale agreements or in agreements between sellers and brokers. In many States a signed writing is required for an agreement to pay a commission to a real estate broker. Such a requirement may be worthy of legislative consideration, but we do not think we should establish such a requirement by judicial decision. Informal agreements fairly made between people of equal skill and understanding serve a useful purpose. But many sellers, unlike brokers, are involved in real estate transactions infrequently, perhaps only once in a lifetime, and are thus unfamiliar with their legal rights. In such cases agreements by the seller to pay a commission even though the purchaser defaults are to be carefully scrutinized. If not fairly made, such agreements may be unconscionable or against public policy.

Smith v. Old Warson Development Co.

479 S.W.2d 795 (Sup. Ct. Mo., 1972)

This was an action brought by Frank and Catherine Smith (plaintiffs) against the Old Warson Development Company (defendant) to recover damages sustained by the abnormal settling of a new house sold to the Smiths by defendant. The trial court granted Old Warson's motion for a directed verdict and the Smiths appealed. Reversed and remanded. The Court of Appeals filed an opinion reversing the trial court and then transferred the case up to the Supreme Court which affirmed the action the Court of Appeals had taken.

Old Warson Development Co. owned a tract of land in St. Louis which it subdivided for sale as residential lots. It had a home constructed on one of the lots which it sold to the Smiths in February of 1963. The sales contract contained the following provisions:

Property to be accepted in its present condition unless otherwise stated in contract. Seller warrants that he has not received any written notification from any governmental agency requiring any repairs, replacements, or alterations to said premises which have not been satisfactorily made. This is the entire contract and neither party shall be bound by representation as to value or otherwise unless set forth in contract.

Within a few months the Smiths noticed that the doors in a section of the house containing a bedroom and bathroom were sticking. Soon they noticed the caulked space between the bathtub and wall was enlarged. Eventually a space developed between the baseboard and the floor, and cracks developed in the wall. All problems were limited to the two rooms, which were constructed on a four-inch concrete slab, completely surrounded by but not attached to, foundation walls. The remainder of the house rested on a foundation and experienced no difficulties. The slab had settled or sunk as much as 1¾ inches. Although the builder made some attempts to repair the visual problems, there was no attempt to correct the basic problem—the settling of the slab.

MORGAN, JUDGE. We accepted transfer of this cause after the filing of an opinion by the Court of Appeals, St. Louis District, because the result reached therein evidenced a departure, although limited, from a strict application of the doctrine of *caveat emptor.* The court's reasoning was expressed in an opinion by Smith, J., which was as follows:

This appeal presents squarely the question of whether implied warranties of merchantable quality and fitness exist in the purchase of a new home by the first purchaser from a vendor-builder. We hold such warranties do exist.

Although considered to be a "real estate" transaction because the ownership to land is transferred, the purchase of a residence is in most cases the purchase of a manufactured product—the house. The land involved is seldom the prime element in such a purchase, certainly not in the urban areas of the state. The structural quality of a house, by its very nature, is nearly impossible to determine by inspection after the house is built, since many of the most important elements of its construction are hidden from view. The ordinary "consumer" can determine little about the soundness of the construction but must rely upon the fact that the vendor-builder holds the structure out to the public as fit for use as a residence, and of being of reasonable quality. Certainly in the case here no determination of the existence of the defect could have been made without ripping out the slab which settled, and maybe not even then. The home here was new and was purchased from the company which built it for sale. The defect here was clearly latent and not capable of discovery by even a careful inspection. Defendant was the developer of the subdivision in which the house was located, and built this home to demonstrate to the public the type of quality residence which could be erected in the subdivision. It was held to the public as "luxurious" and was shown as a model to the public. Common sense tells us that a purchaser under these circumstances should have at least as much protection as the purchaser of a new car, or a gas stove, or a sump pump, or a ladder.

We turn to the "present condition" provision of the contract, and respondent's contention that that provision excluded any implied warranties. On its face it does not indicate that it has reference to implied warranties. Respondent contends that the language "Property to be accepted in its present condition unless otherwise stated in contract" is an exclusion of warranties. We cannot so interpret it. The reasonable interpretation of that provision is that vendor assumes no obligation to do any additional work on the house unless specified. Such a provision would preclude purchasers from insisting that the vendor promised to paint the house a different color, or add a room, or retile a bathroom or correct an obvious defect. We do not believe a reasonable person would interpret that provision as an agreement by the purchaser to accept the house with an unknown latent structural defect.

Public Controls on the Use of Land

While the owner of an interest in real property may generally make such use of his property as he desires, he does not have an unlimited right to do so. Society places a number of restraints on the owner of real property: (1) The owner cannot use his or her property in such a way as to unduly injure others; (2) through the use of the "police power," governmental units have the right to impose reasonable regulations on the use of property; and (3) society retains the right to divest ownership through the power of eminent domain.

Nuisance Control. When different uses are made of separate parcels of land, those uses may come into conflict and one or more of the users may become very unhappy. For example, the owner of a grove of orange trees finds that the dust from a nearby cement mill is forming a crust on his oranges, or the owner of a drive-in movie finds that the spotlights at a nearby auto racetrack are interfering with his patrons' enjoyment of the movies, or a housewife finds the noise from a nearby airport is interfering with her peace of mind. In some cases the courts have granted damages and injunctive relief to such aggrieved persons on the grounds that the use on the other property constitutes a nuisance which interferes substantially with the enjoyment of the property of the aggrieved person.

Nuisances may be divided into private and public. A private nuisance is created when a landowner's use or enjoyment of his land is lessened substantially due to unjustifiable conduct on the part of another. A public nuisance involves a broader class of affected parties and the action to abate it usually must be brought in the name of the public by the government; private parties can normally sue to abate a public nuisance where they can show a unique harm different from that suffered by the public in general. The conduct creating the nuisance may be either intentional or negligent. In a few situations liability may be imposed due to the extra-hazardous activity of the defendant even though neither intent nor negligence are present. The fact that the conduct or use of land by a neighbor hinders an owner from putting his land to a special or "delicate use" does not mean the owner hindered can enjoin the conduct. Nuisance actions involve a balancing of the various interests and rights involved. For example, the courts may weigh the social utility of the objectionable conduct and the burden of abating it versus the degree to which the conduct is infringing on the rights of other property owners.

Zoning and Subdivision Ordinances. State legislatures commonly delegate to political subdivisions the police power to impose reasonable regulations designed to promote the public health, safety, morals, and the general welfare of the community. Zoning ordinances are an exercise of such a power to regulate. Normally, zoning ordinances divide the political subdivision into a number of districts, specify or limit the use to which property in those districts can be put, and restrict improvements and use on the land.

Such restrictions and controls may be of four basis types:

1. Control of Use. Regulation of the activity on the land such as single family dwellings, multi-family dwellings, commercial, light industry or heavy industry.
2. Control of Height and Bulk. Control of the height of buildings, the setback from front, side, and rear lot lines, and the portion of a lot that can be covered by a building.
3. Control of Population Density. Control over the amount of living space that must be provided for each person and specification of the maximum number of persons who can be housed in a given area.
4. Control of Aesthetics. Commonly used to control billboards, but also may be used to enforce similarity and dissimilarity of buildings as well as to preserve historical areas or communities.

When zoning ordinances are passed they have only a prospective effect so that already existing uses and buildings are permitted to continue. However, the ordinance may provide for the gradual phasing out of such uses and buildings that do not conform to the general zoning plan. If a property owner later wants to use his property in a way other than that which is permitted by the zoning ordinance, he must try to have the ordinance amended by showing that his proposed changes are in accordance with the overall plan or by obtaining a variance on the ground the ordinance creates an undue hardship on him by depriving him of the opportunity to make a reasonable use of his land. Such attempts to obtain amendments or variances often conflict with the interests of other nearby property owners who have a vested interest in the zoning status quo and produce heated battles before the zoning authorities.

Many local governments also have ordinances dealing with proposed subdivisions. The ordinances often require that the developer meet certain requirements as to lot size, street and sidewalk layout, and provision for sanitary facilities, and that the city approve the proposed development. In addition, the ordinance may in some cases require the developer to dedicate land to the city for streets, parks, and schools. The purpose of such ordinances is to protect the would-be purchasers in the subdivision as well as the city population as a whole by ensuring that minimum standards are met by the developer.

Some urban planners feel that it is undesirable to totally segregate the living, working, shopping, and entertainment areas as is commonly done with a zoning scheme. They argue that a more livable environment is one that mixes these uses so as to insure the vitality of an area for the vast part of each day. In response to this philosophy, cities and counties are allowing "planned unit developments" and "new towns" which mix such uses so long as the plans are submitted to the authorities and approved pursuant to general guidelines established for such developments.

People are also becoming more aware of the shortcomings of making our land-use decisions on a piecemeal basis at the local level. Airports, major shopping centers, highways, and new towns require a regional, rather than local, planning focus. Moreover, sensitive ecological areas, such as marshes, can readily be destroyed if encroached upon in a piecemeal manner. Accordingly, a number of states and the federal government have passed, or are considering, legislation to put some land-use planning on a regional or a statewide basis.

Eminent Domain. The Constitution provides that private property shall not be taken for public use without just compensation. Implicit in this statement is the power of the state to take property for public use by paying "just compensation" to the owner of the property. This power of eminent domain makes possible our highways, water control projects, municipal and civic centers, public housing, and urban renewal.

Currently, there are several major problems inherent in the use of the eminent domain power. The first is what is meant by "just compensation." A property owner now receives the "fair market value" of his property; but some people feel that this falls short of reimbursing the owner for what he has lost since it does not cover the lost "goodwill" of a business or the emotional attachment a person may have to his home.

A second problem is deciding when a "taking" has occurred. The answer is easy where the owner is completely dispossessed by a governmental unit. It is much more difficult where (1) the zoning power has been utilized to restrict the permissible use of a given piece of property only for a narrow and publicly beneficial use, such as a parking lot, or (2) where the government uses nearby land in such a way as to almost completely destroy the usefulness of adjoining, privately owned land as sometimes occurs in the case of municipal airports.

A third problem is determining when the eminent domain power can be properly exercised. Clearly where the governmental unit itself uses the property, as in the case of municipal building or a public highway, the use of the power is proper. However, where as in the case of urban renewal, the condemned property may be resold to a private developer or the condemned property is not substandard, the use of the power is not so clearly justified.

SUMMARY

Society places a number of restraints on the ownership of real property. First, a person may not create a nuisance on his property such that it unreasonably interferes with another person's enjoyment of his own land. Second, legislative bodies may use the constitutionally provided police power to impose reasonable regulations on property designed to promote the public health, safety, morals and general welfare. Third, the government through the eminent domain power may divest ownership entirely of property it desires to use for public purposes by paying just compensation to the private owner.

Spur Industries, Inc. v. Del E. Webb Development Co.

4 Envir. Rep. Cases 1052 (Sup. Ct. Ariz. 1972)

This was an action brought by Del E. Webb Development Company (plaintiff) against Spur Industries, Inc., (defendant) to enjoin the operation of Spur Industries' feedlot on the grounds it constituted a nuisance substantially interfering with the homeowners' enjoyment of their property in a retirement community developed by Del Webb. A judgment granting a permanent injunction was appealed by Spur and cross appealed by Webb. Judgment was affirmed in part and reversed in part.

In 1956 Spur's predecessor began operating a small cattle-feeding operation of some 6,000 to 7,000 head in an area that included about 25 cattle pens within a 7-mile radius. About one-and-a-half miles away was the city of Youngstown, a retirement community appealing primarily to senior citizens. In 1959 Del Webb acquired some 20,000 acres, a portion of which was located between Youngstown and Spur's predecessor's property, and began to build Sun City, a retirement community. In 1960 Spur acquired the feedlot and began expanding the acreage from 35 to 114 acres and by 1967 was feeding between 20,000 and 30,000 head of cattle. Del Webb in the meantime had acquired additional property between his original acreage and the Spur operation which Webb intended to sell as residential lots. There was considerable sales resistance to about 1,300 lots in the area closest to the Spur operation. Del Webb then brought suit against the Spur feeding operation, complaining that it constituted a public nuisance because of the flies and the odors which drifted or were blown over onto the Webb property. Webb contended that even with good feedlot management the citizens of Sun City were unable to enjoy the outdoor living they had been promised, and that the feedlot should be enjoined.

CAMERON, VICE CHIEF JUSTICE. Although numerous issues are raised, we feel that it is necessary to answer only two questions. They are:

1. Where the operation of a business, such as a cattle feedlot is lawful in the first instance, but becomes a nuisance by reason of a nearby residential area, may the feedlot operation be enjoined in an action brought by the developer of the residential area?
2. Assuming that the nuisance may be enjoined, may the developer of a completely new town or urban area in a previously agricultural area be required to indemnify the operator of the feedlot who must move or cease operation because of the presence of the residential area created by the developer?

The difference between a private nuisance and a public nuisance is generally one of degree. A private nuisance is one affecting a single individual or a definite small number of persons in the enjoyment of private rights not common to the public, while a public nuisance is one affecting the rights enjoyed by citizens as a part of the public. To constitute a public nuisance, the nuisance must affect a considerable number of people or an entire community or neighborhood.

Where the injury is slight, the remedy for minor inconveniences lies in an action for damages rather than in one for an injunction. Moreover, some courts have held, in the "balancing of conveniences" cases, that damages may be the sole remedy.

Thus it would appear from the admittedly incomplete record as developed in the trial court, that, at most, residents of Youngstown would be entitled to damages rather than injunctive relief.

We have no difficulty, however, in agreeing with the conclusion of the trial court that Spur's operation was an enjoinable public nuisance as far as the people in the southern portion of Del Webb's Sun City were concerned.

There was no indication in the instant case at the time Spur and its predecessors located in western Maricopa County that a new city would spring up, full blown, alongside the feeding operation and that the developer of that city would ask the court to order Spur to move because of the new city. Spur is required to move not because of any wrongdoing on the part of Spur, but because of a proper and legitimate regard of the courts for the rights and interests of the public.

Del Webb, on the other hand, is entitled to the relief prayed for (a permanent injunction) not because Webb is blameless, but because of the damage to the people who have been encouraged to purchase homes in Sun City. It does not equitably or legally follow, however, that Webb, being entitled to the injunction, is free of any liability to Spur if Webb has in fact been the cause of damage Spur has sustained. It does not seem harsh to require a developer who has taken advantage of the lesser land values in a rural area as well as the availability of large tracts of land on which to build and develop a new town or city in the area, to indemnify those who are forced to leave as a result.

Having brought people to the nuisance to the foreseeable detriment of Spur, Webb must indemnify Spur for a reasonable amount of the cost of moving or shutting down. It should be noted that this relief to Spur is limited to a case wherein a developer has, with foreseeability, brought into a previously agricultural or industrial area the population which makes necessary the granting of an injunction against a lawful business and for which the business has no adequate relief.

Ferguson v. City of Keene

238 A.2d 1 (Sup. Ct. N.H. 1968)

This was an action by Ferguson (plaintiff) to recover for injury to her property from the noise and vibration emanating from the airport owned by the City of Keene (defendant). The trial court refused to hold as a matter of law that Ferguson had no cause of action in "inverse condemnation." The Supreme Court reversed, holding that no claim of inverse condemnation was stated, but that Ferguson had stated a cause of action in nuisance.

The airport had been established in 1942 and Ferguson acquired her property in 1947. In 1956 the airport was enlarged and part of Ferguson's property was taken for this purpose. Ferguson alleged that the use of a "warm-up apron" located opposite her house resulted in such noise and vibration as to cause windows to break, to make conversation or sleep in the house impossible, and life generally unbearable. She further alleged that this use of the airport constituted a taking of her property for which she was required to be compensated.

DUNCAN, JUSTICE. It is the settled law of this jurisdiction that a municipality, like any property owner, is bound to use its property in a reasonable manner, and is liable if its use results in a private nuisance. The City of Keene contends, however, that no taking of Ferguson's property can properly be alleged, since she admits that the flight path of aircraft does not cross it, and damage alone without an actual taking requires no compensation. The City further argues that its use of the airport is "proper," and that subjection of airports to liability for claims such as this would unduly impede the progress of air transportation in the state. Ferguson asserts that the allegations of its writ include all of the classic elements of nuisance, and also that the City's conduct of the airport gives rise to a cause of action for "inverse condemnation," even though no overflights occur.

Inverse condemnation is a term used to describe "a cause of action against a governmental defendant to recover the value of property which has been taken in fact by the governmental defendant, even though no formal exercise of the power of eminent domain has been attempted by the taking agency."

Pertinent cases decided by the United States Supreme Court have not gone beyond the point of holding that there may be recovery in inverse condemnation for damages occasioned by direct flights of aircraft over a claimant's property. *U.S. v. Causby.* As was pointed out in Dunham, *Griggs v. Allegheny County* in *Perspective: Thirty Years of Supreme Court Expropriation Laws:* "The question whether those (claimants) adjacent to airports, but not in any flight path, should be compensated thus remains an open one so far as the Supreme Court decisions are concerned. But the logic of *Causby* and its idea of fairness would seem to require compensation even where planes do not fly directly over the objector's land." However, in *Batten v. United States,* the Court of Appeals declined to extend the doctrine to a case where overflights did not occur, relying upon the proposition that the federal Constitution requires compensation for a "taking" only.

Since there is hardly a government act which could not cause someone substantial damage, an arbitrary boundary line must be drawn between compensable and noncompensable injury." Under the federal Constitution, the line has been drawn at compensation for a taking of property. "The Fifth Amendment . . . requires just compensation where private property is taken for public use . . . (but) does not undertake . . . to socialize all losses.

A genuine distinction may reasonably be thought to exist between the nature of the injury suffered by the owner whose land is subjected to direct overflight, and that suffered by his neighbor whose land is not beneath the flight path. Only the former has lost the use of the airspace above his land, and he is subjected to risks of physical damage and injury not shared by the latter.

To what extent the nuisance of which Ferguson complains is essential to the public use of the City's airport is a question which is not determinable at this stage of this litigation. The question whether a defendant in circumstances such as these should be compelled by inverse condemnation to acquire an "easement" and compensate Ferguson therefore presents issues of social policy which might well be the subject of legislative study and appropriate enactment.

GRIMES, JUSTICE (dissenting). Ferguson's writ alleges that

the noise from the planes "warming up" for take off, make such a great amount of noise that it is impossible for the people in the house to converse or talk on the telephone, the house vibrates and the glass in the windows shake and that more than 20 panes of glass have been broken by said vibration in the winter of 1963–1964, that it is often times impossible to sleep and there is no peace or quiet in their home and that life has become unbearable because of said noise.

The majority of the court says this declaration does not set forth a cause of action based on inverse condemnation. I disagree.

Our court long ago decided that in our state at least, the term "property" refers to "the right of any person to possess, use, enjoy, and dispose of a thing" and is not limited to the thing itself, and that a person's property is "taken" for public use so as to entitle him to "just compensation" under our Constitution when a physical interference substantially subverts one of these rights even though the thing itself is not taken.

I am unimpressed with the rationale of those cases which confine inverse condemnation to overflights. A person's property rights can be damaged as greatly by sound waves traveling horizontally as by those traveling vertically, and to draw a distinction is to ignore reality.

We are dealing here with an important and fundamental individual right, the roots of which reach back to Magna Carta. It is one which deserves to be stoutly defended and liberally construed. It is one which we should not deny to Ferguson because the means by which her property was taken was neither known to nor foreseen by the Barons of England or the Framers of our Constitution.

The court while denying the constitutional right has at least recognized that Ferguson has set forth a cause of action based on nuisance. This I think is a poor substitute from the standpoint of both parties.

Problem Cases

1. Foskett mortgaged five acres of land that he owned to Commercial Credit Corporation. He then purchased a mobile home, which he placed on the land. He had the wheels removed from the mobile home and placed it on cinder blocks. He also connected it with a well, electric power lines, and septic tank. He subsequently became insolvent and bankruptcy proceedings were begun. The bankruptcy trustee claimed he was entitled to the mobile home because it was personal property and thus subject to seizure as part of the bankruptcy estate. Commercial Credit Corporation claimed the mobile home had become a fixture and was subject to its mortgage lien. Should the home be considered personal property or a fixture?

2. Wolff rented a house from Realty Company. Realty Company gave Wolff written permission to install an oil-burning unit in the furnace, the oil burner to remain the property of Wolff with the right to remove it when he surrendered possession of the house. Realty Company sold the house to Sarafin. When Wolff moved he moved the oil burner and restored the furnace to its original condition. Sarafin sued Wolff to recover the value of the oil burner on the ground that it was a fixture and was his property. Is Sarafin entitled to a judgment?

3. On October 1, 1966, Carl Cantonwine executed five promissory notes, each in the amount of $3,000 and payable on demand "to Frank Fehling and Winniebell Fehling." Frank Fehling was Cantonwine's uncle and was the husband of Winniebell. On October 20, 1966, Frank Fehling executed a will which provided in part that:

   I hereby give, devise and bequeath to my nephew, Carl Cantonwine, his heirs and assigns, of Spotted Horse, Wyoming, if he survives me, the sum of Ten Thousand ($10,000.00) Dollars, and I direct my Executors hereinafter named to forgive any indebtedness which the said, Carl Cantonwine, and/or his wife may owe me at the time of my death and to fully cancel and satisfy said indebtedness.

Frank Fehling died on January 22, 1968, and his will was admitted to probate in the State of Colorado on May 23, 1968. Winnie, the coexecutor of Frank's estate, brought suit against Cantonwine to recover one half of the promissory notes. Winnie claimed that her husband's will had forgiven one half of the indebtedness but that she was entitled to one half which Cantonwine had refused to pay. Cantonwine contended that all the debt was forgiven by the will. How should the court decide?

4. Sewell and Reilly owned adjoining lots. They entered into a written agreement whereby each agreed to allow the other to use the south ten feet of his lot for alley purposes "for so long as the alley" over the other party's lot remained open. Did this agreement create an easement or a license?

5. Flynn and Korsalk own adjoining lots, and a strip of land 11 to 12 feet wide separates the houses on the lots. The distance from Flynn's house to the boundary is 7½ feet. Flynn's predecessor in title, Mrs. Brewer, and her husband owned automobiles from 1927 to 1949 and drove them on the strip, including the portion owned by their neighbors, because it could not be avoided and because it was impossible to tell where the lot line was. Flynn purchased the property from the Brewers in 1949 and continued to drive across the strip. Korsalk purchased the other lot in 1948, began protesting Flynn's driving on his land in 1952, and in 1954 erected a chain link fence on the lot line which effectively prevented Flynn from driving his car across the strip to get to his garage. Flynn seeks an injunction ordering Korsalk to remove the fence and other obstructions in the driveway and to enjoin him from placing obstructions in the future. Should the injunction be granted?

6. The Schlemeyers purchased a frame apartment house in 1954 and discovered shortly after the purchase that there was a substantial termite infestation. They undertook some of the steps suggested by a specialist in pest control but did not take all of the measures he indicated would be necessary to make sure of success. In 1960 the Schlemeyers sold the apartment house to Fred Obde but did not advise him of the termite condition. When Obde later discovered the termite infestation, he brought an action for damages against the Schlemeyers contending that they fraudulently concealed the infestation from him and were under a duty to disclose it. Can Obde recover?

7. In 1956 Mowrer capped an oil well on his property that had previously produced oil but was no longer considered productive. In September 1955, before Mowrer's well was capped, Ashland Oil & Refining Company commenced waterflood operations on land adjacent to Mowrer's, which consisted of injecting salt water at high pressure into the oil strata to force the remaining oil from the oil sands into its operating wells. The waterflood operation had been authorized and approved by the Oil and Gas Division of the Indiana Department of Conservation pursuant to the statutory requirements. In 1958 and again in 1959 or 1960, long after the plugging of the well on Mowrer's land in 1956, crude oil was found seeping out on Mowrer's land at ground level around that well, and in July 1963, crude oil leaked into and contaminated the nearby fresh water well that supplied Mowrer's domestic water. Mowrer brought suit against Ashland, contending that Ashland's action constituted a nuisance. Can Mowrer recover damages on the basis of these facts?

8. In 1971, Buyer acquired a piece of property in the City of Mount Vernon. While the property was surrounded completely by business buildings, it had been zoned for residential use in 1927 and the parking of automobiles allowed as a nonconforming use since that

time. In 1972 the city council amended the zoning ordinance and placed Buyer's property in a zoning category known as "Designated Parking District" which prohibited all uses for the property except the parking and storage of automobiles. Buyer wants to erect a retail shopping center on the property. He claims that the effect of the zoning ordinance is to destroy the greater part of the value of his property and amounts to a taking of private property without just compensation. On these grounds he sues the city to have the ordinance declared unconstitutional. The city claims that the zoning ordinance limiting Buyer's property to the parking of automobiles is necessary because of parking and traffic congestion in the community and that it allows him to make some use of his property. How should the case be decided?

9. Belle Terre is a village on the north shore of Long Island containing about 220 homes inhabited by 700 people in a land area of less than one square mile. Belle Terre has a zoning ordinance which restricts land-use to one-family dwellings and excludes lodging houses, boarding houses, fraternity houses, or multiple family dwellings. The word "family" was defined to mean "one or more persons related by blood or marriage, living and cooking together as a single household unit. A number of persons but not exceeding two (2) living and cooking together as a single housekeeping unit though not related by blood or marriage shall be deemed to constitute a marriage." The Dickmans leased a house in Belle Terre to two students; later four additional students moved into the house. The Village served an order on the Dickmans and the students to remedy the violation of the ordinance. They in turn filed an injunction against the ordinance, contending it was an improper exercise of the "police power" by the Village. How should the court decide the case?

10. The Northcuts bought a lot in North Miami Florida on what was a quiet residential street and constructed a house on it for approximately $40,000. Sometime later the State of Florida began construction of a limited access, federally financed interstate highway very close to their property. The residential side street was used as an access road to the highway by earth moving equipment, dump trucks, cement mixers, and bulldozers. Once the highway was completed, its use caused noise and vibration which the Northcuts claimed caused them to lose sleep, impaired their health, and severely depreciated the value of their property. The Northcuts then brought suit against the State claiming inverse condemnation of their property in that they had been permanently deprived of the benefit and enjoyment of the property without just compensation. Should the Northcuts be awarded compensation for a "taking" of their property?

33

Estates and Trusts

Introduction

Disposition of Property on Death of Owner. When a person dies, the law provides for the payment of his debts and the distribution of any remaining property in his estate to those who are entitled to it. The administration of a person's estate is generally handled under the supervision of a specialized court known as the probate court. If the deceased person does not make a will, his property will be distributed according to state laws known as statutes of descent and distribution or intestate succession. However, if the person makes a valid will that document will generally control the distribution of his or her property.

Dying Intestate. If a person dies without having made a will, or if the will is invalid, then the person is said to have died *intestate.* In that case his real property will be distributed according to the statutes of the state in which it is located, and his personal property will be distributed according to the statutes of the state in which he is domiciled. Generally any debts must be satisfied first out of the personal property.

The laws providing for distribution of an intestate's estate differ from state to state. Theoretically, the rationale of the intestate laws is to distribute the property in a way that reflects the desire of the deceased—that is to distribute it to those persons most closely related to him. In general, the statutes look first to see if the deceased person was survived by a wife, husband, children, or grandchildren and provides for at least some if not total distribution to them. The next focus is on any lineal (blood) descendants such as a mother, father, brother, sister, niece, or nephew. If the estate is not exhausted at this level, then distribution is made to collateral relatives. Collateral relatives are not direct descendants of the deceased person but are related to him through a common ancestor; for example: aunts, uncles, grandfathers, grandmothers, and cousins. Generally those persons who are the same degree removed from the descendant take equal shares. If the entire property is not distributed according to the statutory formula, the property that remains reverts or "escheats" to the state.

Example of Intestacy Law. An example of a statute of descent and distribution is the statute in effect in the District of Columbia. The outline of the D.C. statute is as follows:

(1) If the deceased person left a surviving spouse then:

(a) the spouse takes a ⅓ interest if the deceased person was also survived by children or their descendants;

(b) the spouse takes a ½ interest if the deceased was not survived by children or their descendants but was survived by a father, mother, brother, sister, niece or nephew.

(c) the surviving spouse takes everything if the deceased is not survived by children, grandchildren, father, mother, brother, sister, niece or nephew;

(2) Any surplus left beyond the share of the surviving spouse, or the entire surplus where there is no surviving spouse is distributed as follows:

(a) If there are children, the children take equal shares ("per capita") and children of any deceased children share equally the share their parent would have taken had he or she been alive ("per stirpes"):

(b) If there are no children or their descedants, then the mother and father, or the survivor, take the surplus;

(c) If there are no children, descendants of children, mother or father surviving, then the surplus is divided equally among the surviving brothers and sisters (per capita) with descendants of brothers or sisters splitting equally the share their parent would have taken had he or she been alive;

(3) If none of the previously mentioned persons are alive, then the surplus is distributed equally among the collateral relatives who are the nearest and same degree removed from the deceased. If there are no collateral relatives, the grandparents, or the survivor, take equal shares.

Special Rules. Under the intestacy laws, a person must have a blood relationship to the deceased in order to inherit part or all of his estate. "In-laws"—or persons related through marriage other than as a spouse—are not entitled to share in the estate. State law commonly extends the definition of "children" to include adopted children and treats them the same as natural children. Similarly, half brothers or sisters may be treated the same as those related by whole blood. Illegitimate children may inherit from their mother the same as natural children, but generally do not inherit from their father unless their paternity is either acknowledged or established in a legal proceeding.

Murder Disqualification. Many states provide that a person who is convicted of the homicide (murder or manslaughter) of another person may not inherit any of that person's property either by way of intestate succession or by will. A similar rule frequently applies to the ability of a person to share in the insurance proceeds on the life of a person he murders.

Generally a person must be alive at the time the decedent died in order to claim his statutory share of an intestate's estate: an exception may be made for children or descendants who are born after the intestate's death. If a person who is entitled to a share of another estate dies after the holder of that estate but before receiving his share of it, his share in that estate becomes part of his own estate.

Simultaneous Death. A statute known as the Uniform Simultaneous Death Act provides that where two persons, such as a husband and wife, die under circumstances that make it difficult or impossible to determine who died first, each person's property is to be distributed as though he or she survived.

Advancements. An advancement is a distribution of property during an intestate's lifetime that is intended by him to be a prepayment of the recipient's share of the intestate's property. The property so advanced is considered to be part of the intestate's estate in computing the shares to which the various heirs are entitled and then is deducted in determining the amount to be distributed to the heir who received the advancement.

SUMMARY

If a person dies intestate, that is, dies without having made a valid will, his property will be distributed according to the statutes of descent and distribution. His personal property will be distributed according to the statutes of the state in which he was domiciled, and his real property according to the statutes of the state in which it is located.

Wills

Right of Disposition by Will. The right to dispose of property by will is statutory. Under the feudal system of land tenure in England the king was the title owner of all the land, and the lords and knights held only a life estate in the land. On the death of a landholder, his rights in the land which he held terminated, and no rights in the land descended to his heirs. In 1215 the king granted to the nobility the right to pass their interest in the land which they held to their heirs.

Today, we recognize the theory of basic ownership by the state, and on the basis of this theory the courts have upheld the right of the state and the federal government to tax the estate of a deceased person and to tax an inheritance. Also, the right of the state to prescribe the formalities which must be complied with in the devising of property by will has been firmly established.

Execution of Will. A man who makes a will is known as a "testator" and a woman who makes one is a "testatrix." Although the statutes concerning wills are not uniform in the different states, they are similar in their basic requirements. The courts have been strict in interpreting these statutes, and they will declare a will to be void unless all the requirements of the statute have been complied with in the execution of the will, in which case the property of the deceased will be distributed according to the statutes of descent and distribution.

Only persons of sound mind and of legal age are permitted to dispose of property by will. The required formalities vary with the different states, and the laws of the states which may affect the will should be consulted before the will is executed. Formalities which are required by many states are: (1) The will must be in writing; (2) it must be witnessed by two or three "disinterested" witnesses—persons who do not stand to take any share under the will; (3) it must be signed and sealed by the testator; (4) it must be published by the testator—as a general rule, all that is required for publication is a declaration by the testator, at the time of signing, that the instrument is his will; and (5) the testator must sign in the presence and in the sight of the witnesses, and the witnesses must sign in the presence and in the sight of the testator and in the presence and in the sight of each other. If the statutory formalities are not all complied with, the will is not valid. As a general rule an attestation clause, stating the formalities which have been followed in the execution of the will, is written following the testator's signature. A will procured by fraud or undue influence will not be accepted as a valid will.

Some states recognize the validity of holographic wills, and some recognize the validity of nuncupative wills. A holographic will is one which is wholly written, signed, and sealed in the testator's or testatrix's own hand. The statutes of a few states recognize these wills as valid without formal execution or attestation. A nuncupative will is an oral will. In many states the oral wills made by sailors at sea or by soldiers in actual service are recognized as valid for the purpose of disposing of the personal estate in the actual possession of the testator at the time of the making of the will.

Limitations on Disposition by Will. A person who takes property by will takes it subject to all outstanding claims against the property, both legal and equitable. Also, the rights of creditors are superior to the rights of a beneficiary under the will. If the deceased person is insolvent, persons named as beneficiary take nothing by virtue of the will.

Under the laws of most states the widow or widower of the deceased has statutory rights in the property of the deceased spouse which cannot be defeated by will. As a general rule a widow is given the right to claim certain personal property of the deceased husband, is given the right to the use of the home for a stated period, usually a year, and is given a portion of his real estate or a life estate in a portion of his real estate. In many states the widow's share in the husband's real property is a one-third interest or a life estate in one third of his real property. In some states the husband of a deceased wife is given an interest in her property, and this right cannot be defeated by will. In the community property states, each spouse has a one-half interest in the community property, and the rights of the surviving spouse cannot be defeated by will.

Revocation of Will. One distinguishing feature of a will is that it conveys no interest in the maker's property until his death and the will has been probated. All wills are revocable at the option of the maker; and a will, at the time it is executed, does not confer any present rights in the property devised or bequeathed. A person may revoke his will by destroying or canceling it or by making a later will, duly executed, in which he expressly states that he thereby revokes all former wills executed by him. Under the statutes of the state, certain changes in relationship may operate as a revocation of a will. In some states the marriage of a man or a woman will revoke a will made by such person while single. Similarly, a divorce and property settlement may revoke gifts to the divorced spouse in a previously executed will. The birth of a child after the execution of the will may, under the laws of some states, revoke a will or operate as a partial revocation of a will.

Codicils. A person may amend a will without executing an entire new will by executing a "codicil" to his will with the same formalities that are required for the execution of a will. If validly executed, a codicil has the effect of "republishing" the earlier will.

SUMMARY

A person may dispose of his property by will if he executes it in compliance with the statutory formalities which normally include that it be in writing, that it be witnessed, and that it be published and signed by the testator in the presence of the witnesses. A will procured by fraud or undue influence will not be accepted as a valid will.

There are statutory limitations on a husband's and a wife's right to dispose of their property by will.

A will transfers no interest in property until the death of the maker, and the maker may revoke his or her will at any time. A will may be revoked by operation of law as the result of the change in the status of the maker.

In Re Estate of Weir

475 F.2d 988 (D.C. Cir. 1973)

This was a challenge to a will of Paul Weir brought by his niece, Margaret Weihs. The trial court directed a verdict rejecting the challenge. Affirmed on appeal.

Paul Weir, was a lifelong bachelor who was predeceased by a brother who left two surviving children, a son and a daughter (Margaret Weihs). Weir, an engineer, met Elizabeth Holmead, a widow of approximately the same age, shortly after World War II, and they became close friends until Mr. Weir's death on February 19, 1971. Although they had separate apartments, they shared each other's company, traveled together, took their meals together, and were constant companions until Weir's death. On February 9, 1956, Weir executed a will which left a life estate to Mrs. Holmead and the remainder to his brother, or if he was not living, to his brother's heirs. In 1965, Mr. Weir's brother died. Then, on June 6, 1966, Mr. Weir executed a new will which left $10,000 each to his nephew and niece, and the remainder of his estate to Mrs. Holmead. Upon Weir's death in 1971, the niece challenged the 1966 will, claiming lack of due execution, lack of testamentary capacity, undue influence by Mrs. Holmead and others, and fraud and deceit.

PER CURIAM. The evidence introduced as to lack of testamentary capacity was that Weir dressed conservatively, was occasionally forgetful, sometimes untidy (he left his socks on the floor), and had some strange habits such as picking up dust from the floor and inspecting it. For example, Mrs. Lay, a retired nurse, who lived in an adjoining apartment and had prepared some meals for Weir testified that she believed Weir lacked testamentary capacity at the time of the execution of the 1966 will. Upon cross-examination, it became clear that the only basis for this conclusion was the fact that Weir sometimes picked up dust and wore torn trousers, and her feeling that she "couldn't understand why he wouldn't want to" leave his entire estate to his blood relatives. Mr. Lauten, a trust officer of National Savings & Trust Company, executor of the first (1956) will, testified that he believed Weir didn't have all his "faculties" at the time of the making of the 1966 will. Mr. Lauten testified that he somehow got the impression that Weir was unsatisfied with the 1966 will, but could give no basis for this hunch, or for his bare assertion that the testator didn't have all his "faculties." Weihs testified that she believed Weir lacked testamentary capacity because her middle name was misspelled in the 1966 will and she didn't believe that her uncle would have signed anything with that name misspelled since it was a family name that was very important to him.

Although Weihs's evidence perhaps presented interesting tidbits, the District Court was correct in concluding that there was not enough evidence to go to the jury on the issue of testamentary capacity. In order to make a valid will, testator must be "of sound and disposing mind and capable of executing a valid deed or contract." In this jurisdiction, as in most others, sound and disposing mind simply means that "the decedent must have had, at the time of execution of the instrument, sufficient mental capacity to dispose of his property or estate with judgment and understanding, considering the nature and character of the estate as well as the relative claims of different persons, who would be the natural objects of [his] bounty." In cases where testamentary incapacity has been found there has been a considerably stronger showing that testator lacked a sound and disposing mind. For instance, evidence that testator was extremely ill or under heavy sedation at the time of the execution of the will has been sufficient to allow the issue of testamentary capacity to go to the jury.

Similarly, the evidence presented as to undue influence was insufficient to allow the jury to take that issue. All the witnesses testified without qualification that Weir and Mrs. Holmead had great affection for each other, and that with the exception of Mrs. Holmead, Weir had no close friends. He saw his niece and nephew very infrequently, and only rarely spoke with them on the phone. Although Weir's nephew testified that he believed Mrs. Holmead exercised a "wifely" influence on his uncle, neither nephew or niece could recite anything in particular that Mrs. Holmead ever did or said to unduly influence their uncle.

Unfortunately for Weihs, influence gained by years of mutual affection is not sufficient in law to establish undue influence. Undue influence is influence gained by improper means.

Administration of Estates

Introduction. When a person dies, an orderly procedure is needed to collect his assets, settle his debts, and distribute any remaining assets to those who are entitled to it either under a valid will or by the laws of intestacy. If the decedent did not own any property at his death, or if the property was jointly owned with right of survivorship so that it all passed automatically by operation of law, there is no estate to administer. In addition, summary procedures are sometimes available where the estate is relatively small, for example, where it has assets of less than $1,000.

Executor or Administrator. The first step is to determine whether or not the deceased person left a will. This may require a search of the deceased person's personal papers and his safety deposit box if he has one, and discussions with his attorney or other person who may know whether one was executed. If there is a will, the deceased has likely exercised his right to name the person who he wishes to administer his estate. This person is known as the "executor" if the designee is a man or "executrix" if the designee is a woman. The executor may, for example, be the spouse, a close friend, an attorney, or the trust department of a financial institution.

If there is no will, or if the will fails to name an executor, the court will name an administrator or an administratrix. A surviving spouse or child usually has a statutory right to appointment as administrator, followed by grandchildren, father or mother, brother or sister, or other next of kin. If no relative is available and qualified to serve, a creditor or other person may be appointed by the court.

Both the federal and state governments impose estate or inheritance taxes on estates of a certain size and these returns must be filed. The federal tax is a tax on the deceased's estate, with provision for deducting debts, expenses of administration, and charitable gifts. In addition, an amount equal to the greater of $250,000 or half of the adjusted gross estate may be deducted if at least that amount has been left to the surviving spouse. State inheritance taxes are imposed on the person who receives a gift or statutory share from an estate. However, it is common for a person to include a provision in his will that the estate will pay all taxes, including inheritance taxes, so that his beneficiaries will not have to do so.

When the debts, expenses, and taxes are taken care of, the remainder is distributed to the designated beneficiaries. This may necessitate resorting to rules of interpretation that help affect the distribution intended by the deceased. Other rules govern the distribution when the estate is too small to satisfy all the bequests or when designated beneficiaries are no longer alive.

Most states require that the executor or administrator post a bond in an amount in excess of the estimated value of the estate to insure that he will properly and faithfully perform his duties. However, in drawing a will a person may direct that the executor need not post a bond and the court will usually accept the exemption.

Steps in Administration. If the deceased left a will, it must be "proved" in order to be admitted to probate. Proving the will involves testimony by the witnesses, if they are still alive, to the mental capacity of the deceased at the time he executed the will, that he intended the document to control the disposition of his property, and the circumstances of execution of the will. If the witnesses are no longer alive, the signatures of the deceased and the witnesses will have to be otherwise established.

Whether or not there is a will, the identity of the heirs of the deceased must be established by testimony of witnesses. If the deceased did not make a will, the heirs must be known so that the estate can be distributed pursuant to the intestacy laws. If there is a will, the identity of heirs is necessary so that they can protect their interests. For some heirs this may mean defending a will which provides for them; others may want to try to claim a statutory share or to otherwise challenge the will.

The executor or administrator must also see that an inventory is taken of this estate and that the assets are appraised. Notice must be given to creditors or potential claimants against the estate for them to file and prove their claims within a specified time. Generally, a widow of a deceased is entitled to be paid an allowance during the time the estate is being settled; this allowance has priority over other debts of the estate. The executor must see that any properly payable funeral or burial expenses are paid and that the creditors claims are satisfied. Provision must be made for filing an income tax return, and for paying any income tax due for the partial year prior to decedent's death.

SUMMARY

Estates are administered under the supervision of probate courts. A person may nominate an executor to administer his estate and if he fails to do so or if the person nominated cannot serve, the court will name an administrator. The steps in administration of an estate include taking an inventory of the assets, having them appraised, determining the creditors and persons to whom the estate is to be distributed, paying all proper debts and expenses, and distributing the remainder to those entitled to it.

In Re Estate of Hall

328 F.Supp. 1305 (D.C. D.C. 1971).
aff'd 466 F.2d 340.

This was an action filed by the Navy Relief Society to have a holographic writing of Francesca Ross Hall, admitted to probate as her last will and testament. The court held the will was not properly admissible.

Miss Hall had spend the last 30 years of her life as an inmate of a mental hospital and at the time of her death in 1968 it was assumed that she had died intestate. In the course of administering the estate, however, a handwritten, one-page document was unearthed in a safety deposit box at the Riggs National Bank, conservators of the estates of several members of the Hall family. The document, written in 1932, purported to give all of Miss Hall's estate coming from her grandfather Clapp, approximately 70 percent of her total estate at the time, to "whatever organization cares for the disabled sailors and seamen of the United States Navy and their families." Upon learning of the existence of a will under which it could possibly qualify as a beneficiary, the Navy Relief Society filed an independent action to have the document admitted to probate.

On November 30, 1932, Francesca Ross Hall made a paper writing entitled "Last Will and Testament" handwritten by her on the front and back of a single sheet of paper. The last line on the back side was an incomplete sentence reading, "All personal effects to be left to. . . . Although the writing was not signed by Francesca at the bottom of the back side, her name did appear in her own writing in the body of the document, at the top of the first page: "I, Francesca Ross Hall." The signatures of two witnesses, Robert C. Cousins, Sr., and Henrietta C. Lockner, also appeared at the top of the first page. According to the testimony of Cousins, the only surviving witness, Hall wrote another two pages after the page which was still in existence. According to

Cousins' "best recollection," Hall signed the last page at the bottom and then had Cousins attest the paper as a witness. Cousins declined to read any part of the document.

Although the authenticity of all signatures on the paper were uncontroverted, Cousins testified that neither he nor Lockner, the other witness, were present at the time the other one signed. Moreover, Cousins was not present at the time the first page was written and did not see Hall sign her name on it. According to Cousins' reconstruction of the events of that day in 1932, Lockner could not have been present when any part of the document was written, nor could she have witnessed Hall's signing the missing pages of the purported will.

It was not known what sort of disposition of other property was made in the missing pages which had been detached and destroyed. It was impossible to determine who detached the missing pages, or when they were removed, for the chain of custody of the document was not known. The Bank officials felt that Riggs came into possession of the paper sometime in the early 1940s, before Hall's mother herself was committed to a mental institution, and that it was probable that the mother had control of the document before then.

PRATT, DISTRICT JUDGE. The Court thus is presented with an incomplete document which does not effect a total disposition of all of Hall's estate. The Administrators of the estate contend that because the will is holographic, and not only is incomplete but also not properly signed or attested, the normal presumption of regularity is not operable, and that the Navy Relief Society who has the burden of proof on the issue of its admissibility to probate, cannot sustain this burden. The Administrators urge that the writing in question is not a valid will entitled to be received in probate, specifically challenging probate of the document on three grounds: (1) decedent's name, which appears only in the first line of the text of the writing, while it identifies Miss Hall, is not a valid testamentary signature under District of Columbia law; (2) said writing is not a complete statement of decedent's final intentions; and (3) Mrs. Lockner's signature as an attesting witness was not duly subscribed according to statute.

The District has no special statute dealing with holographic wills. Section 103 of Title 18 of the Code sets forth the general requirements for execution of any valid will. That section provides that:

> A will or testament other than a will executed in the manner provided by 18–107 (noncupative wills), is void unless it is:
>
> (1) in writing and signed by the testator, or by another person in his presence and by his express direction; and
>
> (2) attested and subscribed in the presence of the testator, by at least two credible witnesses.

Of course the burden of proving formal execution of a will rests on the party wishing to have the document admitted to probate, in this case the Navy Relief Society. Where a will appears regular on its face, the normal presumption of regularity would lighten the burden on the moving party.

The document before the Court, however, is not regular on its face. The last two pages of the original document including the page with Francesca's signature, and that of the witness Cousins, are missing under unknown circumstances. It is uncertain whether the second witness, Mrs. Lockner, ever attested the original complete document on the last page. It is certain that Mrs. Lockner did not see Hall sign her name or write any part of the paper. The writing does not effect a complete disposition of Hall's assets. These facts, coupled with Miss Hall's admitted mental problems, place a heavy burden on the Navy Relief Society in its effort to show due execution.

As discussed above, District law requires that even holographic wills be attested and subscribed in the presence of the testator by two witnesses, although they need not sign in each other's presence or physically observe the other's signature. Plaintiff Navy Relief Society urges that the normal presumption of regularity should apply since we have admittedly authentic signatures of the testator and the two witnesses on the present document. It is the Court's view, however, that for all of the reasons discussed above, this document cannot be viewed as being regular on its face, and that therefore due execution cannot be presumed. Plaintiff Navy Relief Society has not and cannot meet its burden of showing that we have a portion of a longer, duly executed document, which should be given present effect.

Because it is manifestly incomplete and because the testator's signature on the first page cannot be viewed as carrying with it any testamentary intent, the Court cannot accept the paper before it as a complete, duly executed document, entitled to be admitted to probate.

Trusts

Introduction. A trust arises when a person who has legal rights to property also has the duty to hold it for the use or benefit of another person. The person benefitted by a trust is considered to have "equitable title" to the property because it is being maintained for his benefit. A trust may be created in a number of different ways, including:

1. The owner of the property may declare that he is holding certain property in trust; for example, a mother might state that she is holding 100 shares of General Motors stock in trust for her daughter;
2. The owner of property may transfer property to another person with the expressed intent that person is not to have the use of it but rather is to hold for the benefit either of the original owner-donor or a third person; for example, Arthur transfers certain stock to First Trust Bank with instructions to pay the income to Arthur's daughter during her lifetime, and after her death to distribute the stock to her children; and
3. By operation of law; for example, where a lawyer representing a client injured in an automobile accident receives a settlement payment from

an insurance company; the lawyer holds the settlement as trustee for his client.

Definitions. A person who creates a trust is known as the "donor" or the "settlor." The person who holds the property in trust is known as the "trustee." The person for whose benefit the property is held is known as the "beneficiary." A single person may occupy more than one of these positions; however, if there is only one beneficiary, he or she cannot be the sole trustee. The property held is sometimes called the "corpus" or "res" and a distinction is made between the property in trust which is known as the "principal" and the "income" that is produced by the principal.

A trust established and effective during the creator's lifetime is known as an *inter vivos* (or living) *trust.* If a trust is established by a will and takes effect on the creator's death, it is known as a *testamentary trust.*

Creation of Express Trusts. Five basic elements are required for the creation of an express trust:

1. The settlor must have the legal capacity to convey; this means the settlor must have the capacity needed to make a contract in the case of a trust created by contract or the testamentary capacity to make a will in the case of a trust created by will;
2. the settlor must intend to create a trust at the present time, and to impose enforceable duties on the trustee, he must do it with the requisite formalities; in the case of a trust of land, the trust must be created in writing so as to meet the Statute of Frauds and in the case of a trust created by a will, it must satisfy the formal requirements for wills;
3. the trust must involve specific property which the settlor has the right to convey;
4. the beneficiary must be sufficiently identified so that he can be ascertained; and
5. the trust must be created for a proper purpose, that is, it cannot be created for a reason contrary to public policy such as the commission of a crime.

Special and somewhat less restrictive rules govern the establishment of charitable trusts.

If the settlor does not name a trustee in a validly created trust, the court will appoint one. Similarly, a court will replace a trustee who resigns, is incompetent or refuses to act.

Creation of Implied Trusts. The law recognizes certain trusts, known as "resulting trusts," which are based on the implied or presumed intent of a person to create a trust. For example, if Ann transfers property to Arthur intending that he be a trustee of it and Ann fails to satisfy the requirements for creating a valid express trust, then Arthur will not be permitted to retain the property for his own use. He holds the property in a resulting trust for Ann or her successors in interest. Another example of a resulting trust would be where Sam transfers property to Ellen to provide for the needs of Grandfather, out of the principal and income, but Grandfather dies before the trust funds are exhausted. Ellen then holds the trust property for the benefit of Sam or his successors.

A "constructive trust" is another type of trust created by operation of law which imposes on the constructive trustee a duty to convey property held by him to another person on the grounds he would be unjustly enriched if he was allowed to retain it. For example, where a person procures the transfer of property by a fraudulent misrepresentation, or duress, he becomes a constructive trustee and is under an obligation to return the property to the original owner.

Transfer of the Beneficiary's Interest. Generally the beneficiary of a trust may voluntarily assign his right to the principal or income from a trust to another person, and his rights are subject to the claims of his creditors. However trusts sometimes contain what are known as "spendthrift" clauses whereby the settlor restricts the voluntary or involuntary transfer of a beneficiary's interest. Such clauses are generally enforced and preclude assignees or creditors from compelling a trustee to recognize their claim to the trust, subject to several exceptions: (1) a person cannot put his own property beyond the claims of his own creditors and thus a spendthrift clause is not effective in a trust where the settlor makes himself a beneficiary; (2) divorced wives and minor children can compel payment for alimony and child support; (3) creditors who have furnished necessaries can compel payment; and (4) once the trustee distributes property to a beneficiary, it can be subject to valid claims of others.

A trust may give the trustee discretion as to the amount of principal or income paid to a beneficiary; in such a case the beneficiary cannot require the trustee to exercise his discretion as desired by the beneficiary.

Termination and Modifications of a Trust. Normally a settlor cannot revoke or modify a trust unless he reserves the power to do so at the time he establishes it. However, a trust may be modified or terminated with the consent of the settlor and all the beneficiaries. Where the settlor is dead or otherwise unable to consent, a trust can be modified or terminated by consent of all persons with a beneficial interest only where it would not frustrate a material purpose of the trust. Because trusts are under the supervisory jurisdiction of the court, the court can permit a deviation from the terms of a trust when unanticipated changes in circumstances threaten accomplishment of the settlor's purpose.

Duties of a Trustee. A trustee must use a reasonable degree of skill, judgment and care in the exercise of his duties unless he holds himself out as having a greater degree of skill, in which case he will be held to the higher standard. A trustee may not comingle the property he holds in trust with his own property or with that of another trust. A trustee owes a duty of loyalty which means he must administer the trust for the benefit of the beneficiaries and must avoid any conflict of interest between his interests and that of the trust. For example, a trustee cannot do business with a trust he administers. A trustee must not prefer one beneficiary's interest to another, he must account to the beneficiaries for all transactions and, unless the trust agreement provides otherwise, he must make the trust productive. A trustee may not delegate discretionary duties to someone else to perform, such as the duty to select investments, but he may delegate the performance of ministerial duties such as the preparation of statements of account.

The powers of a trustee may be defined by the trust agreement, but if they are not, he has all the powers reasonably necessary to carry out the trust. The trustee is personally liable on all contracts made on behalf of a trust, unless the contract specifically provides otherwise; however, he is entitled to reimbursement from the trust property for all legitimate expenditures.

SUMMARY

A trust arises when one person who has legal rights to certain property also has the duty to hold it for the use or benefit of another person. *Inter vivos* trusts are those established during the creator's lifetime and testmentary trusts are those which take effect at death through a will. Trusts may be expressly created or they may arise through implication or operation of law.

Generally the beneficiary of a trust has the right to voluntarily assign the principal or interest in his share of a trust and his rights are subject to the claims of his creditors. Normally a creator of a trust may not revoke or modify a trust unless he reserves the right to do so at the time he establishes; however, there are some exceptions. The trustee owes a duty to use skill, judgment, and care in the exercise of his duties and also owes a duty of loyalty.

American Security and Trust Co. v. Utley
382 F.2d 451 (D.C. Cir. 1967)

This was an action brought by Fred Utley (plaintiff) against Sidney Graves and American Security and Trust Co. (defendants) to attach part of the accrued income of a trust in order to satisfy a debt owing from Graves to Utley. Trial court judgment for Utley. Reversed and remanded on appeal.

Graves was the beneficiary of a testamentary trust by his deceased wife who died on April 11, 1962. The trust contained a "spendthrift" clause. On April 30, 1963 Graves signed a promissory note for $4,500 payable to Utley. When only partial payment was received by the due date on the note, Utley brought suit against Graves and obtained a default judgment. Utley then sought to attach the accrued trust income held by American Security and Trust as trustee.

BURGER, CIRCUIT JUDGE. This appeal presents to us the question whether the income provided for the beneficiary of a spendthrift trust is subject to the claim of a creditor, and if so, to what extent. The District Court determined that because the beneficiary was the trust settlor's spouse, who elected to take under the will creating the trust, rather than under the provisions of the statute, D.C.Code § 19–113 (1961), the income was subject to claims of creditors. [i]n the District of Columbia, as well as in many other jurisdictions, a surviving spouse is entitled by law to a specified share in the decedent's estate. The spouse may renounce a devise or bequest left by will and elect to take such rights as would devolve to him in case of intestacy, D.C.Code, 19–113. On the other hand, if the spouse accepts the benefits of the will, he relinquishes his alternative rights to the wife's or husband's property, as the case may be. In that event the transaction is, in effect, a surrender of his statutory share in the estate in exchange for the benefits under the will, in this instance, the spendthrift trust. The result is that the spendthrift trust under such circumstances is not a free and voluntary gift on the part of the testator or testatrix. The surviving spouse is in effect a purchaser of the benefits, instead of the recipient of a gift. Being a purchaser and in the same position as though he were the creator of the trust, the provisions surrounding the fund with immunity from claims of creditors, become void.

On this premise the District Court then applied the well-known rule that where the settlor-creator of the trust is also the beneficiary, the interest in the trust can be invaded. RESTATEMENT (SECOND) TRUSTS § 156 (1959). We have no quarrel with the rule that one may not create a trust for his own benefit and place the income beyond reach of his creditors. However, the view adopted by the District Court is contrary to the settled weight of authority and we think not warranted as a matter of sound policy.

Professor Scott, while recognizing the criticism of complete immunity for trust income concludes:

> On the whole the better view would seem to be that where a husband creates a trust for his wife by will, the mere fact that she surrenders her right to dower or to a distributive share of his estate does not make her the creator of the trust, even to the extent of the value of the interest which she surrendered. If spendthrift trusts are to be permitted at all, it would seem that a husband should be allowed to create such a trust for his widow, even though she may have power to refuse to accept the provisions of his will and take her dower or distributive share in lieu thereof.

SCOTT, TRUSTS § 156.3, at 1105–1106 (2d Ed. 1956).

We have long recognized the validity of the so-called spendthrift trust, but not without limitation. The historical purpose of a settlor or testator in creating a trust, the income of which was protected from invasion, was to protect the interests of the beneficiary. This purpose has been held to render the income totally immune from claims, including claims for debts incurred by the beneficiary for the necessaries of life. We see no reason for an absolutist "all or nothing" approach. Traditionally, in the absence of a statute, several distinct classes of claimants have been permitted to invade the beneficiary's interest. This court has permitted the interest of a father in a spendthrift trust to be subjected to claims for the support of his minor children. Our holding in *Seidenberg* indicates that it does not necessarily follow from the general validity of spendthrift trusts that trust income is protected from all obligations. We view the primary purpose of such a trust to assure that the beneficiary will be provided for, independent of his own improvidence. To accomplish this the income need not be made immune from debts incurred for the necessities of life; indeed to allow such claims is entirely compatible with the purpose of the trust. This result has been reached in other areas of the law, such as infant's contracts.

The immunity of an infant from liability on his contracts has much in common with the historic basis for the immunity of a spendthrift trust. In each situation the beneficiary of the rule receives sufficient protection if the immunity does not include debts for the necessities of life. What are "necessaries" will obviously vary with the circumstances, income, and background of the beneficiary. We think the law governing contracts of infants will afford adequate guidelines; housing, food, and medical care are examples of the obvious basic necessities of life.

The District Court had no occasion to inquire into the circumstances which gave rise to the indebtedness, and we therefore remand for a determination of the basis of the debt incurred and the purposes to which the proceeds of the loan were devoted. If the District Court finds the debt to have been incurred for necessaries such as those for which an infant would be held liable in contract in otherwise comparable circumstances, the claim may be allowed against the income of the trust; if not, judgment must be for American Security and Trust Co.

Problem Cases

1. In May, 1944, when James D. Cummings was on duty in the South Pacific, as a member of the Marine Corps, he executed the following document and sent it to his father:

   29 May 1944

   Dear Dad:

   "I am writing this today I should have done it a long time ago.

   "This war is a dangerous business at best and while I have been lucky so far one never knows. So I am going to give you all the dope on what you are to do in the event of my getting in the way of a well aimed slug. KEEP THIS LETTER FOR REFERENCE.

"First, I have 10,000 Dollars in Insurance in the VETERANS ADMINISTRATION, WASHINGTON, D.C., this names mother as my next of kin. I have a policy with Phenois Mutual [*sic*] but I think Mildred allowed that to laspe. [*sic*] At the time of our divorce she would not mail it to me, but sent it to a friend of ours. I am having them sent to you. If this policy can be saved without the addition of a war risk clause, I will have it changed.

"Now as my next of kin mom can at my death apply for the insurence [*sic*] which at her age will net around 50 a month for the rest of her life and will revert to you if she should die befor [*sic*] you.

"Also she should apply to the Chief paymaster USMC for my back pay and the six months pay due to her as my next of kin.

"Any money or prorerty [*sic*] which I may have at my death are to be divided equally between you and mom.

"This letter will serve as your authority for the transfer of the money to you. It has been read and my signature witnessed by a Commissionsd [*sic*] Officer of the Marine Crop. [*sic*] serving with the Armed Forcses [*sic*] overseas.

"As ever, love
"your son
"(s) James D. Cummings
"James D. Cummings
"I have Witnessed this signature
"J. M. Venard 2nd Leiut. [*sic*] U SM CR
"Corp J D Cummings
"Engr. Co. 22nd Marines (Reinf.)
co Fleet p.o.
"San Francisco Calif.

"P.S.—If you need any advice on what to do to get the money—see your Local Red Cross Administrator. He or she will have complete information on this."

On July 24, 1944, James Cummings met his death "caused by wounds received in the attack at Guam Island." His mother claimed the letter was a will which granted Cumming's interest in the Phoenix Insurance policy proceeds to her. Is it a valid will?

2. After Boyd Ruff died, his wife found in his wallet a blank check on the back of which was written "I Boyd Ruff request that all I own in the way *of* personal or real estate property to my wife Modene, Boyd Ruff." Ruff had a serious coronary condition which he knew could be fatal at any time, and executed the document shortly before his death and just after a serious heart attack. Ruff was survived by his wife, three brothers and a sister, but left no children. Modene Ruff filed a petition in probate court to admit the document as a will. Ruff's sister, Lois, filed a petition to set the will aside on the grounds: (1) that on its face it was not a valid holographic will and (2) that it did not show a valid intent to make a will. Under Arkansas state law, a holographic will entirely in the handwriting of a testator along with his signature is valid despite the lack of witnesses to it, if the handwriting and signature are later established to be the testator's by three credible disinterested witnesses. Should the petition to admit the will be granted?

3. For 36 years Ward Duchett lived in Washington, D.C., with his sister, Mary, in her home. On numerous occasions Mary had promised Ward she would leave him her real estate if he remained single and continued to live with her. At age 60 Mary became

seriously ill and was put in a hospital. Three weeks later, her sister Maud who was a nurse in Philadelphia came to Washington and took Mary home even though her doctors advised against it and she did not ask to be taken home. Maud took complete charge of Mary, repeatedly prevented other relatives, including Ward, from seeing Mary and told them she was doing it on doctor's orders. That statement was false. Mary was in a very weak physical condition, sometimes could recognize people only by their voices and could not sit up or carry on a conversation. Maud secretly arranged for a lawyer to come and prepare a will which was quickly executed. It left everything to Maud in "consideration of her kindness, untiring devotion and personal service to me during my illness when no other relative offered or came to do for me, and without hope of reward." The Will was witnessed by the lawyer and by a cousin who was very close to Maud. Mary died the next day. There was no evidence that Mary had previously felt any ill-will toward any of her relatives. Ward moves to set the will aside. Should the will be set aside?

4. In 1937, Testator died leaving a will executed in 1928 in which the bulk of his estate was left in trust. The will provided that the trust was to continue during the lifetime of his two sons, Orin Byers and Clifford W. Byers. On the death of either son, if they were survived "by children lawfully begotten of their bodies," the children were to share equally their father's share. If a son died without "leaving surviving children begotten of his body," the trust was to be kept intact until the death of the other son and then divided "among children of said sons who survive him." Orin died in 1941. Clifford died in 1961 leaving a legitimate daughter, Guineveve, and an illegitimate son, Raymond. Both were living when Testator died as was another legitimate daughter who survived Testator by only a few days. Raymond brought an action claiming he was entitled to a one-half interest in trust. Should his claim be granted?

5. On January 18, 1905 Sarah Hume executed a will that provided in part:

   > "Sixth. I will, devise & bequeath to Phillip Russell Hume and Robert Cumberland Hume my farm of one hundred acres (100), if said farm is not sold by me before my death, but they are not to sell said farm before Robert Cumberland Hume is twenty-five (25) years of age, but in event of death of either one of them it is to go to the surviving one."

   She died in 1909 and her will was probated. Phillip and Robert Hume were her grandsons and were teenagers at the time the will was executed. The brothers held the farm of 100 acres until the death of Phillip in 1961 who left his interest in the land to his daughter Louise. Louise claims she is entitled to a half-interest and Robert claims he is entitled to the entire property. What is the basis for each party's claim? How should the court decide?

6. Ellery owned a lot in Wilmington, and Howard owned a lot in San Diego. Ellery and Howard agreed that each would execute a quitclaim deed of his property in favor of the other for the sole purpose of avoiding proceedings in probate. The deeds were executed on November 9, 1950, and were placed by Howard in a safe-deposit box to which only he and his wife had access. In June 1954, the agreement was canceled by mutual consent, and Howard sold his San Diego property. Later, at the request of Ellery, Howard returned Ellery's deed, and Ellery tore it into pieces, twice lengthwise and twice crosswide. Ellery died on August 19, 1956. Ellery left a will devising all his real estate to his nephews and a niece. Two days after Ellery's death, Howard taped the pieces of the torn-up deed together and caused the document to be placed on record on August 21, 1956. Howard claimed that Ellery had stated to him that the deed was torn up accidentally and that Ellery gave the pieces of the deed to Howard. Howard and his wife took possession of the Wilming-

ton property and have lived here ever since. Is Howard the owner of the Wilmington property?

7. In his will, Carl Cross left a sum of money to his brother, Sam, in trust for Sam's life; on Sam's death, it was to go to Marvin Cross in trust for Marvin's life, and on Marvin's death it was to be divided among Carl's brothers and sisters. Sam took the money left to him in trust by Carl along with some money of his own and used it to buy a home for him and his wife, Maggie Cross, as tenants by the entirety. Maggie did not contribute any funds of her own and was aware that trust funds were being used to pay the purchase price. When Sam died, Sam's interest passed to Maggie. Marvin and the other beneficiaries then sued Maggie, seeking a judgment for the amount of the trust funds and to obtain a lien on the property. Are Marvin and the other beneficiaries entitled to a judgment?
8. Prior to 1948 Antonio Petralia was the sole owner of a regular savings account which he had opened in his name at the First National Bank of Chicago. On November 8, 1948, he closed the account and transferred all the funds in it to a savings account entitled "Tony Petralia, Trustee." On the side of the signature card was his signature "Tony Petralia" with the word "Trustee" written beneath it. On the reverse side of the card was the following language: "All deposits in this account are made for the benefit of Domenica Di Maggio to whom or to whose representative said deposits or any part thereof, together with interest thereon, may be paid in the event of the death of the undersigned Trustee." His signature appeared again over a line designated "trustee." Beneath his signature was written "Mrs. Domenica Di Maggio," "July 29, 1909," and "Daughter." From the date the account was opened Petralia alone made numerous deposits to the account and infrequent withdrawls from it. The balance in it steadily increased. When Petralia died, the administrator of his estate claimed that the signature card was insufficient intent to create a trust and also an invalid attempt to dispose of his property after his death without complying with the requirements for wills. Did Petralia create a valid trust?

34

Landlord and Tenant

Leases

Landlord-Tenant Relationship. The relationship of landlord and tenant, which has been with us for a long time, is an area of the law which is rapidly changing. In England and in early America, farms were the most common subjects of leases; the primary object was to lease land on which crops could be grown or cattle grazed. Any buildings on the leased property were frequently of secondary importance to the land itself, and they generally were rather simple structures built without such modern conveniences as plumbing and wiring. The tenant would have dominion over the entire property and would be responsible for its upkeep. The landlord and the tenant would normally have similar knowledge of the condition of the property at the time the lease was entered into. Accordingly, traditional landlord-tenant law looked at a lease mainly as a conveyance of land and gave relatively little attention to its contractual aspects.

Today, the landlord-tenant relationship is typified by the lease of an apartment in a large building located in an urban area. The tenant occupies only a small portion of the total property; he is likely to have signed a form lease dictated by the landlord; and he is less likely than his grandfather to be adept at making the kind of repairs that might be required in the apartment. In the rundown sections of cities the tenant's situation is commonly exacerbated by the presence of rats and filth and by his or her relatively meager economic status.

The law had been slow to recognize the essentially changed nature of the landlord-tenant relationship. The rule of *caveat emptor* in lease situations was eventually grafted with exceptions, and the emphasis changed from focusing on the lease as a conveyance of land to focusing on its contractual aspects. In recent years, the courts, legislatures, and local governing bodies have provided a number of new rules to govern the relationship. Accordingly, this chapter will be concerned not only with the time-developed common law of landlord and tenant but also with recent statutory and case-law developments.

Nature of Lease. A leasehold is an interest in land and is created by a lease which, as a general rule, need not be executed with the same formalities as are followed in the execution of a deed. In some respects a leasehold interest in real property is treated as personal property. In probating an estate after the death of a lessee, any leasehold interest which the lessee held at the time of his or her death is treated as personal property. Also, in some states the courts treat the breach of a lease as a breach of contract and assess damages accordingly.

Execution of Lease. A lease, to be valid, need not conform to any specific formal requirements. Basically, a lease is a contract, and in most states, if the lease is for a term of more than one year from the date it is made, it must under the statute of frauds, be in writing if it is to be enforceable. In some states, however, the statute of frauds expressly provides that leases for a term of three years or less need not be in writing to be enforceable.

The statutes of many states provide for the recording of long-term leases—five or ten years, or longer—and further provide that such leases, to be eligible for recording, must be executed with the same formalities as are used in the execution of a deed. The failure to execute a long-term lease with the formalities set out in the statute does not render it a nullity, the only effect of such failure is to render the lease ineligible for recordation.

In the leasing of real estate, good business practice demands that the parties execute a carefully drafted lease which defines their respective rights. The lease will normally contain covenants covering such essential matters as the use permitted by the tenant, who shall make repairs, the landlord's right to enter the premises, and the purposes for which the landlord may enter, the rent to be paid, warranties as to the condition of the premises, and whether or not the lease may be assigned or the premises sublet.

Rights, Duties, and Liabilities of the Landlord. The rights, duties, and liabilities of the landlord, as well as of the tenant, must be considered in three different situations: (1) where there is no applicable and enforceable lease clause, (2) where there is an applicable and enforceable lease clause, and (3) where there is an applicable statute. The discussion in this section of the text relates primarily to the law which applies in the absence of a lease clause or statute, and it should be kept in mind that a lease clause or statute may supercede the common law rule in any given situation.

When a landlord leases certain premises, the landlord impliedly warrants that he will give the tenant possession of the premises, or at least that the tenant will have the right to possession, and that the tenant's possession will not be interfered with as the result of any act or omission on the part of the landlord or as a result of any defects in the landlord's title. In the absence of covenants in the lease to the contrary, the landlord has no right to enter onto the premises during the term of the lease, and if the landlord does, he or she is a trespasser.

Under traditional law, the landlord does not warrant the condition of the premises, nor does he or she warrant that the premises are suitable for the purposes of the tenant. The tenant takes the premises as he or she finds them. Because the landlord has no duty as to the condition of the premises, the landlord is not liable to the tenant or his or her family for injuries or property damage due to obvious defects or failure to repair. To this general rule, the courts created some very important exceptions: (1) The landlord remains liable to use due care for those common areas of a building in which he or she retains control; (2) the landlord must disclose concealed defects known to him or her and not discoverable on a reasonable inspection by the tenant and is liable for those defects not disclosed that cause injury; (3) the landlord remains liable for the consequences of any negligently made repairs, even though he or she was not obligated to make them; (4) the landlord who rents a fully furnished dwelling for a short period impliedly warrants that the premises are safe and habitable.

Over time many courts have moved away from the traditional rule and have held that an implied warranty of habitability is made in the lease of premises for residential use.

The landlord is entitled to the agreed rent, and at the expiration of the term of the lease, has the right to the surrender of the premises in as good condition as when leased, normal wear and destruction by the elements excepted.

Housing Codes. Many cities and states have enacted housing codes which impose duties on a property-owner with respect to the condition of premises which he rents to others. Typical of these provisions is Section 2304 of the District of Columbia Housing Code which provides that:

> No person shall rent or offer to rent any habitation or the furnishing thereof unless such habitation and its furnishings are in a clean, safe and sanitary condition, in repair and free from rodents or vermin.

Such codes also commonly call for certain minimum temperatures to be maintained in the building, for minimum bathroom and kitchen facilities to be provided along with water heating, for a minimum amount of space per tenant, for certain lighting, ventilation and maintenance to be provided, for stairways, windows, doors, floors, and screens to be in repair, for minimum ceiling heights, for keys and locks to meet certain specifications, for the premises to be kept painted and free of lead paint and for the landlord to issue written receipts for rent payments. The codes may prohibit landlords from retaliating against a tenant who complains to city authorities about conditions in the premises. Buildings of a certain size may be required to have resident custodial care. Some cities have adopted rent control ordinances which limit the amount of rent that may be charged by landlords.

Failure of a landlord to conform to the housing code may result in the landlord losing part or all of his claim to the agreed-upon rent. The landlord who does not make the repairs required by the housing code may become liable for injuries; under a few statutes the tenant may have the right to withhold the rent until the repairs are made or may have the right to move out.

A coming trend of the law is the imposition of a duty on a landlord to safeguard tenants against forseeable criminal conduct. Thus landlords have been found liable for injuries sustained by tenants because the landlord failed to maintain sufficient security control over access to an apartment building and for failure to provide sufficient lighting outside a building in a high crime area. While the landlord is not an insurer of his tenants' safety, he must take reasonable precautions to safeguard his tenants. This means proper locks and lighting, and particularly for larger buildings or ones in high-crime areas, security guards and alarm systems.

Security Deposits. Security deposits or advance payments of rent are commonly required by landlords. Some states and cities limit the amount that can be required to be deposited in advance and require that deposits on leases for more than minimal lengths of time be placed in interest-bearing accounts. They also require landlords to account to tenants for the deposit within a specified period of time—say 30 days—from the termination of the lease; failure of the landlord to do so may result in the inposition of a penalty on him.

Rights and Duties of the Tenant. The tenant may use the leased premises for any lawful purpose which is reasonable and appropriate, unless the purpose for which they may be used is expressly set out in the lease. Under the common law rule the tenant has the exclusive right to the possession and use of the premises during the term of the lease, and if the landlord comes onto the premises without the consent of the tenant, he or she will be guilty of trespass. The tenant is fully responsible for the care and upkeep of the premises and traditionally owed a duty to make all ordinary repairs so that the premises would be returned in the same condition as rented except for normal wear and tear. Again, this duty for the upkeep of residential property has been changed by statute in many jurisdictions and put on the landlord. The tenant has no duty to make major repairs except where he or she was negligent, but the tenant must take steps to prevent damage from the elements as when a window breaks or a roof leaks.

The tenant is normally liable to persons injured or property damaged because of the tenant's negligence on that part of the property over which he or she has control.

The tenant has in the leased premises a property interest which he or she may transfer to another by the assignment of the lease unless the lease expressly provides that it shall not be assigned. However, total prohibitions against assignment are generally considered void as against public policy. Most leases contain a clause that requires the landlord's consent to any assignment and provides that such consent will not be unreasonably withheld.

If the tenant assigns the lease, he does not relieve himself from any contractual obligations under the lease, but the tenant does divest himself of his property interest in the leased premises. The tenant may sublease the premises or a part of them. If the tenant subleases the premises, the tenant does not divest himself of his property interest, and the tenant remains liable to the landlord on all the covenants in the lease. The tenant's relation to his or her sublessee is that of landlord. The tenant cannot grant to a sublessee greater rights than he has under the original lease, and if the original lease contains a provision denying the tenant the right to sublease the premises, such provision is enforceable.

Termination of the Lease. Normally, a lease is ended by "surrender" of the premises by the tenant to the landlord and "acceptance" of the premises by the landlord. However, sometimes the tenant may be forced out by the landlord prior to the end of the lease period or the tenant may vacate the premises before the end of the lease period.

If the premises become uninhabitable because of the acts of the landlord, then under the doctrine of "constructive eviction" the tenant may, after giving the landlord a reasonable opportunity to correct the defect, move out and incur no further liability for rent. The tenant must move out within a reasonable amount of time. For example, if the furnace breaks down in the middle of the winter and the apartment is without heat for February and March, the tenant cannot use this as an excuse for breaking the lease in August.

If the tenant abandons the premises before the end of the lease, the consequences vary from state to state. In some states the landlord is under an obligation to mitigate damages and must attempt to rerent or will lose any claim for further rent against the original tenant. In other states, the landlord may continue to collect rent from the tenant without rerenting, but loses the right if he does rerent. As a result, many leases contain a clause maintaining the landlord's right to the rent whether or not he tries to rerent and continuing the tenant's liability for any difference in rents if the landlord does rerent.

A landlord who desires to evict a tenant for nonpayment of rent or breach of a lease agreement should be careful to comply with any applicable state or city regulation governing evictions. Such regulations may forbid forcible entry to change locks or other self-help measures on the part of landlords. Under landlord lien statutes the landlord may be entitled to remove and hold belongings of a defaulting tenant as security for the rent payment. However, pursuant to the due process clause the tenant must be given notice of the lien and an opportunity to defend and protect his belongings before they can be sold to satisfy the lien.

SUMMARY

As a general rule, no formalities are required for the execution of short-term leases—which may be one to three years depending on the state—but leases for a longer period of time are required by the statute of frauds to be in writing. Long-term leases—five to ten years or longer—are required by the statutes of some states to be recorded, and such leases must be executed with the same formalities as are used in the execution of deeds to real property.

A landlord, in leasing premises, impliedly warrants that the tenant will have possession and quiet enjoyment of the premises. Under the common law rule, the landlord does not warrant the condition of the premises or their suitability for the tenant's purposes but this has been changed by statute or judicial decision in many jurisdictions. Unless the landlord agrees to make ordinary repairs, he or she has no duty to do so under the common law rule; however, many statutes now require landlords to keep residential property in repair.

In the absence of covenants in the lease to the contrary, the tenant has the exclusive right to the possession of the premises and is responsible for the upkeep. The tenant has the right to make any lawful use of the premises he or she wishes, provided the use does not result in permanent injury to them.

Normally a lease is terminated by surrender by the tenant and acceptance by the landlord at the end of the lease term. However, if the premises become uninhabitable through the acts of the landlord, the tenant may move out within a reasonable time after giving the landlord notice to remedy the defects. If the tenant abandons the premises prior to the end of the lease, he or she may remain liable for the rent.

Pines v. Perssion

111 N.W.2d 409 (Sup. Ct. Wisc. 1961)

This was an action brought by Pines and others (plaintiffs) against Perssion (defendant) concerning the lease of the house. Judgment for Pines was affirmed on appeal.

During the 1958–59 school year Pines and the other plaintiffs were tenants in a rooming house owned by Perssion. In May 1959 they asked him if he had a house they could rent for the next schoolyear and he advised them he had one. They looked at the house in June 1959 and found it in filthy condition. Perssion stated he would clean and fix up the house, paint it, provide the necessary furnishings and have the house in suitable condition by the start of the school year in the fall. When the tenants arrived in September it was still in a filthy condition and there were no student furnishings. The tenants began to clean the house themselves and did some painting with paint purchased by Perssion. They became discouraged with their progress and contacted an attorney who advised them to request the Madison building department to inspect the premises. This was done on September 9 and several building code violations were found, including inadequate electrical wiring, kitchen sink and toilet in disrepair, furnace in disrepair, handrail on stairs in disrepair, screens on windows and doors lacking. The city inspector gave Perssion until September 21 to correct the violations, and allowed the tenants to continue to occupy the house. They vacated the premises on September 11.

MARTIN, CHIEF JUSTICE. In our opinion, there was an implied warranty of habitability in the lease and that warranty was breached by Perssion.

The general rule is that there are no implied warranties to the effect that at the time a lease term commences the premises are in a tenantable condition or adapted to the purposes for which leased. A tenant is a purchaser of an estate in land, and is subject to the doctrine of *caveat emptor.* His remedy is to inspect the premises before taking them or to secure an express warranty. Thus, a tenant is not entitled to abandon the premises on the ground of uninhabitability.

There is an exception to this rule, some courts holding that there is an implied warranty of habitability and fitness of the premises where the subject of the lease is a furnished house. This is based on an intention inferred from the fact that under the circumstances the lessee does not have an adequate opportunity to inspect the premises at the time he accepts the lease.

Legislation and administrative rules, such as the safe-place statute, building codes and health regulations, all impose certain duties on a property owner with respect to the condition of his premises. Thus, the legislature has made a policy judgment—that it is socially (and politically) desirable to impose these duties on a property owner—which has rendered the old common law rule obsolete. To follow the old rule of no implied warranty of habitability in leases would, in our opinion, be inconsistent with the current legislative policy concerning housing standards. The need and social desirability of adequate housing for people in this area of rapid population increases is too important to be rebuffed by that obnoxious legal cliche, *caveat emptor.* Permitting landlords to rent "tumbledown" houses is at least a contributing cause of such problems as urban blight, juvenile delinquency and high property taxes for conscientious landowners.

There is no question in this case but that the house was not in a condition reasonably and decently fit for occupation when the lease term commenced. Perssion admitted it was "filthy," and he testified that no cleaning or other work was done in the house before the boys moved in. The filth, of course, was seen by the tenants when they inspected the premises prior to signing the lease. They had no way of knowing, however, that the plumbing, heating and wiring systems were defective. Moreover, on the testimony of the building inspector, it was unfit for occupancy. The state law provides that if the building is not in immediate danger of collapse the owner may board it up so that people cannot enter the building. His second choice is to bring the building up to comply with the safety standards of the code. And his third choice is to tear it down.

The evidence clearly showed that the implied warranty of habitability was breached. The tenants' covenant to pay rent and Perssion's covenant to provide a habitable house were mutually dependent, and thus a breach of the latter by Perssion relieved the tenants of any liability under the former.

Since there was a failure of consideration, the tenants are absolved from liability for rent under the lease and their only liability is for the reasonable rental value of the premises during the time of actual occupancy. We direct the trial court to find what a reasonable rental for that period would be and enter judgment for the tenants in the amount of their deposit plus the amount recoverable for their labor, less the rent so determined by the court.

Brown v. Southall Realty Co.

237 A.2d 834 (Ct. App. D.C. 1968)

This was an action brought by Southall Realty (plaintiff) to evict Mrs. Brown (defendant) for nonpayment of rent. Mrs. Brown contended that no rent was due under the lease because it was an illegal contract. The trial court held for the landlord, Southall Realty. Judgment reversed on appeal, holding that no rent was owed by the tenant.

QUINN, JUDGE. The evidence developed, at the trial, revealed that prior to the signing of the lease agreement, Southall was on notice that certain Housing Code violations existed on the premises in question. An inspector for the District of Columbia Housing Division of the Department of Licenses and Inspections testified that the violations, an obstructed commode, a broken railing, and insufficient ceiling height in the basement, existed at least some months prior to the lease agreement and had not been abated at the time of trial. He also stated that the basement violations prohibited the use of the entire basement as a dwelling place. Counsel for Southall Realty at the trial below elicited an admission from Brown that Southall "told Brown after the lease had been signed that the back room of the basement was habitable despite the Housing Code Violations."

This evidence having been established and uncontroverted, Mrs. Brown contends that the lease should have been declared unenforceable because it was entered into in contravention to the District of Columbia Housing Regulations, and knowingly so.

Section 2304 of the District of Columbia Housing Regulations reads as follows:

> No persons shall rent or offer to rent any habitation, or the furnishings thereof, unless such habitation and its furnishings are in a clean, safe and sanitary condition in repair, and free from rodents or vermin.

Section 2501 of these same Regulations, states:

> Every premises accommodating one or more habitations shall be maintained and kept in repair so as to provide decent living accommodations for the occupants. This part of the Code contemplates more than mere basic repairs, and maintenance to keep out the elements; its purpose is to include repairs and maintenance designed to make a premises or neighborhood healthy and safe.

It appears that the violations known by appellee to be existing on the leasehold at the time of the signing of the lease agreement were of a nature to make the "habitation" unsafe and unsanitary. Neither had the premises been maintained or repaired to the degree contemplated by the regulations, that is, "designed to make a premises . . . healthy and safe." The lease contract was, therefore, entered into in violation of the Housing Regulations requiring that they be safe and sanitary and that they be properly maintained.

In the case of *Hartman v. Lubar,* the court stated that,

> the general rule is that an illegal contract, made in violation of the statutory prohibition designed for police or regulatory purposes, is void and confers no right upon the wrongdoer. . . . To this general rule, however, the courts have found exceptions. For the exception, resort must be had to the intent of the legislature, as well as the subject matter of the legislation.

A reading of Sections 2304 and 2501 infers that the Commissioners of the District of Columbia, in promulgating these Housing Regulations, were endeavoring to regulate the rental of housing in the District and to insure for the prospective tenants that these rental units would be "habitable" and maintained as such. . . . To uphold the validity of this lease agreement, in light of the defects known to be existing on the leasehold prior to the agreement (that is, obstructed commode, broken railing, and insufficient ceiling height in the basement), would be to flout the evident purposes for which Sections 2304 and 2501 were enacted. The more reasonable view is, therefore, that where such conditions exist on a leasehold prior to an agreement to lease, the letting of such premises constitutes a violation of Sections 2304 and 2501 of the Housing Regulations, and that these Sections do indeed "imply a prohibition" so as "to render the prohibited act void."

Garcia v. Freeland Realty, Inc.
314 N.Y.S.2d 215 (Civ. Ct. N.Y.C. 1970)

This was an action brought by Jose Garcia (plaintiff) against Freeland Realty, Inc., (defendant) to recover for materials furnished and labor performed by tenant Garcia in connection with the replastering and painting of rooms in an apartment owned by landlord Freeland Realty. Judgment for Garcia.

Garcia rented the apartment pursuant to an oral lease. He had two small children that he discovered were eating paint and plaster that was flaking off the walls in two of the rooms in the apartment. Garcia complained about the condition to the landlord, and when the landlord did nothing to remedy the situation, Garcia purchased paint and plaster and replastered and repainted the offending walls. He spent $29.53 for materials and also claimed $1.60 an hour (the minimum wage) for ten hours labor.

GOODELL, JUDGE. The issue here, in the light of the uncontested facts, is whether a recovery by Garcia is barred as a matter of law in view of the common-law rule that the landlord, in the absence of an express covenant is not obligated to repair or paint. . . . While statutory duties to repair and paint have been imposed upon the owner by sections 78 and 80 respectively of the Multiple Dwelling Law, it has been held that these duties are enforceable by the municipality only and, therefore, that neither is the basis of a claim by the lessee against the lessor for reimbursement of the cost of repairs made by the lessee.

The court takes judicial notice of the facts, now notorious and a matter of common knowledge in New York City, that in New York City slum apartments "as successive layers of paint peel away, the paint underneath becomes a menace to any young child who can pick off the flakes and put them in his mouth" (*New York Post,* May 15, 1970, p.6); such plaster and paint contain lead; that lead poisoning is limited mainly to the children of the poor in New York City; and that the eating of such plaster and paint flakes by children leads to lead poisoning with the consequences of mental retardation and death.

This, therefore, is not a case involving painting for the sake of comfort or enjoyment of the premises. It is different and more than that. It concerns a situation of emergency and menace to the health and life of children.

The practical question that faced Garcia, a father of small children, in December 1969 and January 1970, was whether he was bound to sit by and do nothing despite the landlord's inactivity and the delays of a municipality beset by a multiplicity of problems and conflicting demands for its attention or whether he should take prompt steps to prevent irreparable damage to his children and charge the cost to his landlord.

In these circumstances, in my view, Garcia had the right to remove the menace to the health and life of his children and to charge the cost, to the extent hereafter noted, to the landlord, for the following reasons.

While it has been held, as noted, that despite sections 78 and 80 of the Multiple Dwelling Law, the making of repairs by a tenant, does not entitle the tenant to reimbursement from the landlord in the absence of an express covenant by the landlord, the landlord is nevertheless liable for injuries suffered by the tenant or members of his family as a result of the landlord's failure to make repairs.

Just as in the case of a falling ceiling or a defective step, so the landlord could foreseeably have been exposed to a tort action for damage had Garcia's children suffered the result of continuing ingestions of plaster and paint because of the landlord's failure to act after notice and demand for action.

Garcia, therefore, by his act, prevented the commission of an actionable tort that might have resulted from inaction.

If damage based upon the commission of a tort is an appropriate award, then in my view, it is proper and desirable to reimburse a plaintiff for the reasonable cost of preventing or averting the commission of a tort after a defendant has had a reasonable opportunity to act and failed to do so in circumstances calling for action on his part. As Prosser has said in his discussion of "prevention":

> The "prophylactic" factor of preventing future harm has been quite important in the field of torts. . . . While the idea of prevention is seldom controlling, it very often has weight as a reason for holding the defendant responsible. (Prosser, *Law of Torts,* (3d ed.), p.23).

In the circumstances of this case involving the concurrent conditions of an immediate threat to the health and life of children and a critical shortage of housing, it is my view that the prevention of an actionable tort by Garcia warrants his reimbursement for the cost of materials and the reasonable value of labor applied to the accomplishment of that result.

Problem Cases

1. Top Dollar Stores occupied certain premises belonging to Smith pursuant to an oral five year lease. Top Dollar submitted a draft written lease to Smith but Smith disagreed with virtually every major provision and demanded revisions. After five months Top Dollar gave notice of termination of the lease to Smith and moved out. Smith then brought suit for specific performance of the five year lease or for damages for its breach. Can Smith recover?

2. Remedco Corporation leased a building at 420 West 121 Street in New York City to the Bryn Mawr Hotel which used the building to operate a hotel. The multi-year lease contained a clause which required that the building not be used "for any business or purpose deemed disreputable." Over a long period of time the hotel rented rooms to anyone who applied and who paid a week's rent in advance even though it had some reason to believe its rooms were being used for assorted illicit purposes. The premises were marked by the police as a focal point for various types of crimes and they made repeated arrests of roomer-occupants for narcotics addiction, prostitution and assorted other crimes. Remedco brought suit to terminate the lease at a time it still had 13 years to run because of the long pattern of conduct by the roomers. Should the court allow Remedco to end the lease?

3. On May 11, Richard Paul, Inc., entered into a written lease for three years beginning June 1 and covering the first three floors of a building in Wilmington, Delaware, which Paul intended to use for the manufacture of a women's sock known as "Peds." The lease provided that the lessor would:

> renovate and put in order the present heating and plumbing system, and the elevator, and immediately after the execution of this Lease, further agrees to spray with lime, the interior of the premises herein demised; to replace all broken glass; and to make such other minor repairs as are necessary to the interior of the premises herein demised, provided, however, that if the costs of the repairs set out in this paragraph exceed the sum of Twelve Hundred Dollars ($1,200.00), the Lessee will pay one half of the costs in excess of the sum of Twelve Hundred Dollars ($1,200.00), but it is mutually agreed and understood that the aforesaid repairs shall in no case exceed the sum of Eighteen Hundred Dollars ($1,800.00). Lessor also agrees to keep the roof of said premises in repair.

   Paul inspected the premises prior to signing the lease and also shortly after June 1 and found them unfit for the use to which it intended to put them. On June 18 it demanded in writing that the landlord make the repairs, on June 23 it had much of the repair work started which was completed on September 9. This included cleaning the premises and a number of minor repairs. Paul then brought suit against the landlord for breach of the lease, claiming as damages: (1) the money expended in making repairs; (2) portions of the rent paid since the premises were not fully occupied; and (3) lost profits which reasonably could have been made had the premises been properly at Paul's disposal. How should the court rule on these claims?

4. Bailey rented an apartment in a building owned by Zlotnick. One of the provisions of the lease was that Bailey would not sublease or assign the lease without the permission of the landlord. One day Bailey was injured by plaster which fell from the ceiling of her kitchen shortly after a new hot water heating system had been installed in the building. Bailey brought an action against Zlotnick to recover for her injuries. Zlotnick defended on the grounds that Bailey was in violation of her lease because she was renting rooms in her apartment to others, a fact which had been known to Zlotnick's agents for some time, although he continued to accept rent from her. Should the court hold Bailey was not rightfully in possession because of the breach and thus barred from any recovery?

5. The toilet bowl in Tenant's apartment had a defective seat. Tenant notified Landlord of the problem but Landlord did not respond in a timely fashion. Tenant tried to fix it by using wire to hold the seat in place. However, Tenant was injured when she fell off when the seat broke. She sued Landlord to recover damages for her injuries, and Landlord claimed he was not liable because she had assumed the risk or had been contributorily negligent. Should Tenant be barred from recovering?

6. Codie Whitman, a young unmarried woman, rented an apartment in the Ritz Apartments which was owned by Gore Properties. William Hickey was the resident manager. One day Hickey saw Harry Porter cleaning paint brushes at a building near the airport, asked him if he would like to make some extra money, and hired him and two other men to paint the interiors of various apartments at the Ritz. Hickey did not inquire into Porter's background. Porter was then assigned to paint the Whitman apartment and given access to it using the landlord's set of keys. During the time he was painting the apartment Porter strangled Miss Whitman. He confessed and was committed to a mental hospital. The Executor of the Whitman estate brought a wrongful death action against Gore Properties and Hickey, claiming that they breached their duty to Miss Whitman and were negligent. Should they be held liable?

7. Tenant rented an apartment from Landlord pursuant to a lease that required him to surrender the premises in "as good a state and condition as reasonable use and wear and tear will permit" and also required him to make a refundable security deposit. After the lease was executed, Landlord notified the tenants in the building that no tenant was to shampoo his wall to wall carpet on surrender of the lease because Landlord had retained a professional carpet cleaner to do it. The cost of the carpet cleaner's services was to be automatically deducted from the security deposit. When Tenant left the building a portion of his security deposit was withheld to cover carpet cleaning and he sued for a refund of the full deposit. Is Tenant entitled to a refund?

8. In early 1952, Colprovia Corporation leased a plant and certain equipment in it from the New Haven Trap Rock Company. New Haven agreed to put the plant in excellent condition. In January 1953, Colprovia acknowledged to New Haven that the plant and equipment had been put in excellent condition and that Colprovia would be responsible for maintaining the equipment and pay for ordinary repairs. In August 1953, one of Colprovia's employees was injured while using some of the equipment which he claimed was in an unsafe, dangerous, and worn condition without adequate safeguards. The employee brought suit against New Haven contending that it should be liable for the injuries he sustained on the premises it owned and using equipment belonging to it. Should he be able to recover against New Haven?

9. Batemore, Inc., leased a store and office building, which had been previously owned by Standard Brands, to Standard Brands for a term of three years. The lease provided that the tenant would maintain the interior of the building and be responsible for the ordinary operating expense; the tenant was also obligated at the expiration of the term to surrender the premises in as good condition as received except for ordinary wear and tear. The building was equipped with an air conditioning system operated by electric power. Because of wartime restrictions, the system contained methyl chloride rather than freon. While freon is comparatively harmless, methyl chloride is dangerous when not properly controlled because it is toxic, inflammable, and subject to ignition and explosion. The air conditioning system was not functioning and a knowledgeable repairman was called to make repairs. However, he and tenant's agents failed to take certain necessary precautions, an explosion and fire resulted, and the building was damaged. Batemore brought suit against Standard Brands to recover damages due to Standard Brand's negligence. Is Standard Brands liable to Batemore?

10. Solomon leased a "building" at 49 South Main in Wilkes-Barre consisting of a store along with part of the storeroom and basement, but specifically excluding the roof, to Neisner Brothers to operate a retail store; nothing was said about land. The lease provided that in the event the premises were destroyed or damaged by fire, the rent would be proportionately abated unless and until the premises were repaired or restored; it provided further that if the premises were not fully repaired or restored within 90 days after the fire, the tenant has the right to terminate the lease. The premises were destroyed by fire through no fault of either party. Solomon showed Neisner the plans for the building he proposed to erect at the site of the fire but Neisner rejected the plans on the grounds they did not conform to the store as it was prior to the fire. Solomon advised Neisner that no space would be provided to it in the building, and Neisner demanded that the store, storeroom and basement be restored for its occupancy for the balance of the term of the lease. The new building was built and then leased to others. Does Neisner have a valid claim for damages against Solomon for an eviction depriving him of the use of the premises?

35

Environmental Law

Introduction

Historical Perspective. In the early 1970s the United States and many other countries in the world became increasingly concerned about damage man was causing to the environment and the possible consequences of further degradation. Historically people have assumed that the air, water, and land around them would absorb their waste products. But in recent times it has become clear that nature's capacity to assimilate people's wastes is not infinite. Burgeoning population, economic growth, affluence, and synthetic products that resist natural decomposition have contributed to environmental deterioration.

Concern about the environment existed long before the 1970s. In medieval England, Parliament passed "smoke control" acts making it illegal to burn soft coal at certain times of the year. Where the owner or operator of a piece of property is using it in such a manner as to unreasonably interfere with another owner's (or the public's) health or enjoyment of his or her property, the courts have long entertained suits to abate the nuisance. Nuisance actions, which are discussed in Chapter 32, are frequently not ideal vehicles for dealing with widespread pollution problems. Rather than a hit-or-miss approach, a comprehensive across-the-board approach is required. Realizing this, the federal government, as well as many state and local governments, had passed air-and-water-pollution abatement laws by the late 1950s and 1960s. As the 1970s began, an explosion of interest and concern over the quality and future of the environment produced new laws and public demands for action.

The Environmental Protection Agency. In December 1970, the President created the Environmental Protection Agency (EPA) to consolidate the federal government's environmental responsibilities. This was an explicit recognition that the problems of air and water pollution, solid waste disposal, water supply, pesticides and radiation control were interrelated and required a coordinated approach. Congress passed comprehensive new legislation covering, among other things, air and water pollution, pesticides, ocean dumping, and noise pollution. Among the factors prompting these laws were: protection of human health, esthetics, economic costs of continued pollution, and protection of natural systems. The next few years will find adjustments being made in our environmental laws and regulations as society decides how clean it wants its environment, how quickly it wants to proceed, and what costs it is willing to bear. Inherent in these societal decisions are questions of which resources to use, and at what rate, and which resources must be protected.

The National Environmental Policy Act. The National Environmental Policy Act (NEPA) was signed into law on January 1, 1970. In addition to creating the Council of Environmental Quality in the Executive Office of the President, the act required that an environmental impact statement be prepared for every recommendation or report on legislation and in every major federal action significantly affecting the quality of the environment. The environmental impact statement must: (1) describe the environmental impact of the proposed action; (2) discuss impacts that cannot be avoided; (3) discuss the alternatives to the proposed action; (4) indicate differences between short- and long-term impacts; and (5) detail any irreversible commitments of resources NEPA requires federal agencies to consider the environmental impact of their actions before they undertake them. And, other federal, state, and local agencies, as well as interested citizens, have an opportunity to comment on the environmental impact of the project before the agency can proceed. Where the process is not followed, citizens can, and have, gone to court to force compliance with NEPA. Adherence by all governmental units, industry, and citizens to the NEPA concept—that the environmental impact of actions should be understood and minimized before they are undertaken—would do much to reduce environmental degradation. A number of states and local governments have passed their own environmental impact laws requiring NEPA-type statements for major public and private developments.

SUMMARY

This decade has seen the passage of many new laws designed to protect the environment and the creation of new administrative agencies to enforce those laws. Older tools for protecting human health and welfare—such as the action to abate a nuisance—have to some extent been supplanted by comprehensive legislation prescribing across-the-board measures to deal with the major kinds and sources of pollution. The NEPA was passed to require the federal government to take into account the environmental effects of actions it proposes to take.

Daly v. Volpe

350 F.Supp. 252 (D.C. Dist. Col. 1972)

This was an action by Daly and others (plaintiffs) against the Secretary of Transportation, John Volpe, and the Washington State Department of Highways (defendants) to enjoin the construction of a federally funded highway on or near plaintiffs' property. Plaintiffs contended, among other things, that defendants had violated the provisions of the National Environmental Policy Act and in particular had failed to take into account the impact the highway would have on a wildlife preserve, Kimball Creek Marsh. Judgment for plaintiffs that the act had not been complied with.

BEEKS, JUDGE. Plaintiffs contend that defendants failed to follow the required procedures with respect to drafting and filing an environmental impact statement. NEPA, which became law on January 1, 1970, requires that

all agencies of the Federal Government shall: . . .

(C) include in every recommendation or report on proposals for legislation and other major Federal actions significantly affecting the quality of the human environment, a detailed statement by the responsible official on—
   (i) the environmental impact of the proposed action.
   (ii) any adverse environmental effects which cannot be avoided should the proposal be implemented.
   (iii) alternatives to the proposed action.
   (iv) the relationship between local short-term uses of man's environment and the maintenance and enhancement of long-term productivity, and
   (v) any irreversible and irretrievable commitments of resources which would be involved in the proposed action should it be implemented.

The state's first-draft environmental impact statement was drafted in the form required by statute, but was ambiguous and self-contradictory. Paragraph one, concerning the environmental impact of the highway, failed to discuss Kimball Creek Marsh, and was too general and ambiguous.

The second paragraph was inadequate. All adverse environmental effects should be listed, and harmful effects which cannot be avoided must be discussed to indicate what measures can be taken to minimize the harm. The state's draft environmental impact statement was far too general and not sufficiently detailed.

The fifth paragraph of the draft impact statement is totally unsatisfactory. It should list, among other things, (1) the cost of land, construction materials, labor, and other economically measurable costs which cannot be retrieved once a highway is constructed; and (2) the resources which may be irretrievably lost, and the nature of each such loss, to which a dollar value cannot be readily assigned—for example, the loss of forested recreational land.

It is the judgment of the court that defendants have failed to conform to the procedural requirements of 42 U.S.C. § 4332 (2)(c). The state must prepare a draft environmental impact statement which conforms to those requirements, circulate it among interested agencies, and make it available to the public prior to another public location hearing. The state shall then prepare a final environmental impact statement, append to it a compilation of the comments received, and submit these, together with a new application for approval of the state's suggested location of I–90, to the Regional Federal Highway Administrator. Federal defendants shall then process the application according to existing regulations. Both the state and federal defendants shall carefully consider the ecological effects of the highway upon Kimball Creek Marsh.

Air Pollution

Introduction. The combustion of fuel, industrial processes, and solid waste disposal are the major contributors to air pollution. People's initial concern with air pollution related to that which they could see—visible or smoke pollution. In the 1880s, Chicago and Cincinnati enacted smoke control ordinances. As the technology became available to deal with smoke and particulate emissions, attention turned to other less visible gasses which impact human health and vegetation. The first federal legislation came in 1955 when Congress authorized $5 million each year for air pollution research. In 1963 the Clean Air Act was passed to provide assistance to the states and to deal with interstate air pollution; it was amended in 1965 and 1967 to provide for among other things, controls on pollution from automobiles. The comprehensive legislation enacted into law in December 1970 now provides the basis for our approach to the air pollution problem; its provisions are central to the discussion that follows. In 1977 Congress made some modifications to the 1970 Act, and enacted provisions designed to prevent deterioration of the air in areas where its quality currently exceeds that required by federal law.

1970 Clean Air Act. The 1970 Clean Air Act separates air pollution controls into essentially two categories: (1) controls on mobile or transportation sources, and (2) controls on stationary sources. The major pollutants from mobile sources such as automobiles and airplanes are carbon monoxide, hydrocarbons, and nitrogen oxides. Carbon monoxide is a colorless, odorless gas which can dull mental performance and even cause death when inhaled in large quantities. Hydrocarbons, which essentially are unburned fuel, combine with nitrogen oxides under the influence of sunlight to become photochemical oxidants—known as smog.

Automobile Pollution. The 1970 Clean Air Act required a reduction by

1975 of 90 percent in the amount of carbon monoxide and hydrocarbons emitted by automobiles and a likewise 90 percent reduction of nitrogen oxides by 1976. The administrator of EPA was empowered to grant a one-year extension of this deadline if technology to achieve the reduction is not available and if the manufacturers made a good-faith effort to meet the deadline. Subsequently Congress has addressed the question of setting even more stringent limits on automobile emissions while at the same time requiring that the new automobiles get better gas mileage. The 1970 act also provided for regulation and registration of fuel additives such as lead, as well as for regulation of emissions from aircraft.

Pollution from Other Sources. The 1970 Clean Air Act established a comprehensive approach for dealing with air pollution from stationary sources. The EPA was required to set national ambient air-quality standards for the major pollutants which have an adverse impact on human health—that is, to set the amount of a given pollutant that could be present in air around us. The ambient air-quality standards were to be set at two levels: (1) *primary* standards which are designed to protect public health from harm; and (2) *secondary* standards which are designed to protect vegetation, materials, climate, visibility, and economic values. Pursuant to this statutory mandate, EPA set ambient air-quality standards for carbon monoxide, nitrogen oxide, sulfur oxide, hydrocarbons, photochemical oxidents, and particulates.

The country was divided into air-quality regions, and each region was required to have an implementation plan for meeting the national ambient air quality standards. This necessitated an inventory of the various sources of air pollution and their contribution to the total air pollution in their air-quality region. The major emitters of pollutants were then required to reduce their emissions to a level that will enable the overall air quality to meet the national standards. The states have the responsibility for deciding which activities must be regulated or curtailed to meet the national standards.

The act also requires that new stationary sources must install the best available technology for reducing air pollution. EPA was required to establish standards to be met by new stationary sources and has done so for the major types of stationary sources of air pollution. The primary responsibility for enforcing the air-quality standards lies with the states, but the federal government also has the right to enforce the standards where the states fail to do so. The Clean Air Act also provides for suits by citizens to force industry or the government to fully comply with the act's provisions.

SUMMARY

The Clean Air Act of 1970, as amended in 1977, separates air pollution controls into two categories (1) mobile sources; and (2) stationary sources.

The act sets out time schedules by which certain control measures must be instituted in order to protect human health and the general welfare from harm attributable to air pollution.

International Harvester Co. v. Ruckelshaus

478 F.2d 615 (D.C. Cir. 1973)

This was an action brought by International Harvester Company, General Motors Corporation, Ford Motors Corporation, and Chrysler Corporation (plaintiffs) against the Administrator of the U.S. Environmental Protection Agency, William D. Ruckelshaus (defendant) challenging the administrator's May 1972 decision not to grant them a one-year postponement of the 1975 standards set by the Clean Air Act of 1970. Judgment for plaintiffs.

LEVENTHAL, CIRCUIT JUDGE. These consolidated petitions of International Harvester and the three major auto companies—Ford, General Motors, and Chrysler—seek review of a decision by the Administrator of the Environmental Protection Agency denying petitioners' applications, filed pursuant to Section 202 of the Clean Air Act, for one-year suspensions of the 1975 emission standards prescribed under the statute for light duty vehicles in the absence of suspension.

The tension of forces presented by the controversy over automobile emission standards may be focused by two central observations:

(1) The automobile is an essential pillar of the American economy. Some 28 percent of the nonfarm workforce draws its livelihood from the automobile industry and its products.
(2) The automobile has had a devastating impact on the American environment. As of 1970, authoritative voices stated that "[a]utomotive pollution constitutes in excess of 60 percent of our national air pollution problem" and more than 80 percent of the air pollutants in concentrated urban areas.

Congressional concern over the problem of automotive emissions dates back to the 1950s, but it was not until the passage of the Clean Air Act in 1965 that Congress established the principle of Federal standards for automobile emissions. Under the 1965 act and its successor, the Air Quality Act of 1967, the Department of Health, Education and Welfare was authorized to promulgate emission limitations commensurate with existing technological feasibility.

The development of emission control technology proceeded haltingly. The Secretary of HEW testified in 1967 that "the state of the art has tended to meander along until some sort of regulation took it by the hand and gave it a good pull. . . . There has been a long period of waiting for it, and it hasn't worked very well."

The legislative background must also take into account the fact that in 1969 the Department of Justice brought suit against the four largest automobile manufacturers on grounds that they had conspired to delay the development of emission control devices.

On December 31, 1970, Congress grasped the nettle and amended the Clean Air Act to set a statutory standard for required reductions in levels of hydrocarbons (HC) and carbon monoxide (CO) which must be achieved for 1975 models of light duty vehicles. Section 202(b) of the Act added by the Clean Air Amendments of 1970, provides that, beginning with the 1975 model year, exhaust emission of hydrocarbons and carbon monoxide from "light duty vehicles" must be reduced at least 90 percent from the permissible emission levels in the 1970 model year. In accordance with the Congressional directives, the administrator on June 23, 1971, promulgated regulations limiting HC and CO emissions from 1975 model light duty vehicles to .41 and 3.4 grams per vehicle mile respectively. At the same time, as required by section 202(b) (2) of the Act, he prescribed the test procedures by which compliance with these standards is measured.

Congress was aware that these 1975 standards were "drastic medicine," designed to "force the state of the art." There was, naturally, concern whether the manufacturers would be able to achieve this goal. Therefore, Congress provided, in Senator Baker's phrase, a "realistic escape hatch": the manufacturers could petition the Administrator of the EPA for a one-year suspension of the 1975 requirements.

This case inevitably presents, to the court as to the administrator, the need for a perspective on the suspension that is informed by an analysis which balances the costs of a "wrong decision" on feasibility against the gains of a correct one. These costs include the risks of grave maladjustments for the technological leader from the eleventh-hour grant of a suspension, and the impact on jobs and the economy from a decision which is only partially accurate, allowing companies to produce cars but at a significantly reduced level of output. Against this must be weighed the environmental savings from denial of suspension. The record indicates that these will be relatively modest. There is also the possibility that failure to grant a suspension may be counterproductive to the environment, if there is significant decline in performance characteristics.

Another consideration is present, that the real cost to granting a suspension arises from the symbolic compromise with the goal of a clean environment. We emphasize that our view of a one-year suspension, and the intent of Congress as to a one-year suspension, is in no sense to be taken as any support for further suspensions. This would plainly be contrary to the intent of Congress to set an absolute standard in 1976. On the contrary, we view the imperative of the Congressional requirement as to the significant improvement that must be wrought no later than 1976, as interrelated with the provision for one-year suspension. The flexibility in the statute provided by the availability of a one-year suspension only strengthens the impact of the absolute standard. Considerations of fairness will support comprehensive and firm, even drastic, regulations, provided a "safety valve" is also provided—ordinarily a provision for waiver, exception or adjustment, in this case a provision for suspension. "The limited safety valve permits a more rigorous adherence to an effective regulation." *WAIT Radio v. FCC, supra,* 418 F.2d at 1159. To hold the safety valve too rigidly is to interfere with the relief that was contemplated as an integral part of the firmness of the overall, enduring program.

Water Pollution

Introduction. History is replete with plague and epidemics brought on by poor sanitation and polluted water. Indeed, preventing waterborne disease has through time been the major reason to combat water pollution. Among the more tragic symbols of our time are the oil-soaked seagull, kepone deposits in the James River, a euthrophying Lake Erie, and a "No Swimming—Water Polluted" sign near a swimming hole. Water pollution can affect public health, recreation, commercial fishing, agriculture, water supplies, and esthetics. Accordingly, our current efforts to combat water pollution have a broad range of reasons to support them.

Federal Legislation. Federal water pollution legislation dates back to the 19th century when Congress enacted the River and Harbor Act of 1886. In fact this act, recodified in the River and Harbor Act of 1899, furnished the legal basis for the EPA's initial enforcement actions against polluters. The act provided that anyone discharging or depositing "refuse" into a navigable waterway had to obtain a discharge permit first from the Corps of Engineers. Under some contemporary court decisions even hot water discharged from nuclear power plants was considered "refuse." The permit system established pursuant to the "Refuse Act" was subsequently been replaced by a permit system set up by the Federal Water Pollution Control Act Amendments of 1972.

The initial Federal Water Pollution Control Act (FWPCA) was passed in 1948. Amendments to the FWPCA in 1956, 1965, 1966, and 1970 increased the federal role in water pollution abatement and strengthened its enforcement powers. Gradually, the federal government has begun to pay a larger and larger share of the costs of building municipal sewage treatment plants; under the 1972 Amendments the federal share is now 75 percent with the remainder being put up by state and local governments.

Clean Waters Act of 1972. The 1972 Amendments to the FWPCA were as comprehensive in the water pollution field as the 1970 Clean Air Act was in the air pollution field. They proclaimed two general goals for this country: (1) to achieve wherever possible by July 1, 1983, water that is clean enough for swimming and other recreational uses, and clean enough for the protection and propagation of fish, shellfish, and wildlife; and (2) by 1985 to have no discharges of pollutants into the nation's waters. The goals reflected a national frustration with the progress made to date in dealing with water pollution and a commitment to end such pollution. The new law set out a series of specific actions to be taken by certain dates by federal, state, and local governments, and by industry and also provided strong enforcement provisions to back up the deadlines. In 1977 Congress enacted some modifications to the 1972 Act which adjusted some of the deadlines and otherwise "finetuned" the Act.

The 1972 Amendments left the primary responsibility for preventing, reducing, and eliminating water pollution with the states but provided that they had to do it within a national framework with the EPA empowered to move in if the states do not fulfill their responsibilities. The law set a number of deadlines to control water pollution from industrial sources: (1) industries discharging wastes into the nation's waterways were required to install the "best practicable" water pollution control technology by July 1, 1977, and must have the "best available" technology on line by July 1, 1983. These deadlines were modified by the 1977 Amendments. New sources of industrial pollution must use the "best available demonstrated control technology." In each instance EPA is responsible for issuing guidelines as to the "best available" and "best practicable" technologies. Industries that discharge their wastes into municipal systems are required to pretreat their wastes so that they will not interfere with the biological operation of the plant or pass through the plant without treatment.

The 1972 law continued and expanded the previously established system of setting water quality standards which define the uses of specific bodies of water—such as recreational, public water supply, propagation of fish and wildlife, and agricultural and industrial water supply. Then the maximum daily loads of various kinds of pollutants are set so that the water will be suitable for the designated type of use. The 1972 law requires that all municipal and industrial dischargers must obtain permits which will spell out the amounts and types of pollutants the permit holder will be allowed to discharge and any steps it must take to reduce its present or anticipated discharge. Polluters are also required to keep records, install and maintain monitoring equipment, and sample their discharges. Penalties for violating the law range from a minimum of $2,500 for a first offense up to $50,000 per day and two years in prison for subsequent violations.

Citizen Suits. Any citizen or group of citizens whose interests are adversely affected has the right to take court action against anyone violating an effluent standard or limitation or an order issued by EPA or a state. Citizens also have the right to take court action against the EPA if it fails to carry out mandatory provisions of the law.

Ocean Dumping. The Marine Protection, Research, and Sanctuaries Act of 1972 set up a permit system regulating the dumping of all types of materials into ocean waters. Thus the nation's concern over the impact of people's actions on the environment is extended to marine areas contiguous to our shores.

SUMMARY

Water pollution has posed potential health problems for people for many years. Federal water pollution control legislation was first passed in 1948 and has been amended five times since then. The 1972 amendments set two major goals for this country: (1) swimmable water wherever possible by 1983, and (2) no discharge of pollutants into the nation's waters by 1985. To facilitate achievement of these goals, the amendments set out a series of strict interim deadlines which must be met by governments and private industry.

United States v. Reserve Mining Co.

8 Envir. Rep. Cases 1978 (D.C. Minn. 1976)

This was an action brought by the United States and a number of cities, states and environmental groups (plaintiffs) against the Reserve Mining Company and others (defendants) to halt the dumping of taconite tailings into Lake Superior. A series of trial and appellate court decisions resulted in a judgment that Reserve Mining's discharge of tailings violated state and federal law, constituted a health hazard and should be enjoined. In this particular decision, the State of Minnesota sought an order imposing penalties against Reserve Mining for violation of the state pollution control laws. The court imposed a penalty of $837,500 against Reserve Mining.

DEVITT, JUDGE. It has been established thet Reserve has violated Minnesota's pollution control laws and regulations. *Reserve Mining Co. v. Environmental Protection Agency,* 514 F.2d 492, (8th Cir. 1975); *United States v. Reserve Mining Co.,* 394 F.Supp. 233; 380 F.Supp. 11 (D. Minn. 1974); Minn. Stat. § 15.071 (1974) authorizes a court to impose a fine of up to $10,000 per day for each violation of, *inter alia,* the laws and regulations violated by Reserve. Minnesota contends that Reserve should be fined for daily violations of these laws and regulations for almost a full year.

The daily dumping of approximately 67,000 tons of carcinogenic waste into Lake Superior polluting public water supplies in violation of its state discharge permits is, by far, Reserve's most serious offense.

In 1947 Reserve obtained from two state agencies, identical permits authorizing it to discharge tailings into Lake Superior. Subsection (d) of those permits prohibits discharges which

> result in any material clouding or discoloration of the water at the surface outside of [the specified discharge] zone . . . nor shall such tailings be discharged so as to result in any material adverse effects on . . . public water supplies. . . .

The district court concluded that "the terms of the permits are being violated" because

> [t]he discharge causes discoloration of the surface waters outside of the zone of discharge, causes an increase in turbidity, and adversely affects the public water supplies of several communities resulting in unlawful pollution of the lake.

The court of appeals agreed, stating that:

> The record shows that Reserve is discharging a substance into Lake Superior waters which under an acceptable but unproved medical theory may be considered as carcinogenic. [T]his discharge gives rise to reasonable medical concern over the public health.

Clearly, these findings justify the conclusion that Reserve violated its discharge permits. The trial court has determined that Reserve was in violation of its state discharge permits every day during the May 20, 1973 to April 20, 1974 period.

Minn. Stat. § 115.45 (1974) requires Reserve to comply with the terms of its state permits or be subject to the penalties authorized by Minn. Stat. § 115.071 subd. 3 (1974). Therefore, because Reserve has violated its permits, the only remaining issue is the amount of the penalty.

In making this determination, the court is aware that, as a result of these discharges, defendants are liable for the costs, expected to be approximately six million dollars, of supplying clean water to the affected communities. In addition, the injunction resulting from this litigation will compel Reserve to either cease operations or expend substantial sums, estimated at over three hundred million dollars, to develop an alternative means of disposing of production wastes.

It is not disputed that Reserve, by supplying needed jobs and services, has revitalized the economy of Northeastern Minnesota and, by adding to the supply of domestically produced raw iron, has contributed to the economy of the entire country. But similar contributions have been made by other corporations while complying with applicable pollution control laws and regulations.

It should be appreciated that Reserve did not set out to spoil the air and water or cause inconvenience to or apprehension among residents of the area. It launched its business venture with the encouragement, even the importuning, of all segments of government and society. But in this business venture, the record shows it returned very substantial profits to its corporate owner-parents, Republic and Armco. It is reasonable to conclude that some of those profits are attributable to operations made less costly by discharging tailings in Lake Superior rather than on land, as is done by its competitors. And, as is discussed later herein, the record shows that Reserve, particularly through its Vice President Haley, frustrated the court in prompt resolution of the controversy by violation of court rules and orders and thus prolonged the status quo.

While the daily discharge of 67,000 tons of tailings into Lake Superior is shocking in these days of improved environmental awareness, those discharges were expressly authorized in 1947 by the State of Minnesota. Hindsight tells us that was a mistake, but the gravity of it has not yet been determined. The court of appeals held that Reserve's discharges have not yet been found to be harmful to the public health and that the danger is potential, not imminent. The court of appeals found that Reserve need not terminate its operations but directed that preventive and precautionary steps be taken. They have been taken. So while the record shows violations of the permits, it has not been shown, and in the view of the court of appeals it is not likely it can be shown, that the past violations have caused actual harm to the public health.

Upon consideration of all the factors and pursuant to authority of Minn. Stat. § 115.071 subd. 3 (1974), the court imposes on defendants a penalty of $2,500 per day for violations of the terms of Reserve's state discharge permits.

Pesticides and Toxic Substances

Introduction. The vast increase in productivity over the past few decades of the American farmer has in large measure been attributable to the farmer's use of chemicals to kill the insects, pests, and weeds that have historically competed with him or her for the farmer's crops. Some of the chemicals, like pesticides, were a mixed blessing. They enabled people to dramatically increase productivity and to conquer disease. On the other hand, dead fish and birds provided evidence that some of the chemicals were building up in the food chain and were proving fatal to some species. Gradually people realized the need to focus on the long term effect of the discharge of chemicals into the environment.

Federal Pesticide Legislation. The federal responsibility for dealing with pesticides was given to the EPA in December of 1970. EPA enforces the Federal Insecticide, Fungicide, and Rodenticide Act of 1947 (FIFRA) as amended recently by the Federal Environmental Pesticide Control Act of 1972 (FEPCA). This act gives EPA the authority to register pesticides before they can be sold, to provide for certification of applicators of pesticides designated for "restrictive" use, to set tolerances on the amount of pesticide residue on crops that provide food for people or animals, and to register and inspect pesticide manufacturing establishments.

Suspension and Cancellation. When the administrator of EPA has reason to believe that continued use of a particular pesticide poses an "imminent hazard" he or she may suspend its registration and remove it from the market. In those situations where the administrator believes there is less than an imminent hazard but where the environmental risks of continuing to use a pesticide outweigh its benefits, the administrator may initiate a cancellation of registration proceeding. This proceeding affords all interested persons—manufacturers, distributors, users, environmentalists, and scientists—an opportunity to present evidence on the proposed cancellation. Cancellation of the registration occurs when the administrator finds that the product will cause "unreasonable adverse effects on the environment."

Toxic Substances. Other current legislation is focused on other toxic substances—such as mercury—and on the new chemical compounds developed each year. In 1976 Congress passed the Toxic Substances Control Act which requires that chemicals be tested by manufacturers or processors to determine their effect on human health or the environment prior to the time they are introduced into commerce. The Act also gives EPA the authority to regulate chemicals, substances or mixtures that present an unreasonable risk of injury to health or the environment and to take action against any such substances or mixtures that pose an imminent hazard. This legislation is in response to the concern that thousands of new substances are released by man into the environment each year, sometimes without adequate consideration of their potential for harm, and it is not until damage from a substance, for example, kepone, occurs that its manufacture or use is properly regulated. At the same time the Act has as a goal that it not unduly impede or create unnecessary economic barriers to technological innovation.

SUMMARY

Use of agricultural chemicals in the last few years has led to vast increases in productivity and at the same time posed increased risks to the environment. The Federal Environmental Pesticide Control Act of 1972 gives the EPA the responsibility to register pesticides before they can be sold, to restrict their use, to set tolerances on residues on food products, and to provide for the certification of applicators. Pesticides whose risks outweigh their benefits may have their registration cancelled or suspended.

Consolidated DDT Hearings
Opinion and Order of the Administrator

37 Fed. Reg. 13369 (1972)

This was an action taken by the administrator of the Environmental Protection Agency cancelling the registration of most of the uses of DDT.

On January 15, 1971, the Environmental Protection Agency commenced formal administrative review of all registrations for DDT products and uses pursuant to section 4(c) of the Federal Insecticide, Fungicide, and Rodenticide Act. Thirty-one companies holding DDT registrations challenged the EPA's cancellation of DDT use registrations. The U.S. Department of Agriculture intervened on the side of the registrants, and the Environmental Defense Fund intervened along with the EPA to help present the case for cancellation.

After a lengthy public hearing, on April 25, 1972, the hearing examiner issued an opinion recommending to the administrator of EPA that all "essential" uses of DDT be retained and that cancellation be lifted. The administrator took the opinion under advisement and received oral and written briefs both supporting and taking exception to the hearing officer's findings of fact and conclusions of law. The administrator then issued his opinion and order cancelling virtually all uses of DDT as of December 31, 1972, except for use on several minor crops and its use for disease control and health-related uses.

WILLIAM D. RUCKELSHAUS, ADMINISTRATOR. This hearing represents the culmination of approximately 3 years of intensive administrative inquiry into the uses of DDT.

Background. DDT is the familiar abbreviation for the chemical (1,1,1,trichlorophenyl ethane), which was for many years the most widely used chemical pesticide in this country. DDT's insecticidal properties were originally discovered, apparently by accident, in 1939, and during World War II it was used extensively for typhus control. Since 1945, DDT has been used for general control of mosquitoes, boll-weevil infestation in cotton-growing areas, and a variety of other uses. Peak use of DDT occurred at the end of the 1950's and present domestic use of DDT in various formulations has been estimated at 6,000 tons per year. According to Admission 7 of the record, approximately 86 percent or 10,277,258 pounds of domestically used DDT is applied to cotton crops. The same admission indicates that 603,053 pounds and 937,901 pounds, or approximately 5 percent and 9 percent of the total formulated by 27 of the petitioners in these hearings, are used respectively on soybean and peanut crops. All other uses of the 11,966,196 pounds amount to 158,833 of the total, or little over 1 percent.

For the above uses it appears that DDT is sold in four different formulations: emulsifiable sprays; dust; wettable powder; and granular form.

Public concern over the widespread use of pesticides was stirred by Rachel Carson's book *Silent Spring* and a natural outgrowth was the investigation of this popular and widely sprayed chemical. DDT, which for many years had been used with apparent safety, was, the critics alleged, a highly dangerous substance which killed beneficial insects, upset the natural ecological balance, and collected in the food chain, thus posing a hazard to man, and other forms of advanced aquatic and avian life.

Application of risk-benefit to crop uses of DDT. The Agency and EDF have established that DDT is toxic to nontarget insects and animals, persistent, mobile, and transferable and that it builds up in the food chain. No label directions for use can completely prevent these hazards. In short, they have established at the very least the risk of the unknown. That risk is compounded where, as is the case with DDT, man and animals tend to accumulate and store the chemical. These facts alone constitute risks that are unjustified where apparently safer alternatives exist to achieve the same benefit. Where, however, there is a demonstrated laboratory relationship between the chemical and toxic effects in man or animals, this risk is, generally speaking, rendered even more unacceptable, if alternatives exist. In the case before us the risk to human health from using DDT cannot be discounted. While these risks might be acceptable were we forced to use DDT, they are not so trivial that we can be indifferent to assuming them unnecessarily.

The evidence of record showing storage in man and magnification in the food chain is a warning to the prudent that man may be exposing himself to a substance that may ultimately have a serious effect on his health.

As Judge Leventhal recently pointed out, cancer is a "sensitive and fright-laden" matter and noted earlier in his opinion that carcinogenic effects are "generally cumulative and irreversible when discovered." *EDF v. EPA.* The possibility that DDT is a carcinogen is at present remote and unquantifiable; but if it is not a siren to panic, it is a semaphore which suggests that an identifiable public benefit is required to justify continued use of DDT. Where one chemical tests tumorigenic in a laboratory and one does not, and both accomplish the same risk, the latter is to be preferred, absent some extenuating circumstances.

The risks to the environment from continued use of DDT are more clearly established. There is no doubt that DDT runoff can cause contamination of waters and given its propensity to volatilize and disperse during application, there is no assurance that curtailed usage on the order of 12 million pounds per year will not continue to affect widespread areas beyond the location of application. The agency staff established as well, the existence of acceptable substitutes for all crop uses of DDT except on onions and sweet potatoes in storage and green peppers.

Registrants attempted but failed to surmount the evidence of established risks and the existence of substitutes by arguing that the buildup of DDT in the environment and its migration to remote areas has resulted from past uses and misuses. There is, however, no persuasive evidence of record to show that the aggregate volume of use of DDT for all uses in question, given the method of application, will not result in continuing dispersal and buildup in the environment and thus add to or maintain the stress on the environment resulting from past use. The Department of Agriculture has, for its part, emphasized DDT's low acute toxicity in comparison to that of alternative chemicals and thus tried to make the risk and benefit equation balance out favorably for the continued use of DDT. While the acute toxicity of methyl parathion must, in the short run, be taken into account, it does not justify continued use of DDT on a long-term basis. Where a chemical can be safely used if label directions are followed, a producer cannot avoid the risk of his own negligence by exposing third parties and the environment to a long-term hazard.

Accordingly, all crop uses of DDT are hereby canceled except for application to onions for control of cutworm, weevils on stored sweet potatoes, and sweet peppers.

Noise Pollution and Radiation Control

Noise Control Act of 1972. Noise pollution—or unwanted sound—has become an undesirable and sometimes dangerous aspect of modern life. Although there is some local and federal legislation now on the books dealing with noise pollution, our efforts to control it are very much in the embryonic stage. In the Noise Control Act of 1972 Congress mandated the Federal Aviation Administration and the Environmental Protection Agency to prescribe standards and regulations for the control and abatement of aircraft noise and sonic boom; the Department of Transportation and the EPA were directed to promulgate standards and regulations relating to noise emissions of interstate railroad and motor carriers. The act further authorizes the administrator of EPA to set regulations for products designated as major noise sources where such standards are feasible.

Local ordinances sometimes specify the hours each day during which construction work on buildings and streets may be performed and commonly require mufflers on motor vehicles. The noise pollution area is of considerable interest to the prospective businessman because it is a factor he is likely to have to take into account in the design of his products and in the operation of his business.

Radiation Control. The rapidly escalating demand for energy combined with the finite availability of fossil fuels has intensified the need for nuclear-fueled power plants. This need has coincided with increased citizen concern with radioactivity. Citizen concerns specifically related to nuclear plants include: possible release of radioactivity into the environment during normal operation of the nuclear reactor, possible accidents through human error or mechanical failure, and the disposal of the radioactive wastes generated by the reactor. There is also concern that the discharge of heated water used to cool the reactor—thermal pollution—may cause irreversible damage to the environment.

Currently, the problems of reactor safety are under the jurisdiction of the Nuclear Regulatory Commission which exercises licensing authority over nuclear power plants. The Environmental Protection Agency has the responsibility for setting standards for radioactivity in the overall environment and for dealing with the radioactive waste disposal problem. The thermal pollution problem is handled by EPA pursuant to its water pollution control authorities.

SUMMARY

As the amount of unwanted noise present in our environment has increased, the federal and local governments have enacted legislation aimed at controlling some of the most offensive sources of noise. As the demand for energy increases, the country is utilizing more and more nuclear energy to satisfy the demand. The regulation of radiation problems occasioned by nuclear reactors is largely done at the federal level by the Environmental Protection Agency and the Nuclear Regulatory Commission.

Problem Cases

1. The General Services Administration, acting as agent for the Department of Justice's Bureau of Prisons, acquired a 206-acre site in a planned, low-density, residential area in San Diego, California, on which it proposed to construct a youth detection facility. The facility would be about one and one half miles from existing residential areas, one half mile from partially constructed residential areas and 350 feet from a proposed elementary school site. The facility would house approximately 250 inmates with a staff of 140 persons. G.S.A. made several environmental assessments of the proposed facility and each time it concluded that the "project was not a major Federal action significantly affecting the human environment." Accordingly, an environmental impact statement was not prepared regarding the proposed youth facility. The local school district and a citizens' association brought suit to require the government to prepare such an impact statement before proceeding with construction of the facility. Should the court enjoin construction until an environmental impact statement is prepared?
2. As part of its iron ore processing operations at Silver Bay, Minnesota, Reserve Mining discharges asbestos fibers into the air. Minnesota air pollution control regulations prohibit the operation of an emission source unless it has filtration equipment which will collect 99 percent, by weight, of the particulate matter discharged by the plant. The Reserve filtration equipment did not comply with this standard, thus resulting in levels of asbestos in the air potentially harmful to public health. The State of Minnesota brought suit to enjoin the asbestos discharges as a public nuisance. Should an injunction be granted?
3. In 1970 Marshall Stacy bought for $40,000 a 240-acre farm with 40,000 Christmas trees on it. He cultivated and pruned the trees and each year cut a number of trees for sale in the Washington, D.C., metropolitan area. He noticed that the trees were not growing as fast as similar trees would normally grow and that many of the trees were discolored. He discovered that the cause of the retarded growth and damage was air pollution, primarily sulfur oxides in the emissions from a large power plant which was located about 22 miles away. Stacy brought suit against the power company, claiming as damages the difference between the value of the damaged trees and the value they would have had if they had not been damaged. Should Stacy be able to recover?
4. In January, 1969 oil began to escape under and near an oil drilling platform operated by the Union Oil Company in the Santa Barbara (California) channel. The crude oil was carried by natural forces of winds and tides over the surface of the ocean and onto the adjacent coast lines, causing damage to property and to the ecology of the area including the fishing potential. A group of commercial fisherman brought suit against Union Oil Claiming that they were entitled to compensation for the injury to commercial fishing attributable to Union Oil's negligence. If the fishermen can show Union Oil was negligent, should they be allowed to recover from Union Oil?
5. From 1939 to 1969 Barnes & Tucker Company operated a bituminous deep coal mine under approximately 6,600 acres in Cambria County, Pennsylvania, near the headwaters of the West Branch of the Susquehanna River. In July 1969 the mine was closed and

sealed. Following the closure the mine became innundated with water and in June 1970 substantial discharges of acid mine drainage were discovered coming from the mine and making their way into the River. The Pennsylvania Clean Streams Law enacted in 1970 provides that: "The discharge of sewage or industrial waste into the waters of this Commonwealth, which causes or contributes to pollution as herein defined or creates a danger of such pollution is hereby declared not to be a reasonable or natural use of such waters, to be against public policy and to be a public nuisance." It further provides: "Any activity or condition declared by this act to be a nuisance, shall be abatable in the manner provided by law or equity for the abatement of nuisances." The Commonwealth brought suit against Barnes & Tucker to require it to abate or treat the acid mine drainage. Should the Court require the drainage be abated or treated?

6. Wilson owned a farm in Jefferson County, Virginia, on which cotton was grown. Three-quarters of a mile away the Elms Company owned land on which it grew rice. The Elms Company had its rice crop carefully dusted by an aviator who was a professional crop duster on a day when no wind was blowing. He used a powerful chemical known as 2-4-D manufactured by Chapman Chemical Company which is very damaging to any broad-leaved plant with which it has contact, but which does no damage to grasses and plants which are not broad leaved. The 2-4-D drifted and settled on the cotton on the Wilson farm, greatly reducing the yield of cotton. Wilson brought suit against Elm and Chapman Chemical to recover compensation for the damage. While Chapman warned users of the damage the product would cause to broad-leaved plants, it had not done any tests to determine what dangers were posed by dusting it by airplane which it knew was a common way of applying agricultural chemicals. In fact it recommended this method for applying 2-4-D. Users of chemicals, like Elm, knew that such agricultural chemicals normally did not float more than 50 to 100 feet beyond the area where they were applied and were given no reason by Chapman to suspect otherwise as to 2-4-D. Should Elm and/or Chapman be liable to Mrs. Wilson for the damage caused to her cotton crop?

7. The New York State Thruway runs through the Village of Pellham Manor. Some of the residents of the Village are concerned about the noise at night emanating from trucks, buses and tractor-trailers traveling the Thruway. They bring suit against the New York State Thruway Authority seeking to prohibit the use of the Thruway by trucks, buses and tractor-trailers through the Village of Pellham Manor between 8 P.M. and 8 A.M. Should an injunction be granted against the Thruway as requested?

PART VIII

Sales

36

Formation and Terms of Sales Contracts

Introduction

Sale of Goods. A sale of goods is the transfer of ownership to tangible personal property, in exchange for money, other goods or the performance of services. The law of sales of goods is codified in Article 2 of the Uniform Commercial Code (Code). While the law of sales is based on the fundamental principles of contract and personal property, it has been modified to accommodate current practices of merchants. In large measure the Code has discarded many technical requirements of earlier law which did not serve any useful purpose in the market place and has replaced them with rules which assure merchants and consumers more just and equitable results that are in keeping with commercial expectations.

Article 2 of the Code applies only to the sale of goods. Thus it does not cover contracts to provide services, contracts to sell real property or contracts to lease personal property. However, some courts have applied the principles set out in the Code to such other transactions which do not specifically involve the sale of goods. When a contract appears to call for the furnishing of both goods and services, a question may arise as to whether the Code applies. For example, the operator of a beauty parlor may use a commercial permanent solution to curl someone's hair which causes injury to that person's head. The injured person might then bring a lawsuit claiming that there was a breach of warranty of the suitability of the permanent solution which resulted in injury to her. In such cases the courts commonly look to see whether the sale of goods is the predominant part of the transaction or is merely an incidental part; where the sale of goods predominates, the Code will normally be applied.

Many of the provisions apply only to merchants or to transactions between merchants. In addition, the Code sets a higher standard of conduct for merchants.[1] The reason for this is that persons who regularly deal in goods should be expected to be familiar with the practices of that trade and with commercial law while ordinary consumers and nonmerchants should not be held to knowledge of these practices.

The Code places considerable emphasis on parties to sales contracts acting in "good faith" and in a "commercially reasonable" manner. When a contract contains an unfair or unconscionable clause, or the contract as a whole is unconscionable, the courts have the right to refuse to enforce the unconscionable clause or contract (2–302).[2]

A number of the Code provisions concerning the sale of goods were discussed in the chapters on contracts. Among the important provisions discussed earlier, together with the section of the Code and the pages in the text where the discussion can be found, are the following:

a. Firm offers. Under the Code an offer in writing by a merchant that gives assurance it will be held open is not revocable for lack of consideration during the time stated, or for a reasonable time if no time is stated, up to a period of three months (Section 2–205) (See pages 111–12).

b. Statute of frauds. The statute of frauds in the Code applies to the sale of goods in the price of $500 of more. Special exceptions are made for written confirmations between merchants, part payment or part delivery, admissions in legal proceedings, and specially manufactured goods (Section 2–201). (See pages 230–31).

c. Formation. Under the Code a contract for the sale of goods may be made in any manner which shows that the parties reached agreement, even though no particular point in time can be pointed to as when the contract was made. Where the parties intended to make a contract, but left one or more terms open, the contract is not invalid for lack of definiteness so long as the court has a basis for giving a remedy (Section 2–204) (See pages 127–28).

d. Additional terms in acceptances. The Code states that an expression of acceptance or written confirmation sent within a reasonable time operates an acceptance even if it states terms additional to or different from those offered, unless acceptance is expressly made conditional on assent to the additional or different terms (Section 2–207) (See page 128).

---

[1] Under the Code, a "merchant" is defined to mean "a person who deals in goods of the kind or otherwise by his occupation holds himself out as having knowledge or skill peculiar to the practices or goods involved in the transaction or to whom such knowledge or skill may be attributed by his employment of an agent or broker or other intermediary who by his occupation holds himself out as having such knowledge or skill." § 2–104(1).

[2] The numbers in the parentheses refer to the sections of the Uniform Commercial Code, 1972.

Terms of the Contract

General terms. Within broad limits the parties to a contract to sell goods may include any terms upon which they agree. In the everyday transactions of business many practices have become common, and under the Code if a particular matter is not specifically covered in a contract or is unclear, common trade practices are used to fill out the terms of the contract.

The Code sets out in some detail the rights of the parties when they use certain terms and those meanings apply unless the parties agrees otherwise. For example, if a contract includes an open-price clause where the price is to be determined later, or if nothing is said about price, the price is what would be considered reasonable at the time of delivery. If the price is to be fixed by either the buyer or seller, that person must act in good faith in setting the price. However, if it is clear from their negotiations that the parties do not intend to be bound unless they agree on a price and the price is not agreed or fixed, no contract results (2–305).

Output and Needs Contracts. In an "output" contract one party is bound to sell, and the other party is bound to buy, the seller's entire output of particular goods. In a "needs" contract the quantity of goods is based on the needs of the buyer. In determining the quantity of goods to be produced or taken pursuant to an output or a needs contract, the rule of good faith applies. Thus no quantity can be demanded or taken that is unreasonably disproportionate to any estimate that was given or to what normally would be expected. For example, Farmer contracts to supply Sam's Grocery with all the apples it requires for sale to customers. If over the past ten years Sam's has sold between 500–700 bushels of apples a year, Farmer would not be liable for delivering 5,000 bushels of apples to Sam's one year because of an unusual demand for them. Similarly if the parties entered into an exclusive dealing contract for certain goods, the seller is obligated to use his best efforts to supply the goods to the buyer and the buyer is obligated to use his best efforts to promote their sale (2–306).

Time for Performance. If no time for performance is stated in the sales contract, a reasonable time for performance is implied. If a contract requires successive performances over an indefinite period of time, the contract is valid for a reasonable time; however, it can be terminated at any time by either party upon the giving of reasonable notice unless the parties have otherwise agreed as to termination (2–309). For example, Farmer Jack agrees to sell his entire output of apples each fall to a cannery at the then current market price. If the contract does not contain a provision spelling out how and when the contract can be terminated, Farmer Jack can terminate it if he gives the cannery a reasonable time to make arrangements to acquire apples from someone else.

Delivery Terms. Standardized shipping terms which through commercial practice have come to have a specific meaning are customarily used in sales contracts. The terms f.o.b. (free on board) and f.a.s. (free alongside) are basic delivery terms. If the delivery term of the contract is f.o.b. or f.a.s. the place the goods originate, the seller is obligated to deliver to the carrier goods which conform to the contract and which are properly prepared for shipment to the buyer, and the seller must make a reasonable contract for transportation of the goods on behalf of the buyer. Under such delivery terms, the goods are at the risk of the buyer during transit and he must pay the shipping charges. If the term is "f.o.b. destination," the seller must deliver the goods to the designated destination and they are at the seller's risk and expense during transit. These terms will be discussed in more detail later in this chapter.

Title

Passage of Title. Title to goods cannot pass from the seller to the buyer until the goods are identified to the contract. For example, if S agrees to sell B 50 chairs and S has 500 chairs in his warehouse, title to 50 chairs will not pass from S to B until the 50 chairs which B has purchased are selected and identified as the chairs sold to B.

The parties may agree between themselves when title to the goods will pass from the seller to the buyer. If there is no agreement, then the general rule is that title to goods passes to the buyer when the seller completes his obligations as to delivery of the goods:

a. If the contract requires the seller to "ship" the goods to the buyer, then the title passes to the buyer when the seller delivers conforming goods to the carrier;

b. If the contract requires the seller to "deliver" the goods to the buyer, title does not pass to the buyer until the goods are delivered to the buyer and tendered to him;

c. If delivery is to be made without moving the goods, then title passes at the time and place of contracting. An exception is made if title to the goods is represented by a document of title such as a warehouse receipt, then title passes when the document of title is delivered to the buyer.

If a buyer rejects goods tendered to him, title reverts to the seller. (2–401).

Importance of Title. At common law most of the problems relating to risks, insurable interests in goods, remedies and other similar rights and liabilities were determined on the basis of who was technical title owner at the particular moment the right of liability arose. However, under the Code the rights of the seller and buyer and of third persons do not depend on the technicality of who has title, and such rights are determined irrespective of such technicality unless the provision of the Code expressly refers to title. Under some circumstances who has title to the goods becomes important, for instance, a situation in which the rights of the seller's or the buyer's creditors in the goods must be determined (2–401).

SUMMARY

Article 2 of the Uniform Commercial Code codifies the law of the sale of goods; it does not apply to contracts to provide services, contracts to sell real property, or contracts to lease personal property, but some courts have applied Code principles by analogy to such contracts.

The Code permits parties considerable flexibility to form a contract to sell goods. It sets out the rights of the parties when certain terms are used and provides certain other provisions to be used if the parties do not specifically agree to the contrary.

Rules as to the passing of title are set out in the Code. Title cannot pass until goods are identified to the contract. Unless otherwise agreed, title passes when the seller has completed his performance. If he is to ship goods, title passes on delivery to the carrier; if he is to deliver the goods, title passes on delivery and tender. If the goods are in the possession of a bailee and a document of title has been issued, title passes on delivery of the document of title. If no document of title has been issued, title passes at the place and time of the making of the contract. Rejection of the goods by the buyer revests title in the seller.

Foster v. Memorial Hospital Association of Charlestown

219 SE 2d 916 (Sup. Ct. of App. West Va. 1975)

This was an action brought by Freeman and Ethel Foster (plaintiffs) against the Memorial Hospital Association of Charlestown (defendant) for breach of warranty arising from a transfusion of impure blood given to Mrs. Foster. She contracted serum hepatitis and was permanently disabled. The trial judge granted summary judgment for the Hospital. Affirmed on Appeal.

NEELY, JUDGE. At first blush this case would appear to be one of first and last impression in West Virginia; however, it presents a theoretical problem with regard to the law of warranty which may have continuing importance in analogous situations.

In 1971 the West Virginia Legislature enacted W Va Code, 16–23–1 which provided that the furnishing of human blood for transfusion is to be considered a service and not a sale, and that no warranties shall be applicable; however the Fosters argue correctly that the facts supporting their cause of action arose in 1968, three years before the enactment of the statute, and therefore the disposition of the case is governed by the general law. Consequently, the Fosters would have this court resolve the cases of the bases of § 2–106, concerning the definition of a "sale," § 2–314 concerning implied warranties and § 2–315 concerning implied warranties for a particular purpose.

The great weight of authority in the United States under the common law, the Uniform Commercial Code, and the old Sales Act, is that a transaction involving blood is not a "sale" creating an implied warranty of fitness. The landmark case on the subject is *Perlmutter v. Beth David Hospital* (1954), in which the court held that the essence of the contractual relationship between hospital and patient is one in which the patient bargains for, and the hospital agrees to make available, the human skill and physical material of medical science to the end that the patient's health is restored. The court said:

> Such a contract is clearly one for services, and, just as clearly, it is not divisible. Concepts of purchase and sale cannot separately be attached to the healing materials—such as medicines, drugs or indeed, blood—supplied by the hospital for a price as part of the medical services it offers. That the property or title to certain items of medical material may be transferred, so to speak, from the hospital to the patient during the course of medical treatment does not serve to make each such transaction a sale. " 'Sale' and 'transfer' are not synonymous," and not every transfer of personal property constitutes a sale. [Citations omitted] It has long been recognized that, when service predominates, and transfer of personal property is but an incidental feature of the transaction, the transaction is not deemed a sale within the Sales Act.

This court agrees with the reasoning of *Perlmutter,* and holds that a court must look to the underlying contract in a close case such as this one in order to discover its implied terms. The provisions of 2–314 create a warranty ". . . if the seller is a merchant with respect to goods of that kind." A hospital or a doctor does not exactly fit into the mold of a "merchant" in the transaction of furnishing blood to a patient in the course of medical treatment. Obviously the ownership of personal property passed for a consideration; however, is it the type of transfer to which the law of warranty applied? There is a reasonable difference between a merchant on the one hand who is engaged in the active promotion and sale of his product such as coca cola bottles, automobile axles, or standardized drugs and a doctor, dentist or lawyer on the other hand who supplied medicine, blood, tooth fillings, or legal briefs in the course of his professional relationship with a patient or client.

We hold that where an individual contracts for *professional* services involving an incidental transfer of personal property as a necessary part of such service, and where the appropriate use of such personal property depends primarily upon the skill and judgment of the person rendering the service, such a transfer of personal property by the professional is not within the contemplation of 2–314 or 2–315 and any injury or damage resulting from such transferred personal property must be recovered by an action grounded in negligence and not by an action grounded in warranty.

Rights of Third Parties

Introduction. A fundamental rule of property law is that a seller cannot pass better title to goods than he has. Thus, if Thief steals a television set from Arthur and sells it to Brown, Brown does not get good title to the television because Thief had no title to it; Arthur would have the right to recover it from Brown. Similarly, if Brown sold the television to Carroll, Carroll could get no better title to it than Brown had; again, Arthur would have the right to recover it from Carroll.

However, under the Code there are several exemptions to the general rule that a buyer cannot get better title to goods than his seller had. The most important exceptions include: (1) a person who has a "voidable title" to goods can pass good title to a bona fide purchaser for value; (2) a person who buys goods in the regular course of a retailer's business take free of any interests in the goods the retailer has given to others; and (3) a person who buys goods in the ordinary course of a dealer's business takes free of any claim of a person who entrusted those goods to the dealer.

Transfer of Voidable Title. A seller having a "voidable title" has the power to pass good title to a good faith purchaser for value (2–403[1]). A seller has a voidable title to goods if he has obtained his title through fraudulent representations. For example, if a person has obtained goods by impersonating another person, or if he has obtained the goods by giving a check in payment for them and the check is dishonored, or if he has obtained the goods without paying the agreed purchase price when it was agreed that the transaction was to be a "cash sale," such a person has a voidable title but can pass good title to a good faith purchaser for value. Under the Code, "good faith" means "honesty in fact in the transaction concerned (1–201[19])" and a buyer has given value if he has given any consideration sufficient to support a simple contract (1–201[44]).

For example, Jones goes to the ABC Appliance Store, convinces the clerk that he is really Clark, who is a good customer of ABC, and leaves with a stereo charged to Clark's account. If Jones sells the stereo to Davis, who gives Jones value for it and has no knowledge of the fraud Jones perpetrated on ABC, Davis get good title to the stereo. ABC cannot recover the stereo from Davis; instead it must look for Jones, the person who deceived it. In this situation both ABC and Davis were innocent of wrongdoing, but the law considers Davis to be the more worthy of its protection because ABC was in a position to have prevented the wrongdoing by Jones. The same result would be reached if Jones had given ABC a check that later "bounced" and then sold the stereo to Davis who was a good faith purchaser for value; Davis would have good title to the stereo, and ABC would have to pursue its right against Jones on the "bounced" check which was not paid by the bank because there were insufficient funds on deposit to cover it.

Buyers in the Ordinary Course of Business. A second exception to the general rule that a buyer of goods can get no better title to the goods than his seller has, is that a person who buys goods in the ordinary course of business from a person dealing in goods of that type takes free of any security interest in the goods given by his seller to other persons (9–307). A "buyer in ordinary course" is a person who in good faith and without knowledge that the sale to him is in violation of the ownership rights of a third party buys goods in the ordinary course of business of a person selling goods of that kind, other than a pawnbroker (1–201[9]).

For example, Brown Buick may borrow money from Bank in order to finance its inventory of new Buicks; in turn, Bank may take a security interest in the inventory to secure repayment of the loan. If Carter buys a new Buick from Brown Buick, he gets good title to the Buick free and clear from the Bank's security interest if he is a buyer in the ordinary course of business. Security interests and the rights of buyers in the ordinary course of business are discussed in more detail in Chapter 45.

Entrusting of Goods. A third exception to the general rule is if goods are entrusted to a merchant who deals in goods of that kind, the merchant has the power to transfer all rights of the entruster to a buyer in the ordinary course of business (2–403[2]). For example, Gail takes her watch to Jeweler, a retail jeweler, to have it repaired, and Jeweler sells the watch to Mary. Mary would acquire good title to the watch and Gail would have to proceed against Jeweler for conversion of her watch. The purpose behind this rule is to protect commerce and give confidence to buyers that they will get good title to goods they buy from merchants in the ordinary course of business. However, a merchant-seller cannot pass good title to stolen goods even if the buyer is a buyer in the ordinary course of business.

SUMMARY

A fundamental rule of property law is that a seller cannot pass better title to goods than he has. Among the exceptions to this general rule are: (1) a person who has voidable title to goods can pass good title to a bona fide purchaser for value; (2) a buyer in the ordinary course of a retailer's business takes free of any interests in the goods the retailer has given to others; and (3) a person who buys goods in the ordinary course of a dealer's business takes free of any claims of a person who entrusted those goods to the dealer.

Maurice Shire, Inc. v. Gerald Modell, Inc.

19 U.C.C. Rep. 1096 (Sup. Ct. N.Y. 1976)

This was an action brought by Maurice Shire, Inc. (plaintiff) against Gerald Modell, Inc. (defendant), to recover possession of a platinum ring containing a 4.58 carat cabochon emerald and 14 oval and 14 round diamonds weighing 3.06 carats. Shire's motion for summary judgment was denied, and the case was set for trial.

On March 10, 1975, Shire, an importer and distributor of jewelry delivered the ring to Walter Gruenstein upon a written memorandum which stated a value of $75,000 for the ring and provided as follows:

> The merchandise described below is delivered to you on memorandum, at your risk from all hazards, regardless of the cause of the loss or damage, only for examination and inspection by prospective purchasers, upon the express condition that all such merchandise shall remain the property of MAURICE SHIRE, INC., and shall be returned on demand, in full in its original form. Until the merchandise is returned and actually received by us, you are fully responsible therefor, and, in the event of damage or loss, whether caused by you or by another, whether or not under your control, you will indemnify us immediately by payment of the stated value which represents the extent of the actual loss and is not intended to constitute a price for the sale of the merchandise. You acquire no right or authority to sell, pledge, hypothecate or otherwise dispose of the merchandise, or any part thereof, by memorandum or otherwise, it being expressly understood that regardless of other transactions or prior trade customs, no credit is extended with respect to this merchandise. A sale of all or any portion of the merchandise shall occur only if and when we agree and you shall have received from us a separate invoice. A subsequent sale of any specific part of the merchandise shall not affect the terms hereof with respect to the balance hereof. Receipt of the merchandise constitutes your agreement to the foregoing terms which represent the entire contract with respect to the merchandise herein described and which cannot be varied by oral statements, dealings with respect to other merchandise or any contrary custom of the trade. This all risk memorandum shall be governed by applicable law of the State of New York.
>
> (This is NOT an INVOICE or BILL OF SALE.)

Gruenstein was a merchant in the trade who bought and sold jewelry. He allegedly took possession of the ring to show to a potential customer. However, Gruenstein took the ring to Gerald Modell, Inc., a pawnbroker and pawned it for $20,000. Shire brought suit against Modell to recover the ring, claiming that it retained title to the ring by virtue of the terms of the memorandum and that Gruenstein's theft or, conversion of the ring could not pass good title to Modell. Modell sought to be reimbursed for the $20,000.

FEIN, JUDGE. The law in this state is clear that, generally, a buyer can acquire only such title as his transferor had power to transfer (§ 2–403). Thus, a thief cannot convey good title, even to a bona fide purchaser for value.

Unlike *Frisch v. Perle,* relied on by Shire, there is no claim there was a theft at the time Shire delivered the ring to Gruenstein. Rather, it is claimed that a limited possessory right was conferred upon Gruenstein, who took possession of the ring on memorandum allegedly for the limited purpose of showing it to a potential customer, in accordance with the custom of the trade. The fraud occurred when he converted the ring when he pledged it to Modell for the sum of $20,000.

Manifestly delivery to Gruenstein did not result in a transfer of title. The memorandum clearly states that title to the jewelry remained with Shire and that Gruenstein acquired "no right or authority to sell, pledge, hypothecate or otherwise dispose of the merchandise."

Modell grounds its claim to good title upon its alleged status as a "good faith purchaser for value" who acquired the property from one with voidable title [§ 2–403(1)], or as a "buyer in the ordinary course of business," who acquired the property from a merchant entrusted with possession [§ 2–403(2)].

Modell cannot be held to be a "buyer in the ordinary course of business" within the terms of § 2–403(2). Modell was not a "buyer" of the ring. U.C.C. § 2–103(1)(a) provides: " 'Buyer' means a person who buys or contracts to buy goods." It is undisputed that the transaction between Modell and Gruenstein involved a pledge of the jewelry for an amount far less than the value stated in the memorandum between Shire and Gruenstein.

Although it is clear from the memorandum agreement that the delivery of the ring by plaintiff to Gruenstein did not effect a transfer of title, the surrender of possession may have created "voidable title" within the meaning of § 2–403(1)(d). Although mere transfer of possession is not sufficient to create "voidable title," additional and surrounding circumstances may be sufficient to create an estoppel to deny such title. For Modell to prevail, it must establish that it was a "good faith purchaser for value" as defined by §§ 1–201(19), (32), (44), and 2–103(1)(b). The term "purchaser" comprehends a pledge transaction, as well as an outright sale [§ 1–201(32) and (33)]. The requirement of good faith for a merchant mandates "honesty in fact and the observance of reasonable commercial standards of fair dealing" [§ 2–103(b)].

Here, there are factual issues as to whether Modell was a good faith purchaser for value and whether the transfer of possession from Shire to Gruenstein was such as to clothe the latter with apparent title or authority to transfer title. In this connection, Modell claims that it had prior similar dealings with Gruenstein. Modell asserts Gruenstein was a diamond dealer, regularly engaged in buying and selling diamonds for his own account and that this was known to the trade and to Shire, who, Modell alleges had prior dealings with Gruenstein as such. Shire disputes this, asserting that Gruenstein was merely a broker, with no inventory of his own. If so, Modell may not have been warranted in relying on Gruenstein's representation of ownership. The ring was apparently pledged for a sum far less than its actual value. Pertinent in this connection is the question as to the occasion for dealers or brokers of diamonds to pledge expensive stones which it would appear should normally be exhibited for sale. However, whether the circumstances were such as to have reasonably caused Modell to be skeptical of Gruenstein's claim of ownership may not be determined upon affidavits alone. The test is whether "the standards of honesty in fact and reasonable commercial standards of fair dealing have . . . been met (§ 2–103)."

Risk of Loss

Introduction. Because goods that are the subject of a contract of sale can readily be lost, stolen or damaged before the buyer takes possession of them, the risk of loss is an important aspect of any sales situation. Under the Code, the risk of loss does not depend on when title to goods passes, but instead is determined by a separate set of rules that are believed to be more realistic and in keeping with reasonable commercial expectations. The Code provisions permit the parties by agreement to shift the allocation of the risk of loss or to divide the risk (2–303) unless the provision in the agreement would be void as to unconscionable clause (See Section 2–302).

General Rules. If the parties do not explicitly agree on an allocation of the risk of loss but do include delivery terms in their agreement requiring or authorizing the seller to ship the goods by carrier, the delivery terms will dictate which party will bear the risk of loss while goods are in transit [2–509(1)]. If the delivery terms are "f.o.b. place of shipment," "f.a.s.," "c.i.f." (which means that the price includes the cost of the goods, insurance and freight) or "c.&f." (which means that the price includes the cost of the goods and the cost of freight to the destination), the risk of loss shifts to the buyer on delivery of the goods to the carrier and the making of a commercially reasonable contract for the goods to be carried to the buyer (2–319; 2–320; 2–509.). However, if the delivery terms are "f.o.b. destination" or "Delivery Ex-Ship," the seller bears the risk of loss while the goods are in transit (2–319(1)(b); (2–322).

Thus, if Seller contracts to sell a quantity of eggs to Buyer f.o.b. the buyer's place of business and the eggs are destroyed en route when the truck carrying them is involved in an accident, the risk of the loss is on the seller and the buyer is not obligated to pay for the eggs. The seller may have the right to recover from the trucking company, but between it and the buyer, the seller has the risk of loss. If the contract calls for delivery f.o.b. the seller's farm, then the risk of loss would be on the buyer. The buyer would have to pay for the eggs and then exert any claims he had against the trucking company.

If the goods are in the possession of a bailee and are to be delivered without being moved, the risk of loss passes to the buyer on delivery to him of a negotiable document of title for the goods; if no negotiable document of title has been issued, the risk of loss passed when the bailee indicated to the buyer that the buyer has the right to the possession of the goods (2–509[1]). For example, if Farmer sells Miller a quantity of grain currently stored at Grain Elevator, the risk of loss of the grain will shift from Farmer to Miller (1) when a negotiable warehouse receipt to the grain is delivered to Miller or (2) when Grain Elevator notifies Miller that it is holding the grain for Miller.

If the transaction is such that it does not fall within the situations discussed above, the risk of loss passes to the buyer on receipt of the goods if the seller is a merchant; if the seller is not a merchant then risk of loss passes to the buyer on the tender of delivery of the goods to the buyer (2–509). For example, if Jones buys a television set from ABC Appliance on Monday intending to pick it up on Thursday and the television is stolen on Wednesday, the risk of loss remained with ABC. However, if Jones had purchased the set from his next door neighbor under this same set of facts and could have taken delivery of the television on Monday, the risk of loss was Jones'.

Effect of Breach on Risk of Loss. When a seller tenders goods which do not conform to the contract and the buyer would have the right to reject the goods, the risk of loss remains with the seller until any defect is cured or until the buyer accepts the goods (2–510[1]). Where the buyer rightfully revokes his acceptance of goods, the risk of loss is with the seller to the extent that any loss is not covered by the buyer's insurance (2–510[2]). This rules gives the seller the benefit of any insurance carried by the buyer. For example, if Arthur bought a new Buick which he later returned to Brown because of serious defects in it and if the automobile was damaged while in Arthur's possession through no fault of his, then the risk of loss would be with Brown. However, if Arthur had insurance on the automobile covering damage to it and recovered from the insurance company, Arthur would have to turn the insurance proceeds over to Brown or use them to fix the car before returning it to Brown.

When a buyer repudiates a contract for goods that have already been set aside by the seller as relating to the contract, the risk of loss stays with the buyer for a commercially reasonable time after the repudiation (2–510[3]). For example, Cannery contracts to buy Farmer's entire crop of peaches. Farmer picks the peaches, crates them and stores them in the barn for Cannery. Cannery then tells Farmer it does not intend to honor the contract. Shortly thereafter, but before Farmer has a chance to find another buyer, the peaches are spoiled by a fire. If Farmer's insurance covers only part of the loss, Cannery must bear the rest of the loss.

Insurable Interest. The general practice of insuring risks is recognized and provided for under the Code. A buyer may protect his interest in goods which are the subject matter of a sales contract before he actually obtains title. The buyer obtains an insurable interest in existing goods when they are identified as the goods covered by the contract even though they are in fact nonconforming. The seller retains an insurable interest in goods so long as he has either title or a security interest in them (2–510[2]).

SUMMARY

Goods which are the subject matter of a sale are sometimes damaged or destroyed and the question of which of the parties to the sales contract must bear the loss frequently arises. The parties to the sales contract may by explicit agreement designate who shall bear such loss or how the risk of loss shall be divided.

The inclusion in the sales contract of delivery terms will indicate which of the parties shall bear the risk of loss during transit. If the delivery term is f.o.b. point of origin, the risk of loss passes to the buyer when goods are delivered to the carrier and a reasonable contract for their carriage is made. If the delivery term is f.o.b. destination, then risk of loss passes on tender of delivery to the buyer. If goods are in the possession of a bailee and not to be moved, the risk passes to the buyer on delivery of a negotiable document of title and, if there is no negotiable document of title, the risk passes when the bailee acknowledges the buyer's rights.

Nonconforming goods are at the risk of the seller. If the buyer repudiates the contract the goods are at the risk of the buyer for a commercially reasonable time. Insurance on the goods inures to the benefit of the party who must bear the loss.

The buyer acquires a property interest in goods identified to the sales contract and has an insurable interest in them even though they may be nonconforming.

Ninth Street East, Ltd. v. Harrison

259 A.2d 772 (Cir. Ct. Conn. 1968)

This was an action brought by Ninth Street East, Ltd. (plaintiff), against Harrison (defendant) to recover the purchase price of merchandise sold by Ninth Street East to Harrison. Judgment for Ninth Street East.

Ninth Street East was the manufacturer of men's clothing with a principal place of business in Los Angeles, California. Harrison was the owner and operator of a men's clothing store, located in Westport, Connecticut, known as "The Rage."

Pursuant to orders received by Ninth Street East in Los Angeles on November 28, 1966, Harrison ordered a variety of clothing items. On November 30, 1966, Ninth Street East delivered the merchandise in Los Angeles to a common carrier known as Denver-Chicago Trucking Company, Inc. (Denver) and received a bill of lading from the trucker. Simultaneously, Ninth Street East mailed Harrison four invoices, all dated November 30, 1966, covering the clothing, in the total sum of $2,216. All the invoices bore the notations that the shipment was made "f.o.b. Los Angeles" and "Via Denver-Chicago" as well as the printed phrase, "Goods Shipped at Purchaser's Risk." Denver's bill of lading disclosed that the shipment was made "collect,"—namely, that Harrison was obligated to pay the freight charges from Los Angeles to Westport. Denver subsequently transferred the shipment to a connecting carrier known as Old Colony Transportation Company (Old Colony) for ultimate delivery at Harrison's store in Westport. The delivery was attempted by Old Colony at Harrison's store on December 12, 1966. Harrison's wife requested the Old Colony truck driver to deliver the merchandise inside the door of Harrison's store. The truck driver refused to do so. The dispute not having been resolved, Old Colony retained possession of the eight cartons comprising the shipment, and the truck thereupon departed from the store premises.

Harrison later reported its refusal to accept delivery. The merchandise was subsequently lost by the carrier. Ninth Street East filed a claim against the carrier but as of the date of the trial, it had not been reimbursed. In his action Harrison claimed that since the merchandise had never been delivered into his place of business, he was not liable for the loss or disappearance of the shipment or its purchase price, and that the risk of loss was on Ninth Street East.

LEVINE, JUSTICE. The basic problem is to determine the terms and conditions of the agreement of the parties to transportation, and the risks and hazards incident thereto. The court finds that the parties had originally agreed that the merchandise would be shipped by common carrier f.o.b. Los Angeles, as the place of shipment, and that Harrison would pay the freight charges between the two points. The notation on the invoices, and the bill of lading, previously described, make this clear. The use of the phrase "f.o.b.," meaning free on board, made this portion of the agreement not only a price term covering Harrison's obligation to pay freight charges between Los Angeles and Westport but also a controlling factor as to risk of loss of the merchandise upon delivery to Denver and subsequently to Old Colony as the carriers, § 2–319, comment 1. Title to the goods, and the right to possession, passed to Harrison at Los Angeles, the f.o.b. point. Upon delivery to the common carrier at the f.o.b. point, the goods thereafter were at Harrison's sole risk § 2–509(1).

It is highly significant that all the invoices sent to Harrison contained the explicit notation "Good Shipped at Purchaser's Risk." This was, initially, a unilateral statement by Ninth Street. The validity of this phrase, as expressing the understanding of both parties, was, however, never actually challenged by Harrison, at the trial or in his brief. The contents of the invoices therefore confirm the statutory allocation of risk of loss on f.o.b. shipments.

The arrangements as to shipment were at the option of Ninth Street as the seller § 2–311(2). Ninth Street duly placed the goods in possession of a carrier, to wit, Denver, and made a reasonable contract for their transportation, having in mind the nature of the merchandise and the remaining circumstances. Notice of the shipment, including the f.o.b. provisions, was properly given to Harrison, as required by law, pursuant to the four invoices § 2–504.

The law erects a presumption in favor of construing the agreement as a "shipment" contract, as opposed to a "destination" contract. Uniform Commercial Code § 2–503, comment 5. Under the presumption of a "shipment" contract, Ninth Street's liability for loss or damage terminated upon delivery to the carrier at the f.o.b. point, to wit, Los Angeles. The court finds that no persuasive evidence was offered to overcome the force of the statutory presumption in the instant case. Thus, as § 2–509(1) indicates, "[w]here the contract requires or authorizes the seller to ship the goods by carrier (a) if it does not require him to deliver them at a particular destination, the risk of loss passes to the buyer when the goods are duly delivered to the carrier." Accordingly, at the f.o.b. point, when the risk of loss shifted, Denver and Old Colony, as carriers, became the agents or bailees of Harrison. The risk of subsequent loss or delay rested on Harrison and not Ninth Street. A disagreement arose between Harrison's wife and the truck driver, resulting in nondelivery of the merchandise, retention thereof by the carrier, and, finally, disappearance of the shipment. The ensuing dispute was fundamentally a matter for resolution between Harrison and the carriers, as his agents. Nothing in the outcome of that dispute could defeat or impair Ninth Street's recovery against Harrison.

Harrison has urged that, since Ninth Street pressed a damage claim against the carrier, this constitutes an assertion of an ownership interest by Ninth Street, and responsibility for loss thereof, inconsistent with Ninth Street's present claim against Harrison. The court does not agree. Even though the risk of loss, subsequent to delivery to the carrier, had passed to Harrison, Ninth Street nevertheless had the privilege of pressing the damage claim against the trucker. Any recovery on the claim would, however, be held by Ninth Street, subject to its own interest, as a fiduciary for Harrison § 2–722(b). In this connection, the evidence demonstrated that Ninth Street first made an effort to secure Harrison's cooperation in asserting the damage claim but was unsuccessful.

The court entertains substantial doubt about the credibility of the defense. Harrison initially professed an urgent need for the merchandise, for holiday sales. When, however, the delivery was tendered, on December 12, 1966, only some two weeks prior to Christmas, Harrison, acting by his wife, saw fit to refuse the merchandise for the alleged reason that the truck driver was obligated to carry the cartons inside Harrison's door. The defense arising out of the refusal is without merit. Harrison knew, or should have known, that his rejection exposed the shipment to time consuming delays and disputes. Hence, delivery in time for holiday business was actually frustrated, not by Ninth Street, but rather by the action of Harrison and his agent, based on a disagreement over a relatively minor item. Wholly apart from the conclusion, previously stated, that such refusal was at the sole risk of Harrison, the court finds that Harrison's conduct was wrongful, arbitrary, and unreasonable, under all the circumstances.

In view of Harrison's wrongful rejection, following the shifting of the risk of loss to him, he is liable to Ninth Street for the entire purchase price of the merchandise. Thus, § 2–709 provides in part; "(1) When the buyer fails to pay the price as it becomes due the seller may recover . . . the price (a) . . . of conforming goods lost or damaged within a commercially reasonable time after risk of their loss has passed to the buyer." In *Lewis v. Scoville* the court said: "Refusal by the defendant to receive the goods did not revest title in the plaintiff, and he is . . . entitled to recover the contract price."

Sales on Trial

Introduction. A common commercial practice is for a seller of goods to entrust possession of goods to a buyer to either give the buyer an opportunity to decide whether or not to buy them or to try to resell them to a third person. The entrusting may be known as a "sale on approval," a "sale or return" or a "consignment," depending on the terms of the entrusting. Occasionally, the goods may be damaged, destroyed, or stolen, or the creditors of the buyer may try to claim them; on such occasions the form of the entrusting will determine whether the buyer or seller had the risk of loss and whether the buyer's creditors can successfully claim the goods.

Sale on Approval. In a sale on approval, the goods are delivered to the buyer with an understanding that he may use or test them for the purpose of determining whether or not he wishes to buy them. In a sale on approval, neither the risk of loss nor title to the goods passes to the buyer until he accepts the goods (2–326). The buyer has the right to use the goods in any manner consistent with the purpose of the trial, but any unwarranted exercise of ownership over the goods is considered to be an acceptance of the goods; similarly, if the buyer fails to notify the seller of his election to return the goods, he is considered to have accepted them. For example, if Dealer agrees to let Hughes take a new automobile home to drive for a day to see if she wants to buy it and Hughes takes the car on a two week vacation trip, Hughes will be considered to have accepted the automobile because in taking it on the trip she used the automobile in a manner beyond that contemplated by the trial and as if she was the owner of it. If Hughes had driven the automobile for a day, decided not to buy it, and parked it in her driveway for two weeks without telling Dealer of her intention to return the automobile, Hughes would also be deemed to have accepted it.

Once the buyer has notified the seller of his election to return the goods, the return is at the seller's expense and risk. Because the title and risk of loss of goods delivered on a sale on approval remain with the seller, goods held on approval are not subject to the claims of the buyer's creditors until the buyer accepts them (2–326 and 2–327).

Sale or Return. In a "sale or return," goods are delivered to a buyer for resale with the understanding that the buyer has the right to return them. Under a sale or return, unless otherwise agreed, the title and risk of loss are in the buyer and while the goods are in the buyer's possession, they are subject to the claims of his creditors (2–326 and 2–327). For example, if Publisher delivers some paperback books to Bookstore on the understanding that Bookstore may return any of the books that remain unsold at the end of six months, the transaction is a sale or return. If the Bookstore is destroyed by a fire, the risk of loss of the paperbacks was Bookstore's and it is responsible to Publisher for the purchase price. Similarly, if Bookstore becomes insolvent and is declared a bankrupt, the paperbacks will be considered part of the bankruptcy estate. If the buyer elects to return goods held on a "sale or return" basis, the return is at the buyer's risk and expense.

Sale on Consignment. Sometimes goods are delivered to a person "on consignment." If the person to whom goods are consigned maintains a place of business dealing in goods of that kind under a name other than that of the person consigning the goods, then the consigner must take certain steps to protect his interest in the goods or they will be subject to the claims of the buyer's creditors. The consignor must either: (1) make sure a sign is prominently posted at the place of business indicating the consignor's interest, or (2) make sure that the buyer's creditors know he is generally in the business of selling goods owned by others, or (3) comply with the filing provisions of Article 9 of the Code—Secured Transactions.[3] For example, Jones operates a retail music store under the name of City Music Store. Baldwin Piano Company delivers some pianos to Jones on consignment. If no notices are posted indicating Baldwin's interest in the pianos, if Jones is not generally known to be selling from a consigned inventory, and if Baldwin does not file its interest with the Recording Office pursuant to Article 9 of the Code, then the goods are subject to the claims of Jones's creditors. This is important to Baldwin because it may think it has retained title. However, the Code treats a "consignment" to a person doing business under a name other than that of the consignor as a "sale or return" (2–326). If Jones did business as the Baldwin Piano Company, Baldwin's interest would be protected from the claims of Jones' creditors without the need for it to post a sign or file under Article 9.

[3] These provisions are discussed in detail in Chapter 45.

SUMMARY

In a sale on approval the goods are delivered to the buyer for use or trial and the risk of loss and title remain in the seller. The goods are not subject to claims of the buyer's creditors and any return of goods is at the seller's risk and expense. A sale or return is one where the goods are sold to the buyer for resale but may be retained at the buyer's option. The risk of loss and title is in the buyer and the goods are subject to the claims of the buyer's creditors. The return of the goods is at the buyer's risk and expense.

Goods delivered "on consignment" are subject to the claims of the creditors of the person to whom they are delivered if he operates a business selling like goods in a name other than that of the party delivering the goods. The person delivering the goods can protect his interest by posting notice as required by the state statute or filing under Article 9. Also, if the person to whom the goods are delivered is known to his creditors to be substantially engaged in selling goods for others the creditors cannot obtain an interest in the goods.

Collier v. B & B Parts Sales, Inc.

471 S.W.2d 151 (Civ. App. Tex. 1971)

This was an action brought by B & B Parts Sales, Inc. (plaintiff), against Collier (defendant) to recover the balance allegedly due on a sale to Collier of stereo tapes, cartridges and equipment. Judgment for B&B Parts Sales, Inc. Affirmed on appeal.

At the time B&B's salesman delivered the stereo tapes, cartridges, and equipment, he gave Collier an invoice that had printed on it "sold to" followed by Collier's name and address in handwriting. Also written in by hand was the notation "Terms 30–60–90 this equipment will be picked up if not sold in 90 days." Collier's store was burglarized shortly afterwards and most of the merchandise was stolen.

Collier maintained that he held the merchandise on consignment and thus the risk of loss was on the consignor. B&B maintained that the transaction was a sale and that Collier was bound to pay for it.

McKAY, JUSTICE. The transaction here was a "sale or return," and under section 2–326(3) and section 2–327(2)(a) and (b) of the Uniform Commercial Code, it became a sale, and therefore title passed to Collier. The notations "Terms 30–60–90" and "this equipment will be picked up if not sold in 90 days" do not constitute a consignment. We construe the language to mean that there was a sale of the items listed on the invoices; but the seller agreed to pick up items which had not been sold in 90 days. In Sec. 2–326:4, p. 260, of Anderson's Uniform Commercial Code is found: "Unless otherwise agreed, a transaction under which goods delivered primarily for resale may be returned to the seller even though they conform to the contract is a sale or return."

Bulk Transfers

Bulk Transfer Legislation. Article 6 of the Uniform Commercial Code—Bulk Transfers—was enacted in order to prevent fraud on creditors. The bulk transfer laws are intended to prevent the commercial fraud where a merchant, owing debts, sells out his stock in trade for cash, pockets the proceeds, and then disappears, leaving his creditors unpaid. The bulk transfer law covers any transfer "in bulk" and not in the ordinary course of the transferor's business of a major part of the materials, supplies, merchandise or other inventory of an enterprise. A transfer of a substantial part of equipment is covered if the transfer is part of a bulk transfer of inventory. The enterprises subject to the bulk transfer law are those whose principal business is the sale of merchandise from stock including retailers, wholesalers and manufacturers (6–102).

The general plan of the bulk transfer law is to give creditors notice in advance of the transfer and to provide a plan for their protection. The seller is required to give the purchaser a schedule of the property to be transferred and a sworn list of the seller's creditors (6–104). The purchaser is required to give the creditors on the list, and any other known creditors, notice of the pending transfer at least ten days before he takes possession of the goods. In some states (New York, for example) the requirement is only that the creditors must receive notice of the proposed transfer; in other states (Pennsylvania, for example), the proceeds of the sale are distributed to the creditors (6–106).

The purchaser must make sure that the requirements of the bulk transfer law are met or he is deemed to hold the goods in trust for the creditors of the seller. A creditor has only six months from the time the transfer took place to file suit to enforce his rights under the bulk transfer law; however, if the parties concealed the transfer, then the creditors have until six months after it was discovered to bring suit (6–111).

SUMMARY

The bulk transfer law is designed to prevent commercial fraud, and anyone who buys substantially all of the materials, supplies, inventory, or equipment of a business, must be concerned with complying with it to make sure he will take title free of claims from the seller's creditors.

Adrian Tabin Corp. v. Climax Boutique, Inc.

338 N.Y.S. 2d 59 (Sup. Ct. N.Y. 1972)

This was an action brought by Adrian Tabin Corp. (plaintiff) against Climax Boutique, Inc. (defendant), to recover money owed to Adrian Tabin by L.D.J. Dresses which had made a bulk sale of its business to Climax Boutique. Trial court found for Adrian Tabin on the ground that Climax Boutique had not satisfied the Bulk Sales provisions of the U.C.C. Reversed on appeal.

Additional facts are stated in the opinion.

SHAPIRO, JUSTICE. The novel issue posed by this appeal is whether a purchaser at a bulk sale, who receives an affidavit of "no creditors" is nevertheless under a duty to make careful inquiry as to the possible existence of creditors, of whom he has no actual knowledge. Adrian Tabin, a creditor of the seller, was not notified of the sale and hence seeks an adjudication that, as to it, the sale is void.

Defendant L.D.J. Dresses, Inc. (hereinafter referred to as "the seller"), operated a dress shop in Jamaica, Queens. The seller was indebted to Adrian Tabin, a garment supplier, at the time it sold its business in bulk to defendant Paul Warman, who in turn sold the business to defendant Climax Boutique, Inc., in which he was a principal. (Warman and Climax will hereafter be referred to as "the purchasers.")

Prior to the consummation of the bulk sale the purchasers received an affidavit from Joseph Marino, the president of the seller, which stated that the seller was not indebted to anyone and had no creditors. The purchasers caused a lien search to be conducted and determined that there were no outstanding liens.

At the trial, the purchasers' attorney testified as follows:

> I knew . . . the attorney for the seller for at least 15 years, knew him well, had seen him in court maybe once a month for 15 years so knew his voice well. In fact I had matters with him too from the past. At the closing . . . (the seller's attorney) and I spoke on the telephone and I said, "What about the general creditors? You have told me already there are none but I think I should have some necessary affidavit to cover." Then he said, "Well, to begin with," he said, "I am going to give you a bill of sale sworn to by the seller and notarized by me as an attorney that there are absolutely no creditors. He has shown me checks that he had sent to all his creditors because I checked it with him in order to close out the business for the end of the year and I am satisfied that there are none and as an attorney I would never let my client sign such an affidavit if I thought there were, and there are no creditors."

The parties stipulated that the purchasers had no knowledge of Adrian Tabin prior to the sale.

In setting aside the sale the court below noted that the purchasers had not requested an examination of the seller's books and had not questioned the source of the garments involved in the sale. It held that the purchasers had not made careful inquiry of the seller as to existing creditors and that, failing such careful inquiry, the purchasers had acted at their peril.

A bulk sale is ineffective against creditors of the seller unless the purchaser requires the seller to furnish a list (signed and sworn to or affirmed) of his existing creditors (Uniform Commercial Code, § 6–104) and notifies such creditors of the impending sale (Uniform Commercial Code, §§ 6–105, 6–107). . . .

Subdivision (3) of § 6–104 of the Uniform Commercial Code provides that "responsibility for the completeness and accuracy of the list of creditors rests on the transferor, and the transfer is not rendered ineffective by errors or omissions therein unless the transferee is shown to have had knowledge." Section 1–201 of the Uniform Commercial Code, the general definitions section of that code, provides, in subdivision (25), that "a person 'knows' or has 'knowledge' of a fact when he has actual knowledge of it." It is therefore apparent that a bulk sale may not be set aside as to creditors not listed by the seller in the affidavit requested by the purchaser, of whom the purchaser had no actual knowledge. As the purchasers concededly had no actual knowledge of Adrian Tabin, the possibility of whose existence as a creditor was denied by the seller in an affidavit (the purchasers having no reason to disbelieve the truthfulness of the affidavit), the bulk sale may not be set aside as to Adrian Tabin.

We note, in passing, that even were the purchasers under a duty to make careful inquiry, they complied with that responsibility in this case by making a lien search and by making inquiry of the seller's attorney, who represented that all creditors had been paid and that he had seen the checks sent out to them in payment of the seller's obligations.

MUNDER, JUSTICE (dissenting). The issue here is simply whether an affidavit of "no creditors" relieves the purchaser at a bulk sale of the duty to make careful inquiry as to the possible existence of creditors of whom he had no actual knowledge, under § 6–104 of the Uniform Commercial Code.

I conclude the answer is no.

A purchaser or transferee of the entire stock of a going business knows the seller more than likely has some creditors. He should at least inquire into the sources of the inventory. Otherwise, the opportunity for fraud upon creditors is too great. Here, the purchasers made no such inquiry. They relied upon an oral assurance by the seller's attorney that there were no general creditors and a statement to the same effect by the seller's president.

Problem Cases

1. Suchy Funeral Home brought suit against Waldenmaier to recover the contracted price for a funeral, including the providing of a casket. Waldenmaier claimed that the lawsuit was commenced more than four years after the funeral and thus was barred by the Code's four-year statute of limitation's (U.C.C. § 2–725). Suchy contended that the Code's

statute of limitations did not apply because no "sale of goods" was involved. Should the court apply the Code provisions to this contract?

2. Mrs. Sheppard purchased several cosmetic products manufactured by Revlon Inc. and received as a promotional bonus a jar of wrinkle creme also produced by Revlon. She applied the creme before going to bed and was later awakened by severe pain in her eye, which she believed to have been caused by the creme. There was no warning on the jar to keep the product away from the eyes. She filed an action based upon breach of warranty. Revlon defended by claiming that because there was no sale, no warranties arose. Should the Court accept this defense?

3. On February 21, 1973, Lawrence Harbach, a farmer, entered into an oral contract to sell 25,000 bushels of soybeans at $3.81 per bushel to Continental Grain Company with delivery in October, November, and December of 1973. Continental mailed a written confirmation to Harbach which Harbach never made any written objection to. Continental claimed that this satisfied the "merchant" exception to the statute of frauds. Harbach refused to honor the contract and Continental brought suit for breach of contract. At the trial, one issue was whether Harbach should be considered a "merchant" within the meaning of the Uniform Commercial Code. For several years Harbach had raised and sold grain as a sole proprietor and as president of a farming corporation; he had sold soybeans for only a few months prior to the alleged sale to Continental. However, his sales of corn had exceeded $100,000 per year from 1970 to 1973. He had also owned or operated three chemical and fertilizer businesses over the past 15 years. Should Harbach be considered a "merchant" for the purpose of applying the Code?

4. On August 3, 1974, a Chevrolet Corvette was stolen from its owner, Location Gallop Leasing of Quebec, Canada. At about the same time, blank registration forms were stolen from the Department of Motor Vehicles in Montreal and used to complete the transfer of the Corvette to a certain Richard Dooust in New York State. At that time New York State issued a certificate of title for the vehicle. Then the auto was transferred by Dooust to Julian LaDuke, another member of the auto theft ring. Thereafter, Patrick D. Elmer, an innocent buyer, purchased the car from LaDuke sometime in early 1975. Thereafter, on May 16, 1975, Johnny Dell, an automobile dealer purchased the Corvette from Elmer for the sum of $5,425. On that date Johnny Dell took physical possession of the automobile and the New York state registration to the vehicle and the certificate of title to it were transferred to Dell. On June 30, 1975, the New York State Police impounded the vehicle. Johnny Dell then sued the New York State Police for the return of the car. Is Dell entitled to possession of the car?

5. Samuel Higgonbottom sold his Mercedes-Benz to Katrina Walters in exchange for a check for $13,500 made out to Walters and gave her the title to the vehicle endorsed over to her. Walters transferred ownership to the vehicle, together with the ownership papers, to an automobile dealership, Benzel-Busch, which in turn sold it to a company known as A-Leet. Higgonbottom discovered that the check given to him was originally issued in the sum of $13.50 and had been fraudulently raised by Walters. Neither Benzel-Busch or A-Leet was aware of the fraud. Higgonbottom then sued A-Leet to recover possession of the vehicle. Is Higgonbottom entitled to recover the vehicle from A-Leet?

6. Eberhard Manufacturing Company entered into a contract to sell certain truck parts to Brown with the parts to be "shipped to" Brown's place of business in Birmingham, Alabama. Eberhard packaged the parts and placed them on board a common carrier with instructions to deliver the goods to Brown. The parts were lost while in transit.

The parties did not expressly agree as to who had the risk of loss and the contract did not contain an f.o.b. term. Between Eberhard and Brown, who had the risk of loss?

7. White Motor Company, a manufacturer of trucks, delivered to Bronx Trucks an autocar truck pursuant to an order placed by Bronx Trucks. White Motor received a signed receipt from the manager of Bronx Trucks for the delivery and also invoiced Bronx Trucks for the agreed purchase price. After the truck had been delivered and invoiced, it was stolen from Bronx Truck's garage. The title papers to the truck were not delivered to Bronx Truck until after the truck was stolen. White Motor sued Bronx Truck for the purchase price of the truck, and Bronx Truck defended on the grounds it did not have title to the truck when it was stolen and thus White Motor was still the owner of it and had the risk of loss. Is Bronx Truck responsible for paying the purchase price to White Motor?
8. The Federal Republic of Germany purchased a sophisticated rocket system and parts from a private munitions manufacturer through the United States government. The delivery terms was "F.O.B. VESSEL." After some of the systems and parts had been loaded on the ship that was to transport the weapons systems to Germany, fire broke out on the ship, partially destroying the system. Had the risk of loss passed to the Federal Republic of Germany?
9. General Electric Company delivered a stock of large lamps to Pettingell Supply Company "as agent to sell or distribute such lamps." Under the agency contract Pettingell could sell the lamps directly to certain customers for their own use or resale; it was also authorized to make deliveries of lamps under contracts of sale entered into by General Electric and the purchasers as well as to make deliveries to other retail agents of General Electric. About 20 percent of Pettingell's sales of General Electric lamps were direct sales to its own customers. Pettingell also wholesaled other electrical supplies, hardware, and housewares. The lamps were its only consignment business. Pettingell had financial difficulties and entered into an assignment for the benefit of creditors. Those creditors claimed the stock of G.E. lamps while G.E. claimed the lamps were its property because it had a principal-agency relationship with Pettingell. Who is entitled to the lamps?
10. Trend House sold its entire business, including stock of merchandise on hand, to Erving's. Erving's failed to obtain a list of creditor's of Trend House and failed to give the prescribed notice of sale to the creditors. The state in which the bulk transfer was made had adopted the "Pennsylvania Plan" (U.C.C. § 6–106) under which the proceeds of the sale are required to be distributed to the transferor's creditors. Darby, as trustee in bankruptcy for Trend House brought an action against Erving's to recover the value of transferred merchandise. Can Erving's be held personally liable for the value of the property transferred in the bulk sale?

37

Product Liability

Introduction

Nature of Product Liability. When a person buys goods he has certain expectations as to the quality of the goods and as to the use that can safely be made of the goods. These expectations may arise in a number of different ways; for example (1) through statements made by the seller in selling the goods or (2) because of express terms in the contract or (3) because the buyer expects the goods to be of the same quality of goods of that kind or (4) because the buyer told the seller what he needed them for and relied on the seller to pick out suitable goods or (5) because the buyer expects the manufacturer of the goods used reasonable care in designing and producing the goods and would warn him if there were any problems to look out for.

In turn a seller or manufacturer to whom a claim is made for a nonconforming or defective product may try in a number of ways to establish that the buyer was not entitled to rely on his expectations as a basis for recovery; for example, (1) that the seller was just engaging in "sales talk" or (2) that the seller expressly limited the statements the buyer could rely on, disclaimed any liability for certain kinds of problems, or limited the buyer's remedies to certain things such as replacement of the defective goods or (3) the manufacturer used normal care in designing and producing the goods and provided careful instructions as to their use and limitations.

When the goods delivered do not conform to the contract description or are defective, the question of the seller's and/or the manufacturer's liability for nonconforming or defective goods arises. Liability for such goods may be asserted on the basis of (a) express or implied warranties under the Code, (b) negligence or (c) strict liability—the bases for so-called "product liability." While each of these legal theories has distinct elements which must be established in order to premise liability, the courts do not always clearly distinguish between the theories in deciding product liability cases. This chapter addresses product liability including express and implied warranties, negligence and strict liability along with such issues as disclaimers, federal warranty requirements and who can sue or be sued for breach of warranty. Because negligence and strict liability have been covered in some detail in Chapter 5, the primary focus of this chapter is on the Code's treatment of warranties.

Representations. When a person is making an effort to sell goods, he usually makes some statements relative to the merits of the goods. Such statements are representations and may range in their legal effect from statements which are mere sales talk to statements which are fraudulent misrepresentations.

In the early period of the development of the law of sales, business was carried on in such a manner that the seller and the buyer negotiated face-to-face in the presence of the goods. Frequently, the seller was an itinerant merchant who would leave for parts unknown as soon as he had sold his wares. Also, the sale was quite often looked upon as a test of wits, the seller doing his best to drive a sharp bargain and the buyer exercising all of the cunning at his command to get a good buy. Under such conditions, neither party placed much faith in the statements of the other. The representations made by a seller were accepted as sales talk and not binding on him unless he clearly and unequivocally assumed responsibility for the quality of the goods he was selling.

With the development of commerce, business methods changed, and there was a shift from the face-to-face sale in the presence of the goods to sales made by the seller's representative, who called on the customer and described or displayed samples of the goods the seller was offering for sale. Since the buyer, under this system of selling, could not examine the goods he was buying before he contracted to buy, he had to rely on the representations of the seller or his agent.

By gradual evolution, merchandising has progressed from a system in which the seller was not held responsible for representations made regarding the goods offered for sale to a system in which a high degree of responsibility is placed on a seller for such representations.

Warranties—General. In its broadest sense a warranty is the assumption of responsibility, by the seller, for the quality, character, or suitability of goods sold. The seller may assume such responsibility by express agreement, in which case the warranty is created by contract and the rights and liabilities are contractual in nature. Such a warranty is called an express warranty.

If the seller has knowingly misrepresented the goods with intent to defraud and the buyer has justifiably relied on the representations to his injury, the seller will be liable to the buyer in damages in an action in tort for deceit.

If the seller is guilty of deceit, the buyer may elect to pursue either his remedy for breach of warranty or his remedy for damages for deceit.

Under some circumstances a degree of responsibility for goods sold is imposed on the seller by operation of law, in which case the nature and extent of the seller's responsibility will be determined by the nature of the transaction. Such responsibility is quasi-contractual in nature. The warranty is included in the sales agreement by operation of law, and such warranties are known as implied warranties.

SUMMARY

Buyers normally have certain expectations as to the quality of the goods they buy and sellers, likewise, have certain expectations as to their liability for the quality of those goods. When delivered goods are nonconforming or defective, including when they cause injury to persons or property, a question of product liability is raised. Product liability may be premised on breach of warranty, negligence or strict liability.

As a result of the change in the method of doing business, we have developed rules of law under which a seller is held responsible for representations made to induce a buyer to purchase goods.

A warranty is the assumption by the seller of goods of the responsibility for the quality, character, and suitability of goods sold. A warranty may result from representations made by the seller, or it may be imposed on the seller by operation of law.

Express Warranties

Nature of Express Warranty. An express warranty is based on contract and is the result of negotiation of the terms of the sales contract. It may be broad in its scope and include all phases of the quality, character, suitability and ownership of the goods involved or it may go to only one or more characteristics of the goods.

Creating an Express Warranty. The seller need not use the words "warrant" or "guarantee" in order to create an express warranty; neither is it necessary that he intend to make a warranty. Any statement of fact or promise made by the seller to the buyer which relates to the goods and becomes a part of the bargain creates an express warranty that the goods will conform to the statement or promise. A statement merely of the value of the goods or a statement which is merely the seller's opinion or commendation of the goods does not create a warranty.

Thus, a seller is not responsible if he, in representing his goods, confines his statements to "sales talk" or "puffing," such as "It is a good buy," "These goods are high class," or "You should be happy with this." Also, the seller is not responsible if he merely expresses an opinion as to the nature or quality of the goods. Whether a statement made by a seller will be interpreted as an opinion or express warranty will depend, in many instances, on the relative experience and knowledge of the parties. If the seller is one who deals in the type of goods he is selling, and the buyer does not deal in such goods and knows little about them, a statement relating to the quality or character of the goods might be interpreted as a warranty; on the other hand if the buyer is a dealer in such goods and has had experience and knowledge substantially equal to that of the seller, the same statements might be interpreted as statements of opinion.

In the negotiation of a sale the seller may use descriptive terms to convey to the buyer an idea of the quality or characteristics of the goods or he may use pictures, drawings, blueprints, or technical specifications. When a seller uses descriptive terms as the basis of the sales contract, he will have expressly warranted that the goods delivered will conform to the description. If a sample or model is made a part of the basis of the bargain, the seller will have expressly warranted that the goods delivered will conform to the sample or model (2–313).[1]

When the express warranty is made orally and the agreement between the buyer and the seller is reduced to writing without including the warranty, a problem may arise as to whether the express warranty became part of the contract. This brings into operation the parole evidence rule contained in Section 2–202, which is discussed in Chapter 13.

SUMMARY

An express warranty is a warranty embodied in the terms of a contract. To expressly warrant goods such words as "warrant" or "guarantee" need not be used. Any affirmation of fact or promise, any description of the goods or a sample or model of the goods used as a basis of the bargain is an express warranty. An affirmation merely of the value of the goods or a statement purporting to be merely the seller's opinion or commendation of the goods does not create an express warranty.

McCarty v. E. J. Korvette, Inc.

18 UCC Rep. 14 (Ct. Sp. App. Mo. 1975)

This was an action brought by Frances and Warren McCarty (plaintiffs) against E. J. Korvette, Inc., and Denman Rubber Manufacturing Co. (defend-

---

[1] The numbers in the parentheses refer to the sections of the Uniform Commercial Code, 1972.

ants) for damages resulting from an alleged breach of express and implied warranties and negligence. The trial court awarded judgment to the defendants. Reversed on appeal.

On February 25, 1971, Frances McCarty bought four tires manufactured by Denman Rubber Manufacturing Co., at Korvette Tire & Auto Centers. On the back side of the invoice given to Mrs. McCarty, under the title "Korvette Tire Centers All-Road-Hazards Tire Guarantee," the following language appeared:

"The tires identified hereon are guaranteed for the number of months (or miles) designated [*36,000 miles*] *against all road hazards* including stone bruises, impact bruises, *blow out,* tread separation, glass cuts and fabric breaks, only when used in normal, non-commercial passenger car service. *If a tire fails to give satisfactory service under the terms of this guarantee,* return it to the nearest Korvette Tire Center. *We will replace the tire* charging only the proportionate part of the sale price for each month elapsed (or mileage used) from date of purchase, plus the full federal tax.

"The above guarantee does not cover tires run flat, or simply worn out; tires injured by a fire, collision, vandalism, misalignment or mechanical defects of the vehicle. Radial or surface fissures, discoloration or ordinary repairable punctures, do not render tires unfit for service. Punctures will be repaired free.

"Neither the manufacturer nor Korvette Tire Centers shall be liable for any consequential damage and our liability is limited solely to replacement of the product." [Emphasis supplied.]

On June 14, 1971, Frances McCarty and her husband were involved in an automobile accident. As a result of a blowout of the right rear tire, their vehicle swerved off the road and turned over several times causing personal injury to each of them as well as property damage to their car.

DAVIDSON, JUDGE. The defendants initially contend that the language contained in the Korvette Tire Centers All-Road-Hazards Tire Guarantee, when read as a whole, does not constitute an express warranty against blowouts, but rather constitutes a guarantee that if a blowout occurs, the tire will be replaced. We do not agree.

Code § 2–313 (1975) defines an express warranty, in pertinent part, as follows:

(1) Express warranties by the seller are created as follows: (a) Any affirmation of fact or promise made by the seller to the buyer which relates to the goods and becomes part of the basis of the bargain creates an express warranty that the goods shall conform to the affirmation or promise.

Here the language on the invoice given to the buyer to the effect that "the tires identified hereon are guaranteed for 36,000 miles . . . against all road hazards, including . . . blow out . . ." constitutes an affirmation that the tires are of such existing quality, capacity and condition as to make them capable of rendering service without blowing out before they have been used for 36,000 miles. This assurance of the serviceability of the tires for a given number of miles, because it is a representation as to the existing quality, capacity and condition of the tires, constitutes an express warranty that the tires will not blow out during the first 36,000 miles of use.

Questions remain as to what impact the additional language appearing on the invoice has upon the scope and extent of the express warranty. Section 2–316 specifically recognizes a right on the part of the warrantor to negate, modify or limit an express or implied warranty under certain circumstances. It also implicitly recognizes that warranties may be limited in two different ways—one by "disclaiming" the warranty or a part of the warranty itself in the manner prescribed by subsections (1)–(3), and the other by "limiting the remedy" available upon breach (subsection (4)) in the manner prescribed by §§ 2–718 and 2–719.

Here the language which says that the guarantee applies only when the tires are used in normal non-commercial passenger car service, and does not apply to tires that are run flat, or simply worn out, injured by a fire, collision, vandalism, misalignment, or mechanical defects of the vehicle, constitutes a disclaimer under § 2–316(1). The language which not only promises to replace the tire if a blowout occurs, but also attempts to avoid consequential damages and restrict the remedies of the buyer solely to replacement, constitutes a limitation of remedies under § 2–316(4), governed by the provisions of § 2–719.

Section 2–719 gives the parties considerable latitude in which to fashion their remedies to their particular requirements. It expressly recognizes that parties may limit their remedies to repair and replacement. The parties, however, must accept the legal consequence that there be some fair remedy for breach of the obligations or duties outlined in the contract. Reasonable agreements which limit or modify remedies will be given effect, but the parties are not free to shape their remedies in an unreasonable or unconscionable way. Section 2–719(3) recognizes the validity of clauses limiting or excluding consequential damages, otherwise available under § 2–714(3), but expressly states that they may not operate in an unconscionable manner. That subsection also establishes that limitation of consequential damages for injury to the person in the case of consumer goods is prima facie unconscionable.

The clause purporting to limit the consumers' remedy solely to replacement of the tire purports to exclude liability for both personal injury and property damage. . .[T]o the extent that the clause purports to limit consequential damages for personal injury, it is unconscionable as a matter of law.

In *Collins v. Uniroyal Inc.*, the Supreme Court of New Jersey held that an express warranty against blowouts had been breached when a blowout occurred, notwithstanding the fact that a defect in the material and workmanship in the tire had not been proved.

The court cogently expressed the reasons for regarding a provision limiting the remedy to replacement of the tire to be "patently" unconscionable, and therefore, invalid by stating:

A tire manufacturer warrants against blowouts in order to increase tire sales. Public advertising by defendant relative to these tires stated: "If it only saves your life once, it's a bargain."

The seller should be held to realize that the purchaser of a tire buying it because so warranted is far more likely to have made the purchase decision in order to protect himself and the passengers in his car from death or personal injury in a blowout accident than to assure himself of a refund of the price of the tire in such an event. That being the natural reliance and the reasonable expectation of the purchaser flowing from the warranty, it appears to us patently unconscionable for the manufacturer to be permitted to limit his damages for a breach of warranty proximately resulting in the purchaser's death to a price refund or a replacement of the tire.

While there is no statutory presumption of unconscionability with respect to a limitation of consequential damages for injury to property in the case of consumer goods, the rationale in *Collins* persuades us that the clause here, which attempts to exclude liability for both personal injury and property damage, is so tainted by unconscionability as to warrant deletion in its entirety. If the defendants do not want to be liable for consequential damages, they should not expressly warrant the tires against blowouts.

Under the present circumstances, the clause purporting to restrict remedies solely to replacement is ineffective. It cannot serve to convert the express warranty against blowouts into a guarantee that if a tire blew out, "the tire would be replaced."

Wat Henry Pontiac Co. v. Bradley

210 P.2d 348 (Sup. Ct. Okla. 1949)

This was an action to recover the sum of $324.56 damages for breach of an express oral warranty of a used car purchased by Mrs. Joe Bradley (plaintiff) from the Wat Henry Pontiac Co. (defendant). The trial resulted in a judgment against the Wat Henry Pontiac Co. in the sum of $279.56. Affirmed on appeal.

JOHNSON, JUSTICE. Mrs. Bradley testified that on October 22, 1944, she went to the Wat Henry Pontiac Company; that she contacted the manager of salesmen in charge of the used cars; that she made a deal for the car; that she was with her brother; and that the brother was present during her negotiations for the purchase of the car; that she asked many questions about the car; that the seller assured her that the car was in good condition; that he had driven the car; that "this is a car we know; this is a car I can recommend"; that "it is in A-1 shape." She informed him that her husband was in Camp Shelby, Mississippi, and that her child was only seven months old; and that she wanted to be sure she was going to get there. Wat Henry further assured her that he knew the car, he knew the man who had brought it in, that it was "mechanically perfect" and that it would get her any place she wanted to go. She asked to drive the car and try it out, but was told that gas rations were very short and they were not allowed to send cars out for trial, but that she had no cause to fear this car, that it was all right; that she could not see the connecting rods or crankshaft or rings; that she was not a mechanic, but was a trained nurse.

The salesman who sold the car testified in substance that he had been an auto mechanic for about twelve years before becoming a salesman; that he was engaged in demonstrating and selling cars; that he did not warrant the car, but explained to the buyer that the sale was without a warranty, but did state that after the deal was closed that he told Bradley, "I would not be afraid to start, and I wouldn't have been afraid to start any place in the car, because it ran as nice as you would expect a car that age to run. There wasn't anything to indicate to me that there was anything wrong with the car, if there was anything wrong with it."

The rule is that to constitute an express warranty no particular form of words is necessary, and any affirmation of the quality or condition of the vehicle, not uttered as a matter of opinion or belief, made by a seller at the time of sale for the purpose of assuring the buyer of the truth of the fact and inducing the buyer to make the purchase, if so received and relied on by the buyer, is an express warranty.

This court in *International Harvester Co. v. Lawyer,* said:

> "Warranty" is a matter of intention. A decisive test is whether the vendor assumes to assert a fact of which the buyer is ignorant, or merely states an opinion, or his judgment, upon a matter of which the vendor has no special knowledge, and on which the buyer may also be expected to have an opinion and to exercise his judgment. In the former case there is a warranty; in the latter case there is not.

The facts in this case bring it squarely within the above well-settled principles of law, and the jury was justified in finding that there was an oral warranty.

The buyer here was ignorant of the facts, and the defects were hidden and not open to discovery by the buyer. The seller was an expert in handling automobiles, having served for a long period of time as an automobile mechanic before becoming a salesman; and his statements as to the condition of the car and where it could be driven constituted a warranty and not mere opinion.

Warranty of Title

Nature and Scope of Warranty of Title. A warranty of title differs from other warranties in that it protects the buyer in his ownership of the goods he has bought whereas other warranties go to the quality of the goods sold. The general rule is that in any contract for the sale of goods the seller warrants that he has good title to the goods and the right to sell them. The seller also impliedly warrants that the goods are free of any liens except those the buyer had knowledge of at the time the contract was made. If the goods are subject to any liens, the contract may provide that the sale is subject to the encumbrance. If no such provision is made, the seller must discharge the lien before the time for delivery of the goods, or the seller will breach the warranty of title.

For example, John puts his used automobile up for sale. John originally borrowed the money from his bank to buy the automobile, and the bank took a security interest or lien on it to secure John's payment of the loan. If John still owes $600 on the automobile at the time he sells the car to Ann, John must either specifically provide in his agreement with Ann that the automobile is being sold subject to the bank's lien, or he must pay off the loan at the bank and obtain a release of the lien prior to the time he is to deliver the automobile to Ann. If John had bought the automobile from Thief, who had stolen it, and the car was later recovered from Ann by the police, then she could go back against John for breach of the warranty of title he made to her when she bought the car from him.

Exclusion or Limitation or Warranty of Title. No warranty of title is given by the seller where the buyer knows from the circumstances that the seller does not have title to the goods but is selling in an official capacity and claims to sell only that title which a third person has. For example, a buyer of goods at a police auction knows that the auctioneer does not have title to the goods he is selling.

A warranty of title may be excluded or modified but only by specific language that makes it clear no warranty of title is being given. The courts have generally held that unless the language of a disclaimer of warranty clearly and unequivocably includes the warranty of title, the buyer is justified in believing that the intent is to disclaim warranties of quality and not warranties of title (2–312[2]).

SUMMARY

The warranty of title differs from other warranties in that it relates to the seller's right to sell the goods rather than to the quality of the goods. In a sale the seller warrants that he is conveying good title and that the goods are not subject to any lien of which the buyer is not aware. The warranty is not made, however, where the buyer knows the seller is acting in some official capacity, that the seller does not have title, or if the warranty of title is excluded or modified in clear and unequivocal language.

Implied Warranties

Nature of Implied Warranty. Under present methods of merchandising and because of the complexity of goods sold, the buyer either has little or no opportunity to examine the goods or is not in a position to adequately test the goods to determine their quality. A merchant dealing in such goods is in a much better position than a buyer to make a thorough examination of the goods or to make tests to determine their quality. Therefore, in the interest of trade certain responsibilities are imposed on the seller, especially if he is a merchant dealing in such goods, for the quality, character and suitability of the goods sold. This responsibility is not assumed by the seller, either by express promise or by the making of representations concerning the goods, but it imposed on him by operation of law. The responsibility imposed is the same, in its general nature, as that assumed by the seller when he expressly warrants goods. In fact the responsibility is a warranty implied in law.

This responsibility is not absolute. It arises only under certain circumstances and the seller may contract against it. The courts, however, favor implied warranties, and if the seller wishes to relieve himself from the responsibility imposed on him by the implied warranties it must be clearly established that the parties to the sale did not intend the implied warranty to be part of the contract of sale.

There are two implied warranties of quality recognized under the Code: the implied warranty of merchantability and the implied warranty of fitness for a particular purpose. These two warranties overlap and under some circumstances the seller may be held liable for breach of both warranties.

Implied Warranty of Merchantability. An implied warranty that the goods are merchantable is made by every seller who is a merchant dealing in goods of the kind sold. Under the Code, the serving for value of food or drink to be consumed either on the premises or elsewhere is a sale, and thus if the food or drink sold in a restaurant is unwholesome, the seller may be held liable for breach of the implied warranty of merchantability.

The Code sets out six tests of merchantability. To be merchantable goods must at least: (1) be acceptable to others in the trade under the contract description; (2) if they are fungible goods such as grain, they must be of fair average quality for the contract description; (3) be fit for the ordinary purpose for which such goods are used; (4) within the variations permitted by the agreement, the goods must be of even kind, quality and quantity within each unit and among all units involved; (5) be adequately contained, packaged, and labeled as the agreement may require; and (6) conform to any promises or statements of fact made on the container or label (2–314[2]).

The common test is, of course, that the goods be fit for the ordinary purpose for which such goods are used. Thus, if a person buys a chair she should be able to reasonably expect that it will be suitable for sitting in and will not collapse under the weight of a normal person who sits down in it; similarly a buyer should be able to expect a baby shampoo can safely be used to shampoo a baby's hair or the buyer of a can of soup should be able to assume it is wholesome and edible.

Implied Warranty of Fitness for Particular Purpose. If at the time a contract for the sale of goods is made, the seller knows the particular purpose for which the buyer needs the goods and that the buyer is relying on the seller to select goods suitable for that purpose, then the seller makes an implied warranty that the goods will be fit for that particular purpose (2–314[2]). For example, a farmer goes to a feed store and tells the clerk that he needs a pesticide that would kill corn borers. If the clerk knows the farmer is depending on the clerk to pick out a suitable pesticide, there is an implied warranty that the product selected will be fit for the farmer's need. If when properly used, the product selected kills the farmer's corn or is ineffective against corn bores, there would be a breach of warranty.

If the buyer gives the seller technical specifications of the goods he wishes to buy or in some other manner clearly indicates the particular goods desired, there would be no evidence of reliance on the seller's judgment and no implied warranty of fitness for a particular purpose. An implied warranty of fitness for a particular purpose may arise whether or not the seller is a merchant dealing in goods of that kind (2–314[2]).

SUMMARY

There are two implied warranties of quality—that of merchantability and that of fitness for a particular purpose. The implied warranty, unless excluded or modified by contract, becomes a part of the sales contract by operation of law.

An implied warranty of merchantability accompanies a sale by a merchant dealing in goods of the kind sold unless the warranty is excluded or modified. The warranty of merchantability imposes liability on the seller if the goods are not fit for the ordinary purpose for which such goods are used. Six tests of merchantability are set out in the Code.

The implied warranty of fitness for a particular purpose is based on the seller's having reason to know the particular purpose for which the buyer wishes the goods and the buyer's reliance on the seller's skill and judgment in selecting the goods suitable for his purpose. The seller need not be a merchant in order for a warranty of fitness for a particular purpose to be created. Both the warranty of merchantability and the warranty of fitness for a particular purpose may be involved in the same sale.

Hunt v. Ferguson-Paulus Enterprises

415 P.2d 13 (Sup. Ct. Ore. 1966)

This was an action by Hunt (plaintiff) against Ferguson-Paulus Enterprises (defendant) to recover damages for injury allegedly sustained through a breach of the warranty of merchantability. Judgment for Ferguson-Paulus and Hunt appealed. Judgment affirmed.

Hunt purchased a cherry pie from Ferguson-Paulus through a vending machine owned and maintained by them. On biting into the pie one of Hunt's teeth was broken when it encountered a cherry pit.

LUSK, JUSTICE. If the cherry pie purchased by Hunt from Ferguson-Paulus was not reasonably fit for human consumption because of the presence of the cherry pit there was a breach of warranty and Hunt was entitled to recover his damages thereby caused.

In the consideration of similar cases some of the courts have drawn a distinction between injury caused by spoiled, impure, or contaminated food or food containing a foreign substance, and injury caused by a substance natural to the product sold. In the latter class of cases, these courts hold there is no liability on the part of the dispenser of the goods. Thus in the leading case of *Mix v. Ingersoll Candy Co.,* the court held that a patron of a restaurant who ordered and paid for chicken pie, which contained a sharp sliver or fragment of chicken bone, and was injured as a result of swallowing the bone, had no cause of action against the restauranter either for breach of warranty or negligence. Referring to cases in which recovery had been allowed the court said:

> All of the cases are instances in which the food was found not to be reasonably fit for human consumption, either by reason of the presence of a foreign substance, or an impure and noxious condition of the food itself, such as for example, glass, stones, wires or nails in the food served, or tainted, diseased, or infected meats or vegetables.

The court went on to say that:

> . . . despite the fact that a chicken bone may occasionally be encountered in a chicken pie, such chicken pie, in the absence of some further defect, is reasonably fit for human consumption. Bones which are natural to the type of meat served cannot legitimately be called a foreign substance, and a consumer who eats meat dishes ought to anticipate and be on guard against the presence of such bones.

Further the court said:

> Certainly no liability would attach to a restaurant keeper for the serving of a T-bone steak, or a beef stew, which contained a bone natural to the type of meat served, or if a fish dish should contain a fish bone, or if a cherry pie should contain a cherry stone—although it be admitted that an ideal cherry pie would be stoneless.

Other courts have rejected the so-called foreign-natural test in favor of what is known as the "reasonable expectation" test, among them the Supreme Court of Wisconsin, which, in *Betehia v. Cape Cod Corp.* held that a person who was injured by a chicken bone in a chicken sandwich served to him in a restaurant, could recover for his injury either for breach of an implied warranty or for negligence. "There is a distinction," the court said, "between what a consumer expects to find in a fish stick and in a baked or fried fish, or in a chicken sandwich made from sliced white meat and in roast chicken. The test should be what is reasonably expected by the consumer in the food as served, not what might be natural to the ingredients of that food prior to preparation. What is to be reasonably expected by the consumer is a jury question in most cases; at least, we cannot say as a matter of law that a patron of a restaurant must expect a bone in a chicken sandwich either because chicken bones are occasionally found there or are natural to chicken."

In view of the judgment for Ferguson-Paulus, we are not required in this case to make a choice between the two rules. Under the foreign-natural test Hunt would be barred from recovery as a matter of law. The reasonable expectation test calls for determination of a question of fact. The Court has found the facts in favor of Ferguson-Paulus and this court has no power to disturb the finding.

Corneliuson v. Arthur Drug Stores, Inc.

214 A.2d 676 (Sup. Ct. Conn. 1965)

This was an action by Corneliuson (plaintiff) against Arthur Drug Stores, Inc. (defendant), for breach of an implied warranty of fitness of a home permanent waving lotion purchased by Corneliuson from Arthur. Corneliuson claimed that, as a result of her use of the lotion, she sustained severe dermatitis with concomitant physical and neurotic injuries. The jury returned a verdict for Corneliuson which the trial court refused to set aside. Reversed on appeal.

HOUSE, JUSTICE. In *Crotty v. Shartenberg's-New Haven, Inc.,* we held that under our statute there may be an implied warranty that the goods sold shall be reasonably fit for a particular purpose, or that the goods shall be of merchantable quality and that the existence, nature and extent of either implied warranty depends on the circumstances of the case. We noted that some jurisdictions hold that if the article sold can be used by a normal person without injury, there is no breach of the implied warranty of reasonable fitness, while others adopt the theory that the seller is not absolved from liability under the implied warranty created by the statute by the mere fact that only a small portion of those who use the product suffer injuries from its use. We concluded that the term "reasonable fitness" must, of necessity, be considered one of degree and that the term must be "related to the subject of the sale."

Rejecting the rule limiting the application of the term "reasonable fitness" to a class or group designated as normal persons, we adopted the test of injurious effect to "an appreciable number of people." We held that not only the causal connection between the product and the injury must be established but also the plaintiff must be a member of a class who would be similarly affected by the product, identifying that class as an appreciable number of people.

In the course of the opinion we used the following language:

To establish a breach of the warranty, the plaintiff must show (1) that the product contains a substance or ingredient which has a tendency to affect injuriously an appreciable number of people, though fewer in number than the number of normal buyers, and (2) that he has, in fact, been injured or harmed by the use of the product. The burden is on the plantiff to establish these facts. Proof of the harmful propensities of the substance and that it can affect injuriously an appreciable number of persons is essential to his case. If a buyer has knowledge, either actual or constructive, that he is allergic to a particular substance and purchases a product which he knows or reasonably should know contains that substance, he cannot recover damages for breach of an implied warranty. Nor can he recover if he suffers harm by reason of his own improper use of the article warranted. When a manufacturer puts into a product to be sold for human use a substance which has deleterious qualities and a tendency to harm an appreciable number of its users, the manufacturer, and not the user, should shoulder the risk of injurious consequences. The same risk should be borne by the retailer who sells the article to a prospective user who, relying on the retailer, is entitled to believe that the article is reasonably fit for the purpose for which it is sold.

Although there was evidence from which the jury could find that the Ogilvie Sisters lotion did cause injury to Corneliuson there was no evidence from which they could find that this lotion as compounded had a tendency to affect injuriously an appreciable number of people. Proof of both injury to Corneliuson and such injurious tendency are necessary for Corneliuson to prevail. Proof that all permanent waving lotions generally contain certain basic chemicals compounded in varying strengths in the different brands and that in the strength used in some of them the chemicals may injuriously affect some people is not alone a reasonable basis for a conclusion that any specific lotion, even though it contains in some form those same basic chemicals, has the injurious tendency requisite to establish liability and that that lotion is not "reasonably fit" or of "merchantable quality" as those terms are used in the statute on implied warranties. The basic test must be applied to the particular product as compounded, which necessarily includes any incorporated substance or ingredient in the strength and quantity used in the particular product, not in the strength and quantity which such substances or ingredients may be used in some other products.

Exclusions, Modification, or Conflict of Warranties

General Rules. Under the Code, the parties to a contract have within certain limits the right to, by agreement, relieve the seller from all or part of his liability arising from express or implied warranties. However, the drafters of the Code and the courts interpreting it generally reflect a determination to protect the buyer from the inclusion in a sales contract of a clause modifying or excluding warranties unless the buyer was fully aware of the clause and freely consented to it. The Code also distinguishes between different types of warranties in providing for modification or exclusion of a particular warranty.

Express Warranties. Because an express warranty is by its terms an explicit part of a sales contract, any other terms of the contract that might tend to limit or negate the warranty are to be construed where possible as consistent with the express warranty; however, to the extent this construction is unreasonable, then the negation or limitation is not given effect (2–316[1]). For example, if a sales contract includes an express warranty and also includes a clause which seeks to exclude "all warranties, express or implied," such clause would be inoperative since it would be unreasonable. Also, if the sales contract is in writing, oral evidence of an agreement to exclude or modify warranties included in the written contract would not be admissible in court to try to prove the exclusion or modification (2–202).

Warranty of Merchantability. In order to exclude the warranty of merchantability, the seller must specifically mention "merchantability" in his oral or written exclusion, and if the exclusion is in writing, the clause that excludes all or part of the warranty of merchantability must be conspicuous. Thus, to exclude or modify an implied warranty of merchantability, where the sales contract is in writing, the exclusion clause would have to be printed or written into the contract in larger type or letters or in ink of a different color so that a person reading the contract would not be likely to overlook it. If the seller wishes added protection he should have the buyer separately sign the exclusion clause (2–316[2]).

Warranty of Fitness for a Particular Purpose. To exclude or modify an implied warranty of fitness for a particular purpose, the exclusion must be in writing and conspicuous. Language to exclude all implied warranties of fitness is sufficient if it states, for example, that "There are no warranties other than those specifically provided in this agreement." However, such clause in the contract, to be effective, would have to be printed or written in conspicuous type or letters (2–316[2]).

Unless circumstances indicate otherwise, all implied warranties are excluded by expressions like "as is," "with all faults," or other language which in common understanding calls the buyer's attention to the exclusion of warranties and makes plain that there are no implied warranties (2–316[3][a]).

Exclusion by Opportunity to Inspect. When the buyer, before entering into the contract, has examined the goods or a sample or model as fully as he desires or has refused to examine the goods, there is no implied warranty with regards to defects which an examination ought to have revealed to him. If the seller merely makes the goods available to the buyer for examination and the buyer neglects to examine them, the seller would not be protected under this provision of the Code. The seller should not only make the goods available for examination but he should demand that the buyer examine the goods (2–316[3][*b*]).

An implied warranty can also be excluded or modified by course of dealings, course of performance or usage of trade (2–316[3][*c*]).

Conflict of Warranties. Frequently in a sales contract implied warranties supplement express warranties. The Code provides that warranties whether express or implied shall be construed as consistent with each other and as cumulative, but if such construction is unreasonable the intention of the parties is used to determine which warranty is dominant. In case of conflict the court must determine from all the facts and circumstances which warranty was intended by the parties to be dominant. The Code also provides that express warranties displace inconsistent implied warranties other than an implied warranty of fitness for a particular purpose (2–317).

Further Limits on Disclaimers. While the Code gives the parties considerable leeway as to the terms they may include in a contract and specifically provides methods for excluding or limiting warranties, there are some further limits on the ability of a seller to shield himself from warranty liability. Under Section 2–302 a court may refuse to enforce a particular clause or an entire contract if it finds the clause or contract was "unconscionable" at the time it was made. While the Section 2–316 requirement that disclaimers of warranty be conspicuous takes care of many of the unfair surprise-type unconscionability cases, the courts may also refuse to enforce a warranty disclaimer as unconscionable where there is a great disparity of bargaining power between the parties and the disclaimer was forced on the buyer without a chance to bargain over its form.

Any limitation by a seller for consequential damages for injury to a person caused by defective consumer goods is prima facie unconscionable (2–719). However, limitations or exclusion of such damages where the loss is commercial is possible as long as the exclusion is not unconscionable.

SUMMARY

Language of a disclaimer in a sales contract is ineffective where such language is inconsistent with an express warranty included in it. To exclude or modify an implied warranty of merchantability, merchantability must be mentioned and in the case of a writing must be conspicuous. To exclude or modify an implied warranty of fitness for a particular purpose the exclusion must be in writing and conspicuous. Implied warranties are excluded by expressions like "as is" or "with all faults." If the buyer examines the goods or a sample or model or if a demand is made that he examine them and he refuses, there is no implied warranty with regards to defects which the examination ought to reveal. An implied warranty can also be excluded or modified by course of dealing, by course of performance or by usage of trade.

Express and implied warranties will be construed as consistent and cumulative unless such construction is unreasonable, and if unreasonable, the intention of the parties as to which warranty is to be dominant is controlling.

Weisz v. Parke-Bernet Galleries, Inc.

325 N.Y.S. 2d 576 (Civ. Ct. N.Y.C. 1971)

This was an action brought by Dr. Arthur Weisz and David and Irene Schwartz (plaintiffs) against the Parke-Bernet Galleries, Inc. (defendant) to recover the purchase prices of paintings that plaintiffs had purchased at a Parke-Bernet auction. Judgment for plaintiffs.

On May 16, 1962, Dr. Arthur Weisz attended an auction conducted by the Parke-Bernet Galleries, Inc., where he ultimately bought for the sum of $3,347.50 a painting listed in the auction catalogue as the work of Raoul Dufy. Some two years later, on May 13, 1964, David and Irene Schwartz bought for $9,360.00 at a Parke-Bernet auction a painting also listed in the catalogue as the work of Raoul Dufy.

Several years after the second auction, as a result of an investigation conducted by the New York County District Attorney's office, the plaintiffs received information that the paintings were in fact forgeries. When this was called to Parke-Bernet's attention, Parke-Bernet denied any legal responsibility, asserting among other things that the conditions of sale for both auctions included a disclaimer of warranty as to genuineness, authorship and the like.

In each instance the auction catalogue contained several pages of print entitled "Conditions of Sale." The second of 15 numbered paragraphs provided as follows:

> The Galleries has endeavored to catalogue and describe the property correctly, but all property is sold "as is" and neither the Galleries nor its consignor warrants or represents, and they shall in no event be responsible for, the correctness of description, genuineness, authorship, provenience or condition of the property, and no statement contained in the catalogue or made orally at the sale or elsewhere shall be deemed to be such a warranty or representation, or an assumption of liability.

SANDLER, JUSTICE. The most substantial of the defenses interposed by Parke-Bernet is that the conditions of sale for the auctions, appearing on a preliminary page of each catalogue, included a disclaimer of any warranty and that the plaintiffs are bound by its terms.

This issue embraces two separate questions, each of which merits careful examination.

First, did the plaintiffs in fact know of the disclaimer, and, if they did not, are they legally chargeable with such knowledge.

Second, if the answer to either part of the first question is yes, was the disclaimer effective, under all the circumstances of the auctions, to immunize Parke-Bernet from the legal consequences that would normally follow where a sale results from a representation of genuineness that is thereafter disclosed to be completely inaccurate.

As to the first auction, I am satisfied that Dr. Weisz did not in fact know of the conditions of sale and may not properly be charged with knowledge of its contents. I accept as entirely accurate his testimony that in his prior appearances at Parke-Bernet auctions he had not made any bids, and that on the occasion of his purchase he did not observe the conditions of sale and was not aware of its existence.

The test proposed for this kind of issue by Williston, quite consistent with the decided cases, is whether "the person . . . should as a reasonable man understand that it contains terms of the contract that he must read at his peril."

The most obvious characteristic of the two Parke-Bernet auctions is that they attracted people on the basis of their interest in owning works of art, not on the basis of their legal experience or business sophistication. Surely it is unrealistic to assume that people who bid at such auctions will ordinarily understand that a gallery catalogue overwhelmingly devoted to descriptions of works of art also includes in its preliminary pages conditions of sale. Even less reasonable does it seem to me to expect a bidder at such an auction to appreciate the possibility that the conditions of sale would include a disclaimer of liability for the accuracy of the basic information presented throughout the catalogue in unqualified form with every appearance of certainty and reliability.

For someone in Dr. Weisz's position to be bound by conditions of sale of which he in fact knew nothing, considerably more was required of Parke-Bernet to call those conditions of sale to his attention than occurred here.

As to the Schwartz case, I am satisfied from the evidence that Mrs. Schwartz knew of the conditions of sale, and that both Schwartz plaintiffs are chargeable with that knowledge since they both participated in the purchase.

This factual conclusion leads to consideration of the extremely interesting question whether the language of disclaimer relied upon as a bar to the actions should be deemed effective for that purpose. No case has come to my attention that squarely presents the issue raised by the underlying realities of this case.

What is immediately apparent from any review of the evidence is that notwithstanding the language of disclaimer, Parke-Bernet expected that bidders at its acutions would rely upon the accuracy of its descriptions, and intended that they should. Parke-Bernet, as the evidence confirms, is an exceedingly well-known gallery, linked in the minds of people with the handling, exhibition and sale of valuable artistic works and invested with an aura of expertness and reliability. The very fact that Parke-Bernet was offering a work of art for sale would inspire confidence that it was genuine and that the listed artist in fact was the creator of the work.

The wording of the catalogue was clearly designed to emphasize the genuineness of the works to be offered. The list of artists followed by catalogue numbers, the black-and-white reproductions of the more important works, the simple listing of the name of the artist with the years of his birth and death could not have failed to impress upon the buyer that these facts could be relied on and that one could safely part with large sums of money in the confident knowledge that a genuine artistic work was being acquired.

Where one party in a contractual relationship occupies a position of superior knowledge and experience, and where the superior knowledge is relied upon and intended to be relied upon by the other, surely more is required for an effective disclaimer than appears here.

After reassuring the reader that Parke-Bernet endeavored to catalogue the works of art correctly, there follow highly technical and legalistic words of disclaimer in a situation in which plain and emphatic words are required. And this provision, in light of the critical importance to the buyer of a warning that he may not rely on the fact that a work attributed to an artist was in fact his creation, is in no way given the special prominence that it clearly requires.

The language used, the understated manner of its presentation, the failure to refer to it explicitly in the preliminary oral announcement of the auction all lead to the conclusion that Parke-Bernet did not expect the bidders to take the disclaimer too seriously or to be too concerned about it. I am convinced that the average reader of this provision would view it as some kind of technicality that should in no way derogate from the certainty that he was buying genuine artistic works, and that this was precisely the impression intended to be conveyed.

In denying legal effect to the disclaimer I am acting consistently with a whole body of law that reflects an increasing sensitivity to the requirements of fair dealing where there is a relationship between parties in which there is a basic inequality of knowledge, expertness or economic power.

Who Benefits from Warranty

General Rule. The courts, in determining who is entitled to the benefit of a warranty, have considered the warranty as contractual. In many situations the seller expressly promises to assume responsibility for the failure of the goods to measure up to certain defined standards. Such a warranty is contractual. However, a warranty may arise as the result of representations which are not promissory in nature, and an implied warranty may attach by operation of law. Nevertheless, all suits for damages for breach of warranty are actions in contract, not in tort. Proceeding from the accepted theory that a warranty is contractual, the courts have applied the general rule of contract law, that one not a party to a contract has no right to enforce the contract. Traditionally, this has meant that a person who did not himself purchase the defective goods did not have a cause of action for breach of warranty and even the purchaser of defective goods could sue only his immediate seller and not the manufacturer with whom he was not in privity of contract.

Demise of the Privity Doctrine. Today there is a growing tendency on the part of courts to allow recovery by an injured purchaser directly from the manufacturer or processor. In most cases the manufacturer or processor has control over the state of the product when it reaches the buyer's control and should be held liable for defects in it. The fact that the ultimate consumer may bring suit against the manufacturer or processor in no way relieves the retailer from his responsibility for the fitness or merchantability of the goods. In many states the buyer has been permitted to sue both the retailer and the manufacturer or processor in the same suit.

The manufacturers of many products give a manufacturer's warranty to the ultimate purchaser of their products in which they warrant their products against certain defined defects and in which they expressly limit their liability for breach of the express warranty. A manufacturer who has given such a warranty is liable on the warranty in a direct suit brought by the ultimate purchaser to whom the warranty is addressed.

Uniform Commercial Code. The drafters of the Code took no position on whether an injured purchaser could directly sue the manufacturer; instead, they left the development of the law on this point open to the courts, which as indicated above tend to allow such direct actions.

The Code, in Section 2–318, does extend warranty protection to "any natural person who is in the family or household of his buyer or who is a guest in his house if it is reasonable to expect that such person may use, consume, or be affected by the goods and who is injured in person by breach of warranty." The Code further provides that the seller may not exclude or limit his liability to the members of the buyer's household or his guests for breach of warranty (2–318). Some states have adopted an alternative Section 2–318 that broadens the class of people who may benefit from a warranty; other states have followed the original 2–318 and would bar recovery for breach of warranty for those persons not specifically covered, for example, employees and some "bystanders."

Henningsen v. Bloomfield Motors, Inc.

161 A.2d 69 (Sup. Ct. N.J. 1960)

This was an action for breach of warranty by Claus and Helen Henningsen (plaintiffs) against Chrysler Corporation and Bloomfield Motors (defendants). The trial court awarded damages to the Henningsens. Affirmed on appeal.

Claus Henningsen purchased a new 1955 Plymouth from Bloomfield Motors as a gift for his wife, Helen. At the time of purchase Claus signed a purchase order that included an express warranty against defects in material and workmanship but which limited Chrysler's obligation to replacing the defective parts. The "warranty clause" went on to say that this warranty was "expressly in lieu of all other warranties expressed or implied, and all other obligations or liabilities on its part." This statement was made in fine print on the reverse side of the purchase order as the seventh of ten paragraphs. Shortly after the purchase and while Helen Henningsen was driving the car on a smooth dry pavement, she heard a loud noise as if something cracked, the steering wheel spun in her hands, and the car veered sharply to the right, crashing into a brick wall. This action was then initiated against Chrysler and Bloomfield Motors, and the trial court awarded judgment to the Henningsens. The defendants appealed, arguing among other things (1) that no implied warranties ran from Chrysler to the Henningsens, (2) that there was an effective disclaimer of the implied warranties, and (3) that Helen Henningsen's lack of privity with the defendants barred a breach of warranty action against them.

FRANCIS, JUSTICE.

I. The Claim of Implied Warranty against the Manufacturer. Preliminarily, it may be said that the express warranty against defective parts and workmanship is not inconsistent with an implied warranty of merchantability. Such warranty cannot be excluded for that reason.

Chrysler points out that an implied warranty of merchantability is an incident of a contract of sale. It concedes, of course, the making of the original sale to Bloomfield Motors, Inc., but maintains that this transaction marked the terminal point of its contractual connection with the car. Then Chrysler urges that since it was not a party to the sale by the dealer to Henningsen, there is no privity of contract between it and the plaintiffs, and the absence of this privity eliminates any such implied warranty.

There is no doubt that under early common-law concepts of contractual liability only those persons who were parties to the bargain could sue for a breach of it. In more recent times a noticeable disposition has appeared in a number of jurisdictions to break through the narrow barrier of privity when dealing with sales of goods in order to give realistic recognition to a universally accepted fact. The fact is that the dealer and the ordinary buyer do not, and are not expected to, buy goods, whether they be foodstuffs or automobiles, exclusively for their own consumption or use. Makers and manufacturers know this and advertise and market their products on that assumption; witness, the "family" car, the baby foods, etc. The limitations of privity in contracts for the sale of goods developed their place in the law when marketing conditions were simple, when maker and buyer frequently met face to face on an equal bargaining plane and when many of the products were relatively uncomplicated and conducive to inspection by a buyer competent to evaluate their quality. With the advent of mass marketing, the manufacturer became remote from the purchaser, sales were accomplished through intermediaries, and the demand for the product was created by advertising media. In such an economy it became obvious that the consumer was the person being cultivated. Manifestly, the connotation of "consumer" was broader than that of "buyer." He signified such a person who, in the reasonable contemplation of the parties to the sale, might be expected to use the product.

As far back as 1932, in the well known case of *Baxter v. Ford Motor Co.*, the Supreme Court of Washington gave recognition to the impact of the existing commercial practices on the straitjacket of privity, saying:

> It would be unjust to recognize a rule that would permit manufacturers of goods to create a demand for their products by representing that they possess qualities which they, in fact, do not possess, and then, because there is no privity of contract existing between the consumer and the manufacturer, deny the consumer the right to recover if damages result from the absence of those qualities, when such absence is not readily noticeable.

Accordingly, we hold that under modern marketing conditions, when a manufacturer puts a new automobile in the stream of trade and promotes its purchase by the public, an implied warranty that it is reasonably suitable for use as such accompanies it into the hands of the ultimate purchaser. Absence of agency between the manufacturer and the dealer who makes the ultimate sale is immaterial.

II. The Effect of the Disclaimer and Limitation of Liability Clauses on the Implied Warranty of Merchantability. What effect should be given to the express warranty in question which seeks to limit the manufacturer's liability to replacement of defective parts, and which disclaims all other warranties, express or implied?

The warranty before us is a standardized form designed for mass use. It is imposed upon the automobile consumer. He takes it or leaves it, and he must take it to buy an automobile. No bargaining is engaged in with respect to it. In fact, the dealer through whom it comes to the buyer is without authority to alter it; his function is ministerial—simply to deliver it. The form warranty is not only standard with Chrysler but, as mentioned above, it is the uniform warranty of the Automobile Manufacturers Association.

The gross inequality of bargaining position occupied by the consumer in the automobile industry is thus apparent. There is no competition among the car makers in the area of the express warranty. Where can the buyer go to negotiate for better protection? Such control and limitation of his remedies are inimical to the public welfare and, at the very least, call for great care by the courts to avoid injustice through application of strict common-law principles of freedom of contract.

V. The Defense of Lack of Privity against Mrs. Henningsen. Both defendants contend that since there was no privity of contract between them and Mrs. Henningsen, she cannot recover for breach of any warranty made by either of them. On the facts, as they were developed, we agree that she was not a party to the purchase agreement. Her right to maintain the action, therefore, depends upon whether she occupies such legal status thereunder as to permit her to take advantage of a breach of defendants' implied warranties.

In the present matter, the basic contractual relationship is between Claus Henningsen, Chrysler, and Bloomfield Motors, Inc. The precise issue presented is whether Mrs. Henningsen, who is not a party to their respective warranties, may claim under them. We are convinced that the cause of justice in this area of the law can be served only by recognizing that she is such a person who, in the reasonable contemplation of the parties to the warranty, might be expected to become a user of the automobile. Accordingly, her lack of privity does not stand in the way of prosecution of the injury suit against the defendant Chrysler.

It is our opinion that an implied warranty of merchantability chargeable to either an automobile manufacturer or a dealer extends to the purchaser of the car, members of his family, and to other persons occupying or using it with his consent. It would be wholly opposed to reality to say that use by such persons is not within the anticipation of parties to such a warranty of reasonable suitability of an automobile for ordinary highway operation. Those persons must be considered within the distributive chain.

Section 2–318 of the Uniform Commercial Code proposes that the warranty be extended to "any natural person who is in the family or household of his buyer or who is a guest in his home if it is reasonable to expect that such person may use, consume or be affected by the goods and who is injured in person by breach of the warranty." And the section provides also that "A seller may not exclude or limit the operation" of the extension. A footnote thereto says that beyond this provision "the section is neutral and is not intended to enlarge or restrict the developing case law on whether the seller's warranties, given to his buyer, who resells, extend to other persons in the distributive chain."

It is not necessary in this case to establish the outside limits of the warranty protection. For present purposes, with respect to automobiles, it suffices to promulgate the principle set forth above.

Federal Trade Commission Warranty Rules

Magnuson-Moss Warranty Act. In the late 1960s and early 1970s Congress conducted a number of investigations into consumer product warranties. It concluded that the warranties were frequently confusing, misleading and frustrating to consumers, that consumer products were typically sold with a form contract dictated by the seller with no real bargaining between the parties, that the remedies were not always meaningful, that the warranty rules should be changed to stimulate manufacturers to market more reliable products for competitive reasons. In 1975, the Magnuson-Moss Warranty Act was signed into law. Its stated purpose was to: (1) provide minimum warranty protection for consumers; (2) increase consumer understanding of warranties; (3) assure warranty performance by providing meaningful remedies; and (4) promote better product reliability by making it easier for consumers to chose between products on the basis of their likely reliability.

Under the Act and the Regulations of the Federal Trade Commission implementing the Act, any seller of a "consumer product"[2] costing the consumer more than $15[3] who gives a written warranty to the consumer[4] is required to "clearly and conspicuously disclose in a single document in simple and understandable language" the following items of information:

1. The identity of the persons to whom the warranty is extended, if the written warranty can be enforced only by the original consumer purchaser or is limited to persons other than every consumer owner of the item during the term of the warranty;
2. A clear description of the products, parts, characteristics, components, and properties covered by the warranty; if necessary for clarity, those items excluded from the warranty must be described;
3. A statement of what the warrantor will do in the event of a defect, malfunction or failure to conform with the written warranty, including those items or services the warrantor will pay for, and if needed for clarity, those items or services he will not pay for;
4. The point in time when the warranty begins (if it begins on a date other than the purchase date) and its duration;
5. A step-by-step explanation of the steps the consumer should follow to obtain performance of the warranty obligation and information regarding any informal dispute settling mechanisms that are available;
6. Any limitations on the duration of implied warranties and any exclusions or limitations on relief, such as incidental or consequential damages, together with a statement that under some state laws the exclusions or limitations may not be allowed; and
7. A statement that the warranty gives the consumer certain legal rights, in addition to his other rights under state law which may vary from state to state.

---

[2] A "consumer product" is in essence defined as tangible personal property distributed in commerce and which is normally used for personal, family, or household purposes. Commercial or industrial products are excluded. 16 Code Federal Regulations § 701.1.

[3] The Act covers consumer products costing more than $5 but the regulations cover only products costing more than $15.

[4] The seller is not required to give a written warranty; however, if the seller does make such a warranty, it must comply with the Act and the Regulations.

The warrantor must designate the warranty as a "full warranty" or as a "limited warranty." A "full warranty" means that: (*a*) any default, malfunction, or failure to conform with the written warranty will be remedied free of charge; (*b*) it is not limited as to duration; (*c*) it has no exclusion or limitation of consequential damages unless printed conspicously on the face of the warranty; (*d*) that if the product contains a defect or malfunctions after a reasonable number of efforts to repair it, the consumer may obtain at his election either a refund or a replacement; (*e*) while the warrantor may impose a duty on the consumer not to modify the product, no other duties can be imposed on the consumer unless they are reasonable; and (*f*) that the warrantor need not perform if the problem was caused by damage to the product or unreasonable use. A "limited warranty" is any other warranty covered by the Act which does not meet the standards for being a "full warranty."

Sellers are required to make the written terms available to a prospective buyer for his review prior to sale. For example, the text of the warranty might be displayed next to the product, or the package on which the text is disclosed can be displayed next to the product. The warrantor of the goods is required to make the texts of the warranties available to sellers in readily usable forms, such as copies of the written warranty with each product, or on a tag, sign, sticker, label, or other attachment to the product, or on a sign or poster. Catalog and door to door sales are also covered. In addition warrantors are encouraged to establish an informal dispute settlement mechanism, which if created must meet certain minimum requirements.

The Act also restricts the manufacturer's or seller's ability to disclaim or modify implied warranties if (*a*) the manufacturer or seller makes any written warranty to the consumer or (*b*) if they enter into a service contract within 90 days of the purchase. Implied warranties may be limited in duration so long as the limit is reasonable; however, any such limitation must be clearly stated and displayed on the face of the warranty. The Act renders ineffective any disclaimer in violation of the Act's terms.

The Act may be enforced by the Federal Trade Commission, the Attorney General, or an injured party, either individually or as part of a class action. The individual suit may be brought to compel performance and for damages.

Negligence and Strict Liability

Product Liability in General. Liability of a manufacturer based on breach of warranty is only one theory of liability included in the area of product liability—the liability of a manufacturer of goods to the user of goods for personal injury or property damage resulting from the use of the goods. Product liability encompasses negligence and so-called strict liability in tort as well as warranty. The scope and nature of the liability of a manufacturer to the user of his product is in a state of continual change and development.

Negligence. The early rule was *caveat emptor,* that the buyer had to make his own inspection, rely on his own judgment and assume the risk of any defect in the goods he purchased. Gradually, American courts came to do away with this rule and to hold that a seller of goods is under a duty to exercise the care of a reasonable man to see that the goods do no harm to a buyer.

An important case in this line of cases was *McPherson v. Buick Motor Co.*[5] decided in 1916 by the New York Court of Appeals. In that case the manufacturer, Buick Motor Company, was held liable to a subpurchaser for injuries sustained when a wheel collapsed. The court found that Buick was negligent in its inspection of the wheel and was liable in tort on a negligence theory.

Subsequent courts have found liability based on negligence not only where there was a failure to inspect but also for (1) misrepresentation as to the character of the goods or their fitness for a particular purpose, (2) failure to disclose known defects or to warn about known dangers, and (3) failure to use due care in designing and preparing the goods for sale.

In many cases, it would be extremely difficult for an injured person to show the circumstances in the seller's plant at the time a defective product was manufactured. At this point, the doctrine of *res ipsa loquitur* often comes to the injured person's aid. To invoke this doctrine he must show that the cause of the injury was something that lay within the responsibility of the defendant-manufacturer, thus putting the burden on the manufacturer to show it did exercise due care in the circumstances. The defendant-manufacturer can prevail against a suit based on negligence if it can show the defect was one that could not be discovered or avoided by the exercise of all reasonable care or that under the facts and circumstances all reasonable care was in fact exercised.

In the earliest cases the courts held that the manufacturer was liable only to the person with whom he contracted. Today a substantial number of courts allow an injured consumer to recover from the manufacturer in a direct suit. The requirement of privity is dispensed with and the decisions have been, as a general rule, based on concepts of public policy or a conduit theory, that is, that the retailer is the conduit through which the product is distributed and that the manufacturer owes the duty of reasonable care directly to the consumer.

Strict Liability. Once negligence became established as a basis for liability

[5] 111 N.E. 1050 (Ct. App. N.Y. 1916).

of sellers to the ultimate consumers, an effort was begun to carry the seller's responsibility even further and to hold the seller liable even though he had exercised reasonable care—in effect making him an insurer of the safety of his product. According to Prosser, the rationale for strict liability which has proved convincing to those courts which have accepted it consists of three main arguments:[6]

1. The public interest in human life and safety demands the maximum possible protection that the law can give against dangerous defects in products which consumers must buy, and against which they are helpless to protect themselves; and it justifies the imposition, upon all suppliers of such products, of full responsibility for the harm they cause, even though the supplier has done his best. This argument, which in the last analysis rests upon public sentiment, has had its greatest force in the cases of food, where there was once popular outcry against an evil industry, injuries and actions have multiplied, and public feeling is most obvious. It is now being advanced as to other products, such as automobiles.

2. The maker, by placing the goods upon the market, represents to the public that they are suitable and safe for use; and by packaging, advertising or otherwise, he does everything that he can to induce that belief. He intends and expects that the product will be purchased and used in reliance upon this assurance of safety; and it is in fact so purchased and used. The middleman is no more than a conduit, a mere mechanical device, through whom the thing sold is to reach the ultimate user. The supplier has invited and solicited the use; and when it leads to disaster, he should not be permitted to avoid the responsibility by saying that he has made no contract with the consumer.

3. It is already possible to enforce strict liability by resort to a series of actions, in which the retailer is first held liable on a warranty to his purchaser, and indemnity on a warranty is then sought successively from other suppliers, until the manufacturer finally pays the damages, with the added costs of repeated litigation. This is an expensive, time-consuming, and wasteful process, and it may be interrupted by insolvency, lack of jurisdication, disclaimers, or the statute of limitations, anywhere along the time.

The essential aspects of strict liability are expressed in Section 402A of the *Restatement of Torts* (Second):

§ 402A. Special Liability of Seller of Product for Physical Harm to User or Consumer.

(1) One who sells any product in a defective condition unreasonably dangerous to the user or consumer or to his property, is subject to liability for physical harm thereby caused to the ultimate user or consumer, or to his property, if

- (a) the seller is engaged in the business of selling such a product, and
- (b) it is expected to and does reach the user or consumer without substantial change in the condition in which it is sold.

(2) The rule stated in Subsection (1) applies although

- (a) the seller has exercised all possible care in the preparation and sale of his product, and
- (b) the user or consumer has not bought the product from or entered into any contractual relation with the seller.

---

[6] William L. Prosser, *Handbook of the Law of Torts* (4th ed.; St. Paul, Minn.: West Publishing Co.), p. 651.

As can be seen from the *Restatement,* the lack of privity of contract is not a defense available to the seller. The crucial elements of strict liability are a "defective condition" at the time the product leaves the seller's hands and which causes harm to a user and which is "unreasonably dangerous" to him or his property—that is, that it is more dangerous than the ordinary consumer would contemplate.

It is important to note that strict liability is presently accepted by more than 40 states but not consistently to all types of products and all types of defects. Strict liability has found its most common acceptance with sales of food and drink, but has been extended to a wide variety of products that can prove to be unreasonably dangerous because of defective manufacture. In addition some states have applied it to situations involving the sale of services, used merchandise and real estate. As presently applied, strict liability can be used against retailers as well as manufacturers of such defective products. Disclaimers of liability in contracts of sale are generally not effective to shield the seller or manufacturer against strict liability.

SUMMARY

Product liability encompasses negligence and strict liability as well as warranties. A seller of goods is under a duty to use due care in the design, manufacture or preparation, inspection, and sale of goods; failure to do so may give rise to a cause of action for negligence by a person injured by a defective product.

Strict liability is imposed by some states on the sellers of some types of products. It arises when a product is sold in a defective condition unreasonably dangerous to a user or consumer or to his property and the defective product results in damage to the person or property. Neither lack of privity nor exercise of all possible due care are defenses to an action for strict liability.

Larsen v. General Motors Corp.

391 F.2d 495 (8th Cir. 1968)

This was an action by Erling David Larsen (plaintiff) against General Motors (defendant) to recover damages resulting from an alleged negligent design of the steering assembly of a Corvair automobile manufactured and sold by defendant. The District Court rendered summary judgment for General Motors and Larsen appealed. Reversed.

Larsen received severe bodily injuries while driving, with the consent of the owner, a 1963 Chevrolet Corvair. A head-on collision, with the impact occurring on the left front corner of the Corvair, caused a severe rearward thrust of the steering mechanism into Larsen's head.

Larsen did not contend that the design caused the accident but that because of the design he received injuries he would not have otherwise received or, in the alternative, his injuries would not have been as severe. The rearward displacement of the steering shaft on the left frontal impact was much greater on the Corvair than it would be in other cars that were designed to protect against such a rearward displacement. Larsen's complaint alleged (1) negligence in design of the steering assembly; (2) negligent failure to warn of the alleged latent or inherently dangerous condition to the user of the steering assembly placement; and (3) breach of express and implied warranties of merchantability of the vehicle's intended use. General Motors contended that it had no duty to design and manufacture a vehicle safe to occupy during collision impacts.

GIBSON, CIRCUIT JUDGE. General Motors contends that it has no duty to produce a vehicle in which it is safe to collide or which is accident-proof or incapable of injurious misuse. It views its duty as extending only to produce a vehicle that is reasonably fit for its intended use or for the purpose for which it was made and that is free from hidden defects; and that the intended use of a vehicle and the purpose for which it is manufactured do not include its participation in head-on collisions or any other type of impact, regardless of the manufacturer's ability to foresee that such collisions may occur.

Larsen maintains that General Motors' view of its duty is too narrow and restrictive and that an automobile manufacturer is under a duty to use reasonable care in the design of the automobile to make it safe to the user for its foreseeable use and that its intended use or purpose is for travel on the streets and highways, including the possibility of impact or collision with other vehicles or stationary objects.

There is a line of cases directly supporting General Motors' contention that negligent design of an automobile is not actionable, where the alleged defective design is not a causative factor in the accident. The latest leading case on this point is *Evans v. General Motors Corp.* A divided court there held that General Motors in designing a "X" body frame without perimeter support, instead of an allegedly more safe perimeter body frame, was not liable for the death of a user allegedly caused by the designed defect because the defendant's design could not have functioned to avoid the collision.

In *Shumard v. General Motors Corp.,* the United States District Court for the Southern District of Ohio held there was no liability where the alleged design defects in a 1962 Corvair automobile caused it to erupt into flames on impact, killing the plaintiff's decedent. That Court said: ". . . No duty exists to make an automobile fireproof, nor does a manufacturer have to make a product which is 'accident-proof' or 'fool-proof.' "

Generally, as noted in 76 A.L.R. 2d 93, Anno.: Products Liability—Duty As to Design, the manufacturer has a duty to use reasonable care under the circumstances in the design of a product but is not an insurer that his product is incapable of producing injury, and this duty of design is met when the article is safe for its intended use and when it will fairly meet any "emergency of use" which is foreseeable.

Accepting, therefore, the principle that a manufacturer's duty of design and construction extends to producing a product that is reasonably fit for its intended use and free of hidden defects that could render it unsafe for such use, the issue narrows on the proper interpretation of "intended use." Automobiles are made for use on the roads and highways in transporting persons and cargo to and from various points. This intended use cannot be carried out without encountering in varying degrees the statistically proved hazard of injury-producing impacts of various types. The manufacturer should not be heard to say that it does not intend its product to be involved in any accident when it can easily foresee and when it knows that the probability over the life of its product is high, that it will be involved in some type of injury-producing accident. O'Connell in his article "Taming the Automobile," 58 *Nw.U.L.Rev.* 299, 348 (1963) cites that between one-fourth to two-thirds of all automobiles during their use at some time are involved in an accident producing injury or death. Other statistics are available showing the frequency and certainty of fatal and injury-producing accidents. It should be recognized that the environment in which a product is used must be taken into consideration by the manufacturer.

We think the "intended use" construction urged by General Motors is much too narrow and unrealistic. Where the manufacturer's negligence in design causes an unreasonable risk to be imposed upon the user of its products, the manufacturer should be liable for the injury caused by its failure to exercise reasonable care in the design. These injuries are readily foreseeable as an incident to the normal and expected use of an automobile. While automobiles are not made for the purpose of colliding with each other, a frequent and inevitable contingency of normal automobile use will result in collisions and injury-producing impacts. No rational basis exists for limiting recovery to situations where the defect in design or manufacture was the causative factor of the accident, as the accident and the resulting injury, usually caused by the so-called "second collison" of the passenger with the interior part of the automobile, all are foreseeable. Where the injuries or enhanced injuries are due to the manufacturer's failure to use reasonable care to avoid subjecting the user of its products to an unreasonable risk of injury, general negligence principles should be applicable. The sole function of an automobile is not just to provide a means of transportation, it is to provide a means of safe transportation or as safe as is reasonably possible under the present state of the art.

Filler v. Rayex Corp.
435 F.2d 336 (7th Cir. 1970)

This was an action brought by Michael Filler and his mother, Barbara Mitchell (plaintiffs) against Rayex Corp. (defendant) to recover damages for loss of Michael's right eye and medical expenses. The U.S. District Court granted judgment for the plaintiffs. Rayex appealed. Judgment affirmed.

The facts are given in the opinion:

CUMMINGS, CIRCUIT JUDGE. When his injury occurred, Michael Filler was a 16-year-old student at Oak Hill High School, near Marion, Indiana. While he was practicing for a varsity baseball game in the late afternoon of June 10, 1966, fungoes were being lofted to him by a fellow player. Filler lost a fly ball in the sun, although he was wearing flipped-down "baseball sunglasses" manufactured by Rayex. After tipping the top of his baseball glove, the ball struck the right side of the sunglasses, shattering the right lens into sharp splinters which pierced his right eye, necessitating its removal nine days later.

Filler's coach was Richard Beck, an experienced ballplayer, whose first baseball season at Oak Hill was in 1965. During that season, Beck would not allow his players to use sunglasses, considering them too dangerous. However, before the 1966 season, he read the following advertisement of Rayex in *Sporting News:*

"PLAY BALL!
and Flip for Instant Eye Protection with
RAYEX
Baseball
SUNGLASSES
Professional
FLIP-SPECS"

The advertisement also stated:

Scientific lenses protect your eyes with a flip from sun and glare anywhere . . . baseball, beach, boat, driving, golfing, fishing, just perfect for Active and Spectator Sports—World's finest sunglasses.

After seeing this material, Beck decided to buy six pairs of Rayex's flip-type baseball sunglasses for use by his outfielders and second basemen. Each pair of sunglasses was in a cardboard box labeled "Baseball Sunglasses—Professional Flip-Specs," stating "simply flip . . . for instant eye protection." The guarantee inside each box provided:

Rayex lenses are guaranteed for life against breakage. If lens breakage occurs mail glasses and 50 cents (Postage Handling Charge) for complete repair service.
Rayex Sunglasses are guaranteed to:

1. Eliminate 96 percent of harmful ultra-violet and infra-red rays.
2. Protect your eyes against reflected glare from smooth surfaces, roads, water, snow, etc.
3. Retain clear, undistorted vision.

Except for the flip feature and elastic tape at the rear of the frame, the glasses resembled ordinary sunglasses. The thinness of the lenses was shielded by the frames and therefore not obvious to users.

These glasses were stored in the glove compartment of coach Beck's car, and in accordance with the custom of his teammates, Filler removed a pair of the sunglasses from the coach's car and was using them at the time of his injury. Neither Filler, nor Beck, nor indeed even Rayex's president knew the lenses would shatter into sharp splinters when hit by a baseball.

After a bench trial, the district judge awarded Filler $101,000 damages and his mother $1,187.75 for her consequential damages. In an unreported memorandum opinion, the district judge supported this result on three independent grounds: implied warranty, strict liability, and negligence.[7] Under any of those theories, privity between the manufacturer and Filler is not required by controlling Indiana law.

We agree that Rayex is liable for breach of an implied warranty of fitness for a particular purpose. Indiana has adopted the implied warranty provision of the Uniform Commercial Code dealing with fitness for a particular purpose:

> Implied Warranty—Fitness for particular purpose—Where the seller at the time of contracting has reason to know any particular purpose for which the goods are required and that the buyer is relying on the seller's skill or judgment to select or furnish suitable goods, there is unless excluded or modified under the next section an implied warranty that the goods shall be fit for such purpose. Burns Indiana Stat Ann § 19–315.

These sunglasses were advertised as baseball sunglasses that would give "instant eye protection." Although they were intended for use by baseball fielders, the thickness of the lenses ranged only from 1.2 mm to 1.5 mm, so that shattering into exceedingly sharp splinters would occur on their breaking. Since they lacked the safety features of plastic or shatterproof glass, the sunglasses were in truth not fit for baseball playing, the particular purpose for which they were sold. Therefore, breach of that implied warranty was properly found.

Indiana has adopted the doctrine of strict liability of sellers of products "in a defective condition unreasonably dangerous to the user," as provided in Section 402A of the Restatement of Torts Second. Here the thinness of the lenses made them unreasonably dangerous to users, so that the doctrine of strict liability is applicable. However, Rayex argues against strict liability, on the ground that the sunglasses were "unavoidably unsafe products" within the exception of Comment k to Section 402A. Even assuming arguendo that the state of the art is not capable of producing a shatter-resistant or splinter-free baseball sunglass as Rayex claims, Comment k furnishes no shelter from liability in this case. The exception applies only when the product is "accompanied by proper . . . warning," which Rayex's product lacked.

Finally, we also agree that Rayex was liable for negligence. Rayex knew that these glasses shattered readily, for a hundred were returned daily for lens replacements. At least it had constructive knowledge that the impact of a baseball would shatter these lenses into sharp splinters, for it must anticipate the reasonably foreseeable risks of the use of the product. Moreover,

---

[7] The court reserved judgment on an express warranty count, and we also do not consider that theory.

despite the obviously physical stresses to which these glasses would be put, inadequate tests were made concerning their physical properties. Accordingly, even if Rayex is not liable for negligence in production and sale of a poorly constructed product, it was properly held liable for its negligent failure to warn users of the danger of its product.

Problem Cases

1. In January, Salk purchased various items of ski equipment from Alpine Ski Shop, including ski bindings manufactured by Cubco. Alpine installed the ski bindings on Salk's skis and adjusted them according to his height, weight and skiing ability. Salk made use of the equipment on four separate occasions without mishap. On the fifth day, Salk fell while skiing and his ski bindings did not release. Salk sued Cubco for breach of express warranty. He contended that Cubco had placed advertisements in national magazines expressly warranting to Salk that its bindings would release in a manner as to guarantee freedom from injury. Representative of the advertisements in question is the following language:

   > Cubco is the precise binding . . . that releases when it's supposed to . . . Both heel and toe release at the exact tension you set. And release whichever way you fall.

   During the course of the trial, uncontroverted evidence was presented to the effect that although no binding could be set at a tension sufficiently low to release during a slow fall and still keep the skier on his skis during normal skiing, Cubco bindings had a multi-directional release which could be adjusted to operate at a variety of tensions and once adjusted would release whenever the selected tension was applied. Should Cubco be found liable for breach of the express warranty asserted by Salk?
2. Welcome bought a new 1973 Buick Le Sabre from Best Buick on August 13, 1973. As part of the transaction, Welcome sold his Mercedes Benz to Best Buick as a trade-in. Welcome had been sold the Mercedes as a 1970 model and it was so registered. Welcome in good faith represented to Best Buick that it was a 1970 model but in fact the Mercedes was a 1968 model. The trade-in allowance for the Mercedes as a 1970 model was $3,900, but as a 1968 model it would have been $2,200. Does Best Buick have any recourse against Welcome?
3. Gillispie, while shopping for groceries, picked up a carton of Coca-Cola and a carton of Sprite, both products manufactured by the Coca-Cola Company. After carrying them normally for about 25 feet, two of the bottles of Sprite exploded, severely cutting his arm. He filed suit against the store which in turn sued Coca-Cola. The basis of the suit was breach of implied warranty of merchantability. Coca-Cola defended claiming that there was no warranty because there had been no sale and secondly that it was not the Sprite that injured Gillispie but the glass bottle. Should Gillispie recover from Coca-Cola for breach of warranty?
4. Siemen owned and operated a sawmill. He was interested in purchasing a particular kind of rip-saw to increase his production of checking pallets. At the suggestion of the manufacturer of the saw in question who said he could not deliver a new saw in less than six months, Siemen went to see Korleski who had a used saw of that type for sale. Korleski was also in sawmill business. Siemen purchased Korleski's eight-year-old saw and was later injured when a piece of wood exploded while being fed through the

saw because the saw could not handle the wood. Siemen sued Korleski to recover for his injuries, claiming that Korleski breached the 2–314 and 2–315 warranties. On these facts does Siemen have a valid claim based on either or both of these warranties?

5. Gates, wishing to purchase a Christmas present for his wife, went to "Penelope's," a women's specialty shop. Although he did not know what sizes his wife wore, he knew that she frequently shopped there and was well known to the sales personnel. He was waited on by the owner of the store who sold him three pants suits and told him that she was certain that they would fit his wife. He was told if there was any problem he could return them. The clothing turned out to be too large for Mrs. Gates and she attempted to exchange it. She could not find anything that was suitable and asked for a refund of the purchase price. She was refused. On what theory should Gates proceed against Penelope's in a small claims action? What are his chances of success?

6. Cohen, through one Griffin, an experienced bricklayer and mason, ordered a large quantity of bricks from Doxey Supply. Griffin was to construct two retaining walls, steps and walkways for Cohen. It was Cohen's desire that the brick to be used match the color and texture of bricks utilized in the construction of his home. Accordingly, Griffin removed a brick from Cohen's home and showed it to Doxey's salesperson, advising him that he wanted a similar brick for the purpose of building retaining walls, walks, and steps. There was no evidence that Griffin asked for the *identical* brick, or that he specified any particular *type* of brick. Nor was there any evidence that Doxey's salesperson knew Griffin to be a mason or that Griffin represented himself as such. A brick, similar in color and texture to the one taken from Cohen's home, was selected and utilized in the construction of retaining walls, walkways, and steps. Within one year, many of the bricks so utilized had badly deteriorated. There was conflicting evidence as to the cause of this deterioration, but it appears either that (1) the type of brick utilized was unsuitable for use in walkways or (2) the particular shipment of brick from which the Cohen's order was drawn was defective. Cohen brought suit to recover damages for breach of warranty. Doxey contended that the warranty was excluded by U.C.C. 2–316(3)(c). Should Cohen recover for breach of warranty?

7. Majors, a farmer, bought a quantity of Triple Noctin, a soybean innoculant, manufactured by Kalo Laboratories, for use on his soybean crop. Prior to purchasing the Triple Noctin, Majors was given a promotional brochure prepared by Kalo which contained the following language:

    100 PERCENT GROWER GUARANTEED Satisfaction guaranteed or the purchase price of this product will be refunded immediately by Kalo Laboratories, Inc. Manufacturer's liability is limited to this refund [*sic*]. There are no warranties which extend beyond the description on the face hereof and the manufacturer is not liable for consequential damages.

    The underlined caption was distinguished by being in larger, capital type and by being printed in red. Other print was black. Upon each package of Triple Noctin sold to Majors appeared the following language:

    GUARANTEE: Satisfaction guaranteed or the purchase price of this product will be refunded immediately by KALO Laboratories, Incorporated. Manufacturer's liability is limited to this refund. There are no warranties which extend beyond the description on the face hereof and the manufacturer is not liable for consequential damages.

    Because of a latent defect in the Triple Noctin it was not effective and Majors' crop failed. The defect was not discoverable until the crop developed. Majors brought an action for damages and at the trial he established evidence that Kalo knew there was some uncertainty as to the effectiveness of its product. Majors also established that the cost of Triple Noctin was about 30 cents per acre while Majors' cost of cultivating, planting, and harvesting his soybean crop was $90 to $100 per acre and that Kalo knew the expenditures would normally be in that range. Kalo contends that its liability is effectively limited by the exclusion clause to refund of the purchase price. Majors contends the clause is unconscionable. What decision should the court reach?

8. Glenn Gray bought a new 1971 Mach I Mustang automobile manufactured by the Ford Motor Company from Pettigrew Motor Company. While Glenn Gray's wife Nancy was driving the automobile, the right front wheel collapsed, causing it to crash and to injure Nancy Gray's mother, Mrs. Browder. Browder filed suit against the Ford Motor Company alleging breach of express and implied warranties and claiming she was a third-party beneficiary of the warranties. Ford Motor Company defended on the ground that there was no privity of contract between Browder and Ford. Is privity a defense to Ford in this case?

9. Weaver was employed by the Reid Furniture Company as a truck driver. One day he obtained gasoline for his employer's truck from the Ralston Service Station and signed a ticket charging the gasoline to his employer. The gasoline apparently contained water which caused the truck to break down on the road. While disabled, the truck was hit by another vehicle causing serious injury to Weaver. Weaver then brought suit against the Ralston Service Station alleging, among other things, breach of the implied warranties of merchantability and fitness for a particular purpose. The Service Station defended on the grounds there was no privity of contract between Weaver and the Service Station. Has the Service Station stated a valid defense?

10. Magnolia Industries purchased from the S&S Zipper Company approximately 35,000 zippers to be installed by it in ladies handbags. S&S Zipper had purchased the zipper tapes which formed part of its zippers from Weiner Industries. The zipper tape material was defective in that it was not colorfast and as a result considerable damage was done to Magnolia's handbags. Magnolia sued Weiner Industries for breach of warranty and negligence. Should Weiner Industries be liable to Magnolia for breach of warranty and/or negligence in producing the defective tapes?

38

Performance

General Rules

Introduction. The rules that govern the performance of contracts for the sale of goods are very similar to the basic rules of performance that are applied to other kinds of contracts. The Code gives the parties great flexibility to expressly provide how a contract will be performed and relies on the usual practices in the trade and any course of dealing between the parties to supplement or interpret a sales contract. The Code also permits the parties to leave to one of the parties the duty to specify some of the particulars of performance, including such things as selecting the assortment of goods or the means of delivery. In the performance of a sales contract each party owes a duty to give the other party reasonable cooperation in performance and must act in good faith and in a commercially reasonable manner (2–311).[1]

Course of Dealing and Usage of Trade. In determining the obligations of the parties, the express terms of the agreement are the primary determinant. The meaning of those terms may be explained by looking to any performance of the contract that has already taken place. For example, if a contract for the sale of goods involves repeated occasions for performance by one party which is acquiesced in without objection by the other party, then that course of performance is relevant to determining the meaning of the agreement (2–208[1]). The performance of any past contract between the parties, and the usual practices in the particular business which the contract concerns, are also relevant. In many kinds of businesses, trade customs and practices have developed which are known by those in the business and are generally assumed

[1] The numbers in the parentheses refer to the sections of the Uniform Commercial Code, 1972.

by the parties to a contract involving goods of that type to be part of the contract.

Under the Code the express terms of the agreement and any course of performance, any past course of dealing and the trade practices are to be construed as consistent with each other if that result can be reached reasonably. If they cannot be reasonably construed as consistent, then the express terms prevail over the other factors. Similarly, the way the parties have performed the current contract prevails over both any past course of dealing between the parties and practices in the trade or business (2–208[2]).

Modification, Rescission, and Waiver. Under the Code, consideration is not required to support a modification or the rescission of a contract for the sale of goods. However, the parties may specify in their agreement that any modification or rescission must be in writing in which case a signed writing is necessary for enforcement of any modification to the contract or its rescission (2–209).

In an installment contract where there are repeated occasions for performance by one or both parties, a party must object to any late performance by the other party or he may be unable to cancel the contract when subsequent performances, such as delivery or payment, are late. Thus a party should be careful to object to any inadequate or late performance by the other party in order to avoid waiving his rights (2–209[4]).

For example, a contract calls for Fish Market to deliver fish to Supermarket every Thursday and for Supermarket to pay on delivery. If Fish Market regularly delivers the fish on Friday and Supermarket does not object, it will be unable to later cancel the contract for that reason. Similarly, if Supermarket does not pay cash but rather sends a check the following week, then Fish Market must object if it may want to rely on the late payment as grounds for later cancelling the contract.

A party who has waived his rights to a portion of a contract not yet performed may retract the waiver by giving reasonable notice to the other party that strict performance will be required. The retraction is effective unless it would be unjust because of a material change of position by the other person in reliance on the waiver (2–209[5]).

Assignment. Under the Code, the duties of either party may be delegated unless the parties agree that the duties are not to be delegated or if there is a strong reason for having the original promisor perform the acts called for by the contract. If a party assigns or delegates his duties, he continues to be responsible to the other party for their performance. Generally, any provision in a contract that prohibits assignment of the contract is construed to mean only that any delegation of performance to some other party is barred; thus a party could still assign his right to receive performance, such as to receive the payment of money or the delivery of goods (2–210).

SUMMARY

The basic rules of contract law regarding the performance of contracts apply to sales contracts. Granting to the buyer and seller options as to performance of a sales contract does not affect the validity of a contract which is otherwise valid. Each party must act in good faith and within the scope of that which is commercially reasonable in exercising his options and must cooperate in a reasonable manner in the performance of the contract.

The conduct of the parties, course of dealing, and trade usage are considered and weighed in determining the duties of performance of the parties to a sales contract. Under the provisions of the Code an agreement to modify or rescind a contract need not be supported by consideration to be valid.

An assignment of a sales contract, unless otherwise agreed, includes the delegation of duties, and a general prohibition of the assignment of a contract bars only the delegation of duties. The assignor does not relieve himself of his liability for the performance of the contract by the delegation of his duties.

Heggblade-Marguleas-Tenneco, Inc. v. Sunshine Biscuit, Inc.

131 Cal. Rptr. 183 (Ct. App. Cal. 1976)

This was an action brought by Heggblade-Marguleas-Tenneco, Inc. (HMT), (plaintiff) against Sunshine Biscuit, Inc. (defendant), seeking damages for breach of contract by two companies owned by Sunshine and referred to as "Bell Brands".[2] The trial court awarded judgment for Sunshine Biscuit, and HMT appealed on the ground the trial court should not have considered evidence of a trade custom. Affirmed on appeal.

On October 15, 1970, Bell Brand entered into a contract with HMT for HMT to deliver 5000 *cwt.* [hundredweight] sacks of Kennebec potatoes between May 15 and July 15, 1971 at $2.60 per sack and another contract to deliver 95,000 cwt. sacks of Kennebec potatoes between May 15 and July 15, 1971 at $2.35 per sack. Only 60,104.9 sacks were accepted by Bell Brand and HMT claimed to have sustained damages of $87,000 because it overplanted.

HMT was a company formed through the merger of a potato grower and a company that marketed agricultural products and had no prior experience marketing processing potatoes. There was testimony at the trial that because the contracts are executed eight or nine months before the harvest season, the custom in the processing potato industry is to treat the quantity solely as a reasonable estimate of the buyers' needs based on their customers' demands

[2] One of the companies was Bell Brand Foods, a wholly-owned subsidiary of Sunshine Biscuit, Inc.; the other was Blue Bell Potato Chip Co., a division of Sunshine Biscuit, Inc. Both companies were referred to as Bell Brand by the Court.

and the growers' ability to supply based on the anticipated yield for the delivery period.

Because of a decline in demand for Bell Brand products in May through July 1971, Bell Brand's sales for the late spring and summer of 1971 were down substantially. As a result, Bell Brand's need for potatoes from its suppliers was severely reduced, and it prorated the reduced demand among its suppliers, including HMT, as fairly as possible. By the end of the harvest season, Bell Brand was able to take only 60,105 cwt. sacks from HMT on the two contracts.

FRANSON, ACTING PRESIDING JUDGE. HMT contends that the quantity terms in the contracts are definite and unambiguous, hence it was error to admit into evidence the custom of the processing potato industry that the amounts specified are reasonable estimates. HMT's contention is without merit.

California Uniform Commercial Code § 2–202 states the parol evidence rule applicable to the sale of personal property:

> Terms with respect to which the confirmatory memoranda of the parties agree or which are otherwise set forth in a writing intended by the parties as a final expression of their agreement with respect to such terms as are included therein may not be contradicted by evidence of any prior agreement or of a contemporaneous oral agreement but may be supplemented
> (a) By course of dealing or usage of trade (Section 1–205) . . . ;

California Uniform Commercial Code § 2–202, subdivision (a), permits a trade usage to be put in evidence "as an instrument of interpretation." The Uniform Commercial Code comment to subdivision (a) of § 2–202 states that evidence of trade usage is admissible ". . . in order that the true understanding of the parties as to the agreement may be reached. Such writings are to be read on the assumption that . . . the usages of trade were taken for granted when the document was phrased. Unless carefully negated they have become an element of the meaning of the words used. Similarly, the course of actual performance by the parties is considered the best indication of what they intended the writing to mean."

A case factually similar to the instant case is *Columbia Nitrogen Corp. v. Royster Co.* (4th Cir. 1971). There the seller sued the buyer for breach of contract for the purchase of a specified quantity of phosphate. The buyer's defense was a trade usage which imposed no duty to accept at the quoted prices the minimum quantity stated in the contract. The trial court had excluded this evidence because ". . . 'custom and usage . . . are not admissible to contradict the express, plain, unambiguous language of a valid written contract, which by virtue of its detail negates the proposition that the contract is open to variances in its terms. . . .' " The Court of Appeals interpreted Virginia Uniform Commercial Code § 2–202, which is identical to California Uniform Commercial Code § 2–202(a), as meaning that where the contract does not expressly state that trade usage cannot be used to explain or supplement the written terms, the evidence of trade usage should be admitted to interpret the contract.

We find *Columbia Nitrogen Corp. v. Royster* persuasive. Under subdivision (a) of § 2–202, established trade usage and custom are a part of the contract unless the parties agree otherwise. Since the contracts in question are silent about the applicability of the usage and custom, evidence of such usage and custom was admissible to explain the meaning of the quantity figures.

Persons carrying on a particular trade are deemed to be aware of prominent trade customs applicable to their industry. The knowledge may be actual or constructive, and it is constructive if the custom is of such general and universal application that the party must be presumed to know of it.

Delivery

General Rules. The duty of the seller is to deliver the goods called for by the contract and the buyer's duty is to accept and pay for the goods if they conform to the contract (2–301). Unless the parties agree otherwise, all of the goods called for by a sales contract must be tendered to the buyer in a single delivery. Where delivery is to be made in lots, then the seller may demand the price of each lot upon delivery unless there has been an agreement for the extension of credit (2–307).

Place of Delivery. Unless the parties specify where delivery is to be made, the goods are to be delivered at the seller's place of business; if the seller does not have a place of business, then delivery is to be made at his home. These rules do not apply when at the time a contract is made the parties know the goods are at some location other than the seller's place of business or house. In such cases the place where the goods are located is the place for delivery (2–308).

Seller's Duties of Delivery. As stated above, the seller owes a duty to tender delivery of goods that conform to the contract to the buyer. Tender of delivery means that the seller must make the goods available to the buyer during reasonable hours and for a reasonable period of time so that the buyer can take possession of them (2–503).

If the contract requires the seller to ship the goods, but does not require the seller to deliver them to the buyer's place of business, then the seller must put the goods in the possession of a carrier—such as a trucking company or railroad—and make a reasonable contract with the carrier to take the goods to the buyer. The seller is also required to notify the buyer that the goods have been shipped. If the seller does not make a reasonable contract or does not notify the buyer and a material delay or loss results, then the buyer has the right to reject the shipment (2–504). For example, if the goods are perishable, such as fresh produce, the seller does not have them shipped in a refrigerated vehicle and the goods deteriorate as a result, the buyer could reject them on the grounds the seller did not make a reasonable contract.

In some situations the goods being sold may be in the possession of a bailee such as a warehouse. If the warehouse has issued a negotiable warehouse receipt, then the seller must endorse the receipt and deliver it to the buyer so that he has the right to obtain the goods from the bailee (2–503[4][a]). A common situation where this might occur is where grain stored at a grain elevator is the subject of a sale. The law of negotiable documents of title is discussed in Chapter 43.

If the goods in the possession of a bailee are not covered by a negotiable warehouse receipt, then the seller must notify the bailee that the goods have been sold to the buyer and obtain the bailee's consent to hold the goods for delivery to the buyer. The risk of loss as to the goods remains with the seller until the bailee agrees to hold them for the buyer (2–503[4][b]).

Nonconforming Delivery. If a seller tries to deliver nonconforming goods to the buyer, the buyer rejects them and the time for delivery has not expired, the seller may notify the buyer that he intends to cure the defect and redeliver conforming goods within the time allowed for delivery (2–508[1]). If the seller had reasonable grounds to believe the buyer would accept the non-conforming goods, then the seller has a reasonable time to cure the defect and ship conforming goods even if the original time for delivery has expired (2–508[2]). For example, Ace Manufacturing contracts to sell 200 red baseball hats to Sam's Sporting Goods with delivery to be made by April 1. On March 1, Sam's receives a package from Ace containing 200 blue baseball hats and refuses to accept them. Ace can notify Sam that it intends to cure the improper delivery by supplying 200 red hats and has until April 1 to deliver the red hats to Sam. If Ace thought Sam's would accept the blue hats because on past shipments it has not objected to the substitution of blue hats for red, then Ace has a reasonable time to deliver the red hats.

SUMMARY

The seller owes a duty to tender conforming goods in fulfillment of the sales contract. Tender must be made at a reasonable time and the buyer must provide reasonable facilities for the acceptance of the goods. If the seller is to ship the goods he must deliver conforming goods to the carrier and make a reasonable contract of transportation. Where delivery of conforming goods is tendered, the buyer owes a duty to accept and make any payment due. If nonconforming goods are tendered and rejected, the seller is given, under certain limitations, the right to cure the defective tender.

Inspection and Payment

Buyer's Right of Inspection. Unless the contract provides otherwise, the buyer has the right to inspect the goods before he accepts or pays for them. The parties may agree as to the time, place and manner in which inspection is to be made. Where no specific agreement is made, the buyer may inspect the goods at any reasonable place and time and in any reasonable manner (2–513[1]).

If the shipping terms are "cash on delivery" (c.o.d.) or "payment against documents" where the buyer must pay first before receiving the goods, then the buyer must pay before inspection unless the goods are marked "inspection allowed" (2–513[3]). Where the contract requires payment before inspection, nonconformity of the goods does not excuse the buyer from his duty to make payment unless the nonconformity is obvious without inspection (2–512). For example, if Farmer contracted to buy a bull and seller delivered a cow, Farmer would be relieved of his duty to make payment. The fact the buyer has to make payment before he has a chance to inspect the goods does not deprive him of any of his remedies against the seller if the goods turn out on inspection to be nonconforming (2–512[2]).

If goods conform to the contract, the buyer must pay the expenses of inspection; however, if the goods are nonconforming he may recover his inspection expenses from the seller (2–513[2]).

Payment. The parties may provide that the price of goods is to be paid in money, goods, real property, services, or otherwise. If all or part of the purchase price of goods is payable in real property, then the transfer of the goods is governed by the law of sales and the transfer of the real property is subject to real estate law (2–304).

Unless the contract provides that the goods are sold on credit, the buyer must pay for the goods on delivery after he has inspected them except where they are shipped c.o.d. in which case he must pay before inspection. The buyer may make payment by personal check or any other method used in the ordinary course of business unless the seller demands payment in money and gives the buyer a reasonable amount of time to procure it. If the buyer makes payment by check, the payment is conditional on the check being paid by the bank when it is presented for payment (2–511). If the bank refuses to pay the check, then the buyer has not satisfied his duty to pay for the goods and does not have the right to retain them.

SUMMARY

In general, the buyer has the right to inspect the goods before acceptance and payment. The place, time, and method of inspection may be fixed by the agreement of the parties. In the absence of agreement, if the goods are to be sent by the seller the place of inspection is the destination of the goods; otherwise at a time, place, and manner reasonable under the circumstances. If the goods are conforming the buyer pays the expense of inspection; if nonconforming, the seller pays the expense.

Unless there is an agreement for credit, payment must be made after inspection of the goods on tender or delivery of the goods or documents of title. Payment may be made by check or any manner current in the ordinary course of business unless the seller demands legal tender.

Acceptance, Revocation, and Rejection

What Constitutes Acceptance. Acceptance of goods occurs when a buyer, once he has inspected the goods or has had a reasonable opportunity to inspect them, either signifies to the seller that he will take the goods or fails to reject the goods. In order for an effective rejection to be made of goods, the buyer must notify the seller and specify the nonconformity. If a buyer does any act that is inconsistent with the seller's ownership of the goods, then he will be considered to have accepted them (2–606). For example, Ace Appliance delivers a new color television set to Bryant. Bryant will have accepted the set if after trying it and finding it to be in working order, he tells Ace that he will keep it. Even if the set is defective, Bryant will be considered to have accepted it if he does not give Ace timely notice that he does not want to keep it because it is not in working order or if he takes the set on a long trip with him even though he knows it does not work properly. In the latter case, the use of it under those circumstances would be inconsistent with a rejection of it and return of ownership to the seller.

If a buyer accepts any part of a commercial unit, he is considered to have accepted the whole unit (2–606[2]). For example, if a bushel of apples is a commercial unit, then a buyer purchasing ten bushels of apples who accepts eight and one-half bushels is considered to have accepted nine bushels.

Effect of Acceptance. Once a buyer has accepted goods, he cannot later reject them unless at the time he accepted them he had reason to believe that the nonconformity would be cured. By accepting goods, the buyer does not forfeit or waive his remedies against the seller for any nonconformities in the goods. However, if he wishes to hold the seller responsible, he must give the seller timely notice that the goods are nonconforming.

The buyer is obligated to pay for those goods he accepts. If he accepts all of the goods sold, he is of course responsible for the full purchase price; if only part of the goods are accepted, he must pay for that part at the contract rate (2–607).

Revocation of Acceptance. Under certain circumstances a buyer is permitted to revoke or undo his acceptance. A buyer may revoke his acceptance of nonconforming goods where (1) the nonconformity substantially impairs the value of the goods and, (2) he accepted them without knowledge of the nonconformity due to the difficulty of discovering the nonconformity or he accepted the goods because of assurances by the seller (2–608).

The right to revoke acceptance must be exercised within a reasonable time after the buyer discovers or should have discovered the nonconformity and before there has been any substantial change in the goods. Revocation is not effective until the buyer notifies the seller of his intention to revoke acceptance. After a buyer revokes acceptance, he has the same rights as if he had rejected the goods when delivery was tendered (2–608).

The right to revoke acceptance could arise, for example, where Arnold buys a new car from Dealer. While driving it home Arnold discovers that the car has a seriously defective transmission. When he returns it to Dealer, Dealer promises to repair it so Arnold decides to keep the car. If the dealer does not fix the transmission after repeated efforts to do so, Arnold could revoke his acceptance on the ground the nonconformity substantially impairs the value of the car, he took delivery of the car without knowledge of the nonconformity, and his acceptance was based on Dealer's assurances that he would fix it. Similarly, revocation of acceptance might be involved where a serious problem with the car not discoverable by inspection shows up in the first month's use. However, revocation would have to be invoked prior to any substantial change in the goods, such as serious damage in an accident or before considerable use is made of the car. What constitutes a "substantial impairment in value" and when there has been a "substantial change in the goods" are questions frequently faced by courts when an attempted revocation of acceptance results in a lawsuit.

Buyer's Rights on Improper Delivery. As a general rule, if goods tendered to the buyer do not conform to the contract he may elect to reject all of the goods, accept all, or accept any commercial unit or units and reject the rest, paying for the units accepted at the contract rate. He will not be permitted to accept part of a commercial unit and reject the rest (2–601).

However, if the contract is an installment contract in that it requires or authorizes delivery in separate lots to be separately accepted, the buyer's options are more limited. The buyer may reject a nonconforming installment if the nonconformity substantially impairs the value of that installment and cannot be cured; but if the nonconformity is not so great as to substantially impair the value of the whole contract and the seller gives assurance that the nonconformity will be cured, then the buyer must accept that installment. Assurance of cure includes an allowance in price for the nonconformity (2–612). This means that by offering an allowance in price for the nonconformity, the seller in an installment contract can force a buyer to accept nonconforming goods.

Where the nonconformity or defect in one installment impairs the value of the whole contract, the buyer may treat it as a breach of the whole contract but must proceed carefully so as not to reinstate the remainder of the contract (2–612).

Manner of Rejection and Duties after Rejection. A buyer, if he elects to reject the goods, must act within a reasonable time after delivery or tender and must give the seller timely notice of the rejection. If the buyer who rejects the goods is a merchant, he is under a duty to follow any reasonable instructions given to him by the seller as to the disposition of goods that are in the buyer's possession or under his control. If the seller refuses or fails to give instructions and the goods are perishable or threaten to rapidly decline in value, the buyer owes a duty to make a reasonable effort to sell the goods for the benefit of the seller. If the seller gives instructions to the buyer, he must reimburse the buyer for expenses incurred in carrying out the instructions (2–603[1]).

If under these circumstances the buyer sells the goods, he must act in good faith in making the sale and will be entitled to reimbursement out of the proceeds for expenses incurred and for a commission if one is usual in that trade (2–603[2] and [3]).

If the rejected goods are not perishable or if there is no reason to believe they will decline in value speedily, the buyer may: (1) store the goods for the seller's account; (2) reship them; or (3) resell them for the seller's account and reimburse himself for expenses plus a commission out of the proceeds (2–604).

After rejection and notice the buyer has no right to exercise ownership over the goods other than to fulfill his rights and duties as set out above. The buyer must exercise reasonable care in handling rejected goods in his possession and must hold them for a time sufficient to permit the seller to remove them. The buyer has no further obligations with regard to goods rightfully rejected. If the buyer wrongfully rejects goods he is liable to the seller for breach of the sales contract (2–602[2] and [3]).

Failure to Particularize. If the buyer fails to state in connection with his rejection a particular defect which is ascertainable by reasonable inspection, he will not be permitted to use the defect to justify his rejection if the seller could have cured the defect had he been given reasonable notice of it. In a transaction taking place between merchants, the seller has, after rejection, a right to a written statement of all the defects in the goods on which the buyer bases his right to reject, and the buyer will not be permitted to set up defects not listed in justification of his rejection (2–605).

SUMMARY

An acceptance of goods occurs when a buyer indicates to the seller, after the buyer has inspected the goods or has had an opportunity to inspect them, that he will keep them in fulfillment of the seller's obligation or when he exercises acts of ownership over them inconsistent with the seller's ownership. Acceptance of any part of a commercial unit is acceptance of the entire unit. The buyer must pay for goods accepted at the contract rate. If the buyer accepts nonconforming goods, he must, if he wishes to hold the seller liable, give him timely notice that the goods are nonconforming.

A buyer may revoke an acceptance where the nonconformity substantially impairs the value of the goods and was not discoverable or if the buyer relied on the seller's assurance. Revocation of acceptance must be exercised before there is a substantial change in the goods. The buyer must act within a reasonable time and give the seller reasonable notice of his revocation.

If the contract is an installment contract, the buyer has the right to reject any nonconforming installment if the nonconformity substantially impairs the value of the installment and cannot be cured. The seller may cure the defect, but if the defect impairs the value of the whole contract it is a breach of the whole contract.

If nonconforming goods are tendered, the buyer may reject all, accept all, or accept any commercial unit and reject the rest. On rejection, if the goods are in the buyer's possession or control, he owes a duty to use reasonable care to protect the goods. He must hold them for a period sufficient to permit the seller to remove them; if the seller does not have a place of business or agent in the market, the buyer must follow the seller's instructions relative to disposition of the goods. If no instructions are given the buyer must, if the goods are perishable or subject to speedy change in value, sell them for the seller's account. If the goods are not perishable he may store, reship, or sell them for the seller's account. The buyer is entitled to reimbursement for the expenses plus commission. If the buyer wrongfully rejects goods he is liable to the seller for breach of contract.

Askco Engineering Corp. v. Mobil Chemical Corp.

535 S.W.2d 893 (Ct. Civ. App. Texas 1976)

This was an action brought by Askco Engineering Corp. (plaintiff) against Mobil Chemical Corp. (defendant) to recover the purchase price of 276,317 pounds of scrap plastic. Mobil contended that it had accepted only 110,212 pounds which it was willing to pay for ($21,510.28) and filed a counterclaim for the cost of warehousing, freight, loading and unloading expense ($14, 079.65) for the remainder which it rejected and which Askco refused to receive.

Judgment for Askco for $21,510.28 less the $14,079.65 due on the counterclaim. Affirmed on appeal.

On April 5, 1975, Robert Feuer, an employee of Mobil, and Al Robbins, Vice President of Askco, signed a purchase order constituting a contract of sale for the purchase of "approximately 250,000 pounds of bulk rolls of low density polyethylene film in warehouse." On the back of the purchase order under the heading "Conditions" were eleven paragraphs. Paragraph 1 provided:

> Seller . . . warrants that such product shall be free from defects in workmanship, material or design . . . and shall conform to the description and specifications. . . .

Paragraph 6 provided:

> Products purchased hereunder are subject to inspection and approval at Buyer's destination. Buyer reserves the right to reject and refuse acceptance of products which are not in accordance with . . . Seller's warranties (express or implied).

Prior to the execution of the purchase order Feuer inspected the material on Askco's premises. The contract agreement required Mobil to transport the material to its plant and it was transported by truck to Mobil's plant in Temple, Texas. This plant was specifically designed to reclaim low density polyethylene and reprocess it into plastic trashcan liners. Mobil attempted to process 45,000 pounds of the material and found that it would not break down properly, causing holes in the film, air losses, and down time. Askco was notified of the problems Mobil was having. Some of the material was received at the Temple plant on April 17, 1974. On May 18, 1974, Robbins went to Temple to discuss the problem. There was testimony that he agreed that Mobil should pay for the goods used and retained and return the remainder to Askco in Pearland, Texas. Thereafter Mobil shipped 166,105 pounds of the material back to Askco and tendered to them a check in the amount of $21,510.28 representing the agreed price of the goods retained. Askco refused to accept the returned goods and the check. The goods were sent back to Mobil and stored by Mobil in a rented warehouse in Temple from approximately June 1, 1974 until April 15, 1975. After the material was returned to Mobil samples representing approximately 75 percent of the material were analyzed. These tests revealed that only 13.7 percent of the samples were low density polyethylene. The remaining 86.3 percent of the samples were various other polymers such as ethylene vinyl acetate, medium density polyethylene, high density polyethylene, ethylene-propylene copolymers or blends, and other materials of varying chemical composition.

COLEMAN, CHIEF JUDGE. The evidence fully supports a finding that Askco expressly warranted the material purchased by Mobil to be low density polyethylene film, and that the material shipped to Mobil and received by them did not conform to the warranty.

Section 2–601 provides that if the goods fail in any respect to conform to the contract, the buyer may accept any commercial unit or units and reject the rest. In a comment to the Uniform Commercial Code, § 2–601, it is stated:

A buyer accepting a nonconforming tender is not penalized by the loss of any remedy otherwise open to him. This policy extends to cover and regulate the acceptance of a part of any lot improperly tendered in any case where the price can reasonably be apportioned. Partial acceptance is permitted whether the part of the goods accepted conforms or not. The only limitation on partial acceptance is that good faith and commercial reasonableness must be used to avoid undue impairment of the value of the remaining portion of the goods . . . In this respect, the test is not only what unit has been the basis of contract, but whether the partial acceptance produces so materially adverse an effect on the remainder as to constitute bad faith.

The crux of this case rests in a determination of what constitutes a "commercial unit" under the circumstances of this case. The term is defined in § 2–105(f) in these words:

"Commercial unit" means such a unit of goods as by commercial usage is a single whole for purposes of sale and division of which materially impairs its character or value on the market or in use. . . .

Askco contends that the entire bulk of the merchandise constituting the subject matter of the contract was a commercial unit. Section 2–606(b) provides that acceptance of a part of any commercial unit is acceptance of the entire unit.

There is evidence that the film was on large, medium, and small rolls: some was loose, some was shredded, some was in boxes, and some was contained on a pallet of rolls. The original purchase order stated the quantity as "All film at Cermetco" and described it as approximately 250,000 pounds of film. The agreed price was not a lot price but was 19 cents per pound. The trial court could reasonably have found that a pound was a "commercial unit" since it appears to be the unit used by the parties and since the evidence does not establish that a division of the material into such units would materially impair its character or value on the market or in use.

Section 2–602 provides that nonconforming goods must be rejected within a reasonable time after their delivery. It further provides that if the buyer has before rejection taken physical possession of goods he is under a duty after rejection to hold them with reasonable care at the seller's disposition for a time sufficient to permit the seller to remove them. Section 2–604 provides that if the seller gives no instructions within a reasonable time after notification of rejection the buyer may store the rejected goods for the seller's account or reship them to him or resell them for the seller's account. Mobil elected to and did reship the goods to Askco, and on failure of Askco to accept such goods incurred additional expense in storing and testing the goods, and thereby acquired a security interest in the goods (Section 2–711). Mobil unsuccessfully attempted to sell the goods and incurred additional expense in disposing of them.

Section 2–602, in paragraph (b) (1) provides that after rejection any exercise of ownership by the buyer with respect to any commercial unit is wrongful as against the seller. There is evidence that the material could not be identified as low density polyethylene by visual or manual inspection. At the time Mobil rejected 166,000 pounds of the merchandise it knew that it was unable to reprocess the material and had identified a small amount of the material as being cellophane. Prior to the rejection of the material Mobil received a letter from Askco in which Mr. Birdsall stated:

> . . . Most of this was low density polyethylene with some laminate material with various interlayers (some nylon and polypropylene). . . .

After Askco was notified that the goods were being rejected Mobil held the goods for a reasonable time for instructions from Askco. When no instructions were received Mobil elected to reship the goods to Askco as authorized by § 2–604. There is no specific provision in the Code governing the action to be taken where returned goods are not accepted by the seller. Mobil elected to store the goods for the seller's benefit for a period of one year. After that period the goods were carted off and buried. There is evidence that at that time the goods had no value.

This course of conduct on the part of Mobil does not constitute an exercise of ownership by the buyer within the meaning of § 2–602. After Askco refused to accept the returned goods, spectrographic tests made by Mobil identified some of the rejected material as being low density polyethylene which would conform to the contract. In view of the difficulty of identifying the various types of chemical compounds in the large mass of materials, Mobil was not required to "cull out" the conforming goods. Nor was Mobil required to again tender the goods to Askco. The goods were worthless and Mobil could reasonably believe that Askco would again refuse to accept them.

Mobil did not accept the goods by reason of § 2–606(a) (1) providing that acceptance of goods occurs when the buyer after a reasonable opportunity to inspect the goods signified to the seller that the goods are conforming or that he will take or retain them in spite of their nonconformity. Askco relies on the fact that Mobil's representative inspected the material before the purchase order was signed, and attempted to use the material after it was delivered. While Mobil's representative had an opportunity to see, scratch and crumble the material, the testimony establishes that such an examination would not enable the representative to determine whether or not the material was low density polyethylene. Making the goods available for such an inspection does not constitute a reasonable opportunity to inspect. Furthermore, the terms of the purchase order provided that the product was subject to inspection and approval at the destination and gave the buyer the right to reject and refuse to accept products which were not in accordance with the specifications.

Rozmus v. Thompson's Lincoln-Mercury Co.

224 A.2d 782 (Super. Ct. Pa. 1966)

This was an action by Rozmus (plaintiff) against Thompson's Lincoln-Mercury (defendant) to recover the sales price of a used automobile that

Rozmus had traded in on a new automobile. Judgment for Thompson's Lincoln-Mercury and Rozmus appealed. Appeals court also held for Thompson's.

On Saturday, June 22, 1963, Rozmus signed an agreement to purchase a new Mercury. He paid $50 down, traded in the old car, and promised to pay the balance within five days. The contract contained a clause acknowledging Rozmus' acceptance of the new car in good order. While driving the automobile home that evening he noticed smoke coming from the exhaust and that the car made a loud, banging and thumping sound. Rozmus immediately called Thompson's salesman and, as it was Saturday, was told to bring the car in on Monday. In accordance with this request, Rozmus returned the car to Thompson's on Monday. Tuesday evening he called for it but upon driving it ascertained that the loud banging and thumping noise persisted. Rozmus immediately returned the car and sought out Stewart, Thompson's general manager, who confirmed the trouble in a test drive. Stewart and Rozmus then returned to the garage where Stewart instructed a mechanic to place the car upon a rack and to see what was causing the noise. Before the mechanic could correct the source of the trouble, which turned out to be two loose engine mounting bolts allowing a misalignment of the drive shaft to occur, Rozmus told Mr. Stewart he wanted another car or the return of the one he had traded in. His demands not being met, he left without taking the new automobile with him. The Mercury automobile was fully adjusted within a few minutes by Thompson's, but Rozmus never returned for it.

Soon after leaving the new automobile with Thompson's, Rozmus brought an action before a justice of the peace for the sale price of the traded Chevrolet car, $361.50. The question before the appeal court in this case was whether Rozmus had the right to revoke acceptance of the new automobile.

MONTGOMERY, JUSTICE. The law on the issue before us is found in § 2–608 which provides that a buyer may revoke his acceptance of goods received if its "non-conformity substantially impairs its value to him." There is no doubt that Rosmus accepted this new automobile. He executed the conditional sales contract which provided that he acknowledged the acceptance of the Mercury in good order, and he drove it from the showroom to his home. Section 2–606 provides that acceptance takes force when the buyer either signifies his acceptance to the seller or does an act inconsistent with the seller's ownership.

The reason why "a substantial impairment of value" must take place before a revocation under § 2–608 may take force is to preclude revocation for trivial defects or defects which may be easily corrected.

It seems clear from reading said § 2–608 that revocation of an acceptance of delivery is now permissible only if the nonconformity substantially impairs the value of the article which has been accepted either (a) on the reasonable assumption that its nonconformity would be cured and it has not been reasonably cured; or (b), without discovery of such nonconformity the acceptance was reasonably induced either by the difficulty of discovery before acceptance or by the seller's assurances. In the present case, Rozmus did not discover the nonconformity before he accepted the automobile as no opportunity to drive it before acceptance was afforded him, and he accepted on the basis of the usual warranties (assurances) which are part of new car sales.

If we review the evidence in the light most favorable to Thompson's, giving it the benefit of all reasonable inferences therefrom by reason of the original decision of Judge McCarthy being in its favor, we would be justified in concluding that the defect did not substantially impair the value of the automobile. The only evidence in the case concerning the defect or nonconformity is that, due to an improper adjustment of the engine supports the drive shaft was moved out of line, which caused a bumping or thumping noise when the rear seat was fully occupied. When the cause was determined it was remedied within a few minutes by Thompson's mechanic. We find nothing in the record to justify a finding that Thompson's agreed to accept the return of the automobile. The evidence is to the contrary, and indicates that Rozmus abandoned the automobile when he left it in Thompson's repair shop.

Assurance, Repudiation, and Excuse

Assurance. If one of the parties to a contract has a reasonable basis for believing that the other party may not be able to perform his obligations, he has the right to demand assurance from the other party that he will perform his obligations. If such assurances are not given within 30 days of a reasonable request for them, then the party is considered to have repudiated the contract (2–609). For example, Farmer contracts to sell 1,000 bushels of apples to Canner with delivery to be made in September. In March, Canner learns that a severe frost has damaged many of the apple blossoms in Farmer's area and that fifty percent of the crop has been lost. Canner has the right, in writing, to demand assurances from Farmer that he will be able to fulfill his obligation in light of the frost. Farmer must provide those assurances within 30 days, for example, by advising Canner that his crop sustained only relatively light damage or that he had only made commitments to sell a small percentage of his total crop and expects to be able to fill his obligations to Canner. If Farmer does not provide such assurances in a timely manner, then he is considered to have repudiated the contract, and Canner has the remedies available to an aggrieved buyer that are discussed in the next chapter.

Anticipatory Repudiation. If one of the parties repudiates a contract, for example by advising the other party that he does not intend to perform his obligations, then the aggrieved party has the right to suspend his own performance and either (1) await performance for a reasonable time or (2) resort to any remedy for breach of contract (2–610).

Until the aggrieved party has either cancelled the contract or has materially changed his position because of the repudiation, the repudiating party may withdraw his repudiation by clearly indicating that he intends to perform his obligations (2–611).

Excuse. Under the Code, the rules for determining when a party is excused from performing his obligations under a contract follow closely the general rules of contract law regarding "impossibility." However, in most situations the Code substitutes the test of commercial impracticability for that of impossibility.

If goods required for performance of a contract and identified to it are destroyed without fault of either party prior to the time and the risk of loss passed to the buyer, then the contract is voided (2–613). For example, Jones agrees to sell and deliver an antique table to Brown, and the table is destroyed when Jones's antique store is hit by lightning and catches fire. The specific table identified to the contract was destroyed without fault of either party prior to the time the risk of loss was to pass to Brown and both parties are relieved of their obligations under the contract. If the table is merely damaged by the fire, then under the Code, Brown has the option of either (1) treating the contract as voided or (2) accepting the table with an allowance in the purchase price to compensate for the damaged condition (2–613).

If the agreed upon means of transportation is not available, but a commercially reasonable substitute means of transportation is available, then it must be used. Similarly, if the agreed upon means of payment is not available, the seller may withhold delivery unless a substitute means is available and used (2–614).

If unforeseen or unforseeable conditions which make performance impractical cause either a delay in delivery or nondelivery in whole or in part, the seller is excused from performance. However, if only part of the seller's capacity to perform is affected, he may allocate his production among his customers; if the seller chooses to do so, he must notify the buyers within a reasonable time of the allocation (2–615). When a buyer receives this notice, he may either terminate the contract or agree to accept the allocation in substitution (2–616).

For example, G.E. contracts to sell certain quantities of fuel rods for nuclear power plants to a number of electric utilities. If the federal government limits the amount of uranium G.E. has access to so that G.E. is unable to fill all of its contracts, G.E. would be excused from full performance on the grounds of commercial impracticability. However, G.E. may allocate its production of fuel rods among its customers and give them notice of the allocation; then each utility can decide whether to cancel or to accept the partial allocation.

SUMMARY

If either party to a sales contract deems himself insecure, as tested by commercial standards, he or she may demand assurance before preceeding with performance. If a party repudiates a sales contract, the aggrieved party may wait or he may bring an action for breach of the contract. In event of repudiation the usual remedies for the breach of the sales contract are available to the aggrieved party. If the party who has repudiated a sales contract wishes to withdraw his repudiation he may do so by giving the aggrieved party notice of his withdrawal before such party has canceled the contract or materially changed his position in reliance on the repudiation.

A party to a sales contract is excused from performance if his performance, due to no fault on his part, becomes commercially impracticable. If the impracticability is as to means of transportation or means of payment, substituted means, if available, may be resorted to. If the impracticability causes delay or ability to perform only partially, the seller may allocate performances among his buyers. A buyer may accept his allotment or cancel the contract.

Publicker Industries, Inc. v. Union Carbide Corp.
17 UCC Rep. 989 (E.D. Pa. 1975)

This was an action brought by Publicker Industries, Inc. (plantiff), against Union Carbide Corp. (defendant) seeking specific performance of a contract. Judgment for Publicker Industries.

In July of 1972 Union Carbide and Publicker entered into a contract whereby Union Carbide would supply Publicker with a substance called "Spirits Grade Ethanol" for a period of three years. The price was to be determined by a detailed formula set forth in the contract. Essentially the price was to be adjusted once at the beginning of each year of the contract to reflect any changes in the seller's costs, primarily of Ethylene, a type of natural gas. However, the contract contained a maximum price that Publicker would have to pay per gallon for the ethanol in any calendar year from 1974 to 1977.

By July of 1974 the price of Ethylene had risen so much that Union Carbide informed Publicker that it would insist on amending the contract to remove the price ceilings and that if Publicker did not agree, Union Carbide would cease supplying it with Ethanol. Publicker then brought an action to require that Union Carbide specifically perform the contract.

WEINER, DISTRICT JUDGE. Union Carbide argues that the very substantial and allegedly unforeseen rise in the price of Ethylene excused it from further performance on two grounds: (1) that it was the type of occurrence which under the "force majeure" clause of the contract relieved it of its duty to perform; and (2) that as a matter of general commercial law, the price rise was of such a nature as to render further performance impracticable (U.C.C. § 2–615).

The "force majeure" clause provided in relevant part that:

> Neither party shall be liable for its failure to perform hereunder if said performance is made impracticable due to any occurrence beyond its reasonable control, including acts of God, fires, floods, wars, sabotage, accidents, labor disputes or shortages, governmental laws, ordinances, rules and regulations . . . inability to obtain material, equipment or transportation, and any other similar or different occurrence. The party whose performance is made impracticable by any such occurrence shall have the right to omit during the period of such occurrence all or any portion of the quantity deliverable during such period.

It is comparable to that portion of the Uniform Commercial Code also relied upon by Union Carbide which provides that:

> Delay or non-delivery in whole or in part by a seller . . . is not a breach of his duty under a contract for sale if performance as agreed has been made impracticable by the occurrence of a contingency the non-occurrence of which was a basic assumption on which the contract was made . . . § 2–615.

Under either of the theories put forth by Union Carbide, the key to success is a finding by us that performance under the terms of the contract would be "impracticable." This would essentially require us to find that increased costs alone are sufficient to render performance impracticable. Comment 4 to § 2–615 quoted above indicates that:

> Increased cost alone does not excuse performance unless the rise in cost is due to some unforeseen contingency which alters the essential nature of the performance. Neither is a rise in the market in itself a justification, for that is exactly the type of business risk which business contracts cover. But a severe shortage of raw materials or of supplies due to a contingency such as war, embargo, local crop failure, unforeseen shutdown of major sources of supply or the like, which either causes a marked increase in cost or altogether prevents the seller from securing supplies necessary to his performance, is within the contemplation of this section.

Union Carbide argues that it has suffered excessive cost increases as a result of allegedly unprecedented Arab price hikes. Testimony was presented to show the connection between oil prices and natural gas prices. Various experts testified that at the time of the contract, it was completely unforeseeable that the oil producing nations would bring about such exorbitant price increases. Union Carbide's experts further testified that the price ceiling established for 1974 in the contract was based upon their forecast that the Ethylene price for 1974 would be 3.75 cents a pound but that is fact by July 1974 the price had risen to 7 cents a pound. As a result, Union Carbines cost per gallon of Ethanol rose from 21.2 cents a gallon in 1973 to 37.2 cents a gallon by the middle of 1974. Confronted with a contract sale price fixed at 26.5 cents a gallon for 1974, Union Carbide was losing over 10 cents a gallon at the time it refused to continue performance. It now alleged that if it is forced to complete performance under the present contract, it will suffer an aggregate loss in excess of $5.8 million.

However, Publicker contends that because the oil producing nations had joined together in 1971 to effect a 25-percent price increase, further price increases of the same kind were not unforeseeable at the time of the contract. Furthermore, it argues that the precise purpose of the ceiling provision in the contract was to place upon Union Carbide the risk of any unusual rise in the price of Ethylene. It is contended that in any event, the mere fact that the cost of performance has doubled does not make such performance impracticable.

We agree with Publicker. We are not aware of any cases where something less than a 100% cost increase has been held to make a seller's performance "impracticable." It is clear that in the present case, the contract contemplated that foreseeable cost increases would be passed on to the buyer. However, the existence of a specific provision which put a ceiling on contract price increases resulting from a rise in the cost of Ethylene impels the conclusion that the parties intended that the risk of a substantial and unforeseen rise in its cost would be born by the seller, Union Carbide.

Problem Cases

1. Knitting Mills sold some goods to Budge pursuant to a written sales contract that provided that no change, modification or waiver of its provisions would be binding unless reduced to writing. The contract also contained a specific disclaimer of warranty of color fastness of the goods. When Budge was sued for the purchase price of the goods he claimed that subsequent to the written contract Knitting Mills had orally warranted the color fastness of the goods. Should Budge be permitted to make this claim?
2. Lewis owned 3,000 pounds of camphor which was stored in the S&S Warehouse on a nonnegotiable warehouse receipt. Lewis sold the camphor to Cundill and delivered to Cundill the warehouse delivery order. Cundill paid Lewis the purchase price of the camphor and sent a check to S&S for the delivery charges. Shortly thereafter the camphor disappeared from the warehouse. Was the camphor ever delivered to Cundill? Who had the risk of loss?
3. Jarstad sold a sporting goods business, Ski Hut Honda, to Tacoma Outdoor Recreation, Inc. The sale included all inventories. A year after the purchase, Tacoma closed the business for two days to conduct an inventory and found the inventory to be unaccountably short by $60,000. Tacoma deducted this amount from the purchase price of the store. Jarstad then brought suit to recover the $60,000, and Tacoma counterclaimed for breach of contract based upon Jarstad's overstatement of inventories. How should the court decide on Tacoma's claim?
4. On November 6, 1973, Rose purchased a used Volkswagen from Epley Motor Sales for $1,020. Before buying it, he took it for a trial drive during which time he did not drive it faster than 55 miles an hour and discovered some minor defects with the brakes and horn. Epley's salesperson advised him that the engine had been "gone through" and "checked" and that some work had been done on it. After Rose purchased the car he

started out on a trip. Enroute the car made a funny racket and blue smoke came out of it; the car sounded as if a piston had broken. Rose stopped the car and got out; the entire back end was engulfed in flames and the car was a total loss. At the time Rose was driving the car at 65–70 miles an hour; he had owned it less than three hours and had driven it less than 100 miles. On November 8, Rose asked Epley Motor Sales to rescind the sale and it refused to do so. Is Rose entitled to revoke his acceptance of the car?

5. Mulcahy purchased a new Oldsmobile from McDavid Oldsmobile and was issued a new car warranty providing that the car and chassis, including all equipment and accessories, were warranted to be free from defects in material and workmanship under normal use and service. Within three months of the purchase of the car and after it had been driven approximately 3,500 miles Mulcahy experienced some trouble with the Delco battery. The battery had to be filled with water every time he filled the car with gasoline, and acid was leaking from the battery onto his driveway. The car had not been in an accident, the battery was well secured in the car, the battery never froze and Mulcany had it checked regularly. While Mulcahy could not see a crack he thought the battery was cracked. Mulcahy took the car to McDavid Oldsmobile which refused to replace the battery under the warranty. Mulcahy then left the car with McDavid and stopped making payments on the car. McDavid brought suit to recover the balance of the purchase price and Mulcahy claimed that he had revoked to acceptance of the car. What result should the court reach?

6. Pollack agreed to sell to Campbell the "contents of Magic Car Wash" for $8,000 and assured Campbell that everything within the four walls of the car wash building was included in the sale. Campbell removed some of the equipment from the premises and then discovered that under the terms of the lease of the building, the boiler, hot-air blowers, and fluorescent lighting could not be removed because they belonged to the landlord. Campbell returned the equipment he had removed and notified Pollack he was rescinding the sale. Pollack claims that Campbell cannot revoke his acceptance because the noninclusion of the boiler, blowers and lighting does not constitute a "substantial breach" since they are worth only about $600. Is Pollack's argument valid?

7. Government Hospital ordered 275 pounds of raw shrimp from Mazar Brothers. Mazur Brothers had the shrimp federally inspected, packed in ice, and delivered to the Hospital. The shrimp were kept refrigerated until the next day when they were put in steam kettles. The cook testified there appeared to be nothing wrong with the appearance of the shrimp in their raw state but after they had boiled for five minutes they had a unwholesome odor and were discolored. The shrimp were not served to patients and were kept refrigerated for four days pending reinspection by the Department of the Interior. Six days after delivery Hospital informed Mazur Brothers that it wanted to reject the shrimp. Could it do so?

8. On April 15, 1959, Motter purchased farm machinery from Wrightstone on a conditional sales contract which provided: "the buyer is not bound to pay any specific amount each month, provided the total balance is paid within twenty-four months." Motter executed a judgment note for the balance which was renewed from time to time as payments were made. The last renewal was on May 5, 1960, in the amount of $590.40. On June 11, 1960, Wrightstone, Inc., repossessed the machinery and, on June 13, 1960, notified Motter that payment must be made in full of the balance. On June 28, 1960, Wrightstone advised Motter that the machinery had been sold and that he owed a balance of $205.90. Judgment was entered for this amount. Wrightstone based its right to repossess the machinery on the ground that it deemed itself insecure. Motter petitioned to have the judgment

opened and the petition was granted. What should Wrightstone have done if it considered itself insecure?

9. In March 1972, a farming corporation entered into a written contract whereby it agreed to sell to Semo Grain Company, a grain dealer, 75,000 bushels of no. 1 yellow soybeans at $3.10 per bushel. Delivery of the soybeans by Olwen Farms was to be made at Semo Grain's elevator during January, 1973. Nothing in the agreement required Olwen Farms to grow the soybeans on any certain lands, and, for that matter, it was not obligated to grow the soybeans. From various farms Olwen Farms either owned or rented, 19,885 bushels of soybeans were produced and harvested. These soybeans were sold by Olwen Farms to other grain purchasers for prices in excess of $3.10 per bushel. Olwen Farms did not deliver any soybeans to Semo Grain. Semo Grain filed a suit in February 1973, seeking to recover the difference between the contract price and market price of soybeans as of January 1973. Olwen Farms claimed it was excused from performing the contract by reason of adverse weather conditions pursuant to § 2–613 and § 2–615. Should Olwin Farms be excused from performance of its contract?

10. In April 1973 Stokes entered into a contract to sell 8,209 bushels of no. 1 yellow soybeans to Gold Kist with delivery to be made no later than December 31, 1973. The contract contained a liquidated damages clause for nondelivery and in addition had the following clause:

    > Notwithstanding the foregoing, if the producer is unable to deliver all or any part of the above quantity as contracted solely because of reasons beyond the producer's control, including an Act of God, the producer and Gold Kist, Inc. agree to settle at the difference between the price stated above for the quantity not delivered and the current cash market price for that quantity at the above Gold Kist facility on the date determined pursuant to (*a*) above, that being the earlier of either the date of notification of intent not to deliver or the first business date after December 31, 1973.

    On November 29, some 9,000 bushels of soybeans owned by Stokes were damaged or destroyed by fire. Stokes thereafter tendered 2,600 bushels of salvage to Gold Kist which refused them as not in conformance with the grade specifications. On December 19, 1973, Gold Kist then brought suit against Stokes, claiming the difference between the contract price and the market price. Is Stokes liable?

39

Remedies for Breach

Remedies in General. If one of the parties to a contract for the sale of goods fails to perform his obligations, the Code provides the injured party with a variety of remedies. The objective of these remedies to put the injured party in as good a position as if the other person had fully performed his contractual obligations. Under the Code an injured party may not recover consequential or penal damages unless such damages are specifically provided for in the Code or in another statute (1–106).[1]

The parties to a contract may provide their own remedies to be applied in event of a default and may also alter or limit the damages available under the Code (2–719[1]). An agreement for liquidated damages will be enforced provided the amount is reasonable. An amount is reasonable if it is not so excessive as to amount to a penalty or so small as to be unconscionable, and provided that in the event of a breach the amount of damages resulting would be difficult to prove and obtaining an adequate remedy otherwise would not be convenient or feasible (2–718[1]).

Consequential damages may also be limited or excluded by agreement between the parties, but such a limitation or exclusion will not be enforced if it would be unconscionable. The Code provides that any attempt to limit consequential damages for injury to a person caused by consumer goods is *prima facie* unconscionable (2–719[3]).

Statute of Limitations. The Code provides that any action for breach of a sales contract must be brought within four years after the breach occurs. The parties, by agreement, may shorten the period to one year but they may not extend it. The cause of action accrues when the breach occurs, whether or not the aggrieved party knows of the breach. The cause of action for

[1] The numbers in the parentheses refer to the sections of the Uniform Commercial Code, 1972.

breach of warranty accrues when the goods are delivered to the buyer unless the warranty pertains to future performance of the goods in which case the cause of action accrues when the buyer should have discovered the breach (2–725).

SUMMARY

The Code remedies for breach of contract are designed to put the injured party in the same position as if the contract had been performed.

As a general rule the courts will enforce an agreement of the parties relating to the damages to which the parties will be entitled, provided the agreement is not void as an unconscionable contract or clause. A liquidated damage provision in a contract is enforceable if the amount is reasonable and the damages for the injury suffered by the injured party are not readily provable. The parties by agreement may provide for additional or supplemental damages, and consequential damages may be limited or excluded except damages for injury to a person from consumer goods.

The statute of limitations on sales contracts is four years from the time the cause of action accrues. The parties may, by agreement, limit the time to one year but they cannot extend it.

Wille v. Southwestern Bell Telephone Co.

19 UCC Rep. 447 (Sup. Ct. Kansas 1976)

This was an action brought by Frank Wille (plaintiff) against Southwestern Bell Telephone Co. (defendant) to recover damages for breach of contract for an omission in the yellow pages of a telephone directory. The trial court granted summary judgment for the telephone company. Affirmed on appeal.

Frank Wille operated a heating and air conditioning sales and service business under the trade names, Frank Wille Company and Frank Wille's Coleman Comfort Center, and for the thirteen years prior to 1974 had purchased some form of yellow page listing for his business in the telephone directory published by Southwestern Bell Telephone Company for Wichita.

In February 1974, Wille signed a contract to list two of his business telephone numbers in the yellow page directory to be published in July 1974. When the new directory came out it omitted one of the numbers. Upon learning of the omission Wille began advertising his business on local television stations and in alternate forms of advertising, with total expenditures being between four and five thousand dollars.

Wille was never billed nor did he pay for the omitted listings. The written contract between the parties was subject to thirteen terms and conditions which were set out on the back of the contract. The fourth paragraph of those conditions provided:

The applicant agrees that the Telephone Company shall not be liable for errors in or omissions of the directory advertising beyond the amount paid for the directory advertising omitted, or in which errors occur, for the issue life of the directory involved.

HARMON, CHIEF JUSTICE. Wille contends the exculpatory clause upon which Bell relies is contrary to public policy and should not be enforced. He asserts unconscionability of contract in two respects: The parties' unequal bargaining position and the form of the contract and the circumstances of its execution.

Although the UCC's application is primarily limited to contracts for the present or future sale of goods (2–102; 2–105), many courts have extended the statute by analogy into other areas of the law or have used the doctrine as an alternative basis for their holdings. The UCC neither defines the concept of unconscionability nor provides the elements or perimeters of the doctrine.

The comment to 2–302 sheds some light on the drafters' intent. It provides in part:

The basic test is whether, in the light of the general commercial background and the commercial needs of the particular trade or case, the clauses involved are so one-sided as to be unconscionable under the circumstances existing at the time of the making of the contract. . . . The principle is one of the prevention of oppression and unfair surprise . . . and not of disturbance of allocation of risks because of superior bargaining power.

One commentator has elaborated on the two types of situations which UCC is designed to deal with:

One type of situation is that involving unfair surprise: where there has actually been no assent to the terms of the contract. Contracts involving unfair surprise are similar to contracts of adhesion. Most often these contracts involve a party whose circumstances, perhaps his inexperience or ignorance, when compared with the circumstances of the other party, make his knowing assent to the fine print terms fictional. Courts have often found in these circumstances an absence of a meaningful bargain.

The other situation is that involving oppression: where, although there has been actual assent, the agreement, surrounding facts, and relative bargaining positions of the parties indicate the possibility of gross over-reaching on the part of either party. Oppression and economic duress in a contract seem to be inseparably linked to an inequality of bargaining power. The economic position of the parties is such that one becomes vulnerable to a grossly unequal bargain.

The leading case on the question of the validity of a Limitation of Liability Clause in a contract for telephone directory advertising is *McTighe v. New England Tel. & Tel. Co.*, where Circuit Judge Medina, speaking for the Court of Appeals for the Second Circuit, said:

The inequality of bargaining power between the telephone company and the businessman desiring to advertise in the yellow pages of the directory is more apparent than real. It is not different from that which exists in any other case in which a potential seller is the only supplier of the particular article or service desired. There are many other modes of advertising to which the businessman may turn if the contract offered him by the telephone company is not attractive. We find in this record no basis for a conclusion that the application of the

Limitation of Liability Clause could lead to a result so unreasonable as to shock the conscience. In the absence of most exceptional circumstances, which do not appear in this record, the insertion of a 'Yellow Page' advertisement under the wrong classification heading will not produce a different result from that which would follow a complete omission of the advertisement from the directory. It would be virtually, if not completely, impossible to determine what portion of the business done by an advertiser is attributable to its use of "Yellow Page" advertising. There are many factors which enter into periodic fluctuations in the volume of business done by a seller of goods. The purpose of the Limitation of Liability Clause is to protect the telephone company from the danger of verdicts primarily speculative in amount. This is not an unreasonable objective. In this respect, the telephone company is not in a different position from the local newspaper, radio or television station, or other advertising media.

In *Steele v. J. I. Case Co.*, we recognized that liability for consequential damages may be limited or excluded contractually unless under all the surrounding facts and circumstances, the limitation or exclusion would be inequitable. Each case of this type must necessarily rest upon its own facts but after examining the terms of the contract, the manner of its execution and the knowledge and experience of Wille we think the contract was neither inequitable nor unconscionable so as to deny its enforcement.

Seller's Remedies

A buyer may breach a contract in a number of ways, including: (1) by wrongfully refusing to accept goods or by wrongfully returning them; (2) by failing to make a payment when due; or (3) by indicating an inability or unwillingness to proceed with the contract. In addition a buyer may become insolvent and thus unable to pay the seller for goods already delivered or for goods which the seller is obligated to deliver.

When a buyer breaches a contract, or when a seller learns of a buyer's insolvency, the seller has a number of remedies under the Code: These remedies include the right to:

1. withhold delivery of undelivered goods (Section 2–703[a]);
2. recover goods from a buyer upon the buyer's insolvency (Section 2–702);
3. stop delivery of goods that are in the possession of a carrier or other bailee (Section 2–705);
4. resell the goods and recover damages (Section 2–706);
5. recover damages for breach of contract (Section 2–708);
6. recover the price (Section 2–709);
7. cancel the contract (Section 2–703[f]).

Damages Based on Resale. When a buyer breaches the contract, the seller has the right to suspend his own performance under the contract and to identify (set aside) as intended for the contract any goods which conform to the contract (2–704). If the seller is in process of manufacturing goods, the seller may exercise reasonable commercial judgment to either complete the manufacture of the goods or to stop manufacturing and sell the uncompleted goods for their scrap or salvage value. In making the decision whether or not to complete the goods, the seller should chose the course which would minimize any loss (2–704[2]). Thus a seller would be justified in completing the manufacture of goods which could readily be resold at the contract price, but would not be justified in completing specially designed goods which would not be saleable to anyone other than the buyer who ordered them. The purpose of the rule is to permit the seller to follow a reasonable course of action to mitigate the damages.

On the buyer's breach of the sales contract, the seller is not obligated to resell the goods but may resell them and recover damages. If the resale is made in good faith and in a commercially reasonable manner, the seller may recover from the buyer the difference between the resale price and the contract price (2–706). If the seller choses this measure of damages, he may also recover "incidential damages" but must give the buyer credit for any expenses the seller saved as a result of the buyer's breach.

Incidental damages include any commercially reasonable charges such as expenses or commissions incurred in stopping delivery or in the transportation of the goods and the expenses incurred in the care and custody of the goods after the buyer's breach (2–710). Expenses saved might be the cost of packaging the goods and of transportation which would be incurred in completing performance of the contract.

If the buyer and seller have agreed as to the manner in which the resale would be made, the courts will enforce the agreement unless it would be found to be unconscionable (2–302). If the parties have not entered into an agreement as to the resale of the goods, the sale may be at public or private sale, but in all events it must be made in good faith and in a commercially reasonable manner. The seller should make it clear that the resale refers to the broken contract.

If the goods are resold at private sale the seller must give the buyer reasonable notification of his intention to resell (2–706[3]). If the sale is a public sale such as at an auction, the seller must give the buyer notice of the time and place of the sale unless the goods are perishable or threaten to decline in value rapidly; the sale must be made at a usual place or market for public sales if one is reasonably available; and, if the goods are not within the view of those attending the sale the notification of the sale must state the place where the goods are located and provide for reasonable inspection by prospective bidders. The seller may bid at a public sale (2–706[4]).

The purchaser at a public sale who buys in good faith takes free from any rights of the original buyer even though the seller has failed to conduct the sale in compliance with the rules set out in the Code (2–706[5]). The seller is not accountable to the buyer for any profit the seller makes on a resale (2–706[6]).

Recovery of Purchase Price. In the normal performance of a contract the seller delivers conforming goods, the buyer accepts them, and the buyer is obligated to pay for them. The seller is entitled to the purchase price of all goods accepted by the buyer and of all conforming goods which are lost or damaged after the risk of loss passed to the buyer. In addition, if a buyer refuses to accept and pay for goods for which he has contracted, the seller is entitled to recover the purchase price of the goods if the seller has made an honest effort to resell and has been unable to do so or if it is apparent that any attempt to resell at a reasonable price would be unsuccessful (2–709). If the seller sues the buyer for the contract price, he must hold the goods for the buyer and deliver them to the buyer when he pays the judgment. If resale becomes possible prior to the time the buyer pays the judgment, the seller may resell but must credit against the judgment the amount received on the sale (2–709[2]).

Damages for Nonacceptance or Rejection. If the buyer refuses to accept conforming goods or repudiates the contract, the seller may recover as damages from the buyer the difference between the market price of the goods at the time and place they were to be delivered to the buyer and the unpaid contract price. The seller is also entitled to recover any incidental expenses incurred but must give the buyer credit for any expenses the seller saved as a result of the buyer's breach of contract (2–708[1]). This measure of damages would most commonly be sought by a seller where the market price of the goods had dropped substantially between the time the contract was made and when the buyer repudiated the contract. For example, on January 1, seller contracts with buyer to sell buyer 100,000 hula hoops at $1.50 each with delivery to be made in Boston on June 1. By June 1 the hula hoop fad has passed and they are selling for $1 each in Boston. If the buyer repudiates the contract on June 1 and refuses to accept delivery of the 100,000 hula hoops, the seller is entitled to the difference between the contract price of $150,000 and the June 1 market price in Boston of $100,000. Thus the seller could recover $50,000 in damages plus any incidental expenses but less any expenses saved by the seller.

If the difference between the market price and the contract price would not put the seller in as good a position as he would have been in had the buyer performed the contract, then the Code provides that the measure of damages is the "profit, including reasonable overhead," which the seller would have made on the contract, plus any incidental expenses incurred but less any expenses saved as a result of the buyer's breach (2–708[2]). Thus, in the hula hoop example discussed above, if the material and direct labor cost to seller of making the hula hoops would have been $0.35 each, the seller could recover from the buyer his lost profit which would be the difference between the contract price of $150,000 and the seller's direct cost of $35,000. The seller would recover $115,000 plus incidental expenses and less any expenses saved.

Seller's Remedies on Discovery of Buyer's Insolvency. If the seller has not agreed to extend credit to the buyer for the purchase price of the goods, the buyer must make payment on delivery of the goods. If the seller tenders delivery of the goods he may withhold delivery unless the agreed payment is made. Where the seller has agreed to extend credit to the buyer for the purchase price of the goods, but discovers before delivery that the buyer is insolvent, the seller may refuse delivery unless the buyer pays cash for the goods together with the unpaid balance for all goods previously delivered under the contract (2–702[1]).

At common law a seller has the right to rescind a sales contract induced by fraud and recover the goods unless they have been sold to a bona fide purchaser for value. Based on this general legal principle, the Code provides that where the seller discovers that the buyer has received goods while insolvent, the seller may reclaim the goods upon demand made within ten days after their receipt. This right granted to the seller is based on constructive deceit on the part of the buyer. The receiving of the goods while insolvent is equivalent to a false representation of solvency. To protect his rights all the seller is required to do is to make a demand within the ten-day period; he need not actually repossess the goods.

If the buyer has misrepresented his solvency to this particular seller in writing within three months before the delivery of the goods, the ten-day limitation on his right to reclaim the goods does not apply. However, the seller's right to reclaim the goods is subject to the prior rights of purchasers in the ordinary course of the buyer's business, good faith purchasers for value, and creditors with a perfected lien on the buyer's inventory (2–702[2] and [3]). Where there is no perfected lien, the goods can be recovered from a trustee in bankruptcy.[2]

Seller's Right to Stop Delivery. If the seller discovers the buyer is insolvent, the seller has the right to stop the delivery of any goods which the seller has shipped to the buyer regardless of the size of the shipment. If a buyer repudiates a sales contract or fails to make a payment due before delivery, the seller also has the right to stop delivery of any shipment of goods where the quantity is a carload, truckload, planeload, or other large shipment (2–705).

To stop delivery the seller must notify the carrier or other bailee in time

[2] In *re National Bellas Hess, Inc.*, 17 UCC Rep. 430 (S.D.N.Y. 1975).

so that by the exercise of reasonable diligence bailee may prevent the delivery of the goods. After receiving notice to stop delivery, the carrier or other bailee owes a duty to hold the goods and deliver them as directed by the seller. The seller is liable to the carrier or other bailee for any expenses incurred or damages resulting from complying with the seller's order to stop delivery. If a nonnegotiable document of title has been issued for the goods, the carrier or other bailee owes no duty to obey a stop-delivery order issued by any person other than the person who consigned the goods to him (2–705[3]).

Liquidated Damages. If the seller has justifiably withheld delivery of the goods because of the buyer's breach, the buyer is entitled to recover any money or goods he has delivered to the seller over and above the agreed amount of liquidated damages. If there is no such agreement, the seller will not be permitted to retain an amount in excess of 20 percent of the value of the total performance for which the buyer is obligated under the contract or $500, whichever is the smaller. This right of restitution is subject to the seller's right to recover damages under other provisions of the Code and to the amount or value of benefits received by the buyer directly or indirectly by reason of the contract (2–718).

SUMMARY

The seller is entitled to the purchase price of conforming goods delivered to and accepted by the buyer. The seller may also recover the purchase price of any conforming goods which were sent to the buyer and were lost or destroyed after the risk of loss had passed to the buyer. Also, if the goods have been identified to the contract and the buyer repudiates the sale, the seller is entitled to the purchase price of the goods that cannot, by a reasonable effort on the part of the seller, be resold for a fair price.

The seller is entitled to recover compensatory damages which were reasonably within the contemplation of the parties. The seller on breach by the buyer is also entitled to incidental damages. If necessary to put the seller in the position he would have held had the buyer performed, the seller may be granted his lost profits, including overhead, as damages. The seller is not obligated to resell on the buyers refusal to accept the goods, but if he does resell in a commercially reasonable manner, he may recover as damages the difference between the sale price and the contract price.

On the buyer's insolvency the seller may reclaim the goods if he makes the demand within ten days after receipt. If written misrepresentation of solvency has been made by the buyer to the particular seller within three months, the ten-day limitation does not apply.

On the buyer's insolvency the seller may stop delivery of the goods by a carrier or other bailee. Delivery of large lots may be stopped on the buyer's repudiation or failure to pay sum due before delivery. Reasonable notice to stop delivery must be given to the carrier or other bailee.

Mott Equity Elevator v. Suihovec

18 UCC Rep. 388 (Sup. Ct. N. Dakota 1975)

This was an action brought by the Mott Equity Elevator (plaintiff) against Rudy Suihovec (defendant) to recover damages for failure to deliver 4,000 bushels of grain. Judgment for Suihovec. Affirmed.

On October 24, 1972, the parties entered a contract whereby Suihovec agreed to sell and deliver in March 4,000 bushels of spring wheat at $1.82 per bushel. Several times a week throughout March, Suihovec contacted the elevator and asked when he could make delivery. Each time he was told that the elevator was filled. Suihovec continued to inquire during April and May and was told there was little or no space for his grain. Finally in June, Suihovec sold and shipped his grain to another buyer for $2.20 per bushel. In mid-September, when the price of grain had risen to $4.00 a bushel, the elevator called Suihovec and asked him to make delivery. He advised the elevator that he was no longer obligated because the elevator had breached the contract. The elevator then brought suit against Suihovec.

VOGEL, JUSTICE. We agree with the trial judge's finding of unreasonable delay by the elevator in making its demand for delivery in September, fully six months after the contract had expired.

The trial judge found that the elevator failed to perform within a reasonable time after a tender of performance by the seller and after the time for performance had expired. The court further concluded that the general conduct of the elevator was such as to justify the seller Suihovec in treating the contract as breached by the elevator.

The elevator strenuously argues that Suihovec was not entitled to resell his grain under Section 2–706, without giving reasonable notice to his intent to resell. The argument also is made that Section 2–309, imposses a duty on Suihovec to give reasonable notice to the other party that he was terminating the contract.

We find these arguments to be without merit. Before discussing these questions, it may be helpful to reiterate the remedies available to the seller following breach by the buyer. Under Section 2–703, the seller is entitled to, among other remedies, withhold delivery, resell and recover damages, recover damages for nonacceptance, or cancel. Suihovec pursued the remedy of cancellation, as was his right. He thereafter resold his grain to another buyer, as was his right. The parties have confused Suihovec's right to dispose of his grain as he wished under a canceled contract with the Code remedy allowing a seller to "resell and recover damages" under Section 2–703, and Section 2–706.

The seller's right to resell and recover damages is, of course, available to a seller in addition to his right to cancel; subsection 1-b of Section 2–719, creates a presumption that clauses prescribing remedies are cumulative rather than exclusive.

The only condition precedent to the seller's right to resell is a breach by the buyer within Section 2–703. The trial judge found that Suihovec had a right to pursue this remedy when he sold his grain directly to the Grain Terminal Association. We would agree that Suihovec did have such a right if it were necessary to apply this section to the seller's conduct in reselling his grain in this case. But the section does not apply. In a falling market Suihovec would probably have desired to resell and recover damages. To recover damages under this section he would be required to act in good faith, sell in a commercially reasonable manner, and give reasonable notice to the buyer of his intention to resell (if the sale was at private sale). Failure to act properly under this section merely deprives the seller of the measure of damages provided in subsection 1. In any event, the seller is not accountable to the buyer for any profit made on any resale under Section 2–706, where, as here, the resale occurred in a rising market and the contract had been canceled. In this case, involving a rising market, Suihovec suffered no damages and thus did not need to resort to this Code remedy.

We hold that the buyer breached the agreement in not accepting delivery within a reasonable time, giving rise to Suihovec's right to cancel under Section 2–703. "Cancellation" is defined in Section 2–106, as follows:

> "Cancellation" occurs when either party puts an end to the contract for breach by the other and its effect is the same as that of "termination" except that the cancelling party also retains any remedy for breach of the whole contract or any unperformed balance.

The elevator makes the argument that Suihovec is not entitled to any "windfall" he might have received when he sold his grain in June to another buyer. The elevator claims that 'Suihovec acted in "bad faith" by failing to notify the elevator of his intention to resell his grain. From the record, we cannot find any evidence that Suihovec acted in bad faith when he trucked his wheat directly to the Grain Terminal Association and sold it for a slightly higher price than provided under the contract. There is no duty to notify of a resale where the contract is cancelled. Suihovec appears to have made every effort to deliver his grain to the elevator. In fact, testimony at trial revealed that he was desperate to deliver his grain to the elevator. It must be remembered that the entire time Suihovec held the grain in storage on his farm, he suffered the risk of loss upon casualty to the grain. In fact, some of the contract grain had to be discarded due to insect damage.

Suihovec was not a seller out to take advantage of a rising market. He made arrangements to market his wheat immediately upon Mott's refusal in late May to accept delivery. When Suihovec sold the grain in June, the market price had risen to only $2.20 per bushel. The elevator, on the other hand, seeks to collect damages at the price of $4.40 per bushel, the market price in September 1973, when it contends Suihovec breached the contract.

We find no bad faith on the part of Suihovec.

E-Z Roll Hardware Mfg. Co., Inc. v. H & H Products & Finishing Corp.

4 UCC Rep. 1045 (N.Y. Sup. Ct., Nassau Cty., 1968)

This was an action for breach of contract by E-Z Roll Hardware (plaintiff) against H&H Products & Finishing Corporation (defendant). Judgment for E-Z Roll Hardware.

The contract, dated October 31, 1963, was in the form of a letter accepting a blanket order for 10,000 sets of "special folding door hardware." Prices were set forth as follows: 2 feet, $0.76; 4 feet, $1.47; 5 feet, $1.54; 6 feet, $1.61; 8 feet, $1.75. There was to be a first shipment of 3,000 sets approximately December 15, 1963. The balance of 7,000 sets was to be shipped as needed by the buyer over a period of not later than nine months.

E-Z commenced shipments in January of 1964 which continued until April 7, 1964. A total of 3,010 sets were shipped for an aggregate price of $4,757.90. E-Z testified that on at least five occasions between June 1964 and January 1966, H&H was contacted about the balance of the order and each time received excuses for delay or promises that there would be larger orders. Finally, in January 1966, H&H stated there would be no additional orders and this action was brought.

E-Z claimed as damages the sum of $11,101 on the theory that this figure represented the purchase price for the balance of the 7,000 sets computed by treating the price of 3,010 sets actually delivered ($4,757.90) as three tenths of the full contract price. Judgement for E-Z for $4,002.40.

LYNDE, JUSTICE. E-Z is entitled to relief, and the question becomes one of measure of damages. E-Z found itself with a large quantity of raw materials on hand which it could not use for any other purpose. Further work would have to be performed before H&H could use the merchandise: metal track would have to be cut to size; plating, assembly and boxing were required. A seller who is in the process of manufacturing goods for the buyer which are not readily saleable when finished and who elects to cease manufacture on repudiation by the buyer does not have an action for the purchase price as such. He does, however, retain his action for damages (U.C.C. § 2–709, sub[3]) which are measured by the difference between costs of performance and contract price and which include losses sustained, such as payments for labor and materials reasonably made in part performance of the contract to the extent that they are wasted if performance is abandoned.

The complicating factor here is that the buyer had the right to control the contract price. The buyer had five alternatives and had the right to demand delivery of the item bearing the lowest price. Its responsibility under the contract would have been fulfilled if it ordered that the balance of the sets (6,990) be delivered in two-foot lengths. In such circumstances the return on the lowest price provides the standard for measuring damages. Assuming completion of the contract on this basis, E-Z would be entitled to $5,312.40 in addition to the amount of $4,757.90 previously received. In order to get that, however, it would have been required to expend an additional $810 in order to identify the material to the contract. H&H may have a credit for that amount plus a credit for $500, the salvage value of the material. The amount, therefore, which is due to E-Z is $4,002.40. This, of course, represents a loss to E-Z but it puts E-Z in the same position as though the contract had been completed. The court cannot remake the contract. Both parties apparently took a business risk when they entered into the agreement. H&H ordered special purpose equipment, hoping that it would have customers for the product and E-Z provided for a loss item in the contract, hoping it would not be a major factor in the entire order.

E-Z's claim for storage is rejected. To qualify for incidental damages as contemplated by U.C.C. § 2–710, there must be compliance with the statutory provisions (U.C.C. §§ 2–709, 2–706) designed to minimize damages. No such action was taken in this case.

In re Units, Inc.

3 UCC Rep. 46 (U.S.D.C. Conn. 1965)

This was a reclamation petition filed by Northern Sash & Door Company (plaintiff) against the trustee in bankruptcy of Units, Inc. (defendant). Reclamation petition was denied.

On December 23, 1964, Units, which owed Northern $16,900 and which was legally insolvent at the time, sent a letter to Northern which read in part:

> Anticipating your anxiety over the status of our account with your company, we felt it wise to acquaint you with our situation at present.
> We are experiencing the typical year end "receivable blues" this coupled with the fact our inventory is extremely heavy and unbalanced has put us in a temporary bind.
> Based on the above we are proposing the following payment schedule to help us through this period.
> December—$4,304.77 (check enclosed)
> January —$4,304.77
> February —$3,856.61
> March —$3,856.60

At that time Units had an unfilled order for merchandise amounting to $8,149.09. On January 13, 1965, Northern's sales manager spoke with Units' treasurer and was allegedly told the January check would be sent if the merchandise was released. Northern sent the merchandise, but the check was never mailed. Northern made no effort to rescind or reclaim until after April 7, 1965, when the petition in bankruptcy was filed.

SEIDMAN, REFEREE. Connecticut General Statutes § 2–702 is controlling. It provides in part:

(2) Where the seller discovers that the buyer has received goods on credit while insolvent he may reclaim the goods upon demand made within ten days after the receipt, but if misrepresentation of solvency has been made to the particular seller in writing within three months before delivery, the ten day limitation does not apply.

(3) The seller's right to reclaim under Subsection (2) is subject to the rights of a buyer in ordinary course . . . or lien creditor under § 2–403.

The reclamation petition alleged a fraudulent misrepresentation of solvency. The trustee pleaded that even if there was a fraudulent misrepresentation the petitioner is not now entitled to reclaim the property since a timely reclamation petition was not made. In reply the petitioner amended its petition by alleging that the bankrupt had made a written misrepresentation of solvency to the petitioner within three months before delivery.

Assuming that a promise that a check would be forthcoming was made, it would be a fraudulent representation that would give the seller a right to reclaim within ten days after delivery. This was not done in the instant case. If the reclaiming creditor is to prevail it is necessary therefore to find there was a misrepresentation of solvency in writing within three months before delivery.

The only evidence of the alleged misrepresentation of solvency is the letter dated December 23, 1964. A careful reading of that letter does not disclose any language which could reasonably be considered a representation of the solvency. The bankrupt in the letter admits that it is unable to pay its bills as they mature and refers to the anxiety which the creditor feels. The letter refers to an unbalanced inventory and a temporary bind. This language might put a reasonably prudent man on further inquiry as to whether or not the debtor is in fact insolvent.

It is impossible for the court to conceive of any reasonable interpretation of the letter of December 23, 1964, to construe it as being a written misrepresentation of solvency.

Buyer's Remedies

The seller may breach a contract in a number of ways, including:

1. repudiation of the contract;
2. failure to make an agreed delivery;
3. delivery of nonconforming goods.

Under the Code, a buyer whose seller breaks the contract is given a number of remedies. Depending on the particular circumstances involved, the buyer may be able to:

1. "cover" and obtain damages based on any additional expense he incurs to acquire the goods (Section 2–712);

2. recover damages for nondelivery plus consequential and incidental damages (Section 2–713);
3. recover damages for nonconforming goods accepted by the buyer, together with consequential and incidental damages (Section 2–714); or
4. obtain specific performance where the goods are unique or unobtainable by "cover" (Section 2–716).

Buyer's Right to Cover. If the seller fails or refuses to deliver the goods called for by the contract, the buyer has the right to "cover" by purchasing substitute goods. He must make the purchase in good faith and without unreasonable delay. If the buyer does purchase or contracts to purchase substitute goods under his right to "cover," he can recover from the seller as damages the difference between the contract price and the cost of the substitute goods plus incidental and consequential damages but less any expenses saved as a result of the seller's breach. The buyer is not obligated to cover and failure to do so will not bar him from any other remedy (2–712).

Incidental Damages. Incidental damages include the expenses reasonably incurred by the buyer in the inspection, receipt, transportation, and care or custody of goods he has rightfully rejected together with any commercially reasonable charges, expenses or commissions he incurs in connection with "cover" (2–715[1]).

Consequential Damages. The buyer is entitled to recover consequential damages if the seller at the time of entering into the contract knew or should have known that a failure to perform the contract would result in special damages due to the buyer's general or special requirements or needs *and* if the damages could not have been prevented by cover (2–715[2][a]).

For example, Seller promises to deliver 1,000 yards of a special fabric to Buyer by September 1, knowing that Buyer wants to acquire the material to make garments suitable for the Christmas season. The Seller also knows that in reliance on his contract with Seller, Buyer will enter into contract with department stores to deliver the finished garments by October 1. If Seller delivers the fabric after September 1, or fails completely to deliver it, he may be liable to the Buyer for any consequential damages Buyer sustains if he is unable to acquire the same material elsewhere in time to fulfill his October 1 contracts.

Consequential damages also include an injury to person or property that is the proximate result of a breach of warranty (2–715[2][b]).

Buyer's Right to Damages for Nondelivery. In the event the seller fails or refuses to deliver the goods he has contracted to deliver, the buyer is entitled to recover as damages the difference between the market price of those goods at the time the buyer learned of the breach and the contract price plus any incidental and consequential damages but less any expenses saved (2–713).

For example, if seller agreed on June 1 to sell and deliver 500 bushels of wheat to buyer on September 1 for $7 per bushel and then refused to deliver on September 1 because the market price was then $8 per bushel, the buyer could recover $500 damages from the seller, plus incidental damages and any consequential damages that could not have been prevented by cover.

Buyer's Right to Specific Performance. The buyer is entitled to the remedy of specific performance and may obtain the specific goods contracted for *only* if they are unique or if the buyer is unable to "cover" or if it is clear that any effort to try to cover by purchasing such goods elsewhere would not be successful (2–716). Thus, a buyer of an antique automobile might have a court order the seller to deliver the specified automobile to the buyer, but the buyer of the grain in a particular storage bin could not get specific performance if he could buy the same kind of grain in the market place.

Damages for Defective Goods. If the buyer accepts defective goods and wishes to hold the seller liable in damages, he must give the seller notice of the breach within a reasonable time after he discovers or should have discovered the breach or he will not be able to recover (2–607[3][a]). If the goods are not as warranted and the buyer has given the required notice, he can recover as damages the difference at the time and place of acceptance between the value of the goods accepted and the value they would have had if they had been as warranted. The buyer may be entitled to incidental or consequential damages, including damages to person or property (2–714).

For example, a seller sells a buyer an automobile tire, warranting it to be "four-ply" construction, but the tire is in fact only only "two-ply." The buyer suffers a flat on the tire when it is punctured by a nail and then discovers that the tire is only two-ply. If the buyer gives seller prompt notice of the breach, he can keep the tire and recover from the seller the difference in value between a "two-ply" and a "four-ply" tire.

Buyer and Seller Agreements as to Remedies. As mentioned earlier in this chapter, the parties to a contract may provide for additional remedies or substitute remedies for those expressly provided in the Code. For example, the buyer's remedies may be limited to the return of the goods and the repayment of the price or to the replacement of nonconforming goods or parts (2–719). However, a court will look to see if such a limitation was freely agreed to or whether it is unconscionable and thus not enforceable.

SUMMARY

The buyer may recover as damages for nondelivery or repudiation on the part of the seller the difference between the market price of the goods and the contract price plus incidental, and under some circumstances consequential, damages. If the buyer covers, the measure of his compensatory damages is the difference between the cost of the cover and the contract price.

The buyer may be entitled to the remedy of specific performance if the goods which are the subject matter of the contract are unique or cannot be obtained by "cover."

In the event the goods are defective and the buyer accepts them, he can, on giving the seller notice of the breach, recover as damages the difference between the value of the goods received and their value had they been conforming goods plus incidental, and under some circumstances consequential, damages.

Keystone Diesel Engine Co. v. Irwin

191 A.2d 376 (Sup. Ct. Pa. 1963)

This was an action by Keystone Diesel Engine Company (plaintiff) against Floyd T. Irwin (defendant) to recover a judgment for the cost of repairs to an engine, and Irwin filed a counterclaim for damages for breach of warranty and loss of profits. Judgment for Keystone Diesel Engine Company and Irwin appealed. Judgment affirmed.

Keystone Diesel Engine Company (Keystone) was a dealer in diesel engines and Irwin operated tractor-trailers as a contract carrier. Keystone sold Irwin a diesel engine which was subsequently installed in a tractor. The engine did not function properly and Keystone performed certain modifications and repairs to it at its own expense. Subsequent repairs were required and Keystone performed the additional work allegedly based upon an oral contract with Irwin to pay Keystone for the additional work and Keystone brought suit. Irwin filed a counterclaim for loss of profits totalling $5,150.

EAGEN, JUSTICE. The Uniform Commercial Code provisions which are appropriate in the instant case read as follows:

> The measure of damages for breach of warranty is the difference at the time and the place of acceptance between the value of the goods accepted and the value they would have had if they had been as warranted, unless *special circumstances* show proximate damages of a different amount (2–714[2]).
>
> In a proper case any incidental and consequential damages under the next section may also be recovered (2–714[3]).
>
> Consequential damages *resulting from the seller's breach* include (a) any loss resulting from general or particular requirements and needs of which the seller at the time of contracting had reason to know and which could not reasonably be prevented by cover or otherwise (2–715[5]).

"Special circumstances" entitling the buyer to damages in excess of the difference between the value as warranted and the value as accepted exist where the buyer has communicated to the seller at the time of entering into the contract sufficient facts to make it apparent that the damages subsequently claimed were within the reasonable contemplation of the parties. The language in *Globe Refining Co. v. Landa Cotton Oil Co.*, gives the rationale of the foregoing rule as follows:

> [O]ne of two contracting parties ought not to be allowed to obtain advantage which he has not paid for. . . . If [a liability for the full profits that might be made by machinery which the defendant was transporting . . .] had been presented to the mind of the ship owner at the time of making the contract, as the basis upon which he was contracting, he would at once have rejected it. . . . The knowledge must be brought home to the party sought to be charged, under such circumstances that he must know that the person he contracts with reasonably believes that he accepts the contract with the special condition attached to it.

In the case at bar, no facts are alleged that would put Keystone on guard to the fact that Irwin would hold Keystone responsible for any loss of profit arising from the inability to use the engine in question. Following Irwin's theory to its logical conclusion, whenever a motor vehicle is sold for use in a profit motivated enterprise and the seller warrants that the vehicle will function properly, the seller will be liable in damages for a breach of warranty to the extent of profits lost on completely unrelated business contracts, where those profits are lost due to the vehicle malfunctioning.

Anticipated profits are not recoverable unless within the contemplation of the parties when the contract was made. Clearly, the claim for loss of profits in the instant case was not within the contemplation of the parties to this contract.

Problem Cases

1. Voth purchased a new Chrysler automobile on August 8, 1969. Chrysler warranted the vehicle against defects in material or workmanship for 12 months or 12,000 miles and stated that it would without charge repair or replace any part of the car defective under the warranty. While driving the vehicle, Voth began experiencing nausea, headaches, vertigo and other physical difficulties in the course of which he incurred substantial medical expenses. Voth had contracted lead poisoning which was attributed to gasoline fumes he inhaled. On July 2, 1970, he discovered that a defective gasoline vent tube was causing gasoline fumes to be gathered and dispersed in the car by the airconditioning system. On June 27, 1974, Voth brought suit for breach of warranty against Chrysler. Chrysler defended on the grounds that the action was barred by the four years statute of limitations in the U.C.C. Is Voth's suit barred by the statute of limitations?
2. On June 3, 1969, Nipkow and Slifka entered into a contract whereby Slifka agreed to buy 7,347 yards of material to be printed in accordance with its instructions. Slifka had until January 1, 1971, to accept the material but never did so. In March 1973, Nipkow made a private resale of the material but did not give Slifka notice of the resale. Nipkow then filed suit against Slifka for breach of contract and claimed as damages the difference between the contract price and the resale price under § 2–706. Is Nipkow entitled to this measure of damages?
3. On July 27, 1973, Henry Linke contracted to sell the Sawyer Farmer's Cooperative 5,000 bushels of wheat at $4.85 per bushel with delivery to be made between July 27, 1973 and October 1, 1973 at the option of the Cooperative. The contract provided that in the

event of default, the damages were to be the difference between the contract price and the market price on the "date this contract is closed by the buyer and the grain ordered in." On August 15, 1973 Linke's wife notified the Cooperative by telephone that Linke did not intend to make delivery of the wheat under the terms of the contract. The Cooperative did not accept or reject the repudiation. On October 1, 1973 the Cooperative contacted Linke and asked when delivery would be made, Linke replied it would not be delivered, maintaining the position taken by his wife on August 15. The Cooperative sued Linke, claiming as damages the difference between the market price on August 15 and the contract price; Linke claimed the market price on October 1 should be used. Which market price should be used?

4. On November 21, 1973, J. E. Littlefield purchased a number of cattle at an auction from the Ranchers Livestock Auction Company of Clovis, New Mexico and paid for the cattle by check drawn on a Colorado bank. The transaction was supposed to be a "cash sale." Littlefield had insufficient funds on deposit to cover the check at the time it was written or at any subsequent time. Littlefield shipped the cattle to the Tulsa Livestock Auction for resale. Rancher's Livestock discovered that Littlefield's bank would not honor his check, and on November 28 Rancher's Livestock put in the mail addressed to the Tulsa Livestock Auction a document entitled "Demand of Seller for Goods Received by Buyer on Credit While Insolvent on November 21, 1973." In the document, Rancher's Livestock claimed the right to return of the cattle under Section 2–702 of the Code. The notice was received by Tulsa Livestock Auction on December 3, 1973. Is Rancher's entitled to reclaim the cattle?
5. In November 1969, Sorenson Orchard Company contracted with Michigan Sugar Company for 800 bags of sugar to be used in processing frozen diced apples. Of the 800 bags, Sorenson returned 68 bags to Michigan Sugar because there was excessive "pan scale" in the bags and the 68 were replaced by Michigan Sugar. Although Sorenson's inspection noticed some "pan scale" in the remaining 732 bags, Sorenson used the bags anyway. Sorenson completed packing the apples for its customers, the apples were put in cold storage and Sorenson was paid for them. In the spring, Sorenson's customers began using the apples and rejected the batch after finding specks of "pan scale" in the apples. Over the next three years Sorenson sold the frozen apples at a great loss. Michigan Sugar sued Sorenson to recover the contract price of the sugar, and Sorenson counterclaimed for breach of warranty, seeking as consequential damages the profits it lost because of its customer's rejection of the frozen apples. Is Sorenson entitled to consequential damages?
6. In the spring of 1973 Cox, who owned a cotton gin, contracted with a number of cotton farmers to buy their 1973 cotton crop. Cox then contracted to sell 1,800 bales of the cotton to Kelly, a cotton broker at 34 to 36 cents per pound, who in turn contracted to sell the cotton to a mill. By the autumn of 1973, the price of cotton had doubled and a number of the farmers defaulted on their contracts because they did not want to sell cotton to Cox at the lower price. As a result, Cox was able to deliver only 1,120 bales to Kelly. Kelly purchased 680 bales of cotton at 78 cents per pound to replace those he was to have obtained from Cox. Kelly then sued Cox to recover as damages the difference between his cost of cover and the contract price. The trial court set the damages as the difference between the market price at the time of breach and the contract price. The court said there was no evidence of the market price at that time so it arbitrarily set it at 40 cents per pound. Kelly appealed, claiming the court incorrectly determined the damages. Is Kelly correct?
7. On September 21, 1970, Laclede Gas Company entered a long-term contract with Amoco Oil Company whereby Amoco was to supply Laclede's propane gas needs. Laclede operated

central propane gas distribution systems for various residential developments in Jefferson County, Missouri, under written agreements with the owners or developers of the developments. Because it was contemplated that the propane systems were eventually to be converted to natural gas, the agreement gave Laclede the right to cancel the contract on 30 days notice to Amoco of this occurrence. Laclede agreed to pay "the Wood River Area Posted Price for propane plus four cents per gallon" for the propane delivered to it under the agreement. During the winter of 1972–73 Amoco experienced a shortage of propane and placed all of its customers, including Laclede, on an allocation basis. Then in May 1973 Laclede inquired about a price increase of which it had been notified, Amoco cancelled the agreement, claiming it had the right to do so because the contract lacked "mutuality." While other sources of propane are available on a short-term basis, Laclede would not be able to find another seller willing to enter a long-term contract like the Amoco agreement. Laclede sued Amoco for breach of contract and sought specific performance. Should the court grant specific performance?

8. Myers purchased a new car from Thompson Chrysler-Plymouth Inc. He paid a total of $4,420.09, including $3,695 for the car, $55.45 in sales tax, $88.87 for life insurance, and $574.72 for finance charges. From the outset the car was faulty. Many of the car's features malfunctioned or did not work at all. After several return trips to the dealer, all of which failed to remedy the problems, it became evident that Myers had a valid claim for a breach of warranty. He then filed a lawsuit against the dealer seeking damages of $4,420.09. The dealer admitted liability but claimed that it was liable for only $3,695, the cash price of the car. How should the judge rule?

Mayor purchased a new car from Thompson Chrysler-Plymouth Inc. He paid a total of $4,420.97, including $3,595 for the car, $85.43 in sales tax, $66.92 for life insurance, and $673.72 for finance charges. From the time the car was in [illegible]. Many of the car's features malfunctioned or did not work at all. After several trips to the dealer, all of which failed to remedy the problems, it became evident that Mayor had a valid claim for a breach of warranty. He then filed a lawsuit against Thompson seeking damages of $4,420.97. The dealer admitted liability but claimed that it was liable only for $3,595, the cash price of the car. How should the judge rule?

PART IX

Commercial Paper

40

Negotiable Instruments

Background

Historical Background. History discloses that every civilization which engaged to an appreciable extent in commerce used some form of commercial paper. Probably the oldest type of commercial paper used in the carrying on of trade was the promissory note. Archaeologists in their excavations found a promissory note of the approximate date 2100 B.C. made payable to bearer. The merchants of Europe used commercial paper, which under the law merchant was negotiable, in the 13th and 14th centuries. However, it appears that such paper was not used in England until about A.D. 1600.

Uniform Commercial Code—Commercial Paper. Today in the United States the law of commercial paper—drafts, checks, certificates of deposit, and promissory notes—is embodied in the Uniform Commercial Code's section on commercial paper. Other negotiable documents, such as investment securities and documents of title, are treated in other sections of the Code. Essentially, the Code makes no drastic changes in those basic rules of commercial paper which have been recognized for centuries, but it has adopted modern terminology and has coordinated, clarified, and simplified the law.

Forms of Commercial Paper

Nature of Commercial Paper. Commercial paper is basically a contract for the payment of money and commonly is used as a substitute for money. A person who pays a debt by check is using commercial paper as a convenient substitute for paying the debt in cash. Commercial paper can also be used as a means of extending credit. For example, a person might give a creditor a promissory note promising to pay a debt in 30 days. Similarly, a bank which gives a depositor a certificate of deposit payable in one year has acknowledged that it owes the depositor a certain amount of money and promised to pay it back to the depositor at the end of the year.

Negotiable paper makes it possible to settle debts without the need to shift money itself between the parties to the debt. For example, A, a retailer in New York, contracts with B, a manufacturer in San Francisco, to purchase $10,000 worth of swim suits. If negotiable instruments did not exist, A would have to send or carry $10,000 in money across the country to B. This would be inconvenient and risky as well, because if the money was stolen along the way, A would be out the $10,000 unless A could locate the thief. The use of a negotiable instrument, such as a check, in which A orders its bank to pay $10,000 from A's account to B or to someone designated by B, allows A to make the payment in a very convenient way by sending a single piece of paper to B. If properly prepared and issued, the negotiable instrument is less risky because if it is stolen en route A's bank may not pay it to anyone but B or someone authorized by B. And, because B has the right to either collect the $10,000 or to transfer the right to do so to someone else, the instrument is a practical substitute for cash to B as well.

This chapter, and the three chapters that follow, will discuss the requirements that are necessary for a "contract" to qualify as a "negotiable instrument" and will develop and explain the characteristics that differentiate a "negotiable instrument" from a simple contract and lead to its widespread use as a substitute for money.

Kinds of Commercial Paper. There are two major classes of commercial paper: (1) promises to pay and (2) orders to pay. Promissory notes and certificates of deposit are promises to pay. Checks and drafts are orders to pay.

Promissory Note. The promissory note is the simplest form of commercial paper and is simply a promise to pay money. In a promissory note one person—known as the "maker"—makes an unconditional promise in writing to pay to another person—known as the "payee"—or at the payee's direction a certain sum of money either on demand or at some particular time in the future.

$ 460.00 July 15 *19* 78

Sixty days *after date* I *promise to pay to*

the order of James Smith

Four hundred sixty and no/100 ***Dollars***

at American National Bank, Chicago, Illinois 60606

Value received.

No. 143 *Due* 9/13/78 Henry Jenkins

The promissory note is primarily a credit instrument and is used in a variety of transactions in which credit is extended. If a person purchases an automobile or a home on time, the probability is that the seller will have the buyer execute a promissory note for the unpaid balance, secured by a security interest in the automobile, or by a real estate mortgage, deed of trust or land contract on the home. The terms of payment of the note will correspond with the terms of payment stated in the sales contract on the automobile or the home. Money also may be loaned on the basis of an unsecured note which evidences the amount of the loan and the terms of repayment.

Certificate of Deposit. A certificate of deposit is an acknowledgment by a bank that it has received a deposit of a specific sum of money and an engagement by the bank to pay the holder of the certificate the sum of money, usually with interest, at a specified time in the future.

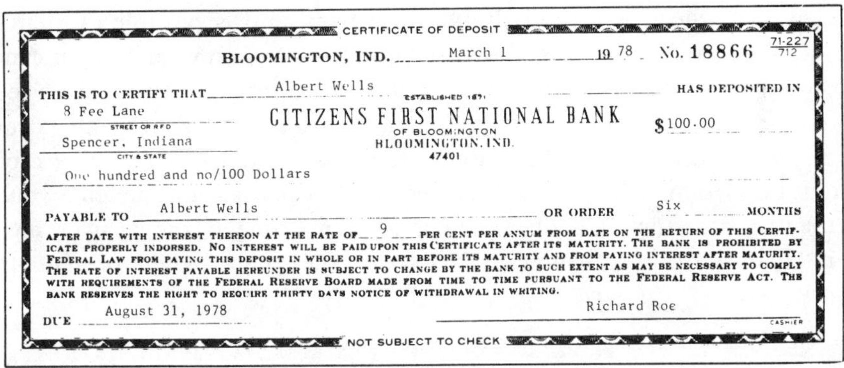

CERTIFICATE OF DEPOSIT

BLOOMINGTON, IND. March 1 19 78 No. 18866 71-227/712

THIS IS TO CERTIFY THAT Albert Wells HAS DEPOSITED IN

8 Fee Lane
STREET OR RFD
Spencer, Indiana
CITY & STATE

ESTABLISHED 1871
CITIZENS FIRST NATIONAL BANK
OF BLOOMINGTON
BLOOMINGTON, IND.
47401

$100.00

One hundred and no/100 Dollars

PAYABLE TO Albert Wells OR ORDER Six MONTHS AFTER DATE WITH INTEREST THEREON AT THE RATE OF 9 PER CENT PER ANNUM FROM DATE ON THE RETURN OF THIS CERTIFICATE PROPERLY INDORSED. NO INTEREST WILL BE PAID UPON THIS CERTIFICATE AFTER ITS MATURITY. THE BANK IS PROHIBITED BY FEDERAL LAW FROM PAYING THIS DEPOSIT IN WHOLE OR IN PART BEFORE ITS MATURITY AND FROM PAYING INTEREST AFTER MATURITY. THE RATE OF INTEREST PAYABLE HEREUNDER IS SUBJECT TO CHANGE BY THE BANK TO SUCH EXTENT AS MAY BE NECESSARY TO COMPLY WITH REQUIREMENTS OF THE FEDERAL RESERVE BOARD MADE FROM TIME TO TIME PURSUANT TO THE FEDERAL RESERVE ACT. THE BANK RESERVES THE RIGHT TO REQUIRE THIRTY DAYS NOTICE OF WITHDRAWAL IN WRITING.

DUE August 31, 1978

Richard Roe
CASHIER

NOT SUBJECT TO CHECK

Draft. A draft is a three-party instrument. In a draft one person—known as the "drawer"—issues an unconditional order in writing to a second person—known as the "drawee"—to pay a third person—known as the "payee"—a certain sum in money. It has a variety of uses. If B owes A a past-due obligation, A may draw a draft for the amount of the debt naming B as drawee and himself or his bank as payee and send the draft to B's bank for presentment and collection. In freight shipments in which the terms are "cash on delivery" it is a common practice for the seller to ship the goods to the buyer on an order bill of lading consigned to himself at the place of delivery, endorse the bill of lading, attach a draft naming the buyer drawee, and then send them through banking channels to the buyer's bank where the draft is presented for payment and where on payment the bill of lading is delivered to the buyer. The result: the buyer gets the goods and the seller gets his money. If credit is extended, the same procedure is followed except a time draft is used, that is, a draft payable at some future time. In such a transaction the buyer will "accept" the draft instead of paying it. To accept the draft he writes his name across its face thereby obligating himself to pay the amount of the draft when due.

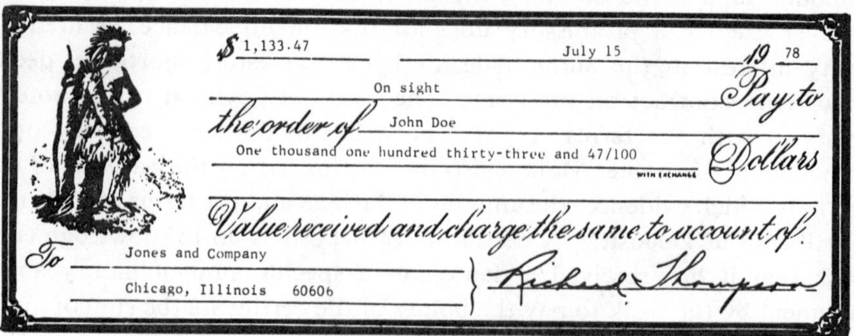
$1,133.47 July 15 19 78
On sight Pay to
the order of John Doe
One thousand one hundred thirty-three and 47/100 Dollars
WITH EXCHANGE
Value received and charge the same to account of
To Jones and Company
Chicago, Illinois 60606
Richard Thompson

Check. A check is a draft drawn on a bank and is payable on demand. It is the most widely used of the various forms of commercial paper, and is used in lieu of money. Neither drafts nor checks are drawn on drawees or banks unless there is some relation existing between the drawer and drawee which justifies the drawer in drawing the draft or check. The check plays such an important role in today's society that each state has enacted statutes making the drawing of a check on a bank a crime if the drawer has no credit balance or one insufficient to cover the check when presented for payment.

No. 1046
CHICAGO, July 15 19 78
PAY TO THE ORDER OF Harry J. Johnson $ 298.00
THE SUM 298 DOL'S 00 CTS DOLLARS
THE TERMINAL NATIONAL BANK OF CHICAGO
Robert Clark

SUMMARY

Commercial paper is basically a promise to pay money. If the instrument satisfies certain formal requirements, it will be negotiable and will have certain characteristics which will distinguish it from simple contracts. Drafts and checks are orders to pay and certificates of deposit and notes are promises to pay.

The note is the simplest form of commercial paper. It is a promise by the maker to pay a sum certain in money to the payee on demand or at some future time. A certificate of deposit is an acknowledgment by a bank of the receipt of money and a promise to repay it. It is used by banks in connection with time deposits. A draft is an order by the drawer addressed to the drawee ordering him to pay the payee a sum certain in money at the sight or at some future time. A check is a draft drawn on a bank and payable on demand. It is used in lieu of money to make all types of payments.

Benefits of Negotiability

Rights of Assignee of Contract. If one party to a contract assigns his rights in the contract to another person, the assignee can acquire no greater rights than the assignor has at the time of the assignment. Thus taking an assignment of a contract involves assuming certain risks because the assignee may not be aware of the nature and scope of any defenses the party liable on the contract may have against the assignor. The assignment of contracts was discussed in detail in Chapter 14.

Rights of Holder of a Negotiable Instrument. If a contract for the payment of money is in the proper form so as to qualify as a "negotiable instrument," then any person to whom the instrument is negotiated and who can qualify as a "holder in due course"[1] takes the instrument free from any "personal" defenses the drawer or maker may have against payment of the instrument.

A holder in due course is still, however, subject to defenses that go to whether the instrument was a valid instrument—such as whether it was induced by extreme duress or whether the maker or drawer had the legal capacity to create a negotiable instrument. In addition, the Federal Trade Commission has recently adopted regulations which have the effect of preserving against even a holder in due course any claim or defense a consumer, who buys goods or services for personal, family or household use, may have against the seller.

The basic holder in due course concept is illustrated by the following example: suppose that wholesaler induces retailer to sign a nonnegotiable contract whereby retailer promises to pay wholesaler $100 in return for some defective goods and wholesaler then assigns the contract to Finch, who pays value for it and takes it without notice or knowledge of the defective goods. When the $100 is due, Finch demands payment, retailer refuses to pay and Finch brings suit. Retailer can set up wholesaler's breach of warranty as a defense, and the defense is good against Finch. Suppose that retailer, instead of executing a nonnegotiable contract for the $100, issues to wholesaler his negotiable promissory note, and wholesaler negotiates the note to Finch, who take it as a holder in due course. Retailer then does not pay the note when due and

[1] The requirements for a holder in due course are set out in Section 3–302 of the Uniform Commercial Code and discussed in detail in the next chapter.

Finch sues on the note. The defense that retailer has against wholesaler for breach of warranty would not be a defense to the instrument in the hands of Finch. Thus Finch would be entitled to collect it from retailer, and Albert would have to make his breach of warranty claim against wholesaler in a separate action.

If Bell should forge Albert's name to a negotiable instrument, and negotiate the instrument to a person who could qualify as a holder in due course, the defense of forgery would be available to Albert in a suit by such holder. However, the holder could sue Bell as Bell is liable on the instrument because he signed it.

A person taking a negotiable instrument as a holder in due course takes it subject to only two major risks: (1) the ability of the holder to collect from the parties to the instrument and (2) the validity of the instrument in its inception. This is a much preferable position to that of the assignee of a nonnegotiable contract who takes the contract subject to all outstanding defenses between the parties.

SUMMARY

The assignee of a contract acquires no greater rights than his assignor has.

If the holder of a negotiable instrument is a holder in due course, he holds the instrument free from personal defenses available to the original parties, but he does not hold the instrument free from real defenses, that is, defenses which go the validity of the instrument in its inception.

Formal Requirements for Negotiability

Basic Requirements. An instrument must satisfy certain formal requirements if it is to be negotiable. If the writing does not fulfill these requirements, it is a nonnegotiable instrument and will be treated as a simple contract rather than as a negotiable instrument. The formal requirements for negotiability may be stated briefly as follows:

1. The instrument must be in writing and signed by the maker (if it is a certificate of deposit or a note) or by the drawer (if it is a draft or check);
2. it must contain an unconditional promise (if it is a note or certificate of deposit) or an unconditional order (if it is a draft or check) to pay a sum certain in money;
3. it must be payable on demand or at a definite time; and
4. it must be payable to order or bearer (3–104[1]).[2]

[2] The numbers in the parentheses refer to the sections of the Uniform Commercial Code, 1972.

Importance of Form. Whether or not an instrument is so drafted that it satisfies these formal requirements is important for one and only one purpose, and that is for the purpose of determining whether the instrument is negotiable or nonnegotiable. Negotiability should not be confused with validity or collectibility. If the instrument is negotiable, the law of negotiable instruments will control in determining the rights and liabilities of the parties to the instrument. If the instrument is nonnegotiable, the general rules of contract law will control.

An instrument which fulfills all of the formal requirements is a negotiable instrument even though it is void, voidable, unenforceable, or uncollectible. Negotiability is a matter of form and nothing else. If a person gives an instrument in payment of a gambling debt in a state which has a statute declaring that any instrument or promise given in payment of a gambling debt is null and void and of no force and effect, the instrument is a negotiable instrument if it is negotiable in form even though it is absolutely void. Also, an instrument which is negotiable in form is a negotiable instrument even though signed by an infant. The fact that the infant may set up infancy as a defense if suit is brought to enforce the instrument is immaterial. The instrument is voidable, but it is negotiable.

An instrument which is negotiable in form although void or voidable may give rise to liability on the part of a person who endorses and negotiates it or transfers it without endorsement whereas if it were nonnegotiable liability to the same extent would not be imposed on an assignor of the instrument.

Language of Negotiable Instrument. In determining the negotiable character of an instrument the language of the instrument must be carefully analyzed to determine whether or not it satisfies all the requirements for negotiability as set out in Article 3 of the Code. There are no technical words which must be used in drafting a negotiable instrument.

I promise to pay Bearer one hundred dollars.
(Signed) Albert Adams

is a negotiable instrument.

This does not follow the phraseology customarily used in the drafting of a promissory note, but it does satisfy all of the requirements of the Code for a negotiable note.

SUMMARY

An instrument, in order to be negotiable, must comply with certain formal requirements which are set out in Section 3–104 of the Code.

The form of the instrument serves only in determining whether the law of negotiable commercial paper or general contract law will control in determining the rights and liabilities of the parties.

No particular technical terms need be used in drafting an instrument which is to be negotiable.

In Writing and Signed

Writing. To be negotiable, an instrument must be in writing and signed by the maker or drawer. An instrument is in writing if it is handwritten, typed, printed or otherwise intentionally reduced to some tangible form (1–201[46]).

The reason for the requirement that an instrument be in writing is that only something having tangible form can be used as a medium of exchange in the business world. Consequently, if a promise to pay is to be easily transferable, it must be given some tangible form, and a writing evidencing the promise is the most convenient way to satisfy the necessity for tangible form. No particular type of writing is required; no particular material is designed to which the writing shall appear; all that is required is that the instrument be in writing. A person could draw a valid negotiable instrument on a piece of wrapping paper in lead pencil. It would be poor business practice, but it would fulfill the statutory requirement that the instrument be in writing.

Signed. The requirement that an instrument be signed can be met by the use of any symbol that the maker or drawer has executed or adopted with the intention to authenticate the instrument as his own. The common practice is for the maker or drawer to write his name on the instrument but this is not required. A typed or rubber stamp signature is sufficient, and a person who cannot write his name might make an "X" and have the act witnessed by someone else.

SUMMARY

To be negotiable, an instrument must be in writing. No particular form of writing is required.

The instrument must be signed by the maker if it is a note or a certificate of deposit or by the drawer if it is a draft or a check. Any mark made on the instrument with the intent of authenticating it is sufficient to satisfy the requirement that the instrument be signed.

Unconditional Promise or Order

Requirement of Promise or Order. If an instrument is a draft or a check, it must contain an order to pay. The courts have held that a simple request to pay, as a favor, to the drawer of the instrument is not an order to pay; however, if the language used connotes a demand, even though framed in polite language, it is sufficient as an order to pay.

If an instrument is a note, or certificate of deposit, it must contain language which connotes an unconditional promise to pay. A mere acknowledgment of a debt is not sufficient to make the instrument negotiable, but an acknowledgment of a debt with words indicating that the debt is to be paid is a sufficient promise to pay. For example, "I owe you $100" has been held not to be a promise to pay, but "Due John Jones or order $100 payable December 1st" has been held to be a promise to pay.

Promise or Order Must Be Unconditional. If the promise does not bind the promisor to pay in all events, it is a conditional promise, and the instrument is nonnegotiable. Likewise, if the order does not demand the drawee to pay in all events, it is conditional, and the instrument is nonnegotiable. Whether or not a promise or order is unconditional must be determined from an interpretation of the language of the instrument. An instrument, to be negotiable, must be so drafted that, by reading it, the nature and extent of the parties' obligations can be determined. If an instrument is so drafted that it is necessary to read some other document, not a part of the instrument but referred to in it, in order to determine the obligations of the parties to the instrument, such instrument is not negotiable.

For example, an instrument which includes a statement such as "payment to be made subject to the terms of a mortgage dated August 30, 1977" is nonnegotiable; but a statement in an instrument such as "This note is secured by a mortgage dated August 30, 1977" does not affect the negotiable character of the instrument. In determining the rights of the parties to the first instrument, a person would have to read the instrument and the mortgage referred to in the instrument.

The reference to the mortgage in the second instrument merely states a fact—the instrument is secured by a mortgage—and the rights and duties of the parties to the instrument are in no way affected by the terms of the mortgage. In determining the rights of the parties, there would in such a case be no reason to refer to the terms of the mortgage.

Express Conditions. If the promise or order is expressly conditioned on the happening of some event, the instrument is nonnegotiable. For example, a promise to pay "if I am elected to Congress" is clearly conditional. If the instrument contains a stipulation which, under the accepted rules of contract law, would be interpreted as an express condition, the instrument is nonnegotiable.

Special Provisions of the Code. The Code sets out certain provisions which may be included in an instrument without affecting the instrument's negotiability.

A statement of the consideration for which the instrument is given, or a statement of the transaction which gave rise to the instrument does not affect its negotiability. For example, a negotiable instrument may contain a notation stating that it was given in payment of last month's rent or next month's rent or a statement that the instrument is given in payment of the purchase price of goods.

Where an instrument indicates a particular fund to be debited or any other fund or source from which reimbursement is expected, such an indication or provision does not make the instrument nonnegotiable. For example checks might contain the notation "payroll account." Such statements on instruments are interpreted as directions for record-keeping purposes and not as conditioning the promise or order. However, a promise or order to pay out of a fund will condition the promise or order since the instrument does not carry the general obligation of the maker or drawer; the obligation to pay is, in effect, conditioned on there being a sufficient balance in the fund to cover the instrument. Because one would have to go outside the instrument to learn whether or not the balance was sufficient, an instrument containing such a provision would not be negotiable even though the fund would be sufficient. This rule does not apply to instruments issued by a government or governmental agency or unit; it is permissible for an instrument issued by a government or governmental agency or unit to contain a provision stating that payment shall be made out of a particular fund or from the proceeds of a particular source (3–105).

SUMMARY

A draft or check, to be negotiable, must contain a promise to pay. The order or promise must be unconditional. Whether a promise or order is or is not unconditional is a matter of the interpretation of the language used. An instrument is not negotiable if the promise or order to pay is expressly conditioned.

A promise or order governed by the terms of another instrument or a promise to pay out of a particular fund is not an unconditional promise.

Holly Hill Acres, Ltd. v. Charter Bank of Gainesville

17 UCC Rep. 144 (Ct. App. Fla. 1975)

This was an action brought by the Charter Bank of Gainesville (plaintiff) as the assignee of a note against the maker of the note, Holly Hill Acres, Ltd. (defendant) to collect the note. Summary judgment granted to the Bank. Reversed on appeal.

On April 28, 1972, Holly Hill executed a promissory note and mortgage and delivered them to Rogers and Blythe. The note contained the following stipulation:

> This note with interest is secured by a mortgage on real estate, of even date herewith, made by the maker hereof in favor of the said payee, and shall be construed and enforced according to the laws of the State of Florida. *The terms of said mortgage are by this reference made a part hereof.* [Emphasis supplied].

Rogers and Blythe assigned the note to the Charter Bank to secure payment of an obligation they owned to the Charter Bank. When the Holly Hill note was not paid, Charter Bank brought suit to collect the note and to foreclose the mortgage. Holly Hill asserted as a defense that fraud on the part of Rogers and Blythe induced the sale which gave rise to the note and mortgage. Charter Bank contended that it was a holder in due course and thus not subject to the defense of fraud. The trial court held that Charter Bank was a holder in due course.

SCHEB, JUDGE. The note having incorporated the terms of the purchase money mortgage was not negotiable. The Bank was not a holder in due course, therefore Holly Hill was entitled to raise against the bank any defenses which could be raised between Holly Hill and Rogers and Blythe.

The note, incorporating by reference the terms of the mortgage, did not contain the unconditional promise to pay required by § 3–104(1)(b). Rather, the note falls within the scope of § 3–105(2)(a). Although negotiability is now governed by the Uniform Commercial Code, this was the Florida view even before the U.C.C. was adopted.

The Bank relies upon *Scott v. Taylor,* as authority for the proposition that its note is negotiable. *Scott,* however, involved a note being secured by mortgage. Mention of a mortgage in a note is a common commercial practice and such reference in itself does not impede the negotiability of the note. There is, however, a significant difference in a note stating that it is "secured by a mortgage" from one which provides, "the terms of said mortgage are by this reference made a part hereof." In the former instance the note merely refers to a separate agreement which does not impede its negotiability, while in the latter instance the note is rendered nonnegotiable. See § § 3–105(2)(a); 3–119.

As a general rule the assignee of a mortgage securing a nonnegotiable note, even though a bona fide purchaser for value, takes subject to all defenses available as against the mortgagees.

Sum Certain in Money

Sum Certain. The promise or order in an instrument must be to pay a sum certain in money. A sum is certain if it is possible to compute from the information stated in the instrument the amount which will be required to discharge the instrument at any given time. The Code permits an instrument to state different rates of interest before or after default; it also allows provisions which provide for a discount or an addition if the note is paid early or if it is paid late. The key element is that a person can compute the amount that is due on the instrument at any given time.

A clause providing for the payment of the costs of collection or an attorney's fee on default does not render the instrument nonnegotiable. Although these charges cannot be predetermined, business practice justifies their inclusion in the instrument without their making the sum payable uncertain (3–106).

Payable in Money. An instrument is payable in money if it is payable in a medium of exchange authorized or adopted by a domestic or foreign government as part of its currency (1–201[24]). If the holder has the option of accepting something other than money, the negotiability of the instrument is not affected, but if the party obligated to pay the instrument has the option of doing something other than paying money, the instrument is not negotiable.

SUMMARY

Under the provisions of the Code a sum is a sum certain if the amount necessary to discharge the instrument at any specific time can be computed from the terms stated in the instrument. Provisions for the payment of collection costs or attorneys' fees are permitted in negotiable instruments.

Payable on Demand or at a Definite Time

Time of Payment. If an instrument is to qualify as a negotiable instrument, it must be payable either on demand or at a definite time. The reason for this requirement is to assure that the time when the instrument will be payable can be determined with certainty. If an instrument is payable only on the happening of some event, the time of occurrence of which is uncertain, then it cannot be a negotiable instrument; it would not matter that the event had already occurred (3–109).

Payable on Demand. An instrument is payable on demand if: (1) it states that it is payable "on demand," "at sight," or "on presentation" (that is when it is presented for payment to the person who is obligated to pay it) or (2) if no time for payment is stated. Because no time of payment is stated on the common check, a check is considered to be payable on demand (3–108).

Payable at a Definite Time. An instrument is payable at a definite time if:

1. it is payable on or before a stated date, such as "on July 1, 1980" or "on or before July 1, 1980";

2. it is payable at a fixed time after a stated date such as "30 days after date," provided that the instrument is dated; or
3. it is payable at a fixed time "after sight" which is in effect a provision that it will be paid at a fixed time after it is presented to the drawee for acceptance.

If an instrument which provides it is payable "30 days after date" is not dated, then it is not payable at a fixed date and is not negotiable; however, this defect may be cured if the holder of the instrument fills in the date before he negotiates it to someone else (3–115).

Under the Code, a provision in an instrument which permits the time for payment to be accelerated at the option of the maker or extended at the option of the holder does not affect negotiability of the instrument so long as the time for payment can be determined with certainty (3–109).

SUMMARY

An instrument is payable on demand if it is stated to be payable on "demand," at "sight," or on "presentment," or if no time of payment is stated. An instrument is payable at a definite time if it is payable on or before a stated date or at a fixed period after sight. A provision in an instrument giving the parties the right to accelerate the time of payment, or giving the holder the right to extend the time of payment does not affect its negotiability. An instrument payable only upon or after the happening of an act or event, the time of occurrence of which is uncertain, is not payable at a definite time.

Payable to Order or Bearer

Necessity of Words of Negotiability. To be negotiable, an instrument must be payable to order or to bearer. Thus an instument that provides "pay to the order of Sarah Smith" or "pay to Sarah Smith or bearer" could be negotiable, while one that provides "pay to Sarah Smith" could not. The use of the words "pay to the order of" and "or bearer" show that the person who executed the instrument intends to issue a negotiable instrument and is not restricting payment of that instrument to Sarah Smith but rather is willing to pay someone else he is ordered by Sarah Smith to pay. In issuing a negotiable instrument, the person who makes or draws the instrument is giving the payee a chance, by negotiating it to a holder in due course, to cut off certain personal defenses the maker or drawer may have against the payee.

Payable to Order. An instrument is payable to order if it is payable "to the order" or "to the assigns" of any person who is specified with reasonable certainty (3–110). For example, an instrument drawn payable "to the order of John Jones" or "to John Jones or order" or "to John Jones or assigns" would be payable to order.

Instruments can be drawn payable to the order of two or more payees together or in the alternative. For example, one could be payable "to the order of John Jones and Henry Smith" in which case the instrument may be negotiated, discharged or inforced only by both of the payees. However, if it was payable "to the order of John Jones or Henry Smith," either payee could negotiate, discharge or inforce it.

Payable to Bearer. An instrument is payable to bearer if it is payable: (1) to "bearer"; (2) to the "order of bearer"; (3) to a specified person or bearer (for example "to John Jones or bearer"); (4) to "cash"; (5) to the "order of cash"; or (6) any other manner that does not indicate a specific person (3–111).

An instrument payable to bearer is known as "bearer paper." As bearer paper it can be negotiated without indorsement (3–202[1]).

SUMMARY

An instrument is payable to order if it is drawn payable "to the order" or "to the assigns" of any person who is specified with reasonable certainty. An instrument is bearer paper if it is payable to bearer or to "cash" or to "the order of cash."

Special Terms

Additional Terms and Omissions. Businesspersons and banks use many special forms of commercial paper drafted to serve their particular needs. Such forms may include terms which have no effect on the negotiability of the instrument. Likewise instruments are sometimes drafted which omit terms customarily included in standard forms of the instrument but their omission in no way affects the validity or negotiability of the instrument.

It is a common practice to state in the instrument the place where the instrument is drawn and/or where it is payable. The place where the instrument is drawn is usually stated together with the date of issue, for example, "Chicago, Ill., Sept. 26, 1978." And the place where it is to be paid is generally noted on the instrument by such a phrase as: "Payable at First Bank of Detroit, Mich." The negotiability of the instrument is not affected, however, by the omission of these details (3–112[1][a]).

A term authorizing the confession of judgment on the instrument when due does not affect the negotiability of the instrument. However, a clause which authorizes confession of judgment prior to the due date of the note and a demand for payment has been held by some courts to render the note nonnegotiable.

The negotiability of a draft or check is not affected by a term providing that the payee by indorsing or cashing the draft or check acknowledges full satisfaction of an obligation of the drawer. Such a term is frequently included in a draft or check issued by an insurance company in payment of a loss claim (3–112[1][f]).

The negotiability of an instrument is not affected by the fact that it is undated, antedated, or postdated. Where the instrument is antedated or postdated, the time when it is payable is determined by the stated date if the instrument is payable on demand or at a fixed period after date (3–114).

Ambiguous Terms. The general rule of interpretation, that handwritten terms control typewritten and printed terms and that typewritten terms control printed terms, applies to commercial paper. If there is a conflict between the amount written on the instrument and the figures, the words control unless the words are ambiguous in which event the figures control.

If an instrument provides for the payment of interest but the rate is not stated, the rate payable is the judgment rate at the place of payment, and the interest is computed from the date of the instrument, or if it is undated from the date of issue of the instrument.

SUMMARY

Printed forms for commercial paper may contain certain clauses for business reasons which do not affect the negotiability of the instruments.

If there are ambiguous terms in a negotiable instrument, the general rule of interpretation is that handwritten terms control typewritten and printed terms and that typewritten terms control printed terms. If there is a conflict between words and figures, the words control unless they are ambiguous in which case the figures control.

Newman v. Manufacturers National Bank

152 N.W.2d 564 (Ct. App. Mich. 1967)

This was an action by Newman (plaintiff) against Manufacturers National Bank (defendant) on the grounds that Manufacturers had improperly paid two of Newman's checks totalling $1,200. Judgment for Manufacturers National Bank and Newman appealed. Affirmed.

In 1955, Newman drew the two checks payable to Belle Epstein but left them undated. There was a printed dateline on the checks which read "Detroit, Mich. ———— 195—" but Newman never filled it in. Newman claimed that over the next four years he had paid all but $400 of the $1,200 debt personally to Epstein and that she told him she had destroyed the two checks. Then on April 17, 1964, the checks were cashed under the endorsement of Belle Epstein. By that time someone had written in the date April 16, 1964 but the original printed figures "195—" remained clearly visible. Newman objected to having his account charged on the grounds the bank had not used ordinary care in paying checks that were stale and altered on their face.

HOLBROOK, JUDGE. The two checks were dated April 16, 1964. It is true that the dates were completed in pen and ink subsequent to the date of issue. However, this was not known by Bank. Bank had a right to rely on the dates appearing on the checks as being correct. Section 3–114 provides in part as follows:

(1) The negotiability of an instrument is not affected by the fact that it is undated, antedated or postdated.

(3) Where the instrument or any signature thereon is dated, the date is presumed to be correct.

Also (3–115) provides in part as follows:

The following rules apply to every instrument: . . .

(b) Handwritten terms control typewritten and printed terms, and typewritten control printed.

Without notice to the contrary, Bank was within its rights to assume that the dates were proper and filled in by Newman or someone authorized by him.

Newman admitted at trial that Bank acted in good faith in honoring the two checks of Newman's in question, and therefore Bank's good faith is not in issue.

In order to determine if defendant bank's action in honoring Newman's two checks under the facts present herein constituted an exercise of proper procedure, we turn to Article 4 of the U.C.C. Section 4–401 provides as follows:

(1) As against its customer, a bank may charge against his account any item which is otherwise properly payable from that account even though the charge creates an overdraft.

(2) A bank which in good faith makes payment to a holder may charge the indicated account of its customer according to

(*a*) the original tenor of his altered item; or

(*b*) the tenor of his completed item, even though the bank knows the item has been completed unless the bank has notice that the completion was improper.

Electronic Banking

The Checkless Society. In recent years developments in the computer and electronics fields have been used with increasing frequency by banks to transfer funds electronically rather than by the use of paper drafts and checks. While the coming of the so-called cashless or checkless society is marked by advances, retreats and shifts in direction, the new forms of conducting monetary transactions have raised many questions regarding the legal rules that will be applied to them. The law in this area is in an embryonic stage and will develop over time as the commercial practices themselves develop. The differences of opinion between the U.S. District Court for the Northern District of Illinois and of the Seventh Circuit Court of Appeals in *State of Illinois v. Continental Illinois National Bank,* which follow this section of the textbook, show conflicting viewpoints as to whether negotiable instruments law should be applied to some of the electronic transactions. Neither court's viewpoint represents the last word on the subject, but they do show several ways the new practices might be treated.

State of Illinois v. Continental Illinois National Bank
19 UCC Rep. 537 (7th Cir. 1976)

This was an action brought by the Illinois State Banking Commissioner (plaintiff) against the Continental Illinois National Bank (defendant) to obtain a declaratory judgment that unmanned computer terminals which permit customers using bank cards to withdraw cash, make deposits, transfer funds or make payments constituted "branch banks." The U.S. District Court held that the terminals amounted to branch banking, but rejected the contention of the Commissioner that use of the machines to withdraw money from a customer's account constituted the "cashing of a check." The Court of Appeals reversed on this question, holding that it did constitute the cashing of a check.

Continental operated several so-called Customer Bank Communication Terminals (CBCTs) which were unmanned terminals connected directly with Continental's main office computer. Customers of the bank insert a specially coded card into the terminal, enter an identification number, and then using keys on the transaction keyboard indicate the type and amounts of the transactions they wish to conduct. The customers may:

a. Withdraw cash (in the amount of $25.00 or any multiple thereof, up to $100.00) from their savings, checking or credit card accounts;

b. Deposit checks or currency in a checking or savings account. At the time of the transaction, the customer is given a receipt at the CBCT indicating the amount and date of the deposit; it is not credited to his account and he may not draw on it until it is received and verified at the main banking premises;

c. Transfer funds between accounts: checking to savings, credit card to checking, or savings to checking; and

d. Make payments on Continental Bank installment loans or credit card charges.

When the transactions are completed the customer receives a receipt and, if he has withdrawn cash from his account, he receives packets containing the cash. A copy of the receipt is retained in the machine and the transactions are later verified by bank employees.

PER CURIAM. The district court here based its conclusion on the functions of CBCT as to the withdrawing of cash and the payment of installments on loans upon the provisions of the Uniform Commercial Code (UCC) and § 3–104(2) which declares a check to be a negotiable instrument drawn on a bank and payable on demand; a writing signed by the maker or drawer and containing an unconditional promise or order to pay a sum certain in money; with negotiability being the essential characteristic of a check. From this the district court concluded that a card inserted into the CBCT machine to secure money was not the cashing of a check within the meaning of UCC or in the common understanding of check cashing. We cannot agree. This is exalting form over substance. The check is merely the means used by the bank to attain the desired objective, i.e., the payment of the money to its customer. The card serves the same purpose as the check. It is an order on the bank. Any order to pay which is properly executed by a customer, whether it be check, card or electronic device, must be recognized as a routine banking function when used as here. The relationship between the bank and its customer is the same. Indeed, the trial court here recognized this when it characterized a CBCT withdrawal as the "functional equivalent" of a written check. And Continental Bank gives the card transaction the same significance:

> The EFTS (Electronic Funds Transfer Systems) at issue in the present case are, *extensions* of the principle of immediate access to customer accounts *in a manner dispensing with underlying paper such a checks.* [Emphasis added. See brief of the Bank supporting its motion for summary judgment, page 8.]

Moreover, although the UCC defines a check as a negotiable instrument, it also provides, § 3–104(3):

> As used in other Articles of this Act, and as the context may require, the terms . . . "check" . . . may refer to instruments which are not negotiable within this Article as well as instruments which are so negotiable.

Just as a transfer of funds by cable or telegraph is in law a check, despite the non-negotiability of the cable, the card here for the purpose of withdrawing cash is a check. What must be remembered is that the foundation of the relationship between the bank and its customer is the former's agreement to pay out the customer's money according to the latter's order. There are many ways in which an order may be given and one way of late is by computer record. And the Ninth Circuit accepts the same concept that computer impulses constitute sufficient writing to meet the order test.

Problem Cases

1. Is the following a negotiable instrument?

   February 26, 1973

   Subject to Approval of Title
   Pay to the Order of Vernon Butterfield $1,997.90.
   The Culver Company
   By A. M. Culver

2. An instrument otherwise negotiable contained the following provision: "This note is given in payment for merchandise and is to be liquidated by payments received on account of sale of such merchandise." Is this a negotiable instrument?

3. A promissory note contains the following language:

   By execution of this document the undersigned hereby acknowledges and promises to pay to the order of Scott Hudgens Realty & Mortgage, Inc., a Delaware corporation, at Atlanta, Georgia, or at such other place or to such other party or parties as the holder hereof may from time to time designate, the principal sum of three thousand dollars ($3,000). This amount is due and payable upon evidence of an acceptable permanent loan of $290,000 for Barton-Ludwig Cains Hill Place Office Building, Atlanta, Georgia, from one of SHRAM's investors and upon acceptance of the commitment by the undersigned.

   Is this note a "negotiable instrument?"

4. An installment sales contract that otherwise would qualify as a negotiable instrument contains a clause stating that the holder of the contract can pay taxes, assessments, and insurance if the obligor does not and then recover what he pays from the obligor. Would this clause make the contract nonnegotiable?

5. Briggs signed a note as maker which contained a clause which permitted acceleration of the maturity date of the note in the event the holder deemed himself insecure and which authorized confession of judgment against the maker "if this note is not paid at any stated or accelerated maturity." Briggs contends that the note is nonnegotiable because of this clause. Is his contention correct?

6. Sylvia signed a note dated May 25, 1963, obligating him to pay to Ferri or to her order $3,000 "within ten (10) years after date." Is this a negotiable instrument?

7. A promissory note reads in part:

   Ninety Days after date, I, we, or either of us, promise to pay to the order of *Three Thousand Four Hundred Ninety Eight and 45/100* ------Dollars."

   The italicized words and symbols are typed in and the remainder is printed. There are no blanks on the face of the instrument as any unused space has been filled in with hyphens. Is this note "order paper" or is it "bearer paper?"

8. Credit Union brought suit to collect $19,896.01 on the following note:

   Note No. 22724 Account No. 3329–99

   $19,896.01 May 7, 1971

   For Value received, I/We jointly and severally, promise to pay to the *EAST TEXAS TEACHERS CREDIT UNION* Credit Union, or order, at *LONGVIEW, TEXAS* the sum of *Nineteen hundred eight hundred ninety-six*—and *01*/100 Dollars, payable in 1 installment of *Seven thousand*—and *No*/100 Dollars, and *1* installment of *Seven thousand*—and *No*/100 Dollars, and 1 installment of $6,803.48 due September 15, 1971

(X) which includes principal and interest

( ) plus interest

on the unpaid balances at the rate of One percent per month, both before and after maturity, the installments to be paid (X) monthly ( ) semi-monthly ( ) weekly ( ) bi-weekly beginning *June 15, 1971*

Collateral: *Shares, 170 head mixed cattle*

* * * * *

Signature of Witnesses	Signature of Maker And Comakers	Address
________	X John L. Wall	________

In his defense Wall contended that there was an ambiguity between the figures and the words of the amount of the note and that it should be resolved so as to reach a principal sum of $2,796.01 ($1,900 plus $896.01). Should the court agree with Wall's construction of the amount of the note?

41

Negotiation and Holder in Due Course

Negotiation

Nature of Negotiation. Negotiation is the transfer of an instrument in such a way that the transferee becomes a "holder." A "holder" of a negotiable instrument is a person who is in possession of an instrument that is either drawn, issued or indorsed to him, to his order, to bearer or in blank (1–201[20]).[1] The formal requirements for negotiation are very simple: If the instrument is payable to order, then it can be negotiated by "delivery" after any necessary indorsements are added; if the instrument is payable to bearer, then it can be negotiated merely by "delivery" (3–302[1]).

Nature of Indorsement. An indorsement of an instrument is made by adding the signature of the holder, either by the holder or on his behalf, on the instrument or on a paper firmly affixed to it (3–202[2]). If the back of an instrument is written full of indorsements, further indorsements should be made on a paper attached firmly to the instrument. Such a paper is called an "allonge."

To be effective as a negotiation an indorsement must convey the entire instrument or any unpaid residue. If it purports to convey less, it operates only as a partial assignment (3–202[3]). This rule is based on consideration of practical business policy. One who has issued a negotiable instrument should not be required to make piecemeal payments to several persons. It is not an uncommon practice for a large obligation to be evidenced by a series of notes, thus enabling the holder to negotiate portions of the debt to different persons. Suppose, for instance, that A borrows $10,000 from B. A might instead of

[1] The numbers in the parentheses refer to the sections of the Uniform Commercial Code, 1972.

giving B a $10,000 note, give him ten $1,000 notes. B would then be in a position to negotiate a $1,000 note to each of ten different persons.

Wrong or Misspelled Name. In indorsing an instrument the indorser should spell the name in the indorsement the same as it appears in the instrument. If the name is misspelled or is one other than his own the indorser may indorse in that name or his own, but a person who is paying or giving value for the instrument may require the indorser to sign both names (3–203).

For example if Joan Ash is issued a check payable to the order of "Joanne Ashe" she may indorse the check either "Joan Ash" or "Joanne Ashe." However if she has taken the check to a bank to cash, the bank may require her to sign both "Joanne Ashe" and "Joan Ash."

Transfer of an Instrument. When an instrument is transferred the transferee obtains those rights the transferor had. However, a transferee who has himself been a party to any fraud or illegality affecting the instrument or who as a prior holder has notice of a defense or claim against it cannot improve his position by taking from a later holder in due course (3–201[1]). For example, suppose that Axe through fraudulent representations induces Bell to execute a negotiable note payable to Axe, and Axe then negotiates the instrument to Clark, who takes as a holder in due course. If Axe thereafter takes the instrument for value from Clark, Axe cannot acquire Clark's rights as a holder in due course. Axe was a party to the fraud which induced the instrument, and the holder of an instrument cannot improve his position by negotiating such instrument and then reacquiring it.

Transfer of Order Instrument. If an order instrument is transferred without indorsement, the instrument has not been negotiated and the transferee does not become a holder in due course because he cannot qualify as a holder. However, unless the parties have otherwise agreed, any transfer for value of an instrument not payable to bearer gives the transferee the right to have the unqualified indorsement of the transferor, and should the transferor refuse to indorse the instrument with an unqualified indorsement the transferee would be entitled to a decree ordering the transferor to so indorse the instrument. The negotiation takes effect only when the indorsement is made and until that time there is no presumption that the transferee is the owner.

Indorsements by Depository Bank. When a customer deposits an instrument with a bank and fails to indorse it, the bank has the right to supply the customer's indorsement unless the instrument specifically requires the payee's signature (4–205). In fact the bank may merely stamp or note on the check that it was deposited by the customer or credited to his account. Insurance and government checks commonly require the signature of the payee.

SUMMARY

Commercial paper may be transferred or negotiated. Only a person to whom a negotiable instrument has been negotiated can qualify as a holder. If an instrument is payable to order it is negotiated by delivery with any necessary indorsement; if payable to bearer it is negotiated by delivery.

An indorsement is made by the holder signing his name on the instrument or on a paper firmly affixed to it. An instrument must be negotiated in its entirety. In indorsing an instrument, if the holder's name is misspelled, the recommended practice is to indorse the name as it appears on the instrument followed by the correct name.

When an instrument is transferred the transferee acquires all the rights his transferor has in the instrument. A person cannot, however, improve his position by reacquiring an instrument. The transferee for value of an unindorsed order instrument has the right, unless otherwise agreed, to have the unqualified indorsement of his transferor.

Indorsements

Effect of Indorsement on Negotiation. The effect of an indorsement on the further negotiation of the instrument will depend in part on whether it is an order instrument or a bearer instrument and in part on the form of the indorsement. It should be remembered that the form of an indorsement can have no effect on the negotiable character of the instrument; if an instrument is a negotiable instrument when issued, it continues to be a negotiable instrument, irrespective of the form of indorsement on the instrument. However, the form of the indorsement is important in determining the right of the holder to negotiate the instrument and in determining what the holder must do to negotiate the instrument.

A negotiable instrument may be indorsed for two distinct reasons. It may be indorsed because the indorsement is necessary to the negotiation of the instrument, or it may be indorsed for the purpose of adding the obligations of the indorser to those of the party primarily liable. When a person indorses a negotiable instrument, he makes contractual promises to the indorsee and, with some exceptions, to subsequent holders of the instrument. The contractual liability of indorsers will be discussed in the next chapter. In this chapter discussion is limited to the effect of the indorsement on further negotiation of the instrument.

Kinds of Indorsements. There are four basic types of indorsements: special, in blank, restrictive, and qualified.

Special Indorsement. A special indorsement contains the signature of the indorser along with words indicating to whom, or to whose order, the instrument is payable. For example, if an instrument drawn "Pay to the order of Marcia Morse" is indorsed by Morse "Pay to the order of Sam Smith, Marcia Morse" or "Pay to Sam Smith, Marcia Morse," it has been indorsed with a special indorsement. An instrument indorsed with a special indorsement remains order paper and can only be negotiated with the indorsement of the person specified (3–204).

Blank Indorsement. If an indorser merely signs his name and does not specify to whom the instrument is payable, the instrument has been indorsed in blank. For example, if an instrument drawn "Pay to the order of Susan Smith" is indorsed "Susan Smith" on the back by Smith, it has been indorsed in blank. The instrument then becomes bearer paper and can be negotiated by delivery alone until it is specially indorsed (3–204).

If an instrument is indorsed in blank and delivered to a holder, he may convert the blank indorsement into a special indorsement by writing over the signature of the indorser in blank any contract which will not in any way alter the obligation imposed by the blank indorsement (3–204[3]). If a negotiable instrument drawn "Pay to the order of Brown" is indorsed "Brown" and delivered to Finch as indorsee, Finch has the right to write over Brown's indorsement "Pay to Finch," thereby converting the blank indorsement into a special indorsement, and the instrument would then have to be indorsed by Finch before it could be further negotiated.

If an instrument indorsed in blank is presented to a bank for collection or payment, the bank normally will ask the presenter to indorse the instrument. It does so, not because an indorsement is necessary for negotiation because it is not, but rather because it wants to gain the presenter's liability as an indorser. This liability is discussed in the next chapter.

Restrictive Indorsement. A restrictive indorsement is one that specifies the purpose of the indorsement or the use to be made of the instrument. Among the more common types of restrictive indorsements are the following:

1. Indorsements for deposit, for example, "For deposit only" or "For deposit only to my account at the First Trust Company."
2. Indorsements for collection which are commonly put on by banks involved in the collection process, for example, "Pay to any bank, banker or trust company" or "For collection only."
3. Indorsements indicating that the indorsement is for the benefit or use of someone other than the person to whom it is payable, for example, "Pay to Arthur Attorney in trust for Mark Minor."
4. Indorsements purporting to prohibit further negotiation, for example, "Pay to Carl Clark only."

5. Conditional indorsements, which indicate they are effective only if a certain condition is satisfied, for example, "Pay to Bernard Builder only if he completes construction of my house by November 1, 1980."

Effect of Restrictive Indorsement. In general, restrictive indorsements do not prevent further transfer or negotiation of the instrument (3–206[1]). An indorsement such as "Pay to Clark only," although recognized as a restrictive indorsement, would have no more effect on the further negotiation of the instrument than would an unrestricted indorsement. However, any transferee[2] under an indorsement which is conditional or includes the words "for collection," "for deposit," "pay any bank," or like terms must pay or apply any value given by him for the instrument consistent with the indorsement and to the extent that he does so he becomes a holder for value.

Suppose that Clark indorses a check payable to his order "for deposit" and deposits it in a bank in which Clark has a commercial account. The bank then credits Clark's account with the amount of the check. The bank is a holder for value to the extent it allows Clark to draw on the credit for the check because it has applied the value it gave for the instrument consistent with the indorsement.

Qualified Indorsements. A qualified indorsement is one in which the indorser disclaims or limits his liability to make the instrument good if the drawer or maker defaults on the instrument. Words such as "without recourse" are used to qualify an indorsement; they can be used with either a special or a blank indorsement and thus make it a qualified special, or a qualified blank, indorsement. The use of a qualified indorsement does not change the negotiable nature of the instrument; its effect is to limit the contractual liability of the indorser. This contractual liability will be discussed in detail in the next chapter.

Grounds for Rescission of Indorsement. Negotiation is effective to transfer an instrument although the negotiation is made by a minor, a corporation exceeding its powers, or any other person without capacity; or it is obtained by fraud, duress or mistake of any kind; or is part of an illegal transaction; or is made in breach of duty. A negotiation made under the above circumstances is in an appropriate case subject to rescission unless the instrument has subsequently been negotiated to a transferee who can qualify as a holder in due course (3–207). The situation discussed above is analogous to a sale of goods where the sale has been induced by fraud or misrepresentation. In such a case the seller may rescind the sale and recover the goods provided seller acts before the goods are resold to a bona fide purchaser for value.

[2] Except an intermediary bank which under § 3–206(2) is not affected by a restrictive endorsement.

SUMMARY

Under the Code there are four basic kinds of indorsements: (1) special, (2) in blank, (3) restrictive, and (4) qualified. The first three have an effect on the negotiation of the instrument; the last one affects the liability of the endorser who qualifies his indorsement.

A special indorsement names a payee, and an instrument specially indorsed must be again indorsed before it is negotiated. A blank indorsement names no indorsee and may be the indorser's signature only. A blank indorsement converts the paper to a bearer instrument.

A restrictive indorsement does not prevent the further negotiation of the instrument but it does impose certain restrictions on the rights of the holder.

If the instrument is indorsed by one not having contractual capacity or authority to endorse or the indorsement is obtained by fraud, duress, or mistake, the indorsement is subject to rescission provided it is rescinded before the instrument is negotiated to a holder in due course.

Westerly Hospital v. Higgins

256 A.2d 506 (Sup. Ct. R.I. 1969)

This was an action brought by the Westerly Hospital (plaintiff) against Higgins (defendant) to recover the unpaid balance due on a promissory note made by Higgins on which the Westerly Hospital was the named payee. Judgment for Westerly Hospital. Affirmed on appeal.

On July 13, 1967, Higgins executed a promissory note in the amount of $527.58 payable to the order of the Westerly Hospital. The note was in consideration for services performed by the hospital in connection with the birth of Higgins' child and was payable in 18 monthly installments of $29.31. An agent of the hospital later indorsed the note in blank and negotiated it to the Industrial National Bank at a discount. The indorsement contained an express clause guaranteeing payment of the principal, interest and late charges in the event of default by the maker.

Higgins made three payments, then failed to make any further payments. The provisions of the note made the entire balance immediately due. Industrial returned the note to the hospital pursuant to the indorsement guarantee. Industrial received payment from the hospital and negotiated the note to it by delivery.

The hospital then brought suit against Higgins on the note. Higgins contended, among other things, that Westerly was not the proper person to bring suit on the note.

ROBERTS, CHIEF JUSTICE. In our opinion, the face of the instrument discloses as a matter of law that Westerly Hospital is the holder of the note in question and, therefore, a proper party to bring this action. The face of the instrument reveals that Westerly Hospital was the payee of the note made by Higgins and his wife as co-makers. It further discloses that an indorsement of guarantee was executed in blank by an authorized representative of plaintiff hospital. The note was then delivered to Industrial. The pertinent provisions of the Uniform Commercial Code provide that where, as in the instant case, there has been a blank indorsement, mere delivery is sufficient to constitute the transferee a holder thereof and is sufficient to make the transfer a valid negotiation. § 3–202; § 3–204. Thereafter when Higgins defaulted, Industrial delivered the note to Westerly in return for the payment of the remaining amount of Higgins' obligation that had been guaranteed by plaintiff hospital.

Higgins argues that this delivery of the note back to Westerly was not sufficient to constitute a valid negotiation. He argues that the attempted special indorsement by Industrial to Westerly Hospital was invalid for the lack of the signature of a duly authorized representative of Industrial and thereby Westerly Hospital was precluded from becoming a holder of the instrument. Thus, according to Higgins, Industrial was the proper party to bring the action on this note. It seems rather obvious that had the transfer of the note from Westerly Hospital to Industrial been other than in blank, this argument would have merit, it being true that an authorized signature of an agent of Industrial would be necessary to negotiate the instrument.

However, § 3–204(2) of the Uniform Commercial Code states, in pertinent part, that "An instrument payable to order and indorsed in blank becomes payable to bearer and may be negotiated by delivery alone until specially indorsed." Here Westerly Hospital as payee of the note caused its indorsement to appear thereon without specifying to whom or to whose order the instrument was payable. Instead, a blank indorsement, one specifying no particular indorsee, was made. The legal effect of such an indorsement and delivery was to authorize Industrial as the transferee and holder of the note to further negotiate the note without indorsement but by mere delivery alone. It is clear that any attempt on its part to achieve negotiation by indorsing the note to Westerly Hospital would have been mere surplusage.

In our opinion, then, the redelivery of the note in question by Industrial to Westerly Hospital accomplished a negotiation of the instrument, and the fact that a purported special indorsement to Westerly Hospital was not legally executed is of no consequence and does not affect Westerly Hospital's status as the holder of the note.

Holder in Due Course

General Requirements. In order to be accorded the special position in negotiable instruments law known as a holder in due course, a person must first be a "holder." As was indicated earlier, a "holder" is a person who is in possession of an instrument drawn, issued or indorsed to him, to his order, to bearer or in blank (1–201[20]). It is important that all indorsements on the instrument at the time it was order paper be authorized indorsements. A forged indorsement is not effective and prevents anyone from becoming a holder unless he obtains a complete chain of authorized indorsements.

To qualify as a holder in due course, the holder must take the instrument (1) for value, (2) in good faith, (3) without notice that it is overdue or has been dishonored, and (4) without notice of any defense against or claim to it (3–302[1]). If the holder cannot comply with all these requirements, he is not a holder in due course and then stands in the same position as an assignee of a simple contract.

Payee as Holder in Due Course. A payee may be a holder in due course if he complies with all the requirements for a holder in due course (3–302[2]). Ordinarily, a payee will have notice or knowledge of defenses to the instrument and will know if it is overdue or has been dishonored; consequently, he could not qualify as a holder in due course. But suppose, for example, that Drew draws a check on First Bank as drawee, payable to the order of Parks but leaves the amount blank. Drew delivers the check to Axe, his agent, and instructs him to fill in $300 as the amount. Axe, instead of filling in $300, fills in $500 as the amount, and Parks gives Axe $500 for the check. Axe gives Drew $300 and absconds with the extra $200. In such a case Parks, as payee, is a holder in due course of the check since he has taken it for value, in good faith, and without notice of defenses.

Purchases of Limited Interest. The purchaser of a limited interest in an instrument can be a holder in due course only to the extent of the interest purchased (3–302[4]). For example, Wells agrees to purchase a note payable to the order of Parks. The note is for the sum of $5,000. Wells pays Parks $1,000 on the negotiation of the note to him (Wells) and agrees to pay the balance of $4,000 in ten days. Before the payment is due Wells learns that Bell, the maker of the note, has a valid defense to it. Wells is a holder in due course for only $1,000.

SUMMARY

To qualify as a holder in due course the holder must take the instrument for value, in good faith and without notice that it is overdue or has been dishonored or of any defense against or claim to it on the part of any other person. A payee may be a holder in due course.

One who purchases a limited interest in an instrument can be a holder in due course only to the extent of the interest purchased.

Stone & Webster Engineering Corp. v. The First National Bank & Trust Co. of Greenfield

184 N.E.2d 358 (Sup. Jud. Ct. Mass. 1962)

This was an action by Stone & Webster Engineering (plaintiff) against The First National Bank & Trust Company of Greenfield (defendant) to recover a judgment for money paid out on checks on which the payee's endorsement was forged.

Stone & Webster had drawn three checks in the total amount of $64,755.44 on The First National Bank of Boston payable to the order of Westinghouse Electric Corporation. An employee of Stone & Webster obtained possession of the checks, forged Westinghouse's endorsement to them, cashed them at the First National Bank & Trust Company of Greenfield, and put the proceeds to his own use. The first two checks were endorsed in typewriting, "For Deposit Only: Westinghouse Electric Corporation By: Mr. O. D. Costine, Treasury Representative" followed by an ink signature "O. D. Costine." The third check was endorsed in typewriting, "Westinghouse Electric Corporation by: (Sgd.) O. D. Costine, Treasury Representative." When Stone & Webster sued the Greenfield Bank for conversion, one of the issues discussed by the court was the status of the Bank. That portion of the opinion follows.

WILKINS, CHIEF JUSTICE. In the case at bar the forged endorsements were "wholly inoperative" as the signatures of the payee, Code §§ 3–404(1), 1–201(43), and equally so both as to the restrictive endorsements for deposits, see § 3–205(c), and as to the endorsement in blank, see § 3–204(2). When the forger transferred the checks to the collecting bank, no negotiation under § 3–202(1) occurred, because there was lacking the necessary endorsement of the payee. For the same reason, the collecting bank could not become a "holder" as defined in § 1–201(20), and so could not become a holder in due course under § 3–202(1).

For Value and in Good Faith

Value. A person, to qualify as a holder in due course of an instrument, must give value for it; a person taking an instrument as a gift would not have given value and not be able to qualify as a holder in due course. "Value" is different from simple consideration. Under the provisions of the Code a holder takes the instrument for value if: (1) the agreed consideration has been performed, for example, if it was given in exchange for a promise to deliver a refrigerator and the refrigerator has been delivered; (2) he acquires a security interest in, or a lien on, the instrument; (3) when he takes the instrument in payment of (or as security for) an antecedent claim; (4) when he gives a negotiable instrument for it; or (5) he makes an irrevocable commitment to a third person (3–303).

A bank or any person who discounts an instrument in the regular course of trade has given value for it. Likewise, if a loan is made and an instrument is pledged as security for the repayment of the loan, the secured party has given value for the instrument to the extent of the amount of the loan. If Axe owes Bell a past-due debt and he indorses and delivers to Bell an instrument issued to him (Axe) in payment of the debt or as security for its repayment, Bell has given value for the instrument.

Suppose that Axe borrows $1,000 from Bell. Axe gives Bell a note for that amount payable in 30 days and Bell indorses and delivers to Axe a check for $1,000 drawn by Clark and payable to Bell. Axe, in issuing his note for $1,000 to Bell, has given value for the Clark check. Also, suppose that Bell and Clark enter into a contract whereby Clark obligates himself to deliver an automobile to Axe and Bell indorses an instrument issued by Drew and delivers it to Clark in payment for the automobile. Clark has given value for the Drew instrument.

Good Faith. Good faith is defined in the Code as follows: "Good faith" means honesty in fact in the conduct or transaction concerned (1–201[19]). Good faith implies commercial honesty. If negotiable instruments are to serve their purpose of facilitating the carrying-on of trade, they must pass freely in the channels of commerce, and a person must be permitted to take a negotiable instrument without first investigating its origin and the intervening transactions whereby the present holder acquired the instrument. Good faith always involves a question of fact and the courts look more carefully at negotiations of instruments issued by consumers. A bank or financing company which buys a lot of negotiable paper from a supplier of consumer goods or services (such as a home repair company) will have its relationship with the supplier scrutinized particularly carefully.

SUMMARY

Value includes the performance of an agreed consideration, such as the delivery of goods purchased, the taking of an instrument as security or as payment or security for an antecedent claim, the giving of a negotiable instrument, or the assuming of an irrevocable obligation to a third person.

Good faith is honesty in fact.

Pazol v. Citizens National Bank of Sandy Springs

138 S.E.2d 442 (Ct. App. Ga. 1964)

This was an action by Citizens National Bank of Sandy Springs (plaintiff) against Sidney Pazol (defendant). Judgment for Citizens National Bank of Sandy Springs and Pazol appealed. Judgment affirmed.

Pazol issued his check for $49,600 drawn on the National Bank of Atlanta and payable to the order of Edison and Seiden Construction Company, Inc. (Edison). Edison wrote "For Deposit" on the check and deposited it in its checking account with the Citizens National Bank of Sandy Springs (Bank). Bank allowed Edison to withdraw all of the credit created by the deposit of the check before it learned that there were defenses to it. When the check was presented for payment it was dishonored. Bank sued Pazol, the drawer of the check, to recover a judgment for the amount of the check. Pazol defended on the ground that Bank was not a holder in due course of the check.

FULTON, CHIEF JUDGE. Bank is at least a holder, as defined by Code § 1–201(20), i.e., "a person who is in possession of a document of title or an instrument or an investment security drawn, *issued or indorsed* to him or to his order or to bearer or in blank." The petition alleges that the payee delivered the check to Bank and "caused the same to be endorsed for deposit." Even if this is construed to mean that the payee did not personally indorse the instrument, as indeed the copy of the check attached as an exhibit shows to be the case, it was issued to Bank. Code § 4–205(1) provides as follows: "A depositary bank which has taken an item for collection may supply any indorsement of the customer which is necessary to title unless the item contains the words 'payee's indorsement required' or the like. In the absence of such a requirement a statement placed on the item by the depositary bank to the effect that the item was deposited by a customer or credited to his account is effective as the customer's indorsement." The comment of the National Conference of Commissioners on Uniform State Laws and the American Law Institute pertaining to this particular section explains that this subsection "is designed to speed up collections by eliminating any necessity to return a *non-bank depositor* any items he may have failed to indorse."

Furthermore, under the allegations of the petition, Bank was a holder in due course as defined by Code § 3–302(1), which requires that the holder take the instrument "(a) for value; and (b) in good faith; and (c) without notice that it is overdue or has been dishonored or of any defense against or claim to it on the part of any person." Regarding requirement (a), Code § 4–209 provides as follows: "For purposes of determining its status as a holder in due course, the bank has given value *to the extent that it has a security interest in an item* provided that the bank otherwise complies with the requirements of 3–302 on what constitutes a holder in due course." Code § 4–208 (1) provides that "[a] bank has a security interest in an item . . . (a) in case of an item deposited in an account to the extent to which credit given for the item has been withdrawn or applied. . . ." By causing the check to be indorsed "for deposit," the payee signified its purpose of deposit and the bank, by applying the value given consistently with this indorsement by crediting the payee-depositor's account with the amount of the check, became a holder for value.

Norman v. World Wide Distributors, Inc.

195 A.2d 115 (Super. Ct. Pa. 1963)

This was an action by Clarence W. Norman and wife (plaintiffs) against World Wide Distributors, Inc., and People National Fund, Inc. (defendants), to have a judgment obtained on a note against Norman and wife declared void. Judgment for Norman and wife, and World Wide Distributors, Inc., and Peoples National Fund, Inc., appealed. Judgment affirmed.

Mancen, agent for World Wide Distributors, Inc. (World Wide), called upon the Normans and outlined to them "a program for direct advertising." He represented to them that if they purchased a breakfront, he would pay them $5 for each letter they wrote to a friend requesting an appointment for World Wide's agent to explain the details of a sound advertising program and $20 for each sale made to any such person. Each friend was to be given the same opportunity to supply names. He persuaded the Normans to sign, without reading, a purchase agreement, and attached judgment note in blank and an "Owners Participation Certificate."

After the note was signed and taken from the home of the Normans it was filled in for $1,079.40 and made payable to H. Waldran T/A State Wide Products at the office of Peoples National Fund (Peoples). The note was purchased by Peoples on January 25, 1961, for $831 and judgment was entered thereon February 7, 1961. World Wide was nowhere to be found. Within approximately a year its principals had operated first under the name of Carpet Industries, then under State Wide, and finally under World Wide Distributors. Peoples dealt with all three companies and its officers had knowledge of the referral plan. The referral plan was a fraudulent scheme based on an operation similar to the chain letter racket. Peoples claims that even though World Wide may have been guilty of fraud, it can collect on the note because it was a holder in due course.

WOODSIDE, JUDGE. "A holder in due course is a holder who takes the instrument (*a*) for value; and (*b*) in good faith; and (*c*) without notice that it is overdue or has been dishonored or of any defense against or claim to it on the part of any person." (3–302[1]).

Section 1–201(19) of the Code defines "good faith" as meaning "honesty in fact in the conduct or transaction concerned." Thus, to be a holder in due course Peoples must have acted in good faith.

He also seeks protection as a holder in due course must have dealt fairly and honestly in acquiring the instrument as to the rights of prior parties, and where circumstances are such as to justify the conclusion that the failure to make inquiry arose from a suspicion that inquiry would disclose a vice or defect in the title, the person is not a holder in due course.

When the defense of fraud appears to be meritorious as to the payee, the burden of showing it was a holder in due course is on the one claiming to be such.

Peoples here had knowledge of circumstances which should have caused it to inquire concerning the payee's method of obtaining the note. Peoples knew enough about the referral plan to require it to inquire further concerning it. The fact that Peoples' vice-president called the makers of the note and denied any connection with the referral plan, indicates his own suspicion concerning it. The frequency with which the principals changed the name under which they were operating—three times in approximately one year—should have added to his suspicion. Furthermore, the People's paid $831 for a $1,079.40 note payable three days after date. Under all the circumstances, Peoples was bound to inquire further into the operation of the seller of these notes, and having made no inquiry, it is held as though it had knowledge of all that inquiry would have revealed.

Notice of Defenses

Nature of Notice. To qualify as a holder in due course, a holder must take the instrument without notice that there are any defenses or adverse claims to it. Notice is something less than knowledge and more than mere suspicion. It is knowledge of facts and circumstances which would prompt an honest person to make inquiry to learn the facts. A person has notice of a fact when (*a*) he has actual knowledge of it; or (*b*) he has received a notice or notification of it; or (*c*) from all the facts and circumstances known to him at the time in question he has reason to know that it exists (1–201[25]).

Incomplete Paper. A person cannot take an instrument as a holder in due course if at the time he takes it the instrument is blank as *to some material term.* The courts have held that the fact that the instrument is incomplete in some material respect puts any person taking it on notice that the holder has limited authority to fill in the blanks, and charges the person with knowledge of facts which a reasonable inquiry would disclose. If the instrument contains blanks, the party taking the instrument takes it subject to all defenses available to the original parties irrespective of whether or not there is any relation between the blank terms and the defense.

To be material, the omitted term must be one which affects the legal obligations of the parties to the instrument. An instrument is incomplete if it is payable to order and the name of the payee is left blank. Similarly, an instrument that has a blank where the amount should be is incomplete. An instrument which was drawn payable "__________ after date" and one drawn "ten __________ after date" were held to be incomplete. Failure to fill in a pronoun does not make the instrument incomplete, as "__________ promise to pay." Likewise, the omission of connective words such as "Pay to Brown order" does not make the instrument incomplete.

Filling in Blanks. When an instrument is signed while still incomplete in any necessary respect, it cannot be enforced until completed. However, when it is completed as authorized it is effective as completed (3–115). A person who takes an instrument which is incomplete in some material respect cannot take as a holder in due course. However, if an incomplete instrument is filled in, a person taking the instrument without notice or knowledge that it was incomplete when delivered or that it was not completed as authorized takes as a holder in due course and can enforce the instrument as completed (3–407[3]). For example, Fred writes a check payable to the order of Sam's Shoes and leaves the amount blank. He gives the check to his friend Alice, asks her to pick up a pair of shoes for him at Sam's, and tells her to fill in the amount of the purchase. If Alice gives the incomplete check to Sam, it cannot be enforced as is. If Sam fills in the check for $19.95, the cost of the shoes, it could be enforced as completed because the completion was authorized. However, if Sam watched as Alice filled the blank in as $30 (and obtained the $10.05 difference in cash), Sam could not take it as a holder in due course as he is deemed to be on notice of the incomplete paper and any defenses that might be made to it. On the other hand, if Alice filled the amount in as $30 before she got to Sam's, Sam could be a holder in due course and enforce the check for $30. In the latter case, Fred who made the unauthorized completion possible must bear the loss until he locates Alice.

Irregular Paper. Anything on the face of an instrument which would put a person on notice that there is something wrong with it makes the instrument irregular. If the instrument is irregular, the person taking it cannot take as a holder in due course and is subject to all defenses available to the parties to the instrument, whether or not there is any relation between the irregularity and the defense to the instrument.

A person is put on notice if one of his experience and training should, in the exercise of reasonable prudence, detect the irregularity. Any noticeable alteration makes an instrument irregular on its face, but a clever alteration does not. However, an alteration might be such as would put a bank cashier on notice but might not put on notice a person who was not accustomed to handling negotiable instruments. The courts have held that the following do not make the instrument irregular on its face: (1) postdating, (2) difference between the handwriting in the body of the instrument and that in the signature, (3) differences in the handwriting in the body of the instrument, and (4) statement of the amount in figures and not in writing.

Instruments stamped "Paid" or "Payment refused," and one made out to an officer of a corporation and signed by the same officer as agent of the corporation have been held to be irregular paper.

Voidable Paper. A holder cannot qualify as a holder in due course if he has notice or knowledge that the obligation of any party is voidable in whole or in part. Notice or knowledge that any signature on the paper was obtained by misrepresentation, fraud, or duress or that the paper was signed by mistake would prevent the holder from qualifying as a holder in due course. If an instrument is paid in full to the holder, all parties are discharged. However, if the party paying an instrument does not take it or have it marked "Paid" or "Canceled" so that it is apparent that it has been discharged, the holder can negotiate it, and any party taking such instrument having no notice can take it as a holder in due course and may be able to demand that the instrument be paid again. (3–304[1][b]).

Negotiation of Fiduciary. Whether or not a purchaser who takes an instrument which has been negotiated to him by a fiduciary takes as a holder in due course will depend on whether such purchaser has notice or knowledge that the fiduciary has negotiated the instrument in violation of his fiduciary duties. If an instrument is payable to a person as trustee or an attorney for someone else, then any attempt by the trustee or attorney to negotiate the instrument for his own benefit gives the purchaser of the instrument knowledge that the beneficiary of the trust may have a claim. For example, a check is drawn "pay to the order of Arthur Adams, Trustee for Mary Minor." If Adams takes the check to an appliance store, indorses his name, and uses it to purchase a television set for himself, then the appliance store would not be a holder in due course because it knew the negotiation was in violation of the fiduciary duty Adams owed to Mary Minor. The purchaser has notice of a claim against the instrument when he has knowledge that a fiduciary has negotiated the instrument in payment of his own debt or in any transaction for his own benefit (3–304[2]).

SUMMARY

A person who takes an instrument which is, at the time he or she takes it, blank in some material respect, cannot take as a holder in due course.

If a person who can qualify as a holder in due course takes an instrument after the blanks have been filled in, he can enforce the instrument as it is filled in.

Anything on the face of the instrument which would put the holder on notice that there is something wrong with the instrument is an irregularity, a person taking such an instrument cannot take as a holder in due course.

A holder cannot qualify as a holder in due course if, at the time he took the paper, he had notice or knowledge that the obligation of any party was voidable in whole or in part or that all parties had been discharged.

A purchaser from a fiduciary cannot take as a holder in due course when purchaser has knowledge that the fiduciary has negotiated the paper for his or her own benefit or otherwise in breach of duty.

Maber, Inc. v. Factor Cab Corp.

244 N.Y.S.2d 768 (App. Div. N.Y. 1963)

This was an action by Maber, Inc. (plaintiff), against Factor Cab Corp. and others (defendants) to recover a judgment on a note. Judgment for Maber, Inc., for less than full amount of note and it appealed. Judgment affirmed.

Factor Cab Corp. issued a series of notes drawn payable to "the order of Donald E. Richel as attorney for Francisco Silvestry." Twenty-one of the notes were indorsed by Richel and his wife and sold to Maber, Inc. Maber, Inc., in purchasing the notes, made its check payable to Richel in his individual name, without qualification or restriction, in the amount of $5,796.24. In addition, it discharged by payment Richel's personal indebtedness to a bank in the amount of $3,903.75. Richel and his wife indorsed the notes as individuals.

Factor Cab Corp. paid some of Silvestry's hospital bills directly and thereby obtained a counter-claim against the notes. Maber, Inc., contended that it took the notes as a holder in due course and free from the counterclaim.

BREITEL, JUSTICE PRESIDING. When Maber took the notes from the attorney, by reason of the descriptive qualification of the named payee (i.e., as attorney for Francisco Silvestry), the holder was on notice that the attorney had received the notes as an agent rather than as a principal, and that the funds might be subject to claims in the right of others. This did not mean that the attorney was not entitled to negotiate the notes. On the contrary, he could (U.C.C. § § 3–117, 3–207, 3–301, 3–304[4][e]). He was even empowered to negotiate them for cash, because it may have been within the fiduciary purpose to convert them into cash, provided, of course, there were no other circumstances to put the holder on notice that the instrument was being diverted from a fiduciary purpose (U.C.C. § 3–304, Comment 5).

But the case is entirely different when it appears, as it did here, that the notes were negotiated for the benefit or individual purpose of the agent. Under such circumstances the holder is charged with bad faith and notice of any defect or infirmity in the instrument, and is not a holder in due course (U.C.C. § § 3–302[1], 3–304[2]). This includes the absence or failure of consideration whether in whole or in part (U.C.C. § 3–408).

Overdue and Dishonored Paper

Paper Payable at Definite Time. A person must take an instrument before it is overdue in order to take as a holder in due course. The courts have based this rule on the reasoning that as a general rule obligations are performed when performance is due, and if an instrument is not paid when due, the nonpayment of the instrument is a circumstance sufficient to put the purchaser on notice that the party primarily liable has a defense to it, and a person taking an overdue instrument takes with notice of all defenses to such instrument.

An instrument payable at a definite date is overdue at the beginning of the day after the due date. An instrument payable at a definite time after date or after presentment is overdue at the beginning of the day after the time state has elapsed. In counting time, the day the instrument is issued is excluded, but the date of payment is included. For example, if an instrument dated January 2 is payable 30 days after date, January 3 is the first day counted, and the instrument is due on February 1 and overdue at the beginning of February 2. A person taking the instrument on February 2 or thereafter cannot take as a holder in due course. If the date of payment falls on a Sunday or a holiday the instrument is payable on the next succeeding business day.

Demand Paper. If an instrument is drawn payable on demand or on presentment, a person taking the instrument an unreasonable time after its issue cannot take as a holder in due course. The Code provides that "reasonable time for a check drawn and payable within the United States is presumed to be 30 days" (3–304[31]). It should be noted that this provision states "is presumed" to be 30 days, not "is" 30 days.

In determining whether a demand instrument is overdue, usage of trade, business practices, the facts and circumstances of the particular case must be considered. In a farming community where the normal period for loans to farmers is six months, a demand note as a general rule can be outstanding a longer period of time before it becomes overdue than could a demand note issued in an industrial community, where the normal period of a loan is 30 to 60 days. In determining when an instrument is overdue, the nature of the transaction in which the instrument is used, the relation of the parties, and all other facts and circumstances must be taken into consideration.

Dishonored Instruments. An instrument has been dishonored when it has been presented for payment or acceptance, and payment or acceptance has been refused. If a demand note has been presented to the maker for payment and payment has been refused, the note has been dishonored. Likewise, if a draft has been presented to the drawee for acceptance or payment, or if a check has been presented to the drawee bank for payment, and acceptance or payment has been refused, the draft or check has been dishonored. Any purchaser taking such note, draft, or check who has reason to know it has been dishonored cannot take as a holder in due course.

SUMMARY

An instrument payable at a definite time or at a stated time after date is overdue at the beginning of the day following the day on which it is payable.

A person taking an instrument when it is overdue cannot take as a holder in due course.

Demand paper is overdue if it is not paid within a reasonable time after issue, and a reasonable time for the payment of a check drawn and payable in the states or territories of the United States or the District of Columbia is presumed to be 30 days.

Demand paper is dishonored when it is presented for payment or acceptance and payment or acceptance is refused.

Rights of Holder in Due Course

Personal Defenses. The keystone of the law of negotiable commercial paper is the rule that a holder in due course of a negotiable instrument takes it free from "personal defenses" or claims which may exist between the original parties to the instrument. The holder in due course takes free of such defenses as lack or failure of consideration, misrepresentation or fraud in the inducement, setoff or counterclaim, breach of warranty of goods sold for which the instrument was issued, and all other defenses which would be available to a promisor in a suit on a contract (3–305[1]). The holder in due course doctrine has, however, been modified to some degree, particularly as to negotiable instruments executed by consumers. These modifications are discussed in some detail in the next section of this chapter.

Real Defenses. From the standpoint of public policy there are certain defenses which do go to the validity of the instrument and which are good against even a holder in due course of a negotiable instrument. These are the so-called "real defenses." The most common "real defenses" which can be asserted even against a holder in due course are:

1. Incapacity of a party to execute a contract, for example, minority.
2. Duress or other illegality which nullifies the obligation of the party.
3. Fraud in the essence or "real" fraud whereby a person was induced to sign the instrument without his realizing or having a chance to discover that it was a negotiable instrument or what its terms were. For example, an illiterate person being asked to sign a document that he is told is a grant of permission to bring a TV set into his house whereas it is in reality a promissory note.
4. Discharge of the party liable in bankruptcy proceedings (3–305[2]).

In regard to minors and others having limited capacity to contract it is basically a matter of social policy whether it is more desirable to protect a holder in due course and thereby facilitate trade or protect the inexperienced and weak from the results of their injudicious acts. As the law has developed the decision has been to protect minors and others having limited contractual capacity. The courts have held that promises made under extreme duress are unenforceable. Similarly, state legislatures by statutory enactment have made promises made in defined illegal transactions totally unenforceable. By logical deduction, if the promise in a negotiable instrument is a nullity it is unenforceable, even by a holder in due course of the instrument. The law also protects those persons who have been "tricked" into signing any paper if they have used a reasonable degree of care.

The objective of our bankruptcy laws and other insolvency laws is to relieve the debtor from his debts and give him a new start. In general, the discharge features of these laws are broad enough to discharge the debtor of all his commercial obligations, including debts owing on negotiable instruments held by holders in due course.

Persons Not Holders in Due Course. Negotiable commercial paper is basically a contract to pay money. If the holder of such paper is not a holder in due course his rights are no greater than are the rights of any promisee or assignee of a simple contract. Such a holder takes the paper subject to all valid claims or the part of any person and subject to all defenses of any party which would be available in an action on a simple contract (3–306).

SUMMARY

A holder in due course of negotiable commercial paper takes free from personal defenses existing between the parties but takes subject to the real defense of minority, and other incapacities available as a defense to a simple contract; duress or illegality of the transaction which renders the obligation a nullity; promises induced by "trickery"; discharge in insolvency proceedings; and discharges of which he has notice.

A holder not a holder in due course takes negotiable commercial paper subject to all the defenses which would be available to a promisor on a simple contract to pay money.

Reading Trust Co. v. Hutchison

35 Pa. D. & C.2d 790 (Ct. of Common Pleas Pa. 1964)

This was an action by Reading Trust Company (plaintiff) to obtain judgment by confession on a note on which the Hutchisons (defendants) were the makers. Judgment was entered and the Hutchisons moved to open the judgment. Motion to open was denied.

On March 7, 1963, an agent of Gracious Living, Inc., called upon the Hutchisons and identified himself as a "demonstrator" of water softening equipment. It was alleged that upon completion of a demonstration the representative explained the cost of purchasing the equipment and indicated that Gracious Living, Inc., would install it on a four months' trial basis if the Hutchisons would give a list of their friends and neighbors and then permit a demonstration in the Hutchison home. The arrangement also provided for compensation to them if sales resulted from such lists. The Hutchisons maintained that the agent "asked them to sign a form which he could show to his boss to prove that he had made the demonstration and also as a bond to cover the unit while it was on the property of the Hutchinsons and until they decided to keep it. The Hutchinsons signed both of these forms." The Hutchisons testified that it was not until they received an installment book from Reading on March 27, 1963 that they realized "that they had been tricked into signing a contract and a judgment note." The Trust Company claimed that it was not a party to the transaction; that it took the note in the normal course of business and that it had no knowledge of the representations made by the agent of Gracious Living.

KOCH, PRESIDING JUDGE. At the outset it must be said that the Hutchinsons have not established that Reading Trust had any knowledge of fraudulent business practices.

The Uniform Commercial Code provides as follows:

(1) A holder in due course is a holder who takes the instrument

(a) for value; and

(b) in good faith including observance of the reasonable commercial standards of any business in which the holder may be engaged; and

(c) without notice that it is overdue or has been dishonored or of any defense against or claim to it on the part of any person.

The crux of the Hutchinsons position is that even though Reading Trust may have had no specific knowledge of the circumstances surrounding the execution of the note, Section 3–305 (2) (c) defeats its rights as a holder in due course. This portion of the Code is as follows:

> To the extent that a holder is a holder in due course he takes the instrument free from
> (1) . . .
> (2) All defenses of any party to the instrument with whom the holder has not dealt except
> (c) Such misrepresentation as has induced the party to sign the instrument with neither knowledge nor reasonable opportunity to obtain knowledge of its character or its essential terms.

The Uniform Commercial Code Comment to the foregoing subsection follows:

> Paragraph (c) of subsection (2) is new. It follows the great majority of the decisions under the original Act in recognizing the defense of "real" or "essential" fraud, sometimes called fraud in the essence or fraud in the factum, as effective against a holder in due course. The

common illustration is that of the maker who is tricked into signing a note in the belief that it is merely a receipt or some other document. The theory of the defense is that his signature on the instrument is ineffective because he did not intend to sign such an instrument at all. Under this provision the defense extends to an instrument signed with knowledge that it is a negotiable instrument, but without knowledge of its essential terms.

The test of the defense here stated is that of excusable ignorance of the contents of the writing signed. The party must not only have been in ignorance, but must also have had no reasonable opportunity to obtain knowledge. In determining what is a reasonable opportunity all relevant factors are to be taken into account, including the age and sex of the party, his intelligence, education and business experience; his ability to read or to understand English, the representations made to him and his reason to rely on them or to have confidence in the person making them; the presence or absence of any third person who might read or explain the instrument to him; or any other possibility of obtaining independent information; and the apparent necessity, or lack of it, for acting without delay.

Unless the misrepresentation meets this test, the defense is cut off by a holder in due course.

We are in accord with the views expressed in this comment. We do not agree the Hutchinsons' contention that this case presents the classic illustration of a maker who was "tricked" into signing a note in the belief that it was another document. While we do not condone some of the high pressure tactics which were used in this case, nevertheless, a reading of the depositions persuades us that upon taking into consideration the factors of excusable ignorance of the contents of the writing signed the judgment should not be opened.

An analysis of the factors shows that the husband petitioner, age 48, is a high school graduate and is employed as a clerk; the wife, age 51, completed her junior year in high school. In addition to their undoubted ability to read and write the English language and their high degree of intelligence as indicated by their depositions neither of them could establish any basis which would indicate that they had any reason to have confidence in the representations made by the agent for Gracious Living, Inc.

In further analyzing the factors we find that there was a third person present on the occasion of the signing, Mr. Albert Mitchell, an uncle of Mrs. Hutchison. He, too, is a high school graduate, and despite his presence, was not asked by the Hutchinsons for advice.

Changes in the Holder in Due Course Doctrine

Consumer Disadvantages. While the fact a subsequent holder in due course of a negotiable instrument takes free of personal defenses between the initial parties to it makes such instruments pass freely in commerce, the holder in due course concept can also result in serious disadvantages to the consumer. When goods or services are sold on credit to consumers in return for negotiable notes, the consumer may effectively lose his right to withhold payment where the goods or services are defective or not delivered if the seller discounts the note to a financial institution for cash and the financial institution becomes a holder in due course. The consumer must pay the note in full to the holder in due course and then pursue the seller, if he can be located. The consumer would be in a far more effective position if he could just withhold payment until the goods or services are delivered or the unsatisfactory performance of the seller is corrected.

State Legislation. Gradually some state legislatures and state courts have limited the holder in due course doctrine, particularly as it relates to consumers. A Uniform Consumer Credit Code was promulgated in 1968 by the National Conference of Commissioners on Uniform State Laws and various consumer organizations have developed model consumer acts. The Uniform Consumer Credit Code, which has been adopted by a relatively small number of states, virtually eliminates negotiable paper in consumer credit sales by prohibiting the seller from taking a negotiable instrument other than a check as evidence of the obligation of the buyer. Some states now require that instruments evidencing consumer indebtedness must carry the legend "consumer paper" and state that instruments carrying the legend are not negotiable instruments. Other states have enacted comprehensive measures which effectively abolish the holder in due course doctrine. The law at the state level is far from uniform and the position of a consumer who has signed a negotiable instrument varies from state to state. The trend, though, is clearly toward limiting the holder in due course doctrine as it adversely affects consumers in consumer transactions.

Federal Trade Commission Regulation. At the federal level, the Federal Trade Commission has, citing its authority to regulate unfair and deceptive trade practices, promulgated a "Trade Regulation Rule Concerning Preservation of Consumers' Claims and Defenses" in consumer credit contracts.[3] The rule makes it an unfair trade practice for a seller, in the course of financing a consumer purchase of goods or services, to employ procedures which make the consumer's duty to pay independent of the seller's duty to fulfill his obligations.

The FTC regulation provides protection to the consumer in those situations where: (1) the buyer executes a sales contract that includes a promissory note; (2) the buyer signs an installment sales contract that includes a "waiver of defenses" clause; or (3) the seller arranges with a third party lender for a direct loan to finance the buyer's purchase.

The FTC regulation deals with the first two situations by requiring that the following statement be included in bold type in any consumer credit contract to be signed by the consumer:

---

[3] *Federal Register,* November 18, 1975 at pages 53,506–14.

ANY HOLDER OF THIS CONSUMER CREDIT CONTRACT IS SUBJECT TO ALL CLAIMS AND DEFENSES WHICH THE DEBTOR COULD ASSERT AGAINST THE SELLER OF THE GOODS OR SERVICES OBTAINED PURSUANT HERETO OR WITH THE PROCEEDS HEREOF. RECOVERY HEREUNDER BY THE DEBTOR SHALL NOT EXCEED AMOUNTS PAID BY THE DEBTOR HEREUNDER.

Where the seller arranges for a direct loan to be made to finance a customer's purchase, the seller may not accept the proceeds of the loan unless the consumer credit contract between the buyer and the lender contains the following statement in bold type:

ANY HOLDER OF THIS CONSUMER CREDIT CONTRACT IS SUBJECT TO ALL CLAIMS AND DEFENSES WHICH THE DEBTOR COULD ASSERT AGAINST THE SELLER OF GOODS OR SERVICES OBTAINED WITH THE PROCEEDS HEREOF. RECOVERY HEREUNDER BY THE DEBTOR SHALL NOT EXCEED AMOUNTS PAID BY THE DEBTOR HEREUNDER.

The required notice will be treated in the same manner as other written terms and conditions in the agreement. The notice must appear without qualification. A contract which includes the Notice in conjunction with other clauses which limit or restrict its application does not satisfy the requirement that the contract "contain the Notice."

The FTC Rule does not eliminate any rights the consumer may have as a matter of federal, state, or local law. Moreover, the Rule creates no new rights or defenses. For example, the Rule would not create a warranty claim or defense where a product is sold "as is." It also does not alter statutes of limitations or other state-created limitations on the consumer's enforcement of claims or defenses. Finally, the claims or defenses relied upon by the consumer must arise from the transaction which he finances.

Failure to comply with the FTC regulation may subject the seller to fines of $10,000 per violation in a civil action brought by the Federal Trade Commission. The FTC has also proposed imposing similar limitations on lenders.

The court decisions, new state laws and the FTC regulations modifying the holder in due course doctrine are an effort to balance the societal interests (1) in protecting the consumer and (2) in assuring the availability of credit along with marketability of commercial paper.

SUMMARY

The holder in due course doctrine as it relates to negotiable instruments signed by consumers has been abolished or modified by new state laws, court decisions, and regulations promulgated by the Federal Trade Commission.

Randolph National Bank v. Vail

308 A.2d 588 (Sup. Ct. Vt. 1970)

This was an action brought by Randolph National Bank (plaintiff) against Carlton Vail (defendant) to recover the balance due on a promissory note held by the bank. Judgment for the bank. Affirmed on appeal.

In October 1968, Carlton Vail entered into an oral agreement with Gerry Smith and Bruce Stearns, pursuant to which Smith and Stearns were to construct a home for Vail and his family in Barnard, Vermont. Smith and Stearns last worked on the house in September 1969; however, several times thereafter, Vail requested Smith and Stearns to correct certain deficiencies and errors made in the construction of the house and to make appropriate corrections in their bill.

On November 1, 1969, Smith went to the Randolph National Bank to inquire about procuring a loan from the bank to pay some of the building suppliers to whom Smith and Stearns owed money. During this meeting, Mr. Smith informed the bank about the debt owed to Smith and Stearns by Carlton Vail arising from the construction of the Vail residence. In view of this debt the bank agreed to make a loan to Smith and Stearns if they would have Vail sign a promissory note made payable to Smith and Stearns that could be endorsed to Randolph National Bank. At the time of the meeting there was no mention made to the bank of any conflict between Smith and Stearns and Vail, or of any dissatisfaction on the part of Vail with the work of Smith and Stearns.

Vail agreed to sign such a note and on November 14, 1969, did so at his residence in Barnard, having no contact with Randolph National Bank prior to that time. The promissory note was made payable to Smith and Stearns at the Randolph National Bank and was in the sum of $4,805.94.

It was signed by Mr. Vail on the assumption that the work on the house would be completed and that the improperly constructed items would be corrected. On November 18, 1969, the promissory note was endorsed in blank by Gerry Smith and Bruce Stearns, doing business as Smith and Stearns, and then presented to the Randolph National Bank so the loan could be made. At no time prior to the receipt of the promissory note did Randolph National Bank have any knowledge tending to indicate there were any defenses or claims against the note. However, after the promissory note became due and the bank contacted Vail about his failure to make payment, it learned of Vail's dissatisfaction with the work of Smith and Stearns.

SHANGRAW, CHIEF JUSTICE. In this appeal Carlton Vail makes an argument in which he contends the Randolph National Bank holds the promissory note subject to all the personal defenses that he had against Smith and Stearns. In so doing, Mr. Vail seeks to have this Court deny Randolph National Bank the rights of a holder in due course provided in § 3–305 that were accorded to the bank by the trial court.

Vail's argument looks to Chapter 63 of Title 9 which he contends applies to this transaction. This chapter was enacted by the legislature to protect the public against unfair methods of competition and unfair or deceptive acts or practices on the part of the business community. In this regard, the legislature sought in part to protect the public against the problems connected with the financing of consumer transactions and enacted 9 V.S.A. § 2455, which provides:

> The holder of a promissory note or instrument or other evidence of indebtedness of a consumer delivered in connection with a contract shall take or hold that note, instrument or evidence subject to all defenses of such consumer which would be available to the consumer in an action on a simple contract, and all rights available to him under this chapter.

The effect of 9 V.S.A. § 2455 is to cut off the rights of a holder in due course of a promissory note found in § 3–305, and to make a subsequent holder subject to all the defenses of a consumer. The protection afforded the consumer through 9 V.S.A. § 2455 is a result of legislative recognition of the substantial differential in bargaining power between the seller and financier on one side and the consumer on the other, and must be viewed as an attempt to equalize that differential by transferring the risk of loss from the note maker to the note holder.

Our inquiry into the argument raised by Mr. Vail must commence with a determination of whether or not 9 V.S.A. § 2455 applies to the unusual facts presented in this case. There can be no doubt that at the time Mr. Vail entered into the agreement with Smith and Stearns he was a consumer contracting for goods and services as defined in 9 V.S.A. § 2454. However, what does remain for our inquiry is whether or not the promissory note was delivered in connection with a contract so as to come within the scope of the protection afforded by 9 V.S.A. § 2455. At the time Mr. Vail signed the promissory note, over a year had passed since the agreement had been entered into, and work on the house had been completed with the exception of those items which Mr. Vail assumed Smith and Stearns would correct. Thus, at the time the note was signed, substantial performance on the agreement had already been effectuated. For this reason, the note must be characterized as security for a pre-existing obligation, and not the type of transaction where the consumer receives the goods and services at the time he signs the contract and promissory note. This difference is critical, for it is apparent Mr. Vail knew what his potential defenses were against Smith and Stearns when he signed the promissory note, as he had received the goods and services prior to that time. Accordingly, Mr. Vail cannot be characterized as the unsuspecting consumer that 9 V.S.A. § 2455 was designed to protect; and consequently, Randolph National Bank cannot be held to hold the promissory note subject to his personal defenses.

Problem Cases

1. Program Aids accepted a number of drafts payable to Bean. The drafts were given as payment in the sale by Bean to Program Aids of catalogs for physical training equipment. Bean negotiated the drafts to Bank which took them as a holder in due course; the Bank later negotiated the drafts back to Bean. Bean brought suit on the drafts against Program Aids. Program Aids sought to defend on the grounds Bean had breached the sales contract by improperly preparing the catalogs. Bean claims he is not subject to the personal defense in this action because he is a transferee from a holder in due course and therefore has the rights of a holder in due course. Is Bean's claim a valid one?
2. A note payable to Petroleum Equipment Leasing Company is indorsed on the reverse side as follows:

   Pay to Equipment Leasing of California
   its successors or assigns
   Petroleum Equipment Leasing Company
   by Richard L. Burns, President

   The note is then assigned without indorsement to Security Pacific National Bank as security for a loan. What kind of indorsement is this? Did the bank acquire the rights of a holder in due course?
3. Charles Joy was the Receiver in Bankruptcy for the Quantuim Development Company. A certified check in the amount of $84,858 was issued payable to the order of "Charles R. Joy, Receiver." Joy indorsed the check on the reverse side as follows: "For Deposit in Quantuim Acct. Quantuim Bankruptcy, Charles R. Joy." He then took the check to the Bank of Nova Scotia and obtained a Certificate of Deposit in the amount of $75,000 issued in the name of "Charles R. Joy" along with a deposit of $9,858 to the Quantuim Bankruptcy Account. On the maturity of the CD the bank paid the funds to Joy who then absconded with the money. What kind of indorsement did Joy put on the check? What is the purpose of such an indorsement? Did the bank comply with its obligation with respect to the indorsement?
4. Davy Crockett Inn purchased a cashiers check payable to "Investments Universal" from the Bank of New Braunfels. Investments Universal was supposed to hold the check until it did certain work for Davy Crockett Inn. However, without performing that work it deposited the check, without indorsement, in its account at the Main Bank. The Main Bank credited the check to Investment Universal's account, stamped the check "credited to account of within named payee, absence of indorsement guaranteed," and sent it to the Bank of New Braunfels where it was paid. Davy Crockett Inn brought suit against the banks claiming the check was improperly paid without Investments Universal's indorsement. Is Davy Crockett's contention correct?
5. On March 27, Maisto purchased a cashier's check in the amount of $3,446 from City National by giving it cash plus a check for $2,585.50 drawn on Maisto's account at the Laurel Bank. Maisto then took the cashier's check, indorsed it along with some other items totaling $9,501, and deposited them in his account at the Laurel Bank. At that time Maisto's account at Laurel Bank was overdrawn by $21,079.43. The Laurel Bank took the $9,501 deposit and provisionally credited Maisto's account, thus reducing the overdrawn balance by $9,501. The next day the Laurel Bank returned the $2,585.50 check to City National which refused to pay it because of insufficient funds in Maisto's account. In turn, when the Laurel Bank presented the cashier's check in the amount of $3,446 to City National for payment, City National refused to honor it, contending that it had stopped payment because it had given the check in return for the N.S.F. check

from Maisto. Laurel Bank then brought suit against City National to recover on the $3,446 cashier's check. Laurel Bank can recover on the check if it can show it was a holder in due course. Has Laurel Bank given "value" so that it can qualify as a holder in due course?

6. Two notes were indorsed by the payee and negotiated to the bank as security for a loan before they were overdue. The payee was a regular depositor of the bank, and the loan was made to enable him to purchase a business. The bank make no inquiry regarding the origin of the notes and had no knowledge of the fact that the two notes had been given in payment for stock in an oil company and that the stock had never been delivered. Is the bank a holder in due course?

7. On March 17, 1966, McQueer purchased some equipment from Johnson's Garage and gave it a note for $10,698 dated March 17, 1966, payable "five days after date." Payee, Johnson's Garage, negotiated the note for value on March 28 to Unadilla National Bank. The bank claims that when it acquired the note, it was payable "45 days after date." On April 1, McQueer who was unaware that the note had been negotiated, paid Johnson's Garage the sum of $10,698. Now the bank seeks to collect on the note from McQueer, and he asserts that he has a personal defense of payment that is good against the bank. Can he assert the defense?

8. At age 90, Geneive Wetmore executed a promissory note payable to her nephew, William DeMint. The note provided "upon my death I promise to pay to the order of William A. DeMint the sum of Twenty Thousand and no/100 Dollars. With interest at no interest from date until paid . . . value received. Interest pays annually. For particular kindness to me and members of the Wetmore family during the course of many years." The provisions relating to interest, time of payment and the final sentence stating the reason for making the note were handwritten onto a printed form promissory note. Wetmore died at age 101, leaving assets totaling less than $10,000. DeMint brought suit against the executor to collect the note, and the executor defended on the grounds the note is not supported by consideration, so shows on its face and is not enforceable under § 3–408 and § 3–406. Is the note enforceable?

9. Gentry applied to James Pair, Inc., an employment agency, for a fee-paid job as a clerk-typist. No fee-paid jobs were available for her, and she was told to go see Kubatsky at Pendley Brothers about a job where "applicant pays fee. Pendley Brothers will refund in six months." Kubatsky interviewed Gentry and advised her that the company would refund the employment fee to her after she had worked for them for six months. Gentry accepted the job at $135 and signed an installment promissory note payable to James Pair, Inc. Gentry worked for two months and paid $163.80 on the note. Then she was advised that Kubatsky had no authority to agree to a refund of the job placement fee and that Pendley Brothers would not do so. Gentry contacted James Pair where she was advised that her contract was with them, not with her employer, and that she owed the full amount of the note. Gentry quit her job and sued James Pair for $163.80. James Pair counterclaimed for the remainder due on the note, claiming it had the rights of a holder in due course. Is James Pair's claim correct?

42

Liability of Parties and Discharge

Signed

Effect of Signing. Under the Code no person is liable on a negotiable instrument unless his signature appears on the instrument. As was indicated in Chapter 41, a signature can include any name, word or mark used in place of a written signature (Section 3–401).[1] An instrument may be signed either by the person himself or by an authorized agent.

The capacity in which a person signs an instrument will, as is discussed later in this chapter, affect his liability on the instrument. For example, a person might be the drawer or maker, drawee or acceptor, or an indorser, each of which has different legal liabilities.

When it is necessary to determine the capacity in which a person has signed an instrument, the position of his signature on the instrument is important but not conclusive. If a signature is placed on the lower right-hand corner of an instrument, the presumption is that he has signed as a maker or drawer. If the drawee named in a draft signs across the face of the instrument, it is a clear indication that he has "accepted" the draft; however his signature on any part of the instrument, front or back, will be held to be an acceptance in the absence of credible evidence of an intent to sign in some other capacity. A signature on the back of an instrument is presumed to be an indorsement (3–402).

Signing by Authorized Agent. A negotiable instrument may be signed by an authorized agent and, if properly signed, the principal will be bound as he would be had he signed it himself. All negotiable paper issued by a corporation is signed by an agent of the corporation. The agent is usually

[1] The numbers in the parentheses refer to the sections of the Uniform Commercial Code, 1972.

an officer of the corporation who is authorized to sign negotiable instruments on its behalf.

Since the liability of the parties to a negotiable instrument is determined by what is on the instrument, and parol evidence is admissible only to clear up ambiguities, the manner of signing in a representative capacity is important. An authorized agent is personally liable if he signs the instrument in his own name and does not indicate on the instrument either the name of the principal or the fact that he is signing in a representative capacity (3–403[2][a]).

If an authorized representative signs a negotiable instrument in his own name in a way that clearly indicates that he has signed in a representative capacity but fails to name the person represented, parol evidence is admissible, between the immediate parties to the instrument, to prove that they intended that the principal be liable and not the party who signed in the representative capacity. For example, if a negotiable instrument is signed, "Axe, agent" and retained by the payee who then sues Axe on the instrument, parol evidence would be admitted to prove that the payee knew that Axe was acting as agent for Parks, his principal, and that the parties intended Parks to be bound rather than Axe. However, if this instrument had been negotiated to a holder in due course, Axe would be personally liable on the instrument (3–403[2][b]).

If a negotiable instrument is signed in the name of an organization and the name of the organization is preceded or followed by the name and office of an authorized individual, the organization and not the officer who has signed the instrument in a representative capacity will be bound (3–403 [3]).

The proper way for a person executing a negotiable instrument in a representative capacity is as follows:

"Parks Corporation
"By Axe, Treasurer." or
"Paul Parks
"By Leonard Axe, his Agent."

Unauthorized Signature. If the name of a person is signed to a negotiable instrument by a person who has no authority to so sign the instrument, the signature is wholly inoperative and does not bind the person whose name is signed. Such a signing is a forgery. For example, if Thief steals Brown's checkbook and signs Brown's name to a check, Brown is not liable on the check because Thief had no authority to sign his name. However, Thief is liable on the check because he signed it (3–404).

SUMMARY

Under the Code no one can be held liable on a negotiable instrument unless his signature appears on the instrument. A person may use any name or symbol as his signature. A person who signs in a representative capacity should make it clear that he is signing as an agent so that the principal, rather than the agent will be liable.

Bell v. Dornan

201 A.2d 324 (Super. Ct. Pa. 1964)

This was an action by James G. Dornan (plaintiff) against Margaret S. Bell, executrix of the estate of William Bell, Jr. (defendant), to have a judgment taken on a judgment note set aside. Judgment for Dornan and Bell appealed. Judgment reversed.

In the lifetime of William Bell, Jr., a note signed as follows:

	"Memma M. Good
(Corporate	"Chet B. Earl Inc., (Seal)
Seal)	"James G. Dornan (Seal)"

and payable to him was issued. After the death of William Bell, Jr., the executrix of his estate took judgment on the note against James G. Dornan.

MONTGOMERY, JUDGE. Under the Uniform Commercial Code § 3–403, it is provided: "(2) An authorized representative who signs his own name to an instrument is also personally obligated unless the instrument names the person represented and shows that the signature is made in a representative capacity. The name of an organization preceded or followed by the name *and office* of an authorized individual is a signature made in a representative capacity."

Mr. Dornan's signature follows the name of the organization but does not show his office. In fact, opposite his name is the word "(SEAL)" as printed on the form of note used, which is in addition to the formal corporate seal imprint which was placed on the note, presumably by the proper custodian. Therefore, we are constrained to hold that under the provision of the code previously set forth he is personally obligated on the instrument. The presence of the corporate seal does not alter our view. The note might very well have been an obligation of the corporation as well as of Dornan.

Pollin v. Mindy Mfg. Co., Inc.

236 A.2d 542 (Sup. Ct. Pa. 1967)

This was an action by Pollin (plaintiff) against Mindy Manufacturing Company and its president, Robert Apfelbaum (defendants) to recover on thirty-six checks drawn in the name of the Company and signed by Apfelbaum. Judgment for Pollin. Apfelbaum appealed. Judgment reversed as to Apfelbaum.

The checks in question had been boldly imprinted at the top with "Mindy Mfg. Co., Inc., 26th & Reed Streets, Philadelphia, Penn., 19146 ________ Payroll Check No. ________" and with "Mindy Mfg. Co., Inc." imprinted above two blank lines appearing at the lower right-hand corner. Under the imprinted name of Mindy Mfg. Co. on the checks was the signature of Robert Apfelbaum without any designation of office or capacity. Pollin contended that Apfelbaum was liable on the checks since his signature was absolute and unqualified. Apfelbaum claimed he had signed in a representative capacity as president of Mindy Manufacturing and not in his individual capacity.

MONTGOMERY, JUDGE. Summary judgment against Apfelbaum was entered by the lower court on the authority of Section 3–403 of the Uniform Commercial Code which provides, "(2) An authorized representative who signs his (own) name to an instrument. . . . (b) except as otherwise established between the immediate parties, is personally obligated if the instrument names the person represented but does not show that the representative signed in a representative capacity . . . ," and our decisions thereunder.

The issue before us, therefore, is whether a third party to the original transaction, the endorsee in the present case, may recover against one who affixes his name to a check in the place where a maker usually signs without indicating he is signing in a representative capacity, without giving consideration to other parts of the instrument or extrinsic evidence. This appears to be a novel question under the Uniform Commercial Code.

If this were an action brought by the payee, parol evidence would be permitted to establish the capacity of the person affixing his signature under Section 3–403 (b) previously recited and our decisions in *Bell v. Dornan* and *Pittsburgh National Bank v. Kemilworth Restaurant Co.*

However, since this is an action brought by a third party our initial inquiry must be for the purpose of determining whether the instrument indicates the capacity of Apfelbaum as a signer. Admittedly, the instrument fails to show the office held by Apfelbaum. However, we do not think this is a complete answer to our problem, since the Code imposes liability on the individual only ". . . if the instrument . . . does not show that the representative signed in a representative capacity. . . ." This implies that the instrument must be considered in its entirety.

Although Section 3–401 (2) of the Uniform Commercial Code provides that "A signature is made by use of any name, including any trade or assumed name, upon an instrument, or by any word or mark used in lieu of a written signature," which would be broad enough to include the printed name of a corporation, we do not believe that a check showing two lines under the imprinted corporate name indicating the signature of one or more corporate officers would be accepted by any reasonably prudent person as a fully executed check of the corporation. It is common to expect that a corporate name placed upon a negotiable instrument in order to bind the corporation as a maker, especially when printed on the instrument, will be accompanied by the signatures of officers authorized by the by-laws to sign the instrument. While we do not rule out the possibility of a printed name being established as an acceptable signature, we hold that such a situation is uncommon, and against a valid corporate signature. Corporations act through officers.

Next we must give consideration to the distinction between a check and a note. A check is an order of a depositor on a bank in the nature of a draft drawn on the bank and payable on demand. It is revokable until paid or accepted for payment. A note is an irrevocable promise to pay on the part of the maker. The maker of a check impliedly engages not only that it will be paid, but that he will have sufficient funds in the bank to meet it. In the present instance the checks clearly showed that they were payable from a special account set up by the corporate defendant for the purpose of paying its employees. This information disclosed by the instrument of itself would refute any contention that Apfelbaum intended to make the instrument his own order on the named bank to pay money to the payee. The money was payable from the account of the corporation defendant over which Apfelbaum as an individual had no control.

Considering the instrument as a whole we conclude that it sufficiently discloses that Apfelbaum signed it in a representative capacity.

Contractual Liability

Primary and Secondary Liability. A party to a negotiable instrument may be either primarily or secondarily liable for the payment of the instrument. The person primarily liable on a negotiable instrument is the person who, by the terms of the instrument, is absolutely required to pay the instrument. For instance, the maker of a note is absolutely required to pay the note and is the person primarily liable. The liability of a party secondarily liable on negotiable commercial paper is comparable in most respects to that of a surety on a simple contract. Secondary liability is a contingent liability and does not arise until the party who is primarily liable has defaulted in his performance.

Contract in General. The terms of the contract of the parties to negotiable commercial paper are not set out on the face of the instrument but are instead written into the contract by operation of law and are as much a part of the contract as though written out in full.

Contract of a Maker. The maker of a note is primarily liable for payment of the note. He has made an unconditional promise to pay a sum certain and is responsible for making good on that promise. The maker's contract is that he will pay the instrument according to its terms at the time he signs it; if the instrument is incomplete when the maker signs it, then his contract is to pay it as completed if it is completed as authorized (3–413).

Contract of Drawee or Acceptor. No person is primarily liable on a draft until it has been accepted by the drawee, after which the drawee becomes the person primarily liable. Usually, a check is paid when presented to the drawee bank, and no person becomes primarily liable on it. However, the drawee bank may, at the request of the drawer or holder, certify the check, in which case the certification of the check makes the certifying bank absolutely liable for the payment of the check. When a drawee accepts a draft he becomes liable on the draft as it reads at the time of his acceptance (3–413).

Contract of a Drawer. The drawer of a check (or other draft) is secondarily liable on the check (or draft). The drawer's contract is that if the check (or draft) is dishonored and if the drawer is given notice of the dishonor, he will pay the amount of the check (or draft) to the holder or to any indorser who takes it back. For example, Jones draws a check on his account at First National Bank payable to the order of Collins. If First National does not pay the check when it is presented for payment by Collins, then Jones is liable to Collins on the basis of his secondary liability.

Because a drawer is secondarily liable on a draft, he may disclaim this liability by drawing "without recourse." (3–413[2]).

Contract of Indorsers. All indorsers are secondarily liable. An indorser may avoid certain liability by qualifying his indorsement, that is, by indorsing "without recourse." Unless the indorsement disclaims liability, the indorser contracts that upon dishonor of the instrument and any necessary notice of dishonor he will pay the instrument according to its terms at the time of his indorsement to the holder or to any subsequent indorser who takes it back (3–414[1]). Indorsers are presumed to be liable in the order in which they have indorsed, from the last indorser back to the first.

An indorser who indorses "without recourse" or other similar qualifying language is not liable to the holder or indorsers for the nonpayment of the instrument by the party primarily liable. By so indorsing he relieves himself from the contractual liability as a guarantor of the instrument.

In addition, by indorsing, an indorser makes certain warranties which are discussed in the next section.

Contract of Accommodation Party. An accommodation party is a person who signs an instrument for the purpose of lending his name to another party to the instrument. For example, a bank may be reluctant to take a promissory note from a certain maker because of his shaky financial condition and may ask that the maker have a friend or relative sign the note as an accommodation maker.

The contract of an accommodation party will depend on the capacity in which he signs the instrument. An accommodation party may sign as a maker, drawer, acceptor or indorser, and thus his liability will be that of a maker, drawer, acceptor or indorser. If an accommodation party pays the instrument, he has a right of recover against the party on whose behalf he signed (3–415[5]).

Example of Contractual Liability in Operation. Suppose that Arch draws a check for $100 on his account at Bank payable to the order of Blum; Blum indorses the check "Pay to the order of Clark, Blum" and negotiates it to Clark; when Clark takes the check to Bank, it refuses to pay the check because there are insufficient funds in Arch's account to cover the check. The check has been presented and dishonored. Clark has two options: (1) first he can proceed against Blum on Blum's secondary liability as an indorser because by putting an unqualified indorsement on the check, Blum contracted to make the check good if it was not honored by the drawee; (2) Clark can proceed against Arch on his drawer's contractual liability because in drawing the check Arch promised to make it good to any holder if it was dishonored and he was given notice. Because Clark dealt with Blum, Clark is probably more likely to return it to Blum for payment; Blum then will have to go against Arch on Arch's contractual liability as drawer.

SUMMARY

Parties to negotiable commercial paper are either primarily or secondarily liable for payment of the instrument.

The terms of the contract of the parties to negotiable commercial paper are written into the instrument by operation of law. The maker of a note and the acceptor of a draft are primarily liable to pay it according to the terms of the instrument. The drawer is secondarily liable; he promises to pay the holder if the instrument is dishonored and he is given notice. Indorsers, who do not qualify their indorsements, contract to pay if the instrument is dishonored on presentment and they are given notice. Indorsers are presumed to be liable in the order in which they have indorsed from the last indorser back to the first.

An accommodation party is liable in the capacity in which he has signed the instrument, as maker, drawer, acceptor or indorser.

Acceptance: Presentment: Dishonor

Introduction. As discussed in the preceding section, primary and secondary liability of a party to a negotiable instrument frequently depends on whether an instrument has been accepted, presented for payment, and/or dishonored.

Acceptance by Drawee. A drawee is not liable on a check or other draft until he accepts it. The drawing of a check or draft on a named drawee is not an assignment of funds in the drawee's hands but is instead an order by the drawer addressed to the drawee ordering him to pay to the payee the sum for which the instrument is drawn. Until the drawee accepts the instrument, there is no contractual relation between the holder of the instrument and the drawee (3–409). The drawee may, and usually does, owe a contractual duty to the drawer of the check or draft to pay or accept it, and if he dishonors the instrument by his failure or refusal to accept or pay it, he will be liable to the drawer for breach of the drawer-drawee contract.

For example, if Jones has $100 in a checking account at First National Bank and writes a check for $10 drawn on First National and payable to Smith, the writing of the check is not an assignment to Smith of $10 of the $100 Jones has in her account. The writing of the check is the issuance of an order by Jones to First National to pay $10 from her account to Smith or to whomever Smith requests it be paid. First National owes no obligation to Smith to pay the $10 to her unless it certifies (accepts) the check. However, if Smith presents the check for payment and First National refuses to pay it even though there are sufficient funds in Jones's account, then First National will be liable to Jones for breaching its contractual obligation to her to pay items properly payable from existing funds in her account. The liability on a bank for wrongful dishonor of checks is discussed in more detail in Chapter 43.

Nature of Acceptance. An acceptance is the drawee's signed commitment to honor the draft as presented. The acceptance must be written on the draft and it may consist of the drawee's signature alone (3–410).

A reasonable time for presentment for acceptance or payment is determined by the nature of the instrument, by trade or bank usage, and by the facts of the particular case. For example, in a farming community a reasonable time to present a promissory note may be six months or within a short time after the crops are sold because it is expected that the payment will be made from the proceeds of the crops.

A reasonable time to present a check to hold the drawer liable is presumed to be 30 days; a reasonable time to present a check in order to hold an indorser liable is to present it within seven days of his indorsement. (3–503).

Rights of Party to Whom Presentment Is Made. The party to whom presentment is made may, without dishonoring the instrument, require the exhibition of the instrument and reasonable identification of the person making presentment and evidence of his authority to make it if he is making it for another person. He is entitled to the surrender of the instrument when it is paid (3–505).

Effect of Unexcused Delay in Presentment. If presentment of a negotiable instrument is delayed beyond the time it is due, and if there is no valid excuse for the delay, then the indorsers are discharged from liability on the instrument. Under certain circumstances a drawer or maker can also be discharged of liability if the bank in which the funds to pay the note or draft were deposited becomes insolvent during the delay (3–502[1]).

Dishonor. An instrument is dishonored when it has been duly presented and acceptance or payment is refused or cannot be obtained within the time prescribed in the Code (3–507[1)]).

When an instrument has been dishonored, the holder has an immediate right of recourse against the parties secondarily liable provided he has given them any necessary notice of dishonor (3–507[2]).

Notice. When a negotiable instrument is dishonored, the holder of the instrument must give notice of the dishonor to any indorsers, drawers, acceptors or makers who he may want to hold liable on the instrument. Such notice may be given in any reasonable manner and may be oral or written. (3–508).

SUMMARY

A draft or check is not an assignment of funds in the hands of the drawee and the drawee is not liable on the instrument until he accepts it. The drawee may accept a draft by signing his name on the draft. An acceptance is a commitment to honor the draft as drawn.

Presentment for payment is necessary to hold parties liable on an instrument and must be made within a reasonable time.

Exhibition of the instrument, indentity and authority of the party presenting, receipt for payment, and surrender of the instrument on payment in full may be demanded. Failure to present the instrument in a timely fashion or when due without excuse discharges the indorsers from their contractual liability to make the instrument good.

An instrument has been dishonored when it has been duly presented and acceptance or payment cannot be obtained within the prescribed time. When an instrument is dishonored and required notices have been given, the holder has a right of recourse against the drawers and indorsers.

Dluge v. Robinson

204 A.2d 279 (Super. Ct. Pa. 1964)

This was an action by Ethel Dluge and Benjamin Rimm, Executors of the estate of Isaac Dluge, deceased (plaintiffs), against Joseph G. Robinson (defendant) to recover a judgment for the amount of a check. Judgment for Dluge and Robinson appealed. Judgment reversed and judgment for Robinson entered.

Robinson indorsed two checks and negotiated them to Isaac Dluge. When presented for payment the drawee bank refused payment because of insufficient funds. Evidence was offered to prove that the checks were returned to Robinson but there was no evidence offered to prove that a demand was made, and the trial court found that demand was not made until nearly seven months after the dishonor of the checks.

FLOOD, JUDGE. If Dluge and Rimm were holders in due course, they would have to prove only (1) that Robinson endorsed the checks and delivered them to Dluge, and (2) that they had been presented to the endorser for payment within a reasonable time. Uniform Commercial Code § 3–501(1) (b). In the case of an uncertified check this is presumed to be within seven days after the endorsement. U.C.C., § 3–503(1) (e), §3–503(2) (b).

"Presentment is a demand for acceptance or payment . . . by or on behalf of the holder," U.C.C., § 3–504(1). The only evidence of any demand was the admission by Robinson that he received a letter from Dluge's attorney demanding payment. Robinson did not state when he received this letter. Dluge did not offer the letter in evidence and there is no way to determine from the record when it was sent except that it was presumably sent before the complaint was filed on September 12, 1960, seven months after the checks were dishonored by the drawee bank. Since Robinson denied any demand at the time the checks were returned to him, and the record is otherwise barren of any evidence of demand within seven days, or any reasonable time, after endorsement, the Dluges did not establish any right to recover even if they had been holders in due course.

Dluge's executors are not holders in due course. Dluge gave the checks to Robinson without any demand for payment, so far as the record shows, and was not in possession of them when the suit was brought. Therefore he was not the holder. " 'Holder' means a person who is in possession of a document of title or an instrument or an investment security drawn, issued or indorsed to him or to his order or to bearer or in blank," U.C.C., § 1–201(20). *A fortiori,* he was not a holder in due course, U.C.C., § 3–302(1).

Warranties of Parties

Whether or not a person signs the instrument he may be liable on the basis of certain implied warranties. These warranties are of two types: (1) those imposed on persons who *transfer* instruments and (2) those imposed on persons who *present* instruments *for payment or acceptance.*

Transferor's Warranties. Any person who transfers an instrument and receives consideration makes five transferor's warranties to his transferee; in addition, if the transfer is by indorsement, they are made to any subsequent holder who takes the instrument in good faith. The five transferor's warranties are:

1. That the transferor has good title to the instrument or is authorized to obtain payment or acceptance on behalf of one who has a good title;
2. That all signatures are genuine or authorized;
3. That the instrument has not been materially altered;
4. That no defense of any party is good against him; and
5. That the transferor has no knowledge of any insolvency proceedings against the maker or acceptor or the drawer of an unaccepted instrument (3–417[2]).

If an indorser endorses an instrument "without recourse," he limits the fourth warranty to a warranty that he has no knowledge of such a defense.

While secondary liability often furnishes a sufficient basis for suing a transferor when the party primarily liable does not pay, warranties are still important. First, they apply even where the transferor did not indorse. Second, unlike secondary liability, they do not depend on presentment, dishonor, and notice, but may be utilized before presentment has been made or after the time for giving notice has expired. Third, it may be easier to return the instrument to a transferor on the grounds of breach of warranty than to prove one's status as a holder in due course against a maker or drawer.

Presentment Warranties. Under commercial law, a distinction as to warranties is made between a person who transfers an instrument to another person and a person who presents the instrument for payment of acceptance to a maker or drawee. The person to whom an instrument is presented for acceptance or payment will not normally pay or accept unless he thinks he is legally obligated to pay or is legally entitled to credit or payment from a third party. As a general rule, when payment or acceptance of an instrument is made, it is final in favor of a holder in due course or a person who in good faith changed his position in reliance on the payment (3–418). Thus if a drawee bank pays a check without checking to see if the drawer's signature is valid, the drawee cannot later obtain repayment from a holder in due course who presented it for payment if the drawee finds the drawer's signature was forged; likewise, the drawee bank that pays a check out of an insufficient funds account cannot obtain repayment from a holder in due course.

However, the general rule of finality of payment or acceptance is subject to three exceptions which are embodied in the Uniform Commercial Code as warranties made by a party presenting an instrument for payment or acceptance and all prior transferors. These warranties, in general, are:

1. That the party has good title to the instrument or is authorized to obtain payment or acceptance on behalf of one who has a good title;

2. That the party has no knowledge that the signature of the maker or the drawer is unauthorized;
3. That the instrument has not been materially altered (3–417[1]).

In certain exceptional cases these warranties do not apply when holders in due course are the presenting parties. For example, a drawer or maker should recognize his own signature and a maker or acceptor should recognize whether the instrument has been materially altered, so they do not get warranties covering these points from a holder in due course.

Operation of Warranties. Following are some examples which show how the transferor's and presentment warranties shift the liability back to a wrongdoer or to the person who dealt immediately with a wrongdoer and thus was in the best position to avert the wrongdoing:

1. Arthur makes a promissory note for $100 payable to the order of Betsy; Carl steals the note from Betsy, indorses her name on the back and gives it to David in exchange for a television set; David negotiates the note for value to Earl who presents the note to Arthur for payment. If Arthur refuses to pay the note because he has been advised by Betsy that it has been stolen, then Earl can proceed to recover the face amount of the note from David on the grounds that as a transferor David warranted that he had good title to the note and that all signatures were genuine. David, in turn, can proceed against Carl on the same basis—if he can find Carl. If he cannot, then David will have to bear the loss caused by Carl's wrongdoing because he was in the best position to ascertain whether Carl was the owner of the note and whether the indorsement of Betsy was genuine. Of course, even though Arthur did not have to pay the note to Earl, Arthur remains liable on his underlying obligation to Betsy.

2. Andrea draws a check for $10 on her checking account at First Bank payable to the order of Brown; Brown cleverly raises the check to $100, indorses it, and negotiates it to Carol; Carol then presents the check for payment to First Bank which pays her $100 and charges Andrea's account for $100; Andrea then asks the Bank to recredit her account for the altered check and it does so; the Bank can proceed against Carol for breach of the presentment warranty that the instrument has not been materially altered which she impliedly made to the Bank when she presented the check for payment; Carol in turn can proceed against Brown for breach of his transferor's warranty that the check had not been materially altered—if she can find him.

3. Bates steals Albert's checkbook and forges Albert's signature to a check for $10 payable to "cash" which he uses to by $10 worth of groceries from Grocer; Grocer presents the check to Albert's bank which pays the amount of the check to Grocer and charges Albert's account; Albert then demands

the bank recredit his account; the Bank can go against Grocer only if Grocer knew the signature of Albert had been forged; otherwise the Bank must look for Bates; the Bank had the responsibility to recognize the true signature of its drawer, Albert, and not to pay the check containing an unauthorized signature.

SUMMARY

The transferor of an instrument warrants title, genuineness of signatures or the authority of one signing, that the instrument has not been materially altered, that no defenses of any party are good against him (if he qualifies his warranty he warrants he has no knowledge of defenses to the instrument) and that he has no knowledge of any insolvency proceedings instituted with respect to the maker or acceptor or the drawer of an unaccepted instrument.

Any person who obtains payment or acceptance of an instrument warrants to a person who in good faith accepts or pays the instrument that he has good title or is authorized to act for a person who has good title to the instrument and that the instrument has not been materially altered. A holder in due course acting in good faith does not warrant to a maker or drawer the genuineness of their signatures.

County Trust Co. v. Cobb

17 UCC Rep. 1077 (2nd Cir. 1975)

This was a third-party action brought by the Franklin County Trust Company (third-party plaintiff) against Willard and Leon Cobb (third-party defendants) to recover for a forged check deposited in the Cobb's partnership account in the Franklin County Trust Co. Judgment for Leon Cobb. Reversed on appeal.

Willard D. Cobb in the course of his operation of the Taylor Insurance Agency in Brattleboro, Vermont, received a check dated March 17, 1968, in the amount of $13,750, issued by The Phoenix of Hartford Insurance Companies ("Phoenix") and payable to the order of R. A. McQuaide Milk Transport ("McQuaide"). The check was issed in payment of a property loss incurred by McQuaide under a policy issued by Phoenix through the Taylor Agency. Willard D. Cobb, without authorization from the payee, fraudulently endorsed the instrument in the name of the payee. He then added his own endorsement "For deposit only—Franklin County Trust Co., Willard D. Cobb."

Willard Cobb left the check with his brother Leon Cobb, who had no connection with the Taylor Agency, and requested him to deposit it in the bank for collection. Leon Cobb deposited the check in the Franklin County Trust Company as the initial deposit to a new account entitled "Econo Car Rental Center," a partnership that had been formed recently by the two brothers. The proceeds of the check were subsequently withdrawn from the partnership account by checks and paid to Willard Cobb for his own use. Franklin County Trust Company was adjudged liable to the drawer of the check. Franklin County Trust Company then brought a third-party action against Willard Cobb and Leon Cobb. Willard admitted his liability.

PER CURIAM. The District Court found that the wrongful act of Willard Cobb in forging the endorsement on the check was not committed in the course of the partnership business, and that Leon Cobb had acted in good faith and was not liable to the bank. We are constrained to reverse.

Section 4–207(2) of the Uniform Commercial Code provides that each "customer" of a bank "who transfers an item and receives a settlement or other consideration for it" warrants to the bank that "he has good title to the item." Section 4–104 of the UCC defines customer as "any person having an account with a bank." § 1–201(30) defines "person" to include any "organization" and §1–201(28) in turn defines "organization" to include a partnership. The partnership "Econo Car Rental Center" was the customer which deposited the check in the partnership account. That partnership was credited with the amount of the check. The partnership thus became liable to the bank under § 4–207(2) on its warranty that it had good title to the check. It did not have good title because of the forged endorsement.

Leon Cobb was a member of the Econo Car Rental partnership. He is therefore liable for the partnership debts under Vt. Stat. Ann. tit. 11, § 1207. The partnership debt arose from its breach of warranty to the bank. That warranty was a partnership warranty and a member of the partnership cannot escape liability even if some of the partners did not participate in the swindle.

It is too bad that Leon was swindled by his brother Willard, but as between two innocent parties, the bank, under the UCC, must prevail over brother Leon.

Conversion of Instruments

Conversion of Instrument. Conversion of an instrument is an unauthorized assumption and exercise of ownership over it. A negotiable instrument can be converted in a number of ways. For example, if it is presented for payment or acceptance and the person to whom it is presented refuses to either pay, accept or return it. An instrument is also converted if a person pays an instrument on a forged indorsement (3–419). For example, Able draws a check on his account at First Bank payable to the order of Barker. If Collins steals the check from Barker, forges Barker's indorsement on it, and cashes it at First Bank, the bank has converted Barker's property because the bank had no right to pay it without her indorsement.

The measure of liability of a drawee who has converted an instrument usually is the face amount of the instrument (3–419[2]).

Harry H. White Lumber Co., Inc., v. Crocker-Citizens National Bank

61 Cal. Rptr. 381 (Ct. App. Cal. 1967)

This was an action by Harry H. White Lumber Company (plaintiff) against Crocker-Citizens National Bank (defendant) to recover for the conversion of a check payable to White Lumber Co. that was paid by Crocker-Citizens Bank on a forged indorsement. White Lumber Company's action was dismissed by the trial court and it appealed. Judgment reversed.

Between December 10, 1964, and January 15, 1965, AIRE-TARE wrote four checks totalling about $4,700 payable to the order of Timberline Roofing Company and Harry H. White Lumber Company and delivered the checks to the joint payee, Timberline Roofing Company. Timberline indorsed its name and then forged the Harry H. White Lumber Company name to each of the checks. Timberline presented them to and received payment for them from Crocker-Citizens National Bank. Harry H. White Lumber claimed it had an interest in the checks, that it was damaged when the bank cashed them for Timberline, and that it was entitled to recover those damages from Crocker National.

McCoy, Judge. The question posed by this appeal is: Does a joint payee of a check have a cause of action against a collecting bank which has paid a check made payable to joint payees bearing an indorsement effected by one joint payee signing his own name and forging that of his joint payee? We hold "yes" under both the Negotiable Instruments Law and the California Commercial Code—Commercial Paper provisions.

The relevant portion of the Commercial Code § 3–116 provides: "An instrument payable to the order of two or more persons . . . (b) if not in the alternative is payable to all of them and may be negotiated, discharged or enforced only by all of them." By the express provisions of § 3–116, subdivision (b) all the joint payees must join not only for negotiation, but also for discharge as well.

Other pertinent sections of the Commercial Code are: § 3–404: "(1) Any unauthorized signature is wholly inoperative as that of the person whose name is signed unless he ratifies it or is precluded from denying it; but it operates as the signature of the unauthorized signer in favor of any person who in good faith pays the instrument or takes it for value. (2) Any unauthorized signature may be ratified for all purposes of this division. Such ratification does not of itself affect any rights of the person ratifying against the actual signer." Section 1–201, subsection 43: " 'Unauthorized' signature or endorsement means one made without actual, implied or apparent authority and includes a forgery." Section 3–306: "Unless he has the rights of a holder in due course any person takes the instrument subject to. . . . (d) The defense that he or a person through whom he holds the instrument acquired it by theft. . . ." Section 3–419: "(1) An instrument is converted when . . . (c) It is paid on a forged indorsement."

The comments under §§ 3–404 and 3–419 indicate that § 3–419 changes the preexisting California law and now gives the payee of a forged check a cause of action for conversion against the drawee (payor) bank. But no change is indicated as to the preexisting California case law permitting the payee to recover from a collecting bank which has paid out on a forged indorsement.

Thus, the Harry H. White Lumber Co. has a cause of action against the Crocker-Citizens National Bank on the check governed by the provisions of the Uniform Commercial Code.

Discharge

Discharge by Payment or Tender. Generally all parties to negotiable commercial paper are discharged when the party primarily liable on it pays the amount due in full to a bona fide holder. The liability of any party is discharged to the extent of his payment or satisfaction to the holder. If a third party claims he is the true owner of the instrument, the party making payment can still be discharged even though he is given notice or has knowledge of the claim. To prevent such payment the claimant must either supply adequate indemnity or obtain a court order enjoining payment (3–603[1]).

A party is not discharged if he pays in bad faith or if he pays a holder who acquired the instrument by theft or who (unless having the rights of a holder in due course) obtained it from someone who acquired it by theft (3–603[1][a]). Also, a party is not discharged if he pays or satisfies a holder of an instrument which has been restrictively indorsed in a manner not consistent with the terms of the restrictive indorsement. For example, Arthur makes a note for $100 payable to the order of Bryan. Bryan indorses the note "Pay to the order of my account no. 16154 at First Bank, Bryan" and entrusts his employee Clark with the note. Clark takes it to Arthur who pays Clark the $100 and Clark runs off with it. Arthur is not discharged from liability because he did not make the payment consistent with the terms of the restrictive indorsement (3–603[1][b]).

Discharge by Cancellation. The holder of a negotiable instrument may discharge the instrument by cancellation. Any destruction or mutilation of a negotiable instrument is a cancellation if the destruction or mutilation is done with the intent that the instrument will no longer evidence an obligation (3–605[1][a]). However, if such destruction or mutilation is by accident, the instrument will not be discharged. In the event the instrument is lost, destroyed, or mutilated, the original terms of the instrument may be established by parol or secondary evidence (3–804).

Discharge by Alteration. Any alteration of an instrument is material if it changes the contract of any of the parties to the instrument in any respect. For example, a change in the number or relation of the parties, or the completing of an incomplete instrument other than as authorized, or the changing of the writing as signed by adding to it or removing any part of it is a material alteration (3–407[1]). A change which in no way affects the contract of the parties such as crossing a "t," dotting an "i" or correcting the grammar in the instrument is not a material alteration.

Generally an alteration by a holder which is both fraudulent and material discharges any party whose contract is changed unless the party consents to the change or is precluded from asserting the defense (3–407[2][a]). For example, Alice draws a check for "one dollar" ($1) in a way that makes it easy for Charles, the payee, to raise it to read "one hundred one" ($101). Charles then negotiates the instrument to Harold. Normally, Alice would be discharged from her drawer's liability by the fraudulent and material alteration made to the check by Charles. Alice had ordered that her bank pay Charles one dollar and he had changed her order, thus relieving her of liability. However, if Alice's negligence contributes to the alteration, she would not be discharged of her liability to a holder in due course to whom the alteration was not obvious and who had no notice of it.

A holder in due course who takes an instrument after it has been altered can enforce it according to its original terms. When an incomplete instrument has been completed after it left the drawer's hands, a holder in due course can enforce it as it is completed (3–407[3]). For example, if Sam draws a check payable to Frank's Nursery, leaving the amount blank, and gives it to his gardener with instructions to purchase some fertilizer at Frank's, filling in the purchase price of the fertilizer when it is known. The gardener fills in the check for $100 and gives it to Frank's in exchange for the fertilizer ($7.25) and the difference in cash ($92.75). The gardener then absconds with the cash. If Frank's had no knowledge of the unauthorized completion, it could enforce the check for $100 against Sam.

Discharge by Impairment of Recourse. If a party to an instrument has posted collateral to secure his or her performance and a holder surrenders the collateral without the consent of parties who would benefit from the collateral, such parties are discharged (3–606). An example of how release of collateral by a holder of a note served to discharge an accommodation maker is shown in the case that follows, *Beneficial Finance v. Marshall.*

SUMMARY

Payment to a bona fide holder at or after the due date of negotiable commercial paper discharges all parties to the instrument. If a third party makes a claim to the instrument, payment to the holder discharges the party making payment unless the party making the claim supplies indemnity or enjoins payment in a suit in which the adverse claimant and the holder are parties. Payment in bad faith to a thief does not discharge the party.

Cancellation must be destruction of the instrument with intent to discharge the parties or by marking it on the face in such a manner that the intent to cancel is apparent.

Any material alteration of an instrument by a holder with fraudulent intent discharges any party whose contract is altered but it does not affect the rights of a holder in due course.

The release of any party or the surrender of collateral discharges any party who has recourse against the discharged party unless all rights are reserved.

Beneficial Finance Co. v. Marshall

18 UCC Rep. 1041 (Ct. App. Okla. 1976)

This was an action brought by the Beneficial Finance Co. (plaintiff), a payee on a note, against the maker, Marshall (defendant), and the accommodation maker, Alva Garren (defendant) to recover the unpaid balance of the note. The trial court awarded judgment to Garren on the grounds he had been discharged. Affirmed on appeal.

Mr. and Mrs. Marshall went to Beneficial Finance to borrow money but were deemed by Beneficial's Office Manager, Puckett, to be bad credit risks. The Marshall's stated their friend Garren would be willing to cosign a note for them if necessary. Puckett advised Garren not to cosign because the Marshall's were bad credit risks. This did not dissuade Garren from cosigning a note for $480, but it prompted him to ask Beneficial to take a lien or security interest in Marshall's custom built Harley Davidson motorcycle, then worth over one thousand dollars. Beneficial took and perfected a security interest on the motorcycle.

Marshall defaulted on the first payment. Beneficial gave notice of the default to Garren and advised him that it was looking to him for payment. Garren then discovered that Beneficial and Marshall had reached agreement whereby Marshall would sell his motorcycle for $700; he was to receive $345 immediately which was to be applied to the loan and he promised to pay the balance of the loan from his pocket. Marshall paid Beneficial $89.50 and left town without giving the proceeds of the sale to Beneficial. Because Beneficial was unable to get the proceeds, it brought suit against Garren. Garren's defense was that he signed the note as an accomodation maker and was entitled to invoke the defense of discharge under § 3–606(1)(b) because the collateral for the loan had been impaired.

Box, Judge. Beneficial concedes Garren's status as an accommodation maker. Its sole contention is that notwithstanding his surety status, Garren is "absolutely liable" to Beneficial since he is a co-maker.

An accommodation party is liable "in the capacity in which he has signed." § 3–415. Since Garren executed the note as a maker he was, as Beneficial urges, jointly and severally liable on the note as a co-maker. § 3–119(e) & (f). This is settled law, but it does not resolve the instant controversy. An accommodation party possesses certain defenses not ordinarily available to the maker or indorser, which can be asserted against all but holders in due course without notice of his accommodation status. The most important of these defenses are found in § 3–606. Under § 3–606(1)(b) the accommodation party is discharged when, without his consent, the holder "unjustifiably impairs any collateral for the instrument." The major question in this appeal is whether Garren was discharged under this section, when the collateral for the loan was sold by the principal debtor and was with the express authority of the creditor.

Beneficial had a security interest in the collateral security (the motorcycle) which had been perfected by filing. Beneficial subsequently gave Marshall, the principal debtor, the express authority to sell the collateral so that it could recover the unpaid balance due on the note. By so doing Beneficial completely relinquished the security interest in the collateral. This is necessarily so because under § 9–306(2) when the debtor sells collateral pursuant to the authority of the creditor, the security interest is immediately cut off. As a consequence Garren's right as surety to be subrogated to the security interest upon payment of Beneficial's claim was likewise destroyed. Obviously when the creditor has lost his security interest in the collateral the surety has also lost his right of recovery against the collateral—a right which more often than not prompted him to enter the agreement in the first place.

The net result of the loss of security in this manner is that the surety's risk is greatly increased, and the law has traditionally held that conduct by the creditor which increases the surety's risk results in a discharge of the surety. Indeed, it appears to have been the common law rule that when the chattel mortgagee or other secured creditor consented to sale or disposition of the collateral, or released the collateral in some manner, the surety was discharged.

The one unifying conclusion that can be drawn from these cases, in our opinion, is that § 3–606(1)(b) will be interpreted broadly to include, in addition to conduct by the creditor which diminishes the value of the collateral, unreasonable acts which make the collateral unavailable to the surety and thus increase his risks. This view seems to be in accord with both the common law of suretyship and the expectations of the parties to a suretyship agreement.

In the instant case the secured creditor (Beneficial) could hardly have made the collateral more unavailable to Garren, the surety. Accordingly, we hold that the sale of the collateral without Garren's express consent constituted an unjustifiable impairment of collateral within the meaning of § 3–606, and that because the value of the collateral exceeded the value of the debt, Garren was totally discharged.

Exceptions to General Liability Rules

General Rules. Normally, a check bearing a forged payee's indorsement is not properly chargeable to a drawer's account nor must a maker pay the note to the current possessor of a note bearing a forged payee's signature. Likewise, the maker or drawer is normally liable for an instrument only according to its tenor at the time he signed it. However, the Code makes several exceptions to these general rules of liability.

Imposter Rule. An imposter is a person who misrepresents his identity to another for the purpose of inducing that person to deal with him in the belief that he is the person he represents himself to be. If a negotiable instrument is drawn payable to the order of or is indorsed to the person whom the imposter represents himself to be or to his confederate, an indorsement of the instrument by any person in the name of such payee or indorsee is effective (3–405[1][a]). For example, suppose that Axe steals Park's automobile. Axe finds the certificate of title in the automobile and then representing himself to be Parks sells the automobile to Berger Used Car Company and it draws its check payable to Parks for the agreed purchase price of the automobile and delivers the check to Axe. Any person can negotiate the check by indorsing it in the name of Parks. The rationale for the imposter rule is to put the responsibility for determining the true identity of the payee on the drawer of a check. The drawer is in a better position to do this than some later holder of the check who may be entirely innocent. The imposter rule allows that later holder to have good title to the check by making the payee's signature valid, even though it is a forgery, and forces the drawer to go after the wrongdoer who tricked him into signing the check.

Fictitious Payee Rule. Where the person signing as or on behalf of a maker or drawer intends the payee to have no interest in the instrument, or where an agent or employee of the maker or drawer has supplied him with the name of the payee intending the latter to have no interest in the instrument, any person can negotiate the instrument by indorsing it in the name of the named payee. For example, suppose that Axe who is employed by the Moore Corporation as an accountant in charge of accounts payable prepares a false invoice naming Parks, Inc., a supplier of the Moore Corporation, as having supplied Moore Corporation with goods and draws a check payable to Parks, Inc., for the amount of the invoice. He then presents it to Temple, treasurer of Moore Corporation, together with other checks with invoices attached, for Temple's signature, all of which Temple signs and returns to Axe for mailing. Axe then withdraws the check payable to Parks, Inc. Anyone can negotiate the check by indorsing it in the name of Parks, Inc. In such a case an employee of the drawer has supplied the drawer with the name of a payee, intending the named payee to have no interest in the check (3–405[1][b] and [c]).

The rationale for the fictitious payee rule is similar to that for the imposter rule. If someone has a dishonest employee or agent who is responsible for the forgery of some checks, the immediate loss on those checks should be placed on the employer of the wrongdoer rather than on some other innocent party. In turn the employer must locate his unfaithful employee or agent and try to recover from him.

Negligence in Signing. A person can be so negligent in drawing or signing a negotiable instrument that he in effect invites an alteration or an unauthorized signature on it. Such a negligent person will be precluded from asserting the alteration or lack of authority against a holder in due course or against a drawee or other payor who pays the instrument in good faith and in accordance with reasonable commercial standards (3–406). For example, if a check or other instrument is drawn for "one dollar" ($1) in such a manner as would easily permit one to alter it to read "One Hundred one dollars" ($101) and it is altered and a person who can qualify as a holder in due course takes the check for $101, the drawer will be held liable for the amount of $101 if under the circumstances the court finds that the negligent manner in which the check was drawn contributed to its alteration.

SUMMARY

Where an imposter has induced a person to issue a negotiable instrument to a named payee whom he intends to have no interest in it, the instrument can be negotiated by an indorsement in the name of the payee made by any person. If the drawer or a person authorized to sign for the drawer makes out a check to a named payee and does not intend that the named payee have any interest in the check, then under the fictitious payee rule any person may sign the name of the named payee and the indorsement will be effective to negotiate the instrument. The drawer of an instrument which is so negligently drawn that it invites alteration or an unauthorized signature and is altered or has a forged signature added may be precluded from asserting the alteration or forgery as a reason why the instrument should not be paid.

Philadelphia Title Insurance Co. v. Fidelity-Philadelphia Trust Co.

212 A.2d 222 (Sup. Ct. Pa. 1965)

This was an action by Philadelphia Title Insurance Company (plaintiff), the drawer of a check, against Fidelity-Philadelphia Trust Company (defendant), the drawee on the check, to have its account recredited. Philadelphia Title argued that one of the payees' signature had been forged so that the check was not properly payable by Fidelity-Philadelphia. Judgment for Fidelity-Philadelphia. Affirmed on appeal.

Mrs. Jezemski was separated from her husband and decided to obtain some money from him by having a mortgage placed on some property her husband held as administrator and heir of his mother's estate and taking the proceeds herself. She went to a lawyer with a gentleman whom she introduced as her husband, and they made out a bond and mortgage on her husband's land. Then she went to a title insurance company which under Philadelphia custom takes care of placing mortgages on property and paying the proceeds to the mortgagor. She told Philadelphia Title's representatives that her husband was too busy to come in that day, but that her husband's signature on the mortgage had been witnessed by her lawyer. Philadelphia Title then placed a mortgage on the property and gave Mrs. Jezemski a check made payable to Edmund and Paula Jezemski and Edmund Jezemski as administrator for his mother's estate. Mrs. Jezemski then forged her husband's signature to the check and negotiated it to a bank. Eventually the check was paid by Fidelity-Philadelphia which then charged the check to Philadelphia Title's account.

COHEN, JUSTICE. The parties do not dispute the proposition that as between payor bank (Fidelity-Philadelphia) and its customer (Title Company), ordinarily, the former must bear the loss occasioned by the forgery of a payee's endorsement (Edmund Jezemski) upon a check drawn by its customer and paid by it, 3–414. The latter provides, inter alia, that "(1) Any unauthorized signature [Edmund Jezemski's] is wholly inoperative as that of the person whose name is signed unless he ratifies it or is precluded from denying it."

However, the banks argue that this case falls within an exception to the above rule, making the forged indorsement of Edmund Jezemski's name effective so that Fidelity-Philadelphia was entitled to charge the account of its customer, the Title Company, who was the drawer of the check. The exception asserted by the banks is found in § 3–405(1)(a) of the Uniform Commercial Code—Commercial Paper which provides:

"An indorsement by any person in the name of a named payee is effective if (a) an imposter by the use of the mails or otherwise has induced the maker or drawer to issue the instrument to him or his confederate in the name of the payee."

The lower court found and the Title Company does not dispute that an imposter appeared before McAllister (attorney) and DiBenefetto (realtor), impersonated Mr. Jezemski, and, in their presence, signed Mr. Jezemski's name to the deed, bond and mortgage; that Mrs. Jezemski was a confederate of the imposter; that the drawer, Title Company, issued the check to Mrs. Jezemski naming her and Mr. Jezemski as payees; and that some person other than Mr. Jezemski indorsed his name on the check.

May Department Stores Co. v. Pittsburgh National Bank

374 F.2d 109 (3d Cir. 1967)

This was an action by May Department Stores Company (plaintiff) against Pittsburgh National Bank (defendant) for allegedly charging May Department Store's checking account with amounts paid on forged indorsements. Summary judgment for National Bank was affirmed on appeal.

An employee of the May Department Stores fraudulently caused it to draw some checks payable to fictitious suppliers. The wrongdoing employee then forged the indorsements of the fictitious payees, cashed the checks at National Bank, and converted the proceeds. The drawee, National Bank, charged the checks paid against the May Department Store account. May Department Stores sued National Bank, claiming the checks were not properly chargeable to the account since they were paid on forged indorsements.

PER CURIAM. The district court properly concluded that the bank was protected by the following provision of the Uniform Commercial Code as in force in Pennsylvania.

> (1) An indorsement by any person in the name of a named payee is effective if . . .
> (a) an agent or employee of the maker or drawer has supplied him with the name of the payee intending the latter to have no such interest, § 3–405(1)(c).

Leonard v. National Bank of West Virginia

145 S.E.2d 23 (Sup. Ct. W. Va. 1965)

This was an action by Leonard (plaintiff) against a drawee bank, National Bank of West Virginia (defendant), to recover money paid by National Bank on an alleged forged check and charged to Leonard's account. The Supreme Court held that National Bank was entitled to a directed verdict in its favor.

On August 3, 1961, Leonard made out a check for $600, signed it as drawer, and also endorsed his signature on the back of the check. He did not date the check nor did he fill in the payee's name. Leonard claimed he gave the check to a man named Santo to whom he owed $600 and that he indorsed the check on the back so that Santo could cash it "at the track." When the check was returned to Leonard by National Bank after it had charged the check to his account, the word "Thrity" [*sic*] had been written in front of the "Six hundred," the name Martin Mattson had been entered as payee, and the indorsement of Martin Mattson appeared on the back of the check above Leonard's signature. Leonard then sued National Bank to have his account recredited for $3,600.

BERRY, JUSTICE. The general rule with regard to altered or raised checks is that if a bank pays such checks it does so at its peril and can only debit the drawer's account for the amount of the check as originally drawn, but there is an exception in the case of altered or raised checks to the effect that if the altering or raising of the check is because of the carelessness of the maker or depositor, the bank cannot be held liable in such case.

It is clear from the evidence in this case and from the check, which was introduced into evidence as an exhibit, that the name of the payee was left blank, that the amount of the check opposite the dollar sign was left blank and a one and one-half inch space to the left of the words "Six hundred" was left blank, and that Leonard's signature on the back of the check as an endorser left a blank space of one inch from the top of the check. As the check was drawn, the blank space for the payee's name could have been made to "cash," any amount could have been placed in the space for the figure opposite the dollar sign and more than enough room was left for words to be filled in before the words "six hundred" in order to alter or raise this check, and all of such blank spaces were filled up in such manner that they could not easily arouse the suspicions of a careful person. It has been repeatedly held in such cases that the drawer is barred from recovery.

The check in question was drawn in such manner that it would be readily raised or altered and such changes could not be detected by the use of ordinary care. In fact, the carelessness of the drawing of the check in question would amount to gross negligence and Leonard would be estopped from any recovery if his were the only negligence involved because such action on his part would amount to negligence as a matter of law.

However, it has been held that the negligence of a depositor in drawing a check which can be altered does not render him liable if the bank fails to exercise due care in paying such check, but if the maker's carelessness is the proximate cause of the payment of such altered check on the part of the bank, the bank is not liable.

The negligence which Leonard endeavors to charge the bank within connection with this transaction is almost entirely based on evidence introduced by Leonard to the effect that the bank was negligent in not having the person who presented the check to the defendant bank for payment identified as the named payee and indorser on the check, Martin Mattson. There is no evidence in this case that the person who presented the check was not Martin Mattson, the named payee and also the person who indorsed the check above the endorsement of Leonard. . . . It would therefore, appear that the question as to whether the bank was guilty of negligence in not having Martin Mattson identified would be immaterial in this case when it was not proved that the signature was a forgery and further the evidence indicated that the bank did perform some identification procedure in this instance. Leonard also contends that the bank was negligent in not having the person who presented the check indorse it after the indorsement of J. P. Leonard. The signature in question speaks for itself and the more than sufficient space for indorsement of a payee above the name of Leonard's signature on the back of the check would constitute negligence on the part of Leonard for having left such space above his indorsement, and the bank could not be charged with negligence in such instance. Leonard further stated that he indorsed the check on the back in order that it could be cashed at the track which would clearly show his intention that the check could be cashed without difficulty, and the fact that he did indorse the check in blank and it was the last indorsement on the back thus made the check easily cashed without difficulty on the part of any person who presented it because it made the check bearer check payable on delivery.

The only other matter in which the defendant Bank could be charged with negligence in connection with the cashing of the check in question was the word evidently intended as thirty which appeared before the words "Six hundred" in a misspelled form as "Thrity." However, the writing is very similar to the words "Six hundred," which the jury found was in the handwriting of Leonard.

Problem Cases

1. Several checks payable to Southeastern Financial Corporation were signed as follows:

   CARRIAGE HOUSE MOBILE HOMES, INC.
   General Account
   By Woody Lacy /s/
   Authorized Signature
   By John Smith /s/
   Authorized Signature

   The checks were subsequently dishonored by the drawee bank. Southeastern then brought an action against John Smith, contending he was personally liable on the checks. Is John Smith personally liable?

2. Arthur Plotkin was the president and treasurer of Creative Travel Inc. which provided services to a company owned by Sumner Boches and Frank Griesing. On March 24, 1973, Boches drew a check for $6,038 payable to Creative Travel; that check was deposited in Creative's checking account at Commonwealth Bank but was returned for insufficient funds on April 2. Then Griesing issued a check dated April 13, 1973, for $6,038 payable to Arthur Plotkin. Plotkin indorsed the check "Arthur Plotkin" and below that was stamped "Creative Travel, Inc., for deposit only in 5–250." This check was also returned for insufficient funds and was charged back to Creative's account but the resulting overdraft in Creative's account exceeded the amount of the check. Commonwealth then brought a lawsuit against Arthur Plotkin as indorser of the check, claiming that he was personally liable on it. Plotkin contended that he had indorsed the check in a representative capacity and that any liability was the liability of the corporation on whose behalf he had signed. Is Plotkin personally liable?

3. On February 1, 1972, a note in the amount of $18,000 payable 30 days from date to P. J. Panzeca was made by Klein Ventures, Ltd., and signed by Llobell in his capacity as president of Klein Ventures. The note was given to Panzeca in payment for labor and materials. The note was signed on the reverse side by Llobell personally. The note was presented for payment, dishonored and protested on March 2, 1972. Panzeca then

brought suit against Llobell to recover the face amount of the note. Llobell claimed he should not be liable because his personal signature was given upon the oral representation of Panzeca that payment would be sought only from Klein Ventures and not from him personally. Is Llobell liable on the note?

4. Moore, a stockbroker, drew a check on its account at Morgan Guaranty Trust payable to Abraham. The check was stolen and Abraham's indorsement was forged on the check. The check was cashed at Bankers Trust which paid the presenter and then forwarded the check for collection to Morgan Guaranty for payment. When the forgery was discovered, Morgan Guaranty recredited Moore's account for the amount of the check and sought repayment from Bankers. Is Bankers liable to Morgan Guaranty?

5. On May 5, 1972, a check for $1,000 drawn by Capezio Philadelphia upon its account with Provident National Bank was issued to Capezio & Things and Michael DePalo. The check was deposited with National Bank of North America although it bore the indorsement of only one of the joint payees, Capezio & Things. Bank of North America credited Capezio & Things' account, indorsed the check, and sent it to Provident Bank for collection. Provident debited Capezio Philadelphia's account. However, the debit was rescinded when Capezio Philadelphia protested that the check had not been properly paid. What recourse does Provident Bank have against the Bank of North America?

6. Mary Hale Dibble was employed as the bookkeeper for a dentist, Dr. Grieshaber. As such she kept track of payments made by his patients, made entries in his ledger book, and made deposits to his account in the National Bank of Detroit often applying the doctor's indorsement stamp to checks. Over a period of a year, Ms. Dibble embezzled receipts of $1,857 from the doctor by forging his indorsement on 15 checks, adding her indorsement and cashing them at National Bank of Detroit. Having discovered Ms. Dibble's actions, does Dr. Grieshaber have any recourse against the National Bank of Detroit?

7. A check dated July 18, 1966 for $4,900 drawn on Bankers Trust Company was payable to the order of "Baiata Enterprises, Inc. & Small Business Administration, N.Y.C. & M. Speigal and Sons Oil Corp. & Tally Petroleum Corp. A.I.M.A." On July 18, 1966, the check was presented to the Chase Manhattan Bank by Rosario Baiata. At that time the check bore indorsements in the name of all the payees. Chase gave Baiata $4,900, indorsed the check and sent it to Bankers Trust who paid Chase for it. Later, it was discovered that the purported signature of "Arthur Dillon, Regional Director, SBA" on behalf of the SBA was a forgery. SBA's claim to the proceeds of the check was based on Baiata Enterprises' default on a loan SBA made to it. Does the SBA have any claim against Chase Manhattan and/or Bankers Trust?

8. Ernest Lee applied for a loan in the amount of $30,000 from the Credit Union for the purpose of purchasing a restaurant. Before approving the application, the Credit Union requested that Lee obtain co-makers as security. James Lee, Susan Lee, Warnetta Gussie and Kwang Rowe signed the promissory note (dated September 1, 1971) as co-makers. The loan became delinquent by June 3, 1972, but no attempt was made to collect the note at that time or to inform the co-makers of the delinquency. On August 8, 1972, Ernest Lee gave the Credit Union a post-dated check for $4,900 payable in October which would have brought the note up to date through October. The Credit Union was told by Lee that sufficient funds would be deposited to pay it in October, but when the Credit Union deposited the check in October it was returned due to insufficient funds. The Credit Union made repeated efforts to collect from Ernest Lee but never gave the co-makers notice of the acceptance of the post-dated check or the delinquency. When

the Credit Union learned Ernest Lee had filed a petition in bankruptcy, it filed suit against the co-makers. Are the co-makers liable on the note?

9. On October 30, 1969, Osborn executed a promissory note in the amount of $2,178 payable to the order of William Thomas on October 30, 1970, with interest at the rate of 7 percent. After the note was signed, Thomas had Osborn's signature notorized by a notary public who had seen him sign the note. The notary's acknowledgment was added to the note. Thomas then took the note to the county auditor's office and had it recorded. Osborn did not pay the note on the due date and when Thomas filed suit to collect it, Osborn claimed that the acknowledgment, notorization and recording violated 3–407 and thus discharged him of liability on the note. Has Osborn stated a valid defense?
10. Clarice Rich was employed by the N.Y. City Board of Education as a clerk. It was her duty to prepare requisitions for checks to be issued by the Board, to prepare the checks, to have them signed by authorized personnel, and to send the checks to the recipients. However, in some instances instead of sending the checks she retained them. Also, on a number of occasions she prepared duplicate requisitions and checks, which, when signed, she likewise retained. She then forged the indorsement of the named payees on the checks she had retained and cashed them at the Chemical Bank where the Board of Education maintained its account. After the Board discovered the forgeries, it demanded that the Chemical Bank credit its account for the amount of the forged checks. Is Chemical Bank required to credit the Board's account as requested?

43

Checks and Documents of Title

Checks

Relation between Drawer and Drawee Bank. A dual relationship exists between the bank and its customer who has a checking account. When the customer makes a deposit in a bank, the relation created between the customer and the bank is that of creditor and debtor, and if the deposit is to a checking account, the relation is also one of principal and agent. The customer is the principal and the bank is the agent. Under banking law as set out in the Code, the bank as agent owes a duty to the customer as principal to honor all checks properly drawn and payable, provided the customer has a balance sufficient to cover the amount of the check. A check is not an assignment of funds in the account (Section 3–409)[1] but is an order to the bank to make payment.

Bank's Duty to Pay. If a bank dishonors a check when the customer has a balance in his account sufficient to cover the check, the bank is liable for damages caused by the wrongful dishonor. If the dishonor occurs through a mistake on the part of the bank, its liability is limited to actual damages. However, consequential damages, such as damages for arrest or prosecution, may be recovered if the customer can prove such damages with reasonable certainty (4–402).

Bank's Right to Charge to Account. The bank has the right to charge any item, properly payable, to a customer's account even though the charge creates an overdraft. If an overdraft is created, the customer becomes indebted

[1] The numbers in parentheses refer to the sections of the Uniform Commercial Code, 1972.

to the bank for the amount of the overdraft, and the bank has the right to charge the next deposit the customer makes with the amount of the overdraft (4–401[1]).

If the bank in good faith pays an altered check, it may charge the customer's account with the amount of the check as originally drawn. Also, if an incomplete check of a customer gets into circulation and is completed and presented to the drawee bank for payment and the bank pays the check, it can charge the amount to the drawer-customer's account, even though the bank knows the check has been completed, unless it has notice that the completion was improper (4–401[2]).

Stop-Payment Orders. Since the bank acts as agent of the drawer in the payment of checks, it must follow all reasonable orders of the drawer relative to payments to be made on his behalf. If the drawer draws a check and then before the check is presented for payment or certification requests the bank not to pay the check—that is he issues a stop-payment order—the bank owes a duty to the drawer not to honor the check when presented. To be effective, the stop-payment order must be received by the bank at such time and in such manner as to afford the bank a reasonable opportunity to act on it prior to the time the bank has paid, certified, or committed itself on the check (4–403[1]).

The stop-payment order may be oral in which case it is binding on the bank for a period of only 14 days unless confirmed in writing within that time. When confirmed in writing, the stop-payment order is good for six months. The time may be extended, however, by renewing the stop-payment order before the expiration of the six months (4–403[2]). The bank is under no obligation to a customer to pay a check, other than a certified check, which is presented more than six months after its date, but may charge its customer's account for payment made thereafter in good faith (4–404).

Bank's Liability for Payment after Stop Payment. The bank is liable to the drawer of a check which it pays while a stop-payment order is in effect for any loss he suffers by reason of such payment, but the drawer has the burden of establishing the amount of the loss. To show a loss the drawer must establish that if the drawee bank had honored the stop-payment order so that the holder of the instrument had to come after the drawer for payment, that the drawer had a valid defense to payment which could have been successfully asserted against that holder of the instrument. To the extent the drawer had such a defense, he has suffered a loss due to the drawee's failure to honor the stop-payment order of the drawer.

For example, Brown buys what is warranted to be a brand new car from Bagley Buick and gives Bagley his check for $5,280 drawn on First Bank. Brown then discovers that the car is in fact a used demonstrator model and calls First Bank ordering it to stop payment on the check. If Bagley Buick presents the check for payment the following day and First Bank pays the check despite the stop payment order, Brown can require the bank to recredit his account because he had a valid defense (breach of warranty) that he could have asserted against Bagley Buick if it had sued him on the check. However, if Bagley Buick had negotiated the check to Sam Smith and Sam qualified as a holder in due course, then if the Bank paid the check to Sam over the stop payment order, Brown would not be able to have his account recredited. The reason for this is that Brown could not show he sustained any loss. If the Bank had refused to pay the check so that Smith came against Brown on his drawer's liability, Brown's personal defense of breach of warranty could not be asserted as a reason for not paying Smith and Brown's only recourse would be to go directly against Bagley Buick.

The bank cannot by agreement disclaim its responsibility for its own lack of good faith or failure to exercise ordinary care nor can it limit the measure of damages for such lack or failure (4–103[1]).

If the bank pays a check after it is given a stop-payment order, it acquires the rights of a transferee of the item and acquires, by subrogation, all of the rights of the person to whom it made payment, including his rights based on the transaction on which the check was based (4–407). In the example above involving Brown and Bagley Buick, if Brown was able to have his account recredited because the First Bank had paid the check to Bagley Buick over his stop payment order, then the Bank would have by subrogation Brown's rights against Bagley Buick for the breach of warranty.

Certified Check. Certification of a check is an acceptance by the drawee bank. Unless otherwise agreed, the bank owes no obligation to certify a check. When the bank certifies a check, it debits the amount of the check to the drawer's account and credits the amount to the certified check account. This certified check account, however, is not a trust fund set up for the payment of such checks, and if the certifying bank becomes insolvent before the certified check is presented for payment, the holder is merely a creditor of the bank.

If a check is certified by the drawee bank at the request of the drawer, the drawer remains secondarily liable on the check. However, if a check is certified by the drawee bank at the request of a holder of the check, then the drawer and any persons who have already indorsed the check are discharged of their secondary liability on the check (3–411). If the holder of a check chooses to have it certified, rather than seeking to have it paid at that time, then the holder has made a conscious decision to look to the certifying bank for payment and is no longer relying on the drawer or the indorsers to make it good.

Death or Incompetence of Customer. Under the general principles of agency law, the authority of an agent to bind his principal is terminated on the death or incompetence of the principal. This rule has been modified by the provisions of the Code relative to a bank's right to honor checks drawn prior to the death or incompetence of the drawer but presented to the drawee bank for payment thereafter. Under the provisions of the Code, the bank has authority to pay checks drawn by an incompetent customer unless the bank knows of the adjudication of incompetence. Neither death nor incompetence of a customer revokes the bank's authority to pay or certify a check until the bank knows of the fact of death or of an adjudication of incompetence and has a reasonable opportunity to act upon it. Even though the bank has knowledge of the death of the customer, it may, for a period of ten days after the date of his death, if it elects to do so, pay or certify checks drawn by him on or prior to that date. However, any person claiming an interest in the deceased customer's estate may order the bank to stop payment (4–405).

Customer's Duty to Report Forgeries and Alterations. The canceled checks drawn by a customer together with a statement of account are usually returned by the bank to the customer once a month, or otherwise made available to him. The customer, on receiving the checks and statement, owes a duty to examine them to discover if any of his signatures on the checks are forgeries or unauthorized or if any of the checks have been altered (4–406[1]).

If the customer fails to examine the checks and statement within a reasonable time, he cannot hold the bank responsible for the payment of checks on which there are forgeries, unauthorized signings or alterations if the bank can show it suffered a loss because of the customer's failure. For example, the bank might show that the forger absconded during that time (4–406[2][a]). In addition, if a series of forgeries, unauthorized signings or alterations are made by the same wrongdoer on any checks paid in good faith by the bank after the first check which had been forged or signed without authority or altered was available to the customer for a reasonable period not exceeding 14 calendar days and before the bank received notification from the customer of any such forgery, unauthorized signature or alteration, the customer cannot hold the bank responsible for paying the check (4–406[2][b]). This rule does not apply if the customer can establish a lack of due care on the part of the bank in paying any item (4–406[3]).

For example, suppose that Axe employs Fell as an accountant and over a period of three months Fell forges Axe's signature to ten checks and cashes them. One of the forged checks is included in the checks returned to Axe at the end of the first month and within 14 calendar days after the return of these checks Fell forges two more checks and cashes them. Axe does not examine the returned checks until a lapse of three months after the checks which included the first forged check were returned to him. The bank would be responsible for the first forged check and the two checks forged and cashed within the 14-day period after the return of the first statement and checks, but it would not be liable for the seven forged checks cashed after the expiration of the 14-day period.

In any event a customer must discover and report to the bank any forgery of his signature, any unauthorized signature, or any alteration within a year from the time the checks are made available to him. If he does not do so, he cannot require the bank to recredit his account for such checks. Similarly, a customer has three years from the time his checks are made available to him to discover and report any unauthorized indorsement; if the customer does not discover the unauthorized indorsement within three years he cannot require the bank to recredit his account for the amount of the check (4–406[4]).

SUMMARY

The relation between a bank and a customer having a commercial account on which checks may be drawn is that of debtor and creditor and principal and agent. In drawing a check the customer as principal authorizes the bank as agent to honor the check. The customer as principal has the right to order the bank to stop payment on a check and if the order to stop payment is received by the bank at such a time and in such form as to give it a reasonable opportunity, the bank owes a duty to refuse payment on an uncertified check. If it pays a check in disregard of a stop-payment order, it is liable to the drawer for any resulting loss.

A bank is not obligated to certify a check, but on certification it becomes primarily liable on the check and, if the check is certified at the request of the holder, the drawer and all prior indorsers are discharged.

A bank may pay checks drawn during a customer's lifetime or while competent and for a period of ten days after death or until the bank learns of an adjudication of incompetence. A customer owes a duty to report to the bank, within a reasonable time after a statement of account and canceled checks are made available, any unauthorized signatures and alterations.

Granite Equipment Leasing Corp. v. Hempstead Bank

9 UCC Rep. 1384 (N.Y. 1971)

This was an action brought by Granite Equipment Leasing Corp. (plaintiff) against Hempstead Bank (defendant) to recover the amount of a check charged to Granite's account. Judgment for Hempstead Bank.

Granite Equipment Leasing Corp. kept a checking account with Hempstead Bank. On October 10, 1968, Granite drew a check payable to Overseas Equipment Co., Inc. Five days later, after Overseas advised that the check had not been received, Granite wrote the Bank on October 15, 1968, to stop payment on the check. On that same day Granite authorized the Bank to wire the payee funds in the same amount as the stopped check and the Bank did so. Granite never renewed its stop payment order between October 1968 and November 10, 1969. On November 10, 1969, without notice or inquiry to Granite, the Bank accepted the original check to Overseas which had been stopped the year before, paid the face amount to a collecting bank, and charged Granite's account.

Granite then sought to recover from the Bank the amount charged because of the check paid to Overseas in November 1969. The Bank defended on the ground that under U.C.C. § 4–403 the stop payment order had expired for want of renewal, and that acting in good faith it was entitled under U.C.C. §4–404 to pay the stale check.

HARNETT, JUDGE. There is no doubt the check is stale. There is no doubt the stop payment order was properly given at the outset, and that it was never renewed. Granite essentially maintains the Bank had a duty to inquire into the circumstances of that stale check, and should not have paid in face of a known lapsed stop order without consulting its depositor.

The Uniform Commercial Code, which became effective in New York on September 27, 1964, provides that:

> (1) A customer may by order to his bank stop payment of any item payable for his account . . . (2) . . . A written [stop] order is effective for only six months unless renewed in writing. U.C.C. § 4–403.

The Official Comment to U.C.C. § 4–403 notes that:

> [t]he purpose of the [six-month limit] is, of course, to facilitate stopping payment by clearing the records of the drawee of accumulated unrevoked stop orders, as where the drawer has found a lost instrument or has settled his controversy with the payee, but has failed to notify the drawee.

Granite cannot be permitted to predicate liability on the part of the Bank on its failure to inquire about and find a stop payment order which had become terminated in default of renewal. *Feller v. Manufacturers Trust Co.,* held that a drawee bank was not liable to a drawer for payment of a check two months after expiration of a stop payment order which had not been renewed. See also, *William Savage, Inc. v. Manufacturers Trust Co.,* holding a bank not liable for payment on an eleven month old check after expiration of a stop payment order.

Neither may Granite predicate a claim of liability upon the Bank's payment of a stale check. The legal principles applicable to this circumstance are codified in U.C.C. § 4–404, which provides that:

> [a] bank is under no obligation . . . to pay a check, other than a certified check, which is presented more than six months after its date, but it may charge its customer's account for a payment made thereafter in good faith.

There is no obligation under the statute on the Bank to search its records to discover old lapsed stop payment orders. The Bank does not have to pay a stale check, but it may pay one in "good faith." Significantly, U.C.C. § 1-201(19) defines "good faith" as "honesty in fact in the conduct or transaction concerned." In the absence of any facts which could justify a finding of dishonesty, bad faith, recklessness, or lack of ordinary care, in the face of circumstances actually known, or which should have been known, the Bank is not liable to Granite for its payment of the check drawn to Overseas.

One statute invalidates stop payment orders not renewed within six months. Another statute allows payment in good faith of stale checks. Granite cannot combine the two statutes to reach a synergistic result not contemplated by either separately.

Granite's complete remedy lies in its pending Florida action against Overseas to recover the extra payment.

Nu-Way Services, Inc. v. Mercantile Trust Co.

530 S.W.2d 743 (Ct. App. Mo. 1975)

This was an action brought by Nu-Way Services, Inc. (plaintiff) against Mercantile Trust Company (defendant) to recover charges against Nu-Way's checking account made by Mercantile on 43 forged and six altered checks. The jury returned a verdict in favor of Nu-Way for $7,903.29 and on Mercantile's motion for a new trial, the trial court granted a new trial as to the amount of damages only. The Missouri Court of Appeals reversed and ordered judgment entered in favor of Nu-Way for $1,438.29 on the altered checks and in favor of Mercantile against Nu-Way on the forged checks.

Nu-Way, a truck repair company, maintained a checking account with Mercantile. The signature card for Nu-Way's president, Mariano Costello, was kept on file by the bank. In a gesture designed for the rehabilitation of a former convict, Mr. Costello hired James Ussery as night manager for Nu-Way. Part of Ussery's duties entailed obtaining automotive parts from parts companies. Mr. Costello would on occasion date and sign checks and fill in the name of the payee (always a parts company) for payment of parts used by Nu-Way, and the amount of the check would be left blank for Ussery to fill in when the cost of the parts was determined at the time they were picked up by him. On seven such checks which Mr. Costello had signed, Ussery made alterations to substitute his name as payee and cashed the checks for his own benefit. Ussery also had unauthorized access to Nu-Way's checkbook and removed a substantial number of blank checks from it. Ussery made use of 43 of the blank checks by forging Mr. Costello's signature on them after making himself the payee. The dates on the altered and forged checks were from July 29, 1971 to January 13, 1972.

Each of the forged checks was returned to Nu-Way by Mercantile along with an itemized statement of account at the end of each month the checks were cashed. And each month Mr. Costello would have a company clerk compare the amount of the checks with the statements looking only for mathematical computation errors by Mercantile. None of the Nu-Way employees, including Mr. Costello, examined any of the checks for forgeries or alterations nor compared the checks with the company checkbook. Ultimately, one of Nu-Way's vendors called Mr. Costello's attention to a check made payable to Ussery, and an investigation revealed the alterations and forgeries. Mercantile was notified of the irregularities and subsequently reimbursed Nu-Way for $231 to cover the amount of the first check altered by Ussery. Nu-Way brought suit to recover the amount paid out on its checking account on the forged and altered checks.

GUNN, JUDGE. In its argument that it has no liability to Nu-Way for the payments made on the altered and forged checks, Mercantile relies on § 4–406, which in pertinent part provides:

(1) When a bank sends to its customer a statement of account accompanied by items paid in good faith in support of the debt entries or holds the statement and items pursuant to a request or instructions of its customer or otherwise in a reasonable manner makes the statement and items available to the customer, the customer must exercise reasonable care and promptness to examine the statement and items to discover his unauthorized signature or any alteration on an item and must notify the bank promptly after discovery thereof.

(2) If the bank establishes that the customer failed with respect to an item to comply with the duties imposed on the customer by subsection (1) the customer is precluded from asserting against the bank

(a) his unauthorized signature or any alteration on the item if the bank also establishes that it suffered a loss by reason of such failure; and

(b) an unauthorized signature or alteration by the same wrongdoer on any other item paid in good faith by the bank after the first item and statement was available to the customer for a reasonable period not exceeding fourteen calendar days and before the bank receives notification from the customer of any such unauthorized signature or alteration.

(3) The preclusion under subsection (2) does not apply if the customer establishes lack of ordinary care on the part of the bank in paying the items.

Nu-Way concedes that under the facts of this case that § 406(3) places the burden upon it of proving that Mercantile lacked ordinary care in paying on the altered and forged checks.

We first consider the question of Mercantile's liability on the 43 forged checks. The fundamental rule in the Uniform Commercial Code regarding unauthorized signatures is stated in § 3–404(1) as follows:

Any unauthorized signature is wholly inoperative as that of the person whose name is signed unless he ratifies it or is precluded from denying it.

It is accepted that Ussery's forgeries of Mr. Costello's signature were unauthorized and would therefore be "wholly inoperative" as to Nu-Way unless Nu-

Way is "precluded from denying it." § 4–406 relates directly to the relationship between depositor and bank and affords an apt guide for determining whether a basis exists for precluding Nu-Way's denial of the signatures.

Initially, we find that Nu-Way failed to meet its obligation under subparagraph (1) of § 4–406, in that it did not "exercise reasonable care and promptness to examine the statement and items to discover [the] unauthorized signatures . . . on an item." In accordance with Mr. Costello's instructions, the Nu-Way clerk in charge of examining the bank statements examined Mercantile's statements to check the accuracy of the mathematics. The "items"—the cancelled checks—were not examined at all. Mr. Costello readily admitted that the checks were not scrutinized for forgeries as required by statute nor was reasonable notice given to Mercantile of any wrongdoing after the first check and statement was made available to Nu-Way within the meaning of § 4–406(a)(b). Hence, Nu-Way failed in its duties to discover and report the forgeries under § 4–406(2) and is precluded from recovering against Mercantile unless it can establish under § 4–406(3) lack of ordinary care on the part of Mercantile in paying the forgeries.

Under § 4–406(3) the burden of establishing Mercantile's lack of ordinary care rests staunchly on Nu-Way. Mercantile presented uncontradicted evidence from one of its officers that the forgery detection method applied by Mercantile was substantially the same as employed by other commercial banks in the St. Louis area. An operations officer of another St. Louis bank testified that the method used by Mercantile to detect forgeries by memorization of the authorized signature card was the same as utilized by his bank.

Nu-Way presented no evidence to refute Mercantile's evidence that the check processing method followed by Mercantile was consistent with general banking usage. By Nu-Way's failure to review its own bank statements when supplied by Mercantile, it had the burden under § 4–406(3) to establish lack of ordinary care by Mercantile. On the record before us we conclude that Nu-Way failed to meet its burden as to the 43 forged checks.

The matter of the altered checks presents a different question. Whereas the forgeries were skillfully written, the alterations were maladroitly performed and the changes so egregious as to call for the reproval of the bank clerk. The alterations should have been readily discovered, and the bank clerk ignored specific instructions to withhold payments on altered checks. Thus, there was substantial evidence to uphold the jury verdict of $1,438.29 on the alterations.

Documents of Title

Introduction. The practice of storing or shipping goods and the giving of a warehouse receipt or bill of lading representing the goods and the transfer of such warehouse receipt or bill of lading as representing the goods is of ancient origin. The warehouseman or the common carrier is a bailee of the goods and he contracts to store or transport the goods and to deliver them to the owner, or to act in accordance with the lawful directions of the owners. The warehouse receipt or the bill of lading may be either negotiable or nonnegotiable. To be negotiable, a warehouse receipt, bill of lading or other document of title must, by its terms, provide that the goods are to be delivered to bearer or to the order of a named person (7–104[1]). The primary difference between the law of negotiable commercial paper and that of negotiable documents of title is based on the difference between the obligation to pay money and the obligation to deliver specific goods.

Warehouse Receipts. A warehouse receipt, to be valid, need not be in any particular form, but if it does not embody within its written or printed form each of the following, the warehouseman is liable for damages caused by the omission to a person injured as a result: (*a*) the location of the warehouse where the goods are stored; (*b*) date of issue; (*c*) consecutive number of the receipt; (*d*) whether goods are to be delivered to bearer or to the order of a named person; (*e*) rate of storage and handling charges;[2] (*f*) description of goods or the packages containing them; (*g*) the signature of the warehouseman or his agent; (*h*) whether the warehouseman is the owner, either solely, jointly, or in common with others, of the goods; and (*i*) statement of the amount of advances made and of liabilities incurred for which the warehouseman claims a lien or security interest. Other terms may be inserted (7–202).

A warehouseman is liable to a purchaser for value in good faith of a warehouse receipt for nonreceipt or misdescription of goods. The receipt may conspicuously qualify the description by a statement such as "contents, condition and quantity unknown" (7–203).

Because a warehouseman is a bailee of the goods, he owes to the holder of the warehouse receipt the duties of a mutual benefit bailee and must exercise reasonable care (7–204). The duties of a bailee are discussed in detail in Chapter 31. The warehouseman may terminate the relation by notification where, for example, the goods are about to deteriorate or cause a threat to other goods in the warehouse (7–206).

Unless the warehouse receipt otherwise provides, the warehouseman must keep separate the goods covered by each receipt; however, different lots of fungible goods, such as grain, may be mingled (7–207).

A warehouseman has a lien against the bailor on the goods covered by his receipt for his storage and other charges incurred in handling the goods (7–209). The Code sets out a detailed procedure for enforcing this lien (7–210).

Bills of Lading. In many respects the right and liabilities of the parties to a negotiable bill of lading are the same as those of the parties to a negotiable

[2] Where goods are stored under a field warehouse arrangement, a statement of that fact is sufficient on a nonnegotiable receipt.

warehouse receipt. The contract of the issuer of a bill of lading is to transport goods whereas the contract of the issuer of a warehouse receipt is to store goods. Like the issuer of a warehouse receipt, the issuer of a bill of lading is liable for nonreceipt or misdescription of the goods, but he may protect himself from liability where he does not know the contents of packages by marking the bill of lading "contents or condition of contents of packages unknown" or similar language. Such terms are ineffective when the goods are loaded by an issuer who is a common carrier unless the goods are concealed by packages (7–301).

A carrier who issues a bill of lading must exercise the same degree of care in relation to the goods as a reasonably careful person would exercise under like circumstances. A liability for damages not caused by the negligence of the carrier may be imposed on it by a special law or rule of law. Under tariff rules a common carrier may limit his liability to a shipper's declaration of value provided the rates are dependent on value (7–309).

Negotiation of Document of Title. A negotiable document of title and a negotiable instrument are negotiated in substantially the same manner. If the document of title provides for the delivery of the goods to bearer, it may be negotiated by delivery. If it provides for delivery of the goods to the order of a named person, it must be indorsed by that person and delivered. If an order document of title is indorsed in blank, it may be negotiated by delivery unless it bears a special indorsement following the blank indorsement, in which event it must be indorsed by the special indorsee and delivered (7–501).

A person taking a negotiable document of title takes as a bona fide holder if he takes in good faith and in the regular course of business. The bona fide holder of a negotiable document of title has substantially the same advantages over a holder who is not a bona fide holder or over a holder of nonnegotiable document of title as a holder in due course of a negotiable instrument has over a holder who is not a holder in due course or over the holder of a nonnegotiable instrument.

Rights Acquired by Negotiation. A person who acquires a negotiable document of title by due negotiation acquires (1) title to the document, (2) title to the goods, (3) the right to the goods delivered to the bailee after the issue of the document, and (4) the direct obligation of the issuer to hold or deliver the goods according to the terms of the document. (7–502[1]).

Under the broad general principle that a person cannot transfer title to goods he does not own, a thief or the owner of goods subject to a valid outstanding security interest cannot, by warehousing or shipping the goods on a negotiable document of title and then negotiating the document of title, transfer to the purchaser of the document of title a better title than such thief or owner has (7–503).

Warranties of Transferor of Document of Title. The transferor of a negotiable document of title warrants to his immediate transferee, in addition to any warranty of goods, only that the document is genuine and that he has no knowledge of any facts that would impair its validity or worth and that his negotiation or transfer is rightful and fully effective with respect to the title to the document and the goods it represents (7–507).

SUMMARY

The warehouseman or common carrier is a bailee of the goods and he contracts to store or transport them. The warehouse receipt or bill of lading may be either negotiable or nonnegotiable. If the warehouse receipt issued by the warehouseman omits in its written or printed terms the information required under the provisions of the Code, the warehouseman is liable to a purchaser in good faith of a warehouse receipt for failure to describe or for misdescription of the goods. He owes to the holder of a warehouse receipt the duties of a mutual benefit bailee. The common carrier's liability on a negotiable bill of lading is the same in most respects as that of the issuer of a negotiable warehouse receipt. His liability may be increased by special law or rule.

The rules of law governing the negotiation of a negotiable document of title are the same in most respects as the rules controlling the negotiation of negotiable commercial paper.

In general, a holder by due negotiation of a negotiable document of title gets good title to the document and the goods and the contractual rights against the bailee. However, a thief or an owner of goods which are subject to a valid perfected security interest cannot, by warehousing or shipping the goods on a negotiable document of title and negotiating it, pass to such transferee greater rights in the goods than such thief or owner has.

A holder who transfers a negotiable document of title warrants to his immediate transferee that the document is genuine and that he has no knowledge of any facts that would impair its validity or worth and that his transfer is rightful and fully effective.

Kimberly-Clark Corp. v. Lake Erie Warehouse

375 N.Y.S.2d 918 (Sup. Ct., App. Div., N.Y. 1975)

This was an action brought by a bailor of paper, Kimberly-Clark Corp. (plaintiff), against the warehouseman, Lake Erie Warehouse (defendant), to recover for water damage alleged to have been caused by Lake Erie Warehouse's negligence. Lake Erie defended on the ground that its Rate Schedule

Agreement provided to Kimberly-Clark contained an exculpatory clause. Judgment for Lake Erie Warehouse. Reversed on appeal.

Additional facts are provided in the opinion.

DEL VECCHIO, JUDGE. The exculpatory provisions were ineffective under § 7–202(3) of the Uniform Commercial Code. The exoneration paragraphs read as follows:

> Sec. 7(c) Warehouseman shall not be liable for damage to customer's goods which are damaged or destroyed by perils insured against by customer; as evidence of which customer waives any and all right of recovery from warehouseman for losses caused by any other perils against which customer has insured.
>
> Sec. 20 Warehouseman's responsibility for storage and handling is limited to "reasonable care as a reasonably careful owner of similar goods would exercise." Warehouseman shall not be liable for any loss or damage to the goods which could not have been avoided by the exercise of such care nor for loss or damage to insured goods as provided in section 7(c).

Individually and together these provisions were an attempt to exempt the warehouseman from liability for damages to stored goods from perils against which the bailor had secured insurance, even when caused by Lake Erie's negligence. However, a warehouseman's liability is fixed by § 7–204(1) of the Uniform Commercial Code, which states:

> A warehouseman is liable for damages for loss of or injury to the goods caused by his failure to exercise such care in regard to them as a reasonably careful man would exercise under like circumstances but unless otherwise agreed he is not liable for damages which could not have been avoided by the exercise of such care.

Subdivision (2) of the same statutory section provides the extent to and manner in which the liability imposed by the preceding subdivision may be modified:

> Damages may be limited by a term in the warehouse receipt or storage agreement *limiting the amount of liability* in case of loss or damage, *and setting forth a specific liability* per article or item, or value per unit of weight, beyond which the warehouseman shall not be liable; provided, however, that such liability may on written request of the bailor at the time of signing such storage agreement or within a reasonable time after receipt of the warehouse receipt be increased on part or all of the goods thereunder, in which event increased rates may be charged based on such increased valuation, but that no such increase shall be permitted contrary to a lawful limitation of liability contained in the warehouseman's tariff, if any. No such limitation is effective with respect to the warehouseman's liability for conversion to his own use. [Emphasis supplied]

Section 7–202 of the Code, relating to terms in a warehouse receipt, provides in part:

> (3) A warehouseman may insert in his receipt any other terms which are not contrary to the provisions of this Act and *do not impair* his obligation of delivery (Section 7–403) or *his duty of care* (Section 7–204). *Any contrary provisions shall be ineffective.* [Emphasis supplied.]

Thus, the statute imposes on the warehouseman a responsibility for breach of a duty of reasonable care, permits a modification of the amount of liability upon prescribed conditions, compliance with which is prerequisite to such modification, and make ineffective any other attempt to alter the warehouseman's obligation.

Problem Cases

1. J. E. B. Stewart received a check in the amount of $185.48 in payment of a fee from a client. The check was that of corporation drawn on an account with the Citizens & Southern National Bank and was indorsed by the client. The check was received in payment of Stewart's services to an employee of the corporation. Stewart presented the check, properly indorsed, to the Citizens & Southern Bank. The bank refused to cash the check even though there were sufficient funds in the drawer's account. Stewart then sued the bank for actual damages of $185.48 and for punitive damages of $50,000 for its failure to cash a valid check drawn against a solvent account in the bank. Does Stewart have a good cause of action against the bank?

2. Sinwellan Corporation maintained a business checking account with Farmer's Bank. P. A. Sinclair set up the account and was authorized to draw on the account. He also was the person who provided Farmer's Bank with the names of persons authorized to draw on the business account and kept his own personal account at the bank. Farmer's wrongfully dishonored certain checks drawn on the business account and signed by P. A. Sinclair. In addition a criminal action was instituted against Sinclair. Sinclair brought suit against Farmer's Bank for damages to compensate him for alleged harmful publicity, loss of reputation and embarrassment suffered as a result of the wrongful dishonor. The Farmer's Bank defended on the grounds that Sinwellan Corporation, not Sinclair, was the "customer" of the bank and thus entitled to sue under Section 4–402. Should Sinclair be considered a customer of the bank?

3. Georgia Motor Club maintained a checking account at the First National Bank. On April 10, 1970, Motor Club's manager notified the bank by telephone that checks numbered 293 through 307 had been stolen in a burglary and gave oral instructions to stop payment on the checks. On April 13, the manager followed the call up with a written stop payment order. The stop payment order indicated that the Motor Club account was never used to write checks payable to individuals and that all checks were signed by a signature stamp, thus any hand signed checks would be forged. During September the bank disregarded the stop payment order and paid checks numbered 294, 297, 300, 302, 305, and 307 drawn on the Motor Club account totaling $1243.56, all of which were hand signed. In January Motor Club notified the bank that it had paid the checks over the stop payment order and requested that it be reimbursed. The bank sought to defend against reimbursement on the grounds that under § 4–406 as enacted in Georgia, a customer has 60 days from the time a statement and checks are made available to him, to notify the bank of any unauthorized signatures. Should Motor Club be reimbursed for the checks paid over the stop payment order?

4. Gunn owned large quantities of fertilizer and Kin Tak, a broker, advised Gunn that he had buyers willing to buy 60,000 tons of fertilizer at $400 per ton. Gunn and Kin Tak then entered into a contract whereby Kin Tak agreed to take for resale not less than 60,000 tons. One provision of the contract required Gunn to make an advance payment of $150,000 to Kin Tak which would be credited against commissions to be earned by Kin Tak as broker. Gunn then purchased a cashier's check in the amount of $150,000

payable to the order of Kin Tak from the Empire Bank. After the check was delivered to Kin Tak, Gunn learned that Kin Tak's customers had cancelled their contracts with him and that Kin Tak did not intend to perform his contract with Gunn. Gunn then asked the Empire Bank to stop payment on the cashier's check; the request was received prior to presentation of the check for payment. Is Gunn entitled to a stop payment order?

5. A check of the Ajax Manufacturing Company dated April 19, 1970, was presented at First National Bank. It had been signed by Smith, known by bank personnel to be a supervisor at Ajax. The check was presented on October 29, 1970. First National paid the check. What could Ajax argue in an effort to have the amount of the check recredited to the account? Would they be successful?

6. Over a period of six years Kiernan's bookkeeper forged checks drawn on Kiernan's account at Union Bank which paid the checks when they were presented for payment. Because the bookkeeper was also responsible for receiving the bank statements and cancelled checks and for reconciling the account, she was able to conceal the fraud from Kiernan. When the fraud was finally discovered, Kiernan brought suit against the Union Bank to recover the amount paid on forged instruments. The court held that Kiernan could not recover on those checks which had been paid and returned to Kiernan more than one year prior to the filing of the complaint. Kiernan argued that the one year provision does not begin to run until he—as opposed to his bookkeeper—actually received the statement of account. Is Kiernan correct?

7. On December 6, 1970, Neo-Tech Systems filed a corporate resolution with the Provident Bank which provided that all checks drawn on Neo-Tech's account in excess of $300 should bear the signature of both Richard Zielasko, president, and Robert Sherwood, treasurer. On November 24, 1971, Robert Sherwood resigned as treasurer of Neo-Tech but no provision was thereafter made to replace him with some other party as signatory on the account with Provident Bank. Between November 24, 1973 and May of 1973 numerous checks in excess of $300 were written on the Provident Bank account by Richard Zielasko. On September 4, 1973, Neo-Tech filed a lawsuit against Provident Bank seeking to recover the proceeds of checks in amounts exceeding $300 written between June 1, 1972 through April 18, 1973, drawn on their account and bearing only the signature of Richard Zielasko. The Provident Bank contended that Neo-Tech was barred from recovering for any of the checks under § 4–406 of the Code because the first check with the unauthorized signature had been made available to Neo-Tech over a year prior to May 31, 1973 when Neo-Tech notified the bank of the lack of authorized signature problem. Is the Provident Bank's contention correct?

8. Quantities of soybean oil were delivered to Lawrence American Field Warehousing Corporation (Lawrence) for which nonnegotiable warehouse receipts were issued. National Dairy Products Corporation (National) held warehouse receipts for some of the soybean oil. On presentation of the receipts it was discovered that no soybean oil was in the storage tanks. No satisfactory explanation was given for the disappearance of the soybean oil—95,233,792 pounds. Either the oil had been stolen or the warehouse receipts had been issued without the receipt of soybean oil. National then sued Lawrence for failure to deliver the goods on presentation of warehouse receipts. Is Lawrence liable to National?

9. United Cargo Corporation issued a negotiable order bill of lading for four large packages consigned to Koreska in New York City. One of the printed terms of the bill of lading was that: "None of the terms of this bill of lading shall be deemed to have been waived by any person unless by express waiver signed by such person or his duly authorized

agent." On arrival in New York the goods were delivered by United to one of Koreska's customers, Park Whitney, supposedly because an agent of Koreska orally advised United to make the delivery to Whitney. When United delivered the goods to Whitney, it did not obtain the negotiable bill of lading. Koreska then sued United for the value of the goods delivered without taking up the negotiable order bill of lading. Is Koreska entitled to recover?

10. On January 14, 1975 Crawford sold two railroad carloads of bulk ammonium nitrate fertilizer to Cunningham and received two checks totalling $30,000 in payment for the fertilizer. On the same day the goods were placed in the care and custody of the Missouri-Kansas-Texas Railroad for shipment to Cuningham's customer, the Eaton Agricultural Center in Indiana. The Railroad issued two nonegotiable bills of lading to cover the goods. On January 23 the checks were returned to Crawford by the bank because there were insufficient funds in Cunningham's account to cover the checks. The goods were in transit at the time and Crawford instructed the Railroad not to deliver them to the Eaton Agricultural Center but rather to another place. The Railroad complied with the instructions. The buyer from Cunningham then sued the Railroad, contending that the Railroad wrongfully breached its obligation to deliver the goods to Cunningham. Was the Railroad correct in following Crawford's instructions?

PART X

Credit

44

Introduction to Security

Introduction

Nature of Credit. In the United States today a substantial portion of the business transacted involves the extension of credit. The term "credit" has many meanings. We shall use it, however, as designating a transaction in which goods are sold and delivered, services are rendered, or money is loaned in exchange for the recipient's promise to pay at some future date.

Unsecured Credit. A multitude of transactions are made which are based on unsecured credit. A common example of such credit is the monthly charge account at the local department store, where goods are sold and delivered to the customer, who promises to pay for them at a later date. Such a transaction is usually called an open-book account. The use of the open-book account or other types of unsecured credit is not confined to consumer transactions but is used extensively by jobbers, suppliers of raw materials, and manufacturers.

This type of credit transaction involves the maximum of risk from the standpoint of the creditor. When goods are delivered, services rendered, or money loaned on unsecured credit, the creditor loses all rights in the goods, services, or money and in return has only a claim against the debtor for the agreed price or for whatever he may have promised in return. If the promise is not fulfilled, the creditor's only course of action is to bring a suit and obtain a judgment. He then may have the sheriff levy an execution on any property subject to the execution, or he may garnish wages or other credits due the debtor which may be subject to garnishment. A person may be execution proof; that is, he may not have any property subject to execution, and at the same time he may not have a steady job or credits due him, in which case garnishment would be of no aid in collecting the judgment. A businessperson may obtain credit insurance and thereby stabilize his credit risk, even though such action does not reduce it. The credit losses of a business extending unsecured credit is reflected in the price the consumer pays for the goods or services, or in the rate of interest paid by a borrower from such businesses.

Secured Credit. If the creditor wishes to minimize his credit risk, he can contract for security; that is, he may require his debtor to convey to him a security interest in property, or he may ask that some person promise to be liable in the event the debtor defaults. If a security interest in property is conveyed to the creditor and the debtor defaults in his payments, the creditor will have the right to sell the property and pay the debt out of the proceeds. If the proceeds are not sufficient to pay the debt, he will have, in the absence of a special agreement, an unsecured claim for the unpaid balance.

Development of Security. Various types of security devices have been developed as social and economic need for them arose. The rights and liabilities of the parties to a secured transaction depend on the nature of the security, that is, whether the security pledged is the promise of another to pay if the debtor does not or whether a security interest in goods, intangibles or real estate is conveyed as security for the payment of a debt or obligation.

If personal credit is pledged, the person may guarantee the payment of the debt, that is, become guarantor, or the person may join the debtor in debtor's promise to pay in which case the person would become surety for the debt.

The oldest and simplest security device was the pledge. To have a pledge valid against third-person claimants it was necessary that the property used as security be delivered to the pledgee or a pledge holder. On default by the pledgor the pledgee had the right to sell the property and apply the proceeds to the payment of the debt.

Situations arose in which it was desirable to leave the property used as security in the possession of the debtor. To accomplish this objective the debtor would give the creditor a bill of sale to the property, thus passing title to the creditor. The bill of sale would provide that if the debtor performed his promise the bill of sale would become null and void, thus revesting title to the property in the debtor. By this device a secret lien on the goods was created and the early courts held that such a transaction was a fraud on third-party claimants and void as to them. Statutes were enacted providing for the recording or filing of the bill of sale which was later designated as a chattel mortgage. These statutes were not uniform in their provisions. Most of them set up formal requirements for the execution of the chattel mortgage and also stated the effect of recording or filing on the rights of third-party claimants.

To avoid the requirements for the execution and filing of the chattel mortgage, sellers of goods would sell the goods on a "conditional sales contract" by the terms of which the seller retained the title to the goods until the purchase price of the goods was paid in full. On default by the buyer the seller could *(a)* repossess the goods or *(b)* pass title and recover a judgment for the unpaid balance of the purchase price. Abuses of this security device gave rise to some regulatory statutes. About one half of the states enacted statutes which provided that the conditional sales contract was void as to third parties unless it was filed or recorded.

No satisfactory device whereby inventory could be used as security was developed. Under the pledge, field warehousing was used and the after-acquired property clause in a chattel mortgage on a stock of goods held for resale partially fulfilled this need. One of the devices which was used was the trust receipt. It was a short-time marketing security arrangement and had its origin in the export-import trade. It was later used extensively as a means of financing retailers of high-unit value consumer goods.

Another method of using inventory as security was that of factoring. The goods involved were delivered to the factor for sale. As a general rule the factor sold the goods in his own name and guaranteed any credit he extended. The factor usually advanced money on the goods, and he had a lien on them for the money advanced and for his charges. Several states enacted factor acts defining the rights and liabilities of the parties involved.

Uniform Commercial Code. The Uniform Commercial Code, Article 9, Secured Transactions, sets out a comprehensive scheme for the regulation of security interests in personal property and fixtures. It does not include security interests in real estate, nor does it replace existing statutory liens such as landlords' liens, artisans' liens, and equipment trusts covering railroad rolling stock, and other listed special liens. The Code abolishes the old formal distinctions between different types of security devices used to create security interests in personal property. Security interests in personal property are covered in Chapter 45.

Security Interests in Real Estate. Three types of contractual security devices have been developed by which real estate may be used as security: (1) the real estate mortgage, (2) the trust deed, and (3) the land contract. In addition to these contract security devices all of the states have enacted statutes granting the right to mechanics' liens on real estate. The real estate mortgage is comparable to the chattel mortgage and the land contract is comparable to the conditional sales contract. The trust deed is used to try to avoid the expense and delay usually accompanying the foreclosure of a mortgage. When it is used the real estate is deeded to a trustee who is empowered to sell it if the debtor does not pay the debt and to apply the proceeds of the sale on the payment of the debt. Under the statutes of some states the trust deed is treated as a real estate mortgage and must be foreclosed as such. Security interests in real property are covered in Chapter 46.

SUMMARY

Credit is a transaction in which goods are sold and delivered, services are rendered, or money is loaned in exchange for the recipient's promise to pay at some future date. When such credit is given on the recipient's unsupported promise to pay, such as, for instance, an open-book account, the credit is unsecured credit. When the credit is supported by the transfer of an interest in property or the supporting promise of a third person to which the creditor can resort for payment if his debtor does not pay, such credit is secured credit.

Various types of security devices were developed to serve the needs of our economy. The development in this area was unorganized and the available security devices were inadequate in many respects. The pledge was the oldest and simplest device. The chattel mortgage was used when it was desirable to leave the goods posted as security in the possession of the debtor. The conditional sales contract could be used only as security for the unpaid balance of the purchase price of the goods. The trust receipt was a short-time marketing device in which high-unit cost goods held as inventory were used as security. Factoring was an inventory security device in which the factor financed the inventory, sold it and repaid the money advanced plus his commissions. The Uniform Commercial Code has replaced these security devices with a unified system of using personal property as security.

Real estate may be used as security. The real estate mortgage is comparable to the old chattel mortgage, and the land contract is comparable to the old conditional sales contract. The deed of trust is used in a limited number of states in lieu of the real estate mortgage.

Common Law and Statutory Liens on Personal Property

Persons Entitled to Common Law Liens. At common law, artisans, innkeepers, and common carriers were entitled to liens to secure the payment of the reasonable value of the services they performed. An artisan, it was reasoned, improved the property of another by his labor and by the addition of his materials, and that improvement became a part of the principal property by accession, and the title of the improved property vested in the owner of the principal property. Therefore the artisan who had enhanced the value of the property was allowed to claim a lien on the property for his reasonable charges.

The innkeeper and the common carrier were bound by law to serve the public. The innkeeper was allowed to claim a lien on his guest's effects for his reasonable charges for food and lodging, and the common carrier was allowed to claim a lien on the goods carried for his reasonable charges for the service. The giving of the common law lien to the innkeeper and common carrier was justified on the ground that since they were obligated to serve the public, they were entitled to the protection of a lien. These common law liens are generally recognized today. Several of the states have incorporated the concept of the common law lien in their statutory liens on personal property, and other states have by statute modified the rights of the common law lienholder.

Characteristics of a Common Law Lien. The common law lien is a possessory lien; it gives the lienholder the right to retain possession of the debtor's property until the debt has been discharged. An artisan is not entitled to a common law lien for his services unless possession of the property has been given to him.

Two essential elements of a common law lien are possession and a debt created by the improvement of the property on which the lien is claimed. If the lienholder surrenders possession to the debtor voluntarily, the lien is lost, but if the debtor obtains possession by fraud, the lien is not extinguished. If the debt is paid, the lien is discharged, because the foundation of the right to the lien is the existence of a debt. However, the discharge of the lien before the debt is paid does not affect the right to recover on the debt.

Statutory Liens on Personal Property. Statutory liens on personal property are liens created by legislative enactment. Many of these statutes are little more than a codification of existing common law liens. However, these statutes have created many additional liens and, at the same time, have provided a procedure for the foreclosure of the lien. Each state has its own lien statutes creating such liens as the needs of the people in the state suggest to the legislators. Carriers' liens and warehousemen's liens are provided for in Article 7, Documents of Title, of the Code.

If the lien created by statute is not recognized at common law, the statute creating the lien is said to be in derogation of the common law. The same is true of a statute providing for a lien which is recognized at common law but which gives to one of the parties rights not recognized under the common law lien. The courts have developed a rule of statutory construction which is generally applied in interpreting and applying such statutes. If the statute is in derogation of the common law, it will be strictly construed; that is, all the provisions of the statute must be complied with before the party can claim benefits under the statute, and the courts will not enlarge the scope of the statute by implication. If one claims a lien on property when he is not entitled to a lien and refuses to surrender possession when demand is made by the owner, he will be liable to the owner either for the conversion of the property or for damages for the unlawful detention.

Foreclosure of Lien. The right of possession of the holder of a common law lien does not give the lienholder the right to sell or claim ownership of the property if his charges are not paid. In the absence of statutes providing for the foreclosure of the lien, the lienholder must bring suit and obtain a judgment for his charges, have the sheriff levy execution on the property, and have the property on which he has a lien sold at execution sale.

Most states have enacted statutes which provide for the sale of the property, after it has been held for a designated period of time, on the giving of notice and on the advertising of the sale by posting or publishing notices of the sale.

SUMMARY

Artisans, innkeepers, and common carriers are entitled to common law liens for their reasonable charges. The common law lien is a possessory lien. An artisan is not entitled to a common law lien on property unless possession of the property on which work is to be done is surrendered to him. The two essential elements of a common law lien are (1) the debt and (2) possession.

Most states have enacted statutes defining the rights to liens on personal property. Many of these statutes are little more than a codification of existing common law liens. However, all states have enlarged, to some extent, the scope of liens on personal property by statutory enactment.

A common law lien gives the lienholder the right of possession of the goods, but if he wishes to foreclose the lien, he must sue the debtor, obtain a judgment, have an execution issued on the judgment and levied on the goods, and have the goods sold at a sheriff's sale. In most states a simplified foreclosure procedure has been provided for by statute.

Beck v. Nutrodynamics, Inc.

186 A.2d 715 (Super. Ct. N.J. 1962)

This was an action in which James S. P. Beck (plaintiff) brought an action in attachment against Nutrodynamics, Inc. (defendant), and attached a quantity of pills. Ivers-Lee intervened, claiming a common-law lien on the pills. The court held that the common-law lien had priority over the attachment and Beck appealed. The Superior Court affirmed the holding.

Prior to the time Beck commenced his suit and attached the pills, Nutrodynamics, Inc., delivered to Ivers-Lee a drug product in completed pill form. Ivers-Lee was to place the pills in foil packages and then in shipping containers suitable for delivery to customers of Nutrodynamics, Inc. The packaged pills were in the possession of Ivers-Lee when Beck instituted his suit by attachment. Approximately 193 cartons of the packaged pills were levied upon and taken into possession by the sheriff. Ivers-Lee claimed an artisan's lien to the goods by virtue of materials, labor and services rendered which had priority over Beck's attachment.

YANCY, JUDGE. A common law lien is the right to retain the possession of personal property until some debt due on or secured by such property is paid or satisfied. This lien is one that arises by implication of law and not from express contract. It is founded on the immemorial recognition of the common law of a right to it in particular cases, or it may result from the established usage of a particular trade or from the mode of dealing between the parties.

The right to this common law lien applies to a bailee, to whom goods have been delivered. To entitle a bailee to a lien on the article bailed, more is necessary than the mere existence of the bailment relationship. The bailee must, by his labor and skill, contribute to the improvement of the article bailed. The bailee having thus performed, the well-settled rule of the common law is that a bailee (artisan) who receives in bailment personal property under an express or implied contract to improve, better, manufacture or repair it for remuneration, and enhances the value of such property by his skill, labor, or materials employed in such undertaking, has a specific lien on such property. This lien may be enforced against the bailor while the property remains in the bailee's possession, and until the reasonable value of his labor, skill, and expenses is paid.

The first question before the court, therefore, is whether the kind of work done by Ivers-Lee is such as to support its assertion to an artisan's lien. The undisputed facts set forth are that Nutrodynamics, Inc. delivered to the claimant a huge quantity of loose, unpackaged capsules so that the same could be rendered salable by having the claimant prepare, mark and package the capsules and place the packages in cardboard mailing containers suitable for delivery to the customers of Nutrodynamics, Inc. The claimant, Ivers-Lee, agreed to render the service and labor and to supply the materials necessary to accomplish the foregoing. The claimant did in fact supply such labor and packaging materials. This work and materials have become assimilated into the final product, and have enhanced the value of the heretofore loose unpackaged pills.

The case of *O'Brien v. Buston* dealt with a lien on goods for personal services rendered and for repairs to the goods. The court stated:

> A workman who by his skill and labor has enhanced the value of a chattel, under an employment . . . has a lien on the chattel for his reasonable charge.

The lien arises from the rendering of the service, and if such service be not paid for, there is a right to detain. The court further stated:

> It is the natural outcome of the transaction wherein one takes his chattel to another with whom he contracts for the performance by the latter of some service upon it for its betterment.

It is to be concluded from the foregoing that the work done by Ivers-Lee did enhance the value of the product.

Suretyship and Guarantee

Surety and Guarantor. A surety, in the broad sense, is a person who is liable for the payment of another person's debt or for the performance of another person's duty. A surety joins the principal in making the promise. Both parties make primary promises to the obligee; however, the relation between the promisors is such that if the surety is required to perform, he will be entitled to reimbursement from his principal for any resulting loss.

A guarantor does not join in making a promise. The guarantor's liability arises on the happening of a stipulated event, such as the failure of the principal to perform his obligation, or the insolvency or bankruptcy of the principal. The guarantor's promise is collateral to the primary promise and is unenforceable, under the statute of frauds, unless evidenced by a writing signed by the guarantor or his duly authorized agent.

The rights and liabilities of a surety and of a guarantor are substantially the same, and we shall not attempt to distinguish between the two in our discussion unless the distinction is of basic importance.

Creation of Relation. The relationship of principal and surety or that of principal and guarantor is created by contract. The rules of contract law apply in determining the existence and nature of the relationship, and the rights and duties of the parties.

As a general rule a corporation does not have the power to bind itself as surety for third persons unless such power is granted to it in its articles of incorporation.

Defenses of Surety. If the principal has a defense which goes to the merits of the primary contract, the defense is available to the surety. Defenses such as lack or failure of consideration, inducement of the contract by fraud or duress, or material breach on the part of the obligee are available to the surety. Defenses such as infancy, insanity, or bankruptcy of the principal, and other defenses which do not go to the merits of the contract but which are personal to the principal are not available to the surety.

The surety contracts to be responsible for the performance of his principal's obligation. If the principal and the creditor by mutual agreement alter the terms of the primary contract and the surety does not consent to the changes, the alteration will operate to relieve the surety of his liability. The surety undertakes to assume the risks incident to the performance of a particular contract, and his obligation cannot be altered without his consent.

Under this rule, if a principal and a creditor enter into an agreement whereby the principal is given an extension of time for the performance of the contract, the surety will be released from his obligation unless he consents. However, mere indulgence on the part of the creditor does not release the surety. If the creditor merely promises the principal that he may have additional time in which to perform, such a promise will not release the surety from his obligation, since it is not a valid agreement to extend the time of performance. The promise to extend the time of performance, if it is to be valid, must be supported by consideration.

In considering whether a surety has been discharged from his contract, the courts commonly distinguish between an "accommodation" surety who has agreed to serve as a surety without compensation and the "compensated" surety, such as a bonding company. The courts are much more protective of the accommodation surety. A compensated surety will not be discharged unless it can show it was harmed by the extension of time and its obligation increased.

Creditor's Duties to Surety. The creditor owes certain duties to the surety in regard to the risk the surety assumes. If creditor induces the surety to assume the risk by fraudulent representations as to the nature of the risk, or if creditor has knowledge of facts which would materially increase the risk and does not disclose such facts to the surety, the surety will be released from liability. If an employer (creditor) knows when he makes application for the bonding of an employee (principal) that such employee has been guilty of fraudulent or criminal misconduct, the employer must disclose this information to the surety. If an employer, after a bonded employee has been guilty of a defalcation covered by the bond, agrees to give the employee another chance and does not report the defalcation to the bonding company (surety), such action will release the bonding company from liability for further defalcations. If the principal has posted security for the performance of his obligation and the creditor surrenders such security without the consent of the surety, the surety will, as a general rule, be released to the extent of the value of the security surrendered. Some states have held, under such circumstances, that the surety is completely discharged.

Subrogation and Contribution. If the surety is compelled to perform the obligation of his principal, the surety acquires, by operation of law, all the rights the creditor had against the principal. This is known as the surety's "right of subrogation."

If two or more persons become sureties for the same principal on the same obligation and one surety, on the principal's default, pays the obligation in full or pays more than his share of the obligation, he is entitled to reimbursement from his cosureties for the amount paid over and above his share. This is known as a surety's "right of contribution." If one or more of the cosureties is insolvent, the loss will be distributed equally among the solvent sureties.

If a surety discharges the obligation for an amount less than the principal sum due, he is entitled to contribution only of the amount actually paid. Cosureties may enter into an express agreement which provides that the risks of the suretyship shall be distributed in unequal portions.

SUMMARY

A surety, in the broad sense, is a person who is liable for the payment of another person's debt. Technically, a surety joins the principal in making the promise to the promisee, whereas a guarantor makes a collateral promise, promising to perform the principal's promise on the happening of a condition precedent.

The relation of surety is created by contract, and the general rules of contract law apply in determining the existence of a contract and in determining the rights and liabilities of the parties. As a general rule, any defense the principal has which goes to the merits of the case is available to the surety. Also, any agreement between the principal and creditor which alters the risks involved in the primary contract will discharge the surety unless he consents or ratifies the agreement, or unless the rights against the surety are reserved.

The creditor owes a duty to use reasonable care in his dealings and not to increase unnecessarily the burden of risk assumed by a surety. If a surety pays his principal's debt, the surety is entitled to all the rights the creditor had against the principal. If there are cosureties and one surety pays more than his share of his principal's debt, he is entitled to contribution from his cosureties.

Phoenix Assurance Co. v. City of Buckner, Missouri

305 F.2d 54 (8th Cir. 1962)

This was an action brought by the Phoenix Assurance Company (plaintiff) against the City of Buckner, Missouri (defendant) seeking a declaration that a performance bond Phoenix had given the City was invalid. Judgment for the City of Buckner. Affirmed on appeal.

On March 30, 1956, the City of Buckner entered into a contract with William Reser, doing business as Continental Construction Company. The contract called for the construction of a sewer system for the City at a cost of $97,036.85. By the terms of the contract, work was to commence at a date to be specified by the City in a written notice to proceed, delivered to the contractor, and was to be completed within 300 days thereafter; the contractor was to "pay the prevailing wage rates in the district pertaining to the trade," and to furnish a performance bond in an amount equal to the contract price, for the faithful carrying out of the contract and the payment of all persons performing labor or furnishing materials.

Reser procured the performance bond from Phoenix by paying a premium of $870.37, in consideration of which Phoenix agreed to indemnify the City for any default by Reser in the performance of his contract. The bond contained the following provision:

PROVIDED FURTHER, That the said Surety, for value received, hereby stipulates and agrees that no change, extension of time, alteration, or addition to the terms of the contract, or the work to be performed thereunder or in the specifications accompanying the same, shall in any wise affect its obligation on this bond and it does hereby waive notice of any change, extension of time, alteration, or addition to the terms of the contract, or to the work, or to the specifications.

Prior to signing the contract with Reser, the City had applied to the federal Housing and Home Finance Agency for financial aid regarding the sewer project. Completion of the paperwork delayed HHFA approval until February 21, 1957, and the City notified Reser two days later to proceed with the work. Reser began the work in April, ran into a dispute with the union in September, and then "quit the job." The City gave notice of default, terminated the contract, and requested Phoenix to take over and complete the job, which it did not do. Instead Phoenix brought suit to have the bond declared void.

Sanborn, Circuit Judge. Phoenix was a compensated surety. One who engages in the business of insurance for compensation may properly be held more rigidly to his obligation to indemnify the insured than one whose suretyship is an undertaking uncompensated the casual.

There is no merit in the contention of Phoenix that because the City did not, at the time contracted with Reser for the construction of the sewer system, have the funds on hand to complete the project, the performance bond in suit was invalid. The City, in order to finance the project, had authorized the issuance of bonds, and had applied to the Housing and Home Finance Agency for their purchase. Neither Reser nor his surety could have had any illusions about how the project was to be financed or could have believed that it was to be an immediate "cash and carry" operation. Moreover, if the performance bond was invalid at the time of its execution, a return or tender back of the completely unearned premium would be a prequisite to the maintenance of this action.

Phoenix contends that it was materially prejudiced by the long delay of the City in giving notice to Reser to proceed with the work—this because prices of material and labor had increased substantially in the interval, thus imposing upon Phoenix a greater risk than it was originally intended to bear—and that the provision in the bond that no change, extension of time, alteration, or addition to the terms of Reser's contract should affect the obligation of the surety, is, for some reason, not apparent to us, inapplicable under the facts of this case.

The general rule relative to extension of time is stated in 50 Am. Jur., Suretyship, § 322, as follows:

In accordance with the rule that a surety company can be relieved from its obligation for suretyship only where a departure from the contract is shown to be a material variance, it is held that an extension of time will not relieve a surety company on a bond unless the extension exceeds the time limited in the bond for bringing suit thereon, or unless the surety company is thereby made to suffer material harm; and that there will be no presumption of injury unless injury is alleged and proved.

It was the obligation of Phoenix to protect the City from any default by Reser in the performance of his contract, and not the obligation of the City to protect Phoenix against loss on account of its assumption of a risk for which it was paid and which turned out badly because of Reser's lack of financial responsibility, and inability to complete his undertaking.

Consumer Credit Laws

Introduction. Because of the widespread use of credit by consumers, the federal government and the states have enacted a series of laws designed to increase the knowledge consumers have before they enter into credit transactions, to extend certain rights to consumers, and to try to assure that they are treated fairly and without discrimination. The number of such laws has grown rapidly in the past few years, and they are generally in the process of being refined and in some cases extended to cover newly discovered problem areas. Both businesspersons and consumers need to be aware of their responsibilities and rights under these laws and the regulations that implement them.

Consumer Credit Protection Act. The Consumer Credit Protection Act, frequently called the Truth-in-Lending Act, requires disclosure of the terms and conditions of credit finance charges prior to the time the consumer signs the contract. The purpose of the act is to provide the consumer with a better opportunity to shop for credit and to avoid its uninformed use. The act requires that the interest rate must be clearly stated in terms of an annual percentage and that the dollar cost of credit be fully described in the "finance charge." The term "finance charge" includes all costs associated with the extension of credit, including loan and finder's fees, and fees for credit reports; charges or premiums for life, health, or accident insurance written in connection with the credit extension must be calculated in the finance charge unless the insurance is not a factor in the extension of credit.

One of the most significant protections in the act is the right of rescission for three business days after the credit transaction is consummated or after the required disclosures are made; the right is limited to credit transactions in which a security interest is acquired in the residence of the person to whom credit is extended. An example of this type of transaction is a contract for home improvements.

The act requires disclosures in advertising when the advertiser mentions some of the terms of credit in an advertisement, *viz,* that no payment is required or the time period during which no finance charge will be imposed.

The act also establishes a $50 maximum liability to the consumer for unauthorized credit card usage and grants, to the consumer a right of action against the creditor for violations involving required disclosures.

Fair Credit Billing Act. In 1974 Congress amended the Truth-In-Lending Act to incorporate specific provisions for the protection of users of credit cards. The Fair Credit Billing Act requires at least semi-annual notice of the cardholder's rights and the specific procedures to be followed in the event he disputes the accuracy of the creditor's statement of the account. The consumer-obligor has 60 days after receiving an account statement from the creditor to notify the creditor of any error. Thereafter the creditor has up to 30 days to notify the consumer of receipt of the dispute notice. The creditor must correct the account, or after undertaking an investigation, must explain its reasons for believing the accuracy of the statement. It must do so within two billing cycles or no more than 90 days.

The act conditions reporting delinquent accounts to credit reporting agencies (such as credit bureaus) on compliance with the act. It also requires that notice be given to the consumer of those persons to whom the creditor reports the delinquency. The creditor forfeits the right to collect up to $50 for noncompliance with the act. Finally, the act clarifies the seller's ability to offer discounts on cash purchases and prohibits surcharges for noncash purchases.

Fair Credit Reporting Act. The Fair Credit Reporting Act was enacted in 1970 to ensure that any information concerning a person's background, supplied by credit agencies and reported to companies who make decisions of whether to grant credit, insurance or employment, is current and accurate. The act entitles a consumer who is denied credit by the recipient of a report to disclosure of the name of the consumer reporting agency which made the report and, upon the consumer's request, the user of the information must disclose its full nature and substance. The consumer may require that the credit agency reinvestigate any disputed material and that any inaccurate or obsolete information be deleted from his file. If the reinvestigation does not resolve the dispute, the consumer may file a brief statement describing the nature of the dispute. Thereafter the consumer reporting agency must disclose the fact that the information is disputed by the consumer. If any inaccurate or unverifiable information is deleted from the consumer's file, the reporting agency must notify at the customer's request, any persons specified by the consumer who received that information within two years for employment purposes or within the prior six months for other purposes (such as credit or insurance).

Equal Credit Opportunity Act. In order to insure equal access to the credit market for all persons, Congress passed the Equal Credit Opportunity

Act which prohibits discrimination in any aspect of a credit transaction on the basis of sex or marital status. Subsequent amendments have extended the act's protection to all persons regardless of race, color, religion, national origin, or age. The act applies to banks, finance companies, department stores, credit card issuers and other firms regularly extending credit. State laws which prohibit separate extensions of credit to each spouse are preempted by the act.

On applications for credit, the creditor may not, on the basis of any of the factors listed above, discourage the application for credit, refuse to grant a separate account to a married woman if she is a credit-worthy applicant, or ask the applicant's marital status if an unsecured separate account is applied for (except in a community property state or where state law requires otherwise).

If the creditor denies the credit application, it must notify the applicant within a reasonable time stating the reasons for the denial. The consumer is also entitled to have creditors report the credit history on any account shared by a husband and wife to credit reporting agencies in the names of both spouses. After November 1, 1976, all accounts opened which both spouses may use for which both spouses are liable, must be reported by creditors in both names.

Fair Debt Collection Practices Act. Congressional concern about late-night phone calls, harrassment, and threats of violence by debt collectors led in 1977 to the Fair Debt Collection Practices Act. At that time some 37 states had laws aimed at debt collection abuses and the federal act allows exemptions for states with debt collection laws similar to the federal law as long as there are adequate provisions for enforcement. The federal act covers only debt collection agencies which collect other companies' bills and excludes department stores, banks, and other businesses that collect their own debts.

Among the prohibitions in the Fair Debt Collection Practices Act are:

1. Debt collectors may not contact consumers at unusual or inconvenient times, or at all, if the consumer is represented by an attorney.
2. Debt collectors may not contact a consumer at his place of employment if the employer objects.
3. Debt collectors may not use harassing or intimidating tactics, including the use of abusive language; and may not engage in false or misleading representations, such as posing as a lawyer or a policeman.
4. Debt collectors may not communicate with third parties—other than a spouse, parent, or financial adviser—about payment of a debt unless authorized by a court.
5. Debt collectors must cease communicating with a consumer after receiving written notice of the consumer's refusal to pay the debt—except to

advise the consumer of further action that may be taken by the collection agent.

6. Debt collectors may not deposit a post-dated check prior to the date on it.

The federal act gives the responsibility for enforcement to the Federal Trade Commission. It also provides for limits on damages and penalties that may be recovered for violation of the act and allows successful plaintiffs, as well as defendants where the suit was harassing in nature, to recover their attorneys' fees.

SUMMARY

Because of the widespread use of credit by consumers, the federal government and the states have enacted a series of laws designed to protect consumers and try to assure that they are treated fairly in credit transactions. The federal Truth-in-Lending Act requires disclosure of the terms, conditions and cost of credit finance charges prior to the time a consumer signs a contract. It also gives the consumer the right to rescind for three business days following his signing a contract that will result in a security interest being acquired in his residence. The Fair Credit Billing Act provides a mechanism for consumers to challenge statements of charge accounts which they believe are incorrect. The Fair Credit Reporting Act was enacted to assure that any information concerning a person's background supplied by credit reporting agencies is current and accurate. The Equal Credit Opportunity Act was enacted to try to assure all persons equal access to the credit market. The Fair Debt Collection Procedure Act protects consumers from abusive tactics of certain debt collectors.

Gardner and North Roofing and Siding Corp. v. Board of Governors of Federal Reserve System

464 F.2d 838 (D.C. Cir. 1972)

This was an action brought by Gardner and North Roofing and Siding Corp. (plaintiff) against the Board of Governors of the Federal Reserve System (defendant) seeking a declaratory judgment that a regulation issued by the Federal Reserve Board pursuant to the "Truth in Lending" Act was invalid. Judgment for Federal Reserve Board. Affirmed on Appeal.

Gardner and North was in the business of renovating, remodeling and repairing homes in the Syracuse, New York area. Its salesmen solicited contracts from homeowners for the repair work and credit was extended to them pursuant to a "deferred payment plan." Although the company did not take a mortgage on the homeowner's property, the laws of New York give home improvement contractors a contractor's or mechanic's lien on the customer's home at the time the work is performed.

Under Section 125a of the Truth in Lending Act in any consumer credit transaction in which a security interest is retained or acquired in any real property which is expected to be used as the residence of the person to whom credit is extended, the consumer has three days following the receipt of certain information from the creditor to rescind the contract. The creditor must inform the prospective consumer that he has such a right to rescind. Pursuant to its responsibility to promulgate regulations to implement the Act, the Federal Reserve Board issued such regulations in which it defined the term *security interest* to include "liens created by operation of law such as mechanic's, materialmen's, artisan's and similar liens."

ROBB, CIRCUIT JUDGE. In general the purpose of the Consumer Credit Protection Act was "to assure a meaningful disclosure of credit terms" to consumers. The specific purpose of section 125(a), was to protect homeowners from the unscrupulous business tactics of certain home improvement contractors. The need for such protection was emphasized in testimony before congressional committees concerning "second mortgage" racketeers who encumbered their customers' houses to secure payment for unneeded or shoddy work. There was also reference to the liens of artisans, materialmen and other arising by operation of law which could subject a consumer's property to loss by foreclosure. Witnesses told of cases in which consumers paid double for work because artisans, unpaid by an unscrupulous contractor, filed mechanic's liens. All this is conceded by Gardner and North in their brief. They also concede that "[i]n either instance, whether the cloud on the homeowner's title was induced by a second mortgage, or by other consensual liens of his own making, or, from liens arising by operation of law, the possibility of loss by foreclosure was evident." As we have said, however, they contend that the "plain language of Section 125(a), as enacted, made rescindable only those contracts [involving] a security interest through a second mortgage or other consensual type lien."

We think Gardner's construction of the statute is too narrow and technical. Being remedial legislation to protect the homeowner, the Act must be broadly construed to effectuate its purpose. So construed, the statute supports the challenged regulation.

A contract to renovate, remodel or repair a house imports that work will be done by mechanics and artisans and that materials will be furnished in connection with that work. Implicit in the contract, therefore, is a provision that a lien will attach to secure payment for the work and materials. In other words, the statutory provision for mechanic's and materialmen's liens must be taken as a part of the contract. This conclusion is fortified by the settled rule that "the laws which subsist at the time and place of the making of a contract . . . enter into and form a part of it, as if they were expressly referred to or incorporated in its terms."

We think it a reasonable construction of the statute that Congress intended to require disclosure of all the consequences flowing from the signing of a home improvement contract, including not only the consequences spelled out in the contract, but also those necessarily inherent therein. Any other construction would expose the homeowner to hidden and perhaps fatal traps; it would lead to precisely the kind of imposition that Congress intended to prevent. Viewed in this light we think the challenged regulation is entirely consistent with the legislative purpose and is a reasonable and proper device for carrying it out.

Millstone v. O'Hanlon Reports, Inc.

383 F.Supp. 269 (E.D. Mo. 1974)

This was an action brought by James Millstone (plaintiff) against O'Hanlon Reports, Inc. (defendant), alleging a violation of the Fair Credit Reporting Act and seeking actual and punitive damages. Judgment for Millstone.

In August 1971, Millstone moved from Washington, D.C., to St. Louis to take a new job with the St. Louis Post Dispatch. He requested and obtained a new automobile insurance policy with Fireman's Fund effective November 15. Shortly afterwards he received a notice saying a personal investigation would be made in connection with the policy. On December 20 he was advised that the policy would be cancelled because of a report made to the insurance company by O'Hanlon Reports.

On December 22, 1971, Millstone went to the office of O'Hanlon Reports where he spoke to O'Connell. Millstone was told that he was entitled to know what was in his report but that O'Hanlon was entitled to reasonable notice of ten (10) days before giving the information. When Millstone protested, O'Connell called the New York Home Office of O'Hanlon and allowed Millstone to speak to a Kenneth Mitchell. Mitchell told Millstone that the information would be available as soon as possible but that he could not give disclosure immediately because the Millstone file was enroute from St. Louis to New York through the mails. After Millstone left the office, the office manager then mailed the file to New York.

On December 28, 1971, Millstone received the disclosure of the information in its file from O'Connell at the O'Hanlon offices. O'Connell read the disclosure from a single sheet of paper which had been prepared by David Slayback, the Vice President of O'Hanlon. The disclosure sheet stated in part that:

> The file shows that you are very much disliked by your neighbors at that location [Millstone's Washington residence], and were considered to be a 'hippy type'. The file indicates that you participated in many demonstrations in Washington, D.C., and that you also housed out-of-town demonstrators during demonstrations. The file indicates that these demonstrators slept on floors, in the basement and wherever else there was room on your property. The file shows that you were strongly suspected of being a drug user by neighbors but they could not positively

substantiate these suspicions. You are shown to have had shoulder length hair and a beard on one occasion while living in Washington, D.C. The file indicates that there were rumors in the neighborhood that you had been evicted by neighbors from three previous residences in Washington, D.C. prior to living at the 48th Street, N.W. location.

This disclosure sheet which Millstone was not allowed to examine was the only item that Millstone was informed of by Mr. O'Connell.

After protesting virtually all the information contained in the disclosure, Millstone asked O'Connell to explain certain facts. O'Connell told Millstone that he had no further information and could not answer the questions. He told Millstone that his instructions from the Home Office were only to read the disclosure sheet prepared in New York and to take careful note of any dispute from the customer. At no time was Millstone allowed to look at the actual consumer report file maintained by O'Hanlon upon him, nor were any actual portions of that file read to Millstone at any time by Mr. O'Connell.

Subsequently, a reinvestigation was made by O'Hanlon, as required by the Fair Credit Reporting Act in the event the consumer disputes information. That report contained similar types of information but Millstone was given only cursory additional information. Only after a Federal Trade Commission investigation was begun did O'Hanlon make some additional disclosures.

WANGELIN, DISTRICT JUDGE. The remainder of this action revolves around the questions of whether or not O'Hanlon is liable under the Fair Credit Reporting Act. Section 1681n allows the recovery of actual damages, costs and reasonable attorneys fees along with punitive damages for willful non-compliance with the Act in question, and Section 1681o allows actual damages along with costs and attorneys fees for negligent non-compliance with this Act. The standard of care imposed by the statutory sections is that:

> Whenever a consumer reporting agency prepares a consumer report it shall follow reasonable procedures to assure maximum possible accuracy of the information concerning the individual about whom the report relates.

It is clear to this Court as the trier of fact that O'Hanlon was in violation of § 1681e(b), in that its procedures of gathering personal information about consumers, such as Millstone, was only from neighbors from the consumer's residence and that these items were not verified. The evidence also shows that O'Hanlon's agent Mayes knowingly included false information in the report which O'Hanlon compiled concerning Millstone. In his report agent Mayes refers to a poll of four neighbors, with full knowledge that he spoke only to three neighbors. Also, the report repeatedly asserts that all of the sources were in agreement when Mayes in fact received information from only one source, Mr. McMillan. Considering the prior unblemished record of Millstone and the fact that O'Hanlon's own operations manual concerning such derogatory information states: "When adverse information is developed, it should be verified by at least one other source to avoid the reporting of any prejudicial or inaccurate information," the actions of O'Hanlons' agent Mayes are so wanton as to be certainly a willful non-compliance with the standard of care imposed by the Act. These actions by O'Hanlon's agent Mayes are so heinous and reprehensible as to justify the harsh damages imposed by Section 1681n. O'Hanlon's methods of reporting on consumer's credit backgrounds as shown at trial were so slipshod and slovenly as to not even approach the realm of reasonable standards of care as imposed by the statute. O'Hanlon's reporting methods were so wanton as to be clearly willful noncompliance with the Fair Credit Reporting Act in the eyes of this Court.

Independent of the previously discussed willful violation of the statute is the defendant's violation of § 1681g(a)(1) in that it failed to disclose, and continued until pretrial discovery forced such disclosure, the nature and substance of all the information contained in its files concerning Millstone. To say that O'Hanlon was parsimonious in its disclosures in this case would be an exercise in understatement. O'Hanlon has stated to the Court that its policy remains not to disclose certain information to consumers which O'Hanlon itself deems appropriate. The previously quoted sections of O'Hanlon's operation Manual are ample evidence of its attitudes and actions concerning this matter. Millstone was forced to return to O'Hanlon's offices on several occasions and each time was able to elicit a little more information from O'Hanlon which concerned him. At no time until this lawsuit and discovery was undertaken did O'Hanlon inform Millstone of the entire amount of information concerning him in O'Hanlon's files.

The actions of O'Hanlon in having the file mailed to its New York office, and instructing its employee in St. Louis to tell Millstone that the file was enroute to New York and that he could not tell Millstone what was in it when the file was actually in St. Louis are further indications of the willful non-compliance of O'Hanlon with this Act. The sole thrust of O'Hanlon's actions was an attempt to withhold from Millstone the information that was rightfully due him under the law. The evidence in the case at bar as a whole is so overwhelming and persuasive as to leave no other conclusion that O'Hanlon was in willful violation of various previously discussed portions of the Fair Credit Reporting Act and should therefore be subject to the liabilities enumerated in Section 1681n.

In regards to damages, the Court further finds that although Millstone suffered no lost wages nor incurred medical expenses on the account of the injuries therein, he suffered by reason of his mental anguish and had symptoms of sleeplessness and nervousness which were amply testified to, and because of the repeated and numerous times in which Millstone had to contact O'Hanlon, in many cases having to leave his employment for meetings on account of O'Hanlon's actions as stated above, Millstone is entitled to actual damages in the amount of $2,500.

Considering the willful noncompliance of O'Hanlon with the requirements of the statute, this Court will assess the sum of $25,000 against defendant O'Hanlon as punitive damages in this action. This Court also finds that the sum of $12,500 will be awarded to Millstone from O'Hanlon for attorneys fees.

Problem Cases

1. O'Brien owned an iceboat which Buxton, as sailing master, sailed for O'Brien. O'Brien did not pay Buxton for his services as sailing master, and Buxton, who had possession of the iceboat, claimed a common law lien on the iceboat for his services. Is Buxton entitled to a common law lien on the iceboat?
2. Bayer was the general contractor on a Massachussetts State highway contract. He hired Deschenes as a subcontractor to do certain excavation work. Deschenes was to start the job by November 24, 1958, and to complete it on or before March 1, 1959. Deschenes was required to furnish a bond of $91,000 to assure his faithful performance of the subcontract, and he purchased such a bond from Aetna Insurance Company. Deschenes began the work on December 1, 1958, and quit on June 22, 1959, after completing only about half of the work. Bayer had made numerous efforts to get Deschenes to do the work and then completed the job himself when Deschenes walked off the job. Bayer then brought a lawsuit against Aetna on the bond, and Aetna claimed it was discharged by the extension of time given to Deschenes. Should Bayer recover on the bond?
3. On November 28, 1933, Dyer joined as a surety with Keyes in executing a promissory note payable on December 1, 1934, to Laney. On January 19, 1946, Dyer paid the note to Laney to satisfy a judgment which Laney had obtained against Dyer. On November 5, 1948, Dyer brought an action for reimbursement against Keyes. Oklahoma had a three year statute of limitations. Keyes claimed that Dyer was bound to bring the lawsuit within three years after the date of the note and was now barred from recovering from him. Should Keyes' contention be accepted by the court?
4. Philbeck bought a new Chevrolet from Timmer's Chevrolet which was financed through General Motors Acceptance Corporation (GMAC). He signed an installment sales contract which included a provision for the purchase of credit life insurance but was in violation of the Truth-In-Lending Act because full disclosure of the total cost of the life insurance was not made. Philbeck brought suit against Timmers and GMAC claiming that both were liable to him for statutory damages as "creditors." Under the Act, a "creditor" is defined as one who regularly extends or arranges for the extension of credit, for which the payment of a finance charge is required, in connection with sales or loans to consumers. Timmers initially extended credit by having Philbeck sign the installment agreement; it then assigned the contract to GMAC. The forms used by Timmers, including the disclosure statement, had been supplied to Timmers by GMAC, and the procedure followed was the same as usually followed between the two companies. Timmers also handled credit arrangements through several banks who supplied the forms to it to use. Should Timmers and GMAC both be deemed "creditors" and liable for the statutory damages?

45

Security Interests in Personal Property

Introduction

Security Interests under Article 9 of U.C.C. Today a large portion of our economy involves the extension of credit with the creditor taking a security interest in personal property of the debtor in order to protect his investment. The law pertaining to security interests in personal property has been codified in Article 9 of the Uniform Commercial Code—Secured Transactions. Article 9 applies to situations frequently encountered by consumers and business persons: for example, the financing of an automobile, the purchase of an appliance on a time-payment plan, or the financing of inventory or business equipment. If the extender of credit wants to retain or attain an interest in the personal property of the debtor to assure the payment of the debt, and wants to be sure that his interest in that personal property will be superior to the claims of other creditors, he must carefully comply with the provisions of Article 9. In the Sales chapters it was pointed out that businessmen often leave out terms in a contract or insert vague terms to be worked out later by mutual agreement of the parties. Such looseness is a luxury that cannot be tolerated when it comes to secured transactions. If a debtor gets into financial difficulties and is unable to meet his financial obligations, it is extremely important from the creditor's standpoint that he have carefully complied with the provisions of Article 9. Even a relatively minor noncompliance can result in the creditor losing his preferred position and finding himself in the same position as an unsecured creditor with little chance of recouping what is owed to him.

Security Interests. Basic to a discussion of secured transactions is the term "security interest" which is broadly defined by the Code to mean "an interest in personal property or fixtures which secures payment or performance of an obligation." (1–201[37]).[1] While it is normal to think of various types of goods as being used for collateral, the Code actually covers secured interests in a much broader grouping of personal property. The Code breaks personal property down into a number of different classifications which are of importance in determining how a creditor goes about getting an enforceable security interest in a particular type of collateral. These Code classifications are:

1. *Instruments.* This category includes checks, notes, drafts, stocks, bonds, and other investment securities.
2. *Documents of Title.* This category includes bills of lading, dock warrants, dock receipts, and warehouse receipts.
3. *Accounts.* This category includes rights to payment for goods sold or leased or for services rendered that are not evidenced by instruments or chattel paper but rather are carried on open account. "Accounts" include such rights to payment whether or not they have been earned by performance. (Revised § 9–106).
4. *Chattel Paper.* This category includes written documents that evidence both an obligation to pay money and a security interest in specific goods. A typical example of chattel paper is what is commonly known as a conditional sales contract: this is the type of contract a consumer might sign when he buys a large appliance such as a refrigerator on a time-payment plan from an appliance store.
5. *General Intangibles.* This is a catchall category which includes, among other things, patents, copyrights, literary royalty rights, franchises, and money (Revised § 9–106).
6. *Goods.* Goods are divided into several classes; the same item of collateral may fall into different classes at different times, depending on its use.

    a. *Consumer Goods.* Goods used or bought for use primarily for personal, family or household use such as automobiles, furniture, and appliances.
    b. *Equipment.* Goods used or bought for use primarily in business, including farming or a profession.
    c. *Farm Products.* Crops, livestock or supplies used or produced in farming operations as long as they are still in the possession of a debtor engaged in farming.

---

[1] The numbers in the parentheses refer to the sections of the Uniform Commercial Code, 1972. In 1972 a number of amendments to Article 9 were proposed by the National Conference of Commissioners on Uniform State Laws; the sections of the Code affected by these proposed amendments are designated "Revised." The proposed amendments must be adopted by the state legislatures before they become law in any given state. The first state to adopt the new amendments was Illinois which made them effective July 1, 1973.

d. *Inventory.* Goods held for sale or lease or to be used under contracts of service as well as raw materials, work in process, or materials used or consumed in a business.
e. *Fixtures.* Goods which will be so affixed to real property so as to be considered a part of the real property.

Obtaining an Enforceable Security Interest. The goal of a creditor is to secure a security interest that will be enforceable against the debtor, other creditors of the debtor, and, in some cases, purchasers of the collateral from the debtor. In general, the obtaining of an enforceable security interest is a two-step process consisting of "attachment" and "perfection."

SUMMARY

A security interest is an interest in personal property or fixtures which secures payment or performance of an obligation. The Code sets out rules for obtaining secured interests in instruments, documents of title, accounts contract rights, chattel paper, general intangibles, and goods. Goods may be consumer goods, equipment, inventory, farm products, or fixtures. To obtain the maximum protection for his security interest the creditor must attach and perfect his security interest.

Attachment of the Security Interest

Attachment. A security interest is not legally enforceable against a debtor until it is "attached" to a particular item or items of the debtor's property (the collateral). In order for a security interest to attach there must be an agreement between the debtor and the creditor in which the debtor grants the creditor a security interest in specified collateral owned by the debtor. The creditor must also give some "value" to the debtor for unless there is a debt owing from the debtor to the creditor there can be no security interest (Revised 9–204). A security interest may also "attach" to collateral if the collateral is the possession of the secured party provided the secured party has given some value to the debtor.

The Security Agreement. As a general rule, the secured party will require that the agreement whereby the debtor grants him a secured interest in the collateral be in writing and signed by the debtor. Such a written agreement is required in all cases except where the collateral is in the possession of the secured party (9–203). The security agreement must describe the collateral with reasonable certainty so as to enable it to be identified.

SAMPLE SECURITY AGREEMENT

Mr. and Mrs.
Mrs.
BUYER Miss ______________________
ADDRESS ______________________
CITY ______________________ TEL. NO.________
DELIVER TO: ______________________

Account No.
Date

SECURITY AGREEMENT
(NAME OF SELLER)

THIS AGREEMENT, executed between (name of Seller), as Secured Party ("Seller"), and Buyer named above, as Debtor ("Buyer"):

Seller agrees to sell and Buyer agrees to purchase, subject to the terms, conditions and agreements herein stated, the goods described below (hereinafter referred to as the "Collateral"), Seller reserving and Buyer granting a purchase money security interest in the Collateral to secure the payment of the balance owed (Item 7) and all other present and future obligations of Buyer to Seller.

DESCRIPTION OF COLLATERAL				TERMS
Quan.	Article	Unit Price	Total	
				(1) Cash Price
				(2) Down Payment
				Trade-in
				Unpaid Principal (3) Balance Owed
				(4) Finance Charge
				Time Balance
				(5) Owed
				(6) Sales Tax
				(7) Balance Owed

Buyer agrees to pay Seller, without relief from valuation and appraisement laws, the balance owed (Item 7) of $______ in ______ successive weekly/monthly installments of $______ each and a final installment of $______, commencing on__________ _____, 19__, and continuing thereafter on the same day of each week/month, until paid, together with all delinquent charges, costs of repossession, collection, disposition, maintenance and other like charges, allowed by law, and reasonable attorneys' fees.

This sale is made subject to the terms, conditions and agreements stated above and on the reverse side hereof. Buyer hereby represents that the correct name and address of Buyer is as stated above, and that all statements made by Buyer as to financial condition and credit information are true.

Buyer hereby acknowledges delivery by Seller to Buyer of a copy of this agreement.

Buyer warrants and represents that the Collateral will be kept at Buyer's address unless otherwise specified as follows: ______________________
______________________; and will be used or is purchased for use primarily for: (check one) family or household purposes ☐; business use ☐; farming operations ☐. The Collateral will not be affixed to real estate unless checked here ☐. If the Collateral is to be affixed to real estate, a description of the real estate is as follows: ______________________
____
____
and the name of the record owner is______________________
______________________.

IN WITNESS WHEREOF, the parties hereto have executed this agreement on this ______ day of __________, 19__.

BUYER'S SIGNATURE

(NAME OF SELLER) Seller, (as Secured Party), Seller's address

______________________ By ______________________

(as Debtor)

____

TERMS, CONDITIONS AND AGREEMENTS

1. The security interest of Seller shall extend to all replacements, proceeds (including tort claims and insurance), and accessories, and shall continue until full performance by Buyer of all conditions and obligations hereunder.

2. Buyer shall maintain the Collateral in good repair, pay all taxes and other charges levied upon the Collateral when due, and shall defend the Collateral against any claims. Buyer shall not permit the Collateral to be removed from the place where kept without the prior written consent of Seller. Buyer shall give prompt written notice to Seller of any transfer, pledge, assignment, or any other process or action taken or pending, voluntary or involuntary, whereby a third party is to obtain or is attempting to obtain possession of or any interest in the Collateral. Seller shall have the right to inspect the Collateral at all reasonable times. At its option, but without obligation to Buyer and without relieving Buyer from any default, Seller may discharge any taxes, liens or other encumbrances levied or placed upon the Collateral for which Buyer agrees to reimburse Seller upon demand.

3. If the Collateral is damaged or destroyed in any manner, the entire balance remaining unpaid under this agreement (hereinafter referred to as the "Agreement Balance") shall immediately become due and payable and Buyer shall first apply any insurance or other receipts compensating for such loss to the Agreement Balance. Buyer shall fully insure the Collateral, for the benefit of both Seller and Buyer, against loss by fire, theft and other casualties by comprehensive extended coverage insurance in an amount equal to the balance owed hereunder.

4. Buyer shall pay all amounts payable hereunder when due at the store of Seller from which this sale is made or at Seller's principal office in __________, Indiana, and upon default shall pay the maximum delinquent charges permitted by law. Upon prepayment of the Agreement Balance, Seller shall allow the minimum discount permitted by law.

5. Time is of the essence of this agreement. Buyer agrees that the following shall constitute an event of default under this Security Agreement: (*a*) the failure of Buyer to perform any condition or obligation contained herein; (*b*) when any statement, representation or warranty made herein by Buyer shall be found to have been untrue in any material respect when made; or (*c*) if Seller in good faith believes that the prospect of payment or performance is impaired. Upon a default, Seller, at its option and without notice or demand to Buyer, shall be entitled to declare the Agreement Balance immediately due and payable, take immediate possession of the Collateral and enter the premises at which the Collateral is located for such purpose or to render the Collateral unusable. Upon request, Buyer shall assemble and make the Collateral available to Seller at a place to be designated by Seller which is reasonably convenient to both parties. Upon repossession, Seller may retain or dispose of any or all of the Collateral in the manner prescribed by the Indiana Uniform Commercial Code and the proceeds of any such disposition shall be first applied in the following order: (*a*) to the reasonable expenses of retaking, holding, preparing for sale, selling and the like; (*b*) to the reasonable attorneys' fees and legal expenses incurred by Seller; and (*c*) to the satisfaction of the indebtedness secured by this security interest. Buyer covenants to release and hold harmless Seller from any and all claims arising out of the repossession of the Collateral. No waiver of any default or any failure or delay to exercise any right or remedy by Seller shall operate as a waiver of any other default or of the same default in the future or as a waiver of any right or remedy with respect to the same or any other occurrence.

6. All rights and remedies of Seller herein specified are cumulative and are in addition to, and shall not exclude, any rights and remedies Seller may have by law.

7. Seller shall not be liable for any damages, including special or consequential damages, for failure to deliver the Collateral or for any delay in delivery of the Collateral to Buyer.

8. Buyer agrees that Seller may carry this agreement, together with any other agreements and accounts, with Buyer in one account upon its records and unless otherwise instructed in writing by Buyer, any payment of less than all amounts then due on all agreements and accounts shall be applied to any accrued delinquent charges, costs of collection and maintenance, and to the balances owing under all agreements or accounts in such order as Seller in its discretion shall determine.

9. Buyer authorizes Seller to execute and file financing statements signed only by Seller covering the Collateral described.

10. Any notice required by this agreement shall be deemed sufficient when mailed to Seller (state Seller's address), or to Buyer at the address at which the Collateral is kept.

11. Buyer shall have the benefit of manufacturers' warranties, if any; however, Seller makes no express warranties (except a warranty of title) and no implied warranties, including any warranty of MERCHANTABILITY or FITNESS. Buyer agrees that there are no promises or agreements between the parties not contained herein. Any modification or rescission of this agreement shall be ineffective unless in writing and signed by both Seller and Buyer.

12. ANY HOLDER OF THIS ~~CONSUMER CREDIT~~ CONTRACT IS SUBJECT TO ALL CLAIMS AND DEFENSES WHICH THE DEBTOR COULD ASSERT AGAINST THE SELLER OF GOODS OR SERVICES OBTAINED WITH THE PROCEEDS HEREOF. RECOVERY HEREUNDER BY THE DEBTOR SHALL NOT EXCEED AMOUNTS PAID BY THE DEBTOR HEREUNDER.

The security agreement usually goes on to spell out the terms of the arrangement between the parties. Thus it will normally contain a promise by the debtor to pay certain amounts of money in a certain way or to perform other obligations and will specify what events will constitute a default. In addition it may contain provisions the secured party deems necessary to protect his interest in the collateral such as requiring the debtor to procure insurance or to periodically report sales of secured inventory goods.

Future Advances. A security agreement may provide that it covers advances of credit to be made at some time in the future. Such later extensions of credit are known as "future advances." Future advances would be involved where, for example, a bank grants a business a line of credit for $10,000 but initially advances only $2,000. When the business draws further against its line of credit, it has received a future advance and the bank is considered to have given additional "value" at that time (Revised 9–204[3]).

After-Acquired Property. A security agreement may also be drafted to grant a creditor a security interest in "after-acquired" property of the debtor—that is property which the debtor does not currently own (or have rights in) but which he may acquire in the future (Revised 9–204[1]). However, the security interest in the after-acquired property cannot "attach" to that property until the debtor obtains some property rights in the new property.[2] For example, Dan's Diner borrows $5,000 from the bank and gives it a security interest in all of the restaurant equipment it currently has as well as all that it may "hereafter acquire." If at the time Dan's owns only a stove then the bank has a security interest only in the stove. However, if a month later Dan's buys a refrigerator, the banks security interest would "attach" to the refrigerator at the time Dan's acquires some rights to it.

A security interest in after-acquired property may be defeated if the debtor acquired his new property subject to what is known as a "purchase money security interest." When the seller of goods retains a security interest in goods until they are paid for, or when money is loaned for the purpose of acquiring certain goods and the lender takes a security interest in those goods, the security interest is known as a "purchase money security interest." The rights of the holder of a purchase money security interest versus the rights of another creditor who had filed earlier on after-acquired property of the debtor are discussed in detail later in this chapter in the section covering "Priorities."

Proceeds. The security agreement may provide that the security interest will cover not only the collateral described in the agreement but will attach to the "proceeds" on the disposal of the collateral by the debtor. For example,

---

[2] The Code imposes an additional requirement as to security interests in after-acquired consumer goods. Security interests do not attach to consumer goods other than accessions unless the consumer acquires them within ten days after the secured party gave value [Revised § 9–204(2); old § 9–204(4)(b)].

if a bank loans money to Dealer to enable Dealer to finance its inventory of new automobiles and the bank takes a security interest in the inventory as well as in the proceeds of the inventory, then the bank would have a security interest in the cash "proceeds" obtained by Dealer when the automobiles are sold to customers. To create a security interest in proceeds all that is necessary is to add the word "proceeds" to the description of the collateral in the security agreement. Under the 1972 proposed amendments to Article 9, proceeds are automatically covered unless the security agreement specifically excludes them. (Revised 9–203[3]).

Assignment. Sales contracts and security agreements for the purchase of consumer goods commonly include a provision that the buyer will not assert against an assignee of the sales contract any claim or defense the buyer may have against the seller. Such a waiver clause makes it easier for a retailer to assign his sales contracts/security agreements to a financing institution because the financing institution then knows it can collect from the buyer without being subject to claims and defenses the buyer might have against the retailer. However, the waiver clause, which is usually given to the buyer as part of a printed form and on a "take it or leave it" basis, can operate to the disadvantage of the buyer. If the merchandise is defective or is not delivered the buyer must continue to make payments to the assignee and cannot stop payment even though he has a legitimate claim against the seller (assignor)

Under the Code, an express or implied waiver of defenses is generally valid and enforceable by an assignee who takes his assignment for value, in good faith, and without notice of a claim or defense (9–206[1]). There are two exceptions to this rule: (1) the waiver is not effective as to any type of defense which could be asserted against a holder in due course of a negotiable instrument; (2) the waiver is not effective if a statute or court decision establishes a different rule for buyers of consumer goods (9–206[1]).

Some states have enacted comprehensive legislation to abolish the waiver of defense clauses in consumer contracts and others have limited their use. The Uniform Consumer Credit Code, which has been adopted by a number of states, gives the adopting states two alternatives regarding waiver of defense clauses: (1) Alternative A provides that an assignee of a consumer sale contract takes subject to all defenses the buyer has against the seller arising out of the sale regardless of whether the contract contains a waiver of defenses clause; and (2) Alternative B permits the enforcement of such clauses only by an assignee who is not related to the seller and who acquires the assignment of the contract in good faith, for value, and gives the buyer notice of the assignment and is not advised by the buyer in writing within three months that the buyer has any claims or defenses against the seller.

In addition the Federal Trade Commission has promulgated regulations (which are discussed in detail in Chapter 41, pages 888 to 889) which apply to those situations where a buyer signs a waiver of defenses clause as part of an installment sales contract. The FTC regulations require that a seller insert in all consumer contracts and direct loan agreements a clause putting any holder of the contract on notice that the holder is subject to all claims and defenses which the buyer-debtor could assert against the seller of the goods or services covered by the contract.

SUMMARY

A security interest is not enforceable until it has been attached to the collateral. To effect this attachment there must be an agreement between the debtor and the secured party that the security interest attach, value must be given to the debtor, and the debtor must have rights in the collateral. A security agreement may cover future advances to be made by the creditor to the debtor. A security agreement may also create a security interest in proceeds of the collateral and in after-acquired property of the debtor.

The Code recognizes clauses by which the buyer on a sales contract/security agreement agrees not to assert any claims or defenses the buyer may have against the seller against any assignee of the sales contract. However, the waiver is not effective where a statute or court decision establishes a different rule for buyers of consumer goods, and a number of states as well as the Federal Trade Commission have limited the use of such waiver of defense clauses in consumer sales contracts.

Perfecting the Security Interest

While "attachment" of the security interest to collateral of a debtor gives a creditor rights vis-a-vis the debtor, the creditor must also be concerned with making sure that he will have a better right to the collateral than any other creditor of the debtor in the event the debtor defaults on his obligations. This protection against other creditors of the debtor and purchasers of the collateral is obtained through the process of "perfecting" the security interest. There are three main means of perfection under the Code:

1. *Public filing* of notice of the security interest;
2. The secured party's taking *possession* of the collateral;
3. Perfection by mere *attachment* of the security interest in certain special situations or for certain limited times.

Public Filing. By far the most common method of perfecting a security interest is by filing a *financing statement* in a public office which then serves as constructive notice to the world that the secured party claims a security interest in collateral belonging to a certain named debtor. The financing state-

UNIFORM COMMERCIAL CODE

STATE OF INDIANA
FINANCING STATEMENT

FORM UCC-1

INSTRUCTIONS

1. Please type this form. Fold only along perforation for mailing.
2. Remove Secured Party and Debtor copies and send other three copies with interleaved carbon paper to the filing officer. Enclose filing fee of $1.00 (plus $ .50 if collateral is or to become a fixture).
3. When filing is to be with more than one office, Form UCC-2 may be placed over this set to avoid double typing.
4. If the space provided for any item(s) is inadequate, the item(s) may be continued on additional sheets, preferably 5"x 8" or sizes convenient to secured party in case of long schedules, indentures, etc. Only one sheet is required. Extra names of debtors may be continued below box "1" in space for description of property.
5. If the collateral is crops or goods which are or are to become fixtures, describe the goods and also the real estate with the name of the record owner if he is other than the debtor.
6. Persons filing a security agreement (as distinguished from a financing statement) are urged to complete this form with or without signature and send with security agreement.
7. If collateral is goods which are or are to become fixtures, use Form UCC-1a over this Form to avoid double typing, and enclose regular fee plus $ .50.
8. The filing officer will return the third page of this Form as an acknowledgment. Secured party at a later time may use third page as a Termination Statement by dating and signing the termination legend on that page.

This Financing Statement is presented to Filing Officer for filing pursuant to the UCC:

3 Maturity Date (if any):

1 Debtor(s) (Last Name First) and Address(es)

2 Secured Party(ies) and Address(es)

For Filing Officer (Date, Time, Number, and Filing Office)

4 This financing statement covers the following types (or items) of property (also describe realty where collateral is crops or fixtures):

Assignee of Secured Party

This statement is filed without the debtor's signature to perfect a security interest in collateral (check ☒ if so)

☐ under a security agreement signed by debtor authorizing secured party to file this statement, or

☐ already subject to a security interest in another jurisdiction when it was brought into this state, or

☐ which is proceeds of the following described original collateral which was perfected:

Check ☒ if covered: ☐ Proceeds of Collateral are also covered. ☐ Products of Collateral are also covered. No. of additional Sheets presented:

Filed with: ☐ Secretary of State ☐ Recorder of ________________ County

By: ______________________ Signature(s) of Debtor(s)

By: ______________________ Signature(s) of Secured Party(ies)

(1) Filing Officer Copy—Alphabetical
FORM UCC-1—INDIANA UNIFORM COMMERCIAL CODE

Approved by: Charles O. Hendricks
Secretary of State

ment will usually consist of a multicopy form available from the state secretary of state's office, although a copy of the security agreement may be filed as a finance statement if it contains the required items of information and has been signed by the debtor.

The financing statement, to be sufficient, must give the names of the debtor and the secured party, be signed by the debtor, must give an address of the secured party from which information concerning the security interest may be obtained, must give a mailing address of the debtor, and must contain a statement indicating the types or describing the items of collateral. If the financing statement covers crops or goods which are to become fixtures, the statement must also contain a description of the real estate concerned (Revised 9–402). The financing statement may be broad in its scope and include all of the debtor's personal property, accounts, contract rights and chattel paper which he owns at the time of its execution or may acquire in the future or it may include a class of property or a few items, or a single item of property.

The requirement as to the place of filing the financing statement is determined by the statutes of the individual state. In all states a security interest in fixtures must be filed in the office where a mortgage on the real estate concerned would be filed or recorded (9–401[1][a]). The secured party acquiring a security interest in property which is a fixture or is to become a fixture, should, in order to obtain maximum security, double file, that is, file as a fixture and as a nonfixture.

In regard to collateral other than fixtures the state may require only central filing, usually in the office of the secretary of state. However, most states require local filing of those transactions which are local in nature, such as when the collateral is equipment used in farming operations, or is farm products, or accounts, contract rights or general intangibles arising from or relating to the sale of farm products by a farmer or consumer goods (9–401).

If no maturity date is stated in the financing statement or if the debt is payable on demand, the filing is valid for five years. If a maturity date is stated in the financing statement, the filing is valid for the stated period plus 60 days but for a period not to exceed five years (9–403[2]). This provision is changed by the 1972 amendments to Article 9 which make financing statements effective for five years unless a continuation statement has been filed prior to the lapse.

A *continuation statement* may be filed within six months before and 60 days after a stated maturity date of five years or less, and otherwise within six months prior to the five-year expiration date. The continuation statement must be signed by the secured party, identify the original statement by file number, and state that the original statement is still effective. Successive continuation statements may be filed (9–403[3]).

When all debts and obligations of the debtor secured by a financing statement are completely fulfilled he is entitled to a *termination statement* signed by the secured party or an assignee of record. Failure to furnish a termination statement after proper demand subjects the affected secured party to a fine of $100 plus damages for any loss caused to the debtor by such failure (9–404).

Possession by the Secured Party as Public Notice. The purpose of public filing of a lien or security interest is to put any interested members of the public on notice of the security interest. This same objective can be reached if the debtor gives up possession of the collateral and delivers it to the secured party or to someone who holds the collateral for the secured party. Under the Code, change of possession of the collateral from the debtor to the secured party or his agent perfects the security interest of the creditor holding a secured interest in the collateral (9–302[1][a]). Generally possession by the secured party is the only means of perfecting a security interest in instruments such as checks or notes.[3] Possession of the collateral by the secured party

[3] Section 9–304(4) and (5) permit a 21-day temporary perfection.

is an alternative and often the most satisfactory means of perfecting a security interest in chattel paper, money and negotiable documents of title.

Possession is also a possible means for perfecting a security interest in inventory. This is sometimes done through the field warehousing arrangement whereby part of the debtor's inventory is fenced off and withdrawals from it permitted only on the approval of the secured party or his on-the-scene representative.

Possession is usually not a practical means for perfecting a security interest in equipment, farm products, and consumer goods and, of course, is not possible at all with accounts or general intangibles.

The person to whom the collateral is delivered holds it as bailee and, he owes the duties of a bailee to the parties in interest (9–207).

Perfection by Attachment. Perfection by mere attachment of the security interest, sometimes known as automatic perfection, is the only form of perfection that occurs without the giving of public notice. It occurs automatically when all the requirements of attachment are complete. This form of perfection is limited to certain classes of collateral and in addition may be only a temporary perfection in some situations.[4]

Permanent perfection by attachment of the security interest alone is valid only with respect to purchase money security interests in consumer goods. Thus, the retailer who sells a television set on a conditional sales contract to a consumer does not have to file a financing statement but is considered to have perfected his security interest just by virtue of its attachment to the television set now in the hands of the consumer.

There are, however, several important exceptions to this permanent perfection by attachment principle. First, it does not apply to those consumer goods which are or will become fixtures or to motor vehicles if they are required to have a certificate of title under state law (Revised 9–302). Thus if a creditor is taking a secured interest in, for example, storm windows purchased by a consumer that will become fixtures, the creditor must file a financing statement to perfect his secured interest. Similarly, if a credit union loans one of its depositors the money to buy a new car in a state that requires certificates of title for cars, the credit union cannot rely on attachment of its security interest but rather must have its security interest noted on the certificate of title. This exception serves to protect the would be buyer or creditor of the vehicle or real estate. By checking the title, in the case of a vehicle, or the

---

[4] Temporary perfection without filing or possession is automatically obtained for 21 days after attachment of the security interest in instruments and negotiable documents (9–304). To get protection beyond the 21-day period, the secured party must perfect by filing or possession. However, during the 21-day period of temporary perfection, any holder in due course of commercial paper or bona fide purchaser of a security or negotiated document will prevail over the secured party relying on temporary perfection (9–309).

real estate records in the case of real property, a potential buyer or creditor can ascertain whether the property is free of liens and can then buy or extend credit with confidence that the vehicle or property is not subject to some undisclosed lien.

Second, although the retailer who relies on attachment for perfection of his security interest in consumer goods will prevail against other creditors of the debtor, he will not prevail over a buyer from the debtor if the buyer buys the collateral without knowledge of the security interest, for value, and for his own personal, family, or household use (9–307[2]). For example, if Appliance Dealer sells a stereo set to Sally on a conditional sales contract reserving a security interest in the stereo until Sally has paid for it in full but does not file a financing statement, then if Sally's credit union tries to claim the stereo as collateral for a later loan to Sally, Appliance Dealer would prevail over the credit union. However, if Sally sells the stereo to her neighbor Susan who gives value to Sally, is not aware that Sally still owes money to the dealer, and buys the set to use in her home, then Appliance Dealer cannot recover the stereo from Susan. To be protected against such a purchaser from the debtor, the secured party must file a financing statement rather than relying on attachment for perfection.

Removal of Collateral. Even where a creditor has a perfected security interest in collateral of his debtor, he needs to be concerned about the possibility that the debtor will remove the collateral from the state where the creditor has filed on it and take the collateral to another state where the creditor does not have his claim filed on the public record. Commonly the security agreement between the creditor and the debtor provides where the collateral is to be kept and that it will not be moved without the debtor giving notice to and/or obtaining the permission of the creditor. There is, however, no absolute assurance that the debtor will be faithful to such an agreement.

Under the Code a secured creditor who has perfected his security interest generally has four months after the collateral is brought into the new state to perfect his security interest in that state. If the creditor does not re-perfect within the four months, his security interest becomes unperfected and he could lose the collateral to a person who purchases it, or takes an interest in it, after it is removed (Revised 9–103[1]). If the creditor has not perfected his security interest by the time collateral is removed, or within the time period the creditor has to perfect in the former location of the collateral, then his interest is unperfected and he does not obtain the advantage of the four month grace period.

The Code rules that govern the removal of collateral covered by a state certificate of title—such as an automobile—are more complicated. If an automobile covered by a certificate of title issued in one state on which a security interest is noted is moved to another state, the perfected secured interest is perfected for four months in the new state, or until the automobile is registered in the new state. If the original state did not require that security interests be noted on the title, and if a new title is issued in the second state without notation of the security interest, then under certain circumstances a buyer of the automobile can take free of the original security interest. To qualify, the buyer must not be in business of buying and selling automobiles and must (1) give value, (2) take delivery after issuance of the new title, and (3) buy without notice of the security interest. (Revised 9–103[2]).[5]

SUMMARY

To protect his security interest against other creditors of the debtor and purchasers of the collateral, the secured party must perfect his security interest. Under the Code there are three means of perfection: public filing of a financing statement; the secured party's taking possession of the collateral; and, in some limited cases, mere attachment of the security interest.

A financing statement is filed at either the secretary of state's office or the local recorder's office, depending on the type of collateral it secures. If no maturity date is stated, the filing is good for five years and may be extended for additional five-year periods by filing a continuation statement. A debtor who has fulfilled his obligations is entitled to a termination statement which removes the financing statement from the records.

Even after a secured party has perfected his security interest he must be concerned about the possible removal of the collateral from the jurisdiction in which the interest was perfected. In general, the secured party will have four months to re-perfect his security interest in the new location of the collateral.

In re Midas Coin Co., Inc.

264 F.Supp. 193 (D.C. Mo. 1967)

This was a bankruptcy proceeding against the Midas Coin Company. St. John's Community Bank filed a petition to foreclose a collateral note which the Bankruptcy Trustee opposed on the grounds the bank had not filed a financing statement and was required to do so in order to protect its security interest. The Bankruptcy Referee refused to allow the foreclosure petition and St. John's Community Bank appealed. Reversed on appeal with directions to approve the foreclosure petition.

Midas Coin was in the business of buying and selling coins and stamps for profit. On January 14, 1966, Midas executed a promissory note to St. John's Bank for $9,637.58 and pledged as collateral security coins from its

[5] Other rules are set out in the Code for accounts, general intangibles, chattel paper and mobile goods removed to other states (Revised 9–103[3] and [4]).

inventory having a face value of $9,750.50. The security agreement provided that the collateral was to secure payment of all other liabilities owed to St. John's Bank as well as the note. At the date of bankruptcy, February 7, 1966, St. John's Bank had coins of a face value of $6,432.50 in its possession and was owed some $9,700 by Midas Coin. St. John's Bank claimed it had a perfected security interest in the coins and the trustee claimed that the security interest was unperfected because no financing statement had been filed.

REGAN, DISTRICT JUDGE. Section 9–302(1)(a) of Article 9 provides that a financing statement must be filed to perfect all security interests, except a security interest in collateral in possession of the secured party under § 9–305. The latter section authorizes the secured party to prefect a security interest in goods, instruments, negotiable documents or chattel paper (as well as letters of credit and advices of credit) by taking possession of the collateral. It is the Bank's position that having taken possession of the collateral, its security interest has thereby been perfected, so that no financing statement was required to be filed.

The trustee contends, and the Referee held, that § 9–305 is not here applicable, upon the theory that coins are money, and that since money is not one of the kinds of property enumerated in that section, the only method of perfecting a security interest therein is by filing a financing statement.

The trustee does not suggest any possible legislative purpose which would be served by differentiating between the transfer of physical possession of coins (or other money of numismatic value) and any other tangible personal property susceptible to such physical possession. If the coins in question are excluded as subject to pledge simply because they fit the statutory definition of "money," in spite of the fact they constitute part of inventory and in any realistic sense are a commodity, the result would be that without any rhyme or reason they would be the only species of tangible personal property in which a security interest could not be perfected without filing a financing statement. We do not believe such was the legislative intent.

Money as such does not customarily serve as commercial collateral. The coins are so in this case solely because of the numismatic value. We hold, therefore, that the coins which were pledged to the Bank under the security agreement constitute "goods," and therefore, the Bank was not required to file a financing statement in order to perfect its security interest.

[*Note: Under the revised Article 9, "money" is specifically included as a "general intangible"* (*See Revised* § *9–106*)].

In re Nicolosi

4 UCC Rep. 111 (S.D. Ohio 1966)

A trustee in bankruptcy filed a petition to sell a diamond ring in his possession free of liens. Pike-Kumber Company claimed it had enforceable lien on the ring. The court held that Pike-Kumber held a perfected security interest in the ring.

Nicolosi purchased the diamond ring from Pike-Kumber on July 7, 1964, as an engagement present for his fiancée. He executed a purchase money security agreement that was not filed; nor was any financing statement filed.

ANDERSON, REFEREE. If the diamond ring, purchased as an engagement ring by the bankrupt, cannot be categorized as consumer goods, and therefore exempted from the notice filing requirements of the Uniform Commercial Code as adopted in Ohio, a perfected security interest does not exist. See U.C.C. § 9–302.

Under the commercial code, collateral is divided into tangible, intangible, and documentary categories. Certainly, a diamond ring falls into the tangible category. The classes of tangible goods are distinguished by the primary use intended. Under U.C.C. § 9–109, the four classes are "consumer goods," "equipment," "farm products" and "inventory."

The difficulty is that the code provisions use terms arising in commercial circles which have different semantical values from legal precedents. Does the fact that the purchaser bought the goods as a special gift to another person signify that it was not for his own "personal, family or household purposes"? The trustee urges that these special facts control under the express provisions of the commercial code.

By a process of exclusion, a diamond engagement ring purchased for one's fiancée is not "equipment" bought or used in business, "farm products" used in farming operations, or "inventory" held for sale, lease or service contracts. When the bankrupt purchased the ring, therefore, it could only have been "consumer goods" bought for use "primarily for personal use."

Priorities

Importance of Determining Priority. Because several creditors may claim a security interest in the same collateral of a debtor, the Code establishes a set of rules for determining which of the conflicting security interests has priority. Determining which creditor has the priority or the best claim takes on particular importance in bankruptcy situations where unless a creditor has a preferred secured interest in collateral that fully protects the obligation owed to him, the creditor may realize only a few cents on every dollar that is owed to him.

Basic Priority Rules. The basic rule established by the Code is that when more than one security interest in the same collateral has been filed (or otherwise perfected), the first security interest to be filed (or perfected) has priority over any that are filed (or perfected) later. If only one security interest has been perfected, for example by filing, then that security interest has priority.

However, if none of the conflicting security interests have been perfected, then the first security interest to be attached to the collateral has priority (Revised 9–312[5]).

Thus, if Bank A filed a financing statement covering Retailer's inventory on February 1, 1969, and Bank B filed such a financing statement on March 1, 1969, covering that same inventory, Bank A would have priority over Bank B even though Bank B might have made its loan and attached its security interest to the inventory prior to the time Bank A did so. However, if Bank A neglected to perfect its security interest by filing and Bank B did perfect, then Bank B as the only perfected security interest in the inventory would prevail.

If both neglected to perfect their security interest, then the first security interest that attached would have priority. For example, if Bank Y has a security agreement covering Dealer's equipment on June 1, 1978 and advances money to Dealer on that date whereas Bank Z does not obtain a security agreement covering that equipment or advance money to Dealer until July 1, 1978, then Bank Y would have priority over Bank Z. In connection with the last situation, it is important to note that unperfected secured creditors do not enjoy a preferred position in bankruptcy proceedings, thus giving additional impetus to the desirability of filing or otherwise perfecting a security interest.

Exceptions to the General Rules. To these general rules there are several very important exceptions which are best discussed in the context of hypothetical situations. First, assume that Bank A takes and perfects a security interest in all present and after-acquired inventory of Debtor. Then Debtor acquires some additional inventory from Wholesaler who retains a security interest in the inventory until Debtor pays for it and Wholesaler perfects this security interest. Wholesaler has a *purchase money security interest* in inventory goods and will have priority over the prior secured creditor (Bank A) if Wholesaler has perfected the security interest by the time the collateral reaches the Debtor and if Wholesaler sends notice of his purchase money security interest to Bank A before Wholesaler ships the goods (Revised 9–312[3]). Thus to protect itself Wholesaler must check the public records to see whether any of Debtor's creditors are claiming an interest in Debtor's inventory; when it discovers that some are claiming an interest, it should file its own security interest and give notice of it to the existing creditors.

Second, assume that Bank B takes and perfects a security interest in all the present and after-acquired equipment belonging to Debtor. Then Supplier sells some equipment to Debtor reserving a security interest in the equipment until it is paid for. If Supplier perfects the purchase money security interest by filing by the time the Debtor obtains the collateral or within ten days thereafter, it will have priority over Bank B because a purchase money security interest in noninventory collateral prevails over a prior perfected security interest if the purchase money security interest is perfected at the time the Debtor takes possession or within ten days afterwards (Revised 9–312[4]).

The preference given to purchase money security interests, provided that their holders comply with the statutory procedure in a timely manner, serves several ends. First, it prevents a single creditor from closing off all other sources of credit to a particular debtor and thus possibly preventing the debtor from obtaining additional inventory or equipment needed to maintain its business. The preference also makes it possible for a supplier of inventory or equipment to have first claim on it until it is paid for, at which time it may become subject to the "after-acquired" property clause of another creditor's security agreement. By requiring that the first perfected creditor be given notice of a purchase money security interest at the time the new inventory comes into the debtor's inventory, the Code serves to alert the first creditor to the fact that some of the inventory on which it may be relying for security is subject to a prior secured interest until it is paid for.

Finally, a buyer in the ordinary course of business (other than a person buying farm products from a person engaged in farming operations) takes free from a security interest created by his seller even though the security interest is perfected and even though the buyer knows of its existence (9–307[1]). For example, Bank loans money to Dealership to finance Dealership's inventory of new automobiles and takes a security interest in the inventory which it perfects by filing. Then Dealership sells an automobile out of inventory to Customer. Customer takes the automobile free of Bank's security interest even though Dealership may be in default on its loan agreement. As long as Customer is a buyer in the ordinary course of business—that is not in the business of buying and selling automobiles—Customer is protected. The reasons for this rule are that Bank really expects to be paid from the proceeds of the sale of the automobiles and it is necessary to the smooth conduct of commerce. Customers would be very reluctant to buy goods if they could not be sure they were getting clear title to them from the merchants from whom they buy.

The Code also provides that certain liens arising by operation of law (such as artisan's liens) have priority over a perfected security interest in the collateral (9–310). For example, Mary takes her automobile, on which Credit Union has a perfected security interest, to Frank's Garage to have it repaired. Under common or statutory law Frank may have a lien on the car to secure payment for his repairwork which permits him to keep the car until he receives payment for his work. If Mary defaults on her loan to the Credit Union, refuses to pay Frank for the repairwork, and the car is sold to satisfy the liens, Frank is entitled to his share of the proceeds before the Credit Union gets anything.

Fixtures. A separate set of problems is raised when the collateral is goods that become fixtures by being so related to particular real estate that an interest in them arises under real estate law. Determining the priorities between a secured party with an interest in the fixtures, subsequent purchasers of the real estate, and those persons who have a secured interest—such as a mortgage—on the real property can involve both real estate law and the Code. However, the Code does set out a number of rules for determining when the holder of a perfected security interest in fixtures has priority over an encumbrancer or owner of the real estate. Some of the Code priority rules are as follows.

First, the holder of the secured interest in a fixture has priority if: (1) his interest is a purchase money security interest which was obtained prior to the time the goods become fixtures; (2) the security interest is perfected by "fixture filing" (that is by filing in the recording office where a mortgage on the real estate would be filed)[6] prior to, or within ten days of, the time when the goods become fixtures (Revised 9–313[4][a]), and (3) the debtor has a recorded interest in the real estate or is in possession of it. For example, Restaurant Supply sells Arnie's Diner a new gas stove on a conditional sales contract, reserving a security interest until it is paid for. The stove is to be installed in a restaurant where Arnie is in possession under a ten-year lease. Restaurant Supply can assure its security interest in the stove will have priority over any claims to it by the owner of the restaurant and anyone holding a mortgage on it if it: (1) enters into a security agreement with Arnie prior to the time the stove is delivered to him and (2) perfects its security interest by "fixture filing" before the stove is hooked up by a plumber or within ten days of that time.

Second, the secured party whose interest in fixtures is perfected will have priority where: (1) the fixtures are removable factory or office machines or readily removable replacements of domestic appliances which are consumer goods; and (2) the security interest was perfected prior to the time the goods became fixtures (Revised 9–313[4][b]). For example, Harriet Homeowner's dishwasher breaks down and she contracts with Appliance Store to buy a new one on a time payment plan. The mortgage on Harriet's house provides that it covers the real property along with all kitchen appliances, or their replacements. Appliance Store's security interest will have priority in the dishwasher against the holder of the mortgage if it perfects its security interest prior to the time the new dishwasher is installed in Harriet's home. Perfection in consumer goods can, of course, be obtained merely by attaching the security interest through the signing of a valid security agreement.

Once a secured party has filed his security interest as a "fixture filing" he will have priority over purchasers or encumbrancers whose interests is filed after that of the secured party (9–313[4][b] and [d]).

---

[6] Revised 9–313(1)(b).

Where the secured party has priority over all owners and encumbrancers of the real estate, he generally has the right on default to remove the collateral from the real estate. However, he must make reimbursement for the cost of any physical injury caused to the property by the removal (9–313[8]).

SUMMARY

The Code sets out a series of rules for determining the priority of conflicting claims of secured creditors to the same collateral. Where more than one security interest has been perfected, then the first security interest to be perfected has priority over any that are perfected later or any that are unperfected. If none of the security interests have been perfected, then the first security interest to attach has priority. However, special rules provide that creditors who have purchase money security interests can prevail over prior secured creditors if they file. In addition a buyer in the ordinary course of business takes free of a security interest created by his seller even though the security interest is perfected and the buyer knows about it.

Special steps must be taken by a secured party holding a security interest in goods that may become fixtures so that his claim is shown on the real estate records.

National Cash Register Co. v. Firestone & Co., Inc.

191 N.E.2d 471 (Sup. Jud. Ct. Mass. 1963)

This was an action by National Cash Register Company (plaintiff) against Firestone & Co., Inc. (defendant), to recover a tort judgment for conversion of a cash register. Judgment for National Cash Register Company and Firestone Co., Inc., appealed. Reversed.

On November 18, 1960, Firestone Co., Inc. (Firestone) made a loan to Edmund Carroll doing business as Kozy Kitchen. To secure the loan a security agreement was executed which listed the items of property included and concluded as follows: "together with all property and articles now, and which may hereafter be, used or mixed with, added or attached to, and/or substituted for any of the described property." A financing statement which included all of the items listed in the security agreement was filed with the town clerk on November 18, 1960, and with the Secretary of State on November 22, 1960. There was no reference to a cash register in either the security agreement or the financing statement and there was no after-acquired property provision in the financing statement. On November 25, 1960, National Cash Register Company (National) delivered a cash register to Carroll, on a conditional sales contract. National filed a financing statement on the cash register with the town clerk on December 20, and with the Secretary of State on December 21, 1960. Carroll defaulted in his payments to both Firestone and National.

Firestone repossessed all of Carroll's fixtures and equipment covered by its security agreement, including the cash register and sold the same. National claimed that it was the title owner of the cash register and brought suit for its conversion.

WILKINS, CHIEF JUSTICE. Under the Uniform Commercial Code, after-acquired property, such as this cash register, might become subject to Firestone's security agreement when delivered, and likewise its delivery under a conditional sale agreement with retention of title in National would not, in and of itself, affect the rights of Firestone. Although National could have completely protected itself by perfecting its interest before or within ten days of the delivery of the cash register to Carroll, it did not try to do so until more than ten days after delivery. Thus the principal issue is whether Firestone's earlier security interest effectively covers the cash register.

First, National argues that the debtor could not have intended to grant security interest to Firestone because the purchase was five months earlier, delivery was about to be made, and the cash register could be repossessed by National for default within the period of twenty-one months provided for instalment payments. It is also urged that, without the cash register, Firestone was well secured for its loan, a fact which cannot be inferred and which, in any event, would not be conclusive. The debtor's intent must be judged by the language of the security agreement.

In § 9–110, it is provided: "For the purposes of this Article any description of personal property or real estate is sufficient whether or not it is specific if it reasonably identifies what is described." In § 9–203 it is provided: (1) . . . a security interest is not enforceable against the debtor or third parties unless . . . (b) the debtor has signed a security agreement which contains a description of the collateral. . . ."

Contrary to National's contention, we are of opinion that the security agreement is broad enough to include the cash register, which concededly did not have to be specifically described. The agreement covers "All contents of luncheonette including equipment such as," which we think covers all those contents and does not mean "equipment, to wit." There is a reference to "all property and articles now, and which may hereafter be, used . . . with [or] added . . . to . . . any of the foregoing described property." We infer that the cash register was used with some of the other equipment even though the case stated does not expressly state that the luncheonette was operated.

Sterling Acceptance Co. v. Grimes

168 A.2d 600 (Super. Ct. Pa. 1961)

This was an action by Sterling Acceptance Co. (plaintiff) against Patrick Grimes (defendant) to recover possession of an automobile. Judgment for Grimes and Sterling Acceptance Co. appealed. Judgment affirmed.

Grimes purchased a new Dodge automobile from Homish, a franchised Dodge dealer. The sale was made in the ordinary course of Homish's business and Grimes paid to Homish the purchase price of the automobile at the time of the sale. Homish had borrowed money from Sterling Acceptance Co. (Sterling) and had given it a perfected security interest in all his inventory. A dealer's certificate of title showing the lien in favor of Sterling was issued and was in the possession of Sterling. Homish did not pay Sterling and it sought to recover the automobile from Grimes.

WOODSIDE, JUDGE. Article 9 of the Uniform Commercial Code deals with secured transactions including liens on personal property intended to be sold in the ordinary course of business. Section 9–307, provides:

(1) In the case of inventory, and in the case of other goods as to which the secured party files a financing statement in which he claims a security interest in proceeds, a buyer in ordinary course of business takes free of a security interest even though perfected and even though the buyer knows of the terms of the security agreement.

According to the comment on § 9–307 of the Uniform Commercial Code, "The theory is that when goods are inventory or when proceeds are claimed the secured party contemplates that his debtor will make sales, and so the debtor has effective power to do so, even though his buyers know the goods they buy were subject to the security interest."

Under the provisions of the Uniform Commercial Code, Sterling must look to Homish for repayment of the loan it made to him, and not to the automobile in the possession of Grimes, who paid the full purchase price to Homish.

National Shawmut Bank of Boston v. Jones

236 A.2d 484 (Sup. Ct. N.H. 1967)

This was an action of replevin by National Shawmut Bank of Boston (plaintiff) against Jones (defendant) to recover possession of a 1964 Dart automobile on which National Shawmut claimed to have an enforceable security interest. The case was transferred to the Supreme Court to have several questions of law answered. The questions were answered and the case was remanded.

On February 15, 1965, Robert Wever purchased the Dart from Wentworth Motor Company on a conditional sales contract for personal, family or household use. Wever executed a "Retail Sales Contract" which was assigned by Wentworth to National Shawmut Bank and which was filed with the town clerk pursuant to 9–401. Without National Shawmut's permission Wever sold the automobile to Hanson-Rock, an automobile dealer in the business of selling new and used cars to the public. Then Jones purchased the car from Hanson-Rock on April 8, 1966, for consideration, in good faith and without any actual knowledge of National Shawmut's security interest. Wever did not complete the payments under the installment plan and National Shawmut sought to foreclose its security interest in the automobile.

GRIMES, JUDGE. Since Wever purchased for personal, family or household purposes, the Dart is classified as consumer goods. (9–109.) National Shawmut's security interest was perfected by filing the financing statement with the town clerk of Hampton where Wever resided (9–401[1][a]), and continues when the collateral is sold without its consent as was the case here unless Article 9 provided otherwise (9–306[2]). In the case of buyers of goods, Article 9–307(1) does provide otherwise in certain instances, as follows:

> A buyer in ordinary course of business [subsection (9) of Section 1–201] other than a person buying farm products from a person engaged in farming operations takes free of a security interest created by his seller even though the security interest is perfected and even though the buyer knows of its existence.

Since Jones purchased in good faith without knowledge that the sale to him was in violation of the security interest of another and bought in the ordinary course from a person in the business of selling automobiles, he was a "buyer in the ordinary course of business" (1–201[9]). However, § 9–307(1) permits him to take free only of "a security interest created by his seller." The security interest of National Shawmut was not created by Hanson-Rock, Inc., Jones's seller, but by Wentworth Motor Co., Inc. Jones, therefore, does not take free of National Shawmut's security interest under this section. Neither does he take free of the security interest by reason of the provisions of § 9–307(2) relating to consumer goods even if he purchased for his own personal, family or household purposes (a fact not agreed upon) because "prior to the purchase, the secured party . . . filed a financing statement. . . ." These are the only two provisions of Article 9 under which a buyer of goods can claim to take free of a security interest where a sale, exchange or other disposition of the collateral was without the consent of the secured party. Jones does not benefit from either one.

Default and Foreclosure

Contract Provisions. Within stated limitations the parties may agree as to the rights of the secured party in the event of default on the part of the debtor. In general, an agreement which deprives the debtor of his right to any surplus after sale of the collateral, his right to redeem before sale, his right to notice of the time and place of sale, his right to hold the secured party liable for breach of his duty, or any other basic right vested in the debtor, will not be enforced. (9–501.) The secured party may, if he so elects, reduce his claim to judgment in which event he will not surrender his right in the collateral and the foreclosure will proceed according to the procedure in judicial sales. The secured party may bid at the sale (9–501[5]).

Right to Possession. On default the secured party is entitled to possession of the collateral. If the collateral is in the possession of the debtor and cannot be repossessed without breach of peace he can institute the possessory court action available under the procedural statutes of the state (9–503). If the collateral is intangible, such as, for instance, accounts, chattel paper, instruments or documents, and performance has been rendered to the debtor, the secured party may give notice and have payments made or performance rendered to him (9–502).

Sale of Collateral. The secured party may dispose of the collateral by sale or lease or in any manner calculated to produce the greatest benefit to all parties concerned; however, the method of disposal must be commercially reasonable. (9–504.) Notice of the time and place of a public sale must be given to the debtor as must notice of a private sale.

Distribution of Proceeds. Proceeds from the liquidation of the collateral are distributed in the following order: (1) expenses of retaking, holding, preparing for sale and the like, and reasonable attorney fees; (2) satisfaction of indebtedness; (3) junior security interests (if written notice of the junior liens is given to the senior lienholder before distribution); and (4) the surplus, if any, to debtor (9–504[1]). In the event the amount received on the liquidation is insufficient to satisfy the obligation, the secured party, in the absence of an agreement to the contrary, is entitled to a deficiency judgment. (9–504[2]).

Consumer Goods. If the security interest is in consumer goods, the secured party must sell if 60 percent of the purchase price or debt has been paid. If less than 60 percent has been paid or if the security interest is in collateral other than consumer goods, the secured party in possession may propose to retain the collateral in satisfaction of the obligation. If no written objection is made to the proposal within 21 days after written notice of the election to retain the collateral is given, the secured party may retain the collateral in satisfaction of the obligation (Revised 9–504).

Duties of Secured Party. The debtor has an absolute right to redeem the collateral at any time before its disposal (9–506). The secured party is liable to injured parties if, in his foreclosure and sale, he has not complied with the provisions of Article 9 (9–507).

Constitutional Requirements Re Repossession. In 1972 in *Fuentes v. Shevin,*[7] the U.S. Supreme Court held that state repossession statutes which authorize summary seizure of goods and chattels by state agents (such as a sheriff) upon an application by some private person who claims he is "lawfully entitled" to the property and posts a bond are unconstitutional because they

[7] 407 U.S. 67 (1972).

deny the current possessor of the property an opportunity to be heard in court before the property is taken from him. The Court did not accept the argument that because the possessors of the property in question had signed conditional sales contracts which authorized the sellers to "take back" or "repossess" the property on default they had waived their rights to a hearing. This decision raised some speculation that the provisions of the Code which permit secured parties to repossess collateral, in some cases without even judicial process, might be constitutionally defective.

Then in 1974 in *Mitchell v. W. T. Grant*[8] the Supreme Court limited the *Fuentes* holding to a requirement that where only property rights are involved there must be some opportunity for a judicial hearing prior to any final determination of the rights of the parties claiming an interest in the property in question. This decision permits property to be seized by state officials, following the filing of an application and the posting of a bond, so long as the person from whom the property is seized later has an opportunity to assert in court his rights to the property.

The repossession provisions of the Code have been attacked in court as lacking in due process, as for example in the case of *Ford Motor Co. v. Milline* which follows this section of the text. However the courts to date have upheld the Code repossession provisions as they relate to private repossession without judicial process.[9] Where judicial process is used, the procedures must conform to the standards laid down in *Fuentes* and *Mitchell.*

SUMMARY

Within stated limitations the parties may agree as to the rights of the secured party if the debtor defaults. Unless otherwise agreed the secured party has the right to possess the collateral. If it is bulky or hard to remove he may render it useless and sell it where located. He may sell the collateral at public or private sale and he may buy the collateral but he must act in good faith and the sale must be commercially reasonable. The proceeds of the sale are distributed as follows: expenses; reasonable attorney fees; satisfaction of indebtedness; junior creditors, if any; and balance to the debtor. Unless otherwise agreed the seller is entitled to a deficiency judgment if the proceeds are not sufficient to cover the debt. If the security interest is in consumer goods the secured party must sell if 60 percent of the debt has been paid. If less than 60 percent has been paid, the secured party may, upon appropriate notice keep the collateral and cancel the debt.

---

[8] 407 U.S. 600 (1974).

[9] See e.g., *Gibbs v. Titelman,* 502 F.2d 1107 (3d Cir. 1974) and cases cited therein.

Ford Motor Credit Co. v. Milline

18 UCC Rep. 1079 (Ga. Ct. App. 1976)

This was an action brought by Milline (plaintiff) against Ford Motor Credit Co. (finance company—defendant) and Leader Lincoln-Mercury, Inc. (dealer—defendant) claiming damages for wrongful repossession of an automobile. Judgment for Milline. Affirmed on appeal subject to Milline's dropping certain of the damages he was awarded.

Milline purchased a new Mercury automobile from Leader Lincoln-Mercury. The transaction was financed through the Ford Motor Credit Co. under an installment loan contract. The purchase price, finance charges and insurance payments were to be paid in 36 monthly installments of $168.83.

On February 28, 1972, the vehicle was involved in a collision. Milline took his automobile to Leader for repairs. During the period of repairs Milline rented a Comet sedan from the dealer. He became indebted for this rental and for damages to the Comet while in his possession. After the repairs had been completed, Ford Credit repossessed the automobile, taking it from the dealer's shop.

On May 8, 1972, when Milline paid Ford Credit $1,235.24 the repossessed vehicle was returned to him. This amount covered three delinquent payments, the forthcoming May installment, insurance deductible, and rental for the Comet plus damage caused to the car while in Milline's possession. Through clerical error by Ford Credit the entire payment was credited on its books to the installment contract so that the account appeared to be prepaid in advance. This error was not discovered until some months after a second repossession of the Mercury and the filing of the law suit on that second taking.

When the Mercury was involved in a second collision it was again brought to the dealer by Milline on August 1, 1972. While the car was there for repairs Ford Credit discovered it had failed to obtain reinstatement of Milline's physical damage insurance after it had been cancelled upon the first repossession. This mistake was admitted by Ford Credit which voluntarily paid $1,913.28 to the dealer for repairs arising out of the "second wreck."

After completion of the repairs caused in the second accident Ford Credit decided to repossess the vehicle. At that time its records showed no payment to have been made in the period intervening since the lump sum payment of May 8th. Thus, the finance company's records showed that on October 27 there was now owed a partial amount of $44.67 for the September installment and the regular installment of $168.83 falling due the next day, October 28. On October 31, 1972, the vehicle was repossessed while in the dealer's possession. This was done without prior written or oral notice to Milline and without notifying Milline of the finance company's decision to declare the entire balance due because of default. When surrendering the automobile to Ford Credit, the dealer obtained an indemnification agreement to protect itself against any claims arising out of the delivery.

On the same date (October 31) Ford Credit mailed Milline a form letter giving him notice of the repossession and acceleration of the balance owing under the contract. This notice also stated "You have a right to redeem the property within ten (10) days from the date of receipt of this notice upon payment of the total balance owing under the contract." It further stated that upon failure to redeem, the car would be sold and any resulting deficiency would be claimed against Milline. Immediately thereafter Milline through his attorney demanded the return of the automobile. The result of conversations with Milline's lawyer was an offer by Ford Credit to return the automobile provided only that the contract was made current by payment of the partial balance for September plus the October payment. This offer was not accepted and Milline filed suit against the dealer and the finance company.

CLARK, JUDGE.

1. Did the Finance Company Have the Right to Repossess the Vehicle Without Notice?

Ford Credit contends its action was permissible under the terms of its contract. The verbiage relied on reads: "In the event buyer defaults in any payment . . . seller shall have all rights and remedies of a secured party under the Uniform Commercial Code, including the right to repossess the property wherever the same may be found with free right of entry, and to recondition and sell the same at public or private sale . . . buyer shall remain liable for any deficiency."

The pertinent section of the Georgia Uniform Commercial Code referred to in the contract is § 9–503 where it is stated that "unless otherwise agreed a secured party has on default the right to take possession of collateral. In taking possession a secured party may proceed without judicial process if this can be done without breach of the peace or may proceed by action. . . ."

Ford Credit cites Georgia authorities and numerous cases from other jurisdictions which have upheld the right of self-help repossession under the U.C.C. Among these are decisions wherein the contention of unconstitutionality has been rejected.

We recognize that self-help repossession has been ruled to be legal in Georgia.

However, the contract at bar also contains additional language which was passed upon by this court in *Chrysler Credit Corp. v. Barnes* and *C & S Motors, Inc. v. Davidson.* That language is an acceleration clause substantially identical to those ruled upon in those two cases. In *C & S Motors, Inc. v. Davidson,* this court concluded that the acceleration clause language "required affirmative action by defendant of notifying plaintiff of its election to declare the contract in default and to accelerate it to maturity. The peremptory taking of the automobile without notice does not suffice." Accordingly, the repossession here without prior notice under the acceleration clause constituted a tort which entitled Milline to sue.

2. Was the Conduct by Defendants of a Nature That Punitive Damages Were Warranted?

"To authorize the imposition of punitive or exemplary damages there must be evidence of willful misconduct, malice, fraud, wantonness, or oppression, or that entire want of care which would raise the presumption of a conscious indifference to consequences." Our reading of the trial transcript does not show evidence of this nature so as to allow punitive damages.

In determining that exemplary damages should not be assessed against Ford Credit we note the following facts favorable to the finance company: Upon the first default the finance company permitted redemption by correction of the default; the finance company voluntarily paid $1,913.28 for repairs on the second wreck in recognition of its mistake in failing to reinstate the cancelled insurance; the contract actually was in arrears for five months even though the company's books erroneously showed only one and one-half months, but even this was after an earlier repossession when the car had been returned to Milline. Furthermore, on the same date as the car was taken and in connection therewith, notice of repossession was given. Thereafter, upon being contacted by Milline's attorney the finance company immediately offered to return the automobile upon the sole condition that the existing delinquency be corrected, which was illustrative of the company's original intent as being limited to collection of the amount which Milline had obligated himself to pay.

Since there is no evidence of willful misconduct, malice, fraud, wantonness, or oppression or that entire want of care which would raise the presumption of indifference to consequences, Milline was not entitled to punitive damages.

Problem Cases

1. On April 12, 1973, ESIC Capital, a finance company loaned Magnum Opus Electronics, Inc. $100,000 and under a signed security agreement took a security interest in "all present and future Accounts and Contract Rights, including all related documents, instruments and chattel papers, and *all General Intangibles.* . . ." A financing statement was properly filed. Magnum defaulted on the agreement. The question then arose whether the name "Magnum Opus" which was a trademark used to identify goods made and sold by Magnum Opus Electronics and which it used in its advertising was to be considered a "general intangible" and thus an asset in which ESIC had a security interest. Does the trademark come within the category "general tangibles?"

2. Metzler owned and operated a chrome and glass furniture manufacturing business under the name Birmingham Occasional Furniture Company. Because Metzler was in arrears with his account, one of his suppliers of chrome plated tubular products, Semco, refused to sell him further goods unless he gave security. A written security agreement was entered into August 29, 1974, and signed by Semco and "Birmingham Occasional Furniture

Company by Robert A. Metzler, Sr." It covered "all machinery, equipment, and inventory maintained in the conduct of the debtor's business to include but not limited to the list attached and all accessories now existing or hereafter acquired." A financing statement was filed on September 3, 1974, giving the debtor's name and business as "Birmingham Occasional Furniture Company, 816 – 19th Street, North Birmingham, Alabama," and covering the same description as above. Metzler also owned and operated a retail furniture business at another location known as Modern Home Furniture where he sold furniture manufactured by Birmingham Occasional Furniture and furniture purchased from other sources. Metzler defaulted on his agreement with Semco and Semco claimed it had a security interest in the machinery, equipment and inventory at both locations because it was "maintained in the conduct of the debtor's business." Is Semco correct?

3. On March 5, 1965, the Princeton Bank filed a financing statement with the New Jersey Secretary of State perfecting the Bank's security interest in the inventory of new and used automobiles owned by Callahan Motors as well as in the proceeds of the sale of automobiles in inventory. On December 29, 1967, the Bank filed a continuation statement along with the appropriate filing fee and was given a copy of the statement marked "filed" by the Secretary of State's Office. On February 23, 1973, Callahan Motors filed a bankruptcy petition. The Bank contends that it has a perfected security in those vehicles in the bankrupt Callahan Motors' inventory which had been purchased from funds advanced by the Bank. Does the Bank have a perfected security interest?

4. Burrows purchased a Utah ranch from Mr. and Mrs. Wilson. The Wilson's retained a purchase money security interest in the livestock involved in the sale. This was perfected by filing a financing statement seven months after the sale. Burrows borrowed $80,000 from Walker Bank immediately after he purchased the ranch. At that time the bank obtained a security interest from Burrows which covered the livestock at the ranch. The bank filed its financing statement two days later. Burrows defaulted on his obligations to both the Wilsons and the bank. Who has priority to the livestock?

5. Pennings Paint Store had been receiving financing for its business from Manufacturers Acceptance Corporation under a valid security agreement that contained an after acquired property clause. In addition, the store received help from Boysen Paint Company by being provided with inventory on a consignment basis. Mr. Pennings decided to incorporate his business and because of this, both parties wanted new security interests. Therefore, on April 4, 1972, a security agreement was executed between Pennings and Boysen in the paint inventory and a financing statement was filed. On April 12, 1972, a security agreement was executed between Pennings and Manufacturer's Acceptance Corporation covering inventory, goods in stock and equipment and then a financing statement was filed. Pennings defaulted on its obligations to both Boysen and Manufacturer's. Which has a priority interest in the inventory.

6. Glatfelter purchased a stereo set under a purchase money security agreement from Mahaley's Store. This agreement was not perfected by filing. She sold the set to Colonial Trading Company which in turn resold it. When Glatfelter did not meet her obligations, Mahaley's sued Colonial Trading for conversion of the stereo set in which it claimed a security interest. Can Mahaley's recover from Colonial Trading?

7. Stroman purchased a car from a used car dealer. Although he took the car, he did not receive a title certificate, but relied upon the dealer to have a certificate processed. The dealer, however, took the title and used it to obtain a loan from a bank. When the dealer defaulted on the loan, the bank attempted to get the car from Stroman. Is the bank entitled to recover the car from Stroman?

8. On April 10, 1969, Benson purchased a new Ford Thunderbird automobile. She traded in her old automobile and financed the balance of $4,326 through the Magnavox Employees Credit Union which took a security interest in the Thunderbird. In July of 1969 the Thunderbird was involved in two accidents and sustained major damage. It was taken to ACM for repairs which took seven months to make and resulted in charges of $2,139.54. Benson was unable to pay the charges and ACM claimed a garageman's lien. Does Magnavox Credit Union's lien or ACM's lien have priority?
9. Nancy Raffa purchased a 1970 Cadillac Eldorado and signed a Retail Installment Contract whereby she was to pay for the automobile over a period of 36 months. The contract was assigned to the Dania Bank by the seller of the automobile. Mrs. Raffa was periodically late with her monthly payments and was more than a month overdue on her 16th payment. The bank authorized a private investigator, who it designated as a "collection agent," to repossess the Cadillac. On September 27, 1972 while Mrs. Raffa and her husband were entertaining friends, the Cadillac was parked unlocked with keys in the ignition, in the driveway of her home. The collection agent walked onto the premises, got into the car and then drove it away. The Retail Installment Contract provided that upon default "seller may without notice or demand for performance, lawfully enter any premises where the motor vehicle may be found and take possession of it." Mrs. Raffa paid off the remainder of the loan and resecured her Cadillac. Then she sued the bank for unlawfully repossessing her automobile. Does she have a valid claim?
10. The Franklin State Bank held a security interest in an automobile owned by Parker. Parker fell behind in his payments and the bank had the automobile repossessed on June 20, 1974, by towing it from Parker's garage. The automobile was not operational at that time because Parker was giving the car a tune-up and had removed the spark plugs, condenser, and air filter. On June 26, 1974, Parker received notice that a private sale of the secured automobile would occur on June 29, 1974, at a designated time and place. On said date Carteret Auto Parts, Inc., was the only party that appeared at the sale which submitted a bid of $50. The Bank feeling that this bid was low, held the automobile until October 1, 1974, waiting for additional bids. Not having received further bids, the Bank sold the automobile to Carteret Auto Parts, Inc., for $50. At no time before or after the repossession did the Bank make any attempts to determine, by inspection or otherwise, why the automobile was not mechanically operational. After the Bank repossessed the automobile on June 20, 1974, Parker inquired of the Bank if he could buy the automobile. The essence of the Bank's response was that Parker could not buy the automobile at the private sale. The Bank sued Parker for the deficiency due after the sale of the automobile. Parker defended on the ground that the notice of the sale was improper and that the sale was not made in a commercially reasonable manner. Should the Bank be awarded a deficiency judgment?

46

Security Interests in Real Property

Real Estate Mortgages

Historical Development. The real estate mortgage, as a form of security, was used in England as early as the middle of the 12th century, but our present-day mortgage law developed from the common law mortgage of the 15th century. The common law mortgage was a deed which conveyed the land to the mortgagee, the title to the land to revest in the mortgagor on payment of the debt secured. The mortgagee was given possession of the land during the term of the mortgage, and if the mortgagor defaulted, the mortgagee's title to the land became absolute. The land was forfeited as a penalty for breach of condition, and the forfeiture did not discharge the debt. The mortgagee could sue on the debt, recover a judgment, and collect the debt, in addition to keeping the land.

The early equity courts did not favor the imposition of penàlties and would relieve from such forfeitures, provided the mortgagor's default was minor in nature and was due to causes beyond his control. By gradual stages the courts became more lenient in permitting redemptions and allowed the mortgagor to redeem if he tendered performance without unreasonable delay. Finally, the courts of equity recognized the mortgagor's right to redeem as an absolute right which would continue until the mortgagee asked the court of equity to decree that the mortgagor's right to redeem be foreclosed and cut off. Our present law regarding the foreclosure of mortgages developed from this practice.

Form, Execution, and Recording. The real estate mortgage is generally recognized as conveying an interest in real property, and it must be executed with the same formality as is a deed. Unless a mortgage is executed as required by the statutes of the state in which the land is located, it is not eligible for recording.

An unrecorded mortgage is not valid against bona fide purchasers or mortgagees for value who have no notice or knowledge of the mortgage, nor is it valid against creditors who acquire a lien on the property. As between the parties the validity of the mortgage does not depend on the fulfillment of the formal requirements. If the transaction is intended as a loan and security for the payment of the loan, the courts will declare it a mortgage, irrespective of the form of the conveyance. The courts jealously guard the mortgagor's right to redeem and will not enforce any contract or agreement cutting off this right. Even though the conveyance is in the form of a warranty deed, the courts will declare it a mortgage if it was given as security.

However, if a deed is given as security for the payment of a loan but the deed is not recorded and the real property is sold by the owner of record (the mortgagee) to an innocent purchaser for value, the innocent purchaser for value acquires good title. The mortgagee will be liable to the mortgagor for any damages the mortgagor has suffered as a result of the sale of the property.

Rights and Liabilities of Mortgagor and Purchasers. The owner (the mortgagor) may sell the property without the consent of the mortgagee (the creditor), but such a sale in no way affects the mortgagee's interest in the property or his claim against the mortgagor on the debt. In case there is a default, the mortgagee may foreclose the mortgage and have the mortgaged property sold. If on foreclosure, sale of the property does not bring enough to pay the costs, interest, and principal, the mortgagee is entitled to a deficiency judgment against the original debtor, the mortgagor, although some courts show reluctance to allow deficiency judgments where real property was used as security for a debt. If the property should sell for more than enough to pay the costs, interest, and principal, the surplus will go to the mortgagor or one who has purchased from him.

The purchaser may buy the mortgaged property "subject to the mortgage," or he may "assume" the mortgage. If he purchases subject to the mortgage and a default and a foreclosure follow, he is not liable for a deficiency; if he assumes the mortgage, he is liable for any deficiency. The property is always liable and may be sold to pay the mortgage debt; and the mortgagor, because he cannot assign his liability, is liable to the mortgagee on the mortgage debt. If the mortgagor sells the mortgaged property to a purchaser who "assumes and agrees to pay the mortgage debt," such purchaser is liable to the mortgagee for the amount of the mortgage debt. In most jurisdictions the mortgagor's liability is that of a surety. If there is a default followed by a foreclosure, the mortgagee in the event of a deficiency may obtain a deficiency judgment against both the mortgagor and the purchaser; and if the mortgagor pays the deficiency, he is entitled to recover the amount paid from the purchaser.

Mortgagee's Right to Assign Mortgage. The mortgagee may assign his interest in the mortgaged property. To do this, he must assign the debt. If the debt is evidenced by a negotiable note, the assignment is usually made by the negotiation of the note plus an assignment of the mortgage; however, in most jurisdictions the negotiation of the note carries with it the right to the security, and the holder of the note is entitled to the benefits of the mortgage.

Foreclosure of Real Estate Mortgage. Foreclosure is the process by which all further rights existing in the mortgagor or persons who have acquired the rights of the mortgagor to redeem the mortgaged real property are defeated and lost. Foreclosure proceedings are usually regulated by the statutes of the state in which the real property is located; and in many states, two or more alternative methods of foreclosure are available to the mortgagee or his assignee. The methods in common use today are (1) strict foreclosure, (2) action and sale, and (3) power of sale.

Under a strict foreclosure, all rights of the mortgagor are cut off by the foreclosure proceedings, and title to the mortgaged property is vested in the mortgagee. There is no sale of the property. Strict foreclosure is used extensively in only a few states, and in those states the right to strict foreclosure is generally confined to those cases where the debt is equal to or exceeds the value of the security, or where the mortgagor or a person who has acquired a right under the mortgagor has only a technical interest in the mortgaged property.

Foreclosure by action and sale is permitted in all states and is the only method of foreclosure permitted in some states. Although the state statutes are not uniform, they are alike in their basic requirements. In a foreclosure by action and sale, suit is brought in a court having jurisdiction. Any party having a property interest which would be cut off by the foreclosure must be made a defendant, and if any such party has a defense, he must enter his appearance and set up his defense. After the case is tried, a judgment is entered and a sale of the property ordered. The proceeds of the sale are applied to the payment of the mortgage debt, and any surplus is paid over to the mortgagor or such other person or persons who would be entitled to it. If there is a deficiency, a deficiency judgment is, as a general rule, entered against the mortgagor and such other persons as would be liable on the debt.

The right to foreclose under a power of sale must be expressly conferred on the mortgagee by the terms of the mortgage. If the procedure for the exercise of the power is set out in the mortgage, such procedure must be followed. Several states have enacted statutes which set out the procedure to be followed in the exercise of a power of sale. No court action is required. As a general rule, notice of the sale must be given to the mortgagor, and the sale must be advertised. The sale must be at auction and must be conducted fairly, and an effort must be made to sell the property at the highest price obtainable. The proceeds of the sale are applied to the payment of costs, interest, and the principal of the debt. Any surplus must be paid to the mortgagor or any other persons as may be entitled to it. If there is a deficiency and the mortgagee wishes to recover a judgment for the deficiency, he must bring suit on the debt.

Right of Redemption. At common law and under existing statutes the mortgagor or an assignee of the mortgagor has an equity of redemption in the mortgaged real estate; that is, he has the absolute right to discharge the mortgage when due and have title to the mortgaged property restored free and clear of the mortgage debt. Under the statutes of all states the mortgagor or any party having an interest in the mortgaged property which will be cut off by the foreclosure may redeem the property after default and before the mortgagee forecloses the mortgage. In several states by statute the mortgagor or any other party in interest is given what is known as a redemption period (usually of six months or one year and either after the foreclosure proceedings are started or after a foreclosure sale of the mortgaged property is made) in which to pay the mortgaged debt, costs and interest and redeem the property.

As a general rule, if a party in interest wishes to redeem, he must, if the redemption period runs after the foreclosure sale, pay to the purchaser at the foreclosure sale the amount the purchaser has paid plus interest up to the time of redemption. If the redemption period runs before the sale, the party in interest must pay the amount of the debt plus the costs and interest. The person who wishes to redeem from a mortgage foreclosure sale must redeem the entire mortgage interest; he cannot redeem a partial interest by paying a proportionate amount of the debt or by paying a proportionate amount of the price bid at the foreclosure sale.

SUMMARY

At common law the mortgaged property was deeded to the mortgagee who took possession of the property. On default by the mortgagor the mortgaged property was forfeited to the mortgagee as a penalty for the default.

At an early date the courts of equity began to relieve from forfeiture immediately on default, and by gradual evolution the time in which the mortgagor had a right to redeem after default was extended until foreclosure of the mortgage.

Mortgages are executed with the same formalities as are deeds and must be recorded to be valid against third persons. Irrespective of the form of a conveyance, if it is made to secure a debt, the courts will declare it to be a mortgage and will permit the mortgagor the right to redeem.

The mortgagor may convey his interest in the mortgaged property, but the purchaser acquires no greater rights than the mortgagor has. Whether or not the purchaser becomes liable to the mortgagee for the payment of the mortgage debt depends on whether the purchaser has assumed and agreed to pay the mortgage debt as part of the purchase price of the property. The mortgagee may assign the mortgage debt and mortgage.

On default by the mortgagor the mortgagee must foreclose the mortgage to cut off the mortgagor's rights in the property. In foreclosing the mortgage, the statutory procedure of the state in which the land is located must be followed.

In most states the mortgagor and other parties in interest are given a period, usually one year, in which to redeem the property from the foreclosure.

City Mortgage Investment Club v. Beh

334 A.2d 183 (Ct. App. D.C. 1973)

This was an action brought by the City Mortgage Investment Club (plaintiff) against Philip and Edith Beh (defendants) to recover on a second deed of trust it held on property purchased by the Behs. Trial court judgment for the Behs. Reversed on appeal.

The Behs purchased the property from Alfred M. Groner and his wife Jeanne. Included in the contract of sale was the Beh's promise "to assume" a second deed of trust of approximately $5,000.00, at 6 percent. The second trust was evidenced by a note. The note originally was payable to the order of Charles H. W. Verbeck, and was signed by Alfred and Jeanne Groner. Verbeck negotiated the note to the order of L. D. Quillian, who held it when the sales contract between the Groners and the Behs was executed. Subsequently, Quillian negotiated the note to the City Mortgage Investment Club.

HARRIS, ASSOCIATE JUDGE. Prior to default and foreclosure the Behs recognized their obligations on the second trust. After acquiring the property in August of 1966, the Behs made regular monthly payments on the second trust note until September of 1970. Foreclosure was had on the first deed of trust but the proceeds of sale left nothing for City Mortgage. The Behs then refused to satisfy the second trust note holder, contending that they had never signed (or even seen) the actual note which was associated with that obligation.

When the Behs purchased the property they contracted to assume the obligation of the Alfred Croners to Verbeck. In other words, the Behs agreed with the Groners to assume that obligation. Verbeck then became the third party creditor beneficiary of the assumption contract between the Behs and the Groners. As such, he was entitled to performance and could enforce that right directly against the Behs. The bona fide assignees of his rights likewise were in position to sue the Behs directly on the contract of assumption, occupying the same status as the originally intended beneficiary.

Trust Deeds and Land Contracts

Trust Deeds. There are three parties to a trust deed transaction: the trustor, who borrows the money; the trustee, who holds legal title to the real property put up as security; and the lender, who is beneficiary of the trust. The purpose of a trust deed transaction is to facilitate the liquidation of the security in the event of default. Most of the states have declared a trust deed to be a mortgage and have required court foreclosure, thereby defeating the purpose of the arrangement.

In a deed-of-trust transaction the borrower deeds to the trustee the real property which is to be put up as security. If the borrower fails to make the required payments on the debt, the trustee is usually given, by the terms of the trust agreement, the power to foreclose or to sell the property. Normally, the trustee does not sell the property until the beneficiary (the lender or his assignee) notifies the trustee that the debtor is in default and demands that the property be sold. The trustee sells the property, usually at public sale, and applies the proceeds to the payment of costs, interest, and principal. If there is a surplus, it is paid over to the trustor. If there is a deficiency and the lender wishes to force collection, he will have to sue on the debt and recover a judgment.

Land Contracts. The land contract, as a security device, is limited in its use to the securing of the payment of the balance of the purchase price of real property. The seller of the property agrees to sell, and the buyer agrees to buy and pay the stipulated purchase price set out in the contract. Usually, the purchaser takes possession of the property, pays all taxes and assessments, keeps the property insured, and assumes all other obligations of an owner. In fact, the purchaser is the equitable owner, but the seller holds the legal title and does not deed the property to the buyer until the purchase price is paid in full. In the event the buyer defaults, the seller has the right to declare a forfeiture and take possession of the property, thereby cutting off all the buyer's rights in the property. The laws of the states vary in regard to the rights of the parties to a land contract, but the trend of the law is toward giving additional protection to a buyer on a land contract by giving him a specific period of time to "redeem" his interest.

As a general rule the procedure for declaration of forfeiting and recovery of property sold on land contract is simpler and less time-consuming than the foreclosure of a real estate mortgage by court action. In some states the procedure to be followed in the event of default on a land contract has been set out by statute. In other states the courts of equity have developed the procedure to be followed in the event of default and forfeiture. If the buyer, after default, voluntarily surrenders possession to the seller, no court procedure is necessary; the seller's title will become absolute, and the buyer's equity will be cut off.

SUMMARY

A trust deed may be used in some states in lieu of a mortgage. In the trust deed transaction the borrower (the trustor) conveys the property to a trustee who, after the default of the trustor and at the request of the lender, sells the property and pays the debt from the proceeds.

The owner of real property may sell on land contract. The seller retains title to the property until the purchase price is paid in full. If the buyer defaults, the seller has the right to reclaim the property.

Mechanic's Lien on Real Estate

Nature of Mechanic's Lien on Real Estate. All rights to a mechanic's lien on real estate must be created by statutory enactment, since the courts have never recognized a common law lien on real property. Consequently, all of the states have enacted statutes pertaining to mechanics' liens on real estate, but the requirements in the various states for obtaining such liens differ so widely and in so many particulars that space does not permit a discussion of these statutes in detail.

Persons Entitled to a Lien. Some statutes set out in detail the classes of persons who are entitled to a mechanic's lien, whereas others set them out in broad general terms. In general, any person whose labor or material has contributed to the improvement of real estate is entitled to a mechanic's lien.

Rights of Subcontractors and Materialmen. A general contractor is a person who has contracted with the owner to build, remodel, or improve real property. A subcontractor is a person who has contracted with the general contractor to perform a stipulated portion of the general contract. A materialman is a person who has contracted to furnish certain materials needed to perform a designated general contract.

Two distinct systems are followed by the several states in allowing mechanics' liens on real estate to subcontractors and materialmen: the New York system and the Pennsylvania system.

The New York system is based on the theory of subrogation, and the subcontractors or materialmen cannot recover more than is owing the contractor at the time they file a lien or give notice of a lien to the owner. Under the Pennsylvania system the subcontractors or materialmen have direct liens and are entitled to liens for the value of labor and material furnished, irrespective of the amount due from the owner to the contractor. Under the New York system the failure of the general contractor to perform his contract or his abandonment of the work has a direct effect on the lien rights of subcontractors and materialmen, whereas under the Pennsylvania system, such breach or abandonment by the general contractor does not directly affect the lien rights of subcontractors and materialmen.

Basis for Mechanic's Lien on Real Estate. In some states, statutes provide that no lien shall be claimed unless the contract for the improvement is in writing and embodies a description of the land on which the improvement is to take place, and of the work to be done, and a statement of the materials to be furnished. Other states permit the contract to be oral, but in no state is a licensee or volunteer entitled to a lien.

No lien can be claimed unless the work is done or the materials are furnished in the performance of a contract to improve specific real property. A sale of materials without reference to the improvement of specific real property does not entitle the person furnishing the material to a lien upon real property which is, in fact, improved by the use of the materials at some time after the sale. Unless the state statute specifically includes submaterialmen, they are not entitled to a lien. For example, if a lumber dealer contracts to furnish the lumber for the erection of a specific building and orders from a sawmill a carload of lumber needed to fulfill the contract, the sawmill will not be entitled to a lien on the building in which the lumber is used unless the state statute expressly provides that submaterialmen are entitled to a lien.

At times the question has arisen as to whether or not materials have been furnished. Some courts have held that the materialmen must prove that the material furnished was actually incorporated into the structure. Under this ruling, if material delivered on the job is diverted by the general contractor or others and not incorporated into the structure, the materialmen will not be entitled to a lien. Other courts have held that the materialman is entitled to a lien if he can furnish proof that the material was delivered on the job under a contract to furnish the material.

Requirements for Obtaining Lien. The requirements for obtaining a mechanic's lien must be complied with strictly. Although there is no uniformity in the statutes as to the requirements for obtaining a lien, they generally require the filing of a notice of lien with a county official, such as the register of deeds or county clerk, which notice sets forth the amount claimed, the name of the owner, the name of the contractor and claimant, and a description of the property. Frequently, the notice of lien must be verified by an affidavit of the claimant. In some states a copy of the notice must be served on the owner or posted on the property.

The notice of lien must be filed within a stipulated time. The time varies from 30 to 90 days, but the favored time is 60 days after the last work is done or after the last materials are furnished. Some statutes distinguish between labor claims, materialmen's claims, and claims of general contractors as to time of filing. The lien, when filed, must be foreclosed within a specified time, which varies from six months to two years.

Priorities and Foreclosure. The provisions for priorities vary widely, but most of the statutes provide that a mechanic's lien has priority over all liens attaching after the first work is performed or after the first materials are furnished. This provision in the statute creates a hidden lien on the property, in that a mechanic's lien, filed within the allotted period of time after completion of the work, attaches as of the time the first work is done or the first material is furnished, but no notice of lien need be filed during this period, and if no notice of lien is filed during this period, third persons would have no means of knowing of the existence of a lien. There are no priorities among lien claimants under the majority of statutes.

The procedure followed in the foreclosure of a mechanic's lien on real estate follows closely the procedure followed in a court foreclosure of a real estate mortgage. The rights acquired by the filing of a lien and the extent of property covered by such lien are set out in some of the mechanic's lien statutes. In general, the lien attaches only to the interest the person has in the property which has been improved at the time the notice is filed. Some statutes provide that the lien attaches to the building and city lot on which the building stands, or if the improvement is to farm property, the lien attaches to a specified amount of land.

Waiver of Lien. The question often arises as to the effect of an express provision in a contract for the improvement of real estate that no lien shall attach to the property for the cost of the improvement. In some states, there are statutes requiring the recording or filing of the contract and making such provision ineffective if the statute is not complied with. In some jurisdictions, it has been held that such a provision is effective against everyone; in other jurisdictions the provision has been held ineffective against all except the contractor; while in still other jurisdictions, such provisions have been held ineffective as to subcontractors, materialmen, and laborers. Whether or not parties have notice of the waiver-of-lien provision plays an important part in several jurisdictions in determining their right to a lien.

SUMMARY

The right to a mechanic's lien on real estate is statutory. The basis of a lien is the improvement of the real estate of one person by the addition of the labor and materials of another.

The persons who are entitled to mechanics' liens on real estate are set out in the statutes, and in this regard the provisions of the statutes vary widely. Under one type of statute the right of a subcontractor or materialman to a mechanic's lien is based on the right of the general contractor, and the total of their claims cannot exceed the amount due the general contractor. Under the other type of statute the subcontractor or materialman is entitled to a direct lien on the improved property for the full value of the work and material furnished. The work and materials must be furnished for the improvement of a particular premise or building. A person is not entitled to a lien for materials sold generally which are not until later incorporated into a building.

To obtain a lien, the lien claimant must comply strictly with the statutory requirements as to the form, content, and time of giving notice of lien, and any other requirements for the obtaining of a lien. As a general rule a lien dates from the time the first labor or materials are furnished and has priority over all subsequent lien claimants.

A lien is foreclosed in the same manner as that followed in a court foreclosure of a real estate mortgage. It attaches to the interest which the person having the improvement made has in the improved property. Under the provisions of some statutes the right to a mechanic's lien may be waived by the insertion of a waiver provision in the contract for the improvement.

Manpower, Inc. v. Phillips

179 N.E.2d 922 (Sup. Ct. Ohio 1962)

This was an action by Manpower, Inc. (plaintiff), against Phillips and Oakley Drive-In Theaters, Inc., and others (defendants) asking for a judgment for labor furnished and the granting of a mechanic's lien. Judgment for Manpower, Inc., and Oakley Drive-In Theaters, Inc., appealed to appellate court where the judgment granting a mechanic's lien was affirmed. Oakley Drive-In Theaters, Inc., appealed to the Supreme Court. Judgment reversed as to mechanic's lien.

Oakley Drive-In Theaters, Inc. (Oakley) engaged Phillips as a general contractor for the construction of an addition to the concession building of Oakley.

Manpower, Inc., had a contract with Phillips to furnish him laborers from time to time. Manpower, Inc., at the request of Phillips, furnished him laborers who worked on the Oakley job and paid the laborers a total of $1,955.45, but Phillips did not pay Manpower, Inc. The trial court granted a judgment against Phillips for $1,955.45 and no appeal was taken from this judgment. It also granted a mechanic's lien on the Oakley building and this appeal was taken from that holding.

GRIFFITH, JUDGE. The question presented in this appeal is whether, under Section 1311.02, Revised Code, a corporation which furnishes laborers to a contractor is entitled to a lien on the property of the owner of real property for labor and work rendered by such laborers, employees of the corporation, in the improvement of such property.

The precise question has never been decided by the courts of this state.

So far as pertinent, Section 1311.02, Revised Code, reads:

> Every person or corporation who does work or labor upon, or furnishes machinery, material, or fuel for constructing, altering . . . repairing, or removing a house . . . or other building . . . by virtue of a contract, express or implied, with the owner, part owner, or lessee of any interest in real estate, or his authorized agent, and every person who as a subcontractor, laborer, or materialman, performs any labor, or furnishes machinery, material or fuel, to an original or principal contractor, or any subcontractor, in carrying forward, performing, or completing any such contract, has a lien to secure the payment thereof. . . .

The first part of that section deals with mechanics' liens for persons who deal directly with the owner or the lessee of the real estate; and the second part deals with those persons at least once removed from the owner or lessee who deal with the contractor or subcontractor.

Clearly, Manpower, Inc., did not have any contract, express or implied, with either the lessee or the fee holder.

The next question presented is: Was Manpower, Inc., a "subcontractor" as that term is used in the statute?

"A subcontractor agrees to do something for another, but it is not controlled or subject to the control of the other in the manner or method of accomplishing the result contracted for."

Clearly Manpower does not meet the statutory definition of a "subcontractor," nor does it meet the pronounced judicial description of such.

Problem Cases

1. Kozan held a first mortgage on a certain piece of real estate on which Levin held a second mortgage. When the owner of the property defaulted on the first mortgage by failing to pay the monthly installments, taxes and water charges as he had agreed to do, Kozan brought foreclosure proceedings. On July 29, 1965, the property was deeded by the owner to Levin. On that date Kozan and Levin entered into a written contract whereby Kozan agreed to forbear foreclosure and Levin agreed to cure the mortgage default and to make the monthly installment payments on the mortgage. Levin paid the default and made the monthly payments for a number of years, but then stopped making them. Kozan

brought suit against him to recover monies due under the agreement, contending that Levin had assumed the mortgage. Should the contract be considered an "assumption of the mortgage" or did Levin take the property "subject to the mortgage?"

2. On July 18, Parker conveyed certain land to Benjamin Coombs and took back a mortgage to secure the payment of $1,616 which was the balance due on the purchase price. The mortgage was recorded on November 11 of that year. Several days earlier, on October 30, Coombs executed a mortgage to Mayham on that same property to secure the payment of $1,269; Mayham recorded his mortgage on October 30. Coombs defaulted on the Mayham mortgage and Mayham brought suit to foreclose it. Parker contended that her mortgage had priority over Mayham's because Mayham knew of it at the time he received his mortgage. The state law provides that mortgages "shall take effect from the time they are recorded." Which mortgage has priority?
3. Pope agreed to sell certain land to Pelz and retained a mortgage on the property to secure the payment of the purchase price. The mortgage contained a clause which provided that if Pelz defaulted, Pope had the "right to enter upon the above-described premises and sell the same at public sale" to pay the purchase price, accounting to Pelz for any surplus. What type of foreclosure does this provision contemplate: (1) strict foreclosure; (2) judicial sale; or (3) private power of sale?
4. Brown hired a contractor to build a house for him, and the contractor hired the Electric Contracting Company to do the electrical work. All of the electrical work was completed by March 10 except that a certain type of ground clamp required by a city ordinance was not then available. The city inspector permitted a different type of clamp to be installed at that time. On April 25 Electric Contracting replaced the clamp with the required type. When Electric Contracting was not paid by the contractor, it filed a materialmen's lien on June 13 and then brought suit against Brown to recover for its work. Brown claimed that the lien was not enforceable because it was not filed within 60 days of the time the work was completed as required by state law. Should the court accept Brown's contention?
5. Field was building a house, and Higginbotham had furnished materials which were used in the construction of the house. On May 18, 1948, Tomlinson loaned Field $2,500 and took a mortgage on the house as security. At this time the house was not completed, and this was known to Tomlinson, who had inspected the house before making the loan and knew that men were working on the house at the time. Field gave Tomlinson an affidavit to the effect that all indebtedness against the house had been paid. No notice of lien was filed against the house at the time the loan was made. Higginbotham was not paid for materials purchased, and within the statutory period, he filed the required notice and affidavit of lien. Tomlinson claims that his mortgage lien is superior to Higginbotham's mechanic's lien. The relevant state statute provides that a person who takes a lien in good faith for a valuable consideration without notice or knowledge of mechanics' liens will be given priority. Is Tomlinson's claim correct?

47

Bankruptcy

Background

Bankruptcy Laws in the United States. The framers of the Constitution gave the federal government the right to regulate and control bankruptcies. This power was first exercised in 1800, when Congress passed a bankruptcy act. Our present federal Bankruptcy Act is the act of 1898 as amended. The act has been amended many times since it was first enacted, but its general plan has not been changed by the amendments. Congress has restudied our bankruptcy legislation following each major depression, and many new features have been added to the Bankruptcy Act of 1898 since the depression of 1929.

Purpose and Scope of the Bankruptcy Act. The purpose of the Bankruptcy Act is (1) to protect creditors from one another, (2) to protect creditors from their debtors, and (3) to protect the honest debtor from his creditors. To accomplish these objectives, a number of insolvency proceedings are available under the federal bankruptcy law. The types of proceedings which will be discussed in this chapter are:

1. Straight Bankruptcy. In straight bankruptcy proceedings, the debtor is required to make a full disclosure of all his property and to surrender it to the trustee. Provisions are made for examination of the debtor and for punishment of the debtor who refuses to make an honest disclosure and surrender of his property. The trustee of the bankrupt's estate administers, liquidates, and distributes the proceeds of the estate to the creditors. Provisions are made for the determination of creditors' rights, the recovery of preferential payments, and the disallowance of preferential liens and encumbrances. If the bankrupt has been honest in his business transactions and in his bankruptcy proceedings, he is granted a discharge.

2. Chapter X Corporate Reorganizations. Chapter X corporate reorganizations are generally intended for use by large corporations with secured creditors and publicly held debt. It is sometimes used where there is a need for an independent investigation of possible corporate mismanagement and for the management of the company to be supervised by a disinterested trustee, under the supervision of a U.S. District Court Judge. Under Chapter X a plan is proposed for settling the claims of creditors. A new corporation is sometimes formed to serve as the vehicle for implementing the plan.

3. Chapter XI Arrangements. Chapter XI provides a proceeding for a business or individual debtor to work out a plan or arrangement for solving the debtor's financial problems under the supervision of a federal court. It is intended primarily for debtors who feel they can solve their financial problems on their own if given sufficient time and if relieved of some pressure. The plan commonly calls for an extension of time or a "composition" arrangement for the unsecured claims. Secured creditors can be restrained from enforcing their claims so long as their rights and interests are not impaired by the debtor's plan or action.

4. Chapter XIII Wage Earner's Plans. Under Chapter XIII of the Bankruptcy Act a wage earner—that is "an individual whose principal income is derived from wages, salary, or commissions"—may file a voluntary petition indicating he is insolvent or unable to pay his debts and stating his desire to effect a composition and/or an extension of his debts to be paid out of his future earnings or wages.

The Bankruptcy Act also has provisions relating to railroad organizations, taxing districts and agencies such as cities, towns, and other municipalities, mortgages on real property owned by individuals or partnerships, and Maritime Commissions liens. These provisions will not be covered in this chapter. Straight bankruptcy will be discussed in some detail, while reorganizations, arrangements, and wage earner plans will be more summarily covered.

Straight Bankruptcy

Bankrupts. Bankruptcy proceedings which seek the liquidation of a bankrupt's assets and their distribution to his creditors under the supervision of a federal district court are initiated either by the filing of (1) a voluntary petition by the debtor or (2) an involuntary petition by his creditor or creditors. Once the debtor is adjudicated a bankrupt, it does not matter whether the bankruptcy proceeding was initiated by a voluntary or an involuntary petition.

Voluntary Petitions. A voluntary petition in bankruptcy may be filed by any person, partnership or corporation (except a municipal, railroad, insurance or banking corporation, or a building and loan association).[1] It is not necessary that the person filing a voluntary petition be insolvent, but he must allege that he has debts. The primary purpose for an individual filing a voluntary petition is to obtain a discharge from some or all of his debts; the discharge of debts will be covered in more detail later in this chapter. It should be noted that normally a discharge in bankruptcy can be obtained only once every six years.

Involuntary Petitions. An involuntary petition in bankruptcy is one filed by a creditor or creditors of a debtor seeking to have him adjudged a bankrupt to have his assets marshalled for distribution to his creditors. Such a petition may be filed against a person (other than a "wage earner," a person who works for wages of less than $1,500 per year, or a farmer) and against any corporation (except a municipal, railroad, insurance or banking corporation, or a building and loan association). If a debtor has twelve or more creditors, at least three must join in filing an involuntary petition. If there are fewer than twelve creditors, then the petition may be filed by a single creditor.

An involuntary petition may be filed by a creditor or creditors only if: (1) the debtor has debts of $1,000 or more; (2) the creditor or creditors who file the petition have provable claims against the debtor that exceed by more than $500 the value of any security held by them; and (3) if the debtor has committed an "act of bankruptcy" within four months of the time the petition is filed.

Acts of Bankruptcy. In order to support the filing of an involuntary petition, it is not enough that a debtor is insolvent; the debtor must have committed an "act of bankruptcy" within four months of the time the petition is filed. Acts of bankruptcy include:

1. Any concealment, removal or fraudulent transfer of the debtor's property by the debtor or with his permission where the purpose of the concealment, removal or transfer is to hinder, delay, or defraud his creditors;
2. Making a preferential transfer, that is a transfer by a debtor, while insolvent, of any portion of his property either to a creditor, or for the benefit of a creditor, relating to an antecedent debt which would have the effect of enabling that creditor to obtain a greater percentage of his debt than some other creditor in the same class (secured or unsecured);
3. A debtor, while insolvent, permitting any creditor to obtain a lien on the debtor's property through legal proceedings;
4. The making of a general assignment for the benefit of creditors;
5. The procuring or permitting the appointment of a receiver or trustee

[1] The insolvency or bankruptcy of these corporations is dealt with under other provisions of the Bankruptcy Act or under other federal statutes.

to take charge of a debtor's property during a time when the debtor is either insolvent or unable to pay his debts as they mature;

6. The admission in writing by a debtor that he is unable to pay his debts and that he is willing to be adjudicated a bankrupt.

SUMMARY

A person who is adjudged a bankrupt on his own petition is a voluntary bankrupt.

Under certain circumstances a debtor may be adjudged bankrupt on the petition of his creditors. Such a debtor is known as an involuntary bankrupt. To be adjudged an involuntary bankrupt, the debtor must have, within four months from the filing of the petition and while insolvent, committed an act of bankruptcy. The Bankruptcy Act sets out what acts are acts of bankruptcy.

Administration of Bankrupt's Estate

Adjudication and Appointment of Trustee. Petitions for both voluntary and involuntary bankruptcy are filed in the federal district court. If the debtor contests an involuntary petition, a trial is held. After an adjudication of bankruptcy, the estate of the bankrupt is referred to the referee for the purpose of administration.

The bankrupt person is required to file detailed schedules that list his property, his creditors, and all persons who have contingent unliquidated or disputed claims against him. It is important that these schedules be carefully prepared so that all creditors will receive notice and so that there is no concealment of assets of the debtor.

The referee in bankruptcy calls the first meeting of creditors between 10 days and 30 days after the adjudication. At the first meeting of creditors the judge or referee presides. The first step in the administration of the estate is the allowance of claims and the election of a trustee or trustees. The trustee is elected by a vote of the claims which have been allowed, and the person who receives the majority vote in number and amount is elected. In determining the number of claims voted, claims of $50 or less are not counted, but such claims are counted in computing the amount. The judge or referee is not bound to appoint the person elected by the creditors as trustee. If the person elected is not qualified or for some other reasons would not be desirable as trustee, the judge or referee may appoint someone of his own selection.

Examination of Bankrupt. The next step is the public examination of the bankrupt. He is examined by the judge or referee who presides at the meeting and, in addition, may be examined by any creditor. This may be done by the creditor himself or by an attorney whom the creditor has employed to conduct the examination on his behalf. The purpose of the examination of the bankrupt is to bring out all the facts relating to his bankruptcy, to determine whether he has made a full and complete disclosure of all his property, to determine whether he has been guilty of any acts which would bar his discharge, and to clear up any questions arising as to claims, assets, or other matters affecting the bankrupt's estate.

Rights and Duties of Trustee. The trustee, as soon as he has qualified, takes possession of all the property of the bankrupt, inventories it, has it appraised, and sets aside the bankrupt's exemptions. He also examines the claims filed, and objects to any claims which are not allowable or which for any reason are improper. The trustee reduces the estate to money as expeditiously as is compatible with the best interests of the parties.

The trustee represents the creditors in the administration of the estate. Title to the bankrupt's property vests in the trustee, and he has all the rights in such property that the bankrupt had at the time of the adjudication. In addition, the trustee has all the rights against the bankrupt's property that a creditor holding an unsatisfied lien on the property of the bankrupt would have. For example, a creditor who has a security interest in certain property of the bankrupt, but whose security interest has not been perfected by compliance with the recording statutes of the state, has a lien on such property which is valid against a creditor with an unsatisfied execution. In such a situation a trustee in bankruptcy would have all the rights of the creditor with the unsatisfied execution.

Under some state and federal laws, certain items of personal property are exempt from the bankruptcy laws and a debtor is permitted by the Bankruptcy Act to retain them. While they vary from state to state, these laws sometimes permit retention of tools of the trade, the family Bible, household goods, or furniture up to a certain amount. However, any such property that has been concealed or fraudulently transferred may not be so protected.

To protect the interests of the creditors, the trustee in bankruptcy is given the right to bring suit in any court in which the bankrupt could have brought suit to enforce claims of the bankrupt's estate. Such suits are brought in the name of the trustee. All such suits are brought under the supervision of the court in which the bankruptcy proceedings are pending. Also, the trustee owes a duty to defend all suits brought against the bankrupt estate.

The trustee must keep an accurate account of all the property and money coming into his hands, deposit all money in the authorized depositories, pay by check or draft all dividends within ten days after they are declared by the referee, and lay before the final meeting of the creditors a detailed statement of the administration of the estate.

SUMMARY

The debtor is adjudged bankrupt by the judge of the federal district court. After adjudication the case is referred to the referee in bankruptcy where, at the first meeting of creditors, a trustee in bankruptcy is elected or appointed. After the election or appointment of the trustee the bankrupt is examined in regard to any matters material to the administration of the estate. The trustee takes possession of all the assets of the bankrupt, collects all claims, sets aside the bankrupt's exemptions, liquidates the assets, and distributes the proceeds among the creditors. Title to the bankrupt's estate vests in the trustee. The trustee must keep accurate accounts and make a final accounting of the administration of the estate.

Debts

Provable Debts. The debts of a bankrupt, for the purpose of the administration of his estate, are classified as "provable debts," "allowable debts," "debts having priority," and "dischargeable debts." If a debt is provable, it is the basis of its owner's right to share in the estate of the bankrupt.

Provable debts include: (1) those founded upon a fixed liability as evidenced by a judgment or an instrument in writing absolutely owing at the time of the filing of the petition; (2) costs of a creditor incurred in good faith trying to recover a provable debt from the debtor; (3) an open account, or an express or implied contract, including quasi-contract; (4) debts reduced to judgment after filing of the petition and before consideration of the bankrupt's discharge; (5) workmen's compensation awards and like awards if the injury occurred prior to adjudication; (6) the right to recover damages in any action for negligence instituted prior to and pending at the time of filing of the petition in bankruptcy; (7) contingent debts and contingent contractual liability; and (8) claims for anticipatory breach of contract, including unexpired leases of personal property or leases; however, landlord's claims may not exceed one year's rent.

Allowable Debts. The fact that a debt is classed as a provable debt does not assure its owner's participation in the distribution of the bankrupt's assets. Before a creditor can participate in the bankruptcy proceedings, he must prove his claim, and the claim must be allowed. The proof of claim is a sworn statement of the amount of the claim, the consideration for it, security held, and so forth; and if it is based on a written instrument, the instrument must be filed with the proof. Claims which are not filed within six months after the first date set for the first meeting of creditors will not be allowed. If the bankrupt has any defense to the debt, such defense will be set up by the trustee, and if established, the claim will not be allowed; or if the defense goes to only part of the claim, the amount of the claim will be reduced. All the defenses which would have been available to the bankrupt will be available to the trustee.

Debts Having Priority. Certain claims are declared by the Bankruptcy Act to have priority over other classes of claims; claims which have priority should not be confused with those claims which are secured. The following claims have priority: Costs and expenses of administration; costs of preserving the estate; filing fees; costs expended by a creditor in the recovery of property which has been transferred or concealed by the bankrupt provided it is recovered for the benefit of the estate; trustee's expenses in opposing the bankrupt's discharge or in his criminal prosecution for violation of the Bankruptcy Act; one reasonable attorney's fee and other professional expenses incurred in connection with a hearing on a voluntary or involuntary petition for the adjudication of bankruptcy if the court adjudges the debtor bankrupt; wages and commissions earned within three months before the commencement of proceedings, due workmen, servants, clerks, or traveling or city salespersons not to exceed $600; and taxes legally owing by the bankrupt to the United States or any state or any subdivision, not to exceed the value of the bankrupt's estate.

Nondischargeable Debts. Certain debts are not affected by the bankrupt's discharge. Section 17 of the Bankruptcy Act provides that a discharge in bankruptcy shall release a bankrupt from all his provable debts, whether allowable in full or in part, except those that: (1) are due as a tax to the United States, or any state, county, district, or municipality; or (2) are liabilities for obtaining money or property by false pretense or false representations; or (3) are due for willful and malicious injuries to the person or property of another; or (4) are due for alimony due or to become due, or for maintenance or support of wife or child, or for seduction of an unmarried female, or for breach of marriage accompanied by seduction, or for criminal conversation; or (5) were not scheduled in time for proof and an allowance even though the name of the creditor was known to the bankrupt (unless that creditor had notice or actual knowledge of the proceedings in bankruptcy); or (6) were created by his fraud, embezzlement, misappropriation, or defalcation while acting as an officer of in any fiduciary capacity; or (7) are for wages which have been earned within three months before the date of commencement of the proceedings in bankruptcy due to "workmen, servants, clerks, or traveling or city salesmen" on salary or commission basis, whole or part-time, whether or not selling exclusively for the bankrupt; or (8) are due for moneys of an employee received or retained by his employer to secure the faithful performance by such employee of the terms of a contract of employment.

These debts are provable debts, and the owner of such a debt has the right to participate in the distribution of the bankrupt's estate; but his right to recover the unpaid balance of the debt is not cut off by the bankrupt's discharge. All provable debts except those listed above are dischargeable debts, that is, the right to recover the unpaid balance is cut off by the bankrupt's discharge.

SUMMARY

Provable debts include substantially all claims except unliquidated tort claims. Contingent claims arising on contracts are provable debts. If a debtor wishes to participate in the bankrupt's estate, he must file a proof of claim in the estate within six months of the first meeting of creditors. Certain debts are given priority by the provisions of the Bankruptcy Act. Certain debts, although provable, are not dischargeable.

Preferences, Liens, and Fraudulent Transfers

Preferential Payments. A preferential payment is a payment made by a debtor (1) while he is insolvent, (2) within four months of the filing of a petition in bankruptcy by or against the debtor, (3) which payment enables the creditor receiving the payment to obtain a greater percentage of his debt than other creditors in the same class, and (4) which creditor, when he received the payment, must have had reasonable grounds to believe that the debtor was insolvent. If a debtor makes a preferential payment, that act is an act of bankruptcy. If a debtor is adjudged bankrupt, the trustee in bankruptcy has the right to recover for the benefit of the estate all preferential payments that have been made by the bankrupt.

One of the purposes of the Bankruptcy Act is to ensure equal treatment for the creditors of an insolvent debtor and to prevent an insolvent debtor from distributing his assets to favored creditors to the detriment of his other creditors. Under the common law, the creditor who first attached or obtained a lien on his debtor's property or who was able to induce a debtor to pay his claim could retain the advantage he had gained, irrespective of the fact that such advantage might deplete the debtor's estate to such a degree that the other creditors could recover nothing. Also, under the common law, if a debtor was solvent but for some reason was temporarily unable to meet his obligations as they matured, one creditor, by starting suit against the debtor, could cause other creditors to rush in and try to salvage as much of their claims as they could, with the result that all persons involved would suffer unnecessary loss due to costs of suit and the inability to realize the full value of assets which would be sold at forced sale. Under the Bankruptcy Act the rights of all persons can be protected.

Even though a debtor is insolvent, he can carry on his business without fear of being adjudged bankrupt if he does not commit an act of bankruptcy. Payments made in the regular course of a business are not preferential payments, and such payments are not acts of bankruptcy. For example, if an insolvent debtor purchases property, paying the purchase price on delivery, such a payment is not a preferential payment. The debtor's estate has been neither increased nor decreased if the property purchased is worth the price paid. Also, the courts have held that if the debtor has purchased goods on credit, the payment of the price of the goods when the account is due is not, under ordinary circumstances, a preferential payment. Such payments are not acts of bankruptcy, and if the debtor is adjudged bankrupt, the trustee in bankruptcy cannot recover such payments even though they have been made while the debtor is insolvent and within four months of the adjudication of bankruptcy.

Preferential Liens. A creditor may attempt to obtain a preference by obtaining a lien on the debtor's property. The lien may be obtained either by legal or equitable process or by contract with the debtor. Any lien which is obtained within four months of the filing of the petition is null and void if the lien is to secure a preexisting debt and if the debtor was insolvent at the time the lien was obtained. A lien which is given as security for present value received is valid against the trustee in bankruptcy.

If an insolvent debtor borrows money or purchases goods and gives a lien on his assets to secure the repayment of the money borrowed or the purchase price of the goods, his assets have not been diminished by the transaction, and the creditor has gained no advantage over existing creditors by the taking of the lien. Such liens are valid against a trustee in bankruptcy of the debtor.

Fraudulent Transfers. Transfers for the purpose of hindering, delaying, or defrauding creditors are null and void. This rule is applied generally throughout the United States. Transfers made by a debtor and every obligation incurred by him within one year of the filing of the petition in bankruptcy are void as to creditors, if made or incurred without fair consideration and while insolvent, or if the transfer or obligation will render him insolvent. If one makes a transfer of property or incurs obligations without fair consideration in contemplation of incurring debts beyond his ability to pay, the transaction is fraudulent to both existing and future creditors. In all the foregoing situations the transfer or obligation may be declared void if made within one year from the date of the filing of the petition in bankruptcy.

All these safeguards are set up to prevent the debtor from concealing or disposing of his property in fraud of his creditors or to prevent him from favoring one creditor at the expense of his other creditors; yet they are so framed that the honest but hard-pressed debtor is not unduly handicapped in continuing the operation of his business. If the debtor "plays fair," he is protected; if he does not, the creditors are protected.

SUMMARY

A preferential payment is a payment made to a creditor by an insolvent debtor within four months of his adjudication as a bankrupt, which payment enables the creditor to realize a greater percentage of his claim than other creditors of the same class; such creditor must have reasonable grounds for believing that the debtor is insolvent. A lien given by an insolvent debtor within four months of his adjudication as a bankrupt, to secure a preexisting debt, is void. Any transfer made or obligation incurred without consideration within one year from the debtor's adjudication as a bankrupt is void as to creditors.

Hanes v. Crown Camera Sales, Inc.

468 F.2d 1318 (5th Cir. 1972)

This was an action brought by Hanes, the trustee in bankruptcy for Television Productions International (TPI), (plaintiff) against Crown Camera Sales (defendant) to recover as voidable preferences three payments totaling $10,-325.33 paid by the bankrupt, TPI, to Crown Camera Sales. Summary judgment for Hanes. Affirmed per curiam.

The facts are given in the Order of the trial court which was attached as an appendix to the per curiam decision of the Court of Appeals.

ORDER. The facts are that TPI had the prospect of getting a contract from the Atlanta Hawks basketball team to provide television lighting for games played at the Georgia Tech coliseum. TPI made arrangements to purchase certain lighting fixtures and lamps from Crown Camera in order to fulfill its contract with the Atlanta Hawks. These arrangements were confirmed in a letter dated September 11, 1970, from TPI to Crown Camera which said in part:

> This is to confirm in writing the order for fixtures and lamps about which we spoke Thursday, Sept. 10, 1970.
>
> It serves as a definite order, in contract, to purchase through Crown Camera Exchange the following items:
>
> * * * * *
>
> It is agreed that the contract monies received from the Atlanta Hawks basketball office for lighting Alexander Memorial Coliseum will be put in full for payment for these fixtures and lamps.

Crown Camera delivered the equipment during October and November, and on December 3, 1970, the Board of Directors of TPI passed a resolution authorizing the officers to assign invoice No. 0370 (to be presented to the

Atlanta Hawks) to Crown Camera. That same day a formal assignment of the invoice was executed by the president of TPI. On December 15, TPI received $1,800 from the Atlanta Hawks as payment in full for invoice No. 0370 and the following day this sum was paid by TPI to Crown Camera. On February 18, 1971, the president of TPI executed an assignment of invoices No. 0433 (presented to the Atlanta Hawks) and No. 1436 (presented to television station WSMW-TV of Worcester, Massachusetts) to Crown Camera. TPI received the amounts due on these invoices, and on February 26 and March 12 made payments of $2,000 and $6,525.33 to Crown Camera, thereby satisfying the account in full for the fixtures and lamps. TPI filed its petition and was adjudged bankrupt on March 18, 1971.

The parties do not dispute that the three payments made by TPI to Crown Camera were transfers of property by a debtor, while insolvent, made within four months before the filing of a petition in bankruptcy, for the benefit of a creditor, who had reasonable cause to believe that the debtor was insolvent, the effect of which was to prefer that creditor. The only question to be determined by this court is whether the transfers were made "for or on account of an antecedent debt." On this issue Crown Camera contends that the letter of September 11, 1970, was an assignment of the proceeds of the Atlanta Hawks contract and that the transfers to Crown Camera of those proceeds, in consequence, were not "for or on account of an antecedent debt." The trustee's position is that the letter was no more than a promise to pay from a particular source, and that the subsequent transfers were payments "for or on account of an antecedent debt," preferential and voidable.

If the letter of September 11, 1970, was a valid assignment, the subsequent three transfers would not be considered preferences because Crown Camera gave fair and present consideration—the fixtures and lamps—for the purported assignment. In such a case the transfers would represent the completion of an exchange of property of equal value rather than payments "for or on account of an antecedent debt. . . ." On the other hand, if the letter was not an assignment but merely a promise to pay from a particular source, the transfers would represent payments in satisfaction of pre-existing debt and would be preferential. The proper construction of the September 11 letter is controlled by Georgia law.

No formal language is necessary under Georgia law to create a legal assignment, and if the language used in a transaction shows the intention of the owner of a right to transfer it instantly so that it becomes the property of the transferee at the time of the transaction, a legal assignment exists. . . . The language of the September 11 letter, however, does not evidence such an intention on the part of TPI. On the contrary, the language shows that TPI intended itself to receive the contract monies from the Atlanta Hawks and then apply such monies as payment for the fixtures and lamps purchased from Crown Camera. It is undisputed that this is exactly what later happened. The court concludes that the September 11th letter did not create a legal assignment.

Discharge

Basis for Granting Discharge. A bankrupt who has not been guilty of serious infractions of the code of business ethics and who has fulfilled his duties as a bankrupt is entitled to a discharge in bankruptcy. The adjudication of bankruptcy of any person, except a corporation, operates as an application for a discharge. A bankrupt may, however, before the hearing on his application, file a written waiver of his right to discharge. A corporation may, within six months after its adjudication, file an application for a discharge in the court in which the proceedings are pending.

Filing Objections to Discharge. After the statutory filing fees have been paid in full, the court makes an order fixing the time for filing objections to the bankrupt's discharge. Notice of the time fixed for filing objections to the discharge is given to all interested parties. If objections have been filed within the time fixed or within any extension of time which may have been granted by the court, the court will hear proofs of the objections at such time as will give the parties a reasonable opportunity to be fully heard. If the court is satisfied that the bankrupt has not committed any of the acts which are a bar to his discharge, the discharge will be granted.

Acts Which Bar Discharge. The acts which are a bar to a bankrupt's discharge are set out in Section 14, Subsection *c*, of the Bankruptcy Act as follows:

> The court shall grant the discharge unless satisfied that the bankrupt has (1) committed an offense punishable by imprisonment as provided under title 18, United States Code Section 152; or (2) destroyed, mutilated, falsified, concealed, or failed to keep or preserve books of account or records, from which his financial condition and business transactions might be ascertained, unless the court deems such acts or failure to have been justified under all the circumstances of the case; or (3) while engaged in business as sole proprietor, partnership or as executive of a corporation, obtained for such business money or property on credit or an extension or renewal of credit by making or publishing or causing to be made or published in any manner whatsoever a materially false statement in writing respecting his financial condition or the financial condition of such partnership or corporation; or (4) at any time subsequent to the first day of the twelve months immediately preceding the filing of the petition in bankruptcy, transferred, removed, destroyed, or concealed, or permitted to be removed, destroyed, or concealed, any of his property, with intent to hinder, delay, or defraud his creditors; or (5) in a proceeding under this Act commenced within six years prior to the date of filing the petition in bankruptcy been granted a discharge, or had a composition or arrangement by way of composition or a wage earner's plan by way of composition confirmed under this Act; or (6) in the course of a proceeding under this Act refused to obey any lawful order of, or to answer any material question approved by, the court; (7) failed to explain satisfactorily any losses of assets or deficiency of assets to meet his liabilities: or (8) failed to pay the filing fees required by this Act in full: *Provided,* that if, upon the hearing of an objection to a discharge, the objector shall show to the satisfaction of the court that there are reasonable grounds for believing that the bankrupt has committed any of the acts which, under this

subdivision *c*, would prevent his discharge in bankruptcy, then the burden of proving that he has not committed any of such acts shall be upon the bankrupt.

Who May File Objections. The trustee, a creditor, the U.S. attorney, or such other attorney as the Attorney General may designate may file objections to and oppose the discharge of a bankrupt. When requested by the court, it is the duty of the U.S. attorney located in the judicial district in which the bankruptcy proceeding is pending to examine into the acts and conduct of the bankrupt. If satisfied that probable ground exists for the denial of a discharge and that public interest warrants the action, it is his duty to oppose the bankrupt's discharge. Also, if the bankrupt fails to appear at the hearing on his discharge or, having appeared, refuses to submit himself to examination at the first meeting of creditors or at any subsequent meeting called for his examination, he is deemed to have waived his right to a discharge.

SUMMARY

A bankrupt is granted a discharge unless he has been guilty of a serious infraction of the code of business ethics or has failed to fulfill his duties as a bankrupt. The time for filing the objections to a bankrupt's discharge is fixed at the first meeting of creditors or at a special meeting called for that purpose.

The grounds for denying a bankrupt's discharge are set out in the Bankruptcy Act. The trustee, a creditor, the U.S. attorney, or an attorney designated by the Attorney General may file objections to a bankrupt's discharge.

Charles Edward & Associates v. England

301 F.2d 572 (9th Cir. 1962)

This was an appeal by Charles P. Trafficante and Paul J. Trafficante from an order of the District Court which set aside the individual discharges in bankruptcy granted by the Referee. Judgment affirmed in part.

The Trafficantes filed individual voluntary petitions in bankruptcy and a short time later Charles Edward & Associates, a partnership composed of the two Trafficantes, was adjudged a bankrupt in an involuntary proceeding. The two individual estates and the partnership estate were consolidated for the purposes of administration. The trustee petitioned the Referee for an extension of time for filing objections to the discharge of the individual bankrupts but through error did not include the partnership. The order extending the time was limited to the individuals. The trustee filed objections to the discharge of both the partnership and the individual partners. The objections were based on the individual partners' failure to keep books, the partnership's transfer of property to the individual partners in fraud of creditors and within one year of the filing of the bankruptcy petition, the individual partners' failure to explain losses in their individual assets amounting to $56,000, and the withdrawal of large amounts of cash within one year of the filing of the petition in bankruptcy and when the partnership was insolvent, with the intent to defraud creditors.

SOLOMON, DISTRICT JUDGE. The failure to keep or preserve books of account or records from which a bankrupt's financial condition and business transactions might be obtained is a ground for the denial of a discharge in bankruptcy under the Bankruptcy Act (Act).

Specification 1 charges:

> 1. That said Bankrupt copartnership and each of the bankrupt individual members thereof failed to keep books or records from which the financial condition of said bankrupt copartnership might be ascertained in that they, and each of them, wholly failed and neglected at all times during the existence of said copartnership to maintain books or records relating to the accounts payable of said copartnership.

The Trafficantes contend that this specification charges misconduct against the partnership and not against the individual partners, and they claim that any other construction would disregard the entity theory of partnership.

Although the Bankruptcy Act of 1938 adopted the entity theory for some purposes and the aggregate theory for other purposes, the entity theory is specifically rejected in ¶ 5, sub. *j* of the Act, which provides that the discharge of a partnership does not discharge the individual partners from partnership debts.

Under either theory, a partner who has engaged in conduct proscribed by the Act, either on behalf of the partnership or on his own behalf, is not entitled to a discharge.

In many cases, as in this one, substantially all of the debts of the individual partners were those of the partnership. The failure of a partner to keep partnership books and records may preclude a creditor or a trustee from ascertaining the true financial condition of a partner.

The Referee's ruling was clearly erroneous, and the District Court was correct in setting it aside.

The transfer of property with intent to hinder, delay or defraud creditors, within 12 months of the filing of a petition in bankruptcy, is also a ground for the denial of a discharge in bankruptcy.

Specification 2 charges:

> 2. That at times subsequent to the first day of the 12 months immediately preceding the filing of the individual partners' petitions in bankruptcy, and also at items [*sic*] subsequent to the first day of the 12 months immediately preceding the filing of the petition in bankruptcy against the said bankrupt copartnership, the said partnership, while continually insolvent, the individual members thereof having full knowledge of such partnership insolvency and with intent to defraud the partnership creditors, transferred to the individual members thereof, property of said partnership, to wit, cash in the sum of $22,819.07 or thereabouts.

Specification 4 is similar to 2, but, in addition, charges that the individual partners made cash withdrawals from partnership funds in the amount of approximately $23,000 and that the partners transferred the money to themselves with intent to defraud partnership creditors.

These two specifications clearly allege improper conduct against the individual partners in personally withdrawing large sums from the partnership with intent to defraud partnership creditors. An individual discharge will be denied a partner who withdraws funds from a partnership with intent to defraud creditors.

Chapter X Reorganizations

Corporate Reorganizations. Chapter X reorganizations are available only to corporations which make a showing in their petition that adequate relief cannot be obtained under Chapter XI (which is discussed later in this chapter). A Chapter X petition may be filed voluntarily by the debtor corporation or it may be filed as an involuntary petition by three or more creditors who have claims aggregating more than $5,000. The petition must allege that the corporation is insolvent or unable to pay its debts as they mature and indicate a desire that a plan be effected. It must also state why the corporation cannot obtain adequate relief under Chapter XI of the Bankruptcy Act. If the petition is an involuntary one filed by creditors they must allege one of the following:

1. That the corporation was adjudged a bankrupt in a bankruptcy proceeding; or
2. That a receiver or trustee has been appointed or has charge of all or the greater portion of the property of the corporation; or
3. That a trustee or mortgagee under a mortgage is, by reason of a default on the mortgage, in possession of all or the greater portion of the property of the corporation; or
4. That a proceeding is pending to foreclose a mortgage or to enforce a lien against all or a greater portion of the property of the corporation; or
5. That the corporation has committed an act of bankruptcy within four months prior to the filing of the petition.

In a Chapter X reorganization, the debtor may be permitted to remain in possession and the court may authorize either the debtor or trustee(s) to run the business. If the indebtedness is more than $250,000, one or more trustees must be appointed by the court. Prior to the approval of a Chapter X petition, the judge may grant a temporary stay of any prior pending bankruptcy, foreclosure or receivership proceeding, pending approval or dismissal of the Chapter X petition.

The Plan. The plan under a Chapter X proceeding may modify the rights of both secured creditors and stockholders of the corporation. Frequently, the plan calls for a new corporation to be formed with the assets of the debtor corporation transferred to it and stock and securities in it are exchanged for those of the debtor corporation. A wide variety of steps may be undertaken to reorganize the debtor's financial affairs, including: (1) sale or transfer of property to other corporations; (2) merger or consolidation in whole or in part with other corporations; (3) liens may be satisfied or modified; (4) indentures may be cancelled or modified; (5) defaults may be cured or waived; (6) maturity dates may be extended and terms of securities, including the interest rates, may be changed; (7) the debtor's corporate charter may be amended; and (8) securities of the debtor may be issued in exchange for existing securities or in satisfaction of claims or stock.

If the scheduled indebtedness of the debtor is more than $3,000,000, the judge must send the plan to the Securities and Exchange Commission for examination and a report; he may do so where the scheduled indebtedness is less. The SEC report is only advisory, but an adverse report may well result in refusal to approve the plan.

The court must first approve the plan. Then it submits it along with the SEC report to shareholders and creditors who are affected by it for their approval. A plan must be accepted by creditors holding two thirds of the claims in each class affected by the plan and, as long as the corporation has not been declared insolvent, then stockholders holding a majority of the stock must also approve it. Then the plan goes back to the court for confirmation. If the plan fails to be approved, accepted, and/or confirmed or if it is not carried out, the judge may dismiss the Chapter X proceeding and, where appropriate, either straight bankruptcy proceedings will continue or the debtor may be adjudged bankrupt.

If a plan is confirmed and consummated, the judge will normally enter an order discharging the debtor from all debts and liabilities covered by the plan.

SUMMARY

Under Chapter X corporations can enter into corporate reorganization proceedings under the supervision of a federal court to reorganize their financial affairs.

Chapter XI Arrangements

Arrangements. Chapter XI of the Bankruptcy Act provides a method by which individual or corporate debtors can make arrangements with their creditors for payment of their debts under the supervision of a federal court. The goal of the debtor in a Chapter XI proceeding is normally to be able to carry on his business without interruption while at the same time reaching a satisfactory agreement with his creditors for the payment of his debts. A Chapter XI proceeding does not affect the rights of secured creditors.

Procedure. A Chapter XI proceeding may be instituted by a debtor filing a petition stating that he is insolvent or unable to pay his debts as they come due and indicating his intent to propose an arrangement. Where a debtor has already filed a voluntary petition in bankruptcy, or even where creditors have filed an involuntary petition in bankruptcy, the debtor may convert a bankruptcy proceeding into a Chapter XI proceeding.

Following the filing of the petition, a meeting of the creditors is held under the supervision of a federal judge or bankruptcy referee. At the meeting creditors' claims are presented, the debtor may be examined, and creditor's acceptances of the arrangement or plan put forward by the debtor are received. Procedures are set out for passing on claims presented by creditors. Commonly the arrangement calls for the debtor to make a deposit of a certain amount which on acceptance of the plan will be distributed to certain creditors and cover the costs and fees entailed in the proceeding. The court can approve the arrangement when it is satisfied that: (1) it has been accepted by a majority of the creditors whose claims have been approved and allowed, or all of the creditors, whether or not their claims have been proved; (2) the debtor has made the required deposit; and (3) the court is satisfied the law has been complied with, it is in the best interest of the creditors, and the debtor is not guilty of any acts that would bar his discharge.

Once the arrangement is confirmed by the court it is binding on the debtor and the unsecured creditors of the debtor. The debtor is then discharged from those unsecured debts except to the extent he must make the payments he agreed to make pursuant to the plan. Arrangements can be set aside within 6 months if the debtor committed fraud which only came to light after confirmation of the arrangement.

Advantages. Among the advantages of a Chapter XI proceeding are:

1. The debtor may be allowed to continue with its business with little court interference;
2. The fairly simple procedure can substantially reduce the fees and expenses of administration that can be involved in a Chapter X reorganization;
3. Arrangement proceedings can be protracted to give the debtor time to earn enough money to make the payments required by the arrangement possible; alternatively they can sometimes be quickly consummated when that is in the interest of the parties;
4. In putting forth the proposed plan, the debtor can deal with preferences,

fraudulent transfers and liens that would be troublesome in a straight bankruptcy proceeding;

5. A debtor who proceeds in good faith and meets the statutory tests can have his plan confirmed even though accepted by only a majority of the filed and allowed claims, and then bind all of the unsecured creditors;
6. Confirmation and fulfillment of the arrangement discharges the debtor from all of his unsecured debts and liabilities except those which under Section 17 of the Bankruptcy Act are not dischargeable.

SUMMARY

Chapter XI provides a means by which individual or corporate debtors can enter into arrangements with their unsecured creditors for the payment of their debts.

In the Matter of Arlan's Department Stores, Inc.

373 F. Supp. 520 (S.D.N.Y. 1974)

The Securities and Exchange Commission (SEC) moved to intervene in pending Chapter XI proceedings of Arlan's Department Stores (the debtor) and to dismiss the Chapter XI petition filed by Arlan's and to require proceedings under Chapter X. The court held that Chapter X proceedings were the appropriate context in which to rehabilitate Arlan's and granted the SEC's motions.

Arlan's Department Stores, a retail store chain spread over several states, was a large public company. Arlan's had three major classes of unsecured creditors as of the filing of the original petition: (1) there were approximately 15,000 trade creditors having claims totalling approximately $35 million; (2) lending institutions were creditors of the debtor in the sum of approximately $21 million, $6 million of which was on a par with trade creditors, the balance having been subordinated to the trade creditors pursuant to various loan agreements; (3) the public held 6 percent convertible subordinated debentures in the sum of $15 million. Those debentures were subordinated to the lending institution debt by virtue of the provisions of the trust indenture. In addition, as a result of the debtor's breach of lease obligations to landlords in connection with stores it formerly operated, there was the possibility of an additional $15 million liability.

Arlan's had outstanding the following issues of securities: (1) the 6 percent convertible subordinated debentures held by approximately 725 widely dispersed public investors, (2) 3,702 shares of preferred stock held by six banks and insurance companies, and (3) 2,775,414 shares of common stock held by approximately 6,000 persons.

A proposed Chapter XI arrangement was promulgated by the various creditor representative groups. In general, the plan provided as follows: the claims of the administration and priority creditors were to be paid in full upon terms agreed upon between Arlan and such creditors. General creditors (including but not limited to trade creditors, senior institutional debt and landlords with breach of lease claims) were to receive 15 percent of their respective claims in cash, payable in percentages varying from 1 percent to 5 percent over a number of years, as well as one share of common stock of Arlan's for each $40 of debt. The subordinated institutional lenders and bankers were to receive one share of the common stock of the debtor for each $27.50 of the indebtedness. The preferred stock owned by those institutional lenders was to be surrendered and exchanged for 66,000 shares of Arlan's common stock. The subordinated debenture holders were to receive one share of common stock for each $27.50 of indebtedness. Present management was to receive common stock equal to 10 percent of the issued and outstanding common stock of Arlan's, and an outside independent investor was to receive common stock equal to 33⅓ percent of the issued and outstanding shares of common stock.

CARTER, DISTRICT JUDGE. At the February 4, 1974, hearing, the court announced that if it determined, after a study of the case law, that it had a wide range of discretion in making the choice between proceedings in Chapter X or XI, the final determination would be based upon the court's view of what would be best for the company and best for the public. It appeared at that point that there were substantial factors here that would favor the choice of Chapter XI. The debtor, being a retail store chain, is highly dependent upon trade credit and there was reason to believe that if it went into Chapter X such credit would not be forthcoming, resulting in the serious possibility of Arlan's complete collapse. Generally, proceedings under Chapter X are slower and more costly and this debtor does have a somewhat urgent need for the infusion of new capital. The proposed Chapter XI arrangement did appear to be acceptable to all segments of the debtor's creditors, and was the result of a private investigation of the company's problems and negotiations among the interested parties. Finally, it is asserted that the public debenture holders were in fact being put in a more advantageous position by the proposed plan than they could ever be under Chapter X. Since they are subordinated to the $21 million of lending institutional debt, under a strict priority doctrine, as often mandated under Chapter X, they could not receive their share until the senior creditors were paid in full. Under the proposed plan, despite their subordinated status, they would receive the same compensation as the senior debt—one share of stock for each $27.50 of indebtedness.

Despite the initial predilection for a proceeding under Chapter XI, I must now conclude that Chapter X is the appropriate context for the rehabilitation of this debtor.

It is not the character of the debtor, but rather the degree and nature of the required reorganization that is determinative. Where the rights of public investor creditors are to be adjusted in more than a minor way, then the safeguards and procedures of Chapter X are required.

The aims of Chapter X as revised were to afford greater protection to creditors and stockholders by providing greater judicial control over the entire proceedings and impartial and expert administrative assistance in corporate reorganization through appointment of a disinterested trustee and the active participation of the SEC.

This is a contrast to the provisions of Chapter XI, which are limited to adjustment of unsecured debt, leave the arrangement and company basically in the hands of the debtor, and do not provide for an independent study by or supervision of a trustee. This procedure is recognized as being primarily concerned with the short-term interests of trade creditors.

In short, Chapter XI provides a summary procedure whereby judicial confirmation is obtained on a plan that has been formulated and accepted with only a bare minimum of independent control or supervision. This, of course, is consistent with the basic purpose of Chapter XI; to provide a quick and economical means of facilitating simple compositions among general creditors who have been deemed by Congress to need only the minimal disinterested protection provided by that chapter."

A simple composition would be one, for example, where there are a small number of public investors who are familiar with the operations of the debtor or even where there are a greater number of investors, but "the adjustment of their debt is relatively minor, consisting, for example, of a short extension of time for payment." Only if public debt is adjusted in such a minor way are the less precautionary proceedings of Chapter XI to be utilized.

Applying these guidelines, it is clear that Chapter X is the necessary context in which to rehabilitate Arlan's. Its debentures are held by approximately 725 widely dispersed public investors who are not closely involved in the operations of the company. The rights of the public debenture holders are being radically adjusted, insofar as publicly held debt is being converted into equity. The capital structure of the company is being subjected to a major reorganization.

Chapter XIII Wage Earners' Plans

Relief for Wage Earners. Chapter XIII of the Bankruptcy Act provides a way for individuals, who do not want to be declared bankrupt, to be given an opportunity to pay their debts in installments under the protection of a federal court free of such problems as garnishments and attachment of their property by creditors. Initially, Congress limited Chapter XIII to wage earners with incomes of less than \$3,600; in 1950 Congress raised it to \$5,000. Under present law, a "wage earner" eligible for Chapter XIII proceedings is defined as "an individual whose principal income is derived from wages, salary or commissions" and there is no upper income limit.

Procedure. Chapter XIII proceedings are initiated by the voluntary petition of a debtor filed in federal court in which the debtor states that he is insolvent or unable to pay his debts as they mature and that he desires to effect a composition or an extension, or both, out of his future earnings or wages. A composition of debts would be an arrangement whereby the amount the person owes is reduced whereas an extension would provide the person a longer period of time to pay them. Commonly the debtor files at the same time a list of his creditors as well as of his assets, liabilities and executory contracts.

Following the filing of the petition, the court usually refers the matter to a referee who calls a meeting of creditors at which time, proof of claims are received and allowed or disallowed. The debtor is examined, and he submits a plan. If the requisite number of creditors accept the plan, and the court is satisfied that it meets the legal requirements it will approve the plan and appoint a trustee to carry out the plan. The plan usually provides for payments over a period of three years or less. Unlike Chapter XI proceedings, a Chapter XIII plan may include provisions dealing with secured debts. When the debtor has completed his performance of the plan, the court will issue an order that discharges him from the debts covered by the plan; the debtor may also be discharged even though he did not complete his payments within the three years if the court is satisfied the failure is due to circumstances for which the debtor cannot justly be held accountable. An active Chapter XIII proceeding stays any straight bankruptcy proceedings; however, if the proceeding is dismissed, for example because the debtor fails to file an acceptable plan or defaults on an accepted plan, straight bankruptcy proceedings may proceed.

Advantages of Chapter XIII. A debtor may chose to file a Chapter XIII proceeding to try to avoid the stigma of bankruptcy or to try to retain more of his property than is exempt from bankruptcy under state law. Chapter XIII can provide some financial discipline to a debtor as well as an opportunity to rehabilitate himself. The debtor's creditors stand to benefit by possibly being able to recover a greater percentage of the debt owed to them than would be true in straight bankruptcy.

SUMMARY

Wage earner plans under Chapter XIII give debtors voluntary opportunity to have a composition or extension of their debts under court supervision while under the protection of a court and free of certain action by their creditors.

Problem Cases

1. After making various assessments for back taxes, the United States obtained on August 20, 1965, a lien on property of Gaines. A number of Gaines' creditors then filed an involuntary petition in bankruptcy on August 27, 1965. The property was sold by the United States on September 8, 1965, to satisfy the lien. Thereafter, an amended petition was filed, alleging that Gaines, while insolvent, had permitted the government to obtain this lien through "distraint." Can Gaines argue that no act of bankruptcy was committed because the government's tax liens arose by statute on the various dates when the taxes were assessed, and not by "distraint" under the bankruptcy statute?
2. Cohen entered into a contract to serve as a high school teacher for "the school year 1966–1967." The contract provided that Cohen's services were to begin on August 20, 1966, and the school year was scheduled to end on June 13, 1967. Although the services under the contract were to be performed during the nine and one-half months of the school year, Cohen's salary was payable in 12 equal monthly installments. Cohen was declared a bankrupt as of February 24, 1967, and on May 5, 1967, the trustee filed an application for a turnover order for amounts due Cohen under the employment contract as of the date of bankruptcy. The trustee claims accrued earnings in the amount of $684 were due Cohen as of that date, based on a pro rata computation of payments to be made during the two and one-half months of summer vacation. Should the turnover order be granted?
3. International Marketing was engaged in buying and selling petroleum and gas products under the direction of sole stockholders Davis, Clark, and Wood. Cooper Petroleum was likewise engaged, and the two companies were in the practice of conducting as much business as possible with each other. Fagan, who was a dominant figure in the management of Cooper Petroleum, acquired one fourth of International's stock, and subsequently transferred it to the members of his family who also occupied executive positions with Cooper Petroleum. Clark served as vice president and director of both companies. On June 2, 1964, and involuntary bankruptcy petition was filed against International. Records of the companies disclosed that during the four-month period preceding bankruptcy, Cooper Petroleum delivered $45,000 worth of goods to International on a running open account and was paid a total of $40,154.94 on that account. Creditors of International sought to recover the $40,154.94 from Cooper Petroleum claiming that these were preferential payments. Can Cooper Petroleum avoid the preferential payment rule by claiming that since the payments did not exceed the value of goods delivered, the net estate of International was thereby enriched by the aggregate transaction and no prejudice resulted to other creditors?
4. Oil Company was adjudged bankrupt. Schneider filed proof of claim with the trustee, claiming to be a creditor of the bankrupt Oil Company. Schneider was the owner of a certificate of Oil Company stock denominated "preferred stock." The certificate provided: "The owners of this stock are entitled to receive and the company is bound to pay on January 1, 1939, the par value thereof, together with all accumulated an unpaid dividends." Should the claim of Schneider be allowed?
5. Gomez acquired a parcel of land from Capital Building and Loan Association on October 10, 1961. Capital retained a vendor's lien and a mortgage on the lot to secure the purchase price of $15,500. On December 16, 1965, Gomez granted a second mortgage on the same land to secure a $5,400 note held by Second Mortgage Company, Inc. Gomez defaulted on both notes, and in a bankruptcy proceeding the property was seized and awarded to Capital as a result of its security interest under the first mortgage. Second Mortgage Company brought suit to recover the balance due on the second mortgage and Gomez pleaded

the prior discharge of bankruptcy as a bar to the suit. Second Mortgage Company contended that Gomez's failure to make payments on the first mortgage, thus allowing foreclosure by the first mortgage holder, constituted a "willful and malicious injury to property" and under the bankruptcy statutes debts arising therefrom are not dischargeable. Can Second Mortgage Company collect?

6. Horace Carpenter had borrowed money from the Kroger Employees Federal Credit Union and on January 21, 1970, when he filed a wage earner plan under Chapter XIII the balance due the Credit Union was approximately $1,100. He had also signed as an accommodation co-maker on five notes payable to the Credit Union executed by other Kroger employees. As many as 20 others had also signed as accommodation parties on some of the notes. In his plan Carpenter listed the Credit Union as a creditor in the amount of $1,100; he offered a plan whereby the Credit Union would receive $50 per month from the plan until the debt was liquidated. On February 11, 1970, the Credit Union filed a proof of claim alleging a debt of $1,055.54 and on March 10 it filed a proof of claim accepting the plan. On May 4, 1972 the Trustee filed a final report showing that the full amount of $1,055.54 had been paid; his debt to the Credit Union was then discharged by Order of the Court. On January 31, 1970, several of Carpenter's fellow employees had defaulted on the notes on which he was an accommodation maker. The Credit Union then charged his account with a pro rata share of the notes he had signed, $150.92 and $108.26. Subsequently, but prior to the discharge, there were other defaults and Carpenter's account was further charged up to a total of $623.66. On August 5, 1972—after discharge—the Credit Union began deducting $39 from Carpenter's weekly salary to apply against the claimed balance. Carpenter then filed a Petition with the court, seeking reimbursement for the moneys deducted and claiming that he had been discharged of his debts to the Credit Union. Should Carpenter's petition be granted?

7. KDI was a large publicly held holding company which had acquired 69 wholly-owned subsidiaries involving more than 50 operating businesses since 1967. Despite net sales of $140,000,000 and earnings of $5.3 million for 1969, KDI was by August 1970 without funds to meet its current obligations. At the time it owed about $31 million to banks, $9 million to debenture holders and $25 million to other creditors. Although it took a number of steps to reduce its cash outflow, including halting further acquisitions and reducing its employees, it had substantial operating losses for 1970. On December 30, 1970, KDI filed a petition under Chapter XI and submitted a proposed plan of arrangement. A creditors committee analyzed the proposed arrangement and strongly recommended that all unsecured creditors file consents to it. A group of stockholders in corporations that had been acquired by KDI filed a motion to transfer the proceedings to Chapter X and to require the appointment of a trustee. The court found that the new management had moved promptly to restore financial stability, the new president of KDI stated he would not stay with the company if a trustee was appointed, and the largest creditors—the banks—indicated that adjustment of their loans was contingent on continued operations under Chapter XI. The court also found that none of the debt subject to the plan of arrangement was evidenced by publicly held securities and that only unsecured debt was affected. Should the court grant the motion to appoint a trustee and transfer the proceedings to Chapter X?

8. On December 8, 1971, Thomas Thompson filed a petition under Chapter XIII to pay his debts through a wage earner plan. After the notice to creditors, Ford Motor Credit Company, a secured creditor to whom Thompson was indebted for payments on a 1970 Ford, filed a proof of claim and rejected the plan. The plan was confirmed over Ford's objections and provided for payments to Ford of $22.90 a week, equivalent to the same

rate and adding up to the same total as in the original sales contract, and enjoined Ford from foreclosing on the automobile. In 1972 Thompson was injured at work and was able to only work part-time. During this time he fell behind in his payments to Ford, even though he was regularly submitting his disability checks to the Trustee. Ford then filed a petition to reclaim the car, alleging that Thompson had failed to make the payments due on the car. Should Ford's petition be granted?

PART XI

Regulation of Business

48

Business and the Constitution

Introduction

Early Regulation. Contrary to popular mythology, the period prior to the Civil War could not accurately be designated as a period of laissez faire. Although the federal government was relatively inactive the states were actively engaged in regulation and even in participation in business activities.[1] Much of the seed capital for private business during this period came from public (state) and foreign investor sources.

Over 80 percent of Americans were self-employed and small proprietorships dominated the business economy. Almost any form of organization was viewed with fear and suspicion. Labor unions were held to be criminal conspiracies and Chief Justice Taney of the Supreme Court reflected the popular view in 1833 when he said:

> It is a fixed principle of our political system to guard against the unnecessary accumulation of power over persons and property in any hands, and no hands are less worthy to be trusted with it than those of the moneyed corporation.[2]

Increasing Government Regulation. As the Industrial Revolution progressed in America near the end of the 19th century, the power of corporations grew and some corporate practices came to be viewed as socially undesirable. Public demands for regulation became insistent. Railroads, in particular, were

---

[1] Lawrence M. Freidman, *A History of American Law* (New York: Simon and Schuster 1973), p. 157.

[2] For a discussion see Arthur Miller, *The Supreme Court and American Capitalism* (New York: Free Press, 1968), p. 4.

heavily criticized for discriminatory rates and policies. There was also a strong trend towards concentration of economic power in all kinds of processing and manufacturing industries through agreements to divide territories, to fix prices, and to combine huge aggregations of capital through the trust device or by corporate mergers. Federal legislation was enacted to deal with these problems, the Interstate Commerce Act in 1887 and then the Sherman Antitrust Act in 1890.[3]

Constitutional Challenges of Government Regulation. The years after the Civil War until the middle 1930s might be called the laissez-faire public policy period. Business firms frequently turned to the courts to resist limitations upon their freedom of action imposed by statutes seeking to regulate certain business activities. Their lawyers often successfully opposed regulation by raising constitutional issues, claiming either that the United States Constitution does not grant power to the Congress to enact such regulatory measures, or that a prohibition in the Constitution prevents either the Congress or the state legislature from passing such legislation.[4]

These constitutional challenges were founded upon the doctrine that the powers of our federal government are limited to those expressly or impliedly delegated to it and not prohibited by the Constitution.[5] Under this doctrine, certain fundamental rights are retained by citizens and by the states. The Constitution and certain of the amendments, especially the first eight, set forth certain specific prohibitions or limits on the exercise of governmental power by the federal government. Therefore, Congressional legislation must both be authorized by the Constitution and not prohibited by it. By interpretation of the Supreme Court, the 14th Amendment has been held not only to impose upon the states the prohibitions contained in that amendment; but also the most important limitations imposed on the federal government by the first ten amendments, usually referred to as the "Bill of Rights."[6]

Insofar as regulation of business is concerned, the most important power granted to the federal government by the Constitution is the Commerce Power, found in Article I, Section 8, Paragraph 3.[7] Most of the important court

---

[3] For a discussion of the Sherman Act, see Chapter 50.

[4] Another common basis for resisting government actions affecting business was the defense that the agency or official has not been properly authorized to take the disputed action.

[5] Some governments having documents called constitutions are not constitutional governments in this sense.

[6] The Tenth Amendment declares that the federal government has no power not delegated to it by the states through the Constitution. The Ninth Amendment declares that the enumeration of certain rights belonging to the United States "shall not be construed to deny or disparage others retained by the people." The important Bill of Rights amendments affecting business will be discussed and are reproduced in the Appendix along with other important parts of the Constitution.

[7] Article I, Section 8, Clause 2 provides: "The Congress shall have Power . . . To regulate Commerce with foreign Nations, and among several States, and with the Indian Tribes."

decisions dealing with the powers of state and federal government to regulate business have arisen under the Commerce Clause, the Due Process Clauses of the Fifth and 14th Amendments, and the Equal Protection Clause of the 14th Amendment.

SUMMARY

In the American system of constitutional government the federal government has only those powers delegated to it by the states through that document. The power that is most important to business is the Commerce Clause. The powers given are limited, however, by specific prohibitions in the Constitution. The most important of these in the past have been the Due Process Clauses of the 5th and 14th Amendments. The Equal Protection Clause of the 14th Amendment has received growing attention from the courts in recent times.

The Commerce Clause

Interstate versus Intrastate Commerce. In the landmark case *Gibbons v. Ogden,*[8] the Supreme Court ruled that New York could not grant Ogden a monopoly to operate coastal steamboats between New York and New Jersey where a competitor, Gibbons, had acquired a federal license to operate steamboats in the same waters. The Court broadly construed the federal commerce power as "complete in itself" which "may be exercised to the utmost extent and acknowledges no limitations other than as prescribed in the Constitution." Thus at first the Commerce power was mainly used by the courts as a *negative* power restricting state regulation of interstate business activities.

Trends in Court Decisions. Although Justice Marshall saw a broad sweep to the federal Commerce power, the post Civil War Court sought to place limits on federal power where the regulation of business was concerned. When Congress passed the Federal Child Labor Act of 1916, which prohibited transportation in interstate commerce of products of factories and mines where children under age of 14 had been permitted to work more than eight hours a day or six days a week, the Court declared the Act unconstitutional by a five to four vote in *Hammer v. Dagenhart.*[9] The majority opinion said that the power over mining and manufacturing within the states was left solely to the states under the Tenth Amendment, and the Commerce Power could not be used to oust the states from the exercise of their powers. However, later, the Court began to expand congressional power under the Commerce

---

[8] 9 Wheat. 1 (1824).

[9] 247 U.S. 251 (1918).

Clause holding, for example, that Congress could prohibit the shipment of stolen vehicles in the channels of interstate commerce.

In 1937 in a landmark decision, the Court upheld the National Labor Relations Act when applied to labor organizing within an individual plant as a valid exercise of the Commerce Power. In this case, *NLRB v. Jones & Laughlin Corp.*,[10] Chief Justice Hughes emphasized the widespread operations of this large corporation, saying that the effect of unfair labor practices upon interstate commerce would be more than indirect and remote. On the same day the Court also upheld the application of the Act to two small companies.

Extent of Commerce Power Today. Once the Commerce Power came to be interpreted as applying to activities having a substantial relationship to commerce, it was difficult to draw a sharp new boundary upon the reach of the Commerce Clause. In our modern highly interdependent economy, few activities do not affect interstate commerce, and federal power to regulate under the clause has been interpreted to extend even to the raising of grain for local consumption on a farm.[11] Thus most important economic activity is within the reach of federal regulation under modern court interpretations of the Commerce Power.

Once an activity is found to be interstate commerce, the power of Congress to legislate with respect to it is very broad. Indeed, the Commerce Power has developed as a kind of "police power" that was not otherwise given to the federal government by the Constitution. The police power in a constitutional sense is the power of a government to promote the health, safety, and general welfare of the people. The Commerce Clause was the basis for the Civil Rights Act of 1964. When application of the Act to a downtown motel which refused to rent rooms to blacks was questioned in *Heart of Atlanta Motel v. United States,* the Court upheld the reach of the Commerce Power saying: "It is said that the operation of the motel here is of a purely local character. But assuming this to be true, 'if it is interstate commerce that feels the pinch it does not matter how local the operations that applies the squeeze.' "[12]

SUMMARY

In an early case the Supreme Court interpreted the Commerce Clause to give to the federal government broad power to regulate interstate commerce but to the states sole power to regulate commerce entirely within their boundaries. Mining and manufacturing were considered to be activities which could

---

[10] 301 U.S. 1 (1937).

[11] *Wickard v. Filburn,* 317 U.S. 111 (1942).

[12] 379 U.S. 241 (1964).

not be reached by federal legislation. Beginning in 1937, the Court broadened its interpretation and now even local activities such as farming and motel-keeping are subject to federal regulation under the Commerce Clause if their operation affects, even indirectly, interstate commerce.

Wickard v. Filburn

317 U.S. 111 (U.S. Sup. Ct. 1942)

Filburn (plaintiff), a farmer, sought an injunction against Wickard (defendant), who was Secretary of Agriculture, to enjoin enforcement of a penalty against Filburn. The District Court held for Filburn, and the case was appealed to the Supreme Court. Reversed.

The Agricultural Adjustment Act of 1938 was passed by Congress in an effort to stabilize agricultural production so as to give farmers reasonable minimum prices. The scheme for wheat involved an annual proclamation by the Secretary of Agriculture of a national acreage allotment which was apportioned to the states and eventually to individual farms. Filburn was a small farmer who kept dairy cattle and chickens and raised a small acreage of winter wheat, some of which was sold but much was used on the farm as livestock feed and for family use. His quota for 1941 was established at 11.1 acres. However, he sowed and harvested 23 acres. For this he was assessed a penalty of $117.11.

MR. JUSTICE JACKSON. Filburn says that this is a regulation of production and consumption of wheat. Such activities are, he urges, beyond the reach of Congressional power under the Commerce Clause, since they are local in character, and their effects upon interstate commerce are at most "indirect."

The Court's recognition of the relevance of the economic effects in the application of the Commerce Clause . . . has made the mechanical application of legal formulas no longer feasible. Once an economic measure of the reach of the power granted to Congress in the Commerce Clause is accepted, questions of federal power cannot be decided simply by finding the activity in question to be "production" nor can consideration of its economic effects be foreclosed by calling them "indirect. . . ."

Whether the subject of the regulation in question was "production," "consumption," or "marketing" is, therefore, not material for purposes of deciding the question of federal power before us. That an activity is of local character may help in a doubtful case to determine whether Congress intended to reach it. The same consideration might help in determining whether in the absence of Congressional action it would be permissible for the state to exert its power on the subject matter, even though in so doing it to some degree affected interstate commerce. But even if Filburn's activity be local and though it may not be regarded as commerce, it may still, whatever its nature, be reached by Congress if it exerts a substantial economic effect on interstate commerce and this irrespective of whether such effect is what might at some earlier time have been defined as "direct" or "indirect."

The effect of consumption of homegrown wheat on interstate commerce is due to the fact that it constitutes the most variable factor in the disappearance of the wheat crop. Consumption on the farm where grown appears to vary in an amount greater than 20 percent of total average production.

. . . One of the primary purposes of the act in question was to increase the market price of wheat and to that end limit the volume thereof that could affect the market. It can hardly be denied that a factor of such volume and variability as home-consumed wheat would have a substantial influence on price and market conditions.

State Regulation

Power and Limitations. The original states forming the United States were considered sovereign while in theory the federal government has only those powers expressly or impliedly delegated to it.[13] The powers of state governments are very broad and include: the power to tax; to own and operate a business; to take private property under eminent domain; and the power to legislate so as to promote the health, safety and general welfare of the citizens of the state. This latter broad power is called the police power. It is limited only by the federal Constitution and by any limitations imposed in the constitution of the particular state.

One of the most important sources for federal constitutional limitations on the police power of the states is the 14th Amendment which applies to action by a state or any of its agencies including local governments. The Supreme Court has incorporated the fundamental Bill of Rights guarantees into the Due Process Clause of the 14th Amendment, thereby expanding the scope of its limitations on state powers. Another limitation on the power of the states arises out of the fact that the Constitution vests plenary power to regulate interstate commerce in the Congress, therefore, any state law which unreasonably obstructs or interferes with the congressional exercise of its power over commerce will be void. The Supremacy Clause makes federal law supreme where the valid exercise of federal power comes into conflict with state power.[14]

---

[13] The Federal Government has some of the inherent powers of sovereignty in international affairs.

[14] Article VI, Paragraph 2: This Constitution, and the Laws of the United States which shall be made in Pursuance thereof; and all Treaties made, or which shall be made, under the Authority of the United States, shall be the supreme Law of the land; and the Judges in every State shall be bound thereby, any Thing in the Constitution or Laws of any State to the Contrary notwithstanding.

State Regulation of Commerce. The Supreme Court held that the Commerce Clause did not by implication exclude the exercise of state power over at least the local aspects of commerce.[15] In three main regulatory areas, however, the Federal power over commerce is exclusive. Those areas are foreign commerce,[16] domestic commerce where the need for national uniformity is essential, and domestic commerce where federal legislation has expressly or impliedly preempted the regulatory area.

The states may have concurrent power to regulate the local aspects of commerce where the federal law has only partially occupied the area, provided: (*a*) the state law is not in conflict with federal law; or (*b*) the state law does not impose an undue burden on commerce; or (*c*) the state law does not discriminate against commerce.[17]

During the height of laissez-faire thinking on the Court, it was quick to find that a state statute imposed an unconstitutional "burden" on interstate commerce. Today a state act would have to substantially impede the free flow of interstate commerce or discriminate in some significant way in favor of local businessmen before the Court would be likely to invalidate it. Not all federal statutes, however, intend to exercise the regulatory power of Congress to the full extent permitted by the Constitution.

In a recent decision the Court may be seeking to place a limit on the reach of the federal commerce power at least where the exercise of such power unduly intrudes on certain aspects of state sovereignty.[18] The Court ruled that Congress could not extend the Fair Labor Standards Act's minimum wage and maximum hour provisions to cover employees of state governments without violating attributes of sovereignty mandated for the states by the Constitution.

SUMMARY

States have full authority to regulate business except to the extent their own constitution and the federal Constitution limit their "police powers." The Commerce Clause of the Constitution has been interpreted as a prohibition of state regulation which obstructs or interferes with the free flow of interstate commerce. Although earlier the Supreme Court was quick to find unconstitutional burdens on interstate commerce, it tends not to do so today unless there is clear interference or discrimination against it. The federal power over

---

[15] *Cooley v. Board of Wardens,* 12 Harv. 299 (1852).

[16] In a few exceptional cases the states have been permitted to exercise some regulatory power over foreign commerce. See, *Boblo Excursion Co. v. Michigan,* 333 U.S. 28 (1948).

[17] For a discussion of state power to tax commerce see Chapter 30.

[18] *National League of Cities v. Usery,* 426 U.S. 833 (1976).

commerce is exclusive in areas where: foreign commerce is involved; national uniformity of regulation is essential; or where federal law has expressly or impliedly preempted the area.

Burbank v. Lockheed Air Terminal, Inc.

411 U.S. 624 (U.S. Sup. Ct. 1973)

Suit brought by Lockheed Air Terminal (plaintiff) against the City of Burbank, California (defendant), seeking an injunction against enforcement of an ordinance adopted by the Burbank City Council. Burbank appealed from the judgment for Lockheed, and this was affirmed by the court of appeals. Affirmed.

The ordinance prohibited "pure jet" aircraft from taking off from the Hollywood-Burbank Airport between 11 P.M. of one day and 7 A.M. the next day and made it unlawful for the operator of the airport to allow such a takeoff. Lockheed was the airport operator. The only regularly scheduled flight affected by the ordinance was an intrastate flight on Pacific Southwest Airlines departing for San Diego every Sunday night at 11:30 P.M. The district court found the ordinance unconstitutional on both Supremacy Clause and Commerce Clause grounds because the Federal Aviation Act of 1958 gave the FAA broad authority to regulate the use of airspace and the Noise Control Act of 1972 obligated the FAA and EPA to develop a comprehensive scheme of federal control of the aircraft noise problem.

MR. JUSTICE DOUGLAS. There is to be sure no express provision of preemption in the 1972 Act. That, however, is not decisive. It is the pervasive nature of the scheme of federal regulation of aircraft noise that leads us to conclude that there is preemption.

Our prior cases on preemption are not precise guidelines in the present controversy, for each case turns on the peculiarities and special features of the federal regulatory scheme in question. Control of noise is, of course, deep seated in the police power of the States. Yet the pervasive control vested in EPA and in FAA under the 1972 Act seems to us to leave no room for local curfews or other local controls. What the ultimate remedy for aircraft noise which plagues many communities and tens of thousands of people is not known. The procedures under the 1972 Act are underway. In addition, the Administrator has imposed a variety of regulations relating to takeoff and landing procedures and runway preferences. The Federal Aviation Act requires a delicate balance between safety and efficiency, and the protection of persons on the ground. Any regulations adopted by the Administrator to control noise pollution must be consistent with the "highest degree of safety." The interdependence of these factors requires a uniform and exclusive system of federal regulation if the congressional objectives underlying the Federal Aviation Act are to be fulfilled.

If we were to uphold the Burbank ordinance and a significant number of municipalities followed suit, it is obvious that fractionalized control of the timing of takeoffs and landings would severly limit the flexibility of the FAA in controlling air traffic flow. The difficulties of scheduling flights to avoid congestion and the concomitant decrease in safety would be compounded. In 1960 the FAA rejected a proposed restriction on jet operations at the Los Angeles airport between 10 P.M. and 7 A.M. because such restrictions could "create critically serious problems to all air transportation patterns."

Great Atlantic and Pacific Tea Company, Inc. v. Cottrell

424 U.S. 366 (U.S. Sup. Ct. 1976)

A&P (plaintiff) brought an action against the State of Mississippi (defendant) to challenge the constitutionality of a Mississippi statute. The law provided that milk and milk products from another state could be sold in Mississippi only if the other state accepts milk produced and processed in Mississippi on a reciprocal basis. The state court ordered A&P not to distribute in Mississippi milk processed in its Louisiana plant. Reversed.

MR. JUSTICE BRENNAN. Mississippi's answer to A&P's Commerce Clause challenge is that the reciprocity requirement is a reasonable exercise of its police power over local affairs, designed to assure the distribution of healthful milk products to the people of its State. We begin our analysis by again emphasizing that "the very purpose of the Commerce Clause was to create an area of free trade among the several states." It has been clear that "the Commerce Clause was not merely an authorization to Congress to enact laws for the protection and encouragement of commerce among the States, but by its own force created an area of trade free from interference by the States. The Commerce Clause even without implementing legislation by Congress is a limitation upon the power of the States." It is no less true, of course, that under our constitutional scheme the States retain broad power to legislate protection for their citizens in matters of local concern such as public health, and that not every exercise of local power is invalid merely because it affects in some way the flow of commerce between the States. Rather, in areas where activities of legitimate local concern overlap with the national interests expressed by the Commerce Clause—where local and national powers are concurrent—the Court in absence of congressional guidance is called upon to make delicate adjustment of the conflicting state and federal claims.

Mississippi's contention that the reciprocity clause serves its vital interests in maintaining the State's health standards borders on the frivolous. The clause clearly does not do so in the sense of furthering Mississippi's established milk quality standards. For according to the State's brief, ". . . Mississippi will do the inspections, will certify them, and will accept a standard below that applicable to domestic producers if the forwarding state will do the same."

Thus, even if Louisiana's standards were lower than Mississippi's, the clause permits Louisiana milk to be admitted to Mississippi if Louisiana enters into a reciprocity agreement. The reciprocity clause thus disserves not promotes any higher Mississippi milk quality standards. Therefore this is a case where the burden imposed on interstate commerce is clearly excessive in relation to the putative local benefits.

Constitutional Restraints on Regulation of Business

First Amendment. The First Amendment provides: "Congress shall make no law . . . abridging freedom of speech, or of the press; or the right of people peaceably to assemble, and to petition the government for a redress of grievances."

Justice Holmes pointed out that none of these rights are absolute when he noted: "The most stringent protection of free speech would not protect a man in falsely shouting, 'Fire!' In a crowded theatre." The "clear and present danger" test is utilized to test whether laws violate First Amendment rights of free speech. This test was sumarized by the Court as follows:

> Whenever the fundamental rights of free speech and assembly are alleged to have been invaded, it must remain open to a defendant to present the issue whether there actually did exist at the time a clear danger; whether the danger, if any, was imminent; and whether the evil apprehended was one so substantial as to justify the . . . restriction interposed by the legislature.[19]

The general rule is that there can be no prior restraint on either freedom of speech or freedom of the press. For example, a court cannot, prior to the act, enjoin peaceful distribution of pamphlets even where the pamphlets are "coercive" or constitute invasion of privacy.[20]

Commercial speech in the form of advertising enjoys at least some First Amendment protection provided it is truthful and the transactions promoted do not violate any laws. Billboard and radio-television advertising may fall under special zoning and regulatory commission rules where public interest considerations in aesthetic or safety factors justify the imposition of reasonable limitations on commercial speech rights.

First Amendment Rights and Property. Peaceable exercise of First Amendment rights on publicly-owned property enjoys wide protection. For example, state trespass laws cannot be invoked arbitrarily to prevent students from assembling to make speeches in the public forums and meeting places of a state university. However, reasonable rules limiting first amendment rights can be enforced for libraries, jails, and military facilities relating to the special

---

[19] *Whitney v. California,* 274 U.S. 357 (1927).

[20] *Better Austin v. Keefe,* 402 U.S. 415 (1971).

purposes and uses of these public institutions. Private property may be dedicated to public uses to such an extent that it becomes quasi-public in character and thereby become subject to various uses by persons exercising First Amendment rights.[21] In general, however, private property owners may restrict or prohibit others from exercising First Amendment rights on their property.[22]

Virginia State Board of Pharmacy v. Virginia Citizens Consumer Council, Inc.

425 U.S. 748 (U.S. Sup. Ct. 1976)

Virginia Citizens Consumer Council (plaintiff) brought suit against the Virginia State Board of Pharmacy (defendant) asking that the court declare that a state statute prohibiting licensed pharmacists from advertising violated the First Amendment. The trial court declared the statute to be unconstitutional and enjoined the Board from enforcing it. The defendant appealed. Affirmed.

MR. JUSTICE BLACKMUN. The question first arises whether, even assuming that First Amendment protection attaches to the flow of drug price information, it is a protection enjoyed by the plaintiffs as recipients of the information, and not solely, if at all, by the advertisers themselves who seek to disseminate that information.

Freedom of speech presupposes a willing speaker. But where a speaker exists, as is the case here, the protection afforded is to the communication, to its source and to its recipients both.

Last Term, in *Bigelow v. Virginia* (1975), the notion of unprotected "commercial speech" all but passed from the scene. We reversed a conviction for violation of a Virginia statute that made the circulation of any publication to encourage or promote the processing of an abortion in Virginia a misdemeanor. The defendant had published in his newspaper the availability of abortions in New York. The advertisement in question, in addition to announcing that abortions were legal in New York, offered the services of a referral agency in that State. We rejected the contention that the publication was unprotected because it was commercial.

If there is a kind of commercial speech that lacks all First Amendment protection, therefore, it must be distinguished by its content. Yet the speech whose content deprives it of protection cannot simply be speech on a commer-

---

[21] *Marsh v. Alabama,* 326 U.S. 501 (1946), held that a corporation which owned and developed a town could not prevent handbills from being distributed within the town.

[22] *Lloyd Corp. v. Tanner,* 407 U.S. 551 (1972), holding that the distribution of anti-war handbills on a privately owned shopping center's property was not protected by the First Amendment; and *Hudgens v. N.L.R.B.,* 424 U.S. 507 (1976), holding that the First Amendment did not protect picketing at a private shopping center.

cial subject. No one would contend that our pharmacist may be prevented from being heard on the subject of whether, in general, pharmaceutical prices should be regulated, or their advertisement forbidden. Nor can it be dispositive that a commercial advertisement is uneditorial, and merely reports a fact. Purely factual matter of public interest may claim protection.

It appears to be feared that if the pharmacist who wishes to provide low cost, and assertedly low quality, services is permitted to advertise, he will be taken up on his offer by too many unwitting customers. They will choose the low-cost, low-quality service and drive the "professional" pharmacist out of business. They will respond only to costly and excessive advertising, and end up paying the price. They will go from one pharmacist to another, following the discount, and destroy the pharmacist-customer relationship. They will lose respect for the profession because its advertises. All this is not in their best interests, and all this can be avoided if they are not permitted to know who is charging what.

There is, of course, an alternative to this highly paternalistic approach. That alternative is to assume that this information is not in itself harmful, that people will perceive their own best interests if only they are well enough informed, and that the best means to that end is to open the channels of communication rather than to close them. If they are truly open, nothing prevents the "professional" pharmacist from marketing his own assertedly superior product, and contrasting it with that of the low-cost, high-volume prescription drug retailer. But the choice among these alternative approaches is not ours to make or the Virginia General Assembly's. It is precisely this kind of choice, between the dangers of suppressing information, and the dangers of its misuse if it is freely available, that the First Amendment makes for us. Virginia is free to require whatever professional standards it wishes of its pharmacists; it may subsidize them or protect them from competition in other ways.

In concluding that commercial speech, like other varieties, is protected, we of course do not hold that it can never be regulated in any way. Some forms of commercial speech regulation are surely permissible. We mention a few only to make clear that they are not before us and therefore are not foreclosed by this case.

There is no claim, for example, that the prohibition on prescription drug price advertising is a mere time, place and manner restriction. We have often approved restrictions of that kind provided that they are justified without reference to the content of the regulated speech, that they serve a significant governmental interest, and that in so doing they leave open ample alternative channels for communication of the information. Whatever may be the proper bounds of time, place, and manner restrictions on commercial speech, they are plainly exceeded by this Virginia statute, which singles out speech of a particular content and seeks to prevent its dissemination completely.

Nor is there any claim that prescription drug price advertisements are forbidden because they are false or misleading in any way. Untruthful speech, commercial or otherwise, has never been protected for its own sake. Obviously, much commercial speech is not provably false, or even wholly false, but only deceptive or misleading. We foresee no obstacle to a State's dealing effectively with this problem. The First Amendment as we construe it today, does not prohibit the State from insuring that the stream of commercial information flows cleanly as well as freely.

Also, there is no claim that the transactions proposed in the forbidden advertisements are themselves illegal in any way. Finally, the special problems of the electronic broadcast media are likewise not in this case.

The Due Process Amendments. The Fifth and 14th Amendments to the United States Constitution (the Fifth applying to activities of the federal government and the 14th to those of the states) have been the sources of the greatest volume of constitutional litigation.[23] The original meaning of due process referred to those procedures due at common law when the government accused, tried, and imprisoned a person for a crime. It was also applied to the procedures used in affecting other rights, such as, for example, taking an individual's property for a public purpose such as a highway. Essentially, it required "fair" procedures including reasonable notice, and a right to be heard before an unbiased tribunal. This is what legal scholars call "procedural due process."[24]

Shortly after the Civil War the Court became heavily influenced by the laissez-faire economic philosophy and on the basis of this philosophical orientation began to declare that virtually all state and federal regulatory laws were arbitrary and unconstitutional under the Due Process Clause. This broadening of the meaning of due process so as to utilize nonprocedural criteria as a basis for testing constitutional validity is known as adopting a "substantive" concept of due process.

It was not until 1937 that this line of cases based upon laissez-faire substantive due process reasoning was overruled. Legislation and actions taken by public officials affecting constitutionally protected rights still must meet procedural due process requirements of basic fairness and also substantive requirements of non-arbitrariness. There is, however, a strong presumption in favor of the constitutional validity of legislation regulating business. In addition, the Court no longer employs economic ideology as a basis for judging whether particular legislation is arbitrary to the extent that it violates Due Process clause standards.

Eminent Domain. The Fifth Amendment also prohibits the taking of pri-

---

[23] For a copy of the Fifth Amendment see Chapter 3, p. 41.

[24] See *Goss v. Lopez,* Chapter 1, p. 11, for a case discussing the application of procedural due process.

vate property for a public use without providing just compensation to the property owner. It imposes the requirement that where any constitutional power is employed as the basis for taking private property, such taking must be for public use and reasonable compensation must be provided. A use is public if the public derives benefits even though the principal beneficiaries may be private. Statutes often authorize private companies such as power companies and railroads to take private property under Eminent Domain.[25]

A direct and immediate interference with the owner's use or enjoyment without a formal taking may require that the Fifth Amendment taking and just compensation conditions be met. For example, low flights of federal aircraft impairing the operation of a poultry farm were held to require compensation. Not all government conduct impairing the value of private property, however, constitutes a "taking" under the Fifth Amendment. A new tax does not constitute a "taking" even though it results in a business becoming unprofitable, forcing the owner to close it down.[26] Likewise, where firemen break down doors during fires no compensation to the owners is required.

Equal Protection. The clause which immediately follows the Due Process Clause of the 14th Amendment, the Equal Protection Clause, prohibits state laws which invidiously discriminate against persons in the same general situation.[27] In recent years, this clause has become a mainspring for cases in the area of civil rights. There is no Equal Protection Clause in the Fifth Amendment which applies to the federal government, but the courts have included prohibitions against invidious discrimination in their interpretations of the Fifth Amendment Due Process Clause.

Under the Equal Protection Clause any statutory classification or differentiation between similarly situated groups or persons must bear a rational relationship to a legitimate state purpose, or be based upon a ground of difference having a fair and substantial relation to the legitimate object of the legislation. The Clause does not prohibit the state from classifying people or corporations for differential treatment so long as there is a *rational basis* for the classification and so long as uniform treatment is provided for all those falling within the same class. Thus chain stores as a group may be subjected to special taxes or regulations which do not apply to individual proprietorships. A sizable number of state regulatory laws have been invalidated because such laws

---

[25] The Fifth Amendment limitations on taking are incorporated into the 14th Amendment via the Due Process Clause.

[26] *City of Pittsburg v. Alco Parking Co.,* 417 U.S. 369 (1974).

[27] Section 1 of the 14th Amendment provides: All persons born or naturalized in the United States and subject to the jurisdiction thereof, are citizens of the United States and of the State wherein they reside. No State shall make or enforce any law which shall abridge the privileges or immunities of citizens of the United States, nor shall any State deprive any person of life, liberty, or property, without the due process of law; nor deny to any person within its jurisdiction the equal protection of the laws.

arbitrarily discriminated against nonresidents or out-of-state businesses in favor of local residents or businesses.

Legislation affecting fundamental rights, however (such as free speech, access to the courts, or voting), or legislation differentiating on the basis of a suspect classification (race, national origin or religion) are subjected to a more rigorous "strict scrutiny" test. Such legislation carries less presumption of validity and will be upheld only if justified by "compelling state interests." For example, various state residency requirements for voting have been successfully challenged under this test.

The 14th Amendment protections only apply to *governmental actions* although this term may include actions taken by private organizations where such organizations have been delegated public functions by any branch of government. Private actions may also be subject to 14th Amendment restraints where government either controls, affirms or to some significant extent becomes involved in the private actions being reviewed. Thus restrictive covenants in deeds which prohibited the purchasers from reselling the property to noncaucasians where invalidated under the Equal Protections Clause. The fact that the parties to such agreement contemplated the use of the courts for enforcing such covenants amounted to sufficient governmental involvement.

Limitations on Governmental Power Today. At present the Supreme Court offers a very limited battleground for business firms seeking to challenge regulation on constitutional grounds. But whereas economic and property rights have been "downgraded" and "upgraded" and narrowed, rights involving political and civil liberties have been expanded. Three principal contributions of the Warren Court were: (1) The "preferred position" theory which holds that where life or liberty are at stake there is less presumption of the validity of regulation than in the case of property; (2) Extension of the Bill of Rights guarantees to bind the states; and (3) Increasing and broadening of the rights of individuals under the Constitution, particularly where rights of the poor and minorities are involved. In the business regulatory area litigation is most apt to occur where federal and state regulation does or may conflict, or where a dispute exists as to the precise meaning of a regulatory rule.

SUMMARY

The Due Process Clauses in the Fifth and 14th Amendments protect natural persons and corporations from governmental laws and actions which are clearly arbitrary or basically unfair. The Due Process protections extend to both governmental procedures and to the nature or substance of the regulatory law itself. There is a strong presumption of validity in favor of properly enacted legislation.

The Equal Protection Clause prohibits invidious discrimination but does not invalidate differential treatment where there is a rational basis for classification. The treatment must be uniform within the class. Some classifications are suspect and must be justified by proof of a compelling state interest.

Construction Ind. Ass'n, Sonoma Co. v. City of Petaluma

522 F.2d 897 (9th Cir. 1975) Cer. den. U.S. Sup. Ct.

Action by Construction Industry Association and certain landowners (plaintiffs) against the City of Petaluma (defendant) challenging the constitutionality of a five-year zoning plan adopted by the City. The City appealed from an adverse decision. Held, reversed.

The City of Petaluma experienced a dramatic increase in its population during the years 1970 and 1971. In order to curb urban sprawl and imbalances between housing developments on the east side of the city and the west side, and between single-family dwellings and multiple residential units, the city council adopted the challenged zoning ordinance to limit the total number of new housing starts and to alleviate the stated imbalances.

CHOY, CIRCUIT JUDGE. Plaintiffs claim that the Plan is arbitrary and unreasonable and, thus, violative of the due process clause of the 14th Amendment. According to plaintiffs the Plan is nothing more than an exclusionary zoning device, designed solely to insulate Petaluma from the urban complex in which it finds itself.

Practically all zoning restrictions have as a purpose and effect the exclusion of some activity or type of structure or a certain density of inhabitants. And in reviewing the reasonableness of a zoning ordinance, our inquiry does not terminate with a finding that it is for an exclusionary purpose. We must determine further whether the exclusion bears any rational relationship to a legitimate state interest. The reasonableness, not the wisdom, of the Petaluma Plan is at issue in this suit.

It is well settled that zoning regulations "must find their justification in some aspect of the police power, asserted for the public welfare." The concept of the public welfare, however, is not limited to the regulation of noxious activities or dangerous structures. As the Court stated in *Berman v. Parker,* (1954):

> The concept of the public welfare is broad and inclusive. The values it represents are spiritual as well as physical, aesthetic as well as monetary. It is within the power of the legislature to determine that the community should be beautiful as well as healthy, spacious as well as clean, well-balanced as well as carefully patrolled.

We conclude therefore that the concept of the public welfare is sufficiently broad to uphold Petaluma's desire to preserve its small town character, its open spaces and low density of population, and to grow at an orderly and deliberate pace.

It is well settled that a state regulation validly based on the police power does not impermissibly burden interstate commerce where the regulation neither discriminates against interstate commerce nor operates to disrupt its required uniformity. As stated by the Supreme Court almost 25 years ago:

> When there is a reasonable basis for legislation to protect the social, as distinguished from the economic, welfare of a community, it is not for this Court because of the Commerce Clause to deny the exercise locally of the sovereign power of the [state].

It is wholly beyond a court's limited authority under the Commerce Clause to review state legislation by balancing reasonable social welfare legislation against its incidental burden on commerce.

Consequently, since the local regulation here is rationally related to the social and environmental welfare of the community and does not discriminate against interstate commerce or operate to disrupt its required uniformity, plaintiffs' claim that the Plan unreasonably burdens commerce must fail.

People v. McDonald

240 N.W.2d 268 (Ct. App. Mich. 1976)

The State of Michigan (plaintiff) commenced criminal charges against John McDonald (defendant) for cutting the hair of a male person in violation of Michigan's Barber Licensing and Regulation Act. McDonald was convicted and now appeals. Reversed.

Section 3 of the Barber Licensing and Regulation Act permits a licensed barber to cut the hair of "any person." However, section 2 of the cosmetology act permits a licensed cosmetologist to cut the hair of "any female." It expressly does not authorize a cosmetologist to cut or clip the hair of any male person, unless he or she has first obtained a barber's license. McDonald, a licensed cosmetologist, was convicted of cutting the hair of a male without having obtained a barber's license. He now challenges the statutory distinction between licensed barbers and licensed cosmetologists as violative of the United States Constitution.

CAVANAGH, JUDGE. Under both equal protection and due process analysis the statutory restriction challenged here fails to pass constitutional muster. Under an equal protection analysis the statutory classification or differentiation between similarly situated groups or persons must bear a rational relationship to a legitimate state purpose or be based upon a ground of difference having a fair and substantial relation to a legitimate object of the legislation. Under a due process analysis the statute, as an exercise of the police power regulating the constitutional right to do business or practice an occupation, must bear a real and substantial relationship (or at least a reasonable relation) to the public health, safety, morals or general welfare. Thus the critical question is whether the restricting of the haircutting activity of cosmetologists is rationally related to a legitimate state objective or reasonably related to the public health, safety, morals, or general welfare.

The purpose of regulating both barbers and cosmetologists is to insure qualified practitioners and insure sanitary facilities. We are unable to perceive any rational or reasonable relation between these objectives and the restriction of the haircutting activity of cosmetologists to female persons. It is certainly not sanitation requirements. Both the cosmetology act and the barbers act prescribe sanitary measures and requirements. There is no showing that different sanitary measures are required to cut men's hair that are not included in the sanitary requirements to cut women's hair.

All hair is created equal—organically and chemically—according to trial testimony. Thus, no difference exists between the hair of males and females which would render one qualified to cut women's hair unqualified to cut men's hair. Cosmetologists are qualified to cut hair; they seek only to render the same services for men's hair that they already provide for women's hair. There is no showing that cosmetologists are unqualified to cut men's hair.

In so far as the statutes prevent cosmetologists from rendering to male patrons the same haircutting services they may lawfully provide to female customers, it violates the equal protection and due process clauses of the state and federal constitutions.

Jackson v. Metropolitan Edison Co.

419 U.S. 345 (U.S. Sup. Ct. 1974)

Jackson (plaintiff) was a resident of York, Pennsylvania, where she received electricity from Metropolitan Edison Co. (defendant). Because of a delinquency in payment of her account, plaintiff's service was disconnected without notice.

Jackson then filed suit against Metropolitan Edison seeking damages for the termination and an injunction requiring Metropolitan to continue providing power to her residence until she has been afforded notice, hearing, and an opportunity to pay for amounts found due. She argued that Metropolitan's termination of her service for alleged nonpayment constituted "state action," depriving her of property in violation of the 14th Amendment's guarantee of due process of law. Affirmed for Metropolitan.

MR. JUSTICE REHNQUIST. Here the action complained of was taken by a utility company which is privately owned and operated, but which in many particulars of its business is subject to extensive state regulation. The mere fact that a business is subject to state regulation does not by itself convert its action into that of the State for purposes of the 14th Amendment. Nor does the fact that the regulation is extensive and detailed, as in the case of most public utilities, do so. It may well be that acts of a heavily regulated utility with at least something of a governmentally protected monopoly will more readily be found to be "state" acts than will the acts of an entity lacking these characteristics. But the inquiry must be whether there is a sufficiently close nexus between the State and the challenged action of the regulated entity so that the action of the latter may be fairly treated as that of the State itself. The true nature of the State's involvement may not be immediately obvious, and detailed inquiry may be required in order to determine whether the test is met.

Jackson first argues that "state action" is present because of the monopoly status allegedly conferred upon Metropolitan by the State of Pennsylvania. As a factual matter, it may well be doubted that the State ever granted or guaranteed Metropolitan a monopoly. But assuming that it had, this fact is not determinative in considering whether Metropolitan's termination of service to Jackson was "state action" for purposes of the 14th Amendment.

Jackson next urges that state action is present because Metropolitan provides an essential public service required to be supplied on a reasonably continuous basis . . . and hence a public function. We have of course found state action present in the exercise by private entity of powers traditionally exclusively reserved to the State. If we were dealing with the exercise by Metropolitan of some power delegated to it by the State which is traditionally associated with sovereignty, such as eminent domain, our case would be quite a different one. But while the Pennsylvania statute imposes an obligation to furnish service on regulated utilities, it imposes no such obligation on the State. The Pennsylvania courts have rejected the contention that the furnishing of utility services are either state functions or municipal duties.

We also reject the notion that Metropolitan's termination is state action because the State "has specifically authorized and approved" the termination practice. In the instant case, Metropolitan filed with the Public Utilities Commission a general tariff—a provision of which states Metropolitan's right to terminate service for nonpayment. This provision has appeared in Metropolitan's previously filed tariffs for many years and has never been the subject of a hearing or other scrutiny by the Commission. Although the Commission did hold hearings on portions of Metropolitan's general tariff relating to a general rate increase, it never even considered the reinsertion of this provision in the newly filed general tariff.

All of Jackson's arguments taken together show no more than that Metropolitan was a heavily regulated private utility, enjoying at least a *partial* monopoly in the providing of electrical service within its territory, and that it elected to terminate service to Jackson in a manner which the Pennsylvania Public Utilities Commission found permissible under State law. Under our decision this is not sufficient to connect the State of Pennsylvania with Metropolitan's action so as to make the latter's conduct attributable to the State for purposes of the 14th Amendment.

Protection of Constitutional Rights By Statute

Section 1983. In 1970 Congress enacted Section 1983 which provides:

Every person who, under color of any statute, ordinance, regulation, custom, or usage, of any State or Territory, subjects, or causes to be subjected, any citizen of the United States or other person within the jurisdiction thereof to the deprivation of any rights, privileges, or immunities secured by the Constitution and laws, shall be liable to the party injured in an action at law, suit in equity, or other proper proceeding for redress.

One of the principle reasons for the legislation is to afford a federal right in federal courts where citizens have been deprived of 14th Amendment rights by state agencies. Violation requires *state action* which involves deprivations of constitutional rights. The applications of the Act and the remedies to be obtained are subject to controversy among legal experts.[28]

Smith v. Brookshire Brothers, Inc.

519 F.2d 93 (5th Cir. 1975)

Action by Smith and McClure (plaintiffs) against Brookshire Brothers, Inc. (defendant), for damages under 42 *U.S.C.* Sec. 1983. Judgment for plaintiffs . . . in the amount of $6,000 and Brookshire appealed. Affirmed.

Smith and McClure entered Brookshire Brothers Store and were arrested by an officer who had been told by Brookshire employees that the plaintiffs had taken a jar of cold cream without paying for it. Brookshire had an arrangement with the local police providing that the police would arrest anyone identified as a shoplifter by the store. The plaintiffs were taken to the police station, finger printed and booked but all charges were ultimately dismissed.

GEE, JUDGE. The district court found that while McClure's deposit of the jar in her bag during shopping created some cause for suspicion, that fact did not create reasonable grounds to detain the woman as a shoplifter before she had been given an opportunity to pay for the item. The court also found that the defendant had acted under color of state law in bringing about the detention of plaintiffs and had thus violated their civil rights within the purview of § 1983.

The police had detained the plaintiffs without independently establishing that there was probable cause to do so—they took them into custody without a valid complaint having been filed and without knowing the facts to believe that a crime had been committed. . . . Instead, they depended on the conclusory assessment of the store officers. These store managers, in turn, did not

[28] Sheldon H. Nahmod, "Section 1983 and the 'Background' of Tort Liability, 50 *Ind. L.J.* 7 (1974).

have probable cause for believing that McClure was a shoplifter and that Smith was an accomplice.

But in order for Brookshire to be liable under § 1983 for fostering a detention without probable cause, the plaintiffs must show that Brookshire was acting under color of law. The police may have made a mistake but they are not defendants here. The store managers may have made a mistake in detaining plaintiffs but that alone would not make them liable under § 1983; it would only create a state tort action, depending on the state's false imprisonment standard. The plaintiffs had to show that the police and the store managers were acting in concert; that Brookshire and the police had a customary plan whose result was the detention in the present case.

The district court decided that such a plan had been evidenced. We do not believe that such a finding is clearly erroneous. Many colloquies at trial gave testimony to the proposition that Brookshire officials knew that they could have people detained merely by calling the police and designating the detainee. Illustrative of the evidence are the following exchanges:

Q: Does Brookshire, to your knowledge, have any type of pre-arranged plan with the Lufkin Police Department to come and assist them when they need help, particularly in the area of shoplifting?

A: (Officer Tooley): Yes, sir, at that time they did.

Q: And shoplifting was part of your job when merchants would call in that they had caught somebody, they would call the police department and you would go out and pick them up?

A: (Officer Tooley): Yes, sir.

Problem Cases

1. The New York Central Railroad was convicted of obstructing a railroad crossing. The applicable state statute allowed a train five minutes to pass; the New York Central took seven minutes. New York Central appeals, claiming that the regulatory statute violated the commerce clause of the U.S. Constitution. Is the statute a valid exercise of the state regulatory power?
2. The city of Barre passed an ordinance to license itinerant photographers. Unlike resident photographers, itinerants were required to post a performance bond and to pay certain licensing fees. Olan Mills, Inc., a corporation employing several itinerant photographers, sues the city, claiming that the ordinance is a violation of the commerce clause and therefore, unconstitutional. Can the city regulate itinerant photographers in this manner?
3. The Louisiana Superdome (a state-owned corporation), had a policy of allowing patrons to smoke tobacco during events held therein. Gasper and a group of nonsmokers filed suit against the Superdome maintaining that the existence of tobacco smoke in the Superdome violated their First Amendment rights as they were forced to breathe the harmful smoke as a precondition to enjoying events there. Gasper also alleges that his due process rights were violated as he has a right to be free from hazardous tobacco smoke while in state buildings. Does the Superdome's smoking policy violate these constitutional rights?
4. An Illinois state statute provides that any employer who, through advertisements, is seeking to hire employees to replace employees currently on strike, must state in such

advertisement that a strike is in progress at that place of business. A violation of this statute is punishable by a fine of not more than $300 for each day of advertising. Federal Tool Company was charged with violating this statute and now claims that this state statute has been preempted by the National Labor Relations Act. The NLRA enacted into law by the United States Congress covers prohibited employer and employee unfair labor practices. Has the Illinois statute been preempted by the NLRA?

5. Willow River Power Co. sued the U.S. Government for damages resulting from reduced generating capacity of Willow's hydroelectric plant caused by government-authorized operations which improved the navigation of Willow River and raised the level of the water of Willow River from which the company obtained its power above the ordinary high-water mark. The U.S. government did not actually take any property from Willow as a result of its operations, but Willow claims that, nonetheless, it is entitled to compensation from the U.S. government for the above-mentioned damages under the 5th Amendment to the U.S. Constitution. Is Willow correct?
6. Hudgens, the owner of a shopping center, threatened to have picketers arrested for picketing inside the shopping center. The picketers brought an action with the NLRB to have Hudgens' actions declared an unfair labor practice since the threat of arrest interfered with their rights of freedom of speech. Will this argument be sustained?
7. Hutton Park Gardens, a landlord organization, challenged the constitutionality of an ordinance promulgated by the Town Council of West Orange that limited the amount by which landlords could raise the rents on single-family apartment units. The ordinance prohibited increases in rents in excess of the annual percentage increase in the Consumer Price Index in the metropolitan area or 15 percent of the existing rent, whichever was less. Does the ordinance violate substantive due process standards?
8. The Township of Mount Laurel enacted an ordinance under a New Jersey enabling statute permitting only single-family, detached houses to be built in residential zones and imposing minimum lot size and floor area requirements. The purpose of the ordinance was to reduce the tax burden on residents, whose property taxes paid for public education. The fewer the school children in a district, the lower the property taxes needed to educate them. The local NAACP, charged that the ordinance perpetuated a critical housing shortage for low and middle income families who cannot afford large lots and homes. Does the housing ordinance violate the Equal Protection guarantees of the 14th Amendment?
9. Metropolitan Co., a nonprofit developer, contracted to buy a tract of land within the boundaries of the Village of Arlington Heights in order to build racially integrated low and moderate-income housing. The obligation to purchase was conditioned on securing rezoning from the Village zoning board. At hearings, opponents mentioned racial factors as well as the fact that the location had always been zoned exclusively for single-family dwelling units. Village denied rezoning and Metropolitan appealed to the courts contending the ruling was racially discriminatory under the Equal Protection Clause of the 14th Amendment. The Court of Appeals ruled that the "ultimate effect" of the ruling was racially discriminatory and, therefore, the ruling had to be set aside even though the court assumed the denial was not motivated by racial considerations. Is this a correct ruling?
10. Remm parked his car in a downtown parking space. His car was subsequently towed away and impounded for allegedly being illegally parked. Remm had to pay towing and storage fees before he could get his car released. The municipal ordinance under which Remm's car was towed provided that the towing and storage charges are to be collected regardless of whether the owner of the vehicle intends to contest the traffic ticket; if

the owner is ultimately found not guilty of the violation, the towing and storage fees are returned to him. Remm now commences suit contending that he was denied due process of law as his property was seized prior to any hearing on the merits of the charge. Is his contention sound?

11. The city of Niles passed an ordinance regulating truck traffic. Trucks intending to discharge cargo within the city were confined to certain roads; trucks not intending to discharge cargo within the city were confined to designated state highways. Dean, a nonresident trucker, was arrested for a violation of the ordinance. Dean contends, however, that the ordinance is a denial of equal protection. Can the city regulate truck traffic in such a manner?
12. Ohrn brought an action against the Rhode Island State Pilotage Commission challenging the constitutionality of Rhode Island's law regulating piloting licenses for registered vessels. Plaintiff claimed that the statute, which requires applicants for a pilot's license to have been residents of Rhode Island for at least five years, violates the right to travel and migrate among the several states as guaranteed by the Equal Protection Clause of the 14th Amendment. The state claims that the law insures safer navigation for vessels entering or leaving its waters. Should the statute be declared unconstitutional?
13. Paul, Chief of Police in Louisville, through honest mistake circulated Davis' picture and name as being an active shoplifter. Davis sued for the harm done him by Paul under Section 1983 of the Civil Rights Act, asserting that the stigma attached to the label of shoplifter denies him his liberty and invaded his constitutional rights. Can Davis prevail?

49

Competitive Torts and the Protection of Ideas

Introduction

Rights Protected. Tort law protecting economic relations from unreasonable interferences developed more recently than did tort law in other areas. However, rights and duties arising out of economic relations now are clearly established in three main categories.

First, business firms are protected against injurious falsehoods or other deceitful practices by competitors which result in diversion of their patronage, or which otherwise injure their goodwill. Second, protection is given to ideas by the law relating to trade secrets, patents, and copyrights. Third, protection is given against certain unjustifiable interferences with contracts or economic expectations. To an important extent, the rights in these areas now are governed by federal and state statutes creating special procedures, rules, and remedies.

Deceitful Diversion of Patronage

Disparagement. The torts of libel and slander, discussed in Chapter 3, afford remedies against competitors who publish defamatory falsehoods charging other businesspersons with personal misconduct. If the falsehood relates to the quality of the product, to the seller's title, or to the type service provided, it is the tort of *disparagement* and proof of actual damage is essential. Although the tort of disparagement originated with cases protecting tangible property rights from injurious falsehoods, protection was later extended to intangible property rights including trademarks, patents, corporate shares, and copyrighted material.

Another form of deceitful diversion of patronage occurs where one firm "palms" its goods off as being those made by a competitor. Although "palming off" is a tort, nearly all actions of this type are now brought under the Lanham Act which affords very extensive protection for trademarks and other product and service identifying marks used by business firms.

Trademarks and Other Marks. A trademark is a distinctive mark, word, design, or picture which is affixed to goods so that purchasers may identify their origin. In general, a trademark must be fanciful, arbitrary, unique, and nondescriptive. Generic terms such as "car" or "ham" and descriptive terms such as "good" or "extra soft" may not be exclusively appropriated as a protectable trademark. This is true even where the user of the term can prove that customers identify the term with the user to the degree that the term has acquired a *secondary meaning.*

A *trade name* is used as the name under which a firm operates. *Service marks* are used to identify services and need only to be registered. *Certification marks* are used by people who do not own the marks but who have a right to identify the product as being approved or authorized by the owner of the mark. The "Good Housekeeping Seal of Approval" is an example of a certification mark. A *collective mark* is employed by an association or group of people to identify the group as being the source of the product or service. Trade union or trade association marks fall into this category.

Since 1946 the Lanham Act (15 U.S.C. Sections 1050–1127) has greatly expanded the scope of registrability and the protection afforded to trademarks, trade names, service marks, certification marks, and collective marks. Such marks are protected against misuse or infringement by Section 1 of the act which states:

> Any person who shall, in commerce, (a) use, without consent of registrant, any reproduction, counterfeit, copy or colorable imitation of any registered mark in connection with the sale, offering for sale, or advertising of any goods or services or in connection with which such use is likely to cause confusion or mistake or to deceive purchasers as to the source of such goods or services shall be . . . [liable for damages and subject to injunction].

Under the Lanham Act there is a Principal Register for the registration of "technical" trademarks. "Technical" trademarks meet all of the requirements in terms of uniqueness and prior use so as to entitle such marks to maximum protection under the act.

There is a Supplemental Register for "all marks capable of distinguishing applicant's goods or services and not registrable on the principal register," including marks which consist of surnames, geographical names, and also distinctive packages and the configuration of goods.

Where a shape or feature of construction of a product is arbitrary and is *basically nonfunctional* (e.g., the Haig and Haig "squeeze" bottle design), such product characteristic is subject to registration and protectable provided its user can establish that the characteristic has acquired *secondary meaning* in the public mind. To establish secondary meaning the user must prove that the particular characteristic causes the public to associate the product with the user.

Registration on the Principal Register carries important presumptions of validity and extends protection beyond that accorded to marks registered on the Supplemental Register. If a firm can establish that a mark has acquired a distinctive secondary meaning identifying its goods, such mark may be registered on the Principal Register. Proof of substantial exclusive continuous use for a period of five years preceding application for registration is prima facie evidence of acquired *secondary meaning.*

Ironically, the more successful a new product becomes, the greater the risk that trademark rights may be lost because the product name acquires a descriptive or generic (popular) meaning. For this reason, Xerox Co. is currently taking national ads urging people not to use "Xerox" as a verb (e.g., "Xerox this for me."). "Aspirin" was a protected trademark until it acquired generic usage.

SUMMARY

The tort of disparagement protects businessmen from injurious falsehoods relating to the quality of their products, their services, or the title to their property. The Lanham Act now gives extensive protection to registered trademarks, trade names, service marks, certification marks, and collective marks. Marks may be lost if they become descriptive or generic.

Testing Systems, Inc. v. Magnaflux Corp.

251 F. Supp. 286 (E.D. Pa. 1966)

This was an action for product disparagement brought by Testing Systems, Inc. (plaintiff), against Magnaflux Corp. (defendant). Judgment for Testing.

Testing and Magnaflux were competitors making equipment and chemical products. Testing Co. sued Magnaflux for damages for having orally and in writing disparaged Testing Co.'s products. This included statements to Testing Co.'s customers and prospective customers that Testing Co.'s products were "no good" and that the "government is throwing them out." It also included a written report falsely stating that the government had tested Testing Co.'s products and found them to be only 40 percent as effective as the products of Magnaflux.

LORD, DISTRICT JUDGE. The fine line that separates healthy competitive effort from underhanded business tactics is frequently difficult to determine.

Apart from the tradesman's right of free speech, which must be vigorously safeguarded, the public has a genuine interest in learning the relative merits of particular products, however that may come about. To advance these interests the law of the marketplace gives the competitor a wide berth in the conduct of his business. As Mr. Justice Maxey of the Pennsylvania Supreme Court said in 1932,

> He may send out circulars, or give information verbally, to customers of other men, knowing they are bound by contract for a definite term, although acting upon the expectation and with the purpose of getting the trade of such persons for himself.
>
> He may use any mode of persuasion with such a customer . . . which appeals to his self-interest, reason, or even his prejudices.
>
> He may descant upon the extent of his rival's facilities compared with his own, his rival's means, his insolvency, if it be a fact, and the benefits which will result to the customer in the future from coming to the solicitor rather than remaining where he is . . . "the law of competition" . . . takes little note of the ordinary rules of good neighborhood or abstract morality.
>
> Nonetheless, there is an outer perimeter to permissible conduct. The tradesman must be assured that his competitors will not be suffered to engage in conduct which falls below the minimum standard of fair dealing.
>
> It is no answer that they can defend themselves by also resorting to disparagement. A self-respecting businessman will not voluntarily adopt, and should not be driven to adopt, a selling method which he regards as undignified, unfair, and repulsive. A competitor should not, by pursuing an unethical practice, force his rival to choose between its adoption and the loss of his trade.

Magnaflux's comments in the case presently before this court do not entitle it to the protection accorded to "unfavorable comparison." There is a readily observable difference between saying that one's product is, in general, better than another's . . . and asserting, as here, that such other's is only 40 percent as effective as one's own. The former, arguably, merely expresses an opinion, the truth or falsity of which is difficult or impossible of ascertainment. The latter, however, is an assertion of fact, not subject to the same frailties of proof, implying that the party making the statement is fortified with the substantive facts necessary to make it. This distinction has never been seriously questioned. Magnaflux in this case admittedly circulated to Testing's present and prospective customers false statements to the effect that the government had tested both products and found the Magnaflux to be 60 percent more effective than Testing's. This is not the sort of "comparison" that courts will protect.

Apart from this, there is at least one additional factor which withdraws Magnaflux's comments from the category of unfavorable comparison. Not content with making the admittedly false statements and allowing them to be evaluated independently of any extraneous influence, Magnaflux here gave added authenticity to its assertions by invoking the reputation of a third party, the United States Government. It is unnecessary to speculate on the additional force Magnaflux's remarks must have had when coupled with the purported approval of so highly credible a source. This, of course, is to say nothing of the statements to the effect that Testing had been "thrown out," which by no stretch of the imagination could be termed mere comparison.

Roto-Rooter Corp. v. O'Neal

513 F.2d 44 (5th Cir. 1975)

Action for damages for trademark infringement brought by Roto-Rooter Corporation (plaintiff) against O'Neal (defendant). Roto-Rooter appealed from an adverse decision. Reversed.

Roto-Rooter was granted a federal registration in 1954 for its service mark "Roto-Rooter" for sewer, pipe, and drain cleaning services. O'Neal started doing business in Texas in 1973 as "Rotary De-Rooting" utilizing an angel operating a sewer cleaning device and a slogan "the sewer man with a conscience."

GODBOLD, CIRCUIT JUDGE. Infringement of a registered mark is governed by 15 U.S.C. § 1114(1) which imposes liability against "use likely to cause confusion, or to cause mistake, or to deceive." Proof of actual confusion is not necessary—likelihood of confusion is the appropriate inquiry. In this circuit likelihood of confusion is determined by evaluating a variety of factors including the type of trademark at issue; similarity of design; similarity of product; identity of retail outlets and purchasers; identity of advertising media utilized; defendant's intent; and actual confusion. While proof of actual confusion is not required to sustain a claim of infringement, the view of this court is that it is the best evidence of likelihood of confusion.

The decision of the trial court must be reversed for two interrelated reasons. The court appears to have employed an incorrect legal standard, and, when examined under correct standards, Roto-Rooter's evidence established the likelihood of confusion required by the law of this circuit. The trial court referred to absence of evidence of statistically significant confusion. The test is, of course, likelihood of confusion. Roto-Rooter presented evidence of actual confusion . . . by the testimony of four persons who had mistakenly employed O'Neal although intending to use the service of Roto-Rooter.

Trade Secrets, Patents, and Copyrights

Trade Secrets. Society's interest in free competition is so strong that copying of a competitor's product is lawful unless trademark, trade secret, patent, or copyright rights are infringed. Copying or product simulation is a widespread practice in American business.

A trade secret is any formula, pattern, device, or compilation of special information which gives the firm developing it a differential advantage over competitors. A firm claiming a trade secret must be able to show that the device or formula was protected and treated as a secret within the firm. This usually means only a few people are allowed access to it and that it is never disclosed to anyone except on a confidential basis. Knowledge generally available in the trade cannot form the basis of trade secrets.

Trade secrets are given only limited protection by the law. It is only where competitors discover the secrets by bribery, theft, commercial espionage, or other wrongful means that injunctions and damages may be granted. If a trade secret is disclosed to someone on a confidential basis, any breach of this confidence will constitute a wrongful misappropriation.

Although a trade secret must confer some special competitive advantage, it need not embody the degree of inventiveness required for patentability. Some owners of patentable trade secrets may elect to run the risk of lawful imitation rather than to make the public disclosure of the invention as is required in order to obtain a patent. The legal monopoly conferred by the patent is only good for 17 years and then anyone can copy the invention.

Patents. A patent may be granted to any person on any new and useful invention of a (1) process, (2) machine, (3) product, (4) composition of matter, (5) new and useful improvement thereof, (6) a growing plant, or (7) a design. The invention must not have been (1) patented or described in any printed publication in this or any foreign country for more than one year prior to application, (2) known or in use by others in this country prior to its invention, and (3) in public use or sale in this country for more than one year prior to application.

Except for design patents, a patentee gets the exclusive right to utilize, make or sell the patented product, machine, or process for a 17-year period. Design patents may be obtained from 3½ to 14 years depending upon the fee paid. The patent monopoly also includes the right to license others, to utilize the patent, and to control the terms and conditions under which such use is made.

The fact that the U.S. Patent Office has issued a patent does not necessarily mean that the patent is valid. About two thirds of all patents challenged in court are held to be invalid or unenforceable for various technical reasons. Infringement of a valid patent renders the infringer liable to the patentee for any profits earned, and also for damages suffered by the patentee. In addition, injunctive relief is available to the patentee to prevent future acts of infringement.

Copyrights. A copyright protects original literary, musical, dramatic, pictorial, audio, and audiovisual works, but it is only the form rather than the ideas, concepts, method of operation, etc., of the work of authorship that is protected. The copyright holder is given exclusive right to reproduce, perform, or display the work, subject to what is known as "fair-use." The 1976 Copyright Act, which became effective January 1, 1978, was the result of 20 years of deliberation in Congress, much of it concerned with fair use in an age of the ubiquitous photocopier. It defines fair use in terms of prior court decisions but it is still quite unclear how far fair use extends. In general, a very limited, noncommercial use of the copyrighted work without the copyright owner's consent in teaching, research, criticism, comment, or news reporting is not an infringement. The application of the fair use doctrine to libraries and performances by nonprofit educational institutions is covered more precisely by the Act.

In general, any form of reproduction of copyrighted material without the consent of the copyright owner may render the copier liable for any actual damages the copyright owner can prove. The court may award from $250 to $10,000 statutory damages if actual damages cannot be proved. Wilful infringements may bring about larger fines and up to one year in prison.

The life of a copyright under the new Act is 50 years beyond the death of the last surviving author of the work, with no provision for renewal. Application for registration of a copyright is made to the Register of Copyright, and one or more copies, depending upon the nature of the work, must be deposited in the Library of Congress. Registration is required for an infringement action, and an innocent infringer has no liability unless notice (usually a © or the word "copyright" or "copr."—but ℗ for phonorecords) is placed upon publicly distributed copies.

The new Act requires cable-TV operators to pay royalties to owners of the programs they broadcast and gives juke-box operators a license to play any record for an annual $8 fee per machine. The Act supercedes state law and the common law copyright for unpublished works. Despite much discussion, Congress did not specify what protection, if any, is gained by copyrighting computer programs.

SUMMARY

In general, in the absence of a patent, copyright, or trade secret the product of others may be imitated or copied. Liability for "palming off" may occur under trademark law if the consumer is being confused. Trade secrets may be duplicated so long as the method of duplication does not involve misappropriation. Patents give a 17-year legal monopoly to the patentee but many patents are held to be invalid. Copyrights confer the exclusive right to reproduce written material for a period of the life of the author plus 50 years. The "fair use" doctrine permits limited duplication of copyrighted works for nonprofit purposes.

Forest Laboratories, Inc. v. Pillsbury Company

452 F.2d 621 (7th Cir. 1971)

Forest Laboratories (plaintiff), a corporation engaged in producing and packaging effervescent sweetener tablets, sued Pillsbury Company (defendant), alleging that Pillsbury had purloined certain Forest trade secrets. Judgment in the amount of $75,000 for Forest and Pillsbury appealed. Affirmed.

Forest had developed a secret process for packing sweetener tablets so as to extend their shelf life. Forest disclosed this secret in confidence to Tidy House Corporation. Pillsbury then purchased the assets of Tidy House and learned the secret.

CUMMINGS, CIRCUIT JUDGE. A trade secret is defined in Section 757, comment (b), of the Restatement as follows:

> A trade secret may consist of any formula, pattern, device, or compilation of information which is used in one's business, and which gives him an opportunity to obtain an advantage over competitors who do not know or use it. It may be a . . . process of . . . treating or preserving materials. . . .

As stated in an authoritative treatise on this subject:

> As distinguished from a patent, a trade secret need not be essentially new, novel or unique; therefore, prior art is a less effective defense in a trade secret case than it is in a patent infringement case. The idea need not be complicated; it may be intrinsically simple and nevertheless qualify as a secret, unless it is in common knowledge and, therefore, within the public domain.

Before finally determining that this tablet-tempering step was a trade secret, the district court weighed the six factors prescribed by *Abbot Laboratories* . . . and the *Restatement.* They are:

1. The extent to which the information is known outside of the claimant's business.
2. The extent to which it is known by employees and others involved in his business.
3. The extent of measures taken by him to guard the secrecy of the information.
4. The value of the information to him and his competitors.
5. The amount of effort or money expended by him in developing the information.
6. The ease or difficulty with which the information could be properly acquired or duplicated by others.

. . . The well settled rule of American jurisdictions, including Wisconsin, is that a corporation which purchases the assets of another corporation does not, by reason of succeeding to the ownership of property, assume the obligations of the transferor corporation.

Exceptions to this rule exist where (*a*) the purchasing corporation expressly or impliedly agrees to assume the liabilities of the seller, (*b*) the transaction amounts to a consolidation or merger of the two companies, (*c*) the purchasing corporation is merely a continuation of the selling corporation, or (*d*) the transaction is entered into fraudulently to escape liability.

Section 758(b) of the Restatement states:

> One who learns another's trade secret from a third person without notice that it is secret and that this person's disclosure is a breach of his duty to the [owner of the trade secret], or who learns the secret through a mistake without notice of the secrecy and the mistake.
>
> (b) is liable to the [owner of the trade secret] for a disclosure or use of the secret after the receipt of such notice unless prior thereto he has in good faith paid value for the secret or has so changed his position that to subject him to liability would be inequitable.

Thus under § 758(b) of the Restatement of Torts, Pillsbury would be liable for its use of the secret after receipt of notice unless prior thereto it had in good faith paid value for the secret.

Sears, Roebuck & Co. v. Stiffel Co.

376 U.S. 225 (U.S. Sup. Ct. 1964)

This was an action for unfair competition brought by Stiffel Co. (plaintiff) against Sears (defendant). Sears appealed from a judgment in favor of Stiffel. Reversed.

Stiffel developed a "pole lamp" which proved to be a commercial success. Sears then brought out a substantially identical lamp at a much lower price and Stiffel sued for unfair competition claiming that Sears had caused confusion in the trade as to the source of the lamps thereby engaging in unfair competition under Illinois law.

MR. JUSTICE BLACK. Pursuant to . . . constitutional authority, Congress in 1790 enacted the first federal patent and copyright law, 1 Stat. 109, and ever since that time has fixed the conditions upon which patents and copyrights shall be granted. These laws, like other laws of the United States enacted pursuant to constitutional authority, are the supreme law of the land. When state law touches upon the area of these federal statutes, it is "familiar doctrine" that the federal policy "may not be set at naught, or its benefits denied" by the state law. This is true, of course, even if the state law is enacted in the exercise of otherwise undoubted state power.

Thus the patent system is one in which uniform federal standards are carefully used to promote invention while at the same time preserving free competition. Obviously a State could not, consistently with the Supremacy Clause of the Constitution, extend the life of a patent beyond its expiration date or give a patent on an article which lacked the level of invention required for federal patents. . . .

In the present case, the "pole lamp" sold by Stiffel has been held not to be entitled to the protection of either a mechanical or a design patent. An unpatentable article, like an article on which the patent has expired, is in the public domain and may be made and sold by whoever chooses to do so. What Sears did was to copy Stiffel's design and to sell lamps almost identical to those sold by Stiffel. This it had every right to do under the federal patent laws. That Stiffel originated the pole lamp and made it popular is immaterial. "Sharing in the goodwill of an article unprotected by patent or trade-mark is the exercise of a right possessed by all—and in the free exercise of which the consuming public is deeply interested." To allow a State by use of its law of unfair competition to prevent the copying of an article which represents too slight an advance to be patented would be to permit the State to block off from the public something which federal law has said belongs to the public. . . .

Sears has been held liable here for unfair competition because of a finding of likelihood of confusion based only on the fact that Sears' lamp was copied from Stiffel's unpatented lamp and that consequently the two looked exactly alike. Of course there could be "confusion" as to who had manufactured these nearly identical articles. But mere inability of the public to tell two identical articles apart is not enough to support an injunction against copying or an award of damages for copying that which the federal patent laws permit to be copied. Doubtless a State may, in appropriate circumstances, require that goods, whether patented or unpatented, be labeled or that other precautionary steps be taken to prevent customers from being misled as to the source, just as it may protect businesses in the use of their trademarks, labels, or distinctive dress in the packaging of goods so as to prevent others, by imitating such markings, from misleading purchasers as to the source of the goods. But because of the federal patent laws a State may not, when the article is unpatented and uncopyrighted, prohibit the copying of the article itself or award damages for such copying. . . .[1]

E. I. Du Pont De Nemours & Co., Inc. v. Christopher

431 F.2d 1012 (5th Cir. 1970)

Rolfe and Gary Christopher (defendants), photographers, were hired by persons unknown to take aerial photographs of new construction at a plant Du Pont (plaintiff) was building. Du Pont employees noticed the airplane circling the construction and tracked down the defendants who refused to disclose the identity of their client. Du Pont claimed it had developed a secret process of making methanol which was being protected as a trade secret and requested that the trial court order the defendants to disclose the identity of their client

[1] The revised copyright laws expand the circumstances where state law and copyright law may afford protection to authors and recording artists. In the *Kawanee Oil* case the Court held that the patent laws had not preempted state protection of trade secret rights under the *Sears v. Stiffle* doctrine even where the particular secret could have been patented. *Kawanee Oil Co. v. Bicron,* 416 U.S. 470 (1974).

and grant other relief including an injunction and damages. The Christophers appealed from an order of disclosure. Affirmed.

GOLDBERG, JUSTICE. The Christophers argued both at trial and before this court that they committed no "actionable wrong" in photographing the Du Pont facility and passing these photographs on to their client because they conducted all of their activities in public airspace, violated no government aviation standard, did not breach any confidential relation, and did not engage in any fraudulent or illegal conduct. In short, the Christophers argue that for an appropriation of trade secrets to be wrong there must be a trespass, other illegal conduct, or breach of a confidential relationship. We disagree.

It is true, as the Christophers assert, that the previous trade secret cases have contained one or more of these elements. However, we do not think that the Texas courts would limit the trade secret protection exclusively to these elements. On the contrary, in *Hyde Corporation v. Huffines,* 1958, the Texas Supreme Court specifically adopted the rule found in the Restatement of Torts which provides:

> One who discloses or uses another's trade secret, without a privilege to do so, is liable to the other if
> (*a*) he discovered the secret by improper means, or
> (*b*) his disclosure or use constitutes a breach of confidence reposed in him by the other in disclosing the secret to him. . . .

Thus, although the previous cases have dealt with a breach of a confidential relationship, a trespass, or other illegal conduct, the rule is much broader than the cases heretofore encountered.

We think, therefore, that the Texas rule is clear. One may use his competitor's secret process if he discovers the process by reverse engineering applied to the finished product; one may use a competitor's process if he discovers it by his own independent research; but one may not avoid these labors by taking the process from the discoverer without his permission at a time when he is taking reasonable precautions to maintain its secrecy. To obtain knowledge of a process without spending the time and money to discover it independently is improper unless the holder voluntarily discloses it or fails to take reasonable precautions to ensure its secrecy.

We note that this view is in perfect accord with the position taken by the authors of the *Restatement.* In commenting on improper means of discovery the savants of the *Restatement* of *Torts* said:

> Improper Means of Discovery. The discovery of another's trade secret by improper means subjects the actor to liability independently of the harm to the interest in the secret. Thus, if one uses physical force to take a secret formula from another's pocket, or breaks into another's office to steal the formula, his conduct is wrongful and subjects him to liability apart from the rule stated in this section. Such conduct is also an improper means of procuring the secret under this rule. But means may be improper under this rule even though they do not cause any other harm than that to the interest in the trade secret. Examples of such means are fraudulent misrepresentations to induce disclosure, tapping of telephone wires, eavesdropping

or other espionage. A complete catalogue of improper means is not possible. In general they are means which fall below the generally accepted standards of commercial morality and reasonable conduct.

In taking this position we realize that industrial espionage of the sort here perpetrated has become a popular sport in some segments of our industrial community. However, our devotion to freewheeling industrial competition must not force us into accepting the law of the jungle as the standard of morality expected in our commercial relations.

Sakraida v. Ag Pro

425 U.S. 273 (U.S. Sup. Ct 1976)

Ag Pro (plaintiff) filed a patent infringement suit against Sakraida (defendant) and Sakraida appealed from an adverse judgment. Reversed.

Ag Pro developed a system for cleaning dairy barns by water flushing and obtained a patent. When sued for infringement Sakraida defended on the ground that Ag Pro's patent was invalid for lack of invention.

MR. JUSTICE BRENNAN. It has long been clear that the Constitution requires that there be some "invention" to be entitled to patent protection. As we explained in *Hotchkiss v. Greenwood,* (1851): "[U]nless more ingenuity and skill . . . were required . . . than were possessed by an ordinary mechanic acquainted with the business, there was an absence of that degree of skill and ingenuity which constitute essential elements of every invention. In other words, the improvement is the work of the skillful mechanic, not that of the inventor."

The Court of Appeals recognized that the patent combined old elements for applying water to a conventional sloped floor in a dairy barn equipped with drains at the bottom of the slope and that the purpose of the storage tank—to accumulate a large volume of water capable of being released in a cascade or surge—was equally conventional. It concluded, however, that the element lacking in the prior art was any evidence of an arrangement of the old elements to effect the abrupt release of a flow of water to wash animal wastes from the floor of a dairy barn. Therefore, "Although Ag Pro's flush system does not embrace a complicated technical improvement, it does achieve a synergistic result through a novel combination."

We cannot agree that the combination of these old elements to produce an abrupt release of water directly on the barn floor from storage tanks or pools can properly be characterized as synergistic, that is "result[ing] in an effect greater than the sum of the several effects taken separately." Rather this patent simply arranges old elements with each performing the same function it had been known to perform although perhaps producing a more striking result than in previous combinations. Such combinations are not patentable under standards appropriate for a combination patent.

Interference with Contract or Economic Expectations

Interference with Contract. In the landmark case *Lumley v. Gye* (1853) a court first ruled that an outsider, who maliciously induced one of the two parties to a contract not to perform the contract, would be liable for damages in tort to the other contracting party who was thereby deprived of the benefits of the contract. The doctrine was later extended to protect all types of business contracts from intentional interferences which were without legal justification. Although the cases are not in complete agreement they seem to make a distinction between those situations where the defendant actively *induced* the breach, and those where the defendant's conduct simply *caused* the breach.

Even where a person induces the breach his conduct might be privileged or justifiable on some ground. For example, it was held that a mother who induced a school to exclude a diseased child from her child's private school was not liable to the parents of the diseased child for having induced the school to breach its contract. Business competition only affords a limited justification for interference with contracts. As Prosser states:

> The courts have held that the sanctity of the existing contract relation takes precedence over any interest in unrestricted competition, and have enforced as law the ethical precept that one competitor must keep his hands off of the contracts of another. This is true of contracts of employment, where workmen are hired away from an employer, as well as competitive business dealings in general; and it has found particular application in cases of offers of better terms to induce the breach of a contract, and of the violation of exclusive agency agreements and the purchase of goods in derogation of a contract limiting their resale.[2]

Interference with Economic Expectations. The early cases of interference with economic expectations usually involved situations where physical violence was employed to drive off customers or workers. Liability was later extended to cover nonviolent malicious interference and then to unjustifiable intentional interference. Where the intent to interfere is present the liability depends upon the motive and purposes of the defendant and upon the means that he utilizes.

SUMMARY

The unjustifiable interference with the contractual relations of others creates tort liability. The cases consider the motive or purpose of the party inducing the breach and make a distinction between actively inducing breach and simply causing breach. Reasonable economic expectations are also protected but the boundaries of this law are ill-defined.

---

[2] William L. Prosser, *Handbook of the Law of Torts*, 4th ed. (St. Paul, Minn.: West Publishing Co., 1971), p. 945.

Carolina Overall Corp. v. East Carolina Linen Supply, Inc.

174 S.E.2d 659 (Ct. App. N.C. 1970)

Carolina Overall Corp. (plaintiff) brought an action against East Carolina Linen Supply, Inc. (defendant) alleging that the latter had wrongfully interfered with one of the plaintiff's employment contracts and with plaintiff's relations with customers. Overall appealed from a judgment for East Carolina. Reversed.

Overall and East Carolina were competitors in the industrial laundry business and East Carolina induced Lowe to breach an employment contract as a route salesman with Overall and to enter the employment of East Carolina. East Carolina, acting through Lowe and other agents, also solicited the business of fourteen of Overall's customers and induced them to breach their contracts with Overall for laundry service.

GRAHAM, JUDGE. It is well established in this jurisdiction that an action lies against one who, without legal justification, knowingly and intentionally causes or induces one party to a contract to breach that contract and cause damage to the other contracting party.

The elements necessary to establish a cause of action for tortious interference with a contract are summarized in *Childress v. Abeles.* . . . The plaintiff must show: (1) that a contract existed between him and a third person which conferred upon plaintiff some contractual right against the third person; (2) that defendant had knowledge of plaintiff's contract with such third person; (3) that defendant intentionally induced the third person not to perform his contract with plaintiff; (4) that in so doing the defendant acted without justification; and (5) that defendant's acts caused plaintiff actual damages.

East Carolina concedes the general principles but argues that competition is legal justification for interference by a party with a contract between his competitor and a third person.

The following general rule is set forth in the Restatement of the Law of Torts, § 768:

> (1) One is privileged purposely to cause a third person not to enter into or continue a business relation with a competitor of the actor if
> (a) the relation concerns a matter involved in the competition between the actor and the competitor, and
> (b) the actor does not employ improper means, and
> (c) the actor does not intend thereby to create or continue an illegal restraint of competition, and
> (d) the actor's purpose is at least in part to advance his interest in his competition with the other.
>
> (2) *The fact that one is a competitor of another for the business of a third person does not create a privilege to cause the third person to commit a breach of contract with the other even under the conditions stated in Subsection* (*1*). [Emphasis added.]

The theory of the doctrine which permits recovery for the tortious interference with a contract is that the right to the performance of a contract and to reap the profits therefrom are property rights which entitle each party to protection and to seek compensation by action in court for an injury to such contract. We see no valid reason for holding that a competitor is privileged to interfere wrongfully with contractual rights. If contracts otherwise binding are not secure from wrongful interference by competitors, they offer little certainty in business relations, and it is security from competition that often gives them value. It is true that a party to a contract which is breached by another has a cause of action for breach of contract. This, however, affords little remedy where the party breaching the contract is insolvent; or where, as alleged here, numerous contracts involving nominal amounts of money are breached as a result of wrongful inducement by a competitor.

In our opinion the complaint states a cause of action for compensatory damages for tortious interference with plaintiff's contracts.

Problem Cases

1. The CES Publishing Corporation began publishing the magazine, *Consumer Electronics Monthly*, in 1972. In 1974, St. Regis Publications began publishing *Consumer Electronics Product News.* CES sues for damages, alleging trademark infringement. Can CES recover?
2. Cook, Inc., processes meat products and seeks to have the notation "Homestead" registered as a trademark under the Lanham Act. Cook's meat products are not subject to the Federal Meat Inspection Act, thus effectively confining its operations to the State of Ohio. However, products are sold to customers from states other than Ohio. The application was denied because the goods were not "in commerce" within the meaning of the Lanham Act. Was this correct?
3. Truck Equipment was engaged in the manufacture of twin hopper bottomed grain semitrailers. The physical appearance of the trailers incorporated two nonfunctional design features that gave it an appearance different than all other grain semitrailers being manufactured. Fruehauf copied the Truck Equipment trailer's design upon its entry into the market, including the nonfunctional features of the design. Truck Equipment sued for trademark infringement under the Lanham Act. Can Truck Equipment prevail?
4. Dudenhoffer, in 1966, sold Crystal, Inc., to Uniservices, Inc., but remained employed as a director and president of Crystal, Inc. Uniservices, for good cause, terminated Dudenhoffer's employment with Crystal, Inc., in 1972 and asked the court to declare that Dudenhoffer could not compete with Crystal, Inc., or utilize or disclose customer lists after the termination. Dudenhoffer argued that the customer lists could be obtained by competitors and were not protectable as trade secrets. Is Dudenhoffer correct?
5. Smith, doing business as Ta'Ron, Inc., advertised a fragrance called "Second Chance" as a duplicate of "Chanel No. 5," at a fraction of the latter's price.

   The advertisement suggested that a "Blindfold Test" be used "on skeptical prospects," challenging them to detect any difference between a well known fragrance and the Ta'Ron "duplicate." One suggested challenge was, "We dare you to try to detect any difference between Chanel #5 ($25.00) and Ta'Ron's 2nd Chance. $7.00."

   In an order blank printed as part of the advertisement each Ta'Ron fragrance was listed with the name of the well known fragrance which it purportedly duplicated immediately beneath. Below "Second Chance" appeared "*(Chanel #5)." The asterisk referred to a statement at the bottom of the form reading "Registered Trade Name of Original Fragrance House." Chanel, Inc., sued claiming damages for trademark infringement and unfair competition. Can Chanel prevail?

6. Fame Publishing Company brought an action for copyright infringement against Alabama Custom Tape, Inc. for selling and distributing "bootleg" tapes. Alabama's policy was to obtain a copy of a "hit" record, duplicate it onto tape thousands or millions of times, and then sell the duplicate to the public for significantly less money than the "original" record published by the record company cost. The applicable federal statute provides that after the first mechanical recording of the statute, others may make "similar use" of the composition upon payment of a token royalty to the record company. Fame argues that "similar use" does not include "pirating" of the record but is merely directed to other artists who wish to perform a certain musical number. Is Alabama guilty of the copyright violation?
7. In prior litigation it was established that the Laitram Corporation held superior patents to Deepsouth Packing Company on machines that would devein shrimp. The court also ruled that Deepsouth could not export its machines unless they were fully assembled. The applicable statute does not prohibit the production or use of a patent product outside the United States. Deepsouth begins to export component parts and Laitram sues for an injunction. Deepsouth contends the patent law protections must be strictly construed. Does Laitram's patent rights extend to the production of component parts?
8. Pavement Salvage Company developed and patented a machine that would help to reduce an aggravating and recurring problem involved in asphalt paving. The machine was a combination of four known processes and its real value came from its convenience in use. Commercially, it was very successful. Anderson's Inc., contests the patent given for the machine. Anderson argues that the machine lacks the necessary element of "invention." Is Pavement's patent valid?
9. Herman Parker, a rhythm and blues singer known as "Little Junior," signed a contract with Sun Record Company giving Sun exclusive recording rights over Parker for two years. During the period of the contract, Parker also agreed to record for Robey. When confronted with the existence of the Sun contract, Robey continued to record Parker's music. Sun brought an action against Robey for wrongful interference with its contractual relationship with Parker. Is Robey liable?
10. Five individuals decided to form a new corporation. It was agreed prior to incorporation that Wilson would be president for a minimum period of five years, while the others would fill the remaining offices. Each individual would be a director of the new corporation and would be required to purchase a certain amount of stock. The agreement was ratified and Wilson became president. At the first meeting of the Board of Directors a by-law was adopted which provided that officers should hold office for one year only, subject to renewal. Wilson signed a contract of employment for one year. During the year, Wilson had a serious drinking problem and had voluntarily committed himself to an institution for alcoholics for 21 days. The Board of Directors refused to renew Wilson's employment contract, even though Wilson had not taken a drink for six to eight months. Wilson sues the directors in tort, alleging wrongful interference with the contractual relationship between himself and the corporation. Are the directors liable to Wilson?

50

The Sherman Act

Introduction

Legal History. In the 1800s, several English steamship companies combined for the purpose of controlling competition in the shipping business. They jointly reduced rates below cost in certain ports, gave rebates to shippers dealing exclusively with their association, and refused to haul for any shipper who dealt anywhere with a competing shipping company. Several competing carriers brought a tort action claiming that the defendants had intentionally caused the plaintiffs great harm without any legal justification.

The English court's ruling in favor of the defendants illustrates how few legal constraints there were on monopolistic business practices at common law. The court ruled that the defendants were only pursuing a "war of competition waged in the interest of their own trade;" and the competitive interest justified the harm inflicted.[1]

With the growth of national markets following the Civil War large industrial combines and trusts engaged in monopolistic practices that soon led to a public outcry for regulation. In 1890, Congress enacted the Sherman Act [26 Stat. 209 (1890) as amended, 15 U.S.C. §§ 1–7] thereby adopting a public policy calling for the preservation and promotion of free competition within the American economy. Although a number of important exceptions or exemptions have been made, and although additional antitrust laws have been added, this basic competitive policy has been maintained since 1890. The Supreme Court summarized the basis for this belief in competition when it said:

> Basic to the faith that a free economy best promotes the public weal is that goods must stand the cold test of competition; that the public, acting through the market's impersonal

[1] *Mogul Steamship Co. Ltd. v. McGregor Gow & Co.,* (1889) 23 Q.B.D. 598, Aff'd. (1892) A.C. 25.

judgment, shall allocate the nation's resources and thus direct the course its economic development will take.[2]

Jurisdiction. The Sherman Act applies only to restraints which have a significant impact upon commerce, either domestic or foreign. Local activities are subject to the act if the anticompetitive effect on commerce is present. For example, restraints affecting the local distribution of goods originating in another state may be subject to the act even where the local retailer purchased the goods from a local wholesaler. Purely local restraints on competition are subject to state antitrust laws; but state regulation of anticompetitive practices has been highly sporadic and largely ineffective.

Over the years, a large number of exceptions or exemptions to the Sherman Act and other antitrust laws have been created by legislation or by court decisions. These exceptions and exemptions are discussed in Chapter 52.

Extra-Territorial Reach of the Sherman Act. The Act prohibits activities of American Nationals abroad where there are such substantial anticompetitive effect on this country's foreign commerce as to constitute unreasonable restraints.[3] Thus when the defendants attempted to monopolize the vanadium market in Canada by having a subsidiary initiate political action which foreclosed the plaintiff from Canadian markets, the Sherman Act was held to apply.[4] Foreign Nationals become subject to our antitrust laws upon proof that they have engaged in "continuous" domestic (local) commercial activities.[5]

SUMMARY

The Sherman Act attempts to promote and protect free competition as the prime regulating mechanism in our economy. The Sherman Act applies only to retraints which have a significant impact on commerce. Purely local restraints are subject to state regulation. The Sherman Act applies to the international activities of American companies where such activities substantially restrain either American, domestic, or foreign commerce.

Hospital Building Co. v. Trustees of the Rex Hospital

425 U.S. 738 (U.S. Sup. Ct. 1976)

Hospital Building Company (plaintiff) brought suit alleging that Trustees of Rex Hospital and others (defendants) conspired to monopolize hospital

---

[2] Times, *Picayune Co. v. U.S.*, 345 U.S. 594, 605 (1953).

[3] 1955 Atty. Gen. Rep. 66–71, 76.

[4] *Continental Ore Co. v. Union Carbide & Carbon Corp.*, 370 U.S. 690 (1962).

[5] *Antitrust Developments, 1955–1968* (ABA, 1968), p. 44.

services in the Raleigh, N.C., area. The district court dismissed the complaint on the basis that the hospital was a purely local activity and therefore only insubstantially affected interstate commerce. Reversed.

MR. JUSTICE MARSHALL. The complaint, fairly read, alleges that if the Trustees and their co-conspirators were to succeed in blocking Hospital Co.'s planned expansion, its purchases of out-of-state medicines and supplies as well as its revenues from out-of-state insurance companies would be thousands and perhaps hundreds of thousands of dollars less than they would otherwise be. Similarly, the management fees that Hospital Co. pays to its out-of-state parent corporation would be less if the expansion were blocked. Moreover, the multimillion dollar financing for the expansion, a large portion of which would be from out of State, would simply not take place if the Trustees succeeded in their alleged scheme. This combination of factors is certainly sufficient to establish a "substantial effect" on interstate commerce under the Act.

The Court of Appeals found two considerations crucial in its refusal to find that the complaint alleged a substantial effect on interstate commerce. The Court's reliance on neither was warranted. First, the Court observed, "The effect [on interstate commerce] here seems to us the indirect and fortuitous consequence of the restraint of the intrastate Raleigh area hospital market, rather than the result of activity purposely directed toward interstate commerce." But the fact that an effect on interstate commerce might be termed "indirect" because the conduct producing it is not "purposely directed" toward interstate commerce does not lead to a conclusion that the conduct at issue is outside the scope of the Sherman Act. For instance, in *Burke v. Ford* (1967), Oklahoma liquor retailers brought a Sherman Act action against liquor wholesalers in the State, alleging that the wholesalers had restrained commerce by dividing up the state market into exclusive territories. While the market division was patently not "purposely directed" toward interstate commerce we held that it nevertheless substantially affected interstate commerce because as a matter of practical economics that division could be expected to reduce significantly the magnitude of purchases made by the wholesalers from out-of-state distillers. "The wholesalers' territorial division . . . almost surely resulted in fewer sales to retailers—hence fewer purchases from out-of-state distillers—than would have occurred had free competition prevailed among the wholesalers."

The Court of Appeals further justified its holding of "no substantial effect" by arguing that "no source of supply or insurance company or lending institution can be expected to go under if Mary Elizabeth doesn't expand, and no market price likely will be affected." While this may be true, it is not of great relevance to the issue of whether the "substantial effect" test is satisfied. An effect can be "substantial" under the Sherman Act even if its impact on interstate commerce falls far short of causing enterprises to fold or affecting market price.

Sanctions and Remedies

Criminal and Civil Proceedings. Persons found guilty of violating either Section 1 or 2 of the Sherman Act are subject to criminal prosecution for a felony and, upon conviction, to a fine not exceeding $1 million in the case of a corporation, or $100,000 for any other person, or imprisonment for three years, or both a fine and imprisonment.[6] The Department of Justice also may institute civil proceedings to restrain conduct in violation of the act and ask the court for various remedies including decrees of divorcement, divestiture or, in extreme cases, dissolution.[7]

Any person injured as a result of violations of the act may bring a suit for treble damages against the violators and also recover reasonable attorney's fees. Once private treble-damage claimants have proven violation of the antitrust laws by the defendants, they then must prove that the violation was the proximate cause of injuries to their businesses and properties in terms of dollars and cents. In regard to proof of damages it was stated in the *Coors* case:

> The general rules relating to antitrust damages are easy to state, but difficult to apply. It is said that, once a plaintiff in a private antitrust action has proved that the defendant violated the law and that this violation caused him injury in fact, the plaintiff is held to a less rigid standard of proof with respect to the actual dollar amount of his damages because "economic harm is tangible and analysis of it is complex. [A] wrongdoer should bear the risk of uncertainty that inheres in measuring the harm he causes."[8]

The classic antitrust conviction against General Electric Co. and other electrical equipment manufacturers resulted in the payment of over $200 million in treble damages claims. Criminal fines are not deductible against federal income taxes, but treble damage claims paid may be deducted as business expenses.

A sizable number of the cases brought by the Department of Justice are settled out of court either by consent decrees in civil suits, or pleas of *nolo contendere* in criminal prosecutions.[9] The court decrees are tailored to meet

---

[6] § .782 (PL93–528) Antitrust Procedures and Penalties Act (1974).

[7] Divorcement means that the company is separated from some operating function. For example, the meat-packers were divorced from owning or controlling retail outlets. A company may be ordered to divest itself of assets or stock. Du Pont was ordered to divest itself of GM stock. Dissolution means that a company must liquidate its assets and go out of business.

[8] *Copper Liquor, Inc. v. Adolph Coors Co.,* 506 F.2d 934, 958 (5th Cir. 1975).

[9] Under the Antitrust Procedures and Penalties Act, any consent judgment proposed by the government must be filed with the appropriate district court and published at least 60 days in advance. During the 60-day period, summaries of the proposed decree and the impact it would be expected to have must be published in various general circulation newspapers seven times in a two-week period. More important, the law provides that defendants would have to make public within ten days of the filing of the decree a description of all the communications they have had with any government employees relating to the proposed judgment.

the competitive ills in each situation. On occasion, the defendants may be ordered to license patents on a royalty free basis, file continuing reports showing compliance, or even give aid in the creation of a new competitive firm in the industry.

If a company is adjudged to have violated the Sherman Act in either civil or criminal proceedings, this judgment may be used as *prima facie* proof of violation by claimants later filing private treble damage suits. Such claimants would still be required to prove the extent of their damage and show that these damages were caused by the conduct adjudged to be in violation of the act. In addition, the trial record with a few exceptions such as confidential trade dates, is available to claimant. The fact that the company charged took a consent decree or filed a plea of *nolo contendere* cannot be used as evidence of violation of the Act in subsequent treble damage suits.

Standing under Antitrust. In order to be able to maintain a private suit for damages or for other remedies under antitrust the person suing must have standing. The test of standing is determined by the directness of injury suffered by the plaintiff. The plaintiff must prove (1) there is a causal connection between an antitrust violation and an injury sufficient to establish the violation as a substantial factor in the occurrence of damage; and (2) that the illegal act is linked to activities of the plaintiff intended to be protected by the antitrust laws.

It has been held that the injury to the particular plaintiffs was too indirect or remote to confer standing in the following cases: a franchisor complaining of an antitrust combination directed at a franchisee; a nonoperating landlord of theaters leased by distributors and exhibitors of films complaining that the lessees were conspiring to limit competition among themselves; a patent owner suing for damages due to restraints directed at his licensees; and stockholders suing for injury directed at their corporation.[10]

In a recent case it was held that indirect ultimate purchasers have no standing under the antitrust laws to sue manufacturers engaged in price fixing. The State of Illinois and various governmental entities contracted with building contractors for the erection of public buildings. It was later discovered that the building contractors had purchased the concrete blocks used from block suppliers that allegedly had engaged in a price-fixing scheme.[11] It appears likely that this decision may be overturned by legislation.

Expansion of Antitrust Enforcement. Congress apparently intends to place more emphasis on antitrust enforcement in the future. The budgets for the antitrust enforcement agencies have been substantially increased and new laws

---

[10] *Appraiser Service Co. v. Association of C.&S. Co.,* 382 F.2d 925 (1967). *Calderone Enter. Corp. v. United Theatre Circuit,* 454 F.2d 1292 (1971); *Productive Inventions v. Trico Products,* 224 F.2d 678 (1955); and *Campo v. National Foodball League,* 334 F. Supp. 1181 (1971).

[11] *Illinois Brick Co. v. Illinois,* 429 U.S. 1087 (1977).

have been enacted to broaden the scope of application and to improve the effectiveness of existing laws.

Under the Antitrust Improvement Act (1976) corporations with assets or sales exceeding $100 million are required to give advanced notice to the Department of Justice and Federal Trade Commission of any acquisition where the assets or sales of the acquired corporation are $10 million or more. In addition, state attorneys general are authorized to file *parens patriae* suits to recover treble damages for the citizens (natural persons) of their states which have been injured by violations of the Sherman Act. In the event the Sherman Act violations involve price fixing the damages may be assessed in the aggregate by statistical or sampling methods. Damages may be distributed to citizens or may be deemed a penalty and deposited with the State as general revenue.

In addition, the investigative powers of the Department of Justice are broadened enabling the department to issue a pre-complaint subpoena, Civil Investigative Demand (CID), not only on the targets of the investigation but also to third parties (suppliers and customers who have information relevant to the investigation). The collection of both oral and documentary evidence is authorized.

SUMMARY

The Sherman Act provides for both civil and criminal proceedings. Treble damage suits may be brought by private parties suffering losses as a result of conduct prohibited under the act. A very large percentage of all cases brought by the government are settled by consent degrees or pleas of *nolo contendere.*

In order to bring a private suit under the antitrust laws the plaintiff must have "standing." The plaintiff must prove that the alleged illegal acts of the defendant(s) were a substantial factor in the occurrence of damage suffered by the plaintiff and the illegal act is linked to activities of the plaintiff intended to be protected by the antitrust laws. Several new laws have been enacted to strengthen and broaden the application of the antitrust laws.

Section 1

Joint Restraints. Section 1 of the Sherman Act provides:

> Every contract, combination in the form of trust or otherwise, or conspiracy, in restraint of trade or commerce among the several states, or with foreign nations is declared to be illegal.

The "contract" is the agreement to restrain competition. A "combination" occurs when two or more persons join together for the purpose of carrying out united action. A "conspiracy" is a continuing partnership in restraint of trade. At least two persons are required under all of these forms of joint activity. The departments or divisions of a company are viewed as being parts of one company and intracompany conduct not directed against a competitor does not violate Section 1. A principal corporation, however, may be found in violation of Section 1 where it conspires with a subsidiary. As will be discussed later, a single company acting alone may violate Section 2 of the Sherman Act.

Per Se Restraints under Section 1

The Nature of Per Se Restraints. Justice Black, speaking for the Court in *Northern Pacific Railway Company v. United States,* discussed the doctrine of a per se Sherman Act violation in the following manner:

> The Sherman Act was designed to be a comprehensive charter of economic liberty aimed at preserving free and unfettered competition as the rule of trade. It rests on the premise that the unrestrained interaction of competitive forces will yield the best allocation of our economic resources, the lowest prices, the highest quality and the greatest material progress, while at the same time providing an environment conducive to the preservation of our democratic political and social institutions. But even were that premise open to question, the policy unequivocally laid down by the Act is competition. And to this end it prohibits "Every contract, combination . . . or conspiracy, in restraint of trade or commerce among the several States." Although this prohibition is literally all-encompassing, the courts have construed it as precluding only those contracts or combinations which "unreasonably" restrain competition.
>
> However, there are certain agreements or practices which because of their pernicious effect on competition and lack of any redeeming virtue are conclusively presumed to be unreasonable and therefore illegal without elaborate inquiry as to the precise harm they have caused or the business excuse for their use. This principle of *per se* unreasonableness not only makes the type of restraints which are proscribed by the Sherman Act more certain to the benefit of everyone concerned, but it also avoids the necessity for an incredibly complicated and prolonged economic investigation into the entire history of the industry involved, as well as related industries, in an effort to determine at large whether a particular restraint has been unreasonable—an inquiry so often wholly fruitless when undertaken. . . .

Some of the most important *per se* restraints include contracts, combinations, or conspiracies to control production, fix or manipulate prices, divide markets or customers, or impose group boycotts.

Restraints on Production. Under competitive theory, the public is supposed to receive the benefit of an optimum production of goods and services at the lowest possible prices. Joint arrangements among competitors which seek to manipulate production for anticompetitive purposes are per se violations.

Restraints on Pricing. A majority of the antitrust cases brought by the government under Section 1 involve charges of price fixing. As a general rule, any joint activities fixing or attempting to control prices either horizontally (between competitors) or vertically (between suppliers and distributors) are illegal per se. This prohibition applies regardless of the motive of those fixing, stabilizing, or manipulating prices and applies to setting maximum prices to protect consumers as well as setting minimum prices to protect small firms in a distress industry.

The antitrust agencies often use circumstantial evidence to establish the existence of illegal pricing arrangements. Nor need there be proof of an outright agreement. As the Supreme Court stated in one case:

> It is elementary that an unlawful conspiracy may be and often is formed without simultaneous action or agreement on the part of the conspirators. . . . Acceptance by competitors without previous agreement, of an invitation to participate in a plan, the necessary consequence of which, if carried out, is restraint of interstate commerce, is sufficient to establish an unlawful conspiracy under the Sherman Act. . . .[12]

On the other hand, the mere fact that competitors may charge the same prices does not of itself prove a violation. In another case, the Supreme Court stated:

> . . . But this Court has never held that proof of parallel business behavior conclusively establishes agreement or, phrased differently, that such behavior itself constitutes a Sherman Act offense. Circumstantial evidence of consciously parallel behavior may have made heavy inroads into the traditional judicial attitude toward conspiracy; but "conscious parallelism" has not yet read conspiracy out of the Sherman Act entirely.[13]

A manufacturer acting unilaterally, is not prohibited from selling to a dealer and *suggesting* a resale price. Such a manufacturer may, subject to supply contract obligations, discontinue selling to any dealer who refuses to abide by the suggested prices. However, if the manufacturer tries to obtain a price maintenance agreement from any dealer or in any way collaborates with other dealers in seeing that the suggested prices are maintained, Section 1 is violated.

Division of Markets or Customers. In one of the earliest antitrust cases, several pipe manufacturers were held guilty of per se violations when they apportioned out their market geographically among themselves.[14] It is likewise illegal per se for competitors to allocate customers and agree not to solicit each other's customers.

Until the 1977 *Sylvania* decision, which follows, a manufacturer or supplier

---

[12] *Interstate Circuit Inc. v. U.S.,* 306 U.S. 208, 227 (1939). In dictum in *FTC v. Cement Institute,* 333 U.S. 683, 716 n. 17 (1948), the Supreme Court said: "It is enough to warrant a finding of a 'combination' within the meaning of the Sherman Act, if there is evidence that persons, with knowledge that concerted action was contemplated and invited, give adherence to and then participate in a scheme."

[13] *Theatre Enterprises Inc. v. Paramount Film Distributing Corp.,* 346 U.S. 537, 540 (1954).

[14] *U.S. v. Addyston Pipe & Steel Co.,* 85 F.271 (6th Cir. 1898), Aff'd. 175 U.S. 211 (1899).

could not legally impose vertical market area or customer restriction agreements on his distributors who were buying goods for resale. The legality of such vertical restrictions is now uncertain; but it appears that at least some types of vertical restraints no longer fall into the per se category.

Group Boycotts. Joint activities by competitors designed to foreclose any competitor's access to a market or to a source of supply are illegal per se. This was held to be true even where dress manufacturers combined to prevent retail stores throughout the nation from dealing with design "pirate" manufacturers who were copying the dress patterns of the "legitimate" dress manufacturers.[15]

Reciprocal Dealing Arrangements. Large firms typically buy large quantities of goods from suppliers. In many cases, these supplying companies have need of goods of the type manufactured by companies which they supply. Under these circumstances, a large firm may find it very advantageous to use its buying power as a means of "encouraging" its suppliers to purchase all or most of their requirements from the large firm. This use of purchasing power to promote sales is called "reciprocity" and may involve serious antitrust consequences.

The case law on reciprocity is very limited. In the 1930s, the FTC found that the coercive use of reciprocity was an unfair method of competition which violated Section 5 of the Federal Trade Commission Act. Reciprocity and even the possibility of reciprocity were important considerations in recent cases brought under the merger prohibitions of the Clayton Act (Section 7).[16]

In *United States v. General Dynamics*[17] the court indicated that either coercive or mutual patronage reciprocity agreements could constitute per se violations of Section 1 of the Sherman Act. The court stated:

> the actual or potential implementation of coercive reciprocity, which presupposes the existence of leverage (i.e., large purchases from, and currently small sales to, the prospect), is inimical to a competitive economic society. "Mutual patronage" reciprocity, on the other hand, occurs when both parties stand on equal footing with reference to purchasing power inter se, yet agree to purchase from one another. While the former practice certainly is the more offensive the latter arrangements are equally disruptive of the competitive processes.[18]

Other Per Se Restraints. Other per se restraints include joint action by competitors to pool profits and losses, refrain from advertising prices, and to refrain from bidding against each other at auctions. Marketing arrangements otherwise legal (i.e., agency distribution or reciprocal dealing) may become

---

[15] *Fashion Originator's Guild v. FTC,* 312 U.S. 457 (1941).

[16] *FTC v. Consolidated Foods,* 380 U.S. 592 (1965).

[17] 258 F. Supp. 36 (S.D.N.Y. 1966).

[18] *Id.* at 59.

illegal per se if a dominant firm exercises coercive control over other firms in creating or operating such arrangements. Also illegal per se are virtually all tying contracts or any activities attempting to extend the antitrust immunities granted in any exceptions or exemptions to the Act beyond the strict limitations afforded for such exceptions or exemptions. The exemptions to the antitrust laws are discussed in Chapter 53.

SUMMARY

Section 1 of the act prohibits joint conduct in restraint of competition. Major per se restraints include agreements to: control production; fix or stabilize prices; divide markets or allocate customers; boycott other competitors; and most tying contracts. Where per se restraints are involved no defenses or justifications for the conduct will be permitted.

Esco Corp. v. United States

340 F.2d 1000 (9th Cir. 1965)

Esco and three other distributors of stainless steel pipe were prosecuted for a criminal conspiracy to fix prices under Section 1 of the Sherman Act. The three other defendants filed pleas of *nolo contendere* and only Esco chose to stand trial. Esco appealed from a jury verdict finding Esco guilty. Affirmed.

BARNES, CIRCUIT JUDGE. While particularly true of price-fixing conspiracies, it is well recognized law that any conspiracy can ordinarily only be proved by inferences drawn from relevant and competent circumstantial evidence, including the conduct of the defendants charged. A knowing wink can mean more than words. Let us suppose five competitors meet on several occasions, discuss their problems, and one finally states—"I won't fix prices with any of you, but here is what I am going to do—put the price of my gidget at X dollars; now you all do what you want." He then leaves the meeting. Competitor number two says—"I don't care whether number one does what he says he's going to do or not; nor do I care what the rest of you do, but I am going to price my gidget at X dollars." Number three makes a similar statement—"My price is X dollars." Number four says not one word. All leave and fix "their" prices at "X" dollars.

We do not say the foregoing illustration *compels* an inference in this case that the competitors' conduct constituted a price-fixing conspiracy, *including an agreement to so conspire,* but neither can we say, as a matter of law, that an inference of no agreement is compelled. As in so many other instances, it remains a question for the trier of fact to consider and determine what inference appeals to it (the jury) as most logical and persuasive, after it has heard all the evidence as to what these competitors had done before such meeting, and what actions they took thereafter, or what actions they did not take.

An accidental or incidental price uniformity, or even "pure" conscious parallelism of prices is, standing alone, not unlawful. Nor is an individual competitor's sole decision to follow a price leadership, standing alone, a violation of law. But we do not find that factual situation here.

Esco then adds a definition to "mutual consent," *i.e.,* "an exchange of assurances to take or refrain from a given course of conduct." With this we disagree, if by it Esco means the existence of specific assurances. Written assurances it concedes, are unnecessary. So are oral assurances, if a course of conduct, or a price schedule, once suggested or outlined by a competitor in the presence of other competitors, is followed by all—generally and customarily—and continuously for all practical purposes, even though there be slight variations.

It is not necessary to find an express agreement, either oral or written, in order to find a conspiracy, but it is sufficient that a concert of action be contemplated and that defendants conform to the arrangement. Mutual consent need not be bottomed on express agreement, for any conformance to an agreed or contemplated pattern of conduct will warrant an inference of conspiracy. Thus not only action, but even a lack of action, may be enough from which to infer a combination or conspiracy.

Applying these rules to the facts at hand, the jury came to an opposite conclusion from that which Esco urges, and the fact that Esco's involvement was in but two of ten allegedly conspirational situations does not absolve Esco from participation in the entire conspiracy if its involvement in the two was unlawful and knowingly and purposely performed.

United States v. General Motors Corp.

384 U.S. 127 (U.S. Sup. Ct. 1966)

Civil action by the United States (plaintiff) against General Motors Corp. and others (defendants) for violation of Section 1 of the Sherman Act. The United States appealed from an adverse decision below. Reversed.

In the late 1950s discount houses began offering to sell new cars to the public at "bargain" prices. By 1960, a number of Chevrolet dealers were working with discount houses. In some instances the discount houses would act simply as a referral service and would direct their customers to certain dealers where "bargains" might be obtained. In other cases, the new cars were actually sold by and through the discount houses to customers.

In most cases, the dealers dealing with and through the discounters did not deal with discounters in their own primary market areas. The cars were discounted into other dealer markets where local customers expected those dealers to perform warranty and repair services. The local dealers, losing the profitable sales and gaining the service headaches, joined forces and acting through their trade association sent hundreds of letters and wires to Detroit—with telling effect. Within a week Chevrolet's zone manager, O'Connor, was directed to furnish his superiors in Detroit with "a detailed report of the discount house operations as well as what action we in the zone are taking to curb such sales."

MR. JUSTICE FORTAS. We have here a classic conspiracy in restraint of trade: joint, collaborative action by dealers, the defendant associations, and General Motors to eliminate a class of competitors by terminating business dealings between them and a minority of Chevrolet dealers and to deprive franchised dealers of their freedom to deal through discounters if they so choose.

These findings by the trial judge compel the conclusion that a conspiracy to restrain trade was proved. The error of the trial court lies in its failure to apply the correct and established standard for ascertaining the existence of a combination or conspiracy under §1 of the Sherman Act. The trial court attempted to justify its conclusion on the following reasoning: That each defendant and alleged co-conspirator acted to promote its own self-interest. . . .

It is of no consequence, for purposes of determining whether there has been a combination or conspiracy under §1 of the Sherman Act, that each party acted in its own lawful interest. . . . And although we regard as clearly erroneous and irreconcilable with its other findings the trial court's conclusory "finding" that there had been no "agreement" among the defendants and their alleged co-conspirators, it has long been settled that explicit agreement is not a necessary part of a Sherman Act conspiracy—certainly not where, as here, joint and collaborative action was pervasive in the initiation, execution, and fulfillment of the plan.

Neither individual dealers nor the associations acted independently or separately. The dealers collaborated, through the associations and otherwise, among themselves and with General Motors, both to enlist the aid of General Motors and to enforce dealers' promises to forsake the discounters. The associations explicitly entered into a joint venture to assist General Motors in policing the dealers' promises, and their joint proffer of aid was accepted and utilized by General Motors.

Nor did General Motors confine its activities to the contractual boundaries of its relationships with individual dealers. As the trial court found General Motors at no time announced that it would terminate the franchise of any dealer which furnished cars to the discounters. The evidence indicates that it had no intention of acting in this unilateral fashion. On the contrary, overriding corporate policy with respect to proper dealer relations dissuaded General Motors from engaging in this sort of wholly unilateral conduct, the validity of which under the antitrust laws was assumed, without being decided, in *Parke, Davis, supra.*

There can be no doubt that the effect of the combination or conspiracy here was to restrain trade and commerce within the meaning of the Sherman

Act. Elimination, by joint collaborative action, of discounters from access to the market is a *per se* violation of the Act.

The principle of these cases is that where businessmen concert their actions in order to deprive others of access to merchandise which the latter wish to sell to the public, we need not inquire into the economic motivation underlying their conduct.

We note, moreover, that inherent in the success of the combination in this case was a substantial restraint upon price competition—a goal unlawful *per se* when sought to be effected by combination or conspiracy.

Rule of Reason Restraints

Some Examples. Other types of activities are found to be illegal only if the purpose or effect of such activities, in light of all of the economic circumstances, is found to be unreasonably restrictive of competition. Activities of this type include: ancillary covenants not to compete found in employment contracts or in contracts for the purchase of a business; price, customer and marketing territory restrictions imposed by a manufacturer in bona fide consignee-agency selling arrangements; various grantback, pooling, marketing restrictions contained in patent licensing contracts; and exclusive dealing and requirement contract arrangements.

Simpson v. Union Oil Co. of California

377 U.S. 13 (U.S. Sup. Ct. 1964)

This was an action for treble damages under Section 1 of the Sherman Act brought by Simpson (plaintiff) against Union Oil (defendant). Judgment for Union Oil and Simpson appealed. Reversed.

Disturbed by price wars, Union Oil required lessees of its retail outlets (including Simpson) to sign product consignment agreements which were one year in duration. The station leases were also for one year. Under the consignment agreement Union retained the title to the gasoline delivered and controlled the retail prices charged. Simpson, however, had the burden of risks, except for acts of God, for gasoline in his possession. Simpson sold some of the gasoline below the price set by Union and Union refused to renew his lease and consignment agreement. Simpson sued claiming that the consignment arrangement was forced on him in violation of Section 1 of the Sherman Act.

MR. JUSTICE DOUGLAS. We are enlightened on present-day marketing methods by recent congressional investigations. In the automobile field the price is "the manufacturer's suggested retail price," not a price coercively exacted; nor do automobiles go on consignment; they are sold. Resale price maintenance of gasoline through the "consignment" device is increasing. The "consignment" device in the gasoline field is used for resale price maintenance.

Dealers, like Simpson, are independent businessmen; and they have all or most of the indicia of entrepreneurs, except for price fixing. The risk of loss of the gasoline is on them, apart from acts of God. Their return is affected by the rise and fall in the market price, their commissions declining as retail prices drop. Practically the only power they have to be wholly independent businessmen, whose service depends on their own initiative and enterprise, is taken from them by the proviso that they must sell their gasoline at prices fixed by Union Oil. By reason of the lease and "consignment" agreement dealers are coercively laced into an arrangement under which their supplier is able to impose noncompetitive prices on thousands of persons who otherwise might be competitive. The evil of this resale price maintenance program, like that of the requirements contracts held illegal by *Standard Oil Co. of California and Standard Stations v. United States,* is its inexorable potentiality for and even certainty in destroying competition in retail sales of gasoline by these nominal "consignees" who are in reality small struggling competitors seeking retail gas customers.

As we have said, an owner of an article may send it to a dealer who may in turn undertake to sell it only at a price determined by the owner. There is nothing illegal about that arrangement. When, however, a "consignment" device is used to cover a vast gasoline distribution system, fixing prices through many retail outlets, the antitrust laws prevent calling the "consignment" an agency, for then the end result of *United States v. Socony Vacuum Oil Co.* would be avoided merely by clever manipulation of words, not by differences in substance. The present, coercive "consignment" device, if successful against challenge under the anti-trust laws, furnishes a wooden formula for administering prices on a vast scale.

To allow Union Oil to achieve price fixing in this vast distribution system through this "consignment" device would be to make legality for antitrust purposes turn on clever draftsmanship. We refuse to let a matter so vital to a competitive system rest on such easy manipulation.

Hence on the issue of resale price maintenance under the Sherman Act there is nothing left to try, for there was an agreement for resale price maintenance, coercively employed.

Continental T.V., Inc. v. GTE Sylvania, Inc.

429 U.S. 1070 (U.S. Sup. Ct. 1977)

Treble damage suit by Continental T.V., Inc., against GTE Sylvania, Inc. Continental requested review of an adverse decision below. Affirmed.

In the early 1950s Sylvania's share of the national TV market had declined to about 1%. In attempts to remedy this situation, Sylvania phased out all wholesalers and limited the number of retail franchises it granted for a given area. Sylvania also required that each franchisee sell Sylvania products only from the sales location described in each franchise. This strategy apparently contributed to increasing sales by Sylvania, but led to friction with some dealers when Sylvania shuffled sales location areas and refused to grant requests for expansion of some sales areas. Continental, a Sylvania dealer, became unhappy when Sylvania franchised another dealer in part of Continental's market, and then refused a request by Continental for permission to expand into another market area. As the dispute developed, Sylvania first reduced Continental's credit line and then cancelled Continental's franchise. Continental sued and the District Court ruled that the sales location limitation clauses in the franchise were illegal *per se* under the *Schwinn* case. The Court of Appeals reversed saying the clause had to be judged under the "rule of reason."

MR. JUSTICE POWELL. In the present case, it is undisputed that title to the televisions passed from Sylvania to Continental. Thus, the *Schwinn per se* rule applies unless Sylvania's restriction on locations falls outside *Schwinn's* prohibition against a manufacturer attempting to restrict a "retailer's freedom as to where and to whom it will resell the products." As the Court of Appeals conceded, the language of *Schwinn* is clearly broad enough to apply to the present case. Unlike the Court of Appeals, however, we are unable to find a principled basis for distinguishing *Schwinn* from the case now before us.

Schwinn itself was an abrupt and largely unexplained departure from *White Motor Co. v. United States,* where only four years earlier the Court had refused to endorse a *per se* rule for vertical restrictions. Since its announcement, *Schwinn* has been the subject of continuing controversy and confusion, both in the scholarly journals and in the federal courts. The great weight of scholarly opinion has been critical of the decision, and a number of the federal courts confronted with analogous vertical restrictions have sought to limit its reach. In our view, the experience of the past ten years should be brought to bear on this subject of considerable commercial importance.

The market impact of vertical restrictions is complex because of their potential for a simultaneous reduction of intrabrand competition and stimulation of interbrand competition. Significantly, the Court in *Schwinn* did not distinguish among the challenged restrictions on the basis of their individual potential for intrabrand harm or interbrand benefit. Restrictions that completely eliminated intrabrand competition among Schwinn distributors were analyzed no differently than those that merely moderated intrabrand competition among retailers. The pivotal factor was the passage of title: All restrictions were held to be *per se* illegal where title had passed, and all were evaluated and sustained under the rule of reason where it had not. The location restriction at issue here would be subject to the same pattern of analysis under *Schwinn.*

It appears that this distinction between sale and nonsale transactions resulted from the Court's effort to accommodate the perceived intrabrand harm and interbrand benefit of vertical restrictions. The *per se* rule for sale transactions reflected the view that vertical restrictions are "so obviously destructive" of intrabrand competition that their use would "open the door to exclusivity of outlets and limitations of territory further than prudence permits." Conversely, the continued adherence to the traditional rule of reason for nonsale transactions reflected the view that the restrictions have too great a potential for the promotion of interbrand competition to justify complete prohibition. The Court's opinion provides no analytical support for these contrasting positions. Nor is there even an assertion in the opinion that the competitive impact of vertical restrictions is significantly affected by the form of the transaction. Nonsale transactions appear to be excluded from the *per se* rule, not because of a greater danger of intrabrand harm or a greater promise of interbrand benefit, but rather because of the Court's unexplained belief that a complete *per se* prohibition would be too "inflexible."

Vertical restrictions reduce intrabrand competition by limiting the number of sellers of a particular product competing for the business of a given group of buyers. Location restrictions have this effect because of practical constraints on the effective marketing area of retail outlets. Although intrabrand competition may be reduced, the ability of retailers to exploit the resulting market may be limited both by the ability of consumers to travel to other franchised locations and, perhaps more importantly, to purchase the competing products of other manufacturers. None of these key variables, however, is affected by the form of the transaction by which a manufacturer conveys his products to the retailers.

Vertical restrictions promote interbrand competition by allowing the manufacturer to achieve certain efficiencies in the distribution of his products. These "redeeming virtues" are implicit in every decision sustaining vertical restrictions under the rule of reason. Economists have identified a number of ways in which manufacturers can use such restrictions to compete more effectively against other manufacturers. For example, new manufacturers and manufacturers entering new markets can use the restrictions in order to induce competent and aggressive retailers to make the kind of investment of capital and labor that is often required in the distribution of products unknown to the consumer. Established manufacturers can use them to induce retailers to engage in promotional activities or to provide service and repair facilities necessary to the efficient marketing of their products. Service and repair are vital for many products, such as automobiles and major household appliances. The availability and quality of such services affect a manufacturer's good will and the competitiveness of his product. Because of market imperfections such as the so-called free rider effect, these services might not be provided by retailers in a purely competitive situation, despite the fact that each retailer's benefit would be greater if all provided services than if none did.

Economists also have argued that manufacturers have an economic interest in maintaining as much intrabrand competition as is consistent with the efficient distribution of their products. Although the view that the manufacturer's interest necessarily corresponds with that of the public is not universally shared, even the leading critic of vertical restrictions concedes that *Schwinn's* distinction between sale and nonsale transactions is essentially unrelated to any relevant economic impact. Comanor, Vertical Territoral and Customer Restrictions: White Motor and Its Aftermath, 81 *Harv. L. Rev.* 1419, 1422 (1968). Indeed, to the extent that the form of the transaction is related to interbrand benefits, the Court's distinction is inconsistent with its articulated concern for the ability of smaller firms from using the exception for nonsale transactions.

We conclude that the distinction drawn in *Schwinn* between sale and nonsale transactions is not sufficient to justify the application of a *per se* rule in one situation and a rule of reason in the other. The question remains whether the *per se* rule stated in *Schwinn* should be expanded to include nonsale transactions or abandoned in favor of a return to the rule of reason. We have found no persuasive support for expanding the rule. As noted above, the *Schwinn* Court recognized the undesirability of "prohibit[ing] all vertical restrictions of territory and all franchising. . . ." And even Continental does not urge us to hold that all such restrictions are *per se* illegal.

We revert to the standard articulated in *Northern Pac. R. Co.*, and reiterated in *White Motor,* for determining whether vertical restrictions must be "conclusively presumed to be unreasonable and therefore illegal without elaborate inquiry as to the precise harm they have caused or the business excuse for their use." Such restrictions, in varying forms, are widely used in our free market economy. As indicated above, there is substantial scholarly and judicial authority supporting their economic utility. There is relatively no showing in this case, either generally or with respect to Sylvania's agreements, that vertical restrictions have or are likely to have a "pernicious effect on competition" or that they "lack . . . any redeeming virtue." Accordingly, we conclude that the *per se* rule stated in *Schwinn* must be overruled. In so holding we do not foreclose the possibility that particular applications of vertical restrictions might justify *per se* prohibition under *Northern Pac. R. Co.* But we do make clear that departure from the rule of reason standard must be based upon demonstrable economic effect rather than—as in *Schwinn*—upon formalistic line drawing.

In sum, we conclude that the appropriate decision is to return to the rule of reason that governed vertical restrictions prior to *Schwinn.* When competitive effects are shown to result from particular vertical restrictions they can be adequately policed under the rule of reason, the standard traditionally applied for the majority of anticompetitive practices challenged under § 1 of the Act.

United States Steel Corp. v. Fortner Enterprises, Inc.,

429 U.S. 610 (U.S. Sup. Ct. 1977)

Private treble damage action brought by Fortner Enterprises, Inc. (plaintiff) against U.S. Steel Corporation (defendant). U.S. Steel appealed from an adverse decision. Reversed.

Fortner needed capital for both land acquisition and development. In exchange for Fortner's promise to purchase 210 prefabricated steel homes from U.S. Steel, U.S. Steel agreed to lend Fortner $2 million at 6 percent through its wholly owned Credit Corporation subsidiary. Difficulties arose after the development started, and Fortner sued alleging U.S. Steel was violating Sec. 1 of the Sherman Act by using the credit as a tying product in order to sell the houses, the tied product.

MR. JUSTICE STEVENS. . . . [T]he District Court concluded "that all of the required elements of an illegal tie-in agreement did exist since the tie-in itself was present, a not insubstantial amount of interstate commerce in the tied product was restrained and the Credit Corporation did possess sufficient economic power or leverage to effect such restraint."

Although the Credit Corporation is owned by one of the nation's largest manufacturing corporations, there is nothing in the record to indicate that this enabled it to borrow funds on terms more favorable than those available to competing lenders, or that it was able to operate more efficiently than other lending institutions. In short, the affiliation between the defendants does not appear to have given the Credit Corporation any cost advantage over its competitors in the credit market.

The same may be said about the fact that loans from the Credit Corporation were used to obtain house sales from Fortner and others. In some tying situations a disproportionately large volume of sales of the tied product resulting from only a few strategic sales of the tying product may reflect a form of economic "leverage" that is probative of power in the market for the tying product. But in this case Fortner was only required to purchase houses for the number of lots for which it received financing.

The most significant finding made by the District Court related to the unique character of the credit extended to Fortner. This finding is particularly important because the unique character of the tying product has provided critical support for the finding of illegality in prior cases. Thus, the statutory grant of a patent monopoly in *International Salt Co. v. United States,* the copyright monopolies in *United States v. Paramount Pictures, Inc.,* and the extensive land holdings in *Northern Pacific R. Co. v. United States,* represented tying products that the Court regarded as sufficiently unique to give rise to a presumption of economic power.

As the Court plainly stated in its prior opinion in this case, these decisions do not require that the defendant have a monopoly or even a dominant position throughout the market for a tying product. They do, however, focus attention on the question whether the seller has the power within the market for the tying product, to raise prices or to require purchasers to accept burdensome terms that could not be exacted in a completely competitive market. In short, the question is whether the seller has some advantage not shared by his competitors in the market for the tying product.

Quite clearly, if the evidence merely shows that credit terms are unique because the seller is willing to accept a lesser profit—or to incur greater risks—than its competitors, that kind of uniqueness will not give rise to any inference of economic power in the credit market. Yet this is, in substance, all that the record in this case indicates.

The unusual credit bargain offered to Fortner proves nothing more than a willingness to provide cheap financing in order to sell expensive houses. Without any evidence that the Credit Corporation had some cost advantage over its competitors—or could offer a form of financing that was significantly differentiated from that which other lenders could offer if they so elected—the unique character of its financing does not support the conclusion that defendants had the kind of economic power which Fortner had the burden of proving in order to prevail in this litigation.

Section 2

Statutory Wording. Section 2 provides:

> Every person who shall monopolize, or attempt to monopolize, or combine or conspire with any other person or persons to monopolize any part of the trade or commerce among the several states, or with foreign nations shall be deemed guilty of a misdemeanor. . . .

A single firm (or person) may monopolize or attempt to monopolize. Two or more firms are required in order to combine or conspire to monopolize.

Monopolizing. Monopolizing takes place where a firm acting singly, or a group of firms acting together, have the power to control prices or to exclude competitors from a market. This power to monopolize must be coupled with the intent to exercise it.

Illegal power to control prices or to exclude competitors is measured in relation to the relevant market. The relevant market is determined by defining the product line being monopolized and then by fixing the geographic market for the product line as defined. The product line is determined by including those products which are competitive substitutes for the defendant's products. The geographic scope of the market is measured in terms of the area where the products are customarily made available for purchases. A similar determination of the relevant market is made where services are monopolized rather than products. Economically related services are classed as a "cluster" or trade grouping, and then a geographic market is determined. The two cases that follow illustrate how the Supreme Court determined relevant markets so as to rationalize contrasting results.

The mere existence of monopoly power is not of itself illegal, for a firm may have achieved the power by lawful means such as through a patent or through sheer efficiency. However, the existence of monopolizing power acquired, maintained or used in ways from which an *intent* to exercise such power can be inferred creates the basis for a violation. The acts from which the intent may be inferred need not necessarily be illegal. As was stated in the *Alcoa* Case:

> Alcoa insists that it never excluded competitors; but we can think of no more effective exclusion than progressively to embrace each new opportunity as it opened, and to face each newcomer with new capacity already geared to a great organization, having the advantage of experience trade connections and an elite of personnel. Only in case we interpret "exclusion" as limited to maneuvers not honestly industrial, but actuated solely by a desire to prevent competition, can such a course, indefatigably pursued, be deemed not exclusionary. So to limit it would in our judgment emasculate the act.[19]

SUMMARY

Section 2 of the act relates to the crime of monopolizing and may involve one or more firms. Monopolizing entails the power to control prices or exclude competitors in relation to the relevant market. The intent to exercise this monopolizing power must also be proven. This intent must be inferred from conduct aimed at either creating or preserving the power.

United States v. E. I. Du Pont de Nemours & Co.

351 U.S. 377 (U.S. Sup. Ct. 1956).

Civil action by the United States (plaintiff) against E. I. Du Pont (defendant) for violation of Sec. 2 of the Sherman Act. The U.S. appealed from a judgement below for Du Pont. Affirmed.

Du Pont had produced almost 75% of all cellophane marketed in the United States for a number of years but argues that the relevant market was the entire market for flexible packaging materials and that cellophane accounted for only 18 percent of that market.

MR. JUSTICE REED. If cellophane is the "market" that Du Pont is found to dominate, it may be assumed it does have monopoly power over that "market." Monopoly power is the power to control prices or exclude competition. It seems apparent that Du Pont's power to set the price of cellophane has been limited only by the competition afforded by other flexible packaging materials. Moreover, it may be practically impossible for anyone to commence manufacturing cellophane without full access to Du Pont's technique. However, Du Pont has no power to prevent competition from other wrapping materials. The trial court consequently had to determine whether competition from the other wrappings prevented Du Pont from possessing monopoly power in violation of § 2. Price and competition are so intimately entwined that any discussion of theory must treat them as one. It is inconceivable that

[19] *U.S. v. Alcoa,* 148 F.2d 416, 431 (2d Cir. 1945).

price could be controlled without power over competition or vice versa. This approach to the determination of monopoly power is strengthened by this Court's conclusion in prior cases that, when an alleged monopolist has power over price and competition, an intention to monopolize in a proper case may be assumed.

When a product is controlled by one interest, without substitutes available in the market, there is monopoly power. Because most products have possible substitutes, we cannot . . . give "that infinite range" to the definition of substitutes. Nor is it a proper interpretation of the Sherman Act to require that products be fungible to be considered in the relevant market.

But where there are market alternatives that buyers may readily use for their purposes, illegal monopoly does not exist merely because the product said to be monopolized differs from others. If it were not so, only physically identical products would be a part of the market. To accept the Government's argument, we would have to conclude that the manufacturers of plain as well as moistureproof cellophane were monopolists, and so with films such as Pliofilm, foil, glassine, polyethylene, and Saran, for each of these wrapping materials is distinguishable. These were all exhibits in the case. New wrappings appear, generally similar to cellophane: is each a monopoly? What is called for is an appraisal of the "cross-elasticity" of demand in the trade. . . . In considering what is the relevant market for determining the control of price and competition, no more definite rule can be declared than that commodities reasonably interchangeable by consumers for the same purposes make up that "part of the trade or commerce," monopolization of which may be illegal.

In determining the market under the Sherman Act, it is the use or uses to which the commodity is put that control. The selling price between commodities with similar uses and different characteristics may vary, so that the cheaper product can drive out the more expensive. Or, the superior quality of higher priced articles may make dominant the more desirable. Cellophane costs more than many competing products and less than a few. But whatever the price, there are various flexible wrapping materials that are bought by manufacturers for packaging their goods in their own plants or are sold to converters who shape and print them for use in the packaging of the commodities to be wrapped. . . .

It may be admitted that cellophane combines the desirable elements of transparency, strength and cheapness more definitely than any of the others.

But, despite cellophane's advantages, it has to meet competition from other materials in every one of its uses. The Government makes no challenge that cellophane furnishes less than 7 percent of wrappings for bakery products, 25 percent for candy, 32 percent for snacks, 35 percent for meats and poultry, 27 percent for crackers and biscuits, 47 percent for fresh produce, and 34 percent for frozen foods. Seventy-five to 80 percent of cigarettes are wrapped in cellophane. Thus, cellophane shares the packaging market with others. The over-all result is that cellophane accounts for 17.9 percent of flexible wrapping materials, measured by the wrapping surface.

An element for consideration as to cross-elasticity of demand between products is the responsiveness of the sales of one product to price changes of the other. If a slight decrease in the price of cellophane causes a considerable number of customers of other flexible wrappings to switch to cellophane, it would be an indication that a high cross-elasticity of demand exists between them; that the products compete in the same market. The court below held that the "[g]reat sensitivity of customers in the flexible packaging markets to price or quality changes" prevented Du Pont from possessing monopoly control over price.

We conclude that cellophane's interchangeability with the other materials mentioned suffices to make it a part of this flexible packaging material market.[20]

United States v. Grinnell Corp.

384 U.S. 563 (U.S. Sup. Ct. 1966)

This was a civil suit brought by the United States (plaintiff) against Grinnell Corp. (defendant) under Section 2 of the Sherman Act. The district court held for the Government but both Grinnell and the Government appealed. The Government asked for additional relief. Judgment for the Government affirmed and additional relief granted.

Grinnell manufactures plumbing supplies and fire sprinkler systems. It also owns 76 percent of the stock of ADT, 89 percent of the stock of AFA, and 100 percent of the stock of Holmes. ADT provides both burglary and fire protection services; Holmes provides burglary services alone; AFA supplies only fire protection service. Each offers a central station service under which hazard-detecting devices installed on the protected premises automatically transmit an electric signal to a central station. There are other forms of protective services. But the record shows that subscribers to accredited central station service (i.e., that approved by the insurance underwriters) receive reductions in their insurance premiums that are substantially greater than the reduction received by the users of other kinds of protection service. In 1961 accredited companies in the central station service business grossed $65 million. ADT, Holmes, and AFA, all controlled by Grinnell, are the three largest companies in the business in terms of revenue with about 87 percent of the business.

In 1907 Grinnell entered into a series of agreements with the other defendant companies which allocated the major cities and markets for central station alarm services in the United States. Each defendant agreed not to compete outside of the market areas allocated.

Over the years the defendants purchased the stock or assets of 30 companies engaged in the business of providing burglar or fire alarm services. After Grinnell acquired control of the other defendants, the latter continued in

[20] There were four dissenting Justices.

their attempts to acquire central station companies—offers being made to at least eight companies between the years 1955 and 1961, including four of the five largest nondefendant companies in the business. When the present suit was filed, each of those defendants had outstanding an offer to purchase one of the four largest nondefendant companies.

ADT over the years reduced its minimum basic rates to meet competition and renewed contracts at substantially increased rates in cities where it had a monopoly of accredited central station service. ADT threatened retaliation against firms that contemplated inaugurating central station service.

MR. JUSTICE DOUGLAS. The offense of monopoly under Section 2 of the Sherman Act has two elements: (1) the possession of monopoly power in the relevant market and (2) the willful acquisition or maintenance of that power as distinguished from growth or development as a consequence of a superior product, business acumen, or historic accident. We shall see that this second ingredient presents no major problem here, as what was done in building the empire was done plainly and explicitly for a single purpose. In *United States v. E. I. Du Pont De Nemours & Co.,* we defined monopoly power as "the power to control prices or exclude competition." The existence of such power ordinarily may be inferred from the predominant share of the market. In *American Tobacco Co. v. United States,* we said that "over two thirds of the entire domestic field of cigarettes, and . . . over 80 percent of the field of comparable cigarettes" constituted "a substantial monopoly." In *United States v. Aluminum Co. of America,* 90 percent of the market constituted monopoly power. In the present case, 87 percent of the accredited central station service business leaves no doubt that the congeries of these defendants have monopoly power—power which, as our discussion of the record indicates, they did not hesitate to wield—if that business is the relevant market. The only remaining question therefore is, what is the relevant market?

In case of a product it may be of such a character that substitute products must also be considered, as customers may turn to them if there is a slight increase in the price of the main product. That is the teaching of the *Du Pont* case, that commodities reasonably interchangeable make up that "part" of trade or commerce which Section 2 protects against monopoly power.

The District Court treated the entire accredited central station service business as a single market and we think it was justified in so doing. Defendants argue that the different central station services offered are so diverse that they cannot under *Du Pont* be lumped together to make up the relevant market. For example, burglar alarm services are not interchangeable with fire alarm services. They further urge that *Du Pont* requires that protective services other than those of the central station variety be included in the market definition.

But there is here a single use, i.e., the protection of property, through a central station that receives signals. It is that service, accredited, that is unique and that competes with all the other forms of property protection. We see no barrier to combining in a single market a number of different products or services where that combination reflects commercial realities. To repeat, there is here a single basic service—the protection of property through use of a central service station—that must be compared with all other forms of property protection.

There are, to be sure, substitutes for the accredited central station service. But none of them appears to operate on the same level as the central station service so as to meet the interchangeability test of the *Du Pont* case.

Defendants earnestly urge that despite these differences, they face competition from these other modes of protection. They seem to us seriously to overstate the degree of competition, but we recognize that (as the District Court found) they "do not have unfettered power to control the price of their services . . . due to the fringe competition of other alarm or watchmen services." What defendants overlook is that the high degree of differentiation between central station protection and the other forms means that for many customers, only central station protection will do.

As the District Court found, the relevant market for determining whether the defendants have monopoly power is not the several local areas which the individual stations serve, but the broader national market that reflects the reality of the way in which they built and conduct their business.

We have said enough about the great hold that the defendants have on this market. The percentage is so high as to justify the finding of monopoly. And, as the facts already related indicate, this monopoly was achieved in large part by unlawful and exclusionary practices. The restrictive agreements that pre-empted for each company a segment of the market where it was free of competition of the others were one device. Pricing practices that contained competitors were another. The acquisition by Grinnell of ADT, AFA, and Holmes were still another. Its control of the three other defendants eliminated any possibility of an outbreak of competition that might have occurred when the 1907 agreements terminated. By those acquisitions it perfected the monopoly power to exclude competitors and fix prices.

[*The court further indicated that the district court should have granted the government relief beyond requiring Grinnell to divest itself of stock in ADT, Holmes and AFA. The monopoly power of ADT in certain cities would have to be broken by divestiture, and the request of the Government for continuing inspection reports, and an injunction was granted.*]

Problem Cases

1. Page Publishing Company owned and published the *Commercial News,* a general business newspaper serving the Los Angeles area. Page brought an antitrust action against a number of community newspapers serving small neighborhoods in and around Los Angeles and the Los Angeles Newspaper Service Bureau together with several of its officers. The Bureau was owned substantially by the defendant newspapers and represented them in the solicitation of legal advertising.

Page claimed that collusive and illegal bidding by defendants caused the *Commercial News* to lose printing contracts for the 1951 and 1954 Los Angeles delinquent tax lists. Page argued that newspapers by their nature engage in interstate commerce and therefore are subject to the federal antitrust laws. Is Page correct?

2. Eastex Aviation brought a private antitrust action against Sperry & Hutchinson Co., distributors of S&H "Green Stamps." Sperry & Hutchinson had a policy of providing a retailer with the stamps, promotional advertising signs, and a supply of books to be distributed to and used by customers for collecting the stamps. S&H agreed not to supply green stamps to retailers wanting stamps in similar businesses and geographic areas to retailers already distributing S&H's stamps. Retailers agreed not to sell or distribute stamps except to their retail customers. Are these restrictions on distributing stamps violations of the Sherman Act?
3. The National Society of Professional Engineers (NSPE) promulgated a Code of Ethics which stated that an engineer "will not compete unfairly with another engineer by attempting to obtain employment . . . by competitive bidding. . . ." The United States attacks this mandate as violative of § 1 of the Sherman Act as a conspiracy in restraint of trade. The NSPE urges the application of the rule of reason test to the activities. Will the court apply the rule of reason?
4. Carpa, Inc., acquired a franchised restaurant from Ward Foods operated under the trademark "Zuider Zee." In order to obtain the franchise Carpa was obligated to purchase equipment and supplies from Ward Foods. The "Zuider Zee" franchise market was well advertised and fast growing, with at least seven such franchises established throughout the Southwest in four years. Was a jury justified in concluding that this was an illegal tying contract?
5. Socony-Vacuum Oil Company and several other major oil companies agreed to maintain a purchasing program to absorb the large amounts of "distress" gasoline being marketed as a result of overproduction in the gasoline industry. The plan was effectuated by means of a committee of the various major companies which would designate the distress supplies each major company would purchase on the open market. The plan, however, was wholly voluntary. Is this a violation of § 1 of the Sherman Act?
6. Response of Carolina entered into a contract with Leasco Response to become a franchisee of a time-sharing computer system. The contract contained an "Area of Primary Responsibility" (APR) Clause for the franchisee. Royalties of 15 percent of sales were to be paid by Response of Carolina to Leasco Response for the franchisee's sales within the APR, but royalties of 70 percent for sales to customers outside the APR. Is this an objectionable contract under the Sherman Act § 1?
7. Miller and others purchased condominiums from Granados, who as developer had sold $40 million worth of condominiums. The condominium association entered into an agreement requiring the manager of the complex to provide goods, services and administration pursuant to an exclusive six-year contract, obligating the condominium owners to pay $120 per quarter for such services. The purchase of the condominiums was conditioned upon acceptance of the management contract. Is this an illegal tying contract?
8. Prior to 1968, Reed Brothers had been a farm chemical distributor under contract with Monsanto Co. After terminating its contract with Monsanto, Reed Brothers continued to purchase Monsanto products from Monsanto dealers. In 1967, Monsanto established new policies concerning the distribution of its goods to wholesalers such as the Reed Brothers, making it economically unfeasible for the dealers to sell to wholesalers who were located outside a specified geographic area. These policies were enforced strictly

by Monsanto by suggesting that those dealers not complying would be terminated. Is this a valid refusal to deal by Monsanto?

9. De Filippo and Fleishman, partners in a Ford automobile dealership, contracted with Ford for the lease of a new site for the dealership. The terms of the agreement were to include a deferral of a substantial portion of the first and second years' rent until the fourth and fifth years. Other Ford dealers in the area objected to the provision allowing the deferral of income, which objection eventually caused Ford, after conferring with the other dealers, to refuse to grant De Filippo a franchise based on the original terms. Is this a *per se* violation of the Sherman Act, § 1?

10. Boddicker was a dentist licensed to practice in Arizona. He alleged that the American Dental Association (ADA), the Arizona State Dental Association (ASDA), and the Central Arizona Dental Society (CADS) conspired to require membership in the ADA as a condition precedent to membership in the ASDA and CADS. While membership in the ASDA and CADS is not a prerequisite to practicing dentistry in Arizona, member dentists derive benefits from membership including participation in continuing education programs, group insurance, the exchange of information with and referral of patients by fellow members, etc. The ADA provides similar services to its members. Boddicker now claims that the requirement of ASDA and CADS that membership in them is conditional upon membership in the ADA creates an anticompetitive tying arrangement in violation of Sections 1 and 2 of the Sherman Act. Has there been a violation?

11. Todhunter-Mitchell & Co., a Bahamian beer importer, brought an antitrust action against Anheuser-Busch, Inc. for alleged violations of the Sherman Act. Plaintiff's principal competitor, Bahama Blenders, was the only licensed distributor in Bahama of Anheuser-Busch beers, and its wholesalers in Miami and New Orleans were prohibited from selling to Todhunter-Mitchell. Todhunter-Mitchell alleged that Anheuser-Bush was attempting to eliminate price competition of Budweiser beer in the Bahama Islands. Anheuser-Busch claimed that a refusal to deal is not in violation of the Sherman Act. How should the court rule in this case?

51

The Clayton Act

Introduction

History. The continued expansion of large firms after the passage of the Sherman Act led critics of the act, mainly supporters of small local businesses, to argue that additional antitrust legislation was needed. Some believed that the prohibitions in the Sherman Act were too general and vague and others felt that court interpretations had weakened the act. Still others argued for prohibitions that would stop monopoly in its incipiency. The Sherman Act could be brought to bear only against accomplished restraints after the "blood was on the ground."

With the passage of the Clayton Act in 1914 [38 Stat. 730 (1914), as amended, 15 U.S.C. §§ 12–27], Congress attempted to strike at specific monopolistic practices in their incipiency. Section 2 of the act made certain forms of price discriminations illegal, but since this section was amended and strengthened with the passage of the Robinson-Patman Act in 1936, price discrimination will be treated when that act is discussed in the next chapter. The major prohibitions in the Clayton Act other than those in Section 2 are found in Section 3 (exclusive dealing, requirement and tying contracts), and Section 7 (antimerger).[1]

[1] Section 8 of the Clayton Act provides that . . . "no person at the same time shall be a director in any two or more corporations, any one of which has capital, surplus, and undivided profits aggregating more than $1 million . . . if such corporations are or shall have been theretofore competitors, so that the elimination of competition by agreement between them would constitute a violation of any of the provisions of the antitrust laws." The FTC filed only 13 complaints under this section prior to 1964. Only one cease-and-desist order resulted because in other cases the executives simply resigned. There have been a few court cases. See *U.S. v. Sears, Roebuck and Co.,* 111 F. Supp. 614 (1953). In recent years both Congress and the Commission have indicated increasing interest in this area. The Commission has accepted consent decrees involving Section 8 violations in more than a dozen cases and has several investigations under way at the time of this writing.

Section 3

This section makes it unlawful for any person *in interstate or foreign commerce,* to lease or sell commodities for use, consumption or resale within the United States or its territories, or to fix a price charged therefore:

> . . . on condition, agreement, or understanding that the lessee or purchaser thereof shall not use or deal in the goods . . . or other commodities of a competitor or competitors of the lessor or seller, where the effect of such lease, sale or contract for sale or such conditions, agreement, or understanding may be to substantially lessen competition or tend to create a monopoly in any line of commerce.

A sizable number of limitations on the application of Section 3 are to be found in the language employed. First, Section 3 applies only to sales of commodities and not to sales of services. An actual sale or leasing arrangement must have been made. The section does not apply to situations where a seller (or lessor) has refused to deal because the buyer (or lessee) was unwilling to accept otherwise illegal tying or exclusive dealing conditions. The section does not apply where goods are shipped by a principal to an agent on consignment since no sale or lease of commodities would be involved. Nor does it apply unless the agreements or understandings involve conditions designed to prevent buyers (or lessees) from dealing with competing sellers (or lessors). There must be a *probability* that the agreements or understandings will lessen competition or tend to create a monopoly in a line of commerce (product market). Lastly, the transaction must be *in commerce* and not merely bear some "substantial relation to commerce" as is the less stringent jurisdictional test under the Sherman Act.

SUMMARY

The Clayton Act was enacted to strengthen antitrust enforcement and to stop certain anticompetitive practices in their incipiency before harm was done to competition. Section 3 of the act applies to exclusive dealing contracts and to tying contracts.

Gulf Oil Corp. v. Copp Paving Co., Inc.

419 U.S. 186 (U.S. Sup. Ct. 1974)

Copp Paving Co., Inc. (plaintiff), a plant where asphaltic concrete for surfacing highway was manufactured and sold entirely intra state, brought a private antitrust action under the Clayton and Robinson-Patman Acts against Gulf Oil Corp. (defendant), a producer of liquid petroleum asphalt used on interstate highways. Gulf claimed that the fact that its products were sold only within a state meant that its products were not "in commerce" for purposes of the

Clayton and Robinson-Patman Acts. Judgment for Copp and Gulf appealed. Reversed.

MR. JUSTICE POWELL. Copp's "in commerce" argument rests essentially on a purely formal "nexus" to commerce: the highways are instrumentalities of interstate commerce; therefore, any conduct of Gulf with respect to an ingredient of a highway is *per se* "in commerce." Copp thus would have us expand the concept of the flow of commerce by incorporating categories of activities that are perceptibly connected to its instrumentalities. But whatever merit this catagorical inclusion and exclusion approach may have when dealing with the language and purposes of other regulatory enactments, it does not carry over to the context of the Robinson-Patman and Clayton Acts. The chain of connection has no logical endpoint. The universe of arguably included activities would be broad and its limits nebulous in the extreme.

In short, assuming that the facially narrow language of the Clayton and Robinson-Patman Acts was intended to denote something more than the relatively restrictive flow of commerce concept, we think the nexus approach would be an irrational way to proceed. The justification for an expansive interpretation of the "in commerce" language, if such an interpretation is viable at all, must rest on a congressional intent that the Acts reach all practices, even those of local character, harmful to the national marketplace.

Standard Oil of California v. United States

337 U.S. 293 (U.S. Sup. Ct. 1949)

The United States brought a suit under Section 3 of the Clayton Act against Standard Oil of California (defendant). Standard appealed from an adverse decision. Affirmed.

Standard operated in eight western states where it was the largest seller of gasoline with about 23 percent of the total gallonage. Sales by company-owned stations was 6.8 percent of this total and by "independent" dealer operated outlets 6.7 percent, with the balance going to industrial users.

Standard sold over $57 million in gasoline and $8 million in other products through its dealer-operated outlets. Some 2,777 dealers contracted to buy all of their requirements (petroleum products and TBA) from Standard while another 4,368 dealers agreed to only buy all of their petroleum products requirements from Standard.

MR. JUSTICE FRANKFURTER. Section 3 of the Clayton Act prohibits specific practices not covered by the broad terms of the Sherman Act. The issue before us, therefore, is whether the requirement of showing that the effect of the agreements "may be to substantially lessen competition" can be satisfied simply by proof that a substantial portion of commerce is affected or whether it must also be proven that competitive activity has actually diminished or probably will diminish.

Requirements contracts may be of economic advantage to buyers as well as to sellers, and thus indirectly of advantage to the consuming public. In the case of the buyer, they may assure supply, afford protection against rises in price, enable long-term planning on the basis of known costs, and reduce the expense and risk of storage in the quantity necessary for a commodity having a fluctuating demand. From the seller's point of view, requirements contracts may lessen selling expenses, give protection against price fluctuations, and offer the possibility of a predictable market. They may be useful to a seller trying to establish a foothold against counterattacks of entrenched competitors.

But these advantages do not offset the illegality of such contracts.

We conclude that Section 3 is satisfied by proof that competition has been reduced in a substantial share of the line of commerce affected. Standard's competitors cannot sell their products to dealers subject to these contracts, and the value of retail sales covered by these contracts is substantial. In view of the widespread use of such contracts by Standard's competitors and the lack of alternative ways to market petroleum products, there is evidence that competitive activity has been reduced. Standard's use of the contracts creates just such a potential clog on competition as it was the purpose of Section 3 to remove wherever it would impede a substantial amount of competitive activity.

Tampa Electric Co. v. Nashville Coal Co.

365 U.S. 320 (U.S. Sup. Ct. 1961)

Tampa Electric Co. (plaintiff) brought this action for a declaratory judgment establishing the validity of a contract whereby Tampa agreed to purchase all of its coal requirements for a 20-year period from Nashville Coal Co. (defendant). Tampa appealed from a decision ruling that the contract was illegal under Section 3 of the Clayton Act. Reversed.

Tampa Electric is a public utility serving an area of about 1,800 square miles around Tampa, Florida. Tampa Electric entered a 20-year contract whereby it agreed to buy its total requirements of coal for its Gannon Station from Nashville Coal Co. This purchase obligation also extended to any additional coal using plants Tampa might build at the Gannon Station during the life of the contract. A minimum price for the coal was set with a cost escalation clause. After Tampa had spent approximately $7.5 million preparing to burn coal instead of oil, Nashville notified Tampa that it would not perform because the contract violated Section 3 of the Clayton Act.

MR. JUSTICE CLARK. In practical application, even though a contract is found to be an exclusive-dealing arrangement, it does not violate the section unless the court believes it probable that performance of the contract will foreclose competition in a substantial share of the line of commerce affected. Following the guidelines of earlier decisions, certain considerations must be taken. *First,* the line of commerce, i.e., the type of goods, wares, or merchandise, etc., involved must be determined, where it is in controversy, on the basis of the facts peculiar to the case. *Second,* the area of effective competition in the known line of commerce must be charted by careful selection of the market area in which the seller operates, and to which the purchaser can practicably turn for supplies. In short, the threatened foreclosure of competition must be substantial in relation to the market affected.

To determine substantiality in a given case, it is necessary to weigh the probable effect of the contract on the relevant area of effective competition, taking into account the relative strength of the parties, the proportionate volume of commerce involved in relation to the total volume of commerce in the relevant market area, and the probable immediate and future effects which preemption of that share of the market might have on effective competition therein. It follows that a mere showing that the contract itself involves a substantial number of dollars is ordinarily of little consequence.

In applying these considerations to the facts of the case before us, it appears clear that both the Court of Appeals and the District Court have not given the required effect to a controlling factor in the case—the relevant competitive market area.

Neither the Court of Appeals nor the District Court considered in detail the question of the relevant market. They do seem, however, to have been satisfied with inquiring only as to competition within "Peninsular Florida." By far the bulk of the overwhelming tonnage marketed from the same producing area as serves Tampa is sold outside of Georgia and Florida, and the producers were "eager" to sell more coal in those States. While the relevant competitive market is not ordinarily susceptible to a "metes and bounds" definition, it is of course the area in which respondents and the other 700 producers effectively compete. The record shows that, like the respondents, they sold bituminous coal "suitable for [Tampa's] requirements," mined in parts of Pennsylvania, Virginia, West Virginia, Kentucky, Tennessee, Alabama, Ohio and Illinois. . . . it clearly appears that the proportionate volume of the total relevant coal product as to which the challenged contract pre-empted competition, less than 1 percent, is, conservatively speaking, quite insubstantial. A more accurate figure, even assuming preemption to the extent of the maximum anticipated total requirements, 2,250,000 tons a year, would be .77 percent.

Section 7

Statutory Wording. As amended in 1950, Section 7 of the Clayton Act prohibits the acquisition by a corporation, in interstate or foreign commerce, unless solely for investment, of:

. . . the whole or any part of the stock . . . or assets of another corporation engaged also in commerce, where in any line of commerce in any section of the country, the effect of such acquisition may be substantially to lessen competition, or to tend to create a monopoly.[2]

Interpretation. In order to determine the legality of a given acquisition under this section the court first must define the product line (line of commerce) and the relevant market area (section of the country) involved utilizing the same analysis discussed in relation to Section 2 of the Sherman Act. There need only be a *reasonable probability* that anticompetitive effects will be the result of the merger. The Supreme Court has permitted the FTC to define submarkets within both product and area markets. In the *Brown Shoe* case a merger involving only 5 percent of the shoe industry's sales volume was held illegal where the relevant market was defined to include only sales of men's, women's, and children's shoes in cities of 10,000 or more in population.[3]

An acquisition has been invalidated where there are concentration trends in an industry even though fierce and fragmented competition persisted after the acquisition. A merger might be invalidated because of its effect on *potential* competition; or because a large firm might, by a product extension merger, enter a different industry and endanger the existing competitive balance within the industry. The possibility that reciprocal trading exchanges arising out of a merger might foreclose other firms from a significant market might be another factor given weight by the court. The Burger Court now appears to require more proof of probable anticompetitive effects than did the Warren Court.

Reports on "conglomerate" mergers dominated the business news during the 1960s. There is some confusion as to definition, but the term conglomerate is usually applied to acquisitions where there is no discernible relationship in the nature of the business between the acquiring and the acquired firms.[4] It seems apparent, however, that a large firm will not be permitted to make an acquisition in an already concentrated industry which might confront "existing competitors and such potential competitors as existed with an even more formidable opponent."[5]

SUMMARY

Section 7 of the act can be enforced against all types of mergers and acquisitions. The U.S. Supreme Court has taken the position that any additional

---

[2] 38 Stat. 731 (1914), as amended 15 U.S.C. Sec. 18 (1952).

[3] *Brown Shoe Co. v. United States,* 370 U.S. 294 (1962).

[4] Sometimes a conglomerate merger is defined as one being neither vertical nor horizontal. See *Antitrust Developments* (Supplement to Report of Attorney General's National Committee to Study the Antitrust Laws, American Bar Association, 1968).

[5] *General Foods v. FTC,* 386 F.2d 936, 944 (3d Cir. 1967). The *General Dynamics* case which follows, however, demonstrates pitfalls of making generalizations in this highly complex area.

concentration in most industries poses a potential threat to the working of our competitive system. Section 7 has been applied to stop acquisitions even in highly fragmented industries provided concentration trends are found to exist.

United States v. Phillipsburg National Bank

399 U.S. 350 (U.S. Sup. Ct. 1970)

Action by the United States to enjoin a merger between Phillipsburg National Bank and Second National Bank (defendants). The United States appealed from an adverse decision. Reversed.

The Phillipsburg Bank (PNB) and the Second National Bank (SNB) operate in the Phillipsburg-Eaton area although the bulk of their business is done in Phillipsburg. There were seven commercial banks in the area but the merger left only two banks in Phillipsburg. The Comptroller of Currency had approved the merger.

MR. JUSTICE BRENNAN. *The product market.* The cluster of products (various kinds of credit) and services (such as checking accounts and trust administration) called commercial banking is the line of commerce. Commercial banks are the only financial institutions in which a wide variety of financial products and services are gathered together in one place. The clustering of financial products and services in banks makes it easier for all banking customers. Customers of small banks need and use this cluster of services and products. Full-service banking in one institution may be significant to the economy of communities whose populations are too small to support a large array of differentiated savings and credit businesses.

The geographic market. In determining the relevant geographic market, the proper question to be asked is not where the parties to the merger do business or even where they compete, but where, within the area of competitive overlap, the effect of the merger on competition will be direct and immediate. This depends on the geographic structure of supplier-customer relations. More specifically, we stated that the area of effective competition in the line of commerce must be charted by careful selection of the market area in which the seller operates and to which the purchaser can practicably turn for supplies.

Commercial realities in the banking industry make clear that banks generally have a very localized business. Convenience of location is essential to effective competition. Most individuals bank in their local community; they find it impractical to conduct their banking business at a distance. In locating the market area in which companies compete, it is important to consider the places from which they draw business, the location of their offices, and where they seek business. Here, the banks drew over 85 percent of their business from the Phillipsburg-Easton area and only about ten percent from Easton itself. The entire Lehigh Valley is too broad for a geographic market; it is Phillipsburg only. [The merger was held to violate Section 7 of the Clayton Act.]

FTC v. Procter & Gamble Co.

386 U.S. 568 (U.S. Sup. Ct. 1967)

This was an action brought by the Federal Trade Commission charging that Procter & Gamble Co. had acquired the assets of Clorox Chemical Co. in violation of Section 7 of the Clayton Act. The FTC ordered divestiture but the Court of Appeals reversed and dismissed the action. The FTC appealed. Reversed.

MR. JUSTICE DOUGLAS. As indicated by the Commission in its painstaking and illuminating report, it does not particularly aid analysis to talk of this merger in conventional terms, namely, horizontal or vertical or conglomerate. This merger may most appropriately be described as a "product-extension merger," as the Commission stated. The facts are not disputed, and a summary will demonstrate the correctness of the Commission's decision.

At the time of the merger, Clorox was the leading manufacturer in the heavily concentrated household liquid bleach industry. It is agreed that household liquid bleach is the relevant line of commerce. The product is used in the home as a germicide and disinfectant, and more importantly, as a whitening agent in washing clothes and fabrics. It is a distinctive product with no close substitutes. Liquid bleach is a low-price, high-turnover consumer product sold mainly through grocery stores and supermarkets. The relevant geographical market is the Nation and a series of regional markets. Because of high shipping costs and low sales price, it is not feasible to ship the product more than 300 miles from its point of manufacture. Most manufactures are limited to competition within a single region since they have but one plant. Clorox is the only firm selling nationally; it has 13 plants distributed throughout the Nation. Purex, Clorox's closest competitor in size, does not distribute its bleach in the northeast or middle-Atlantic States; in 1957, Purex's bleach was available in less than 50 percent of the national market.

At the time of the acquisition, Clorox was the leading manufacturer of household liquid bleach, with 48.8 percent of the national sales—annual sales of slightly less than $40 million. Its market share had been steadily increasing for the five years prior to the merger. The industry is highly concentrated; in 1957, Clorox and Purex accounted for almost 65 percent of the Nation's household liquid bleach sales, and, together with four other firms, for almost 80 percent. The remaining 20 percent was divided among over 200 small producers. Clorox had total assets of $12 million; only eight producers had assets in excess of $1 million and very few had assets of more than $75,000.

In light of the territorial limitations on distribution, national figures do not give an accurate picture of Clorox's dominance in the various regions. Thus, Clorox's seven principal competitors did no business in New England, the mid-Atlantic States, or metropolitan New York.

Since all liquid bleach is chemically identical, advertising and sales promotion is vital. In 1957 Clorox spent almost $3.7 million on advertising, imprinting the value of its bleach in the mind of the consumer. In addition, it spent $1.7 million for other promotional activities.

Procter is a large, diversified manufacturer of low-price, high-turnover household products sold through grocery, drug and department stores. Prior to its acquisition of Clorox, it did not produce household liquid bleach. Its 1957 sales were in excess of $1.1 billion from which it realized profits of more than $67 million; its assets were over $500 million. Procter has been marked by rapid growth and diversification. It has successfully developed and introduced a number of new products. Its primary activity is in the general area of soaps, detergents, and cleansers; in 1957, of total domestic sales, more than one-half (over $500 million) were in this field. Procter was the dominant factor in this area. It accounted for 54.4 percent of all packaged detergent sales. The industry is heavily concentrated—Procter and its nearest competitors, Colgate-Palmolive and Lever Brothers, account for 80 percent of the market.

In the marketing of soaps, detergents, and cleansers, as in the marketing of household liquid bleach, advertising and sales promotion are vital. In 1957, Procter was the Nation's largest advertiser, spending more than $80 million on advertising and an additional $47 million on sales promotion. Due to its tremendous volume, Procter receives substantial discounts from the media. As a multi-product producer Procter enjoys substantial advantages in advertising and sales promotion. Thus, it can and does feature several products in its promotions, reducing the printing, mailing, and other costs for each product. It also purchases network programs on behalf of several products, enabling it to give each product network exposure at a fraction of the cost per product that a firm with only one product to advertise would incur.

Prior to the acquisition, Procter was in the course of diversifying into product lines related to its basic detergent-soap-cleanser business. Liquid bleach was a distinct possibility since packaged detergents—Procter's primary product line—and liquid bleach are used complementarily in washing clothes and fabrics, and in general household clothing.

The decision to acquire Clorox was the result of a study conducted by Procter's promotion department designed to determine the advisability of entering the liquid bleach industry. The initial report noted the ascendancy of liquid bleach in the large and expanding household bleach market, and recommended that Procter purchase Clorox rather than enter independently. Since a large investment would be needed to obtain a satisfactory market share, acquisition of the industry's leading firm was attractive.

The Commission found that the acquisition might substantially lessen competition. The findings and reasoning of the Commission need be only briefly summarized. The Commission found that the substitution of Procter with its huge assets and advertising advantages for the already dominant Clorox would dissuade new entrants and discourage active competition from the firms already in the industry due to fear of retaliation by Procter. The Commission thought it relevant that retailers might be induced to give Clorox preferred shelf space since it would be manufactured by Procter, which also produced a number of other products marketed by the retailers. There was also the danger that Procter might underprice Clorox in order to drive out competition, and subsidize the underpricing with revenue from other products. The Commission carefully reviewed the effect of the acquisition on the structure of the industry, noting that "the practical tendency of the . . . merger . . . is to transform the liquid bleach industry into an arena of big business competition only, with the few small firms falling by the wayside, unable to compete with their giant rivals." Further, the merger would seriously diminish potential competition by eliminating Procter as a potential entrant into the industry. Prior to the merger, the Commission found that Procter was the most likely prospective entrant, and absent the merger would have remained on the periphery, restraining Clorox from exercising its market power. If Procter had actually entered, Clorox's dominant position would have been eroded and the concentration of the industry reduced.

Section 7 of the Clayton Act was intended to arrest the anticompetitive effects of market power in their incipiency. The core question is whether a merger may substantially lessen competition, and necessarily requires a prediction of the merger's impact on competition, present and future. And there is certainly no requirement that the anticompetitive power manifest itself in anticompetitive action before § 7 can be called into play. If the enforcement of § 7 turned on the existence of actual anticompetitive practices, the congressional policy of thwarting such practices in their incipiency would be frustrated.

United States v. General Dynamics Corp.

415 U.S. 486 (U.S. Sup. Ct. 1974)

Action by the government (plaintiff) to require the divestiture of a subsidiary of General Dynamics (defendant). The district court gave a judgment for General Dynamics which the government appealed. Affirmed.

Material Service Corp. was a producer of building materials and coal. All of its coal production, amounting to 15.1 percent of the Illinois market's production, was from deep-shaft mines. Material Service acquired effective control of United Electric's stock in 1959. United Electric was a coal producer operating open-pit mining operations and had a market share in the Illinois market of 8.1 percent. General Dynamics subsequently acquired 100 percent of the Material Service stock and was sued by the government as successor to Material Service.

MR. JUSTICE STEWART. At trial controversy focused on three basic issues: the propriety of coal as a "line of commerce," the definition of Illinois or the Eastern Interior Coal Province Sales Area as a relevant "section of the country," and the probability of a lessening of competition within these or any other product and geographic markets resulting from the acquisition. The District Court decided against the Government on each of these issues.

As to the relevant product market, the court found that coal faced strong and direct competition from other sources of energy such as oil, natural gas, nuclear energy, and geothermal power which created a cross-elasticity of demand among those various fuels. As a result, it concluded that coal, by itself, was not a permissible product market and that the "energy market" was the sole "line of commerce" in which anticompetitive effects could properly be canvassed.

Similarly, the District Court rejected the Government's proposed geographic markets on the ground that they were "based essentially on past and present production statistics and do not relate to actual coal consumption patterns." The court found that a realistic geographic market should be defined in terms of transportation arteries and freight charges that determine the cost of delivered coal to purchasers and thus the competitive position of various coal producers.

Finally, and for purposes of this appeal most significantly, the District Court found that the evidence did not support the Government's contention that the 1959 acquisition of United Electric substantially lessened competition in any product or geographic market. This conclusion was based on four determinations made in the court's opinion. First, the court noted that while the number of coal producers in the Eastern Interior Coal Province declined from 144 to 39 during the period of 1957–1967, this reduction "occurred not because small producers have been acquired by others, but as the inevitable result of the change in the nature of demand for coal."

The court noted that United Electric and Material were "predominantly complementary in nature" since "United Electric is a strip mining company with no experience in deep mining nor likelihood of acquiring it [and] Material is a deep mining company with no experience or expertise in strip mining." Finally, the court found that United Electric's coal reserves were so low that its potential to compete with other coal producers in the future was far weaker than the aggregate production statistics relied on by the Government might otherwise have indicated. In particular, the court found that virtually all of United Electric's proved coal reserves were either depleted or already committed by long-term contracts with large customers, and that United Electric's power to affect the price of coal was thus severely limited and steadily diminishing. On the basis of these considerations, the court concluded: "Under these circumstances, continuation of the affiliation between United Electric and Material is not adverse to competition, nor would divestiture benefit competition even were this court to accept the Government's unrealistic product and geographic market definitions."

Evidence of past production does not, as a matter of logic, necessarily give a proper picture of a company's future ability to compete. In most situations, of course, the unstated assumption is that a company that has maintained a certain share of a market in the recent past will be in a position to do so in the immediate future. Thus, companies that have controlled sufficiently large shares of a concentrated market are barred from merger by § 7, not because of their past acts, but because their past performances imply an ability to continue to dominate with at least equal vigor.

The focus of competition in a given time frame is not on the disposition of coal already produced but on the procurement of new long-term supply contracts.

Since we agree with the District Court that the Government's reliance on production statistics in the context of this case was insufficient, it follows that the judgment before us may be affirmed without reaching the issues of geographic and product markets.[6]

Brunswick Corp. v. Pueblo Bowl-O-Mat, Inc.

429 U.S. 477 (U.S. Sup. Ct. 1977)

Suit by Pueblo Bowl-O-Mat, Inc. (plaintiff), against Brunswick Corp. (defendant) for treble damages and injunctive relief under Sec. 4 and Sec. 7 of the Clayton Act. Brunswick petitioned the court to reverse an adverse decision. Reversed.

Pueblo operated bowling centers in three markets in competition with other bowling centers, some of whom had purchased equipment on credit from Brunswick but later defaulted on the accounts. Brunswick was one of the two largest equipment manufacturers and by far the largest operator of bowling centers in the United States. Brunswick acquired some 222 of these defaulting centers in the seven years prior to 1977, but still controlled only 2 percent of all bowling centers.

Pueblo contends that by these acquisitions Brunswick lessened competition in all three markets in which Pueblo operated and that had Brunswick allowed the defaulting centers to close, Pueblo would have made more profits. The trial jury brought in a verdict for Pueblo for $2,358,030, which was later adjusted and trebled.

MR. JUSTICE MARSHALL. The issue for decision is a narrow one. Brunswick does not presently contest the Court of Appeals' conclusion that a properly instructed jury could have found the acquisitions unlawful. Nor does Brunswick challenge the Court of Appeals' determination that the evidence would support a finding that had Brunswick not acquired these centers, they would have gone out of business and Pueblo's income would have increased. Bruns-

[6] Four justices dissented.

wick questions only whether antitrust damages are available where the sole injury alleged is that competitors were continued in business, thereby denying Pueblo an anticipated increase in market shares.

To answer that question it is necessary to examine the antimerger and treble damage provisions of the Clayton Act. Section 7 of the Act proscribes mergers whose effect "may be substantially to lessen competition, or to tend to create a monopoly." It is, as we have observed many times, a prophylactic measure, intended "primarily to arrest apprehended consequences of intercorporate relationships before those relationships could work their evil. . . ."

Section 4, in contrast, is in essence a remedial provision. It provides treble damages to "any person who shall be injured in his business or property by reason of anything forbidden in the antitrust laws. . . ." Of course, treble damages also play an important role in penalizing wrong-doers and deterring wrongdoing, as we also have frequently observed. It nevertheless is true that the treble damage provision, which makes awards available only to injured parties, and measures the awards by a multiple of the injury actually proved, is designed primarily as a remedy.

Intermeshing a statutory prohibition against acts with a potential to cause certain harms with a damage action intended to remedy those harms is not without difficulty. Plainly, to recover damages Pueblo must prove more than that Brunswick violated § 7, since such proof establishes only that injury may result. Pueblo contends that the only additional element they need demonstrate is that they are in a worse position than they would have been had Brunswick not committed those acts. The Court of Appeals agreed, holding compensable any loss "causally linked" to "the mere presence of the violator in the market." Because this holding divorces antitrust recovery from the purposes of the antitrust laws without clear statutory command to do so, we cannot agree with it.

Every merger of two existing entities into one, whether lawful or unlawful, has the potential for producing economic readjustments that adversely affect some persons. But Congress has not condemned mergers on that account; it has condemned them only when they may produce anticompetitive effects. Yet under the Court of Appeals' holding, once a merger is found to violate § 7, all dislocations caused by the merger are actionable, regardless of whether those dislocations have anything to do with the reason the merger was condemned. This holding would make § 4 recovery entirely fortuitous, and would authorize damages for losses which are of no concern to the antitrust laws.

Both of these consequences are well illustrated by the facts of this case. If the acquisitions here were unlawful, it is because they brought a "deep pocket" parent into a market of "pygmies." Yet Pueblo's injury—the loss of income that would have accrued had the acquired centers gone bankrupt—bears no relationship to the size of either the acquiring company or its competitors. Pueblo would have suffered the identical "loss"—but no compensable injury—had the acquired centers instead obtained refinancing or been purchased by "shallow pocket" parents, as the Court of Appeals itself acknowledged. Thus Pueblo's injury was not of "the type that the statute was intended to forestall."

But the antitrust laws are not merely indifferent to the injury claimed here. At base, Pueblo complains that by acquiring the failing centers Brunswick preserved competition, thereby depriving Pueblo of the benefits of increased concentration. The damages Pueblo obtained are designed to provide them with the profits they would have realized had competition been reduced. The antitrust laws, however, were enacted for "the protection of competition, not competitors." It is inimical to the purposes of these laws to award damages for the type of injury claimed here.

Problem Cases

1. IBM leased its punching, sorting, and tabulating machines for a specified rental period upon condition that the lease would terminate if any punch cards not manufactured by IBM are used in the lease machines. IBM maintains that such a provision is necessary since the cards used must conform to exacting quality specifications concerning the thickness and quality of paper. Is this a valid defense to a charge of a violation of § 3 of the Clayton Act making unlawful tying clauses which tend to create a monopoly?
2. Window Company issued franchises which required all distributors and dealers of its patented combination storm and screen windows to maintain a sales organization devoted exclusively to the sale of such windows. Distributors and dealers also were required not to offer for sale merchandise competitive with any article manufactured or distributed by the Window Co., and to purchase from Window Co. materials necessary for the manufacture of special units. A terminated dealer sued Window Co. alleging that this plan caused him losses and that he was terminated for handling competitive goods. Has the dealer stated a valid claim under the antitrust laws?
3. Serum Company was the nation's largest producer of hog serum and had exclusive requirement franchises with all 16 of its wholesalers. The wholesalers could buy from other sources provided they gave up the use of the word "Anchor" in their business. The FTC brought an action under Section 3 of the Clayton Act asking that these restrictions on the use of the word "Anchor" be held illegal. Can Serum Co. impose such restrictions?
4. Carvel franchised dealers to sell soft ice cream. The franchise provided that Carvel would suggest retail prices. Each dealer was required to buy or lease a number of items of equipment in the franchise package. Some of this equipment was patented and much of it was not. There was evidence that the franchise package as a whole was desired by the retailers as distinguished from patented equipment and the restrictions were aimed at protecting the quality of the food and service. One dealer sued Carvel for treble damages claiming that the leasing or selling of the patented equipment as a package constituted a per se violation of Section 3 of the Clayton Act (illegal tie-in sale). Were the franchise restrictions included as a package with the patent illegal?
5. Red Kap, the largest supplier of industrial rental garments to unaffiliated laundries, with a market share of 23 percent, acquired all the assets of Hayes Co. Hayes was engaged in the same line of commerce and accounted for 7.5 percent of the sales in the market. Prior to the acquisition, 44.7 percent of all industrial rental sales were accounted for by

the two largest firms, 69.7 percent by the four largest firms and 80.9 percent by the eight largest firms. Does the acquisition violate Section 7 of the Clayton Act?

6. Ford Motor Co. made a substantial portion of its own parts, although it did not make spark plugs or batteries but purchased these parts from independent companies. The original equipment of new cars, insofar as spark plugs are concerned, is referred to as the "OE." The replacement market is referred to as the "aftermarket." Independent companies, such as Autolite, furnished the auto manufacturers with OE spark plugs at cost or less, intending to recover their losses on OE sales by profitable sale in the aftermarket. Ford was anxious to participate in this aftermarket and so it acquired certain assets of Autolite in 1961. General Motors had entered the spark plug manufacturing field, making the AC brand, whose market share was about 30 percent. When Ford acquired Autolite, whose market share was 15 percent, only one major competitor was left and that was Champion whose market share declined from 50 percent in 1960 to just under 40 percent in 1964, and to just about 33 percent in 1966. The government brought a divestiture action under Section 7 of the Celler-Kefauver Antimerger Act claiming Ford's acquisition of certain of Autolite's assets may have the effect of substantially lessening competition. Was Ford's acquisition permissible?

7. Reynolds Metals Co. acquired Arrow Brand, Inc., in 1956. At that time, Reynolds was the major supplier of aluminum foil to large quantity buyers. Arrow, who purchased its supply from Reynolds, was the major supplier of aluminum foil to florist shops. The FTC brings suit to require that Reynolds divest itself of Arrow. The FTC claims that the Arrow acquisition would substantially lessen competition in the florist trade for aluminum foil. Reynolds counters, claiming that the relevant "line of commerce" is not simply the florist trade, but all trades that require the specialized use of aluminum foil. Is the FTC correct in narrowly defining "line of commerce?"

8. In 1958, Pabst, the nation's 10th largest brewer, acquired Blatz, which ranked 18th. The merger made Pabst fifth largest with 4.5 percent of the industry's total sales. By 1961, they ranked third with 5.8 percent of the market. In Wisconsin before the merger Blatz was the leading seller and Pabst ranked fourth. The merger made Pabst first with 24 percent and by 1961 this had grown to 27.4 percent. In the three-state area of Wisconsin, Illinois, and Michigan in 1957 Blatz ranked sixth with 5.8 percent of the market and Pabst was seventh with 5.4 percent. The government sued Pabst alleging that the acquisition violated Section 7 of the Clayton Act. The District Court dismissed the government's case on the ground that they failed to show that the effect of the acquisition ". . . may be substantially to lessen competition or to tend to create monopoly in the continental United States, the only relevant geographic market." Should the decision stand on appeal?

9. The product market of the combined glass and metal container industry was dominated by six firms with Continental Can ranking second and Hazel-Atlas ranking sixth. In 1956 Continental acquired the assets of Hazel-Atlas, the third largest producer of glass containers, giving the combined firms 25 percent of the combined container market. There was evidence of concentration trends in both the glass and metal container industries. The U.S. challenged the acquisition under Section 7 and Continental defended on the ground that metal and glass were two separate product lines and hence acquisition had no real anticompetitive tendency. Is Continental correct?

52

The Robinson-Patman Act

Introduction

Objectives. The two primary objectives of the Robinson-Patman Act (49 Stat. 1526, as amended, 15 U.S.C. § 13) are: (1) To prevent suppliers from attempting to gain an unfair advantage over their competitors by discriminating among buyers either in price or in providing allowances or services, and (2) to prevent buyers from using their economic power to gain discriminatory prices from suppliers so as to gain an advantage over their own competitors. The overall objective is to promote equality of economic opportunity for business selling and buying goods in the channels of commerce.

History. The Robinson-Patman Act amendment of Section 2 of the Clayton Act was enacted in 1936 because of increasing congressional concern for the plight of small retailers confronted with the growth of chain-store competition. The original Section 2 of the Clayton Act was drafted primarily to prohibit the practice, early used by the Standard Oil Company and others, of employing local and territorial price discrimination to drive out competitors in a given area. However, the complaint of grocers, druggists and other retailers, and the wholesalers who supplied them, was that suppliers discriminated in price between different customers, sometimes charging chain stores even less than they did the wholesalers who sold to the small independent stores. The Clayton Act had been interpreted to require an examination only into the competitive effect at the seller's level—not at the customer's level. Furthermore, it was interpreted to permit a seller to meet the price of a competitor even if the competitor's price itself was discriminatory and to permit different prices for different quantities without regard to the cost savings of the seller.

Concern had been brought to a head in 1934 by the report of a thorough investigation of chain stores conducted by the Federal Trade Commission upon the request of Congress. It publicized not only the fact that chains were buying their goods more cheaply than their smaller competitors but that they also frequently received advertising and promotional allowances, payments in lieu of brokerage and other inducements to buy not available to their competitors and often given secretly.

Recently, criticism of the Act seems to have intensified, but efforts to persuade Congress to repeal it have had little success. FTC enforcement activity has been reduced to a minimum. However, private treble damage suits are not uncommon.

The Statute. Section 2(a) of the amended Clayton Act provides:

> That it shall be unlawful for any person engaged in commerce, in the course of such commerce, either directly or indirectly, to discriminate in price between different purchasers of commodities of like grade and quality, where either or any of the purchases involved in such discrimination are in commerce, where such commodities are sold for use, consumption, or resale within the United States or any Territory thereof or the District of Columbia or any insular possession or other place under the jurisdiction of the United States, and where the effect of such discrimination may be substantially to lessen competition or tend to create a monopoly in any line of commerce, or to injure, destroy, or prevent competition with any person who either grants or knowingly receives the benefit of such discrimination, or with customers of either of them: *Provided,* That nothing herein contained shall prevent differentials which make only due allowance for differences in the cost of manufacture, sale, or delivery resulting from the differing methods or quantities in which such commodities are to such purchasers sold or delivered: *Provided, however,* That the Federal Trade Commission may, after due investigation and hearing to all interested parties, fix and establish quantity limits, and revise the same as it finds necessary, as to particular commodities or classes of commodities, where it finds that available purchasers in greater quantities are so few as to render differentials on account thereof unjustly discriminatory or promotive of monopoly in any line of commerce; and the foregoing shall then not be construed to permit differentials based on differences in quantities greater than those so fixed and established: *And provided further,* That nothing herein contained shall prevent persons engaged in selling goods, wares, or merchandise in commerce from selecting their own customers in bona fide transactions and not in restraint of trade: *And provided further,* That nothing herein contained shall prevent price changes from time to time where in response to changing conditions affecting the market for or the marketability of the goods concerned, such as but not limited to actual or imminent deterioration of perishable goods, obsolescence of seasonal goods, distress sales under court process, or sales in good faith in discontinuance of business in the goods concerned.

Commerce. The price discrimination must have a tendency to diminish competition and must occur in interstate commerce. Unlike the Sherman Act definition of commerce, however, the courts have interpreted this provision to require that the transaction in question involve two or more states or the District of Columbia and a state. The fact that the customers who are discriminated against are located in the same state as those who are favored does not make the act inapplicable if the goods are shipped in from another state. The act also applies where one of the competing buyers is in another state even though the seller and other buyers are in the same state. However, the act does not apply, for example, to an Indiana manufacturer selling to Indiana customers, although if the Indiana manufacturer is part of an interstate enterprise and uses resources from out of state to finance local price-cutting, a violation may be found. Only domestic commerce involving transactions by American businesspersons is covered by the act.

Discrimination in Price. A price discrimination under the act must involve two or more sales to different purchasers at different prices. One who sells to all buyers at a fixed f.o.b. price would clearly not violate Section 2(a) of the act. The price to be considered is the delivered price—that is, the price at the point where the buyer takes the goods. For two or more sales to be treated as discriminatory, they must be fairly close in point of time. How close depends upon the commodity—longer for pianos than meat or corn, which tend to fluctuate rapidly in price due to perishability or rapidly changing supply and demand factors.

Section 2(a) applies only to different prices between different actual purchasers. Merely quoting a discriminatory price or refusing to sell except at a discriminatory price is not a violation under this section. An actual sale at a discriminatory price must occur before the section applies.

Under certain conditions sales will be attributed, for purposes of the act, to a seller which are not made directly by him. For example, sales by a subsidiary will be attributed to the parent if there is a high degree of control exercised by the parent—likewise, a manufacturer who controls the sales of its customer, a wholesaler, by having its own sales people take the order and referring it to the wholesaler is the seller.

Commodities of Like Grade and Quality. Section 2's prohibition of price discrimination applies only to goods. It does not cover services. Discriminatory pricing practices in selling advertising space or leasing real estate are not prohibited by the act. What goods are of like grade and quality is a more difficult issue. Different prices cannot be justified merely because the labels on the product are different. It has been held that private labeling of merchandise, such as food products and appliances, does not make them different from the same goods carrying the seller's house brand. If a seller can establish that there is an actual physical difference in grade or quality between two products, then he can justify any differential in price between them he wishes. For this reason establishing a lower priced "fighting" brand is not illegal. The differential in price between different grades or qualities of goods need not, under the act, be proportionate to actual differences in the seller's costs. The magnitude of the difference in quality necessary to permit differential pricing is not clear, although courts have tended to require less difference than has the FTC, nor is it clear the extent to which differences in design permit price differentials. Of course, so long as the seller offers all designs, styles, and qualities to all purchasers, he forecloses questions with respect to discrimination when he establishes different prices.

Competitive Effect. Section 2(a) applies only to discriminations which have the reasonable probability of lessening competition. Such an injury may occur to the competition between the sellers, which is called the *primary* level. A classic case was the early Standard Oil practice of cutting prices in one area to drive out a competitor. It is often claimed that a big national firm can finance this "predatory" price cutting by raising prices elsewhere. In such a case there might be no competition between the customers in the price-cutting market and those in the other areas. Or the injury to competition may be at the buyer or *secondary* level, as between a chain grocery and an independent. Often a price discrimination will cause the requisite injury at both levels. Indeed, a third level or *tertiary* competitive injury may occur, as where the effect is on the competition between customers of customers of the seller granting the lower price.

The act does not specifically deal with functional discounts, that is, discounts granted to a buyer, such a wholesaler, performing certain functions in the distribution system. Therefore, whether a functional price differential is prohibited depends upon its competitive effect. So long as the distribution system is the same for all of the seller's goods distributed in a given area (for example, a manufacturer sells only to wholesalers who in turn supply the retailers) there is little likelihood of violation. However, where a seller sells to a buyer who serves both as a wholesaler and a retailer, injury to competition at the retail level may occur. A competitive advantage may also arise when a wholesaler customer of the seller sells to retailers at a lower price than the seller himself sells to retailers in the same market. Generally, however, the FTC has not questioned lower prices granted to bona fide wholesalers and jobbers.

Defenses. There are two primary defenses a seller may use to justify price differentials. The first is to show that a differential can be justified on the basis of differences in cost to the seller in manufacture, sale, or delivery arising from differences in method or quantities involved. The second defense, appearing in Section 2(b), is to show that a price differential was made in good faith to meet a price of a competitor. In addition, the last of the provisos of Section 2(a) specifically permits differentials in price in response to changing market conditions or changes in the marketability of the goods such as the danger of imminent deterioration of perishable goods or of the obsolescence of seasonal goods. The burden of proving a defense is specifically laid by Section 2(b) upon the person claiming the defense.

Cost Justification. If one buyer purchases the seller's product in reusable containers which may be handled by lift truck and in carload lots at his own warehouse and another buyer requires store door delivery of a few units at a time in small cartons, obviously the cost to the seller will be lower in the first case, although the exact amount of the price differential may be extremely difficult to justify. It is quite unlikely that quantity discounts based upon the annual volume of purchases can be justified on a cost-saving basis.

Nor is a seller likely to be able to justify pricing a favored customer on something near to a marginal cost basis because the economies of the additional business would vanish if the other customers were lost. However, the difficulties of cost accounting for a specific product have been recognized and averaging of costs is permitted both by the FTC and the Supreme Court.

Meeting Competition. Section 2(b) states:

> Upon proof being made, at any hearing on a complaint under this section, that there has been discrimination in price or services or facilities furnished, the burden of rebutting the prima facie case thus made by showing justification shall be upon the person charged with a violation of this section, and unless justification shall be affirmatively shown, the Commission is authorized to issue an order terminating the discrimination: *Provided, however,* That nothing herein contained shall prevent a seller rebutting the prima facie case thus made by showing that his lower price or the furnishing of services or facilities to any purchaser or purchasers was made in good faith to meet an equally low price of a competitor, or the services or facilities furnished by a competitor.

Although meeting a competitor's price is an absolute defense, the FTC has taken a very strict view toward it and has been successful in persuading the courts to limit its application. For example, a seller cannot claim the defense if he knows or should know that the competitor's price which he met was itself an unlawful price discrimination. The seller can only meet, not undercut, the lower price of his competitor, and he cannot use the defense to meet a competitor's price for goods of lower quality or in a larger quantity than those involved in the seller's quotation. Nor can he use a price necessary to meet a specific competitive situation to charge systematically lower prices to a certain customer or customers. The FTC has taken the position that the defense is available only to meet a specific competitor's price in order to keep a specific customer and not to gain new customers by meeting the price of a competitor. This view was rejected by the Seventh Circuit Court, however.[1] Although the seller usually cannot prove that a competitor actually did offer the lower price, he must act upon reasonable belief, and merely taking the word of a customer or even one's own salesman may be held not to be sufficient grounds.

SUMMARY

The objectives of the Robinson-Patman Act, amending the Clayton Act, are to prevent discrimination in price or services by sellers which affect competition among their customers and to prevent discriminatory prices which a seller might use to gain an advantage over his own competitors.

Other discriminatory practices which involve two or more states are covered

---

[1] *Sunshine Biscuits, Inc. v. FTC,* 306 F.2d 48 (7th Cir. 1962).

by the act, either discrimination between buyers located in different states or discrimination by a seller between customers in a state different from the one in which he is located.

Differences in prices are unlawful under Section 2(a) only if: (1) there are two or more contemporaneous sales by the same seller, (2) at different prices, (3) of commodities of like grade and quality, (4) where at least of one the sales is made in interstate commerce, (5) the discrimination tends to diminish competition, and (6) causes injury to the plaintiff.

A seller has two defenses to justify differences in price between customers—(1) that the difference in price reflects differences in cost to the seller in manufacture, sale or delivery and (2) that the discriminatory price merely meets a nondiscriminatory price of a competitor for goods of the same quantity and quality.

Utah Pie Co. v. Continental Baking Co.

386 U.S. 685 (U.S. Sup. Ct. 1967)

Suit for treble damages and injunction brought by Utah Pie Company (plaintiff) against Continental Baking Company, Carnation Company and Pet Milk Company (defendants) charging conspiracy under the Sherman Act and price discrimination under the Robinson-Patman Act. The jury found for Utah Pie on the price discrimination charge. The circuit court reversed on appeal. Reversed.

Utah Pie had been baking pies in its plant in Salt Lake City and selling them in the surrounding area for 30 years. It had entered the frozen pie business in late 1957 and it was immediately successful. It was a small company having 18 employees at the time of the trial. The defendant companies were large and each was a major factor in the frozen pie market in one or more regions of the country. All three entered the Utah frozen pie market before Utah Pie did. None of them had a plant in Utah and most of their pies were shipped in from California. This gave Utah Pie a natural advantage.

The number of frozen pies sold in the Salt Lake market during the time covered by the suit—1958 through the first eight months of 1961—increased nearly five-fold. Utah Pie's share of the market in those years was 66.5, 34.3, 45.5, and 45.3 percent, and its net worth increased from $31,651 on October 31, 1957 to $68,802 on October 31, 1961.

For most of the period covered by the suit Utah Pie's prices were the lowest in the market, but this was challenged by each of the defendant competitors at one time or another for varying periods. The level of prices for frozen pies in the market dropped during this period of intense competition, with Utah Pie's prices falling from $4.15 per dozen to $2.75 per dozen. Each of the defendant competitors sold frozen pies in the Salt Lake City market during parts of this period at prices lower than they were selling comparable pies in other markets considerably closer to their plants.

MR. JUSTICE WHITE. We disagree with the Court of Appeals in several respects. First, there was evidence from which the jury could have found considerably more price discrimination by Pet with respect to "Pet-Ritz" and "Swiss Miss' pies than was considered by the Court of Appeals. In addition to the seven months during which Pet's prices in Salt Lake were lower than prices in the California markets, there was evidence from which the jury could reasonably have found than in ten additional months the Salt Lake City prices for "Pet-Ritz" pies were discriminatory as compared with sales in western markets other than California. Likewise, with respect to "Swiss Miss" pies, there was evidence in the record from which the jury could have found that in 5 of the 13 months during which the "Swiss Miss" pies were sold prior to the filing of this suit, prices in Salt Lake City were lower than those charged by Pet in either California or some other western market.

. . . [T]he Court of Appeals almost entirely ignored other evidence which provides material support for the jury's conclusion that Pet's behavior satisfied the statutory test regarding competitive injury. This evidence bore on the issue of Pet's predatory intent to injure Utah Pie. As an initial matter, the jury could have concluded that Pet's discriminatory pricing was aimed at Utah Pie; Pet's own management, as early as 1959, identified Utah Pie as an "unfavorable factor," one which "d[u]g holes in our operation" and posed a constant "check" on Pet's performance in the Salt Lake City market. Moreover, Pet candidly admitted that during the period when it was establishing its relationship with Safeway, it sent into Utah Pie's plant an industrial spy to seek information that would be of use to Pet in convincing Safeway that Utah Pie was not worthy of its custom. Pet denied that it ever in fact used what it had learned against Utah Pie in competing for Safeway's business. The parties, however, are not the ultimate judges of credibility. But even giving Pet's view of the incident a measure of weight does not mean the jury was foreclosed from considering the predatory intent underlying Pet's mode of competition. Finally, Pet does not deny that the evidence showed it suffered substantial losses on its frozen pie sales during the greater part of the time involved in this suit. . . .

Utah Pies' case against Continental is not complicated. Continental was a substantial factor in the market in 1957. But its sales of frozen 22-ounce dessert pies, sold under the "Morton" brand amounted to only 1.3 percent of the market in 1958, 2.9 percent in 1959, and 1.8 percent in 1960. . . . Then in June 1961, it took the steps which are the heart of Utah Pie's complaint against it. Effective for the last two weeks of June it offered its 22-ounce frozen apple pies in the Utah area at $3.85 per dozen. It was then selling the same pies at substantially higher prices in other markets. The Salt Lake City price was less than its direct cost plus an allocation for overhead. Utah's going price at the time for its 24-ounce "Frost'N'Flame" apple pie sold to

Associated Grocers was \$3.10 per dozen, and for its "Utah" brand \$3.40 per dozen.

We need not dwell long upon the case against Carnation. . . . After Carnation's temporary setback in 1959 it instituted a new pricing policy to regain business in the Salt Lake City market. The new policy involved a slash in price of 60 cents per dozen pies, which brought Carnation's price to a level admittedly well below its costs, and well below the other prices prevailing in the market. The impact of the move was felt immediately, and the two other major sellers in the market reduced their prices. Carnation's banner year, 1960, in the end involved eight months during which the prices in Salt Lake City were lower than prices charged in other markets.

Section 2(a) does not forbid price competition which will probably injure or lessen competition by eliminating competitors, discouraging entry into the market or enhancing the market shares of the dominant sellers. But Congress has established some ground rules for the game. Sellers may not sell like goods to different purchasers at different prices if the result may be to injure competition in either the sellers' or the buyers' market unless such discriminations are justified as permitted by the Act. This case concerns the sellers market. In this context, the Court of Appeals placed heavy emphasis on the fact that Utah Pie constantly increased its sales volume and continued to make a profit. But we disagree with its apparent view that there is no reasonably possible injury to competition as long as the volume of sales in a particular market is expanding and at least some of the competitors in the market continue to operate at a profit. Nor do we think that the Act only comes into play to regulate the conduct of price discriminators when their discriminatory prices consistently undercut other competitors. . . . Courts and commentators alike have noted that the existence of predatory intent might bear on the likelihood of injury to competition. In this case there was some evidence of predatory intent with respect to each of these respondents. There was also other evidence upon which the jury could rationally find the requisite injury to competition. The frozen pie market in Salt Lake City was highly competitive. At times Utah Pie was a leader in moving the general level of prices down, and at other times each of the respondents also bore responsibility for the downward pressure on the price structure. We believe that the Act reaches price discrimination that erodes competition as much as it does price discrimination that is intended to have immediate destructive impact. In this case, the evidence shows a drastically declining price structure which the jury could rationally attribute to continued or sporadic price discrimination. The jury was entitled to conclude that "the effect of such discrimination," by each of the respondents, "may be substantially to lessen competition . . . or to injure, destroy, or prevent competition with any person who either grants or knowingly receives the benefit of such discrimination. . . ." The statutory test is one that necessarily looks forward on the basis of proven conduct in the past. Proper application of that standard here requires reversal of the judgment of the Court of Appeals.

MR. JUSTICE STEWART (DISSENTING). There is only one issue in this case in its present posture: . . . did the respondents' actions have the anticompetitive effect required by the statute as an element of a cause of action?

The Court's own description of the Salt Lake City frozen pie market from 1958 through 1961, shows that the answer to that question must be no. In 1958 Utah Pie had a quasi-monopolistic 66.5 percent of the market. In 1961—after the alleged predations of the respondents—Utah Pie still had a commanding 45.3 percent, Pet had 29.4 percent, and the remainder of the market was divided almost equally between Continental, Carnation, and other small local bakers. . . . Thus, if we assume that the price discrimination proven against the respondents had any effect on competition, that effect must have been beneficent.

. . . [T]he Court has fallen into the error of reading the Robinson-Patman Act as protecting competitors, instead of competition. . . . [L]ower prices are the hallmark of intensified competition.

U.S. v. U.S. Gypsum Co.

550 F.2d 115 (3d Cir. 1977)

The Government obtained an indictment against U.S. Gypsum Company (USG), five other major gypsum board producing companies, and a number of top executives of these firms (defendants), charging a violation of Section 1 of the Sherman Act. The principal defense was that the practice of the competitors in verifying between each other the quotations of prices made to customers, upon which the Government relied as evidence of a price fixing conspiracy, was permitted under Section 2(a) of the Robinson-Patman Act. The defendants appealed their convictions. Reversed and remanded.

The production of gypsum board, the principal component of interior walls in all types of buildings, is concentrated. During the period relevant to the case eight sellers accounted for more than 94% of national sales. The Government's case centered on a practice the sellers called "verification." An officer of one manufacturer would telephone a competing firm's officer to determine the price at which the competitor was offering gypsum board to a specific customer. The Government contended that the purpose of the practice was to stabilize prices and to "police" agreed-upon increases. The sellers insisted that the only purpose was to ensure compliance with the Section 2(b) of the Robinson-Patman, which permits a seller to meet the price of a competitor.

The sellers asserted that almost all discounting off list prices was not reflected on invoices so that checking invoices was ineffective and that purchasers often lied about competitor's offers in order to "whipsaw" a price cut. They argued that, therefore, they had three choices: (1) offer the reduced price on the basis of the purchaser's unconfirmed report and risk Robinson-Patman liability; (2) forego the price cut and risk losing the sale; or (3) call the competitor, verify his offer, and establish a section 2(b) defense to any Robinson-Patman charge concerning the price cut. They alleged error in the court's instructions with respect to the purpose of "verification."

HUNTER, CIRCUIT JUDGE. The Supreme Court has drawn a narrow line in deciding the data dissemination cases under section 1 of the Sherman Act. The difficulty derives from the fact that in competitive markets, information exchanges promote competition, while in oligopolistic markets, they depress competition.

The Supreme Court, 6–3, found [in *U.S. v. Container Corp.*] a combination or conspiracy proscribed by the Sherman Act. The freedom to supply information only if each defendant so chose was described merely as the freedom to withdraw from the agreement. From the concentrated nature of the industry, the majority concluded that the information exchanges must have set a floor under prices. The Court distinguished *Cement Manufacturers,* by pointing out that *Container* revealed no "controlling circumstance, viz., that cement manufacturers . . . exchanged price information as a means of protecting their legal rights from fraudulent inducements. . . ."

The question before us is whether sellers' alleged desire to establish a defense, to price discrimination charges, of compliance with section 2(b) of the Robinson-Patman Act would create a similar "controlling circumstance" that would legitimate an agreement otherwise prohibited by section 1 of the Sherman Act. If it would, then the trial court's instruction was improper in permitting the jury to convict sellers merely by finding an effect on prices, with no consideration of purpose. The Government denies that compliance with section 2(b) amounts to a "controlling circumstance." *Container,* claims the Government, limited "controlling circumstances" to prevention of fraud.

We do not read that case so narrowly. If the *Container* Court had sought to restrict the exception to "prevention of fraud," it could have distinguished *Cement Manufacturers* by noting simply that the *Container* case did not involve an attempt to thwart fraudulent purchasing practices, as had *Cement Manufacturers.* Instead, the Court used that much broader term "controlling circumstance. . . ."

Price verification, insist the sellers, must be considered a controlling circumstance. They claim that otherwise the very activity dictated by the Robinson-Patman Act could be used as evidence of conspiracy to convict under the Sherman Act. This conflict between the two acts would leave them with their three unappealing alternatives: (1) forego the price cut and probably lose a sale; (2) cut the price and risk a Robinson-Patman charge, if the buyer was lying; or (3) verify the price and risk the Sherman Act charge involved here.

The Government replies that nothing in the Robinson-Patman Act condones discussions about prices among competitors, nor has any court ever required such discussions as a condition of establishing a section 2(b) defense. Section 2(b), says the Government, does not force Sellers to verify. The Government poses its alternatives for the sellers: (1) refrain from cutting prices to the single buyer; (2) cut prices as to all buyers. In neither event will the seller break either antitrust law.

. . . We fear that so limiting sellers' alternatives would discourage price competition in industries like gypsum board, where the fact that price cutting occurs off list prices and invoices makes corroboration of reported competitor's offers difficult or impossible. In such industries, the Government's alternatives would eliminate the section 2(b) defense. This, it seems to us, would be more likely to put a floor under prices than to induce wholesale cutting . . . since a firm in a concentrated industry would be unlikely to reduce prices across the board simply to close a single sale. And it is through isolated price reductions that established price levels are eroded, precipitating widespread price cuts.

. . . Several witnesses testified that the purpose of the "verification" calls was to establish a Robinson-Patman defense and that their scope was confined by that purpose. There was also testimony concerning the unreliability of purchasers in the gypsum board market. Therefore, sellers were entitled to an instruction that their verification practice would not violate the Sherman Act if the jury found: (1) the sellers engaged in the practice solely to comply with the strictures of Robinson-Patman; (2) they had first resorted to all other reasonable means of corroboration, without success; (3) they had good, independent reason to doubt the buyer's truthfulness; and (4) their communication with competitors was strictly limited to the one price and one buyer at issue.

Brokerage Payments

Unlawful Brokerage. Section 2(c) establishes a per se violation of the act in that any type of dummy brokerage payment is prohibited, whether or not paid directly to the buyer. Unlike Section 2(a), no effect on competition need be shown to prove the violation. The section was aimed at price discrimination granted by means of brokerage payments to the buyer or his nominee. To accomplish this objective some courts have, by their interpretation of the section, eliminated the words "except for services rendered," and this is the position which has been taken by the FTC.[2] Even when a buyer's broker renders a service such as warehousing or breaking bulk, payment to him as been held to be a violation. Therefore, any commission or allowance to a person directly or indirectly controlled by the buyer is prohibited whether or not any of the payment ever reaches the buyer. Section 2(c) has been interpreted to prohibit commercial bribery or "kickbacks" to agents of customers if they have an anticompetitive effect. It has also been held to be a violation

[2] *Cf. Southgate Brokerage Co. v. FTC,* 150 F.2d 607 (4th Cir. 1945) with *Thomasville Chair Co. v. FTC,* 306 F.2d 541 (5th Cir. 1962).

of Section 2(c) if a seller's broker accepts a lower commission and passes the savings to the buyer. Independent grocers' buying cooperatives have found this subsection an obstacle to their operations although it was aimed at their major competitors, the large food chains.

Grace v. E. J. Kozin Co.

538 F.2d 170 (7th Cir. 1976)

Gerald Grace (plaintiff), as Trustee in Bankruptcy of S.I. Greene Co., brought a treble damage action against E. J. Kozin Co. and Bernard Kane (defendants) to recover damages alleged to have resulted from violation of Section 2(c) of the Robinson-Patman Act. Judgment for the Trustee was appealed. Affirmed as to the Robinson-Patman Act violation.

S. I. Greene Co. was a wholesaler of frozen and prepared seafood products. E. J. Kozin Co. was a corporation formed subsequent to the events complained of to take over a seafood business competing with Greene Co. that had been operated as a proprietorship by Erwin Kozin, a principal shareholder, director, and officer of the corporation. Bernard Kane was the son-in-law of Greene's president and sales manager of Greene. At a time subsequent to the events complained of but prior to suit, Kane left Greene and became principle shareholder, director and president of Kozin Co.

In October 1969 Kane convinced Greene to begin purchasing substantial quantities of seafood from Kozin. Kozin paid Kane $19,780 in commissions on those sales. The trial court awarded the Trustee for Greene Co. treble damages in the amount of $59,342.

CUMMINGS, CIRCUIT JUDGE. [Kozin and Kane] contend, and we agree, that [they] had embarked upon a joint enterprise whereby they purchased seafood products and resold them to Greene and other companies. Under this analysis, the district court was clearly correct in concluding that Kane breached his fiduciary duty to his employer by not offering Greene the opportunity to participate in the joint venture. Our duty is to determine the legal consequences of that breach of duty.

From this viewpoint, the district court correctly concluded that Kozin's inducement to Kane to participate in the joint venture constituted "commercial bribery." In Section 2(c) of the Robinson-Patman Act, Congress concluded that under certain circumstances it is an unfair trade practice for an agent to serve two masters. One of the purposes of this section is to protect the integrity of the principal-agent relationship where a violation has an anti-competitive effect. Therefore, although defendants argue that Section 2(c) of the Robinson-Patman Act does not reach commercial bribery cases such as this, we agree with the Sixth and Ninth Circuits that it does.

Defendants next contend that plaintiff failed to prove that Greene suffered an injury to its business cognizable under the antitrust laws. However, had Greene participated in the joint venture instead of Kane, Greene would have received the commissions. Quite logically, the district court concluded that as a result of Kozin's payments to Kane of commissions on sales to Greene, Greene paid a price for the products it purchased from Kozin which was higher than it would otherwise have paid except for the $19,780.64 in illegal commissions which Kozin paid Kane. From this evidence, the court could reasonably infer an injury to Greene. The presence of the kickback effectively precluded the realization of Greene's maximum profit potential, so that the fact of damage was adequately established. Further, the net effect of Kozin's bribery was indirect price discrimination with regard to the prices charged Greene by suppliers potentially common to Kozin and Greene.

Discriminatory Payments and Services

Introduction. Sellers and their customers both benefit from merchandising activities carried on by the customer to promote the sale of the goods. These would include such activities as advertising, displays of the goods, demonstrations and distribution of samples or premiums. Section 2(d) applies primarily to payments made by the seller to his customers to encourage such activities by them. Section 2(e) applies primarily to furnishing such services to the customer by the seller. These sections make either the payment for or the furnishing of a service illegal unless it is made available to all competing customers on proportionately equal terms. Many more enforcement actions have been brought under these sections than under Section 2(a).

Section 2(d) states:

> That it shall be unlawful for any person engaged in commerce to pay or contract for the payment of anything of value to or for the benefit of a customer of such person in the course of such commerce as compensation or in consideration for any services or facilities furnished by or through such customer in connection with the processing, handling, sale or offering for sale of any products or commodities manufactured, sold, or offered for sale by such person, unless such payment or consideration is available on proportionally equal terms to all other customers competing in the distribution of such products or commodities.

Section 2(e) declares:

> That it shall be unlawful for any person to discriminate in favor of one purchaser against another purchaser or purchasers of a commodity bought for resale, without or with processing, by contracting to furnish or furnishing, or by contributing to the furnishing of, any services or facilities connected with the processing, handling, sale, or offering for sale of such commodity so purchased upon terms not accorded to all purchasers on proportionally equal terms.

Both sections define per se violations. That is, whether the discriminatory allowance or service has the effect of injuring competition is immaterial. However, Section 2(b) of the act specifically includes the furnishing of services as part of the meeting competition defense, and this has been interpreted to apply to the payment of allowances under Section 2(d).

Competing Customers. It will be noted that the language of the two sections differs in some respects but they have been interpreted as having substantially the same meaning. For example, the requirement that the customers be competing in Section 2(d) has been read into 2(e).[3]

One may be considered a customer under the act although not buying directly from the seller offering services or payments. A buyer such as a food market buys for resale from a wholesaler is treated as a customer of the manufacturer or processer selling to the wholesaler.

Available. The requirement of availability demands of the seller offering promotional payments or services more than merely not denying the request of a customer to be given a similar payment or service. For example, to encourage a customer to include the seller's branded product in the customer's regular newspaper advertising, the seller may offer a cooperative advertising contract paying the buyer at some prescribed rate for such advertising. The seller must actually make known to its other customers the availability of a subsidy on a proportional basis.

To be available the service must be something appropriate to the customer. It is not enough for a seller of coffee to make a payment available only to customers who advertise in newspapers. The cooperative advertising plan must be flexible enough to permit all competing customers to participate—with handbills or other types of advertising or perhaps even other kinds of promotional devices such as window or counter displays.

On Proportionately Equal Terms. The most common method of proportionalizing is relating payments or services to the quantity of goods purchased. An example would be a payment of 50 cents per case of coffee or for each $5 worth of merchandise purchased. It has been suggested that payments or services, such as furnishing a display case, could be proportionalized by furnishing one case for each of the buyer's stores or payments could be related to the square feet of window space devoted to a display of the seller's product. The fact that it is impracticable to furnish a cosmetics demonstrator for one hour to a small drug store when one is furnished for a full day to a store selling eight times as much of the cosmetics firm's products does not excuse the offering of a proportional service. However, it need not be the same service; it might be quite a different sort of promotional device, such as a demonstration kit.

The seller who makes payments for customer's merchandising services has, according to the FTC, a duty to ensure that the payments are actually used for that purpose.

---

[3] *FTC v. Simplicity Pattern Co.*, 360 U.S. 55 (1959).

SUMMARY

Section 2(d) prohibits payments by a seller to a customer for furnishing any service or facility unless such payments are made available on proportionately equal terms to all competing customers. Section 2(e) prohibits the seller from himself furnishing services or facilities which are not available on a proportionalized basis. "Competing customers" has been held to include those buying for resale from a seller's customer such as a wholesaler. The requirement of availability requires that the seller actually make known the offer of the payment of service.

FTC v. Fred Meyer, Inc.

390 U.S. 341 (U.S. Sup. Ct. 1968)

This was a proceeding on petition of Fred Meyer, Inc. (petitioner), to review and set aside an order of the Federal Trade Commission (respondent) requiring Meyer to cease and desist from inducing certain suppliers to engage in discriminatory sales promotional activities prohibited by Section 2(d) of the Clayton Act as amended by the Robinson-Patman Act. The Court of Appeals for the Ninth Circuit disagreed in part with the Commission's interpretation of Section 2(d) and directed it to modify the order. Reversed and remanded to the FTC.

Fred Meyer, Inc., operating a chain of 13 supermarkets in the Portland, Oregon, area and making one fourth of the retail food sales in the area, conducted a four week promotional campaign each year. The promotion involved the distribution of a 72-page coupon book to its customers, each coupon good for a special price, often a one-third reduction from the regular price on a specified item carried in the Meyer stores. The coupon book was sold by Meyer to consumers for 10 cents and, in addition, Meyer charged each supplier joining in the promotion $3.50 for each coupon page. The suppliers usually underwrote the promotion further by redeeming coupons for cash or replacing without charge some proportion of the goods sold by Meyer during the promotion.

The proceeding before the commission involved Tri-Valley Packing Association and Idaho Canning Co. as suppliers who, it was alleged, had violated Section 2(d) in participating in the 1957 promotion. Both paid Meyer $3.50 for the coupon and each agreed to replace for Meyer every third can sold under the offer. Both suppliers also sold to two wholesalers, Hudson House and Wadhams, who resold to a number of Meyer's retail competitors. No comparable promotional allowances had been accorded either of the wholesalers.

Meyer argued that there had been no violation of Section 2(d) because Meyer was not competing with the wholesalers and that the retailers who were competing with Meyer were not customers of Tri-Valley and Idaho

Canning but were customers of the wholesalers. The FTC took the view that Meyer's retail competitors buying through the wholesalers were indirect customers of Tri-Valley and Idaho Canning. The FTC ruled that Section 2(d) prohibits a supplier from granting promotional allowances to a direct-buying retailer, such as Meyer, unless the allowances are also made available to wholesalers who purchase from the supplier and resell to retailers who compete with the direct buyer.

MR. CHIEF JUSTICE WARREN. We agree with the Commission that the proscription of Section 2(d) reaches the kind of discriminatory promotional allowances granted Meyer by Tri-Valley and Idaho Canning. Therefore, we reverse the judgment of the Court of Appeals on this point. However, because we have concluded that Meyer's retail competitors, rather than the two wholesalers, were competing customers under the statute, we also remand the case to the Commission for appropriate modification of its order.

For reasons stated below, we agree with Meyer that, on the facts of this case, Section 2(d) reaches only discrimination between customers competing for resales at the same functional level and, therefore, does not mandate proportional equality between Meyer and the two wholesalers.

Of course, neither the Committee Report nor other parts of the legislative history in so many words defines "customer" to include retailers who purchase through wholesalers and compete with direct buyers in resales. But a narrower reading of Section 2(d) would lead to the following anomalous result. On the one hand, direct-buying retailers like Meyer, who resell large quantities of their suppliers' products and therefore find it feasible to undertake the traditional wholesaling functions for themselves, would be protected by the provision from the granting of discriminatory promotional allowances to their direct-buying competitors. On the other hand, smaller retailers whose only access to suppliers is through independent wholesalers would not be entitled to this protection. Such a result would be diametrically opposed to Congress' clearly stated intent to improve the competitive position of small retailers by eliminating what was regarded as an abusive form of discrimination. If we were to read "customer" as excluding retailers who buy through wholesalers and compete with direct buyers, we would frustrate the purpose of Section 2(d). We effectuate it by holding that the section includes such competing retailers within the protected class.

Given these findings, it was unnecessary for the Commission to resort to the indirect customer doctrine. Whether suppliers deal directly with disfavored competitors or not, they can, and here did, afford a direct buyer the kind of competitive advantage which Section 2(d) was intended to eliminate. In light of our holding that "customer" in Section 2(d) includes retailers who buy through wholesalers and compete with a direct buyer in the resale of the supplier's product, the requirement of direct dealing between the supplier and disfavored competitors imposed by the Court of Appeals rests on too narrow a reading of the statute.

Although we approach the Commission's ruling with the deference due the agency charged with day-to-day administration of the Act, we hold that, at least on the facts before us, Section 2(d) does not require proportional equality between Meyer and the two wholesalers.

We recognize that it would be both inappropriate and unwise to attempt to formulate an all-embracing rule applying the elusive language of the section to every system of distribution a supplier might devise for getting his product to the consumer. But, on the concrete facts here presented, it is clear that the direct impact of Meyer's receiving discriminatory promotional allowances is felt by the disfavored retailers with whom Meyer competes in resales. We cannot assume without a clear indication from Congress that Section 2(d) was intended to compel the supplier to pay the allowances to a reseller further up the distributive chain who might or might not pass them on to the level where the impact would be felt directly. We conclude that the most reasonable construction of Section 2(d) is one which places on the supplier the responsibility for making promotional allowances available to those resellers who compete directly with the favored buyer.

The Commission argues here that the view we take of Section 2(d) is impracticable because suppliers will not always find it feasible to bypass their wholesalers and grant promotional allowance directly to their numerous retail outlets. Our decision does not necessitate such bypassing. We hold only that, when a supplier gives allowances to a direct-buying retailer, he must also make them available on comparable terms to those who buy his products through wholesalers and compete with the direct buyer in resales. Nothing we have said bars a supplier, consistently with other provisions of the anti-trust laws, from utilizing his wholesalers to distribute payments or administer a promotional program, so long as the supplier takes responsibility, under rules and guides promulgated by the Commission for the regulation of such practices, for seeing that the allowances are made available to all who compete in the resale of his product.

Buyer Inducement of Discrimination

Inducements Prohibited. Section 2(f) is directed at the buyer and makes it illegal for him to induce or receive knowingly a discrimination in price prohibited by Section 2(a). It states:

> That it shall be unlawful for any person engaged in commerce, in the course of such commerce, knowingly to induce or receive a discrimination in price which is prohibited by this section.

It does not apply to promotional payments or services prohibited by Sections 2(d) and 2(e). A violation occurs only when the buyer knows that the price he receives is lower than that which the seller charges other customers. However, he need not have knowledge that the discrimination actually violates Section 2(a). For example, to be in violation of Section 2(f) the buyer need not be aware of the injury to competition necessary for a violation of Section 2(a).

Problem Cases

1. Jim and Bill Beam, d/b/a Beam Brothers Contractors, operated an asphalt cement mixing plant primarily for their own use in constructing, repairing and resurfacing highways within the state of Arkansas. From 1966 to 1969 they purchased the asphalt and oil used in their plant from the Lion Oil Division of Monsanto Company, Inc., at Eldorado, Arkansas. Monsanto quoted a price for asphaltic products on a job-by-job basis, continuing the same price until the job was completed. Prices quoted differed from job to job and, therefore, different contractors received different prices. The Beams experienced financial problems and eventually suffered the loss of all of their equipment and were forced out of business.

   They brought a treble damage suit against Monsanto, claiming damages of $15,000 by reason of being charged higher prices on their jobs than were charged other contractors. One of Monsanto's defenses was that the Robinson-Patman Act did not apply because interstate commerce was not involved. Is this a good defense?

2. FLM Collision Parts, Inc., a small company in Yonkers, N.Y., was selling "crash parts" for automobiles manufactured by the Ford Motor Company to independent automobile repair shops. Ford sold the parts only to franchised Ford and Lincoln-Mercury dealers either to use in their own repair work or to resell to independent repair shops, and it refused to sell directly to FLM. In 1968 Ford established a wholesale incentive allowance for parts purchased for resale, and the dealer from whom FLM purchased its requirements passed substantially all of this discount on to FLM. Beginning in 1972 Ford discontinued the allowance (in order to reduce competition for resale of parts between companies like FLM and Ford dealers, FLM alleged). The result was that Ford charged its dealers who sold to middlemen like FLM a higher price than it charged Ford dealers who sold the parts directly to an independent body shop.

   FLM brought a treble damage action under Section 2(a) of the Robinson-Patman Act. Ford's defense was that the price differential is not prohibited by Section 2(a) because it involves a "functional discount." Is this a good defense?

3. American Can Company granted quantity discounts on a scale ranging from 1 percent to 5 percent of annual purchases. The 1-percent discount was granted to customers who purchased between $500,000 and $1 million worth of cans annually. Bruce's Juices purchased approximately $350,000 worth of cans per year and received no discount. Two of its competitors had canneries nearby which used about the same volume of cans but these customers were permitted to pool their purchases with the result that one qualified for the 5-percent discount and the other for a 4-percent discount. The purchases of 98 percent of the customers of American Can were too small to qualify them for any discount. Only three customers received the 5-percent discount. Bruce's brought an action for treble damages against American Can. Is the discount policy a violation of Section 2(a)?

4. Forster, a manufacturer of wooden clothespins, gave a number of distributors in the Pittsburgh market one case of clothespins free for each ten cases purchased, a deal not

available elsewhere. When charged by the FTC with a violation of Section 2(a), Forster's executives testified to the effect that 10 of the 125 clothespin buyers in the Pittsburgh area "reported" that Penley, a competitor seeking to enter the market, was "quoting" or "offering" a 10-percent price concession. There was no testimony that any of these buyers had themselves been made the price reduction offer. Is this a good defense under Section 2(b)?

5. Vebco, Inc., had been a distributor in the El Paso, Texas, and Arizona market for AMXCO, Inc., formerly American Excelsior Company. AMXCO manufactured pads for evaporative type air conditioners and sold them throughout the Southwest through distributors. After a change in AMXCO's price to Vebco for the pads, Vebco began manufacturing competitive pads by hand. In January 1971 Vebco cut its price to discount houses in the El Paso area to 14.5 percent below list price and was able to take the large K-Mart account away from an AMXCO distributor. In March AMXCO established a 25-percent discount. However, no sales were made at that price because Vebco verified the price quotations and notified its customers that it would also give a 25-percent discount. AMXCO then lowered its price to a 32.5-percent discount, and Vebco again met this price. Vebco couldn't hold to this price and soon went back to the 25-percent discount. AMXCO then made one sale to K-Mart at a 39-percent discount but announced a 25-percent discount for the 1972 season.

   Vebco filed a treble damage suit charging a violation of Section 2(a) of the Robinson-Patman Act.

   As evidence of predatory intent by AMXCO, it produced a memo by an AMXCO manager who suggested four alternative ways of dealing with the intense competition, one of these being to offer prices low enough in El Paso that Vebco would lose money at a competitive price. AMXCO's evidence showed that at its lowest price quoted in El Paso it made a slight manufacturing profit and a higher profit in its sale division. Vebco's cooler pad sales had increased every year since 1968 except for a slight decline in 1972, and AMXCO's share of the national market had declined steadily since 1969.

   The jury trial ended in a verdict for AMXCO. Vebco appealed, claiming the court erred in failing to direct a verdict in Vebco's favor because of AMXCO's predatory intent. Should the judgment be affirmed?

6. Haveg Industries had entered into a contract to sell certain goods to Republic Packaging Corporation at a price higher than it had sold such goods to one of Republic's competitors. Haveg then refused to complete the sale or to sell to Republic at any price. Did Haveg violate the Robinson-Patman Act?

7. Broch, a broker for Canada Foods and several other food products manufacturers, tried to make a sale to Smucker of apple concentrate processed by Canada Foods. The regular price was $1.30 per gallon in 50-gallon drums and Canada Foods usually paid Broch a 5-percent commission. Smucker wanted 500 gallons but was willing to pay only $1.25 per gallon. Canada Foods agreed to make the sale at that price if Broch would agree to reduce its brokerage to 3 percent. Thus, in effect, the seller and broker equally shared the price reduction. The sale was completed and subsequent sales were made to Smucker on the same basis. Sales by Broch to other customers continued at $1.30 and 5-percent commission. The FTC charged Broch with a violation of Section 2(c) of the amended Clayton Act. Broch defended on the grounds that it was an independent selling agent, was not covered by Section 2(c), and had not paid anything of value as a commission or other compensation to the buyer. Is Broch's defense good?

8. Vanity Fair Paper Mills used a standard cooperative advertising agreement in selling its household paper products to retail and wholesale grocers and druggists in the Texas-

Louisiana area. Also, because it did not have funds available for extensive advertising, it occasionally participated in special promotions by its customers that featured its products along with other suppliers. Weingarten, a large retail grocery chain operating in the area, requested Vanity Fair to participate in its 57th Anniversary Sale. It offered Vanity Fair a schedule of promotional services combining an advertisement of Vanity Fair's products in Weingarten's newspaper advertising and special product displays and the "personal enthusiasm" of Weingarten store personnel in one or more of the geographical areas covered by Weingarten stores. The cost of participation, according to the schedule, ranged from \$56.05 to \$3,995.90. Vanity Fair chose the \$215 item which gave it the promotional service in all of Weingarten's Texas and Louisiana stores plus 1/16 page in the newspapers in Houston, Freeport, Baytown, and Texas City.

Childs Big Chain was the only other customer of Vanity Fair which competed with Weingarten in southeastern Texas and southwestern Louisiana which received a special promotional allowance. None of the other customers requested such an allowance. The combined payments from the standard cooperative advertising contract and the special promotional allowances gave Weingarten 3.4 percent and Childs 2.2 percent on Vanity Fair's gross sales to them. The other customers who received no special allowance received allowances ranging from 1.9 percent to zero.

Did the allowance to Weingarten violate Section 2(d)?

9. For two years Blass and Cohn, competing department stores, carried Elizabeth Arden Cosmetics. Arden paid Blass an allowance equal to one half the salary of a clerk-demonstrator to push the products and an allowance equal to the full amount of a demonstrator's salary to Cohn. Sales of Arden's products by the two stores fluctuated—for some periods Blass's sales exceed Cohn's although for the full two years Cohn bought \$11,251 and Blass \$8,788 of Arden's products. Blass sued Arden, alleging violation of Sections 2(d) and 2(e) of the amended Clayton Act and asked for treble damages based on the difference in allowances made between Blass and Cohn. Arden argued that Section 2(e) was unconstitutional because it was not expressly limited to transactions in interstate commerce and that Blass had made no showing that its business had been injured as a result of the discrimination. Should Blass recover three times the amount of the difference the allowances to Blass and those to Cohn?

10. A number of small firms organized themselves into a buying group in order to obtain the economies and volume discounts available to large-scale buyers. The member firms would place their individual orders in the name of their buying group, the American Motor Specialties Company. These orders were sent either directly to the manufacturer or were sent through the group office without any consolidation of member orders. Shipments were made directly to the individual firms, and the rebates were shared on the basis of the proportion the individual members' purchases bore to the group's total purchases. When this arrangement was attacked, American Motors Specialists defended on the ground that the FTC failed to prove that they had *knowingly* induced or received discriminatory prices. Did American Motors Specialties' buying practice violate Section 2(f)?

53

The Federal Trade Commission, Consumer Protection, and Antitrust Exemptions

The Federal Trade Commission Act

The Federal Trade Commission Act [38 Stat. 717 (1914) as amended, 15 U.S.C. §§ 41–58] like the Clayton Act was enacted because its proponents felt that the Sherman Act had not sufficiently curtailed certain monopolistic practices and tendencies in the American economy. The act created a special bipartisan administrative agency charged with giving expert and continuing enforcement of antitrust policies. Under Section 5 of the act the FTC is given very broad powers to police "unfair methods of competition in commerce, and unfair or deceptive acts or practices in commerce."

The Commission has described the factors it considers in determining whether a practice that is neither in violation of the antitrust laws nor deceptive is nonetheless unfair:

1. Whether the practice, without necessarily having been previously considered unlawful, offends public policy;
2. Whether it is immoral, unethical, oppressive, or unscrupulous;
3. Whether it causes substantial injury to consumers.

In 1977, the Commission had a budget of $52 million, employed 1,700 staff people, and had 759 investigations underway including proceedings against Exxon, General Motors, Sears, Kellogg, General Foods, ITT, and the American Medical Association. Each day the FTC receives a large number of wires and letters from private business firms and the general public reporting alleged violations of various federal laws. Nearly all FTC investigations and cease and desist orders are a byproduct of these communications.

While the Federal Trade Commission Act is not technically a part of the antitrust laws and private treble damage actions cannot be brought under Section 5, the act overlaps the Sherman Act in that it also makes illegal as "unfair methods of competition," any of the restraints of trade which are illegal under the Sherman Act. In addition, the powers of the FTC reach incipient anticompetitive practices, false advertising, and other deceptive practices which are not reached by the Sherman Act. The FTC has concurrent jurisdiction with the Department of Justice to enforce the Clayton Act. In practice, the FTC alone has brought the cases under the Robinson-Patman Act amendments to the Clayton Act. The FTC also has jurisdiction in regard to various other acts including: the Webb-Pomerene Act; Wool Products Labeling Act; Federal Drug and Cosmetic Act; Fur Products Labeling Act; Flammable Fabric Act; Lanham Trade-Mark Act; and the Fair Packaging and Labeling Act; and several consumer credit laws.

The FTC issues "cease and desist" orders against violations of the FTC Act which become final unless appealed to the courts. Businesses which violate these orders are subject to $10,000 fines for each day of continuing violation. Special penalties vary in regard to the other laws enforced.

Trade Regulation Rules. The FTC started issuing trade regulation rules in the early 1960s. Nearly all of these rules have been issued in the area of consumer protection but more recently rules are under consideration related to competition and competitive practices.[1] Hearings are now being held in regard to trade regulation rules dealing with lease covenants restricting competition in shopping centers, pricing and other practices by funeral directors, and termination clauses in gasoline dealer leases. After a trade rule has been issued such rule has the effect of law and violators can receive fines up to $10,000 per day.

SUMMARY

The FTC has broad powers to stop anticompetitive and deceptive practices. The Commission issues cease and desist orders and also has the power to levy fines. Private treble damage suits are not permitted for violations of the FTC Act. Trade Regulations rules have the effect of law and are being issued in increasing numbers by the FTC.

---

[1] See Chapter 41 for a discussion of the new FTC "Holder-in-Due-Course" Trade Regulation Rule designed to afford more protection for consumers.

FTC v. Sperry and Hutchinson Co.

405 U.S. 233 (U.S. Sup.Ct 1972)

Cease-and-desist order brought by the FTC (plaintiff) against the Sperry and Hutchinson Co. (S&H) (defendant). The FTC appealed from an adverse judgment. Reversed and remanded to the FTC.

S&H, the trading stamp concern, sought to limit unauthorized commercial exchanges and redemptions of its stamps. The S&H company believed that commercial 'trafficking' in the stamps would seriously impair the consumer interest and consequently, adversely affect their stamp business. Between 1957 and 1965, the company threatened or instituted various legal action in 258 instances where it felt there existed unauthorized trading, and the FTC found that such actions violated Section 5 of the FTC Act. S&H conceded that it had acted in such a manner, but argued that its conduct was beyond the scope of Section 5.

MR. JUSTICE WHITE. In reality, the question is a double one: First, does Section 5 empower the Commission to define and proscribe an unfair competitive practice, even though the practice does not infringe either the letter or spirit of the antitrust laws? Second, does Section 5 empower the Commission to proscribe practices as unfair or deceptive in their effect upon consumers regardless of their nature or quality as competitive practices or their effect on competition? We think the statute, its legislative history, and prior cases compel an affirmative answer to both questions.

Unfair competive practices (are) not limited to those likely to have anticompetitive consequences after the manner of the antitrust laws; nor (are) unfair practices in commerce confined to purely competitive behavior.

Legislative and judicial authorities alike convince us that the Federal Trade Commission does not arrogate excessive power to itself if, in measuring a practice against the elusive, but congressionally mandated standard of fairness, it, like a court of equity, considers public values beyond simply those enshrined in the letter or encompassed in the spirit of the antitrust laws.

The general conclusion just enunciated requires us to hold that the Court of Appeals erred in its construction of Section 5 of the Federal Trade Commission Act.

Resort Car Rental System, Inc. v. FTC

518 F.2d 962 (9th Cir. 1975)

Action to review cease and desist order by the FTC (plaintiff) against Resort Car Rental System, Inc. (defendant) to eliminate false advertising by Resort. Cease and desist order affirmed.

Defendant consisted of several companies, all using the term "Dollar-A-Day" in their names. The FTC found that the term so used misled consumers and was a misrepresentation since the actual charges included the base rate plus a mileage charge, a minimum mileage requirement and insurance charges. Defendant maintains that the consumer is informed of the rates and charges before entering the contract, and therefore takes exception to the FTC ruling.

PER CURIAM. We review the evidence to determine whether it was sufficient to reasonably support the Commission's conclusions. The Federal Trade Commission's judgment is entitled to great deference here because deceptive advertising cases necessarily require "inference and pragmatic judgment."

Contrary to Resort's assertions, the public is not under any duty to make reasonable inquiry into the truth of advertising. The Federal Trade Commission Act is violated if it induces the first contact through deception, even if the buyer later becomes fully informed before entering the contract. Advertising capable of being interpreted in a misleading way should be construed against the advertiser.

Resort further complain that the Commission's order exceeded its lawful authority to proscribe unlawful trade practices. They argue that excision of the trade name "Dollar-A-Day" destroyed the valuable good will vested in that slogan when less drastic means could have achieved the desired end.

The Federal Trade Commission has broad discretion to fashion orders appropriate to prevent unfair trade practices. That was not abused here. The order was reasonably related to its goals. As the order stated, "[t]he trade name, 'dollar-a-day' by its nature has a decisive connotation for which any qualifying language would result in a contradiction in terms."

Fedders Corp. v. FTC

529 F.2d 1398 (2nd Cir. 1976)

Cease and desist action filed by the FTC (plaintiff) against Fedders Corp. (defendant). Judgment granting order appealed. Affirmed.

Fedders, an air conditioning equipment manufacturer, advertised that its products were "unique" because they have "reserve cooling power," a term intended to imply an unusual ability to cool in extreme conditions of heat and humidity.

OAKES, CIRCUIT JUDGE. A cease and desist order was entered by the Commission which prohibits Fedders from:

1. Representing, directly or by implication, that any air conditioner, on the basis of a comparison thereof with the air conditioners of other manufacturers then being marketed in the United States in commercial quantities, is unique in any material respect, unless such is the fact;

2. Making, directly or indirectly, any statement or representation in any advertising or sales promotional material as to the air cooling, dehumidification, or circulation characteristics, capacity or capabilities of any air conditioner, unless at the time of such representation respon-

ent has a reasonable basis for such statement or representation, which shall consist of competent scientific, engineering or other similar objective material or industry-wide standards based on such material.

Fedders does not challenge the Commission's finding that Fedders' advertising involved misrepresentations. Instead, it contends that the Commission's order is impermissibly broad in that it prohibits practices which are not sufficiently related to the unlawful practice actually found by the Commission and that these practices are, therefore, outside the proper scope of the Commission's remedial order. More specifically the claim is, as it has been all along, that the order appealed from covers not only "uniqueness" claims of the type which has been found false by the administrative law judge, but also covers advertising claims with respect to "performance characteristics" of the product, i.e., air cooling, dehumidification and circulation, which Fedders claims were not involved in the FTC proceeding. Since Fedders quite properly agrees that the Commission has the power within its discretion to enjoin "like and related acts" to the one condemned, the question before us is whether the Commission's order is sufficiently narrow to come within that standard. We hold that it is and deny the petition for modification of the order.

There is much broad language in the cases that the Commission has a wide discretion in its choice of a remedy to "cope with the unlawful practices" disclosed by the record. The Commission

. . . is not limited to prohibiting "the illegal practice in the precise form" existing in the past. This agency, like others, may fashion its relief to restrain "other like or related unlawful acts" (1941).

At the same time we take full cognizance of the petitioner's point that, as we expressed it in *Country Tweeds, Inc. v. FTC,* the overall concept of "reasonableness" has required the narrowing of deceptive advertising orders so that they more closely relate to the offending conduct while "still sufficiently prohibiting 'variations on the basic theme.' "

There is no dispute that paragraph 1 of the Commission's order is reasonably related to the unlawful misrepresentations Fedders has engaged in.

Paragraph 2 of the FTC order, we think, stands on no different footing. This part of the order, which forbids petitioner from making advertising claims as to the "air cooling, dehumidification, or circulation characteristics, capacity or capabilities of any air conditioner" unless substantiated is also reasonably related to the prior misrepresentations which Fedders employed in its sales program.

FTC v. National Comm'n on Egg Nutrition

517 F.2d 485 (7th Cir. 1975)

Action by the FTC (plaintiff) to enjoin the National Commission on Egg Nutrition (defendant) from making false statements in advertising. Judgment for National Commission appealed. Reversed.

The National Commission on Egg Nutrition (NCEN) had published advertising representing that there is no scientific evidence that eating eggs increases the risk of heart disease or heart attack. The FTC sought to enjoin such representations as false and violative of the Federal Trade Commission Act, Sections 5 and 12.

TONE, CIRCUIT JUDGE. NCEN argues that the issuance of an injunction would at least raise a serious First Amendment question. As Chief Judge Fairchild's concurring opinion suggests, the First Amendment is not "wholly irrelevant if government selectively seeks to prohibit commercial advertising because it espoused one side of a genuine controversy." NCEN has done more than espouse one side of a genuine controversy, however. It has made statements denying the existence of scientific evidence which the record clearly shows does exist. These statements are, therefore, false and misleading. "There is no constitutional right to disseminate false or misleading advertisements."

Regardless of the reach of the First Amendment in this area, we think the injunction should not go so far as to prohibit NCEN from making a fair presentation of its side of the controversy. NCEN should, as the Commission contends, be enjoined from disseminating in commerce or by mail advertising containing statements to the effect that there is no scientific evidence that increased intake of dietary cholesterol resulting from eating eggs increases the risk of heart disease or attendant or related conditions or other statements tending to misrepresent the state of scientific evidence on the subject in question. The injunction should not, however, prohibit NCEN from stating that there is scientific evidence supporting the theory that dietary cholesterol intake is not harmful, or from describing that evidence, provided that it also states that there is substantial contrary evidence.

FTC v. Texaco, Inc.

393 U.S. 223 (U.S. Sup. Ct. 1968)

The FTC (plantiff) brought this proceeding against Texaco (defendant) under Section 5 of the FTC Act charging that Texaco's sales commission plan with its dealers constituted an unfair method of competition. The Circuit Court set aside a cease and desist order issued by the Commission and the Commission appealed. Reversed.

MR. JUSTICE BLACK. The question presented by this case is whether the FTC was warranted in finding that it was an unfair method of competition in violation of § 5 of the Federal Trade Commission Act for respondent Texaco to undertake to induce its service station dealers to purchase Goodrich tires, batteries, and accessories (hereafter referred to as TBA) in return for a commission paid by Goodrich to Texaco.

The Commission and Texaco agreed that the Texaco-Goodrich arrangement for marketing TBA will fall under the rationale of our *Atlantic* decision if the Commission was correct in its three ultimate conclusions that (1) Texaco has dominant economic power over its dealers; (2) that Texaco exercises that power over its dealers in fulfilling its agreement to promote and sponsor Goodrich products; and (3) that anticompetitive effects result from the exercise of that power.

That Texaco holds dominant economic power over its dealers is clearly shown by the record in this case. In fact, Texaco does not contest the conclusion of the Court of Appeals below and the Fifth Circuit Court of Appeals in *Shell* that such power is "inherent in the structure and economics of the petroleum distribution system." Nearly 40% of the Texaco dealers lease their stations from Texaco. These dealers typically hold a one-year lease on their stations, and these leases are subject to termination at the end of any year on 10 days' notice. At any time during the year a man's lease on his service station may be immediately terminated by Texaco without advance notice if in Texaco's judgment any of the "house-keeping" provisions of the lease, relating to the use and appearance of the station, are not fulfilled. The contract under which Texaco dealers receive their vital supply of gasoline and other petroleum products also runs from year to year and is terminable on 30 days' notice under Texaco's standard form contract. The average dealer is a man of limited means who has what is for him a sizable investment in his station. He stands to lose much if he incurs the ill will of Texaco. As Judge Wisdom wrote in *Shell,* "A man operating a gas station is bound to be overawed by the great corporation that is his supplier, his banker, and his landlord."

It is against the background of this dominant economic power over the dealers that the sales commission arrangement must be viewed. The Texaco-Goodrich agreement provides that Goodrich will pay Texaco a commission of 10 percent on all purchases by Texaco service station dealers of Goodrich TBA. In return, Texaco agrees to "promote the sale of Goodrich products" to Texaco dealers. During the five-year period studied by the Commission (1952–1956) $245 million of the Goodrich and Firestone TBA sponsored by Texaco was purchased by Texaco dealers, for which Texaco received almost $22 million in commissions. Evidence before the Commission showed that Texaco carried out its agreement to promote Goodrich products through constantly reminding its dealers of Texaco's desire that they stock and sell the sponsored Goodrich TBA. Texaco emphasizes the importance of TBA and the recommended brands as early as its initial interview with a prospective dealer and repeats its recommendation through a steady flow of campaign materials utilizing Goodrich products. Texaco salesmen, the primary link between Texaco and the dealers, promote Goodrich products in their day-to-day contact with the Texaco dealers. The evaluation of a dealer's station by the Texaco salesman is often an important factor in determining whether a dealer's contract or lease with Texaco will be renewed. Thus the Texaco salesmen, whose favorable opinion is so important to every dealer, are the key men in the promotion of Goodrich products, and on occasion accompany the Goodrich salesmen in their calls on the dealers. Finally, Texaco receives regular reports on the amount of sponsored TBA purchased by each dealer. Texaco contends, however, that these reports are used only for maintaining its accounts with Goodrich and not for policing dealer purchases.

The sales commission system for marketing TBA is inherently coercive. A service station dealer whose very livelihood depends upon the continuing good favor of a major oil company is constantly aware of the oil company's desire that he stock and sell the recommended brand of TBA.

We are similarly convinced that the Commission was correct in determining that this arrangement has an adverse effect on competition in the marketing of TBA. Service stations play an increasingly important role in the marketing of tires, batteries, and other automotive accessories. With five major companies supplying virtually all of the tires that come with new cars, only in the replacement market can the smaller companies hope to compete. Ideally, each service station dealer would stock the brands of TBA that in his judgment were most favored by customers for price and quality. To the extent that dealers are induced to select the sponsored brand in order to maintain the good favor of the oil company upon which they are dependent, to that extent the operation of the competitive market is adversely affected. The nonsponsored brands do not compete on the even terms of price and quality competition; they must overcome, in addition, the influence of the dominant oil company that has been paid to induce its dealers to buy the recommended brand. While the success of this arrangement in foreclosing competitors from the TBA market has not matched that of the direct coercion employed by Atlantic, we feel that the anticompetitive tendencies of such a system are clear, and that the Commission was properly fulfilling the task that Congress assigned it in halting this practice in its incipiency. The Commission is not required to show that a practice it condemns has totally eliminated competition in the relevant market.

The Commission was justified in concluding that more than an insubstantial amount of commerce was involved. Texaco is one of the nation's largest petroleum companies. It sells its products to approximately 30,000 service stations, or about 16.5 percent of all service stations in the United States. The volume of sponsored TBA purchased by Texaco dealers in the five-year period 1952–1956 was $245 million, five times the amount involved in the *Atlantic* case.

Consumer Protection and Public Safety Laws

Health Protection. The Food, Drug, and Cosmetic Act[2] was passed to protect the health of the consuming public and to guard it against economic exploitation. These objectives are accomplished by regulating dangerous foods, drugs, and cosmetics, by prohibiting misleading and false labeling, by establish-

[2] 21 U.S.C.A. Section 301 et seq.

ing standards of quality, and by requiring that any of the products marketed be proven safe and effective. The Act specifically prohibits mislabeling and adulteration. Violations of the Act can result in seizure or destruction of the product.

The Fair Packaging and Labeling Act[3] seeks to protect consumers from inaccurate information regarding a products' quantity, and to encourage and facilitate consumer evaluation of comparable goods. Alcohol, tobacco, prescription drugs, meats, and poultry products are specifically excluded from coverage because they are regulated under other statutes. The Act requires that a product's label conform to a number of regulations; penalties for violations include product seizure.

Product Safety. Created by the Consumer Product Safety Act of 1972,[4] the Consumer Product Safety Commission is given broad powers to regulate the production and sale of consumer goods that are potentially dangerous. The commission has the power to formulate rules and to ban or seize hazardous products. The Act has four major purposes:

1. Protection against unreasonable risks from products.
2. Development of uniform safety standards.
3. Research into causes and prevention of product related injuries.
4. Assistance to consumers in evaluating comparable product safety features.

Civil and possible criminal penalties can be applied for violations of the Act.

Freedom of Information Act. The Freedom of Information Act[5] was enacted so as to provide citizens with information concerning the activities and determinations of governmental agencies, as well as the character and type of information compiled by such agencies relating to citizens.

The act has five key provisions: (1) it provides that agencies will publish or make available descriptions of its central and field organization, rules of procedure, statements of general policy, adjudicatory opinions, and administrative staff and instruction manuals, with exceptions in such matters as national defense, trade secrets, law enforcement, personal privacy, and commercial or financial information; (2) it provides that, with exceptions, agency meetings will be open to the public with prior notice given of such meetings in regards to the time, place and subject matter of the meetings, with provisions made for the availability of transcripts and minutes of meetings; (3) it provides that individuals can request to review their records and any information kept on them, and to request corrections for inaccurate, irrelevant, untimely or incomplete information and it establishes intra-agency and civil review proce-

---

[3] 15 U.S.C.A. Section 1451 et seq.

[4] 15 U.S.C.A. Section 2051 et seq.

[5] 5 U.S.C.A. 552.

dures to facilitate such requests; (4) it provides that an individual's name and address may not be sold or rented by an agency unless specifically authorized by law; and (5) it conditions disclosure of matters relating to individuals between agencies and other individuals.

Sunshine Act. The "Government in the Sunshine Act"[6] was enacted so as to entitle the public to information regarding the decision-making processes of the federal government. This act has five key features: (1) it requires that meetings of the members of multiheaded executive agencies be open to public observation, with specified exceptions; (2) it establishes procedures for closing certain meetings to the public; (3) it provides for judicial review of agency action regarding open meetings and related provisions; (4) it prohibits ex parte communications in certain administrative hearings; and (5) it amends the Freedom of Information and Federal Advisory Committee Acts.

Exceptions and Exemptions to Antitrust

In general. The 1914 Clayton Act created a broad exemption to the antitrust laws so as to permit the formation of agricultural cooperatives. A similar exemption was created for those engaged in commercial fishing in 1934.

The Clayton Act likewise attempted to exempt the activities of labor unions from the antitrust law but restrictive court interpretations left the unions subject to the laws until the exemption was reinterpreted after the passage of the Norris-LaGuardia Act in 1932.[7] Union activities are now largely exempted from the antitrust laws except where unions combine with or exert economic pressure on businesses for the purpose of fixing prices or imposing other illegal restraints on competition.[8]

The Webb-Pomerene Act exempts the activity of exporters engaged in foreign trade provided such activity does not "artificially or intentionally enhance or depress prices within the United States." It is argued that this exemption is necessary so that American firms can compete on an even foot with the many cartels operating in foreign markets.

Many industries are "affected with the public interest" and are subject to

[6] Public Law 94–409.

[7] The landmark case exempting unions for most purposes was *U.S. v. Hutchenson,* 312 U.S. 219 (1941).

[8] The *Pennington* case which follows illustrates a union (U.M.W.) with an employer group (union mine operators) for the purpose of injuring nonunion mine operators. In *Connell Construction Co. v. Plumber and Steamfitters Local,* 421 U.S. 616 (U.S. Sup. Ct. 1975) a closely divided court held the union in violation of the Sherman Act where the union picketed a general contractor with whom the union had no dispute in order to force the contractor not to deal with nonunion subcontractors.

varying degrees of regulation by state and federal agencies. Some of these industries including insurance, banking, electric power, airline, telephone, radio and television broadcasting, railroad, pipeline, stock exchange, and ocean shipping are permitted to compete within the varying limits set by the various regulatory commissions; but in general, regulation rather than competition is relied upon to protect the public interest.[9] In recent years there have been efforts to promote more competition, and to reduce the amount of regulation in many of these industries.

State Unfair Practice Acts. Thirty-one states have enacted "unfair practices" acts aimed at preventing sales below cost "for the purpose of injuring competitors or destroying competition." The acts usually attempt to define cost so as to include all costs including all overhead expenses. Some statutes require a definite percentage markup—such as 12 percent over the invoice or replacement cost and provide that any sale below such a figure is *prima facie* a sale below cost.

These statutes have been successfully challenged on constitutional grounds in a number of states. On the whole they have been rarely enforced and are of little importance.

***Noerr* and *Parker* Doctrines.** In the *Noerr* case (1961) the Supreme Court held that "the Sherman Act does not prohibit two or more persons from associating together in an attempt to persuade the legislature or the executive to take particular action with respect to a law that would produce a restraint or a monopoly." As has generally been true of other sweeping pronouncements made by the Court, the later cases begin to define limits and to make exceptions to this broad rule.[10]

In the *Trucking Unlimited* case several large trucking companies joined a conspiracy for the purpose of blocking the granting or transfer of the certificates of public convenience and necessity to all potential competitions. One or more of the members of the group would appear before the state regulatory commission and oppose each new application with or without cause and regardless of its merits and continue to do so throughout all stages of appeal. The Supreme Court Ruled that this conduct violated the Sherman Act saying that it fell within the "sham exception" to the *Noerr* case. The Court stated:

> A combination of entrepreneurs to harass and deter their competitors from having "free and unlimited access" to the agencies and courts, to defeat that right by massive, concerted and purposeful activities of the group are ways of building up one empire and destroying another. As stated in the concurring opinion, that is the essence of those parts of the complaint to

---

[9] The doctrine of "*primary jurisdiction*" often requires that the appropriate regulatory agency pass on public policy questions relating to competition in regulated industries before such issues can be presented in the courts.

[10] *Eastern R.R. President's Conference v. Noerr Motor Freight, Inc.*, 365 U.S. 127 (1961).

which we refer. If these facts are proved, a violation of the antitrust laws has been established. If the end result is unlawful, it matters not that the means used in violation may be lawful.[11]

Under the *Parker* doctrine "state actions" are exempt from the antitrust laws.[12] In order to find shelter under this exemption the acts must be those of state officials acting under authority of state law, or those of private individuals acting under the "active supervision of authorized state officials." The *Detroit Edison* case which follows apparently narrows the scope of the *Parker* exemption and may prove to be a landmark case in terms of antitrust exemption laws and policies.

SUMMARY

There are numerous major exceptions or exemptions to the application of the antitrust laws including: most union activities; agricultural cooperatives; exporters; public utilities and other regulated businesses; and state unfair practices acts, which prohibit sales below cost. On the whole unfair practice acts have been of little importance.

The *Noerr-Pennington* doctrine gives a broad antitrust immunity to political activities aimed at influencing the legislative branches of government even where the purpose and effect of such activities is to lessen competition. The *Parker* doctrine permits the states to replace competition with state regulation under an antitrust immunity given to "state action." There is a "sham" exception to these immunities where attempts are made to subvert the functions of the courts or the functions of regulatory agencies.

United Mine Workers v. Pennington

381 U.S. 657 (U.S. Sup. Ct. 1964)

The United Mine Workers of America (plaintiff) sued the Pennington partners (defendants) for royalty payments under the National Bituminous Coal Wage Agreement of 1950. Pennington filed a cross claim for damages under the antitrust laws. The Court of Appeals affirmed a trial court ruling in favor of Pennington. UMW appealed. Affirmed except as to the amount of damages awarded Pennington.

In its cross claim Pennington alleged that the UMW and certain large coal operators had conspired to restrain and monopolize commerce in violation of §§ 1 and 2 of the Sherman Act. It was alleged that, to eradicate overproduction in the coal industry, the UMW and large operators agreed to eliminate

[11] *California Transport Co. v. Trucking Unlimited,* 404 U.S. 508 (1972).

[12] *Parker v. Brown,* 317 U.S. 341 (1943).

the smaller companies, by imposing the terms of the 1950 Agreement on all companies regardless of ability to pay, by increasing royalties due the welfare fund, by excluding the marketing, production and sale of nonunion coal, by refusing to lease coal lands to nonunion operators and refusing to buy or sell coal mined by such operators, by obtaining from the Secretary of Labor the establishment of a minimum wage under the Walsh-Healey Act higher than that in other industries, by urging TVA to curtail spot market purchases which were exempt from the Walsh-Healey order, and by waging a price-cutting campaign to drive small companies out of the spot market.

MR. JUSTICE WHITE. The question presented . . . is whether in the circumstances of this case the union is exempt from liability under the antitrust laws. We think the answer is clearly in the negative and that the union's motions were correctly denied.

Hutchenson stated:

> So long as a union acts in its self-interest *and does not combine with non-labor groups,* the licit and the illicit under § 20 are not to be distinguished by any judgment regarding the wisdom or unwisdom, the rightness or wrongness, the selfishness or unselfishness of the end of which the particular union activities are the means. . . . [Emphasis added.]

And in *Allen Bradley Co. v. Union* . . . this Court made explicit what had been merely a qualifying expression in *Hutcheson* and held that "when the unions participated with a combination of business men who had complete power to eliminate all competition among themselves and to prevent all competition from others, a situation was created not included within the exemptions of the Clayton and Norris-LaGuardia Acts." . . . Subsequent cases have applied the *Allen Bradley* doctrine to such combinations without regard to whether they found expression in a collective bargaining agreement, and even though the mechanism for effectuating the purpose of the combination was an agreement on wages.

. . . We think it beyond question that a union may conclude a wage agreement with the multi-employer bargaining unit without violating the antitrust laws and that it may as a matter of its own policy, and not by agreement with all or part of the employers of that unit, seek the same wages from other employers.

But we think a union forfeits its exemption from the antitrust laws when it is clearly shown that it has agreed with one set of employers to impose a certain wage scale on other bargaining units.

We agree with the UMW that both the Court of Appeals and the trial court failed to take proper account of the *Noerr* case. In approving the instructions of the trial court with regard to the approaches of the union and the operators to the Secretary of Labor and to the TVA officials, the Court of Appeals considered *Noerr* as applying only to conduct "unaccompanied by a purpose or intent to further a conspiracy to violate a statute. It is the illegal purpose or intent inherent in the conduct which vitiates the conduct which would otherwise be legal." . . . *Noerr* shields from the Sherman Act a concerted effort to influence public officials regardless of intent or purpose. . . . It is clear under *Noerr* that Pennington could not collect any damages under the Sherman Act for any injury which it suffered from the action of the Secretary of Labor. The conduct of the union and the operators did not violate the Act, the action taken to set a minimum wage for government purchases of coal was the act of a public official who is not claimed to be a co-conspirator, and the jury should have been instructed, as UMW requested, to exclude any damages which *Pennington* may have suffered as a result of the Secretary's Walsh-Healey determinations.[13]

Cantor v. Detroit Edison Co.

428 U.S. 583 (U.S. Sup. Ct. 1976)

Treble damage antitrust action brought by Cantor, a retail druggist (plaintiff), against Detroit Edison Co. (defendant). Cantor was granted a review of an adverse lower court decisions.

Cantor alleged that Detroit Edison used its monopoly power in the distribution of electricity to restrain competition in the sale of light bulbs in violation of Sec. 2 of the Sherman Act and Sec. 3 of the Clayton Act. Detroit Edison had been providing "free" light bulbs to its customers since 1886. In 1916 the Michigan Public Service Commission (MPSC) approved a tariff filed by Detroit Edison setting forth the light bulb program. Thereafter, the Commission's approval of tariffs has included implicit approval of the "free" lamp exchange program.

MR. JUSTICE STEVENS. In this case we are asked to hold that private conduct required by state law is exempt from the Sherman Act. Two quite different reasons might support such a rule. First, if a private citizen has done nothing more than obey the command of his state sovereign, it would be unjust to conclude that he has thereby offended federal law. Second, if the State is already regulating an area of the economy, it is arguable that Congress did not intend to superimpose the antitrust laws as an additional, and perhaps conflicting, regulatory mechanism. We consider these two reasons separately.

We may assume that it would be unacceptable ever to impose statutory liability on a party who had done nothing more than obey a state command. Such an assumption would not decide this case, if, indeed, it would decide any actual case. For typically cases of this kind involve a blend of private and public decision making. The Court has already decided that state authorization, approval, encouragement, or participation in restrictive private conduct confers no antitrust immunity.

[13] The case was remanded to have the damages in the amount of $270,000 awarded Pennington scaled downward in accordance with the *Noerr* Doctrine.

The case before us also discloses a program which is the product of a decision in which both Detroit Edison and the Commission participated. Detroit Edison could not maintain the lamp exchange program without the approval of the Commission, and now may not abandon it without such approval. Nevertheless, there can be no doubt that the option to have, or not to have, such a program is primarily Detroit's, not the Commission's. Indeed, Detroit initiated the program years before the regulatory agency was even created. There is nothing unjust in a conclusion that Detroit's participation in the decision is sufficiently significant to require that its conduct implementing the decision, like comparable conduct by unregulated businesses, conform to applicable federal law. Accordingly, even though there may be cases in which the State's participation in a decision is so dominant that it would be unfair to hold a private party responsible for his conduct implementing it, this record discloses no such unfairness.

Apart from the question of fairness to the individual who must conform not only to state regulation but to the federal antitrust laws as well, we must consider whether Congress intended to superimpose antitrust standards on conduct already being regulated under a different standard. *Amici curiae* forcefully contend that the competitive standard imposed by antitrust legislation is fundamentally inconsistent with the "public interest" standard widely enforced by regulatory agencies, and that the essential teaching of *Parker v. Brown* is that the federal antitrust laws should not be applied in areas of the economy pervasively regulated by state agencies.

There are at least three reasons why this argument is unacceptable. First, merely because certain conduct may be subject both to state regulation and to the federal antitrust laws does not necessarily mean that it must satisfy inconsistent standards; second, even assuming inconsistency, we could not accept the view that the federal interest must inevitably be subordinated to the State's; and finally, even if we were to assume that Congress did not intend the antitrust laws to apply to areas of the economy primarily regulated by a State, that assumption would not foreclose the enforcement of the antitrust laws in an essentially unregulated area such as the market for electric light bulbs.

Unquestionably there are examples of economic regulation in which the very purpose of the government control is to avoid the consequences of unrestrained competition. Agricultural marketing programs, such as that involved in *Parker,* were of that character. But all economic regulation does not necessarily suppress competition. On the contrary, public utility regulation typically assumes that the private firm is a natural monopoly and that public controls are necessary to protect the consumer from exploitation. There is no logical inconsistency between requiring such a firm to meet regulatory criteria insofar as it is exercising its natural monopoly powers and also to comply with antitrust standards to the extent that it engages in business activity in competitive areas of the economy.

The mere possibility of conflict between state regulatory policy and federal antitrust policy is an insufficient basis for implying an exemption from the federal antitrust laws. Congress could hardly have intended state regulatory agencies to have broader power than federal agencies to exempt private conduct from the antitrust laws. Therefore, assuming that there are situations in which the existence of state regulation should give rise to an implied exemption, the standards for ascertaining the existence and scope of such an exemption surely must be at least as severe as those applied to federal regulatory legislation.

The separate opinions in this case make much of the obvious fact that *Parker v. Brown* implicitly held that California's raisin marketing program was not a violation of the Sherman Act. That is, of course, perfectly true. But the only way the legality of any program may be tested under the Sherman Act is by determining whether the persons who administer it have acted lawfully. The federal statute proscribes the conduct of persons, not programs, and the narrow holding in *Parker* concerned only the legality of the conduct of the state officials charged by law with the responsibility for administering California's program.

Problem Cases

1. The lease between a developer landlord—Tyson's Corner Regional Shopping Center, and a tenant—a large department store, gave the store a "sole and absolute" right to disapprove of other tenants' entry into the large suburban center. The Federal Trade Commission charged that these "prior approval provisions" restrained trade in violation of Section 5 of the Federal Trade Commission Act, not only by restricting competition from prospective tenants and competitors, but also by limiting the floor space available to new entries and prohibiting their use of "discount" advertising and their sale of certain brands of merchandise. How should the court rule on the Commissioner's allegations?
2. Firestone Tire Co., in promoting one of its tire products, used the following two advertisements. The first one claimed that the tires were "safe tires" which were custom built and personally inspected by skilled craftsmen. Firestone's own consumer survey showed that 15.3 percent of a scientifically selected sample of tire purchasers thought the advertisement meant that the tires were absolutely safe and absolutely free from any defects. The second advertisement claimed that the tire "stops 25 percent quicker." Firestone had performed one set of tests on one surface to substantiate this claim. The FTC ordered Firestone to cease and desist the use of these advertisements saying the first advertisement was deceptive and the second one unfair and deceptive because it was without substantial scientific test data to support it. Will the FTC order be overturned on appeal?
3. The Colgate-Palmolive Co. marketed and advertised a product called Rapid Shave. The television commercials showed the shaving cream being applied to sandpaper, with a razor immediately shaving the area clean. In actuality, it required 80 minutes for the sandpaper to soak before it could be shaved. Evidence also indicated that the sandpaper, as shown on television, was in fact plexiglass with sand applied. Colgate claimed that these misrepresentations are not so material as to mislead the public. The FTC claimed that any misrepresentation, if it induces the public to buy, is an illegal deception. The FTC issues a cease and desist order. Must Colgate comply?

4. The FBI received a letter in April 1976 requesting access under the Freedom of Information Act (FOIA) on all FBI files on the American Civil Liberties Union. The ACLU sued because the FBI failed to respond within the time allowed by the FOIA. The FBI asked the court to stay further proceedings under Section 552(a)(6)(C) of the FOIA which provides: "If the Government can show exceptional circumstances exist and that the agency is exercising due diligence in responding to the request, the court may retain jurisdiction and allow the agency additional time to complete its review of the records." The FBI claims that the large number of FOIA requests that they have received constitutes such "exceptional circumstances" and that the inability of their staff to respond to such a large volume demonstrates the "due diligence" required by the statute. Is the FBI entitled to a stay?

5. Ashland filed suit seeking an injunction ordering the FTC not to turn over to a congressional investigating subcommittee certain data concerning Ashland's natural gas holdings which the FTC had obtained. Ashland argued that "trade secret" information is exempt from disclosure under the Freedom of Information Act and that the same rule protecting trade secrets applies to data obtained by the FTC. Is Ashland correct?

6. St. Paul Title Insurance Corp. sold title insurance in the state of Missouri. Lawyers Title Co., a competitor, alleged that St. Paul had unfairly restrained competition through predatory pricing of title insurance by charging lower title insurance rates in St. Louis than in other areas of Missouri. The State of Missouri has enacted statutes which empower the state superintendent of insurance to conduct periodic examinations of accounts, to require reports and to hold public hearings to determine whether title insurance carriers are complying with all statutory duties. Lawyers Title Co. brings an action under the Sherman and Clayton Acts against St. Paul Title Corp. St. Paul claims that the McCarran-Ferguson Act exempts it from federal antitrust regulation as the Missouri statutes "regulate" pricing practices within the meaning of the Act. Is St. Paul's claim valid?

7. The City of Lafayette, Louisiana, brought a Sherman Act suit against the Louisiana Power and Light Company. Power and Light counterclaims, alleging the City itself was guilty of antitrust violations, by including anticompetitive covenants in its debentures and conspiring to extend power services beyond the lawful limit. The City defends on the basis that it is automatically exempt from the antitrust laws on the basis of the state action exemption. Is this a good defense?

8. Local 189 and Jewel Tea Company came to the agreement, after extended collective bargaining negotiations, that meat department operating hours "shall be 9 A.M. to 6 P.M. Monday through Saturday, inclusive. No customer shall be served who comes into the market before or after the hours set for the above." The restriction on marketing hours for fresh meat was in response to the desire by butchers to maintain shorter hours, and to eliminate the possibility that unskilled workers might conduct butchering operations. Jewel seeks to have the agreement set aside as violative of §§ 1 and 2 of the Sherman Act. Will Jewel prevail?

9. Plumbers Local, representing the plumbing and mechanical trades in Dallas, was a party to a multiemployer collective-bargaining contract with a mechanical contractors association. The agreement contained a "most favored nation" clause, by which the union agreed that if it granted a more favorable contract to any other employer, it would extend the same terms to all association members. The union picketed Connell Construction Co., a building contractor who subcontracted all of its plumbing and mechanical work, even though Connell had no employees the union wished to represent. The Union demanded that Connell agree to deal only with subcontractors that had current contracts in force

with the Union. Connell sued for treble damages under Section 1 of the Sherman Act. The union contends its activities are exempt. Is the union correct?

10. Armco Steel Corp. brought a private antitrust suit against the United Mine Workers of America. UMW had signed a no-strike agreement with Armco, but refused to cross picket lines when "unidentified pickets" appeared at the gates to Armco's mines. Armco alleged that the UMW had circumvented the provisions of the contract by arranging for picketing and then pretending to honor the illegal picket lines. UMW's defense was that none of the alleged actions on its part constituted a cause of action under the Sherman Act. Should the court dismiss the suit?
11. Meicler, a resident of Texas, purchased an automobile insurance policy from Aetna Casualty and Surety Co. Upon renewal, the insurer notified Meicler of his reclassification to a higher rate category because of an accident charged to him. Meicler found, in contacting other insurance companies, that they too refused to insure him at the previous rate. The State of Texas has a comprehensive insurance rate regulation program that each insurer must follow in establishing rates, which are established with reference to good or bad driving "points." Has the Aetna, along with other insurers, violated federal antitrust laws?
12. The Goldfarbs contracted to buy a home in Virginia. The lender who financed the purchase required them to secure title insurance necessitating a title examination of the property. The Goldfarbs found that a title search could only legally be performed by a member of the Virginia State Bar and no member of the bar would examine the title for less than the minimum fee prescribed by the County Bar Association and enforced by Virginia Bar Association. The fee amounted to 1 percent of the value of the property involved.

    The Goldfarbs brought a class action seeking injunctive relief and damages on the ground that the minimum fee schedule, as published by the County Bar Association and enforced by the state Bar, violated Section 1 of the Sherman Act. Can the Goldfarbs prevail?

Appendixes

Uniform Commercial Code

ARTICLE 1. General Provisions

PART 1

SHORT TITLE, CONSTRUCTION, APPLICATION AND SUBJECT MATTER OF THE ACT

§ 1–101. Short Title.

This Act shall be known and may be cited as Uniform Commercial Code.

§ 1–102. Purposes; Rules of Construction; Variation by Agreement.

(1) This Act shall be liberally construed and applied to promote its underlying purposes and policies.

(2) Underlying purposes and policies of this Act are

(a) to simplify, clarify and modernize the law governing commercial transactions;

(b) to permit the continued expansion of commercial practices through custom, usage and agreement of the parties;

(c) to make uniform the law among the various jurisdictions.

(3) The effect of provisions of this Act may be varied by agreement, except as otherwise provided in this Act and except that the obligations of good faith, diligence, reasonableness and care prescribed by this Act may not be disclaimed by agreement but the parties may by agreement determine the standards by which the performance of such obligations is to be measured if such standards are not manifestly unreasonable.

(4) The presence in certain provisions of this Act of the words "unless otherwise agreed" or words of similar import does not imply that the effect of other provisions may not be varied by agreement under subsection (3).

(5) In this Act unless the context otherwise requires

(a) words in the singular number include the plural, and in the plural include the singular;

General note: One asterisk (*) connotates "sections of the U.C.C. where the draftsmen offered the states a choice between several alternative provisions but only one of the alternatives is provided." Two asterisks (**) connotate "those sections of Article 9 which were changed by the 1972 amendments to the Code."

(b) words of the masculine gender include the feminine and the neuter, and when the sense so indicates words of the neuter gender may refer to any gender.

§ 1–103. Supplementary General Principles of Law Applicable.

Unless displaced by the particular provisions of this Act, the principles of law and equity, including the law merchant and the law relative to capacity to contract, principal and agent, estoppel, fraud, misrepresentation, duress, coercion, mistake, bankruptcy, or other validating or invalidating cause shall supplement its provisions.

§ 1–104. Construction Against Implicit Repeal.

This Act being a general act intended as a unified coverage of its subject matter, no part of it shall be deemed to be impliedly repealed by subsequent legislation if such construction can reasonably be avoided.

§ 1–105. Territorial Application of the Act; Parties' Power to Choose Applicable Law.

(1) Except as provided hereafter in this section, when a transaction bears a reasonable relation to this state and also to another state or nation the parties may agree that the law either of this state or of such other state or nation shall govern their rights and duties. Failing such agreement this Act applies to transactions bearing an appropriate relation to this state.

(2) Where one of the following provisions of this Act specifies the applicable law, that provision governs and a contrary agreement is effective only to the extent permitted by the law (including the conflict of laws rules) so specified:

Rights of creditors against sold goods. Section 2–402.

Applicability of the Article on Bank Deposits and Collections. Section 1–102.

Bulk transfers subject to the Article on Bulk Transfers. Section 6–102.

Applicability of the Article on Investment Securities. Section 8–106.

Perfection provisions of the Article on Secured Transactions. Section 9–103.

§ 1–106. Remedies to Be Liberally Administered.

(1) The remedies provided by this Act shall be liberally administered to the end that the aggrieved party may be put in as good a position as if the other party had fully performed but neither consequential or special nor penal damages may be had except as specifically provided in this Act or by other rule of law.

(2) Any right or obligation declared by this Act is enforceable by action unless the provision declaring it specifies a different and limited effect.

§ 1–107. Waiver or Renunciation of Claim or Right After Breach.

Any claim or right arising out of an alleged breach can be discharged in whole or in part without consideration by a written waiver or renunciation signed and delivered by the aggrieved party.

§ 1–108. Severability.

If any provision or clause of this Act or application thereof to any person or circumstances is held invalid, such invalidity shall not affect other provisions or applications of the Act which can be given effect without the invalid provision or application, and to this end the provisions of this Act are declared to be severable.

§ 1–109. Section Captions.

Section captions are parts of this Act.

PART 2
GENERAL DEFINITIONS AND PRINCIPLES OF INTERPRETATION

§ 1–201. General Definitions.

Subject to additional definitions contained in the subsequent Articles of this Act which are applicable to specific Articles or Parts thereof, and unless the context otherwise requires, in this Act:

(1) "Action" in the sense of a judicial proceeding includes recoupment, counterclaim, set-off, suit in equity and any other proceedings in which rights are determined.

(2) "Aggrieved party" means a party entitled to resort to a remedy.

(3) "Agreement" means the bargain of the parties in fact as found in their language or by implication from other circumstances including course of dealing or usage of trade or course of performance as provided in this Act (Sections 1–205 and 2–208). Whether an agreement has legal consequences is determined by the provisions of this Act, if applicable; otherwise by the law of contracts (Section 1–103). (Compare "Contract.")

(4) "Bank" means any person engaged in the business of banking.

(5) "Bearer" means the person in possession of an instrument, document of title, or security payable to bearer or indorsed in blank.

(6) "Bill of lading" means a document evidencing the receipt of goods for shipment issued by a person engaged in the business of transporting or forwarding goods, and includes an airbill. "Airbill" means a document serving for air transportation as a bill of lading does for marine or rail transportation, and includes an air consignment note or air waybill.

(7) "Branch" includes a separately incorporated foreign branch of a bank.

(8) "Burden of establishing" a fact means the burden of persuading the triers of fact that the existence of the fact is more probable than its non-existence.

(9) "Buyer in ordinary course of business" means a person who in good faith and without knowledge that the sale to him is in violation of the ownership rights or security interest of a third party in the goods buys in ordinary course from a person in the business of selling goods of that kind but does not include a pawnbroker. All persons who sell minerals or the like (including oil and gas) at wellhead or minehead shall be deemed to be persons in the business of selling goods of that kind. "Buying" may be for cash or by exchange of other property or on secured or unsecured credit and includes receiving goods or documents of title under a pre-existing contract for sale but does not include a transfer in bulk or as security for or in total or partial satisfaction of a money debt.

(10) "Conspicuous": A term or clause is conspicuous when it is so written that a reasonable person against whom it is to operate ought to have noticed it. A printed heading in capitals (as: NON-NEGOTIABLE BILL OF LADING) is conspicuous. Language in the body of a form is "conspicuous" if it is in larger or other contrasting type or color. But in a telegram any stated term is "conspicuous." Whether a term or clause is "conspicuous" or not is for decision by the court.

(11) "Contract" means the total legal obligation which results from the parties' agreement as affected by this Act and any other applicable rules of law. (Compare "Agreement.")

(12) "Creditor" includes a general creditor, a secured creditor, a lien creditor and any representative of creditors, including an assignee for the benefit of creditors, a trustee in bankruptcy, a receiver in equity and an executor or administrator of an insolvent debtor's or assignor's estate.

(13) "Defendant" includes a person in the position of defendant in a cross-action or counterclaim.

(14) "Delivery" with respect to instruments, documents of title, chattel paper or securities means voluntary transfer of possession.

(15) "Document of title" includes bill of lading, dock warrant, dock receipt, warehouse receipt or order for the delivery of goods, and also any other document which in the regular course of business or financing is treated as adequately evidencing that the person in possession of it is entitled to receive, hold and dispose of the document and the goods it covers. To be a document of title a document must purport to be issued by or addressed to a bailee and purport to cover goods in the bailee's possession which are either identified or are fungible portions of an identified mass.

(16) "Fault" means wrongful act, omission or breach.

(17) "Fungible" with respect to goods or securities means goods or securities of which any unit is, by nature or usage of trade, the equivalent of any other like unit. Goods which are not fungible shall be deemed fungible for the purposes of this Act to the extent that under a particular agreement of document unlike units are treated as equivalents.

(18) "Genuine" means free of forgery or counterfeiting.

(19) "Good faith" means honesty in fact in the conduct or transaction concerned.

(20) "Holder" means a person who is in possession of a document of title or an instrument or an investment security drawn, issued or indorsed to him or to his order or to bearer or in blank.

(21) To "honor" is to pay or to accept and pay, or where a credit so engages to purchase or discount a draft complying with the terms of the credit.

(22) "Insolvency proceedings" includes any assignment for the benefit of creditors or other proceedings intended to liquidate or rehabilitate the estate of the person involved.

(23) A person is "insolvent" who either has ceased to pay his debts in the ordinary course of business or cannot pay his debts as they become due or is insolvent within the meaning of the federal bankruptcy law.

(24) "Money" means a medium of exchange authorized or adopted by a domestic or foreign government as a part of its currency.

(25) A person has "notice" of a fact when

(a) he has actual knowledge of it; or

(b) he has received a notice or notification of it; or

(c) from all the facts and circumstances known to him at the time in question he has reason to know that it exists.

A person "knows" or has "knowledge" of a fact when he has actual knowledge of it. "Discover" or "learn" or a word or phrase of similar import refers to knowledge rather than to reason to know. The time and circumstances under which a notice or notification may cease to be effective are not determined by this Act.

(26) A person "notifies" or "gives" notice or notification to another by taking such steps as may be reasonably required to inform the other in ordinary course whether or not such other actually comes to know of it. A person "receives" a notice or notification when

(a) it comes to his attention; or

(b) it is duly delivered at the place of business through which the contract was made or at any other place held out by him as the place for receipt of such communications.

(27) Notice, knowledge or a notice or notification received by an organization is effective for a particular transaction from the time when it is brought to the attention of the individual conducting that transaction, and in any event from the time when it would have been brought to his attention if the organization had exercised due diligence. An organization exercises due diligence if it maintains reasonable routines for communicating significant information to the person conducting the transaction and there is reasonable compliance with the routines.

Due diligence does not require an individual acting for the organization to communicate information unless such communication is part of his regular duties or unless he has reason to know of the transaction and that the transaction would be materially affected by the information.

(28) "Organization" includes a corporation, government or governmental subdivision or agency, business trust, estate, trust, partnership or association, two or more persons having a joint or common interest, or any other legal or commercial entity.

(29) "Party," as distinct from "third party," means a person who has engaged in a transaction or made an agreement within this Act.

(30) "Person" includes an individual or an organization (See Section 1–102).

(31) "Presumption" or "presumed" means that the trier of fact must find the existence of the fact presumed unless and until evidence is introduced which would support a finding of its non-existence.

(32) "Purchase" includes taking by sale, discount, negotiation, mortgage, pledge, lien, issue or re-issue, gift or any other voluntary transaction creating an interest in property.

(33) "Purchaser" means a person who takes by purchase.

(34) "Remedy" means any remedial right to which an aggrieved party is entitled with or without resort to a tribunal.

(35) "Representative" includes an agent, an officer of a corporation or association, and a trustee, executor or administrator of an estate, or any other person empowered to act for another.

(36) "Rights" includes remedies.

(37) "Security interest" means an interest in personal property or fixtures which secures payment or performance of an obligation. The retention or reservation of title by a seller of goods notwithstanding shipment or delivery to the buyer (Section 2–401) is limited in effect to a reservation of a "security interest." The term also includes any interest of a buyer of accounts or chattel paper which is subject to Article 9. The special property interest of a buyer of goods on identification of such goods to a contract for sale under Section 2–401 is not a "security interest," but a buyer may also acquire a "security interest" by complying with Article 9. Unless a lease or consignment is intended as security, reservation of title thereunder is not a "security interest" but a consignment is in any event subject to the provisions on consignment sales (Section 2–326). Whether a lease is intended as security is to be determined by the facts of each case; however, (a) the inclusion of an option to purchase does not of itself make the lease one intended for security, and (b) an agreement that upon compliance with the terms of the lease the lessee shall become or has the option to become the owner of the property for no additional consideration or for a nominal consideration does make the lease one intended for security.

(38) "Send" in connection with any writing or notice means to deposit in the mail or deliver for transmission by any other usual means of communication with postage or cost of transmission provided for and properly addressed and in the case of an instrument to an address specified thereon or otherwise agreed, or if there be none to any address reasonable under the circumstances. The receipt of any writing or notice within the time at which it would have arrived if properly sent his the effect of a proper sending.

(39) "Signed" includes any symbol executed or adopted by a party with present intention to authenticate a writing.

(40) "Surety" includes guarantor.

(41) "Telegram" includes a message transmitted by radio, teletype, cable, any mechanical method of transmission, or the like.

(42) "Term" means that portion of an agreement which relates to a particular matter.

(43) "Unauthorized" signature or indorsement means one made without actual, implied or apparent authority and includes a forgery.

(44) "Value." Except as otherwise provided with respect to negotiable instruments and bank collections (Sections 3–303, 4–208 and 4–209) a person gives "value" for rights if he acquires them

(a) in return for a binding commitment to extend credit or for the extension of immediately available credit whether or not drawn upon and whether or not a chargeback is provided for in the event of difficulties in collection; or

(b) as security for or in total or partial satisfaction of a pre-existing claim; or

(c) by accepting delivery pursuant to a pre-existing contract for purchase; or

(d) generally, in return for any consideration sufficient to support a simple contract.

(45) "Warehouse receipt" means a receipt issued by a person engaged in the business of storing goods for hire.

(46) "Written" or "writing" includes printing, typewriting or any other intentional reduction to tangible form. As amended 1962 and 1972.

§ 1–202. Prima Facie Evidence by Third Party Documents.

A document in due form purporting to be a bill of lading, policy or certificate of insurance, official weigher's or inspector's certificate, consular invoice, or any other document authorized or required by the contract to be issued by a third party shall be prima facie evidence of its own authenticity and genuineness and of the facts stated in the document by the third party.

§ 1–203. Obligation of Good Faith.

Every contract or duty within this Act imposes an obligation of good faith in its performance or enforcement.

§ 1–204. Time; Reasonable Time; "Seasonably."

(1) Whenever this Act requires any action to be taken within a reasonable time, any time which is not manifestly unreasonable may be fixed by agreement.

(2) What is a reasonable time for taking any action depends on the nature, purpose and circumstances of such action.

(3) An action is taken "seasonably" when it is taken at or within the time agreed or if no time is agreed at or within a reasonable time.

§ 1–205. Course of Dealing and Usage of Trade.

(1) A course of dealing is a sequence of previous conduct between the parties to a particular transaction which is fairly to be regarded as establishing a common basis of understanding for interpreting their expressions and other conduct.

(2) A usage of trade is any practice or method of dealing having such regularity of observance in a place, vocation or trade as to justify an expectation that it will be observed with respect to the transaction in question. The existence and scope of such a usage are to be proved as facts. If it is established that such a usage is embodied in a written trade code or similar writing the interpretation of the writing is for the court.

(3) A course of dealing between parties and any usage of trade in the vocation or trade in which they are engaged or of which they are or should be aware give particular meaning to and supplement or qualify terms of an agreement.

(4) The express terms of an agreement and an applicable course of dealing or usage of trade shall be construed wherever reasonable as consistent with each other; but when such construction is unreasonable express terms control both course of dealing and usage of trade and course of dealing controls usage of trade.

(5) An applicable usage of trade in the place where any part of performance is to occur shall be used in interpreting the agreement as to that part of the performance.

(6) Evidence of a relevant usage of trade offered by one party is not admissible unless and until he has given the other party such notice as the court finds sufficient to prevent unfair surprise to the latter.

§ 1–206. Statute of Frauds for Kinds of Personal Property Not Otherwise Covered.

(1) Except in the cases described in subsection (2) of this section a contract for the sale of personal property is not enforceable by way of action or defense beyond five thousand dollars in amount or value of remedy unless there is some writing which indicates that a contract for sale has been made between the parties at a defined or stated price, reasonably identifies the subject matter, and is signed by the party against whom enforcement is sought or by his authorized agent.

(2) Subsection (1) of this section does not apply to contracts for the sale of goods (Section 2–201) nor of securities (Section 8–319) nor to security agreements (Section 9–203).

§ 1–207. Performance or Acceptance Under Reservation of Rights.

A party who with explicit reservation of rights performs or promises performance or assents to performance in a manner demanded or offered by the other party does not thereby prejudice the rights reserved. Such words as "without prejudice," "under protest" or the like are sufficient.

§ 1–208. Option to Accelerate at Will.

A term providing that one party or his successor in interest may accelerate payment or performance or require collateral or additional collateral "at will" or "when he deems himself insecure" or in words of similar import shall be construed to mean that he shall have power to do so only if he in good faith believes that the prospect of payment or performance is impaired. The burden of establishing lack of good faith is on the party against whom the power has been exercised.

§ 1–209. Subordinated Obligations.

An obligation may be issued as subordinated to payment of another obligation of the person obligated, or a creditor may subordinate his right to payment of an obligation by agreement with either the person obligated or another creditor of the person obligated. Such a subordination does not create a security interest as against either the common debtor or a subordinated creditor. This section shall be construed as declaring the law as it existed prior to the enactment of this section and not as modifying it.

ARTICLE 2. Sales

PART 1
SHORT TITLE, GENERAL CONSTRUCTION AND SUBJECT MATTER

§ 2–101. Short Title.

This Article shall be known and may be cited as Uniform Commercial Code—Sales.

§ 2–102. Scope; Certain Security and Other Transactions Excluded From This Article.

Unless the context otherwise requires, this Article applies to transactions in goods; it does not apply to any transaction which although in the form of an unconditional contract to sell or present sale is intended to operate only as a security transaction nor does this Article impair or repeal any statute regulating sales to consumers, farmers or other specified classes of buyers.

§ 2–103. Definitions and Index of Definitions.

(1) In this Article unless the context otherwise requires

(a) "Buyer" means a person who buys or contracts to buy goods.

(b) "Good faith" in the case of a merchant means honesty in fact and the observance of reasonable commercial standards of fair dealing in the trade.

(c) "Receipt" of goods means taking physical possession of them.

(d) "Seller" means a person who sells or contracts to sell goods.

(2) Other definitions applying to this Article or to specified Parts thereof, and the sections in which they appear are:

"Acceptance." Section 2–606.
"Banker's credit." Section 2–325.
"Between merchants." Section 2–104.
"Cancellation." Section 2–106(4).
"Commercial unit." Section 2–105.
"Confirmed credit." Section 2–325.
"Conforming to contract." Section 2–106.
"Contract for sale." Section 2–106.
"Cover." Section 2–712.
"Entrusting." Section 2–403.
"Financing agency." Section 2–104.
"Future goods." Section 2–105.
"Goods." Section 2–105.
"Identification." Section 2–501.
"Installment contract." Section 2–612.
"Letter of Credit." Section 2–325.
"Lot." Section 2–105.
"Merchant." Section 2–104.
"Overseas." Section 2–323.
"Person in position of seller." Section 2–707.
"Present sale." Section 2–106.
"Sale." Section 2–106.
"Sale on approval." Section 2–326.
"Sale or return." Section 2–326.
"Termination." Section 2–106.

(3) The following definitions in other Articles apply to this Article:

"Check." Section 3–104.
"Consignee." Section 7–102.
"Consignor." Section 7–102.
"Consumer goods." Section 9–109.
"Dishonor." Section 3–507.
"Draft." Section 3–104.

(4) In addition Article 1 contains general definitions and principles of construction and interpretation applicable throughout this Article.

§ 2–104. Definitions: "Merchant"; "Between Merchants"; "Financing Agency."

(1) "Merchant" means a person who deals in goods of the kind or otherwise by his occupation holds himself out as having knowledge or skill peculiar to the practices or goods involved in

the transaction or to whom such knowledge or skill may be attributed by his employment of an agent or broker or other intermediary who by his occupation holds himself out as having such knowledge or skill.

(2) "Financing agency" means a bank, finance company or other person who in the ordinary course of business makes advances against goods or documents of title or who by arrangement with either the seller or the buyer intervenes in ordinary course to make or collect payment due or claimed under the contract for sale, as by purchasing or paying the seller's draft or making advances against it or by merely taking it for collection whether or not documents of title accompany the draft. "Financing agency" includes also a bank or other person who similarly intervenes between persons who are in the position of seller and buyer in respect to the goods (Section 2–707).

(3) "Between merchants" means in any transaction with respect to which both parties are chargeable with the knowledge or skill of merchants.

§ 2–105. Definitions: Transferability; "Goods"; "Future" Goods; "Lot"; "Commercial Unit."

(1) "Goods" means all things (including specially manufactured goods) which are movable at the time of identification to the contract for sale other than the money in which the price is to be paid, investment securities (Article 8) and things in action. "Goods" also includes the unborn young of animals and growing crops and other identified things attached to realty as described in the section on goods to be severed from realty (Section 2–107).

(2) Goods must be both existing and identified before any interest in them can pass. Goods which are not both existing and identified are "future" goods. A purported present sale of future goods or of any interest therein operates as a contract to sell.

(3) There may be a sale of a part interest in existing identified goods.

(4) An undivided share in an identified bulk of fungible goods is sufficiently identified to be sold although the quantity of the bulk is not determined. Any agreed proportion of such a bulk or any quantity thereof agreed upon by number, weight or other measure may to the extent of the seller's interest in the bulk be sold to the buyer who then becomes an owner in common.

(5) "Lot" means a parcel or a single article which is the subject matter of a separate sale or delivery, whether or not it is sufficient to perform the contract.

(6) "Commercial unit" means such a unit of goods as by commercial usage is a single whole for purposes of sale and division of which materially impairs its character or value on the market or in use. A commercial unit may be a single article (as a machine) or a set of articles (as a suite of furniture or an assortment of sizes) or a quantity (as a bale, gross, or carload) or any other unit treated in use or in the relevant market as a single whole.

§ 2–106. Definitions: "Contract"; "Agreement"; "Contract for Sale"; "Sale"; "Present Sale"; "Conforming" to Contract; "Termination"; "Cancellation."

(1) In this Article unless the context otherwise requires "contract" and "agreement" are limited to those relating to the present or future sale of goods. "Contract for sale" includes both a present sale of goods and a contract to sell goods at a future time. A "sale" consists in the passing of title from the seller to the buyer for a price (Section 2–401). A "present sale" means a sale which is accomplished by the making of the contract.

(2) Goods or conduct including any part of a performance are "conforming" or conform to the contract when they are in accordance with the obligations under the contract.

(3) "Termination" occurs when either party pursuant to a power created by agreement or law puts an end to the contract otherwise than for its breach. On "termination" all obligations

which are still executory on both sides are discharged but any right based on prior breach or performance survives.

(4) "Cancellation" occurs when either party puts an end to the contract for breach by the other and its effect is the same as that of "termination" except that the cancelling party also retains any remedy for breach of the whole contract or any unperformed balance.

§ 2–107. Goods to Be Severed From Realty: Recording.

(1) A contract for the sale of minerals or the like (including oil and gas) or a structure or its materials to be removed from realty is a contract for the sale of goods within this Article if they are to be severed by the seller but until severance a purported present sale thereof which is not effective as a transfer of an interest in land is effective only as a contract to sell.

(2) A contract for the sale apart from the land of growing crops or other things attached to realty and capable of severance without material harm thereto but not described in subsection (1) or of timber to be cut is a contract for the sale of goods within this Article whether the subject matter is to be severed by the buyer or by the seller even though it forms part of the realty at the time of contracting, and the parties can by identification effect a present sale before severance.

(3) The provisions of this section are subject to any third party rights provided by the law relating to realty records, and the contract for sale may be extended and recorded as a document transferring an interest in land and shall then constitute notice to third parties of the buyer's rights under the contract for sale.

PART 2
FORM, FORMATION AND READJUSTMENT OF CONTRACT

§ 2–201. Formal Requirements; Statute of Frauds.

(1) Except as otherwise provided in this section a contract for the sale of goods for the price of $500 or more is not enforceable by way of action or defense unless there is some writing sufficient to indicate that a contract for sale has been made between the parties and signed by the party against whom enforcement is sought or by his authorized agent or broker. A writing is not insufficient because it omits or incorrectly states a term agreed upon but the contract is not enforceable under this paragraph beyond the quantity of goods shown in such writing.

(2) Between merchants if within a reasonable time a writing in confirmation of the contract and sufficient against the sender is received and the party receiving it has reason to know its contents, it satisfies the requirements of subsection (1) against such party unless written notice of objection to its contents is given within 10 days after it is received.

(3) A contract which does not satisfy the requirements of subsection (1) but which is valid in other respects is enforceable

(a) if the goods are to be specially manufactured for the buyer and are not suitable for sale to others in the ordinary course of the seller's business and the seller, before notice of repudiation is received and under circumstances which reasonably indicate that the goods are for the buyer, has made either a substantial beginning of their manufacture or commitments for their procurement; or

(b) if the party against whom enforcement is sought admits in his pleading, testimony or otherwise in court that a contract for sale was made, but the contract is not enforceable under this provision beyond the quantity of goods admitted; or

(c) with respect to goods for which payment has been made and accepted or which have been received and accepted (Section 2–606).

§ 2–202. Final Written Expression: Parol or Extrinsic Evidence.

Terms with respect to which the confirmatory memoranda of the parties agree or which are otherwise set forth in a writing intended by the parties as a final expression of their agreement with respect to such terms as are included therein may not be contradicted by evidence of any prior agreement or of a contemporaneous oral agreement but may be explained or supplemented

(a) by course of dealing or usage of trade (Section 1–205) or by course of performance (Section 2–208); and

(b) by evidence of consistent additional terms unless the court finds the writing to have been intended also as a complete and exclusive statement of the terms of the agreement.

§ 2–203. Seals Inoperative.

The affixing of a seal to a writing evidencing a contract for sale or an offer to buy or sell goods does not constitute the writing a sealed instrument and the law with respect to sealed instruments does not apply to such a contract or offer.

§ 2–204. Formation in General.

(1) A contract for sale of goods may be made in any manner sufficient to show agreement, including conduct by both parties which recognizes the existence of such a contract.

(2) An agreement sufficient to constitute a contract for sale may be found even though the moment of its making is undetermined.

(3) Even though one or more terms are left open a contract for sale does not fail for indefiniteness if the parties have intended to make a contract and there is a reasonably certain basis for giving an appropriate remedy.

§ 2–205. Firm Offers.

An offer by a merchant to buy or sell goods in a signed writing which by its terms gives assurance that it will be held open is not revocable, for lack of consideration, during the time stated or if no time is stated for a reasonable time, but in no event may such period of irrevocability exceed three months; but any such term of assurance on a form supplied by the offeree must be separately signed by the offeror.

§ 2–206. Offer and Acceptance in Formation of Contract.

(1) Unless otherwise unambiguously indicated by the language or circumstances

(a) an offer to make a contract shall be construed as inviting acceptance in any manner and by any medium reasonable in the circumstances;

(b) an order or other offer to buy goods for prompt or current shipment shall be construed as inviting acceptance either by a prompt promise to ship or by the prompt or current shipment of conforming or non-conforming goods, but such a shipment of non-conforming goods does not constitute an acceptance if the seller seasonably notifies the buyer that the shipment is offered only as an accommodation to the buyer.

(2) Where the beginning of a requested performance is a reasonable mode of acceptance an offeror who is not notified of acceptance within a reasonable time may treat the offer as having lapsed before acceptance.

§ 2–207. Additional Terms in Acceptance or Confirmation.

(1) A definite and seasonable expression of acceptance or a written confirmation which is sent within a reasonable time operates as an acceptance even though it states terms additional

to or different from those offered or agreed upon, unless acceptance is expressly made conditional on assent to the additional or different terms.

(2) The additional terms are to be construed as proposals for addition to the contract. Between merchants such terms become part of the contract unless:

(a) the offer expressly limits acceptance to the terms of the offer;

(b) they materially alter it; or

(c) notification of objection to them has already been given or is given within a reasonable time after notice of them is received.

(3) Conduct by both parties which recognizes the existence of a contract is sufficient to establish a contract for sale although the writings of the parties do not otherwise establish a contract. In such case the terms of the particular contract consist of those terms on which the writings of the parties agree, together with any supplementary terms incorporated under any other provisions of this Act.

§ 2–208. Course of Performance or Practical Construction.

(1) Where the contract for sale involves repeated occasions for performance by either party with knowledge of the nature of the performance and opportunity for objection to it by the other, any course of performance accepted or acquiesced in without objection shall be relevant to determine the meaning of the agreement.

(2) The express terms of the agreement and any such course of performance, as well as any course of dealing and usage of trade, shall be construed whenever reasonable as consistent with each other; but when such construction is unreasonable, express terms shall control course of performance and course of performance shall control both course of dealing and usage of trade (Section 1–205).

(3) Subject to the provisions of the next section on modification and waiver, such course of performance shall be relevant to show a waiver or modification of any term inconsistent with such course of performance.

§ 2–209. Modification, Rescission and Waiver.

(1) An agreement modifying a contract within this Article needs no consideration to be binding.

(2) A signed agreement which excludes modification or rescission except by a signed writing cannot be otherwise modified or rescinded, but except as between merchants such a requirement on a form supplied by the merchant must be separately signed by the other party.

(3) The requirements of the statute of frauds section of this Article (Section 2–201) must be satisfied if the contract as modified is within its provisions.

(4) Although an attempt at modification or rescission does not satisfy the requirements of subsection (2) or (3) it can operate as a waiver.

(5) A party who has made a waiver affecting an executory portion of the contract may retract the waiver by reasonable notification received by the other party that strict performance will be required of any term waived, unless the retraction would be unjust in view of a material change of position in reliance on the waiver.

§ 2–210. Delegation of Performance; Assignment of Rights.

(1) A party may perform his duty through a delegate unless otherwise agreed or unless the other party has a substantial interest in having his original promisor perform or control the acts required by the contract. No delegation of performance relieves the party delegating of any duty to perform or any liability for breach.

(2) Unless otherwise agreed all rights of either seller or buyer can be assigned except where the assignment would materially change the duty of the other party, or increase materially

the burden or risk imposed on him by his contract, or impair materially his chance of obtaining return performance. A right to damages for breach of the whole contract or a right arising out of the assignor's due performance of his entire obligation can be assigned despite agreement otherwise.

(3) Unless the circumstances indicate the contrary a prohibition of assignment of "the contract" is to be construed as barring only the delegation to the assignee of the assignor's performance.

(4) An assignment of "the contract" or of "all the rights under the contract" or an assignment in similar general terms is an assignment of rights and unless the language or the circumstances (as in an assignment for security) indicate the contrary, it is a delegation of performance of the duties of the assignor and its acceptance by the assignee constitutues a promise by him to perform those duties. This promise is enforceable by either the assignor or the other party to the original contract.

(5) The other party may treat any assignment which delegates performance as creating reasonable grounds for insecurity and may without prejudice to his rights against the assignor demand assurances from the assignee (Section 2–609).

PART 3
GENERAL OBLIGATION AND CONSTRUCTION OF CONTRACT

§ 2–301. General Obligations of Parties.

The obligation of the seller is to transfer and deliver and that of the buyer is to accept and pay in accordance with the contract.

§ 2–302. Unconscionable Contract or Clause.

(1) If the court as a matter of law finds the contract or any clause of the contract to have been unconscionable at the time it was made the court may refuse to enforce the contract, or it may enforce the remainder of the contract without the unconscionable clause, or it may so limit the application of any unconscionable clause as to avoid any unconscionable result.

(2) When it is claimed or appears to the court that the contract or any clause thereof may be unconscionable the parties shall be afforded a reasonable opportunity to present evidence as to its commercial setting, purpose and effect to aid the court in making the determination.

§ 2–303. Allocation or Division of Risks.

Where this Article allocates a risk or a burden as between the parties "unless otherwise agreed," the agreement may not only shift the allocation but may also divide the risk or burden.

§ 2–304. Price Payable in Money, Goods, Realty, or Otherwise.

(1) The price can be made payable in money or otherwise. If it is payable in whole or in part in goods each party is a seller of the goods which he is to transfer.

(2) Even though all or part of the price is payable in an interest in realty the transfer of the goods and the seller's obligations with reference to them are subject to this Article, but not the transfer of the interest in realty or the transferor's obligations in connection therewith.

§ 2–305. Open Price Term.

(1) The parties if they so intend can conclude a contract for sale even though the price is not settled. In such a case the price is a reasonable price at the time for delivery if

(a) nothing is said as to price; or

(b) the price is left to be agreed by the parties and they fail to agree; or

(c) the price is to be fixed in terms of some agreed market or other standard as set or recorded by a third person or agency and it is not so set or recorded.

(2) A price to be fixed by the seller or by the buyer means a price for him to fix in good faith.

(3) When a price left to be fixed otherwise than by agreement of the parties fails to be fixed through fault of one party the other may at his option treat the contract as cancelled or himself fix a reasonable price.

(4) Where, however, the parties intend not to be bound unless the price be fixed or agreed and it is not fixed or agreed there is no contract. In such a case the buyer must return any goods already received or if unable so to do must pay their reasonable value at the time of delivery and the seller must return any portion of the price paid on account.

§ 2–306. Output, Requirements and Exclusive Dealings.

(1) A term which measures the quantity by the output of the seller or the requirements of the buyer means such actual output or requirements as may occur in good faith, except that no quantity unreasonably disproportionate to any stated estimate or in the absence of a stated estimate to any normal or otherwise comparable prior output or requirements may be tendered or demanded.

(2) A lawful agreement by either the seller or the buyer for exclusive dealing in the kind of goods concerned imposes unless otherwise agreed an obligation by the seller to use best efforts to supply the goods and by the buyer to use best efforts to promote their sale.

§ 2–307. Delivery in Single Lot or Several Lots.

Unless otherwise agreed all goods called for by a contract for sale must be tendered in a single delivery and payment is due only on such tender but where the circumstances give either party the right to make or demand delivery in lots the price if it can be apportioned may be demanded for each lot.

§ 2–308. Absence of Specified Place for Delivery.

Unless otherwise agreed

(a) the place for delivery of goods is the seller's place of business or if he has none his residence; but

(b) in a contract for sale of identified goods which to the knowledge of the parties at the time of contracting are in some other place, that place is the place for their delivery; and

(c) documents of title may be delivered through customary banking channels.

§ 2–309. Absence of Specific Time Provisions; Notice of Termination.

(1) The time for shipment or delivery or any other action under a contract if not provided in this Article or agreed upon shall be a reasonable time.

(2) Where the contract provides for successive performances but is indefinite in duration it is valid for a reasonable time but unless otherwise agreed may be terminated at any time by either party.

(3) Termination of a contract by one party except on the happening of an agreed event requires that reasonable notification be received by the other party and an agreement dispensing with notification is invalid if its operation would be unconscionable.

§ 2–310. Open Time for Payment or Running of Credit; Authority to Ship Under Reservation.

Unless otherwise agreed

(a) payment is due at the time and place at which the buyer is to receive the goods even though the place of shipment is the place of delivery; and

(b) if the seller is authorized to send the goods he may ship them under reservation, and may tender the documents of title, but the buyer may inspect the goods after their arrival before payment is due unless such inspection is inconsistent with the terms of the contract (Section 2–513); and

(c) if delivery is authorized and made by way of documents of title otherwise than by subsection (b) then payment is due at the time and place at which the buyer is to receive the documents regardless of where the goods are to be received; and

(d) where the seller is required or authorized to ship the goods on credit the credit period runs from the time of shipment but post-dating the invoice or delaying its dispatch will correspondingly delay the starting of the credit period.

§ 2–311. Options and Cooperation Respecting Performance.

(1) An agreement for sale which is otherwise sufficiently definite (subsection (3) of Section 2–204) to be a contract is not made invalid by the feact that it leaves particulars of performance to be specified by one of the parties. Any such specification must be made in good faith and within limits set by commercial reasonableness.

(2) Unless otherwise agreed specifications relating to assortment of the goods are at the buyer's option and except as otherwise provided in subsections (1) (c) and (3) of Section 2–319 specifications or arrangements relating to shipment are at the seller's option.

(3) Where such specification would materially affect the other party's performance but is not seasonably made or where one party's cooperation is necessary to the agreed performance of the other but is not seasonably forthcoming, the other party in addition to all other remedies

(a) is excused for any resulting delay in his own performance; and

(b) may also either proceed to perform in any reasonable manner or after the time for a material part of his own performance treat the failure to specify or to cooperate as a breach by failure to deliver or accept the goods.

§ 2–312. Warranty of Title and Against Infringement; Buyer's Obligation Against Infringement.

(1) Subject to subsection (2) there is in a contract for sale a warranty by the seller that

(a) the title conveyed shall be good, and its transfer rightful; and

(b) the goods shall be delivered free from any security interest or other lien or encumbrance of which the buyer at the time of contracting has no knowledge.

(2) A warranty under subsection (1) will be excluded or modified only by specific language or by circumstances which give the buyer reason to know that the person selling does not claim title in himself or that he is purporting to sell only such right or title as he or a third person may have.

(3) Unless otherwise agreed a seller who is a merchant regularly dealing in goods of the kind warrants that the goods shall be delivered free of the rightful claim of any third person by way of infringement or the like but a buyer who furnishes specifications to the seller must hold the seller harmless against any such claim which arises out of compliance with the specifications.

§ 2–313. Express Warranties by Affirmation, Promise, Description, Sample.

(1) Express warranties by the seller are created as follows:

(a) Any affirmation of fact or promise made by the seller to the buyer which relates to the goods and becomes part of the basis of the bargain creates an express warranty that the goods shall conform to the affirmation or promise.

(b) Any description of the goods which is made part of the basis of the bargain creates an express warranty that the goods shall conform to the description.

(c) Any sample or model which is made part of the basis of the bargain creates an express warranty that the whole of the goods shall conform to the sample or model.

(2) It is not necessary to the creation of an express warranty that the seller use formal words such as "warrant" or "guarantee" or that he have a specific intention to make a warranty, but an affirmation merely of the value of the goods or a statement purporting to be merely the seller's opinion or commendation of the goods does not create a warranty.

§ 2–314. Implied Warranty: Merchantability; Usage of Trade.

(1) Unless excluded or modified (Section 2–316), a warranty that the goods shall be merchantable is implied in a contract for their sale if the seller is a merchant with respect to goods of that kind. Under this section the serving for value of food or drink to be consumed either on the premises or elsewhere is a sale.

(2) Goods to be merchantable must be at least such as

(a) pass without objection in the trade under the contract description; and

(b) in the case of fungible goods, are of fair average quality within the description; and

(c) are fit for the ordinary purposes for which such goods are used; and

(d) run, within the variations permitted by the agreement, of even kind, quality and quantity within each unit and among all units involved; and

(e) are adequately contained, packaged, and labeled as the agreement may require; and

(f) conform to the promises or affirmations of fact made on the container or label if any.

(3) Unless excluded or modified (Section 2–316) other implied warranties may arise from course of dealing or usage of trade.

§ 2–315. Implied Warranty: Fitness for Particular Purpose.

Where the seller at the time of contracting has reason to know any particular purpose for which the goods are required and that the buyer is relying on the seller's skill or judgment to select or furnish suitable goods, there is unless excluded or modified under the next section an implied warranty that the goods shall be fit for such purpose.

§ 2–316. Exclusion or Modification of Warranties.

(1) Words or conduct relevant to the creation of an express warranty and words or conduct tending to negate or limit warranty shall be construed wherever reasonable as consistent with each other; but subject to the provisions of this Article on parol or extrinsic evidence (Section 2–202) negation or limitation is inoperative to the extent that such construction is unreasonable.

(2) Subject to subsection (3), to exclude or modify the implied warranty of merchantability or any part of it the language must mention merchantability and in case of a writing must be conspicuous, and to exclude or modify any implied warranty of fitness the exclusion must be by a writing and conspicuous. Language to exclude all implied warranties of fitness is sufficient if it states, for example, that "There are no warranties which extend beyond the description on the face hereof."

(3) Notwithstanding subsection (2)

(a) unless the circumstances indicate otherwise, all implied warranties are excluded by expressions like "as is," "with all faults" or other language which in common understanding calls the buyer's attention to the exclusion of warranties and makes plain that there is no implied warranty; and

(b) when the buyer before entering into the contract has examined the goods or the sample or model as fully as he desired or has refused to examine the goods there is no implied warranty with regard to defects which an examination ought in the circumstances to have revealed to him; and

(c) an implied warranty can also be excluded or modified by course of dealing or course of performance or usage of trade.

(4) Remedies for breach of warranty can be limited in accordance with the provisions of this Article on liquidation or limitation of damages and on contractual modification of remedy (Sections 2–718 and 2–719).

§ 2–317. Cumulation and Conflict of Warranties Express or Implied.

Warranties whether express or implied shall be construed as consistent with each other and as cumulative, but if such construction is unreasonable the intention of the parties shall determine which warranty is dominant. In ascertaining that intention the following rules apply:

(a) Exact or technical specifications displace an inconsistent sample or model or general language of description.

(b) A sample from an existing bulk displaces inconsistent general language of description.

(c) Express warranties displace inconsistent implied warranties other than an implied warranty of fitness for a particular purpose.

§ 2–318. Third Party Beneficiaries of Warranties Express or Implied.

A seller's warranty whether express or implied extends to any natural person who is in the family or household of his buyer or who is a guest in his home if it is reasonable to expect that such person may use, consume or be affected by the goods and who is injured in person by breach of the warranty. A seller may not exclude or limit the operation of this section.

§ 2–319. F.O.B. and F.A.S. Terms.

(1) Unless otherwise agreed the term F.O.B. (which means "free on board") at a named place, even though used only in connection with the stated price, is a delivery term under which

(a) when the term is F.O.B. the place of shipment, the seller must at that place ship the goods in the manner provided in this Article (Section 2–504) and bear the expense and risk of putting them into the possession of the carrier; or

(b) when the term is F.O.B. the place of destination, the seller must at his own expense and risk transport the goods to that place and there tender delivery of them in the manner provided in this Article (Section 2–503);

(c) when under either (a) or (b) the term is also F.O.B. vessel, car or other vehicle, the seller must in addition at his own expense and risk load the goods on board. If the term is F.O.B. vessel the buyer must name the vessel and in an appropriate case the seller must comply with the provisions of this Article on the form of bill of lading (Section 2–323).

(2) Unless otherwise agreed the term F.A.S. vessel (which means "free alongside") at a named port, even though used only in connection with the stated price, is a delivery term under which the seller must

(a) at his own expense and risk deliver the goods alongside the vessel in the manner usual in that port or on a dock designated and provided by the buyer; and

(b) obtain and tender a receipt for the goods in exchange for which the carrier is under a duty to issue a bill of lading.

(3) Unless otherwise agreed in any case falling within subsection (1) (a) or (c) or subsection (2) the buyer must seasonably give any needed instructions for making delivery, including when the term is F.A.S. or F.O.B. the loading berth of the vessel and in an appropriate case its name and sailing date. The seller may treat the failure of needed instructions as a failure

of cooperation under this Article (Section 2–311). He may also at his option move the goods in any reasonable manner preparatory to delivery or shipment.

(4) Under the term F.O.B. vessel or F.A.S. unless otherwise agreed the buyer must make payment against tender of the required documents and the seller may not tender nor the buyer demand delivery of the goods in substitution for the documents.

§ 2–320. C.I.F. and C. & F. Terms.

(1) The term C.I.F. means that the price includes in a lump sum the cost of the goods and the insurance and freight to the named destination. The term C. & F. or C.F. means that the price so includes cost and freight to the named destination.

(2) Unless otherwise agreed and even though used only in connection with the stated price and destination, the term C.I.F. destination or its equivalent requires the seller at his own expense and risk to

(a) put the goods into the possession of a carrier at the port for shipment and obtain a negotiable bill or bills of lading covering the entire transportation to the named destination; and

(b) load the goods and obtain a receipt from the carrier (which may be contained in the bill of lading) showing that the freight has been paid or provided for; and

(c) obtain a policy or certificate of insurance, including any war risk insurance, of a kind and on terms then current at the port of shipment in the usual amount, in the currency of the contract, shown to cover the same goods covered by the bill of lading and providing for payment of loss to the order of the buyer or for the account of whom it may concern; but the seller may add to the price the amount of the premium for any such war risk insurance; and

(d) prepare an invoice of the goods and procure any other documents required to effect shipment or to comply with the contract; and

(e) forward and tender with commercial promptness all the documents in due form and with any indorsement necessary to perfect the buyer's rights.

(3) Unless otherwise agreed the term C. & F. or its equivalent has the same effect and imposes upon the seller the same obligations and risks as a C.I.F. term except the obligation as to insurance.

(4) Under the term C.I.F. or C. & F. unless otherwise agreed the buyer must make payment against tender of the required documents and the seller may not tender nor the buyer demand delivery of the goods in substitution for the documents.

§ 2–321. C.I.F. or C. & F.: "Net Landed Weights"; "Payment on Arrival"; Warranty of Condition on Arrival.

Under a contract containing a term C.I.F. or C. & F.

(1) Where the price is based on or is to be adjusted according to "net landed weights," "delivered weights," "out turn" quantity or quality or the like, unless otherwise agreed the seller must reasonably estimate the price. The payment due on tender of the documents called for by the contract is the amount so estimated, but after final adjustment of the price a settlement must be made with commercial promptness.

(2) An agreement described in subsection (1) or any warranty of quality or condition of the goods on arrival places upon the seller the risk of ordinary deterioration, shrinkage and the like in transportation but has no effect on the place or time of identification to the contract for sale or delivery or on the passing of the risk of loss.

(3) Unless otherwise agreed where the contract provides for payment on or after arrival of the goods the seller must before payment allow such preliminary inspection as is feasible;

but if the goods are lost delivery of the documents and payment are due when the goods should have arrived.

§ 2–322. Delivery "Ex-Ship."

(1) Unless otherwise agreed a term for delivery of goods "ex-ship" (which means from the carrying vessel) or in equivalent language is not restricted to a particular ship and requires delivery from a ship which has reached a place at the named port of destination where goods of the kind are usually discharged.

(2) Under such a term unless otherwise agreed

(a) the seller must discharge all liens arising out of the carriage and furnish the buyer with a direction which puts the carrier under a duty to deliver the goods; and

(b) the risk of loss does not pass to the buyer until the goods leave the ship's tackle or are otherwise properly unloaded.

§ 2–323. Form of Bill of Lading Required in Overseas Shipment; "Overseas."

(1) Where the contract contemplates overseas shipment and contains a term C.I.F. or C. & F. or F.O.B. vessel, the seller unless otherwise agreed must obtain a negotiable bill of lading stating that the goods have been loaded on board or, in the case of a term C.I.F. or C. & F., received for shipment.

(2) Where in a case within subsection (1) a bill of lading has been issued in a set of parts, unless otherwise agreed if the documents are not to be sent from abroad the buyer may demand tender of the full set; otherwise only one part of the bill of lading need be tendered. Even if the agreement expressly requires a full set

(a) due tender of a single part is acceptable within the provisions of this Article on cure of improper delivery (subsection (1) of Section 2–508); and

(b) even though the full set is demanded, if the documents are sent from abroad the person tendering an incomplete set may nevertheless require payment upon furnishing an indemnity which the buyer in good faith deems adequate.

(3) A shipment by water or by air or a contract contemplating such shipment is "overseas" insofar as by usage of trade or agreement it is subject to the commercial, financing or shipping practices characteristic of international deep water commerce.

§ 2–324. "No Arrival, No Sale" Term.

Under a term "no arrival, no sale" or terms of like meaning, unless otherwise agreed,

(a) the seller must properly ship conforming goods and if they arrive by any means he must tender them on arrival but he assumes no obligation that the goods will arrive unless he has caused the non-arrival; and

(b) where without fault of the seller the goods are in part lost or have so deteriorated as no longer to conform to the contract or arrive after the contract time, the buyer may proceed as if there had been casualty to identified goods (Section 2–613).

§ 2–325. "Letter of Credit" Term; "Confirmed Credit."

(1) Failure of the buyer seasonably to furnish an agreed letter of credit is a breach of the contract for sale.

(2) The delivery to seller of a proper letter of credit suspends the buyer's obligation to pay. If the letter of credit is dishonored, the seller may on seasonable notification to the buyer require payment directly from him.

(3) Unless otherwise agreed the term "letter of credit" or "banker's credit" in a contract for sale means an irrevocable credit issued by a financing agency of good repute and, where the shipment is overseas, of good international repute. The term "confirmed credit" means

that the credit must also carry the direct obligation of such an agency which does business in the seller's financial market.

§ 2–326. Sale on Approval and Sale or Return; Consignment Sales and Rights of Creditors.

(1) Unless otherwise agreed, if delivered goods may be returned by the buyer even though they conform to the contract, the transaction is

(a) a "sale on approval" if the goods are delivered primarily for use, and

(b) a "sale or return" if the goods are delivered primarily for resale.

(2) Except as provided in subsection (3), goods held on approval are not subject to the claims of the buyer's creditors until acceptance; goods held on sale or return are subject to such claims while in the buyer's possession.

(3) Where goods are delivered to a person for sale and such person maintains a place of business at which he deals in goods of the kind involved, under a name other than the name of the person making delivery, then with respect to claims of creditors of the person conducting the business the goods are deemed to be on sale or return. The provisons of this subsection are applicable even though an agreement purports to reserve title to the person making delivery until payment or resale or uses such words as "on consignment" or "on memorandum." However, this subsection is not applicable if the person making delivery

(a) complies with an applicable law providing for a consignor's interest or the like to be evidenced by a sign, or

(b) establishes that the person conducting the business is generally known by his creditors to be substantially engaged in selling the goods of others, or

(c) complies with the filing provisions of the Article on Secured Transactions (Article 9).

(4) Any "or return" term of a contract for sale is to be treated as a separate contract for sale within the statute of frauds section of this Article (Section 2–201) and as contradicting the sale aspect of the contract within the provisions of this Article on parol or extrinsic evidence (Section 2–202).

§ 2–327. Special Incidents of Sale on Approval and Sale or Return.

(1) Under a sale on approval unless otherwise agreed

(a) although the goods are identified to the contract the risk of loss and the title do not pass to the buyer until acceptance; and

(b) use of the goods consistent with the purpose of trial is not acceptance but failure seasonably to notify the seller of election to return the goods is acceptance, and if the goods conform to the contract acceptance of any part is acceptance of the whole; and

(c) after due notification of election to return, the return is at the seller's risk and expense but a merchant buyer must follow any reasonable instructions.

(2) Under a sale or return unless otherwise agreed

(a) the option to return extends to the whole or any commercial unit of the goods while in substantially their original condition, but must be exercised seasonably; and

(b) the return is at the buyer's risk and expense.

§ 2–328. Sale by Auction.

(1) In a sale by auction if goods are put in lots each lot is the subject of a separate sale.

(2) A sale by auction is complete when the auctioneer so announces by the fall of the hammer or in other customary manner. Where a bid is made while the hammer is falling in acceptance of a prior bid the auctioneer may in his discretion reopen the bidding or declare the goods sold under the bid on which the hammer was falling.

(3) Such a sale is with reserve unless the goods are in explicit terms put up without reserve. In an auction with reserve the auctioneer may withdraw the goods at any time until he announces completion of the sale. In an auction without reserve, after the auctioneer calls for bids on an article or lot, that article or lot cannot be withdrawn unless no bid is made within a reasonable time. In either case a bidder may retract his bid until the auctioneer's announcement of completion of the sale, but a bidder's retraction does not revive any previous bid.

(4) If the auctioneer knowingly receives a bid on the seller's behalf or the seller makes or procures such a bid, and notice has not been given that liberty for such bidding is reserved, the buyer may at his option avoid the sale or take the goods at the price of the last good faith bid prior to the completion of the sale. This subsection shall not apply to any bid at a forced sale.

PART 4
TITLE, CREDITORS AND GOOD FAITH PURCHASERS

§ 2–401. Passing of Title; Reservation for Security; Limited Application of This Section.

Each provision of this Article with regard to the rights, obligations and remedies of the seller, the buyer, purchasers or other third parties applies irrespective of title to the goods except where the provision refers to such title. Insofar as situations are not covered by the other provisions of this Article and matters concerning title become material the following rules apply:

(1) Title to goods cannot pass under a contract for sale prior to their identification to the contract (Section 2–501), and unless otherwise explicitly agreed the buyer acquires by their identification a special property as limited by this Act. Any retention or reservation by the seller of the title (property) in goods shipped or delivered to the buyer is limited in effect to a reservation of a security interest. Subject to these provisions and to the provisions of the Article on Secured Transactions (Artile 9), title to goods passes from the seller to the buyer in any manner and on any conditions explicitly agreed on by the parties.

(2) Unless otherwise explicitly agreed title passes to the buyer at the time and place at which the seller completes his performance with reference to the physical delivery of the goods, despite any reservation of a security interest and even though a document of title is to be delivered at a different time or place; and in particular and despite any reservation of a security interest by the bill of lading

(a) if the contract requires or authorizes the seller to send the goods to the buyer but does not require him to deliver them at destination, title passes to the buyer at the time and place of shipment; but

(b) if the contract requires delivery at destination, title passes on tender there.

(3) Unless otherwise explicitly agreed where delivery is to be made without moving the goods,

(a) if the seller is to deliver a document of title, title passes at the time when and the place where he delivers such documents; or

(b) if the goods are at the time of contracting already identified and no documents are to be delivered, title passes at the time and place of contracting.

(4) A rejection or other refusal by the buyer to receive or retain the goods, whether or not justified, or a justified revocation of acceptance revests title to the goods in the seller. Such revesting occurs by operation of law and is not a "sale."

§ 2–402. Rights of Seller's Creditors Against Sold Goods.

(1) Except as provided in subsections (2) and (3), rights of unsecured creditors of the seller with respect to goods which have been identified to a contract for sale are subject to the buyer's rights to recover the goods under this Article (Sections 2–502 and 2–716).

(2) A creditor of the seller may treat a sale or an identification of goods to a contract for sale as void if as against him a retention of possession by the seller is fraudulent under any rule of law of the state where the goods are situated, except that retention of possession in good faith and current course of trade by a merchant-seller for a commercially reasonable time after a sale or identification is not fraudulent.

(3) Nothing in this Article shall be deemed to impair the rights of creditors of the seller

(a) under the provisions of the Article on Secured Transactions (Article 9); or

(b) where identification to the contract or delivery is made not in current course of trade but in satisfaction of or as security for a pre-existing claim for money, security or the like and is made under circumstances which under any rule of law of the state where the goods are situated would apart from this Article constitute the transaction a fraudulent transfer or voidable preference.

§ 2–403. Power to Transfer; Good Faith Puchase of Goods; "Entrusting."

(a) A purchaser of goods acquires all title which his transferor had or had power to transfer except that a purchaser of a limited interest acquires rights only to the extent of the interest purchased. A person with voidable title has power to transfer a good title to a good faith purchaser for value. When goods have been delivered under a transaction of purchase the purchaser has such power even though

(a) the transferor was deceived as to the identity of the purchaser, or

(b) the delivery was in exchange for a check which is later dishonored, or

(c) it was agreed that the transaction was to be a "cash sale," or

(d) the delivery was procured through fraud punishable as larcenous under the criminal law.

(2) Any entrusting of possession of goods to a merchant who deals in goods of that kind gives him power to transfer all rights of the entruster to a buyer in ordinary course of business.

(3) "Entrusting" includes any delivery and any acquiescence in retention of possession regardless of any condition expressed between the parties to the delivery or acquiescence and regardless of whether the procurement of the entrusting or the possessor's disposition of the goods have been such as to be larcenous under the criminal law.

(4) The rights of other purchasers of goods and of lien creditors are governed by the Articles of Secured Transactions (Article 9), Bulk Transfers (Article 6) and Documents of Title (Article 7).

PART 5

PERFORMANCE

§ 2–501. Insurable Interest in Goods; Manner of Identification of Goods.

(1) The buyer obtains a special property and an insurable interest in goods by identification of existing goods as goods to which the contract refers even though the goods so identified are non-conforming and he has an option to return or reject them. Such identification can be made at any time and in any manner explicitly agreed to by the parties. In the absence of explicit agreement identification occurs

(a) when the contract is made if it is for the sale of goods already existing and identified;

(b) if the contract is for the sale of future goods other than those described in paragraph (c), when goods are shipped, marked or otherwise designated by the seller as goods to which the contract refers;

(c) when the crops are planted or otherwise become growing crops or the young are conceived if the contract is for the sale of unborn young to be born within twelve months after contracting or for the sale of crops to be harvested within twelve months or the next normal harvest season after contracting whichever is longer.

(2) The seller retains an insurable interest in goods so long as title to or any security interest in the goods remains in him and where the identification is by the seller alone he may until default or insolvency or notification to the buyer that the identification is final substitute other goods for those identified.

(3) Nothing in this section impairs any insurable interest recognized under any other statute or rule of law.

§ 2–502. Buyer's Right to Goods on Seller's Insolvency.

(1) Subject to subsection (2) and even though the goods have not been shipped a buyer who has paid a part or all of the price of goods in which he has a special property under the provisions of the immediately preceding section may on making and keeping good a tender of any unpaid protion of their price recover them from the seller if the seller becomes insolvent within ten days after receipt of the first installment on their price.

(2) If the identification creating his special property has been made by the buyer he acquires the right to recover the goods only if they conform to the contract for sale.

§ 2–503. Manner of Seller's Tender of Delivery.

(1) Tender of delivery requires that the seller put and hold conforming goods at the buyer's disposition and give the buyer any notification reasonably necessary to enable him to take delivery. The manner, time and place for tender are determined by the agreement and this Article, and in particular

(a) tender must be at a reasonable hour, and if it is of goods they must be kept available for the period reasonably necessary to enable the buyer to take possession; but

(b) unless otherwise agreed the buyer must furnish facilities reasonably suited to the receipt of the goods.

(2) Where the case is within the next section respecting shipment tender requires that the seller comply with its provisions.

(3) Where the seller is required to deliver at a particular destination tender requires that he comply with subsection (1) and also in any appropriate case tender documents as described in subsections (4) and (5) of this section.

(4) Where goods are in the possession of a bailee and are to be delivered without being moved

(a) tender requires that the seller either tender a negotiable document of title covering such goods or procure acknowledgment by the bailee of the buyer's right to possession of the goods; but

(b) tender to the buyer of a non-negotiable document of title or of a written direction to the bailee to deliver is sufficient tender unless the buyer seasonably objects, and receipt by the bailee of notification of the buyer's rights fixes those rights as against the bailee and all third persons; but risk of loss of the goods and of any failure by the bailee to honor the non-negotiable document of title or to obey the direction remains on the seller until the buyer has had a reasonable time to present the document or direction, and a refusal by the bailee to honor the document or to obey the direction defeats the tender.

(5) Where the contract requires the seller to deliver documents

(a) he must tender all such documents in correct form, except as provided in this Article with respect to bills of lading in a set (subsection (2) of Section 2–323); and

(b) tender through customary banking channels is sufficient and dishonor of a draft accompanying the documents constitutes non-acceptance or rejection.

§ 2–504. Shipment by Seller.

Where the seller is required or authorized to send the goods to the buyer and the contract does not require him to deliver them at a particular destination, then unless otherwise agreed he must

(a) put the goods in the possession of such a carrier and make such a contract for their transportation as may be reasonable having regard to the nature of the goods and other circumstances of the case; and

(b) obtain and promptly deliver or tender in due form any document necessary to enable the buyer to obtain possession of the goods or otherwise required by the agreement or by usage of trade; and

(c) promptly notify the buyer of the shipment.

Failure to notify the buyer under paragraph (c) or to make a proper contract under paragraph (a) is a ground for rejection only if material delay or loss ensues.

§ 2–505. Seller's Shipment Under Reservation.

(1) Where the seller has identified goods to the contract by or before shipment:

(a) his procurement of a negotiable bill of lading to his own order or otherwise reserves in him a security interest in the goods. His procurement of the bill to the order of a financing agency or of the buyer indicates in addition only the seller's expectation of transferring that interest to the person named.

(b) a non-negotiable bill of lading to himself or his nominee reserves possession of the goods as security but except in a case of conditional delivery (subsection (2) of Section 2–507) a non-negotiable bill of lading naming the buyer as consignee reserves no security interest even though the seller retains possession of the bill of lading.

(2) When shipment by the seller with reservation of a security interest is in violation of the contract for sale it constitutes an improper contract for transportation within the preceding section but impairs neither the rights given to the buyer by shipment and identification of the goods to the contract nor the seller's powers as a holder of a negotiable document.

§ 2–506. Rights of Financing Agency.

(1) A financing agency by paying or purchasing for value a draft which relates to a shipment of goods acquires to the extent of the payment or purchase and in addition to its own rights under the draft and any document of title securing it any rights of the shipper in the goods including the right to stop delivery and the shipper's right to have the draft honored by the buyer.

(2) The right to reimbursement of a financing agency which has in good faith honored or purchased the draft under commitment to or authority from the buyer is not impaired by subsequent discovery of defects with reference to any relevant document which was apparently regular on its face.

§ 2–507. Effect of Seller's Tender; Delivery on Condition.

(1) Tender of delivery is a condition to the buyer's duty to accept the goods and, unless otherwise agreed, to his duty to pay for them. Tender entitles the seller to acceptance of the goods and to payment according to the contract.

(2) Where payment is due and demanded on the delivery to the buyer of goods or documents of title, his right as against the seller to retain or dispose of them is conditional upon his making the payment due.

§ 2–508. Cure by Seller of Improper Tender or Delivery; Replacement.

(1) Where any tender or delivery by the seller is rejected because non-conforming and the time for performance has not yet expired, the seller may seasonably notify the buyer of

his intention to cure and may then within the contract time make a conforming delivery.

(2) Where the buyer rejects a non-conforming tender which the seller had reasonable grounds to believe would be acceptable with or without money allowance the seller may if he seasonably notifies the buyer have a further reasonable time to substitute a conforming tender.

§ 2–509. Risk of Loss in the Absence of Breach.

(1) Where the contract requires or authorizes the seller to ship the goods by carrier

(a) if it does not require him to deliver them at a particular destination, the risk of loss passes to the buyer when the goods are duly delivered to the carrier even though the shipment is under reservation (Section 2–505); but

(b) if it does require him to deliver them at a particular destination and the goods are there duly tendered while in the possession of the carrier, the risk of loss passes to the buyer when the goods are there duly so tendered as to enable the buyer to take delivery.

(2) Where the goods are held by a bailee to be delivered without being moved, the risk of loss passes to the buyer

(a) on his receipt of a negotiable document of title covering the goods; or

(b) on acknowledgment by the bailee of the buyer's right to possession of the goods; or

(c) after his receipt of a non-negotiable document of title or other written direction to deliver, as provided in subsection (4) (b) of Section 2–503.

(3) In any case not within subsection (1) or (2), the risk of loss passes to the buyer on his receipt of the goods if the seller is a merchant; otherwise the risk passes to the buyer on tender of delivery.

(4) The provisions of this section are subject to contrary agreement of the parties and to the provisions of this Article on sale on approval (Section 2–327) and on effect of breach on risk of loss (Section 2–510).

§ 2–510. Effect of Breach on Risk of Loss.

(1) Where a tender or delivery of goods so fails to conform to the contract as to give a right of rejection the risk of their loss remains on the seller until cure or acceptance.

(2) Where the buyer rightfully revokes acceptance he may to the extent of any deficiency in his effective insurance coverage treat the risk of loss as having rested on the seller from the beginning.

(3) Where the buyer as to conforming goods already identified to the contract for sale repudiates or is otherwise in breach before risk of their loss has passed to him, the seller may to the extent of any deficiency in his effective insurance coverage treat the risk of loss as resting on the buyer for a commercially reasonable time.

§ 2–511. Tender of Payment by Buyer; Payment by Check.

(1) Unless otherwise agreed tender of payment is a condition to the seller's duty to tender and complete any delivery.

(2) Tender of payment is sufficient when made by any means or in any manner current in the ordinary course of business unless the seller demands payment in legal tender and gives any extension of time reasonably necessary to procure it.

(3) Subject to the provisions of this Act on the effect of an instrument on an obligation (Section 3–802), payment by check is conditional and is defeated as between the parties by dishonor of the check on due presentment.

§ 2–512. Payment by Buyer Before Inspection.

(1) Where the contract requires payment before inspection non-conformity of the goods does not excuse the buyer from so making payment unless

(a) the non-conformity appears without inspection; or

(b) despite tender of the required documents the circumstances would justify injunction against honor under the provisions of this Act (Section 5–114).

(2) Payment pursuant to subsection (1) does not constitute an acceptance of goods or impair the buyer's right to inspect or any of his remedies.

§ 2–513. Buyer's Right to Inspection of Goods.

(1) Unless otherwise agreed and subject to subsection (3), where goods are tendered or delivered or identified to the contract for sale, the buyer has a right before payment or acceptance to inspect them at any reasonable place and time and in any reasonable manner. When the seller is required or authorized to send the goods to the buyer, the inspection may be after their arrival.

(2) Expenses of inspection must be borne by the buyer but may be recovered from the seller if the goods do not conform and are rejected.

(3) Unless otherwise agreed and subject to the provisions of this Article on C.I.F. contracts (subsection (3) of Section 2–321), the buyer is not entitled to inspect the goods before payment of the price when the contract provides

(a) for delivery "C.O.D." or on other like terms; or

(b) for payment against documents of title, except where such payment is due only after the goods are to become available for inspection.

(4) A place or method of inspection fixed by the parties is presumed to be exclusive but unless otherwise expressly agreed it does not postpone identification or shift the place for delivery or for passing the risk of loss. If compliance becomes impossible, inspection shall be as provided in this section unless the place or method fixed was clearly intended as an indispensable condition failure of which avoids the contract.

§ 2–514. When Documents Deliverable on Acceptance; When on Payment.

Unless otherwise agreed documents against which a draft is drawn are to be delivered to the drawee on acceptance of the draft if it is payable more than three days after presentment; otherwise, only on payment.

§ 2–515. Preserving Evidence of Goods in Dispute.

In furtherance of the adjustment of any claim or dispute

(a) either party on reasonable notification to the other and for the purpose of ascertaining the facts and preserving evidence has the right to inspect, test and sample the goods including such of them as may be in the possession or control of the other; and

(b) the parties may agree to a third party inspection or survey to determine the conformity or condition of the goods and may agree that the findings shall be binding upon them in any subsequent litigation or adjustment.

PART 6

BREACH, REPUDIATION AND EXCUSE

§ 2–601. Buyer's Rights on Improper Delivery.

Subject to the provisions of this Article on breach in installment contracts (Section 2–612) and unless otherwise agreed under the sections on contractual limitations of remedy

(Sections 2–718 and 2–719), if the goods or the tender of delivery fail in any respect to conform to the contract, the buyer may

(a) reject the whole; or
(b) accept the whole; or
(c) accept any commercial unit or units and reject the rest.

§ 2–602. Manner and Effect of Rightful Rejection.

(1) Rejection of goods must be within a reasonable time after their delivery or tender. It is ineffective unless the buyer seasonably notifies the seller.

(2) Subject to the provisions of the two following sections on rejected goods (Sections 2–603 and 2–604),

(a) after rejection any exercise of ownership by the buyer with respect to any commercial unit is wrongful as against the seller; and
(b) if the buyer has before rejection taken physical possession of goods in which he does not have a security interest under the provisions of this Article (subsection (3) of Section 2–711), he is under a duty after rejection to hold them with reasonable care at the seller's disposition for a time sufficient to permit the seller to remove them; but
(c) the buyer has no further obligations with regard to goods rightfully rejected.

(3) The seller's rights with respect to goods wrongfully rejected are governed by the provisions of this Article on Seller's remedies in general (Section 2–703).

§ 2–603. Merchant Buyer's Duties as to Rightfully Rejected Goods.

(1) Subject to any security interest in the buyer (subsection (3) of Section 2–711), when the seller has no agent or place of business at the market of rejection a merchant buyer is under a duty after rejection of goods in his possession or control to follow any reasonable instructions received from the seller with respect to the goods and in the absence of such instructions to make reasonable efforts to sell them for the seller's account if they are perishable or threaten to decline in value speedily. Instructions are not reasonable if on demand indemnity for expenses is not forthcoming.

(2) When the buyer sells goods under subsection (1), he is entitled to reimbursement from the seller or out of the proceeds for reasonable expenses of caring for and selling them, and if the expenses include no selling commission then to such commission as is usual in the trade or if there is none to a reasonable sum not exceeding ten per cent on the gross proceeds.

(3) In complying with this section the buyer is held only to good faith and good faith conduct hereunder is neither acceptance nor conversion nor the basis of an action for damages.

§ 2–604. Buyer's Options as to Salvage of Rightfully Rejected Goods.

Subject to the provisions of the immediately preceding section on perishables if the seller gives no instructions within a reasonable time after notification of rejection the buyer may store the rejected goods for the seller's account or reship them to him or resell them for the seller's account with reimbursement as provided in the preceding section. Such action is not acceptance or conversion.

§ 2–605. Waiver of Buyer's Objections by Failure to Particularize.

(1) The buyer's failure to state in connection with rejection a particular defect which is ascertainable by reasonable inspection precludes him from relying on the unstated defect to justify rejection or to establish breach

(a) where the seller could have cured if it stated seasonably; or
(b) between merchants when the seller has after rejection made a request in writing

for a full and final written statement of all defects on which the buyer proposes to rely.

(2) Payment against documents made without reservation of rights precludes recovery of the payment for defects apparent on the face of the documents.

§ 2–606. What Constitutes Acceptance of Goods.

(1) Acceptance of goods occurs when the buyer

(a) after a reasonable opportunity to inspect the goods signifies to the seller that the goods are conforming or that he will take or retain them in spite of their nonconformity; or

(b) fails to make an effective rejection (subsection (1) of Section 2–602), but such acceptance does not occur until the buyer has had a reasonable opportunity to inspect them; or

(c) does any act inconsistent with the seller's ownership; but if such act is wrongful as against the seller it is an acceptance only if ratified by him.

(2) Acceptance of a part of any commercial unit is acceptance of that entire unit.

§ 2–607. Effect of Acceptance; Notice of Breach; Burden of Establishing Breach After Acceptance; Notice of Claim or Litigation to Person Answerable Over.

(1) The buyer must pay at the contract rate for any goods accepted.

(2) Acceptance of goods by the buyer precludes rejection of the goods accepted and if made with knowledge of a non-conformity cannot be revoked because of it unless the acceptance was on the reasonable assumption that the non-conformity would be seasonably cured but acceptance does not of itself impair any other remedy provided by this Article for non-conformity.

(3) Where a tender has been accepted

(a) the buyer must within a reasonable time after he discovers or should have discovered any breach notify the seller of breach or be barred from any remedy; and

(b) if the claim is one for infringement or the like (subsection (3) of Section 2–312) and the buyer is sued as a result of such a breach he must so notify the seller within a reasonable time after he receives notice of the litigation or be barred from any remedy over for liability established by the litigation.

(4) The burden is on the buyer to establish any breach with respect to the goods accepted.

(5) Where the buyer is sued for breach of a warranty or other obligation for which his seller is answerable over

(a) he may give his seller written notice of the litigation. If the notice states that the seller may come in and defend and that if the seller does not do so he will be bound in any action against him by his buyer by any determination of fact common to the two litigations, then unless the seller after seasonable receipt of the notice does come in and defend he is so bound.

(b) if the claim is one for infringement or the like (subsection (3) of Section 2–312) the original seller may demand in writing that his buyer turn over to him control of the litigation including settlement or else be barred from any remedy over and if he also agrees to bear all expense and to satisfy any adverse judgment, then unless the buyer after seasonable receipt of the demand does turn over control the buyer is so barred.

(6) The provisions of subsections (3), (4) and (5) apply to any obligation of a buyer to hold the seller harmless against infringement or the like (subsection (3) of Section 2–312).

§ 2–608. Revocation of Acceptance in Whole or in Part.

(1) The buyer may revoke his acceptance of a lot or commercial unit whose non-conformity substantially impairs its value to him if he has accepted it

(a) on the reasonable assumption that its non-conformity would be cured and it has not been seasonably cured; or

(b) without discovery of such non-conformity if his acceptance was reasonably induced either by the difficulty of discovery before acceptance or by the seller's assurances.

(2) Revocation of acceptance must occur within a reasonable time after the buyer discovers or should have discovered the ground for it and before any substantial change in condition of the goods which is not caused by their own defects. It is not effective until the buyer notifies the seller of it

(3) A buyer who so revokes has the same rights and duties with regard to the goods involved as if he had rejected them.

§ 2–609. Right to Adequate Assurance of Performance.

(1) A contract for sale imposes an obligation on each party that the other's expectation of receiving due performance will not be impaired. When reasonable grounds for insecurity arise with respect to the performance of either party the other may in writing demand adequate assurance of due performance and until he receives such assurance may if commercially reasonable suspend any performance for which he has not already received the agreed return.

(2) Between merchants the reasonableness of grounds for insecurity and the adequacy of any assurance offered shall be determined according to commercial standards.

(3) Acceptance of any improper delivery or payment does not prejudice the aggrieved party's right to demand adequate assurance of future performance.

(4) After receipt of a justified demand failure to provide within a reasonable time not exceeding thirty days such assurance of due performance as is adequate under the circumstances of the particular case is a repudiation of the contract.

§ 2–610. Anticipatory Repudiation.

When either party repudiates the contract with respect to a performance not yet due the loss of which will substantially impair the value of the contract to the other, the aggrieved party may

(a) for a commercially reasonable time await performance by the repudiating party; or

(b) resort to any remedy for breach (Section 2–703 or Section 2–711), even though he has notified the repudiating party that he would await the latter's performance and has urged retraction; and

(c) in either case suspend his own performance or proceed in accordance with the provisions of this Article on the seller's right to identify goods to the contract notwithstanding breach or to salvage unfinished goods (Section 2–704).

§ 2–611. Retraction of Anticipatory Repudiation.

(1) Until the repudiating party's next performance is due he can retract his repudiation unless the aggrieved party has since the repudiation cancelled or materially changed his position or otherwise indicated that he considers the repudiation final.

(2) Retraction may be by any method which clearly indicates to the aggrieved party that the repudiating party intends to perform, but most include any assurance justifiably demanded under the provisions of this Article (Section 2–609).

(3) Retraction reinstates the repudiating party's rights under the contract with due excuse and allowance to the aggrieved party for any delay occasioned by the repudiation.

§ 2–612. "Installment Contract"; Breach.

(1) An "installment contract" is one which requires or authorizes the delivery of goods in separate lots to be separately accepted, even though the contract contains a clause "each delivery is a separate contract" or its equivalent.

(2) The buyer may reject any installment which is non-conforming if the non-conformity substantially impairs the value of that installment and cannot be cured or if the non-conformity is a defect in the required documents; but if the non-conformity does not fall within subsection (3) and the seller gives adequate assurance of its cure the buyer must accept that installment.

(3) Whenever non-conformity or default with respect to one or more installments substantially impairs the value of the whole contract there is a breach of the whole. But the aggrieved party reinstates the contract if he accepts a non-conforming installment without seasonably notifying of cancellation or if he brings an action with respect only to past installments or demands performance as to future installments.

§ 2–613. Casualty to Identified Goods.

Where the contract requires for its performance goods identified when the contract is made, and the goods suffer casualty without fault of either party before the risk of loss passes to the buyer, or in a proper case under a "no arrival, no sale" term (Section 2–324) then

(a) if the loss is total the contract is avoided; and

(b) if the loss is partial or the goods have so deteriorated as no longer to conform to the contract the buyer may nevertheless demand inspection and at his option either treat the contract as avoided or accept the goods with due allowance from the contract price for the deterioration or the deficiency in quantity but without further right against the seller.

§ 2–614. Substituted Performance.

(1) Where without fault of either party the agreed berthing, loading, or unloading facilities fail or an agreed type of carrier becomes unavailable or the agreed manner of delivery otherwise becomes commercially impracticable but a commercially reasonable substitute is available, such substitute performance must be tendered and accepted.

(2) If the agreed means or manner of payment fails because of domestic or foreign governmental regulation, the seller may withhold or stop delivery unless the buyer provides a means or manner of payment which is commercially a substantial equivalent. If delivery has already been taken, payment by the means or in the manner provided by the regulation discharges the buyer's obligation unless the regulation is discriminatory, oppressive or predatory.

§ 2–615. Excuse by Failure of Presupposed Conditions.

Except so far as a seller may have assumed a greater obligation and subject to the preceding section on substituted performance:

(a) Delay in delivery or non-delivery in whole or in part by a seller who complies with paragraphs (b) and (c) is not a breach of his duty under a contract for sale if performance as agreed has been made impracticable by the occurrence of a contingency the non-occurrence of which was a basic assumption on which the contract was made or by compliance in good faith with any applicable foreign or domestic governmental regulation or order whether or not it later proves to be invalid.

(b) Where the causes mentioned in paragraph (a) affect only a part of the seller's capacity to perform, he must allocate production and deliveries among his customers but may at his option include regular customers not then under contract as well as his own requirements for further manufacture. He may so allocate in any manner which is fair and reasonable.

(c) The seller must notify the buyer seasonably that there will be delay or non-delivery and, when allocation is required under paragraph (b), of the estimated quota thus made available for the buyer.

§ 2–616. Procedure on Notice Claiming Excuse.

(1) Where the buyer receives notification of a material or indefinite delay or an allocation justified under the preceding section he may be written notification to the seller as to any delivery concerned, and where the prospective deficiency substantially impairs the value of the whole contract under the provisions of this Article relating to breach of installment contracts (Section 2–612), then also as to the whole,

(a) terminate and thereby discharge any unexecuted portion of the contract; or

(b) modify the contract by agreeing to take his available quota in substitution.

(2) If after receipt of such notification from the seller the buyer fails so to modify the contract within a reasonable time not exceeding thirty days the contract lapses with respect to any deliveries affected.

(3) The provisions of this section may not be negated by agreement except in so far as the seller has assumed a greater obligation under the preceding section.

PART 7
REMEDIES

§ 2–701. Remedies for Breach of Collateral Contracts Not Impaired.

Remedies for breach of any obligation or promise collateral or ancillary to a contract for sale are not impaired by the provisions of this Article.

§ 2–702. Seller's Remedies on Discovery of Buyer's Insolvency.

(1) Where the seller discovers the buyer to be insolvent he may refuse delivery except for cash including payment for all goods theretofore delivered under the contract, and stop delivery under this Article (Section 2–705).

(2) Where the seller discovers that the buyer has received goods on credit while insolvent he may reclaim the goods upon demand made within ten days after the receipt, but if misrepresentation of solvency has been made to the particular seller in writing within three months before delivery the ten day limitation does not apply. Except as provided in this subsection the seller may not base a right to reclaim goods on the buyer's fraudulent or innocent misrepresentation of solvency or of intent to pay.

(8) The seller's right to reclaim under subsection (2) is subject to the rights of a buyer in ordinary course or other good faith purchaser under this Article (Section 2–403). Successful reclamation of goods excludes all other remedies with respect to them.

§ 2–703. Seller's Remedies in General.

Where the buyer wrongfully rejects or revokes acceptance of goods or fails to make a payment due on or before delivery or repudiates with respect to a part or the whole, then with respect to any goods directly affected and, if the breach is of the whole contract (Section 2–612), then also with respect to the whole undelivered balance, the aggrieved seller may

(a) withhold delivery of such goods;

(b) stop delivery by any bailee as hereafter provided (Section 2–705);

(c) proceed under the next section respecting goods still unidentified to the contract;

(d) resell and recover damages as hereafter provided (Section 2–706);

(e) recover damages for non-acceptance (Section 2–708) or in a proper case the price (Section 2–709);

(f) cancel.

§ 2–704. Seller's Right to Identify Goods to the Contract Notwithstanding Breach or to Salvage Unfinished Goods.

(1) An aggrieved seller under the preceding section may

(a) identify to the contract conforming goods not already identified if at the time he learned of the breach they are in his possession or control;

(b) treat as the subject of resale goods which have demonstrably been intended for the particular contract even though those goods are unfinished.

(2) Where the goods are unfinished an aggrieved seller may in the exercise of reasonable commercial judgment for the purposes of avoiding loss and of effective realization either complete the manufacture and wholly identify the goods to the contract or cease manufacture and resell for scrap or salvage value or proceed in any other reasonable manner.

§ 2–705. Seller's Stoppage of Delivery in Transit or Otherwise.

(1) The seller may stop delivery of goods in the possession of a carrier or other bailee when he discovers the buyer to be insolvent (Section 2–702) and may stop delivery of carload, truckload, planeload or larger shipments of express or freight when the buyer repudiates or fails to make a payment due before delivery or if for any other reason the seller has a right to withhold or reclaim the goods.

(2) As against such buyer the seller may stop delivery until

(a) receipt of the goods by the buyer; or

(b) acknowledgment to the buyer by any bailee of the goods except a carrier that the bailee holds the goods for the buyer; or

(c) such acknowledgment to the buyer by a carrier by reshipment or as warehouseman; or

(d) negotiation to the buyer of any negotiable document of title covering the goods.

(3) (a) To stop delivery the seller must so notify as to enable the bailee by reasonable diligence to prevent delivery of the goods.

(b) After such notification the bailee must hold and deliver the goods according to the directions of the seller but the seller is liable to the bailee for any ensuing charges or damages.

(c) If a negotiable document of title has been issued for goods the bailee is not obliged to obey a notification to stop until surrender of the document.

(d) A carrier who has issued a non-negotiable bill of lading is not obliged to obey a notification to stop received from a person other than the consignor.

§ 2–706. Seller's Resale Including Contract for Resale.

(1) Under the conditions stated in Section 2–703 on seller's remedies, the seller may resell the goods concerned or the undelivered balance thereof. Where the resale is made in good faith and in a commercially reasonable manner the seller may recover the difference between the resale price and the contract price together with any incidental damages allowed under the provisions of this Article (Section 2–710), but less expenses saved in consequence of the buyer's breach.

(2) Except as otherwise provided in subsection (3) or unless otherwise agreed resale may be at public or private sale including sale by way of one or more contracts to sell or of identification to an existing contract of the seller. Sale may be as a unit or in parcels and at any time and place and on any terms but every aspect of the sale including the method, manner, time, place and terms must be commercially reasonable. The resale must be reasonably identified as referring to the broken contract, but it is not necessary that the goods be in existence or that any or all of them have been identified to the contract before the breach.

(3) Where the resale is at private sale the seller must give the buyer reasonable notification of his intention to resell.

(4) Where the resale is at public sale

(a) only identified goods can be sold except where there is a recognized market for a public sale of futures in goods of the kind; and

(b) it must be made at a usual place or market for public sale if one is reasonably available and except in the case of goods which are perishable or threaten to decline in value speedily the seller must give the buyer reasonable notice of the time and place of the resale; and

(c) if the goods are not to be within the view of those attending the sale the notification of sale must state the place where the goods are located and provide for their reasonable inspection by prospective bidders; and

(d) the seller may buy.

(5) A purchaser who buys in good faith at a resale takes the goods free of any rights of the original buyer even though the seller fails to comply with one or more of the requirements of this section.

(6) The seller is not accountable to the buyer for any profit made on any resale. A person in the position of a seller (Section 2–707) or a buyer who has rightfully rejected or justifiably revoked acceptance must account for any excess over the amount of his security interest, as hereinafter defined (subsection (3) of Section 2–711).

§ 2–707. "Person in the Position of a Seller."

(1) A "person in the position of a seller" includes as against a principal an agent who has paid or become responsible for the price of goods on behalf of his principal or anyone who otherwise holds a security interest or other right in goods similar to that of a seller.

(2) A person in the position of a seller may as provided in this Article withhold or stop delivery (Section 2–705) and resell (Section 2–706) and recover incidental damages (Section 2–710).

§ 2–708. Seller's Damages for Non-acceptance or Repudiation.

(1) Subject to subsection (2) and to the provisions of this Article with respect to proof of market price (Section 2–723), the measure of damages for non-acceptance or repudiation by the buyer is the difference between the market price at the time and place for tender and the unpaid contract price together with any incidental damages provided in this Article (Section 2–710), but less expenses saved in consequence of the buyer's breach.

(2) If the measure of damages provided in subsection (1) is inadequate to put the seller in as good a position as performance would have done then the measure of damages is the profit (including reasonable overhead) which the seller would have made from full performance by the buyer, together with any incidental damages provided in this Article (Section 2–710), due allowance for costs reasonably incurred and due credit for payments or proceeds of resale.

§ 2–709. Action for the Price.

(1) When the buyer fails to pay the price as it becomes due the seller may recover, together with any incidental damages under the next section, the price

(a) of goods accepted or of conforming goods lost or damaged within a commercially reasonable time after risk of their loss has passed to the buyer; and

(b) of goods identified to the contract if the seller is unable after reasonable effort to resell them at a reasonable price or the circumstances reasonably indicate that such effort will be unavailing.

(2) Where the seller sues for the price he must hold for the buyer any goods which have been identified to the contract and are still in his control except that if resale becomes possible he may resell them at any time prior to the collection of the judgment. The net proceeds of any such resale must be credited to the buyer and payment of the judgment entitles him to any goods not resold.

(3) After the buyer has wrongfully rejected or revoked acceptance of the goods or has failed to make a payment due or has repudiated (Section 2–610), a seller who is held not entitled to the price under this section shall nevertheless be awarded damages for non-acceptance under the preceding section.

§ 2–710. Seller's Incidental Damages.

Incidental damages to an aggrieved seller include any commercially reasonable charges, expenses or commissions incurred in stopping delivery, in the transportation, care and custody of goods after the buyer's breach, in connection with return or resale of the goods or otherwise resulting from the breach.

§ 2–711. Buyer's Remedies in General; Buyer's Security Interest in Rejected Goods.

(1) Where the seller fails to make delivery or repudiates or the buyer rightfully rejects or justifiably revokes acceptance then with respect to any goods involved, and with respect to the whole if the breach goes to the whole contract (Section 2–612), the buyer may cancel and whether or not he has done so may in addition to recovering so much of the price as has been paid

(a) "cover" and have damages under the next section as to all the goods affected whether or not they have been identified to the contract; or

(b) recover damages for non-delivery as provided in this Article (Section 2–713).

(2) Where the seller fails to deliver or repudiates the buyer may also

(a) if the goods have been identified recover them as provided in this Article (Section 2–502); or

(b) in a proper case obtain specific performance or replevy the goods as provided in this Article (Section 2–716).

(3) On rightful rejection or justifiable revocation of acceptance a buyer has a security interest in goods in his possession or control for any payments made on their price and any expenses reasonably incurred in their inspection, receipt, transportation, care and custody and may hold such goods and resell them in like manner as an aggrieved seller (Section 2–706).

§ 2–712. "Cover"; Buyer's Procurement of Substitute Goods.

(1) After a breach within the preceding section the buyer may "cover" by making in good faith and without unreasonable delay any reasonable purchase of or contract to purchase goods in substitution for those due from the seller.

(2) The buyer may recover from the seller as damages the difference between the cost of cover and the contract price together with any incidental or consequential damages as hereinafter defined (Section 2–715), but less expenses saved in consequence of the seller's breach.

(3) Failure of the buyer to effect cover within this section does not bar him from any other remedy.

§ 2–713. Buyer's Damages for Non-Delivery or Repudiation.

(1) Subject to the provisions of this Article with respect to proof of market price (Section 2–723), the measure of damages for non-delivery or repudiation by the seller is the difference

between the market price at the time when the buyer learned of the breach and the contract price together with any incidental and consequential damages provided in this Article (Section 2–715), but less expenses saved in consequence of the seller's breach.

(2) Market price is to be determined as of the place for tender or, in cases of rejection after arrival or revocation of acceptance, as of the place of arrival.

§ 2–714. Buyer's Damages for Breach in Regard to Accepted Goods.

(1) Where the buyer has accepted goods and given notification (subsection (3) of Section 2–607) he may recover as damages for any non-conformity of tender the loss resulting in the ordinary course of events from the seller's breach as determined in any manner which is reasonable.

(2) The measure of damages for breach of warranty is the difference at the time and place of acceptance between the value of the goods accepted and the value they would have had if they had been as warranted, unless special circumstances show proximate damages of a different amount.

(3) In a proper case any incidental and consequential damages under the next section may also be recovered.

§ 2–715. Buyer's Incidental and Consequential Damages.

(1) Incidental damages resulting from the seller's breach include expenses reasonably incurred in inspection, receipt, transportation and care and custody of goods rightfully rejected, any commercially reasonable charges, expenses or commissions in connection with effecting cover and any other reasonable expense incident to the delay or other breach.

(2) Consequential damages resulting from the seller's breach include

(a) any loss resulting from general or particular requirements and needs of which the seller at the time of contracting had reason to know and which could not reasonably be prevented by cover or otherwise; and

(b) injury to person or property proximately resulting from any breach of warranty.

§2–716. Buyer's Right to Specific Performance or Replevin.

(1) Specific performance may be decreed where the goods are unique or in other proper circumstances.

(2) The decree for specific performance may include such terms and conditions as to payment of the price, damages, or other relief as the court may deem just.

(3) The buyer has a right of replevin for goods identified to the contract if after reasonable effort he is unable to effect cover for such goods or the circumstances reasonably indicate that such effort will be unavailing or if the goods have been shipped under reservation and satisfaction of the security interest in them has been made or tendered.

§ 2–717. Deduction of Damages From the Price.

The buyer on notifying the seller of his intention to do so may deduct all or any part of the damages resulting from any breach of the contract from any part of the price still due under the same contract.

§ 2–718. Liquidation or Limitation of Damages; Deposits.

(1) Damages for breach by either party may be liquidated in the agreement but only at an amount which is reasonable in the light of the anticipated or actual harm caused by the breach, the difficulties of proof of loss, and the inconvenience or nonfeasibility of otherwise obtaining an adequate remedy. A term fixing unreasonably large liquidated damages is void as a penalty.

(2) Where the seller justifiably withholds delivery of goods because of the buyer's breach, the buyer is entitled to restitution of any amount by which the sum of his payments exceeds

(a) the amount to which the seller is entitled by virtue of terms liquidating the seller's damages in accordance with subsection (1), or

(b) in the absence of such terms, twenty per cent of the value of the total performance for which the buyer is obligated under the contract or $500, whichever is smaller.

(3) The buyer's right to restitution under subsection (2) is subject to offset to the extent that the seller establishes

(a) a right to recover damages under the provisions of this Article other than subsection (1), and

(b) the amount of value of any benefits received by the buyer directly or indirectly by reason of the contract.

(4) Where a seller has received payment in goods their reasonable value or the proceeds of their resale shall be treated as payments for the purposes of subsection (2); but if the seller has notice of the buyer's breach before reselling goods received in part performance, his resale is subject to the conditions laid down in this Article on resale by an aggrieved seller (Section 2–706).

§ 2–719. Contractual Modification or Limitation of Remedy.

(1) Subject to the provisions of subsections (2) and (3) of this section and of the preceding section on liquidation and limitation of damages,

(a) the agreement may provide for remedies in addition to or in substitution for those provided in this Article and may limit or alter the measure of damages recoverable under this Article, as by limiting the buyer's remedies to return of the goods and repayment of the price or to repair and replacement of non-conforming goods or parts; and

(b) resort to a remedy as provided is optional unless the remedy is expressly agreed to be exclusive, in which case it is the sole remedy.

(2) Where circumstances cause an exclusive or limited remedy to fail of its essential purpose, remedy may be had as provided in this Act.

(3) Consequential damages may be limited or excluded unless the limitation or exclusion is unconscionable. Limitation of consequential damages for injury to the person in the case of consumer goods is prima facie unconscionable but limitation of damages where the loss is commercial is not.

§ 2–720. Effect of "Cancellation" or "Rescission" on Claims for Antecedent Breach.

Unless the contrary intention clearly appears, expressions of "cancellation" or "rescission" of the contract or the like shall not be construed as a renunciation or discharge of any claim in damages for an antecedent breach.

§ 2–721. Remedies for Fraud.

Remedies for material misrepresentation or fraud include all remedies available under this Article for non-fraudulent breach. Neither rescission or a claim for rescission of the contract for sale nor rejection or return of the goods shall bar or be deemed inconsistent with a claim for damages or other remedy.

§ 2–722. Who Can Sue Third Parties for Injury to Goods.

Where a third party so deals with goods which have been identified to a contract for sale as to cause actionable injury to a party to that contract

(a) a right of action against the third party is in either party to the contract for sale who has title to or a security interest or a special property or an insurable interest in the goods; and if the goods have been destroyed or converted a right of action is also in the party who either bore the risk of loss under the contract for sale or has since the injury assumed that risk as against the other;

(b) if at the time of the injury the party plaintiff did not bear the risk of loss as against the other party to the contract for sale and there is no arrangement between them for disposition of the recovery, his suit or settlement is, subject to his own interest, as a fiduciary for the other party to the contract;

(c) either party may with the consent of the other sue for the benefit of whom it may concern.

§ 2–723. Proof of Market Price: Time and Place.

(1) If an action based on anticipatory repudiation comes to trial before the time for performance with respect to some or all of the goods, any damages based on market price (Section 2–708 or Section 2–713) shall be determined according to the price of such goods prevailing at the time when the aggrieved party learned of the repudiation.

(2) If evidence of a price prevailing at the times or places described in this Article is not readily available the price prevailing within any reasonable time before or after the time described or at any other place which in commercial judgment or under usage of trade would serve as a reasonable substitute for the one described may be used, making any proper allowance for the cost of transporting the goods to or from such other place.

(3) Evidence of a relevant price prevailing at a time or place other than the one described in this Article offered by one party is not admissible unless and until he has given the other party such notice as the court finds sufficient to prevent unfair surprise.

§ 2–724. Admissibility of Market Quotations.

Whenever the prevailing price or value of any goods regularly bought and sold in any established commodity market is in issue, reports in official publications or trade journals or in newspapers or periodicals of general circulation published as the reports of such market shall be admissible in evidence. The circumstances of the preparation of such a report may be shown to affect its weight but not its admissibility.

§ 2–725. Statute of Limitations in Contracts for Sale.

(1) An action for breach of any contract for sale must be commenced within four years after the cause of action has accrued. By the original agreement the parties may reduce the period of limitation to not less than one year but may not extend it.

(2) A cause of action accrues when the breach occurs, regardless of the aggrieved party's lack of knowledge of the breach. A breach of warranty occurs when tender of delivery is made, except that where a warranty explicitly extends to future performance of the goods and discovery of the breach must await the time of such performance the cause of action accrues when the breach is or should have been discovered.

(3) Where an action commenced within the time limited by subsection (1) is so terminated as to leave available a remedy by another action for the same breach such other action may be commenced after the expiration of the time limited and within six months after the termination of the first action unless the termination resulted from voluntary discontinuance or from dismissal for failure or neglect to prosecute.

(4) This section does not alter the law on tolling of the statute of limitations nor does it apply to causes of action which have accrued before this Act becomes effective.

ARTICLE 3. Commercial Paper

PART 1
SHORT TITLE, FORM AND INTERPRETATION

§ 3–101. Short Title.

This Article shall be known and may be cited as Uniform Commercial Code—Commercial Paper.

§ 3–102. Definitions and Index of Definitions.

(1) In this Article unless the context otherwise requires

(a) "Issue" means the first delivery of an instrument to a holder or a remitter.

(b) An "order" is a direction to pay and must be more than an authorization or request. It must identify the person to pay with reasonable certainty. It may be addressed to one or more such persons jointly or in the alternative but not in succession.

(c) A "promise" is an undertaking to pay and must be more than an acknowledgment of an obligation.

(d) "Secondary party" means a drawer or endorser.

(e) "Instrument" means a negotiable instrument.

(2) Other definitions applying to this Article and the sections in which they appear are:

"Acceptance." Section 3–410.
"Accommodation party." Section 3–415.
"Alteration." Section 3–407.
"Certificate of deposit." Section 3–104.
"Certification." Section 3–411.
"Check." Section 3–104.
"Definite time." Section 3–109.
"Dishonor." Section 3–507.
"Draft." Section 3–104.
"Holder in due course." Section 3–302.
"Negotiation." Section 3–202.
"Note." Section 3–104.
"Notice of dishonor." Section 3–508.
"On demand." Section 3–108.
"Presentment." Section 3–504.
"Protest." Section 3–509.
"Restrictive Indorsement." Section 3–205.
"Signature." Section 3–401.

(3) The following definitions in other Articles apply to this Article:

"Account." Section 4–104
"Banking Day." Section 4–104.
"Clearing house." Section 4–104.
"Collecting bank." Section 4–105.
"Customer." Section 4–104.
"Depositary Bank." Section 4–105.
"Documentary Draft." Section 4–104.
"Intermediary Bank." Section 4–105.
"Item." Section 4–104.
"Midnight deadline." Section 4–104.
"Payor bank." Section 4–105.

(4) In addition Article 1 contains general definitions and principles of construction and interpretation applicable throughout this Article.

§ 3–103. Limitations on Scope of Article.

(1) This Article does not apply to money, documents of title or investment securities.

(2) The provisions of this Article are subject to the provisions of the Article on Bank Deposits and Collections (Article 4) and Secured Transactions (Article 9).

§ 3–104. Form of Negotiable Instruments; "Draft"; "Check"; "Certificate of Deposit"; "Note."

(1) Any writing to be a negotiable instrument within this Article must

(a) be signed by the maker or drawer; and

(b) contain an unconditional promise or order to pay a sum certain in money and no other promise, order, obligation or power given by the maker or drawer except as authorized by this Article; and

(c) be payable on demand or at a definite time; and

(d) be payable to order or to bearer.

(2) A writing which complies with the requirements of this section is

(a) a "draft" ("bill of exchange") if it is an order;

(b) a "check" if it is a draft drawn on a bank and payable on demand;

(c) a "certificate of deposit" if it is an acknowledgment by a bank of receipt of money with an engagement to repay it;

(d) a "note" if it is a promise other than a certificate of deposit.

(3) As used in other Articles of this Act, and as the context may require, the terms "draft," "check," "certificate of deposit" and "note" may refer to instruments which are not negotiable within this Article as well as to instruments which are so negotiable.

§ 3–105. When Promise or Order Unconditional.

(1) A promise or order otherwise unconditional is not made conditional by the fact that the instrument

(a) is subject to implied or constructive conditions; or

(b) states its consideration, whether performed or promised, or the transaction which gave rise to the instrument, or that the promise or order is made or the instrument matures in accordance with or "as per" such transaction; or

(c) refers to or states that it arises out of a separate agreement or refers to a separate agreement for rights as to prepayment or acceleration; or

(d) states that it is drawn under a letter of credit; or

(e) states that it is secured, whether by mortgage, reservation of title or otherwise; or

(f) indicates a particular account to be debited or any other fund or source from which reimbursement is expected; or

(g) is limited to payment out of a particular fund or the proceeds of a particular source, if the instrument is issued by a government or governmental agency or unit; or

(h) is limited to payment out of the entire assets of a partnership, unincorporated association, trust or estate by or on behalf of which the instrument is issued.

(2) A promise or order is not unconditional if the instrument

(a) states that it is subject to or governed by any other agreement; or

(b) states that it is to be paid only out of a particular fund or source except as provided in this section.

§ 3–106. Sum Certain.

(1) The sum payable is a sum certain even though it is to be paid

(a) with stated interest or by stated installments; or

(b) with stated different rates of interest before and after default or a specified date; or
(c) with a stated discount or addition if paid before or after the date fixed for payment; or
(d) with exchange or less exchange, whether at a fixed rate or at the current rate; or
(e) with costs of collection or an attorney's fee or both upon default.

(2) Nothing in this section shall validate any term which is otherwise illegal.

§ 3–107. Money.

(1) An instrument is payable in money if the medium of exchange in which it is payable is money at the time the instrument is made. An instrument payable in "currency" or "current funds" is payable in money.

(2) A promise or order to pay a sum stated in a foreign currency is for a sum certain in money and, unless a different medium of payment is specified in the instrument, may be satisfied by payment of that number of dollars which the stated foreign currency will purchase at the buying sight rate for that currency on the day on which the instrument is payable or, if payable on demand, on the day of demand. If such an instrument specifies a foreign currency as the medium of payment the instrument is payable in that currency.

§ 3–108. Payable on Demand.

Instruments payable on demand include those payable at sight or on presentation and those in which no time for payment is stated.

§ 3–109. Definite Time.

(1) An instrument is payable at a definite time if by its terms it is payable

(a) on or before a stated date or at a fixed period after a stated date; or
(b) at a fixed period after sight; or
(c) at a definite time subject to any acceleration; or
(d) at a definite time subject to extension at the option of the holder, or to extension to a further definite time at the option of the maker or acceptor or automatically upon or after a specified act or event.

(2) An instrument which by its terms is otherwise payable only upon an act or event uncertain as to time of occurrence is not payable at a definite time even though the act or event has occurred.

§ 3–110. Payable to Order.

(1) An instrument is payable to order when by its terms it is payable to the order or assigns of any person therein specified with reasonable certainty, or to him or his order, or when it is conspicuously designated on its face as "exchange" or the like and names a payee. It may be payable to the order of

(a) the maker or drawer; or
(b) the drawee; or
(c) a payee who is not maker, drawer or drawee; or
(d) two or more payees together or in the alternative; or
(e) an estate, trust or fund, in which case it is payable to the order of the representative of such estate, trust or fund or his successors; or
(f) an office, or an officer by his title as such in which case it is payable to the principal but the incumbent of the office or his successor may act as if he or they were the holder; or
(g) a partnership or unincorporated association, in which case it is payable to the partnership or association and may be indorsed or transferred by any person thereto authorized.

(2) An instrument not payable to order is not made so payable by such words as "payable upon return of this instrument properly indorsed."

(3) An instrument made payable both to order and to bearer is payable to order unless the bearer words are handwritten or typewritten.

§ 3–111. Payable to Bearer.

An instrument is payable to bearer when by its terms it is payable to

(a) bearer or the order of bearer; or

(b) a specified person or bearer; or

(c) "cash" or the order of "cash," or any other indication which does not purport to designate a specific payee.

§ 3–112. Terms and Omissions Not Affecting Negotiability.

(1) The negotiability of an instrument is not affected by

(a) the omission of a statement of any consideration or of the place where the instrument is drawn or payable; or

(b) a statement that collateral has been given to secure obligations either on the instrument or otherwise of an obligor on the instrument or that in case of default on those obligations the holder may realize on or dispose of the collateral; or

(c) a promise or power to maintain or protect collateral or to give additional collateral; or

(d) a term authorizing a confession of judgment on the instrument if it is not paid when due; or

(e) a term purporting to waive the benefit of any law intended for the advantage or protection of any obligor; or

(f) a term in a draft providing that the payee by indorsing or cashing it acknowledges full satisfaction of an obligation of the drawer; or

(g) A statement in a draft drawn in a set of parts (Section 3–801) to the effect that the order is effective only if no other part has been honored.

(2) Nothing in this section shall validate any term which is otherwise illegal.

§ 3–113. Seal.

An instrument otherwise negotiable is within this Article even though it is under a seal.

§ 3–114. Date, Antedating, Postdating.

(1) The negotiability of an instrument is not affected by the fact that it is undated, antedated or postdated.

(2) Where an instrument is antedated or postdated the time when it is payable is determined by the stated date if the instrument is payable on demand or at a fixed period after date.

(3) Where the instrument or any signature thereon is dated, the date is presumed to be correct.

§ 3–115. Incomplete Instruments.

(1) When a paper whose contents at the time of signing show that it is intended to become an instrument is signed while still incomplete in any necessary respect it cannot be enforced until completed, but when it is completed in accordance with authority given it is effective as completed.

(2) If the completion is unauthorized the rules as to material alteration apply (Section 3–407), even though the paper was not delivered by the maker or drawer; but the burden of establishing that any completion is unauthorized is on the party so asserting.

§ 3–116. Instruments Payable to Two or More Persons.

An instrument payable to the order of two or more persons

(a) if in the alternative is payable to any one of them and may be negotiated, discharged or enforced by any of them who has possession of it;

(b) if not in the alternative is payable to all of them and may be negotiated, discharged or enforced only by all of them.

§ 3–117. Instruments Payable With Words of Description.

An instrument made payable to a named person with the addition of words describing him

(a) as agent or officer of a specified person is payable to his principal but the agent or officer may act as if he were the holder;

(b) as any other fiduciary for a specified person or purpose is payable to the payee and may be negotiated, discharged or enforced by him;

(c) in any other manner is payable to the payee unconditionally and the additional words are without effect on subsequent parties.

§ 3–118. Ambiguous Terms and Rules of Construction.

The following rules apply to every instrument:

(a) Where there is doubt whether the instrument is a draft or a note the holder may treat it as either. A draft drawn on the drawer is effective as a note.

(b) Handwritten terms control typewritten and printed terms, and typewritten control printed.

(c) Words control figures except that if the words are ambiguous figures control.

(d) Unless otherwise specified a provision for interest means interest at the judgment rate at the place of payment from the date of the instrument, or if it is undated from the date of issue.

(e) Unless the instrument otherwise specifies two or more persons who sign as maker, acceptor or drawer or indorser and as a part of the same transaction are jointly and severally liable even though the instrument contains such words as "I promise to pay."

(f) Unless otherwise specified consent to extension authorizes a single extension for not longer than the original period. A consent to extension, expressed in the instrument, is binding on secondary parties and accommodation makers. A holder may not exercise his option to extend an instrument over the objection of a maker or acceptor or other party who in accordance with Section 3–604 tenders full payment when the instrument is due.

§ 3–119. Other Writings Affecting Instrument.

(1) As between the obligor and his immediate obligee or any transferee the terms of an instrument may be modified or affected by any other written agreement executed as a part of the same transaction, except that a holder in due course is not affected by any limitation of his rights arising out of the separate written agreement if he had no notice of the limitation when he took the instrument.

(2) A separate agreement does not affect the negotiability of an instrument.

§ 3–120. Instruments "Payable Through" Bank.

An instrument which states that it is "payable through" a bank or the like designates that bank as a collecting bank to make presentment but does not of itself authorize the bank to pay the instrument.

§ 3–121. Instruments Payable at Bank.*

A note or acceptance which states that it is payable at a bank is the equivalent of a draft drawn on the bank payable when it falls due out of any funds of the maker or acceptor in current account or otherwise available for such payment.

§ 3–122. Accrual of Cause of Action.

(1) A cause of action against a maker or an acceptor accrues

(a) in the case of a time instrument on the day after maturity;

(b) in the case of a demand instrument upon its date or, if no date is stated, on the date of issue.

(2) A cause of action against the obligor of a demand or time certificate of deposit accrues upon demand, but demand on a time certificate may not be made until on or after the date of maturity.

(3) A cause of action against a drawer of a draft or an indorser of any instrument accrues upon demand following dishonor of the instrument. Notice of dishonor is a demand.

(4) Unless an instrument provides otherwise, interest runs at the rate provided by the law for a judgment

(a) in the case of a maker, acceptor or other primary obligor of a demand instrument, from the date of demand;

(b) in all other cases from the date of accrual of the cause of action.

PART 2
TRANSFER AND NEGOTIATION

§ 3–201. Transfer: Right to Indorsement.

(1) Transfer of an instrument vests in the transferee such rights as the transferor has therein, except that a transferee who has himself been a party to any fraud or illegality affecting the instrument or who as a prior holder had notice of a defense or claim against it cannot improve his position by taking from a later holder in due course.

(2) A transfer of a security interest in an instrument vests the foregoing rights in the transferee to the extent of the interest transferred.

(3) Unless otherwise agreed any transfer for value of an instrument not then payable to bearer gives the transferee the specifically enforceable right to have the unqualified indorsement of the transferor. Negotiation takes effect only when the indorsement is made and until that time there is no presumption that the transferee is the owner.

§ 3–202. Negotiation.

(1) Negotiation is the transfer of an instrument in such form that the transferee becomes a holder. If the instrument is payable to order it is negotiated by delivery with any necessary indorsement; if payable to bearer it is negotiated by delivery.

(2) An indorsement must be written by or on behalf of the holder and on the instrument or on a paper so firmly affixed thereto as to become a part thereof.

(3) An indorsement is effective for negotiation only when it conveys the entire instrument or any unpaid residue. If it purports to be of less it operates only as a partial assignment.

(4) Words of assignment, condition, waiver, guaranty, limitation or disclaimer of liability and the like accompanying an indorsement do not affect its character as an indorsement.

§ 3–203. Wrong or Misspelled Name.

Where an instrument is made payable to a person under a misspelled name or one other than his own he may indorse in that name or his own or both; but signature in both names may be required by a person paying or giving value for the instrument.

§ 3–204. Special Indorsement; Blank Indorsement.

(1) A special indorsement specifies the person to whom or to whose order it makes the instrument payable. Any instrument specially indorsed becomes payable to the order of the special indorsee and may be further negotiated only by his indorsement.

(2) An indorsement in blank specifies no particular indorsee and may consist of a mere signature. An instrument payable to order and indorsed in blank becomes payable to bearer and may be negotiated by delivery alone until specially indorsed.

(3) The holder may convert a blank indorsement into a special indorsement by writing over the signature of the indorser in blank any contract consistent with the character of the indorsement.

§ 3–205. Restrictive Indorsements

An indorsement is restrictive which either

(a) is conditional; or

(b) purports to prohibit further transfer of the instrument; or

(c) includes the words "for collection," "for deposit," "pay any bank," or like terms signifying a purpose of deposit or collection; or

(d) otherwise states that it is for the benefit or use of the indorser or of another person.

§ 3–206. Effect of Restrictive Indorsement.

(1) No restrictive indorsement prevents further transfer or negotiation of the instrument.

(2) An intermediary bank, or a payor bank which is not the depositary bank, is neither given notice nor otherwise affected by a restrictive indorsement of any person except the bank's immediate transferor or the person presenting for payment.

(3) Except for an intermediary bank, any transferee under an indorsement which is conditional or includes the words "for collection," "for deposit," "pay any bank," or like terms (subparagraphs (a) and (c) of Section 3–205) must pay or apply any value given by him for or on the security of the instrument consistently with the indorsement and to the extent that he does so he becomes a holder for value. In addition such transferee is a holder in due course if he otherwise complies with the requirements of Section 3–302 on what constitutes a holder in due course.

(4) The first take under an indorsement for the benefit of the indorser or another person (subparagraph (d) of Section 3–205) must pay or apply any value given by him for or on the security of the instrument consistently with the indorsement and to the extent that he does so he becomes a holder for value. In addition such taker is a holder in due course if he otherwise complies with the requirements of Section 3–302 on what constitutes a holder in due course. A later holder for value is neither given notice nor otherwise affected by such restrictive indorsement unless he has knowledge that a fiduciary or other person has negotiated the instrument in any transaction for his own benefit or otherwise in breach of duty (subsection (2) of Section 3–304).

§ 3–207. Negotiation Effective Although It May Be Rescinded.

(1) Negotiation is effective to transfer the instrument although the negotiation is

(a) made by an infant, a corporation exceeding its powers, or any other person without capacity; or

(b) obtained by fraud, duress or mistake of any kind; or

(c) part of an illegal transaction; or

(d) made in breach of duty.

(2) Except as against a subsequent holder in due course such negotiation is in an appropriate case subject to rescission, the declaration of a constructive trust or any other remedy permitted by law.

§ 3–208. Reacquisition.

Where an instrument is returned to or reacquired by a prior party he may cancel any indorsement which is not necessary to his title and reissue or further negotiate the instrument, but any intervening party is discharged as against the reacquiring party and subsequent holders not in due course and if his indorsement has been cancelled is discharged as against subsequent holders in due course as well.

PART 3
RIGHTS OF A HOLDER

§ 3–301. Rights of a Holder.

The holder of an instrument whether or not he is the owner may transfer or negotiate it and, except as otherwise provided in Section 3–603 on payment or satisfaction, discharge it or enforce payment in his own name.

§ 3–302. Holder in Due Course.

(1) A holder in due course is a holder who takes the instrument
- (a) for value; and
- (b) in good faith; and
- (c) without notice that it is overdue or has been dishonored or of any defense against or claim to it on the part of any person.

(2) A payee may be a holder in due course.

(3) A holder does not become a holder in due course of an instrument:
- (a) by purchase of it at judicial sale or by taking it under legal process; or
- (b) by acquiring it in taking over an estate; or
- (c) by purchasing it as part of a bulk transaction not in regular course of business of the transferor.

(4) A purchaser of a limited interest can be a holder in due course only to the extent of the interest purchased.

§ 3–303. Taking for Value.

A holder takes the instrument for value
- (a) to the extent that the agreed consideration has been performed or that he acquires a security interest in or a lien on the instrument otherwise than by legal process; or
- (b) when he takes the instrument in payment of or as security for an antecedent claim against any person whether or not the claim is due; or
- (c) when he gives a negotiable instrument for it or makes an irrevocable commitment to a third person.

§ 3–304. Notice to Purchaser.

(1) The purchaser has notice of a claim or defense if
- (a) the instrument is so incomplete, bears such visible evidence of forgery or alteration, or is otherwise so irregular as to call into question its validity, terms or ownership or to create an ambiguity as to the party to pay; or
- (b) the purchaser has notice that the obligation of any party is voidable in whole or in part, or that all parties have been discharged.

(2) The purchaser has notice of a claim against the instrument when he has knowledge that a fiduciary has negotiated the instrument in payment of or as security for his own debt or in any transaction for his own benefit or otherwise in breach of duty.

(3) The purchaser has notice that an instrument is overdue if he has reason to know

(a) that any part of the principal amount is overdue or that there is an uncured default in payment of another instrument of the same series; or

(b) that acceleration of the instrument has been made; or

(c) that he is taking a demand instrument after demand has been made or more than a reasonable length of time after its issue. A reasonable time for a check drawn and payable within the states and territories of the United States and the District of Columbia is presumed to be thirty days.

(4) Knowledge of the following facts does not of itself give the purchaser notice of a defense or claim

(a) that the instrument is antedated or postdated;

(b) that it was issued or negotiated in return for an executory promise or accompanied by a separate agreement, unless the purchaser has notice that a defense or claim has arisen from the terms thereof;

(c) that any party has signed for accommodation;

(d) that an incomplete instrument has been completed, unless the purchaser has notice of any improper completion;

(e) that any person negotiating the instrument is or was a fiduciary;

(f) that there has been default in payment of interest on the instrument or in payment of any other instrument, except one of the same series.

(5) The filing or recording of a document does not of itself constitute notice within the provisions of this Article to a person who would otherwise be a holder in due course.

(6) To be effective notice must be received at such time and in such manner as to give a reasonable opportunity to act on it.

§ 3–305. Rights of a Holder in Due Course.

To the extent that a holder is a holder in due course he takes the instrument free from

(1) all claims to it on the part of any person; and

(2) all defenses of any party to the instrument with whom the holder has not dealt except

(a) infancy, to the extent that it is a defense to a simple contract; and

(b) such other incapacity, or duress, or illegality of the transaction, as renders the obligation of the party a nullity; and

(c) such misrepresentation as has induced the party to sign the instrument with neither knowledge nor reasonable opportunity to obtain knowledge of its character or its essential terms; and

(d) discharge in insolvency proceedings; and

(e) any other discharge of which the holder has notice when he takes the instrument.

§ 3–306. Rights of One Not Holder in Due Course.

Unless he has the rights of a holder in due course any person takes the instrument subject to

(a) all valid claims to it on the part of any person; and

(b) all defenses of any party which would be available in an action on a simple contract; and

(c) the defenses of want or failure of consideration, non-performance of any condition precedent, non-delivery, or delivery for a special purpose (Section 3–408); and

(d) the defense that he or a person through whom he holds the instrument acquired it by theft, or that payment or satisfaction to such holder would be inconsistent with the terms of a restrictive indorsement. The claim of any third person to the instrument is not otherwise available as a defense to any party liable thereon unless the third person himself defends the action for such party.

§ 3–307. Burden of Establishing Signatures, Defenses and Due Course.

(1) Unless specifically denied in the pleadings each signature on an instrument is admitted. When the effectiveness of a signature is put in issue

(a) the burden of establishing it is on the party claiming under the signature; but

(b) the signature is presumed to be genuine or authorized except where the action is to enforce the obligation of a purported signer who has died or become incompetent before proof is required.

(2) When signatures are admitted or established, production of the instrument entitles a holder to recover on it unless the defendant establishes a defense.

(3) After it is shown that a defense exists a person claiming the rights of a holder in due course has the burden of establishing that he or some person under whom he claims is in all respects a holder in due course.

PART 4
LIABILITY OF PARTIES

§ 3–401. Signature.

(1) No person is liable on an instrument unless his signature appears thereon.

(2) A signature is made by use of any name, including any trade or assumed name, upon an instrument, or by any word or mark used in lieu of a written signature.

§ 3–402. Signature in Ambiguous Capacity.

Unless the instrument clearly indicates that a signature is made in some other capacity it is an indorsement.

§3–403. Signature by Authorized Representative.

(1) A signature may be made by an agent or other representative, and his authority to make it may be established as in other cases of representation. No particular form of appointment is necessary to establish such authority.

(2) An authorized representative who signs his own name to an instrument

(a) is personally obligated if the instrument neither names the person represented nor shows that the representative signed in a representative capacity;

(b) except as otherwise established between the immediate parties, is personally obligated if the instrument names the person represented but does not show that the representative signed in a representative capacity, or if the instrument does not name the person represented but does show that the representative signed in a representative capacity.

(3) Except as otherwise established the name of an organization preceded or followed by the name and office of an authorized individual is a signature made in a representative capacity.

§ 3–404. Unauthorized Signatures.

(1) Any unauthorized signature is wholly inoperative as that of the person whose name is signed unless he ratifies it or is precluded from denying it; but it operates as the signature

of the unauthorized signer in favor of any person who in good faith pays the instrument or takes it for value.

(2) Any unauthorized signature may be ratified for all purposes of this Article. Such ratification does not of itself affect any rights of the person ratifying against the actual signer.

§ 3–405. Impostors; Signature in Name of Payee.

(1) An indorsement by any person in the name of a named payee is effective if

(a) an impostor by use of the mails or otherwise has induced the maker or drawer to issue the instrument to him or his confederate in the name of the payee; or

(b) a person signing as or on behalf of a maker or drawer intends the payee to have no interest in the instrument; or

(c) an agent or employee of the maker or drawer has supplied him with the name of the payee intending the latter to have no such interest.

(2) Nothing in this section shall affect the criminal or civil liability of the person so indorsing.

§ 3–406. Negligence Contributing to Alteration or Unauthorized Signature.

Any person who by his negligence substantially contributes to a material alteration of the instrument or to the making of an unauthorized signature is precluded from asserting the alteration or lack of authority against a holder in due course or against a drawee or other payor who pays the instrument in good faith and in accordance with the reasonable commercial standards of the drawee's or payor's business.

§ 3–407. Alteration.

(1) Any alteration of an instrument is material which changes the contract of any party thereto in any respect, including any such change in

(a) the number or relations of the parties; or

(b) an incomplete instrument, by completing it otherwise than as authorized; or

(c) the writing as signed, by adding to it or by removing any part of it.

(2) As against any person other than a subsequent holder in due course.

(a) Alteration by the holder which is both fraudulent and material discharges any party whose contract is thereby changed unless that party assents or is precluded from asserting the defense;

(b) no other alteration discharges any party and the instrument may be enforced according to its original tenor, or as to incomplete instruments according to the authority given.

(3) A subsequent holder in due course may in all cases enforce the instrument according to its original tenor, and when an incomplete instrument has been completed, he may enforce it as completed.

§ 3–408. Consideration.

Want or failure of consideration is a defense as against any person not having the rights of a holder in due course (Section 3–305), except that no consideration is necessary for an instrument or obligation thereon given in payment of or as security for an antecedent obligation of any kind. Nothing in this section shall be taken to displace any statute outside this Act under which a promise is enforceable notwithstanding lack or failure of consideration. Partial failure of consideration is a defense pro tanto whether or not the failure is in an ascertained or liquidated amount.

§ 3–409. Draft Not an Assignment.

(1) A check or other draft does not of itself operate as an assignment of any funds in the hands of the drawee available for its payment, and the drawee is not liable on the instrument until he accepts it.

(2) Nothing in this section shall affect any liability in contract, tort or otherwise arising from any letter of credit or other obligation or representation which is not an acceptance.

§ 3–410. Definition and Operation of Acceptance.

(1) Acceptance is the drawee's signed engagement to honor the draft as presented. It must be written on the draft, and may consist of his signature alone. It becomes operative when completed by delivery or notification.

(2) A draft may be accepted although it has not been signed by the drawer or is otherwise incomplete or is overdue or has been dishonored.

(3) Where the draft is payable at a fixed period after sight and the acceptor fails to date his acceptance the holder may complete it by supplying a date in good faith.

§ 3–411. Certification of a Check.

(1) Certification of a check is acceptance. Where a holder procures certification the drawer and all prior indorsers are discharged.

(2) Unless otherwise agreed a bank has no obligation to certify a check.

(3) A bank may certify a check before returning it for lack of proper indorsement. If it does so the drawer is discharged.

§ 3–412. Acceptance Varying Draft.

(1) Where the drawee's proffered acceptance in any manner varies the draft as presented the holder may refuse the acceptance and treat the draft as dishonored in which case the drawee is entitled to have his acceptance cancelled.

(2) The terms of the draft are not varied by an acceptance to pay at any particular bank or place in the United States, unless the acceptance states that the draft is to be paid only at such bank or place.

(3) Where the holder assents to an acceptance varying the terms of the draft each drawer and indorser who does not affirmatively assent is discharged.

§ 3–413. Contract of Maker, Drawer and Acceptor.

(1) The maker or acceptor engages that he will pay the instrument according to its tenor at the time of his engagement or as completed pursuant to Section 3–115 on incomplete instruments.

(2) The drawer engages that upon dishonor of the draft and any necessary notice of dishonor or protest he will pay the amount of the draft to the holder or to any indorser who takes it up. The drawer may disclaim this liability by drawing without recourse.

(3) By making, drawing or accepting the party admits as against all subsequent parties including the drawee the existence of the payee and his then capacity to indorse.

§ 3–414. Contract of Indorser; Order of Liability.

(1) Unless the indorsement otherwise specifies (as by such words as "without recourse") every indorser engages that upon dishonor and any necessary notice of dishonor and protest he will pay the instrument according to its tenor at the time of his indorsement to the holder or to any subsequent indorser who takes it up, even though the indorser who takes it up was not obligated to do so.

(2) Unless they otherwise agree indorsers are liable to one another in the order in which they indorse, which is presumed to be the order in which their signatures appear on the instrument.

§ 3–415. Contract of Accommodation Party.

(1) An accommodation party is one who signs the instrument in any capacity for the purpose of lending his name to another party to it.

(2) When the instrument has been taken for value before it is due the accommodation party is liable in the capacity in which he has signed even though the taker knows of the accommodation.

(3) As against a holder in due course and without notice of the accommodation oral proof of the accommodation is not admissible to give the accommodation party the benefit of discharges dependent on his character as such. In other cases the accommodation character may be shown by oral proof.

(4) An indorsement which shows that it is not in the chain of title is notice of its accommodation character.

(5) An accommodation party is not liable to the party accommodated, and if he pays the instrument has a right of recourse on the instrument against such party.

§ 3–416. Contract of Guarantor.

(1) "Payment guaranteed" or equivalent words added to a signature mean that the signer engages that if the instrument is not paid when due he will pay it according to its tenor without resort by the holder to any other party.

(2) "Collection guaranteed" or equivalent words added to a signature mean that the signer engages that if the instrument is not paid when due he will pay it according to its tenor, but only after the holder has reduced his claim against the maker or acceptor to judgment and execution has been returned unsatisfied, or after the maker or acceptor has become insolvent or it is otherwise apparent that it is useless to proceed against him.

(3) Words of guaranty which do not otherwise specify guarantee payment.

(4) No words of guaranty added to the signature of a sole maker or acceptor affect his liability on the instrument. Such words added to the signature of one of two or more makers or acceptors create a presumption that the signature is for the accommodation of the others.

(5) When words of guaranty are used presentment, notice of dishonor and protest are not necessary to charge the user.

(6) Any guaranty written on the instrument is enforcible notwithstanding any statute of frauds.

§ 3–417. Warranties on Presentment and Transfer.

(1) Any person who obtains payment or acceptance and any prior transferor warrants to a person who in good faith pays or accepts that

- (a) he has a good title to the instrument or is authorized to obtain payment or acceptance on behalf of one who has a good title; and
- (b) he has no knowledge that the signature of the maker or drawer is unauthorized, except that this warranty is not given by a holder in due course acting in good faith
  - (i) to a maker with respect to the maker's own signature; or
  - (ii) to a drawer with respect to the drawer's own signature, whether or not the drawer is also the drawee; or
  - (iii) to an acceptor of a draft if the holder in due course took the draft after the acceptance or obtained the acceptance without knowledge that the drawer's signature was unauthorized; and
- (c) the instrument has not been materially altered, except that this warranty is not given by a holder in due course acting in good faith

(i) to the maker of a note; or
(ii) to the drawer of a draft whether or not the drawer is also the drawee; or
(iii) to the acceptor of a draft with respect to an alteration made prior to the acceptance if the holder in due course took the draft after the acceptance, even though the acceptance provided "payable as originally drawn" or equivalent terms; or
(iv) to the acceptor of a draft with respect to an alteration made after the acceptance.

(2) Any person who transfers an instrument and receives consideration warrants to his transferee and if the transfer is by indorsement to any subsequent holder who takes the instrument in good faith that

(a) he has a good title to the instrument or is authorized to obtain payment or acceptance on behalf of one who has a good title and the transfer is otherwise rightful; and
(b) all signatures are genuine or authorized; and
(c) the instrument has not been materially altered; and
(d) no defense of any party is good against him; and
(e) he has no knowledge of any insolvency proceeding instituted with respect to the maker or acceptor or the drawer of an unaccepted instrument.

(3) By transferring "without recourse" the transferor limits the obligation stated in subsection (2) (d) to a warranty that he has no knowledge of such a defense.

(4) A selling agent or broker who does not disclose the fact that he is acting only as such gives the warranties provided in this section, but if he makes such disclosure warrants only his good faith and authority.

§ 3–418. Finality of Payment or Acceptance.

Except for recovery of bank payments as provided in the Article on Bank Deposits and Collections (Article 4) and except for liability for breach of warranty on presentment under the preceding section, payment or acceptance of any instrument is final in favor of a holder in due course, or a person who has in good faith changed his position in reliance on the payment.

§ 3–419. Conversion of Instrument; Innocent Representative.

(1) An instrument is converted when

(a) a drawee to whom it is delivered for acceptance refuses to return it on demand; or
(b) any person to whom it is delivered for payment refuses on demand either to pay or to return it; or
(c) it is paid on a forged indorsement.

(2) In an action against a drawee under subsection (1) the measure of the drawee's liability is the face amount of the instrument. In any other action under subsection (1) the measure of liability is presumed to be the face amount of the instrument.

(3) Subject to the provisions of this Act concerning restrictive indorsements a representative, including a depositary or collecting bank, who has in good faith and in accordance with the reasonable commercial standards applicable to the business of such representative dealt with an instrument or its proceeds on behalf of one who was not the true owner is not liable in conversion or otherwise to the true owner beyond the amount of any proceeds remaining in his hands.

(4) An intermediary bank or payor bank which is not a depositary bank is not liable in conversion solely by reason of the fact that proceeds of an item indorsed restrictively (Sections 3–205 and 3–206) are not paid or applied consistently with the restrictive indorsement of an indorser other than its immediate transferor.

PART 5
PRESENTMENT, NOTICE OF DISHONOR AND PROTEST

§ 3–501. When Presentment, Notice of Dishonor, and Protest Necessary or Permissible.

(1) Unless excused (Section 3–511) presentment is necessary to charge secondary parties as follows:

(a) presentment for acceptance is necessary to charge the drawer and indorsers of a draft where the draft so provides, or is payable elsewhere than at the residence or place of business of the drawee, or its date of payment depends upon such presentment. The holder may at his option present for acceptance any other draft payable at a stated date;

(b) presentment for payment is necessary to charge any indorser;

(c) in the case of any drawer, the acceptor of a draft payable at a bank or the maker of a note payable at a bank, presentment for payment is necessary, but failure to make presentment discharges such drawer, acceptor or maker only as stated in Section 3–502(1) (b).

(2) Unless excused (Section 3–511)

(a) notice of any dishonor is necessary to charge any indorser;

(b) in the case of any drawer, the acceptor of a draft payable at a bank or the maker of a note payable at a bank, notice of any dishonor is necessary, but failure to give such notice discharges such drawer, acceptor or maker only as stated in Section 3–502(1) (b).

(3) Unless excused (Section 3–511) protest of any dishonor is necessary to charge the drawer and indorsers of any draft which on its face appears to be drawn or payable outside of the states, territories, dependencies and possessions of the United States, the District of Columbia and the Commonwealth of Puerto Rico. The holder may at his option make protest of any dishonor of any other instrument and in the case of a foreign draft may on insolvency of the acceptor before maturity make protest for better security.

(4) Notwithstanding any provision of this section, neither presentment nor notice of dishonor nor protest is necessary to charge an indorser who has indorsed an instrument after maturity.

§ 3–502. Unexcused Delay; Discharge.

(1) Where without excuse any necessary presentment or notice of dishonor is delayed beyond the time when it is due

(a) any indorser is discharged; and

(b) any drawer or the acceptor of a draft payable at a bank or the maker of a note payable at a bank who because the drawee or payor bank becomes insolvent during the delay is deprived of funds maintained with the drawee or payor bank to cover the instrument may discharge his liability by written assignment to the holder of his rights against the drawee or payor bank in respect of such funds, but such drawer, acceptor or maker is not otherwise discharged.

(2) Where without excuse a necessary protest is delayed beyond the time when it is due any drawer or indorser is discharged.

§ 3–503. Time of Presentment.

(1) Unless a different time is expressed in the instrument the time for any presentment is determined as follows:

(a) where an instrument is payable at or a fixed period after a stated date any presentment for acceptance must be made on or before the date it is payable:

(b) where an instrument is payable after sight in must either be presented for acceptance or negotiated within a reasonable time after date or issue whichever is later;

(c) where an instrument shows the date on which it is payable presentment for payment is due on that date;

(d) where an instrument is accelerated presentment for payment is due within a reasonable time after the acceleration;

(e) with respect to the liability of any secondary party presentment for acceptance or payment of any other instrument is due within a reasonable time after such party becomes liable thereon.

(2) A reasonable time for presentment is determined by the nature of the instrument, any usage of banking or trade and the facts of the particular case. In the case of an uncertified check which is drawn and payable within the United States and which is not a draft drawn by a bank the following are presumed to be reasonable periods within which to present for payment or to initiate bank collection:

(a) with respect to the liability of the drawer, thirty days after date or issue whichever is later; and

(b) with respect to the liability of an indorser, seven days after his indorsement.

(3) Where any presentment is due on a day which is not a full business day for either the person making presentment or the party to pay or accept, presentment is due on the next following day which is a full business day for both parties.

(4) Presentment to be sufficient must be made at a reasonable hour, and if at a bank during its banking day.

§ 3–504. How Presentment Made.

(1) Presentment is a demand for acceptance or payment made upon the maker, acceptor, drawee or other payor by or on behalf of the holder.

(2) Presentment may be made

(a) by mail, in which event the time of presentment is determined by the time of receipt of the mail; or

(b) through a clearing house; or

(c) at the place of acceptance or payment specified in the instrument or if there be none at the place of business or residence of the party to accept or pay. If neither the party to accept or pay nor anyone authorized to act for him is present or accessible at such place presentment is excused.

(3) It may be made

(a) to any one of two or more makers, acceptors, drawees or other payors; or

(b) to any person who has authority to make or refuse the acceptance or payment.

(4) A draft accepted or a note made payable at a bank in the United States must be presented at such bank.

(5) In the cases described in Section 4–210 presentment may be made in the manner and with the result stated in that section.

§ 3–505. Rights of Party to Whom Presentment Is Made.

(1) The party to whom presentment is made may without dishonor require

(a) exhibition of the instrument; and

(b) reasonable indentification of the person making presentment and evidence of his authority to make it if made for another; and

(c) that the instrument be produced for acceptance or payment at a place specified in it, or if there be none at any place reasonable in the circumstances; and

(d) a signed receipt on the instrument for any partial or full payment and its surrender upon full payment.

(2) Failure to comply with any such requirement invalidates the presentment but the person presenting has a reasonable time in which to comply and the time for acceptance or payment runs from the time of compliance.

§ 3–506. Time Allowed for Acceptance or Payment.

(1) Acceptance may be deferred without dishonor until the close of the next business day following presentment. The holder may also in a good faith effort to obtain acceptance and without either dishonor of the instrument or discharge of secondary parties allow postponement of acceptance for an additional business day.

(2) Except as a longer time is allowed in the case of documentary drafts drawn under a letter of credit, and unless an earlier time is agreed to by the party to pay, payment of an instrument may be deferred without dishonor pending reasonable examination to determine whether it is properly payable, but payment must be made in any event before the close of business on the day or presentment.

§ 3–507. Dishonor; Holder's Right of Recourse; Term Allowing Re-Presentment.

(1) An instrument is dishonored when

(a) a necessary or optional presentment is duly made and due acceptance or payment is refused or cannot be obtained within the prescribed time or in case of bank collections the instrument is seasonably returned by the midnight deadline (Section 4–301); or

(b) presentment is excused and the instrument is not duly accepted or paid.

(2) Subject to any necessary notice of dishonor and protest, the holder has upon dishonor an immediate right of recourse against the drawers and indorsers.

(3) Return of an instrument for lack of proper indorsement is not dishonor.

(4) A term in a draft or an indorsement thereof allowing a stated time for re-presentment in the event of any dishonor of the draft by nonacceptance if a time draft or by nonpayment if a sight draft gives the holder as against any secondary party bound by the term an option to waive the dishonor without affecting the liability of the secondary party and he may present again up to the end of the stated time.

§ 3–508. Notice of Dishonor.

(1) Notice of dishonor may be given to any person who may be liable on the instrument by or on behalf of the holder or any party who has himself received notice, or any other party who can be compelled to pay the instrument. In addition an agent or bank in whose hands the instrument is dishonored may give notice to his principal or customer or to another agent or bank from which the instrument was received.

(2) Any necessary notice must be given by a bank before its midnight deadline and by any other person before midnight of the third business day after dishonor or receipt of notice of dishonor.

(3) Notice may be given in any reasonable manner. It may be oral or written and in any terms which identify the instrument and state that it has been dishonored. A misdescription which does not mislead the party notified does not vitiate the notice. Sending the instrument bearing a stamp, ticket or writing stating that acceptance or payment has been refused or sending a notice of debit with respect to the instrument is sufficient.

(4) Written notice is given when sent although it is not received.

(5) Notice to one partner is notice to each although the firm has been dissolved.

(6) When any party is in insolvency proceedings instituted after the issue of the instrument notice may be given either to the party or to the representative of his estate.

(7) When any party is dead or incompetent notice may be sent to his last known address or given to his personal representative.

(8) Notice operates for the benefit of all parties who have rights on the instrument against the party notified.

§ 3–509. Protest; Noting for Protest.

(1) A protest is a certificate of dishonor made under the hand and seal of a United States consul or vice consul or a notary public or other person authorized to certify dishonor by the law of the place where dishonor occurs. It may be made upon information satisfactory to such person.

(2) The protest must identify the instrument and certify either that due presentment has been made or the reason why it is excused and that the instrument has been dishonored by nonacceptance or nonpayment.

(3) The protest may also certify that notice of dishonor has been given to all parties or to specified parties.

(4) Subject to subsection (5) any necessary protest is due by the time that notice of dishonor is due.

(5) If, before protest is due, an instrument has been noted for protest by the officer to make protest, the protest may be made at any time thereafter as of the date of the noting.

§ 3–510. Evidence of Dishonor and Notice of Dishonor.

The following are admissible as evidence and create a presumption of dishonor and of any notice of dishonor therein shown:

(a) a document regular in form as provided in the preceding section which purports to be a protest;

(b) the purported stamp or writing of the drawee, payor bank or presenting bank on the instrument or accompanying it stating that acceptance or payment has been refused for reasons consistent with dishonor;

(c) any book or record of the drawee, payor bank, or any collecting bank kept in the usual course of business which shows dishonor, even though there is no evidence of who made the entry.

§ 3–511. Waived or Excused Presentment, Protest or Notice of Dishonor or Delay Therein.

(1) Delay in presentment, protest or notice of dishonor is excused when the party is without notice that it is due or when the delay is caused by circumstances beyond his control and he exercises reasonable diligence after the cause of the delay ceases to operate.

(2) Presentment or notice or protest as the case may be is entirely excused when

(a) the party to be charged has waived it expressly or by implication either before or after it is due; or

(b) such party has himself dishonored the instrument or has countermanded payment or otherwise has no reason to expect or right to require that the instrument be accepted or paid; or

(c) by reasonable diligence the presentment or protest cannot be made or the notice given.

(3) Presentment is also entirely excused when

(a) the maker, acceptor or drawee of any instrument except a documentary draft is dead or in insolvency proceedings instituted after the issue of the instrument; or

(b) acceptance or payment is refused but not for want of proper presentment.

(4) Where a draft has been dishonored by nonacceptance a later presentment for payment and any notice of dishonor and protest for nonpayment are excused unless in the meantime the instrument has been accepted.

(5) A waiver of protest is also a waiver of presentment and of notice of dishonor even though protest is not required.

(6) Where a waiver of presentment or notice or protest is embodied in the instrument itself it is binding upon all parties; but where it is written above the signature of an indorser it binds him only.

PART 6
DISCHARGE

§ 3–601. Discharge of Parties.

(1) The extent of the discharge of any party from liability on an instrument is governed by the sections on

(a) payment or satisfaction (Section 3–603); or
(b) tender of payment (Section 3–604); or
(c) cancellation or renunciation (Section 3–605); or
(d) impairment of right of recourse or of collateral (Section 3–606); or
(e) reacquisition of the instrument by a prior party (Section 3–208); or
(f) fraudulent and material alteration (Section 3–407); or
(g) certification of a check (Section 3–411); or
(h) acceptance varying a draft (Section 3–412); or
(i) unexcused delay in presentment or notice of dishonor or protest (Section 3–502).

(2) Any party is also discharged from his liability on an instrument to another party by any other act or agreement with such party which would discharge his simple contract for the payment of money.

(3) The liability of all parties is discharged when any party who has himself no right of action or recourse on the instrument

(a) reacquires the instrument in his own right; or
(b) is discharged under any provision of this Article, except as otherwise provided with respect to discharge for impairment of recourse or of collateral (Section 3–606).

§ 3–602. Effect of Discharge Against Holder in Due Course.

No discharge of any party provided by this Article is effective against a subsequent holder in due course unless he has notice thereof when he takes the instrument.

§ 3–603. Payment or Satisfaction.

(1) The liability of any party is discharged to the extent of his payment or satisfaction to the holder even though it is made with knowledge of a claim of another person to the instrument unless prior to such payment or satisfaction the person making the claim either supplies indemnity deemed adequate by the party seeking the discharge or enjoins payment or satisfaction by order of a court of competent jurisdiction in an action in which the adverse claimant and the holder are parties. This subsection does not, however, result in the dscharge of the liability

(a) of a party who in bad faith pays or satisfies a holder who acquired the instrument by theft or who (unless having the rights of a holder in due course) holds through one who so acquired it; or
(b) of a party (other than an intermediary bank or a payor bank which is not a depositary bank) who pays or satisfies the holder of an instrument which has been restrictively indorsed in a manner not consistent with the terms of such restrictive indorsement.

(2) Payment or satisfaction may be made with the consent of the holder by any person including a stranger to the instrument. Surrender of the instrument to such a person gives him the rights of a transferee (Section 3–201).

§ 3–604. Tender of Payment.

(1) Any party making tender of full payment to a holder when or after it is due is discharged to the extent of all subsequent liability for interest, costs and attorney's fees.

(2) The holder's refusal of such tender wholly discharges any party who has a right of recourse against the party making the tender.

(3) Where the maker or acceptor of an instrument payable otherwise than on demand is able and ready to pay at every place of payment specified in the instrument when it is due, it is equivalent to tender.

§ 3–605. Cancellation and Renunciation.

(1) The holder of an instrument may even without consideration discharge any party

(a) in any manner apparent on the face of the instrument or the indorsement, as by intentionally cancelling the instrument or the party's signature by destruction or mutilation, or by striking out the party's signature; or

(b) by renouncing his rights by a writing signed and delivered or by surrender of the instrument to the party to be discharged.

(2) Neither cancellation nor renunciation without surrender of the instrument affects the title thereto.

§ 3–606. Impairment of Recourse or of Collateral.

(1) The holder discharges any party to the instrument to the extent that without such party's consent the holder

(a) without express reservation of rights releases or agrees not to sue any person against whom the party has to the knowledge of the holder a right of recourse or agrees to suspend the right to enforce against such person the instrument or collateral or otherwise discharges such person, except that failure or delay in effecting any required presentment, protest or notice of dishonor with respect to any such person does not discharge any party as to whom presentment, protest or notice of dishonor is effective or unnecessary; or

(b) unjustifiably impairs any collateral for the instrument given by or on behalf of the party or any person against whom he has a right to recourse.

(2) By express reservation of rights against a party with a right of recourse the holder preserves

(a) all his rights against such party as of the time when the instrument was originally due; and

(b) the right of the party to pay the instrument as of that time; and

(c) all rights of such party to recourse against others.

PART 7
ADVICE OF INTERNATIONAL SIGHT DRAFT

§ 3–701. Letter of Advice of International Sight Draft.

(1) A "letter of advice" is a drawer's communication to the drawee that a described draft has been drawn.

(2) Unless otherwise agreed when a bank receives from another bank a letter of advice of an international sight draft the drawee bank may immediately debit the drawer's account

and stop the running of interest pro tanto. Such a debit and any resulting credit to any account covering outstanding drafts leaves in the drawer full power to stop payment or otherwise dispose of the amount and creates no trust or interest in favor of the holder.

(3) Unless otherwise agreed and except where a draft is drawn under a credit issued by the drawee, the drawee of an international sight draft owes the drawer no duty to pay an unadvised draft but if it does so and the draft is genuine, may appropriately debit the drawer's account.

PART 8
MISCELLANEOUS

§ 3–801. Drafts in a Set.

(1) Where a draft is drawn in a set of party, each of which is numbered and expressed to be an order only if no other part has been honored, the whole of the parts constitutes one draft but a taker of any part may become a holder in due course of the draft.

(2) Any person who negotiates, indorses or accepts a single part of a draft drawn in a set thereby becomes liable to any holder in due course of that part as if it were the whole set, but as between different holders in due course to whom different parts have been negotiated the holder whose title first accrues has all rights to the draft and its proceeds.

(3) As against the drawee the first presented part of a draft drawn in a set is the part entitled to payment, or if a time draft to acceptance and payment. Acceptance of any subsequently presented part renders the drawee liable thereon under subsection (2). With respect both to a holder and to the drawer payment of a subsequently presented part of a draft payable at sight has the same effect as payment of a check notwithstanding an effective stop order (Section 4–407).

(4) Except as otherwise provided in this section, where any part of a draft in a set is discharged by payment or otherwise the whole draft is discharged.

§ 3–802. Effect of Instrument on Obligation for Which It Is Given.

(1) Unless otherwise agreed where an instrument is taken for an underlying obligation

(a) the obligation is pro tanto discharged if a bank is drawer, maker or acceptor of the instrument and there is no recourse on the instrument against the underlying obligor; and

(b) in any other case the obligation is suspended pro tanto until the instrument is due or if it is payable on demand until its presentment. If the instrument is dishonored action may be maintained on either the instrument or the obligation; discharge of the underlying obligor on the instrument also discharges him on the obligation.

(2) The taking in good faith of a check which is not postdated does not of itself so extend the time on the original obligation as to discharge a surety.

§ 3–803. Notice to Third Party.

Where a defendant is sued for breach of an obligation for which a third person is answerable over under this Article he may give the third person written notice of the litigation, and the person notified may then give similar notice to any other person who is answerable over to him under this Article. If the notice states that the person notified may come in and defend and that if the person notified does not do so he will in any action against him by the person giving the notice be bound by any determination of fact common to the two litigations, then unless after seasonable receipt of the notice the person notified does come in and defend he is so bound.

§ 3–804. Lost, Destroyed or Stolen Instruments.

The owner of an instrument which is lost, whether by destruction, theft or otherwise, may maintain an action in his own name and recover from any party liable thereon upon due proof of his ownership, the facts which prevent his production of the instrument and its terms. The court may require security indemnifying the defendant against loss by reason of further claims on the instrument.

§ 3–805. Instruments Not Payable to Order or to Bearer.

This Article applies to any instrument whose terms do not preclude transfer and which is otherwise negotiable within this Article but which is not payable to order or to bearer, except that there can be no holder in due course of such an instrument.

ARTICLE 4. Bank Deposits and Collections

PART 1

GENERAL PROVISIONS AND DEFINITIONS

§ 4–101. Short Title.

This Article shall be known and may be cited as Uniform Commercial Code—Bank Deposits and Collections.

§ 4–102. Applicability.

(1) To the extent that items within this Article are also within the scope of Articles 3 and 8, they are subject to the provisions of those Articles. In the event of conflict the provisions of this Article govern those of Article 3 but the provisions of Article 8 govern those of this Article.

(2) The liability of a bank for action or non-action with respect to any item handled by it for purposes of presentment, payment or collection is governed by the law of the place where the bank is located. In the case of action or non-action by or at a branch or separate office of a bank, its liability is governed by the law of the place where the branch or separate office is located.

§ 4–103. Variation by Agreement; Measure of Damages; Certain Action Constituting Ordinary Care.

(1) The effect of the provisions of this Article may be varied by agreement except that no agreement can disclaim a bank's responsibility for its own lack of good faith or failure to exercise ordinary care or can limit the measure of damages for such lack or failure; but the parties may by agreement determine the standards by which such responsibility is to be measured if such standards are not manifestly unreasonable.

(2) Federal Reserve regulations and operating letters, clearing house rules, and the like, have the effect of agreements under subsection (1), whether or not specifically assented to by all parties interested in items handled.

(3) Action or non-action approved by this Article or pursuant to Federal Reserve regulations or operating letters constitutes the exercise of ordinary care and, in the absence of special instructions, action or non-action consistent with clearing house rules and the like or with a general banking usage not disapproved by this Article, prima facie constitutes the exercise of ordinary care.

(4) The specification or approval of certain procedures by this Article does not constitute disapproval of other procedures which may be reasonable under the circumstances.

(5) The measure of damages for fialure to exercise ordinary care in handling an item is the amount of the item reduced by an amount which could not have been realized by the use of ordinary care, and where there is bad faith it includes other damages, if any, suffered by the party as a proximate consequence.

§ 4–104. Definitions and Index of Definitions.

(1) In this Article unless the context otherwise requires

(a) "Account" means any account with a bank and includes a checking, time, interest or savings account;

(b) "Afternoon" means the period of a day between noon and midnight;

(c) "Banking day" means that part of any day on which a bank is open to the public for carrying on substantially all of its banking functions;

(d) "Clearing house" means any association of banks or other payors regularly clearing items;

(e) "Customer" means any person having an account with a bank or for whom a bank has agreed to collect items and includes a bank carrying an account with another bank;

(f) "Documentary draft" means any negotiable or non-negotiable draft with accompanying documents, securities or other papers to be delivered against honor of the draft;

(g) "Item" means any instrument for the payment of money even though it is not negotiable but does not include money;

(h) "Midnight deadline" with respect to a bank is midnight on its next banking day following the banking day on which it receives the relevant item or notice or from which the time for taking action commences to run, whichever is later;

(i) "Properly payable" includes the availability of funds for payment at the time of decision to pay or dishonor;

(j) "Settle" means to pay in cash, by clearing house settlement, in a charge or credit or by remittance, or otherwise as instructed. A settlement may be either provisional or final;

(k) "Suspends payments" with respect to a bank means that it has been closed by order of the supervisory authorities, that a public officer has been appointed to take it over or that it ceases or refuses to make payments in the ordinary course of business.

(2) Other definitions applying to this Article and the sections in which they appear are:

"Collecting bank"	Section 4–105.
"Depositary bank"	Section 4–105.
"Intermediary bank"	Section 4–105.
"Payor bank"	Section 4–105.
"Presenting bank"	Section 4–105.
"Remitting bank"	Section 4–105.

(3) The following definitions in other Articles apply to this Article:

"Acceptance"	Section 3–410.
"Certificate of deposit"	Section 3–104.
"Certification"	Section 3–411.
"Check"	Section 3–104.
"Draft"	Section 3–104.
"Holder in due course"	Section 3–302.
"Notice of dishonor"	Section 3–508.
"Presentment"	Section 3–504.
"Protest"	Section 3–509.
"Secondary party"	Section 3–102.

(4) In addition Article 1 contains general definitions and principles of construction and interpretation applicable throughout this Article.

§ 4–105. "Depositary Bank"; "Intermediary Bank"; "Collecting Bank"; "Payor Bank"; "Presenting Bank"; "Remitting Bank."

In this Article unless the context otherwise requires:

(a) "Depositary bank" means the first bank to which an item is transferred for collection even though it is also the payor bank;

(b) "Payor bank" means a bank by which an item is payable as drawn or accepted;

(c) "Intermediary bank" means any bank to which an item is transferred in course of collection except the depositary or payor bank;

(d) "Collecting bank" means any bank handling the item for collection except the payor bank;

(e) "Presenting bank" means any bank presenting an item except a payor bank;

(f) "Remitting bank" means any payor or intermediary bank remitting for an item.

§ 4–106. Separate Office of a Bank.*

A branch or separate office of a bank is a separate bank for the purpose of computing the time within which and determining the place at or to which action may be taken or notices or orders shall be given under this Article and under Article 3.

§ 4–107. Time of Receipt of Items.

(1) For the purpose of allowing time to process items, prove balances and make the necessary entries on its books to determine its position for the day, a bank may fix an afternoon hour of 2 P.M. or later as a cut-off hour for the handling of money and items and the making of entries on its books.

(2) Any item or deposit of money received on any day after a cut-off hour so fixed or after the close of the banking day may be treated as being received at the opening of the next banking day.

§ 4–108. Delays.

(1) Unless otherwise instructed, a collecting bank in a good faith effort to secure payment may, in the case of specific items and with or without the approval of any person involved, waive, modify or extend time limits imposed or permitted by this Act for a period not in excess of an additional banking day without discharge of secondary parties and without liability to its transferor or any prior party.

(2) Delay by a collecting bank or payor bank beyond time limits prescribed or permitted by this Act or by instructions is excused if caused by interruption of communication facilities, suspension of payments by another bank, war, emergency conditions or other circumstances beyond the control of the bank provided it exercises such diligence as the circumstances require.

§ 4–109. Process of Posting.

The "process of posting" means the usual procedure followed by a payor bank in determining to pay an item and in recording the payment including one or more of the following or other steps as determined by the bank:

(a) verification of any signature;

(b) ascertaining that sufficient funds are available;

(c) affixing a "paid" or other stamp;

(d) entering a charge or entry to a customer's account;

(e) correcting or reversing an entry or erroneous action with respect to the item.

PART 2

COLLECTION OF ITEMS: DEPOSITARY AND COLLECTING BANKS

§ 4–201. Presumption and Duration of Agency Status of Collecting Banks and Provisional Status of Credits; Applicability of Article; Item Indorsed "Pay Any Bank."

(1) Unless a contrary intent clearly appears and prior to the time that a settlement given by a collecting bank for an item is or becomes final (subsection (3) of Section 4–211 and Sections 4–212 and 4–213) the bank is an agent or sub-agent of the owner of the item and any settlement given for the item is provisional. This provision applies regardless of the form of indorsement or lack of indorsement and even though credit given for the item is subject to immediate withdrawal as of right or is in fact withdrawn; but the continuance of ownership of an item by its owner and any rights of the owner to proceeds of the item are subject to rights of a collecting bank such as those resulting from outstanding advances on the item and valid rights of setoff. When an item is handled by banks for purposes of presentment, payment and collection, the relevant provisions of this Article apply even though action of parties clearly establishes that a particular bank has purchased the item and is the owner of it.

(2) After an item has been indorsed with the words "pay any bank" or the like, only a bank may acquire the rights of a holder

(a) until the item has been returned to the customer initiating collection; or

(b) until the item has been specially indorsed by a bank to a person who is not a bank.

§ 4–202. Responsibility for Collection; When Action Seasonable.

(1) A collecting bank must use ordinary care in

(a) presenting an item or sending it for presentment; and

(b) sending notice of dishonor or non-payment or returning an item other than a documentary draft to the bank's transferor [or directly to the depositary bank under subsection (2) of Section 4–212] (*see note to Section 4–212*) after learning that the item has not been paid or accepted, as the case may be; and

(c) settling for an item when the bank receives final settlement; and

(d) making or providing for any necessary protest; and

(e) notifying its transferor of any loss or delay in transit within a reasonable time after discovery thereof.

(2) A collecting bank taking proper action before its midnight deadline following receipt of an item, notice or payment acts seasonably; taking proper action within a reasonably longer time may be seasonable but the bank has the burden of so establishing.

(3) Subject to subsection (1) (a), a bank is not liable for the insolvency, neglect, misconduct, mistake or default of another bank or person or for loss or destruction of an item in transit or in the possession of others.

§ 4–203. Effect of Instructions.

Subject to the provisions of Article 3 concerning conversion of instruments (Section 3–419) and the provisions of both Article 3 and this Article concerning restrictive indorsements only a collecting bank's transferor can give instructions which affect the bank or constitute notice to it and a collecting bank is not liable to prior parties for any action taken pursuant to such instructions or in accordance with any agreement with its transferor.

§ 4–204. Methods of Sending and Presenting; Sending Direct to Payor Bank.

(1) A collecting bank must send items by reasonably prompt method taking into consideration any relevant instructions, the nature of the item, the number of such items on hand,

and the cost of collection involved and the method generally used by it or others to present such items.

(2) A collecting bank may send

(a) any item direct to the payor bank;

(b) any item to any non-bank payor if authorized by its transferor; and

(c) any item other than documentary drafts to any nonbank payor, if authorized by Federal Reserve regulation or operating letter, clearing house rule or the like.

(3) Presentment may be made by a presenting bank at a place where the payor bank has requested that presentment be made.

§ 4–205. Supplying Missing Indorsement; No Notice from Prior Indorsement.

(1) A depositary bank which has taken an item for collection may supply any indorsement of the customer which is necessary to title unless the item contains the words "payee's indorsement required" or the like. In the absence of such a requirement a statement placed on the item by the depositary bank to the effect that the item was deposited by a customer or credited to his account is effective as the customer's indorsement.

(2) An intermediary bank, or payor bank which is not a depositary bank, is neither given notice nor otherwise affected by a restrictive indorsement of any person except the bank's immediate transferor.

§ 4–206. Transfer Between Banks.

Any agreed method which identifies the transferor bank is sufficient for the item's further transfer to another bank.

§ 4–207. Warranties of Customer and Collecting Banks on Transfer or Presentment of Items; Time for Claims.

(1) Each customer or collecting bank who obtains payment or acceptance of an item and each prior customer and collecting bank warrants to the payor bank or other payor who in good faith pays or accepts the item that

(a) he has a good title to the item or is authorized to obtain payment or acceptance on behalf of one who has a good title; and

(b) he has no knowledge that the signature of the maker or drawer is unauthorized, except that this warranty is not given by any customer or collecting bank that is a holder in due course and acts in good faith

(i) to a maker with respect to the maker's own signature; or

(ii) to a drawer with respect to the drawer's own signature, whether or not the drawer is also the drawee; or

(iii) to an acceptor of an item if the holder in due course took the item after the acceptance or obtained the acceptance without knowledge that the drawer's signature was unauthorized; and

(c) the item has not been materially altered, except that this warranty is not given by any customer or collecting bank that is a holder in due course and acts in good faith

(i) to the maker of a note; or

(ii) to the drawer of a draft whether or not the drawer is also the drawee; or

(iii) to the acceptor of an item with respect to an alteration made prior to the acceptance if the holder in due course took the item after the acceptance, even though the acceptance provided "payable as originally drawn" or equivalent terms; or

(iv) to the acceptor of an item with respect to an alteration made after the acceptance.

(2) Each customer and collecting bank who transfers an item and received a settlement

or other consideration for it warrants to his transferee and to any subsequent collecting bank who takes the item in good faith that

(a) he has a good title to the item or is authorized to obtain payment or acceptance on behalf of one who has a good title and the transfer is otherwise rightful; and
(b) all signatures are genuine or authorized; and
(c) the item has not been materially altered; and
(d) no defense of any party is good against him; and
(e) he has no knowledge of any insolvency proceeding instituted with respect to the maker or acceptor or the drawer of an unaccepted item.

In addition each customer and collecting bank so transferring an item and receiving a settlement or other consideration engages that upon dishonor and any necessary notice of dishonor and protest he will take up the item.

(3) The warranties and the engagement to honor set forth in the two preceding subsections arise notwithstanding the absence of indorsement or words of guaranty or warranty in the transfer or presentment and a collecting bank remains liable for their breach despite remittance to its transferor. Damages for breach of such warranties or engagement to honor shall not exceed the consideration received by the customer or collecting bank responsible plus finance charges and expenses related to the item, if any.

(4) Unless a claim for breach of warranty under this section is made within a reasonable time after the person claiming learns of the breach, the person liable is discharged to the extent of any loss caused by the delay in making claim.

§ 4–208. Security Interest of Collecting Bank in Items, Accompanying Documents and Proceeds.

(1) A bank has a security interest in an item and any accompanying documents or the proceeds of either

(a) in case of an item deposited in an account to the extent to which credit given for the item has been withdrawn or applied;
(b) in case of an item for which it has given credit available for withdrawal as of right, to the extent of the credit given whether or not the credit is drawn upon and whether or not there is a right of charge-back; or
(c) if it makes an advance on or against the item.

(2) When credit which has been given for several items received at one time or pursuant to a single agreement is withdrawn or applied in part the security interest remains upon all the items, any accompanying documents or the proceeds of either. For the purpose of this section, credits first given are first withdrawn.

(3) Receipt by a collecting bank of a final settlement for an item is a realization on its security interest in the item, accompanying documents and proceeds. To the extent and so long as the bank does not receive final settlement for the item or give up possession of the item or accompanying documents for purposes other than collection, the security interest continues and is subject to the provisions of Artile 9 except that

(a) no security agreement is necessary to make the security interest enforceable (subsection (1) (b) of Section 9–203); and
(b) no filing is required to perfect the security interest; and
(c) the security interest has priority over conflicting perfected security interests in the item, accompanying documents or proceeds.

§ 4–209. When Bank Gives Value for Purposes of Holder in Due Course.

For purposes of determining its status as a holder in due course, the bank has given value to the extent that it has a security interest in an item provided that the bank otherwise complies with the requirements of Section 3–302 on what constitutes a holder in due course.

§ 4–210. Presentment by Notice of Item Not Payable by, Through or at a Bank; Liability of Secondary, Parties.

(1) Unless otherwise instructed, a collecting bank may present an item not payable by, through or at a bank by sending to the party to accept or pay a written notice that the bank holds the item for acceptance or payment. The notice must be sent in time to be received on or before the day when presentment is due and the bank must meet any requirement of the party to accept or pay under Section 3–505 by the close of the bank's next banking day after it knows of the requirement.

(2) Where presentment is made by notice and neither honor nor request for compliance with a requirement under Section 3–505 is received by the close of business on the day after maturity or in the case of demand items by the close of business on the third banking day after notice was sent, the presenting bank may treat the item as dishonored and charge any secondary party by sending him notice of the facts.

§ 4–211. Media of Remittance; Provisional and Final Settlement in Remittance Cases.

(1) A collecting bank may take in settlement of an item

(a) a check of the remitting bank or of another bank on any bank except the remitting bank; or

(b) a cashier's check or similar primary obligation of a remitting bank which is a member of or clears through a member of the same clearing house or group as the collecting bank; or

(c) appropriate authority to charge an account of the remitting bank or of another bank with the collecting bank; or

(d) if the item is drawn upon or payable by a person other than a bank, a cashier's check, certified check or other bank check or obligation.

(2) If before its midnight deadline the collecting bank properly dishonors a remittance check or authorization to charge on itself or presents or forwards for collection a remittance instrument of or on another bank which is of a kind approved by subsection (1) or has not been authorized by it, the collecting bank is not liable to prior parties in the event of the dishonor of such check, instrument or authorization.

(3) A settlement for an item by means of a remittance instrument or authorization to charge is or becomes a final settlement as to both the person making and the person receiving the settlement

(a) if the remittance instrument or authorization to charge is of a kind approved by subsection (1) or has not been authorized by the person receiving the settlement and in either case the person receiving the settlement acts seasonably before its midnight deadline in presenting, forwarding for collection or paying the instrument or authorization,—at the time the remittance instrument or authorization is finally paid by the payor by which it is payable;

(b) if the person receiving the settlement has authorized remittance by a non-bank check or obligation or by a cashier's check or similar primary obligation of or a check upon the payor or other remitting bank which is not a kind approved by subsection (1) (b),—at the time of the receipt of such remittance check or obligation; or

(c) if in a case not covered by sub-paragraphs (a) or (b) the person receiving the settlement fails to seasonably present, forward for collection, pay or return a remittance instrument or authorization to it to charge before its midnight deadline,—at such midnight deadline.

§ 4–212. Right of Charge-Back or Refund.

(1) If a collecting bank has made provisional settlement with its customer for an item and itself fails by reason of dishonor, suspension of payments by a bank or otherwise to

receive a settlement for the item which is or becomes final, the bank may revoke the settlement given by it, charge back the amount of any credit given for the item to its customer's account or obtain refund from its customer whether or not is is able to return the items if by its midnight deadline or within a longer reasonable time after it learns the facts it returns the item or sends notification of the facts. These rights to revoke, charge-back and obtain refund terminate if and when a settlement for the item received by the bank is or becomes final (subsection (3) of Section 4–211 and subsections (2) and (3) of Section 4–213).

(2) Within the time and manner prescribed by this section and Section 4–301, an intermediary or payor bank, as the case may be, may return an unpaid item directly to the depositary bank and may send for collection a draft on the depositary bank and obtain reimbursement. In such case, if the depositary bank has received provisional settlement for the item, it must reimburse the bank drawing the draft and any provisional credits for the item between banks shall become and remain final.

(3) A depositary bank which is also the payor may charge-back the amount of an item to its customer's account or obtain refund in accordance with the section governing return of an item received by a payor bank for credit on its books. (Section 4–301).

(4) The right to charge-back is not affected by

(a) prior use of the credit given for the item; or

(b) failure by any bank to exercise ordinary care with respect to the item but any bank so failing remains liable.

(5) A failure to charge-back or claim refund does not affect other rights of the bank against the customer or any other party.

(6) If credit is given in dollars as the equivalent of the value of an item payable in a foreign currency the dollar amount of any charge-back or refund shall be calculated on the basis of the buying sight rate for the foreign currency prevailing on the day when the person entitled to the charge-back or refund learns that it will not receive payment in ordinary course.

§ 4–213. Final Payment of Item by Payor Bank; When Provisional Debits and Credits Become Final; When Certain Credits Become Available for Withdrawal.

(1) An item is finally paid by a payor bank when the bank has done any of the following, whichever happens first:

(a) paid the item in cash; or

(b) settled for the item without reserving a right to revoke the settlement and without having such right under statute, clearing house rule or agreement; or

(c) completed the process of posting the item to the indicated account of the drawer, maker or other person to be charged therewith; or

(d) made a provisional settlement for the item and failed to revoke the settlement in the time and manner permitted by statute, clearing house rule or agreement.

Upon a final payment under subparagraphs (b), (c) or (d) the payor bank shall be accountable for the amount of the item.

(2) If provisional settlement for an item between the presenting and payor banks is made through a clearing house or by debits or credits in an account between them, then to the extent that provisional debits or credits for the item are entered in accounts between the presenting and payor banks or between the presenting and successive prior collecting banks seriatim, they become final upon final payment of the item by the payor bank.

(3) If a collecting bank receives a settlement for an item which is or becomes final (subsection (3) of Section 4–211, subsection (2) of Section 4–213) the bank is accountable to its customer for the amount of the item and any provisional credit given for the item in an account with its customer becomes final.

(4) Subject to any right of the bank to apply the credit to an obligation of the customer,

credit given by a bank for an item in an account with its customer becomes available for withdrawal as of right

(a) in any case where the bank has received a provisional settlement for the item,—when such settlement becomes final and the bank has had a reasonable time to learn that the settlement is final;

(b) in any case where the bank is both a depositary bank and a payor bank and the item is finally paid,—at the opening of the bank's second banking day following receipt of the item.

(5) A deposit of money in a bank is final when made but, subject to any right of the bank to apply the deposit to an obligation of the customer, the deposit becomes available for withdrawal as of right at the opening of the bank's next banking day following receipt of the deposit.

§ 4–214. Insolvency and Preference.

(1) Any item in or coming into the possession of a payor or collecting bank which suspends payment and which item is not finally paid shall be returned by the receiver, trustee or agent in charge of the closed bank to the presenting bank or the closed bank's customer.

(2) If a payor bank finally pays an item and suspends payments without making a settlement for the item with its customer or the presenting bank which settlement is or becomes final, the owner of the item has a preferred claim against the payor bank.

(3) If a payor bank gives or a collecting bank gives or receives a provisional settlement for an item and thereafter suspends payments, the suspension does not prevent or interfere with the settlement becoming final if such finality occurs automatically upon the lapse of certain time or the happening of certain events (subsection (3) of Section 4–211, subsections (1) (d), (2) and (3) of Section 4–213).

(4) If a collecting bank receives from subsequent parties settlement for an item which settlement is or becomes final and suspends payments without making a settlement for the item with its customer which is or becomes final, the owner of the item has a preferred claim against such collecting bank.

PART 3

COLLECTION OF ITEMS: PAYOR BANKS

§ 4–301. Deferred Posting; Recovery of Payment by Return of Items; Time of Dishonor.

(1) Where an authorized settlement for a demand item (other than a documentary draft) received by a payor bank otherwise than for immediate payment over the counter has been made before midnight of the banking day of receipt the payor bank may revoke the settlement and recover any payment if before it has made final payment (subsection (1) of Section 4–213) and before its midnight deadline it

(a) returns the item; or

(b) sends written notice of dishonor or nonpayment if the item is held for protest or is otherwise unavailable for return.

(2) If a demand item is received by a payor bank for credit on its books it may return such item or send notice of dishonor and may revoke any credit given or recover the amount thereof withdrawn by its customer, if it acts within the time limit and in the manner specified in the preceding subsection.

(3) Unless previous notice of dishonor has been sent an item is dishonored at the time when for purposes of dishonor it is returned or notice sent in accordance with this section.

(4) An item is returned:

(a) as to an item received through a clearing house, when it is delivered to the presenting or last collecting bank or to the clearing house or is sent or delivered in accordance with its rules; or

(b) in all other cases, when it is sent or delivered to the bank's customer or transferor or pursuant to his instructions.

§ 4–302. Payor Bank's Responsibility for Late Return of Item.

In the absence of a valid defense such as breach of a presentment warranty (subsection (1) of Section 4–207), settlement effected or the like, if an item is presented on and received by a payor bank the bank is accountable for the amount of

(a) a demand item other than a documentary draft whether properly payable or not if the bank, in any case where it is not also the depositary bank, retains the item beyond midnight of the banking day of receipt without settling for it or, regardless of whether it is also the depositary bank, does not pay or return the item or send notice of dishonor until after its midnight deadline; or

(b) any other properly payable item unless within the time allowed for acceptance or payment of that item the bank either accepts or pays the item or returns it and accompanying documents.

§ 4–303. When Items Subject to Notice, Stop-Order, Legal Process or Setoff; Order in Which Items May Be Charged or Certified.

(1) Any knowledge, notice or stop-order received by, legal process served upon or setoff exercised by a payor bank, whether or not effective under other rules of law to terminate, suspend or modify the bank's right or duty to pay an item or to charge its customer's account for the item, comes too late to so terminate, suspend or modify such right or duty if the knowledge, notice, stop-order or legal process is received or served and a reasonable time for the bank to act thereon expires or the setoff is exercised after the bank has done any of the following:

(a) accented or certified the item:

(b) paid the item in cash;

(c) settled for the item without reserving a right to revoke the settlement and without having such right under statute, clearing house rule or agreement;

(d) completed the process of posting the item to the indicated account of the drawer, maker or other person to be charged therewith or otherwise has evidenced by examination of such indicated account and by action its decision to pay the item; or

(e) become accountable for the amount of the item under subsection (1) (d) of Section 4–213 and Section 4–302 dealing with the payor bank's responsibility for late return of items.

(2) Subject to the provisions of subsection (1) items may be accepted, paid, certified or charged to the indicated account of its customer in any order convenient to the bank.

PART 4

RELATIONSHIP BETWEEN PAYOR BANK AND ITS CUSTOMER

§ 4–401. When Bank May Charge Customer's Account.

(1) As against its customer, a bank may charge against his account any item which is otherwise properly payable from that account even though the charge creates an overdraft.

(2) A bank which in good faith makes payment to a holder may charge the indicated account of its customer according to

(a) the original tenor of his altered item; or

(b) the tenor of his completed item, even though the bank knows the item has been completed unless the bank has notice that the completion was improper.

§ 4–402. Bank's Liability to Customer for Wrongful Dishonor.

A payor bank is liable to its customer for damages proximately caused by the wrongful dishonor of an item. When the dishonor occurs through mistake liability is limited to actual damages proved. If so proximately caused and proved damages may include damages for an arrest or prosecution of the customer or other consequential damages. Whether any consequential damages are proximately caused by the wrongful dishonor is a question of fact to be determined in each case.

§ 4–403. Customer's Right to Stop Payment; Burden of Proof of Loss.

(1) A customer may by order to his bank stop payment of any item payable for his account but the order must be received at such time and in such manner as to afford the bank a reasonable opportunity to act on it prior to any action by the bank with respect to the item described in Section 4–303.

(2) An oral order is binding upon the bank only for fourteen calendar days unless confirmed in writing within that period. A written order is effective for only six months unless renewed in writing.

(3) The burden of establishing the fact and amount of loss resulting from the payment of an item contrary to a binding stop payment order is on the customer.

§ 4–404. Bank Not Obligated to Pay Check More Than Six Months Old.

A bank is under no obligation to a customer having a checking account to pay a check, other than a certified check, which is presented more than six months after its date, but it may charge its customer's account for a payment made thereafter in good faith.

§ 4–405. Death or Incompetence of Customer.

(1) A payor or collecting bank's authority to accept, pay or collect an item or to account for proceeds of its collection if otherwise effective is not rendered ineffective by incompetence of a customer of either bank existing at the time the item is issued or its collection is undertaken if the bank does not know of an adjudication of incompetence. Neither death nor incompetence of a customer revokes such authority to accept, pay, collect or account until the bank knows of the fact of death or of an adjudication of incompetence and has reasonable opportunity to act on it.

(2) Even with knowledge a bank may for 10 days after the date of death pay or certify checks drawn on or prior to that date unless ordered to stop payment by a person claiming an interest in the account.

§ 4–406. Customer's Duty to Discover and Report Unauthorized Signature or Alteration.

(1) When a bank sends to its customer a statement of account accompanied by items paid in good faith in support of the debit entries or holds the statement and items pursuant to a request or instructions of its customer or otherwise in a reasonable manner makes the statement and items available to the customer, the customer must exercise reasonable care and promptness to examine the statement and items to discover his unauthorized signature or any alteration on an item and must notify the bank promptly after discovery thereof.

(2) If the bank establishes that the customer failed with respect to an item to comply with the duties imposed on the customer by subsection (1) the customer is precluded from asserting against the bank

(a) his unauthorized signature or any alteration on the item if the bank also establishes that it suffered a loss by reason of such failure; and

(b) an unauthorized signature or alteration by the same wrongdoer on any other item paid in good faith by the bank after the first item and statement was available to the customer for a reasonable period not exceeding fourteen calendar days and before the bank receives notification from the customer of any such unauthorized signature or alteration.

(3) The preclusion under subsection (2) does not apply if the customer establishes lack of ordinary care on the part of the bank in paying the item(s).

(4) Without regard to care or lack of care of either the customer or the bank a customer who does not within one year from the time the statement and items are made available to the customer (subsection (1)) discover and report his unauthorized signature or any alteration on the face or back of the item or does not within 3 years from that time discover and report any unauthorized indorsement is precluded from asserting against the bank such unauthorized signature or indorsement or such alteration.

(5) If under this section a payor bank has a valid defense against a claim of a customer upon or resulting from payment of an item and waives or fails upon request to assert the defense the bank may not assert against any collecting bank or other prior party presenting or transferring the item a claim based upon the unauthorized signature or alteration giving rise to the customer's claim.

§ 4–407. Payor Bank's Right to Subrogation on Improper Payment.

If a payor bank has paid an item over the stop payment order of the drawer or maker or otherwise under circumstances giving a basis for objection by the drawer or maker, to prevent unjust enrichment and only to the extent necessary to prevent loss to the bank by reason of its payment of the item, the payor bank shall be subrogated to the rights

(a) of any holder in due course on the item against the drawer or maker; and

(b) of the payee or any other holder of the item against the drawer or maker either on the item or under the transaction out of which the item arose; and

(c) of the drawer or maker against the payee or any other holder of the item with respect to the transaction out of which the item arose.

PART 5
COLLECTION OF DOCUMENTARY DRAFTS

§ 4–501. Handling of Documentary Drafts; Duty to Send for Presentment and to Notify Customer of Dishonor.

A bank which takes a documentary draft for collection must present or send the draft and accompanying documents for presentment and upon learning that the draft has not been paid or accepted in due course must seasonably notify its customer of such fact even though it may have discounted or bought the draft or extended credit available for withdrawal as of right.

§ 4–502. Presentment of "On Arrival" Drafts.

When a draft or the relevant instructions require presentment "on arrival," "when goods arrive" or the like, the collecting bank need not present until in its judgment a reasonable time for arrival of the goods has expired. Refusal to pay or accept because the goods have not arrived is not dishonor; the bank must notify its transferor of such refusal but need not present the draft again until it is instructed to do so or learns of the arrival of the goods.

§ 4–503. Responsibility of Presenting Bank for Documents and Goods; Report of Reasons for Dishonor; Referee in Case of Need.

Unless otherwise instructed and except as provided in Article 5 a bank presenting a documentary draft

(a) must deliver the documents to the drawee on acceptance of the draft if it is payable more than three days after presentment; otherwise, only on payment; and

(b) upon dishonor, either in the case of presentment for acceptance or presentment for payment, may seek and follow instructions from any referee in case of need designated in the draft or if the presenting bank does not choose to utilize his services it must use diligence and good faith to ascertain the reason for dishonor, must notify its transferor of the dishonor and of the results of its effort to ascertain the reasons therefor and must request instructions.

But the presenting bank is under no obligation with respect to goods represented by the documents except to follow any reasonable instructions seasonably received; it has a right to reimbursement for any expense incurred in following instructions and to prepayment of or indemnity for such expenses.

§ 4–504. Privilege of Presenting Bank to Deal With Goods; Security Interest for Expenses

(1) A presenting bank which, following the dishonor of a documentary draft, has seasonably requested instructions but does not receive them within a reasonable time may store, sell, or otherwise deal with the goods in any reasonable manner.

(2) For its reasonable expenses incurred by action under subsection (1) the presenting bank has a lien upon the goods or their proceeds, which may be foreclosed in the same manner as an unpaid seller's lien.

ARTICLE 6. Bulk Transfers

§ 6–101. Short Title.

This Article shall be known and may be cited as Uniform Commercial Code—Bulk Transfers.

§ 6–102. "Bulk Transfers"; Transfers of Equipment; Enterprises Subject to This Article; Bulk Transfers Subject to This Article

(1) A "bulk transfer" is any transfer in bulk and not in the ordinary course of the transferor's business of a major part of the materials, supplies, merchandise or other inventory (Section 9–109) of an enterprise subject to this Article.

(2) A transfer of a substantial part of the equipment (Section 9–109) of such an enterprise is a bulk transfer if it is made in connection with a bulk transfer of inventory, but not otherwise.

(3) The enterprises subject to this Article are all those whose principal business is the sale of merchandise from stock, including those who manufacture what they sell.

(4) Except as limited by the following section all bulk transfers of goods located within this state are subject to this Article.

§ 6–103. Transfers Excepted From This Article.

The following transfers are not subject to this Article:

(1) Those made to give security for the performance of an obligation;

(2) General assignments for the benefit of all the creditors of the transferor, and subsequent transfers by the assignee thereunder;

(3) Transfers in settlement of a lien or other security interests;

(4) Sales by executors, administrators, receivers, trustees in bankruptcy, or any public officer under judicial process;

(5) Sales made in the course of judicial or administrative proceedings for the dissolution or reorganization of a corporation and of which is sent to the creditors of the corporation pursuant to order of the court or administrative agency;

(6) Transfers to a person maintaining a known place of business in this State who becomes

bound to pay the debts of the transferor in full and gives public notice of that fact, and who is solvent after becoming so bound;

(7) A transfer to a new business enterprise organized to take over and continue the business, if public notice of the transaction is given and the new enterprise assumes the debts of the transferor and he receives nothing from the transaction except an interest in the new enterprise junior to the claims of creditors;

(8) Transfers of property which is exempt from execution.

Public notice under subsection (6) or subsection (7) may be given by publishing once a week for two consecutive weeks in a newspaper of general circulation where the transferor had its principal place of business in this state an advertisement including the names and addresses of the transferor and transferee and the effective date of the transfer.

§ 6–104. Schedule of Property, List of Creditors.

(1) Except as provided with respect to auction sales (Section 6–108), a bulk transfer subject to this Article is ineffective against any creditor of the transferor unless:

(a) The transferee requires the transferor to furnish a list of his existing creditors prepared as stated in this section; and

(b) The parties prepare a schedule of the property transferred sufficient to identify it; and

(c) The transferee preserves the list and schedule for six months next following the transfer and permits inspection of either or both and copying therefrom at all reasonable hours by any creditor of the transferor, or files the list and schedule in (*a public office to be here identified*).

(2) The list of creditors must be signed and sworn to or affirmed by the transferor or his agent. It must contain the names and business addresses of all creditors of the transferor, with the amounts when known, and also the names of all persons who are known to the transferor to assert claims against him even though such claims are disputed. If the transferor is the obligor of an outstanding issue of bonds, debentures or the like as to which there is an indenture trustee, the list of creditors need include only the name and address of the indenture trustee and the aggregate outstanding principal amount of the issue.

(3) Responsibility for the completeness and accuracy of the list of creditors rests on the transferor, and the transfer is not rendered ineffective by errors or omissions therein unless the transferee is shown to have had knowledge.

§ 6–105. Notice to Creditors.

In addition to the requirements of the preceding section, any bulk transfer subject to this Article except one made by auction sale (Section 6–108) is ineffective against any creditor of the transferor unless at least ten days before he takes possession of the goods or pays for them, whichever happens first, the transferee gives notice of the transfer in the manner and to the persons hereafter provided (Section 6–107).

§ 6–106. Application of the Proceeds.

In addition to the requirements of the two preceding sections:

(1) Upon every bulk transfer subject to this Article for which new consideration becomes payable except those made by sale at auction it is the duty of the transferee to assure that such consideration is applied so far as necessary to pay those debts of the transferor which are either shown on the list furnished by the transferor (Section 6–104) or filed in writing in the place stated in the notice (Section 6–107) within thirty days after the mailing of such notice. This duty of the transferee runs to all the holders of such debts, and may be enforced by any of them for the benefit of all.

(2) If any of said debts are in dispute the necessary sum may be withheld from distribution until the dispute is settled or adjudicated.

(3) If the consideration payable is not enough to pay all of the said debts in full distribution shall be made pro rata.

(4) The transferee may within ten days after he takes possession of the goods pay the consideration into the (specify court) in the county where the transferor had its principal place of business in this state and thereafter may discharge his duty under this section by giving notice by registered or certified mail to all the persons to whom the duty runs that the consideration has been paid into that court and that they should file their claims there. On motion of any interested party, the court may order the distribution of the consideration to the persons entitled to it.

§ 6–107. The Notice.

(1) The notice to creditors (Section 6–105) shall state:

(a) that a bulk transfer is about to be made; and

(b) the names and business addresses of the transferor and transferee, and all other business names and addresses used by the transferor within three years last past so far as known to the transferee; and

(c) whether or not all the debts of the transferor are to be paid in full as they fall due as a result of the transaction, and if so, the address to which creditors should send their bills.

(2) If the debts of the transferor are not to be paid in full as they fall due or if the transferee is in doubt on that point then the notice shall state further:

(a) the location and general description of the property to be transferred and the estimated total of the transferor's debts;

(b) the address where the schedule of property and list of creditors (Section 6–104) may be inspected;

(c) whether the transfer is to pay existing debts and if so the amount of such debts and to whom owing;

(d) whether the transfer is for new consideration and if so the amount of such consideration and the time and place of payment; [and]

[(e) if for new consideration the time and place where creditors of the transferor are to file their claims.]

(3) The notice in any case shall be delivered personally or sent by registered or certified mail to all the persons shown on the list of creditors furnished by the transferor (Section 6–104) and to all other persons who are known to the transferee to hold or assert claims against the transferor.

§ 6–108. Auction Sales; "Auctioneer."

(1) A bulk transfer is subject to this Article even though it is by sale at auction, but only in the manner and with the results stated in this section.

(2) The transferor shall furnish a list of his creditors and assist in the preparation of a schedule of the property to be sold, both prepared as before stated (Section 6–104).

(3) The person or persons other than the transferor who direct, control or are responsible for the auction are collectively called the "auctioneer." The auctioneer shall:

(a) receive and retain the list of creditors and prepare and retain the schedule of property for the period stated in this Article (Section 6–104);

(b) give notice of the auction personally or by registered or certified mail at least ten days before it occurs to all persons shown on the list of creditors and to all other persons who are known to him to hold or assert claims against the transferor; [and]

[(c) assure that the net proceeds of the auction are applied as provided in this Article (Section 6–106).]

(4) Failure of the auctioneer to perform any of these duties does not affect the validity of the sale or the title of the purchasers, but if the auctioneer knows that the auction constitutes a bulk transfer such failure renders the auctioneer liable to the creditors of the transferor as a class for the sums owing to them from the transferor up to but not exceeding the net proceeds of the auction. If the auctioneer consists of several persons their liability is joint and several.

§ 6–109. What Creditors Protected; Credit for Payment to Particular Creditors.

(1) The creditors of the transferor mentioned in this Article are those holding claims based on transactions or events occurring before the bulk transfer, but creditors who become such after notice to creditors is given (Sections 6–105 and 6–107) are not entitled to notice.

(2) Against the aggregate obligation imposed by the provisions of this Article concerning the application of the proceeds (Section 6–106 and subsection (3) (c) of 6–108) the transferee or auctioneer is entitled to credit for sums paid to particular creditors of the transferor, not exceeding the sums believed in good faith at the time of the payment to be properly payable to such creditors.

§ 6–110. Subsequent Transfers.

When the title of a transferee to property is subject to a defect by reason of his non-compliance with the requirements of this Article, then:

(1) a purchaser of any of such property from such transferee who pays no value or who takes with notice of such non-compliance takes subject to such defect, but

(2) a purchaser for value in good faith and without such notice takes free of such defect.

§ 6–111. Limitation of Actions and Levies.

No action under this Article shall be brought nor levy made more than six months after the date on which the transferee took possession of the goods unless the transfer has been concealed. If the transfer has been concealed, actions may be brought or levies made within six months after its discovery.

ARTICLE 7. Warehouse Receipts, Bills of Lading and Other Documents of Title

PART 1

GENERAL

§ 7–101. Short Title.

This Article shall be known and may be cited as Uniform Commercial Code—Documents of Title.

§ 7–102. Definitions and Index of Definitions.

(1) In this Article, unless the context otherwise requires:

(a) "Bailee" means the person who by a warehouse receipt, bill of lading or other document of title acknowledges possession of goods and contracts to deliver them.

(b) "Consignee" means the person named in a bill to whom or to whose order the bill promises delivery.

(c) "Consignor" means the person named in a bill as the person from whom the goods have been received for shipment.

(d) "Delivery order" means a written order to deliver goods directed to a warehouseman, carrier or other person who in the ordinary course of business issues warehouse receipts or bills of lading.

(e) "Document" means document of title as defined in the general definitions in Article 1 (Section 1–201).

(f) "Goods" means all things which are treated as movable for the purposes of a contract of storage or transportation.

(g) "Issuer" means a bailee who issues a document except that in relation to an unaccepted delivery order it means the person who orders the possessor of goods to deliver. Issuer includes any person for whom an agent or employee purports to act in issuing a document if the agent or employee has real or apparent authority to issue documents, notwithstanding that the issuer received no goods or that the goods were misdescribed or that in any other respect the agent or employee violated his instructions.

(h) "Warehouseman" is a person engaged in the business of storing goods for hire.

(2) Other definitions applying to this Article or to specified Parts thereof, and the sections in which they appear are:

"Duly negotiate." Section 7–501.

"Person entitled under the document." Section 7–403(4).

(3) Definitions in other Articles applying to this Article and the sections in which they appear are:

"Contract for sale." Section 2–106.

"Overseas." Section 2–323.

"Receipt" of goods. Section 2–103.

(4) In addition Article 1 contains general definitions and principles of construction and interpretation applicable throughout this Article.

§ 7–103. Relation of Article to Treaty, Statute, Tariff, Classification or Regulation.

To the extent that any treaty or statute of the United States, regulatory statute of this State or tariff, classification or regulation filed or issued pursuant thereto is applicable, the provisions of this Article are subject thereto.

§ 7–104. Negotiable and Non-Negotiable Warehouse Receipt, Bill of Lading or Other Document of Title.

(1) A warehouse receipt, bill of lading or other document of title is negotiable

(a) if by its terms the goods are to be delivered to bearer or to the order of a named person; or

(b) where recognized in overseas trade, if it runs to a named person or assigns.

(2) Any other document is non-negotiable. A bill of lading in which it is stated that the goods are consigned to a named person is not made negotiable by a provision that the goods are to be delivered only against a written order signed by the same or another named person.

§ 7–105. Construction Against Negative Implication.

The omission from either Part 2 or Part 3 of this Article of a provision corresponding to a provision made in the other Part does not imply that a corresponding rule of law is not applicable.

PART 2

WAREHOUSE RECEIPTS: SPECIAL PROVISIONS

§ 7–201. Who May Issue a Warehouse Receipt; Storage Under Government Bond.

(1) A warehouse receipt may be issued by any warehouseman.

(2) Where goods including distilled spirits and agricultural commodities are stored under a statute requiring a bond against withdrawal or a license for the issuance of receipts in the

nature of warehouse receipts, a receipt issued for the goods has like effect as a warehouse receipt even though issued by a person who is the owner of the goods and is not a warehouseman.

§ 7–202. Form of Warehouse Receipt; Essential Terms; Optional Terms.

(1) A warehouse receipt need not be in any particular form.

(2) Unless a warehouse receipt embodies within its written or printed terms each of the following, the warehouseman is liable for damages caused by the omission to a person injured thereby:

(a) the location of the warehouse where the goods are stored:
(b) the date of issue of the receipt;
(c) the consecutive number of receipt;
(d) a statement whether the goods received will be delivered to the bearer, to a specified person, or to a specified person or his order;
(e) the rate of storage and handling charges, except that where goods are stored under a field warehousing arrangement a statement of that fact is sufficient on a non-negotiable receipt;
(f) a description of the goods or of the packages containing them;
(g) the signature of the warehouseman, which may be made by his authorized agent;
(h) if the receipt is issued for goods of which the warehouseman is owner, either solely or jointly or in common with others, the fact of such ownership; and
(i) a statement of the amount of advances made and of liabilities incurred for which the warehouseman claims a lien or security interest (Section 7–209). If the precise amount of such advances made or of such liabilities incurred is, at the time of the issue of the receipt, unknown to the warehouseman or to his agent who issues it, a statement of the fact that advances have been made or liabilities incurred and the purpose thereof is sufficient.

(3) A warehouseman may insert in his receipt any other terms which are not contrary to the provisions of this Act and do not impair his obligation of delivery (Section 7–403) or his duty of care (Section 7–204). Any contrary provisions shall be ineffective.

§ 7–203. Liability for Non-Receipt or Misdescription.

A party to or purchaser for value in good faith of a document of title other than a bill of lading relying in either case upon the description therein of the goods may recover from the issuer damages caused by the non-receipt or misdescription of the goods, except to the extent that the document conspicuously indicates that the issuer does not know whether any part or all of the goods in fact were received or conform to the description, as where the description is in terms of marks or labels or kind, quantity or condition, or the receipt or description is qualified by "contents, condition and quality unknown," "said to contain" or the like, if such indication be true, or the party or purchaser otherwise has notice.

§ 7–204. Duty of Care; Contractual Limitation of Warehouseman's Liability.*

(1) A warehouseman is liable for damages for loss of or injury to the goods caused by his failure to exercise such care in regard to them as a reasonably careful man would exercise under like circumstances but unless otherwise agreed he is not liable for damages which could not have been avoided by the exercise of such care.

(2) Damages may be limited by a term in the warehouse receipt or storage agreement limiting the amount of liability in case of loss or damage, and setting forth a specific liability per article or item, or value per unit of weight, beyond which the warehouseman shall not be liable; provided, however, that such liability may on written request of the bailor at the time of signing such storage agreement or within a reasonable time after receipt of the warehouse

receipt be increased on part or all of the goods thereunder, in which event increased rates may be charged based on such increased valuation, but that no such increase shall be permitted contrary to a lawful limitation of liability contained in the warehouseman's tariff, if any. No such limitation is effective with respect to the warehouseman's liability for conversion to his own use.

(3) Reasonable provisions as to the time and manner of presenting claims and instituting actions based on the bailment may be included in the warehouse receipt or tariff.

§ 7–205. Title Under Warehouse Receipt Defeated in Certain Cases.

A buyer in the ordinary course of business of fungible goods sold and delivered by a warehouseman who is also in the business of buying and selling such goods takes free of any claim under a warehouse receipt even though it has been duly negotiated.

§ 7–206. Termination of Storage at Warehouseman's Option.

(1) A warehouseman may on notifying the person on whose account the goods are held and any other person known to claim an interest in the goods require payment of any charges and removal of the goods from the warehouse at the termination of the period of storage fixed by the document, or, if no period is fixed, within a stated period not less than thirty days after the notification. If the goods are not removed before the date specified in the notification, the warehouseman may sell them in accordance with the provisions of the section on enforcement of a warehouseman's lien (Section 7–210).

(2) If a warehouseman in good faith believes that the goods are about to deteriorate or decline in value to less than the amount of his lien within the time prescribed in subsection (1) for notification, advertisement and sale, the warehouseman may specify in the notification any reasonable shorter time for removal of the goods and in case the goods are not removed, may sell them at public sale held not less than one week after a single advertisement or posting.

(3) If as a result of a quality or condition of the goods of which the warehouseman had no notice at the time of deposit the goods are a hazard to other property or to the warehouse or to persons, the warehouseman may sell the goods at public or private sale without advertisement on reasonable notification to all persons known to claim an interest in the goods. If the warehouseman after a reasonable effort is unable to sell the goods he may dispose of them in any lawful manner and shall incur no liability by reason of such disposition.

(4) The warehouseman must deliver the goods to any person entitled to them under this Article upon due demand made at any time prior to sale or other disposition under this section.

(5) The warehouseman may satisfy his lien from the proceeds of any sale or disposition under this section but must hold the balance for delivery on the demand of any person to whom he would have been bound to deliver the goods.

§ 7–207. Goods Must Be Kept Separate; Fungible Goods.

(1) Unless the warehouse receipt otherwise provides, a warehouseman must keep separate the goods covered by each receipt so as to permit at all times identification and delivery of those goods except that different lots of fungible goods may be commingled.

(2) Fungible goods so commingled are owned in common by the persons entitled thereto and the warehouseman is severally liable to each owner for that owner's share. Where because of overissue a mass of fungible goods is insufficient to meet all the receipts which the warehouseman has issued against it, the persons entitled include all holders to whom overissued receipts have been duly negotiated.

§ 7–208. Altered Warehouse Receipts.

Where a blank in a negotiable warehouse receipt has been filled in without authority, a purchaser for value and without notice of the want of authority may treat the insertion as authorized. Any other unauthorized alteration leaves any receipt enforceable against the issuer according to its original tenor.

§ 7–209. Lien of Warehouseman.

(1) A warehouseman has a lien against the bailor on the goods covered by a warehouse receipt or on the proceeds thereof in his possession for charges for storage or transportation (including demurrage and terminal charges), insurance, labor, or charges present or future in relation to the goods, and for expenses necessary for preservation of the goods or reasonably incurred in their sale pursuant to law. If the person on whose account the goods are held is liable for like charges or expenses in relation to other goods whenever deposited and it is stated in the receipt that a lien is claimed for charges and expenses in relation to other goods, the warehouseman also has a lien against him for such charges and expenses whether or not the other goods have been delivered by the warehouseman. But against a person to whom a negotiable warehouse receipt is duly negotiated a warehouseman's lien is limited to charges in an amount or at a rate specified on the receipt or if no charges are so specified then to a reasonable charge for storage of the goods covered by the receipt subsequent to the date of the receipt.

(2) The warehouseman may also reserve a security interest against the bailor for a maximum amount specified on the receipt for charges other than those specified in subsection (1), such as for money advanced and interest. Such a security interest is governed by the Article on Secured Transactions (Article 9).

(3) (a) A warehouseman's lien for charges and expenses under subsection (1) or a security interest under subsection (2) is also effective against any person who so entrusted the bailor with possession of the goods that a pledge of them by him to a good faith purchaser for value would have been valid but is not effective against a person as to whom the document confers no right in the goods covered by it under Section 7–503.

(b) A warehouseman's lien on household goods for charges and expenses in relation to the goods under subsection (1) is also effective against all persons if the depositor was the legal possessor of the goods at the time of deposit. "Household goods" means furniture, furnishings and personal effects used by the depositor in a dwelling.

(4) A warehouseman loses his lien on any goods which he voluntarily delivers or which he unjustifiably refuses to deliver.

§ 7–210. Enforcement of Warehouseman's Lien.

(1) Except as provided in subsection (2), a warehouseman's lien may be enforced by public or private sale of the goods in block or in parcels, at any time or place and on any terms which are commercially reasonable, after notifying all persons known to claim an interest in the goods. Such notification must include a statement of the amount due, the nature of the proposed sale and the time and place of any public sale. The fact that a better price could have been obtained by a sale at a different time or in a different method from that selected by the warehouseman is not of itself sufficient to establish that the sale was not made in a commercially reasonable manner. If the warehouseman either sells the goods in the usual manner in any recognized market therefor, or if he sells at the price current in such market at the time of his sale, or if he has otherwise sold in conformity with commercially reasonable practices among dealers in the type of goods sold, he has sold in a commercially reasonable

manner. A sale of more goods than apparently necessary to be offered to insure satisfaction of the obligation is not commercially reasonable except in cases covered by the preceding sentence.

(2) A warehouseman's lien on goods other than goods stored by a merchant in the course of his business may be enforced only as follows:

(a) All persons known to claim an interest in the goods must be notified.

(b) The notification must be delivered in person or sent by registered or certified letter to the last known address of any person to be notified.

(c) The notification must include an itemized statement of the claim, a description of the goods subject to the lien, a demand for payment within a specified time not less than ten days after receipt of the notification, and a conspicuous statement that unless the claim is paid within that time the goods will be advertised for sale and sold by auction at a specified time and place.

(d) The sale must conform to the terms of the notification.

(e) The sale must be held at the nearest suitable place to that where the goods are held or stored.

(f) After the expiration of the time given in the notification, an advertisement of the sale must be published once a week for two weeks consecutively in a newspaper of general circulation where the sale is to be held. The advertisement must include a description of the goods, the name of the person on whose account they are being held, and the time and place of the sale. The sale must take place at least fifteen days after the first publication. If there is no newspaper of general circulation where the sale is to be held, the advertisement must be posted at least ten days before the sale in not less than six conspicuous places in the neighborhood of the proposed sale.

(3) Before any sale pursuant to this section any person claiming a right in the goods may pay the amount necessary to satisfy the lien and the reasonable expenses incurred under this section. In that event the goods must not be sold, but must be retained by the warehouseman subject to the terms of the receipt and this Article.

(4) The warehouseman may buy at any public sale pursuant to this section.

(5) A purchaser in good faith of goods sold to enforce a warehouseman's lien takes the goods free of any rights of persons against whom the lien was valid, despite noncompliance by the warehouseman with the requirements of this section.

(6) The warehouseman may satisfy his lien from the proceeds of any sale pursuant to this section but must hold the balance, if any, for delivery on demand to any person to whom he would have been bound to deliver the goods.

(7) The rights provided by this section shall be in addition to all other rights allowed by law to a creditor against his debtor.

(8) Where a lien is on goods stored by a merchant in the course of his business the lien may be enforced in accordance with either subsection (1) or (2).

(9) The warehouseman is liable for damages caused by failure to comply with the requirements for sale under this section and in case of willful violation is liable for conversion.

PART 3

BILLS OF LADING: SPECIAL PROVISIONS

§ 7–301. Liability for Non-Receipt or Misdescription; "Said to Contain"; "Shipper's Load and Count"; Improper Handling.

(1) A consignee of a non-negotiable bill who has given value in good faith or a holder to whom a negotiable bill has been duly negotiated relying in either case upon the description

therein of the goods, or upon the date therein shown, may recover from the issuer damages caused by the misdating of the bill or the nonreceipt or misdescription of the goods, except to the extent that the document indicates that the issuer does not know whether any part or all of the goods in fact were received or conform to the description, as where the description is in terms of marks or labels or kind, quantity, or condition or the receipt or description is qualified by "contents or condition of contents of packages unknown," "said to contain," "shipper's weight, load and count" or the like, if such indication be true.

(2) When goods are loaded by an issuer who is a common carrier, the issuer must count the packages of goods if package freight and ascertain the kind and quantity if bulk freight. In such cases "shipper's weight, load and count" or other words indicating that the description was made by the shipper are ineffective except as to freight concealed by packages.

(3) When bulk freight is loaded by a shipper who makes available to the issuer adequate facilities for weighing such freight, an issuer who is a common carrier must ascertain the kind and quantity within a reasonable time after receiving the written request of the shipper to do so. In such cases "shipper's weight" or other words of like purport are ineffective.

(4) The issuer may be inserting in the bill the words "shipper's weight, load and count" or other words of like purport indicate that the goods were loaded by the shipper; and if such statement be true the issuer shall not be liable for damages caused by the improper loading. But their omission does not imply liability for such damages.

(5) The shipper shall be deemed to have guaranteed to the issuer the accuracy at the time of shipment of the description, marks, labels, number, kind, quantity, condition and weight, as furnished by him; and the shipper shall indemnify the issuer against damage caused by inaccuracies in such particulars. The right of the issuer to such indemnity shall in no way limit his responsibility and liability under the contract of carriage to any person other than the shipper.

§ 7–302. Through Bills of Lading and Similar Documents.

(1) The issuer of a through bill of lading or other document embodying an undertaking to be performed in part by persons acting as its agents or by connecting carriers is liable to anyone entitled to recover on the document for any breach by such other persons or by a connecting carrier of its obligation under the document but to the extent that the bill covers an undertaking to be performed overseas or in territory not contiguous to the continental United States or an undertaking including matters other than transportation this liability may be varied by agreement of the parties.

(2) Where goods covered by a through bill of lading or other document embodying an undertaking to be performed in part by persons other than the issuer are received by any such person, he is subject with respect to his own performance while the goods are in his possession to the obligation of the issuer. His obligation is discharged by delivery of the goods to another such person pursuant to the document, and does not include liability for breach by any other such persons or by the issuer.

(3) The issuer of such through bill of lading or other document shall be entitled to recover from the connecting carrier or such other person in possession of the goods when the breach of the obligation under the document occurred, the amount it may be required to pay to anyone entitled to recover on the document therefor, as may be evidenced by any receipt, judgment, or transcript thereof, and the amount of any expense reasonably incurred by it in defending any action brought by anyone entitled to recover on the document therefor.

§ 7–303. Diversion; Reconsignment; Change of Instructions.

(1) Unless the bill of lading otherwise provides, the carrier may deliver the goods to a person or destination other than that stated in the bill or may otherwise dispose of the goods on instructions from

(a) the holder of a negotiable bill; or
(b) the consignor on a non-negotiable bill notwithstanding contrary instructions from the consignee; or
(c) the consignee on a non-negotiable bill in the absence of contrary instructions from the consignor, if the goods have arrived at the billed destination or if the consignee is in possession of the bill; or
(d) the consignee on a non-negotiable bill if he is entitled as against the consignor to dispose of them.

(2) Unless such instructions are noted on a negotiable bill of lading, a person to whom the bill is duly negotiated can hold the bailee according to the original terms.

§ 7–304. Bills of Lading in a Set.

(1) Except where customary in overseas transportation, a bill of lading must not be issued in a set of parts. The issuer is liable for damages caused by violation of this subsection.

(2) Where a bill of lading is lawfully drawn in a set of parts, each of which is numbered and expressed to be valid only if the goods have not been delivered against any other part, the whole of the parts constitute one bill.

(3) Where a bill of lading is lawfully issued in a set of parts and different parts are negotiated to different persons, the title of the holder to whom the first due negotiation is made prevails as to both the document and the goods even though any later holder may have received the goods from the carrier in good faith and discharged the carrier's obligation by surrender of his part.

(4) Any person who negotiates or transfers a single part of a bill of lading drawn in a set is liable to holders of that part as if it were the whole set.

(5) The bailee is obliged to deliver in accordance with Part 4 of this Article against the first presented part of a bill of lading lawfully drawn in a set. Such delivery discharges the bailee's obligation on the whole bill.

§ 7–305. Destination Bills.

(1) Instead of issuing a bill of lading to the consignor at the place of shipment a carrier may at the request of the consignor procure the bill to be issued at destination or at any other place designated in the request.

(2) Upon request of anyone entitled as against the carrier to control the goods while in transit and on surrender of any outstanding bill of lading or other receipt covering such goods, the issuer may procure a substitute bill to be issued at any place designated in the request.

§ 7–306. Altered Bills of Lading.

An unauthorized alteration or filling in of a blank in a bill of lading leaves the bill enforceable according to its original tenor.

§ 7–307. Lien of Carrier.

(1) A carrier has a lien on the goods covered by a bill of lading for charges subsequent to the date of its receipt of the goods for storage or transportation (including demurrage and terminal charges) and for expenses necessary for preservation of the goods incident to their transportation or reasonably incurred in their sale pursuant to law. But against a purchaser for value of a negotiable bill of lading a carrier's lien is limited to charges stated in the bill or the applicable tariffs, or if no charges are stated then to a reasonable charge.

(2) A lien for charges and expenses under subsection (1) on goods which the carrier was required by law to receive for transportation is effective against the consignor or any person entitled to the goods unless the carrier had notice that the consignor lacked authority to subject the goods to such charges and expenses. Any other lien under subsection (1) is effective

against the consignor and any person who permitted the bailor to have control or possession of the goods unless the carrier had notice that the bailor lacked such authority.

(3) A carrier loses his lien on any goods which he voluntarily delivers or which he unjustifiably refuses to deliver.

§ 7–308. Enforcement of Carrier's Lien.

(1) A carrier's lien may be enforced by public or private sale of the goods, in block or in parcels, at any time or place and on any terms which are commercially reasonable, after notifying all persons known to claim an interest in the goods. Such notification must include a statement of the amount due, the nature of the proposed sale and the time and place of any public sale. The fact that a better price could have been obtained by a sale at a different time or in a different method from that selected by the carrier is not of itself sufficient to establish that the sale was not made in a commercially reasonable manner. If the carrier either sells the goods in the usual manner in any recognized market therefor or if he sells at the price current in such market at the time of his sale or if he has otherwise sold in conformity with commercially reasonable practices among dealers in the type of goods sold he has sold in a commercially reasonable manner. A sale of more goods than apparently necessary to be offered to ensure satisfaction of the obligation is not commercially reasonable except in cases covered by the preceding sentence.

(2) Before any sale pursuant to this section any person claiming a right in the goods may pay the amount necessary to satisfy the lien and the reasonable expenses incurred under this section. In that event the goods must not be sold, but must be retained by the carrier subject to the terms of the bill and this Article.

(3) The carrier may buy at any public sale pursuant to this section.

(4) A purchaser in good faith of goods sold to enforce a carrier's lien takes the goods free of any rights of persons against whom the lien was valid, despite noncompliance by the carrier with the requirements of this section.

(5) The carrier may satisfy his lien from the proceeds of any sale pursuant to this section but must hold the balance, if any, for delivery on demand to any person to whom he would have been bound to deliver the goods.

(6) The rights provided by this section shall be in addition to all other rights allowed by law to a creditor against his debtor.

(7) A carrier's lien may be enforced in accordance with either subsection (1) or the procedure set forth in subsection (2) of Section 7–210.

(8) The carrier is liable for damages caused by failure to comply with the requirements for sale under this section and in case of willful violation is liable for conversion.

§ 7–309. Duty of Care; Contractual Limitation of Carrier's Liability.

(1) A carrier who issues a bill of lading whether negotiable or non-negotiable must exercise the degree of care in relation to the goods which a reasonably careful man would exercise under like circumstances. This subsection does not repeal or change any law or rule of law which imposes liability upon a common carrier for damages not caused by its negligence.

(2) Damages may be limited by a provision that the carrier's liability shall not exceed a value stated in the document if the carrier's rates are dependent upon value and the consignor by the carrier's tariff is afforded an opportunity to declare a higher value or a value as lawfully provided in the tariff, or where no tariff is filed he is otherwise advised of such opportunity; but no such limitation is effective with respect to the carrier's liability for conversion to its own use.

(3) Reasonable provisions as to the time and manner of presenting claims and instituting actions based on the shipment may be included in a bill of lading or tariff.

PART 4

WAREHOUSE RECEIPTS AND BILLS OF LADING: GENERAL OBLIGATIONS

§ 7–401. Irregularities in Issue of Receipt or Bill or Conduct of Issuer.

The obligations imposed by this Article on an issuer apply to a document of title regardless of the fact that

(a) the document may not comply with the requirements of this Article or of any other law or regulation regarding its issue, form or content; or
(b) the issuer may have violated laws regulating the conduct of his business; or
(c) the goods covered by the document were owned by the bailee at the time the document was issued; or
(d) The person issuing the document does not come within the definition of warehouseman if it purports to be a warehouse receipt.

§ 7–402. Duplicate Receipt or Bill; Overissue.

Neither a duplicate nor any other document of title purporting to cover goods already represented by an outstanding document of the same issuer confers any right in the goods, except as provided in the case of bills in a set, overissue of documents for fungible goods and substitutes for lost, stolen or destroyed documents. But the issuer is liable for damages caused by his overissue or failue to identify a duplicate document as such by conspicuous notation on its face.

§ 7–403. Obligation of Warehouseman or Carrier to Deliver; Excuse.*

(1) The bailee must deliver the goods to a person entitled under the document who complies with subsections (2) and (3), unless and to the extent that the bailee establishes any of the following:

(a) delivery of the goods to a person whose receipt was rightful as against the claimant;
(b) damage to or delay, loss or destruction of the goods for which the bailee is not liable, but the burden of establishing negligence in such cases is on the person entitled under the document;
(c) previous sale or other disposition of the goods in lawful enforcement of a lien or on warehouseman's lawful termination of storage;
(d) the exercise by a seller of his right to stop delivery pursuant to the provisions of the Article on Sales (Section 2–705);
(e) a diversion, reconsignment or other disposition pursuant to the provisions of this Article (Section 7–303) or tariff regulating such right;
(f) release, satisfaction or any other fact affording a personal defense against the claimant;
(g) any other lawful excuse.

(2) A person claiming goods covered by a document of title must satisfy the bailee's lien where the bailee so requests or where the bailee is prohibited by law from delivering the goods until the charges are paid.

(3) Unless the person claiming is one against whom the document confers no right under Section 7–503(1), he must surrender for cancellation or notation of partial deliveries any outstanding negotiable document covering the goods, and the bailee must cancel the document or conspicuously note the partial delivery thereon or be liable to any person to whom the document is duly negotiated.

(4) "Person entitled under the document" means holder in the case of a negotiable document, or the person to whom delivery is to be made by the terms of or pursuant to written instructions under a non-negotiable document.

§ 7–404. No Liability for Good Faith Delivery Pursuant to Receipt or Bill.

A bailee who in good faith including observance of reasonable commercial standards has received goods and delivered or otherwise disposed of them according to the terms of the document of title or pursuant to this Article is not liable therefor. This rule applies even though the person from whom he received the goods had no authority to procure the document or to dispose of the goods and even though the person to whom he delivered the goods had no authority to receive them.

PART 5

WAREHOUSE RECEIPTS AND BILLS OF LADING: NEGOTIATION AND TRANSFER

§ 7–501. Form of Negotiation and Requirements of "Due Negotiation."

(1) A negotiable document of title running to the order of a named person is negotiated by his indorsement and delivery. After his indorsement in blank or to bearer any person can negotiate it by delivery alone.

(2) (a) A negotiable document of title is also negotiated by delivery alone when by its original terms it runs to bearer.

(b) When a document running to the order of a named person is delivered to him the effect is the same as if the document had been negotiated.

(3) Negotiation of a negotiable document of title after it has been indorsed to a specified person requires indorsement by the special indorsee as well as delivery.

(4) A negotiable document of title is "duly negotiated" when it is negotiated in the manner stated in this section to a holder who purchases it in good faith without notice of any defense against or claim to it on the part of any person and for value, unless it is established that the negotiation is not in the regular course of business or financing or involves receiving the document in settlement or payment of a money obligation.

(5) Indorsement of a non-negotiable document neither makes it negotiable nor adds to the transferee's rights.

(6) The naming in a negotiable bill of a person to be notified of the arrival of the goods does not limit the negotiability of the bill nor constitute notice to a purchaser thereof of any interest of such person in the goods.

§ 7–502. Rights Acquired by Due Negotiation.

(1) Subject to the following section and to the provisions of Section 7–205 on fungible goods, a holder to whom a negotiable document of title has been duly negotiated acquires thereby:

(a) title to the document;

(b) title to the goods;

(c) all rights accruing under the law of agency or estoppel, including rights to goods delivered to the bailee after the document was issued; and

(d) the direct obligation of the issuer to hold or deliver the goods according to the terms of the document free of any defense or claim by him except those arising under the terms of the document or under this Article. In the case of a delivery order the bailee's obligation accrues only upon acceptance and the obligation acquired by the holder is that the issuer and any indorser will procure the acceptance of the bailee.

(2) Subject to the following section, title and rights so acquired are not defeated by any stoppage of the goods represented by the document or by surrender of such goods by the bailee, and are not impaired even though the negotiation or any prior negotiation constituted

a breach of duty or even though any person has been deprived of possession of the document by misrepresentation, fraud, accident, mistake, duress, loss, theft or conversion, or even though a previous sale or other transfer of the goods or document has been made to a third person.

§ 7–503. Document of Title to Goods Defeated in Certain Cases.

(1) A document of title confers no right in goods against a person who before issuance of the document had a legal interest or a perfected security interest in them and who neither

(a) delivered or entrusted them or any document of title covering them to the bailor or his nominee with actual or apparent authority to ship, store or sell or with power to obtain delivery under this Article (Section 7–403) or with power of disposition under this Act (Sections 2–403 and 9–307) or other statute or rule of law; nor

(b) acquiesced in the procurement by the bailor or his nominee of any document of title.

(2) Title to goods based upon an unaccepted delivery order is subject to the rights of anyone to whom a negotiable warehouse receipt or bill of lading covering the goods has been duly negotiated. Such a title may be defeated under the next section to the same extent as the rights of the issuer or a transferee from the issuer.

(3) Title to goods based upon a bill of lading issued to a freight forwarder is subject to the rights of anyone to whom a bill issued by the freight forwarder is duly negotiated; but delivery by the carrier in accordance with Part 4 of this Article pursuant to its own bill of lading discharges the carrier's obligation to deliver.

§ 7–504. Rights Acquired in the Absence of Due Negotiation; Effect of Diversion; Seller's Stoppage of Delivery.

(1) A transferee of a document, whether negotiable or non-negotiable, to whom the document has been delivered but not duly negotiated, acquires the title and rights which his transferor had or had actual authority to convey.

(2) In the case of a non-negotiable document, until but not after the bailee receives notification of the transfer, the rights of the transferee may be defeated.

(a) by those creditors of the transferor who could treat the sale as void under Section 2–402; or

(b) by a buyer from the transferor in ordinary course of business if the bailee had delivered the goods to the buyer or received notification of his rights; or

(c) as against the bailee by good faith dealings of the bailee with the transferor.

(3) A diversion or other change of shipping instructions by the consignor in a non-negotiable bill of lading which causes the bailee not to deliver to the consignee defeats the consignee's title to the goods if they have been delivered to a buyer in ordinary course of business and in any event defeats the consignee's rights against the bailee.

(4) Delivery pursuant to a non-negotiable document may be stopped by a seller under Section 2–705, and subject to the requirement of due notification there provided. A bailee honoring the seller's instructions is entitled to be indemnified by the seller against any resulting loss or expense.

§ 7–505. Indorser Not a Guarantor for Other Parties.

The indorsement of a document of title issued by a bailee does not make the indorser liable for any default by the bailee or by previous indorsers.

§ 7–506. Delivery Without Indorsement: Right to Compel Indorsement.

The transferee of a negotiable document of title has a specifically enforceable right to have his transferor supply any necessary indorsement but the transfer becomes a negotiation only as of the time the indorsement is supplied.

§ 7–507. Warranties on Negotiation or Transfer of Receipt or Bill.

Where a person negotiates or transfers a document of title for value otherwise than as a mere intermediary under the next following section, then unless otherwise agreed he warrants to his immediate purchaser only in addition to any warranty made in selling the goods

(a) that the document is genuine; and

(b) that he has no knowledge of any fact which would impair its validity or worth; and

(c) that his negotiation or transfer is rightful and fully effective with respect to the title to the document and the goods it represents.

§ 7–508. Warranties of Collecting Bank as to Documents.

A collecting bank or other intermediary known to be entrusted with documents on behalf of another or with collection of a draft or other claim against delivery of documents warrants by such delivery of the documents only its own good faith and authority. This rule applies even though the intermediary has purchased or made advances against the claim or draft to be collected.

PART 6

WAREHOUSE RECEIPTS AND BILLS OF LADING: MISCELLANEOUS PROVISIONS

§ 7–601. Lost and Missing Documents.

(1) If a document has been lost, stolen or destroyed, a court may order delivery of the goods or issuance of a substitute document and the bailee may without liability to any person comply with such order. If the document was negotiable the claimant must post security approved by the court to indemnify any person who may suffer loss as a result of non-surrender of the document. If the document was not negotiable, such security may be required at the discretion of the court. The court may also in its discretion order payment of the bailee's reasonable costs and counsel fees.

(2) A bailee who without court order delivers goods to a person claiming under a missing negotiable document is liable to any person injured thereby, and if the delivery is not in good faith becomes liable for conversion. Delivery in good faith is not conversion if made in accordance with a filed classification or tariff or, where no classification or tariff is filed, if the claimant posts security with the bailee in an amount at least double the value of the goods at the time of posting to indemnify any person injured by the delivery who files a notice of claim within one year after the delivery.

§ 7–602. Attachment of Goods Covered by a Negotiable Document.

Except where the document was originally issued upon delivery of the goods by a person who had no power to dispose of them, no lien attaches by virtue of any judicial process to goods in the possession of a bailee for which a negotiable document of title is outstanding unless the document be first surrendered to the bailee or its negotiation enjoined, and the bailee shall not be compelled to deliver the goods pursuant to process until the document is surrendered to him or impounded by the court. One who purchases the document for value without notice of the process or injunction takes free of the lien imposed by judicial process.

§ 7–603. Conflicting Claims; Interpleader.

If more than one person claims title or possession of the goods, the bailee is excused from delivery until he has had a reasonable time to ascertain the validity of the adverse claims or to bring an action to compel all claimants to interplead and may compel such interpleader, either in defending an action for non-delivery of the goods, or by original action, whichever is appropriate.

ARTICLE 9. Secured Transactions; Sales of Accounts and Chattel Paper

PART 1

SHORT TITLE, APPLICABILITY AND DEFINITIONS

§ 9–101. Short Title.

This Article shall be known and may be cited as Uniform Commercial Code—Secured Transactions.

§ 9–102. Policy and Subject Matter of Article.**

(1) Except as otherwise provided in Section 9–104 on excluded transactions, this Article applies

(a) to any transaction (regardless of its form) which is intended to create a security interest in personal property or fixtures including goods, documents, instruments, general intangibles, chattel paper or accounts; and also

(b) to any sale of accounts or chattel paper.

(2) This Article applies to security interests created by contract including pledge, assignment, chattel mortgage, chattel trust, trust deed, factor's lien, equipment trust, conditional sale, trust receipt, other lien or title retention contract and lease or consignment intended as security. This Article does not apply to statutory liens except as provided in Section 9–310.

(3) The application of this Article to a security interest in a secured obligation is not affected by the fact that the obligation is itself secured by a transaction or interest to which this Article does not apply.

§ 9–103. Perfection of Security Interests in Multiple State Transactions.**

(1) Documents, instruments and ordinary goods.

(a) This subsection applies to documents and instruments and to goods other than those covered by a certificate of title described in subsection (2), mobile goods described in subsection (3), and minerals described in subsection (5).

(b) Except as otherwise provided in this subsection, perfection and the effect of perfection or non-perfection of a security interest in collateral are governed by the law of the jurisdiction where the collateral is when the last event occurs on which is based the assertion that the security interest is perfected or unperfected.

(c) If the parties to a transaction created a purchase money security interest in goods in one jurisdiction understand at the time that the security interest attaches that the goods will be kept in another jurisdiction, then the law of the other jurisdiction governs the perfection and the effect of perfection or non-perfection of the security interest from the time it attaches until thirty days after the debtor receives possession of the goods and thereafter if the goods are taken to the other jurisdiction before the end of the thirty-day period.

(d) When collateral is brought into and kept in this state while subject to a security interest perfected under the law of the jurisdiction from which the collateral was removed, the security interest remains perfected, but if action is required by Part 3 of this Article to perfect the security interest,

(i) if the action is not taken before the expiration of the period of perfection in the other jurisdiction or the end of four months after the collateral is brought into this state, whichever period first expires, the security interest becomes unperfected at the end of that period and is thereafter deemed to have been unperfected as against a person who became a purchaser after removal;

(ii) if the action is taken before the expiration of the period specified in subparagraph (i), the security interest continues perfected thereafter;

(iii) for the purpose of priority over a buyer of consumer goods (subsection (2) of Section 9–307), the period of the effectiveness of a filing in the jurisdiction from which the collateral is removed is governed by the rules with respect to perfection in subparagraphs (i) and (ii).

(2) Certificate of title.

(a) This subsection applies to goods covered by a certificate of title issued under a statute of this state or of another jurisdiction under the law of which indication of a security interest on the certificate is required as a condition of perfection.

(b) Except as otherwise provided in this subsection, perfection and the effect of perfection or non-perfection of the security interest are governed by the law (including the conflict of laws rules) of the jurisdiction issuing the certificate until four months after the goods are removed from that jurisdiction and thereafter until the goods are registered in another jurisdiction, but in any event not beyond surrender of the certificate. After the expiration of that period, the goods are not covered by the certificate of title within the meaning of this section.

(c) Except with respect to the rights of a buyer described in the next paragraph, a security interest, perfected in another jurisdiction otherwise than by notation on a certificate of title, in goods brought into this state and thereafter covered by a certificate of title issued by this state is subject to the rules stated in paragraph (d) of subsection (1).

(d) If goods are brought into this state while a security interest therein is perfected in any manner under the law of the jurisdiction from which the goods are removed and a certificate of title is issued by this state and the certificate does not show that the goods are subject to the security interest or that they may be subject to security interests not shown on the certificate, the security interest is subordinate to the rights of a buyer of the goods who is not in the business of selling goods of that kind to the extent that he gives value and receives delivery of the goods after issuance of the certificate and without knowledge of the security interest.

(3) Accounts, general intangibles and mobile goods.

(a) This subsection applies to accounts (other than an account described in subsection (5) on minerals) and general intangibles and to goods which are mobile and which are of a type normally used in more than one jurisdiction, such as motor vehicles, trailers, rolling stock, airplanes, shipping containers, road building and construction machinery and commercial harvesting machinery and the like, if the goods are equipment or are inventory leased or held for lease by the debtor to others, and are not covered by a certificate of title described in subsection (2).

(b) The law (including the conflict of laws rules) of the jurisdiction in which the debtor is located governs the perfection and the effect of perfection or non-perfection of the security interest.

(c) If, however, the debtor is located in a jurisdiction which is not a part of the United States, and which does not provide for perfection of the security interest by filing or recording in that jurisdiction, the law of the jurisdiction in the United States in which the debtor has its major executive office in the United States governs the perfection and the effect of perfection or non-perfection of the security interest through filing. In the alternative, if the debtor is located in a jurisdiction which is not a part of the United States or Canada and the collateral is accounts or general intangibles for money due or to become due, the security interest may be perfected by notification to the account debtor. As used in this paragraph, "United States" includes its territories and possessions and the Commonwealth of Puerto Rico.

(d) A debtor shall be deemed located at his place of business if he has one, at his chief executive office if he has more than one place of business, otherwise at his residence. If, however, the debtor is a foreign air carrier under the Federal Aviation Act of 1958, as amended, it shall be deemed located at the designated office of the agent upon whom service of process may be made on behalf of the foreign air carrier.

(e) A security interest perfected under the law of the jurisdiction of the location of the debtor is perfected until the expiration of four months after a change of the debtor's location to another jurisdiction, or until perfection would have ceased by the law of the first jurisdiction, whichever period first expires. Unless perfected in the new jurisdiction before the end of that period, it becomes unperfected thereafter and is deemed to have been unperfected as against a person who became a purchaser after the change.

(4) Chattel paper.

The rules stated for goods in subsection (1) apply to a possessory security interest in chattel paper. The rules stated for accounts in subsection (3) apply to a non-possessory security interest in chattel paper, but the security interest may not be perfected by notification to the account debtor.

(5) Minerals.

Perfection and the effect of perfection or non-perfection of a security interest which is created by a debtor who has an interest in minerals or the like (including oil and gas) before extraction and which attaches thereto as extracted, or which attaches to an account resulting from the sale thereof at the wellhead or minehead are governed by the law (including the conflict of laws rules) of the jurisdiction wherein the wellhead or minehead is located.

§ 9–104. Transactions Excluded From Article.

This Article does not apply

(a) to a security interest subject to any statute of the United States, to the extent that such statute governs the rights of parties to and third parties affected by transactions in particular types of property; or

(b) to a landlord's lien; or

(c) to a lien given by statute or other rule of law for services or materials except as provided in Section 9–310 on priority of such liens; or

(d) to a transfer of a claim for wages, salary or other compensation of an employee; or

(e) to a transfer by a government or governmental subdivision or agency; or

(f) to a sale of accounts or chattel paper as part of a sale of the business out of which they arose, or an assignment of accounts or chattel paper which is for the purpose of collection only, or a transfer of a right to payment under a contract to an assignee who is also to do the performance under the contract or a transfer of a single account to an assignee in whole or partial satisfaction of a preexisting indebtedness; or

(g) to a transfer of an interest in or claim in or under any policy of insurance, except as provided with respect to proceeds (Section 9–306) and priorities in proceeds (Section 9–312); or

(h) to a right represented by a judgment (other than a judgment taken on a right to payment which was collateral); or

(i) to any right of set-off; or

(j) except to the extent that provision is made for fixtures in Section 9–313, to the creation or transfer of an interest in or lien on real estate, including a lease or rents thereunder; or

(k) to a transfer in whole or in part of any claim arising out of tort; or

(l) to a transfer of an interest in any deposit account (subsection (1) of Section 9–105), except as provided with respect to proceeds (Section 9–306) and priorities in proceeds (Section 9–312).

§ 9–105. Definitions and Index of Definitions.**

(1) In this Article unless the context otherwise requires:

(a) "Account debtor" means the person who is obligated on an account, chattel paper or general intangible;

(b) "Chattel paper" means a writing or writings which evidence both a monetary obligation and a security interest in or a lease of specific goods, but a charter or other contract involving the use or hire of a vessel is not chattel paper. When a transaction is evidenced both by such a security agreement or a lease and by an instrument or a series of instruments, the group of writings taken together constitutes chattel paper;

(c) "Collateral" means the property subject to a security interest, and includes accounts and chattel paper which have been sold;

(d) "Debtor" means the person who owes payment or other performance of the obligation secured, whether or not he owns or has rights in the collateral, and includes the seller of accounts or chattel paper. Where the debtor and the owner of the collateral are not the same person, the term "debtor" means the owner of the collateral in any provision of the Article dealing with the collateral, the obligor in any provision dealing with the obligation, and may include both where the context so requires;

(e) "Deposit account" means a demand, time, savings, passbook or like account maintained with a bank, savings and loan association, credit union or like organization, other than an account evidenced by a certificate of deposit;

(f) "Document" means document of title as defined in the general definitions of Article 1 (Section 1–201), and a receipt of the kind described in subsection (2) of Section 7–201;

(g) "Encumbrance" includes real estate mortgages and other liens on real estate and all other rights in real estate that are not ownership interests;

(h) "Goods" includes all things which are movable at the time the security interest attaches or which are fixtures (Section 9–313), but does not include money, documents, instruments, accounts, chattel paper, general intangibles, or minerals or the like (including oil and gas) before extraction. "Goods" also includes standing timber which is to be cut and removed under a conveyance or contract for sale, the unborn young of animals, and growing crops;

(i) "Instrument" means a negotiable instrument (defined in Section 3–104), or a security (defined in Section 8–102) or any other writing which evidences a right to the payment of money and is not itself a security agreement or lease and is of a type which is in ordinary course of business transferred by delivery with any necessary indorsement or assignment;

(j) "Mortgage" means a consensual interest created by a real estate mortgage, a trust deed on real estate, or the like;

(k) An advance is made "pursuant to commitment" if the secured party has bound himself to make it, whether or not a subsequent event of default or other event not within his control) has relieved or may relieve him from his obligation;

(l) "Security agreement" means an agreement which creates or provides for a security interest;

(m) "Secured party" means a lender, seller or other person in whose favor there is a security interest, including a person to whom accounts or chattel paper have been sold. When the holders of obligations issued under an indenture of trust, equipment trust agreement or the like are represented by a trustree or other person, the representative is the secured party;

(n) ""Transmitting utility" means any person primarily engaged in the railroad, street railway or trolley bus business, the electric or electronics communications transmission business, the transmission of goods by pipeline, or the transmission or the production and transmission of electricity, steam, gas or water, or the provision of sewer service.

(2) Other definitions applying to this Article and the sections in which they appear are:

"Account." Section 9–106.
"Attach." Section 9–203.
"Construction mortgage." Section 9–313(1).
"Consumer goods." Section 9–109(1).
"Equipment." Section 9–109(2).
"Farm products." Section 9–109(3).
"Fixture." Section 9–313(1).
"Fixture filing." Section 9–313(1).
"General intangibles." Section 9–106.
"Inventory." Section 9–109(4).
"Lien creditor." Section 9–301(3).
"Proceeds." Section 9–306(1).
"Purchase money security interest." Section 9–107.
"United States." Section 9–103.

(3) The following definitions in other Articles apply to this Article:

"Check." Section 3–104.
"Contract for sale." Section 2–106.
"Holder in due course." Section 3–302.
"Note." Section 3–104.
"Sale." Section 2–106.

(4) In addition Article 1 contains general definitions and principles of construction and interpretation applicable throughout this Article.

§ 9–106. Definitions: "Account"; "General Intangibles."**

"Account" means any right to payment for goods sold or leased or for services rendered which is not evidenced by an instrument or chattel paper, whether or not it has been earned by performance. "General intangibles" means any personal property (including things in action) other than goods, accounts, chattel paper, documents, instruments, and money. All rights to payment earned or unearned under a charter or other contract involving the use or hire of a vessel and all rights incident to the charter or contract are accounts.

§ 9–107. Definitions: "Purchase Money Security Interest."

A security interest is a "purchase money security interest" to the extent that it is

(a) taken or retained by the seller of the collateral to secure all or part of its price; or

(b) taken by a person who by making advances or incurring an obligation gives value to enable the debtor to acquire rights in or the use of collateral if such value is in fact so used.

§ 9–108. When After-Acquired Collateral Not Security for Antecedent Debt.

Where a secured party makes an advance, incurs an obligation, releases a perfected security interest, or otherwise gives new value which is to be secured in whole or in part by after-acquired property his security interest in the after-acquired collateral shall be deemed to be taken for new value and not as security for an antecedent debt if the debtor acquires his rights in such collateral either in the ordinary course of his business or under a contract of purchase made pursuant to the security agreement within a reasonable time after new value is given.

§ 9–109. Classification of Goods; "Consumer Goods"; "Equipment"; "Farm Products"; "Inventory."

Goods are

(1) "consumer goods" if they are used or bought for use primarily for personal, family or household purposes;

(2) "equipment" if they are used or bought for use primarily in business (including farming or a profession) or by a debtor who is a non-profit organization or a governmental subdivision or agency or if the goods are not included in the definitions of inventory, farm products or consumer goods;

(3) "farm products" if they are crops or livestock or supplies used or produced in farming operations or if they are products of crops or livestock in their unmanufactured states (such as ginned cotton, wool-clip, maple syrup, milk and eggs), and if they are in the possession of a debtor engaged in raising, fattening, grazing or other farming operations. If goods are farm products they are neither equipment nor inventory;

(4) "inventory" if they are held by a person who holds them for sale or lease or to be furnished under contracts of service or if he has so furnished them, or if they are raw materials, work in process or materials used or consumed in a business. Inventory of a person is not to be classified as his equipment.

§ 9–110. Sufficiency of Description.

For the purposes of this Article any description of personal property or real estate is sufficient whether or not it is specific if it reasonably identifies what is described.

§ 9–111. Applicability of Bulk Transfer Laws.

The creation of a security interest is not a bulk transfer under Article 6 (see Section 6–103).

§ 9–112. Where Collateral Is Not Owned by Debtor.

Unless otherwise agreed, when a secured party knows that collateral is owned by a person who is not the debtor, the owner of the collateral is entitled to receive from the secured party any surplus under Section 9–502(2) or under Section 9–504(1), and is not liable for the debt or for any deficiency after resale, and he has the same right as the debtor

(a) to receive statements under Section 9–208;

(b) to receive notice of and to object to a secured party's proposal to retain the collateral in satisfaction of the indebtedness under Section 9–505;

(c) to redeem the collateral under Section 9–506;

(d) to obtain injunctive or other relief under Section 9–507(1); and

(e) to recover losses caused to him under Section 9–208(2).

§ 9–113. Security Interests Arising Under Article on Sales.

A security interest arising solely under the Article on Sales (Article 2) is subject to the provisions of this Article except that to the extent that and so long as the debtor does not have or does not lawfully obtain possession of the goods

(a) no security agreement is necessary to make the security interest enforceable; and
(b) no filing is required to perfect the security interest; and
(c) the rights of the secured party on default by the debtor are governed by the Article on Sales (Article 2).

§ 9–114. Consignment.**

(1) A person who delivers goods under a consignment which is not a security interest and who would be required to file under this Article by paragraph (3) (c) of Section 2–326 has priority over a secured party who is or becomes a creditor of the consignee and who would have a perfected security interest in the goods if they were the property of the consignee, and also has priority with respect to identifiable cash proceeds received on or before delivery of the goods to a buyer, if

(a) the consignor complies with the filing provision of the Article on Sales with respect to consignments (paragraph (3) (c) of Section 2–326) before the consignee receives possession of the goods; and
(b) the consignor gives notification in writing to the holder of the security interest if the holder has filed a financing statement covering the same types of goods before the date of the filing made by the consignor; and
(c) the holder of the security interest receives the notification within five years before the consignee receives possession of the goods; and
(d) the notification states that the consignor expects to deliver goods on consignment to the consignee, describing the goods by item or type.

(2) In the case of a consignment which is not a security interest and in which the requirements of the preceding subsection have not been met, a person who delivers goods to another is subordinate to a person who would have a perfected security interest in the goods if they were the property of the debtor.

PART 2

VALIDITY OF SECURITY AGREEMENT AND RIGHTS OF PARTIES THERETO

§ 9–201. General Validity of Security Agreement.

Except as otherwise provided by this Act a security agreement is effective according to its terms between the parties, against purchasers of the collateral and against creditors. Nothing in this Article validates any charge or practice illegal under any statute or regulation thereunder governing usury, small loans, retail installment sales, or the like, or extends the application of any such statute or regulation to any transaction not otherwise subject thereto.

§ 9–202. Title to Collateral Immaterial.

Each provision of this Article with regard to rights, obligations and remedies applies whether title to collateral is in the secured party or in the debtor.

§ 9–203. Attachment and Enforceability of Security Interest; Proceeds; Formal Requisites.**

(1) Subject to the provisions of Section 4–208 on the security interest of a collecting bank and Section 9–113 on a security interest arising under the Article on Sales, a security interest is not enforceable against the debtor or third parties with respect to the collateral and does not attach unless

(a) the collateral is in the possession of the secured party pursuant to agreement, or the debtor has signed a security agreement which contains a description of the collateral and in addition, when the security interest covers crops growing or to be grown or timber to be cut, a description of the land concerned; and

(b) value has been given; and

(c) the debtor has rights in the collateral.

(2) A security interest attaches when it becomes enforceable against the debtor with respect to the collateral. Attachment occurs as soon as all of the events specified in subsection (1) have taken place unless explicit agreement postpones the time of attaching.

(3) Unless otherwise agreed a security agreement gives the secured party the rights to proceeds provided by Section 9–306.

(4) A transaction, although subject to this Article, is also subject to . . . .*, and in the case of conflict between the provisions of this Article and any such statute, the provisions of such statute control. Failure to comply with any applicable statute has only the effect which is specified therein.

§ 9–204. After-Acquired Property; Future Advances.**

(1) Except as provided in subsection (2), a security agreement may provide that any or all obligations covered by the security agreement are to be secured by after-acquired collateral.

(2) No security interest attaches under an after-acquired property clause to consumer goods other than accessions (Section 9–314) when given as additional security unless the debtor acquires rights in them within ten days after the secured party gives value.

(3) Obligations covered by a security agreement may include future advances or other value whether or not the advances or value are given pursuant to commitment (subsection (1) of Section 9–105).

§ 9–205. Use or Disposition of Collateral Without Accounting Permissible.**

A security interest is not invalid or fraudulent against creditors by reason of liberty in the debtor to use, commingle or dispose of all or part of the collateral (including returned or repossessed goods) or to collect or compromise accounts or chattel paper, or to accept the return of goods or make repossessions, or to use, commingle or dispose of proceeds, or by reason of the failure of the secured party to require the debtor to account for proceeds or replace collateral. This section does not relax the requirements of possession where perfection of a security interest depends upon possession of the collateral by the secured party or by a bailee.

§ 9–206. Agreement Not to Assert Defenses Against Assignee; Modification of Sales Warranties Where Security Agreement Exists.

(1) Subject to any statute or decision which establishes a different rule for buyers or lessees of consumer goods, an agreement by a buyer or lessee that he will not assert against an assignee any claim or defense which he may have against the seller or lessor is enforceable by an assignee who takes his assignment for value, in good faith and without notice of a claim or defense, except as to defenses of a type which may be asserted against a holder in due course of a negotiable instrument under the Article on Commercial Paper (Article 3). A buyer who as part of one transaction signs both a negotiable instrument and a security agreement makes such an agreement.

(2) When a seller retains a purchase money security interest in goods the Article on Sales (Article 2) governs the sale and any disclaimer, limitation or modification of the seller's warranties.

§ 9–207. Rights and Duties When Collateral is in Secured Party's Possession.

(1) A secured party must use reasonable care in the custody and preservation of collateral in his possession. In the case of an instrument or chattel paper reasonable care includes taking necessary steps to preserve rights against prior parties unless otherwise agreed.

(2) Unless otherwise agreed, when collateral is in the secured party's possession

(a) reasonable expenses (including the cost of any insurance and payment of taxes or other charges) incurred in the custody, preservation, use or operation of the collateral are chargeable to the debtor and are secured by the collateral;

(b) the risk of accidental loss or damage is on the debtor to the extent of any deficiency in any effective insurance coverage;

(c) the secured party may hold as additional security any increase or profits (except money) received from the collateral, but money so received, unless remitted to the debtor, shall be applied in reduction of the secured obligation;

(d) the secured party must keep the collateral identifiable but fungible collateral may be commingled;

(e) the secured party may repledge the collateral upon terms which do not impair the debtor's right to redeem it.

(3) A secured party is liable for any loss caused by his failure to meet any obligation imposed by the preceding subsections but does not lose his security interest.

(4) A secured party may use or operate the collateral for the purpose of preserving the collateral or its value or pursuant to the order of a court of appropriate jurisdiction or, except in the case of consumer goods, in the manner and to the extent provided in the security agreement.

§ 9–208. Request for Statement of Account or List of Collateral.

(1) A debtor may sign a statement indicating what he believes to be the aggregate amount of unpaid indebtedness as of a specified date and may send it to the secured party with a request that the statement be approved or corrected and returned to the debtor. When the security agreement or any other record kept by the secured party identifies the collateral a debtor may similarly request the secured party to approve or correct a list of the collateral.

(2) The secured party must comply with such a request within two weeks after receipt by sending a written correction or approval. If the secured party claims a security interest in all of a particular type of collateral owned by the debtor he may indicate that fact in his reply and need not approve or correct an itemized list of such collateral. If the secured party without reasonable excuse fails to comply he is liable for any loss caused to the debtor thereby; and if the debtor has properly included in his request a good faith statement of the obligation or a list of the collateral or both the secured party may claim a security interest only as shown in the statement against persons misled by his failure to comply. If he no longer has an interest in the obligation or collateral at the time the request is received he must disclose the name and address of any successor in interest known to him and he is liable for any loss caused to the debtor as a result of failure to disclose. A successor in interest is not subject to this section until a request is received by him.

(3) A debtor is entitled to such a statement once every six months without charge. The secured party may require payment of a charge not exceeding $10 for each additional statement furnished.

PART 3

RIGHTS OF THIRD PARTIES; PERFECTED AND UNPERFECTED SECURITY INTERESTS; RULES OF PRIORITY

§ 9–301. Persons Who Take Priority Over Unperfected Security Interests; Rights of "Lien Creditor."**

(1) Except as otherwise provided in subsection (2), an unperfected security interest is subordinate to the rights of

(a) persons entitled to priority under Section 9–312;
(b) a person who becomes a lien creditor before the security interest is perfected;
(c) in the case of goods, instruments, documents, and chattel paper, a person who is not a secured party and who is a transferee in bulk or other buyer not in ordinary course of business or is a buyer of farm products in ordinary course of business, to the extent that he gives value and receives delivery of the collateral without knowledge of the security interest and before it is perfected;
(d) in the case of accounts and general intangibles, a person who is not a secured party and who is a transferee to the extent that he gives value without knowledge of the security interest and before it is perfected.

(2) If the secured party files with respect to a purchase money security interest before or within ten days after the debtor receives possession of the collateral, he takes priority over the rights of a transferee in bulk or of a lien creditor which arise between the time the security interest attaches and the time of filing.

(3) A "lien creditor" means a creditor who has acquired a lien on the property involved by attachment, levy or the like and includes an assignee for benefit of creditors from the time of assignment, and a trustee in bankruptcy from the date of the filing of the petition or a receiver in equity from the time of appointment.

(4) A person who becomes a lien creditor while a security interest is perfected takes subject to the security interest only to the extent that it secures advances made before he becomes a lien creditor or within 45 days thereafter or made without knowledge of the lien or pursuant to a commitment entered into without knowledge of the lien.

§ 9–302. When Filing Is Required to Perfect Security Interest; Security Interests to Which Filing Provisions of This Article Do Not Apply.

(1) A financing statement must be filed to perfect all security interests except the following:
(a) a security interest in collateral in possession of the secured party under Section 9–305;
(b) a security interest temporarily perfected in instruments or documents without delivery under Section 9–304 or in proceeds for a 10 day period under Section 9–306;
(c) a security interest created by an assignment of a beneficial interest in a trust or a decedent's estate;
(d) a purchase money security interest in consumer goods; but filing is required for a motor vehicle required to be registered; and fixture filing is required for priority over conflicting interests in fixtures to the extent provided in Section 9–313;
(e) an assignment of accounts which does not alone or in conjunction with other assignments to the same assignee transfer a significant part of the outstanding accounts of the assignor;
(f) a security interest of a collecting bank (Section 4–208) or arising under the Article on Sales (see Section 9–113) or covered in subsection (3) of this section;
(g) an assignment for the benefit of all the creditors of the transferor, and subsequent transfers by the assignee thereunder.

(2) If a secured party assigns a perfected security interest, no filing under this Article is required in order to continue the perfected status of the security interest against creditors of and transferees from the original debtor.

(3) The filing of a financing statement otherwise requried by this Article is not necessary or effective to perfect a security interest in property subject to
(a) a statute or treaty of the United States which provides for a national or international registration or a national or international certificate of title or which specifies a

place of filing different from that specified in this Article for filing of the security interest; or

(b) the following statutes of this state; [list any certificate of title statute covering automobiles, trailers, mobile homes, boats, farm tractors, or the like, and any central filing statute*.]; but during any period in which collateral is inventory held for sale by a person who is in the business of selling goods of that kind, the filing provisions of this Article (Part 4) apply to a security interest in that collateral created by him as debtor; or

(c) a certificate of title statute of another jurisdiction under the law of which indication of a security interest on the certificate is required as a condition of perfection (subsection (2) of Section 9–103).

(4) Compliance with a statute or treaty described in subsection (3) is equivalent to the filing of a financing statement under this Article, and a security interest in property subject to the statute or treaty can be perfected only by compliance therewith except as provided in Section 9–103 on multiple state transactions. Duration and renewal of perfection of a security interest perfected by compliance with the statute or treaty are governed by the provisions of the statute or treaty; in other respects the security interest is subject to this Article.

§ 9–303. When Security Interest Is Perfected; Continuity of Perfection.

(1) A security interest is perfected when it has attached and when all of the applicable steps required for perfection have been taken. Such steps are specified in Sections 9–302, 9–304, 9–305 and 9–306. If such steps are taken before the security interest attaches, it is perfected at the time when it attaches.

(2) If a security interest is originally perfected in any way permitted under this Article and is subsequently perfected in some other way under this Article, without an intermediate period when it was unperfected, the security interest shall be deemed to be perfected continuously for the purposes of this Article.

§ 9–304. Perfection of Security Interest in Instruments, Documents, and Goods Covered by Documents; Perfection by Permissive Filing; Temporary Perfection Without Filing or Transfer of Possession.**

(1) A security interest in chattel paper or negotiable documents may be perfected by filing. A security interest in money or instruments (other than instruments which constitute part of chattel paper) can be perfected only by the second party's taking possession, except as provided in subsections (4) and (5) of this section and subsections (2) and (3) of Section 9–306 on proceeds.

(2) During the period that goods are in the possession of the issuer of a negotiable document therefor, a security interest in the goods is perfected by perfecting a security interest in the document, and any security interest in the goods otherwise perfected during such period is subject thereto.

(3) A security interest in goods in the possession of a bailee other than one who has issued a negotiable document therefor is perfected by issuance of a document in the name of the secured party or by the bailee's receipt of notification of the secured party's interest or by filing as to the goods.

(4) A security interest in instruments or negotiable documents is perfected without filing or the taking of possession for a period of 21 days from the time it attaches to the extent that it arises for new value given under a written security agreement.

(5) A security interest remains perfected for a period of 21 days without filing where a secured party having a perfected security interest in an instrument, a negotiable document or goods in possession of a bailee other than one who has issued a negotiable document therefor

(a) makes available to the debtor the goods or documents representing the goods for the purpose of ultimate sale or exchange or for the purpose of loading, unloading, storing, shipping, transshipping, manufacturing, processing or otherwise dealing with them in a manner preliminary to their sale or exchange, but priority between conflicting security interests in the goods is subject to subsection (3) of Section 9–312; or

(b) delivers the instrument to the debtor for the purpose of ultimate sale or exchange or of presentation, collection, renewal or registration of transfer.

(6) After the 21 day period in subsections (4) and (5) perfection depends upon compliance with applicable provisions of this Article.

§ 9–305. When Possession by Secured Party Perfects Security Interest Without Filing.**

A security interest in letters of credit and advices of credit (subsection (2) (a) of Section 5–116), goods, instruments, money, negotiable documents or chattel paper may be perfected by the secured party's taking possession of the collateral. If such collateral other than goods covered by a negotiable document is held by a bailee, the secured party is deemed to have possession from the time the bailee receives notification of the secured party's interest. A security interest is perfected by possession from the time possession is taken without relation back and continues only so long as possession is retained, unless otherwise specified in this Article. The security interest may be otherwise perfected as provided in this Article before or after the period of possession by the secured party.

§ 9–306. "Proceeds"; Secured Party's Rights on Disposition of Collateral.**

(1) "Proceeds" includes whatever is received upon the sale, exchange, collection or other disposition of collateral or proceeds. Insurance payable by reason of loss or damage to the collateral is proceeds, except to the extent that it is payable to a person other than a party to the security agreement. Money, checks, deposit accounts, and the like are "cash proceeds." All other proceeds are "non-cash proceeds".

(2) Except where this Article otherwise provides, a security interest continues in collateral notwithstanding sale, exchange or other disposition thereof unless the disposition was authorized by the secured party in the security agreement or otherwise, and also continues in any identifiable proceeds including collections received by the debtor.

(3) The security interest in proceeds is a continuously perfected security interest if the interest in the original collateral was perfected but it ceases to be a perfected security interest and becomes unperfected ten days after receipt of the proceeds by the debtor unless

(a) a filed financing statement covers the original collateral and the proceeds are collateral in which a security interest may be perfected by filing in the office or offices where the financing statement has been filed and, if the proceeds are acquired with cash proceeds, the description of collateral in the financing statement indicates the types of property constituting the proceeds; or

(b) a filed financing statement covers the original collateral and the proceeds are identifiable cash proceeds; or

(c) the security interest in the proceeds is perfected before the expiration of the ten day period.

Except as provided in this section, a security interest in proceeds can be perfected only by the methods or under the circumstances permitted in this Article for original collateral of the same type.

(4) In the event of insolvency proceedings instituted by or against a debtor, a secured party with a perfected security interest in proceeds has a perfected security interest only in the following proceeds:

(a) in identifiable non-cash proceeds and in separate deposit accounts containing only proceeds;
(b) in identifiable cash proceeds in the form of money which is neither commingled with other money nor deposited in a deposit account prior to the insolvency proceedings;
(c) in identifiable cash proceeds in the form of checks and the like which are not deposited in a deposit account prior to the insolvency proceedings; and
(d) in all cash and deposit accounts of the debtor in which proceeds have been commingled with other funds, but the perfected security interest under this paragraph (d) is
 (i) subject to any right to set-off; and
 (ii) limited to an amount not greater than the amount of any cash proceeds received by the debtor within ten days before the institution of the insolvency proceedings less the sum of (I) the payments to the secured party on account of cash proceeds received by the debtor during such period and (II) the cash proceeds received by the debtor during such period to which the secured party is entitled under paragraphs (a) through (c) of this subsection (4).

(5) If a sale of goods results in an account or chattel paper which is transferred by the seller to a secured party, and if the goods are returned to or are repossessed by the seller or the secured party, the following rules determine priorities:

(a) If the goods were collateral at the time of sale, for an indebtedness of the seller which is still unpaid, the original security interest attaches again to the goods and continues as a perfected security interest if it was perfected at the time when the goods were sold. If the security interest was originally perfected by a filing which is still effective, nothing further is required to continue the perfected status; in any other case, the secured party must take possession of the returned or repossessed goods or must file.
(b) An unpaid transferee of the chattel paper has a security interest in the goods against the transferor. Such security interest is prior to a security interest asserted under paragraph (a) to the extent that the transferee of the chattel paper was entitled to priority under Section 9–308.
(c) An unpaid transferee of the account has a security interest in the goods against the transferor. Such security interest is subordinate to a security interest asserted under paragraph (a).
(d) A security interest of an unpaid transferee asserted under paragraph (b) or (c) must be perfected for protection against creditors of the transferor and purchasers of the returned or repossessed goods.

§ 9–307. Protection of Buyers of Goods.**

(1) A buyer in ordinary course of business (subsection (9) of Section 1–201) other than a person buying farm products from a person engaged in farming operations takes free of a security interest created by his seller even though the security interest is perfected and even though the buyer knows of its existence.

(2) In the case of consumer goods, a buyer takes free of a security interest even though perfected if he buys without knowledge of the security interest, for value and for his own personal, family or household purposes unless prior to the purchase the secured party has filed a financing statement covering such goods.

(3) A buyer other than a buyer in ordinary course of business (subsection (1) of this section) takes free of a security interest to the extent that it secures future advances made after the secured party acquires knowledge of the purchase, or more than 45 days after the purchase,

whichever first occurs, unless made pursuant to a commitment entered into without knowledge of the purchase and before the expiration of the 45 day period.

§ 9–308. Purchase of Chattel Paper and Instruments.**

A purchaser of chattel paper or an instrument who gives new value and takes possession of it in the ordinary course of his business has priority over a security interest in the chattel paper or instrument

(a) which is perfected under Section 9–304 (permissive filing and temporary perfection) or under Section 9–306 (perfection as to proceeds) if he acts without knowledge that the specific paper or instrument is subject to a security interest; or

(b) which is claimed merely as proceeds of inventory subject to a security interest (Section 9–306) even though he knows that the specific paper or instrument is subject to the security interest.

§ 9–309. Protection of Purchasers of Instruments and Documents.

Nothing in this Article limits the rights of a holder in due course of a negotiable instrument (Section 3–302) or a holder to whom a negotiable document of title has been duly negotiated (Section 7–501) or a bona fide purchaser of a security (Section 8–301) and such holders or purchasers take priority over an earlier security interest even though perfected. Filing under this Article does not constitute notice of the security interest to such holders or purchasers.

§ 9–310. Priority of Certain Liens Arising by Operation of Law.

When a person in the ordinary course of his business furnishes services or materials with respect to goods subject to a security interest, a lien upon goods in the possession of such person given by statute or rule of law for such materials or services takes priority over a perfected security interest unless the lien is statutory and the statute expressly provides otherwise.

§ 9–311. Alienability of Debtor's Rights: Judicial Process.

The debtor's rights in collateral may be voluntarily or involuntarily transferred (by way of sale, creation of a security interest, attachment, levy, garnishment or other judicial process) notwithstanding a provision in the security agreement prohibiting any transfer or making the transfer constitute a default.

§ 9–312. Priorities Among Conflicting Security Interests in the Same Collateral.**

(1) The rules of priority stated in other sections of this Part and in the following sections shall govern when applicable: Section 4–208 with respect to the security interests of collecting banks in items being collected, accompanying documents and proceeds; Section 9–103 on security interests related to other jurisdictions; Section 9–114 on consignments.

(2) A perfected security interest in crops for new value given to enable the debtor to produce the crops during the production season and given not more than three months before the crops become growing crops by planting or otherwise takes priority over an earlier perfected security interest to the extent that such earlier interest secures obligations due more than six months before the crops become growing crops by planting or otherwise, even though the person giving new value had knowledge of the earlier security interest.

(3) A perfected purchase money security interest in inventory has priority over a conflicting security interest in the same inventory and also has priority in identifiable cash proceeds received on or before the delivery of the inventory to a buyer if

(a) the purchase money security interest is perfected at the time the debtor receives possession of the inventory; and

(b) the purchase money secured party gives notification in writing to the holder of the conflicting security interest if the holder had filed a financing statement covering the same types of inventory (i) before the date of the filing made by the purchase money secured party, or (ii) before the beginning of the 21 day period where the purchase money security interest is temporarily perfected without filing or possession (subsection (5) of Section 9–304); and

(c) the holder of the conflicting security interest receives the notification within five years before the debtor receives possession of the inventory; and

(d) the notification states that the person giving the notice has or expects to acquire a purchase money security interest in inventory of the debtor, describing such inventory by item or type.

(4) A purchase money security interest in collateral other than inventory has priority over a conflicting security interest in the same collateral or its proceeds if the purchase money security interest is perfected at the time the debtor receives possession of the collateral or within ten days thereafter.

(5) In all cases not governed by other rules stated in this section (including cases of purchase money security interests which do not qualify for the special priorities set forth in subsections (3) and (4) of this section), priority between conflicting security interests in the same collateral shall be determined according to the following rules:

(a) Conflicting security interests rank according to priority in time of filing or perfection. Priority dates from the time a filing is first made covering the collateral or the time the security interest is first perfected, whichever is earlier, provided that there is no period thereafter when there is neither filing nor perfection.

(b) So long as conflicting security interests are unperfected, the first to attach has priority.

(6) For the purposes of subsection (5) a date of filing or perfection as to collateral is also a date of filing or perfection as to proceeds.

(7) If future advances are made while a security interest is perfected by filing or the taking of possession, the security interest has the same priority for the purposes of subsection (5) with respect to the future advances as it does with respect to the first advance. If a commitment is made before or while the security interest is so perfected, the security interest has the same priority with respect to advances made pursuant thereto. In other cases a perfected security interest has priority from the date the advance is made.

§ 9–313. Priority of Security Interests in Fixtures.**

(1) In this section and in the provisions of Part 4 of this Article referring to fixture filing, unless the context otherwise requires

(a) goods are "fixtures" when they become so related to particular real estate that an interest in them arises under real estate law

(b) a "fixture filing" is the filing in the office where a mortgage on the real estate would be filed or recorded of a financing statement covering goods which are or are to become fixtures and conforming to the requirements of subsection (5) of Section 9–402

(c) a mortgage is a "construction mortgage" to the extent that it secures an obligation incurred for the construction of an improvement on land including the acquisition cost of the land, if the recorded writing so indicates.

(2) A security interest under this Article may be created in goods which are fixutres or may continue in goods which become fixtures, but no security interest exists under this Article in ordinary building materials incorporated into an improvement on land.

(3) This Article does not prevent creation of an encumbrance upon fixtures pursuant to real estate law.

(4) A perfected security interest in fixtures has priority over the conflicting interest of an encumbrancer or owner of the real estate where

(a) the security interest is a purchase money security interest, the interest of the encumbrancer or owner arises before the goods become fixtures, the security interest is perfected by a fixture filing before the goods become fixtures or within ten days thereafter, and the debtor has an interest of record in the real estate or is in possession of the real estate; or

(b) the security interest is perfected by a fixture filing before the interest of the encumbrancer or owner is of record, the security interest has priority over any conflicting interest of a precedessor in title of the encumbrancer or owner, and the debtor has an interest of record in the real estate or is in possession of the real estate; or

(c) the fixtures are readily removable factory or office machines or readily removable replacements of domestic appliances which are consumer goods, and before the goods become fixtures the security interest is perfected by any method permitted by this Article; or

(d) the conflicting interest is a lien on the real estate obtained by legal or equitable proceedings after the security interest was perfected by any method permitted by this Article.

(5) A security interest in fixtures, whether or not perfected, has priority over the conflicting interest of an encumbrancer or owner of the real estate where

(a) the encumbrancer or owner has consented in writing to the security interest or has disclaimed an interest in the goods as fixtures; or

(b) the debtor has a right to remove the goods as against the encumbrancer or owner. If the debtor's right terminates, the priority of the security interest continues for a reasonable time.

(6) Notwithstanding paragraph (a) of subsection (4) but otherwise subject to subsections (4) and (5), a security interest in fixtures is subordinate to a construction mortgage recorded before the goods become fixtures if the goods become fixtures before the completion of the construction. To the extent that it is given to refinance a construction mortgage, a mortgage has this priority to the same extent as the construction mortgage.

(7) In cases not within the preceding subsections, a security interest in fixtures is subordinate to the conflicting interest of an encumbrancer or owner of the related real estate who is not the debtor.

(8) When the secured party has priority over all owners and encumbrancers of the real estate, he may, on default, subject to the provisions of Part 5, remove his collateral from the real estate but he must reimburse any encumbrancer or owner of the real estate who is not the debtor and who has not otherwise agreed for the cost of repair of any physical injury, but not for any diminution in value of the real estate caused by the absence of the goods removed or by any necessity of replacing them. A person entitled to reimbursement may refuse permission to remove until the secured party gives adequate security for the performance of this obligation.

§ 9–314. Accessions.

(1) A security interest in goods which attaches before they are installed in or affixed to other goods takes priority as to the goods installed or affixed (called in this section "accessions") over the claims of all persons to the whole except as stated in subsection (3) and subject to Section 9–315(1).

(2) A security interest which attaches to goods after they become part of a whole is valid against all persons subsequently acquiring interests in the whole except as stated in subsection (3) but is invalid against any person with an interest in the whole at the time the security interest attaches to the goods who has not in writing consented to the security interest or disclaimed an interest in the goods as part of the whole.

(3) The security interests described in subsections (1) and (2) do not take priority over

(a) a subsequent purchaser for value of any interest in the whole; or

(b) a creditor with a lien on the whole subsequently obtained by judicial proceedings; or

(c) a creditor with a prior perfected security interest in the whole to the extent that he makes subsequent advances

if the subsequent purchase is made, the lien by judicial proceedings obtained or the subsequent advance under the prior perfected security interest is made or contracted for without knowledge of the security interest and before it is perfected. A purchaser of the whole at a foreclosure sale other than the holder of a perfected security interest purchasing at his own foreclosure sale is a subsequent purchaser within this section.

(4) When under subsections (1) or (2) and (3) a secured party has an interest in accessions which has priority over the claims of all persons who have interests in the whole, he may on default subject to the provisions of Part 5 remove his collateral from the whole but he must reimburse any encumbrancer or owner of the whole who is not the debtor and who has not otherwise agreed for the cost of repair of any physical injury but not for any diminution in value of the whole caused by the absence of the goods removed or by any necessity for replacing them. A person entitled to reimbursement may refuse permission to remove until the secured party gives adequate security for the performance of this obligation.

§ 9–315. Priority When Goods Are Commingled or Processed.

(1) If a security interest in goods was perfected and subsequently the goods or a part thereof have become part of a product or mass, the security interest continues in the product or mass if

(a) the goods are so manufactured, processed, assembled or commingled that their identity is lost in the product or mass; or

(b) a financing statement covering the original goods also covers the product into which the goods have been manufactured, processed or assembled.

In a case to which paragraph (b) applies, no separate security interest in that part of the original goods which has been manufactured, processed or assembled into the product may be claimed under Section 9–314.

(2) When under subsection (1) more than one security interest attaches to the product or mass, they rank equally according to the ratio that the cost of the goods to which each interest originally attached bears to the cost of the total product or mass.

§ 9–316. Priority Subject to Subordination.

Nothing in this Article prevents subordination by agreement by any person entitled to priority.

§ 9–317. Secured Party Not Obligated on Contract of Debtor.

The mere existence of a security interest or authority given to the debtor to dispose of or use collateral does not impose contract or tort liability upon the secured party for the debtor's acts or omissions.

§ 9–318. Defenses Against Assignee; Modification of Contract After Notification of Assignment; Term Prohibiting Assignment Ineffective; Identification and Proof of Assignment.**

(1) Unless an account debtor has made an enforceable agreement not to assert defenses or claims arising out of a sale as provided in Section 9–206 the rights of an assignee are subject to

(a) all the terms of the contract between the account debtor and assignor and any defense or claim arising therefrom; and

(b) any other defense or claim of the account debtor against the assignor which accrues before the account debtor receives notification of the assignment.

(2) So far as the right to payment or a part thereof under an assignment contract has not been fully earned by performance, and notwithstanding notification of the assignment, any modification of or substitution for the contract made in good faith and in accordance with reasonable commercial standards is effective against an assignee unless the account debtor has otherwise agreed but the assignee acquires corresponding rights under the modified or substituted contract. The assignment may provide that such modification or substitution is a breach by the assignor.

(3) The account debtor is authorized to pay the assignor until the account debtor receives notification that the amount due or to become due has been assigned and that payment is to be made to the assignee. A notification which does not reasonably identify the rights assigned is ineffective. If requested by the account debtor, the assignee must seasonably furnish reasonable proof that the assignment has been made and unless he does so the account debtor may pay the assignor.

(4) A term in any contract between an account debtor and an assignor is ineffective if it prohibits assignment of an account or prohibits creation of a security interest in a general intangible for money due or to become due or requires the account debtor's consent to such assignment or security interest.

PART 4

FILING

§ 9–401. Place of Filing; Erroneous Filing; Removal of Collateral.* **

(1) The proper place to file in order to perfect a security interest is as follows:

(a) when the collateral is timber to be cut or is minerals or the like (including oil and gas) or accounts subject to subsection (5) of Section 9–103, or when the financing statement is filed as a fixture filing (Section 9–313) and the collateral is goods which are or are to become fixtures, then in the office where a mortgage on the real estate would be filed or recorded;

(b) in all other cases, in the office of the Secretary of State.

(2) A filing which is made in good faith in an improper place or not in all of the places required by this section is nevertheless effective with regard to any collateral as to which the filing complied with the requirements of this Article and is also effective with regard to collateral covered by the financing statement against any person who has knowledge of the contents of such financing statement.

(3) A filing which is made in the proper place in this state continues effective even though the debtor's residence or place of business or the location of the collateral or its use, whichever controlled the original filing, is thereafter changed.

(4) The rules stated in Section 9–103 determine whether filing is necessary in this state.

(5) Notwithstanding the preceding subsections, and subject to subsection (3) of Section 9–302, the proper place to file in order to perfect a security interest in collateral, including

fixtures, of a transmitting utility is the office of the [Secretary of State]. This filing constitutes a fixture filing (Section 9–313) as to the collateral described therein which is or is to become fixtures.

(6) For the purposes of this section, the residence of an organization is its place of business if it has one or its chief executive office if it has more than one place of business.

§ 9–402. Formal Requisites of Financing Statement; Amendments; Mortgage as Financing Statement.**

(1) A financing statement is sufficient if it gives the names of the debtor and the secured party, is signed by the debtor, gives an address of the secured party from which information concerning the security interest may be obtained, gives a mailing address of the debtor and contains a statement indicating the types, or describing the items, of collateral. A financing statement may be filed before a security agreement is made or a security interest otherwise attaches. When the financing statement covers crops growing or to be grown, the statement must also contain a description of the real estate concerned. When the financing statement covers timber to be cut or covers minerals or the like (including oil and gas) or accounts subject to subsection (5) of Section 9–103, or when the financing statement is filed as a fixture filing (Section 9–313) and the collateral is goods which are or are to become fixtures, the statement must also comply with subsection (5). A copy of the security agreement is sufficient as a financing statement if it contains the above information and is signed by the debtor. A carbon, photographic or other reproduction of a security agreement or a financing statement is sufficient as a financing statement if the security agreement so provides or if the original has been filed in this state.

(2) A financing statement which otherwise complies with subsection (1) is sufficient when it is signed by the secured party instead of the debtor if it is filed to perfect a security interest in

(a) collateral already subject to a security interest in another jurisdiction when it is brought into this state, or when the debtor's location is changed to this state. Such a financing statement must state that the collateral was brought into this state or that the debtor's location was changed to this state under such circumstances; or

(b) proceeds under Section 9–306 if the security interest in the original collateral was perfected. Such a financing statement must describe the original collateral; or

(c) collateral as to which the filing has lapsed; or

(d) collateral acquired after a change of name, identity or corporate structure of the debtor (subsection (7)).

(3) A form substantially as follows is sufficient to comply with subsection (1):

Name of debtor (or assignor) ______________________________

Address ______________________________

Name of secured party (or assignee) ______________________________

Address ______________________________

1. This financing statement covers the following types (or items) of property:
   (Describe) ______________________________
2. (If collateral is crops) The above described crops are growing or are to be grown on:
   (Describe Real Estate) ______________________________
3. (If applicable) The above goods are to become fixtures on[1]
   (Describe Real Estate) __________ and this financing statement is to be filed [for

---

[1] Where appropriate substitute either "The above timber is standing on. . . ." or "The above minerals or the like (including oil and gas) or accounts will be financed at the wellhead or minehead of the well or mine located on. . . ."

record] in the real estate records. (If the debtor does not have an interest of record) The name of a record owner is ____________________

4. (If products of collateral are claimed) Products of the collateral are also covered.

(use whichever is applicable) ____________________
Signature of Debtor (or Assignor)

____
Signature of Secured Party (or Assignee)

(4) A financing statement may be amended by filing a writing signed by both the debtor and the secured party. An amendment does not extend the period of effectiveness of a financing statement. If any amendment adds collateral, it is effective as to the added collateral only from the filing date of the amendment. In this Article, unless the context otherwise requires, the term "financing statement" means the original financing statement and any amendments.

(5) A financing statement covering timber to be cut or covering minerals or the like (including oil and gas) or accounts subject to subsection (5) of Section 9–103, or a financing statement filed as a fixture filing (Section 9–313) where the debtor is not a transmitting utility, must show that it covers this type of collateral, must recite that it is to be filed [for record] in the real estate records, and the financing statement must contain a description of the real estate [sufficient if it were contained in a mortgage of the real estate to give constructive notice of the mortgage under the law of this state]. If the debtor does not have an interest of record in the real estate, the financing statement must show the name of a record owner.

(6) A mortgage is effective as a financing statement filed as a fixture filing from the date of its recording if

(a) the goods are described in the mortgage by item or type; and

(b) the goods are or are to become fixtures related to the real estate described in the mortgage; and

(c) the mortgage complies with the requirements for a financing statement in this section other than a recital that it is to be filed in the real estate records; and

(d) the mortgage is duly recorded.

No fee with reference to the financing statement is required other than the regular recording and satisfaction fees with respect to the mortgage.

(7) A financing statement sufficiently shows the name of the debtor if it gives the individual, partnership or corporate name of the debtor, whether or not it adds other trade names or names of partners. Where the debtor so changes his name or in the case of an organization its name, identity or corporate structure that a filed financing statement becomes seriously misleading, the filing is not effective to perfect a security interest in collateral acquired by the debtor more than four months after the change, unless a new appropriate financing statement is filed before the expiration of that time. A filed financing statement remains effective with respect to collateral transferred by the debtor even though the secured party knows of or consents to the transfer.

(8) A financing statement substantially complying with the requirements of this section is effective even though it contains minor errors which are not seriously misleading.

§ 9–403. What Constitutes Filing; Duration of Filing; Effect of Lapsed Filing; Duties of Filing Officer.**

(1) Presentation for filing of a financing statement and tender of the filing fee or acceptance of the statement by the filing officer constitutes filing under this Article.

(2) Except as provided in subsection (6) a filed financing statement is effective for a period of five years from the date of filing. The effectiveness of a filed financing statement lapses on the expiration of the five year period unless a continuation statement is filed prior to the

lapse. If a security interest perfected by filing exists at the time insolvency proceedings are commenced by or against the debtor, the security interest remains perfected until termination of the insolvency proceedings and thereafter for a period of sixty days or until expiration of the five year period, whichever occurs later. Upon lapse the security interest becomes unperfected, unless it is perfected without filing. If the security interest becomes unperfected upon lapse, it is deemed to have been unperfected as against a person who became a purchaser or lien creditor before lapse.

(3) A continuation statement may be filed by the secured party within six months prior to the expiration of the five year period specified in subsection (2). Any such continuation statement must be signed by the secured party, identify the original statement by file number and state that the original statement is still effective. A continuation statement signed by a person other than the secured party of record must be accompanied by a separate written statement of assignment signed by the secured party of record and complying with subsection (2) of Section 9–405, including payment of the required fee. Upon timely filing of the continuation statement, the effectiveness of the original statement is continued for five years after the last date to which the filing was effective whereupon it lapses in the same manner as provided in subsection (2) unless another continuation statement is filed prior to such lapse. Succeeding continuation statements may be filed in the same manner to continue the effectiveness of the original statement. Unless a statute on disposition of public records provides otherwise, the filing officer may remove a lapsed statement from the files and destroy it immediately if he has retained a microfilm or other photographic record, or in other cases after one year after the lapse. The filing officer shall so arrange matters by physical annexation of financing statements to continuation statements or other related filings, or by other means, that if he physically destroys the financing statements of a period more than five years past, those which have been continued by a continuation statement or which are still effective under subsection (6) shall be retained.

(4) Except as provided in subsection (7) a filing officer shall mark each statement with a file number and with the date and hour of filing and shall hold the statement or a microfilm or other photographic copy thereof for public inspection. In addition the filing officer shall index the statement according to the name of the debtor and shall note in the index the file number and the address of the debtor given in the statement.

(5) The uniform fee for filing and indexing and for stamping a copy furnished by the secured party to show the date and place of filing for an original financing statement or for a continuation statement shall be $__________ if the statement is in the standard form prescribed by the [Secretary of State] and otherwise shall be $__________, plus in each case, if the financing statement is subject to subsection (5) of Section 9–402, $__________. The uniform fee for each name more than one required to be indexed shall be $__________. The secured party may at his option show a trade name for any person and an extra uniform indexing fee of $__________ shall be paid with respect thereto.

(6) If the debtor is a transmitting utility (subsection (5) of Section 9–401) and a filed financing statement so states, it is effective until a termination statement is filed. A real estate mortgage which is effective as a fixture filing under subsection (6) of Section 9–402 remains effective as a fixture filing until the mortgage is released or satisfied of record or its effectiveness otherwise terminates as to the real estate.

(7) When a financing statement covers timber to be cut or covers minerals or the like (including oil and gas) or accounts subject to subsection (5) of Section 9–103, or is filed as a fixture filing, the filing officer shall index it under the names of the debtor and any owner of record shown on the financing statement in the same fashion as if they were the mortgagors in a mortgage of the real estate described, and, to the extent that the law of this state provides

for indexing of mortgages under the name of the mortgagee, under the name of the secured party as if he were the mortgagee thereunder, or where indexing is by description in the same fashion as if the financing statement were a mortgage of the real estate described.

§ 9–404. Termination Statement.**

(1) If a financing statement covering consumer goods is filed on or after __________, then within one month or within ten days following written demand by the debtor after there is no outstanding secured obligation and no commitment to make advances, incur obligations or otherwise give value, the secured statement must file with each filing officer with whom the financing statement was filed, a termination statement to the effect that he no longer claims a security interest under the financing statement, which shall be identified by file number. In other cases whenever there is no outstanding secured obligation and no commitment to make advances, incur obligations or otherwise give value, the secured party must on written demand by the debtor send the debtor, for each filing officer with whom the financing statement was filed, a termination statement to the effect that he no longer claims a security interest under the financing statement, which shall be identified by file number. A termination statement signed by a person other than the secured party of record must be accompanied by a separate written statement of assignment signed by the secured party of record complying with subsection (2) of Section 9–405, including payment of the required fee. If the affected secured party fails to file such a termination statement as required by this subsection, or to send such a termination statement within ten days after proper demand therefor, he shall be liable to the debtor for one hundred dollars, and in addition for any loss caused to the debtor by such failure.

(2) On presentation to the filing officer of such a termination statement he must note it in the index. If he has received the termination statement in duplicate, he shall return one copy of the termination statement to the secured party stamped to show the time of receipt thereof. If the filing officer has a microfilm or other photographic record of the financing statement, and of any related continuation statement, statement of assignment and statement of release, he may remove the originals from the files at any time after receipt of the termination statement, or if he has no such record, he may remove them from the files at any time after one year after receipt of the termination statement.

(3) If the termination statement is in the standard form prescribed by the [Secretary of State], the uniform fee for filing and indexing the termination statement shall be $__________, and otherwise shall be $__________, plus in each case an additional fee of $__________ for each name more than one against which the termination statement is required to be indexed.

§ 9–405. Assignment of Security Interest; Duties of Filing Officer; Fees.**

(1) A financing statement may disclose an assignment of a security interest in the collateral described in the financing statement by indication in the financing statement of the name and address of the assignee or by an assignment itself or a copy thereof on the face or back of the statement. On presentation to the filing officer of such a financing statement the filing officer shall mark the same as provided in Section 9–403(4). The uniform fee for filing, indexing and furnishing filing data for a financing statement so indicating an assignment shall be $__________ if the statement is in the standard form prescribed by the [Secretary of State] and otherwise shall be $__________, plus in each case an additional fee of $__________ for each name more than one against which the financing statement is required to be indexed.

(2) A secured party may assign of record all or part of his rights under a financing statement by the filing in the place where the original financing statement was filed of a separate written statement of assignment signed by the secured party of record and setting forth the name of the secured party of record and the debtor, the file number and the date of filing of the financing statement and the name and address of the assignee and containing a description

of the collateral assigned. A copy of the assignment is sufficient as a separate statement if it complies with the preceding sentence. On presentation to the filing officer of such a separate statement, the filing officer shall mark such separate statement with the date and hour of the filing. He shall note the assignment on the index of the financing statement, or in the case of a fixture filing, or a filing covering timber to be cut, or covering minerals or the like (including oil and gas) or accounts subject to subsection (5) of Section 9–103, he shall index the assignment under the name of the assignor as grantor and, to the extent that the law of this state provides for indexing the assignment of a mortgage under the name of the assignee, he shall index the assignment of the financing statement under the name of the assignee. The uniform fee for filing, indexing and furnishing filing data about such a separate statement of assignment shall be $__________ if the statement is in the standard form prescribed by the [Secretary of State] and otherwise shall be $__________, plus in each case an additional fee of $__________ for each name more than one against which the statement of assignment is required to be indexed. Notwithstanding the provisions of this subsection, an assignment of record of a security interest in a fixture contained in a mortgage effective as a fixture filing (subsection (6) of Section 9–402) may be made only by an assignment of the mortgage in the manner provided by the law of this state other than this Act.

(3) After the disclosure or filing of an assignment under this section, the assignee is the secured party of record.

§ 9–406. Release of Collateral; Duties of Filing Officer; Fees.**

A secured party of record may by his signed statement release all or a part of any collateral described in a filed financing statement. The statement of release is sufficient if it contains a description of the collateral being released, the name and address of the debtor, the name and address of the secured party, and the file number of the financing statement. A statement of release signed by a person other than the secured party of record must be accompanied by a separate written statement of assignment signed by the secured party of record and complying with subsection (2) of Section 9–405, including payment of the required fee. Upon presentation of such a statement of release to the filing officer he shall mark the statement with the hour and date of filing and shall note the same upon the margin of the index of the filing of the financing statement. The uniform fee for filing and noting such a statement of release shall be $__________ if the statement is in the standard form prescribed by the [Secretary of State] and otherwise shall be $__________, plus in each case an additional fee of $__________ for each name more than one against which the statement of release is required to be indexed.

§ 9–407. Information From Filing Officer.* **

(1) If the person filing any financing statement, termination statement, statement of assignment, or statement of release, furnishes the filing officer a copy thereof, the filing officer shall upon request note upon the copy the file number and date and hour of the filing of the original and deliver or send the copy to such person.

(2) Upon request of any person, the filing officer shall issue his certificate showing whether there is on file on the date and hour stated therein, any presently effective financing statement naming a particular debtor and any statement of assignment thereof and if there is, giving the date and hour of filing of each such statement and the names and addresses of each secured party therein. The uniform fee for such a certificate shall be $__________ if the request for the certificate is in the standard form prescribed by the Secretary of State and otherwise shall be $__________. Upon request the filing officer shall furnish a copy of any filed financing statement or statement of assignment for a uniform fee of $__________ per page.

§ 9–408. Financing Statements Covering Consigned or Leased Goods.**

A consignor or lessor of goods may file a financing statement using the terms "consignor," "consignee," "lessor," "lessee" or the like instead of the terms specified in Section 9–402. The provisions of this Part shall apply as appropriate to such a financing statement but its filing shall not of itself be a factor in determining whether or not the consignment or lease is intended as security (Section 1–201(37)). However, if it is determined for other reasons that the consignment or lease is so intended, a security interest of the consignor or lessor which attaches to the consigned or leased goods is perfected by such filing.

PART 5

DEFAULT

§ 9–501. Default; Procedure When Security Agreement Covers Both Real and Personal Property.**

(1) When a debtor is in default under a security agreement, a secured party has the rights and remedies provided in this Part and except as limited by subsection (3) those provided in the security agreement. He may reduce his claim to judgment, foreclose or otherwise enforce the security interest by any available judicial procedure. If the collateral is documents the secured party may proceed either as to the documents or as to the goods covered thereby. A secured party in possession has the rights, remedies and duties provided in Section 9–207. The rights and remedies referred to in this subsection are cumulative.

(2) After default, the debtor has the rights and remedies provided in this Part, those provided in the security agreement and those provided in Section 9–207.

(3) To the extent that they give rights to the debtor and impose duties on the secured party, the rules stated in the subsections referred to below may not be waived or varied except as provided with respect to compulsory disposition of collateral (subsection (3) of Section 9–504 and Section 9–505) and with respect to redemption of collateral (Section 9–506) but the parties may by agreement determine the standards by which the fulfillment of these rights and duties is to be measured if such standards are not manifestly unreasonable:

(a) subsection (2) of Section 9–502 and subsection (2) of Section 9–504 insofar as they require accounting for surplus proceeds of collateral;

(b) subsection (3) of Section 9–504 and subsection (1) of Section 9–505 which deal with disposition of collateral;

(c) subsection (2) of Section 9–505 which deals with acceptance of collateral as discharge of obligation;

(d) Section 9–506 which deals with redemption of collateral; and

(e) subsection (1) of Section 9–507 which deals with the secured party's liability for failure to comply with this Part.

(4) If the security agreement covers both real and personal property, the secured party may proceed under this Part as to the personal property or he may proceed as to both the real and the personal property in accordance with his rights and remedies in respect of the real property in which case the provisions of this Part do not apply.

(5) When a secured party has reduced his claim to judgment the lien of any levy which may be made upon his collateral by virtue of any execution based upon the judgment shall relate back to the date of the perfection of the security interest in such collateral. A judicial sale, pursuant to such execution, is a foreclosure of the security interest by judicial procedure within the meaning of this section, and the secured party may purchase at the sale and thereafter hold the collateral free of any other requirements of this Article.

§ 9–502. Collection Rights of Secured Party.**

(1) When so agreed and in any event on default the secured party is entitled to notify an account debtor or the obligor on an instrument to make payment to him whether or not the assignor was theretofore making collections on the collateral, and also to take control of any proceeds to which he is entitled under Section 9–306.

(2) A secured party who by agreement is entitled to charge back uncollected collateral or otherwise to full or limited recourse against the debtor and who undertakes to collect from the account debtors or obligors must proceed in a commercially reasonable manner and may deduct his reasonable expenses of realization from the collections. If the security agreement secures an indebtedness, the secured party must account to the debtor for any surplus, and unless otherwise agreed, the debtor is liable for any deficiency. But, if the underlying transaction was a sale of accounts or chattel paper, the debtor is entitled to any surplus or is liable for any deficiency only if the security agreement so provides.

§ 9–503. Secured Party's Right to Take Possession After Default.

Unless otherwise agreed a secured party has on default the right to take possession of the collateral. In taking possession a secured party may proceed without judicial process if this can be done without breach of the peace or may proceed by action. If the security agreement so provides the secured party may require the debtor to assemble the collateral and make it available to the secured party at a place to be designated by the secured party which is reasonably convenient to both parties. Without removal a secured party may render equipment unusable, and may dispose of collateral on the debtor's premises under Section 9–504.

§ 9–504. Secured Party's Right to Dispose of Collateral After Default; Effect of Disposition.**

(1) A secured party after default may sell, lease or otherwise dispose of any or all of the collateral in its then condition or following any commercially reasonable preparation or processing. Any sale of goods is subject to the Article on Sales (Article 2). The proceeds of disposition shall be applied in the order following to

(a) the reasonable expenses of retaking, holding, preparing for sale or lease, selling, leasing and the like and, to the extent provided for in the agreement and not prohibited by law, the reasonable attorneys' fees and legal expenses incurred by the secured party;

(b) the satisfaction of indebtedness secured by the security interest under which the disposition is made;

(c) the satisfaction of indebtedness secured by any subordinate security interest in the collateral if written notification of demand therefor is received before distribution of the proceeds is completed. If requested by the secured party, the holder of a subordinate security interest must seasonably furnish reasonable proof of his interest, and unless he does so, the secured party need not comply with his demand.

(2) If the security interest secures an indebtedness, the secured party must account to the debtor for any surplus, and, unless otherwise agreed, the debtor is liable for any deficiency. But if the underlying transaction was a sale of accounts or chattel paper, the debtor is entitled to any surplus or is liable for any deficiency only if the security agreement so provides.

(3) Disposition of the collateral may be by public or private proceedings and may be made by way of one or more contracts. Sale or other disposition may be as a unit or in parcels and at any time and place and on any terms but every aspect of the disposition including the method, manner, time, place and terms must be commercially reasonable. Unless collateral is perishable or threatens to decline speedily in value or is of a type customarily sold on a recognized market, reasonable notification of the time and place of any public sale or reasonable notification of the time after which any private sale or other intended disposition is to be

made shall be sent by the secured party to the debtor, if he has not signed after default a statement renouncing or modifying his right to notification of sale. In the case of consumer goods no other notification need be sent. In other cases notification shall be sent to any other secured party from whom the secured party has received (before sending his notification to the debtor or before the debtor's renunciation of his rights) written notice of a claim of an interest in the collateral. The secured party may buy at any public sale and if the collateral is of a type customarily sold in a recognized market or is of a type which is the subject of widely distributed standard price quotations he may buy at private sale.

(4) When collateral is disposed of by a secured party after default, the disposition transfers to a purchaser for value all of the debtor's rights therein, discharges the security interest under which it is made and any security interest or lien subordinate thereto. The purchaser takes free of all such rights and interests even though the secured party fails to comply with the requirements of this Part or of any judicial proceedings

(a) in the case of a public sale, if the purchaser has no knowledge of any defects in the sale and if he does not buy in collusion with the secured party, other bidders or the person conducting the sale; or

(b) in any other case, if the purchaser acts in good faith.

(5) A person who is liable to a secured party under a guaranty, indorsement, repurchase agreement or the like and who receives a transfer of collateral from the secured party or is subrogated to his rights has thereafter the rights and duties of the secured party. Such a transfer of collateral is not a sale or disposition of the collateral under this Article.

§ 9–505. Compulsory Disposition of Collateral; Acceptance of the Collateral as Discharge of Obligation.

(1) If the debtor has paid sixty per cent of the cash price in the case of a purchase money security interest in consumer goods or sixty per cent of the loan in the case of another security interest in consumer goods, and has not signed after default a statement renouncing or modifying his rights under this Part a secured party who has taken possession of collateral must dispose of it under Section 9–504 and if he fails to do so within ninety days after he takes possession the debtor at his option may recover in conversion or under Section 9–507(1) on secured party's liability.

(2) In any other case involving consumer goods or any other collateral a secured party in possession may, after default, propose to retain the collateral in satisfaction of the obligation. Written notice of such proposal shall be sent to the debtor if he has not signed after default a statement renouncing or modifying his rights under this subsection. In the case of consumer goods no other notice need be given. In other cases notice shall be sent to any other secured party from whom the secured party has received (before sending his notice to the debtor or before the debtor's renunciation of his rights) written notice of a claim of an interest in the collateral. If the secured party receives objection in writing from a person entitled to receive notification within twenty-one days after the notice was sent, the secured party must dispose of the collateral under Section 9–504. In the absence of such written objection the secured party may retain the collateral in satisfaction of the debtor's obligation.

§ 9–506. Debtor's Right to Redeem Collateral.

At any time before the secured party has disposed of collateral or entered into a contract for its disposition under Section 9–504 or before the obligation has been discharged under Section 9–505(2) the debtor or any other secured party may unless otherwise agreed in writing after default redeem the collateral by tendering fulfillment of all obligations secured by the collateral as well as the expenses reasonably incurred by the secured party in retaking, holding and preparing the collateral for disposition, in arranging for the sale, and to the extent provided in the agreement and not prohibited by law, his reasonable attorneys' fees and legal expenses.

§ 9–507. Secured Party's Liability for Failure to Comply With This Part.

(1) If it is established that the secured party is not proceeding in accordance with the provisions of this Part disposition may be ordered or restrained on appropriate terms and conditions. If the disposition has occurred the debtor or any person entitled to notification or whose security interest has been made known to the secured party prior to the disposition has a right to recovery from the secured party any loss caused by a failure to comply with the provisions of this Part. If the collateral is consumer goods, the debtor has a right to recover in any event an amount not less than the credit service charge plus ten per cent of the principal amount of the debt or the time price differential plus 10 per cent of the cash price.

(2) The fact that a better price could have been obtained by a sale at a different time or in a different method from that selected by the secured party is not of itself sufficient to establish that the sale was not made in a commercially reasonable manner. If the secured party either sells the collateral in the usual manner in any recognized market therefor or if he sells at the price current in such market at the time of his sale or if he has otherwise sold in conformity with reasonable commercial practices among dealers in the type of property sold he has sold in a commercially reasonable manner. The principles stated in the two preceding sentences with respect to sales also apply as may be appropriate to other types of disposition. A disposition which has been approved in any judicial proceeding or by any bona fide creditors' committee or representative of creditors shall conclusively be deemed to be commercially reasonable, but this sentence does not indicate that any such approval must be obtained in any case nor does it indicate that any disposition not so approved is not commercially reasonable.

Uniform Partnership Act

PART I
PRELIMINARY PROVISIONS

Sec. 1. (Name of Act.) This act may be cited as Uniform Partnership Act.

Sec. 2. (Definition of Terms.) In this act, "Court" includes every court and judge having jurisdiction in the case.

"Business" includes every trade, occupation, or profession.

"Person" includes individuals, partnerships, corporation, and other associations.

"Bankrupt" includes bankrupt under the Federal Bankruptcy Act or insolvent under any state insolvent act.

"Conveyance" includes every assignment, lease, mortgage, or encumbrance.

"Real property" includes land and any interest or estate in land.

Sec. 3. (Interpretation of Knowledge and Notice.) (1) A person has "knowledge" of a fact within the meaning of this act not only when he has actual knowledge thereof, but also when he has knowledge of such other facts as in the circumstances shows bad faith.

(2) A person has "notice" of a fact within the meaning of this act when the person who claims the benefit of the notice

(a) States the fact to such person, or

(b) Delivers through the mail, or by other means of communication, a written statement of the fact to such person or to a proper person at his place of business or residence.

Sec. 4. (Rules of Construction.) (1) The rule that statutes in derogation of the common law are to be strictly construed shall have no application to this act.

(2) The law of estoppel shall apply under this act.

(3) The law of agency shall apply under this act.

(4) This act shall be so interpreted and construed as to effect its general purpose to make uniform the law of those states which enact it.

(5) This act shall not be construed so as to impair the obligations of any contract existing when the act goes into effect, nor to affect any action or proceedings begun or right accrued before this act takes effect.

Sec. 5. (Rules for Cases Not Provided for in this Act.) In any case not provided for in this act the rules of law and equity, including the law merchant, shall govern.

PART II
NATURE OF PARTNERSHIP

Sec. 6. (Partnership Defined.) (1) A partnership is an association of two or more persons to carry on as co-owners a business for profit.

(2) But any association formed under any other statute of this state, or any statute adopted by authority, other than the authority of this state, is not a partnership under this act, unless such association would have been a partnership in this state prior to the adoption of this act; but this act shall apply to limited partnerships except in so far as the statutes relating to such partnerships are inconsistent herewith.

Sec. 7. (Rules for Determining the Existence of a Partnership.) In determining whether a partnership exists, these rules shall apply:

(1) Except as provided by Section 16 persons who are not partners as to each other are not partners as to third persons.

(2) Joint tenancy, tenancy in common, tenancy by the entireties, joint property, common property, or part ownership does not of itself establish a partnership, whether such co-owners do or do not share any profits made by the use of the property.

(3) The sharing of gross returns does not of itself establish a partnership, whether or not the persons sharing them have a joint or common right or interest in any property from which the returns are derived.

(4) The receipt by a person of a share of the profits of a business is prima facie evidence that he is a partner in the business, but no such inference shall be drawn if such profits were received in payment:

(a) As a debt by installments or otherwise,

(b) As wages of an employee or rent to a landlord,

(c) As an annuity to a widow or representative of a deceased partner,

(d) As interest on a loan, though the amount of payment vary with the profits of the business,

(e) As the consideration for the sale of a good-will of a business or other property by installments or otherwise.

Sec. 8. (Partnership Property.) (1) All property originally brought into the partnership stock or subsequently acquired by purchase or otherwise, on account of the partnership, is partnership property.

(2) Unless the contrary intention appears, property acquired with partnership funds is partnership property.

(3) Any estate in real property may be acquired in the partnership name. Title so acquired can be conveyed only in the partnership name.

(4) A conveyance to a partnership in the partnership name, though without words of inheritance, passes the entire estate of the grantor unless a contrary intent appears.

PART III
RELATIONS OF PARTNERS TO PERSONS DEALING WITH THE PARTNERSHIP

Sec. 9. (Partner Agent of Partnership as to Partnership Business.) (1) Every partner is an agent of the partnership for the purpose of its business, and the act of every partner, including the execution in the partnership name of any instrument, for apparently carrying on in the usual way the business of the partnership of which he is a member binds the partnership, unless the partner so acting has in fact no authority to act for the partnership in the particular matter, and the person with whom he is dealing has knowledge of the fact that he has no such authority.

(2) An act of a partner which is not apparently for the carrying on of the business of the partnership in the usual way does not bind the partnership unless authorized by the other partners.

(3) Unless authorized by the other partners or unless they have abandoned the business, one or more but less than all the partners have no authority to:

(a) Assign the partnership property in trust for creditors or on the assignee's promise to pay the debts of the partnership,

(b) Dispose of the good-will of the business,

(c) Do any other act which would make it impossible to carry on the ordinary business of a partnership,

(d) Confess a judgment,

(e) Submit a partnership claim or liability to arbitration or reference.

(4) No act of a partner in contravention of a restriction on authority shall bind the partnership to persons having knowledge of the restriction.

Sec. 10. (Conveyance of Real Property of the Partnership.) (1) Where title to real property is in the partnership name, any partner may convey title to such property by a conveyance executed in the partnership name; but the partnership may recover such property unless the partner's act binds the partnership under the provisions of paragraph (1) of section 9 or unless such property has been conveyed by the grantee or a person claiming through such grantee to a holder for value without knowledge that the partner, in making the conveyance, has exceeded his authority.

(2) Where title to real property is in the name of the partnership, a conveyance executed by a partner, in his own name, passes the equitable interest of the partnership, provided the act is one within the authority of the partner under the provisions of paragraph (1) of section 9.

(3) Where title to real property is in the name of one or more but not all the partners, and the record does not disclose the right of the partnership, the partners in whose name the title stands may convey title to such property, but the partnership may recover such property if the partners' act does not bind the partnership under the provisions of paragraph (1) of section 9, unless the purchaser or his assignee, is a holder for value, without knowledge.

(4) Where the title to real property is in the name of one or more or all the partners, or in a third person in trust for the partnership, a conveyance executed by a partner in the partnership name, or in his own name, passes the equitable interest of the partnership, provided the act is one within the authority of the partner under the provisions of paragraph (1) of section 9.

(5) Where the title to real property is in the names of all the partners a conveyance executed by all the partners passes all their rights in such property.

Sec. 11. (Partnership Bound by Admission of Partner.) An admission or representation made by any partner concerning partnership affairs within the scope of his authority as conferred by this act is evidence against the partnership.

Sec. 12. (Partnership Charged with Knowledge of or Notice to Partner.) Notice to any partner of any matter relating to partnership affairs, and the knowledge of the partner acting in the particular matter, acquired while a partner or then present to his mind, and the knowledge of any other partner who reasonably could and should have communicated it to the acting partner, operate as notice to or knowledge of the partnership, except in the case of a fraud on the partnership committed by or with the consent of that partner.

Sec. 13. (Partnership Bound by Partner's Wrongful Act.) Where, by any wrongful act or omission of any partner acting in the ordinary course of the business of the partnership or with the authority of his co-partners, loss or injury is caused to any person, not being a partner in the partnership, or any penalty is incurred, the partnership is liable therefor to the same extent as the partner so acting or omitting to act.

Sec. 14. (Partnership Bound by Partner's Breach of Trust.) The partnership is bound to make good the loss:

(a) Where one partner acting within the scope of his apparent authority receives money or property of a third person and misapplies it; and

(b) Where the partnership in the course of its business receives money or property of a third person and the money or property so received is misapplied by any partner while it is in the custody of the partnership.

Sec. 15. (Nature of Partner's Liability.) All partners are liable:

(a) Jointly and severally for everything chargeable to the partnership under sections 13 and 14,

(b) Jointly for all other debts and obligations of the partnership; but any partner may enter into a separate obligation to perform a partnership contract.

Sec. 16. (Partner by Estoppel.) (1) When a person, by words spoken or written or by conduct, represents himself, or consents to another representing him to any one, as a partner in an existing partnership or with one or more persons not actual partners, he is liable to any such person to whom such representation has been made, who has, on the faith of such representation, given credit to the actual or apparent partnership, and if he has made such representation or consented to its being made in a public manner he is liable to such person, whether the representation has or has not been made or communicated to such person so giving credit by or with the knowledge of the apparent partner making the representation or consenting to its being made.

(a) When a partnership liability results, he is liable as though he were an actual member of the partnership.

(b) When no partnership liability results, he is liable jointly with other persons, if any, so consenting to the contract or representation as to incur liability, otherwise separately.

(2) When a person has been thus represented to be a partner in an existing partnership, or with one or more persons not actual partners, he is an agent of the persons consenting to such representation to bind them to the same extent and in the same manner as though he were a partner in fact, with respect to persons who rely upon the representation. Where all

the members of the existing partnership consent to the representation, a partnership act or obligation results; but in all other cases it is the joint act or obligation of the person acting and the persons consenting to the representation.

Sec. 17. (Liability of Incoming Partner.) A person admitted as a partner into an existing partnership is liable for all the obligations of the partnership arising before his admission as though he had been a partner when such obligations were incurred, except that this liability shall be satisfied only out of partnership property.

PART IV
RELATIONS OF PARTNERS TO ONE ANOTHER

Sec. 18. (Rules Determining Rights and Duties of Partners.) The rights and duties of the partners in relation to the partnership shall be determined, subject to any agreement between them, by the following rules:

(a) Each partner shall be repaid his contributions, whether by way of capital or advances to the partnership property and share equally in the profits and surplus remaining after all liabilities, including those to partners, are satisfied; and must contribute towards the losses, whether of capital or otherwise, sustained by the partnership according to his share in the profits.

(b) The partnership must indemnify every partner in respect of payments made and personal liabilities reasonably incurred by him in the ordinary and proper conduct of its business, or for the preservation of its business or property.

(c) A partner, who in aid of the partnership makes any payment or advance beyond the amount of capital which he agreed to contribute, shall be paid interest from the date of the payment or advance.

(d) A partner shall receive interest on the capital contributed by him only from the date when repayment should be made.

(e) All partners have equal rights in the management and conduct of the partnership business.

(f) No partner is entitled to remuneration for acting in the partnership business, except that a surviving partner is entitled to reasonable compensation for his services in winding up the partnership affairs.

(g) No person can become a member of a partnership without the consent of all the partners.

(h) Any difference arising as to ordinary matters connected with the partnership business may be decided by a majority of the partners; but no act in contravention of any agreement between the partners may be done rightfully without the consent of all the partners.

Sec. 19. (Partnership Books.) The partnership books shall be kept, subject to any agreement between the partners, at the principal place of business of the partnership, and every partner shall at all times have access to and may inspect and copy any of them.

Sec. 20. (Duty of Partners to Render Information.) Partners shall render on demand true and full information of all things affecting the partnership to any partner or the legal representative of any deceased partner or partner under legal disability.

Sec. 21. (Partner Accountable as a Fiduciary.) (1) Every partner must account to the partnership for any benefit, and hold as trustee for it any profits derived by him without the consent of the other partners from any transaction connected with the formation, conduct, or liquidation of the partnership or from any use by him of its property.

(2) This section applies also to the representatives of a deceased partner engaged in the liquidation of the affairs of the partnership as the personal representatives of the last surviving partner.

Sec. 22. (Right to an Account.) Any partner shall have the right to a formal account as to partnership affairs:

(a) If he is wrongfully excluded from the partnership business or possession of its property by his co-partners,

(b) If the right exists under the terms of any agreement,

(c) As provided by section 21,

(d) Whenever other circumstances render it just and reasonable.

Sec. 23. (Continuation of Partnership Beyond Fixed Term.) (1) When a partnership for a fixed term or particular undertaking is continued after the termination of such term or particular undertaking without any express agreement, the rights and duties of the partners remain the same as they were at such termination, so far as is consistent with a partnership at will.

(2) A continuation of the business by the partners or such of them as habitually acted therein during the term, without any settlement or liquidation of the partnership affairs, is prima facie evidence of a continuation of the partnership.

PART V
PROPERTY RIGHTS OF A PARTNER

Sec. 24. (Extent of Property Rights of a Partner.) The property rights of a partner are (1) his rights in specific partnership property, (2) his interest in the partnership, and (3) his right to participate in the management.

Sec. 25. (Nature of a Partner's Right in Specific Partnership Property.) (1) A partner is co-owner with his partners of specific partnership property holding as a tenant in partnership.

(2) The incidents of this tenancy are such that:

(a) A partner, subject to the provisions of this act and to any agreement between the partners, has an equal right with his partners to possess specific partnership property for partnership purposes; but he has no right to possess such property for any other purpose without the consent of his partners.

(b) A partner's right in specific partnership property is not assignable except in connection with the assignment of rights of all the partners in the same property.

(c) A partner's right in specific partnership property is not subject to attachment or execution, except on a claim against the partnership. When partnership property is attached for a partnership debt the partners, or any of them, or the representatives of a deceased partner, cannot claim any right under the homestead or exemption laws.

(d) On the death of a partner his right in specific partnership property vests in the surviving partner or partners, except where the deceased was the last surviving partner, when his right in such property vests in his legal representative. Such surviving partner or partners, or the legal representative of the last surviving partner, has no right to possess the partnership property for any but a partnership purpose.

(e) A partner's right in specific partnership property is not subject to dower, curtesy, or allowances to widows, heirs, or next of kin.

Sec. 26. (Nature of Partner's Interest in the Partnership.) A partner's interest in the partnership is his share of the profits and surplus, and the same is personal property.

Sec. 27. (Assignment of Partner's Interest.) (1) A conveyance by a partner of his interest in the partnership does not of itself dissolve the partnership, nor, as against the other partners in the absence of agreement, entitle the assignee, during the continuance of the partnership to interfere in the management or administration of the partnership business or affairs, or to require any information or account of partnership transactions, or to inspect the partnership books; but it merely entitles the assignee to receive in accordance with his contract the profits to which the assigning partner would otherwise be entitled.

(2) In case of a dissolution of the partnership, the assignee is entitled to receive his assignor's interest and may require an account from the date only of the last account agreed to by all the partners.

Sec. 28. (Partner's Interest Subject to Charging Order.) (1) On due application to a competent court by any judgment creditor of a partner, the court which entered the judgment, order, or decree, or any other court, may charge the interest of the debtor partner with payment of the unsatisifed amount of such judgment debt with interest thereon; and may then or later appoint a receiver of his share of the profits, and of any other money due or to fall due to him in respect of the partnership, and make all other orders, directions, accounts and inquiries which the debtor partner might have made, or which the circumstances of the case may require.

(2) The interest charged may be redeemed at any time before foreclosure, or in case of a sale being directed by the court may be purchased without thereby causing a dissolution:

(a) With separate property, by any one or more of the partners, or

(b) With partnership property, by any one or more of the partners with the consent of all the partners whose interests are not so charged or sold.

(3) Nothing in this act shall be held to deprive a partner of his right, if any, under the exemption laws, as regards his interest in the partnership.

PART VI
DISSOLUTION AND WINDING UP

Sec. 29. (Dissolution Defined.) The dissolution of a partnership is the change in the relation of the partners caused by any partner ceasing to be associated in the carrying on as distinguished from the winding up of the business.

Sec. 30. (Partnerhip Not Terminated by Dissolution.) On dissolution the partnership is not terminated, but continues until the winding up of partnership affairs is completed.

Sec. 31. (Causes of Dissolution.) Dissolution is caused: (1) Without violation of the agreement between the partners,

(a) By the termination of the definite term or particular undertaking specified in the agreement,

(b) By the express will of any partner when no definite term or particular undertaking is specified,

(c) By the express will of all the partners who have not assigned their interest or suffered them to be charged for their separate debts, either before or after the termination of any specified term or particular undertaking,

(d) By the expulsion of any partner from the business bona fide in accordance with such a power conferred by the agreement between the partners;

(2) In contravention of the agreement between the partners, where the circumstances do not permit a dissolution under any other provision of this section, by the express will of any partner at any time;

(3) By any event which makes it unlawful for the business of the partnership to be carried on or for the members to carry it on in partnership;

(4) By the death of any partner;

(5) By the bankruptcy of any partner or the partnership;

(6) By decree of court under section 32.

Sec. 32. (Dissolution by Decree of Court.) (1) On application by or for a partner the court shall decree a dissolution whenever:

(a) A partner has been declared a lunatic in any judicial proceeding or is shown to be of unsound mind,

(b) A partner becomes in any other way incapable of performing his part of the partnership contract,

(c) A partner has been guilty of such conduct as tends to affect prejudicially the carrying on of the business,

(d) A partner wilfully or persistently commits a breach of the partnership agreement, or otherwise so conducts himself in matters relating to the partnership business that it is not reasonably practicable to carry on the business in partnership with him,

(e) The business of the partnership can only be carried on at a loss,

(f) Other circumstances render a dissolution equitable.

(2) On the application of the purchaser of a partner's interest under section 27 or 28:

(a) After the termination of the specified term or particular undertaking,

(b) At any time if the partnership was a partnership at will when the interest was assigned or when the charging order was issued.

Sec. 33. (General Effect of Dissolution on Authority of Partner.) Except so far as may be necessary to wind up partnership affairs or to complete transactions begun but not then finished, dissolution terminates all authority of any partner to act for the partnership,

(1) With respect to the partners,

(a) When the dissolution is not by the act, bankruptcy or death of a partner; or

(b) When the dissolution is by such act, bankruptcy or death of a partner, in cases where section 34 so requires.

(2) With respect to persons not partners, as declared in section 35.

Sec. 34. (Right of Partner to Contribution From Copartners After Dissolution.) Where the dissolution is caused by the act, death or bankruptcy of a partner, each partner is liable to his copartners for his share of any liability created by any partner acting for the partnership as if the partnership had not been dissolved unless:

(a) The dissolution being by act of any partner, the partner acting for the partnership had knowledge of the dissolution, or

(b) The dissolution being by the death or bankruptcy of a partner, the partner acting for the partnership had knowledge or notice of the death or bankruptcy.

Sec. 35. (Power of Partner to Bind Partnership to Third Persons After Dissolution.) (1) After dissolution a partner can bind the partnership except as provided in Paragraph (3):

(a) By any act appropriate for winding up partnership affairs or completing transactions unfinished at dissolution;

(b) By any transaction which would bind the partnership if dissolution had not taken place, provided the other party to the transaction:

(I) Had extended credit to the partnership prior to dissolution and had no knowledge or notice of the dissolution; or

(II) Though he had not so extended credit, had nevertheless known of the partnership prior to dissolution, and, having no knowledge or notice of dissolution, the fact of dissolution had not been advertised in a newspaper of general circulation in the place (or in each place if more than one) at which the partnership business was regularly carried on.

(2) The liability of a partner under paragraph (1b) shall be satisfied out of partnership assets alone when such partner had been prior to dissolution:

(a) Unknown as a partner to the person with whom the contract is made; and

(b) So far unknown and inactive in partnership affairs that the business reputation of the partnership could not be said to have been in any degree due to his connection with it.

(3) The partnership is in no case bound by any act of a partner after dissolution:

(a) Where the partnership is dissolved because it is unlawful to carry on the business, unless the act is appropriate for winding up partnership affairs; or

(b) Where the partner has become bankrupt; or

(c) Where the partner has no authority to wind up partnership affairs; except by a transaction with one who:

(I) Had extended credit to the partnership prior to dissolution and had no knowledge or notice of his want of authority; or

(II) Had not extended credit to the partnership prior to dissolution, and, having no knowledge or notice of his want of authority, the fact of his want of authority has not been advertised in the manner provided for advertising the fact of dissolution in paragraph (1bII).

(4) Nothing in this section shall affect the liability under section 16 of any person who after dissolution represents himself or consents to another representing him as a partner in a partnership engaged in carrying on business.

Sec. 36. (Effect of Dissolution on Partner's Existing Liability.) (1) The dissolution of the partnership does not of itself discharge the existing liability of any partner.

(2) A partner is discharged from any existing liability upon dissolution of the partnership by an agreement to that effect between himself, the partnership creditor and the person or partnership continuing the business; and such agreement may be inferred from the course of dealing between the creditor having knowledge of the dissolution and the person or partnership continuing the business.

(3) Where a person agrees to assume the existing obligations of a dissolved partnership, the partners whose obligations have been assumed shall be discharged from any liability to any creditor of the partnership who, knowing of the agreement, consents to a material alteration in the nature or time of payment of such obligations.

(4) The individual property of a deceased partner shall be liable for all obligations of the partnership incurred while he was a partner but subject to the prior payment of his separate debts.

Sec. 37. (Right to Wind Up.) Unless otherwise agreed the partners who have not wrongfully dissolved the partnership or the legal representative of the last surviving partner, not bankrupt, has the right to wind up the partnership affairs; provided, however, that any partner, his legal representative or his assignee, upon cause shown, may obtain winding up by the court.

Sec. 38. (Rights of Partners to Application of Partnership Property.) (1) When dissolution is caused in any way, except in contravention of the partnership agreement, each partner as against his co-partners and all persons claiming through them in respect of their interests in the partnership, unless otherwise agreed, may have the partnership property applied to discharge its liabilities, and the surplus applied to pay in cash the net amount owing to the respective partners. But if dissolution is caused by expulsion of a partner, bona fide under the partnership agreement and if the expelled partner is discharged from all partnership liabilities, either by payment or agreement under section 36(2), he shall receive in cash only the net amount due him from the partnership.

(2) When dissolution is caused in contravention of the partnership agreement the rights of the partners shall be as follows:

(a) Each partner who has not caused dissolution wrongfully shall have:

(I) All the rights specified in paragraph (1) of this section, and

(II) The right, as against each partner who has caused the dissolution wrongfully, to damages for breach of the agreement.

(b) The partners who have not caused the dissolution wrongfully, if they all desire to continue the business in the same name, either by themselves or jointly with others, may do so, during the agreed term for the partnership and for that purpose may possess the partnership property, provided they secure the payment by bond approved by the court, or pay to any partner who has caused the dissolution wrongfully, the value of his interest in the partnership at the dissolution, less any damages recoverable under clause (2aII) of the section, and in like manner indemnify him against all present or future partnership liabilities.

(c) A partner who has caused the dissolution wrongfully shall have:

(I) If the business is not continued under the provisions of paragraph (2b) all the rights of a partner under paragraph (1), subject to clause (2aII), of this section.

(II) If the business is continued under paragraph (2b) of this section the right as against his co-partners and all claiming through them in respect of their interests in the partnership, to have the value of his interest in the partnership, less any damages caused to his co-partners by the dissolution, ascertained and paid to him in cash, or the payment secured by bond approved by the court, and to be released from all existing liabilities of the partnership; but in ascertaining the value of the partner's interest the vale of the good-will of the business shall not be considered.

Sec. 39. (Rights Where Partnership is Dissolved for Fraud or Misrepresentation.) Where a partnership contract is rescinded on the ground of the fraud or misrepresentation of one of the parties thereto, the party entitled to rescind is, without prejudice to any other right, entitled,

(a) To a lien on, or right of retention of, the surplus of the partnership property after satisfying the partnership liabilities to third persons for any sum of money paid by him for the purchase of an interest in the partnership and for any capital or advances contributed by him; and

(b) To stand, after all liabilities to third persons have been satisfied, in the place of the creditors of the partnership for any payments made by him in respect of the partnership liabilities; and

(c) To be indemnified by the person guilty of the fraud or making the representation against all debts and liabilities of the partnership.

Sec. 40. (Rules for Distribution.) In settling accounts between the partners after dissolution, the following rules shall be observed, subject to any agreement to the contrary:

(a) The assets of the partnership are:

(I) The partnership property,

(II) The contributions of the partners necessary for the payment of all the liabilities specified in clause (b) of this paragraph.

(b) The liabilities of the partnership shall rank in order of payment, as follows:
 (I) Those owing to creditors other than partners,
 (II) Those owing to partners other than for capital and profits,
 (III) Those owing to partners in respect of capital,
 (IV) Those owing to partners in respect of profits.

(c) The assets shall be applied in the order of their declaration in clause (a) of this paragraph to the satisfaction of the liabilities.

(d) The partners shall contribute, as provided by section 18(a) the amount necessary to satisfy the liabilities; but if any, but not all, of the partners are insolvent, or, not being subject to process, refuse to contribute, the other parties shall contribute their share of the liabilities, and, in the relative proportions in which they share the profits, the additional amount necessary to pay the liabilities.

(e) An assignee for the benefit of creditors or any person appointed by the court shall have the right to enforce the contributions specified in clause (d) of this paragraph.

(f) Any partner or his legal representative shall have the right to enforce the contributions specified in clause (d) of this paragraph, to the extent of the amount which he has paid in excess of his share of the liability.

(g) The individual property of a deceased partner shall be liable for the contributions specified in clause (d) of this paragraph.

(h) When partnership property and the individual properties of the partners are in possession of a court for distribution, partnership creditors shall have priority on partnership property and separate creditors on individual property saving the rights of lien or secured creditors as heretofore.

(i) Where a partner has become bankrupt or his estate is insolvent the claims against his separate property shall rank in the following order:
 (I) Those owing to separate creditors,
 (II) Those owing to partnership creditors,
 (III) Those owing to partners by way of contribution.

Sec. 41. (Liability of Persons Continuing the Business in Certain Cases.) (1) When any new partner is admitted into an existing partnership, or when any partner retires and assigns (or the representative of the deceased partner assigns) his rights in partnership property to two or more of the partners, or to one or more of the partners and one or more third persons, if the business is continued without liquidation of the partnership affairs, creditors of the first or dissolved partnership are also creditors of the partnership so continuing the business.

(2) When all but one partner retire and assign (or the representative of a deceased partner assigns) their rights in partnership property to the remaining partner, who continues the business without liquidation of partnership affairs, either alone or with others, creditors of the dissolved partnership are also creditors of the person or partnership so continuing the business.

(3) When any partner retires or dies and the business of the dissolved partnership is continued as set forth in paragraphs (1) and (2) of this section, with the consent of the retired partners or the representative of the deceased partner, but without any assignment of his right in partnership property, rights of creditors of the dissolved partnership and of the creditors of the person or partnership continuing the business shall be as if such assignment had been made.

(4) When all the partners or their representatives assign their rights in partnership property to one or more third persons who promise to pay the debts and who continue the business of the dissolved partnership, creditors of the dissolved partnership are also creditors of the person or partnership continuing the business.

(5) When any partner wrongfully causes a dissolution and the remaining partners continue the business under the provisions of section 38(2b), either alone or with others, and without

liquidation of the partnership affairs, creditors of the dissolved partnership are also creditors of the person or partnership continuing the business.

(6) When a partner is expelled and the remaining partners continue the business either alone or with others, without liquidation of the partnership affairs, creditors of the dissolved partnership are also creditors of the person or partnership continuing the business.

(7) The liability of a third person becoming a partner in the partnership continuing the business, under this section, to the creditors of the dissolved partnership shall be satisfied out of partnership property only.

(8) When the business of a partnership after dissolution is continued under any conditions set forth in this section the creditors of the dissolved partnership, as against the separate creditors of the retiring or deceased partner or the representative of the deceased partner, have a prior right to any claim of the retired partner or the representative of the deceased partner against the person or partnership continuing the business, on account of the retired or deceased partner's interest in the dissolved partnership or on account of any consideration promised for such interest or for his right in partnership property.

(9) Nothing in this section shall be held to modify any right of creditors to set aside any assignment on the ground of fraud.

(10) The use by the person or partnership continuing the business of the partnership name, or the name of a deceased partner as part thereof, shall not of itself make the individual property of the deceased partner liable for any debts contracted by such person or partnership.

Sec. 42. (Rights of Retiring or Estate of Deceased Partner When the Business is Continued.) When any partner retires or dies, and the business is continued under any of the conditions set forth in section 41(1, 2, 3, 5, 6), or section 38(2b), without any settlement of accounts as between him or his estate and the person or partnership continuing the business, unless otherwise agreed, he or his legal representative as against such persons or partnership may have the value of his interest at the date of dissolution ascertained, and shall receive as an ordinary creditor an amount equal to the value of his interest in the dissolved partnership with interest, or, at his option or at the option of his legal representative, in lieu of interest, the profits attributable to the use of his right in the property of the dissolved partnership; provided that the creditors of the dissolved partnership as against the separate creditors, or the representative of the retired or deceased partner, shall have priority on any claim arising under this section, as provided by section 41(8) of this act.

Sec. 43. (Accrual of Actions.) The right to an account of his interest shall accrue to any partner, or his legal representative, as against the winding up partners or the surviving partners or the person or partnership continuing the business, at the date of dissolution, in the absence of any agreement to the contrary.

PART VII
MISCELLANEOUS PROVISIONS

Sec. 44. (When Act Takes Effect.) This act shall take effect on the __________ day of __________ one thousand nine hundred and __________.

Sec. 45. (Legislation Repealed.) All acts or parts of acts inconsistent with this act are hereby repealed.

Model Business Corporation Act

(1969 Text as Amended to 1977)

§ 1. Short Title.

This Act shall be known and may be cited as the ". . . . . . Business Corporation Act."

§ 2. Definitions.

As used in this Act, unless the context otherwise requires, the term:

(a) "Corporation" or "domestic corporation" means a corporation for profit subject to the provisions of this Act, except a foreign corporation.

(b) "Foreign corporation" means a corporation for profit organized under laws other than the laws of this State for a purpose or purposes for which a corporation may be organized under this Act.

(c) "Articles of incorporation" means the original or restated articles of incorporation or articles of consolidation and all amendments thereto including articles of merger.

(d) "Shares" means the units into which the proprietary interests in a corporation are divided.

(e) "Subscriber" means one who subscribes for shares in a corporation, whether before or after incorporation.

(f) "Shareholder" means one who is a holder of record of shares in a corporation. If the articles of incorporation or the by-laws so provide, the board of directors may adopt by resolution a procedure whereby a shareholder of the corporation may certify in writing to the corporation that all or a portion of the shares registered in the name of such shareholder are held for the account of a specified person or persons. The resolution shall set forth (1) the classification of shareholder who may certify, (2) the purpose or purposes for which the certification may be made, (3) the form of certification and information to be contained therein, (4) if the certification is with respect to a record date or closing of the stock transfer books within which the certification must be received by the corporation and (5) such other provisions with respect to the procedure as are deemed necessary or desirable. Upon receipt by the corporation of a certification complying with the procedure, the persons specified in the certification shall be deemed, for the purpose or purposes set forth in the certification, to be the holders of record of the number of shares specified in place of the shareholder making the certification.

(g) "Authorized shares" means the shares of all classes which the corporation is authorized to issue.

(h) "Treasury shares" means shares of a corporation which have been issued, have been subsequently acquired by and belong to the corporation, and have not, either by reason of the acquisition or thereafter, been cancelled or restored to the status of authorized but unissued shares. Treasury shares shall be deemed to be "issued" shares, but not "outstanding" shares.

(i) "Net assets" means the amount by which the total assets of a corporation exceed the total debts of the corporation.

(j) "Stated capital" means, at any particular time, the sum of (1) the par value of all shares of the corporation having a par value that have been issued, (2) the amount of the consideration received by the corporation for all shares of the corporation without par value that have been issued, except such part of the consideration therefor as may have been allocated to capital surplus in a manner permitted by law, and (3) such amounts not included in clauses (1) and (2) of this paragraph as have been transferred to stated capital of the corporation, whether upon the issue of shares as a share dividend or otherwise, minus all reductions from such sum as have been effected in a manner permitted by law. Irrespective of the manner of designation thereof by the laws under which a foreign corporation is organized, the stated capital of a foreign corporation shall be determined on the same basis and in the same manner as the stated capital of a domestic corporation, for the purpose of computing fees, franchise taxes and other charges imposed by this Act.

(k) "Surplus" means the excess of the net assets of a corporation over its stated capital.

(l) "Earned surplus" means the portion of the surplus of a corporation equal to the balance of its net profits, income, gains and losses from the date of incorporation, or from the latest date when a deficit was eliminated by an application of its capital surplus or stated capital or otherwise, after deducting subsequent distributions to shareholders and transfers to stated capital and capital surplus to the extent such distributions and transfers are made out of earned surplus. Earned surplus shall include also any portion of surplus allocated to earned surplus in mergers, consolidations or acquisitions of all or substantially all of the outstanding shares or of the property and assets of another corporation, domestic or foreign.

(m) "Capital surplus" means the entire surplus of a corporation other than its earned surplus.

(n) "Insolvent" means inability of a corporation to pay its debts as they become due in the usual course of its business.

(o) "Employee" includes officers but not directors. A director may accept duties which make him also an employee.

§ 3. Purposes.

Corporations may be organized under this Act for any lawful purpose or purposes, except for the purpose of banking or insurance.

§ 4. General Powers.

Each corporation shall have power:

(a) To have perpetual succession by its corporate name unless a limited period of duration is stated in its articles of incorporation.

(b) To sue and be sued, complain and defend, in its corporate name.

(c) To have a corporate seal which may be altered at pleasure, and to use the same by causing it, or a facsimile thereof, to be impressed or affixed or in any other manner reproduced.

(d) To purchase, take, receive, lease, or otherwise acquire, own, hold, improve, use and otherwise deal in and with, real or personal property, or any interest therein, wherever situated.

(e) To sell, convey, mortgage, pledge, lease, exchange, transfer and otherwise dispose of all or any part of its property and assets.

(f) To lend money and use its credit to assist its employees.

(g) To purchase, take, receive, subscribe for, or otherwise acquire, own, hold, vote, use, employ, sell, mortgage, lend, pledge, or otherwise dispose of, and otherwise use and deal in and with, shares or other interests in, or obligations of, other domestic or foreign corporations, associations, partnerships or individuals, or direct or indirect obligations of the United States or of any other government, state, territory, governmental district or municipality or of any instrumentality thereof.

(h) To make contracts and guarantees and incur liabilities, borrow money at such rates of interest as the corporation may determine, issue its notes, bonds, and other obligations, and secure any of its obligations by mortgage or pledge of all or any of its property, franchises and income.

(i) To lend money for its corporate purposes, invest and reinvest its funds, and take and hold real and personal property as security for the payment of funds so loaned or invested.

(j) To conduct its business, carry on its operations and have offices and exercise the powers granted by this Act, within or without this State.

(k) To elect or appoint officers and agents of the corporation, and define their duties and fix their compensation.

(l) To make and alter by-laws, not inconsistent with its articles of incorporation or with the laws of this State, for the administration and regulation of the affairs of the corporation.

(m) To make donations for the public welfare or for charitable, scientific or educational purposes.

(n) To transact any lawful business which the board of directors shall find will be in aid of governmental policy.

(o) To pay pensions and establish pension plans, pension trusts, profit sharing plans, stock bonus plans, stock option plans and other incentive plans for any or all of its directors, officers and employees.

(p) To be a promoter, partner, member, associate, or manager of any partnership, joint venture, trust or other enterprise.

(q) To have and exercise all powers necessary or convenient to effect its purposes.

§ 5. Indemnification of Officers, Directors, Employees and Agents.

(a) A corporation shall have power to indemnify any person who was or is a party or is threatened to be made a party to any threatened, pending or completed action, suit or proceeding, whether civil, criminal, administrative or investigative (other than an action by or in the right of the corporation) by reason of the fact that he is or was a director, officer, employee or agent of the corporation, or is or was serving at the request of the corporation as a director, officer, employee or agent of another corporation, partnership, joint venture, trust or other enterprise, against expenses (including attorneys' fees), judgments, fines and amounts paid in settlement actually and reasonably incurred by him in connection with such action, suit or proceeding if he acted in good faith and in a manner he reasonably believed to be in or not opposed to the best interests of the corporation, and, with respect to any criminal action or proceeding, had no reasonable cause to believe his conduct was unlawful. The termination of any action, suit or proceeding by judgment, order, settlement, conviction, or upon a plea of nolo contendere or its equivalent, shall not, of itself, create a presumption that the person did not act in good faith and in a manner which he reasonably believed to be in or not opposed to the best interests of the corporation, and, with respect to any criminal action or proceeding, had reasonable cause to believe that his conduct was unlawful.

(b) A corporation shall have power to indemnify any person who was or is a party or is threatened to be made a party to any threatened, pending or completed action or suit by or in the right of the corporation to procure a judgment in its favor by reason of the fact that he is or was a director, officer, employee or agent of the corporation, or is or was serving at the request of the corporation as a director, officer, employee or agent of another corporation, partnership, joint venture, trust or other enterprise against expenses (including attorneys' fees) actually and reasonably incurred by him in connection with the defense or settlement of such action or suit if he acted in good faith and in a manner he reasonably believed to be in or not opposed to the best interests of the corporation and except that no indemnification shall be made in respect of any claim, issue or matter as to which such person shall have been adjudged to be liable for negligence or misconduct in the performance of his duty to the corporation unless and only to the extent that the court in which such action or suit was brought shall determine upon application that, despite the adjudication of liability but in view of all circumstances of the case, such person is fairly and reasonably entitled to indemnity for such expenses which such court shall deem proper.

(c) To the extent that a director, officer, employee or agent of a corporation has been successful on the merits or otherwise in defense of any action, suit or proceeding referred to in subsections (a) or (b), or in defense of any claim, issue or matter therein, he shall be indemnified against expenses (including attorneys' fees) actually and reasonably incurred by him in connection therewith.

(d) Any indemnification under subsections (a) or (b) (unless ordered by a court) shall be made by the corporation only as authorized in the specific case upon a determination that indemnification of the director, officer, employee or agent is proper in the circumstances because he has met the applicable standard of conduct set forth in subsections (a) or (b). Such determination shall be made (1) by the board of directors by a majority vote of a quorum consisting of directors who were not parties to such action, suit or proceeding, or (2) if such a quorum is not obtainable, or, even if obtainable a quorum of disinterested directors so directs, by independent legal counsel in a written opinion, or (3) by the shareholders.

(e) Expenses (including attorneys' fees) incurred in defending a civil or criminal action, suit or proceeding may be paid by the corporation in advance of the final disposition of such action, suit or proceeding as authorized in the manner provided in subsection (d) upon receipt of an undertaking by or on behalf of the director, officer, employee or agent to repay such amount unless it shall ultimately be determined that he is entitled to be indemnified by the corporation as authorized in this section.

(f) The indemnification provided by this section shall not be deemed exclusive of any other rights to which those indemnified may be entitled under any by-law, agreement, vote of shareholders or disinterested directors or otherwise, both as to action in his official capacity and as to action in another capacity while holding such office, and shall continue as to a person who has ceased to be a director, officer, employee or agent and shall inure to the benefit of the heirs, executors and administrators of such a person.

(g) A corporation shall have power to purchase and maintain insurance on behalf of any person who is or was a director, officer, employee or agent of the corporation, or is or was serving at the request of the corporation as a director, officer, employee or agent of another corporation, partnership, joint venture, trust or other enterprise against any liability asserted against him and incurred by him in any such capacity or arising out of his status as such, whether or not the corporation would have the power to indemnify him against such liability under the provisions of this section.

§ 6. Right of Corporation to Acquire and Dispose of Its Own Shares.

A corporation shall have the right to purchase, take, receive or otherwise acquire, hold, own, pledge, transfer or otherwise dispose of its own shares, but purchases of its own shares, whether direct or indirect, shall be made only to the extent of unreserved and unrestricted earned surplus available therefor, and, if the articles of incorporation so permit with the affirmative vote of the holders of a majority of all shares entitled to vote thereon, to the extent of unreserved and unrestricted capital surplus available therefor.

To the extent that earned surplus or capital surplus is used as the measure of the corporation's right to purchase its own shares, such surplus shall be restricted so long as such shares are held as treasury shares, and upon the disposition or cancellation of any such shares the restriction shall be removed pro tanto.

Notwithstanding the foregoing limitation, a corporation may purchase or otherwise acquire its own shares for the purpose of:

(a) Eliminating fractional shares.

(b) Collecting or compromising indebtedness to the corporation.

(c) Paying dissenting shareholders entitled to payment for their shares under the provisions of this Act.

(d) Effecting, subject to the other provisions of this Act, the retirement of its redeemable shares by redemption or by purchase at not to exceed the redemption price.

No purchase of or payment for its own shares shall be made at a time when the corporation is insolvent or when such purchase or payment would make it insolvent.

§ 7. Defense of Ultra Vires.

No act of a corporation and no conveyance or transfer of real or personal property to or by a corporation shall be invalid by reason of the fact that the corporation was without capacity or power to do such act or to make or receive such conveyance or transfer, but such lack of capacity or power may be asserted:

(a) In a proceeding by a shareholder against the corporation to enjoin the doing of any act or the transfer of real or personal property by or to the corporation. If the unauthorized act or transfer sought to be enjoined is being, or is to be, performed or made pursuant to a contract to which the corporation is a party, the court may, if all of the parties to the contract are parties to the proceeding and if it deems the same to be equitable, set aside and enjoin the performance of such contract, and in so doing may allow to the corporation or to the other parties to the contract, as the case may be, compensation for the loss or damage sustained by either of them which may result from the action of the court in setting aside and enjoining the performance of such contract, but anticipated profits to be derived from the performance of the contract shall not be awarded by the court as a loss or damage sustained.

(b) In a proceeding by the corporation, whether acting directly or through a receiver, trustee, or other legal representative, or through shareholders in a representative suit, against the incumbent or former officers or directors of the corporation.

(c) In a proceeding by the Attorney General, as provided in this Act, to dissolve the corporation, or in a proceeding by the Attorney General to enjoin the corporation from the transaction of unauthorized business.

§ 8. Corporate Name.

The corporate name:

(a) Shall contain the word "corporation," "company," "incorporated" or "limited," or shall contain an abbreviation of one of such words.

(b) Shall not contain any word or phrase which indicates or implies that it is organized for any purpose other than one or more of the purposes contained in its articles of incorporation.

(c) Shall not be the same as, or deceptively similar to, the name of any domestic corporation existing under the laws of this State or any foreign corporation authorized to transact business in this State, or a name the exclusive right to which is, at the time, reserved in the manner provided in this Act, or the name of a corporation which has in effect a registration of its corporate name as provided in this Act, except that this provision shall not apply if the applicant files with the Secretary of State either of the following: (1) the written consent of such other corporation or holder of a reserved or registered name to use the same or deceptively similar name and one or more words are added to make such name distinguishable from such other name, or (2) a certified copy of a final decree of a court of competent jurisdiction establishing the prior right of the applicant to the use of such name in this State.

A corporation with which another corporation, domestic or foreign, is merged, or which is formed by the reorganization or consolidation of one or more domestic or foreign corporations or upon a sale, lease or other disposition to or exchange with, a domestic corporation of all or substantially all the assets of another corporation, domestic or foreign, including its name, may have the same name as that used in this State by any of such corporations if such other corporation was organized under the laws of, or is authorized to transact business in, this State.

§ 9. Reserved Name.

The exclusive right to the use of a corporate name may be reserved by:

(a) Any person intending to organize a corporation under this Act.

(b) Any domestic corporation intending to change its name.

(c) Any foreign corporation intending to make application for a certificate of authority to transact business in this State.

(d) Any foreign corporation authorized to transact business in this State and intending to change its name.

(e) Any person intending to organize a foreign corporation and intending to have such corporation make application for a certificate of authority to transact business in this State.

The reservation shall be made by filing with the Secretary of State an application to reserve a specified corporate name, executed by the applicant. If the Secretary of State finds that the name is available for corporate use, he shall reserve the same for the exclusive use of the applicant for a period of one hundred and twenty days.

The right to the exclusive use of a specified corporate name so reserved may be transferred to any other person or corporation by filing in the office of the Secretary of State a notice of such transfer, executed by the applicant for whom the name was reserved, and specifying the name and address of the transferee.

§ 10. Registered Name.

Any corporation organized and existing under the laws of any state or territory of the United States may register its corporate name under this Act, provided its corporate name is not the same as, or deceptively similar to, the name of any domestic corporation existing under the laws of this State, or the name of any foreign corporation authorized to transact business in this State, or any corporate name reserved or registered under this Act.

Such registration shall be made by:

(a) Filing with the Secretary of State (1) an application for registration executed by the corporation by an officer thereof, setting forth the name of the corporation, the state or territory under the laws of which it is incorporated, the date of its incorporation, a statement that it is carrying on or doing business, and a brief statement of the business in which it is engaged, and (2) a certificate setting forth that such corporation is in good standing under the laws of the state or territory wherein it is organized, executed by the Secretary of State of such state or territory or by such other official as may have custody of the records pertaining to corporations, and

(b) Paying to the Secretary of State a registration fee in the amount of . . . .

for each month, or fraction thereof, between the date of filing such application and December 31st of the calendar year in which such application is filed.

Such registration shall be effective until the close of the calendar year in which the application for registration is filed.

§ 11. Renewal of Registered Name. [*Text Omitted.*]

§ 12. Registered Office and Registered Agent.

Each corporation shall have and continuously maintain in this State:

(a) A registered office which may be, but need not be, the same as its place of business.

(b) A registered agent, which agent may be either an individual resident in this State whose business office is identical with such registered office, or a domestic corporation, or a foreign corporation authorized to transact business in this State, having a business office identical with such registered office.

§ 13. Change of Registered Office or Registered Agent. [*Text Omitted.*]

§ 14. Service of Process on Corporation.

The registered agent so appointed by a corporation shall be an agent of such corporation upon whom any process, notice or demand required or permitted by law to be served upon the corporation may be served.

Whenever a corporation shall fail to appoint or maintain a registered agent in this State, or whenever its registered agent cannot with reasonable diligence be found at the registered office, then the Secretary of State shall be an agent of such corporation upon whom any such process, notice, or demand may be served. Service on the Secretary of State of any such process, notice, or demand shall be made by delivering to and leaving with him, or with any clerk having charge of the corporation department of his office, duplicate copies of such process, notice or demand. In the event any such process, notice or demand is served on the Secretary of State, he shall immediately cause one of the copies thereof to be forwarded by registered mail, addressed to the corporation at its registered office. Any service so had on the Secretary of State shall be returnable in not less than thirty days.

The Secretary of State shall keep a record of all processes, notices and demands served upon him under this section, and shall record therein the time of such service and his action with reference thereto.

Nothing herein contained shall limit or affect the right to serve any process, notice or demand required or permitted by law to be served upon a corporation in any other manner now or hereafter permitted by law.

§ 15. Authorized Shares.

Each corporation shall have power to create and issue the number of shares stated in its articles of incorporation. Such shares may be divided into one or more classes, any or all of which classes may consist of shares with par value or shares without par value, with such designations, preferences, limitations, and relative rights as shall be stated in the articles of incorporation. The articles of incorporation may limit or deny the voting rights of or provide special voting rights for the shares of any class to the extent not inconsistent with the provisions of this Act.

Without limiting the authority herein contained, a corporation, when so provided in its articles of incorporation, may issue shares of preferred or special classes:

(a) Subject to the right of the corporation to redeem any of such shares at the price fixed by the articles of incorporation for the redemption thereof.

(b) Entitling the holders thereof to cumulative, noncumulative or partially cumulative dividends.

(c) Having preference over any other class or classes of shares as to the payment of dividends.

(d) Having preference in the assets of the corporation over any other class or classes of shares upon the voluntary or involuntary liquidation of the corporation.

(e) Convertible into shares of any other class or into shares of any series of the same or any other class, except a class having prior or superior rights and preferences as to dividends or distribution of assets upon liquidation, but shares without par value shall not be converted into shares with par value unless that part of the stated capital of the corporation represented by such shares without par value is, at the time of conversion, at least equal to the aggregate par value of the shares into which the shares without par value are to be converted or the amount of any such deficiency is transferred from surplus to stated capital.

§ 16. Issuance of Shares of Preferred or Special Classes in Series.

If the articles of incorporation so provide, the shares of any preferred or special class may be divided into and issued in series. If the shares of any such class are to be issued in series, then each series shall be so designated as to distinguish the shares thereof from the shares of all other series and classes. Any or all of the series of any such class and the variations in the relative rights and preferences as between different series may be fixed and determined by the articles of incorporation, but all shares of the same class shall be identical except as to the following relative rights and preferences, as to which there may be variations between different series:

(A) The rate of dividend.

(B) Whether shares may be redeemed and, if so, the redemption price and the terms and conditions of redemption.

(C) The amount payable upon shares in event of voluntary and involuntary liquidation.

(D) Sinking fund provisions, if any, for the redemption or purchase of shares.

(E) The terms and conditions, if any, on which shares may be converted.

(F) Voting rights, if any.

If the articles of incorporation shall expressly vest authority in the board of directors, then, to the extent that the articles of incorporation shall not have established series and fixed and determined the variations in the relative rights and preferences as between series, the board of directors shall have authority to divide any or all of such classes into series and, within the limitations set forth in this section and in the articles of incorporation, fix and determine the relative rights and preferences of the shares of any series so established.

In order for the board of directors to establish a series, where authority so to do is contained in the articles of incorporation, the board of directors shall adopt a resolution setting forth the designation of the series and fixing and determining the relative rights and preferences thereof, or so much thereof as shall not be fixed and determined by the articles of incorporation.

Prior to the issue of any shares of a series established by resolution adopted by the board of directors, the corporation shall file in the office of the Secretary of State a statement setting forth:

(a) The name of the corporation.

(b) A copy of the resolution establishing and designating the series, and fixing and determining the relative rights and preferences thereof.

(c) The date of adoption of such resolution.

(d) That such resolution was duly adopted by the board of directors.

Such statement shall be executed in duplicate by the corporation by its president or a vice president and by its secretary or an assistant secretary, and verified by one of the officers signing such statement, and shall be delivered to the Secretary of State. If the Secretary of State finds that such statement conforms to law, he shall, when all franchise taxes and fees have been paid as in this Act prescribed:

(1) Endorse on each of such duplicate originals the word "Filed," and the month, day, and year of the filing thereof.

(2) File one of such duplicate originals in his office.

(3) Return the other duplicate original to the corporation or its representative.

Upon the filing of such statement by the Secretary of State, the resolution establishing and designating the series and fixing and determining the relative rights and preferences thereof shall become effective and shall constitute an amendment of the articles of incorporation.

§ 17. Subscriptions for Shares.

A subscription for shares of a corporation to be organized shall be irrevocable for a period of six months, unless otherwise provided by the terms of the subscription agreement or unless all of the subscribers consent to the revocation of such subscription.

Unless otherwise provided in the subscription agreement, subscriptions for shares, whether made before or after the organization of a corporation, shall be paid in full at such time, or in such installments and at such times, as shall be determined by the board of directors. Any call made by the board of directors for payment on subscriptions shall be uniform as to all shares of the same class or as to all shares of the same series, as the case may be. In case of default in the payment of any installment or call when such payment is due, the corporation may proceed to collect the amount due in the same manner as any debt due the corporation. The by-laws may prescribe other penalties for failure to pay installments or calls that may become due, but no penalty working a forfeiture of a subscription, or of the amounts paid thereon, shall be declared as against any subscriber unless the amount due thereon shall remain unpaid for a period of twenty days after written demand has been made therefor. If mailed, such written demand shall be deemed to be made when deposited in the United States mail in a sealed envelope addressed to the subscriber at his last post-office address known to the corporation, with postage thereon prepaid. In the event of the sale of any shares by reason of any forfeiture, the excess of proceeds realized over the amount due and unpaid on such shares shall be paid to the delinquent subscriber or to his legal representative.

§ 18. Consideration for Shares.

Shares having a par value may be issued for such consideration expressed in dollars, not less than the par value thereof, as shall be fixed from time to time by the board of directors.

Shares without par value may be issued for such consideration expressed in dollars as may be fixed from time to time by the board of directors unless the articles of incorporation reserve to the shareholders the right to fix the consideration. In the event that such right be reserved as to any shares, the shareholders shall, prior to the issuance of such shares, fix the consideration to be received for such shares, by a vote of the holders of a majority of all shares entitled to vote thereon.

Treasury shares may be disposed of by the corporation for such consideration expressed in dollars as may be fixed from time to time by the board of directors.

That part of the surplus of a corporation which is transferred to stated capital upon the issuance of shares as a share dividend shall be deemed to be the consideration for the issuance of such shares.

In the event of the issuance of shares upon the conversion or exchange of indebtedness or shares, the consideration for the shares so issued shall be (1) the principal sum of, and accrued interest on, the indebtedness so exchanged or converted, or the stated capital then represented by the shares so exchanged or converted, and (2) that part of surplus, if any, transferred to stated capital upon the issuance of shares for the shares so exchanged or converted, and (3) any additional consideration paid to the corporation upon the issuance of shares for the indebtedness or shares so exchanged or converted.

§ 19. Payment for Shares.

The consideration for the issuance of shares may be paid, in whole or in part, in money, in other property, tangible or intangible, or in labor or services actually performed for the corporation. When payment of the consideration for which shares are to be issued shall have been received by the corporation, such shares shall be deemed to be fully paid and nonassessable.

Neither promissory notes nor future services shall constitute payment or part payment for the issuance of shares of a corporation.

In the absence of fraud in the transaction, the judgment of the board of directors or the shareholders, as the case may be, as to the value of the consideration received for shares shall be conclusive.

§ 20. Stock Rights and Options.

Subject to any provisions in respect thereof set forth in its articles of incorporation, a corporation may create and issue, whether or not in connection with the issuance and sale of any of its shares or other securities, rights or options entitling the holders thereof to purchase from the corporation shares of any class or classes. Such rights or options shall be evidenced in such manner as the board of directors shall approve and, subject to the provisions of the articles of incorporation, shall set forth the terms upon which, the time or times within which and the price or prices at which such shares may be purchased from the corporation upon the exercise of any such right or option. If such rights or options are to be issued to directors, officers or employees as such of the corporation or of any subsidiary thereof, and not to the shareholders generally, their issuance shall be approved by the affirmative vote of the holders of a majority of the shares entitled to vote thereon or shall be authorized by and consistent with a plan approved or ratified by such a vote of shareholders. In the absence of fraud in the transaction, the judgment of the board of directors as to the adequacy of the consideration received for such rights or options shall be conclusive. The price or prices to be received for any shares having a par value, other than treasury shares to be issued upon the exercise of such rights or options, shall not be less than the par value thereof.

§ 21. Determination of Amount of Stated Capital.

In case of the issuance by a corporation of shares having a par value, the consideration received therefor shall constitute stated capital to the extent of the par value of such shares, and the excess, if any, of such consideration shall constitute capital surplus.

In case of the issuance by a corporation of shares without par value, the entire consideration received therefor shall constitute stated capital unless the corporation shall determine as provided in this section that only a part thereof shall be stated capital. Within a period of sixty days after the issuance of any shares without par value, the board of directors may allocate to capital surplus any portion of the consideration received for the issuance of such shares. No such allocation shall be made of any portion of the consideration received for shares without par value having a preference in the assets of the corporation in the event of involuntary liquidation except the amount, if any, of such consideration in excess of such preference.

If shares have been or shall be issued by a corporation in merger or consolidation or in acquisition of all or substantially all of the outstanding shares or of the property and assets of another corporation, whether domestic or foreign, any amount that would otherwise constitute capital surplus under the foregoing provisions of this section may instead be allocated to earned surplus by the board of directors of the issuing corporation except that its aggregate earned surplus shall not exceed the sum of the earned surpluses as defined in this Act of the issuing corporation and of all other corporations, domestic or foreign, that were merged or consolidated or of which the shares or assets were acquired.

The stated capital of a corporation may be increased from time to time by resolution of the board of directors directing that all or a part of the surplus of the corporation be transferred to stated capital. The board of directors may direct that the amount of the surplus so transferred shall be deemed to be stated capital in respect of any designated class of shares.

§ 22. Expenses of Organization, Reorganization and Financing.

The reasonable charges and expenses of organization or reorganization of a corporation, and the reasonable expenses of and compensation for the sale or underwriting of its shares, may be paid or allowed by such corporation out of the consideration received by it in payment for its shares without thereby rendering such shares not fully paid or assessable.

§ 23. Certificates Representing Shares.

The shares of a corporation shall be represented by certificates signed by the president or a vice president and the secretary or an assistant secretary of the corporation, and may be sealed with the seal of the corporation or a facsimile thereof. The signatures of the president or vice president and the secretary or assistant secretary upon a certificate may be facsimiles if the certificate is manually signed on behalf of a transfer agent or a registrar, other than the corporation itself or an employee of the corporation. In case any officer who has signed or whose facsimile signature has been placed upon such certificate shall have ceased to be such officer before such certificate is issued, it may be issued by the corporation with the same effect as if he were such officer at the date of its issue.

Every certificate representing shares issued by a corporation which is authorized to issue shares of more than one class shall set forth upon the face or back of the certificate, or shall state that the corporation will furnish to any shareholder upon request and without charge, a full statement of the designtions, preferences, limitations, and relative rights of the shares of each class authorized to be issued, and if the corporation is authorized to issue any preferred or special class in series, the variations in the relative rights and preferences between the shares of each such series so far as the same have been fixed and determined and the authority of the board of directors to fix and determine the relative rights and preferences of subsequent series.

Each certificate representing shares shall state upon the face thereof:

(a) That the corporation is organized under the laws of this State.

(b) The name of the person to whom issued.

(c) The number and class of shares, and the designation of the series, if any, which such certificate represents.

(d) The par value of each share represented by such certificate, or a statement that the shares are without par value.

No certificate shall be issued for any share until such share is fully paid.

§ 24. Fractional Shares.

A corporation may (1) issue fractions of a share, (2) arrange for the disposition of fractional interests by those entitled thereto, (3) pay in cash the fair value of fractions of a share as of the time when those entitled to receive such fractions are determined, or (4) issue scrip in registered or bearer form which shall entitle the holder to receive a certificate for a full share upon the surrender of such scrip aggregating a full share. A certificate for a fractional share shall, but scrip shall not unless otherwise provided therein, entitle the holder to exercise voting rights, to receive dividends thereon, and to participate in any of the assets of the corporation in the event of liquidation. The board of directors may cause scrip to be issued subject to the condition that it shall become void if not exchanged for certificates representing full shares before a specified date, or subject to the condition that the shares for which scrip is exchangeable may be sold by the corporation and the proceeds thereof distributed to the holders of scrip, or subject to any other conditions which the board of directors may deem advisable.

§ 25. Liability of Subscribers and Shareholders.

A holder of or subscriber to shares of a corporation shall be under no obligation to the corporation or its creditors with respect to such shares other than the obligation to pay to the corporation the full consideration for which such shares were issued or to be issued.

Any person becoming an assignee or transferee of shares or of a subscription for shares in good faith and without knowledge or notice that the full consideration therefor has not been paid shall not be personally liable to the corporation or its creditors for any unpaid portion of such consideration.

An executor, administrator, conservator, guardian, trustee, assignee for the benefit of creditors, or receiver shall not be personally liable to the corporation as a holder of or subscriber to shares of a corporation but the estate and funds in his hands shall be so liable.

No pledgee or other holder of shares as collateral security shall be personally liable as a shareholder.

§ 26. Shareholders' Preemptive Rights.

The shareholders of a corporation shall have no preemptive right to acquire unissued or treasury shares of the corporation, or securities of the corporation convertible into or carrying a right to subscribe to or acquire shares, except to the extent, if any, that such right is provided in the articles of incorporation.

§ 26A. Shareholders' Preemptive Rights [Alternative].

Except to the extent limited or denied by this section or by the articles of incorporation, shareholders shall have a preemptive right to acquire unissued or treasury shares or securities convertible into such shares or carrying a right to subscribe to or acquire shares.

Unless otherwise provided in the articles of incorporation,

(a) No preemptive right shall exist

(1) to acquire any shares issued to directors, officers or employees pursuant to approval by the affirmative vote of the holders of a majority of the shares entitled to vote thereon or when authorized by and consistent with a plan theretofore approved by such a vote of shareholders; or

(2) to acquire any shares sold otherwise than for cash.

(b) Holders of shares of any class that is preferred or limited as to dividends or assets shall not be entitled to any preemptive right.

(c) Holders of shares of common stock shall not be entitled to any preemptive right to shares of any class that is preferred or limited as to dividends or assets or to any obligations, unless convertible into shares of common stock or carrying a right to subscribe to or acquire shares of common stock.

(d) Holders of common stock without voting power shall have no preemptive right to shares of common stock with voting power.

(e) The preemptive right shall be only an opportunity to acquire shares or other securities under such terms and conditions as the board of directors may fix for the purpose of providing a fair and reasonable opportunity for the exercise of such right.

§ 27. By-Laws.

The initial by-laws of a corporation shall be adopted by its board of directors. The power to alter, amend or repeal the bylaws or adopt new by-laws, subject to repeal or change by action of the shareholders, shall be vested in the board of directors unless reserved to the shareholders by the articles of incorporation. The by-laws may contain any provisions for the regulation and management of the affairs of the corporation not inconsistent with law or the articles of incorporation.

§ 27A. By-Laws and Other Powers in Emergency [Optional].

The board of directors of any corporation may adopt emergency by-laws, subject to repeal or change by action of the shareholders, which shall, notwithstanding any different provision elsewhere in this Act or in the articles of incorporation or bylaws, be operative during any emergency in the conduct of the business of the corporation resulting from an attack on the United States or any nuclear or atomic disaster. The emergency by-laws may make any provision that may be practical and necessary for the circumstances of the emergency, including provisions that:

(a) A meeting of the board of directors may be called by any officer or director in such manner and under such conditions as shall be prescribed in the emergency by-laws;

(b) The director or directors in attendance at the meeting, or any greater number fixed by the emergency by-laws, shall constitute a quorum; and

(c) The officers or other persons designated on a list approved by the board of directors before the emergency, all in such order of priority and subject to such conditions, and for such period of time (not longer than reasonably necessary after the termination of the emergency) as may be provided in the emergency by-laws or in the resolution approving the list shall, to the extent required to provide a quorum at any meeting of the board of directors, be deemed directors for such meeting.

The board of directors, either before or during any such emergency, may provide, and from time to time modify, lines of succession in the event that during such an emergency any or all officers or agents of the corporation shall for any reason be rendered incapable of discharging their duties.

The board of directors, either before or during any such emergency, may, effective in the emergency, change the head office or designate several alternative head offices or regional offices, or authorize the officers so to do.

To the extent not inconsistent with any emergency by-laws so adopted, the by-laws of the corporation shall remain in effect during any such emergency and upon its termination the emergency by-laws shall cease to be operative.

Unless otherwise provided in emergency by-laws, notice of any meeting of the board of directors during any such emergency may be given only to such of the directors as it may be feasible to reach at the time and by such means as may be feasible at the time, including publication or radio.

To the extent required to constitute a quorum at any meeting of the board of directors during any such emergency, the officers of the corporation who are present shall, unless otherwise provided in emergency by-laws, be deemed, in order of rank and within the same rank in order of seniority, directors for such meeting.

No officer, director or employee acting in accordance with any emergency by-laws shall be liable except for willful misconduct. No officer, director or employee shall be liable for any action taken by him in good faith in such an emergency in furtherance of the ordinary business affairs of the corporation even though not authorized by the by-laws then in effect.

§ 28. Meetings of Shareholders.

Meetings of shareholders may be held at such place within or without this State as may be stated in or fixed in accordance with the by-laws. If no other place is stated or so fixed, meetings shall be held at the registered office of the corporation.

An annual meeting of the shareholders shall be held at such time as may be stated in or fixed in accordance with the by-laws. If the annual meeting is not held within any thirteen-month period the Court of . . . . may, on the application of any shareholder, summarily order a meeting to be held.

Special meetings of the shareholders may be called by the board of directors, the holders of not less than one-tenth of all the shares entitled to vote at the meeting, or such other persons as may be authorized in the articles of incorporation or the by-laws.

§ 29. Notice of Shareholders' Meetings.

Written notice stating the place, day and hour of the meeting and, in case of a special meeting, the purpose or purposes for which the meeting is called, shall be delivered not less than ten nor more than fifty days before the date of the meeting, either personally or by mail, by or at the direction of the president, the secretary, or the officer or persons calling the meeting, to each shareholder of record entitled to vote at such meeting. If mailed, such notice shall be deemed to be delivered when deposited in the United States mail addressed to the shareholder at his address as it appears on the stock transfer books of the corporation, with postage thereon prepaid.

§ 30. Closing of Transfer Books and Fixing Record Date.

For the purpose of determining shareholders entitled to notice of or to vote at any meeting of shareholders or any adjournment thereof, or entitled to receive payment of any dividend, or in order to make a determination of shareholders for any other proper purpose, the board of directors of a corporation may provide that the stock transfer books shall be closed for a stated period but not to exceed, in any case, fifty days. If the stock transfer books shall be closed for the purpose of determining shareholders entitled to notice of or to vote at a meeting of shareholders, such books shall be closed for at least ten days immediately preceding such meeting. In lieu of closing the stock transfer books, the by-laws, or in the absence of an applicable by-law the board of directors, may fix in advance a date as the record date for any such determination of shareholders, such date in any case to be not more than fifty days and, in case of a meeting of shareholders, not less than ten days prior to the date on which the particular action, requiring such determination of shareholders, is to be taken. If the stock transfer books are not closed and no record date is fixed for the determination of shareholders entitled to notice of or to vote at a meeting of shareholders, or shareholders entitled to receive payment of a dividend, the date on which notice of the meeting is mailed or the date on which the resolution of the board of directors declaring such dividend is adopted, as the case may be, shall be the record date for such determination of shareholders. When a determination of shareholders entitled to vote at any meeting of shareholders has been made as provided in this section, such determination shall apply to any adjournment thereof.

§ 31. Voting Record.

The officer or agent having charge of the stock transfer books for shares of a corporation shall make a complete record of the shareholders entitled to vote at such meeting or any adjournment thereof, arranged in alphabetical order, with the address of and the number of shares held by each. Such record shall be produced and kept open at the time and place of the meeting and shall be subject to the inspection of any shareholder during the whole time of the meeting of the purposes thereof.

Failure to comply with the requirements of this section shall not affect the validity of any action taken at such meeting.

An officer or agent having charge of the stock transfer books who shall fail to prepare the record of shareholders, or produce and keep it open for inspection at the meeting, as provided in this section, shall be liable to any shareholder suffering damage on account of such failure, to the extent of such damage.

§ 32. Quorum of Shareholders.

Unless otherwise provided in the articles of incorporation, a majority of the shares entitled to vote, represented in person or by proxy, shall constitute a quorum at a meeting of shareholders, but in no event shall a quorum consist of less than one-third of the shares entitled to vote at the meeting. If a quorum is present, the affirmative vote of the majority of the shares represented at the meeting and entitled to vote on the subject matter shall be the act of the shareholders, unless the vote of a greater number or voting by classes is required by this Act or the articles of incorporation or by-laws.

§ 33. Voting of Shares.

Each outstanding share, regardless of class, shall be entitled to one vote on each matter submitted to a vote at a meeting of shareholders, except as may be otherwise provided in the articles of incorporation. If the articles of incorporation provide for more or less than one vote for any share, on any matter, every reference in this Act to a majority or other proportion of shares shall refer to such a majority or other proportion of votes entitled to be cast.

Neither treasury shares, nor shares held by another corporation if a majority of the shares entitled to vote for the election of directors of such other corporation is held by the corporation, shall be voted at any meeting or counted in determining the total number of outstanding shares at any given time.

A shareholder may vote either in person or by proxy executed in writing by the shareholder or by his duly authorized attorney-in-fact. No proxy shall be valid after eleven months from the date of its execution, unless otherwise provided in the proxy.

[Either of the following prefatory phrases may be inserted here: "The articles of incorporation may provide that" or "Unless the articles of incorporation otherwise provide"] . . . at each election for directors every shareholder entitled to vote at such election shall have the right to vote, in person or by proxy, the number of shares owned by him for as many persons as there are directors to be elected and for whose election he has a right to vote, or to cumulate his votes by giving one candidate as many votes as the number of such directors multiplied by the number of his shares shall equal, or by distributing such votes on the same principle among any number of such candidates.

Shares standing in the name of another corporation, domestic or foreign, may be voted by such officer, agent or proxy as the by-laws of such other corporation may prescribe, or, in the absence of such provision, as the board of directors of such other corporation may determine.

Shares held by an administrator, executor, guardian or conservator may be voted by him, either in person or by proxy, without a transfer of such shares into his name. Shares standing in the name of a trustee may be voted by him, either in person or by proxy, but no trustee shall be entitled to vote shares held by him without a transfer of such shares into his name.

Shares standing in the name of a receiver may be voted by such receiver, and shares held by or under the control of a receiver may be voted by such receiver without the transfer thereof into his name if authority so to do be contained in an appropriate order of the court by which such receiver was appointed.

A shareholder whose shares are pledged shall be entitled to vote such shares until the shares have been transferred into the name of the pledgee, and thereafter the pledgee shall be entitled to vote the shares so transferred.

On and after the date on which written notice of redemption of redeemable shares has been mailed to the holders thereof and a sum sufficient to redeem such shares has been deposited with a bank or trust company with irrevocable instruction and authority to pay the redemption price to the holders thereof upon surrender of certificates therefor, such shares shall not be entitled to vote on any matter and shall not be deemed to be outstanding shares.

§ 34. Voting Trusts and Agreements Among Shareholders.

Any number of shareholders of a corporation may create a voting trust for the purpose of conferring upon a trustee or trustees the right to vote or otherwise represent their shares, for a period of not to exceed ten years, by entering into a written voting trust agreement specifying the terms and conditions of the voting trust, by depositing a counterpart of the agreement with the corporation at its registered office, and by transferring their shares to such trustee or trustees for the purposes of the agreement. Such trustee or trustees shall keep a record of the holders of voting trust certificates evidencing a beneficial interest in the voting trust, giving the names and addresses of all such holders and the number and class of the shares in respect of which the voting trust certificates held by each are issued, and shall deposit a copy of such record with the corporation at its registered office. The counterpart of the voting trust agreement and the copy of such record so deposited with the corporation shall be subject to the same right of examination by a shareholder of the corporation, in person or by agent or attorney, as are the books and records of the corporation, and such counterpart and such copy of such record shall be subject to examination by any holder of record of voting trust certificates, either in person or by agent or attorney, at any reasonable time for any proper purpose.

Agreements among shareholders regarding the voting of their shares shall be valid and enforceable in accordance with their terms. Such agreements shall not be subject to the provisions of this section regarding voting trusts.

§ 35. Board of Directors.

All corporate powers shall be exercised by or under authority of, and the business and affairs of a corporation shall be managed under the direction of, a board of directors except as may be otherwise provided in this Act or the articles of incorporation. If any such provision is made in the articles of incorporation, the powers and duties conferred or imposed upon the board of directors by this Act shall be exercised or performed to such extent and by such person or persons as shall be provided in the articles of incorporation. Directors need not be residents of this State or shareholders of the corporation unless the articles of incorporation or by-laws so require. The articles of incorporation or by-laws may prescribe other qualifications for directors. The board of directors shall have authority to fix the compensation of directors unless otherwise provided in the articles of incorporation.

A director shall perform his duties as a director, including his duties as a member of any committee of the board upon which he may serve, in good faith, in a manner he reasonably believes to be in the best interests of the corporation, and with such care as an ordinarily prudent person in a like position would use under similar circumstances. In performing his duties, a director shall be entitled to rely on information, opinions, reports or statements, including financial statements and other financial data, in each case prepared or presented by:

(a) one or more officers or employees of the corporation whom the director reasonably believes to be reliable and competent in the matters presented,

(b) counsel, public accountants or other persons as to matters which the director reasonably believes to be within such person's professional or expert competence, or

(c) a committee of the board upon which he does not serve, duly designated in accordance with a provision of the articles of incorporation or the by-laws, as to matters within its designated authority, which committee the director reasonably believes to merit confidence,

but he shall not be considered to be acting in good faith if he has knowledge concerning the matter in question that would cause such reliance to be unwarranted. A person who so performs his duties shall have no liability by reason of being or having been a director of the corporation.

A director of a corporation who is present at a meeting of its board of directors at which action on any corporate matter is taken shall be presumed to have assented to the action taken unless his dissent shall be entered in the minutes of the meeting or unless he shall file his written dissent to such action with the secretary of the meeting before the adjournment thereof or shall forward such dissent by registered mail to the secretary of the corporation immediately after the adjournment of the meeting. Such right to dissent shall not apply to a director who voted in favor of such action.

§ 36. Number and Election of Directors.

The board of directors of a corporation shall consist of one or more members. The number of directors shall be fixed by, or in the manner provided in, the articles of incorporation or the by-laws, except as to the number constituting the initial board of directors, which number shall be fixed by the articles of incorporation. The number of directors may be increased or decreased from time to time by amendment to, or in the manner provided in, the articles of incorporation or the by-laws, but no decrease shall have the effect of shortening the term of any incumbent director. In the absence of a by-law providing for the number of directors, the number shall be the same as that provided for in the articles of incorporation. The names and addresses of the members of the first board of directors shall be stated in the articles of incorporation. Such persons shall hold office until the first annual meeting of shareholders, and until their successors shall have been elected and qualified. At the first annual meeting of shareholders and at each annual meeting thereafter the shareholders shall elect directors to hold office until the next succeeding annual meeting, except in case of the classification of directors as permitted by this Act. Each director shall hold office for the term for which he is elected and until his successor shall have been elected and qualified.

§ 37. Classification of Directors.

When the board of directors shall consist of nine or more members, in lieu of electing the whole number of directors annually, the articles of incorporation may provide that the directors be divided into either two or three classes, each class to be as nearly equal in number as possible, the term of office of directors of the first class to expire at the first annual meeting of shareholders after their election, that of the second class to expire at the second annual meeting after their election, and that of the third class, if any, to expire at the third annual meeting after their election. At each annual meeting after such classification the number of directors equal to the number of the class whose term expires at the time such meeting shall be elected to hold office until the second succeeding annual meeting, if there be two classes, or until the third succeeding annual meeting, if there be three classes. No classification of directors shall be effective prior to the first annual meeting of shareholders.

§ 38. Vacancies.

Any vacancy occurring in the board of directors may be filled by the affirmative vote of a majority of the remaining directors though less than a quorum of the board of directors. A director elected to fill a vacancy shall be elected for the unexpired term of his predecessor in office. Any directorship to be filled by reason of an increase in the number of directors may be filled by the board of directors for a term of office continuing only until the next election of directors by the shareholders.

§ 39. Removal of Directors.

At a meeting of shareholders called expressly for that purpose, directors may be removed in the manner provided in this section. Any director or the entire board of directors may be removed, with or without cause, by a vote of the holders of a majority of the shares then entitled to vote at an election of directors.

In the case of a corporation having cumulative voting, if less than the entire board is to be removed, no one of the directors may be removed if the votes cast against his removal would be sufficient to elect him if then cumulatively voted at an election of the entire board of directors, or, if there be classes of directors, at an election of the class of directors of which he is a part.

Whenever the holders of the shares of any class are entitled to elect one or more directors by the provisions of the articles of incorporation, the provisions of this section shall apply, in respect to the removal of a director or directors so elected, to the vote of the holders of the outstanding shares of that class and not to the vote of the outstanding shares as a whole.

§ 40. Quorum of Directors.

A majority of the number of directors fixed by or in the manner provided in the by-laws or in the absence of a by-law fixing or providing for the number of directors, then of the number stated in the articles of incorporation, shall constitute a quorum for the transaction of business unless a greater number is required by the articles of incorporation or the by-laws. The act of the majority of the directors present at a meeting at which a quorum is present shall be the act of the board of directors, unless the act of a greater number is required by the articles of incorporation or the by-laws.

§ 41. Director Conflicts of Interest.

No contract or other transaction between a corporation and one or more of its directors or any other corporation, firm, association or entity in which one or more of its directors are directors or officers or are financially interested, shall be either void or voidable because of such relationship or interest or because such director or directors are present at the meeting of the board of directors or a committee thereof which authorizes, approves or ratifies such contract or transaction or because his or their votes are counted for such purpose, if:

(a) the fact of such relationship or interest is disclosed or known to the board of directors or committee which authorizes, approves or ratifies the contract or transaction by a vote or consent sufficient for the purpose without counting the votes or consents of such interested directors; or

(b) the fact of such relationship or interest is disclosed or known to the shareholders entitled to vote and they authorize, approve or ratify such contract or transaction by vote or written consent; or

(c) the contract or transaction is fair and reasonable to the corporation.

Common or interested directors may be counted in determining the presence of a quorum at a meeting of the board of directors or a committee thereof which authorizes, approves or ratifies such contract or transaction.

§ 42. Executive and Other Committees.

If the articles of incorporation or the by-laws so provide, the board of directors, by resolution adopted by a majority of the full board of directors, may designate from among its members an executive committee and one or more other committees each of which, to the extent provided in such resolution or in the articles of incorporation or the by-laws of the corporation, shall have and may exercise all the authority of the board of directors, except that no such committee shall have authority to (i) declare dividends or distributions, (ii) approve or recommend to shareholders actions or proposals required by this Act to be approved by shareholders, (iii) designate candidates for the office of director, for purposes of proxy solicitation or otherwise, or fill vacancies on the board of directors or any committee thereof, (iv) amend the by-laws, (v) approve a plan of merger not requiring shareholder approval, (vi) reduce earned or capital surplus, (vii) authorize or approve the reacquisition of shares unless pursuant to a general formula or method specified by the board of directors, or (viii) authorize or approve the issuance or sale of, or any contract to issue or sell, shares or designate the terms of a series of a class of shares, provided that the board of directors, having acted regarding general authorization for the issuance or sale of shares, or any contract therefor, and, in the case of a series, the designation thereof, may, pursuant to a general formula or method specified by the board by resolution or by adoption of a stock option or other plan, authorize a committee to fix the terms of any contract for the sale of the shares and to fix the terms upon which such shares may be issued or sold, including, without limitation, the price, the dividend rate, provisions for redemption, sinking fund, conversion, voting or preferential rights, and provisions for other features of a class of shares, or a series of a class of shares, with full power in such committee to adopt any final resolution setting forth all the terms thereof and to authorize the statement of the terms of a series for filing with the Secretary of State under this Act.

Neither the designation of any such committee, the delegation thereto of authority, nor action by such committee pursuant to such authority shall alone constitute compliance by any member of the board of directors, not a member of the committee in question, with his responsibility to act in good faith, in a manner he reasonably believes to be in the best interests of the corporation, and with such care as an ordinarily prudent person in a like position would use under similar circumstances.

§ 43. Place and Notice of Directors' Meetings; Committee Meetings

Meetings of the board of directors, regular or special, may be held either within or without this State.

Regular meetings of the board of directors or any committee designated thereby may be held with or without notice as prescribed in the by-laws. Special meetings of the board of directors or any committee designated thereby shall be held upon such notice as is prescribed in the by-laws. Attendance of a director at a meeting shall constitute a waiver of notice of such meeting, except where a director attends a meeting for the express purpose of objecting to the transaction of any business because the meeting is not lawfully called or convened. Neither the business to be transacted at, nor the purpose of, any regular or special meeting of the board of directors or any committee designated thereby need be specified in the notice or waiver of notice of such meeting unless required by the by-laws.

Except as may be otherwise restricted by the articles of incorporation or by-laws, members of the board of directors or any committee designated thereby may participate in a meeting of such board or committee by means of a conference telephone or similar communications equipment by means of which all persons participating in the meeting can hear each other at the same time and participation by such means shall constitute presence in person at a meeting.

§ 44. Action by Directors Without a Meeting.

Unless otherwise provided by the articles of incorporation or by-laws, any action required by this Act to be taken at a meeting of the directors of a corporation, or any action which may be taken at a meeting of the directors or of a committee, may be taken without a meeting if a consent in writing, setting forth the action so taken, shall be signed by all of the directors, or all of the members of the committee, as the case may be. Such consent shall have the same effect as a unanimous vote.

§ 45. Dividends.

The board of directors of a corporation may, from time to time, declare and the corporation may pay dividends in cash, property, or its own shares, except when the corporation is insolvent or when the payment thereof would render the corporation insolvent or when the declaration or payment thereof would be contrary to any restriction contained in the articles of incorporation, subject to the following provisions:

(a) Dividends may be declared and paid in cash or property only out of the unreserved and unrestricted earned surplus of the corporation, except as otherwise provided in this section.

[Alternative] (a) Dividends may be declared and paid in cash or property only out of the unreserved and unrestricted earned surplus of the corporation, or out of the unreserved and unrestricted net earnings of the current fiscal year and the next preceding fiscal year taken as a single period, except as otherwise provided in this section.

(b) If the articles of incorporation of a corporation engaged in the business of exploiting natural resources so provide, dividends may be declared and paid in cash out of the depletion reserves, but each such dividend shall be identified as a distribution of such reserves and the amount per share paid from such reserves shall be disclosed to the shareholders receiving the same concurrently with the distribution thereof.

(c) Dividends may be declared and paid in its own treasury shares.

(d) Dividends may be declared and paid in its own authorized but unissued shares out of any unreserved and unrestricted surplus of the corporation upon the following conditions:

(1) If a dividend is payable in its own shares having a par value, such shares shall be issued at not less than the par value thereof and there shall be transferred to stated capital at the time such dividend is paid an amount of surplus equal to the aggregate par value of the shares to be issued as a dividend.

(2) If a dividend is payable in its own shares without par value, such shares shall be issued at such stated value as shall be fixed by the board of directors by resolution adopted at the time such dividend is declared, and there shall be transferred to stated capital at the time such dividend is paid an amount of surplus equal to the aggregate stated value so fixed in respect of such shares; and the amount per share so transferred to stated capital shall be disclosed to the shareholders receiving such dividend concurrently with the payment thereof.

(e) No dividend payable in shares of any class shall be paid to the holders of shares of any other class unless the articles of incorporation so provide or such payment is authorized by the affirmative vote or the written consent of the holders of at least a majority of the outstanding shares of the class in which the payment is to be made.

A split-up or division of the issued shares of any class into a greater number of shares of the same class without increasing the stated capital of the corporation shall not be construed to be a share dividend within the meaning of this section.

§ 46. Distributions from Capital Surplus.

The board of directors of a corporation may, from time to time, distribute to its shareholders out of capital surplus of the corporation a portion of its assets, in cash or property, subject to the following provisions:

(a) No such distribution shall be made at a time when the corporation is insolvent or when such distribution would render the corporation insolvent.

(b) No such distribution shall be made unless the articles of incorporation so provide or such distribution is authorized by the affirmative vote of the holders of a majority of the outstanding shares of each class whether or not entitled to vote thereon by the provisions of the articles of incorporation of the corporation.

(c) No such distribution shall be made to the holders of any class of shares unless all cumulative dividends accrued on all preferred or special classes of shares entitled to preferential dividends shall have been fully paid.

(d) No such distribution shall be made to the holders of any class of shares which would reduce the remaining net assets of the corporation below the aggregate preferential amount payable in event of involuntary liquidation to the holders of shares having preferential rights to the assets of the corporation in the event of liquidation.

(e) Each such distribution, when made, shall be identified as a distribution from capital surplus and the amount per share disclosed to the shareholders receiving the same concurrently with the distribution thereof.

The board of directors of a corporation may also, from time to time, distribute to the holders of its outstanding shares having a cumulative preferential right to receive dividends, in discharge of their cumulative dividend rights, dividends payable in cash out of the capital surplus of the corporation, if at the time the corporation has no earned surplus and is not insolvent and would not thereby be rendered insolvent. Each such distribution when made, shall be identified as a payment of cumulative dividends out of capital surplus.

§ 47. Loans to Employees and Directors.

A corporation shall not lend money to or use its credit to assist its directors without authorization in the particular case by its shareholders, but may lend money to and use its credit to assist any employee of the corporation or of a subsidiary, including any such employee who is a director of the corporation, if the board of directors decides that such loan or assistance may benefit the corporation.

§ 48. Liability of Directors in Certain Cases.

In addition to any other liabilities, a director shall be liable in the following circumstances unless he complies with the standard provided in this Act for the performance of the duties of directors:

(a) A director who votes for or assents to the declaration of any dividend or other distribution of the assets of a corporation to its shareholders contrary to the provisions of this Act or contrary to any restrictions contained in the articles of incorporation, shall be liable to the corporation, jointly and severally with all other directors so voting or assenting, for the amount of such dividend which is paid or the value of such assets which are distributed in excess of the amount of such dividend or distribution which could have been paid or distributed without a violation of the provisions of this Act or the restrictions in the articles of incorporation.

(b) A director who votes for or assents to the purchase of the corporation's own shares contrary to the provisions of this Act shall be liable to the corporation, jointly and severally with all other directors so voting or assenting, for the amount of consideration paid for such shares which is in excess of the maximum amount which could have been paid therefor without a violation of the provisions of this Act.

(c) A director who votes for or assents to any distribution of assets of a corporation to its shareholders during the liquidation of the corporation without the payment and discharge of, or making adequate provision for, all known debts, obligations, and liabilities of the corporation shall be liable to the corporation, jointly and severally with all other directors so voting or assenting, for the value of such assets which are distributed, to the extent that such debts, obligations and liabilities of the corporation are not thereafter paid and discharged.

Any director against whom a claim shall be asserted under or pursuant to this section shall be asserted under or pursuant to this section for the payment of a dividend or other distribution of assets of a corporation and who shall be held liable thereon, shall be entitled to contribution from the shareholders who accepted or received any such dividend or assets, knowing such dividend or distribution to have been made in violation of this Act, in proportion to the amounts received by them.

Any director against whom a claim shall be asserted under or pursuant to this section shall be entitled to contribution from the other directors who voted for or assented to the action upon which the claim is asserted.

§ 49. Provisions Relating to Actions by Shareholders.

No action shall be brought in this State by a shareholder in the right of a domestic or foreign corporation unless the plaintiff was a holder of record of shares or of voting trust certificates therefor at the time of the transaction of which he complains, or his shares or voting trust certificates thereafter devolved upon him by operation of law from a person who was a holder of record at such time.

In any action hereafter instituted in the right of any domestic or foreign corporation by the holder or holders of record of shares of such corporation or of voting trust certificates therefor, the court having jurisdiction, upon final judgment and a finding that the action was brought without reasonable cause, may require the plaintiff or plaintiffs to pay to the parties named as defendant the reasonable expenses, including fees of attorneys, incurred by them in the defense of such action.

In any action now pending or hereafter instituted or maintained in the right of any domestic or foreign corporation by the holder or holders of record of less than five per cent of the outstanding shares of any class of such corporation or of voting trust certificates therefor, unless the shares or voting trust certificates so held have a market value in excess of twenty-five thousand dollars, the corporation in whose right such action is brought shall be entitled at any time before final judgment to require the plaintiff or plaintiffs to give security for the reasonable expenses, including fees of attorneys, that may be incurred by it in connection with such action or may be incurred by other parties named as defendant for which it may become legally liable. Market value shall be determined as of the date that the plaintiff institutes the action or, in the case of an intervenor, as of the date that he becomes a party to the action. The amount of such security may from time to time be increased or decreased, in the discretion of the court, upon showing that the security provided has or may become inadequate or is excessive. The corporation shall have recourse to such security in such amount as the court having jurisdiction shall determine upon the termination of such action, whether or not the court finds the action was brought without reasonable cause.

§ 50. Officers.

The officers of a corporation shall consist of a president, one or more vice presidents as may be prescribed by the by-laws, a secretary, and a treasurer, each of whom shall be elected by the board of directors at such time and in such manner as may be prescribed by the by-laws. Such other officers and assistant officers and agents as may be deemed necessary may be elected or appointed by the board of directors or chosen in such other manner as may be prescribed by the by-laws. Any two or more offices may be held by the same person, except the offices of president and secretary.

All officers and agents of the corporation, as between themselves and the corporation, shall have such authority and perform such duties in the management of the corporation as may be provided in the by-laws, or as may be determined by resolution of the board of directors not inconsistent with the by-laws.

§ 51. Removal of Officers.

Any officer or agent may be removed by the board of directors whenever in its judgment the best interests of the corporation will be served thereby, but such removal shall be without prejudice to the contract rights, if any, of the person so removed. Election or appointment of an officer or agent shall not of itself create contract rights.

§ 52. Books and Records.

Each corporation shall keep correct and complete books and records of account and shall keep minutes of the proceedings of its shareholders and board of directors and shall keep at its registered office or principal place of business, or at the office of its transfer agent or registrar, a record of its shareholders, giving the names and addresses of all shareholders and the number and class of the shares held by each. Any books, records and minutes may be in written form or in any other form capable of being converted into written form within a reasonable time.

Any person who shall have been a holder of record of shares or of voting trust certificates therefor at least six months immediately preceding his demand or shall be the holder of record of, or the holder of record of voting trust certificates for, at least five per cent of all the outstanding shares of the corporation, upon written demand stating the purpose thereof, shall have the right to examine, in person, or by agent or attorney, at any reasonable time or times, for any proper purpose its relevant books and records of account, minutes, and record of shareholders and to make extracts therefrom.

Any officer or agent who, or a corporation which, shall refuse to allow any such shareholder or holder of voting trust certificates, or his agent or attorney, so to examine and make extracts from its books and records of account, minutes, and record of shareholders, for any proper purpose, shall be liable to such shareholder or holder of voting trust certificates in a penalty of ten per cent of the value of the shares owned by such shareholder, or in respect of which such voting trust certificates are issued, in addition to any other damages or remedy afforded him by law. It shall be a defense to any action for penalties under this section that the person suing therefor has within two years sold or offered for sale any list of shareholders or of holders of voting trust certificates for shares of such corporation or any other corporation or has aided or abetted any person in procuring any list of shareholders or of holders of voting trust certificates for any such purpose, or has improperly used any information secured through any prior examination of the books and records of account, or minutes, or record of shareholders or of holders of voting trust certificates for shares of such corporation or any other corporation, or was not acting in good faith or for a proper purpose in making his demand.

Nothing herein contained shall impair the power of any court of competent jurisdiction, upon proof by a shareholder or holder of voting trust certificates of proper purpose, irrespective of the period of time during which such shareholder or holder of voting trust certificates shall have been a shareholder of record or a holder of record of voting trust certificates, and irrespective of the number of shares held by him or represented by voting trust certificates held by him, to compel the production for examination by such shareholder or holder of voting trust certificates of the books and records of account, minutes and record of shareholders of a corporation.

Upon the written request of any shareholder or holder of voting trust certificates for shares of a corporation, the corporation shall mail to such shareholder or holder of voting trust certificates its most recent financial statements showing in reasonable detail its assets and liabilities and the results of its operations.

§ 53. Incorporators.

One or more persons, or a domestic or foreign corporation, may act as incorporator or incorporators of a corporation by signing and delivering in duplicate to the Secretary of State articles of incorporation for such corporation.

§ 54. Articles of Incorporation.

The articles of incorporation shall set forth:

(a) The name of the corporation.

(b) The period of duration, which may be perpetual.

(c) The purpose or purposes for which the corporation is organized which may be stated to be, or to include, the transaction of any or all lawful business for which corporations may be incorporated under this Act.

(d) The aggregate number of shares which the corporation shall have authority to issue; if such shares are to consist of one class only, the par value of each of such shares, or a statement that all of such shares are without par value; or, if such shares are to be divided into classes, the number of shares of each class, and a statement of the par value of the shares of each such class or that such shares are to be without par value.

(e) If the shares are to be divided into classes, the designation of each class and a statement of the preferences, limitations and relative rights in respect of the shares of each class.

(f) If the corporation is to issue the shares of any preferred or special class in series, then the designation of each series and a statement of the variations in the relative rights and preferences as between series insofar as the same are to be fixed in the articles of incorporation, and a statement of any authority to be vested in the board of directors to establish series and fix and determine the variations in the relative rights and preferences as between series.

(g) If any preemptive right is to be granted to shareholders, the provisions therefor.

(h) Any provision, not inconsistent with law, which the incorporators elect to set forth in the articles of incorporation for the regulation of the internal affairs of the corporation, including any provision restricting the transfer of shares and any provision which under this Act is required or permitted to be set forth in the by-laws.

(i) The address of its initial registered office, and the name of its initial registered agent at such address.

(j) The number of directors constituting the initial board of directors and the names and addresses of the persons who are to serve as directors until the first annual meeting of shareholders or until their successors be elected and qualify.

(k) The name and address of each incorporator.

It shall not be necessary to set forth in the articles of incorporation any of the corporate powers enumerated in this Act.

§ 55. Filing of Articles of Incorporation.

Duplicate originals of the articles of incorporation shall be delivered to the Secretary of State. If the Secretary of State finds that the articles of incorporation conform to law, he shall, when all fees have been paid as in this Act prescribed:

(a) Endorse on each of such duplicate originals the word "Filed," and the month, day and year of the filing thereof.

(b) File one of such duplicate originals in his office.

(c) Issue a certificate of incorporation to which he shall affix the other duplicate original.

The certificate of incorporation, together with the duplicate original of the articles of incorporation affixed thereto by the Secretary of State, shall be returned to the incorporators or their representative.

§ 56. Effect of Issuance of Certificate of Incorporation.

Upon the issuance of the certificate of incorporation, the corporate existence shall begin, and such certificate of incorporation shall be conclusive evidence that all conditions precedent required to be performed by the incorporators have been complied with and that the corporation has been incorporated under this Act, except as against this State in a proceeding to cancel or revoke the certificate of incorporation or for involuntary dissolution of the corporation.

§ 57. Organization Meeting of Directors.

After the issuance of the certificate of incorporation an organization meeting of the board of directors named in the articles of incorporation shall be held, either within or without this State, at the call of a majority of the directors named in the articles of incorporation, for the purpose of adopting by-laws, electing officers and transacting such other business as may come before the meeting. The directors calling the meeting shall give at least three days' notice thereof by mail to each director so named, stating the time and place of the meeting.

§ 58. Right to Amend Articles of Incorporation.

A corporation may amend its articles of incorporation, from time to time, in any and as many respects as may be desired, so long as its articles of incorporation as amended contain only such provisions as might be lawfully contained in original articles of incorporation at the time of making such amendment, and, if a change in shares or the rights of shareholders, or an exchange, reclassification or cancellation of shares or rights of shareholders is to be made, such provisions as may be necessary to effect such change, exchange, reclassification or cancellation.

In particular, and without limitation upon such general power of amendment, a corporation may amend its articles of incorporation, from time to time, so as:

(a) To change its corporate name.

(b) To change its period of duration.

(c) To change, enlarge or diminish its corporate purposes.

(d) To increase or decrease the aggregate number of shares, or shares of any class, which the corporation has authority to issue.

(e) To increase or decrease the par value of the authorized shares of any class having a par value, whether issued or unissued.

(f) To exchange, classify, reclassify or cancel all or any part of its shares, whether issued or unissued.

(g) To change the designation of all or any part of its shares, whether issued or unissued, and to change the preferences, limitations, and the relative rights in respect of all or any part of its shares, whether issued or unissued.

(h) To change shares having the par value, whether issued or unissued, into the same or a different number of shares without par value, and to change shares without par value, whether issued or unissued, into the same or a different number of shares having a par value.

(i) To change the shares of any class, whether issued or unissued and whether with or without par value, into a different number of shares of the same class or into the same or a different number of shares, either with or without par value, of other classes.

(j) To create new classes of shares having rights and preferences either prior and superior or subordinate and inferior to the shares of any class then authorized, whether issued or unissued.

(k) To cancel or otherwise affect the right of the holders of the shares of any class to receive dividends which have accrued but have not been declared.

(l) To divide any preferred or special class of shares, whether issued or unissued, into series and fix and determine the designations of such series and the variations in the relative rights and preferences as between the shares of such series.

(m) To authorize the board of directors to establish, out of authorized but unissued shares, series of any preferred or special class of shares and fix and determine the relative rights and preferences of the shares of any series so established.

(n) To authorize the board of directors to fix and determine the relative rights and preferences of the authorized but unissued shares of series theretofore established in respect of which either the relative rights and preferences have not been fixed and determined or the relative rights and preferences theretofore fixed and determined are to be changed.

(o) To revoke, diminish, or enlarge the authority of the board of directors to establish series out of authorized but unissued shares of any preferred or special class and fix and determine the relative rights and preferences of the shares of any series so established.

(p) To limit, deny or grant to shareholders of any class the preemptive right to acquire additional or treasury shares of the corporation, whether then or thereafter authorized.

§ 59. Procedure to Amend Articles of Incorporation.

Amendments to the articles of incorporation shall be made in the following manner:

(a) The board of directors shall adopt a resolution setting forth the proposed amendment and, if shares have been issued, directing that it be submitted to a vote at a meeting of shareholders, which may be either the annual or a special meeting. If no shares have been issued, the amendment shall be adopted by resolution of the board of directors and the provisions for adoption by shareholders shall not apply. The resolution may incorporate the proposed amendment in restated articles of incorporation which contain a statement that except for the designated amendment the restated articles of incorporation correctly set forth without change the corresponding provisions of the articles of incorporation as theretofore amended, and that the restated articles of incorporation together with the designated amendment supersede the original articles of incorporation and all amendments thereto.

(b) Written notice setting forth the proposed amendment or a summary of the changes to be effected thereby shall be given to each shareholder of record entitled to vote thereon within the time and in the manner provided in this Act for the giving of notice of meetings of shareholders. If the meeting be an annual meeting, the proposed amendment of such summary may be included in the notice of such annual meeting.

(c) At such meeting a vote of the shareholders entitled to vote thereon shall be taken on the proposed amendment. The proposed amendment shall be adopted upon receiving the affirmative vote of the holders of a majority of the shares entitled to vote thereon, unless any class of shares is entitled to vote thereon as a class, in which event the proposed amendment shall be adopted upon receiving the affirmative vote of the holders of a majority of the shares of each class of shares entitled to vote thereon as a class and of the total shares entitled to vote thereon.

Any number of amendments may be submitted to the shareholders, and voted upon by them, at one meeting.

§ 60. Class Voting on Amendments.

The holders of the outstanding shares of a class shall be entitled to vote as a class upon a proposed amendment, whether or not entitled to vote thereon by the provisions of the articles of incorporation, if the amendment would:

(a) Increase or decrease the aggregate number of authorized shares of such class.

(b) Increase or decrease the par value of the shares of such class.

(c) Effect an exchange, reclassification or cancellation of all or part of the shares of such class.

(d) Effect an exchange, or create a right of exchange, of all or any part of the shares of another class into the shares of such class.

(e) Change the designations, preferences, limitations or relative rights of the shares of such class.

(f) Change the shares of such class, whether with or without par value, into the same or a different number of shares, either with or without par value, of the same class or another class or classes.

(g) Create a new class of shares having rights and preferences prior and superior to the shares of such class, or increase the rights and preferences or the number of authorized shares, of any class having rights and preferences prior or superior to the shares of such class.

(h) In the case of a preferred or special class of shares, divide the shares of such class into series and fix and determine the designation of such series and the variations in the relative rights and preferences between the shares of such series, or authorize the board of directors to do so.

(i) Limit or deny any existing preemptive rights of the shares of such class.

(j) Cancel or otherwise affect dividends on the shares of such class which have accrued but have not been declared.

§ 61. Articles of Amendment.

The articles of amendment shall be executed in duplicate by the corporation by its president or a vice president and by its secretary or an assistant secretary, and verified by one of the officers signing such articles, and shall set forth:

(a) The name of the corporation.

(b) The amendments so adopted.

(c) The date of the adoption of the amendment by the shareholders, or by the board of directors where no shares have been issued.

(d) The number of shares outstanding, and the number of shares entitled to vote thereon, and if the shares of any class are entitled to vote thereon as a class, the designation and number of outstanding shares entitled to vote thereon of each such class.

(e) The number of shares voted for and against such amendment, respectively, and, if the shares of any class are entitled to vote thereon as a class, the number of shares of each such class voted for and against such amendment, respectively, or if no shares have been issued, a statement to that effect.

(f) If such amendment provides for an exchange, reclassification or cancellation of issued shares, and if the manner in which the same shall be effected is not set forth in the amendment, then a statement of the manner in which the same shall be effected.

(g) If such amendment effects a change in the amount of stated capital, then a statement of the manner in which the same is effected and a statement, expressed in dollars, of the amount of stated capital as changed by such amendment.

§ 62. Filing of Articles of Amendment.

Duplicate originals of the articles of amendment shall be delivered to the Secretary of State. If the Secretary of State finds that the articles of amendment conform to law, he shall, when all fees and franchise taxes have been paid as in this Act prescribed:

(a) Endorse on each of such duplicate originals the word "Filed," and the month, day and year of the filing thereof.

(b) File one of such duplicate originals in his office.

(c) Issue a certificate of amendment to which he shall affix the other duplicate original.

The certificate of amendment, together with the duplicate original of the articles of amendment affixed thereto by the Secretary of State, shall be returned to the corporation or its representative.

§ 63. Effect of Certificate of Amendment.

The amendment shall become effective upon the issuance of the certificate of amendment by the Secretary of State, or on such later date, not more than thirty days subsequent to the filing thereof with the Secretary of State, as shall be provided for in the articles of amendment.

No amendment shall affect any existing cause of action in favor of or against such corporation, or any pending suit to which such corporation shall be a party, or the existing rights of persons other than shareholders; and, in the event the corporate name shall be changed by amendment, no suit brought by or against such corporation under its former name shall abate for that reason.

§ 64. Restated Articles of Incorporation.

A domestic corporation may at any time restate its articles of incorporation as theretofore amended, by a resolution adopted by the board of directors.

Upon the adoption of such resolution, restated articles of incorporation shall be executed in duplicate by the corporation by its president or a vice president and by its secretary or assistant secretary and verified by one of the officers signing such articles and shall set forth all of the operative provisions of the articles of incorporation as theretofore amended together with a statement that the restated articles of incorporation correctly set forth without change the corresponding provisions of the articles of incorporation as theretofore amended and that the restated articles of incorporation supersede the original articles of incorporation and all amendments thereto.

Duplicate originals of the restated articles of incorporation shall be delivered to the Secretary of State. If the Secretary of State finds that such restated articles of incorporation conform to law, he shall, when all fees and franchise taxes have been paid as in this Act prescribed:

(1) Endorse on each of such duplicate originals the word "Filed," and the month, day and year of the filing thereof.

(2) File one of such duplicate originals in his office.

(3) Issue a restated certificate of incorporation, to which he shall affix the other duplicate original.

The restated certificate of incorporation, together with the duplicate original of the restated articles of incorporation affixed thereto by the Secretary of State, shall be returned to the corporation or its representative.

Upon the issuance of the restated certificate of incorporation by the Secretary of State, the restated articles of incorporation shall become effective and shall supersede the original articles of incorporation and all amendments thereto.

§ 65. Amendment of Articles of Incorporation in Reorganization Proceedings.

Whenever a plan of reorganization of a corporation has been confirmed by degree or order of a court of competent jurisdiction in proceedings for the reorganization of such corporation, pursuant to the provisions of any applicable statute of the United States relating to reorganizations of corporations, the articles of incorporation of the corporation may be amended, in the manner provided in this section, in as many respects as may be necessary to carry out the plan and put it into effect, so long as the articles of incorporation as amended contain only such provisions as might be lawfully contained in original articles of incorporation at the time of making such amendment.

In particular and without limitation upon such general power of amendment, the articles of incorporation may be amended for such purpose so as to:

(A) Change the corporate name, period of duration or corporate purposes of the corporation;

(B) Repeal, alter or amend the by-laws of the corporation;

(C) Change the aggregate number of shares or shares of any class, which the corporation has authority to issue;

(D) Change the preferences, limitations and relative rights in respect of all or any part of the shares of the corporation, and classify, reclassify or cancel all or any part thereof, whether issued or unissued;

(E) Authorize the issuance of bonds, debentures or other obligations of the corporation, whether or not convertible into shares of any class or bearing warrants or other evidences of optional rights to purchase or subscribe for shares of any class, and fix the terms and conditions thereof; and

(F) Constitute or reconstitute and classify or reclassify the board of directors of the corporation, and appoint directors and officers in place of or in addition to all or any of the directors or officers then in office.

Amendments to the articles of incorporation pursuant to this section shall be made in the following manner:

(a) Articles of amendment approved by decree or order of such court shall be executed and verified in duplicate by such person or persons as the court shall designate or appoint for the purpose, and shall set forth the name of the corporation, the amendments of the articles of incorporation approved by the court, the date of the decree or order approving the articles of amendment, the title of the proceedings in which the decree or order was entered, and a statement that such decree or order was entered by a court having jurisdiction of the proceedings for the reorganization of the corporation pursuant to the provisions of an applicable statute of the United States.

(b) Duplicate originals of the articles of amendment shall be delivered to the Secretary of State. If the Secretary of State finds that the articles of amendment conform to law, he shall, when all fees and franchise taxes have been paid as in this Act prescribed:

(1) Endorse on each of such duplicate originals the word "Filed," and the month, day and year of the filing thereof.

(2) File one of such duplicate originals in his office.

(3) Issue a certificate of amendment to which he shall affix the other duplicate original.

The certificate of amendment, together with the duplicate original of the articles of amendment affixed thereto by the Secretary of State, shall be returned to the corporation or its representative.

The amendment shall become effective upon the issuance of the certificate of amendment by the Secretary of State, or on such later date, not more than thirty days subsequent to the filing thereof with the Secretary of State, as shall be provided for in the articles of amendment without any action thereon by the directors or shareholders of the corporation and with the same effect as if the amendments had been adopted by unanimous action of the directors and shareholders of the corporation.

§ 66. Restriction on Redemption or Purchase of Redeemable Shares.

No redemption or purchase of redeemable shares shall be made by a corporation when it is insolvent or when such redemption or purchase would render it insolvent, or which would reduce the net assets below the aggregate amount payable to the holders of shares having prior or equal rights to the assets of the corporation upon involuntary dissolution.

§ 67. Cancellation of Redeemable Shares by Redemption or Purchase.

When redeemable shares of a corporation are redeemed or purchased by the corporation, the redemption or purchase shall effect a cancellation of such shares, and a statement of cancellation shall be filed as provided in this section. Thereupon such shares shall be restored to the status of authorized but unissued shares, unless the articles of incorporation provide that such shares when redeemed or purchased shall not be reissued, in which case the filing of the statement of cancellation shall constitute an amendment to the articles of incorporation and shall reduce the number of shares of the class so cancelled which the corporation is authorized to issue by the number of shares so cancelled.

The statement of cancellation shall be executed in duplicate by the corporation by its president or a vice president and by its secretary or an assistant secretary, and verified by one of the officers signing such statement, and shall set forth:

(a) The name of the corporation.

(b) The number of redeemable shares cancelled through redemption or purchase, itemized by classes and series.

(c) The aggregate number of issued shares, itemized by classes and series, after giving effect to such cancellation.

(d) The amount, expressed in dollars, of the stated capital of the corporation after giving effect to such cancellation.

(e) If the articles of incorporation provide that the cancelled shares shall not be reissued, the number of shares which the corporation will have authority to issue itemized by classes and series, after giving effect to such cancellation.

Duplicate originals of such statement shall be delivered to the Secretary of State. If the Secretary of State finds that such statement conforms to law, he shall, when all fees and franchise taxes have been paid as in this Act prescribed:

(1) Endorse on each of such duplicate originals the word "Filed," and the month, day and year of the filing thereof.

(2) File one of such duplicate originals in his office.

(3) Return the other duplicate original to the corporation or its representative.

Upon the filing of such statement of cancellation, the stated capital of the corporation shall be deemed to be reduced by that part of the stated capital which was, at the time of such cancellation, represented by the shares so cancelled.

Nothing contained in this section shall be construed to forbid a cancellation of shares or a reduction of stated capital in any other manner permitted by this Act.

§ 68. Cancellation of Other Reacquired Shares.

A corporation may at any time, by resolution of its board of directors, cancel all or any part of the shares of the corporation of any class reacquired by it, other than redeemable shares redeemed or purchased, and in such event a statement of cancellation shall be filed as provided in this section. [*Remainder of Text Omitted.*]

§ 69. Reduction of Stated Capital in Certain Cases.

A reduction of the stated capital of a corporation, where such reduction is not accompanied by any action requiring an amendment of the articles of incorporation and not accompanied by a cancellation of shares, may be made in the following manner: [*Remainder of Text Omitted.*]

§ 70. Special Provisions Relating to Surplus and Reserves.

The surplus, if any, created by or arising out of a reduction of the stated capital of a corporation shall be capital surplus.

The capital surplus of a corporation may be increased from time to time by resolution of the board of directors directing that all or a part of the earned surplus of the corporation be transferred to capital surplus.

A corporation may, by resolution of its board of directors, apply any part or all of its capital surplus to the reduction or elimination of any deficit arising from losses, however incurred, but only after first eliminating the earned surplus, if any, of the corporation by applying such losses against earned surplus and only to the extent that such losses exceed the earned surplus, if any. Each such application of capital surplus shall, to the extent thereof, effect a reduction of capital surplus.

A corporation may, by resolution of its board of directors, create a reserve or reserves out of its earned surplus for any proper purpose or purposes, and may abolish any such reserve in the same manner. Earned surplus of the corporation to the extent so reserved shall not be available for the payment of dividends or other distributions by the corporation except as expressly permitted by this Act.

§ 71. Procedure for Merger.

Any two or more domestic corporations may merge into one of such corporations pursuant to a plan of merger approved in the manner provided in this Act.

The board of directors of each corporation shall, by resolution adopted by each such board, approve a plan of merger setting forth:

(a) The names of the corporations proposing to merge, and the name of the corporation into which they propose to merge, which is hereinafter designated as the surviving corporation.

(b) The terms and conditions of the proposed merger.

(c) The manner and basis of converting the shares of each corporation into shares, obligations or other securities of the surviving corporation or of any other corporation or, in whole or in part, into cash or other property.

(d) A statement of any changes in the articles of incorporation of the surviving corporation to be effected by such merger.

(e) Such other provisions with respect to the proposed merger as are deemed necessary or desirable.

§ 72. Procedure for Consolidation.

Any two or more domestic corporations may consolidate into a new corporation pursuant to a plan of consolidation approved in the manner provided in this Act.

The board of directors of each corporation shall, by a resolution adopted by each such board, approve a plan of consolidation setting forth:

(a) The names of the corporations proposing to consolidate, and the name of the new corporation into which they propose to consolidate, which is hereinafter designated as the new corporation.

(b) The terms and conditions of the proposed consolidation.

(c) The manner and basis of converting the shares of each corporation into shares, obligations or other securities of the new corporation or of any other corporation or, in whole or in part, into cash or other property.

(d) With respect to the new corporation, all of the statements required to be set forth in articles of incorporation for corporations organized under this Act.

(e) Such other provisions with respect to the proposed consolidation as are deemed necessary or desirable.

§ 72A. Procedure for Share Exchange.

All the issued or all the outstanding shares of one or more classes of any domestic corporation may be acquired through the exchange of all such shares of such class or classes by another domestic or foreign corporation pursuant to a plan of exchange approved in the manner provided in this Act.

The board of directors of each corporation shall, by resolution adopted by each such board, approve a plan of exchange setting forth:

(a) The name of the corporation the shares of which are proposed to be acquired by exchange and the name of the corporation to acquire the shares of such corporation in the exchange, which is hereinafter designated as the acquiring corporation.

(b) The terms and conditions of the proposed exchange.

(c) The manner and basis of exchanging the shares to be acquired for shares, obligations or other securities of the acquiring corporation or any other corporation, or, in whole or in part, for cash or other property.

(d) Such other provisions with respect to the proposed exchange as are deemed necessary or desirable.

The procedure authorized by this Section shall not be deemed to limit the power of a corporation to acquire all or part of the shares of any class or classes of a corporation through a voluntary exchange or otherwise by agreement with the shareholders.

§ 73. Approval by Shareholders.

The board of directors of each corporation in the case of a merger or consolidation, and the board of directors of the corporation the shares of which are to be acquired in the case of an exchange, upon approving such plan of merger, consolidation or exchange, shall, by resolution, direct that the plan be submitted to a vote at a meeting of its shareholders, which may be either an annual or a special meeting. Written notice shall be given to each shareholder of record, whether or not entitled to vote at such meeting, not less than twenty days before such meeting, in the manner provided in this Act for the giving of notice of meetings of shareholders, and, whether the meeting be an annual or a special meeting, shall state that the purpose or one of the purposes is to consider the proposed plan of merger, consolidation or exchange. A copy or a summary of the plan of merger, consolidation or exchange, as the case may be, shall be included in or enclosed with such notice.

At each such meeting, a vote of the shareholders shall be taken on the proposed plan. The plan shall be approved upon receiving the affirmative vote of the holders of a majority of the shares entitled to vote thereon of each such corporation, unless any class of shares of any such corporation is entitled to vote thereon as a class, in which event, as to such corporation, the plan shall be approved upon receiving the affirmative vote of the holders of a majority of the shares of each class of shares entitled to vote thereon as a class and of the total shares entitled to vote thereon. Any class of shares of any such corporation shall be entitled to vote as a class if any such plan contains any provision which, if contained in a proposed amendment to articles of incorporation, would entitle such class of shares to vote as a class and, in the case of an exchange, if the class is included in the exchange.

After such approval by a vote of the shareholders of each such corporation, and at any time prior to the filing of the articles of merger, consolidation or exchange, the merger, consolidation or exchange may be abandoned pursuant to provisions therefor, if any, set forth in the plan.

§ 74. Articles of Merger, Consolidation or Exchange.

Upon such approval, articles of merger, articles of consolidation or articles of exchange shall be executed in duplicate by each corporation by its president or a vice president and by its secretary or an assistant secretary, and verified by one of the officers of each corporation signing such articles, and shall set forth:

(a) The plan of merger, consolidation or exchange.

(b) As to each corporation the shareholders of which were required to vote thereon, the number of shares outstanding, and, if the shares of any class were entitled to vote as a class, the designation and number of outstanding shares of each such class.

(c) As to each corporation the shareholders of which were required to vote thereon, the number of shares voted for and against such plan, respectively, and, if the shares of any class were entitled to vote as a class, the number of shares of each such class voted for and against such plan, respectively.

(d) As to the acquiring corporation in a plan of exchange, a statement that the adoption of the plan and performance of its terms were duly approved by its board of directors and such other requisite corporate action, if any, as may be required of it.

Duplicate originals of the articles of merger, consolidation or exchange shall be delivered to the Secretary of State. If the Secretary of State finds that such articles conform to law, he shall, when all fees and franchise taxes have been paid as in this Act prescribed:

(1) Endorse on each of such duplicate originals the word "Filed," and the month, day and year of the filing thereof.

(2) File one of such duplicate originals in his office.

(3) Issue a certificate of merger, consolidation or exchange to which he shall affix the other duplicate original.

The certificate of merger, consolidation or exchange together with the duplicate original of the articles affixed thereto by the Secretary of State, shall be returned to the surviving, new or acquiring corporation, as the case may be, or its representative.

§ 75. Merger of Subsidiary Corporation.

Any corporation owning at least ninety percent of the outstanding shares of each class of another corporation may merge such other corporation into itself without approval by a vote of the shareholders of either corporation. Its board of directors shall, by resolution, approve a plan of merger setting forth:

(A) The name of the subsidiary corporation and the name of the corporation owning at least ninety percent of its shares, which is hereinafter designated as the surviving corporation.

(B) The manner and basis of converting the shares of the subsidiary corporation into shares, obligations or other securities of the surviving corporation or of any other corporation or, in whole or in part, into cash or other property.

A copy of such plan of merger shall be mailed to each shareholder of record of the subsidiary corporation.

Articles of merger shall be executed in duplicate by the surviving corporation by its president or a vice president and by its secretary or an assistant secretary, and verified by one of its officers signing such articles, and shall set forth:

(a) The plan of merger;

(b) The number of outstanding shares of each class of the subsidiary corporation and the number of such shares of each class owned by the surviving corporation; and

(c) The date of the mailing to shareholders of the subsidiary corporation of a copy of the plan of merger.

On and after the thirtieth day after the mailing of a copy of the plan of merger to shareholders of the subsidiary corporation or upon the waiver thereof by the holders of all outstanding shares duplicate originals of the articles of merger shall be delivered to the Secretary of State. If the Secretary of State finds that such articles conform to law, he shall, when all fees and franchise taxes have been paid as in this Act prescribed:

(1) Endorse on each of such duplicate originals the word "Filed," and the month, day and year of the filing thereof,

(2) File one of such duplicate originals in his office, and

(3) Issue a certificate of merger to which he shall affix the other duplicate original.

The certificate of merger, together with the duplicate original of the articles of merger affixed thereto by the Secretary of State, shall be returned to the surviving corporation or its representative.

§ 76. Effect of Merger, Consolidation or Exchange.

A merger, consolidation or exchange shall become effective upon the issuance of a certificate of merger, consolidation or exchange by the Secretary of State, or on such later date, not more than thirty days subsequent to the filing thereof with the Secretary of State, as shall be provided for in the plan.

When a merger or consolidation has become effective:

(a) The several corporations parties to the plan of merger or consolidation shall be a single corporation, which, in the case of a merger, shall be that corporation designated in the plan of merger as the surviving corporation, and, in the case of a consolidation, shall be the new corporation provided for in the plan of consolidation.

(b) The separate existence of all corporations parties to the plan of merger or consolidation, except the surviving or new corporation, shall cease.

(c) Such surviving or new corporation shall have all the rights, privileges, immunities and powers and shall be subject to all the duties and liabilities of a corporation organized under this Act.

(d) Such surviving or new corporation shall thereupon and thereafter possess all the rights, privileges, immunities, and franchises, of a public as well as of a private nature, of each of the merging or consolidating corporations; and all property, real, personal and mixed, and all debts due on whatever account, including subscriptions to shares, and all other choses in action, and all and every other interest of or belonging to or due to each of the corporations so merged or consolidated, shall be taken and deemed to be transferred to and vested in such single corporation without further act or deed; and the title to any real estate, or any interest therein, vested in any of such corporations shall not revert or be in any way impaired by reason of such merger or consolidation.

(e) Such surviving or new corporation shall thenceforth be responsible and liable for all the liabilities and obligations of each of the corporations so merged or consolidated; and any claim existing or action or proceeding pending by or against any of such corporations may be prosecuted as if such merger or consolidation had not taken place, or such surviving or new corporation may be substituted in its place. Neither the rights of creditors nor any liens upon the property of any such corporation shall be impaired by such merger or consolidation.

(f) In the case of a merger, the articles of incorporation of the surviving corporation shall be deemed to be amended to the extent, if any, that changes in its articles of incorporation are stated in the plan of merger; and, in the case of a consolidation, the statements set forth in the articles of consolidation and which are required or permitted to be set forth in the articles of incorporation of corporations organized under this Act shall be deemed to be the original articles of incorporation of the new corporation.

When a merger, consolidation or exchange has become effective, the shares of the corporation or corporations party to the plan that are, under the terms of the plan, to be converted or exchanged, shall cease to exist, in the case of a merger or consolidation, or be deemed to be exchanged in the case of an exchange, and the holders of such shares shall thereafter be entitled only to the shares, obligations, other securities, cash or other property into which they shall have been converted or for which they shall have been exchanged, in accordance with the plan, subject to any rights under Section 80 of this Act.

§ 77. Merger, Consolidation or Exchange of Shares Between Domestic and Foreign Corporations.

One or more foreign corporations and one or more domestic corporations may be merged or consolidated, or participate in an exchange, in the following manner, if such merger, consolidation or exchange is permitted by the laws of the state under which each such foreign corporation is organized:

(a) Each domestic corporation shall comply with the provisions of this Act with respect to the merger, consolidation or exchange, as the case may be, of domestic corporations and each foreign corporation shall comply with the applicable provisions of the laws of the state under which it is organized.

(b) If the surviving or new corporation in a merger or consolidation is to be governed by the laws of any state other than this State, it shall comply with the provisions of this Act with respect to foreign corporations if it is to transact business in this State, and in every case it shall file with the Secretary of State of this State:

(1) An agreement that it may be served with process in this State in any proceeding for the enforcement of any obligation of any domestic corporation which is a party to such merger or consolidation and in any proceeding for the enforcement of the rights of a dissenting shareholder of any such domestic corporation against the surviving or new corporation;

(2) An irrevocable appointment of the Secretary of State of this State as its agent to accept service of process in any such proceeding; and

(3) An agreement that it will promptly pay to the dissenting shareholders of any such domestic corporation, the amount, if any, to which they shall be entitled under provisions of this Act with respect to the rights of dissenting shareholders.

§ 78. Sale of Assets in Regular Course of Business and Mortgage or Pledge of Assets.

The sale, lease, exchange, or other disposition of all, or substantially all, the property and assets of a corporation in the usual and regular course of its business and the mortgage or pledge of any or all property and assets of a corporation whether or not in the usual and regular course of business may be made upon such terms and conditions and for such consideration, which may consist in whole or in part of cash or other property, including shares, obligations or other securities of any other corporation, domestic or foreign, as shall be authorized by its board of directors; and in any such case no authorization or consent of the shareholders shall be required.

§ 79. Sale of Assets Other Than in Regular Course of Business.

A sale, lease, exchange, or other disposition of all, or substantially all, the property and assets, with or without the good will, of a corporation, if not in the usual and regular course of its business, may be made upon such terms and conditions and for such consideration, which may consist in whole or in part of cash or other property, including shares, obligations or other securities of any other corporation, domestic or foreign, as may be authorized in the following manner:

(a) The board of directors shall adopt a resolution recommending such sale, lease, exchange, or other disposition and directing the submission thereof to a vote at a meeting of shareholders, which may be either an annual or a special meeting.

(b) Written notice shall be given to each shareholder of record, whether or not entitled to vote at such meeting, not less than twenty days before such meeting, in the manner provided in this Act for the giving of notice of meetings of shareholders, and, whether the meeting be an annual or a special meeting, shall state that the purpose, or one of the purposes is to consider the proposed sale, lease, exchange, or other disposition.

(c) At such meeting the shareholders may authorize such sale, lease, exchange, or other disposition and may fix, or may authorize the board of directors to fix, any or all of the terms and conditions thereof and the consideration to be received by the corporation therefor. Such authorization shall require the affirmative vote of the holders of a majority of the shares of the corporation entitled to vote thereon, unless any class of shares is entitled to vote thereon as a class, in which event such authorization shall require the affirmative vote of the holders of a majority of the shares of each class of shares entitled to vote as a class thereon and of the total shares entitled to vote thereon.

(d) After such authorization by a vote of shareholders, the board of directors nevertheless, in its discretion, may abandon such sale, lease, exchange, or other disposition of assets, subject to the rights of third parties under any contracts relating thereto, without further action or approval by shareholders.

§ 80. Right of Shareholders to Dissent.

Any shareholder of a corporation shall have the right to dissent from any of the following corporate actions:

(a) Any plan of merger or consolidation to which the corporation is a party; or

(b) Any sale or exchange of all or substantially all of the property and assets of the corporation not made in the usual and regular course of its business, including a sale in dissolution, but not including a sale pursuant to an order of a court having jurisdiction in the premises or a sale for cash on terms requiring that all or substantially all of the net proceeds of sale be distributed to the shareholders in accordance with their respective interests within one year after the date of sale.

(c) Any plan of exchange to which the corporation is a party as the corporation the shares of which are to be acquired.

A shareholder may dissent as to less than all of the shares registered in his name. In that event, his rights shall be determined as if the shares as to which he has dissented and his other shares were registered in the names of different shareholders.

This section shall not apply to the shareholders of the surviving corporation in a merger if a vote of shareholders of such corporation is not necessary to authorize such merger. Nor shall it apply to the holders of shares of any class or series if the shares of such class or series were registered on a national securities exchange on the date fixed to determine the shareholders entitled to vote at the meeting of shareholders at which the plan of merger, consolidation or exchange or the proposed sale or exchange of property and assets is to be acted upon unless the articles of incorporation of the corporation shall otherwise provide.

§ 81. Rights of Dissenting Shareholders.

Any shareholder electing to exercise such right of dissent shall file with the corporation, prior to or at the meeting of shareholders at which such proposed corporate action is submitted to a vote, a written objection to such proposed corporate action. If such proposed corporate action be approved by the required vote and such shareholder shall not have voted in favor thereof, such shareholder may, within ten days after the date on which the vote was taken or if a corporation is to be merged without a vote of its shareholders into another corporation, any of its shareholders may, within fifteen days after the plan of such merger shall have been mailed to such shareholders, make written demand on the corporation, or, in the case of a merger or consolidation, on the surviving or new corporation, domestic or foreign, for payment of the fair value of such shareholder's shares, and, if such proposed corporate action is effected, such corporation shall pay to such shareholder, upon surrender of the certificate or certificates representing such shares, the fair value thereof as of the day prior to the date on which the vote was taken approving the proposed corporate action, excluding any appreciation or depreciation in anticipation of such corporate action. Any shareholder failing to make demand within the applicable ten-day or fifteen-day period shall be bound by the terms of the proposed corporate action. Any shareholder making such demand shall thereafter be entitled only to payment as in this section provided and shall not be entitled to vote or to exercise any other rights of a shareholder.

No such demand may be withdrawn unless the corporation shall consent thereto. If, however, such demand shall be withdrawn upon consent, or if the proposed corporate action shall be abandoned or rescinded or the shareholders shall revoke the authority to effect such action, or if, in the case of a merger, on the date of the filing of the articles of merger the surviving corporation is the owner of all the outstanding shares of the other corporations, domestic and foreign, that are parties to the merger, or if no demand or petition for the determination of fair value by a court shall have been made or filed within the time provided in this section, or if a court of competent jurisdiction shall determine that such shareholder is not entitled to the relief provided by this section, then the right of such shareholder to be paid the fair value of his shares shall cease and his status as a shareholder shall be restored, without prejudice to any corporate proceedings which may have been taken during the interim.

Within ten days after such corporate action is effected, the corporation, or, in the case of a merger or consolidation, the surviving or new corporation, domestic or foreign, shall give written notice thereof to each dissenting shareholder who has made demand as herein provided, and shall make a written offer to each such shareholder to pay for such shares at a specified price deemed by such corporation to be the fair value thereof. Such notice and offer shall be accompanied by a balance sheet of the corporation the shares of which the dissenting shareholder holds, as of the latest available date and not more than twelve months prior to the making of such offer, and a profit and loss statement of such corporation for the twelve months' period ended on the date of such balance sheet.

If within thirty days after the date on which such corporate action was effected the fair value of such shares is agreed upon between any such dissenting shareholder and the corporation, payment therefor shall be made within ninety days after the date on which such corporate action was effected, upon surrender of the certificate or certificates representing such shares. Upon payment of the agreed value the dissenting shareholder shall cease to have any interest in such shares.

If within such period of thirty days a dissenting shareholder and the corporation do not so agree, then the corporation, within thirty days after receipt of written demand from any dissenting shareholder given within sixty days after the date on which such corporate action was effected, shall, or at its election at any time within such period of sixty days may, file a petition in any court of competent jurisdiction in the county in this State where the registered office of the corporation is located requesting that the fair value of such shares be found and determined. If, in the case of a merger or consolidation, the surviving or new corporation is a foreign corporation without a registered office in this State, such petition shall be filed in the county where the registered office of the domestic corporation was last located. If the corporation shall fail to institute the proceeding as herein provided, any dissenting shareholder may do so in the name of the corporation. All dissenting shareholders, wherever residing, shall be made parties to the proceeding as an action against their shares quasi in rem. A copy of the petition shall be served on each dissenting shareholder who is a resident of this State and shall be served by registered or certified mail on each dissenting shareholder who is a nonresident. Service on nonresidents shall also be made by publication as provided by law. The jurisdiction of the court shall be plenary and exclusive. All shareholders who are parties to the proceeding shall be entitled to judgment against the corporation for the amount of the fair value of their shares. The court may, if it so elects, appoint one or more persons as appraisers to receive evidence and recommend a decision on the question of fair value. The appraisers shall have such power and authority as shall be specified in the order of their appointment or an amendment thereof. The judgment shall be payable only upon and concurrently with the surrender to the corporation of the certificate or certificates representing such shares. Upon payment of the judgment, the dissenting shareholder shall cease to have any interest in such shares.

The judgment shall include an allowance for interest at such rate as the court may find to be fair and equitable in all the circumstances, from the date on which the vote was taken on the proposed corporate action to the date of payment.

The costs and expenses of any such proceeding shall be determined by the court and shall be assessed against the corporation, but all or any part of such costs and expenses may be apportioned and assessed as the court may deem equitable against any or all of the dissenting shareholders who are parties to the proceeding to whom the corporation shall have made an offer to pay for the shares if the court shall find that the action of such shareholders in failing to accept such offer was arbitrary or vexatious or not in good faith. Such expenses shall include reasonable compensation for and reasonable expenses of the appraisers, but shall exclude the fees and expenses of counsel for and experts employed by any party; but if the fair value of the shares as determined materially exceeds the amount which the corporation offered to pay therefor, or if no offer was made, the court in its discretion may award to any shareholder who is a party to the proceeding such sum as the court may determine to be reasonable compensation to any expert or experts employed by the shareholder in the proceeding.

Within twenty days after demanding payment for his shares, each shareholder demanding payment shall submit the certificate or certificates representing his shares to the corporation for notation thereon that such demand has been made. His failure to do so shall, at the option of the corporation, terminate his rights under this section unless a court of competent jurisdiction, for good and sufficient cause shown, shall otherwise direct. If shares represented by a certificate on which notation has been so made shall be transferred, each new certificate issued therefor shall bear similar notation, together with the name of the original dissenting holder of such shares, and a transferee of such shares shall acquire by such transfer no rights in the corporation other than those which the original dissenting shareholder had after making demand for payment of the fair value thereof.

Shares acquired by a corporation pursuant to payment of the agreed value therefor or to payment of the judgment entered therefor, as in this section provided, may be held and disposed of by such corporation as in the case of other treasury shares, except that, in the case of a merger or consolidation, they may be held and disposed of as the plan of merger or consolidation may otherwise provide.

§ 82. Voluntary Dissolution by Incorporators.

A corporation which has not commenced business and which has not issued any shares, may be voluntarily dissolved by its incorporators at any time in the following manner:

(a) Articles of dissolution shall be executed in duplicate by a majority of the incorporators, and verified by them, and shall set forth:

(1) The name of the corporation.

(2) The date of issuance of its certificate of incorporation.

(3) That none of its shares has been issued.

(4) That the corporation has not commenced business.

(5) That the amount, if any, actually paid in on subscriptions for its shares, less any part thereof disbursed for necessary expenses, has been returned to those entitled thereto.

(6) That no debts of the corporation remain unpaid.

(7) That a majority of the incorporators elect that the corporation be dissolved.

(b) Duplicate originals of the articles of dissolution shall be delivered to the Secretary of State. If the Secretary of State finds that the articles of dissolution conform to law, he shall, when all fees and franchise taxes have been paid as in this Act prescribed:

(1) Endorse on each of such duplicate originals the word "Filed," and the month, day and year of the filing thereof.

(2) File one of such duplicate originals in his office.

(3) Issue a certificate of dissolution to which he shall affix the other duplicate original.

The certificate of dissolution, together with the duplicate original of the articles of dissolution affixed thereto by the Secretary of State, shall be returned to the incorporators or their representative. Upon the issuance of such certificate of dissolution by the Secretary of State, the existence of the corporation shall cease.

§ 83. Voluntary Dissolution by Consent of Shareholders.

A corporation may be voluntarily dissolved by the written consent of all of its shareholders. Upon the execution of such written consent, a statement of intent to dissolve shall be executed in duplicate by the corporation by its president or a vice president and by its secretary or an assistant secretary, and verified by one of the officers signing such statement, which statement shall set forth:

(a) The name of the corporation.

(b) The names and respective addresses of its officers.

(c) The names and respective addresses of its directors.

(d) A copy of the written consent signed by all shareholders of the corporation.

(e) A statement that such written consent has been signed by all shareholders of the corporation or signed in their names by their attorneys thereunto duly authorized.

§ 84. Voluntary Dissolution by Act of Corporation.

A corporation may be dissolved by the act of the corporation, when authorized in the following manner:

(a) The board of directors shall adopt a resolution recommending that the corporation be dissolved, and directing that the question of such dissolution be submitted to a vote at a meeting of shareholders, which may be either an annual or a special meeting.

(b) Written notice shall be given to each shareholder of record entitled to vote at such meeting within the time and in the manner provided in this Act for the giving of notice of meetings of shareholders, and, whether the meeting be an annual or special meeting, shall state that the purpose, or one of the purposes, of such meeting is to consider the advisability of dissolving the corporation.

(c) At such meeting a vote of shareholders entitled to vote thereat shall be taken on a resolution to dissolve the corporation. Such resolution shall be adopted upon receiving the affirmative vote of the holders of a majority of the shares of the corporation entitled to vote thereon, unless any class of shares is entitled to vote thereon as a class, in which event the resolution shall be adopted upon receiving the affirmative vote of the holders of a majority of the shares of each class of shares entitled to vote thereon as a class and of the total shares entitled to vote thereon.

(d) Upon the adoption of such resolution, a statement of intent to dissolve shall be executed in duplicate by the corporation by its president or a vice president and by its secretary or an assistant secretary, and verified by one of the officers signing such statement, which statement shall set forth:

(1) The name of the corporation.

(2) The names and respective addresses of its officers.

(3) The names and respective addresses of its directors.

(4) A copy of the resolution adopted by the shareholders authorizing the dissolution of the corporation.

(5) The number of shares outstanding, and, if the shares of any class are entitled to vote as a class, the designation and number of outstanding shares of each such class.

(6) The number of shares voted for and against the resolution, respectively, and, if the shares of any class are entitled to vote as a class, the number of shares of each such class voted for and against the resolution, respectively.

§ 85. Filing of Statement of Intent to Dissolve.

Duplicate originals of the statement of intent to dissolve, whether by consent of shareholders or by act of the corporation, shall be delivered to the Secretary of State. If the Secretary of State finds that such statement conforms to law, he shall, when all fees and franchise taxes have been paid as in this Act prescribed:

(a) Endorse on each of such duplicate originals the word "Filed," and the month, day and year of the filing thereof.

(b) File one of such duplicate originals in his office.

(c) Return the other duplicate original to the corporation or its representative.

§ 86. Effect of Statement of Intent to Dissolve.

Upon the filing by the Secretary of State of a statement of intent to dissolve, whether by consent of shareholders or by act of the corporation, the corporation shall cease to carry on its business, except insofar as may be necessary for the winding up thereof, but its corporate existence shall continue until a certificate of dissolution has been issued by the Secretary of State or until a decree dissolving the corporation has been entered by a court of competent jurisdiction as in this Act provided.

§ 87. Procedure after Filing of Statement of Intent to Dissolve.

After the filing by the Secretary of State of a statement of intent to dissolve:

(a) The corporation shall immediately cause notice thereof to be mailed to each known creditor of the corporation.

(b) The corporation shall proceed to collect its assets, convey and dispose of such of its properties as are not to be distributed in kind to its shareholders, pay, satisfy and discharge its liabilities and obligations and do all other acts required to liquidate its business and affairs, and, after paying or adequately providing for the payment of all its obligations, distribute the remainder of its assets, either in cash or in kind, among its shareholders according to their respective rights and interests.

(c) The corporation, at any time during the liquidation of its business and affairs, may make application to a court of competent jurisdiction within the state and judicial subdivision in which the registered office or principal place of business of the corporation is situated, to have the liquidation continued under the supervision of the court as provided in this Act.

§ 88. Revocation of Voluntary Dissolution Proceedings by Consent of Shareholders.

By the written consent of all of its shareholders, a corporation may, at any time prior to the issuance of a certificate of dissolution by the Secretary of State, revoke voluntary dissolution proceedings theretofore taken, in the following manner:

Upon the execution of such written consent, a statement of revocation of voluntary dissolution proceedings shall be executed in duplicate by the corporation by its president or a vice president and by its secretary or an assistant secretary, and verified by one of the officers signing such statement, which statement shall set forth:

(a) The name of the corporation.

(b) The names and respective addresses of its officers.

(c) The names and respective addresses of its directors.

(d) A copy of the written consent signed by all shareholders of the corporation revoking such voluntary dissolution proceedings.

(e) That such written consent has been signed by all shareholders of the corporation or signed in their names by their attorneys thereunto duly authorized.

§ 89. Revocation of Voluntary Dissolution Proceedings by Act of Corporation. [*Text Omitted.*]

§ 90. Filing of Statement of Revocation of Voluntary Dissolution Proceedings. [*Text Omitted.*]

§ 91. Effect of Statement of Revocation of Voluntary Dissolution Proceedings.

Upon the filing by the Secretary of State of a statement of revocation of voluntary dissolution proceedings, whether by consent of shareholders or by act of the corporation, the revocation of the voluntary dissolution proceedings shall become effective and the corporation may again carry on its business.

§ 92. Articles of Dissolution.

If voluntary dissolution proceedings have not been revoked, then when all debts, liabilities and obligations of the corporation have been paid and discharged, or adequate provision has been made therefor, and all of the remaining property and assets of the corporation have been distributed to its shareholders, articles of dissolution shall be executed in duplicate by the corporation by its president or a vice president and by its secretary or an assistant secretary, and verified by one of the officers signing such statement, which statement shall set forth:

(a) The name of the corporation.

(b) That the Secretary of State has theretofore filed a statement of intent to dissolve the corporation, and the date on which such statement was filed.

(c) That all debts, obligations and liabilities of the corporation have been paid and discharged or that adequate provision has been made therefor.

(d) That all the remaining property and assets of the corporation have been distributed among its shareholders in accordance with their respective rights and interests.

(e) That there are no suits pending against the corporation in any court, or that adequate provision has been made for the satisfaction of any judgment, order or decree which may be entered against it in any pending suit.

§ 93. Filing of Articles of Dissolution.

Duplicate originals of such articles of dissolution shall be delivered to the Secretary of State. If the Secretary of State finds that such articles of dissolution conform to law, he shall, when all fees and franchise taxes have been paid as in this Act prescribed:

(a) Endorse on each of such duplicate originals the word "Filed," and the month, day and year of the filing thereof.

(b) File one of such duplicate originals in his office.

(c) Issue a certificate of dissolution to which he shall affix the other duplicate original.

The certificate of dissolution, together with the duplicate original of the articles of dissolution affixed thereto by the Secretary of State, shall be returned to the representative of the dissolved corporation. Upon the issuance of such certificate of dissolution the existence of the corporation shall cease, except for the purpose of suits, other proceedings and appropriate corporate action by shareholders, directors and officers as provided in this Act.

§ 94. Involuntary Dissolution.

A corporation may be disolved involuntarily by a decree of the .... court in an action filed by the Attorney General when it is established that:

(a) The corporation has failed to file its annual report within the time required by this Act, or has failed to pay its franchise tax on or before the first day of August of the year in which such franchise tax becomes due and payable; or

(b) The corporation procured its articles of incorporation through fraud; or

(c) The corporation has continued to exceed or abuse the authority conferred upon it by law; or

(d) The corporation has failed for thirty days to appoint and maintain a registered agent in this State; or

(e) The corporation has failed for thirty days after change of its registered office or registered agent to file in the office of the Secretary of State a statement of such change.

§ 95. Notification to Attorney General.

The Secretary of State, on or before the last day of December of each year, shall certify to the Attorney General the names of all corporations which have failed to file their annual reports or to pay franchise taxes in accordance with the provisions of this Act, together with the facts pertinent thereto. He shall also certify, from time to time, the names of all corporations which have given other cause for dissolution as provided in this Act, together with the facts pertinent thereto. Whenever the Secretary of State shall certify the name of a corporation to the Attorney General as having given any cause for dissolution, the Secretary of State shall concurrently mail to the corporation at its registered office a notice that such certification has been made. Upon the receipt of such certification, the Attorney General shall file an action in the name of the State against such corporation for its dissolution. Every such certificate from the Secretary of State to the Attorney General pertaining to the failure of a corporation to file an annual report or pay a franchise tax shall be taken and received in all courts as prima facie evidence of the facts therein stated. If, before action is filed, the corporation shall file its annual report or pay its franchise tax, together with all penalties thereon, or shall appoint or maintain a registered agent as provided in this Act, or shall file with the Secretary of State the required statement of change of registered office or registered agent, such fact shall be forthwith certified by the Secretary of State to the Attorney General and he shall not file an action against such corporation for such cause. If, after action is filed, the corporation shall file its annual report or pay its franchise tax, together with all penalties thereon, or shall appoint or maintain a registered agent as provided in this Act, or shall file with the Secretary of State the required statement of change of registered office or registered agent, and shall pay the costs of such action, the action for such cause shall abate.

§ 96. Venue and Process.

Every action for the involuntary dissolution of a corporation shall be commenced by the Attorney General either in the .... court of the county in which the registered office of the corporation is situated, or in the .... court of .... county. Summons shall issue and be served as in other civil actions. If process is returned not found, the Attorney General shall cause publication to be made as in other civil cases in some newspaper published in the county where the registered office of the corporation is situated, containing a notice of the pendency of such action, the title of the court, the title of the action, and the date on or after which default may be entered. The Attorney General may include in one notice the names of any number of corporations against which actions are then pending in the same court. The Attorney General shall cause a copy of such notice to be mailed to the corporation at its registered office within ten days after the first publication thereof. The certificate of the Attorney General of the mailing of such notice shall be prima facie evidence thereof. Such notice shall be published at least once each week for two successive weeks, and the first publication thereof may begin at any time after the summons has been returned. Unless a corporation shall have been served with summons, no default shall be taken against it earlier than thirty days after the first publication of such notice.

§ 97. Jurisdiction of Court to Liquidate Assets and Business of Corporation.

The .... courts shall have full power to liquidate the assets and business of a corportion:

(a) In an action by a shareholder when it is established:

(1) That the directors are deadlocked in the management of the corporate affairs and the shareholders are unable to break the deadlock, and that irreparable injury to the corporation is being suffered or is threatened by reason thereof; or

(2) That the acts of the directors or those in control of the corporation are illegal, oppressive or fraudulent; or

(3) That the shareholders are deadlocked in voting power, and have failed, for a period which includes at least two consecutive annual meeting dates, to elect successors to directors whose terms have expired or would have expired upon the election of their successors; or

(4) That the corporate assets are being misapplied or wasted.

(b) In an action by a creditor:

(1) When the claim of the creditor has been reduced to judgment and an execution thereon returned unsatisfied and it is established that the corporation is insolvent; or

(2) When the corporation has admitted in writing that the claim of the creditor is due and owing and it is established that the corporation is insolvent.

(c) Upon application by a corporation which has filed a statement of intent to dissolve, as provided in this Act, to have its liquidation continued under the supervision of the court.

(d) When an action has been filed by the Attorney General to dissolve a corporation and it is established that liquidation of its business and affairs should precede the entry of a decree of dissolution.

Proceedings under clause (a), (b) or (c) of this section shall be brought in the county in which the registered office or the principal office of the corporation is situated.

It shall not be necessary to make shareholders parties to any such action or proceeding unless relief is sought against them personally.

§ 98. Procedure in Liquidation of Corporation by Court.

In proceedings to liquidate the assets and business of a corporation the court shall have power to issue injunctions, to appoint a receiver or receivers pendente lite, with such powers and duties as the court, from time to time, may direct, and to take such other proceedings as may be requisite to preserve the corporate assets wherever situated, and carry on the business of the corporation until a full hearing can be had.

After a hearing had upon such notice as the court may direct to be given to all parties to the proceedings and to any other parties in interest designated by the court, the court may appoint a liquidating receiver or receivers with authority to collect the assets of the corporation, including all amounts owing to the corporation by subscribers on account of any unpaid portion of the consideration for the issuance of shares. Such liquidating receiver or receivers shall have authority, subject to the order of the court, to sell, convey and dispose of all or any part of the assets of the corporation wherever situated, either at public or private sale. The assets of the corporation or the proceeds resulting from a sale, conveyance or other disposition thereof shall be applied to the expenses of such liquidation and to the payment of the liabilities and obligations of the corporation, and any remaining assets or proceeds shall be distributed among its shareholders according to their respective rights and interests. The order appointing such liquidating receiver or receivers shall state their powers and duties. Such powers and duties may be increased or diminished at any time during the proceedings.

The court shall have power to allow from time to time as expenses of the liquidation compensation to the receiver or receivers and to attorneys in the proceeding, and to direct the payment thereof out of the assets of the corporation or the proceeds of any sale or disposition of such assets.

A receiver of a corporation appointed under the provisions of this section shall have authority to sue and defend in all courts in his own name as receiver of such corporation. The court appointing such receiver shall have exclusive jurisdiction of the corporation and its property, wherever situated.

§ 99. Qualifications of Receivers.

A receiver shall in all cases be a natural person or a corporation authorized to act as receiver, which corporation may be a domestic corporation or a foreign corporation authorized to transact business in this State, and shall in all cases give such bond as the court may direct with such sureties as the court may require.

§ 100. Filing of Claims in Liquidation Proceedings.

In proceedings to liquidate the assets and business of a corporation the court may require all creditors of the corporation to file with the clerk of the court or with the receiver, in such form as the court may prescribe, proofs under oath of their respective claims. If the court requires the filing of claims it shall fix a date, which shall be not less than four months from the date of the order, as the last day for the filing of claims, and shall prescribe the notice that shall be given to creditors and claimants of the date so fixed. Prior to the date so fixed, the court may extend the time for the filing of claims. Creditors and claimants failing to file proofs of claim on or before the date so fixed may be barred, by order of court, from participating in the distribution of the assets of the corporation.

§ 101. Discontinuance of Liquidation Proceedings.

The liquidation of the assets and business of a corporation may be discontinued at any time during the liquidation proceedings when it is established that cause for liquidation no longer exists. In such event the court shall dismiss the proceedings and direct the receiver to redeliver to the corporation all its remaining property and assets.

§ 102. Decree of Involuntary Dissolution.

In proceedings to liquidate the assets and business of a corporation, when the costs and expenses of such proceedings and all debts, obligations and liabilities of the corporation shall have been paid and discharged and all of its remaining property and assets distributed to its shareholders, or in case its property and assets are not sufficient to satisfy and discharge such costs, expenses, debts and obligations, all the property and assets have been applied so far as they will go to their payment, the court shall enter a decree dissolving the corporation, whereupon the existence of the corporation shall cease.

§ 103. Filing of Decree of Dissolution.

In case the court shall enter a decree dissolving a corporation, it shall be the duty of the clerk of such court to cause a certified copy of the decree to be filed with the Secretary of State. No fee shall be charged by the Secretary of State for the filing thereof.

§ 104. Deposit with State Treasurer of Amount Due Certain Shareholders.

Upon the voluntary or involuntary dissolution of a corporation, the portion of the assets distributable to a creditor or shareholder who is unknown or cannot be found, or who is under disability and there is no person legally competent to receive such distributive portion, shall be reduced to cash and deposited with the State Treasurer and shall be paid over to such creditor or shareholder or to his legal representative upon proof satisfactory to the State Treasurer of his right thereto.

§ 105. Survival of Remedy after Dissolution.

The dissolution of a corporation either (1) by the issuance of a certificate of dissolution by the Secretary of State, or (2) by a decree of court when the court has not liquidated the assets and business of the corporation as provided in this Act, or (3) by expiration of its period of duration, shall not take away or impair any remedy available to or against such corporation, its directors, officers, or shareholders, for any right or claim existing, or any liability incurred, prior to such dissolution if action or other proceeding thereon is commenced within two years after the date of such dissolution. Any such action or proceeding by or against the corporation may be prosecuted or defended by the corporation in its corporate name. The shareholders, directors and officers shall have power to take such corporate or other action as shall be appropriate to protect such remedy, right or claim. If such corporation was dissolved by the expiration of its period of duration, such corporation may amend its articles of incorporation at any time during such period of two years so as to extend its period of duration.

§ 106. Admission of Foreign Corporation.

No foreign corporation shall have the right to transact business in this State until it shall have procured a certificate of authority so to do from the Secretary of State. No foreign corporation shall be entitled to procure a certificate of authority under this Act to transact in this State any business which a corporation organized under this Act is not permitted to transact. A foreign corporation shall not be denied a certificate of authority by reason of the fact that the laws of the state or country under which such corporation is organized governing its organization and internal affairs differ from the laws of this State, and nothing in this Act contained shall be construed to authorize this State to regulate the organization or the internal affairs of such corporation.

Without excluding other activities which may not constitute transacting business in this State, a foreign corporation shall not be considered to be transacting business in this State, for the purposes of this Act, by reason of carrying on in this State any one or more of the following activities:

(a) Maintaining or defending any action or suit or any administrative or arbitration proceeding, or effecting the settlement thereof or the settlement of claims or disputes.

(b) Holding meetings of its directors or shareholders or carrying on other activities concerning its internal affairs.

(c) Maintaining bank accounts.

(d) Maintaining offices or agencies for the transfer, exchange and registration of its securities, or appointing and maintaining trustees or depositaries with relation to its securities.

(e) Effecting sales through independent contractors.

(f) Soliciting or procuring orders, whether by mail or through employees or agents or otherwise, where such orders require acceptance without this State before becoming binding contracts.

(g) Creating as borrower or lender, or acquiring, indebtedness or mortgages or other security interests in real or personal property.

(h) Securing or collecting debts or enforcing any rights in property securing the same.

(i) Transacting any business in interstate commerce.

(j) Conducting an isolated transaction completed within a period of thirty days and not in the course of a number of repeated transactions of like nature.

§ 107. Powers of Foreign Corporation.

A foreign corporation which shall have received a certificate of authority under this Act shall, until a certificate of revocation or of withdrawal shall have been issued as provided in this Act, enjoy the same, but no greater, rights and privileges as a domestic corporation organized for the purposes set forth in the application pursuant to which such certificate of authority is issued; and, except as in this Act otherwise provided, shall be subject to the same duties, restrictions, penalties and liabilities now or hereafter imposed upon a domestic corporation of like character.

§ 108. Corporate Name of Foreign Corporation.

No certificate of authority shall be issued to a foreign corporation unless the corporate name of such corporation:

(a) Shall contain the word "corporation," "company," "incorporated," or "limited," or shall contain an abbreviation of one of such words, or such corporation shall, for use in this State, add at the end of its name one of such words or an abbreviation thereof.

(b) Shall not contain any word or phrase which indicates or implies that it is organized for any purpose other than one or more of the purposes contained in its articles of incorporation or that it is authorized or empowered to conduct the business of banking or insurance.

(c) Shall not be the same as, or deceptively similar to, the name of any domestic corporation existing under the laws of this State or any foreign corporation authorized to transact business in this State, or a name the exclusive right to which is, at the time, reserved in the manner provided in this Act, or the name of a corporation which has in effect a registration of its name as provided in this Act, except that this provision shall not apply if the foreign corporation applying for a certificate of authority files with the Secretary of State any one of the following:

(1) a resolution of its board of directors adopting a fictitious name for use in transacting business in this State which fictitious name is not deceptively similar to the name of any domestic corporation or of any foreign corporation authorized to transact business in this State or to any name reserved or registered as provided in this Act, or

(2) the written consent of such other corporation or holder of a reserved or registered name to use the same or deceptively similar name and one or more words are added to make such name distinguishable from such other name, or

(3) a certified copy of a final decree of a court of competent jurisdiction establishing the prior right of such foreign corporation to the use of such name in this State.

§ 109. Change of Name by Foreign Corporation.

Whenever a foreign corporation which is authorized to transact business in this State shall change its name to one under which a certificate of authority would not be granted to it on application therefor, the certificate of authority of such corporation shall be suspended and it shall not thereafter transact any business in this State until it has changed its name to a name which is available to it under the laws of this State or has otherwise complied with the provisions of this Act.

§ 110. Application for Certificate of Authority.

A foreign corporation, in order to procure a certificate of authority to transact business in this State, shall make application therefore to the Secretary of State, which application shall set forth:

(a) The name of the corporation and the state or country under the laws of which it is incorporated.

(b) If the name of the corporation does not contain the word "corporation," "company," "incorporated," or "limited," or does not contain an abbreviation of one of such words, then the name of the corporation with the word or abbreviation which it elects to add thereto for use in this State.

(c) The date of incorporation and the period of duration of the corporation.

(d) The address of the principal office of the corporation in the state or country under the laws of which it is incorporated.

(e) The address of the proposed registered office of the corporation in this State, and the name of its proposed registered agent in this State at such address.

(f) The purpose or purposes of the corporation which it proposes to pursue in the transaction of business in this State.

(g) The names and respective addresses of the directors and officers of the corporation.

(h) A statement of the aggregate number of shares which the corporation has authority to issue, itemized by classes, par value of shares, shares without par value, and series, if any, within a class.

(i) A statement of the aggregate number of issued shares itemized by classes, par value of shares, shares without par value, and series, if any, within a class.

(j) A statement, expressed in dollars, of the amount of stated capital of the corporation, as defined in this Act.

(k) An estimate, expressed in dollars, of the value of all property to be owned by the corporation for the following year, wherever located, and an estimate of the value of the property of the corporation to be located within this State during such year, and an estimate, expressed in dollars, of the gross amount of business which will be transacted by the corporation during such year, and an estimate of the gross amount thereof which will be transacted by the corporation at or from places of business in this State during such year.

(1) Such additional information as may be necessary or appropriate in order to enable the Secretary of State to determine whether such corporation is entitled to a certificate of authority to transact business in this State and to determine and assess the fees and franchise taxes payable as in this Act prescribed.

Such application shall be made on forms prescribed and furnished by the Secretary of State and shall be executed in duplicate by the corporation by its president or a vice president and by its secretary or an assistant secretary, and verified by one of the officers signing such application.

§ 111. Filing of Application for Certificate of Authority.

Duplicate originals of the application of the corporation for a certificate of authority shall be delivered to the Secretary of State, together with a copy of its articles of incorporation and all amendments thereto, duly authenticated by the proper officer of the state or country under the laws of which it is incorporated.

If the Secretary of State finds that such application conforms to law, he shall, when all fees and franchise taxes have been paid as in this Act prescribed:

(a) Endorse on each of such documents the word "Filed," and the month, day and year of the filing thereof.

(b) File in his office one of such duplicate originals of the application and the copy of the articles of incorporation and amendments thereto.

(c) Issue a certificate of authority to transact business in this State to which he shall affix the other duplicate original application.

The certificate of authority, together with the duplicate original of the application affixed thereto by the Secretary of State, shall be returned to the corporation or its representative.

§ 112. Effect of Certificate of Authority

Upon the issuance of a certificate of authority by the Secretary of State, the corporation shall be authorized to transact business in this State for those purposes set forth in its application, subject, however, to the right of this State to suspend or to revoke such authority as provided in this Act.

§ 113. Registered Office and Registered Agent of Foreign Corporation.

Each foreign corporation authorized to transact business in this State shall have and continuously maintain in this State:

(a) A registered office which may be, but need not be, the same as its place of business in this State.

(b) A registered agent, which agent may be either an individual resident in this State whose business office is identical with such registered office, or a domestic corporation, or a foreign corporation authorized to transact business in this State, having a business office identical with such registered office.

§ 114. Change of Registered Office or Registered Agent of Foreign Corporation. [*Text Omitted.*]

§ 115. Service of Process on Foreign Corporation.

The registered agent so appointed by a foreign corporation authorized to transact business in this State shall be an agent of such corporation upon whom any process, notice or demand required or permitted by law to be served upon the corporation may be served.

Whenever a foreign corporation authorized to transact business in this State shall fail to appoint or maintain a registered agent in this State, or whenever any such registered agent cannot with reasonable diligence be found at the registered office, or whenever the certificate of authority of a foreign corporation shall be suspended or revoked, then the Secretary of State shall be an agent of such corporation upon whom any such process, notice, or demand may be served. Service on the Secretary of State of any such process, notice or demand shall be made by delivering to and leaving with him, or with any clerk having charge of the corporation department of his office, duplicate copies of such process, notice or demand. In the event any such process, notice or demand is served on the Secretary of State, he shall immediately cause one of such copies thereof to be forwarded by registered mail, addressed to the corporation at its principal office in the state or country under the laws of which it is incorporated. Any service so had on the Secretary of State shall be returnable in not less than thirty days.

The Secretary of State shall keep a record of all processes, notices and demands served upon him under this section, and shall record therein the time of such service and his action with reference thereto.

Nothing herein contained shall limit or affect the right to serve any process, notice or demand, required or permitted by law to be served upon a foreign corporation in any other manner now or hereafter permitted by law.

§ 116. Amendment to Articles of Incorporation of Foreign Corporation. [*Text Omitted.*]

§ 117. Merger of Foreign Corporation Authorized to Transact Business in This State. [*Text Omitted.*]

§ 118. Amended Certificate of Authority. [*Text Omitted.*]

§ 119. Withdrawal of Foreign Corporation. [*Text Omitted.*]

§ 120. Filing of Application for Withdrawal. [*Text Omitted.*]

§ 121. Revocation of Certificate of Authority. [*Text Omitted.*]

§ 122. Issuance of Certificate of Revocation. [*Text Omitted.*]

§ 123. Application to Corporations Heretofore Authorized to Transact Business in this State. [*Text Omitted.*]

§ 124. Transacting Business Without Certificate of Authority.

No foreign corporation transacting business in this State without a certificate of authority shall be permitted to maintain any action, suit or proceeding in any court of this State, until such corporation shall have obtained a certificate of authority. Nor shall any action, suit or proceeding be maintained in any court of this State by any successor or assignee of such corporation on any right, claim or demand arising out of the transaction of business by such corporation in this State, until a certificate of authority shall have been obtained by such corporation or by a corporation which has acquired all or substantially all of its assets.

The failure of a foreign corporation to obtain a certificate of authority to transact business in this State shall not impair the validity of any contract or act of such corporation, and shall not prevent such corporation from defending any action, suit or proceeding in any court of this State.

A foreign corporation which transacts business in this State without a certificate of authority shall be liable to this State, for the years or parts thereof during which it transacted business in this State without a certificate of authority, in an amount equal to all fees and franchise taxes which would have been imposed by this Act upon such corporation had it duly applied for and received a certificate of authority to transact business in this State as required by this Act and thereafter filed all reports required by this Act, plus all penalities imposed by this Act for failure to pay such fees and franchise taxes. The Attorney General shall bring proceedings to recover all amounts due this State under the provisions of this Section.

§ 125. Annual Report of Domestic and Foreign Corporations.

Each domestic corporation, and each foreign corporation authorized to transact business in this State, shall file, within the time prescribed by this Act, an annual report setting forth:

(a) The name of the corporation and the state or country under the laws of which it is incorporated.

(b) The address of the registered office of the corporation in this State, and the name of its registered agent in this State at such address, and, in case of a foreign corporation, the address of its principal office in the state or country under the laws of which it is incorporated.

(c) A brief statement of the character of the business in which the corporation is actually engaged in this State.

(d) The names and respective addresses of the directors and officers of the corporation.

(e) A statement of the aggregate number of shares which the corporation has authority to issue, itemized by classes, par value of shares, shares without par value, and series, if any, within a class.

(f) A statement of the aggregate number of issued shares, itemized by classes, par value of shares, shares without par value, and series, if any, within a class.

(g) A statement, expressed in dollars, of the amount of stated capital of the corporation, as defined in this Act.

(h) A statement, expressed in dollars, of the value of all the property owned by the corporation, wherever located, and the value of the property of the corporation located within this State, and a statement, expressed in dollars, of the gross amount of business transacted by the corporation for the twelve months ended on the thirty-first day of December preceding the date herein provided for the filing of such report and the gross amount thereof transacted by the corporation at or from places of business in this State. If, on the thirty-first day of December preceding the time herein provided for the filing of such report, the corporation had not been in existence for a period of twelve months, or in the case of a foreign corporation had not been authorized to transact business in this State for a period of twelve months, the statement with respect to business transacted shall be furnished for the period between the date of incorporation or the date of its authorization to transact business in this State, as the case may be, and such thirty-first day of December. If all the property of the corporation is located in this State and all of its business is transacted at or from places of business in this State, or if the corporation elects to pay the annual franchise tax on the basis of its entire stated capital, then the information required by this subparagraph need not be set forth in such report.

(i) Such additional information as may be necessary or appropriate in order to enable the

Secretary of State to determine and assess the proper amount of franchise taxes payable by such corporation.

Such annual report shall be made on forms prescribed and furnished by the Secretary of State, and the information therein contained shall be given as of the date of the execution of the report, except as to the information required by subparagraphs (g), (h) and (i) which shall be given as of the close of business on the thirty-first day of December next preceding the date herein provided for the filing of such report. It shall be executed by the corporation by its president, a vice president, secretary, an assistant secretary, or treasurer, and verified by the officer executing the report, or, if the corporation is in the hands of a receiver or trustee, it shall be executed on behalf of the corporation and verified by such receiver or trustee.

§ 126. Filing of Annual Report of Domestic and Foreign Corporations. [*Text Omitted.*]

§ 127. Fees, Franchise Taxes and Charges to Be Collected by Secretary of State. [*Text Omitted.*]

§ 128. Fees for Filing Documents and Issuing Certificates. [*Text Omitted.*]

§ 129. Miscellaneous Charges. [*Text Omitted.*]

§ 130. License Fees Payable by Domestic Corporations. [*Text Omitted.*]

§ 131. License Fees Payable by Foreign Corporations. [*Text Omitted.*]

§ 132. Franchise Taxes Payable by Domestic Corporations. [*Text Omitted.*]

§ 133. Franchise Taxes Payable by Foreign Corporation. [*Text Omitted.*]

§ 134. Assessment and Collection of Annual Franchise Taxes. [*Text Omitted.*]

§ 135. Penalties Imposed upon Corporations.

Each corporation, domestic or foreign, that fails or refuses to file its annual report for any year within the time prescribed by this Act shall be subject to a penalty of ten per cent of the amount of the franchise tax assessed against it for the period beginning July 1 of the year in which such report should have been filed. Such penalty shall be assessed by the Secretary of State at the time of the assessment of the franchise tax. If the amount of the franchise tax as originally assessed against such corporation be thereafter adjusted in accordance with the provisions of this Act, the amount of the penalty shall be likewise adjusted to ten per cent of the amount of the adjusted franchise tax. The amount of the franchise tax and the amount of the penalty shall be separately stated in any notice to the corporation with respect thereto.

If the franchise tax assessed in accordance with the provisions of this Act shall not be paid on or before the thirty-first day of July, it shall be deemed to be delinquent, and there shall be added a penalty of one per cent for each month or part of month that the same is delinquent, commencing with the month of August.

Each corporation, domestic or foreign, that fails or refuses to answer truthfully and fully within the time prescribed by this Act interrogatories propounded by the Secretary of State in accordance with the provisions of this Act, shall be deemed to be guilty of a misdemeanor and upon conviction thereof may be fined in any amount not exceeding five hundred dollars.

§ 136. Penalties Imposed upon Officers and Directors.

Each officer and director of a corporation, domestic or foreign, who fails or refuses within the time prescribed by this Act to answer truthfully and fully interrogatories propounded to him by the Secretary of State in accordance with the provisions of this Act, or who signs any articles, statement, report, application or other document filed with the Secretary of State which is known to such officer or director to be false in any material respect, shall be deemed to be guilty of a misdemeanor, and upon conviction thereof may be fined in any amount not exceeding . . . . dollars.

§ 137. Interrogatories by Secretary of State

The Secretary of State may propound to any corporation, domestic or foreign, subject to the provisions of this Act, and to any officer or director thereof, such interrogatories as may be reasonably necessary and proper to enable him to ascertain whether such corporation has complied with all the provisions of this Act applicable to such corporation. Such interrogatories shall be answered within thirty days after the mailing thereof, or within such additional time as shall be fixed by the Secretary of State, and the answers thereto shall be full and complete and shall be made in writing and under oath. If such interrogatories be directed to an individual they shall be answered by him, and if directed to a corporation they shall be answered by the president, vice president, secretary or assistant secretary thereof. The Secretary of State need not file any document to which such interrogatories relate until such interrogatories be answered as herein provided, and not then if the answers thereto disclose that such document is not in conformity with the provisions of this Act. The Secretary of State shall certify to the Attorney General, for such action as the Attorney General may deem appropriate, all interrogatories and answers thereto which disclose a violation of any of the provisions of this Act.

§ 138. Information Disclosed by Interrogatories.

Interrogatories propounded by the Secretary of State and the answers thereto shall not be open to public inspection nor shall the Secretary of State disclose any facts or information obtained therefrom except insofar as his official duty may require the same to be made public or in the event such interrogatories or the answers thereto are required for evidence in any criminal proceedings or in any other action by this State.

§ 139. Powers for Secretary of State

The Secretary of State shall have the power and authority reasonably necessary to enable him to administer this Act efficiently and to perform the duties therein imposed upon him.

§ 140. Appeal from Secretary of State. [*Text Omitted.*]

§ 141. Certificates and Certified Copies to be Received in Evidence. [*Text Omitted.*]

§ 142. Forms to be Furnished by Secretary of State. [*Text Omitted.*]

§ 143. Greater Voting Requirements.

Whenever, with respect to any action to be taken by the shareholders of a corporation, the articles of incorporation require the vote or concurrence of the holders of a greater proportion of the shares, or of any class or series thereof, then required by this Act with respect to such action, the provisions of the articles of incorporation shall control.

§ 144. Waiver of Notice.

Whenever any notice is required to be given to any shareholder or director of a corporation under the provisions of this Act or under the provisions of the articles of incorporation or by-laws of the corporation, a wavier thereof in writing signed by the person or persons entitled to such notice, whether before or after the time stated therein, shall be equivalent to the giving of such notice.

§ 145. Action by Shareholders Without a Meeting.

Any action required by this Act to be taken at a meeting of the shareholders of a corporation, or any action which may be taken at a meeting of the shareholders, may be taken without a meeting if a consent in writing, setting forth the action so taken, shall be signed by all of the shareholders entitled to vote with respect to the subject matter thereof.

Such consent shall have the same effect as a unanimous vote of shareholders, and may be stated as such in any articles or document filed with the Secretary of State under this Act.

§ 146. Unauthorized Assumption of Corporate Powers.

All persons who assume to act as a corporation without authority so to do shall be jointly and severally liable for all debts and liabilities incurred or arising as a result thereof.

§ 147. Application to Existing Corporations. [*Text Omitted.*]

§ 148. Application to Foreign and Interstate Commerce. [*Text Omitted.*]

§ 149. Reservation of Power. [*Text Omitted.*]

§ 150. Effect of Repeal of Prior Acts. [*Text Omitted.*]

§ 151. Effect of Invalidity of Part of This Act. [*Text Omitted.*]

§ 152. Repeal of Prior Acts.

Selected Parts of the U.S. Constitution*

ARTICLE I

Section 8. The Congress shall have Power: To lay and collect Taxes, Duties, Imposts and Excises, to pay the Debts and provide for the common Defence and general Welfare of the United States; but all Duties, Imposts and Excises shall be uniform throughout the United States.

To borrow Money on the credit of the United States;

To regulate Commerce with foreign Nations, and among the several States, and with the Indian Tribes;

To establish an uniform Rule of Naturalization, and uniform Laws on the subject of Bankruptcies throughout the United States;

To coin Money, regulate the Value thereof, and of foreign Coin, and fix the Standard of Weights and Measures;

To provide for the Punishment of counterfeiting the Securities and current Coin of the United States;

To establish Post Offices and post Roads;

To promote the Progress of Science and useful Arts, by securing for limited Times to Authors and Inventors the exclusive Right to their respective Writings and Discoveries;

To constitute Tribunals inferior to the Supreme Court;

* * * * *

And

To make all Laws which shall be necessary and proper for carrying into Execution the foregoing Powers, and all other Powers vested by this Constitution in the Government of the United States, or in any Department or Officer thereof.

*** Article 1, Section 8 and the Amendments that follow were thought to be the most important in regard to business. Except for those selected, the first ten Amendments (referred to as the Bill of Rights) have little application to business.**

AMENDMENT I.

(*The First Ten Amendments were proposed by Congress on September 25, 1789; ratified and adoption certified on December 15, 1791.*)

Congress shall make no law respecting an establishment of religion, or prohibiting the free exercise thereof; or abridging the freedom of speech, or of the press; or the right of the people peaceably to assemble, and to petition the Government for a redress of grievances.

AMENDMENT IV.

The right of the people to be secure in their persons, houses, papers, and effects, against unreasonable searches and seizures, shall not be violated, and no Warrants shall issue, but upon probable cause, supported by Oath or affirmation, and particularly describing the place to be searched, and the persons or things to be seized.

AMENDMENT V.

No person shall be held to answer for a capital, or other infamous crime, unless on a presentment or indictment of a Grand Jury, except in cases arising in the land or naval forces, or in the Militia, when in actual service in time of War or public danger; nor shall any person be subject for the same offence to be twice put in jeopardy of life or limb; nor shall be compelled in any criminal case to be a witness against himself, nor be deprived of life, liberty, or property, without due process of law; nor shall private property be taken for public use, without just compensation.

AMENDMENT XIV.

(Ratified July 28, 1868)

Section 1. All persons born or naturalized in the United States, and subject to the jurisdiction thereof, are citizens of the United States and of the State wherein they reside. No State shall make or enforce any law which shall abridge the privileges or immunities of citizens of the United States; nor shall any State deprive any person of life, liberty, or property, without due process of law; nor deny to any person within its jurisdiction the equal protection of the laws.

AMENDMENT XVI.

(Ratified February 25, 1913)

The Congress shall have the power to lay and collect taxes on incomes, from whatever source derived, without apportionment among the several States, and without regard to any census or enumeration.

Glossary of Legal Terms and Definitions

abatement of nuisance. Removal of a nuisance by court action.

ab initio. From the beginning. A contract which is void ab initio is void from its inception.

absque injuria. Without violation of a legal right.

abstract of title. A summary of the conveyances, transfers, and other facts relied on as evidence of title, together with all such facts appearing of record which may impair its validity. It should contain a brief but complete history of the title.

abutting owners. Those owners whose lands touch.

acceleration. The shortening of the time for the performance of a contract or the payment of a note by the operation of some provision in the contract or note itself.

acceptance. The actual or implied receipt and retention of that which is tendered or offered. The acceptance of an offer is the assent to an offer which is requisite to the formation of a contract. It is either express or evidenced by circumstances from which such assent may be implied.

accession. In its legal meaning it is generally used to signify the acquisition of property by its incorporation or union with other property.

accommodation paper. A negotiable instrument signed without consideration by a party as acceptor, drawer, or endorser for the purpose of enabling the payee to obtain credit.

accord and satisfaction. The adjustment of a disagreement as to what is due from one person to another, and the payment of the agreed amount.

account stated. An account which has been rendered by one to another and which purports to state the true balance due and which balance is either expressly or impliedly admitted to be due by the debtor.

acknowledgment. A form for authenticating instruments conveying property or otherwise conferring rights. It is a public declaration by the grantor that the act evidenced by the instrument is his act and deed. Also an admission or confirmation.

acquit. To set free or judicially to discharge from an accusation; to release from a debt, duty, obligation, charge or suspicion of guilt.

act of God. An occurrence resulting exclusively from natural forces which could not have been prevented or whose effects could not have been avoided by care or foresight.

actionable. Remedial by an action at law.

action ex contractu. An action arising out of the breach of a contract.

action ex delicto. An action arising out of the violation of a duty or obligation created by positive law independent of contract. An action in tort.

ad litem. During the pendency of the action or proceeding.

adjudge. To give judgment; to decide; to sentence.

adjudicate. To adjudge; to settle by judicial decree; to hear or try and determine, as a court.

administrator. A man appointed by a probate court to settle the estate of a decreased person. His duties are customarily defined by statute. If a woman is appointed she is called the administratrix.

adverse possession. Open and notorious possession of real property over a given length of time which denies ownership in any other claimant.

advisement. When a court takes a case under advisement it delays its decision until it has examined and considered the questions involved.

affidavit. A statement or declaration reduced to writing and sworn or affirmed to before an officer who has authority to administer an oath or affirmation.

affirm. To confirm a former judgment or order of a court. Also to declare solemnly instead of making a sworn statement.

agent. An agent is the substitute or representative of his principal and derives his authority from him.

aggrieved. One whose legal rights have been invaded by the act of another is said to be aggrieved. Also one whose pecuniary interest is directly affected by a judgment, or whose right of property may be divested thereby, is to be considered a party aggrieved.

alienation. The voluntary act or acts by which one person transfers his or her own property to another.

aliquot. Strictly, forming an exact proper divisor, but treated as meaning fractional when applied to trusts, etc.

allegation. A declaration, a formal averment or statement of a party to an action in a declaration or pleading of what the party intends to prove.

allege. To make a statement of fact; to plead.

amortize. In modern usage the word means to provide for the payment of a debt by creating a sinking fund or paying in installments.

ancillary. Auxiliary to. An ancillary receiver is a receiver who has been appointed in aid of, and in subordination to, the primary receiver.

answer. The pleading of a defendant in which he or she may deny any or all the facts set out in the plaintiff's declaration or complaint.

anticipatory breach. The doctrine of the law of contracts that when the promisor has repudiated the contract before the time of performance has arrived the promisee may sue forthwith.

appearance. The first act of the defendant in court.

appellant. A person who files an appeal.

appellate jurisdiction. Jurisdiction to revise or correct the work of a subordinate court.

appellee. A party against whom a cause is appealed from a lower court to a higher court, called the "respondent" in some jurisdictions.

applicant. A petitioner; one who files a petition or application.

appurtenances. An accessory; something that belongs to another thing; e.g., buildings are appurtenant to the land and a bar would be appurtenant to a tavern.

arbitrate. To submit some disputed matter to selected persons and to accept their decision or award as a substitute for the decision of a judicial tribunal.

argument. The discussion by counsel for the respective parties of their contentions on the law and the facts of the case being tried in order to aid the jury in arriving at a correct and just conclusion.

assent. To give or express one's concurrence or approval of something done. Assent does not include consent.

assignable. Capable of being lawfully assigned or transferred; transferable; negotiable. Also capable of being specified or pointed out as an assignable error.

assignee. A person to whom an assignment is made.

assignment. A transfer or setting over of property or some right or interest therein, from one person to another. In its ordinary application the word is limited to the transfer of choses in action, e.g., the assignment of a contract.

assignor. The maker of an assignment.

assumpsit. An action at common law to recover damages for breach of contract.

attachment. Taking property into the legal custody of an officer by virtue of the directions contained in a writ of attachment. A seizure under a writ of a debtor's property.

attest. To bear witness to; to affirm; to be true or genuine.

attorney-in-fact. A person who is authorized by his principal, either for some particular purpose, or to do a particular act, not of a legal character.

authentication. Such official attestation of a written instrument as will render it legally admissible in evidence.

authority. Judicial or legislative precedent; delegated power; warrant.

averment. A positive statement of fact made in a pleading.

avoidable. Capable of being nullified or made void.

bad faith. The term imports a person's actual intent to mislead or deceive another; an intent to take an unfair and unethical advantage of another.

bailee. The person to whom a bailment is made.

bailment. A delivery of personal property by one person to another in trust for a specific purpose, with a contract, express or implied, that the trust shall be faithfully executed and the property returned or duly accounted for when the special purpose is accomplished, or kept until the bailor reclaims it.

bailor. The maker of a bailment; one who delivers personal property to another to be held in bailment.

bankruptcy. The state of a person who is unable to pay his or her debts without respect to time; one whose liabilities exceed his or her assets.

bar. As a collective noun it is used to include those persons who are admitted to practice law, members of the bar. The court itself. A plea or peremptory exception of a defendant sufficient to destroy the plaintiff's action.

barratry. The habitual stirring up of quarrels and suits; a single act would not constitute the offense.

bearer. The designation of the bearer as the payee of a negotiable instrument signifies that the instrument is payable to the person who seems to be the holder.

bench. A court; the judges of a court; the seat upon which the judges of a court are accustomed to sit while the court is in session.

beneficiary. The person for whose benefit an insurance policy, trust, will, or contract is established but not the promisee. In the case of a contract, the beneficiary is called a *third-party beneficiary.* A *donee beneficiary* is one who is not a party to a contract but who receives the promised performance as a gift. A *creditor beneficiary* is one who is not a party to a contract but receives the performance in discharge of a debt owed by the promisee to him.

bequeath. Commonly used to denote a testamentary gift of real estate; synonymous with "to devise."

bid. To make an offer at an auction or at a judicial sale. As a noun it means an offer.

bilateral contract. A contract in which the promise of one of the parties forms the consideration for the promise of the other; a contract formed by an offer requiring a reciprocal promise.

bill of exchange. An unconditional order in writing by one person to another, signed by the person giving it, requiring the person to whom it is addressed to pay on demand or at a fixed or determinable future time a sum certain in money to order or to bearer.

bill of lading. A written acknowledgment of the receipt of goods to be transported to a designated place and delivery to a named person or to his or her order.

bill of sale. A written agreement by which one person assigns or transfers interests or rights in personal property to another.

binder. Also called a binding slip—a brief memorandum or agreement issued by an insurer as a temporary policy for the convenience of all the parties, constituting a present insurance in the amount specified, to continue in force until the execution of a formal policy.

"blue sky" laws. A popular name for statutes regulating the sale of securities and intended to protect investors against fraudulent and visionary schemes.

bona fide. Good faith.

bond. A promise under seal to pay money.

breaking bulk. The division or separation of the contents of a package or container.

brief. A statement of a party's case; usually an abridgment of either the plaintiff's or defendant's case prepared by his or her attorneys for use of counsel on a trial at law. Also an abridgment of a reported case.

broker. An agent who bargains or carries on negotiations in behalf of the principal as an intermediary between the latter and third persons in transacting business relative to the acquisition of contractual rights, or to the sale or purchase of property the custody of which is not intrusted to him or her for the purpose of discharging the agency.

bulk transfer. The sale or transfer of a major part of the stock of goods of a merchant at one time and not in the ordinary course of business.

burden of proof. The necessity or obligation of affirmatively proving the fact or facts in dispute on an issue raised in a suit in court.

bylaw. A rule or law of a corporation for its government. It includes all self-made regulations of a corporation affecting its business and members which do not operate on third persons, or in any way affect their rights.

c.i.f. An abbreviation for cost, freight, and insurance, used in mercantile transactions, especially in import transactions.

c.o.d. **"Cash on delivery."** When goods are delivered to a carrier for a cash on delivery shipment the carrier must not deliver without receiving payment of the amount due.

call. A notice of a meeting to be held by the stockholders or board of directors of a corporation. Also a demand for payment. In securities trading, a negotiable option contract granting the bearer the right to buy a certain quantity of a particular security at the agreed price on or before the agreed date.

cancellation. The act of crossing out a writing. The operation of destroying a written instrument.

caption. The heading or title of a document.

carte blanche. A signed blank instrument intended by the signer to be filled in and used by another person without restriction.

case law. The law as laid down in the decisions of the courts. The law extracted from decided cases.

cashier's check. A bill of exchange, drawn by a bank upon itself, and accepted by the act of issuance.

cause of action. A right of action at law arises from the existence of a primary right in the plaintiff, and an invasion of that right by some civil wrong on the part of the defendant, and that the facts which establish the existence of that right and that civil wrong constitute the cause of action.

caveat emptor. Let the buyer beware. This maxim expresses the general idea that the buyer purchases at his peril, and that there are no warranties, either express or implied, made by the seller.

caveat venditor. Let the seller beware. It is not accepted as a rule of law in the law of sales.

certification. The return of a writ; a formal attestation of a matter of fact; the appropriate marking of a certified check.

certified check. A check which has been "accepted" by the drawee bank and has been so marked or certified that it indicates such acceptance.

cestui que trust. The person for whose benefit property is held in trust by a trustee.

champerty. The purchase of an interest in a matter in dispute so as to take part in the litigation.

chancellor. A judge of a court of chancery.

chancery. Equity or a court of equity.

charge. To charge a jury is to instruct the jury as to the essential law of the case. The first step in the prosecution of a crime is to formally accuse the offender or charge him with the crime.

charter. An instrument or authority from the sovereign power bestowing the right or power to do business under the corporate form of organization. Also the organic law of a city or town, and representing a portion of the statute law of the state.

chattel mortgage. An instrument whereby the owner of chattels transfers the title to such property to another as security for the performance of an obligation subject to be defeated on the performance of the obligation. Under the U.C.C. called merely a security interest.

chattel real. Interests in real estate less than a freehold, such as an estate for years.

chattels. Goods both movable and immovable except such as are in the nature of freehold or a part of a freehold.

check. A written order on a bank or banker payable on demand to the person named or his order or bearer and drawn by virtue of credits due the drawer from the bank created by money deposited with the bank.

chose in action. A personal right not reduced to possession but recoverable by a suit at law.

citation. A writ issued out of a court of competent jurisdiction, commanding the person therein named to appear on a day named to do something therein mentioned.

citation of authorities. The reference to legal authorities such as reported cases or treatises to support propositions advanced.

civil action. An action brought to enforce a civil right; in contrast to a criminal action.

class action. An action brought on behalf of the plaintiff and others similarly situated.

close corporation. A corporation in which directors and officers, rather than the shareholders, have the right to fill vacancies occurring in their ranks. Also used to refer to any corporation whose stock is not freely traded and whose shareholders are personally known to each other.

code. A system of law; a systematic and complete body of law.

codicil. Some addition to or qualification of one's last will and testament.

cognovit. To acknowledge an action. A cognovit note is a promissory note which contains an acknowledgment clause.

collateral attack. An attempt to impeach a decree, a judgment or other official act in a proceeding which has not been instituted for the express purpose of correcting or annulling or modifying the decree, judgment or offical act.

comaker. A person who with another or others signs a negotiable instrument on its face and thereby becomes primarily liable for its payment.

commercial law. The law which relates to the rights of property and persons engaged in trade or commerce.

commission merchant. A person who sells goods in his own name at his own store, and on commission, from sample. Also one who buys and sells goods for a principal in his own name and without disclosing his principal.

common carrier. One who undertakes, for hire or reward, to transport the goods of such of the public as choose to employ him.

compensatory damages. See damages.

complaint. A form of legal process which usually consists of a formal allegation or charge against a party, made or presented to the appropriate court or officer. The technical name of a bill in equity by which the complainant sets out his cause of action.

composition with creditors. An agreement between creditors and their common debtor and between themselves whereby the creditors agree to accept the sum or security stipulated in full payment of their claims.

concurrent. Running with, simultaneously with. The word is used in different senses. In contracts concurrent conditions are conditions which must be performed simultaneously by the mutual acts required by each of the parties.

condemn. To appropriate land for public use. To adjudge a person guilty; to pass sentence upon a person convicted of a crime.

condition. A provision or clause in a contract which operates to suspend or rescind the principal obligation. A qualification or restriction annexed to a conveyance of lands, whereby it is provided that in the case a particular event does or does not happen, or in case the grantor or grantees do or omit to do a particular act, an estate shall commence, be enlarged or be defeated.

condition precedent. A condition which must happen before either party is bound by the principal obligation of a contract; e.g., one agrees to purchase goods if they are delivered before a stated day. Delivery before the stated day is a condition precedent to one's obligation to purchase.

condition subsequent. A condition which operates to relieve or discharge one from his obligation under a contract.

conditional acceptance. An acceptance of a bill of exchange containing some qualification limiting or altering the acceptor's liability on the bill.

conditional sale. The term is most frequently applied to a sale wherein the seller reserves the title to the goods, though the possession is delivered to the buyer, until the purchase price is paid in full.

confession of judgment. An entry of judgment upon the admission or confession of the debtor without the formality, time, or expense involved in an ordinary proceeding.

conservator (of an insane person). A person appointed by a court to take care of and oversee the person and estate of an idiot or other incompetent person.

consignee. A person to whom goods are consigned, shipped, or otherwise transmitted, either for sale or for safekeeping.

consignment. A bailment for sale. The consignee does not undertake the absolute obligation to sell or pay for the goods.

consignor. One who sends goods to another on consignment; a shipper or transmitter of goods.

construe. To read a statute or document for the purpose of ascertaining its meaning and effect but in doing so the law must be regarded.

contempt. Conduct in the presence of a legislative or judicial body tending to disturb its proceedings, or impair the respect due to its authority or a disobedience to the rules or orders of such a body which interferes with the due administration of law.

contra. Otherwise; disagreeing with; contrary to.

contra bonos moris. Contrary to good morals.

contribution. A payment made by each, or by any, of several having a common interest or liability of his share in the loss suffered, or in the money necessarily paid by one of the parties in behalf of the others.

conversion. Any distinct act of dominion wrongfully exerted over another's personal property in denial of or inconsistent with his rights therein. That tort which is committed by a person who deals with chattels not belonging to him in a manner which is inconsistent with the ownership of the lawful owner.

conveyance. In its common use it refers to a written instrument transferring the title to land or some interest therein from one person to another. It is sometimes applied to the transfer of the property in personalty.

copartnership. A partnership.

corporation. An artificial being, invisible, intangible and existing only in contemplation of law. It is exclusively the work of the law, and the best evidence of its existence is the grant of corporate powers by the commonwealth.

corporeal. Possessing physical substance; tangible; perceptible to the senses.

counterclaim. A claim which, if established, will defeat or in some way qualify a judgment to which the plaintiff is otherwise entitled.

counter-offer. A cross offer made by the offeree to the offeror.

covenant. The word is used in its popular sense as synonymous to contract. In its specific sense it ordinarily imparts an agreement reduced to writing, and executed by a sealing and delivery.

covenantor. A person who covenants; the maker of a covenant.

coverture. The condition of a married woman.

credible. As applied to a witness the word means competent.

cross-action. Cross-complaint; an independent action brought by a defendant against the plaintiff.

culpable. Blameworthy; denotes breach of legal duty but not criminal conduct.

cumulative voting. A method of voting by which an elector entitled to vote for several candidates for the same office may cast more than one vote for the same candidate, distributing among the candidates as he chooses a number of votes equal to the number of candidates to be elected.

custody. The bare control or care of a thing as distinguished from the possession of it.

d/b/a/. Doing business as; indicates the use of a trade name.

damages. Indemnity to the person who suffers loss or harm from an injury; a sum recoverable as amends for a wrong. An adequate compensation for the loss suffered or the injury sustained.

compensatory. Damages that will compensate a party for direct losses due to an injury suffered.

consequential. Damages which are not produced without the concurrence of some other event attributable to the same origin or cause.

liquidated. Damages made certain by the prior agreement of the parties.

nominal. Damages which are recoverable where a legal right is to be vindicated against an invasion which has produced no actual present loss.

special. Actual damages that would not necessarily but because of special circumstances do in fact flow from an injury.

date of issue. As the term is applied to notes, bonds, etc., of a series, it usually means the arbitrary date fixed as the beginning of the term for which they run, without reference to the precise time when convenience or the state of the market may permit of their sale or delivery.

deal. To engage in mutual intercourse or transactions of any kind.

debenture. A written acknowledgment of a debt; specifically an instrument under seal for the repayment of money lent.

debtor. A person who owes another anything, or who is under obligation, arising from express agreement, implication of law, or from the principles of natural justice, to render and pay a sum of money to another.

deceit. A type of fraud; actual fraud consisting of any false representations or contrivance whereby one person overreaches and misleads another to his hurt.

decision. A decision is the judgment of a court, while the opinion represents merely the reasons for that judgment.

declaration. The pleadings by which a plaintiff in an action at law sets out his cause of action. An admission or statement subsequently used as evidence in the trial of an action.

declaratory judgment. One which expresses the opinion of a court on a question of law without ordering anything to be done.

decree. An order or sentence of a court of equity determining some right or adjudicating some matter affecting the merits of the cause.

deed. A writing, sealed and delivered by the parties; an instrument conveying real property.

de facto. In fact as distinguished from "de jure," by right.

de jure. By right; complying with the law in all respects.

de minimis non curat lex. The law is not concerned with trifles. The maxim has been applied to exclude the recovery of nominal damages where no unlawful intent or disturbance of a right of possession is shown, and where all possible damage is expressly disproved.

de novo, trial. Anew; over again; a second time. A trial de novo is a new trial in which the entire case is retried in all its detail.

defalcation. The word includes both embezzlement and misappropriation and is a broader term than either.

default. Fault; neglect; omission; the failure of a party to an action to appear when properly served with process; the failure to perform a duty or obligation; the failure of a person to pay money when due or when lawfully demanded.

defeasible (of title to property). Capable of being defeated. A title to property which is open to attack or which may be defeated by the performance of some act.

defend. To oppose a claim or action; to plead in defense of an action; to contest an action suit or proceeding.

defendant. A party sued in a personal action.

defendant in error. Any of the parties in whose favor a judgment was rendered which the losing party seeks to have reversed or modified by writ of error and whom he names as adverse parties.

deficiency. That part of a debt which a mortgage was made to secure, not realized by the liquidation of the mortgaged property. Something which is lacking.

defraud. To deprive another of a right by deception or artifice. To cheat; to wrong another by fraud.

dehors. Outside of; disconnected with; unrelated to.

del credere agent. An agent who guarantees his principal against the default of those with whom contracts are made.

deliver. To surrender property to another person.

demand. A claim; a legal obligation; a request to perform an alleged obligation; a written statement of a claim.

demurrage. A compensation for the delay of a vessel beyond the time allowed for loading, unloading, or sailing. It is also applied to the compensation for the similar delay of a railroad car.

demurrer. A motion to dismiss; an allegation in pleading to the effect that even if the facts alleged by the opposing party are true, they are insufficient to require an answer.

dependent covenants. Covenants made by two parties to a deed or agreement which are such that the thing covenanted or promised to be done on each part enters into the whole consideration for the covenant or promise on the part of the other, or such covenants as are concurrent, and to be performed at the same time. Neither party to such a covenant can maintain an action against the other without averring and proving performance on his part.

deposition. An affidavit; an oath; the written

testimony of a witness given in the course of a judicial proceeding, either at law or in equity, in response to interrogatories either oral or written, and where an opportunity is given for cross-examination.

deputy. A person subordinate to a public officer whose business and object is to perform the duties of the principal.

derivative action. A suit by a shareholder to enforce a corporate cause of action.

descent. Hereditary succession. It is the title whereby a man on the death of his ancestor acquires his estate by right of representation as his heir at law, an heir being one upon whom the law casts the estate immediately at the death of the ancestor, the estate so descending being the inheritance.

detinue. A common-law action, now seldom used, which lies where a party claims the specific recovery of goods and chattels unlawfully detained from him.

detriment. A detriment is any act or forebearance by a promisee. A loss or harm suffered in person or property.

dictum. The opinion of a judge which does not embody the resolution or determination of the court and is made without argument, or full consideration of the point, and is not the professed deliberation of the judge himself.

directed verdict. A verdict which the jury returns as directed by the court. The court may thus withdraw the case from the jury whenever there is no competent, relevant and material evidence to support the issue.

discharge in bankruptcy. An order or decree rendered by a court in bankruptcy proceedings, the effect of which is to satisfy all debts provable against the estate of the bankrupt as of the time when the bankruptcy proceedings were initiated.

discount. A loan upon an evidence of debt, where the compensation for the use of the money until the maturity of the debt is deducted from the principal and retained by the lender at the time of making the loan.

dismiss. To order a cause, motion, or prosecution to be discontinued or quashed.

diverse citizenship. A term of frequent use in the interpretation of the federal constitutional provision for the jurisdiction of the federal courts which extends it to controversies between citizens of different states.

divided court. A court is so described when there has been a division of opinion between its members on a matter which has been submitted to it for decision.

dividend. A gain or profit. A fund which a corporation sets apart from its profits to be divided among its members.

domain. The ownership of land; immediate or absolute ownership. The public lands of a state are frequently termed the public domain.

domicile. A place where a person lives or has his home; in a strict legal sense, the place where he has his true, fixed, permanent home and principal establishment, and to which place he has whenever he is absent, the intention of returning.

dominion (property). The rights of dominion or property are those rights which a man may acquire in and to such external things as are unconnected with his body.

donee. A person to whom a gift is made.

donor. A person who makes a gift.

dower. The legal right or interest which his wife acquires by marriage in the real estate of her husband.

draft. A written order drawn upon one person by another, requesting him to pay money to a designated third person. A bill of exchange payable on demand.

drawee. A person upon whom a draft or bill of exchange is drawn by the drawer.

drawer. The maker of a draft or bill of exchange.

due bill. An acknowledgment of a debt in writing, not made payable to order.

dummy. One posing or represented as acting for himself, but in reality acting for another. A tool or "straw man" for the real parties in interest.

duress. Overpowering of the will of a person by force or fear.

earnest. Something given as part of the purchase price to bind the bargain.

easement. A liberty, privilege or advantage in land without profit, existing distinct from the ownership of the soil; the right which one person has to use the land of another for a specific purpose.

edict. A command or prohibition promulgated by a sovereign and having the effect of law.

effects. As used in wills, the word is held equivalent to personal property. It denotes property in a more extensive sense than goods and includes all kinds of personal property but will be held not to include real property, unless the context discloses an intention on the part of the testator to dispose of his realty by the use of the word.

e.g. An abbreviation for "exempli gratia," meaning for or by the way of example.

ejectment. By statute in some states, it is an action to recover the immediate possession of real property. At common law, it was a purely possessory action, and as modified by statute, though based upon title, it is still essentially a possessory action.

eleemosynary corporation. A corporation created for a charitable purpose or for charitable purposes.

emancipate. To release; to set free. Where a father expressly or impliedly by his conduct waives his right generally to the services of his minor child, the child is said to be emancipated and he may sue on contracts made by him for his services.

embezzlement. A statutory offense consisting of the fraudulent conversion of another's personal property by one to whom it has been intrusted, with the intention of depriving the owner thereof, the gist of the offense being usually the violation of relations of fiduciary character.

encumbrance. An encumbrance on land is a right in a third person in the land to the diminuition of the value of the land, though consistent with the passing of the fee by the deed of conveyance.

endorsement. See indorsement.

entry. Recordation; noting in a record; going upon land; taking actual possession of land. Literally, the act of going into a place after a breach has been effected.

eo nominee. By or in that name or designation.

equity. A system of justice that developed in England separate from the common-law courts. Few states in the U.S. still maintain separate equity courts though most apply equity principles and procedures when remedies derived from the equity courts are sought. A broader meaning denotes fairness and justice.

error. A mistake of law or fact; a mistake of the court in the trial of an action.

escheat. The revision of land to the state in the event there is no person competent to inherit it.

estate. Technically the word refers only to an interest in land.

estate at will. A lease of lands or tenements to be held at the will of the lessor. Such can be determined by either party.

estate for a term. An estate less than a freehold which is in fact a contract for the possession of land or tenements for some determinate period.

estate for life. An estate created by deed or grant conveying land or tenements to a person to hold for the term of his own life or for the life of any other person or for more lives than one.

estate in fee simple. An absolute inheritance, clear of any conditions, limitations or restrictions to praticular heirs. It is the highest estate known to the law and necessarily implies absolute dominion over the land.

estate per autre vie. An estate which is to endure for the life of another person than the grantee, or for the lives of more than one, in either of which cases the grantee is called the tenant for life.

estoppel. That state of affairs which arises when one is forbidden by law from alleging or denying a fact because of his previous action or inaction.

et al. An abbreviation for the Latin "et alius" meaning "and another" also of "et alii" meaning "and others."

et ux. An abbreviation for the Latin "et uxor" meaning "and his wife."

eviction. Originally, as applied to tenants, the word meant depriving the tenant of the possession of the demised premises, but technically, it is the disturbance of his possession, depriving him of the enjoyment of the premises demised or any portion thereof by title paramount or by entry and act of the landlord.

evidence. That which makes clear or ascertains the truth of the fact or point in issue either on the one side or the other; those rules of law whereby we determine what testimony is to be admitted and what rejected in each case and what is the weight to be given to the testimony admitted.

exception. An objection; a reservation; a contradiction.

ex contractu. From or out of a contract.

ex delicto. From or out of a wrongful act; tortious; tortiously.

executed. When applied to written instruments the word is sometimes used as synonymous with the word "signed" and means no more than that, but more frequently it imports that everything has been done to complete the transaction; that is that the instrument has been signed, sealed, and delivered. An executed contract is one in which the object of the contract is performed.

execution. A remedy in the form of a writ or process afforded by law for the enforcement of a judgment. The final consummation of a contract of sale, including only those acts which are necessary to the full completion of an instrument, such as the signature of the seller, the affixing of his seal and its delivery to the buyer.

executor. A person who is designated in a will as one who is to administer the estate of the testator.

executory. Not yet executed; not yet fully performed, completed, fulfilled or carried out; to be performed wholly or in part.

executrix. Feminine of executor.

exemption. A release from some burden, duty or obligation; a grace; a favor; an immunity; taken out from under the general rule, not to be like others who are not exempt.

exhibit. A copy of a written instrument on which a pleading is founded, annexed to the pleading and by reference made a part of it. Any paper or thing offered in evidence and marked for identification.

f.a.s. An abbreviation for the expression "free alongside steamer."

f.o.b. An abbreviation of "free on board."

face value. The nominal or par value of an instrument as expressed on its face; in the case of a bond this is the amount really due, including interest.

factor. An agent who is employed to sell goods for a principal, usually in his own name, and who is given possession of the goods.

fee simple absolute. Same as fee simple. See estate in fee simple.

felony. As a general rule all crimes punishable by death or by imprisonment in a state prison are felonies.

feme covert. A married woman.

feme sole. An unmarried woman.

fiction. An assumption made by the law that something is true which is or may be false.

fiduciary. One who holds goods in trust for another or one who holds a position of trust and confidence.

fieri facias. You cause to be made—an ordinary writ of execution whereby the officer is commanded to levy and sell and to "make," if he can, the amount of the judgment creditors demand.

fixture. A thing which was originally a personal chattel and which has been actually or constructively affixed to the soil itself or to some structure legally a part of such soil; an article which was once a chattel, but which by being physically annexed or affixed to the realty has become accessory to it and part and parcel of it.

forwarder. A person who, having no interest in goods and no ownership or interest in the means of their carriage, undertakes, for hire, to forward them by a safe carrier to their destination.

franchise. A special privilege conferred by government upon individuals, and which does not belong to the citizens of a country generally, of common right. Also a contractual relationship establishing a means of marketing goods or services giving certain elements of control to the supplier (franchiser) in return for the right of the franchisee to use the supplier's tradename or trademark, usually in a specific marketing area.

fungible goods. Goods any unit of which is from its nature or by mercantile custom treated as the equivalent of any other unit.

futures. Contracts for the sale and future delivery of stocks or commodities, wherein either party may waive delivery, and receive or pay, as the case may be, the difference in market price at the time set for delivery.

garnishee. As a noun, the term signifies the person upon whom a garnishment is served, usually a debtor of the defendant in the action. Used as a verb, the word means to institute garnishment proceedings; to cause a garnishment to be levied on the garnishee.

garnishment. The term denotes a proceeding whereby property, money, or credits of a debtor in possession of another, the garnishee, are applied to the payment of the debts by means of process against the debtor and the garnishee. It is a statutory proceeding based upon contract relations, and can only be resorted to where it is authorized by statute.

general issue. A plea of the defendant amounting to a denial of every material allegation of fact in the plaintiff's complaint or declaration.

going business. An establishment which is still continuing to transact its ordinary business, though it may be insolvent.

good faith. An honest intention to abstain from taking an unfair advantage of another.

grantee. A person to whom a grant is made.

grantor. A person who makes a grant.

gravamen. Gist, essence; substance. The grievance complained of; the substantial cause of the action.

guarantor. A person who promises to answer for the debt, default or miscarriage of another.

guaranty. An undertaking by one person to be answerable for the payment of some debt, or the due performance of some contract or duty by another person, who remains liable to pay or perform the same.

guardian. A person (in some rare cases a corporation) to whom the law has entrusted the custody and control of the person, or estate, or both, of an infant, lunatic or incompetent person.

habeas corpus. Any of several common-law writs having as their object to bring a party before the court or judge. The only issue it presents is whether the prisoner is restrained of his liberty by due process.

habendum. The second part of a deed or conveyance following that part which names the grantee. It describes the estate conveyed and to what use. It is no longer essential and if included in a modern deed is a mere useless form.

hearing. The supporting of one's contentions by argument and if need be by proof. It is an absolute right and if denied to a contestant it would amount to the denial of one of his constitutional rights.

hedging. A market transaction in which a party buys a certain quantity of a given commodity at the price current on the date of the purchase and sells an equal quantity of the same commodity for future delivery for the purpose of getting protection against loss due to fluctuation in the market.

heirs. Those persons appointed by law to succeed to the real estate of a decedent, in case of intestacy.

hereditaments. A larger and more comprehensive word than either "land" or "tenements," and meaning anything capable of being inherited, whether it be corporeal, incorporeal, real, personal, or mixed.

holder in due course. A holder who has taken a negotiable instrument under the following conditions;

(1) That it is complete and regular on its face; (2) that he became the holder of it before it was overdue, and without notice that it had been previously dishonored, if such was the fact; (3) that he took it in good faith and for value; (4) that at the time it was negotiated to him he had no notice of any infirmity in the instrument or defect in the title of the person negotiating it.

holding company. A corporation whose purpose or function is to own or otherwise hold the shares of other corporations either for investment or control.

homestead. In a legal sense the word means the real estate occupied as a home and also the right to have it exempt from levy and forced sale. It is the land, not exceeding the prescribed amount, upon which the dwelling house, or residence, or habitation, or abode of the owner thereof and his family resides, and includes the dwelling house as an indispensable part.

illusory. Deceiving or intending to deceive, as by false appearances; fallacious. An illusory promise is a promise which appears to be binding but which in fact does not bind the promisor.

immunity. A personal favor granted by law, contrary to the general rule.

impanel. To place the names of the jurors on a panel; to make a list of the names of those persons who have been selected for jury duty; to go through the process of selecting a jury which is to try a cause.

implied warranty. An implied warranty arises by operation of law and exists without any intention of the seller to create it. It is a conclusion or inference of law, pronounced by the court, on facts admitted or proved before the jury.

inalienable. Incapable of being alienated, transferred, or conveyed; nontransferrable.

in banc. With all the judges of the court sitting.

in camera. In the judge's chambers; in private.

in pari delicto. Equally at fault in tort or crime; in equal fault or guilt.

in personam. Against the person.

in re. In the matter; in the transaction.

in rem. Against a thing and not against a person; concerning the condition or status of a thing.

in statu quo. In the existing state of things.

in toto. In the whole, altogether; wholly.

in transitu. On the journey. Goods are as a rule considered as in transitu while they are in the possession of a carrier, whether by land or water, until they arrive at the ultimate place of their destination and are delivered into the actual possession of the buyer, whether or not the carrier has been named or designated by the buyer.

incapacity. In its legal meaning it applies to one's legal disability, such as infancy, want of authority, or other personal incapacity to alter legal relationship.

inception. Initial stage. The word does not refer to a state of actual existence but to a condition of things or circumstances from which the thing may develop; as the beginning of work on a building.

inchoate. Imperfect; incipient; not completely formed.

indemnify. To hold harmless against loss or damage.

indemnity. An obligation or duty resting on one person to make good any loss or damage another has incurred while acting at his request or for his benefit. By a contract of indemnity one may agree to save another from a legal consequence of the conduct of one of the parties or of some other person.

indenture. Identures were deeds which originally were made in two parts formed by cutting or tearing a single sheet across the middle in a jagged or indented line, so that the two parts might be subsequently matched; and they were executed by both grantor and grantee. Later the indenting of the deed was discontinued, yet the term came to be applied to all deeds which were executed by both parties.

independent contractor. One who, exercising an independent employment, contracts to do a piece of work according to his or her own methods, and without being subject to the control of the employer except as to result. The legal effect is to insulate the employing party from liability for the misconduct of employees of the independent contractor.

indictment. An accusation founded on legal testimony of a direct and positive character, and the concurring judgment of at least 12 of the grand jurors that upon the evidence presented to them the defendant is guilty.

indorsement. Writing on the back of an instrument; the contract whereby the holder of a bill or note transfers to another person his right to such instrument and incurs the liabilities incident to the transfer.

infant. See minor.

information. A written accusation of crime preferred by a public prosecuting officer without the intervention of a grand jury.

injunction. A restraining order issued by a court of equity; a prohibitory writ restraining a person from committing or doing an act, other than a criminal act, which appears to be against equity and conscience. There is also the mandatory injunction which commands an act to be done or undone and compels the performance of some affirmative act.

insolvency. The word has two distinct meanings. It may be used to denote the insufficiency of the entire property and assets of an individual to pay his or her debts, which is its general meaning and its meaning as used in the Bankruptcy Act; but in a more restricted sense, it expresses the inability of a party to pay his debts as they become due in the regular course of his business, and it is so used when traders and merchants are said to be insolvent.

instrument. In its broadest sense, the term includes formal or legal documents in writing, such as contracts, deeds, wills, bonds, leases, and mortgages. In the law of evidence it has still a wider meaning and includes not merely documents, but witnesses and things animate and inanimate which may be presented for inspection.

insurable interest. Any interest in property the owner of which interest derives a benefit from the existance of the property or would suffer a loss from its destruction. It is not necessary, to constitute an insurable interest, that the interest is such that the event insured against would necessarily subject the insured to loss; it is sufficient that it might do so.

inter alia. Among other things or matters.

interlocutory. Something not final but deciding only some subsidiary matter raised while a law suit is pending.

interpleader. An equitable remedy applicable where one fears injury from conflicting claims. Where a person does not know which of two or more persons claiming certain property held by him or her has a right to it, filing a bill of interpleader forces the claimants to litigate the title between themselves.

intervention. A proceeding by which one not originally made a party to an action or suit is permitted, on his own application, to appear therein and join one of the original parties in maintaining his cause of action or defense, or to assert some cause of action against some or all of the parties to the proceeding as originally instituted.

intestate. A person who has died without leaving a valid will disposing of his or her property and estate.

ipso facto. By the fact itself; by the very fact; by the act itself.

joint bank account. A bank account of two persons so fixed that they shall be joint owners thereof during their mutual lives, and the survivor shall take the whole on the death of other.

jointly. Acting together or in concert or cooperating; holding in common or interdependently, not separately. Persons are "jointly bound" in a bond or note when both or all must be sued in one action for its enforcement, not either one at the election of the creditor.

jointly and severally. Persons who find themselves "jointly and severally" in a bond or note may all be sued together for its enforcement, or the creditor may select any one or more as the object of his suit.

joint tenancy. An estate held by two or more jointly, with an equal right in all to share in the enjoyments of the land during their lives. Four requisites must exist to constitute a joint tenancy, viz: the tenants must have one and the same interest; the interest must accrue by one and the same conveyance; they must commence at one and the same time; and the property must be held by one and the same undivided possession. If any one of these four elements is lacking, the estate will not be one of joint tenancy. An incident of joint tenancy is the right of survivorship.

judgment. The sentence of the law upon the record; the application of the law to the facts and pleadings. The last word in the judicial controversy; the final consideration and determination of a court of competent jurisdiction upon matters submitted to it in an action or proceeding.

judgment lien. The statutory lien upon the real property of a judgment debtor which is created by the judgment itself. At common law a judgment imposes no lien upon the real property of the judgment debtor, and to subject the property of the debtor to the judgment it was necessary to take out a writ called an elegit.

judgment n.o.v. (judgment non obstante veredicto). Judgment notwithstanding the verdict. Under certain circumstances the judge has the power to enter a judgment which is contrary to the verdict of the jury. Such a judgment is a judgment non obstante veredicto.

jurisdiction. The right to adjudicate concerning the subject matter in a given case. The modern tendency is to make the word include not only the power to hear and determine, but also the power to render the particular judgment in the particular case.

jury. A body of lay persons, selected by lot, or by some other fair and impartial means, to ascertain, under the guidance of the judge, the truth in questions of fact arising either in civil litigation or a criminal process.

kite. To secure the temporary use of money by issuing or negotiating worthless paper and then redeeming such paper with the proceeds of similar paper. The word is also used as a noun, meaning the worthless paper thus employed.

laches. The established doctrine of equity that, apart from any question of statutory limitation, its courts will discourage delay and sloth in the enforcement of rights. Equity demands conscience, good faith, and reasonable diligence.

law merchant. The custom of merchants, or lex mercatorio, which grew out of the necessity and convenience of business, and which, although different from the general rules of the common law, was engrafted into it and became a part of it. It was founded on the custom and usage of merchants.

leading case. A case often referred to by the courts and by counsel as having finally settled and determined a point of law.

leading questions. Those questions which suggest to the witness the answer desired, those which assume a fact to be proved which is not proved, or which, embodying a material fact, admit of an answer by a simple negative or affirmative.

lease. A contract for the possession and use of land on one side, and a recompense of rent or other income on the other, a conveyance to a person for life, or years, or at will in consideration of a return of rent or other recompense.

legacy. A bequest; a testamentary gift of personal property. Sometimes incorrectly applied to a testamentary gift of real property.

legal. According to the principles of law; according to the method required by statute; by means of judicial proceedings; not equitable.

legitimacy. A person's status embracing his right to inherit from his ancestors, to be inherited from, and to bear the name and enjoy the support of his father.

letter of credit. An instrument containing a request (general or special) to pay to the bearer or person named money, or sell him or her some commodity on credit or give something of value and look to the drawer of the letter for recompense.

levy. At common law a levy on goods consisted of an officer's entering the premises where they were and either leaving an assistant in charge of them or removing them after taking an inventory. Today courts differ as to what is a valid levy, but by the weight of authority there must be an actual or constructive seizure of the goods. In most states, a levy on land must be made by some unequivocal act of the officer indicating the intention of singling out certain real estate for the satisfaction of the debt.

license. A personal privilege to do some act or series of acts upon the land of another, without possessing any estate therein. A permit or authorization to do what, without a license, would be unlawful.

lien. In its most extensive meaning it is a charge upon property for the payment or discharge of a debt or duty; a qualified right; a proprietary interest which, in a given case, may be exercised over the property of another.

life estate. See estate for life.

lis pendens. A pending suit. As applied to the doctrine of lis pendens it is the jurisdiction, power, or control which courts acquire over property involved in a suit, pending the continuance of the action, and until its final judgment therein.

listing contract. A so-called contract whereby an owner of real property employs a broker to procure a purchaser without giving the broker exclusive right to sell. Under such an agreement, it is generally held that the employment may be terminated by the owner at will, and that a sale of the property by the owner terminates the employment.

litigant. A party to a lawsuit.

long arm statute. A statute subjecting a foreign corporation to jurisdiction although it may have committed only a single within the state.

magistrate. A word commonly applied to the lower judicial officers, such as justices of the peace, police judges, town recorders, and other local judicial functionaries. In a broader sense, a magistrate is a public civil officer invested with some part of the legislative, executive, or judicial power given by the Constitution. The President of the United States is the chief magistrate of the nation.

maker. A person who makes or executes an instrument, the signer of an instrument.

mala fides. Bad faith.

malfeasance. The doing of an act which a person ought not to do at all. It is to be distinguished from misfeasance, which is the improper doing of an act which a person might lawfully do.

malum in se. Evil in and of itself. An offense or act which is naturally evil as adjudged by the senses of a civilized community. Acts malum in se are usually criminal acts, but not necessarily so.

malum prohibitum. An act which is wrong because it is made so by statute.

mandamus. We command. It is a command issuing from a competent jurisdiction, in the name of the state or sovereign, directed to some inferior court, officer, corporation, or person, requiring the performance of a particular duty therein specified, which duty results from the official station of the party to whom it is directed, or from operation of law.

margin. A deposit by a buyer in stocks with a seller or a stockbroker, as security to cover fluctuations in the market in reference to stocks which the buyer has purchased, but for which he has not paid. Commodities are also traded on margin.

marshals. Ministerial officers belonging to the executive department of the federal government, who with their deputies have the same powers of executing the laws of the United States in each state as the sheriffs and their deputies in such state may have in executing the laws of that state.

mechanic's lien. A claim created by law for the purpose of securing a priority of payment of the price of value of work performed and materials furnished in erecting or repairing a building or other structure; as such it attaches to the land as well as to the buildings erected therein.

mens rea. A guilty mind, criminal intent.

merchantable. Of good quality and salable, but not necessarily the best. As applied to articles sold, the word requires that the article shall be such as is usually sold in the market, of medium quality and bringing the average price.

minor. A person who has not reached the age at which the law recognizes a general contractual capacity (called majority), formerly 21 years; recently changed to 18 in many states.

misdemeanor. Any crime which is punishable neither by death nor by imprisonment in a state prison.

mistrial. An invalid trial due to lack of jurisdiction, error in selection of jurors or some other fundamental requirement.

mitigation of damages. A term relating only to exemplary damages and their reduction by extenuating circumstances such as provocation or malice. The theory of such mitigation is based on the regard of the law for the frailty of human passions, since it looks with some indulgence upon violations of good order which are committed in a moment of irritation and excitement.

moiety. One half.

mortgage. A conveyance of property to secure the performance of some obligation, the conveyance to be void on the due performance thereof.

motive. The cause or reason that induced a person to commit a crime.

movables. A word derived from the civil law and usually understood to signify the utensils which are to furnish or ornament a house, but it would seem to comprehend personal property generally.

mutuality. Reciprocal obligations of the parties required to make a contract binding on either party.

necessaries. With reference to a minor, the word includes whatever is reasonably necessary for his or her proper and suitable maintenance, in view of the income level and social position of the minor's family.

negligence. The word has been defined as the omission to do something which a reasonable man, guided by those considerations which ordinarily regulate human affairs, would do, or doing something which a prudent and reasonable man would not do.

negotiable. Capable of being transferred by indorsement or delivery so as to give the holder a right to sue in his or her own name and to avoid certain defenses against the payee.

negotiable instrument. An instrument which may be transferred or negotiated, so that the holder may maintain an action thereon in his own name.

no arrival, no sale. A sale of goods "to arrive" or "on arrival," per or ex a certain ship, has been construed to be a sale subject to a double condition precedent, namely, that the ship arrives in port and that when it arrives the goods are on board, and if either of these conditions fails, the contract becomes nugatory.

no-par value stock. Stock of a corporation having no face or par value.

nolo contendere. A plea in a criminal action which has the same effect as a guilty plea except that it does not bind the defendant in a civil suit on the same wrong.

nominal damages. Damages which are recoverable where a legal right is to be vindicated against an invasion that has produced no actual present loss of any kind, or where there has been a breach of a contract and no actual damages whatever have been or can be shown, or where, under like conditions, there has been a breach of legal duty.

non compos mentis. Totally and positively incompetent. The term denotes a person entirely destitute or bereft of his memory or understanding.

nonfeasance. In the law of agency, it is the total omission or failure of an agent to enter upon the performance of some distinct duty or undertaking which he or she has agreed with the principal to do.

non obstante veredicto. See judgment non obstante veredicto.

nonsuit. A judgment given against a plaintiff who is unable to prove a case, or when the plaintiff refuses or neglects to proceed to trial.

noting protest. The act of making a memorandum on a bill or note at the time of, and embracing the principal facts attending, its dishonor. The object is to have a record from which the instrument of protest may be written, so that a notary need not rely on his memory for the fact.

novation. A mutual agreement, between all parties concerned, for the discharge of a valid existing obligation by the substitution of a new valid obligation on the part of the debtor or another, or a like agreement for the discharge of a debtor to his creditor by the substitution of a new creditor.

nudum pactum. A naked promise, a promise for which there is no consideration.

nuisance. In legal parlance, the word extends to everything that endangers life or health, gives offense to the senses, violates the laws of decency, or obstructs the reasonable and comfortable use of property.

oath. Any form of attestation by which a person signifies that he is bound in conscience to perform an act faithfully and truthfully. It involves the idea of calling on God to witness what is averred as truth, and it is supposed to be accompanied with an invocation of His vengeance, or a renunciation of His favor, in the event of falsehood.

obiter dictum. That which is said in passing; a rule of law set forth in a court's opinion, but not involved in the case; what is said by the court outside the record or on a point not necessarily involved therein.

objection. In the trial of a case it is the formal remonstrance made by counsel to something which has been said or done, in order to obtain the court's ruling thereon; and when the court has ruled, the alleged error is preserved by the objector's exception to the ruling, which exception is noted in the record.

obligee. A person to whom another is bound by a promise or other obligation; a promisee.

obligor. A person who is bound by a promise or other obligation; a promisor.

offer. A proposal by one person to another which is intended of itself to create legal relations on acceptance by the person to whom it is made.

offeree. A person to whom an offer is made.

offeror. A person who makes an offer.

opinion. The opinion of the court represents merely the reasons for its judgment, while the decision of the court is the judgment itself.

option. A contract whereby the owner of property agrees with another person that such person shall have the right to buy the property at a fixed price within a certain time. There are two independent elements in an option contract: First, the offer to sell, which does not become a contract until accepted; second, the completed contract to leave the offer open for a specified time.

ordinance. A legislative enactment of a county or an incorporated city or town.

ostensible authority. Such authority as a principal, either intentionally or by want of ordinary care, causes or allows a third person to believe the agent to possess.

ostensible partners. Members of a partnership whose names are made known and appear to the world as partners.

overdraft. The withdrawal from a bank by a depositor of money in excess of the amount of money he or she has on deposit there.

overplus. That which remains; a balance left over.

owner's risk. A term employed by common carriers in bills of lading and shipping receipts to signify that the carrier does not assume responsibility for the safety of the goods.

par. Par means equal, and par value means a value equal to the face of a bond or a stock certificate.

parol. Oral; verbal; by word of mouth; spoken as opposed to written.

parties. All persons who are interested in the subject matter of an action and who have a right to make defense, control the proceedings, examine and cross-examine witnesses, and appeal from the judgment.

partition. A proceeding the object of which is to enable those who own property as joint tenants or tenants in common, to put an end to the tenancy so as to vest in each a sole estate in specific property or an allotment of the lands and tenements. If a division of the estate is impracticable the estate ought to be sold, and the proceeds divided.

partners. Those persons who contribute property, money, or services to carry on a joint business for their common benefit, and who own and share the profits thereof in certain proportions; the members of a partnership.

patent. A patent for land is a conveyance of title to government lands by the government; a patent of an invention is the right of monopoly secured by statute to those who invent or discover new and useful devices and processes.

pawn. A pledge; a bailment of personal property as security for some debt or engagement, redeemable on certain terms, and with an implied power of sale on default.

payee. A person to whom a payment is made or is made payable.

pecuniary. Financial; pertaining or relating to money; capable of being estimated, computed, or measured by money value.

per curiam. By the court; by the court as a whole.

per se. The expression means by or through itself; simply, as such; in its own relations.

peremptory challenge. A challenge to a proposed juror which a defendant in a criminal case may make as an absolute right, and which cannot be questioned by either opposing counsel or the court.

performance. As the word implies, it is such a thorough fulfillment of a duty as puts an end to obligations by leaving nothing to be done. The chief requisite of performance is that it shall be exact.

perjury. The willful and corrupt false swearing or affirming, after an oath lawfully administered, in the course of a judicial or quasi judicial proceeding as to some matter material to the issue or point in question.

petition. In equity pleading, a petititon is in the nature of a pleading (at least when filed by a stranger to the suit) and forms a basis for independent action.

plaintiff. A person who brings a suit, action, bill, or complaint.

plaintiff in error. The unsuccessful party to the action who prosecutes a writ of error in a higher court.

plea. A plea is an answer to a declaration or complaint or any material allegation of fact therein which if untrue would defeat the action. In criminal procedure, a plea is the matter which the accused, on his arraignment, alleges in answer to the charge against him.

pledge. A pawn; a bailment of personal property as security for some debt or engagement, redeemable on certain terms, and with an implied power of sale on default.

pledgee. A person to whom personal property is pledged by a pledgor.

pledgor. A person who makes a pledge of personal property to a pledgee.

positive law. Laws actually and specifically enacted or adopted by proper authority for the government of a jural society as distinguished from principles of morality or laws of honor.

possession. Respecting real property, possession involves exclusive dominion and control such as owners of like property usually exercise over it. The existence of such possession is largely a question of fact dependent on the nature of the property and the surrounding circumstances.

power of attorney. A written authorization to an agent to perform specified acts in behalf of his or her principal. The writing by which the authority is evidenced is termed a letter of attorney and is dictated by the convenience and certainty of business.

precedent. A previous decision relied upon as authority.

preference. The act of a debtor in paying or securing one or more of his creditors in a manner more favorable to them than to other creditors or to the exclusion of such other creditors. In the absence of statute, a preference is perfectly good, but to be legal it must be bona fide, and not a mere subterfuge of the debtor to secure a future benefit to himself or to prevent the application of his property to his debts.

prerogative. A special power, privilege, or immunity, usually used in reference to an official or his office.

presumption. A term used to signify that which may be assumed without proof, or taken for granted. It is asserted as a self-evident result of human reason and experience.

prima facie. At first view or appearance of the business, as a holder of a bill of exchange, endorsed in blank, is prima facie its owner. Prima facie evidence of fact is in law sufficient to establish the fact, unless rebutted.

privilege. A right peculiar to an individual or body.

privity. A mutual or successive relationship as, for example, between the parties to a contract.

pro rata. According to the rate, proportion, or allowance.

pro tanto. For so much; to such an extent.

probate. A term used to include all matters of which probate courts have jurisdiction, which in many states are the estates of deceased persons and of persons under guardianship.

process. In law, generally the summons or notice of beginning of suit.

proffer. To offer for acceptance or to make a tender of.

promisee. The person to whom a promise is made.

promisor. A person who makes a promise to another; a person who promises.

promissory estoppel. An estoppel arising on account of a promise that the promissor should expect to and which does induce an action or forbearance of a substantial nature.

promoters. The persons who bring about the incorporation and organization of a corporation.

prospectus. An introductory proposal for a contract in which the representations may or may not form the basis of the contract actually made; it may contain promises which are to be treated as a sort of floating obligation to take effect when appropriated by persons to whom they are addressed, and amount to a contract when assented to by any person who invests his money on the faith of them.

proximate cause. That cause of an injury which, in natural and continuous sequence, unbroken by any efficient intervening cause, produces the injury, and without which the injury would not have occurred.

qualified acceptance. A conditional or modified acceptance. In order to create a contract an acceptance must accept the offer substantially as made; hence a qualified acceptance is no acceptance at all, is treated by the courts as a rejection of the offer made, and is in effect an offer by the offeree, which the offeror may, if he chooses, accept and thus create a contract.

quantum meruit. As much as is deserved. A part of a common law action in assumpsit for the value of services rendered.

quash. To vacate or make void.

quasi contract. An obligation arising not from an agreement between the parties but from the voluntary act of one of them or some relation between them which will be enforced by a court.

quasi judicial. Acts of public officers involving investigation of facts and drawing conclusions from them as a basis of official action.

quitclaim deed. A deed conveying only the right, title, and interest of the grantor in the property described, as distinguished from a deed conveying the property itself.

quo warranto. By what authority. The name of a writ (and also of the whole pleading) by which the government commences an action to recover an office or franchise from the person or corporation in possession of it.

quorum. That number of persons, shares represented, or officers who may lawfully transact the business of a meeting called for that purpose.

ratification. The adoption by one in whose name an unauthorized act has been performed by another upon the assumption of authority to act as his or her agent, even though without any precedent authority whatever, which adoption or ratification relates back, supplies the original authority to do the act, binding the principal so adopting or ratifying to the same extent as if the act had been done in the first instance—by previous authority. The act of a minor upon reaching majority affirming a voidable contract made during infancy and giving it the same force and effect as if it had been valid from the beginning.

rebuttal. Testimony addressed to evidence

produced by the opposite party; rebutting evidence.

receiver. An indifferent person between the parties to a cause, appointed by the court to receive and preserve the property or funds in litigation, and receive its rents, issues, and profits, and apply or dispose of them at the direction of the court, when it does not seem reasonable that either party should hold them.

recognizance. At common law, an obligation entered into before some court of record or magistrate duly authorized, with a condition to do some particular act, usually to appear and answer to a criminal accusation. Being taken in open court and entered upon the order book, it was valid without the signature or seal of any of the obligors.

recorder. A public officer of a town or county charged with the duty of keeping the record books required by law to be kept in his or her office and of receiving and causing to be copied in such books such instruments as by law are entitled to be recorded.

redemption. The buying back of one's property after it has been sold. The right to redeem property sold under an order or decree of court is purely a privilege conferred by, and does not exist independently of, statute.

redress. Remedy; indemnity; reparation.

release. The giving up or abandoning of a claim or right to a person against whom the claim exists or the rights is to be enforced or exercised. It is the discharge of a debt by the act of the party in distinction from an extinguishment which is a discharge by operation of law.

remainderman. One who is entitled to the remainder of the estate after a particular estate carved out of it has expired.

remand. An action of an appellate court returning a case to the trial court to take further action.

remedy. The appropriate legal form of relief by which a remediable right may be enforced.

remittitur. The certificate of reversal issued by an appellate court upon reversing the order or judgment appealed from.

replevin. A common-law action by which the owner recovers possession of his own goods.

res. The thing; the subject matter of a suit; the property involved in the litigation; a matter; property; the business; the affair; the transaction.

res adjudicata. A matter which has been adjudicated; that which is definitely settled by a judicial decision.

rescind. As the word is applied to contracts, to rescind in some cases means to terminate the contract as to future transactions, while in others it means to annul the contract from the beginning.

residue. All that portion of the estate of a testator of which no effectual disposition has been made by his will otherwise than in the residuary clause.

respondent. The defendant in an action; a party adverse to an appellant in an action which is appealed to a higher court. The person against whom a bill in equity was exhibited.

restitution. Indemnification.

reversion. The residue of a fee simple remaining in the grantor, to commence in possession after the determination of some particular estate granted out by him. The estate of a landlord during the existence of the outstanding leasehold estate.

reversioner. A person who is entitled to a reversion.

right. When we speak of a person having a right, we must necessarily refer to a civil right as distinguished from the elemental idea of a right absolute. We must have in mind a right given and protected by law, and a person's enjoyment thereof is regulated entirely by the law which creates it.

riparian. Pertaining to or situated on the bank of a river. The word has reference to the bank and not to the bed of the stream.

sanction. The penalty that will be incurred by a wrongdoer for the breach of law.

satisfaction. A performance of the terms of an accord. If such terms require a payment of a sum of money, then "satisfaction" means that such payment has been made.

scienter. In cases of fraud and deceit, the word means knowledge on the part of the person making the representations, at the time when they are made, that they are false. In an action for deceit it is generally held that scienter must be proved.

seal. At common law, a seal is an impression on wax or some other tenacious material, but in modern practice the letters "l.s." (locus sigilli) or the word "seal" enclosed in a scroll, either written, or printed, and acknowledged in the body of the instrument to be a seal, are often used as substitutes.

security. That which makes the enforcement of a promise more certain than the mere personal obligation of the debtor or promisor, whatever may be his possessions or financial standing. It may be a pledge of property or an additional personal obligation; but it means more than the mere promise of the debtor with property liable to general execution.

security agreement. An agreement which creates or provides a security interest or lien on personal property. A term used in the U.C.C. including a wide range of transactions in the nature of chattel mortgages, conditional sales, etc.

seizin. In a legal sense, the word means possession of premises with the intention of asserting a claim to a freehold estate therein; it is practically the same thing as ownership; it is a possession of a freehold estate, such as by the common law is created by livery of seizin.

service. As applied to a process of courts, the word ordinarily implies something in the nature of an act or proceeding adverse to the party served, or of a notice to him.

setoff. A setoff both at law and in equity is that right which exists between two parties, each of whom, under an independent contract, owes an ascertained amount to the other, to set off their respective debts by way of mutual deduction, so that, in any action brought for the larger debt, the residue only, after such deduction, shall be recovered.

severable contract. A contract which is not entire or indivisible. If the consideration is single, the contract is entire; but if it is expressly or by necessary implication apportioned, the contract is severable. The question is ordinarily determined by inquiring whether the contract embraces one or more subject matters, whether the obligation is due at the same time to the same person, and whether the consideration is entire or apportioned.

shareholder. It is generally held that one who holds shares on the books of the corporation is a shareholder and that one who merely holds a stock certificate is not. Shareholders may become such either by original subscription, by direct purchase from the corporation, or by subsequent transfer from the original holder.

share of stock. The right which its owner has in the management, profits and ultimate assets of the corporation. The tangible property of a corporation and the shares of stock therein are separate and distinct kinds of property and belong to different owners, the first being the property of an artificial person—the corporation—the latter the property of the individual owner.

sight. A term signifying the date of the acceptance or that of protest for the nonacceptance of a bill of exchange; for example, ten days after sight.

sinking fund. A fund accumulated by an issuer to redeem corporate securities.

situs. Location; local position; the place where a person or thing is, is his situs. Intangible property has no actual situs, but it may have a legal situs, and for the purpose of taxation its legal situs is at the place where it is owned and not at the place where it is owed.

specific performance. Performance of a contract precisely as agreed upon; the remedy that arose in equity law to compel the defendant to do what he agreed to do.

stare decisis. The doctrine or principle that the decisions of the court should stand as precedents for future guidance.

stated capital. Defined specifically in the Model Business Corporation Act; generally, the amount received by a corporation upon issuance of its shares except that assigned to capital surplus.

status quo. The existing state of things.

stipulation. An agreement between opposing counsel in a pending action, usually required to be made in open court and entered on the minutes of the court, or else to be in writing and filed in the action, ordinarily entered into for the purpose of avoiding delay, trouble, or expense in the conduct of the action.

stockholder. See shareholder.

stoppage in transitu. A right which the vendor of goods on credit has to recall them, or retake them, on the discovery of the insolvency of the vendee. It continues so long as the carrier remains in the possession and control of the goods or until there has been an actual or constructive delivery to the vendee, or some third person has acquired a bona fide right in them.

subpoena. A process the purpose of which is to compel the attendance of a person whom it is desired to use as a witness.

subrogation. The substitution of one person in the place of another with reference to a lawful claim or right, frequently referred to as the doctrine of substitution. It is a device adopted or invented by equity to compel the ultimate discharge of a debt or obligation by the person who in good conscience ought to pay it.

sui generis. Of its own kind; peculiar to itself.

summary judgment. A decision of a trial court without hearing evidence.

summary proceedings. Proceedings, usually statutory, in the course of which many formalities are dispensed with. But such proceedings are not concluded without proper investigation of the facts, or without notice, or an opportunity to be heard by the person alleged to have committed the act, or whose property is sought to be affected.

summons. A writ or process issued and served upon a defendant in a civil action for the purpose of securing his appearance in the action.

supra. Above; above mentioned; in addition to.

surety. One who by accessory agreement called a contract of suretyship binds himself with another, called the principal, for the performance of an obligation in respect to which such other person is already bound and primarily liable for such performance.

T/A. Trading as, indicating the use of a trade name.

tacking. The adding together of successive periods of adverse possession of persons in privity with each other, in order to constitute one continuous adverse possession for the time required by the statute, to establish title.

tangible. Capable of being possessed or realized; readily apprehensible by the mind; real; substantial; evident.

tenancy. A tenancy exists when one has let real estate to another to hold of him as landlord. When duly created and the tenant put into possession, he is the owner of an estate for the time being, and has all the usual rights and remedies to defend his possession.

tender. An unconditional offer of payment, consisting in the actual production in money or legal tender of a sum not less than the amount due.

tender offer. An offer to security holders to acquire their securities in exchange for money or other securities.

tenement. A word commonly used in deeds which passes not only lands and other inheritances but also offices, rents, commons, and profits arising from lands. Usually it is applied exclusively to land, or what is ordinarily denominated real property.

tenor. The tenor of an instrument is an exact copy of the instrument. Under the rule that an indictment for forgery must set out in the instrument according to its "tenor," the word means an exact copy—that the instrument is set forth in the very words and figures.

tenure. The manner of holding or occupying lands or offices. The most common estate in land is tenure in "fee simple." With respect to offices tenure imports time, e.g. "tenure for life" or "during good behavior."

testament. A last will and testament is the disposition of one's property to take effect after death.

testator. A deceased person who died leaving a will.

testatrix. Feminine of testator.

testimony. In some contexts the word bears the same import as the word "evidence," but in most connections it has a much narrower meaning. Testimony is the words heard from the witness in court, and evidence is what the jury considers it worth.

tort. An injury or wrong committed, either with or without force, to the person or property of another. Such injury may arise by nonfeasance, or by the malfeasance or the misfeasance of the wrongdoer.

tort-feasor. A person who commits a tort; a wrongdoer.

tortious. Partaking of the nature of a tort; wrongful; injurious.

trade fixtures. Articles of personal property which have been annexed to the freehold and which are necessary to the carrying on of a trade.

transcript. A copy of a writing.

transferee. A person to whom a transfer is made.

transferor. A person who makes a transfer.

treasury shares. Shares of stock of a corporation which have been issued as fully paid to shareholders and subsequently acquired by the corporation.

treble damages. Three times provable damages, as may be granted to private parties bringing an action under the antitrust laws.

trespass. Every unauthorized entry on another's property is a trespass and any person who makes such an entry is a trespasser. In its widest signification, trespass means any violation of law. In its most restricted sense, it signifies an injury intentionally inflicted by force either on the person or property of another.

trial. An examination before a competent tribunal, according to the law of the land, of the facts or law put in issue in a cause, for the purpose of determining such issue. When the court hears and determines any issue of fact or law for the purpose of determining the rights of the parties, it may be considered a trial.

trover. A common-law action for damages due to a conversion of personal property.

trust. A confidence reposed in one person, who is termed trustee, for the benefit of another, who is called the cestui que trust, respecting property, which is held by the trustee for the benefit of the cestui que trust. As the word is used in the law pertaining to unlawful combinations and monopolies, a trust in its original and typical form is a combination formed by an agreement among the shareholders in a number of competing corporations to transfer their shares to an unincorporated board of trustees, and to receive in exchange trust certificates in some agreed proportion to their shareholdings.

trustee. A person in whom property is vested in trust for another.

trustee in bankruptcy. The federal bankruptcy act defines the term as an officer, and he is an officer of the courts in a certain restricted sense, but not in any such sense as a receiver. He takes the legal title to the property of the bankrupt and in respect to suits stands in the same general position as a trustee of an express trust or an executor. His duties are fixed by statute. He is to collect and reduce to money the property of the estate of the bankrupt.

ultra vires act. An act of a corporation which is beyond the powers conferred upon the corporation.

unilateral contract. A contract formed by an offer or a promise on one side for an act to be done on the other, and a doing of the act by the other by way of acceptance of the offer or promise; that is, a contract wherein the only acceptance of the offer that is necessary is the performance of the act.

usury. The taking more than the law allows upon a loan or for forbearance of a debt. Illegal interest; interest in excess of the rate allowed by law.

utter. As applied to counterfeiting, to utter and publish is to declare or assert, directly or indirectly, by words or action, that the money or note is good. Thus to offer it in payment is an uttering or publishing.

valid. Effective; operative; not void; subsisting; sufficient in law.

vendee. A purchaser of property. The word is more commonly applied to a purchaser of real property, the word "buyer" being more commonly applied to the purchaser of personal property.

vendor. A person who sells property to a vendee. The words "vendor" and "vendee" are more commonly applied to the seller and purchaser of real estate, and the words "seller" and "buyer" are more commonly applied to the seller and purchaser of personal property.

venire. The name of a writ by which a jury is summoned.

venue. The word originally was employed to indicate the county from which the jurors were to come who were to try a case, but in modern times it refers to the county in which a case is to be tried.

verdict. The answer of a jury given to the court concerning the matters of fact committed to their trial and examination; it makes no precedent, and settles nothing but the present controversy to which it relates. It is the decision made by the jury and reported to the court, and as such it is an elemental entity which cannot be divided by the judge.

verification. The affidavit of a party annexed to his pleadings which states that the pleading is true of his own knowledge except as to matters which are therein stated on his information or belief, and as to those matters, that he believes it to be true. A sworn statement of the truth of the facts stated in the instrument verified.

versus. Against. Versus, vs., and v. have become ingrafted upon the English language; their meaning is as well understood and their use quite as appropriate as the word "against" could be.

vest. To give an immediate fixed right of present or future enjoyment.

void. That which is entirely null. A void act is one which is not binding on either party, and which is not susceptible of ratification.

voidable. Capable of being made void; not utterly null, but annullable, and hence that may be either voided or confirmed.

waive. To throw away; to relinquish voluntarily, as a right which one may enforce, if he chooses.

waiver. The intentional relinquishment of a known right. It is a voluntary act and implies an election by the party to dispense with something of value, or to forego some advantage which he or she might have demanded and insisted on.

warrant. An order authorizing a payment of money by another person to a third person. Also an option to purchase a security. As a verb, the word means to defend; to guarantee; to enter into an obligation of warranty.

warrant of arrest. A legal process issued by competent authority, usually directed to regular officers of the law, but occasionally issued to private persons named in it, directing the arrest of a person or persons upon grounds stated therein.

warranty. In the sale of a commodity, an undertaking by the seller to answer for the defects therein is construed as a warranty. In a contract of insurance, as a general rule, any statement or description, or any undertaking on the part of the insured on the face of the policy or in another instrument properly incorporated in the policy, which relates to the risk, is a warranty.

waste. The material alteration, abuse, or destructive use of property by one in rightful possession of it which results in injury to one having an underlying interest in it.

watered stock. Stock issued by a corporation as fully paid up, when in fact it is not fully paid up.

writ. A commandment of a court given for the purpose of compelling a defendant to take certain action, usually directed to a sheriff or other officer to execute it.

Indexes

Case Index

T

U

V–W

General Index

M

N

O

P

T

This book has been set in 10 and 9 point Times Roman, leaded 2 points. Part numbers are 12 and 32 point Times Roman and part titles are 22 point Times Roman. Chapter numbers are 32 point Compano and chapter titles are 18 point Times Roman. The size of the type page is 30 by 46½ picas.